The Broadview Anthology of
Social and Political Thought

VOLUME 2
The Twentieth Century and Beyond

The Broadview Anthology of
Social and Political Thought

VOLUME 2
The Twentieth Century and Beyond

GENERAL EDITORS

Andrew Bailey
Samantha Brennan
Will Kymlicka
Jacob Levy
Alex Sager
Clark Wolf

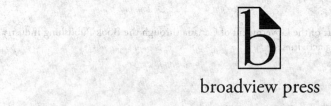

broadview press

Library and Archives Canada Cataloguing in Publication

    The Broadview anthology of social and political thought / general editors, Andrew Bailey ... [et al.].

Includes bibliographical references and index.
Complete contents: v. 1. From Plato to Nietzsche - v. 2. The twentieth century and beyond.
ISBN 978-1-55111-742-3 (v. 1).—ISBN 978-1-55111-899-4 (v. 2)

    1. Social sciences—Philosophy—Textbooks. 2. Political science—Philosophy—Textbooks. 1. Sciences sociales—Philosophie—Manuels d'enseignement supérieur. 2. Science politique—Philosophie—Manuels d'enseignement supérieur.
I. Bailey, Andrew, 1969- II. Title: Anthology of social and political thought.

B72.B76 2008   300.1   C2008-900804-9

Broadview Press is an independent, international publishing house, incorporated in 1985. Broadview believes in shared ownership, both with its employees and with the general public; since the year 2000 Broadview shares have traded publicly on the Toronto Venture Exchange under the symbol BDP.

We welcome comments and suggestions regarding any aspect of our publications—please feel free to contact us at the addresses below or at broadview@broadviewpress.com.

North America   PO Box 1243, Peterborough, Ontario, Canada K9J 7H5
2215 Kenmore Ave., Buffalo, New York, USA 14207
Tel: (705) 743-8990; Fax: (705) 743-8353
email: customerservice@broadviewpress.com

UK, Ireland, and continental Europe   NBN International, Estover Road, Plymouth, UK PL6 7PY
Tel: 44 (0) 1752 202300; Fax: 44 (0) 1752 202330
email: enquiries@nbninternational.com

Australia and New Zealand   UNIREPS, University of New South Wales
Sydney, NSW, 2052 Australia
Tel: 61 2 9664 0999; Fax: 61 2 9664 5420
email: info.press@unsw.edu.au

www.broadviewpress.com

Broadview Press acknowledges the financial support of the Government of Canada through the Book Publishing Industry Development Program (BPIDP) for our publishing activities.

PRINTED IN CANADA

Contributing Editors and Writers

Contents

PART III Rights-Based Liberalism and its Critics

Preface

In recent decades anthologies of social and political thought have generally taken one of two directions. One approach has been to deal with the major figures, stopping more or less at the beginning of the twentieth century— "Plato to Nietzsche" has been a common configuration. The other has been to focus on the period starting around 1970—the era of Rawls and rights-based liberalism, and the reaction to this work, of course, but also the era of powerful new waves in feminist thought. The two approaches have existed largely in isolation from each other, and to a large extent that has reflected pedagogical practice, with separate courses or groups of courses at many universities covering classical and contemporary political thought.

This anthology bridges that divide in one obvious respect, through the inclusion of material from the period 1900 to 1970. It also breaks new ground in a variety of ways. Readers will notice, for example, that the range of figures included in every era is broader than is customary. Along with Plato and Aristotle one may find Thucydides, Seneca and Cicero; along with Augustine and Aquinas one may find Al-Farabi, Marsilius of Padua, and de Pisan; along with Locke, Rousseau and Wollstonecraft one may find de Gouges and Constant. Noteworthy throughout is the extent to which women are included; this anthology recognizes as few other general collections have done the degree to which thinkers ranging from de Pisan, Wollstonecraft and Astell to de Beauvoir, Okin, and Nussbaum have made vitally important contributions.

In giving appropriate space to figures such as these, the general editors have had no wish to displace figures traditionally acknowledged as central. Indeed, we have endeavoured with these central figures not only to include complete (when possible) or substantial selections from core readings, but also to provide some material rarely or never previously included in this type of anthology. Along with selections from the *Republic*, the complete *Apology*, and the complete *Crito*, for example, we include selections from Plato's *Laws* (in a new translation); along with selections from Rawls's *Theory of Justice* we include his important essay "The Idea of an Overlapping Consensus"; and so on.

To have attempted all this within the compass of a single volume would have resulted in a book that was very unwieldy; with this in mind, we have from its early stages conceived of the project as a two-volume work. Our hope is that publishing in this way will allow for a high degree of pedagogical flexibility. Courses focusing either on "Plato to Nietzsche" or on the twentieth and twenty-first centuries will obviously require only one of the two volumes. For courses covering the full range of political thought the volumes are available packaged together at a special price. And for special situations it is also possible to make special arrangements; if, for example, a course focuses on several figures included in volume 1, together with a limited amount from volume 2, the publisher can prepare a course pack of the needed material from the second volume, and ship that together with the bound-book volume 1 at a special price for the student.

If *The Broadview Anthology* fills in many gaps in covering the full range of political thought, it also recognizes that there may often be good reasons for approaching twentieth- and twenty-first-century political thought rather differently than is the norm for earlier periods. Notably, a thematic organization is often felt to be suitable for the later period, a chronological organization for earlier periods. With that in mind, we present the figures in volume 1 in this anthology in chronological order, but group the selections in volume 2 under three broad thematic headings, each with its own substantial introduction. In these sections, we have included many early- and mid-twentieth-century writings to reflect the importance of sometimes neglected themes such as power, the state, gender, race, and post-colonialism. Inevitably, there is overlap between these sections, and certainly some selections could equally well have been included in a section other than the one in which they appear. It should be emphasized that the sectional divisions are intended to provide a loose framework, not to impose a prescriptive view as to how the material should be taught; the present arrangement in no way precludes instructors from discussing a particular selection in conjunction with those in other sections. But we hope it will provide for the second volume a pedagogically more useful structure than would a strictly chronological arrangement.

All too often with anthologies it is assumed that what is important is *only* the selections themselves, and how they are arranged. Our working principle with *The Broadview Anthology* has been very different. We believe issues of translation are of real importance, and we have made substantial efforts to include in these pages translations that are both accurate and accessible to the reader. We also believe that thorough annotation and extensive introductory material are vital to the success of an anthology with twenty-first-century readers. Whereas most anthologies of political thought include only minimal annotations, we make it a practice to gloss any reference not likely to be familiar to undergraduate readers. Rather than brief headnotes, we provide substantial introductions even to figures not generally acknowledged as occupying a central place in political thought. For the figures who have been generally acknowledged to be of central importance,[1] we go further, providing extended introductions designed to help students place the figure in a broad context of history and intellectual history as well as of political thought, and to steer them clear of common misconceptions. And, for virtually all figures included within the anthology, we provide something that one might not imagine in this age

of the visual would be as unusual as it is in anthologies of political thought—illustration.

All in all, *The Broadview Anthology* is a project as ambitious as it is wide-ranging. With a view to the great challenges involved, we have conceived of the project from the outset as a broadly collaborative effort. The general editors have taken the lead in setting out the general shape of the anthology and in choosing the individual selections; the general editors have also reviewed and had a hand in shaping the introductory materials. But a large number of others have played vitally important roles—offering their advice as to what should and should not be included, commenting on texts and translations, and in many cases drafting annotations and superb introductory material. Their very substantial contributions are acknowledged following the title page; without their help it would surely have been impossible to produce this anthology in a timely fashion, and to them both the general editors and the publishers extend profound thanks.

---

1   There is of course substantial room for disagreement as to which figures *are* of central importance, particularly in the context of an anthology designed for undergraduate teaching. Though no choice of selections will be entirely free from controversy, we have consulted with many professors in the philosophy and political science departments to construct a complete as possible table of contents that gives each figure her or his appropriate weight.

Acknowledgments

To a much greater extent than most anthologies, *The Broadview Anthology of Social and Political Thought* is a collaborative effort. The many who contributed by drafting introductory material, preparing annotations, or editing texts are listed immediately following the listing of the general editors on the title page. Special mention should here be made of the contributions of Prof. Robert M. Martin of Dalhousie University, who not only led the way in the drafting of introductions and notes but also assisted significantly in the preliminary editing of material drafted by others; of Victoria Kamsler of Princeton University, who has made very significant contributions both to the medieval and to the twentieth-century sections; and of Dr. Janet Sisson of Mount Royal College, whose contributions to the anthology's first section have been extensive and invaluable. Several others in-house at Broadview—notably, former Broadview Philosophy editors Tania Therien and Ryan Chynces—made significant contributions that should also be acknowledged.

Invaluable too has been the assistance of the dozens of academics who have been kind enough to offer their advice at one time or another during the preparation of the anthology on the specifics as to what should or should not be included, on various issues relating to translation, on the nuances of titling the anthology, and on a number of other matters. Following is a partial list; we apologize to any we have inadvertently omitted.

❖ ❖ ❖ ❖ ❖

Barbara Arneil, University of British Columbia
Farid Abdel-Nour, San Diego State University
Terence Ball, Arizona State University
Nandita Biswas Mellamphy, University of Western Ontario
William Buschert, University of Saskatchewan
Don Carmichael, University of Alberta
William Chaloupka, Colorado State University (Fort Collins)
B. Cooper, University of Calgary
Jack Crittenden, Arizona State University
Richard Dagger, Arizona State University
Shadia Drury, University of Regina
Allison Dube, University of Calgary
Avigail Eisenberg, University of Victoria
Cecil L Eubanks, Louisiana State University
Catherine Frost, McMaster University
Joshua D. Goldstein, University of Calgary
Thomas Heilke, University of Kansas

Peter Ives, University of Winnipeg
Catherine Kellogg, University of Alberta
Ed King, Concordia University
Jennet Kirkpatrick, University of Michigan
Mika LaVaque-Manty, University of Michigan
Douglas G Long, University of Western Ontario
Allan MacLeod, University of Saskatchewan
Anne Manuel, University of Michigan
Kirstie McClure, University of California, Los Angeles
Dennis McKerlie, University of Calgary
Margaret Ogrodnick, University of Manitoba
Anthony Parel, University of Calgary
John Seaman, McMaster University
Richard Sigurdson, University of Manitoba
Travis Smith, Concordia University
Christina Tarnopolsky, McGill University
Richard Vernon, University of Western Ontario
Ann Ward, University of Regina

PART 1

Power and the State

INTRODUCTION TO *POWER AND THE STATE*
Victoria Kamsler

By the end of the twentieth century, a single political ideology had come to dominate the Western world: there was near universal support for some form of liberal-democratic political order. But for most of the period between 1900 and 1945, the Western world was riven by intense ideological struggles between anarchists, Marxists, fascists, and liberal-democrats. All of these ideologies viewed themselves as self-consciously "modern" ideologies, emerging to fill the vacuum left by the discrediting of earlier pre-modern ideologies of feudalism, absolutist monarchy, or theocracy. Each suggested it was well-suited to liberate and fulfill the potential created by modern industrialized societies. They differed profoundly, however, on how they saw the nature and role of the state and of state power.

It is at times difficult to understand the rise of ideologies such as anarchism, Marxism, or fascism in today's climate. This puzzle is not likely to be dispelled by reading the texts included below, many of which may appear surprisingly weak in their argumentation and evidence. For this reason, it is helpful to give a brief historical sketch of the conditions under which these ideologies arose. Though they have earlier, sometimes ancient, roots, they came into their own in the early decades of the twentieth century.

Much of the most significant social and political thought from the American and French Revolutions to the beginning of World War I has its roots in the philosophy of the Enlightenment. Intellectuals believed in the power of reason and empirical investigation to transform society, liberate humanity, and progress toward a better world. Kant had imagined a world of republican governments at peace joining together in a federation of free states. John Stuart Mill had argued that freedom of opinion, speech and assembly, protected from state interference and the tyranny of the majority, would allow truth to win out. Even Marx (who, as we see below, left an ambiguous legacy) had been convinced that humanity liberated from class-domination and material necessity would be able to freely regulate people's interactions and environment for the common good. Eventually, according to Marx, this would result in the withering away of the state, leaving in its place a free, communist society.

Toward the end of the nineteenth century some began to question the enlightenment ideals. Friedrich Nietzsche sought to deflate the pretenses of reason and claimed to reveal the perverse underside of Enlightenment morality. Max Weber worried that the increasing use of end-means reasoning would trap society in an "iron cage"—a rule-based system exercising rational control of every aspect of society under an increasingly dominant bureaucracy. Marx disparaged liberal rights as tools for bourgeoisie domination and argued that capitalism contained the seeds of its own destruction.

Enlightenment thinkers had connected science and technology with progress; they had viewed the unprecedented growth of global trade as a guarantee of increasing prosperity and peace. World War I (1914-18) introduced trench warfare, the use of poison gas, and an unprecedented death toll—approximately ten million soldiers and another ten million civilians—mainly casualties of famine and disease. Though some philosophers (such as John Dewey) called for a deepening of enlightenment values, many intellectuals adopted an apocalyptic tone in the wake of World War I. The war devastated the economy of Europe, causing widespread discontent. Social and political institutions proved unable to deal with lowered standards of living and increased unemployment. Famine in Russia from 1916-17 contributed to the overthrow of the Russian Czar and to the Bolshevik-led October Revolution, in which Lenin established the ruling communist party that would last until the dissolution of the USSR in 1991. Germany faced hyperinflation in 1922-23, an economic catastrophe that contributed to the eventual rise of the National Socialist party ten years later under Hitler. A worldwide economic downturn began in 1928, and the Great Depression lasted through the 1930s. Many liberals began to question the efficacy of the free market; could it really work for the greater good? The planned economy of the Soviet Union appealed to many. (At the time, little information of Stalin's purges was available.)

Economic and social unrest gave many people reason to question the adequacy of liberal, democratic, and capitalist institutions. Conservatives questioned the ideals of democracy and equality and looked back in nostalgia to aristocratic hierarchies. Democratic socialists argued that capitalism could never realize the ideals of equality and genuine freedom. Radical socialists expressed skepticism about democracy, and some advocated temporary dictatorship to transform the relations of production. Fascists turned to an all-embracing state and authoritarian nationalism to escape the work of modernity. Much of the colonial world identified liberalism with the imperial regimes they sought to overthrow. Even the most enlightened in such regimes had disparaged the abilities of colonial subjects; John Stuart Mill, for example, an official in the British East India Company as well as a philosopher and political economist, was very much of his time when he argued in *Considerations on Representative Government* (1861) that only citizens of a commercial society had the capacity for self-government. Though in some ways he was critical of colonial government, Mill nevertheless concluded that imperialism could be justified as a paternalistic civilizing mission that should be left in place until colonial subjects were able to rule themselves. The persistence of such attitudes led many postcolonial states to reject liberalism in favor of Marxism.

This leads us to our theme: power and the state. Though some have argued that globalization has begun to erode state sovereignty, it is still very much the case that the state is today's central political agent. Theorists typically understand the state as a set of unified institutions over a specific territory and population. The state also typically claims to exert a legitimate monopoly over the use of force. As a result, the state is a system of power that exercises a significant, if not fully determinate, role over who gets what. The state provides the framework for many of people's actions and place in society. It determines benefits and burdens. It fixes social hierarchies and plays a role in the formation of values. The centrality of the state poses central problems in social and political philosophy. What roles should the state play? What limits should be placed on its power? What relationship should the state have to society as a whole? What is the source of state authority and legitimacy?

From anarchists, who believe that the state is illegitimate; to communists, who believe that the state should eventually "wither away"; to totalitarians, who believe that the power of the state should penetrate every aspect of people's lives, even their thoughts; to constitutional democrats, who hold that the state is the people's representative; almost every logically possible view about power and the state has been defended. In this section, we include readings that reflect all of these contending ideological perspectives from the pre-1945 period.

In such cases, while noting the central themes and tendencies of a work, it is often best to treat them as historical documents, significant for the influence they have had. How did these works come to exercise such influence, and command the allegiance that they did? Why were people moved by them, and why did they believe them?

These are questions for historians, and perhaps for cognitive psychologists. But they also raise important questions for political theory. As we will see, one of the central issues at stake in these ideological disputes was precisely the capacity of individual citizens to engage in reasoned public debate. When political ideologues and demagogues address themselves to subordinated, excluded, or otherwise angry, frustrated, and disenfranchised people, they evoke powerful passions and interests. By contrast, democracy depends on the capacity of a free people to reason together, on their own behalf, to weigh evidence and to make valid judgments. Democratic citizens need an ability to recognize false premises and specious reasoning, sophistry, and deception. One central point at issue in these ideological struggles is whether such democratic public reasoning is possible.

Our discussion of power and the state will begin with anarchism and its arguments for the abolition of the state. We will then consider various forms of increasing concentrations of state power.

Anarchism

Anarchism has a long, if discontinuous history. The presence of an anarchist tradition is a distinctive feature of Western political thought, and there are few examples of anarchist thought outside the Western political tradition. Among the very few are some early Taoists and a handful of medieval Islamic theorists. For example, Muslim political theory of the ninth century included a significant school of anarchists, if by that we mean thinkers who held that Muslim society could do without the existence of the state. The Mu'tazilite anarchists held that government was not inherently illegitimate. However, they observed that the imamate had always tended to become a kingship, and thus had come to be based upon the rule of force. This kind of rule was neither prescribed by the Koran nor required by reason; therefore it should be strictly optional for Muslim societies. "All the anarchists came from Basra in southern Iraq, or had their intellectual roots there ..."[1] These thinkers

---

1   Patricia Crone, "Ninth-Century Muslim Anarchists" *Past and Present*, No. 167. (May, 2000), pp. 3-28, p. 2. The discussion of Muslim anarchism, and of the early history of Western anarchism, is indebted to this work.

"denied the necessity of the imamate (roughly translatable as legitimate government)."[1]

How did anarchism later become a strain of Western political thought? One early source of Western anarchist thought is the natural law tradition of the Stoics, who imagined a golden age of society before the state came into existence. Unlike Plato and Aristotle before them, who had thought of state and society as arising together and as being functionally inseparable, the Stoics made it possible to conceive of the state as unnecessary, indeed as a kind of afterthought. Later, medieval natural law theorists would reconcile this account of the golden age, or earthly paradise, with an account of the Fall of Man. Earthly rulers, then, were given by God to bring order to humanity's debased and fallen nature, thus rendering political obedience legitimate. But the Stoic heritage remained, and created the imaginative possibility of a society, governed by right reason, existing without the institutions of the state. As Patricia Crone puts it:

> Westerners have always found it possible to think away the state. Some would think away society along with it, to illustrate how nasty, brutish and short life would be in the state of nature; but many would dream up societies from which the structures of domination had been removed, with reference to the remote past, the millenarian future, real or alleged primitive societies, or by way of construing utopias based on natural law or its socio-economic successor. In short, Western anarchism is in essence the belief that we can return to the condition of innocence from which we have fallen, or to some secularized version of it.[2]

But how accurate is it to claim that anarchism calls for a "return to innocence"? Most modern anarchist thought does not call for a return to any pre-existing state—in fact, it is self-consciously innovative and "vanguardist." Indeed, as we noted earlier, this is a defining feature of the ideological struggles of the pre-war period—they were all attempting to define the nature and requirements of "modernity."

A Short History of Modern Anarchism

In 1793, William Godwin's *Inquiry Concerning Political Justice* provided the first modern theoretical statement of anarchist ideas. Godwin argued that humans, as reasoning beings, must live according to the light of their own reason; and that governmental power, based on force and not reason, was inherently tyrannical and must be abolished. In the nineteenth century, Pierre-Joseph Proudhon—best known for his slogan "Property is theft!"—revived interest in anarchism by placing claims for justice (with reference principally to ending exploitation of the poor), at the center of all questions of political legitimacy. Arguing that both the church and state failed the test of justice, he proposed in their place a framework of economic mutualism, free credit, and freedom of exchange. This made possible a system of individual sovereignty and voluntary cooperation, the twin pillars of every system of anarchism.[3] Another important early variant of anarchism was Max Stirner's "egotistical anarchism." Stirner expanded upon the theme of individual sovereignty, drawing from it a kind of anti-morality of individualism, discarding all conventions of ethics and social norms: "A fig for good and evil! I am I, and I am neither good nor evil. Neither has any meaning for me.... For me, there is nothing above myself."[4]

In the 1860s, Mikhail Bakunin propounded the first leftist revolutionary doctrine of anarchism, incorporating into it an atheistic foundation; a call for the overthrow of the state; and an agenda of revolutionary social transformation. Like other anarchists before him, he tied the illegitimacy of the state to the violence of its history. For Bakunin, the state

> was born in all countries of the marriage of violence, rapine, pillage, in a word, war and conquest.... Even when it commands what is good, it hinders and spoils it, just because it commands it, and because every command provokes and excites the legitimate revolts of liberty.[5]

Despite his critique of the violent origins of the state, Bakunin's elitist, vanguardist variant of anarchism called for social revolution to be brought about through a violent overthrow of the state:

---

1 Ibid., p. 3.
2 Ibid., p. 8.

3 Ibid., p. 47.
4 Max Stirner, *The Ego and His Own* (1845; tr. New York, 1907) pp. 7-8. Quoted in Charles A. Madison (1945). "Anarchism in the United States," *Journal of the History of Ideas* 6 (1), p. 48.
5 *God and the State*, quoted by Bertrand Russell, *Proposed Roads to Freedom* (New York, 1919), p. 49. In Charles A. Madison, op. cit. p. 48.

He rejected political action as a means of abolishing the state and developed the doctrine of revolutionary conspiracy under autocratic leadership—disregarding the conflict of this principle with his philosophy of anarchism.... His approval of violence as a weapon against the agents of oppression led to nihilism in Russia and to individual acts of terrorism elsewhere—with the result that anarchism became generally synonymous with assassination and chaos.[1]

It is to the anarchism of Bakunin, the Russian anarchism of terrorism and assassination, that we must look for the sources of Emma Goldman's variety of anarchism.

Two American Anarchisms

Anarchism in America has historically taken two forms: individualist anarchism and communist anarchism.[2] Individualist anarchism has its roots in aspects of Enlightenment political philosophy. The social contract tradition, in particular, imagined the possibility of people living together in society (or out of society, in the case of Rousseau) without any formal government. But some roots of individualist anarchism lie simply in the experience of the American frontier. American settlers had to make shift without the framework of the state, and cultural habits of self-reliance and individualism, celebrated by Emerson and Thoreau, were a part of what was distinctive about the American experience. In Europe, centuries of traditional authority of the Church and various political entities brought the controlling, violent, and oppressive character of state action to the forefront of anarchist thought. But American individualist anarchism had a utopian flavor, and a notable degree of faith in man's inherently good nature. Its faith in the self-governing powers of the individual and its disdain for regulation was to find a home in libertarian thought and the defense of free-market capitalism. Individualist anarchists imagined life without the state. Communist anarchists instead envisioned a socialist, stateless society run by horizontally organized, voluntary associations. They advocated the collectivization of the means of production and of individual labor, which they believed would allow a system of distribution according to need—following the second half of Karl Marx's slogan, "from each according to his ability, to each according to his need" (*Critique of the Gotha Program* [1875]). Peter Kropotkin, perhaps the most significant theorist of communist anarchism, wrote in *The Conquest of Bread* (1892) that "houses, fields, and factories will no longer be private property, and that they will belong to the commune or the nation and money, wages, and trade would be abolished."

Another difference between individualist anarchist and communist anarchist thought is that the latter often advocated the violent overthrow of the state. *Prominent communist anarchists published handbooks on the making of bombs and other incendiary devices, and in 1901 anarchists assassinated both President William McKinley of the United States and King Humbert of Italy.

Emma Goldman

Conceptual innovation is central to the development and spread of modern democratic movements. By reframing basic political concepts and ideas about social and political identity, democratic movements widened the scope of political representation. Conceptual innovation also plays a central role in the work of the anarchist Emma Goldman. However, in Goldman's case it is the perpetual innovation of vanguardism—the efforts of a revolutionary organization to take center stage in a political movement and guide it according to its ideology. For Goldman, vanguardism and the destruction of all conventional authority become ends in themselves, apart from any consequences they may have for those caught up in their wake.

Goldman begins her famous essay, "Anarchism," with an appeal to conceptual innovation:

> The history of human growth and development is at the same time the history of the terrible struggle of every new idea heralding the approach of a brighter dawn ...

She defines anarchism as follows:

> The philosophy of a new social order based on liberty unrestricted by man-made law; the theory that all forms of government rest on violence, and are therefore wrong and harmful, as well as unnecessary.

Goldman's anarchism displays many attractive ideals:

---

1 Charles A. Madison, op.cit. p. 48.

2 This discussion of American anarchism is indebted to Charles A. Madison, "Anarchism in the United States," *Journal of the History of Ideas*, Vol. 6, No. 1 (Jan., 1945), pp. 46-66.

Anarchism stands for a social order based on the free grouping of individuals for the purpose of producing real social wealth; an order that will guarantee to every human being free access to the earth and enjoyment of the necessities of life, according to individual desires, tastes and inclinations.

At the same time, there is tension in Goldman's writing between the ideal of a stateless, self-ordering society composed of ordinary people, and an elitism that occasionally verges on contempt for the masses. Anarchist society is only possible if ordinary people are morally and intellectually capable of producing real social wealth independently of the use of state power. Authoritarians and conservatives who have little faith in people's capacity to reason often doubt that ordinary people will ever be so capable. Lack of confidence in the ability of ordinary people to function without the state may also be expressed by liberals; they tend to be more optimistic about ordinary citizens' capacity to participate in the public process, but still acknowledge that conflicting interests and finite resources require state power.

Marxism

In the early twentieth century Marx's ideas had been circulating in radical circles for over 50 years, but the groups espousing them remained on the fringe, far removed from power. The possibility of a revolutionary overthrow of the state became more real in the ferment of the First World War in countries such as Germany, and revolution took place in Russia in 1917. The sudden prospect of achieving power forced Marxists throughout Europe and beyond to clarify their views about the nature of the state, and about the role of revolutionary elites in achieving state power. A central issue for Marxists was the relationship between the Communist movement and the broader population. While Communists foresaw the possibility of seizing power, they realized they did not have the broad support of the majority of the population for a communist revolution, and that the pursuit of communism would therefore require a "vanguard" willing to seize power and rule forcefully, even against the hesitation or resistance of ordinary citizens. Much of the intellectual work of early twentieth-century Marxists was devoted to explaining and justifying this sort of "vanguardism" and "democratic centralism"—e.g., by appeals to the superior knowledge of

the Communist elite, or to the moral superiority of their long-term ends, which could then justify their coercive pursuit of revolution.

One of the principal differences between Marxists and anarchists of a communist stripe concerns the nature of revolution and its goal. Where communist anarchists of the early twentieth century sought the violent overthrow of the state and its replacement with freely cooperating voluntary associations, Marxists believed in the power and uses of centralized authority in the hands of the Communist Party. Trotsky and Lenin both differed from Emma Goldman and the communist anarchists in their belief that the state itself could be a crucial instrument of revolution. Lenin shared with Emma Goldman a belief in the importance of a vanguard to lead the revolution, but for Lenin it should be a Party vanguard: uniform, disciplined, and exceptionless.

Trotsky is most famously the theorist of "permanent revolution." Unlike mainstream Marxists, who believed that revolution would come in distinct stages, and that a "bourgeois revolution" must be completed prior to the final triumph of socialism, Trotsky contended that Russian workers were capable of bringing the revolution all the way to its socialist fruition in one uninterrupted sequence of revolutionary activity. After the Revolution of 1917, there was some convergence in their views. Trotsky came to accept vanguardism, and Lenin (perforce) came to accept the idea of Russian exceptionalism, that conditions in Russia were such that an intervening stage of bourgeois democracy was not needed in the march to state socialism.

In "What is to be Done?" (1902), Lenin develops his view that the Russian workers are themselves incapable of bringing about the socialist transformation. Class political consciousness can be brought to the workers *only from without, from an elite "vanguard" of party doctrinaires*. Lenin describes a bifurcated political world, where all theories and movements either adhere to the correct interpretation of social democracy (communism), or they support "bourgeois democracy" (reformist socialism). It is important to stress that Lenin's view of social democracy is very different from modern social democracy, which combines a commitment to liberal rights with a mixed economy, significant regulation of private enterprise in the interest of workers, and extensive social security. For Lenin, social democracy required Marxist class struggle and revolution to establish a socialist state with the eventual abolition of private property and class, to be replaced with the equal and common ownership of the means of production. For Lenin, "bourgeois democracy" would assimilate spontaneous worker movements and traditional unions to liberalism and the status quo: "to belittle the socialist ideology *in any way, to turn aside from it in the slightest degree* means to strengthen bourgeois ideology." According to Lenin,

> Social Democracy is always found to be in advance of all others in furnishing the most revolutionary appraisal of every given event and in championing every protest against tyranny. It does not lull itself with arguments that the economic struggle brings the workers to realize that they have no political rights and that the concrete conditions unavoidably impel the working-class movement on to the path of revolution. It intervenes in every sphere and in every question of social and political life.

Lenin's main views may be summarized as follows:

1) *The rejection of spontaneity*: Spontaneous democratic opposition to economic inequalities is at best a preliminary to true social democratic consciousness; the "spontaneous element," in essence, represents nothing more nor less than "consciousness in an *embryonic form*."

2) *Vanguardism*: Lenin emphasized the need for a vanguard party to bring about the revolution and wrote that "*there could not have been* Social-Democratic consciousness among the workers. It would have to be brought to them from without. The history of all countries shows that the working class, exclusively by its own effort, is able to develop only trade union consciousness."

3) *Propaganda*: Lenin held that the task of the vanguard is not education, but propaganda: "The principal thing, of course, is *propaganda* and *agitation* among all strata of the people." This view stemmed from Lenin's conviction that the working class could not achieve class consciousness except through the vanguard. Thus, he claimed that "there can be no talk of an independent ideology formulated by the working masses themselves in the process of their movement."

Dewey Meets Trotsky

John Dewey, an American Pragmatist, was among the most significant democratic philosophers of the first half of the twentieth century. Although his theoretical influence was eclipsed in the latter part of that century by the work of John Rawls and others, Dewey's practical influence has lived on, most notably in the formation of educational policy in the United States, Japan and China, where his emphasis on engaged learning-by-doing, and freely experienced problem-solving, challenged accepted models that conceived of learning more as a passive process, and emphasized memorization.

Dewey was an engaged and high-profile public advocate. In addition to his famous lecture tours of China and Japan, Dewey was directly involved in the public critique and assessment of contemporary Marxism. Dewey spent the better part of half a century reflecting upon Marxism, his views evolving in response to fresh evidence about the nature of the Soviet regime. At first somewhat sympathetic to the great social experiment of Lenin and the Russian Revolution, like many others he later became disenchanted with Stalinist absolutism. His most concentrated reflections on the subject arose from his own direct involvement in the international subcommission convened in Mexico to hear Trotsky's responses to the charges brought against him in the Soviet Union at the Moscow Trials of 1936-37.[1]

According to one school of thought, Dewey's thinking evolved as he came to identify what he viewed as two fundamental flaws in Marxist theory, flaws that arguably showed Stalinist totalitarianism to be not an unfortunate aberration or corruption, but entirely consistent with certain basic Marxist views. The first error has to do with the terrifying window for abuse laid open by the Marxist belief in the justification of revolutionary means by revolutionary ends. A second fundamental flaw concerns the instrumentalization of the relation between man and nature; the brutalism that characterized Soviet industrialization may be seen as a physical manifestation of that tendency in Marxist thought.[2]

Marxism played a significant role in much of Europe during the twentieth century and influenced many of the European social democratic and labor parties. The United States, however, (despite offering some haven to anarchism in the early part of the twentieth century) never developed any substantial Marxist movement. Despite the wild allegations of the anti-communist witch-hunts of the McCarthy era, in the 1950s, actual associations of Marxists in America were few and far between. Some have suggested that the spirit of individualism was too powerful in the United

---

1   This discussion is indebted to "Dewey's Critique of Marxism," by Jonathan D. Moreno and R. Scott Frey, *The Sociological Quarterly*, Vol. 26, No. 1. (Spring, 1985), pp. 21-34.

2   Ibid., p. 21-22.

States to allow Marxism to put down deep roots. Another view is that Marxism never flourished in America because Dewey provided his own distinctive and influential alternative to it:

> Before World War II there could be a comparatively simple answer to the question why Marxism, almost everywhere the principal framework for expressing radical philosophical discontent with the existing order, had only a peripheral effect on the American scene. The answer was that America had already possessed a developed and influential philosophy for the criticism and reconstruction of a social theory and practice. That philosophy was John Dewey's.[1]

The selections in this section from Dewey and Trotsky were written following their encounter in Mexico. The 78 year-old Dewey, at the time hard at work on his *Logic: the Theory of Inquiry* (1938), took time off to serve on the commission. The final report of the Commission, *Not Guilty*, exonerated Trotsky of Stalin's charges. An eyewitness account of this extraordinary political event was written by the novelist James T. Farrell. Farrell records:

> The hearings told part of the tragic story of how the state founded by Lenin and Trotsky, and by many of their brave, noble, and dedicated coworkers, evolved or was transformed (Trotsky at Coyoacan insisted on the word *transformed* in this context) into the Soviet totalitarian regime with which the world is now familiar. When Trotsky told of the democratic slogans and of the struggle of the Left Opposition which he led against Stalin, and some of the men who were executed as "Trotskyites," his explanation of his defeat was basically necessitarian. Quoting from Trotsky's book, *The Revolution Betrayed*, Dewey asked Trotsky if the dictatorship, in its early stage, were "a matter of iron necessity." Trotsky's answer was: "To a certain degree, not an absolute degree, but to a certain degree it is a historical necessity."[2]

Farrell adds:

Shortly after his ninetieth birthday, I talked with Dewey about Trotsky. Dewey said: "He was tragic. To see such brilliant native intelligence locked up in absolutes."

He considered Trotsky as a writer to be the best of the dogmatic Marxists, but he looked upon him as a dogmatist.[3]

Farrell further quotes Dewey from a December 19, 1937 *Washington Post* interview:

> The great lesson to be derived from these amazing revelations [at Coyoacan] is the complete breakdown of revolutionary Marxism. Nor do I think that a confirmed Communist is going to get anywhere by concluding that because he can no longer believe in Stalin he must now pin his faith in Trotsky. The great question for all American radicals is that they must go back and reconsider the whole question of means of inquiry about social change and of truly democratic methods of approach to social progress. ... During the trial [the Coyoacan hearings] I asked Trotsky whether there was any reason to believe that a proletarian revolution in any other country would be more successful than that of Russia. His reply was evasive.[4]

The only other direct encounter between Dewey and Trotsky was literary; it is found in the pages of *The New International* of 1938. Trotsky's "Their Morals and Ours" and Dewey's "Means and Ends" help to focus the immediate issues. Trotsky argues that only the end being pursued can justify the means, but he denies that all means of class struggle are justified in realizing the Marxian goal of human liberation: "Permissable and obligatory are those and only those means ... which unite the revolutionary proletariat ..." The "great revolutionary end" is incompatible with means that alienate the workers from one another, for example. Not all means are justified by the end, but only some.

Dewey analyzes the basic logic and assumptions of Trotsky's revolutionary ideology. Trotsky claimed that his theory both rejects the distinction between means and ends, and shows how the end of human emancipation justifies the means of revolution. Dewey shows that Trotsky, in a sense, has got his own methodology backwards; because what he is really arguing is not that means and ends are interrelated,

---

1 Charles Frankel, 1977, "John Dewey's social philosophy," in Steven M. Cahn (ed.), *New Studies in the Philosophy of John Dewey* (Hanover, N.H.: University Press of New England) p. 30.

2 "Dewey in Mexico," in James T. Farrell, *Reflections at Fifty and other essays* (London: Neville Spearman Limited, 1956) p. 118.

3 Ibid., p. 119.

4 Ibid., p. 116.

but that the revolutionary means justify whatever ends they bring about. Trotsky deduces, as if from a natural law, that revolutionary ends alone can and will bring about human emancipation. But Dewey points out that our relation to natural laws is one of investigation, not formal deduction. By analogy, he reminds us that medicine and biology could not proceed by asserting the existence of a natural law and deducing its consequences for the contents of the natural world. Instead, we must examine that world first hand to understand how it works and how it can be healed. Trotsky claimed that either one must adhere to an idealist or absolutist form of ethics or one must adopt his own version of the relationship between means and ends. However, Dewey shows this to be a false dichotomy. Dewey's own pragmatism is a counter-example to Trotsky's neat division of the world into them and us: the absolutists versus the revolutionaries.

Weber

In "Politics as a Vocation" Max Weber also sounds several critical notes concerning the foundations of Marxist revolutionary thought. In one respect Weber resembles both Dewey and Trotsky: he is no admirer of moral absolutism. But the reasons for his critique and the conclusions that he draws are quite different. For Weber, moral absolutists of all stripes fail to acknowledge the fundamental relation of political power and violence. The legitimate use of force is the feature that distinguishes politics from all other endeavors, and for this reason the exercise of political power needs a distinctive kind of justification. Instead of requiring purity of intention from political actors, politics requires a capacity for judgment in the face of moral complexity.

Weber begins "Politics as a Vocation" by reflecting on the personal qualities needed by one who seeks to wield political power. Weber is concerned to set out an ethic of statecraft, which will turn out to be different from the requirements of personal morality, but which is an ethic nevertheless. It sets forth terms by which one ought to judge and act, but these terms are not universal; rather, they are tailored to the particular demands of political leadership. As such, the command of moral absolutes gives way to the consideration of consequences, at least in part because the scale of political consequences is potentially so vast.

Weber is not only important for his views on political leadership; he is also arguably the preeminent theorist of power and the state:

Just like the political associations which preceded it historically, the state is a relationship of rule (*Herrschaft*) by human beings over human beings, and one that rests on the legitimate use of violence (that is, violence that is held to be legitimate). For the state to remain in existence, those who are ruled must submit to the authority claimed by whoever rules at a given time. When do people do this, and why? What inner justifications and what external means support this rule?[1]

As a sociologist, Weber is interested in state as an empirical organization. Like Aristotle, Weber believes humans to be political animals; but with Hobbes, he holds that politics is irreducibly characterized by the struggle for power and the clash of interests. Legitimacy is not a normative concept, providing an ideal standard for just rule. Rather, it is what makes people accept rule. Weber realizes that no regime can remain in power merely through the use of force. Even the worst tyrants must attempt to justify their position through some means. Much of Weber's political works is dedicated to this question. He finds the answer in his ideal-types of "traditional rule" based on the authority derived from custom, the "charismatic rule" of extraordinary leaders, and the "legal rule" defined by the bureaucratic order.

Weber's focus on bureaucracy in fact cuts across political ideologies. Weber held that industrial societies of all political stripes become increasingly bureaucratized:

The objective indispensability of the once-existing apparatus, with its peculiar, "impersonal" character, means that the mechanism—in contrast to feudal orders based upon personal piety—is easily made to work for anybody who knows how to gain control over it. A rationally ordered system of officials continues to function smoothly after the enemy has occupied the area; he merely needs to change the top officials.[2]

The modern state is bureaucratic and Weber realizes the danger of bureaucratic officials, who possess superior technical and specialized knowledge, overstepping their bounds. Weber's analysis of bureaucracy provides a powerful tool for

1   Max Weber, *Political Writings*, ed. Peter Lassman and Ronald Speirs (Cambridge: Cambridge University Press, 1994) p. 311.

2   Max Weber, *From Max Weber: Essays in Sociology*, translated and edited by H.H. Gerth and C. Wright Mills (New York: Oxford University Press, Inc., 1946) p. 229.

understanding not only the terrors of the fascist and communist state—made possible by a dedicated administration—but also the apparatus of legal experts, accountants, and mid-level managers whose influence is so apparent in the modern corporation around most of the globe.

Fascism

Marxists were not the only ones to believe that the violent seizure of state power by a vanguard elite could be ideologically justified. Similar ideas can be seen amongst fascist theorists, such as Carl Schmitt and Giovanni Gentile, although of course they differed significantly from Marxists about the nature of the society that should then be constructed. For fascists, the key to transforming society was to build an overriding sense of belonging to a (typically) racially defined nation.

The rise of fascism had many sources.[1] The Treaty of Versailles symbolized for Germans the humiliation of World War I and brought with it the punitive war debts. The democratic Weimar Republic in Germany was torn by economic depression, mass unemployment, and political fragmentation. Italy was ravaged by similar conditions. When combined with the Bolshevik revolution in Russia, these factors led many to believe that communism would soon spread across Europe—and eventually the globe. As a result, many industrialists actively supported fascism as a bulwark against socialist revolution. Fascism did indeed provide a non-Marxist alternative for disaffected populations, swayed by organic nationalist mythology and militarist ambitions. Despite Mussolini's threats to march on Rome and seize power (an event which never occurred but was later mythologized as a *coup d'état* in fascist propaganda), fascism in Italy and Germany came to power largely through official channels.

Mussolini was appointed premier in 1922 and quickly worked to build a totalitarian state—a state that penetrated every aspect of private citizens' lives. Children were indoctrinated into the state ideology through education and compulsory recreation. The National Leisure Time Organization was formed to occupy adults when not at work. Networks of informers arose in conjunction with special police forces endowed with arbitrary powers. Similar institutions were created in Germany—the paramilitary Hitler

Youth organization prominent among them, as is vividly illustrated in Leni Riefenstahl's famous 1934 propaganda film *Triumph of the Will*. The SS gained increasing power, infiltrating private life and murdering dissenters. The Nuremberg laws of 1935 put into place a racist legal system that progressively stripped Jews of their positions, their rights, and their property—and led to the Holocaust.

Unlike Marxism, which has produced much work (beginning with Marx) of intellectual value, fascism has for the most part been intellectually barren. Fascism as a political ideology is characterized by extreme nationalism, statism, anti-communism, and corporatism. Under fascism, the nation is identified completely with the state. Individual autonomy is relentlessly subordinated to the state. Indeed, all organizations are viewed as organic extensions of the state—fascist corporatism does not abolish private property, but rather directs production through bureaucracy, often toward militaristic ends. Similarly, fascism rejects the socialist identification with social class, thought to divide loyalty from the nation (a plausible view, given the communist movement's internationalism). The fascist state is frequently identified with a charismatic leader. The state propaganda machine creates a cult of personality from which the state gains much of its authority. And finally, the fascist state tends to define nationalism in exclusionary, racial terms. Such was most notoriously the case, of course, with the virulent anti-Semitism of Nazi Germany. *Blut und boden* (blood and soil) was a rallying cry for the German fascists. Irrational appeals to the Spirit of the *Volk* (folk) personified by Hitler promoted the grotesque fantasy of racial purity that resulted in concentration camps, gas chambers, and six million deaths.

Schmitt

Carl Schmitt was best known during his own lifetime as the theorist of the Nazi state, and of the Nazi legal order in particular. Schmitt was an early supporter of the Nazi overthrow of the constitutional order of Weimar Germany, and wrote in support of Hitler's rise to power in 1933 and his use of violent means to consolidate that power. His work was also distinctly flavored with the anti-Semitism characteristic of the Nazi regime. If Hitler himself was Nazism's propagandist in chief (as author of *Mein Kampf*) and Martin Heidegger its philosopher, then Schmitt more than anyone was responsible for Nazi jurisprudence and political theory.

Schmitt's death in 1985 brought a renewal of interest in his work, not as the theorist of Nazism but as one of

---

1   Here we mainly discuss the German and Italian fascist regimes. Two other significant fascist states were Spain under Franco (1939–75), and Argentina under Peron (1946–55).

the twentieth century's most challenging critics of modern liberal democracy. Schmitt opposed the romantic individualism of early twentieth-century German culture. He saw in its pluralism a neglect of traditional authority and a reliance upon the whims of individual egos. Liberal individualism was, for Schmitt, a kind of aesthetic self-indulgence, embellishing individual identity with endless indeterminate conversations. Similarly, he saw parliamentary government as undisciplined in its reliance on open-ended deliberation, and falsely democratic, because only an educated elite would be capable of the free-ranging reasoning called for by public discussion of political ends. To genuinely include the disparate and conflicting interests of political society at large would undo the cultural and class affinities of elite parliamentarians that made polite discussion possible.

For Schmitt, what is distinctive about politics is not the accommodation and reciprocity of public deliberation, but the fundamental clash of friend and enemy. In other words, in order to define the political, Schmitt identifies a bi-polar contrast in one dimension of value: "friend" and "enemy" in politics is like "beautiful" and "ugly" in aesthetics. Though he acknowledges that this contrast is "not exhaustive," that other factors may come into play, nevertheless this is the core idea behind Schmitt's political thought.

The political enemy need not be morally evil or aesthetically ugly; he need not appear as an economic competitor, and it may even be advantageous to engage with him in business transactions. But he is, nevertheless, the other, the stranger, and it is sufficient for his nature that he is, in a specially intense way, something existentially different and alien.

Gentile

Just as Schmitt was the theorist of Nazism who later became known for his critique of liberalism, Giovanni Gentile was known as the philosopher of Italian fascism, but his philosophical writings are now remembered for other reasons. Gentile served as a supporter and apologist for Mussolini's regime, but his theoretical views had little influence on the course of fascist thought, and his renown as a philosopher came largely through his development of a version of Hegelian idealism that influenced the subsequent course of Italian philosophy.

Gentile himself was aware of the limited role of theory in the practice of fascism: "The truth is that the significance of Fascism is not to be measured in the special theoretical or practical theses that it takes up at one or another time."

In fact, the use of theoretical pronouncements in fascism simply serves as an expression of the will of the leader or party elite, and does not constitute an ideal standpoint from which to critique the success or shortcomings of political action. Political language takes the form of a directive, rather than expressing intellectual reflection or speculation:

> "intellectualism" [as "intellectualism" is understood by Fascists] divorces thought from action, science from life, the brain from the heart, and theory from practice. It is the posture of the talker and the skeptic, of the person who entrenches himself behind the maxim that it is one thing to say something and another thing to do it....

The role of centralized leadership in fascism strongly resembles the role of the Führer in Nazism, but the insistence by Gentile on the leadership role of a party vanguard to unify and subdue the plural interests of the "masses" echoes the vanguardism of Lenin: "it is almost impossible to conform the masses to the demands of an elite Party of vanguard morality. Such a conformity could only happen slowly, through education and reform." The totalitarian nature of fascism, like its Nazi and Marxist counterparts, is made explicit in Gentile's description of the scope and penetration of Fascist discipline and party structure into ordinary people's lives from childhood onward. A central goal of fascist organization is "to bring into the Party, and into the institutions created by the Party, all the people—commencing from their most tender years." Just as the Party extends into the details of ordinary life, it expands to fill all the public space, leaving no room for opposition or any institutional division of powers: "the Party's organization expands almost to the full extent of the State."

How then does fascism view the role of the people who it seeks to control? Individuals exist for the state as functional parts of a machinelike "whole" in a specialized division of labor by categories of production:

> The organic State sought to reach the individual as it could only find him, as he in fact is: as a specialized producer whose tasks moved him to associate himself with others of the same category, all belonging to the same unitary economic organism that is the nation.

Italian fascism was thus a form of corporatism, a way of thinking about the state as an organic unity of functionally distinct productive groupings. In the preceding passage, we see some echo of the roots of fascism in anarcho-syndicalism, the idea that organizations should be spontaneously self-forming according to their own criteria and interests. However, fascism constructs an overarching system of control that regulates these groups within the body politic so that all come under the unified will of the Party, as expressed in the dictates of Mussolini, *il Duce*.

Hayek

Given the range of ideologies discussed so far, it might seem that political debates in the first half of the twentieth century were divided between those who favored abolishing the state (anarchists) and those who wished to give it total control (Marxists and fascists). But in fact many theorists were concerned to defend the possibility of a constitutionally limited state, and to identify the dangers of all forms of totalitarian thinking. Two such thinkers were Friedrich von Hayek and Hannah Arendt. Both wrote in response to the horrors they witnessed emerging under Nazism and Communism, although they offered very different diagnoses and remedies.

After the trio of totalitarian ideologies—Marxism, Nazism, and Leninism—the work of Friedrich von Hayek provides a strikingly different view of the nature of order in a political system. Unlike totalitarian accounts of the centralization of power under the will of a supreme leader or party vanguard, Hayek provides an account of the rule of law in which abstract and impartial rules create a framework for personal freedom. Hayek is perhaps best known for his critique of socialism and defense of free markets, but the legal and political theory represented in this volume is part of a blistering critique of Carl Schmitt. Schmitt had distinguished between two contrasting approaches to law: normativism and decisionism. Normativism is the rule of abstract laws that do not take account of particular circumstances or objectives. Decisionism is a concept of government by will, by the specific dictates of a supreme authority. Not surprisingly, in his totalitarian arguments against liberalism and the rule of law, Schmitt developed a defense of "decisionism."

Hayek was profoundly opposed to Schmitt's view. He saw Schmitt as a principal engineer of Nazi legal doctrine and held him partly responsible for the spread of totalitarian ideas in Germany. But Hayek himself adopted a recognizable variant of Schmitt's distinction between normativism and decisionism, and made his mark by inverting Schmitt's

argument, and defending the rule of law against the commands of a central authority.[1] Hayek believed that Schmitt's defense of decisionism rested on a fundamental mistake about the nature of political order and how it is constituted. Hayek wrote that Schmitt's

> central belief, as he finally formulated it, is that ... law is not to consist of abstract rules which make possible the formation of a spontaneous order by the free action of individuals through limiting the range of their actions, but is to be the instrument of arrangement or organization by which the individual is made to serve concrete purposes. This is the inevitable outcome of an intellectual development in which the self-ordering forces of society and the role of law in an ordering mechanism are no longer understood.[2]

By contrast, Hayek argued that economic theory provided abundant evidence of the emergence of order through freely coordinated actions, "without deliberate organization by a commanding intelligence":

> The enemies of liberty have always based their arguments on the contention that order in human affairs requires that some should give orders and others obey. Much of the opposition to a system of freedom under general laws arises from the inability to conceive of an effective co-ordination of human activities without deliberate organization by a commanding intelligence. One of the achievements of economic theory has been to explain how such a mutual adjustment of the spontaneous activities of individuals is brought about by the market, provided that there is a known delimitation of the sphere of control of each individual. An understanding of that mechanism of mutual adjustment of individuals forms the most important part of the knowledge that ought to enter into the making of general rules limiting individual action.

1   See F. R. Cristi, "Hayek and Schmitt on the Rule of Law," *Canadian Journal of Political Science / Revue canadienne de science politique*, Vol. 17, No. 3. (Sep., 1984), pp. 521-35.

2   Friedrich von Hayek, *Law, Legislation and Liberty*, vol. 1: *Rules and Order* (Chicago: University of Chicago Press. 1971) p. 71. Quoted in Ibid., p. 530.

By making certain aspects of the practical environment pre-dictable, by protecting the interests of individuals from the incursions of others, and by denying the right of command concerning the particulars of human action, the rule of law enhances freedom. A system of law differs from a system of command by protecting individuals from unpredictable interference and thus creating conditions under which they can use their knowledge to enhance and pursue their indi-vidual interests. By tapping into the resources of experience and judgment of a whole people, a system of laws is more effective, more rational, and ultimately more orderly than rule by specific directives imposed from above.

Arendt

Totalitarians argue for the concentration of power in the hands of a leader or vanguard party; Hayek believed that or-der freely arises in the space for individual action created by a system of laws. Though their approaches are essentially op-posed, they share a common discourse of the relative merits of systems of law versus systems of command. It is fitting to close with a consideration of Hannah Arendt, whose work stands apart from all of them. Arendt distinguished between power, a capacity to implement political action that flows from the will of the people, and authority, a source of judg-ment that refers laws and political action to the founding principles of a society. The Roman Senate and the Supreme Court of the United States for Arendt were paradigmatic sources of authority. She believed that Marxism went wrong (among other ways) in failing to distinguish between power and authority; such a distinction was needed to uphold the legitimate founding principles of a stable political order. Marxists believed that they were witnessing the inevitable demise of an existing political order, and that the revolu-tion would reveal a new order, immanent in the ruins of the old, without any act of political establishment. The idea of "permanent revolution," for Arendt, indicated a fluid dynamic of change without the solid framework of a con-stituted political order, and thus there would be no space for public life. Continuous revolutionary movement would be a kind of endless pointlessness. By contrast, political order creates the conditions in which human meaning may emerge, by creating a shared public space in which words and deeds can be freely expressed and remembered:

> Power preserves the public realm and the space of appearance, and as such it is also the lifeblood of

the human artifice, which, unless it is the scene of action and speech, of the web of human affairs and relationships and the stories engendered by them, lacks its ultimate raison d'être. Without being talked about by men and without housing them, the world would not be a human artifice but a heap of unrelated things to which each iso-lated individual was at liberty to add one more object; without the human artifice to house them, human affairs would be as floating, as futile and vain, as the wanderings of nomad tribes.[1]

If authority is concerned with the preservation of the found-ing order of a political society, then power is concerned with its public activity. A distinctive feature of Arendt's political thought is the importance she placed upon political words and deeds, and not the policy intentions or consequences that flowed from them:

> the innermost meaning of the acted deed and the spoken word is independent of victory and defeat and must remain untouched by any eventual out-come, by their consequences for better or worse.[2]

The public realm for Arendt is a world of appearances, where words and deeds come into being and are judged and remembered. Authority and power are closely related, because the act of founding, and the authority to preserve it, is needed to create the public space where the drama of political action may take place and the experience of it be shared. The idea of political power as creating a public drama is not so far off the mark, and Arendt's critics often note the theatrical qualities, and lack of policy substance, inherent in her ideas. However, her focus on free public expression found a willing audience in Soviet-era Eastern Europe, where her work was widely read in samizdat, or underground, publications. The extraordinary wave of public protests and demonstrations that marked the Velvet Revolution in 1968 in the former Czechoslovakia, the fall of the Berlin Wall, and the collapse of communist regimes in 1989 was in some sense a manifestion of her ideas of public freedom, and may indeed have owed something to her idea of political power.

---

1   Hannah Arendt, *The Human Condition* (Chicago, IL: The Univer-sity of Chicago Press, 1956) p. 179.
2   Ibid., p. 187.

EMMA GOLDMAN
(1869–1940)

Born to a lower middle-class family in Russian-dominated Lithuania, Emma Goldman was educated in Russia and emigrated to Rochester, New York, in 1885 to escape increasing anti-Semitism and political repression. The hanging of four anarchists after the Haymarket Riot in Chicago in 1886 drew her attention to the international anarchist movement, and soon she became a leading writer and speaker on its behalf, constantly in trouble with the authorities. In 1893 she was jailed for inciting a riot in a speech in which she urged unemployed workers: "Ask for work. If they do not give you work, ask for bread. If they do not give you work or bread, take bread." In 1901 she was again arrested, this time for having had two brief conversations with Leon Czolgosz, the anarchist assassin of President McKinley—a man much more in the spirit of the cartoon image of the anarchist, and one whose values were quite far from those of Goldman. On that occasion, she was not convicted, but in 1916 she served a jail sentence for distributing birth control literature. In 1917 she began two years imprisonment for conspiring to obstruct the World War I draft; on her release, she was deported to the newly created Soviet Union. The director of her deportation hearing, J. Edgar Hoover, called her "one of the most dangerous anarchists in America." When not in jail, she lectured widely in the US, denouncing conventional morality, agitating for freedom of speech, defending the rights of homosexuals, denouncing the oppression of women in the traditional monogamous patriarchal marriage, and advocating sexual freedom.

In the Soviet Union she soon became disillusioned with the Bolshevik revolutionary movement's penchant for violence and intolerance of political dissent. Leaving there for England and France, she became an ardent anti-Soviet agitator during the 1920s. During the 30s she acted as publicist and fund-raiser for the anarcho-syndicalists in the Spanish civil war (one of the many groups on the Republican side who resisted the fascist Nationalist army of Francisco Fran-

co), blaming their defeat on the Communists. She died in Toronto in 1940 while on a trip raising money for Spanish and other refugees from Fascism.

Goldman's political views were not the result of an overarching theory, but were rather the result of strong predilections and feelings, directed toward particular concrete social matters. Anarchism, the position with which she is most closely identified, came in many forms, and Goldman's is not easily placed within any of them. She does share with all anarchists a strong distaste for authority and a rejection of the political state, and, with many of them, a moral condemnation of the repressive and inegalitarian features of capitalism. The ideal society, she thought, would provide maximum freedom for individualistic self-expression. In her view, authoritarian society is responsible for antisocial reactions; the minimal social organization that was necessary for collective activity would arise from the natural tendency to cooperate of people freed from the artificial strictures of strong government.

Her influence was strong in several directions. As a socialist who rejected both capitalism and, as it was applied in the Soviet Union under Lenin and Stalin, Marxism, she became a hero of the New Left, who often looked to her in their periodic attempts to find an ideology that would provide fresh expression for principles of liberty, equality, and social justice. She was an early crusader against many of the repressive aspects of conventional morality, and a revolutionary especially in the cause of sexual freedom. And she is rightly seen as a central figure in early twentieth-century feminism.

◆　◆　◆　◆　◆

from Anarchism: What It Really Stands For (1910)

Anarchy

Ever reviled, accursed, ne'er understood,
　　Thou art the grisly terror of our age.
"Wreck of all order," cry the multitude,
　　"Art thou, and war and murder's endless rage."
O, let them cry. To them that ne'er have striven
　　The truth that lies behind a word to find,
To them the word's right meaning was not given.
　　They shall continue blind among the blind.
But thou, O word, so clear, so strong, so pure,
　　Thou sayest all which I for goal have taken.
I give thee to the future! Thine secure
　　When each at least unto himself shall waken.
Comes it in sunshine? In the tempest's thrill?
　　I cannot tell—but it the earth shall see!
I am an Anarchist! Wherefore I will
　　Not rule, and also ruled I will not be I

　　　　　　　　　　　　　　John Henry MacKay[1]

The history of human growth and development is at the same time the history of the terrible struggle of every new idea heralding the approach of a brighter dawn. In its tenacious hold on tradition, the Old has never hesitated to make use of the foulest and cruelest means to stay the advent of the New, in whatever form or period the latter may have asserted itself. Nor need we retrace our steps into the distant past to realize the enormity of opposition, difficulties, and hardships placed in the path of every progressive idea. The rack, the thumbscrew, and the knout are still with us; so are the convict's garb and the social wrath, all conspiring against the spirit that is serenely marching on.

Anarchism could not hope to escape the fate of all other ideas of innovation. Indeed, as the most revolutionary and uncompromising innovator, Anarchism must needs meet with the combined ignorance and venom of the world it aims to reconstruct.

To deal even remotely with all that is being said and done against Anarchism would necessitate the writing of a whole volume. I shall therefore meet only two of the principal objections. In so doing, I shall attempt to elucidate what Anarchism really stands for.

The strange phenomenon of the opposition to Anarchism is that it brings to light the relation between so-called intelligence and ignorance. And yet this is not so very strange when we consider the relativity of all things. The ignorant mass has in its favor that it makes no pretense of knowledge or tolerance. Acting, as it always does, by mere impulse, its reasons are like those of a child. "Why?" "Because." Yet the opposition of the uneducated to Anarchism deserves the same consideration as that of the intelligent man.

What, then, are the objections? First, Anarchism is impractical, though a beautiful ideal. Second, Anarchism stands for violence and destruction, hence it must be repudiated as vile and dangerous. Both the intelligent man and the ignorant mass judge not from a thorough knowledge of the subject, but either from hearsay or false interpretation.

A practical scheme, says Oscar Wilde, is either one already in existence, or a scheme that could be carried out under the existing conditions; but it is exactly the existing conditions that one objects to, and any scheme that could accept these conditions is wrong and foolish.[2] The true criterion of the practical, therefore, is not whether the latter can keep intact the wrong or foolish; rather is it whether the scheme has vitality enough to leave the stagnant waters of the old, and build, as well as sustain, new life. In the light of this conception, Anarchism is indeed practical. More than any other idea, it is helping to do away with the wrong and foolish; more than any other idea, it is building and sustaining new life.

1　*John Henry Mackay*　(1864–1933) Scottish-born anarchist, who spent most of his life in Germany. Known for his political writing and his advocacy of gay rights.

2　*A practical scheme … wrong and foolish*　In "The Soul of Man Under Socialism" by Oscar Wilde (1854–1900), Irish author known for his barbed wit: "It will, of course, be said that such a scheme as is set forth here [freeing artists from governmental control] is quite unpractical, and goes against human nature. This is perfectly true. It is unpractical, and it goes against human nature. This is why it is worth carrying out, and that is why one proposes it. For what is a practical scheme? *A practical scheme is either a scheme that is already in existence, or a scheme that could be carried out under existing conditions.* But it is exactly the existing conditions that one objects to, and any scheme that could accept these conditions is wrong and foolish. The conditions will be done away with, and human nature will change."

The emotions of the ignorant man are continuously kept at a pitch by the most blood-curdling stories about Anarchism. Not a thing too outrageous to be employed against this philosophy and its exponents. Therefore Anarchism represents to the unthinking what the proverbial bad man does to the child,—a black monster bent on swallowing everything; in short, destruction and violence.

Destruction and violence! How is the ordinary man to know that the most violent element in society is ignorance; that its power of destruction is the very thing Anarchism is combating? Nor is he aware that Anarchism, whose roots, as it were, are part of nature's forces, destroys, not healthful tissue, but parasitic growths that feed on the life's essence of society. It is merely clearing the soil from weeds and sagebrush, that it may eventually bear healthy fruit.

Someone has said that it requires less mental effort to condemn than to think. The widespread mental indolence, so prevalent in society, proves this to be only too true. Rather than to go to the bottom of any given idea, to examine into its origin and meaning, most people will either condemn it altogether, or rely on some superficial or prejudicial definition of non-essentials.

Anarchism urges man to think, to investigate, to analyze every proposition; but that the brain capacity of the average reader be not taxed too much, I also shall begin with a definition, and then elaborate on the latter.

ANARCHISM:—The philosophy of a new social order based on liberty unrestricted by man-made law; the theory that all forms of government rest on violence, and are therefore wrong and harmful, as well as unnecessary.

The new social order rests, of course, on the materialistic basis of life; but while all Anarchists agree that the main evil today is an economic one, they maintain that the solution of that evil can be brought about only through the consideration of *every phase* of life,—individual, as well as the collective; the internal, as well as the external phases.

A thorough perusal of the history of human development will disclose two elements in bitter conflict with each other; elements that are only now beginning to be understood, not as foreign to each other, but as closely related and truly harmonious, if only placed in proper environment: the individual and social instincts. The individual and society have waged a relentless and bloody battle for ages, each striving for supremacy, because each was blind to the value and importance of the other. The individual and social instincts,—the one a most potent factor for individual endeavor, for growth, aspiration, self-realization; the other an equally potent factor for mutual helpfulness and social well-being.

The explanation of the storm raging within the individual, and between him and his surroundings, is not far to seek. The primitive man, unable to understand his being, much less the unity of all life, felt himself absolutely dependent on blind, hidden forces ever ready to mock and taunt him. Out of that attitude grew the religious concepts of man as a mere speck of dust dependent on superior powers on high, who can only be appeased by complete surrender. All the early sagas rest on that idea, which continues to be the *Leitmotiv*[1] of the biblical tales dealing with the relation of man to God, to the State, to society. Again and again the same motif, *man is nothing, the powers are everything*. Thus Jehovah would only endure man on condition of complete surrender. Man can have all the glories of the earth, but he must not become conscious of himself. The State, society, and moral laws all sing the same refrain: Man can have all the glories of the earth, but he must not become conscious of himself.

Anarchism is the only philosophy which brings to man the consciousness of himself; which maintains that God, the State, and society are non-existent, that their promises are null and void, since they can be fulfilled only through man's subordination. Anarchism is therefore the teacher of the unity of life; not merely in nature, but in man. There is no conflict between the individual and the social instincts, any more than there is between the heart and the lungs: the one the receptacle of a precious life essence, the other the repository of the element that keeps the essence pure and strong. The individual is the heart of society, conserving the essence of social life; society is the lungs which are distributing the element to keep the life essence—that is, the individual—pure and strong.

"The one thing of value in the world," says Emerson, "is the active soul; this every man contains within him. The soul active sees absolute truth and utters truth and creates."[2] In other words, the individual instinct is the thing of value in the world. It is the true soul that sees and creates the truth alive, out of which is to come a still greater truth, the re-born social soul.

---

1 *Leitmotiv* German: A recurring theme.

2 *The one thing … truth and creates* From the speech "The American Scholar," delivered in Cambridge MA in 1837 by Ralph Waldo Emerson (1803–82), American writer and philosopher.

Anarchism is the great liberator of man from the phantoms that have held him captive; it is the arbiter and pacifier of the two forces for individual and social harmony. To accomplish that unity, Anarchism has declared war on the pernicious influences which have so far prevented the harmonious blending of individual and social instincts, the individual and society.

Religion, the dominion of the human mind; Property, the dominion of human needs; and Government, the dominion of human conduct, represent the stronghold of man's enslavement and all the horrors it entails. Religion! How it dominates man's mind, how it humiliates and degrades his soul. God is everything, man is nothing, says religion. But out of that nothing God has created a kingdom so despotic, so tyrannical, so cruel, so terribly exacting that naught but gloom and tears and blood have ruled the world since gods began. Anarchism rouses man to rebellion against this black monster. Break your mental fetters, says Anarchism to man, for not until you think and judge for yourself will you get rid of the dominion of darkness, the greatest obstacle to all progress.

Property, the dominion of man's needs, the denial of the right to satisfy his needs. Time was when property claimed a divine right, when it came to man with the same refrain, even as religion, "Sacrifice! Abnegate! Submit!" The spirit of Anarchism has lifted man from his prostrate position. He now stands erect, with his face toward the light. He has learned to see the insatiable, devouring, devastating nature of property, and he is preparing to strike the monster dead.

"Property is robbery," said the great French Anarchist Proudhon.[1] Yes, but without risk and danger to the robber. Monopolizing the accumulated efforts of man, property has robbed him of his birthright, and has turned him loose a pauper and an outcast. Property has not even the time-worn excuse that man does not create enough to satisfy all needs. The A B C student of economics knows that the productivity of labor within the last few decades far exceeds normal demand. But what are normal demands to an abnormal institution? The only demand that property recognizes is its own gluttonous appetite for greater wealth, because wealth means power; the power to subdue, to crush, to exploit, the power to enslave, to outrage, to degrade. America is particularly boastful of her great power, her enormous national wealth. Poor America, of what avail is all her wealth, if the individuals comprising the nation are wretchedly poor? If they live in squalor, in filth, in crime, with hope and joy gone, a homeless, soilless army of human prey.

It is generally conceded that unless the returns of any business venture exceed the cost, bankruptcy is inevitable. But those engaged in the business of producing wealth have not yet learned even this simple lesson. Every year the cost of production in human life is growing larger (50,000 killed, 100,000 wounded in America last year); the returns to the masses, who help to create wealth, are ever getting smaller. Yet America continues to be blind to the inevitable bankruptcy of our business of production. Nor is this the only crime of the latter. Still more fatal is the crime of turning the producer into a mere particle of a machine, with less will and decision than his master of steel and iron. Man is being robbed not merely of the products of his labor, but of the power of free initiative, of originality, and the interest in, or desire for, the things he is making.

Real wealth consists in things of utility and beauty, in things that help to create strong, beautiful bodies and surroundings inspiring to live in. But if man is doomed to wind cotton around a spool, or dig coal, or build roads for thirty years of his life, there can be no talk of wealth. What he gives to the world is only gray and hideous things, reflecting a dull and hideous existence,—too weak to live, too cowardly to die. Strange to say, there are people who extol this deadening method of centralized production as the proudest achievement of our age. They fail utterly to realize that if we are to continue in machine subserviency, our slavery is more complete than was our bondage to the King. They do not want to know that centralization is not only the death-knell of liberty, but also of health and beauty, of art and science, all these being impossible in a clock-like, mechanical atmosphere.

Anarchism cannot but repudiate such a method of production: its goal is the freest possible expression of all the latent powers of the individual. Oscar Wilde defines a perfect personality as "one who develops under perfect conditions, who is not wounded, maimed, or in danger."[2] A perfect personality, then, is only possible in a state of society where

---

1   *Proudhon*   Pierre-Joseph Proudhon (1809–65), French political philosopher, considered the founder of philosophical anarchism and the first to call himself an "anarchist." This famous quotation, more usually translated "property is theft," is from *Qu'est-ce que la propriété? Recherche sur le principe du droit et du gouvernement* (*What is Property? Or, an Inquiry into the Principle of Right and Government*, 1840).

2   *one who develops … in danger*   In Wilde, "The Soul of Man Under Socialism."

man is free to choose the mode of work, the conditions of work, and the freedom to work. One to whom the making of a table, the building of a house, or the tilling of the soil, is what the painting is to the artist and the discovery to the scientist,—the result of inspiration, of intense longing, and deep interest in work as a creative force. That being the ideal of Anarchism, its economic arrangements must consist of voluntary productive and distributive associations, gradually developing into free communism, as the best means of producing with the least waste of human energy. Anarchism, however, also recognizes the right of the individual, or numbers of individuals, to arrange at all times for other forms of work, in harmony with their tastes and desires.

Such free display of human energy being possible only under complete individual and social freedom, Anarchism directs its forces against the third and greatest foe of all social equality; namely, the State, organized authority, or statutory law,—the dominion of human conduct.

Just as religion has fettered the human mind, and as property, or the monopoly of things, has subdued and stifled man's needs, so has the State enslaved his spirit, dictating every phase of conduct. "All government in essence," says Emerson, "is tyranny." It matters not whether it is government by divine right or majority rule. In every instance its aim is the absolute subordination of the individual.

Referring to the American government, the greatest American Anarchist, David Thoreau, said: "Government, what is it but a tradition, though a recent one, endeavoring to transmit itself unimpaired to posterity, but each instance losing its integrity; it has not the vitality and force of a single living man. Law never made man a whit more just; and by means of their respect for it, even the well disposed are daily made agents of injustice."[1]

Indeed, the keynote of government is injustice. With the arrogance and self-sufficiency of the King who could do no wrong, governments ordain, judge, condemn, and punish the most insignificant offenses, while maintaining themselves by the greatest of all offenses, the annihilation of individual liberty. Thus Ouida[2] is right when she maintains that "the State only aims at instilling those qualities in its public by which its demands are obeyed, and its exchequer is filled. Its highest attainment is the reduction of mankind to clockwork. In its atmosphere all those finer and more delicate liberties, which require treatment and spacious expansion, inevitably dry up and perish. The State requires a taxpaying machine in which there is no hitch, an exchequer in which there is never a deficit, and a public, monotonous, obedient, colorless, spiritless, moving humbly like a flock of sheep along a straight high road between two walls."

Yet even a flock of sheep would resist the chicanery of the State, if it were not for the corruptive, tyrannical, and oppressive methods it employs to serve its purposes. Therefore Bakunin[3] repudiates the State as synonymous with the surrender of the liberty of the individual or small minorities,—the destruction of social relationship, the curtailment, or complete denial even, of life itself, for its own aggrandizement. The State is the altar of political freedom and, like the religious altar, it is maintained for the purpose of human sacrifice.

In fact, there is hardly a modern thinker who does not agree that government, organized authority, or the State, is necessary *only* to maintain or protect property and monopoly. It has proven efficient in that function only.

Even George Bernard Shaw, who hopes for the miraculous from the State under Fabianism,[4] nevertheless admits that "it is at present a huge machine for robbing and slave-driving of the poor by brute force." This being the case, it is hard to see why the clever prefacer wishes to uphold the State after poverty shall have ceased to exist.

Unfortunately there are still a number of people who continue in the fatal belief that government rests on natural laws, that it maintains social order and harmony, that it diminishes crime, and that it prevents the lazy man from fleecing his fellows. I shall therefore examine these contentions.

A natural law is that factor in man which asserts itself freely and spontaneously without any external force, in harmony with the requirements of nature. For instance, the demand for nutrition, for sex gratification, for light, air, and

1   *Government, what is it … agents of injustice*   From "Civil Disobedience," part 1.

2   *Ouida*   The pen name of Maria Louise Ramé (1839–1908), English writer known primarily as a novelist, but also author of libertarian essays during the 1880s. This quotation is from her essay "The State as an Immoral Teacher," *North American Review*, Volume 153, pp. 193–204.

3   *Bakunin*   Mikhail Alexandrovich Bakunin (1814–76), Russian revolutionary, important early figure in modern anarchism and libertarian socialism.

4   *George Bernard Shaw … Fabianism*   Shaw (1856–1950) was an Irish dramatist, also known for his writings advocating socialism, women's rights, and vegetarianism. He was among the founders of the British Fabian Society, a moderate middle-class socialist movement advocating non-violent gradual change.

exercise, is a natural law. But its expression needs not the machinery of government, needs not the club, the gun, the handcuff, or the prison. To obey such laws, if we may call it obedience, requires only spontaneity and free opportunity. That governments do not maintain themselves through such harmonious factors is proven by the terrible array of violence, force, and coercion all governments use in order to live. Thus Blackstone[1] is right when he says, "Human laws are invalid, because they are contrary to the laws of nature."

Unless it be the order of Warsaw after the slaughter of thousands of people, it is difficult to ascribe to governments any capacity for order or social harmony. Order derived through submission and maintained by terror is not much of a safe guaranty; yet that is the only "order" that governments have ever maintained. True social harmony grows naturally out of solidarity of interests. In a society where those who always work never have anything, while those who never work enjoy everything, solidarity of interests is non-existent; hence social harmony is but a myth. The only way organized authority meets this grave situation is by extending still greater privileges to those who have already monopolized the earth, and by still further enslaving the disinherited masses. Thus the entire arsenal of government—laws, police, soldiers, the courts, legislatures, prisons,—is strenuously engaged in "harmonizing" the most antagonistic elements in society.

The most absurd apology for authority and law is that they serve to diminish crime. Aside from the fact that the State is itself the greatest criminal, breaking every written and natural law, stealing in the form of taxes, killing in the form of war and capital punishment, it has come to an absolute standstill in coping with crime. It has failed utterly to destroy or even minimize the horrible scourge of its own creation.

Crime is naught but misdirected energy. So long as every institution of today, economic, political, social, and moral, conspires to misdirect human energy into wrong channels; so long as most people are out of place doing the things they hate to do, living a life they loathe to live, crime will be inevitable, and all the laws on the statutes can only increase, but never do away with, crime. What does society, as it exists today, know of the process of despair, the poverty, the horrors, the fearful struggle the human soul must pass on its way to crime and degradation. Who that knows this terrible process can fail to see the truth in these words of Peter Kropotkin:[2]

"Those who will hold the balance between the benefits thus attributed to law and punishment and the degrading effect of the latter on humanity; those who will estimate the torrent of depravity poured abroad in human society by the informer, favored by the Judge even, and paid for in clinking cash by governments, under the pretext of aiding to unmask crime; those who will go within prison walls and there see what human beings become when deprived of liberty, when subjected to the care of brutal keepers, to coarse, cruel words, to a thousand stinging, piercing humiliations, will agree with us that the entire apparatus of prison and punishment is an abomination which ought to be brought to an end."

The deterrent influence of law on the lazy man is too absurd to merit consideration. If society were only relieved of the waste and expense of keeping a lazy class, and the equally great expense of the paraphernalia of protection this lazy class requires, the social tables would contain an abundance for all, including even the occasional lazy individual. Besides, it is well to consider that laziness results either from special privileges, or physical and mental abnormalities. Our present insane system of production fosters both, and the most astounding phenomenon is that people should want to work at all now. Anarchism aims to strip labor of its deadening, dulling aspect, of its gloom and compulsion. It aims to make work an instrument of joy, of strength, of color, of real harmony, so that the poorest sort of a man should find in work both recreation and hope.

To achieve such an arrangement of life, government, with its unjust, arbitrary, repressive measures, must be done away with. At best it has but imposed one single mode of life upon all, without regard to individual and social variations and needs. In destroying government and statutory laws, Anarchism proposes to rescue the self-respect and independence of the individual from all restraint and invasion by authority. Only in freedom can man grow to his full stature. Only in freedom will he learn to think and move, and give the very best in him. Only in freedom will he realize

---

1   *Blackstone* Sir William Blackstone (1723–80), English lawyer and legal scholar; his *Commentaries on the Laws of England* (first published 1765–69) remains an important history and analysis of English common law.

2   *Peter Kropotkin* Prince Peter (Pyotr) Alexeyevich Kropotkin (1842–1921), leading Russian anarchist theorist, one of the first to advocate anarchist communism, and an important influence on Goldman. He considers prisons in his book *In Russian and French Prisons* (1887).

the true force of the social bonds which knit men together, and which are the true foundation of a normal social life.

But what about human nature? Can it be changed? And if not, will it endure under Anarchism?

Poor human nature, what horrible crimes have been committed in thy name! Every fool, from king to policeman, from the flatheaded parson to the visionless dabbler in science, presumes to speak authoritatively of human nature. The greater the mental charlatan, the more definite his insistence on the wickedness and weaknesses of human nature. Yet, how can any one speak of it today, with every soul in a prison, with every heart fettered, wounded, and maimed?

John Burroughs[1] has stated that experimental study of animals in captivity is absolutely useless. Their character, their habits, their appetites undergo a complete transformation when torn from their soil in field and forest. With human nature caged in a narrow space, whipped daily into submission, how can we speak of its potentialities?

Freedom, expansion, opportunity, and, above all, peace and repose, alone can teach us the real dominant factors of human nature and all its wonderful possibilities.

Anarchism, then, really stands for the liberation of the human mind from the dominion of religion; the liberation of the human body from the dominion of property; liberation from the shackles and restraint of government. Anarchism stands for a social order based on the free grouping of individuals for the purpose of producing real social wealth; an order that will guarantee to every human being free access to the earth and full enjoyment of the necessities of life, according to individual desires, tastes, and inclinations.

---

1   *John Burroughs* American naturalist and writer of extremely popular essays on nature (1837–1921).

V.I. LENIN
(1870–1924)

Vladimir Ilyich Lenin was one of the most significant political figures of the twentieth century; by radicalizing the Russian Revolution, he became the first leader of the Soviet Union. Over the course of his life, Lenin wrote many books and hundreds of articles. His early composition "What Is To Be Done?" served as a blueprint for adapting ideas derived from the works of Marx and Engels to the specific circumstances of Russia in the early twentieth century. As an expression of how to make Marx's theoretical ideas more practical, it inspired revolutionaries not only in Russia, but also around the world.

Lenin was born Vladimir Ilyich Ulyanov in Simbirsk, Russia (now named Ulyanovsk in his honor) on 22 April 1870. His father was a prosperous and highly ranked bureaucrat in the education system. Despite his position within the Czar's autocratic government, he was a supporter of a more democratic system. When Lenin was fifteen, his father died suddenly. A year later Lenin's older brother was arrested, convicted, and executed for plotting to kill Czar Alexander III. At age seventeen Lenin began university, but was expelled within a few months for his involvement in protests against the government. He then enrolled in St. Petersburg University, from which he received a law degree in 1891. It was during this time that he first read the writings of Karl Marx, as well as Chernyshevsky's socialist novel *What Is To Be Done?* Over the next several years Lenin became more politically involved; he founded the League of Struggle in 1895, and from 1897-1900 he was exiled to Siberia for his anti-government activities.

After his return from Siberia, Lenin produced a number of political writings, founded a newspaper, and, like many other revolutionary figures, adopted a pseudonym. As V.I. Lenin, he published "What Is To Be Done?" in March 1902. He became the leader of the Bolshevik political party and played a leading role in the overthrow of Czar Nicholas II in 1917. Shortly thereafter Lenin officially became the leader of the new Soviet Union. During this period until his death on 21 January 1924, Lenin erected the foundations of a totalitarian state based on his interpretation of Marxist ideas. Though some have portrayed the early Soviet Union as having been more or less free of the brutal cruelty that characterized the later Stalin era, recent archival research has shown beyond dispute that it was Lenin who established the prison camps, crushed the intelligentsia, and eliminated any trace of a free press. He also pioneered the use of murderous purges and famine as a political weapon—a weapon that Josef Stalin would later perfect.

Like Marx, Lenin rejected non-revolutionary forms of socialism that argued for democratic reform from within capitalism. Unlike Marx, Lenin had little faith in the proletariat achieving class consciousness on their own and spontaneously rising up against the bourgeoisie. Instead, Lenin advocated a revolution led by a vanguard party—an intellectual class of professional, full-time political activists. This vanguard would establish a centralized government with rigid party discipline to educate the proletariat and dispel capitalist indoctrination.

Lenin's views about the vanguard were connected to his theory of imperialism, which is perhaps his most lasting contribution to political theory. Marx argued that communism could only arise after a capitalist society had provided the necessary abundance. Once the workers realized that they were contributing the labor, but not reaping its riches, they would revolt. In contrast, Lenin argued that capitalism's highest stage was in fact imperialism, under which capitalist, industrial states dominated foreign territories, expropriated their resources, and exploited their workers. In Lenin's view, imperialism served to appease at least part of the working class in industrial states, and thus allowed the capitalists to retain power. As long as imperialism endured, Lenin believed, a proletarian revolution would not occur in developed states. Rather, proletarian revolution could happen in an underdeveloped state—such as early twentieth-century Russia—under the lead of a vanguard party.

Lenin's views have been centrally important to revolutionary movements and to communist governments in many countries (including China, Cuba, Vietnam, and Laos). How much longer their influence will extend is still unclear; in recent years, many formerly communist regimes have been moving toward capitalism and democracy. Lenin's analyses of capitalism and imperialism still contain important insights, though relatively few social and political theorists openly endorse his authoritarianism or his political methods.

◆ ◆ ◆ ◆ ◆

from *What is to Be Done?* (1902)

1: *Dogmatism and "Freedom of Criticism"*

D. Engels on the Importance of Theoretical Struggle

… Without revolutionary theory there can be no revolutionary movement. This idea cannot be insisted upon too strongly at a time when the fashionable preaching of opportunism goes hand in hand with an infatuation for the narrowest forms of practical activity. Yet, for Russian Social-Democrats the importance of theory is enhanced by three other circumstances, which are often forgotten: first, by the fact that our Party is only in process of formation, its features are only just becoming defined, and it has as yet far from settled accounts with the other trends of revolutionary thought that threaten to divert the movement from the correct path. On the contrary, precisely the very recent past was marked by a revival of non-Social-Democratic revolutionary trends (an eventuation regarding which Axelrod[1] long ago warned the Economists). Under these circumstances, what at first sight appears to be an "unimportant" error may lead to most deplorable consequences, and only short-sighted people can consider factional disputes and a strict

differentiation between shades of opinion inopportune or superfluous. The fate of Russian Social-Democracy for very many years to come may depend on the strengthening of one or the other "shade."

Secondly, the Social-Democratic movement is in its very essence an international movement. This means, not only that we must combat national chauvinism, but that an incipient movement in a young country can be successful only if it makes use of the experiences of other countries. In order to make use of these experiences it is not enough merely to be acquainted with them, or simply to copy out the latest resolutions. What is required is the ability to treat these experiences critically and to test them independently. He who realises how enormously the modern working-class movement has grown and branched out will understand what a reserve of theoretical forces and political (as well as revolutionary) experience is required to carry out this task.

Thirdly, the national tasks of Russian Social-Democracy are such as have never confronted any other socialist party in the world. We shall have occasion further on to deal with the political and organisational duties which the task of emancipating the whole people from the yoke of autocracy imposes upon us. At this point, we wish to state only that the *role of vanguard fighter can be fulfilled only by a party that is guided by the most advanced theory.*

…

2: *The Spontaneity of the Masses and the Consciousness of the Social-Democrats*

A. The Beginning of the Spontaneous Upsurge

… In the previous chapter we pointed out how *universally* absorbed the educated youth of Russia was in the theories of Marxism in the middle of the nineties. In the same period the strikes that followed the famous St. Petersburg industrial war of 1896[2] assumed a similar general character. Their spread over the whole of Russia clearly showed the depth of the newly awakening popular movement, and if we are to speak of the "spontaneous element" then, of course, it is this strike movement which, first and foremost,

---

1   *Axelrod* Lyubov Isaakovna Axelrod (1868–1946), Marxist philosopher and Russian revolutionary.

2   *St. Petersburg industrial war of 1896* Strikes occasioned in May-June 1896 when employers refused to pay wages for holidays for the coronation of Emperor Nicholas II (who was executed along with his family by the Bolsheviks after the Russian Revolution of 1917).

must be regarded as spontaneous. But there is spontaneity and spontaneity. Strikes occurred in Russia in the seventies and sixties (and even in the first half of the nineteenth century), and they were accompanied by the "spontaneous" destruction of machinery, etc. Compared with these "revolts," the strikes of the nineties might even be described as "conscious," to such an extent do they mark the progress which the working-class movement made in that period. This shows that the "spontaneous element," in essence, represents nothing more nor less than consciousness in an *embryonic form*. Even the primitive revolts expressed the awakening of consciousness to a certain extent. The workers were losing their age-long faith in the permanence of the system which oppressed them and began—I shall not say to understand, but to sense—the necessity for collective resistance, definitely abandoning their slavish submission to the authorities. But this was, nevertheless, more in the nature of outbursts of desperation and vengeance than of *struggle*. The strikes of the nineties revealed far greater flashes of consciousness; definite demands were advanced, the strike was carefully timed, known cases and instances in other places were discussed, etc. The revolts were simply the resistance of the oppressed, whereas the systematic strikes represented the class struggle in embryo, but only in embryo. Taken by themselves, these strikes were simply trade union struggles, not yet Social Democratic struggles. They marked the awakening antagonisms between workers and employers; but the workers, were not, and could not be, conscious of the irreconcilable antagonism of their interests to the whole of the modern political and social system, i.e., theirs was not yet Social Democratic consciousness. In this sense, the strikes of the nineties, despite the enormous progress they represented as compared with the "revolts," remained a purely spontaneous movement.

We have said that *there could not have been* Social-Democratic consciousness among the workers. It would have to be brought to them from without. The history of all countries shows that the working class, exclusively by its own effort, is able to develop only trade union consciousness, i.e., the conviction that it is necessary to combine in unions, fight the employers, and strive to compel the government to pass necessary labour legislation, etc.[1] The theory of socialism, however, grew out of the philosophic, historical, and eco-

nomic theories elaborated by educated representatives of the propertied classes, by intellectuals. By their social status the founders of modern scientific socialism, Marx and Engels, themselves belonged to the bourgeois intelligentsia. In the very same way, in Russia, the theoretical doctrine of Social Democracy arose altogether independently of the spontaneous growth of the working-class movement; it arose as a natural and inevitable outcome of the development of thought among the revolutionary socialist intelligentsia....

[...]

B. Bowing to Spontaneity

Since there can be no talk of an independent ideology formulated by the working masses themselves in the process of their movement,[2] the only choice is—either bourgeois or socialist ideology. There is no middle course (for mankind has not created a "third" ideology, and, moreover, in a society torn by class antagonisms there can never be a non-class or an above-class ideology). Hence, to belittle the socialist ideology *in any way, to turn aside from it in the slightest degree* means to strengthen bourgeois ideology. There is much talk of spontaneity. But the *spontaneous* development of the working-class movement leads to its subordination to bourgeois ideology, *to its development along the lines of the Credo programme;* for the spontaneous working-class movement is trade-unionism, is *Nur-Gewerkschaftlerei*,[3] and trade unionism means the ideological enslavement of the workers by the bourgeoisie. Hence, our task, the task of Social-Dem-

---

1   *the conviction ... labour legislation, etc.*   [Lenin's note] Trade-unionism does not exclude "politics" altogether, as some imagine. Trade unions have always conducted some political (but not So-cial-Democratic) agitation and struggle.

2   *working masses ... their ideology* [Lenin's note] This does not mean, of course, that the workers have no part in creating such an ideology. They take part, however, not as workers, but as socialist theoreticians, as Proudhons and Weitlings; in other words, they take part only when they are able, and to the extent that they are able, more or less, to acquire the knowledge of their age and develop that knowledge. But in order that working men *may succeed in this more often*, every effort must be made to raise the level of the consciousness of the workers in general; it is necessary that the workers do not confine themselves to the artificially restricted limits of *literature for workers* but that they learn to an increasing degree to master the *general literature*. It would be even truer to say "are not confined," instead of "do not confine themselves," because the workers themselves wish to read and do read all that is written for the intelligentsia, and only a few (bad) intellectuals believe that it is enough for workers to be told a few things about factory conditions and to have repeated to them over and over again what has long been known.

3   *Nur-Gewerkschaftlerei* German: Mere trade unionism.

ocracy, is *to combat spontaneity, to divert* the working-class movement from this spontaneous, trade-unionist striving to come under the wing of the bourgeoisie, and to bring it under the wing of revolutionary Social Democracy....

3: *Trade-Unionist Politics and Social-Democratic Politics*

E. The Working Class As Vanguard Fighter For Democracy

We have seen that the conduct of the broadest political agitation and, consequently, of all-sided political exposures is an absolutely necessary and a *paramount* task of our activity, if this activity is to be truly Social-Democratic. However, we arrived at this conclusion solely on the grounds of the pressing needs of the working class for political knowledge and political training. But such a presentation of the question is too narrow, for it ignores the general democratic tasks of Social-Democracy, in particular of present-day Russian Social-Democracy. In order to explain the point more concretely we shall approach the subject from an aspect that is "nearest" to the Economist, namely, from the practical aspect. "Everyone agrees" that it is necessary to develop the political consciousness of the working class. The question is, *how* that is to be done and what is required to do it. The economic struggle merely "impels" the workers to realise the government's attitude towards the working class. Consequently, *however much we may try* to "lend the economic, struggle itself a political character," *we shall never be able to* develop the political consciousness of the workers (to the level of Social-Democratic political consciousness) by keeping within the framework of the economic struggle, for *that framework is too narrow*. The Martynov formula[1] has some value for us, not because it illustrates Martynov's aptitude for confusing things, but because it pointedly expresses the basic error that all the Economists commit, namely, their conviction that it is possible to develop the class political consciousness of the workers *from within*, so to speak, from their economic struggle, i.e., by making this struggle the exclusive (or, at least, the main) starting-point, by making it the exclusive (or, at least, the main) basis. Such a view is

radically wrong. Piqued by our polemics against them, the Economists refuse to ponder deeply over the origins of these disagreements, with the result that we simply cannot understand one another. It is as if we spoke in different tongues.

Class political consciousness can be brought to the workers *only from without*, that is, only from outside the economic struggle, from outside the sphere of relations between workers and employers. The sphere from which alone it is possible to obtain this knowledge is the sphere of relationships of *all* classes and strata to the state and the government, the sphere of the interrelations between *all* classes. For that reason, the reply to the question as to what must be done to bring political knowledge to the workers cannot be merely the answer with which, in the majority of cases, the practical workers, especially those inclined towards Economism, mostly content themselves, namely: "To go among the workers." To bring political knowledge to the *workers* the Social Democrats must *go among all classes of the population*; they must dispatch units of their army *in all directions*.

…

… We said that a Social Democrat, if he really believes it necessary to develop comprehensively the political consciousness of the proletariat, must "go among all classes of the population." This gives rise to the questions: how is this to be done? have we enough forces to do this? is there a basis for such work among all the other classes? will this not mean a retreat, or lead to a retreat, from the class point of view? Let us deal with these questions.

We must "go among all classes of the population" as theoreticians, as proagandists, as agitators, and as organisers. No one doubts that the theoretical work of Social Democrats should aim at studying all the specific features of the social and political condition of the various classes. But extremely little is done in this direction as compared with the work that is done in studying the specific features of factory life. In the committees and study circles, one can meet people who are immersed in the study even of some special branch of the metal industry; but one can hardly ever find members of organisations (obliged, as often happens, for some reason or other to give up practical work) who are especially engaged in gathering material on some pressing question of social and political life in our country which could serve as a means for conducting Social-Democratic work among other strata of the population. In dwelling upon the fact that the majority of the present-day leaders of the working-class movement lack training, we cannot refrain from

---

1   *Martynov formula*   Lenin refers to Alexander Martynov (1865–1935), who held (with Marx and against Lenin and the Bolsheviks) that capitalism had to run its course before socialism could be achievable.

mentioning training in this respect also, for it too is bound up with the Economist conception of "close organic connection with the proletarian struggle." The principal thing, of course, is *propaganda* and *agitation* among all strata of the people. The work of the West European Social-Democrat is in this respect facilitated by the public meetings and rallies which *all* are free to attend, and by the fact that in parliament he addresses the representatives of *all* classes. We have neither a parliament nor freedom of assembly; nevertheless, we are able to arrange meetings of workers who desire to listen to *a Social Democrat*. We must also find ways and means of calling meetings of representatives of all social classes that desire to listen to *a democrat*; for he is no Social Democrat who forgets in practice that "the Communists support every revolutionary movement," that we are obliged for that reason to expound and emphasise *general democratic tasks before the whole people*, without for a moment concealing our socialist convictions. He is no Social Democrat who forgets in practice his obligation to be *ahead of all* in raising, accentuating, and solving *every* general democratic question.

3. Trade-unionist Politics and Social Democratic Politics

F. Once More "Slanderers," Once More "Mystifiers"

These polite expressions, as the reader will recall, belong to *Rabocheye Dyelo*,[1] which in this way answers our charge that it "is indirectly preparing the ground for converting the working-class movement into an instrument of bourgeois democracy." In its simplicity of heart *Rabocheye Dyelo* decided that this accusation was nothing more than a polemical sally: these malicious doctrinaires are bent on saying all sorts of unpleasant things about us, and, what can be more unpleasant than being an instrument of bourgeois democracy? And so they print in bold type a "refutation": "Nothing but downright slander," "mystification," "mummery." Like Jove,[2] *Rabocheye Dyelo* (although bearing little resemblance

to that deity) is wrathful because it is wrong, and proves by its hasty abuse that it is incapable of understanding its opponents' mode of reasoning. And yet, with only a little reflection it would have understood why *any* subservience to the spontaneity of the mass movement and *any* degrading of Social Democratic politics to the level of trade unionist politics mean preparing the ground for converting the working-class movement into an instrument of bourgeois democracy. The spontaneous working-class movement is by itself able to create (and inevitably does create) only trade unionism, and working-class trade unionist politics is precisely working-class bourgeois politics. The fact that the working class participates in the political struggle, and even in the political revolution, does not in itself make its politics Social Democratic politics. Will *Rabocheye Dyelo* make bold to deny this? Will it, at long last, publicly, plainly, and without equivocation explain how it understands the urgent questions of international and of Russian Social Democracy? Hardly. It will never do anything of the kind, because it holds fast to the trick, which might be described as the "not here" method—"It's not me, it's not my horse, I'm not the driver. We are not Economists; *Rabochaya Mysl*[3] does not stand for Economism; there is no Economism at all in Russia." This is a remarkably adroit and "political" trick, which suffers from the slight defect, however, that the publications practising it are usually nicknamed, "At your service, sir."

Rabocheye Dyelo imagines that bourgeois democracy in Russia is, in general, merely a "phantom."[4] Happy people! Ostrich-like, they bury their heads in the sand and imagine that everything around has disappeared. Liberal publicists who month after month proclaim to the world their triumph over the collapse and even the disappearance of Marxism; liberal newspapers (*S. Peterburgskiye Vedomosti*,[5] *Russkiye*

---

1   *Rabocheye Dyelo*   Russian: *The Worker's Cause*. *Rabocheye Dyelo* was an economic journal published in Geneva between April 1899 and February 1902 by the Union of Russian Social-Democrats Abroad.

2   *Jove*   Jupiter, chief of the Roman gods and patron deity of the Roman state. He had the same role as Zeus did in Greek mythology.

3   *Rabochaya Mysl*   Russian: *Workers' Thought*, economic journal published from 1897 to 1902.

4   *Rabochaya Dyelo … phantom*   [Lenin's note] There follows a reference to the "concrete Russian conditions which fatalistically impel the working-class movement on to the revoutionary path." But these people refuse to understand that the revolutionary path of the working-class movement might not be a Social Democratic path. When absolutism reigned, the entire West-European bourgeoisie impelled, deliberately impelled, the workers on to the path of revolution. We Social Democrats, however, cannot be satisfied with that. And if we, by any means whatever, degrade Social Democratic politics to the level of spontaneous trade unionist politics, we thereby play into the hands of bourgeois democracy.

5   *S. Peterburgskiye Vedomosti*   Russian: *St. Petersburg Recorder*, a newspaper that began publication in St. Petersburg in 1728 as a

Vedomosti,[1] and many others) which encourage the liberals who bring to the workers the Brentano conception of the class struggle and the trade unionist conception of politics; the galaxy of critics of Marxism, whose real tendencies were so very well disclosed by the *Credo* and whose literary products alone circulate in Russia without let or hindrance; the revival of revolutionary *non*-Social-Democratic tendencies, particularly after the February and March events—all these, apparently, are just phantoms! All these have nothing at all to do with bourgeois democracy!

Rabocheye Dyelo and the authors of the Economist letter published in *Iskra*,[2] No. 12, should "ponder over the reason why the events of the spring brought about such a revival of revolutionary non-Social Democratic tendencies instead of increasing the authority and the prestige of Social-Democracy."

The reason lies in the fact that we failed to cope with our tasks. The masses of the workers proved to be more active than we. We lacked adequately trained revolutionary leaders and organisers possessed of a thorough knowledge of the mood prevailing among all the opposition strata and able to head the movement, to turn a spontaneous demonstration into a political one, broaden its political character, etc. Under such circumstances, our backwardness will inevitably be utilised by the more mobile and more energetic non-Social Democratic revolutionaries, and the workers, however energetically and self-sacrificingly they may fight the police and the troops, however revolutionary their actions may be, will prove to be merely a force supporting those revolutionaries, the rearguard of bourgeois democracy, and not the Social Democratic vanguard. Let us take, for example, the German Social Democrats, whose weak aspects alone our Economists desire to emulate. Why is there *not a single* political event in Germany that does not add to the authority and prestige of Social Democracy? Because Social Democracy is always found to be in advance of all others in furnishing the most revolutionary appraisal of every given event and in championing every protest against tyranny. It does not lull itself with arguments that the economic struggle brings the workers to realise that they have no political rights and that the concrete conditions unavoidably impel the working-class movement on to the path of revolution. It intervenes in every sphere and in every question of social and political life; in the matter of Wilhelm's refusal to endorse a bourgeois progressist as city mayor (our Economists have not yet managed to educate the Germans to the understanding that such an act is, in fact, a compromise with liberalism!); in the matter of the law against "obscene" publications and pictures; in the matter of governmental influence on the election of professors, etc. Everywhere the Social Democrats are found in the forefront, rousing political discontent among all classes, rousing the sluggards, stimulating the laggards, and providing a wealth of material for the development of the political consciousness and the political activity of the proletariat. As a result, even the avowed enemies of socialism are filled with respect for this advanced political fighter, and not infrequently an important document from bourgeois, and even from bureaucratic and Court circles, makes its way by some miraculous means into the editorial office of *Vorwarts*.[3]

This, then, is the resolution of the seeming "contradiction" that surpasses *Rabocheye Dyelo's* powers of understanding to such an extent that it can only throw up its hands and cry, "Mummery!" Indeed, just think of it: We, *Rabocheye Dyelo*, regard the *mass* working class movement as the *cornerstone* (and say so in bold type!); we warn all and sundry against belittling the significance of the element of spontaneity; we desire to lend the economic struggle itself—*itself*—a political character; we desire to maintain close and organic contact with the proletarian struggle. And yet we are told that we are preparing the ground for the conversion of the working-class movement into an instrument of bourgeois democracy! And who are they that presume to say this? People who "compromise" with liberalism by intervening in every "liberal" issue (what a gross misunderstanding of "organic contact with the proletarian struggle!"), by devoting so much attention to the students and even (oh horror!) to the Zemstvos! People who in general wish to devote a greater percentage (compared with the Economists) of their efforts to activity among non-proletarian classes of the population! What is this but "mummery"?

Poor *Rabocheye Dyelo*! Will it ever find the solution to this perplexing puzzle?

continuation of the first Russian newspaper, *Vedomosti*, founded in 1703.

1 *Russkiye Vedomosti* Russian: *Russian Recorder*, a newspaper published in Moscow from 1863 onwards by a group of Moscow University liberal professors and reformers.

2 *Iskra* Russian: *Spark*. Political newspaper published by Russian socialist emigrants.

3 *Vorwarts* German: *Forwards*. German Social Democratic newspaper.

LEON TROTSKY
(1879-1940)

Born Lev Davidovich Bronstein, Leon Trotsky was one of the chief Bolshevik revolutionaries in Russia, and one of the twentieth century's most significant Marxist theorists. Involved in revolutionary activity from the age of 17, Trotsky organized socialist parties and published pamphlets, newspapers, and books. This earned him several prison terms; he was exiled to Siberia in 1900, where he studied Voltaire, Kant and Darwin. He escaped in 1902, borrowing the name "Trotsky" from one of his jailers.

The next decade and a half were spent in journalism and political activity, in Russia and on the continent. During this time, Trotsky wrote *Results and Prospects* (published in 1919) on the 1905 Russian Revolution. Among the leaders of the 1917 Bolshevik revolution, he was second in importance only to Lenin. Trotsky played a key role in the formation of the Politburo, the central governing body in the Soviet Union, and served in the 1918-20 civil war as the People's Commissar of Army and Navy Affairs, successfully commanding the Red army.

From 1923 onward Lenin was largely incapacitated following a series of strokes, and in the late 1920s a power struggle developed in the Soviet leadership; Stalin outmaneuvered Trotsky, who was sent into exile in February 1929. Trotsky spent time in the Turkish island of Prinkipo, France, and Norway, before settling in Mexico. During this period he wrote *The Permanent Revolution* (1930), a work of revolutionary theory; a three-volume *History of the Russian Revolution* (1930); and *The Revolution Betrayed* (1936), documenting his criticisms of Stalin. It had been a struggle over ideology as well as power; whereas Stalin defended the expansion of his own notoriously brutal authority and the centralization of power through bureaucracy, Trotsky predicted that unless overthrown and replaced by a workers' democracy, the bureaucracy would eventually degenerate into a new capitalist class.

In the late 1930s Stalin set up show trials, condemning and executing anyone perceived as a threat to his authority. The court convicted Trotsky *in absentia* for crimes including plotting to kill Stalin, slaughtering workers, and treason. To answer these charges, American philosopher John Dewey chaired the "Commission of Inquiry into the Charges Made Against Leon Trotsky in the Moscow Trials" in Coyoacan, Mexico, in April 1937. The commission returned with a "not guilty" verdict. On 20 August 1940, however, the Stalinist agent Ramón Mercader assassinated Trotsky.

Marx, in his *Theses on Feuerbach*, wrote, "The philosophers have only interpreted the world, in various ways; the point is to change it." Trotsky put this advice into practice; it is difficult to draw a sharp line between his political activity and his philosophy.

For orthodox Marxists, the economic structure forms the "base" of society, largely determining the social, political and intellectual relations. The political economy polarizes social classes, with a few controlling the means of production and others excluded. Marx saw history as necessarily entailing a struggle between classes, which would culminate in the working class, the proletariat, taking control of the means of production. A temporary "dictatorship of the proletariat" would form in this transitional period, but eventually a classless communist society would evolve.

Lenin, in *What Is To Be Done?* argued that the workers would never spontaneously revolt. Instead, a vanguard of trained revolutionaries was necessary to lead the workers. Trotsky initially rejected Lenin's ideas, predicting in *Our Political Tasks* (1904) that "the party organization at first substitutes itself for the party as a whole; the Central Committee substitutes itself for the organization; and finally a single 'dictator' substitutes himself for the Central Committee." Though he later accepted the establishment of a "vanguard party," history has given credence to his earlier view.

Intellectually, Trotsky is best known for his theory of permanent revolution, which he developed from Marx and Engels. Orthodox Marxists held that conditions in semi-feudal countries such as Russia at the turn of the century were not ripe for socialist revolution, since peasants, not industrial workers, made up most of the population. Trotsky rejected this brand of historical determinism, arguing the international situation, imperialism, the specific dynamics of the class struggle, and the initiative of individuals could all alter the situation. In certain historical circumstances the proletariat could and should take the initiative, leading the peasants. In his view, the stage of bourgeois capitalism that Marx had regarded as a necessary stage on the way to socialism could be entirely bypassed; the proletariat and peasantry could begin to eliminate private property, and proceed directly on the road to socialism. This revolution would trigger revolution in more developed countries, eventually spreading socialism to the entire world.

◆ ◆ ◆ ◆ ◆

Their Morals and Ours: The Class Foundations of Moral Practice (1938)

In memory of Leon Sedoff

Moral Effluvia

During an epoch of triumphant reaction, Messrs. democrats, social-democrats, anarchists, and other representatives of the "left" camp begin to exude double their usual amount of moral effluvia, similar to persons who perspire doubly in fear. Paraphrasing the Ten Commandments or the Sermon on the Mount, these moralists address themselves not so much to triumphant reaction[1] as to those revolutionists suffering under its persecution, who with their "excesses" and "amoral" principles "provoke" reaction and give it moral justification. Moreover they prescribe a simple

but certain means of avoiding reaction: it is necessary only to strive and morally to regenerate oneself. Free samples of moral perfection for those desirous are furnished by all the interested editorial offices.

The class basis of this false and pompous sermon is—the intellectual petty bourgeoisie. The political basis—their impotence and confusion in the face of approaching reaction. Psychological basis—their effort at overcoming the feeling of their own inferiority through masquerading in the beard of a prophet.

A moralizing Philistine's[2] favorite method is the lumping of reaction's conduct with that of revolution. He achieves success in this device through recourse to formal analogies. To him czarism and Bolshevism are twins. Twins are likewise discovered in fascism and communism. An inventory is compiled of the common features in Catholicism—or more specifically, Jesuitism—and Bolshevism. Hitler and Mussolini, utilizing from their side exactly the same method, disclose that liberalism, democracy, and Bolshevism represent merely different manifestations of one and the same evil. The conception that Stalinism and Trotskyism are "essentially" one and the same now enjoys the joint approval of liberals, democrats, devout Catholics, idealists, pragmatists, and anarchists. If the Stalinists are unable to adhere to this "People's Front," then it is only because they are accidentally occupied with the extermination of Trotskyists.

The fundamental feature of these *approchements*[3] and similitudes lies in their completely ignoring the material foundation of the various currents, that is, their class nature and by that token their objective historical role. Instead they evaluate and classify different currents according to some external and secondary manifestation, most often according to their relation to one or another abstract principle which for the given classifier has a special professional value. Thus to the Roman pope Freemasons[4] and Darwinists, Marxists and anarchists are twins because all of them sacrilegiously deny the immaculate conception. To Hitler, liberalism and Marxism are twins because they ignore

---

1 *reaction* The noun *reaction* and the adjective *reactionary* are frequently found in the writings of socialist authors. They are generally used to refer to the conservatives and conservative forces in society who react against progressive or revolutionary leftist ideas and activities.

2 *Philistine* Someone indifferent to culture and intellect and its achievements. The term originally referred to the people of ancient Philistia (on the coast of the Mediterranean) who warred with the Hebrews. (Today the word is commonly spelled with a lower-case p.)

3 *approchements* French: approximations.

4 *Freemasons* Members of the secret society of Masons, a fraternal group. Historically, the Catholic Church was a bitter enemy of the Freemasons.

"blood and honor." To a democrat, fascism and Bolshevism are twins because they do not bow before universal suffrage. And so forth.

Undoubtedly the currents grouped above have certain common features. But the gist of the matter lies in the fact that the evolution of mankind exhausts itself neither by universal suffrage, nor by "blood and honor," nor by the dogma of the immaculate conception. The historical process signifies primarily the class struggle; moreover, different classes in the name of different aims may in certain instances utilize similar means. Essentially it cannot be otherwise. Armies in combat are always more or less symmetrical; were there nothing in common in their methods of struggle they could not inflict blows upon each other.

If an ignorant peasant or shopkeeper, understanding neither the origin nor the sense of the struggle between the proletariat and the bourgeoisie,[1] discovers himself between the two fires, he will consider both belligerent camps with equal hatred. And who are all these democratic moralists? Ideologists of intermediary layers who have fallen, or are in fear of falling between the two fires. The chief traits of the prophets of this type are alienism[2] to great historical movements, a hardened conservative mentality, smug narrowness, and a most primitive political cowardice. More than anything moralists wish that history should leave them in peace with their petty books, little magazines, subscribers, common sense, and moral copy books. But history does not leave them in peace. It cuffs them now from the left, now from the right. Clearly—revolution and reaction, Czarism and Bolshevism, communism and fascism, Stalinism and Trotskyism—are all twins. Whoever doubts this may feel the symmetrical skull bumps upon both the right and left sides of these very moralists.

Marxist Amoralism and Eternal Truths

The most popular and most imposing accusation directed against Bolshevik "amoralism" bases itself on the so-called Jesuitical maxim of Bolshevism: "The end justifies the means." From this it is not difficult to reach the further conclusion: since the Trotskyists, like all Bolsheviks (or Marxists) do not recognize the principles of morality, there

is, consequently, no "principled" difference between Trotskyism and Stalinism. Q.E.D.

One completely vulgar and cynical American monthly conducted a questionnaire on the moral philosophy of Bolshevism. The questionnaire, as is customary, was to have simultaneously served the ends of ethics and advertisement. The inimitable H.G. Wells,[3] whose high fancy is surpassed only by his Homeric self-satisfaction was not slow in solidarizing himself with the reactionary snobs of *Common Sense*. Here everything fell into order. But even those participants who considered it necessary to defend Bolshevism did so, in the majority of cases, not without timid evasions (Eastman) [4]: the principles of Marxism are, of course, bad, but among the Bolsheviks there are, nevertheless, worthy people. Truly, such "friends" are more dangerous than enemies.

Should we care to take Messrs. Unmaskers seriously, then first of all we would ask them: what are your own moral principles? Here is a question which will scarcely receive an answer. Let us admit for the moment that neither personal nor social ends can justify the means. Then it is evidently necessary to seek criteria outside of historical society and those ends which arise in its development. But where? If not on earth, then in the heavens. In divine revelation popes long ago discovered faultless moral criteria. Petty secular popes speak about eternal moral truths without naming their original source. However, we are justified in concluding: since these truths are eternal, they should have existed not only before the appearance of half-monkey-half-man upon the earth but before the evolution of the solar system. Whence then did they arise? The theory of eternal morals can in nowise survive without god.

Moralists of the Anglo-Saxon type, in so far as they do not confine themselves to rationalist utilitarianism, the ethics of bourgeois bookkeeping, appear conscious or unconscious students of Viscount Shaftesbury,[5] who—at the

---

1   *Proletariat … bourgeoisie* The former is the working class; the latter the middle class (or more specifically, for many socialists, land, property, and factory owners).

2   *alienism* Isolation, dissociation from.

---

3   *H.G. Wells* (1866–1946), English writer now known primarily for his science fiction (*The Time Machine, The War of the Worlds*), though he was also a historian and an anti-Marxist socialist theorist.

4   *Common Sense … Eastman Common Sense* was a liberal/socialist/non-Marxist magazine founded in 1932. Max Eastman (1888–1969), an American socialist writer, was a contributor.

5   *Viscount Shaftesbury* Trotsky is probably referring to Anthony Ashley Cooper, Third Earl of Shaftesbury (1671–1713). Shaftesbury is often thought to have been the first philosopher to use the term "moral sense," referring to the capacity to feel "second-order" affections of right or wrong.

beginning of the 18th century!—deduced moral judgments from a special "moral sense" supposedly once and for all given to man. Supra-class morality inevitably leads to the acknowledgment of a special substance, of a "moral sense," "conscience," some kind of absolute which is nothing more than the philosophic-cowardly pseudonym for god. Independent of "ends," that is, of society, morality, whether we deduce it from eternal truths or from the "nature of man," proves in the end to be a form of "natural theology." Heaven remains the only fortified position for military operations against dialectic materialism.[1]

At the end of the last century in Russia there arose a whole school of "Marxists" (Struve, Berdyaev, Bulgakov,[2] and others) who wished to supplement the teachings of Marx with a self-sufficient, that is, supra-class moral principle. These people began, of course, with Kant and the categorical imperative. But how did they end? Struve is now a retired minister of the Crimean baron Wrangel, and a faithful son of the church; Bulgakov is an orthodox priest; Berdyaev expounds the Apocalypse in sundry languages. These metamorphoses which seem so unexpected at first glance are not at all explained by the "Slavic soul"—Struve has a German soul—but by the sweep of the social struggle in Russia. The fundamental trend of this metamorphosis is essentially international.

Classical philosophic idealism in so far as it aimed in its time to secularize morality, that is, to free it from religious sanction, represented a tremendous step forward (Hegel). But having torn from heaven, moral philosophy had to find earthly roots. To discover these roots was one of the tasks of materialism. After Shaftesbury came Darwin, after Hegel—Marx. To appeal now to "eternal moral truths" signifies attempting to turn the wheels backward. Philosophic idealism is only a stage: from religion to materialism, or, contrariwise, from materialism to religion.

---

1   *dialectic materialism*   General name for the philosophical basis of Marxism. This approach aims to combine the "dialectical" account of change from Hegel's "dialectical idealism" with a "materialistic" basis, in which the *material* forces of production are the real causes of social and historical phenomena, and of change.

2   *Struve, Berdyaev, Bulgakov*   Pyotr Berngardovich Struve (1870–1944), liberal Russian economist and political scientist; Nikolai Alexandrovich Berdyaev (1874–1948), Russian religious and political philosopher; Mikhail Bulgakov (1891–1940), Russian journalist, playwright, novelist, and short story writer.

"The End Justifies the Means"

The Jesuit order, organized in the first half of the 16th century for combating Protestantism, never taught, let it be said, that *any* means, even though it be criminal from the point of view of the Catholic morals, was permissible if only it led to the "end," that is, to the triumph of Catholicism. Such an internally contradictory and psychologically absurd doctrine was maliciously attributed to the Jesuits by their Protestant and partly Catholic opponents who were not shy in choosing the means for achieving their ends. Jesuit theologians who, like the theologians of other schools, were occupied with the question of personal responsibility, actually taught that the means in itself can be a matter of indifference but that the moral justification or judgment of the given means flows from the end. Thus shooting in itself is a matter of indifference; shooting a mad dog that threatens a child—a virtue; shooting with the aim of violation or murder—a crime. Outside of these commonplaces the theologians of this order made no promulgations.

In so far as their practical moral philosophy is concerned the Jesuits were not at all worse than other monks or Catholic priests, on the contrary, they were superior to them; in any case, more consistent, bolder, and perspicacious. The Jesuits represented a militant organization, strictly centralized, aggressive, and dangerous not only to enemies but also to allies. In his psychology and method of action the Jesuit of the "heroic" period distinguished himself from an average priest as the warrior of a church from its shopkeeper. We have no reason to idealize either one or the other. But it is altogether unworthy to look upon a fanatic-warrior with the eyes of an obtuse and slothful shopkeeper.

If we are to remain in the field of purely formal or psychological similitudes, then it can, if you like, be said that the Bolsheviks appear in relation to the democrats and social-democrats of all hues as did the Jesuits—in relation to the peaceful ecclesiastical hierarchy. Compared to revolutionary Marxists, the social-democrats and centrists appear like morons, or a quack beside a physician: they do not think one problem through to the end, believe in the power of conjuration and cravenly avoid every difficulty, hoping for a miracle. Opportunists are peaceful shopkeepers in socialist ideas while Bolsheviks are its inveterate warriors. From this comes the hatred and slander against Bolsheviks from those who have an abundance of their historically conditioned faults but not one of their merits.

However, the juxtaposition of Bolshevism and Jesuitism still remains completely one-sided and superficial, rather of a literary than historical kind. In accordance with the character and interests of those classes upon which they based themselves, the Jesuits represented reaction, the Protestants—progress. The limitedness of this "progress" in its turn found direct expression in the morality of the Protestants. Thus the teachings of Christ "purified" by them did not at all hinder the city bourgeois, Luther, from calling for the execution of revolting peasants as "mad dogs." Dr. Martin[1] evidently considered that the "end justifies the means" even before that maxim was attributed to the Jesuits. In turn the Jesuits, competing with Protestantism, adapted themselves ever more to the spirit of bourgeois society, and of the three vows: poverty, chastity, and obedience, preserved only the third, and at that in an extremely attenuated form. From the point of view of the Christian ideal, the morality of the Jesuits degenerated the more they ceased to be Jesuits. The warriors of the church became its bureaucrats and, like all bureaucrats, passable swindlers.

Jesuitism and Utilitarianism

This brief discussion is sufficient, perhaps, to show what ignorance and narrowness are necessary to consider seriously the contraposition of the "Jesuit" principle, "the end justifies the means," to another seemingly higher moral, in which each "means" carries its own moral tag like merchandise with fixed prices in a department store. It is remarkable that the common sense of the Anglo-Saxon Philistine has managed to wax indignant at the "Jesuit" principle and simultaneously to find inspiration in the utilitarian morality, so characteristic of British philosophy. Moreover, the criterion of Bentham-John Mill,[2] "the greatest possible happiness for the greatest possible number," signifies that those means are moral which lead to the common welfare as the higher end. In its general philosophical formulations Anglo-Saxon utilitarianism thus fully coincides with the "Jesuit" principle, "the end justifies the means." Empiricism, we see, exists in the world only to free us from the necessity of making both ends meet.

Herbert Spencer,[3] into whose empiricism Darwin inculcated the idea of "evolution," as a special vaccine, taught that in the moral sphere evolution proceeds from "sensations" to "ideas." Sensations conform to the criterion of immediate pleasure, while ideas permit one to be guided by the criterion of *future, lasting and higher pleasure*. Thus the moral criterion here too is "pleasure" and "happiness." But the content of this criterion acquires breadth and depth depending upon the level of "evolution." In this way Herbert Spencer too, through the methods of his own "evolutionary" utilitarianism, showed that the principle, "the end justifies the means," does not embrace anything immoral.

It is naïve, however, to expect from this abstract "principle" an answer to the practical question: what may we, and what may we not do? Moreover, the principle, the end justifies the means, naturally raises the question: and what justifies the end? In practical life as in the historical movement the end and the means constantly change places. A machine under construction is an "end" of production only that upon entering the factory it may become the "means." Democracy in certain periods is the "end" of the class struggle only that later it may be transformed into its "means." Not embracing anything immoral, the so-called "Jesuit" principle fails, however, to resolve the moral problem.

The "evolutionary" utilitarianism of Spencer likewise abandons us half-way without an answer, since, following Darwin, it tries to dissolve the concrete historical morality in the biological needs or in the "social instincts" characteristic of a gregarious animal, and this at a time when the very understanding of morality arises only in an antagonistic milieu, that is, in a society torn by classes.

Bourgeois evolutionism halts impotently at the threshold of historical society because it does not wish to acknowledge the driving force in the evolution of social forms: *the class struggle*. Morality is one of the ideological functions in this struggle. The ruling class forces *its* ends upon society and habituates it into considering all those means which contradict its ends as immoral. That is the chief function of official morality. It pursues the idea of the "greatest possible happiness" not for the majority but for a small and ever diminishing minority. Such a régime could

---

1   *Dr. Martin*   I.e., Martin Luther.
2   *Bentham-John Mill*   Jeremy Bentham (1748–1832), English philosopher, early advocate of utilitarianism; John Stuart Mill (1806–73), English philosopher who developed and applied Bentham's theories.

---

3   *Herbert Spencer*   English philosopher (1820–1903); he extended his version of evolution to many social and cultural phenomena, developing the theory called "Social Darwinism."

not have endured for even a week through force alone. It needs the cement of morality. The mixing of this cement constitutes the profession of the petty bourgeois theoreticians and moralists. They dabble in all colors of the rainbow but in the final instance remain apostles of slavery and submission.

"Moral Precepts Obligatory Upon All"

Whoever does not care to return to Moses, Christ or Mohammed; whoever is not satisfied with eclectic *hodge-podges* must acknowledge that morality is a product of social development; that there is nothing invariable about it; that it serves social interests; that these interests are contradictory; that morality more than any other form of ideology has a class character.

But do not elementary moral precepts exist, worked out in the development of mankind as an integral element necessary for the life of every collective body? Undoubtedly such precepts exist but the extent of their action is extremely limited and unstable. Norms "obligatory upon all" become the less forceful the sharper the character assumed by the class struggle. The highest pitch of the class struggle is civil war which explodes into mid-air all moral ties between the hostile classes.

Under "normal" conditions a "normal" man observes the commandment: "Thou shalt not kill!" But if he murders under exceptional conditions for self-defense, the judge condones his action. If he falls victim to a murderer, the court will kill the murderer. The necessity of the court's action, as that of the self-defense, flows from antagonistic interests. In so far as the state is concerned, in peaceful times it limits itself to individual cases of legalized murder so that in time of war it may transform the "obligatory" commandment, "Thou shalt not kill!" into its opposite. The most "humane" governments, which in peaceful times "detest" war, proclaim during war that the highest duty of their armies is the extermination of the greatest possible number of people.

The so-called "generally recognized" moral precepts in essence preserve an algebraic, that is, an indeterminate character. They merely express the fact that man, in his individual conduct, is bound by certain common norms that flow from his being a member of society. The highest generalization of these norms is the "categorical imperative" of Kant. But in spite of the fact that it occupies a high position upon the philosophic Olympus this imperative does not embody anything categoric[1] because it embodies nothing concrete. It is a shell without content.

This vacuity in the norms obligatory upon all arises from the fact that in all decisive questions people feel their class membership considerably more profoundly and more directly than their membership in "society." The norms of "obligatory" morality are in reality charged with class, that is, antagonistic content. The moral norm becomes the more categoric the less it is "obligatory" upon all. The solidarity of workers, especially of strikers or barricade fighters, is incomparably more "categoric" than human solidarity in general.

The bourgeoisie, which far surpasses the proletariat in the completeness and irreconcilability of its class consciousness, is vitally interested in imposing *its* moral philosophy upon the exploited masses. It is exactly for this purpose that the concrete norms of the bourgeois catechism are concealed under moral abstractions patronized by religion, philosophy, or that hybrid which is called "common sense." The appeal to abstract norms is not a disinterested philosophic mistake but a necessary element in the mechanics of class deception. The exposure of this deceit which retains the tradition of thousands of years is the first duty of a proletarian revolutionist.

The Crisis in Democratic Morality

In order to guarantee the triumph of their interests in big questions, the ruling classes are constrained to make concessions on secondary questions, naturally only so long as these concessions are reconciled in the bookkeeping. During the epoch of capitalistic upsurge especially in the last few decades before the World War these concessions, at least in relation to the top layers of the proletariat, were of a completely genuine nature. Industry at that time expanded almost uninterruptedly. The prosperity of the civilized nations, partially, too, that of the toiling masses increased. Democracy appeared solid. Workers' organizations grew. At the same time reformist tendencies deepened. The relations between the classes softened, at least outwardly. Thus certain elementary moral precepts in social relations were established along with the norms of democracy and the

---

1   *categoric*   For Kant, a "categoric[al]" imperative is a directive to action that holds for all rational beings at all times—as opposed to "hypothetical" imperatives which advise different actions depending on circumstances and aims.

habits of class collaboration. The impression was created of an ever more free, more just, and more humane society. The rising line of progress seemed infinite to "common sense."

Instead, however, war broke out with a train of convulsions, crises, catastrophes, epidemics, and bestiality. The economic life of mankind landed in an *impasse*. The class antagonisms became sharp and naked. The safety valves of democracy began to explode one after the other. The elementary moral precepts seemed even more fragile than the democratic institutions and reformist illusions. Mendacity, slander, bribery, venality, coercion, murder grew to unprecedented dimensions. To a stunned simpleton all these vexations seem a temporary result of war. Actually they are manifestations of imperialist decline. The decay of capitalism denotes the decay of contemporary society with its right and its morals.

The "synthesis" of imperialist turpitude is fascism directly begotten of the bankruptcy of bourgeois democracy before the problems of the imperialist epoch. Remnants of democracy continue still to exist only in the rich capitalist aristocracies: for each "democrat" in England, France, Holland, Belgium there is a certain number of colonial slaves; "60 Families"[1] dominate the democracy of the United States, and so forth. Moreover, shoots of fascism grow rapidly in all democracies. Stalinism in its turn is the product of imperialist pressure upon a backward and isolated workers' state, a symmetrical complement in its own *genre* to fascism.

While idealistic Philistines—anarchists of course occupy first place—tirelessly unmask Marxist "amoralism" in their press, the American trusts, according to John L. Lewis (C.I.O.)[2] are spending not less than $80,000,000 a year[3] on the practical struggle against revolutionary "demoralization," that is, espionage, bribery of workers, frame-ups, and dark-alley murders. The categorical imperative sometimes chooses circuitous ways for its triumph!

Let us note in justice that the most sincere and at the same time the most limited petty bourgeois moralists still

---

1   *60 Families*   Ferdinand Lundberg (1905–95), American economist and journalist, published a book in 1936 called *America's Sixty Families*—a study of the enormously powerful sixty richest families in the US.

2   *John L. Lewis (C.I.O.)*   John L. Lewis (1880–1969), American labor leader, a central figure in the founding of the Congress of Industrial Organizations (C.I.O.), an alliance of trade unions, during the 1930s. It was designed as a more radical alternative to the American Federation of Labor (A.F.L.).

3   *not less than $80,000,000 a year*   Adjusting for inflation, this amounts to approximately $1,085,000,000 in 2009.

live even today in the idealized memories of yesterday and hope for its return. They do not understand that morality is a function of the class struggle; that democratic morality corresponds to the epoch of liberal and progressive capitalism; that the sharpening of the class struggle in passing through its latest phase definitively and irrevocably destroyed this morality; that in its place came the morality of fascism on one side, on the other the morality of proletarian revolution.

"Common Sense"

Democracy and "generally recognized" morality are not the only victims of imperialism. The third suffering martyr is "universal" common sense. This lowest form of the intellect is not only necessary under all conditions but under certain conditions is also adequate. Common sense's basic capital consists of the elementary conclusions of universal experience: not to put one's fingers in fire, whenever possible to proceed along a straight line, not to tease vicious dogs ... and so forth and so on. Under a stable social milieu common sense is adequate for bargaining, healing, writing articles, leading trade unions, voting in parliament, marrying and reproducing the race. But when that same common sense attempts to go beyond its valid limits into the arena of more complex generalizations, it is exposed as just a clot of prejudices of a definite class and a definite epoch. No more than a simple capitalist crisis brings common sense to an *impasse*; and before such catastrophes as revolution, counter-revolution and war, common sense proves a perfect fool. In order to realize the catastrophic transgressions against the "normal" course of events higher qualities of intellect are necessary, philosophically expressed as yet only by dialectic materialism.

Max Eastman, who successfully attempts to endow "common sense" with a most attractive literary style, has fashioned out of the struggle against dialectics nothing less than a profession for himself. Eastman seriously takes the conservative banalities of common sense wedded to good style as "the science of revolution." Supporting the reactionary snobs of *Common Sense*, he expounds to mankind with inimitable assurance that if Trotsky had been guided not by Marxist doctrine but by common sense then he would not ... have lost power. That inner dialectic which until now has appeared in the inevitable succession of determined stages in all revolutions does not exist for Eastman. Reaction's displacing revolution, to him, is determined through insufficient respect for common sense. Eastman does not understand that it is Stalin who in a historical sense fell *victim* to common sense, that is, its inadequacy, since that power which he possesses serves ends hostile to Bolshevism. Marxist doctrine, on the other hand, permitted us to tear away in time from the Thermidorian[1] bureaucracy and to continue to serve the ends of international socialism.

Every science, and in that sense also the "science of revolution" is controlled by experience. Since Eastman well knows how to maintain revolutionary power under the condition of world counter-revolution, then he also knows, we may hope, how to conquer power. It would be very desirable that he finally disclose his secrets. Best of all that it be done in the form of a *draft program for a revolutionary party* under the title: How to Conquer and Hold Power. We fear, however, that it is precisely common sense which will urge Eastman to refrain from such a risky undertaking. And this time common sense will be right.

Marxist doctrine, which Eastman, alas, never understood, permitted us to foresee the inevitability under certain historic conditions of the Soviet Thermidor with all its coil of crimes. That same doctrine long ago predicted the inevitability of the downfall of bourgeois democracy and its morality. However the doctrinaires of "common sense" were caught unaware by fascism and Stalinism. Common sense operates on invariable magnitudes in a world where only change is invariable. Dialectics, on the contrary, takes all phenomena, institutions, and norms in their rise, development and decay. The dialectical consideration of morals as a subservient and transient product of the class struggle seems to common sense an "amoralism." But there is nothing more flat, stale, self-satisfied and cynical than the moral rules of common sense!

Moralists and the G.P.U.[2]

The Moscow trials[3] provided the occasion for a crusade against Bolshevik "amoralism." However, the crusade was not opened at once. The truth is that in their majority the moralists, directly or indirectly, were friends of the Kremlin. As such they long attempted to hide their amazement and even feigned that nothing unusual had occurred.

But the Moscow trials were not at all an accident. Servile obedience, hypocrisy, the official cult of mendacity, bribery, and other forms of corruption had already begun to blossom ostentatiously in Moscow by 1924-1925. The future judicial frame-ups were being prepared openly before the eyes of the whole world. There was no lack of warning. The "friends," however, did not wish to notice anything. No wonder: the majority of these gentlemen, in their time irreconcilably hostile to the October Revolution, became friends of the Soviet Union merely at the rate of its Thermidorian degeneration—the petty bourgeois democrats of the West recognized in the petty bourgeois bureaucracy of the East a kindred soul.

Did these people really believe the Moscow accusations? Only the most obtuse. The others did not wish to alarm themselves by verification. Is it reasonable to infringe upon the flattering, comfortable, and often well-paying friendship with the Soviet embassies? Moreover—oh, they did not forget this!—indiscreet truth can injure the prestige of the U.S.S.R. These people screened the crimes by utilitarian considerations, that is, frankly applied the principle, "the end justifies the means."

The King's Counselor, Pritt,[4] who succeeded with timeliness in peering under the chiton of the Stalinist Themis[5] and there discovered everything in order, took upon himself the shameless initiative. Romain Rolland,[6] whose moral authority is highly evaluated by the Soviet publishing house bookkeepers, hastened to proclaim one of his manifestos where melancholy lyricism unites with senile cynicism. The French League for the Rights of Man, which thundered

---

1   *Thermidorian*   "Thermidore" was a month of the reformed calendar newly established by the French Revolution. The "Thermidorian Reaction" was a revolt (initiated on "9 Thermadore Year II"—27 July 1794) against the excesses of the Reign of Terror, marking the end of the radical phase of the French Revolution.

2   *G.P.U.*   The State Political Directorate, an early Soviet political police force, the forerunner of the K.G.B. Founded in 1922, it gradually assumed more power and, renamed the OGPU, became active in the battles during the late 20s and early 30s among political factions and in state-sponsored repression and terror.

3   *The Moscow trials*   A series of trials in Russia, 1936–38; opponents of Stalin (including Trotsky and some of his followers)

were convicted of counter-revolution; many were executed as a result. (Trotsky, out of the country in exile, was sentenced to death in absentia.) Information revealed much later (under Nikolai Khrushchev) showed what had widely been suspected—that these were show trials, with falsified evidence, forced confessions, and predetermined verdicts.

4   *Pritt*   Denis Nowell Pritt (1887–1972), English leftist lawyer, investigated the Moscow Trials and wrote various articles defending their procedures.

5   *chiton of the Stalinist Themis*   Themis, the Greek mythological titan, was the embodiment of divine order, law, and custom. Her "chiton" is her tunic.

6   *Romain Rolland*   (1866–1944), French idealistic writer, admirer of the Soviet social experiment.

about the "amoralism of Lenin and Trotsky" in 1917 when they broke the military alliance with France, hastened to screen Stalin's crimes in 1936 in the interests of the Franco-Soviet pact.[1] A patriotic end justifies, as is known, any means. *The Nation and The New Republic*[2] closed their eyes to Yagoda's exploits[3] since their "friendship" with the U.S.S.R. guaranteed their own authority. Yet only a year ago these gentlemen did not at all declare Stalinism and Trotskyism to be one and the same. They openly stood for Stalin, for his realism, for his justice and for his Yagoda. They clung to this position as long as they could.

Until the moment of the execution of Tukhachevsky, Yakir,[4] and the others, the big bourgeoisie of the democratic countries, not without pleasure, though blanketed with fastidiousness, watched the execution of the revolutionists in the U.S.S.R. In this sense *The Nation* and *The New Republic*, not to speak of Duranty, Louis Fischer,[5] and their kindred prostitutes of the pen, fully responded to the interests of "democratic" imperialism. The execution of the generals alarmed the bourgeoisie, compelling them to understand that the advanced disintegration of the Stalinist apparatus lightened the tasks of Hitler, Mussolini and the Mikado.[6] *The New York Times* cautiously but insistently began to correct its own Duranty. The Paris *Le Temps* opened its columns slightly to shedding light upon the actual situation in the U.S.S.R. As for the petty bourgeois moralists and sycophants, they were never anything but servile echoes of the capitalist class. Moreover, after the International Commission of Inquiry, headed by John Dewey, brought out its verdict it became clear to every person who thought even a trifle that further open defense

of the G.P.U. signified peril of political and moral death. Only at this moment did the "friends" decide to bring the eternal moral truths into god's world, that is, to fall back to the second line trench.

Frightened Stalinists and semi-Stalinists occupy not the last place among moralists. Eugene Lyons during several years cohabited nicely with the Thermidorian clique, considering himself almost-a-Bolshevik. Withdrawing from the Kremlin—for a reason that is to us a matter of indifference—he rose, of course, immediately into the clouds of idealism. Liston Oak until recently enjoyed such confidence from the Comintern that it entrusted him with conducting the English propaganda for republican Spain. This did not, naturally, hinder him, once he had relinquished his post, from likewise relinquishing the Marxist alphabet. Expatriate Walter Krivitsky, having broken with the G.P.U., immediately joined the bourgeois democracy. Evidently this too is the metamorphosis of the very aged Charles Rappoport.[7] Having tossed Stalinism overboard, people of such ilk—they are many—cannot help seeking indemnification in the postulates of abstract morality for the disillusionment and abasement of ideals they have experienced. Ask them: "Why have you switched from the Comintern[8] or G.P.U. ranks to the camp of the bourgeoisie?" They have a ready answer: "Trotskyism is no better than Stalinism."

The Disposition of Political Chessmen

"Trotskyism is revolutionary romanticism; Stalinism—practical politics." Of this banal contraposition with which the average Philistine until yesterday justified his friendship with Thermidor against the revolution, there remains not a trace today. Trotskyism and Stalinism are in general no longer counterpoised but identified. They are identified, however, only in form not in essence. Having recoiled to the meridian of the "categorical imperative," the democrats actually continue to defend the G.P.U. except with greater camouflage

---

1   *Franco-Soviet pact* Short-lived agreement between France and the Soviets in 1935, promising France military aid in case it was invaded by Germany.

2   *The Nation and The New Republic* Left-leaning American magazines, both of which were generally initially sympathetic to the Soviet Union. *The Nation* was founded in 1865 and *The New Republic* in 1914. Both continue to be published today.

3   *Yagoda's exploits* Genrikh Grigoryevich Yagoda (1891–1938), head of the NKVD, the Soviet secret police, 1934 to 1936; in charge of the initial phase of Stalin's purges; helped run the Moscow show trials.

4   *Tukhachevsky, Yakir* Mikhail Tukhachevsky (1893–1937), and Iona Yakir (1896–1937), Soviet officials associated with reform movements, both convicted in the Moscow trials and executed.

5   *Duranty, Louis Fischer* Walter Duranty (1884–1957), British journalist; Louis Fischer (1896–1970), American journalist. Both were sympathetic, for a time, to Stalin's rule.

6   *Mikado* Title (used only in the West) for the Emperor of Japan.

7   *Eugene Lyons ... Charles Rappoport* Lyons (1898–1985) and Oak (1910–70) were American journalist/writers. Krivitsky (1899–1941) was a Soviet spy who defected to the west in 1938. Rappoport (1865–1941) was a Russian-born French communist. All became disillusioned with Stalinism.

8   *Comintern* The Communist International (otherwise known as the Third International), an organization with members in many countries, dedicated to the ideals of communism. Formed in 1919, it was dissolved in 1943.

and perfidy. He who slanders the victim aids the executioner. In this case, as in others, morality serves politics.

The democratic Philistine and Stalinist bureaucrat are, if not twins, brothers in spirit. In any case they belong politically to the same camp. The present governmental system of France and—if we add the anarchists—of republican Spain is based on the collaboration of Stalinists, social-democrats and liberals. If the British Independent Labour Party appears roughed up it is because for a number of years it has not withdrawn from the embrace of the Comintern. The French Socialist Party expelled the Trotskyists from their ranks exactly when it prepared to fuse with the Stalinists. If the fusion did not materialize, it was not because of principled divergences—what remains of them?—but only because of the fear of the social-democratic careerists over their posts. Having returned from Spain, Norman Thomas[1] declared that "objectively" the Trotskyists help Franco,[2] and with this subjective absurdity he gave "objective" service to the G.P.U. executioners. This righteous man expelled the American "Trotskyists" from his party precisely as the G.P.U. shot down their co-thinkers in the U.S.S.R. and in Spain. In many democratic countries, the Stalinists in spite of their "amoralism" have penetrated into the government apparatus not without success. In the trade unions they cohabit nicely with bureaucrats of other hues. True, the Stalinists have an extremely lightminded attitude toward the criminal code and in that way frighten away their "democratic" friends in peaceful times; but in exceptional circumstances, as indicated by the example of Spain, they more surely become the leaders of the petty bourgeoisie against the proletariat.

The Second and Amsterdam Internationals[3] naturally did not take upon themselves the responsibility for the frame-ups; this work they left to the Comintern. They themselves kept quiet. Privately they explained that from a "moral" point of view they were against Stalin, but from a political point of view—for him. Only when the People's Front in France cracked irreparably and forced the socialists to think about tomorrow did Léon Blum[4] find at the bottom of his inkwell the necessary formulas for moral abhorrence.

If Otto Bauer[5] mildly condemned Vyshinsky's[6] justice it was only in order to support Stalin's politics with greater "impartiality." The fate of socialism, according to Bauer's recent declaration, is tied with the fate of the Soviet Union. "And the fate of the Soviet Union," he continues, "is the fate of Stalinism so long as [!] the inner development of the Soviet Union itself does not overcome the Stalinist phase of development." All of Bauer is contained in this remarkable sentence, all of Austro-Marxism, the whole mendacity and rot of the social-democracy! "So long as" the Stalinist bureaucracy is sufficiently strong to murder the progressive representatives of the "inner development," until then Bauer sticks with Stalin. When in spite of Bauer the revolutionary forces overthrow Stalin, then Bauer will generously recognize the "inner development"—with not more than ten years delay.

Behind the old Internationals, the London Bureau[7] of the centrists trails along, happily combining in itself the characteristics of a kindergarten, a school for mentally arrested adolescents, and a home for invalids. The secretary of the Bureau, Fenner Brockway,[8] began with the declaration that an inquiry into the Moscow trials could "harm the U.S.S.R." and proposed instead an investigation into ... the political activity of Trotsky through an "impartial" Commission of five irreconcilable enemies of Trotsky. Brandler and Lovestone[9] publicly solidarized with Yagoda;

---

1   *Norman Thomas* (1884–1968), American socialist; an important figure in the non-communist left, he ran for president six times on the Socialist Party ticket.

2   *Franco* General Francisco Franco (1892–1975). He led a coup d'état against the left-wing republican government elected in Spain in 1938; after winning the civil war that followed, he ran a fascist state until his death in 1975.

3   *Second and Amsterdam Internationals* The Second International was an organization founded by socialist and labor parties in 1889 to further the growth of socialism. It disbanded in 1916. The so-called "Amsterdam International" (the International Federation of Trade Unions) was established by reformist European trade union leaders in Amsterdam in 1919, in explicit opposition to revolutionary socialism.

4   *Léon Blum* (1872–1950), Socialist Prime Minister of France, serving three times between 1936 and 1947.

5   *Otto Bauer* (1881–1931), Austrian Social Democrat, leading theoretician of the Austro-Marxist school.

6   *Vyshinsky* Andrei Vyshinsky (1883–1955), Soviet official who led the prosecution at all the Moscow Trials.

7   *London Bureau* Popular name of the International Revolutionary Marxist Center, an international association of left-socialist parties formed in 1932 in opposition both to social democracy and to the Third International.

8   *Fenner Brockway* Baron Brockway (1888–1988) was a British pacifist and socialist politician.

9   *Brandler and Lovestone* Heinrich Brandler (1881–1967), German communist politician; Jay Lovestone (1897–1990) leader of the Communist Party USA, later an anti-Communist and secret worker for the CIA.

they retreated only from Yezhov.[1] Jacob Walcher,[2] upon an obviously false pretext, refused to give testimony which was unfavorable to Stalin before the International Commission headed by John Dewey. The putrid morals of these people is only a product of their putrid politics.

But perhaps the most lamentable role is that played by the anarchists. If Stalinism and Trotskyism are one and the same, as they affirm in every sentence, then why do the Spanish anarchists assist the Stalinists in revenging themselves upon the Trotskyists and at the same time upon the revolutionary anarchists? The more frank anarchist theoreticians respond: this is payment for armaments. In other words: the end justifies the means. But what is their *end*? Anarchism? Socialism? No, merely the salvaging of this very same bourgeois democracy which prepared fascism's success. To base ends correspond base means.

That is the real disposition of the figures on the world political board!

Stalinism—A Product of the Old Society

Russia took the greatest leap in history, a leap in which the most progressive forces of the country found their expression. Now in the current reaction, the sweep of which is proportionate to the sweep of the revolution, backwardness is taking its revenge. Stalinism embodies this reaction. The barbarism of old Russian history upon new social bases seems yet more disgusting since it is constrained to conceal itself in hypocrisy unprecedented in history.

The liberals and the social-democrats of the West, who were constrained by the Russian Revolution into doubt about their rotted ideas, now experienced a fresh influx of courage. The moral gangrene of the Soviet bureaucracy seemed to them the rehabilitation of liberalism. Stereotyped copybooks are drawn out into the light: "every dictatorship contains the seeds of its own degeneration"; "only democracy guarantees the development of personality"; and so forth. The contrasting of democracy and dictatorship, including in the given case a condemnation of socialism in favor of the bourgeois régime, stuns one from the point of view of theory by its illiterateness and unscrupulousness. The Stalinist pollution, a historical reality, is counterposed to democracy—a supra-historical abstraction. But democracy also possesses a history in which there is no lack of pollution. In order to characterize Soviet bureaucracy we have borrowed the names of "Thermidor" and "Bonapartism"[3] from the history of bourgeois democracy because—let this be known to the retarded liberal doctrinaires—*democracy came into the world not at all through the democratic road*. Only a vulgar mentality can satisfy itself by chewing on the theme that Bonapartism was the "natural offspring" of Jacobinism,[4] the historical punishment for infringing upon democracy, and so on. Without the Jacobin retribution upon feudalism, bourgeois democracy would have been absolutely unthinkable. Contrasting to the concrete historical stages of Jacobinism, Thermidor, Bonapartism the idealized abstraction of "democracy," is as vicious as contrasting the pains of childbirth to a living infant.

Stalinism in turn is not an abstraction of "dictatorship," but an immense bureaucratic reaction against the proletarian dictatorship in a backward and isolated country. The October Revolution[5] abolished privileges, waged war against social inequality, replaced the bureaucracy with self-government of the toilers, abolished secret diplomacy, strove to render all social relationships completely transparent. Stalinism reëstablished the most offensive forms of privileges, imbued inequality with a provocative character, strangled mass self-activity under police absolutism, transformed administration into a monopoly of the Kremlin oligarchy and regenerated the fetishism of power in forms that absolute monarchy dared not dream of.

Social reaction in all forms is constrained to mask its real aims. The sharper the transition from revolution to reaction; the more the reaction is dependent upon the traditions of revolution, that is, the greater its fear of the masses—the more is it forced to resort to mendacity and frame-up in the struggle against the representatives of the revolution. Stalinist frame-ups are not a fruit of Bolshevik

---

1   *Yezhov*   Nikolai Yezhov (1895–1940) was a senior figure in the Soviet secret police during the period of Stalin's Purge.

2   *Jacob Walcher*   (1887–1970), one of the founders of the German Communist party.

3   *Bonapartism*   The movement in post-1815 France in favor of a return of a powerful emperor, on the model of Napoleon Bonaparte. More generally, any political movement promoting the idea of an authoritarian leader.

4   *Jacobinism*   Advocacy of extreme revolutionary views; the reference is to the Jacobins, radical French Revolution republicans.

5   *October Revolution*   After the February (1917) Revolution overthrew the Russian Czar, the October Revolution gave power to the Bolsheviks. Civil war followed.

"amoralism"; no, like all important events in history, they are a product of the concrete social struggle, and the most perfidious and severest of all at that: the struggle of a new aristocracy against the masses that raised it to power.

Verily boundless intellectual and moral obtuseness is required to identify the reactionary police morality of Stalinism with the revolutionary morality of the Bolsheviks. Lenin's party has long ceased to exist—it was shattered between inner difficulties and world imperialism. In its place rose the Stalinist bureaucracy, transmissive mechanism of imperialism. The bureaucracy substituted class collaboration for the class struggle on the world arena, social-patriotism for internationalism. In order to adapt the ruling party to the tasks of reaction, the bureaucracy "renewed" its composition through executing revolutionists and recruiting careerists.

Every reaction regenerates, nourishes and strengthens those elements of the historic past which the revolution struck but which it could not vanquish. The methods of Stalinism bring to the highest tension, to a culmination and at the same time to an absurdity all those methods of untruth, brutality and baseness which constitute the mechanics of control in every class society including also that of democracy. Stalinism is a single clot of all monstrosities of the historical State, its most malicious caricature and disgusting grimace. When the representatives of old society puritanically counterpoise a sterilized democratic abstraction to the gangrene of Stalinism, we can with full justice recommend to them, as to all of old society, that they fall enamored of themselves in the warped mirror of Soviet Thermidor. True, the G.P.U. far surpasses all other régimes in the nakedness of its crimes. But this flows from the immense amplitude of events shaking Russia under the influence of world imperialist demoralization.

Among the liberals and radicals there are not a few individuals who have assimilated the methods of the materialist interpretation of events and who consider themselves Marxists. This does not hinder them, however, from remaining bourgeois journalists, professors or politicians. A Bolshevik is inconceivable, of course, without the materialist method, in the sphere of morality too. But this method serves him not solely for the interpretation of events but rather for the creation of a revolutionary party of the proletariat. It is impossible to accomplish this task without complete independence from the bourgeoisie and their morality. Yet bourgeois public opinion actually now reigns in full sway over the official workers' movement from Wil-

liam Green[1] in the United States, Léon Blum and Maurice Thorez in France, to Garcia Oliver[2] in Spain. In this fact the reactionary character of the present period reaches its sharpest expression.

A revolutionary Marxist cannot begin to approach his historical mission without having broken morally from bourgeois public opinion and its agencies in the proletariat. For this, moral courage of a different caliber is required than that of opening wide one's mouth at meetings and yelling, "Down with Hitler!" "Down with Franco!" It is precisely this resolute, completely-thought-out, inflexible rupture of the Bolsheviks from conservative moral philosophy not only of the big but of the petty bourgeoisie which mortally terrorizes democratic phrase-mongers, drawing room prophets and lobbying heroes. From this is derived their complaints about the "amoralism" of the Bolsheviks.

Their identification of bourgeois morals with morals "in general" can best of all, perhaps, be verified at the extreme left wing of the petty bourgeoisie, precisely in the centrist parties of the so-called London Bureau. Since this organization "recognizes" the program of proletarian revolution, our disagreements with it seem, at first glance, secondary. Actually their "recognition" is valueless because it does not bind them to anything. They "recognize" the proletarian revolution as the Kantians recognized the categorical imperative, that is, as a holy principle but not applicable to daily life. In the sphere of practical politics they unite with the worst enemies of the revolution (reformists and Stalinists) for the struggle against us. All their thinking is permeated with duplicity and falsehood. If the centrists, according to a general rule, do not raise themselves to imposing crimes it is only because they forever remain in the byways of politics: they are, so to speak, petty pick-pockets of history. For this reason they consider themselves called upon to regenerate the workers' movement with a new morality.

At the extreme left wing of this "left" fraternity stands a small and politically completely insignificant grouping of German émigrés who publish the paper *Neuer Weg* (The New Road). Let us bend down lower and listen to these "revolutionary" indicters of Bolshevik amoralism. In a tone of ambiguous pseudo-praise the *Neuer Weg* proclaims that the Bolsheviks are distinguished advantageously from other parties by their absence of hypocrisy—they openly declare

---

1 *William Green* (1873–1952), politically moderate president of the AFL (American Federation of Labor), 1924–52.

2 *Garcia Oliver* Juan García Oliver (1901–80), Spanish anarchist and labor leader.

what others quietly apply in fact, that is, the principle: "the end justifies the means." But according to the convictions of *Newer Weg* such a "bourgeois" precept is incompatible with a "healthy socialist movement." "Lying and worse are not permissible means of struggle, as Lenin still considered." The word "still" evidently signifies that Lenin did not succeed in overcoming his delusions only because he failed to live until the discovery of *The New Road*.

In the formula, "lying and worse," "worse" evidently signifies—violence, murder, and so on, since under equal conditions violence is worse than lying; and murder—the most extreme form of violence. We thus come to the conclusion that lying, violence, murder are incompatible with a "healthy socialist movement." What, however, is our relation to revolution? Civil war is the most severe of all forms of war. It is unthinkable not only without violence against tertiary figures but, under contemporary technique, without murdering old men, old women and children. Must one be reminded of Spain? The only possible answer of the "friends" of republican Spain sounds like this: civil war is better than fascist slavery. But this completely correct answer merely signifies that the *end* (democracy or socialism) justifies, under certain conditions, such *means* as violence and murder. Not to speak about lies! Without lies war would be as unimaginable as a machine without oil. In order to safeguard even the session of the Cortes[1] (February 1, 1938) from Fascist bombs the Barcelona government several times deliberately deceived journalists and their own population. Could it have acted in any other way? Whoever accepts the end: victory over Franco, must accept the means: civil war with its wake of horrors and crimes.

Nevertheless, lying and violence "in themselves" warrant condemnation? Of course, even as does the class society which generates them. A society without social contradictions will naturally be a society without lies and violence. However there is no way of building a bridge to that society save by revolutionary, that is, violent means. The revolution itself is a product of class society and of necessity bears its traits. From the point of view of "eternal truths" revolution is of course "anti-moral." But this merely means that idealist morality is counter-revolutionary, that is, in the service of the exploiters.

"Civil war," will perhaps respond the philosopher caught unawares, "is however a sad exception. But in peaceful times a healthy socialist movement should man-

age without violence and lying." Such an answer however represents nothing less than a pathetic evasion. There is no impervious demarcation between "peaceful" class struggle and revolution. Every strike embodies in an unexpanded form all the elements of civil war. Each side strives to impress the opponent with an exaggerated representation of its resoluteness to struggle and its material resources. Through their press, agents, and spies the capitalists labor to frighten and demoralize the strikers. From their side, the workers' pickets, where persuasion does not avail, are compelled to resort to force. Thus "lie and worse" are an inseparable part of the class struggle even in its most elementary form. It remains to be added that the very conception of *truth* and *lie* was born of social contradictions.

Revolution and the Institution of Hostages

Stalin arrests and shoots the children of his opponents after these opponents have been themselves executed under false accusations. With the help of the institution of family hostages Stalin compels those Soviet diplomats to return from abroad who permitted themselves an expression of doubt upon the infallibility of Yagoda or Yezhov. The moralists of *Neuer Weg* consider it necessary and timely to remind us on this occasion of the fact that Trotsky in 1919[2] "also" introduced a law upon hostages. But here it becomes necessary to quote literally: "The detention of innocent relatives by Stalin is disgusting barbarism. But it remains a barbarism as well when it was dictated by Trotsky (1919)." Here is the idealistic moralist in all his beauty! His criteria are as false as the norms of bourgeois democracy—in both cases *parity* is supposed where in actuality there is not even a trace of it.

We will not insist here upon the fact that the Decree of 1919 led scarcely to even one execution of relatives of those commanders whose perfidy not only caused the loss of innumerable human lives but threatened the revolution itself with direct annihilation. The question in the end does not concern that. If the revolution had displayed less superfluous generosity from the very beginning, hundreds of thousands of lives would have been saved. Thus or otherwise I carry full responsibility for the Decree of 1919. It was a necessary

---

1   *Cortes*   Spanish parliament.

2   *1919*   Date of a secret decision by the Bolsheviks to move against the Don Cossacks (a strongly counter-revolutionary community with a large armed force, living along the Don River). Widespread deportations and executions were reported to have resulted.

measure in the struggle against the oppressors. Only in the historical content of the struggle lies the justification of the decree as in general the justification of the whole civil war which, too, can be called, not without foundation, "disgusting barbarism."

We leave to some Emil Ludwig[1] or his ilk the drawing of Abraham Lincoln's portrait with rosy little wings. Lincoln's significance lies in his not hesitating before the most severe means once they were found to be necessary in achieving a great historic aim posed by the development of a young nation. The question lies not even in which of the warring camps caused or itself suffered the greatest number of victims. History has different yardsticks for the cruelty of the Northerners and the cruelty of the Southerners in the Civil War. A slave-owner who through cunning and violence shackles a slave in chains, and a slave who through cunning or violence breaks the chains—let not the contemptible eunuchs tell us that they are equals before a court of morality!

After the Paris Commune[2] had been drowned in blood and the reactionary knaves of the whole world dragged its banner in the filth of vilification and slander, there were not a few democratic Philistines who, adapting themselves to reaction, slandered the Communards for shooting 64 hostages headed by the Paris archbishop. Marx did not hesitate a moment in defending this bloody act of the Commune. In a circular[3] issued by the General Council of the First International,[4] in which seethes the fiery eruption of lava, Marx first reminds us of the bourgeoisie adopting the institution of hostages in the struggle against both colonial peoples and their own toiling masses and afterwards refers to the systematic execution of the Commune captives by the frenzied reactionaries, continuing: "... the Commune, to protect their [the captives'] lives, was obliged to resort to the Prussian practice of securing hostages. The lives of the hostages had been forfeited over and over again by the continued shoot-ing of prisoners on the part of the Versaillese.[5] How could they be spared any longer after the carnage with which MacMahon's Prætorians[6] celebrated their entry into Paris? Was even the last check upon the unscrupulous ferocity of bourgeois governments—the taking of hostages—to be made a mere sham of?" Thus Marx defended the execution of hostages although behind his back in the General Council sat not a few Fenner Brockways, Norman Thomases and other Otto Bauers. But so fresh was the indignation of the world proletariat against the ferocity of the Versaillese that the reactionary moralistic bunglers preferred to keep silent in expectation of times more favorable to them which, alas, were not slow in appearing. Only after the definite triumph of reaction did the petty bourgeois moralists, together with the trade union bureaucrats and the anarchist phrase-mongers destroy the First International.

When the October Revolution was defending itself against the united forces of imperialism on a 5,000 mile front, the workers of the whole world followed the course of the struggle with such ardent sympathy that in their forums it was extremely risky to indict the "disgusting barbarism" of the institution of hostages. Complete degeneration of the Soviet State and the triumph of reaction in a number of countries was necessary before the moralists crawled out of their crevices ... to aid Stalin. If it is true that the repressions safeguarding the privileges of the new aristocracy have the same moral value as the revolutionary measures of the liberating struggle, then Stalin is completely justified, if ... if the proletarian revolution is not completely condemned.

Seeking examples of immorality in the events of the Russian Civil War,[7] Messrs. Moralists find themselves at the same time constrained to close their eyes to the fact that the Spanish revolution also produced an institution of hostages, at least during that period when it was a genuine revolution of the masses. If the indicters dare not attack the

---

1   *Emil Ludwig* (1881–1948) German author, known for his popular biographies, including one of Stalin.

2   *Paris Commune* Government that controlled the district (French: *commune*) of Paris for two months in 1871, and that followed anarchist or socialist policies.

3   *a circular* "The Civil War in France" (1871).

4   *First International* Popular name for the International Working-men's Association (IWA), an international socialist organization founded in London in 1864, with the aim of uniting leftist political groups and trade unions. After a period of factional conflict and decline, it was succeeded by the Second International in 1889.

5   *the Versaillese* French government forces that invaded Paris in 1871 and dissolved the Paris Commune.

6   *MacMahon's Prætorians* Marie-Edmé-Patrice-Maurice de MacMahon (1808–93), French military commander and politician, led the final victorious assault of the government troops against the Paris Commune. The "Praetorians" (the praetorian guard) was the troop of bodyguards used by Roman Emperors (originally used to guard the praetor—the commanding general of a Roman Army). Eventually the term "praetorian guard" came to carry with it associations of venality, corruption, and cruelty.

7   *Russian Civil War* War (1917–22) between the Bolsheviks—the Red Army—and an alliance of domestic and foreign forces—the White Army.

Spanish workers for their "disgusting barbarism," it is only because the ground of the Pyrennean peninsula[1] is still too hot for them. It is considerably more convenient to return to 1919. This is already history, the old men have forgotten and the young ones have not yet learned. For the same reason Pharisees[2] of various hues return to Kronstadt[3] and Makhno[4] with such obstinacy—here exists a free outlet for moral effluvia!

"Morality of the Kaffirs "[5]

It is impossible not to agree with the moralists that history chooses grievous pathways. But what type of conclusion for practical activity is to be drawn from this? Leo Tolstoy[6] recommended that we ignore the social conventions and perfect ourselves. Mahatma Ghandi advises that we drink goat's milk. Alas, the "revolutionary" moralists of *Neuer Weg* did not drift far from these recipes. "We should free ourselves," they preach, "from those morals of the Kaffirs to whom only what the enemy does is wrong." Excellent advice! "We should free ourselves...." Tolstoy recommended in addition that we free ourselves from the sins of the flesh. However, statistics fail to confirm the success of his recommendation. Our centrist mannikins have succeeded in elevating themselves to supra-class morality in a class society. But almost 2,000 years have passed since it was stated: "Love your enemies," "Offer also the other cheek...." However, even the holy Roman father[7] so far has not "freed himself" from hatred against his enemies. Truly, Satan, the enemy of mankind, is powerful!

---

1   *Pyrennean peninsula*   Spain.

2   *Pharisees*   Ancient Jewish religious group which endorsed a strict interpretation of the Mosaic Law. In the New Testament, Jesus frequently accused them of self-righteousness, pride, and hypocrisy. Thus, the term is often used to refer to a self-righteous and sanctimonious person.

3   *Kronstadt*   Town near St. Petersburg, site of the 1921 Kronstadt Rebellion against Bolshevik repressive policies. The Rebellion was quickly and brutally suppressed by the Red Army under Trotsky's direction.

4   *Makhno*   Nestor Makhno (1888–1934), anarcho-communist Ukrainian revolutionary and political leader; after a period of alliance with the Bolsheviks, his anarchist politics drew Russian opposition. Trotsky was instrumental in forcing Makhno into exile and in convicting many of his followers as criminals.

5   *Kaffirs*   Racist term for black South Africans.

6   *Leo Tolstoy*   (1828–1910), Russian writer and essayist, famous for his novels; he was also a pacifist Christian anarchist.

7   *the holy Roman father*   The Pope.

To apply different criteria to the actions of the exploiters and the exploited signifies, according to these pitiful mannikins, standing on the level of the "morals of the Kaffirs." First of all such a contemptuous reference to the Kaffirs is hardly proper from the pen of "socialists." Are the morals of the Kaffirs really so bad? Here is what the *Encyclopædia Britannica* says upon the subject:

"In their social and political relations they display great tact and intelligence; they are remarkably brave, warlike, and hospitable, and were honest and truthful until through contact with the whites they became suspicious, revengeful and thievish, besides acquiring most European vices." It is impossible not to arrive at the conclusion that white missionaries, preachers of eternal morals, participated in the corruption of the Kaffirs.

If we should tell the toiler-Kaffir how the workers arose in a part of our planet and caught their exploiters unawares, he would be very pleased. On the other hand, he would be chagrined to discover that the oppressors had succeeded in deceiving the oppressed. A Kaffir who has not been demoralized by missionaries to the marrow of his bones will never apply one and the same abstract moral norms to the oppressors and the oppressed. Yet he will easily comprehend an explanation that it is the function of these abstract norms to prevent the oppressed from arising against their oppressors.

What an instructive coincidence: in order to slander the Bolsheviks, the missionaries of *Neuer Weg* were compelled at the same time to slander the Kaffirs; moreover in both cases the slander follows the line of the official bourgeois lie: against revolutionists and against the colored races. No, we prefer the Kaffirs to all missionaries, both spiritual and secular!

It is not necessary in any case, however, to overestimate the conscientiousness of the moralists of *Neuer Weg* and other *cul-de-sacs*. The intentions of these people are not so bad. But despite these intentions they serve as levers in the mechanics of reaction. In such a period as the present when the petty bourgeois parties who cling to the liberal bourgeoisie or its shadow (the politics of the "Peoples' Front"[8]) paralyze the proletariat and pave the road for Fascism (Spain, France ...), the Bolsheviks, that is, revolutionary Marxists,

---

8   *Peoples' Front*   Otherwise known as "Popular Front," referring to any of several alliances bringing together communist and socialist parties with left-leaning bourgeois groups (liberals, etc.). The best-known examples of this were in France and Spain in the 1930s. They generally failed due to factional divisions.

become especially odious figures in the eyes of bourgeois public opinion. The fundamental political pressure of our time shifts from right to left. In the final analysis the whole weight of reaction bears down upon the shoulders of a tiny revolutionary minority. This minority is called the Fourth International.[1] *Voila l'ennemi!* There is the enemy!

In the mechanics of reaction Stalinism occupies many leading positions. All groupings of bourgeois society, including the anarchists, utilize its aid in the struggle against the proletarian revolution. At the same time the petty bourgeois democrats attempt, at least to the extent of fifty percent, to cast the repulsiveness of the crimes of its Moscow ally upon the indomitable revolutionary minority. Herein lies the sense of the now stylish dictum: "Trotskyism and Stalinism are one and the same." The adversaries of the Bolsheviks and the Kaffirs thus aid reaction in slandering the party of revolution.

The "Amoralism" of Lenin

The Russian "Socialist Revolutionaries" were always the most moral individuals: essentially they were composed of ethics alone. This did not prevent them, however, at the time of revolution from deceiving the Russian peasants. In the Parisian organ of Kerensky,[2] that very ethical socialist who was the forerunner of Stalin in manufacturing spurious accusations against the Bolsheviks, another old "Socialist Revolutionary" Zenzinov[3] writes: "Lenin, as is known, taught that for the sake of gaining the desired ends communists can, and sometimes must 'resort to all sorts of devices, manœuvres and subterfuge' ..." (*New Russia*, February 17, 1938, p. 3). From this they draw the ritualistic conclusion: Stalinism is the natural offspring of Leninism.

Unfortunately, the ethical indicter is not even capable of quoting honestly. Lenin said: "It is necessary to be able ... to

resort to all sorts of devices, manœuvres, and illegal methods, to evasion and subterfuge, *in order to penetrate into the trade unions, to remain in them, and to carry on communist work in them at all costs.*" The necessity for evasion and manœuvres, according to Lenin's explanation, is called forth by the fact that the reformist bureaucracy, betraying the workers to capital, baits revolutionists, persecutes them, and even resorts to turning the bourgeois police upon them. "Manœuvres" and "subterfuge" are in this case only methods of valid self-defense against the perfidious reformist bureaucracy.

The party of this very Zenzinov once carried on illegal work against Czarism, and later—against the Bolsheviks. In both cases it resorted to craftiness, evasion, false passports and other forms of "subterfuge." All these *means* were considered not only "ethical" but also heroic because they corresponded to political *aims* of the petty bourgeoisie. But the situation changes at once when proletarian revolutionists are forced to resort to conspirative measures against the petty bourgeois democracy. The key to the morality of these gentlemen has, as we see, a class character!

The "amoralist" Lenin openly, in the press, gives advice concerning military craftiness against perfidious leaders. And the moralist Zenzinov maliciously chops both ends from the quotation in order to deceive the reader: the ethical indicter is proved as usual a petty swindler. Not for nothing was Lenin fond of repeating: it is very difficult to meet a conscientious adversary!

A worker who does not conceal the "truth" about the strikers' plans from the capitalists is simply a betrayer deserving contempt and boycott. The soldier who discloses the "truth" to the enemy is punished as a spy. Kerensky tried to lay at the Bolsheviks' door the accusation of having disclosed the "truth" to Ludendorff's[4] staff. It appears that even the "holy truth" is not an end in itself. More imperious criteria which, as analysis demonstrates, carry a class character, rule over it.

The life and death struggle is unthinkable without military man proletariat then not deceive Hitler's police? Or perhaps Soviet Bolsheviks have an "immoral" attitude when they deceive the G.P.U.? Every pious bourgeois applauds the cleverness of police who succeed through craftiness in seizing a dangerous gangster. Is military craftiness really permissible when the question concerns the overthrow of the gangsters of imperialism?

---

1   *Fourth International*   Organization founded by Trotsky in 1938, to counter the Third International which was controlled by Stalinists. Opposed by just about every leftist group, they remained divided and ineffectual, though some groups today claim to be their legitimate successors.

2   *Kerensky*   Alexander Kerensky (1881–1970), Russian revolutionary leader, an important figure in the initial overthrow of the Czarist regime, was second Prime Minister in the Provisional Government that ruled for a few months in 1917, until Lenin and the Bolsheviks seized power during the October Revolution.

3   *Zenzinov*   Vladimir Zenzinov (1880–1953), Russian revolutionary activist, who was later exiled due to his anti-Bolshevism, and spent much of his life writing from exile.

---

4   *Ludendorff*   Erich Friedrich Wilhelm Ludendorff (1865–1937), German Army officer.

Norman Thomas speaks about "that strange communist amorality in which nothing matters but the party and its power" (*Socialist Call*, March 12, 1938, p. 5). Moreover, Thomas throws into one heap the present Comintern, that is, the conspiracy of the Kremlin bureaucracy against the working class, with the Bolshevik party which represented a conspiracy of the advanced workers against the bourgeoisie. This thoroughly dishonest juxtaposition has already been sufficiently exposed above. Stalinism merely screens itself under the cult of the party; actually it destroys and tramples the party in filth. It is true, however, that to a Bolshevik the party is everything. The drawing-room socialist, Thomas, is surprised by and rejects a similar relationship between a revolutionist and revolution because be himself is only a bourgeois with a socialist "ideal." In the eyes of Thomas and his kind the party is only a secondary instrument for electoral combinations and other similar uses, not more. His personal life, interests, ties, moral criteria exist outside the party. With hostile astonishment he looks down upon the Bolshevik to whom the party is a weapon for the revolutionary reconstruction of society, including also its morality. To a revolutionary Marxist there can be no contradiction between personal morality and the interests of the party, since the party embodies in his consciousness the very highest tasks and aims of mankind. It is naïve to imagine that Thomas has a higher understanding of morality than the Marxists. He merely has a base conception of the party.

"All that arises is worthy of perishing," says the dialectician, Goethe.[1] The destruction of the Bolshevik party—an episode in world reaction—does not, however, disparage its world-wide historic significance. In the period of its revolutionary ascendance, that is, when it actually represented the proletarian vanguard, it was the most honest party in history. Wherever it could, it, of course, deceived the class enemies; on the other hand it told the toilers the truth, the whole truth, and nothing but the truth. Only thanks to this did it succeed in winning their trust to a degree never before achieved by any other party in the world.

The clerks of the ruling classes call the organizers of this party "amoralists." In the eyes of conscious workers this accusation carries a complimentary character. It signifies: Lenin refused to recognize moral norms established by slave-owners for their slaves and never observed by the slave-owners themselves; he called upon the proletariat to extend the class struggle into the moral sphere too. Whoever fawns before precepts established by the enemy will never vanquish that enemy!

The "amoralism" of Lenin, that is, his rejection of supraclass morals, did not hinder him from remaining faithful to one and the same ideal throughout his whole life; from devoting his whole being to the cause of the oppressed; from displaying the highest conscientiousness in the sphere of ideas and the highest fearlessness in the sphere of action, from maintaining an attitude untainted by the least superiority to an "ordinary" worker, to a defenseless woman, to a child. Does it not seem that "amoralism" in the given case is only a pseudonym for higher human morality?

An Instructive Episode

Here it is proper to relate an episode which, in spite of its modest dimensions, does not badly illustrate the difference between *their* morals and *ours*. In 1935, through a letter to my Belgian friends, I developed the conception that the attempt of a young revolutionary party to organize "its own" trade unions is equivalent to suicide. It is necessary to find the workers where they are. But this means paying dues in order to sustain an opportunist apparatus? "Of course," I replied, "for the right to undermine the reformists it is necessary temporarily to pay them a contribution." But reformists will not permit us to undermine them? "True," I answered, "undermining demands conspirative measures. Reformists are the political police of the bourgeoisie within the working class. We must act without their permission, and against their interdiction...." Through an accidental raid on comrade D.'s home in connection, if I am not mistaken, with the matter of supplying arms for the Spanish workers, the Belgian police seized my letter. Within several days it was published. The press of Vandervelde, De Man, and Spaak[2] did not of course spare lightning against my "Machiavellianism" and "Jesuitism." And who are these accusers? Vandervelde, president for many years of the Second International, long ago became a trusted servant of Belgian capital. De Man, who in a series of ponderous tomes ennobled socialism with idealistic morals, making overtures to

---

1   *the dialectician Goethe* Johann Wolfgang von Goethe (1749–1832) poet, writer, essayist, artist. A dialectician is a philosopher who argues by weighing conflicting or opposite facts, attempting to resolve apparent contradictions.

2   *Vandervelde ... Spaak* Emile Vandervelde (1866–1938), Henri (Hendrik) De Man (1885–1953), Paul-Henri Charles Spaak (1899–1972). All three were Belgian socialist leaders. Vandervelde and Spaak each held a variety of political positions.

religion, seized the first suitable occasion in which to betray the workers and became a common bourgeois minister. Even more lovely is Spaak's case. A year and a half previously this gentleman belonged to the left-socialist opposition and came to me in France for advice upon the methods of struggle against Vandervelde's bureaucracy. I set forth the same conceptions which later constituted my letter. But within a year after his visit, Spaak rejected the thorns for the roses. Betraying his comrades of the opposition, he became one of the most cynical ministers of Belgian capital. In the trade unions and in their own party these gentlemen stifle every critical voice, systematically corrupt and bribe the most advanced workers and just as systematically expel the refractory ones. They are distinguished from the G.P.U. only by the fact that they have not yet resorted to spilling blood—as good patriots they husband the workers' blood for the next imperialist war. Obviously—one must be a most hellish abomination, a moral deformation, a "Kaffir," a Bolshevik, in order to advise the revolutionary workers to observe the precepts of conspiracy in the struggle against these gentlemen!

From the point of view of the Belgian laws, my letter did not of course contain anything criminal. The duty of the "democratic" police was to return the letter to the addressee with an apology. The duty of the socialist party was to protest against the raid which had been dictated by concern over General Franco's interests. But Messrs. Socialists were not at all shy at utilizing the indecent police service—without this they could not have enjoyed the happy occasion of once more exposing the superiority of their morals over the amoralism of the Bolsheviks.

Everything is symbolical in this episode. The Belgian social-democrats dumped the buckets of their indignation upon me exactly while their Norwegian co-thinkers held me and my wife under lock and key in order to prevent us from defending ourselves against the accusations of the G.P.U. The Norwegian government well knew that the Moscow accusations were spurious—the social-democratic semi-official newspaper affirmed this openly during the first days. But Moscow touched the Norwegian shipowners and fish merchants on the pocketbook—and Messrs. Social-Democrats immediately flopped down on all fours. The leader of the party, Martin Tranmæl,[1] is not only an author-

ity in the moral sphere but openly a righteous person: he does not drink, does not smoke, does not indulge in meat and in winter bathes in an ice-hole. This did not hinder him, after he had arrested us upon the order of the G.P.U., from especially inviting a Norwegian agent of the G.P.U., one Jacob Fries—a bourgeois without honor or conscience, to calumniate me. But enough....

The morals of these gentlemen consists of conventional precepts and turns of speech which are supposed to screen their interests, appetites and fears. In the majority they are ready for any baseness—rejection of convictions, perfidy, betrayal—in the name of ambition or cupidity. In the holy sphere of personal interests the end to them justifies any means. But it is precisely because of this that they require special codes of morals, durable, and at the same time elastic, like good suspenders. They detest anyone who exposes their professional secrets to the masses. In "peaceful" times their hatred is expressed in slander—in Billingsgate or "philosophical" language. In times of sharp social conflicts, as in Spain, these moralists, hand in hand with the G.P.U., murder revolutionists. In order to justify themselves, they repeat: "Trotskyism and Stalinism are one and the same."

Dialectic Interdependence of End and Means

A means can be justified only by its end. But the end in its turn needs to be justified. From the Marxist point of view, which expresses the historical interests of the proletariat, the end is justified if it leads to increasing the power of man over nature and to the abolition of the power of man over man.

"We are to understand then that in achieving this end anything is permissible?" sarcastically demands the Philistine, demonstrating that he understood nothing. That is permissible, we answer, which *really* leads to the liberation of mankind. Since this end can be achieved only through revolution, the liberating morality of the proletariat of necessity is endowed with a revolutionary character. It irreconcilably counteracts not only religious dogma but every kind of idealistic fetish, these philosophic gendarmes of the ruling class. It deduces a rule for conduct from the laws of the development of society, thus primarily from the class struggle, this law of all laws.

"Just the same," the moralist continues to insist, "does it mean that in the class struggle against capitalists all

---

1   *Martin Tranmæl* (1879–1967) was leader of the more radical left wing of the Norwegian Labor Party, and a long-time Soviet sympathizer.

means are permissible: lying, frame-up, betrayal, murder, and so on?" Permissible and obligatory are those and only those means, we answer, which unite the revolutionary proletariat, fill their hearts with irreconcilable hostility to oppression, teach them contempt for official morality and its democratic echoers, imbue them with consciousness of their own historic mission, raise their courage and spirit of self-sacrifice in the struggle. Precisely from this it flows that *not* all means are permissible. When we say that the end justifies the means, then for us the conclusion follows that the great revolutionary end spurns those base means and ways which set one part of the working class against other parts, or attempt to make the masses happy without their participation; or lower the faith of the masses in themselves and their organization, replacing it by worship for the "leaders." Primarily and irreconcilably, revolutionary morality rejects servility in relation to the bourgeoisie and haughtiness in relation to the toilers, that is, those characteristics in which petty bourgeois pedants and moralists are thoroughly steeped.

These criteria do not, of course, give a ready answer to the question as to what is permissible and what is not permissible in each separate case. There can be no such automatic answers. Problems of revolutionary morality are fused with the problems of revolutionary strategy and tactics. The living experience of the movement under the clarification of theory provides the correct answer to these problems.

Dialectic materialism does not know dualism between means and end, The end flows naturally from the historical movement. Organically the means are subordinated to the end. The immediate end becomes the means for a further end. In his play, *Franz von Sickingen*, Ferdinand Lassalle[1] puts the following words into the mouth of one of the heroes:

> "... Show not the *goal*
> But show also the *path*. So closely interwoven
> Are path and goal that each with other
> Ever changes, and other *paths* forthwith
> Another *goal* set up."

Lassalle's lines are not at all perfect. Still worse is the fact that in practical politics Lassalle himself diverged from the above expressed precept—it is sufficient to recall that he went as far as secret agreements with Bismark! But the

dialectic inter-dependence between means and end is expressed entirely correctly in the above-quoted sentences. Seeds of wheat must be sown in order to yield an ear of wheat.

Is individual terror, for example, permissible or impermissible from the point of view of "pure morals"? In this abstract form the question does not exist at all for us. Conservative Swiss bourgeois even now render official praise to the terrorist William Tell.[2] Our sympathies are fully on the side of Irish, Russian, Polish or Hindu terrorists in their struggle against national and political oppression. The assassinated Kirov, a rude satrap, does not call forth any sympathy. Our relation to the assassin remains neutral only because we know not what motives guided him. If it became known that Nikolayev[3] acted as a conscious avenger for workers' rights trampled upon by Kirov, our sympathies would be fully on the side of the assassin. However, not the question of subjective motives but that of objective expediency has for us the decisive significance. Are the given means really capable of leading to the goal? In relation to individual terror, both theory and experience bear witness that such is not the case. To the terrorist we say: it is impossible to replace the masses; only in the mass movement can you find expedient expression for your heroism. However, under conditions of civil war, the assassination of individual oppressors ceases to be an act of individual terror. If, we shall say, a revolutionist bombed General Franco and his staff into the air, it would hardly evoke moral indignation even from the democratic eunuchs. Under the conditions of civil war a similar act would be politically completely expedient. Thus, even in the sharpest question—murder of man by man—moral absolutes prove futile. Moral evaluations, together with those political, flow from the inner needs of struggle.

The liberation of the workers can come only through the workers themselves. There is, therefore, no greater crime than deceiving the masses, palming off defeats as victories, friends as enemies, bribing workers' leaders, fabricating

---

1 *Ferdinand Lassalle* German jurist and socialist political activist (1825–64). The play Trotsky mentions was published in 1859.

---

2 *William Tell* Legendary hero of fourteenth-century Switzerland. In the famous story, he was forced by the local tyrant, to whom he refused to pay his respects, to shoot an apple off his son's head with his crossbow; later he shot the tyrant.

3 *Kirov … Nikolayev* Sergei Kirov (1886–1934) was a prominent early Bolshevik leader assassinated by Leonid Nikolaev (1904–34). Trotsky's followers were accused of the assassination, and Stalin responded with massive purges. It is sometimes suggested that Stalin himself was behind the killing.

legends, staging false trials, in a word, doing what the Stalinists do. These means can serve only one end: lengthening the domination of a clique already condemned by history. But they cannot serve to liberate the masses. That is why the Fourth International leads against Stalinism a life and death struggle.

The masses, of course, are not at all impeccable. Idealization of the masses is foreign to us. We have seen them under different conditions, at different stages and in addition in the biggest political shocks. We have observed their strong and weak sides. Their strong side—resoluteness, self-sacrifice, heroism—has always found its clearest expression in times of revolutionary upsurge. During this period the Bolsheviks headed the masses. Afterward a different historical chapter loomed when the weak side of the oppressed came to the forefront: heterogeneity, insufficiency of culture, narrowness of world outlook. The masses tired of the tension, became disillusioned, lost faith in themselves—and cleared the road for the new aristocracy. In this epoch the Bolsheviks ("Trotskyists") found themselves isolated from the masses. Practically we went through two such big historic cycles: 1897-1905, years of flood tide; 1907-1913 years of the ebb; 1917-1923, a period of upsurge unprecedented in history; finally, a new period of reaction which has not ended even today. In these immense events the "Trotsky-

ists" learned the rhythm of history, that is, the dialectics of the class struggle. They also learned, it seems, and to a certain degree successfully, how to subordinate their subjective plans and programs to this objective rhythm. They learned not to fall into despair over the fact that the laws of history do not depend upon their individual tastes and are not subordinated to their own moral criteria. They learned to subordinate their individual desires to the laws of history. They learned not to become frightened by the most powerful enemies, if their power is in contradiction to the needs of historical development. They know how to swim against the stream in the deep conviction that the new historic flood will carry them to the other shore. Not all will reach that shore, many will drown. But to participate in this movement with open eyes and with an intense will—only this can give the highest moral satisfaction to a thinking being!

COYOACAN, D. F, *February 16, 1938.*
Leon TROTSKY

P.S.—I wrote these lines during those days when my son struggled unknown to me, with death. I dedicate to his memory this small work which, I hope, would have met with his approval—Leon Sedoff was a genuine revolutionist and despised the Pharisees.

L.T.

JOHN DEWEY
(1859-1952)

As one of the three major American pragmatists (along with Charles Sanders Peirce and William James), Dewey contributed to most areas of philosophy. His work ranged from political philosophy and ethics to philosophy of education, metaphysics, epistemology, logic, philosophy of religion, and aesthetics. Dewey was an important American public intellectual, with a career that spanned nearly 70 years. As a political philosopher he was particularly influential for the links he forged between political and educational theory. Dewey's moral and political works include *The School and Society* (1899), *Democracy and Education* (1916), *Human Nature and Conduct* (1922), *The Public and its Problems* (1927), *Liberalism and Social Action* (1935), and *Freedom and Culture* (1939).

Born and raised in Burlington, Vermont, Dewey attended the University of Vermont for his undergraduate studies and received his PhD from John Hopkins University in 1884. At John Hopkins, he fell under the influence of George Sylvester Morris, a prominent Hegelian, and G. Stanley Hall, the experimental psychologist. After a stint of teaching at the University of Michigan (1884-94), he moved to the University of Chicago (1894-1904), where he founded the progressive Laboratory School. Disagreements with the administration led him to resign and move to Columbia University, where he taught from 1904 until his retirement in 1930.

Beyond his philosophical contributions, Dewey was active in public life, advocating women's suffrage and workers' rights. Dewey (albeit unsuccessfully) defended Bertrand Russell in 1940 when religious leaders protested the appointment of the radical atheist divorcé to the College of the City of New York. Later, he chaired the "Commission of Inquiry into the Charges Made Against Leon Trotsky in the Moscow Trials" in Coyoacan, Mexico in April 1937. The Commission was formed to investigate Stalin's show trials, particularly his charges against the exiled Trotsky, convicted in absentia of plotting to assassinate Stalin, slaughtering workers, and treason. The trial lasted a week and the commission returned with a "not guilty" verdict.

Aside from William James, the German idealist Georg Wilhelm Hegel and Charles Darwin were the great influences on Dewey's philosophy. In his autobiographical piece, "From Absolutism to Experimentalism," Dewey noted that his "acquaintance with Hegel" had "left a permanent deposit" in his thinking. From Hegel, Dewey took the notion of people as irreducibly social beings, as well as the view that there is no sharp divide between individuals and their environment. This led him to an organic view of society, rejecting forms of individualism that fail to acknowledge our social character, as well as metaphysical and epistemological views that place us apart from nature.

Unlike the Marxists, many of whom Hegel also inspired, Dewey remained a liberal throughout his life, though his experience in the Great Depression led him to reject rampant individualism for a form of social democracy. James's *Principles of Psychology* and its naturalist approach, along with his interest in experimental psychology, eventually led Dewey away from Hegel's idealism. It encouraged him to adopt Darwin's conception of development, and a dynamic vision of human nature emphasizing growth.

Dewey's political philosophy begins with concrete problems faced by individuals and society. Like Plato, Aristotle, and Rousseau, Dewey regarded education as central to political philosophy. Unlike some philosophers who posit a fixed, human nature, Dewey believed that our capacities and identity are formed through interaction with the environment. Humans participate in nature (which includes society) as part of nature, where they face problems that thwart their aims and demand solutions. Many philosophers have attempted to discover basic, universal ethical or political principles independent of any particular community and use these to evaluate our actual society. Dewey rejects this approach and insists that ethics involves what the title of his well-known essay calls, "The Construction of the Good." We encounter a problematic situation which we are unequipped to address. This leads us to propose hypotheses and test them experimentally. This process is open-ended and continues indefinitely, as we actively "construct" social arrangements and institutions in a critical, reflective manner.

This approach naturally demands a philosophy of education and democracy. The Laboratory School, which Dewey ran with his wife, Alice, inspired the twentieth century's progressive education movement, emphasizing experimentation, problem solving and critical thinking. Dewey viewed education as a process, crucially linked to the formation of critical citizens capable of functioning in a democracy. Only through education can we attack the problems that beset us. *The Public and its Problems* (1927) defended democracy against Walter Lippmann's elitist *The Phantom Public* (1925), which dismissed ordinary citizens' ability to participate competently in public affairs. Dewey argued for a free press providing accurate information on public affairs, and for a better educated public. Where Lippmann dismissed participatory democracy, Dewey called for democratic reform.

Dewey has continued to influence political philosophers and democratic theorists, including North American communitarian philosophers such as Michael Sandel and Charles Taylor and continental thinkers such as Jürgen Habermas.

◆ ◆ ◆ ◆ ◆

Means and Ends: Their Interdependence, and Leon Trotsky's Essay on "Their Morals and Ours" (1938)

The relation of means and ends has long been an outstanding issue in morals. It has also been a burning issue in political theory and practice. Of late the discussion has centered about the later developments of Marxism in the U.S.S.R. The course of the Stalinists has been defended by many of his adherents in other countries on the ground that the purges and prosecutions, perhaps even with a certain

amount of falsification, was necessary to maintain the alleged socialistic régime of that country. Others have used the measures of the Stalinist bureaucracy to condemn the Marxist policy on the ground that the latter leads to such excesses as have occurred in the U.S.S.R. precisely because Marxism holds that the end justifies the means. Some of these critics have held that since Trotsky is also a Marxian he is committed to the same policy and consequently if he had been in power would also have felt bound to use any means whatever that seemed necessary to achieve the end involved in dictatorship by the proletariat.

The discussion has had at least one useful theoretical result. It has brought out into the open for the first time, as far as I am aware, an explicit discussion by a consistent Marxian of the relation of means and ends in social action. At the courteous invitation of one of the editors of this review, I propose to discuss this issue in the light of Mr. Trotsky's discussion of the interdependence of means and ends. Much of the earlier part of his essay does not, accordingly, enter into my discussion, though I may say that on the ground of *tu quoque argument*[1] (suggested by the title) Trotsky has had no great difficulty in showing that some of his critics have acted in much the same way they attribute to him. Since Mr. Trotsky also indicates that the only alternative position to the idea that the end justifies the means is some form of absolutistic ethics based on the alleged deliverances of conscience, or a moral sense, or some brand of eternal truths, I wish to say that I write from a standpoint that rejects all such doctrines as definitely as does Mr. Trotsky himself, and that I hold that the end in the sense of consequences provides the only basis for moral ideas and action, and therefore provides the only justification that can be found for means employed.

The point I propose to consider is that brought up toward the end of Mr. Trotsky's discussion in the section headed "Dialectic Interdependence of Means and Ends." The following statement is basic: "A means can be justified only by its end. But the end in turn needs to be justified. From the Marxian point of view, which expresses the historic interests of the proletariat, the end is justified if it leads to increasing the power of man over nature and to the abolition of the power of man over man." This increase of the power of man over nature, accompanying the abolition

---

1   *tu quoque argument*   Latin: *you also*. A *tu quoque* argument is one that attempts to refute someone's criticism by pointing out that the criticizer is also guilty of the same fault. It does not show that the criticism is not valid.

of the power of man over man, seems accordingly to be *the* end—that is, an end which does not need itself to be justified but which is the justification of the ends that are in turn means to it. It may also be added that others than Marxians might accept this formulation of *the* end and hold that it expresses the moral interest of society—if not the historic interest—and not merely and exclusively that of the proletariat.

But for my present purpose, it is important to note that the word "*end*" is here used to cover two things—the final justifying end and ends that are themselves means to this final end. For while it is not said in so many words that some ends are but means, that proposition is certainly implied in the statement that some ends "*lead* to increasing the power of man over nature, etc." Mr. Trotsky goes on to explain that the principle that the end justifies the means does not mean that every means is permissible. "That is permissible, we answer, which really leads to the liberation of mankind."

Were the latter statement consistently adhered to and followed through it would be consistent with the sound principle of interdependence of means and end. Being in accord with it, it would lead to scrupulous examination of the means that are used, to ascertain what their actual objective consequences will be as far as it is humanly possible to tell—to show that they do "really" lead to the liberation of mankind. It is at this point that the double significance of *end* becomes important. As far as it means consequences actually reached, it is clearly dependent upon means used, while measures in their capacity of means are dependent upon the end in the sense that they have to be viewed and judged on the ground of their actual objective results. On this basis, an *end-in-view* represents or is an *idea* of the final consequences, in case the idea is formed *on the ground of the means that are judged to be most likely to produce the end*. The end in view is thus itself a means for directing action—just as a man's *idea* of health to be attained or a house to be built is not identical with end in the sense of actual outcome but is a means for directing action to achieve that end.

Now what has given the maxim (and the practice it formulates) that the end justifies the means a bad name is that the end-in-view, the end professed and entertained (perhaps quite sincerely) justifies the use of certain means, and so justifies the latter that it is not necessary to examine what the actual consequences of the use of chosen means will be. An individual may hold, and quite sincerely as far as his personal opinion is concerned that certain means will "really" lead to a professed and desired end. But the real question is not one of personal belief but of the objective grounds upon which it is held: namely, the consequences that will actually be produced by them. So when Mr. Trotsky says that "dialectical materialism knows no dualism between means and end," the natural interpretation is that he will recommend the use of means that can be shown by their own nature to lead to the liberation of mankind as an objective consequence.

One would expect, then, that with the idea of the liberation of mankind as the end-in-view, there would be an examination of *all* means that are likely to attain this end without any fixed preconception as to what they *must* be, and that every suggested means would be weighed and judged on the express ground of the consequences it is likely to produce.

But this is *not* the course adopted in Mr. Trotsky's further discussion. He says: "The liberating morality of the proletariat is of a revolutionary character.... It *deduces* a rule of conduct from the laws of the development of society, thus primarily from the class struggle, the law of all laws." (Italics are mine.) As if to leave no doubt of his meaning he says: "The end flows from the historical movement"—that of the class struggle. The principle of interdependence of means and end has thus disappeared or at least been submerged. For the choice of means is not decided upon on the ground of an independent examination of measures and policies with respect to their actual objective consequences. On the contrary, means are "*deduced*" from an independent source, an alleged law of history which is *the* law of all laws of social development. Nor does the logic of the case change if the word "alleged" is stricken out. For even so, it follows that means to be used are not derived from consideration of the end, the liberation of mankind, but from another outside source. The professed end—the end-in-view—the liberation of mankind, is thus subordinated to the class struggle as the means by which it is to be attained. Instead of *inter*dependence of means and end, the end is dependent upon the means but the means are not derived from the end. Since the class struggle is regarded as the *only* means that will reach the end, and since the view that it is the only means is reached deductively and not by an inductive examination of the means-consequences in their interdependence, the means, the class struggle, does not need to be critically examined with respect to its actual objective consequences. It is automatically absolved from all need for critical examination. If we are not back in the position that the *end-in-view* (as distinct from objective consequences) justifies the use of any means in line with the class struggle and that it justifies the neglect of all other means, I fail to understand the logic of Mr. Trotsky's position.

The position that I have indicated as that of genuine interdependence of means and ends does not automatically rule out class struggle as one means for attaining the end. But it does rule out the deductive method of arriving at it as a means, to say nothing of its being the *only* means. The selection of class struggle as a means has to be justified, on the ground of the interdependence of means and end, by an examination of actual consequences of its use, not deductively. Historical considerations are certainly relevant to this examination. But the assumption of a *fixed law* of social development is not relevant. It is as if a biologist or a physician were to assert that a certain law of biology which he accepts is so related to the end of health that the means of arriving at health—and the only means—can be deduced from it, so that no further examination of biological phenomena is needed. The whole case is prejudged.

It is one thing to say that class struggle is a means of attaining the end of the liberation of mankind. It is a radically different thing to say that there is an absolute *law* of class struggle which determines the means to be used. For if it determines the means, it also determines the end—the actual consequences, and upon the principle of genuine interdependence of means and end it is arbitrary and subjective to say that that consequence will be the liberation of mankind. The liberation of mankind is the end to be striven for. In any legitimate sense of "moral," it is a moral end. No scientific law can determine a moral end save by deserting the principle of interdependence of means and end. A Marxian may sincerely believe that class struggle is *the* law of social development. But quite aside from the fact that the belief closes the doors to further examination of history—just as an assertion that the Newtonian laws are the final laws of physics would preclude further search for physical laws—it would not follow, even if it were the scientific law of history, that it is the means to the moral goal of the liberation of mankind. That it is such a means has to be shown not by "deduction" from a law but by examination of the actual relations of means and consequences; an examination in which given the liberation of mankind as end, there is free and unprejudiced search for the means by which it can be attained.

One more consideration may be added about class struggle as a means. There are presumably several, perhaps many, different ways by means of which the class struggle may be carried on. How can a choice be made among these different ways except by examining their consequences in relation to the goal of liberation of mankind? The belief that a law of history determines the particular way in which the struggle is to be carried on certainly seems to tend toward a fanatical and even mystical devotion to use of certain ways of conducting the class struggle to the exclusion of all other ways of conducting it. I have no wish to go outside the theoretical question of the interdependence of means and ends but it is conceivable that the course actually taken by the revolution in the U.S.S.R. becomes more explicable when it is noted that means were deduced from a supposed scientific law instead of being searched for and adopted on the ground of their relation to the moral end of the liberation of mankind.

The only conclusion I am able to reach is that in avoiding one kind of absolutism Mr. Trotsky has plunged into another kind of absolutism. There appears to be a curious transfer among orthodox Marxists of allegiance from the ideals of socialism and scientific *methods* of attaining them (scientific in the sense of being based on the objective relations of means and consequences) to the class struggle as the law of historical change. Deduction of ends set up, of means and attitudes, from this law as the primary thing makes all moral questions, that is, all questions of the end to be finally attained, meaningless. To be scientific about ends does not mean to read them out of laws, whether the laws are natural or social. Orthodox Marxism shares with orthodox religionism and with traditional idealism the belief that human ends are interwoven into the very texture and structure of existence—a conception inherited presumably from its Hegelian[1] origin.

New York City, July 3, 1938

---

1   *Hegelian* Marx (and Marxism) was heavily influenced by the German idealist philosopher Georg Wilhelm Friedrich Hegel (1770–1831), who held that the world is the continuous development of Mind or Spirit (*Geist*) towards an end or goal. Marx is generally taken to have substituted materialism for Hegel's idealism, but to have retained the view that history develops towards a rational end. His own theory of history is based on economic relations of production.

MAX WEBER
(1864-1920)

Max Weber is widely regarded as one of the greatest figures in the social sciences. Though today he is most prominently associated with sociology, a discipline he arguably created, he also contributed to economics, political theory, law, history, and religious studies. In political and social philosophy, he is one of the central representatives of political realism, a school of thought whose roots may be traced from Thucydides, through Machiavelli and Hobbes, to later scholars such as E.H. Carr, Hans Morgenthau, Reinhold Niebuhr, George F. Kennan, and Henry Kissinger.

Born in 1864 in Berlin to an academic and political family, Weber was a precocious child who began to write at an early age about history, philosophy, and politics. He received his law degree and passed the bar in 1887, followed by a doctorate in 1889; his dissertation was on medieval trading companies and his habilitation (a further requirement in German universities in order to qualify for a teaching position) on law and Roman agrarian history. After a brief legal career, he taught from 1894 to 1897 at Freiburg and at Heidelberg until 1902, when a mental breakdown led him to resign his professorship. He continued to work as a scholar; his most important early work was *The Protestant Ethic and the Spirit of Capitalism* (1904-05), in which he argued that the Calvinist ethic with its notion of a "calling" strongly influenced the development of capitalism—an argument that provided an alternative to the Marxist view that the economic base determines the intellectual superstructure. Weber followed this work with studies of the economics of Confucianism, Taoism, Hinduism, Buddhism, and Judaism.

During this time, he acted as journal editor, hospital administrator, and political consultant. He also acted as a consultant in the drafting of the Weimar constitution and was a member of the German delegation to the Versailles peace conference of 1919. Right-wing opposition led him

to abandon politics in 1918; he became professor of economics in Munich in 1818, but died only two years later, with much of his greatest work unpublished. This included a series of influential methodological essays (gathered in *Collected Essays in Scientific Theory* in 1922) and *Economy and Society* (also published posthumously in 1922). His lecture notes on the origin and history of capitalism were published as *General Economic History* in 1923.

Weber argued that fact and value are sharply distinguished, and that the natural sciences discover facts, but have nothing whatever to say about values. Social science is different from natural science, since it involves agents with an understanding of what they are doing, requiring a science which supplements value-free objective-fact-collection with interpretation (*Verstehen*). This view led to Weber's theory of "ideal types," conceptual schemes of a priori categories, values, and interests that structure and give meaning to phenomena.

According to Weber, modernization has led to the "disenchantment" of the world, so that there is no principled way of deciding between ultimate ends. On this view, a rational political science can tell us whether a policy is suitable to achieving one's ends, but not whether those ends themselves are justified. Politics, for Weber, has a tragic aspect to it. It is characterized by power struggles, the "rule of man over man"; individuals strive for power either for its own sake or to achieve certain ends. It is tragic in large part because sometimes a politician must be prepared to do evil in order to achieve good.

Here Weber introduces the distinction between an "ethics of conviction" and an "ethics of responsibility." Adherents of an ethics of conviction believe in absolute moral principles that must be acted upon regardless of the consequences. (Jesus' Sermon on the Mount is a paradigmatic example.) Politicians, according to Weber, must adapt an ethics of responsibility, one which allows for compromise, along with a full acceptance of responsibility for the foreseeable consequences. But Weber also believed that the political vocation requires passion; Luther's assertion "Here I stand, I can do no other," in which the leader takes responsibility for his or her value commitments, was for Weber a model.

Weber famously defined the state as having a monopoly on the legitimate use of force. But no regime can rule for long by force alone, so some means is necessary through which people may be brought to accept the regime. Weber distinguishes three sources of political legitimacy—a term that should here be understood in terms of what leads people to accept an order of rules, not in the normative sense of whether or not they *ought* to accept them. *Traditional rule* relies on custom, for example royal lineages; *charismatic rule* depends on the exceptional character of the leader; *rational-legal rule* uses legal statute and judicial action to enforce rationally designed rules.

The modern state (in contrast to earlier familial, religious, patriarchal, or feudal structures) does this chiefly by means of law and bureaucracy. Bureaucracy, because of its technical superiority (i.e., it achieves the ends set out for it better than do earlier forms of organization) dominates capitalist and socialist states. Though Weber often argues for a "value-free" science, he contrasts the *Kulturmensch* (the cultured man) with the *Fachmensch* (the expert specialist), and expresses horror at the notion of people transformed into cogs in the bureaucratic machine, unable to choose their own goals.

Weber's political legacy is controversial. Though traditionally identified as politically left of center (in consequence largely of his strong rejection of authoritarianism and his advocacy of democratic parliamentary reform), his formulation of charismatic rule, along with his (disputed) role in Article 48 of the Weimar constitution (giving the president extraordinary powers in times of crisis) disturbingly anticipate the rise of Hitler. Weber endorsed extreme nationalism as a means of transcending the factions that characterized post-World War I politics. His views have been related to the work of Carl Schmitt, who concluded that Weimar parliamentarianism could not cope with the conflict between totalizing parties, and who endorsed the National Socialists. He has also been widely criticized—by Jürgen Habermas, among others—for his "value-free" approach to politics, an approach in which functional analysis takes precedence over normative debate concerning political ends.

◆ ◆ ◆ ◆ ◆

Politics as a Vocation (1919)

What can politics as a vocation offer in the way of inner satisfaction, and which personal qualities does it presuppose in anyone who devotes himself to it?

Well, it offers first of all the sense of power. Even in positions which are, formally speaking, modest, the professional politician can feel himself elevated above the everyday level by the sense of exercising influence over men, of having a share in power over their lives, but above all by the sense of having his finger on the pulse of historically important events. But the question which he has to face is this: through which personal qualities can he hope to do justice to this power (however narrow its limits in his particular case) and so to the responsibility it lays on him? At this point we enter the domain of ethical questions; for it is in this domain that the question arises: what kind of man must one be to venture to lay hands on the spokes of the wheel of history?

Three qualities above all, it might be said, are of decisive importance for the politician: passion, a sense of responsibility and judgment. By "passion" I mean *realistic* passion—a passionate commitment to a realistic cause, to the god or demon in whose domain it lies. I do not mean "passion" in the sense of that state of mind which my late friend Georg Simmel used to call "sterile excitement"—a state which is characteristic of a certain kind of intellectual, especially of Russian intellectuals (though not perhaps all of them!), and which now plays such a large part amongst our own intellectuals in this carnival which is dignified with the proud name of a "revolution." It is a kind of romanticism of the intellectually "interesting" which lacks any realistic sense of responsibility and runs away to nothing. For it is not enough merely to have the passion, however genuinely felt. That alone does not make a politician, unless it is used to further some real cause and so makes a *sense of responsibility* towards this cause the ultimate guide of his behavior. And that requires the, decisive psychological quality of the politician—*judgment*—the ability to contemplate things as they are with inner calm and composure before allowing them to affect one's actions, or in other words, an attitude of *detachment* towards things and people. Lack of detachment, purely as such, is one of the mortal sins for every politician, and one of those qualities which would condemn our rising generation of intellectuals to political impotence if they were to cultivate it. The problem, therefore, is simply how hot passion and cool judgment can be made to combine within the same personality. Politics is made with the head, not with other parts of the body or mind. And dedication to politics can only be born from passion and nourished by it, if it is not to be a frivolous intellectual game but an authentic human activity. But that firm discipline of the personality which is the hallmark of the passionate politician and distinguishes him from the political dilettante who is merely possessed by "sterile excitement" is achievable only through the habit of detachment, in every sense of that word. The "strength" of a political "personality" is to be found above all in the possession of these qualities.

The politician has daily, even hourly, to overcome in himself a wholly banal and all-too-human enemy: the *vanity* which is so common and which is the deadly enemy of all concrete commitment and of all detachment (in this case, detachment towards oneself). Vanity is a very widespread characteristic, and perhaps no one is altogether free of it. In academic and scholarly circles, indeed, it is a kind of occupational disease. But equally, in the case of a scholar, however distasteful its manifestations may be, it is relatively harmless in the sense that it does not, as a rule, interfere with his scholarly activity. In the politician's case, things are quite different. In his work, the urge for *power* plays an inescapable part. The 'power instinct', as it is often called, belongs therefore among his normal attributes.

The point at which someone in his profession begins to sin against the Holy Ghost, however, is the point at which this urge for power becomes *detached from reality*, and becomes a means of purely personal self-intoxication instead of being applied exclusively in the service of some realistic cause. For there are ultimately only two sorts of mortal sin in die political world: lack of realism and lack of responsibility (which is often, though not always, identical with it). At its most powerful, vanity—the need to occupy the limelight as much as possible—tempts the politician to commit one or both of these sins. The temptation is all the greater, in that the demagogue is forced to take into account the "effect" which he produces: indeed just because of this he runs a constant risk of becoming a play-actor, making light of the responsibility for the Consequences of his actions and asking only what "impression" he is making. His lack of realism leads him to seek the glittering semblance of power rather than the reality of it, while his lack of responsibility leads him to enjoy power purely for its own sake, without any substantive purpose. For although, or rather precisely *because*, power is the inescapable instrument of all politics, and the urge to power is therefore one of the driving forces behind all politics, there is no more pernicious way to distort the political drive than for a politician to boast of his power like a parvenu and luxuriate conceitedly in the sensation of power—in short, to worship power for its own sake. The pure "power-politician" extolled in the cult which has its zealous adherents even in our own society, may operate with impressive effect, but in the event his operations lead only into a meaningless void. In that respect, the critics of "power politics" are absolutely right. In the sudden inner collapse of some, typical representatives of this way of thinking we have been able to see, what inner weakness and impotence is concealed behind their ostentatious but totally empty posturing. It results from an utterly cheap, superficial and *blase* attitude towards the *meaning* of human activity—an attitude lacking all awareness of the tragic element with which all action, but especially political action, is in fact intertwined.

It is undeniably true, indeed a fundamental truth of all history (though not one to be explored more closely here), that the final result of political: activity often, nay, regularly, bears very little relation to the original intention: often, indeed, it is quite the opposite of what was first intended. But, for this very reason, if the activity is to have any kind of inner balance, the intention of serving some real cause must be present. It is a matter for the politician's own fundamental beliefs what *form* this cause; for the sake of which he seeks power and uses power, should take. He can seek to promote national or universal, social-cum-ethical or cultural, secular or religious causes. He can be carried away by enthusiasm for "progress" (in whatever sense) or he can coolly reject this sort of belief. He can insist on standing firm in the service of an "ideal," or he can reject such pretensions on principle and choose to serve the more external goals of everyday life. At all events, some belief or other must always be there. Otherwise, there will weigh on him in the event, it is perfectly correct to point out, the curse of futility to which all finite creatures are subject, even in what seem from the outside to be his greatest successes.

With what has just been said we have already begun to consider the last problem which concerns us this evening: the *ethos* of politics as a "cause." What sense of vocation can we find in the profession of politics itself, quite independently of any goals it may serve within the general moral economy of life? In which area of ethics, so to speak, is it at home. Here, to be sure, we find a confrontation of ultimate conceptions of life between which in the end a *choice* must be made. Let us resolutely approach this problem, which has recently been reopened, although in my view in an extremely distorted form.

But let us first rid the question of an utterly trivial attempt to cloud the issue. Ethics can, of course, first appear on the scene playing a part which, from the moral point of view, is absolutely fatal. Let us consider some examples. You will seldom find a man who has fallen out of love with one woman and in love with another who does not feel the need to justify his action to himself. He will say that the first was not worthy of his love, or that she deceived him, or whatever other "reasons" of the same general kind there may be. There is a lack of gallantry here; which is still further compounded by the "justification" which he invents for the unfortunate fact that he doesn't love her any more and that the woman must simply put up with it. In virtue of this justification, he claims to exonerate himself and tries to shift not only the suffering but also the blame on to her. The man who is successful in winning a woman's love behaves in exactly the same way: his rival must be less worthy than himself, otherwise he would not have lost. And of course the case is no different when after a victorious war the victor claims, in an unworthy desire for self-justification: "I won, because I was in the right." Or take the case of someone who suffers a mental breakdown because of the sheer horror of war and then, instead of straightforwardly admitting that it was indeed too much for him, feels the need to justify his war-weariness to himself by substituting the feeling that he could not bear the war because he had to fight for a morally evil cause. It is the same with the defeated in war. Instead of looking, like old women, for the guilty men after a war (and, after all, it is the structure of the society which led to the war), it would be more manly and austere to say to the enemy: "We lost the war, you have won it. All that is now over and done with: now let us talk about the conclusions to be drawn, as far as they concern the *real* interests involved, and, most importantly, in the light of the responsibility towards the *future*, which concerns the victor above all." Everything else is undignified and one only has to pay for it in the end. Damage to its interests a nation will forgive, but not damage to its honor, least of all when caused by a canting self-righteousness. Every new document which comes to light decades later leads to the revival of the undignified howls, the hatred and the anger, instead of allowing the war and its outcome to be at least

morally buried. This can be done only if we adopt a realistic and chivalrous, but above all a *dignified* attitude. It cannot be done by insisting on "morality": that really means no more than a lack of dignity on both sides. Those who do so are occupying themselves not with the true concerns of the politician—the future and his responsibility towards it—but instead with politically sterile, because undecidable, questions of past guilt. It is *here*, if anywhere, that political guilt lies. In so doing, moreover, such people overlook the inevitable distortion of the whole issue by thoroughly material interests—the interest of the victors in extracting the greatest possible advantage, both material and moral, and the hope of the defeated that they may gain some advantage by acknowledging their guilt. If anything is "vulgar," that is, and it is the result of using "morality" in this way as a means of "getting one's due."

But what is the nature of the real relation between ethics and politics? Have they, as has sometimes been said, nothing whatever to do with each other? Or, on the contrary, is it correct to say that the *same* ethical standards apply in political life as in every other area of activity? The view has sometimes been taken that these two propositions present us with mutually exclusive alternatives: either the one or the other is correct. But is it true that any ethical system in the world could impose *identical* rules of conduct on sexual, commercial, familial and professional relationships; on one's relations with one's wife, greengrocer, son, competitor, friend and defendant? Should it really matter so little, in deciding on the ethical standards required in politics, that the specific instrument of politics is power, backed up by *violence*? Don't we see that the Bolshevist and Spartacist ideologues achieve exactly the *same* results as any military dictator you care to mention, precisely because they use this essential instrument of politics? What difference is there between domination by the Workers' and Soldiers' Soviets and that by any ruler of the old regime, apart from the persons of the power holders and their dilettantism? What difference is there between the polemics of most of the representatives of the so-called "new morality" themselves against the opponents whom they criticise and those of any demagogue you care to mention? Someone will say: the nobility of their intentions. Fine! But what we are talking about here is the means which they use; and the opponents whom they attack claim likewise, with equal honesty from their point of view, that their ultimate intentions are noble. "They that take the sword shall perish with the sword," and war is war wherever it is fought.

Well then, what about the ethics of the Sermon on the Mount?[1] The Sermon on the Mount, or, in other words, the absolute ethics of the Gospel, is a more serious matter than it is believed to be by those who are nowadays so keen to cite its requirements. It is not something to trifle with. What has been said about the causal principle in science holds equally good of it too: it is not a cab which one can hail at will, to get in or out of as one thinks fit. What it really means, if it is not to be reduced to a set of trivialities, is: all or nothing. Take, for example, the rich young man who "went away grieved: for he had great possessions."[2] The commandment of the Gospel is unconditional and clear: give what thou hast—*everything*, categorically. The politician will say that this is a socially meaningless demand, so long as it does not apply to *everyone*. So we must have taxes, tolls, confiscations—in short, compulsion and regulation applied to *everyone*. The ethical commandment simply pays attention to that: that is its very essence. Or what about "Turn the other cheek?"[3] The commandment is unconditional: we are not to ask questions about the other's right to strike the blow. It is an ethic which denies all self-respect—except for a saint. That is the point: one must be a saint in everything, at least in intention: one must live like Jesus or the Apostles or St Francis[4] or their like, and *then* this code of ethics will have meaning and express value. Otherwise, it will not. For if the consequence to be drawn from the other-worldly ethics of love is "Resist not evil with force," the contrary proposition is true for the politician: "Thou *shalt* resist evil with force" (otherwise you are *responsible* for the victory of evil). Anyone who wants to act according to the ethics of the Gospel should not go on strike, since strikes are a form of coercion: he should join one of the unaffiliated trades unions. But above all he should not talk about "revolution." For the ethic of the Gospel certainly does not teach that civil war is the one legitimate kind of war. The pacifist who lives by the Gospel will refuse to bear arms or will throw them away, as pacifists were recommended to do in Germany, as a moral duty, in order to put an end to the war and so to

all wars. The politician will say that the only sure means of discrediting war for all *foreseeable* time would have been to make peace on the basis of the *status quo*. Then the combatant peoples would have asked what the war was all for. It would have been reduced *ad absurdum*[5]—which is not now possible. For there will have been political gains for the victors, or at least for some of them. And the responsibility for that lies with the attitude which made all resistance impossible for us. Now—once the period of exhaustion is past—it will be *peace* which is discredited, *not* war: that is the result of absolute ethics.

Finally, the duty to tell the truth. For absolute ethics this is unconditional. The conclusion has therefore been drawn that all documents should be published, especially those which lay the blame on one's own country, and that on the basis of this one-sided publication guilt should be acknowledged unilaterally, unconditionally, and without regard for the consequences. The politician will find that the result of this is not that truth is advanced, but rather that it is obscured by the misuses to which it is put and the passions which are unleashed; that the only approach which could be fruitful is for impartial umpires methodically to set out the evidence in a way which takes all sides into account. Every other procedure can have consequences for the nation which adopts it which would be impossible to make good even after several decades. But absolute ethics is not even *concerned* with "consequences."

That is the decisive point. We must be clear that all activity which is governed by ethical standards can be subsumed under one of two maxims, which are fundamentally different from, and irreconcilably opposed to, each other. The ethical standards may either be based on *intentions* or on *responsibility*. Not that an ethic of intentions is the same as irresponsibility or an ethic of responsibility the same as indifference to intentions. Naturally, there is no question of either of these two things.

But there is a profound antithesis between actions governed by the ethics of intention, where to put it in religious language "The Christian acts rightly and leaves the outcome to God," and actions governed by the ethics of responsibility, where one is answerable for the (foreseeable) *consequences* of one's actions. You may put a very plausible case to a Syndicalist who is a convinced believer in the

---

1   *Sermon on the Mount*   First sermon given by Jesus (in which he lays out his central teachings), recorded in Matthew 5–7 and Luke 6.20–49.

2   *went away grieved … great possessions*   See Matthew 19.22.

3   *Turn the other cheek*   See Matthew 5.39: "But I say unto you, That ye resist not evil: but whosoever shall smite thee on thy right cheek, turn to him the other also" (King James Version).

4   *St. Francis*   St. Francis of Assisi (1181–1226), founder of the Order of Friars Minor (also known as the Franciscans).

5   *reduced ad absurdum*   From *reductio ad absurdum*, Latin for "reduction to the absurd." The phrase refers to a form of argument in which the premises are assumed and it is shown that they lead to an absurd conclusion, thus allowing the premises to be rejected.

ethics of intention, to the effect that the consequences of his actions will be an increase in the chances for reaction, increased oppression of his class, retardation of its progress; and all this will make not the slightest impression on him. If an action which results from a pure intention has evil consequences, then the responsibility lies not with the man who performed the action but, with the world in general, the stupidity of other men—or the will of God, who created them as they are. The man who acts according to the ethics of responsibility, on the other hand, takes into account just those ordinary faults in men; he has, as Fichte[1] has justly said, no right whatever to assume their goodness or perfection and doesn't feel himself in any position to shift on to others the consequences of his own action, insofar as he could foresee them. He will say: "These are the consequences to be imputed to my action." The man who bases his ethics on intentions feels that he is "responsible" only for seeing that the flame of pure intention, the flame of protest against the injustice of the social order, is not extinguished. The aim of his action, which, considered from the point of view of its possible consequences, is totally irrational, is to keep fanning this flame; the action can and should have only the value of an example.

But even here we have not finished with the problem. No system of ethics in the world can avoid facing the fact that good ends in many cases can be achieved only at the price of morally dubious or at least, dangerous means and the possibility, or even the probability, of evil side-effects. No system of ethics in the world can make it possible to decide when and to what extent the morally good end "sanctifies" the morally dangerous means and side-effects.

For politics, the essential means is violence. The significance of the tension between means and ends from the ethical point of view can be judged from the fact that, as is well known, the revolutionary Socialists of the Zimmerwald faction, even during the war, professed a principle, which could be formulated in the following pregnant words: "If the choice which faces us is between several more years of war followed by revolution and immediate peace with no revolution, then we choose several more years of war!" If one had gone on to ask what this revolution was supposed to achieve, every scientifically trained Socialist would have replied that there was no question of a transition to an economic order which could be called "socialist" in *his* sense;

rather a bourgeois economy would arise yet again, rid only of its feudal elements and the remains of dynasticism. For this modest result, then, they were willing to face "several more years of war!" One could well be excused for thinking that even someone with very firm socialist convictions might well reject an end which can only be achieved by such means. Exactly the same applies to Bolshevism and Spartacism, and in general to every kind of revolutionary Socialism. It is, of course, simply ridiculous for those on this side to express *moral* revulsion for the "power-politicians" of the old regime on account of their use of the same means—however completely justified the rejection of their *ends* may be.

It is on this very problem of the sanctification of the means by the end that the ethics of intention in general seems to have run aground. Indeed, the only logical course open to it is to *repudiate all* activity which involves the use of morally dangerous means. I repeat, this is the only *logical* course. In the real world we do indeed constantly have the experience of seeing the believer in the ethics of intention suddenly turn into a millenarian prophet. For example, those who have just been preaching "Love against Force," suddenly urge their followers to use force—for the *last* time, so as to bring about a situation in which *all* violence will be abolished—just as our military commanders said to their men before every offensive, "This is the last one: it will bring victory and so peace." The believer in the ethics of intention cannot accept the ethical irrationality of the world. He is a cosmic "rationalist" in his ethical views. All of you who know your Dostoyevsky[2] will remember the scene with the Grand Inquisitor,[3] where this problem is admirably analysed. It is impossible to reconcile the requirements of the ethics of intention and the ethics of responsibility, and equally impossible to lay down a moral rule for deciding which end is to sanctify which means, if one makes any concessions at all to this principle.

My colleague F.W. Foerster,[4] whom I respect very much as a man for the undoubted purity of his intentions, but whose political views, I confess, I totally reject, believes that in his book he has circumvented this difficulty by the simple thesis that from good only good can come and from

---

1   *Fichte*   Johann Gottlieb Fichte (1762–1814), German idealist philosopher.

2   *Dostoyevsky*   Fyodor Mikhailovich Dostoevsky (1821–81), Russian novelist, author of *The Brothers Karamazov* (1879–80) and many other works.

3   *Grand Inquisitor*   Parable in *The Brothers Karamazov*.

4   *F.W. Foerster*   Catholic moral and political philosopher (1869–1966), author of *Weltpolitik und Weltgewissen*.

bad only bad. If this were so, then this whole set of problems would not exist. But it is truly amazing that 2,500 years after the Upanishads[1] such a thesis can still see the light of day. Not only the whole course of world history, but every incontrovertible test of everyday experience makes it plain that the opposite is true. The development of all the world religions is due to this fact. The age-old problem of theodicy comes down precisely to this question: how is it that a power which is depicted as being at the same time all-powerful and loving has been able to create an irrational world like this one of unmerited suffering, unpunished injustice and irredeemable folly? Either the omnipotence or the benevolence must be lacking: or else life is governed by wholly different principles of compensation and retribution, principles which we can explain metaphysically or which are even hidden for ever from our understanding. This problem posed by the experience of the irrationality of the world has been the driving force behind all religious development. The Indian doctrine of Karma,[2] Persian Dualism,[3] Original Sin,[4] Predestination,[5] and the *deus absconditus*[6] have all grown out of this experience. The ancient Christians, too, knew very well that this world is ruled by demons, and that he who meddles with politics, who in other words makes use of the instruments of power and violence, concludes a pact with the infernal powers. They knew too that for such a man's actions it is *not* the case that from good only good, from bad only bad can come, but that often the opposite holds true. Anyone who cannot see that is indeed politically a child.

Religious ethics have come to terms in various ways with the fact that we are involved in different ways of life, gov-erned by different sets of rules. Hellenic[7] polytheism sacrificed to Aphrodite as well as to Hera, to Dionysus as well as Apollo, knowing full well that they were not infrequently in conflict with each other. The Hindu way of life made each of the different callings subject to a separate ethical code, a Dharma,[8] and divided them off permanently as castes from each other. These castes were, moreover, organised into a strict hierarchy of rank, from which there was no escape for anyone born into it, except by rebirth in the next: life, and by which different castes were placed at varying distances from the highest religious blessings of salvation. This made it possible to cultivate the Dharma of each individual caste, from the ascetics and Brahmins[9] to the thieves and prostitutes, in a manner appropriate to the specific inherent laws of each calling. These included the professions both of war and of politics. You can find a classification of war within the total; system of ways of life in the Bhagavad-gita,[10] in the dialogue between Krishna and Arjuna. "Do thou what must be done"—that is, do what is required by the Dharma of the warrior caste and its rules, that which, is specifically necessary to achieve the aim of war. In this system of beliefs, work does not obstruct religious salvation but promotes it. From time immemorial, Indra's heaven[11] was as sure a fate for those Indian warriors who met a hero's death as was Valhalla[12] for the Germans: The Indian warrior would, however, have felt as much contempt for Nirvana[13] as the Germans would have felt for the Christian Heaven with its choirs of angels. This specialisation of ethical codes made it possible for Indian ethics to treat this royal art in a wholly consistent way, by following only, the inherent laws of politics and even radically strengthening them. Truly radical "Machia-

---

1   *Upanishads*   Hindu sacred texts on philosophy and on the nature of God, dating from the eighth century BCE.

2   *Karma*   The universal law of cause and effect in the Hindu, Buddhist, and Jain religions in which one's actions give rise to one's future states or experiences.

3   *Persian Dualism*   Weber refers to Zoroastrianism, which dates from perhaps the tenth century BCE and which was once the dominant religion of what is today Iran. The founder, Zoroaster, held that the universe is a struggle between the dual forces of truth and lie.

4   *Original Sin*   The Christian view that humanity is born into a "fallen" state as a result of Adam and Eve eating from the tree of the knowledge of good and evil.

5   *Predestination*   The Calvinist view that God has appointed some people for salvation through grace (and condemned others to damnation for their sins); and that one's actions have no effect on one's fate.

6   *deus absconditus*   Latin: hidden God.

7   *Hellenic*   Synonomous with "Greek."

8   *Dharma*   Religious and moral law governing individual and group conduct. In Hinduism, it also refers to the obligations one has as a member of one of the five castes. The caste system determines one's social status, and mobility between castes was traditionally not permitted.

9   *Brahmins*   Members of the highest caste, responsible for religious functions.

10   *Bhagavad-gita*   Sanskrit text from the Mahabharata epic, consisting of a conversation before a war between the warrior-prince Arjuna and the deity Krishna.

11   *Indra's heaven*   Indra is the Hindu god of weather and war.

12   *Valhalla*   Hall of the Norse deity Odin, to which the Valkyries escorted valiant warriors slain in battle.

13   *Nirvana*   State of enlightenment, in which desire and suffering are extinguished.

vellianism,"[1] in the popular sense of that word is classically expressed in Indian literature in the Arthashastra of Kautilya[2] (written long before the birth of Christ, ostensibly in the time of Chandragupta[3]): compared to it, Macchiavelli's *The Prince* is harmless.

In Catholic ethics, with which Professor Foerster has close connections, the *consilia evangelica*,[4] as is well known, are recognised as a special code for those blessed with the charisma of the saindy life. A contrast is drawn between the monk on the one hand, who may neither shed blood nor pursue profit, and the pious knight or citizen on the other, of whom the first may shed blood and the second pursue profit. The way in which this ethic is reconciled with, and finds a place in, the system of salvation is less consistent than in India: this is a consequence, indeed a necessary consequence, of the basic presuppositions of the Christian faith. The idea that the world has been corrupted by original sin made it relatively easy to incorporate the use of force into ethics as a corrective against sin and the heretics endangering men's souls. But the purely otherworldly requirements of the Sermon on the Mount, according to which a man's intentions were of supreme importance, and the religious conception of Natural Law as an absolute requirement which was based on it, retained their revolutionary power and emerged with elemental energy at almost all times of social upheaval. They gave rise in particular to the radical pacifist sects. One of these in Pennsylvania made the experiment of a state in which there was no external power; but the outcome was tragic, in that when the War of Independence broke out the Quakers could not take up arms in defence of their own ideals for which the war was being fought.

Ordinary Protestantism, on the other hand, legitimised the state, and therewith violence as a means, as a divine institution in general and specifically as the legitimate government. Luther took the burden of moral responsibility for war away from the individual and transferred it to the government, which it could never be a sin to obey on any

matter other than a question of faith. Calvinism, again, recognised in principle that force might be used in order to defend the faith, and so sanctioned the religious war which was from the beginning a vital element in Islamic life. Evidently, then, the problem of political ethics is definitely *not* simply a modern phenomenon arising out of the rejection of religious belief which originated in the hero-cult of the Renaissance. All religions have grappled with it, with very different degrees of success, and after what has been said it could not have been otherwise. It is the specific use by groups of human beings of the means of legitimate violence as such which determines the particular character of all ethical problems of politics. Anyone who accepts the use of this means, to whatever ends (and every politician does so) is thereby committed to accepting its specific consequences. This is particularly true of the warrior of faith—religious or revolutionary. Let us steel ourselves to consider the present situation as an example. Anyone who wants to establish absolute justice on earth by *force*, requires for this purpose a following—a human "apparatus." To these followers he must hold out the prospect of the necessary internal and external rewards—a reward in heaven or on earth—or else the apparatus will cease to function. Take the internal rewards first: in the conditions of modern class-warfare, these are gratification of hatred and the desire for vengeance, and especially of feelings of resentment and the need for pseudo-moral self-righteousness and therefore of the need to slander and abuse the enemy. The external rewards are adventure, victory, plunder, power, and the spoils of office. The leader, once successful, is totally dependent on the functioning of this apparatus which he creates. Thus he is dependent on *its* motives, not his own. And he is dependent therefore on his ability to guarantee these rewards to his followers—the Red Guard, the secret police, the agitators, whom he needs—*over a long period of time*. What he in fact achieves under such conditions is never in his own hands: it is dictated to him by the motives which inspire the actions of his followers, and from the moral point of view these are predominantly vulgar. His followers are only held in check as long as at least some of them (perhaps never, in this world, the majority of them) are moved by an honest belief in his person and his cause. But in the first place, this belief, even where it is sincerely felt, is very often in reality only a means of giving moral "legitimacy" to the passion for vengeance, power, plunder and office: let us not labour under any illusions about that, for the materialist interpretation of history is also not a cab to be hailed at will, and it does

---

1 *Machiavellianism* The view, based upon Italian political theorist Machiavelli's *The Prince* (as popularly understood), that any means is justifiable in maintaining power.

2 *Arthashàstra of Kautily* Treatise on statecraft and military strategy by Kautilya—usually thought to be the professor Chānaka (c. 350–283 BCE), who later became prime minister of the ancient Indian Maurya Empire.

3 *Chandragupta* Chandragupta Maurya (c.340–298 BCE), founder of the Maurya Empire.

4 *consilia evangelica* Latin: Evangelic Counsels.

not come to a halt just for revolutionaries! In the second place, and most important of all, emotional revolution is followed by traditionalist routine. The hero of faith, and, even more, faith itself fades away or becomes (which is even more effective) part of the conventional jargon of political philistines and technicians. This development takes place with especial speed in ideological struggles, because it is usually conducted or inspired by true *leaders,* the prophets of the revolution. For, as with every apparatus of leadership, so here, one of the necessary conditions of success is to empty the ideas of all content, to concentrate on matters of fact, and to carry through a process of intellectual "proletarization"[1] in the interests of "discipline." The followers of a warrior of faith, once they have achieved power, tend to degenerate with particular ease into a thoroughly commonplace class of office-holders.

Anyone who wants to take up politics in general, and especially politics as a vocation, must be conscious of these ethical paradoxes and of his own responsibility for the changes which may be brought about in *himself* under pressure from them. I repeat, he is meddling with the infernal powers which lie in wait for him in every use of violence. The great virtuosi of other-worldly love of mankind and saintliness, whether from Nazareth or Assisi or the castles of Indian kings, have not employed the instrument of politics, force. Their kingdom was "not of this world,"[2] although they worked and still work in this world: the figures of Platon Karatayev[3] and the saintly characters in Dostoyevsky are still the closest approximations to them. The man who is concerned for the welfare of his soul and the salvation of the souls of others does not seek these aims along the path of politics. Politics has quite different goals, which can only be achieved by force. The genius, or demon, of politics lives in a state of inner tension with the God of love, even with the Christian God as the Church depicts Him, and this tension may at any time erupt into irresoluble conflict. This was known to men even in the time when the Church was dominant. The interdict in those days represented an enormously greater power over men and their souls' salvation than the (to use Fichte's words) "cold sanction" of Kantian moral judgment: it lay time after time on Florence, but still the citizens of Florence fought against the Papal states. And it is with such situations in mind that Macchiavelli, in a beautiful passage in (if I am not mistaken) his *History of Florence*, makes one of his heroes extol those citizens to whom the greatness of their native city is more important than the salvation of their souls.

If, for native city or "native land," which not everyone nowadays may consider to represent clear values, you substitute "the future of Socialism" or even "international peace," then you have the problem in its current form. For to seek to achieve all such ends by *political* activity, using force as a means and acting in accordance with the ethics of responsibility, is to endanger the "welfare of the soul." But when the goal is pursued in accordance with the pure ethics of intention in a war of faith, it can be damaged and discredited for generations to come, since no one takes responsibility for the consequences. For then the infernal powers which are involved remain unrecognised. These powers are inexorable: they create consequences for a man's activity, even for his own inner personality, to which he is helplessly surrendered if he does not see them. "The Devil is an old man" (and it is not age in years of life that the proverb refers to), "so become old in order to understand him." I have never allowed myself to be trumped in debate by the date on a birth certificate: the sheer fact that someone is twenty, while I am over fifty, can certainly never lead me to think that that alone was an achievement before which I should swoon with awe. It is not age that counts. What matters is the disciplined dispassionateness with which one looks at the realities of life, and the capacity to endure them and inwardly to cope with them.

It is true: politics is made with the head, but certainly not *only* with the head. In that respect those who advocate the ethics of intention are absolutely right. No one can tell anyone else whether they *ought* to act according to the ethics of intention or the ethics of responsibility, or when they should follow the one and when the other. One thing only can be said. In these days of an excitement which, in your opinion, is *not* "sterile" (though excitement is certainly not always the same thing as genuine passion), when suddenly the politicians of intention come forward *en masse*[4] with the watchword, "It is the world which is stupid and vulgar, not

---

1   *proletarization* Transformation of people (e.g., the bourgeoisie or the middle class) so that they become members of the proletariat (the working class which, in Marxist theory, do not own the means of production and thus must work for a wage).

2   *not of this world* See John 18.36: "Jesus answered, My kingdom is not of this world: if my kingdom were of this world, then would my servants fight, that I should not be delivered to the Jews: but now is my kingdom not from hence" (King James Version).

3   *Platon Karatayev* Character in Russian writer Leo Tolstoy's *War and Peace* (1865–69).

4   *en masse* French: all together.

me; the responsibility for the consequences doesn't concern me, it concerns the others whom I serve and whose stupidity and vulgarity I shall eradicate," then, I often think, we have to ask first how much *inner strength* lies behind this ethics of intention. I have the impression that, in nine cases out of ten, I have to do with windbags, who do not really feel what they profess to feel, but are simply intoxicating themselves with romantic sensations. This does not interest me very much from the human point of view and impresses me not at all. But it is enormously impressive if a *more mature* man (whether old or young in years) who feels his responsibility for the consequences genuinely and with all his heart and acts according to the ethics of responsibility, says at whatever point it may be: "Here I stand: I can no other." That is an expression of authentic humanity and stirs one's feelings. For the *possibility* of this sort of situation occurring at some time or other must indeed exist for *any one* of us who is not inwardly dead. To that extent, the ethics of intention and the ethics of responsibility are not diametrically opposed, but complementary: together they make the true man, the man who can have the "vocation of politics."

And now, ladies and gentlemen, let us agree to discuss this point again *ten years from now*. If by that time, as I am sorry to say I cannot help but fear will be the case, for a whole series of reasons, the period of reaction will have long set in and little—perhaps not nothing at all, but at least little that is visible—of what certainly many of you and, as I freely confess, I too have wished and hoped for will have been achieved—if, as is very probable, that is what happens, it will not demoralise me, but it is to be sure an inner burden to be aware of it. In that event, I should very much like to see what has "become" (inwardly) of those of you who now feel that you are genuine followers of "the politics of intention" and share in the frenzy which this revolution amounts to. It would be nice if the situation were such that Shakespeare's Sonnet 102 were true:

> Our love was new, and then but in the spring,
> When I was wont to greet it with my lays;
> As Philomel[1] in summer's front doth sing
> And stops her pipe in growth of riper days.

But that is not how things are. It is not "summer's front" which lies before us, but first of all a Polar night of icy darkness and severity, whichever group may be outwardly victorious at present. For where there is nothing, it is not only the Kaiser but the proletarian too who has lost his rights. When this night begins slowly to fade, who will be left still living of those whose spring has now, to all appearances, been clad in such luxuriant blossom? And what will by then have become of the inner lives of you all? Embitterment or philistinism, simple apathetic acceptance of the world and of one's profession or, third and far from least common, mystical escapism in those who are gifted in that direction or, as is frequently and regrettably the case, force themselves into it to follow the fashion? In every such case I shall conclude that such people were not suited to their field of activity, not able to cope with the world as it really is and with the routine of their daily lives. Objectively and factually, in their innermost hearts, they did not have the vocation for politics which they thought they had. They would have done better to promote brotherly love between man and man in a simple, straightforward way; and for the rest to have worked in a purely down-to-earth way at their everyday tasks.

Politics is a matter of boring down strongly and slowly through hard boards with passion and judgment together. It is perfectly true, and confirmed by all historical experience, that the possible cannot be achieved without continually reaching out towards that which is impossible in this world. But to do that a man must be a leader, and furthermore, in a very straightforward sense of the word, a hero. Even those who are not both must arm themselves with that stoutness of heart which is able to confront even the shipwreck of all their hopes, and they must do this now—otherwise they will not be in a position even to accomplish what is possible today. Only someone who is confident that he will not be shattered if the world, seen from his point of view, is too stupid or too vulgar for what he wants to offer it; someone who can say, in spite of that, "but still!"—only he has the "vocation" for politics.

---

1   *Philomel*   Often spelled "Philomela," identified with the nightingale. In Ovid's *Metamorphosis*, Philomela was raped by king Tereus of Thrace, her sister Procne's husband, who cut out her tongue when she threatened to tell her sister. At the end of the tale, the three are transformed into birds, with Philomela becoming a nightingale.

CARL SCHMITT
(1888-1985)

Carl Schmitt is one of the most controversial figures in social and political philosophy. He is among the foremost critics of the liberal state and its legal order, but his work remains tainted by his support for and membership in the Nazi Party (an affiliation he never renounced). Despite this repugnant assocation, he has exerted a wide influence, not only on conservative thought, but also on left-wing thinkers who sympathize with his diagnosis of liberalism, and on liberals, who have recognized the need to respond to his criticisms.

Born in 1888 into a petit-bourgeois family in Westphalia, Germany, Schmitt studied law and politics in Berlin, Munich, and Strasbourg, graduating in 1915. He acted as legal counselor to the German army during World War I. In the years that followed, he wrote many important works, including *Political Romanticism* (1919), *Political Theology: Four Chapters on the Concept of Sovereignty* (1922), *The Crisis of Parliamentary Democracy* (1923) and, perhaps his best known essay, *The Concept of the Political* (1927). He was appointed professor of law at the University of Berlin in 1933, the same year he entered the Nazi Party. After the war he was interned at Nuremberg in 1945, but was never brought to trial. Unlike many other important intellectuals associated with the Nazi party, he was banned from teaching for the rest of his life; he returned to his hometown of Plettenberg, where he lived until 1985, writing, and talking to frequent admiring visitors.

In *The Concept of the Political* Schmitt argued that every area of inquiry is structured by a duality. Thus morality contrasts good with evil and aesthetics centers on the opposition between beauty and ugliness. What defines politics, according to Schmitt, is the friend/enemy distinction, rallying strong feeling and often force against the demonized other. Liberalism, however, is apolitical in its denial of this distinction; it is characterized by a commitment to neutrality and the rule of law. It attempts to constrain conflict by binding individuals with institutions such as parliamentary democracy and legal procedures. But, according to Schmitt, liberalism cannot resolve the inevitable conflict between private interest groups. In fact, any attempt at neutrality is simply the victory of one faction over another; the practice of party politics in fact shows that liberalism conflicts with democracy (understood as rule of the people).

Moreover, liberalism with its commitment to the rule of law cannot deal with the "state of exception"—charactertized by unforeseen emergencies and sudden crises (such as war, civil unrest or natural disasters) that may paralyze states that rely on stable law and fixed rules of political procedure. Schmitt argues that such circumstances require the abolition of the rule of law and of parliaments, and their replacement by a dictatorial sovereign who will guide the country through crises, and define friends and enemies. This leader would then reconstruct the political order based on a vision of a homogenous nation.

Schmitt's work has attracted the attention of some leftists, including Water Benjamin and Jacques Derrida. The critical theorist Jürgen Habermas has had a productive, though critical dialogue with Schmitt's work. The communitarian challenge to liberalism sometimes raises criticisms of liberalism similar to Schmitt's, especially his argument that liberalism and democracy conflict, and has sometimes shared both his attraction to organic metaphors for society and his commitment to nationalism.

◆ ◆ ◆ ◆ ◆

from *The Concept of the Political* (1932)

1

The concept of the state presupposes the concept of the political.

According to modern linguistic usage, the state is the political status of an organized people in an enclosed territorial unit. This is nothing more than a general paraphrase, not a definition of the state. Since we are concerned here with the nature of the political, such a definition is unwarranted. It may be left open what the state is in its essence—a machine or an organism, a person or an institution, a society or a community, an enterprise or a beehive, or perhaps even a basic procedural order. These definitions and images anticipate too much meaning, interpretation, illustration, and construction, and therefore cannot constitute any appropriate point of departure for a simple and elementary statement.

In its literal sense and in its historical appearance the state is a specific entity of a people. Vis-à-vis the many conceivable kinds of entities, it is in the decisive case the ultimate authority. More need not be said at this moment. All characteristics of this image of entity and people receive their meaning from the further distinctive trait of the political and become incomprehensible when the nature of the political is misunderstood.

One seldom finds a clear definition of the political. The word is most frequently used negatively, in contrast to various other ideas, for example in such antitheses as politics and economy, politics and morality, politics and law; and within law there is again politics and civil law and so forth. By means of such negative, often also polemical confrontations, it is usually possible, depending upon the context and concrete situation, to characterize something with clarity. But this is still not a specific definition. In one way or another "political" is generally juxtaposed to "state" or at least is brought into relation with it. The state thus appears as something political, the political as something pertaining to the state—obviously an unsatisfactory circle.

…

The equation *state* = *politics* becomes erroneous and deceptive at exactly the moment when state and society penetrate each other. What had been up to that point affairs of state become thereby social matters, and, vice versa, what had been purely social matters become affairs of state—as must necessarily occur in a democratically organized unit. Heretofore ostensibly neutral domains—religion, culture, education, the economy—then cease to be neutral in the sense that they do not pertain to state and to politics. As a polemical concept against such neutralizations and depoliticalizations of important domains appears the total state, which potentially embraces every domain. This results in the identity of state and society. In such a state, therefore, everything is at least potentially political, and in referring to the state it is no longer possible to assert for it a specifically political characteristic.

…

2

A definition of the political can be obtained only by discovering and defining the specifically political categories. In contrast to the various relatively independent endeavors of human thought and action, particularly the moral, aesthetic, and economic, the political has its own criteria which express themselves in a characteristic way. The political must therefore rest on its own ultimate distinctions, to which all action with a specifically political meaning can be traced. Let us assume that in the realm of morality the final distinctions are between good and evil, in aesthetics beautiful and ugly, in economics profitable and unprofitable. The question then is whether there is also a special distinction which can serve as a simple criterion of the political and of what it consists. The nature of such a political distinction is surely different from that of those others. It is independent of them and as such can speak clearly for itself.

The specific political distinction to which political actions and motives can be reduced is that between friend and enemy. This provides a definition in the sense of a criterion and not as an exhaustive definition or one indicative of substantial content. Insofar as it is not derived from other criteria, the antithesis of friend and enemy corresponds to the relatively independent criteria of other antitheses: good and evil in the moral sphere, beautiful and ugly in the aesthetic sphere, and so on. In any event it is independent, not in the sense of a distinct new domain, but in that it can neither be based on any one antithesis or any combination of other antitheses, nor can it be traced to these. If the antithesis of good and evil is not simply identical with that of beautiful and ugly, profitable and unprofitable, and cannot be directly reduced to the others, then the antithesis of friend and enemy must even less be confused with or mistaken for the others. The distinction of friend and enemy denotes the utmost degree of intensity of a union or separation, of an association or dissociation. It can exist theoretically and practically, without having simultaneously to draw upon all those moral, aesthetic, economic, or other distinctions. The political enemy need not be morally evil or aesthetically ugly; he need not appear as an economic competitor, and it may even be advantageous to engage with him in business transactions. But he is, nevertheless, the other, the stranger; and it is sufficient for his nature that he is, in a specially intense way, existentially something different and alien, so that in the extreme case conflicts with him are possible. These can neither be decided by a previously determined general norm nor by the judgment of a disinterested and therefore neutral third party.

Only the actual participants can correctly recognize, understand, and judge the concrete situation and settle the extreme case of conflict. Each participant is in a position to judge whether the adversary intends to negate his opponent's way of life and therefore must be repulsed or fought in order to preserve one's own form of existence. Emotionally the enemy is easily treated as being evil and ugly, because every distinction, most of all the political, as the strongest and most intense of the distinctions and categorizations, draws upon other distinctions for support. This does not alter the autonomy of such distinctions. Consequently, the reverse is also true: the morally evil, aesthetically ugly or economically damaging need not necessarily be the enemy; the morally good, aesthetically beautiful, and economically profitable need not necessarily become the friend in the specifically political sense of the word. Thereby the inherently objective nature and autonomy of the political becomes evident by virtue of its being able to treat, distinguish, and comprehend the friend-enemy antithesis independently of other antitheses.

3

The friend and enemy concepts are to be understood in their concrete and existential sense, not as metaphors or symbols, not mixed and weakened by economic, moral, and other conceptions, least of all in a private-individualistic sense as a psychological expression of private emotions and tendencies. They are neither normative nor pure spiritual antitheses. Liberalism in one of its typical dilemmas (to be treated further under Section 8) of intellect and economics has attempted to transform the enemy from the viewpoint of economics into a competitor and from the intellectual point into a debating adversary. In the domain of economics there are no enemies, only competitors, and in a thoroughly moral and ethical world perhaps only debating adversaries. It is irrelevant here whether one rejects, accepts, or perhaps finds it an atavistic remnant of barbaric times that nations continue to group themselves according to friend and enemy, or hopes that the antithesis will one day vanish from the world, or whether it is perhaps sound pedagogic reasoning to imagine that enemies no longer exist at all. The concern here is neither with abstractions nor with normative ideals, but with inherent reality and the real possibility of such a distinction. One mayor may not share these hopes and pedagogic ideals. But, rationally speaking, it cannot be denied that nations continue to group themselves according to the friend and enemy antithesis, that the distinction still remains actual today, and that this is an ever present possibility for every people existing in the political sphere. The enemy is not merely any competitor or just any partner of a conflict in general. He is also not the private adversary whom one hates. An enemy exists only when, at least potentially, one fighting collectivity of people confronts a similar collectivity. The enemy is solely the public enemy, because everything that has a relationship to such a collectivity of men, particularly to a whole nation, becomes public by virtue of such a relationship....

The political is the most intense and extreme antagonism, and every concrete antagonism becomes that much more political the closer it approaches the most extreme point, that of the friend-enemy grouping. In its entirety the state as an organized political entity decides for itself the friend-enemy distinction. Furthermore, next to the primary political decisions and under the protection of the decision taken, numerous secondary concepts of the political emanate. As to the equation of politics and state discussed under Section 1, it has the effect, for example, of contrasting a political attitude of a state with party politics so that one can speak of a state's domestic religious, educational, communal, social policy, and so on. Notwithstanding, the state encompasses and relativizes all these antitheses. However an antithesis and antagonism remain here within the state's domain which have relevance for the concept of the political. Finally even more banal forms of politics appear, forms which assume parasite- and caricature-like configurations. What remains here from the original friend-enemy grouping is only some sort of antagonistic moment, which manifests itself in all sorts of tactics and practices, competitions and intrigues; and the most peculiar dealings and manipulations are called politics. But the fact that the substance of the political is contained in the context of a concrete antagonism is still expressed in everyday language, even where the awareness of the extreme case has been entirely lost.

This becomes evident in daily speech and can be exemplified by two obvious phenomena. First, all political concepts, images, and terms have a polemical meaning. They are focused on a specific conflict and are bound to a concrete situation; the result (which manifests itself in war or revolution) is a friend-enemy grouping, and they turn into empty and ghostlike abstractions when this situation disappears. Words such as state, republic, society, class, as well as sovereignty, constitutional state, absolutism, dictatorship, economic planning, neutral or total state, and so on, are incomprehensible if one does not know exactly who is to be affected, combated, refuted, or negated by such a term. Above all the polemical character determines the use of the word political regardless of whether the adversary is designated as nonpolitical (in the sense of *harmless*), or vice versa if one wants to disqualify or denounce him as political in order to portray oneself as nonpolitical (in the sense of purely scientific, purely moral, purely juristic, purely aesthetic, purely economic, or on the basis of similar purities) and thereby superior.

Secondly, in usual domestic polemics the word political is today often used interchangeably with party politics. The inevitable lack of objectivity in political decisions, which is only the reflex to suppress the politically inherent friend-enemy antithesis, manifests itself in the regrettable forms and aspects of the scramble for office and the politics of patronage. The demand for depoliticalization which arises in this context means only the rejection of party politics, etc. The equation politics = party politics is possible whenever antagonisms among domestic political parties succeed in weakening the all-embracing political unit, the state. The intensification of internal antagonisms has the effect of weakening the common identity vis-à-vis another state. If domestic conflicts among political parties have become the sole political difference, the most extreme degree of internal political tension is thereby reached; i.e., the domestic, not the foreign friend-and-enemy groupings are decisive for armed conflict. The ever present possibility of conflict must

always be kept in mind. If one wants to speak of politics in the context of the primacy of internal politics, then this conflict no longer refers to war between organized nations but to civil war.

For to the enemy concept belongs the ever present possibility of combat. All peripherals must be left aside from this term, including military details and the development of weapons technology. War is armed combat between organized political entities; civil war is armed combat within an organized unit. A self-laceration endangers the survival of the latter. The essence of a weapon is that it is a means of physically killing human beings. Just as the term enemy, the word combat, too, is to be understood in its original existential sense. It does not mean competition, nor does it mean pure intellectual controversy nor symbolic wrestlings in which, after all, every human being is somehow always involved, for it is a fact that the entire life of a human being is a struggle and every human being symbolically a combatant. The friend, enemy, and combat concepts receive their real meaning precisely because they refer to the real possibility of physical killing. War follows from enmity. War is the existential negation of the enemy. It is the most extreme consequence of enmity. It does not have to be common, normal, something ideal, or desirable. But it must nevertheless remain a real possibility for as long as the concept of the enemy remains valid.

It is by no means as though the political signifies nothing but devastating war and every political deed a military action, by no means as though every nation would be uninterruptedly faced with the friend-enemy alternative vis-à-vis every other nation. And, after all, could not the politically reasonable course reside in avoiding war? The definition of the political suggested here neither favors war nor militarism, neither imperialism nor pacifism. Nor is it an attempt to idealize the victorious war or the successful revolution as a "social ideal," since neither war nor revolution is something social or something ideal. The military battle itself is not the "continuation of politics by other means" as the famous term of Clausewitz[1] is generally incorrectly cited.[2] War has its own strategic, tactical, and other rules and points of view, but they all presuppose that

1   *Clausewitz* Carl Philipp Gottfried von Clausewitz (1780–1831), Prussian military theorist and historian, best known for his treatise *On War* (1832).
2   *Clausewitz is generally incorrectly cited* Carl von Clausewitz writes: "War is nothing but a continuation of political intercourse with a mixture of other means."

the political decision has already been made as to who the enemy is. In war the adversaries most often confront each other openly; normally they are identifiable by a uniform, and the distinction of friend and enemy is therefore no longer a political problem which the fighting soldier has to solve. A British diplomat correctly stated in this context that the politician is better schooled for the battle than the soldier, because the politician fights his whole life whereas the soldier does so in exceptional circumstances only. War is neither the aim nor the purpose nor even the very content of politics. But as an ever present possibility it is the leading presupposition which determines in a characteristic way human action and thinking and thereby creates a specifically political behavior.

The criterion of the friend-and-enemy distinction in no way implies that one particular nation must forever be the friend or enemy of another specific nation or that a state of neutrality is not possible or could not be politically reasonable. As with every political concept, the neutrality concept too is subject to the ultimate presupposition of a real possibility of a friend-and-enemy grouping. Should only neutrality prevail in the world, then not only war but also neutrality would come to an end. The politics of avoiding war terminates, as does all politics, whenever the possibility of fighting disappears. What always matters is the possibility of the extreme case taking place, the real war, and the decision whether this situation has or has not arrived.

…

A world in which the possibility of war is utterly eliminated, a completely pacified globe, would be a world without the distinction of friend and enemy and hence a world without politics. It is conceivable that such a world might contain many very interesting antitheses and contrasts, competitions and intrigues of every kind, but there would not be a meaningful antithesis whereby men could be required to sacrifice life, authorized to shed blood, and kill other human beings. For the definition of the political, it is here even irrelevant whether such a world without politics is desirable as an ideal situation. The phenomenon of the political can be understood only in the context of the ever present possibility of the friend-and-enemy grouping, regardless of the aspects which this possibility implies for morality, aesthetics, and economics.

War as the most extreme political means discloses the possibility which underlies every political idea, namely, the distinction of friend and enemy. This makes sense only as long as this distinction in mankind is actually present or at least potentially possible. On the other hand, it would be senseless to wage war for purely religious, purely moral, purely juristic, or purely economic motives. The friend-and-enemy grouping and therefore also war cannot be derived from these specific antitheses of human endeavor. A war need be neither something religious nor something morally good nor something lucrative. War today is in all likelihood none of these. This obvious point is mostly confused by the fact that religious, moral, and other antitheses can intensify to political ones and can bring about the decisive friend-or-enemy constellation. If, in fact, this occurs, then the relevant antithesis is no longer purely religious, moral, or economic, but political. The sole remaining question then is always whether such a friend-and-enemy grouping is really at hand, regardless of which human motives are sufficiently strong to have brought it about.

Nothing can escape this logical conclusion of the political. If pacifist hostility toward war were so strong as to drive pacifists into a war against non pacifists, in a war against war, that would prove that pacifism truly possesses political energy because it is sufficiently strong to group men according to friend and enemy. If, in fact, the will to abolish war is so strong that it no longer shuns war, then it has become a political motive, i.e., it affirms, even if only as an extreme possibility, war and even the reason for war. Presently this appears to be a peculiar way of justifying wars. The war is then considered to constitute the absolute last war of humanity. Such a war is necessarily unusually intense and inhuman because, by transcending the limits of the political framework, it simultaneously degrades the enemy into moral and other categories and is forced to make of him a monster that must not only be defeated but also utterly destroyed. In other words, he is an enemy who no longer must be compelled to retreat into his borders only. The feasibility of such war is particularly illustrative of the fact that war as a real possibility is still present today, and this fact is crucial for the friend-and-enemy antithesis and for the recognition of politics.

7

…

I have pointed out several times that the antagonism between the so-called authoritarian and anarchist theories can be traced to these formulas. A part of the theories and postulates which presuppose man to be good is liberal. Without being actually anarchist they are polemically directed against the intervention of the state. Ingenuous anarchism reveals that the belief in the natural goodness of man is closely tied to the radical denial of state and government. One follows from the other, and both foment each other. For the liberals, on the other hand, the goodness of man signifies nothing more than an argument with whose aid the state is made to serve society. This means that society determines its own order and that state and government are subordinate and must be distrustingly controlled and bound to precise limits. The classical formulation by Thomas Paine says: society is the result of our reasonably regulated needs, government is the result of our wickedness. The radicalism vis-à-vis state and government grows in proportion to the radical belief in the goodness of man's nature. Bourgeois liberalism was never radical in a political sense. Yet it remains self-evident that liberalism's negation of state and the political, its neutralizations, depoliticalizations, and declarations of freedom have likewise a certain political meaning, and in a concrete situation these are polemically directed against a specific state and its political power. But this is neither a political theory nor a political idea. Although liberalism has not radically denied the state, it has, on the other hand, neither advanced a positive theory of state nor on its own discovered how to reform the state, but has attempted only to tie the political to the ethical and to subjugate it to economics. It has produced a doctrine of the separation and balance of powers, i.e., a system of checks and controls of state and government. This cannot be characterized as either a theory of state or a basic political principle.

8

Liberalism has changed all political conceptions in a peculiar and systematic fashion. Like any other significant human movement liberalism too, as a historical force, has failed to elude the political. Its neutralizations and depoliticalizations (of education, the economy, etc.) are, to be sure, of political significance. Liberals of all countries have engaged in politics just as other parties and have in the most different ways coalesced with non-liberal elements and ideas. There are national liberals, social liberals, free conservatives, liberal Catholics, and so on. In particular they have tied themselves to very illiberal, essentially political, and even democratic movements leading to the total state. But the question is whether a specific political idea can be derived

from the pure and consequential concept of individualistic liberalism. This is to be denied.

The negation of the political, which is inherent in every consistent individualism, leads necessarily to a political practice of distrust toward all conceivable political forces and forms of state and government, but never produces on its own a positive theory of state, government, and politics. As a result, there exists a liberal policy in the form of a polemical antithesis against state, church, or other institutions which restrict individual freedom. There exists a liberal policy of trade, church, and education, but absolutely no liberal politics, only a liberal critique of politics. The systematic theory of liberalism concerns almost solely the internal struggle against the power of the state. For the purpose of protecting individual freedom and private property, liberalism provides a series of methods for hindering and controlling the state's and government's power. It makes of the state a compromise and of its institutions a ventilating system and, moreover, balances monarchy against democracy and vice versa. In critical times—particularly 1848—this led to such a contradictory position that all good observers, such as Lorenz von Stein,[1] Karl Marx, Friedrich Julius Stahl, Donoso Cortés, despaired of trying to find here a political principle or an intellectually consistent idea.

In a very systematic fashion liberal thought evades or ignores state and politics and moves instead in a typical always recurring polarity of two heterogeneous spheres, namely ethics and economics, intellect and trade, education and property. The critical distrust of state and politics is easily explained by the principles of a system whereby the individual must remain *terminus a quo*[2] and *terminus ad quem*.[3] In case of need, the political entity must demand the sacrifice of life. Such a demand is in no way justifiable by the individualism of liberal thought. No consistent individualism can entrust to someone other than to the individual himself the right to dispose of the physical life of the individual. An individualism in which anyone other than the free individual himself were to decide upon the substance and dimension of his freedom would be only an empty phrase. For the individual as such there is no enemy with whom he must enter into a life-and-death struggle if he personally does not want to do so. To compel him to fight against his will is, from the viewpoint of the private individual, lack

---

1   *Lorenz von Stein*   German economist and sociologist (1815–90).
2   *terminus a quo*   Latin: starting point; origin.
3   *terminus ad quem*   Latin: final limiting point; aim; goal.

of freedom and repression. All liberal pathos turns against repression and lack of freedom. Every encroachment, every threat to individual freedom and private property and free competition is called repression and is *eo ipso*[1] something evil. What this liberalism still admits of state, government, and politics is confined to securing the conditions for liberty and eliminating infringements on freedom.

We thus arrive at an entire system of demilitarized and depoliticized concepts. A few may here be enumerated in order to show the incredibly coherent systematics of liberal thought, which, despite all reversals, has still not been replaced in Europe today [1932]. These liberal concepts typically move between ethics (intellectuality) and economics (trade). From this polarity they attempt to annihilate the political as a domain of conquering power and repression. The concept of private law serves as a lever and the notion of private property forms the center of the globe, whose poles ethics and economics—are only the contrasting emissions from this central point.

Ethical or moral pathos and materialist economic reality combine in every typical liberal manifestation and give every political concept a double face. Thus the political concept of battle in liberal thought becomes competition in the domain of economics and discussion in the intellectual realm. Instead of a clear distinction between the two different states, that of war and that of peace, there appears the dynamic of perpetual competition and perpetual discussion. The state turns into society: on the ethical-intellectual side into an ideological humanitarian conception of humanity, and on the other into an economic-technical system of production and traffic. The self-understood will to repel the enemy in a given battle situation turns into a rationally constructed social ideal or program, a tendency or an economic calculation. A politically united people becomes, on the one hand, a culturally interested public, and, on the other, partially an industrial concern and its employers, partially a mass of consumers. At the intellectual pole, government and power turns into propaganda and mass manipulation, and at the economic pole, control.

These dissolutions aim with great precision at subjugating state and politics, partially into an individualistic domain of private law and morality, partially into economic notions. In doing so they deprive state and politics of their specific meaning. Outside of the political, liberalism not only recognizes with self-evident logic the autonomy of different human realms but drives them toward specialization and even toward complete isolation. That art is a daughter of freedom, that aesthetic value judgment is absolutely autonomous, that artistic genius is sovereign—all this is axiomatic of liberalism. In some countries a genuine liberal pathos came to the fore only when this autonomous freedom of art was endangered by moralistic apostles of tradition. Morality became autonomous vis-à-vis metaphysics and religion, science vis-à-vis religion, art, and morality, etc. The most important example of such an autonomy is the validity of norms and laws of economics. That production and consumption, price formation and market have their own sphere and can be directed neither by ethics nor aesthetics, nor by religion, nor, least of all, by politics was considered one of the few truly unquestionable dogmas of this liberal age. With great passion political viewpoints were deprived of every validity and subjugated to the norms and orders of morality, law, and economics. In the concrete reality of the political, no abstract orders or norms but always real human groupings and associations rule over the other human groupings and associations. Politically, the rule of morality, law, and economics always assumes a concrete political meaning.

...

The extraordinarily intricate coalition of economy, freedom, technology, ethics, and parliamentarianism has long ago finished off its old enemy: the residues of the absolute state and a feudal aristocracy; and with the disappearance of the enemy it has lost its original meaning. Now new groupings and coalitions appear. Economy is no longer *eo ipso* freedom; technology does not serve comforts only, but just as much the production of dangerous weapons and instruments. Progress no longer produces *eo ipso* the humanitarian and moral perfection which was considered progress in the eighteenth century. A technological rationalization can be the opposite of an economic rationalization. Nevertheless, Europe's spiritual atmosphere continues to remain until this very day under the spell of this nineteenth-century historical interpretation. Until recently its formulas and concepts retained a force which appeared to survive the death of its old adversary.

...

State and politics cannot be exterminated. The world will not become depoliticized with the aid of definitions

---

1 *eo ipso* Latin: by that very fact.

and constructions, all of which circle the polarity of ethics and economics. Economic antagonisms can become political, and the fact that an economic power position could arise proves that the point of the political may be reached from the economic as well as from any other domain. The often quoted phrase by Walter Rathenau,[1] namely that the destiny today is not politics but economics, originated in this context. It would be more exact to say that politics continues to remain the destiny, but what has occurred is that economics has become political and thereby the destiny.

It is also erroneous to believe that a political position founded on economic superiority is "essentially unwarlike," as Joseph Schumpeter[2] says in his *Zur Soziologie der Imperialismen*. Essentially unwarlike is the terminology based on the essence of liberal ideology. An imperialism based on pure economic power will naturally attempt to sustain a worldwide condition which enables it to apply and manage, unmolested, its economic means, e.g., terminating credit, embargoing raw materials, destroying the currencies of others, and so on. Every attempt of a people to withdraw itself from the effects of such "peaceful" methods is considered by this imperialism as extra-economic power. Pure economic imperialism will also apply a stronger, but still economic, and therefore (according to this terminology) nonpolitical, essentially peaceful means of force. A 1921 League of Nations resolution 40 enumerates as examples: economic sanctions and severance of the food supply from the civilian population. Finally, it has sufficient technical means to brings about violent death. Modern means of annihilation have been produced by enormous investments of capital and intelligence, surely to be used if necessary.

For the application of such means, a new and essentially pacifist vocabulary has been created. War is condemned but executions, sanctions, punitive expeditions, pacifications, protection of treaties, international police, and measures to assure peace remain. The adversary is thus no longer called an enemy but a disturber of peace and is thereby designated to be an outlaw of humanity. A war waged to protect or expand economic power must, with the aid of propaganda, turn into a crusade and into the last war of humanity. This is implicit in the polarity of ethics and economics, a polarity astonishingly systematic and consistent. But this allegedly nonpolitical and apparently even antipolitical system serves existing or newly emerging friend-and-enemy groupings and cannot escape the logic of the political.

---

1   *Walter Rathenau*   German industrialist and writer who served as Foreign Minister of Germany during the Weimar Republic (1867–1922).

2   *Joseph Schumpeter*   German economist, sociologist and political scientist (1883–1950). Schmitt refers to *Zur Soziologie der Imperialismen* (*The Sociology of Imperialism*), 1919.

F.A. HAYEK
(1899-1992)

Friedrich August von Hayek, Austrian-born British economist and political philosopher, is known for his defense of free-market capitalism and of classical liberalism. He won the Nobel Prize in Economics in 1974 (shared with Gunnar Myrdal). At a meeting shortly after Margaret Thatcher became Leader of the British Conservative Party, she banged a copy of Hayek's *The Constitution of Liberty* down on a table, saying "This is what we believe." When presenting Hayek with the Presidential Medal of Freedom in 1991, George H.W. Bush said of him that he "has done more than any thinker of our age to explore the promise and contours of liberty. He grew up in the shadow of Hitler's tyranny and devoted himself at an early age to the nurture of institutions that preserve and expand freedom, the lifeblood of a full life…. Professor von Hayek has revolutionized the world's intellectual and political life." Not all political philosophers would rate Hayek's importance so highly, but he is universally acknowledged as having exerted a significant influence on the direction of politics and economics in Britain and America in the late twentieth century.

Hayek was born in Vienna into an intellectual family. Serving during World War I in the Austrian artillery, he experienced ferocious fighting, witnessed horrible carnage and vowed to work for a better world. In the early 1920s he received doctorates in law and political science from the University of Vienna, while also studying psychology and economics. After a couple of years as a research assistant at New York University, he worked in Austria on the treaty ending World War I, and directed an economics institute. Postwar Europe was a shambles; poverty and hunger were spreading, and with them socialist ideas. Hayek was at first receptive to socialism's concern for the poor, and its arguments for government intervention in the interests of equity and justice. But then he met Ludwig van Mises, the famous "Austrian School" economist and passionate libertarian, who convinced him that markets work, governments do not.

Hayek's economic views motivate his political views. Hayek was one of the early contributors to the economics of information. Many economic theories artificially assume that agents have access to full and correct information. Hayek raised the problem of social coordination under conditions where agents possess different, possibly incorrect, and tacit (rather than explicit) information under constantly changing conditions. According to Hayek, social coordination was possible because market prices contain information about the intentions of market participants and the abundance or scarcity of goods and services. Markets allow agents to coordinate their plans and correct errors. They also provide the opportunity for entrepreneurs to exploit market inefficiencies and the incentive for innovators to discover and sell new products.

Hayek connected his theory of information and markets to his views about freedom. Planned economies, in which prices are fixed by some central body, are unable to gather or process all of the necessary resources to allocate resources—hence the shortage or overproduction of resources in many communist and ex-communist states. On Hayek's account, if governments were to justify planning economies and distributing resources, they would have to do so on the basis of universally shared values. If—as Hayek believed was the case—values such as egalitarianism were not universally shared, for a government to act on the basis of such values would represent an imposition on at least some of the population. Hayek argued for a free market system tied to democratic government in which property rights and rule of law protected the private sphere from state interference. This would allow individuals to pursue their own values with the help of information provided by market prices.

In 1931 Hayek took a job teaching at the London School of Economics. He and John Maynard Keynes, at Cambridge, were regarded as the leading economic theorists of the day. They were friends personally, but poles apart in political and economic philosophy. Keynes argued for government intervention in the economy; Hayek advocated a perfectly free market, even at times of economic distress such as the Great Depression. Government intervention, he claimed, would lead to increased government power, which would lead to a totalitarian state. Economic problems should thus be left alone to work themselves out in the long run. (Keynes's famous reply: "In the long run, we'll all be dead.")

Keynesian thinking very clearly gained the upper hand in the late 1930s and 1940s, and in 1947 (at a conference Hayek organized at Mt. Pelerin in Austria, also attended by the young libertarian Milton Friedman), Hayek predicted a long battle before the world changed its mind. In 1950, he moved to the University of Chicago, but was excluded from their Economics Department—because he believed, of his unpopular views. By 1970, when Hayek returned to Austria, it seemed that Keynesian mixed economies were successful everywhere, and that nobody would pay attention to him again. But the tide was already turning, particularly due to stagflation—a combination of high inflation and high unemployment—in the United Kingdom in the 1960s and 1970s and the United States in the 1970s. In 1974, when Hayek won the Nobel Prize, much of academic economic opinion and many of the western nations' economies were shifting away from Keynes's ideas and towards those of Hayek. For the next twenty years the political and economic orthodoxy in most Western countries was to call for less government intervention in economic activity. Not until the century's end did the pendulum begin to swing again in the opposite direction.

◆ ◆ ◆ ◆ ◆

from *The Constitution of Liberty* (1960)

Chapter 10: Law, Commands, and Order

Order is not a pressure imposed upon society from without, but an equilibrium which is set up from within.[1]

José Ortega y Gasset[2]

1. "The rule whereby the indivisible border line is fixed within which the being and activity of each individual obtain a secure and free sphere is the law."[3] Thus one of the great legal scholars of the last century stated the basic conception of the law of liberty. This conception of the law which made it the basis of freedom has since been largely lost. It will be the chief aim of this chapter to recover and make more precise the conception of the law on which the ideal of freedom under the law was built and which made it possible to speak of the law as "the science of liberty."[4]

Life of man in society, or even of the social animals in groups, is made possible by the individuals acting according to certain rules. With the growth of intelligence, these rules tend to develop from unconscious habits into explicit and articulated statements and at the same time to become more abstract and general. Our familiarity with the institutions of law prevents us from seeing how subtle and complex a

1 *Order is not a pressure ... from within* [Unless otherwise indicated, all notes to this selection are by the author, rather than the editors of this anthology] The quotation at the head of the chapter is taken from José Ortega y Gasset, *Mirabeau o el político* (*Mirabeau or politics*) (1928). See J.C. Carter, "The Ideal and the Actual in the Law," Report of the Thirteenth Annual Meeting of the American Bar Association (1890), p.234: "Law is not a body of commands imposed upon society from without, either by an individual sovereign or superior, or by a sovereign body constituted by representatives of society itself. It exists at all times as one of the elements of society springing directly from habit and custom. It is therefore the unconscious creation of society, or in other words, a growth." The stress on the law being prior to the state, which is the organized effort to create and enforce it, goes back at least to David Hume (see his *Treatise*, Book III, Part II).

2 *José Ortega y Gasset* [editors' note] José Ortega y Gasset was an influential Spanish philosopher (1883–1955).

3 *The rule whereby ... is the law* F.C. von Savigny, *System des heutigen römischen Rechts*, 1840.

4 *the science of liberty* Charles Beudant, *Le Droit individuel et l'état*, 1891.

device the delimitation of individual spheres by abstract rules is. If it had been deliberately designed, it would deserve to rank among the greatest of human inventions. But it has, of course, been as little invented by anyone mind as language or money or most of the practices and conventions on which social life rests.

A kind of delimitation of individual spheres by rules appears even in animal societies. A degree of order, preventing too frequent fights or interference with the search for food, etc., here arises often from the fact that the individual, as it strays farther from its lair, becomes less ready to fight. In consequence, when two individuals meet at some intermediate place, one of them will usually withdraw without an actual trial of strength. Thus a sphere belonging to each individual is determined, not by the demarcation of a concrete boundary, but by the observation of a rule—a rule, of course, that is not known as such by the individual but that is honored in action. The illustration shows how even such unconscious habits will involve a sort of abstraction: a condition of such generality as that of distance from home will determine the response of any individual on meeting another. If we tried to define any of the more truly social habits that make possible the life of animals in groups, we should have to state many of them in terms of abstract rules.

That such abstract rules are regularly observed in action does not mean that they are known to the individual in the sense that it could communicate them. Abstraction occurs whenever an individual responds in the same manner to circumstances that have only some features in common.[1] Men generally act in accordance with abstract rules in this sense long before they can state them.[2] Even when they

have acquired the power of conscious abstraction, their conscious thinking and acting are probably still guided by a great many such abstract rules which they obey without being able to formulate them. The fact that a rule is generally obeyed in action therefore does not mean that it does not still have to be discovered and formulated in words.

2. The nature of these abstract rules that we call "laws" in the strict sense is best shown by contrasting them with specific and particular commands. If we take the word "command" in its widest sense, the general rules governing human conduct might indeed also be regarded as commands. Laws and commands differ in the same way from statements of fact and therefore belong to the same logical category. But a general rule that everybody obeys, unlike a command proper, does not necessarily presuppose a person who has issued it. It also differs from a command by its generality and abstractness.[3] The degree of this generality or abstractness ranges continuously from the order that tells a man to do a particular thing here and now to the instruction that, in such and such conditions, whatever he does will have to satisfy certain requirements. Law in its ideal form might be described as a "once-and-for-all" command that is directed to unknown people and that is abstracted from all particular circumstances of time and place and refers only to such conditions as may occur anywhere and at any time. It is advisable, however, not to confuse laws and commands, though we must recognize that laws shade gradually into commands as their content becomes more specific.

The important difference between the two concepts lies in the fact that, as we move from commands to laws, the source of the decision on what particular action is to be taken shifts progressively from the issuer of the command or law to the acting person. The ideal type of command determines uniquely the action to be performed and leaves

---

1 *Abstraction occurs … in common* "Abstraction" does not appear only in the form of verbal statements. It manifests itself also in the way in which we respond similarly to any one of a class of events which in most respects may be very different from one another, and in the feelings which are evoked by these events and which guide our action, be it a sense of justice or of moral or aesthetic approval or disapproval. Also there are probably always more general principles governing our minds which we cannot formulate, yet which guide our thinking—laws of the structure of the mind which are too general to be formulated within that structure. Even when we speak of an abstract rule guiding decisions, we need not mean a rule expressed in words but merely one which could be so formulated. On all these problems compare my book, *The Sensory Order*, 1952.

2 *Men generally act … they can state them* See E. Saprit, *Selected Writings*, 1949, p.548: "It is easy for an Australian native, for instance, to say by what kinship term he calls so and so or whether or not he may undertake such and such relations with a given

individual. It is exceedingly difficult for him to give a general rule of which these specific examples of behavior are but illustrations, though all the while he acts as though the rule were perfectly well known to him. *In a sense it is well known to him.* But this knowledge is not capable of conscious manipulation in terms of word symbols. It is, rather, a very delicately nuanced feeling of subtle relations, both experienced and possible."

3 *It also differs … abstractness* The treatment of law as a species of command (deriving from Thomas Hobbes and John Austin) was originally intended to stress the logical similarity of these two kinds of sentences as distinguished from, say, a statement of fact. It should not, however, obscure, as it has done, the essential differences.

those to whom it is addressed no chance to use their own knowledge or follow their own predilections. The action performed according to such commands serves exclusively the purposes of him who has issued it. The ideal type of law, on the other hand, provides merely additional information to be taken into account in the decision of the actor.

The manner in which the aims and the knowledge that guide a particular action are distributed between the authority and the performer is thus the most important distinction between general laws and specific commands. It can be illustrated by the different ways in which the chief of a primitive tribe, or the head of a household, may regulate the activities of his subordinates. At the one extreme will be the instance where he relies entirely on specific orders and his subjects are not allowed to act at all except as ordered. If the chief prescribes on every occasion every detail of the actions of his subordinates, they will be mere tools, without an opportunity of using their own knowledge and judgment, and all the aims pursued and all the knowledge utilized will be those of the chief. In most circumstances, however, it will better serve his purposes if he gives merely general instructions about the kinds of actions to be performed or the ends to be achieved at certain times, and leaves it to the different individuals to fill in the details according to circumstances—that is, according to their knowledge. Such general instructions will already constitute rules of a kind, and the action under them will be guided partly by the knowledge of the chief and partly by that of the acting persons. It will be the chief who decides what results are to be achieved, at what time, by whom, and perhaps by which means; but the particular manner in which they are brought about will be decided by the individuals responsible. The servants of a big household or the employees of a plant will thus be mostly occupied with the routine of carrying out standing orders, adapting them all the time to particular circumstances and only occasionally receiving specific commands.

In these circumstances the ends toward which all activity is directed are still those of the chief. He may, however, also allow members of the group to pursue, within certain limits, their own ends. This presupposes the designation of the means that each may use for his purposes. Such an allocation of means may take the form of the assignment of particular things or of times that the individual may use for his own ends. Such a listing of the rights of each individual can be altered only by specific orders of the chief. Or the sphere of free action of each individual may be determined and altered in accordance with general rules laid down in advance for longer periods, and such rules can make it possible for each individual by his own action (such as bartering with other members of the group or earning premiums offered by the head for merit) to alter or shape the sphere within which he can direct his action for his own purposes. Thus, from the delimitation of a private sphere by rules, a right like that of property will emerge.

3. A similar transition from specificity and concreteness to increasing generality and abstractness we also find in the evolution from the rules of custom to law in the modern sense. Compared with the laws of a society that cultivates individual freedom, the rules of conduct of a primitive society are relatively concrete. They not merely limit the range within which the individual can shape his own action but often prescribe specifically how he must proceed to achieve particular results, or what he must do at particular times and places. In them the expression of the factual knowledge that certain effects will be produced by a particular procedure and the demand that this procedure be followed in appropriate conditions are still undifferentiated. To give only one illustration: the rules which the Bantu observes when he moves between the fourteen huts of his village along strictly prescribed lines according to his age, sex, or status greatly restrict his choice. Though he is not obeying another man's will but impersonal custom, having to observe a ritual to reach a certain point restricts his choice of method more than is necessary to secure equal freedom to others.

The "compulsion of custom" becomes an obstacle only when the customary way of doing things is no longer the only way that the individual knows and when he can think of other ways of achieving a desirable object. It was largely with the growth of individual intelligence and the tendency to break away from the habitual manner of action that it became necessary to state explicitly or reformulate the rules and gradually to reduce the positive prescriptions to the essentially negative confinement to a range of actions that will not interfere with the similarly recognized spheres of others.

The transition from specific custom to law illustrates even better than the transition from command to law what, for lack of a better term, we have called the "abstract character" of true law.[1] Its general and abstract rules specify that

---

1   *The transition ... true law*   If there were no danger of confusion with the other meanings of those terms, it would be preferable to speak of "formal" rather than of "abstract" laws, in the same sense as that in which the term "formal" is used in logical discussions. (See K.R. Popper, *Logik der Forschung*, 1935.) Unfortunately, "for-

in certain circumstances action must satisfy certain conditions; but all the many kinds of action that satisfy these conditions are permissible. The rules merely provide the framework within which the individual must move but within which the decisions are his. So far as his relations with other private persons are concerned, the prohibitions are almost entirely of a negative character, unless the person to whom they refer has himself, by his actions, created conditions from which positive obligations arise. They are instrumental, they are means put at his disposal, and they provide part of the data which, together with his knowledge of the particular circumstances of time and place, he can use as the basis for his decisions.

Since the laws determine only part of the conditions that the actions of the individual will have to satisfy, and apply to unknown people whenever certain conditions are present, irrespective of most of the facts of the particular situation, the lawgiver cannot foresee what will be their effect on particular people or for what purposes they will use them. When we call them "instrumental," we mean that in obeying them the individual still pursues his own and not the lawgiver's ends. Indeed, specific ends of action, being always particulars, should not enter into general rules. The law will prohibit killing another person or killing except under conditions so defined that they may occur at any time or place, but not the killing of particular individuals.

In observing such rules, we do not serve another person's end, nor can we properly be said to be subject to his will. My action can hardly be regarded as subject to the will of another person if I use his rules for my own purposes as I might use my knowledge of a law of nature, and if that person does not know of my existence or of the particular circumstances in which the rules will apply to me or of the effects they will have on my plans. At least in all those instances where the coercion threatened is avoidable, the law merely alters the means at my disposal and does not determine the ends I have to pursue. It would be ridiculous to say that I am obeying another's will in fulfilling a contract, when I could not have concluded it had there not been a recognized rule that promises must be kept, or in accepting

the legal consequence of any other action that I have taken in full knowledge of the law.

The significance for the individual of the knowledge that certain rules will be universally applied is that, in consequence, the different objects and forms of action acquire for him new properties. He knows of man-made cause-and-effect relations which he can make use of for whatever purpose he wishes. The effects of these man-made laws on his actions are of precisely the same kind as those of the laws of nature: his knowledge of either enables him to foresee what will be the consequences of his actions, and it helps him to make plans with confidence. There is little difference between the knowledge that if he builds a bonfire on the floor of his living room his house will burn down, and the knowledge that if he sets his neighbor's house on fire he will find himself in jail. Like the laws of nature, the laws of the state provide fixed features in the environment in which he has to move; though they eliminate certain choices open to him, they do not, as a rule, limit the choice to some specific action that somebody else wants him to take.

4. The conception of freedom under the law that is the chief concern of this book rests on the contention that when we obey laws, in the sense of general abstract rules laid down irrespective of their application to us, we are not subject to another man's will and are therefore free. It is because the lawgiver does not know the particular cases to which his rules will apply, and it is because the judge who applies them has no choice in drawing the conclusions that follow from the existing body of rules and the particular facts of the case, that it can be said that laws and not men rule. Because the rule is laid down in ignorance of the particular case and no man's will decides the coercion used to enforce it, the law is not arbitrary.[1] This, however, is true only if

---

mal" is also applied to everything that is enacted by the legislature, while only if such an enactment takes the form of an abstract rule, such a law in the formal sense is a law also in the substantive or material sense. For example, when Max Weber, in his *Law in Economy and Society*, 1954, pp.226–29, speaks of "formal justice," he means justice determined by law, not merely in the formal but in the substantive sense.

1   *Because the rule … is not abitrary*   See G.C. Lewis, *An Essay on the Government of Dependencies*, 1841, p.16, n.: "When a person voluntarily regulates his conduct according to a rule or maxim which he has previously announced his intention of conforming to, he is thought to deprive himself of *arbitrium*, free will, discretion, or *willkür*, in the individual act. Hence, when a government acts in an individual case, not in conformity with a pre-existing law or a rule of conduct, laid down by itself, its act is said to be arbitrary." Also *ibid.*, p.24: "Every government, whether monarchical, aristocratical, or democratical, may be conducted arbitrarily, and not in accordance with general rules. There is not, and cannot be, anything in the form of government, which will afford its subjects a legal security against an improper arbitrary exercise of sovereign power. This security is to be found only in the influence of public

by "law" we mean the general rules that apply equally to everybody. This generality is probably the most important aspect of that attribute of law which we have called its "abstractness." As a true law should not name any particulars, so it should especially not single out any specific persons or group of persons.

The significance of a system in which all coercive action of government is confined to the execution of general abstract rules is often stated in the words of one of the great historians of the law: "The movement of progressive societies has hitherto been a movement *from Status to Contract*."[1] The conception of status, of an assigned place that each individual occupies in society, corresponds, indeed, to a state in which the rules are not fully general but single out particular persons or groups and confer upon them special rights and duties. The emphasis on contract as the opposite of status is, however, a little misleading, as it singles out one, albeit the most important, of the instruments that the law supplies to the individual to shape his own position. The true contrast to a reign of status is the reign of general and equal laws, of the rules which are the same for all, or, we might say, of the rule of *leges* in the original meaning of the Latin word for laws—*leges* that is, as opposed to the *privi-leges*.[2]

The requirement that the rules of true law be general does not mean that sometimes special rules may not apply to different classes of people if they refer to properties that only some people possess. There may be rules that can apply only to women or to the blind or to persons above a certain age. (In most such instances it would not even be necessary to name the class of people to whom the rule applies: only a woman, for example, can be raped or got with child.) Such distinctions will not be arbitrary, will not subject one group to the will of others, if they are equally recognized as justified by those inside and those outside the group. This does not mean that there must be unanimity as to the desirability of the distinction, but merely that individual views will not depend on whether the individual is in the group or not. So long as, for instance, the distinction is favored by the majority both inside and outside the group, there is a strong presumption that it serves the ends of both. When, however, only those inside the group favor the distinction, it is clearly privilege; while if only those outside favor it, it is discrimination. What is privilege to some is, of course, always discrimination to the rest.

5. It is not to be denied that even general, abstract rules, equally applicable to all, may possibly constitute severe restrictions on liberty. But when we reflect on it, we see how very unlikely this is. The chief safeguard is that the rules must apply to those who lay them down and those who apply them—that is, to the government as well as the governed—and that nobody has the power to grant exceptions. If all that is prohibited and enjoined is prohibited and enjoined for all without exception (unless such exception follows from another general rule) and if even authority has no special powers except that of enforcing the law, little that anybody may reasonably wish to do is likely to be prohibited. It is possible that a fanatical religious group will impose upon the rest restrictions which its members will be pleased to observe but which will be obstacles for others in the pursuit of important aims. But if it is true that religion has often provided the pretext for the establishing of rules felt to be extremely oppressive and that religious liberty is therefore regarded as very important for freedom, it is also significant that religious beliefs seem to be almost the only ground on which general rules seriously restrictive of liberty have ever been universally enforced. But how comparatively innocuous, even if irksome, are most such restrictions imposed on literally everybody, as, for instance, the Scottish Sabbath, compared with those that are likely to be imposed only on some! It is significant that most restrictions on what we regard as private affairs, such as sumptuary legislation, have usually been imposed only on selected groups of people or, as in the case of prohibition, were practicable only because the government reserved the right to grant exceptions.

It should also be remembered that, so far as men's actions toward other persons are concerned, freedom can never mean more than that they are restricted only by general rules. Since there is no kind of action that may not interfere with another person's protected sphere, neither speech, nor the press, nor the exercise of religion can be completely free. In all these fields (and, as we shall see later, in that of contract) freedom does mean and can mean only that what we may do is not dependent on the approval of any person or authority and is limited only by the same abstract rules that apply equally to all.

---

opinion, and the other moral restraints which create the main difference in the goodness of supreme governments."

1   *The movement ... from Status to Contract*   Sir Henry Maine, *Ancient Law*, 1861, p.151; see R.H. Graveson, "The Movement from Status to Contract," *Modern Law Review*, vol. 4 (1940–41).

2   *privi-leges*   "Privilege" derives from the Latin *privilegium*, literally, "a private law." In law, this refers to a law affecting a special person, a special right or an exemption from liability.

But if it is the law that makes us free, this is true only of the law in this sense of abstract general rule, or of what is called "the law in the material meaning," which differs from law in the merely formal sense by the character of the rules and not by their origin. The "law" that is a specific command, an order that is called a "law" merely because it emanates from the legislative authority, is the chief instrument of oppression. The confusion of these two conceptions of law and the loss of the belief that laws can rule, that men in laying down and enforcing laws in the former sense are not enforcing their will, are among the chief causes of the decline of liberty, to which legal theory has contributed as much as political doctrine.

We shall have to return later to the manner in which modern legal theory has increasingly obscured these distinctions. Here we can only indicate the contrast between the two concepts of law by giving examples of the extreme positions taken on them. The classical view is expressed in Chief Justice John Marshall's famous statement: "Judicial power, as contradistinguished from the power of laws, has no existence. Courts are mere instruments of law, and can will nothing."[1] Hold against this the most frequently quoted statement of a modern jurist, that has found the greatest favor among so-called progressives, namely, Justice Holmes's that "general propositions do not decide concrete cases."[2] The same position has been put by a contemporary political scientist thus: "The law cannot rule. Only men can exercise power over other men. To say that the law rules and not men, may consequently signify that the fact is to be hidden that men rule over men."[3]

The fact is that, if "to rule" means to make men obey another's will, government has no such power to rule in a free society. The citizen as citizen cannot be ruled in this sense, cannot be ordered about, no matter what his position may be in the job he has chosen for his own purposes or while, in accordance with the law, he temporarily becomes the agent of government. He can be ruled, however, in the sense in which "to rule" means the enforcement of general rules, laid down irrespective of the particular case and equally applicable to all. For here no human decision will be required in the great majority of cases to which the rules apply; and even when a court has to determine how the general rules may be applied to a particular case, it is the implications of the whole system of accepted rules that decide, not the will of the court.

6. The rationale of securing to each individual a known range within which he can decide on his actions is to enable him to make the fullest use of his knowledge, especially of his concrete and often unique knowledge of the particular circumstances of time and place.[4] The law tells him what facts he may count on and thereby extends the range within which he can predict the consequences of his actions. At the same time it tells him what possible consequences of his actions he must take into account or what he will be held responsible for. This means that what he is allowed or required to do must depend only on circumstances he can be presumed to know or be able to ascertain. No rule can be effective, or can leave him free to decide, that makes his range of free decisions dependent on remote consequences of his actions beyond his ability to foresee. Even of those effects which he might be presumed to foresee, the rules will single out some that he will have to take into account while allowing him to disregard others. In particular, such rules will not merely demand that he must not do anything that will damage others but will be—or should be—so expressed that, when applied to a particular situation, they will clearly decide which effects must be taken into account and which need not.

If the law thus serves to enable the individual to act effectively on his own knowledge and for this purpose adds to his knowledge, it also embodies knowledge, or the results of past experience, that are utilized so long as men act under these rules. In fact, the collaboration of individuals under

1   *Judicial power … can will nothing*   Chief Justice John Marshall in *Osborn v. Bank of United States*, 22 U.S. (9 Wheaton) 736, 866 (1824). [Editors' note] John Marshall (1755–1835) was an American statesman and Chief Justice of the United States from 1801–35. He changed the shape of American constitutional law, establishing the right of the Supreme Court to strike down laws that are deemed to violate the US Constitution.

2   *general propositions … concrete cases*   O.W. Holmes, Jr., *Lochner v. New York*, 198 U.S. 45, 76 (1905). [Editors' note] Oliver Wendell Holmes, Jr. (1841–1935) served on the US supreme court from 1902 to 1932.

3   *The laws … men rule over men*   F. Neumann, "The Concept of Political Freedom," *Columbia Law Review*, LIII (1953), 910, reprinted in his *The Democratic and the Authoritarian State*, 1957, pp.160–200.

4   *The rationale … time and place*   See Adam Smith, *The Wealth of Nations*: "What is the species of domestic industry which his capital can employ, and of which the product is likely to be of the greatest value, every individual, it is evident, can *in his local situation*, judge much better than any statesman or lawgiver can do for him." (Italics added.)

common rules rests on a sort of division of knowledge,[1] where the individual must take account of particular circumstances but the law ensures that their action will be adapted to certain general or permanent characteristics of their society. This experience, embodied in the law, that individuals utilize by observing rules, is difficult to discuss, since it is ordinarily not known to them or to anyone person. Most of these rules have never been deliberately invented but have grown through a gradual process of trial and error in which the experience of successive generations has helped to make them what they are. In most instances, therefore, nobody knows or has ever known all the reasons and considerations that have led to a rule being given a particular form. We must thus often endeavor to *discover* the functions that a rule actually serves. If we do not know the rationale of a particular rule, as is often the case, we must try to understand what its general function or purpose is to be if we are to improve upon it by deliberate legislation.

Thus the rules under which the citizens act constitute an adaptation of the whole of society to its environment and to the general characteristics of its members. They serve, or should serve, to assist the individuals in forming plans of action that they will have a good chance of carrying through. The rules may have come to exist merely because, in a certain type of situation, friction is likely to arise among individuals about what each is entitled to do, which can be prevented only if there is a rule to tell each clearly what his rights are. Here it is necessary merely that some known rule cover the type of situation, and it may not matter greatly what its contents are.

There will, however, often be several possible rules which satisfy this requirement but which will not be equally satisfactory. What exactly is to be included in that bundle of rights that we call "property," especially where land is concerned, what other rights the protected sphere is to include, what contracts the state is to enforce, are all issues in which only experience will show what is the most expedient arrangement. There is nothing "natural" in any particular definition of rights of this kind, such as the Roman conception of property as a right to use or abuse an object as one pleases, which, however often repeated, is in fact hardly practicable in its strict form. But the main features of all somewhat more advanced legal orders are sufficiently similar to appear as mere elaborations of what David Hume called the "three fundamental laws of nature, *that of the stability of possession, of transference by consent, and of the performance of promises.*"[2]

Our concern here cannot be, however, the particular content but only certain general attributes which these rules ought to possess in a free society. Since the lawgiver cannot foresee what use the persons affected will make of his rules, he can only aim to make them beneficial on the whole or in the majority of cases. But, as they operate through the expectations that they create, it is essential that they be always applied, irrespective of whether or not the consequences in a particular instance seem desirable.[3] That the legislator

---

1   *In fact, the collaboration … division of knowledge* See Lionel Robbins, *The Theory of Economic Policy*, 1952, p.193: The classical liberal "proposes, as it were, a division of labor: the state shall prescribe what individuals shall not do, if they are not to get in each other's way, while the citizen shall be left free to do anything which is not so forbidden. To the one is assigned the task of establishing formal rules, to the other responsibility for the substance of specific action."

2   *three fundamental laws of nature … performance of promises* See Hume, *Treatise*, Part 2, sec. 6; see also John Walter Jones, *Historical Introduction to the Theory of Law*, 1940, p.114: "In looking through the French Code and leaving out of account the law of the family, Duguit finds only three fundamental rules and no more—freedom of contract, the inviolability of property, and the duty to compensate another for damage due to one's fault. All the rest resolve themselves into subsidiary directions to some State agent or other."

3   *But, as they operate … seem desirable* See Hume, *Treatise*, Book 3, Part 2, sections 2–6, which still contains perhaps the most satisfactory discussion of the problems considered here: "A single act of justice is frequently contrary to *public interest*; and were it to stand alone, without being followed by other acts, may, in itself, be very prejudicial to society … Nor is every single act of justice, considered apart, more conducive to private interest than to public; … But however single acts of justice may be contrary, either to public or private interest, 'tis certain, that the whole plan or scheme is highly conducive, or indeed absolutely requisite, both to the support of society and the well-being of every individual. 'Tis impossible to separate the good from the ill. Property must be stable, and must be fixed by general rules. Though in one instance the public be a sufferer, this momentary ill is amply compensated by the steady prosecution of the rule, and by the peace and order which it establishes in society." See also the *Enquiry Concerning the Principles of Morals*: "The benefit, resulting from [the social virtues of justice and fidelity] is not the consequence of every individual single act; but arises from the whole scheme or system, concurred in by the whole, or the great part of the society … The result of the individual acts is here, in many instances, directly opposite to that of the whole system of actions; and the former may be extremely hurtful, while the latter is, to the highest degree, advantageous. Riches, inherited from a parent, are, in a bad man's hand, the instrument of mischief. The right of succession may, in one instance, be hurtful. Its benefit arises only from the observance of

confines himself to general rules rather than particular commands is the consequence of his necessary ignorance of the special circumstances under which they apply; all he can do is to provide some firm data for the use of those who have to make plans for particular actions. But in fixing for them only some of the conditions of their actions, he can provide opportunities and chances, but never certainties so far as the results of their efforts are concerned.

The necessity of emphasizing that it is of the essence of the abstract rules of law that they will only be likely to be beneficial in most cases to which they apply and, in fact, are one of the means by which man has learned to cope with his constitutional ignorance, has been imposed on us by certain rationalist interpretations of utilitarianism. It is true enough that the justification of any particular rule of law must be its usefulness—even though this usefulness may not be demonstrable by rational argument but known only because the rule has in practice proved itself more convenient than any other. But, generally speaking, only the rule as a whole must be so justified, not its every application.[1] The idea that each conflict, in law or in morals, should be so decided as would seem most expedient to somebody who could comprehend all the consequences of that decision involves the denial of the necessity of any rules. "Only a society of omniscient individuals could give each person complete liberty to weigh every particular action on general

utilitarian grounds."[2] Such an "extreme" utilitarianism leads to absurdity; and only what has been called "restricted" utilitarianism has therefore any relevance to our problem. Yet few beliefs have been more destructive of the respect for the rules of law and of morals than the idea that a rule is binding only if the beneficial effect of observing it in the particular instance can be recognized.

The oldest form of this misconception has been associated with the (usually misquoted) formula "salus populi suprema lex esto" ("the welfare of the people ought to be—not 'is'—the highest law"[3]). Correctly understood, it means that the end of the law ought to be the welfare of the people, that the general rules should be so designed as to serve it, but *not* that any conception of a particular social end should provide a justification for breaking those general rules. A specific end, a concrete result to be achieved, can never be a law.

7. The enemies of liberty have always based their arguments on the contention that order in human affairs requires that some should give orders and others obey.[4] Much of the opposition to a system of freedom under general laws arises from the inability to conceive of an effective co-ordination of human activities without deliberate organization by a commanding intelligence. One of the achievements of economic theory has been to explain how such a mutual adjustment of the spontaneous activities of individuals is brought about by the market, provided that there is a known delimitation of the sphere of control of each individual. An understanding of that mechanism of mutual adjustment of individuals forms the most important part

---

the general rule; and it is sufficient, if compensation be thereby made for all the ills and inconveniences, which form particular characters and situations." Also, *ibid*.: "All the laws of nature, which regulate property, as well as all civil laws, are general, and regard alone some essential circumstances of the case, without taking into consideration the characters, situations, and connexions of the person concerned, or any particular consequences which may result from the determination of these laws, in any particular case which offers. They deprive, without scruple, a beneficent man of all his possessions, if acquired by mistake, without a good title; in order to bestow them on a selfish miser, who has already heaped up immense stores of superfluous riches. Public utility requires, that property should be regulated by general inflexible rules; and though such rules are adopted as best serve the same end of public utility, it is impossible for them to prevent all particular hardships, or make beneficial consequences result from every individual case. It is sufficient, if the whole plan or scheme be necessary to the support of civil society, and if the balance of good, in the main, do thereby preponderate much above that of evil." I would like in this connection to acknowledge my indebtedness to Sir Arnold Plant, who many years ago first drew my attention to the importance of Hume's discussion of these issues.

1 *But, generally speaking ... its every application* See John Stuart Mill, *On Liberty*, 1869.

2 *Only a society ... general utilitarian grounds* See John Rawls, "Two Concepts of Rules," *Philosophical Review*, Volume 66 (1955); J.J.C. Smart, "Extreme and Restricted Utilitarianism," *Philosophical Quarterly*, Volume 6 (1956); H.J. McCloskey, "An Examination of Restricted Utilitarianism," *Philosophical Review*, Volume 66 (1957); J.O. Urmson, "The Interpretation of the Moral Philosophy of J.S. Mill's Utilitarianism," *Philosophical Quarterly*, Volume 6 (1956); and S.E. Toulmin, *An Examination of the Place of Reason in Ethics*, 1950.

3 *The oldest form ... highest law* John Selden in his *Table Talk* (1892) observes: "There is not anything in the world so much abused as this sentence, *salus populi suprema lex est*." Latin: The good of the people in the highest law.

4 *The enemies of liberty ... others obey* See, e.g., the opinion of James I, quoted by F.D. Wormuth, *The Origins of Modern Constitutionalism*, 1949, that "order was dependent upon the relationship of command and obedience. All organization derived from superiority and subordination."

of the knowledge that ought to enter into the making of general rules limiting individual action.

The orderliness of social activity shows itself in the fact that the individual can carry out a consistent plan of action that, at almost every stage, rests on the expectation of certain contributions from his fellows. "That there is some kind of order, consistency and constancy, in social life is obvious. If there were not, none of us would be able to go about his affairs or satisfy his most elementary wants."[1] This orderliness cannot be the result of a unified direction if we want individuals to adjust their actions to the particular circumstances largely known only to them and never known in their totality to anyone mind. Order with reference to society thus means essentially that individual action is guided by successful foresight, that people not only make effective use of their knowledge but can also foresee with a high degree of confidence what collaboration they can expect from others.

Such an order involving an adjustment to circumstances, knowledge of which is dispersed among a great many people, cannot be established by central direction. It can arise only from the mutual adjustment of the elements and their response to the events that act immediately upon them. It is what M. Polanyi has called the spontaneous formation of a "polycentric order": "When order is achieved among human beings by allowing them to interact with each other on their own initiative-subject only to the laws which uniformly apply to all of them—we have a system of spontaneous order in society. We may then say that the efforts of these individuals are coordinated by exercising their individual initiative and that this self-coordination justifies this liberty on public grounds. The actions of such individuals are said to be free, for they are not determined by any *specific* command, whether of a superior or a public authority; the compulsion to which they are subject is impersonal and general."[2]

Though people more familiar with the manner in which men order physical objects often find the formation of such spontaneous orders difficult to comprehend, there are, of course, many instances in which we must similarly rely on the spontaneous adjustments of individual elements to produce a physical order. We could never produce a crystal or a complex organic compound if we had to place each individual molecule or atom in the appropriate place in relation to the others. We must rely on the fact that in certain conditions they will arrange themselves in a structure possessing certain characteristics. The use of these spontaneous forces, which in such instances is our only means of achieving the desired result, implies, then) that many features of the process creating the order will be beyond our control; we cannot, in other words, rely on these forces and at the same time make sure that particular atoms will occupy specific places in the resulting structure.

Similarly, we can produce the conditions for the formation of an order in society, but we cannot arrange the manner in which its elements will order themselves under appropriate conditions. In this sense the task of the lawgiver is not to set up a particular order but merely to create conditions in which an orderly arrangement can establish and ever renew itself. As in nature, to induce the establishment of such an order does not require that we be able to predict the behavior of the individual atom—that will depend on the unknown particular circumstances in which it finds itself. All that is required is a limited regularity in its behavior; and the purpose of the human laws we enforce is to secure such limited regularity as will make the formation of an order possible.

Where the elements of such an order are intelligent human beings whom we wish to use their individual capacities as successfully as possible in the pursuit of their own ends, the chief requirement for its establishment is that each know which of the circumstances in his environment he can count on. This need for protection against unpredictable interference is sometimes represented as peculiar to "bourgeois society."[3] But, unless by "bourgeois society" is meant any society in which free individuals co-operate under conditions of division of labor, such a view confines the need to far too few social arrangements. It is the essential condition of individual freedom, and to secure it is the main function of law.[4]

---

1   *That there is some kind of order ... elementary wants*   I apologize to the author whose words I quote but whose name I have forgotten.

2   *When order is achieved ... impersonal and general*   M. Polanyi, *The Logic of Liberty,* 1951, p.159.

3   *bourgeois society*   Max Weber, *Theory of Social and Economic Organization,* 1947, tends to treat the need for "calculability and reliability in the functioning of the legal order" as a peculiarity of "capitalism" or the "bourgeois phase" of society. This is correct only if these terms are regarded as descriptive of any free society based on the division of labor.

4   *It is the essential condition ... it is the main function of law*   See E. Brunner, *Justice and the Social Order,* 1945, p.22: "Law is order by foresight. With regard to human beings, that is the service it renders; it is also its burden and its danger. It offers protection from the arbitrary, it gives a feeling of reliability, of security, it takes from the future its ominous darkness."

GIOVANNI GENTILE
(1875-1944)

Gentile (pronounced jane-TEE-luh) was an Italian philosopher best known under the description he gave himself: "the philosopher of Fascism." He also, however, is noteworthy as the creator of "actual idealism," a Hegelian philosophical system that dominated Italian philosophy for the first half of the twentieth century. Gentile attempted to derive his political views from this abstract philosophical standpoint.

Gentile was born in Sicily, and studied philosophy at the University of Pisa. His thesis was on the nineteenth-century Italian philosophers Rosmini and Gioberti, though he also did work on Kant and Hegel. His thesis was published a year after his graduation, and another book—a Hegelian treatment of Marx—followed the next year. While writing it, he became acquainted with Benedetto Croce, with whom he collaborated in Croce's journal *La critica*; the journal attacked the dominant positivist tradition in Italy, and was instrumental in the revival of Italian Hegelian idealism.

In 1906 Gentile became professor of philosophy at the university in Palermo, and began producing, at a great rate, what would become a huge body of philosophical writing. His major work, written after he had moved to Pisa, was *Teoria generale dello spirito come atto puro* (1916, tr. *The Theory of Mind as Pure Act*, 1922).

In 1922 Gentile was made a senator and minister of education in Mussolini's first cabinet; in 1924, he moved on to become the first president of the National Fascist Institute of Culture; by this time, he had become an enthusiastic defender and ideologist of fascism. After Mussolini's fall in 1943, Gentile went into retirement. He was assassinated by Italian communist partisans in 1944.

Gentile's philosophical system was called "actual idealism." It adopts Hegel's idea of the dialectical process, placing it inside the pure act of thinking; for Gentile, the

act of the thinking subject was the sole basis for human knowledge. Critics remark that this standpoint runs the risk of degenerating into solipsism or at least subjectivism, but Gentile insisted that it could provide a basis for objectivity and realism.

Marx's influence on Gentile is evident in the latter's view of the unity of theory and practice: thinking and acting—comprehending and transforming the world—are both conceived of as part of the same activity of "self-constitution" or "self-affirmation." This emphasis on action connected Gentile's abstract philosophical system with practical political and economic activity. He rejected individualism and advocated instead a powerful collectivism that would embody the virtues of fascist totalitarianism—a term he is said to have coined: "Nothing above the State, nothing against the State, nothing outside the State." The will of the state is thought to acquire a moral force—thereby blurring the dividing line between might and right, and offering a justification for repressions: "[it is impossible] to distinguish moral force from material force…. Every force is a moral force, for it is always an expression of will, and whatever method of argument it uses—from sermon to cudgel—its efficacy cannot be other than that of entreating the inner man and persuading him to agree." In 1932, the *Italian Encyclopedia* (of which Gentile was editor) contained an article called "A Doctrine of Fascism" signed by Mussolini, but written by Gentile. The article described and endorsed the central characteristics of Italian fascism: the replacement of parliamentary rule by "corporatism"—legislation by civic assemblies representing economic, industrial, agrarian, and professional groups—and the "*führerprinzip*"—a Nazi-style strictly hierarchical state leadership.

With the demise of fascism, much of Gentile's political influence disappeared; however, divorced from what he took to be its political consequences, his version of Hegelian idealism remains important in Italian philosophy, and has had an influence on the English idealist philosophers such as R.G. Collingwood.

• • • • •

from *Origins and Doctrine of Fascism* (1929)

8: Squadrism

The four year period 1919-1922 was characterized, in the development of the Fascist revolution, by the deployment of Fascist squads. The action squads were the military force of a virtual State. [They were the military arm of a State] in the process of realizing itself—which in order to create a superior regime, violated the controlling laws of a moribund State system—understood as inadequate to the demands of the national State sought by the revolution. The March on Rome[1] of the 28th of October 1922 was not the beginning, but the conclusion of that revolutionary movement, which on that date, with the consequent constitution of the Mussolini ministry, assumed full legality. From that point, Fascism, as the directive idea of the State, underwent evolution, slowly creating the institutions necessary for its actuation and its investment of all the economic, juridical, and political arrangements which make up the State, and which the State guarantees.

After the 28th of October 1922, Fascism no longer confronted a State that was to be destroyed; Fascism became the State and proceeded against those internal factions that opposed and resisted the development of those Fascist principles that were expected to animate the new State. Fascism was no longer a revolution against the State, but a revolutionary State mobilized against the residue and internal debris that obstructed its evolution and organiza-

tion. The period of violence and revolutionary illegality had ended—although the activity of the squads continued for a time to flicker here and there—in spite of the iron discipline imposed by the Duce of Fascism and Head of the Government.[2] Mussolini sought to have reality conform to the logic that governed the development of his idea and that of the Party that incarnated that idea. Fascism possessed all the means necessary for reconstruction: it transformed its own illegal action squads into the legal voluntary militia—in which the spirit of the revolution would be maintained until the fulfillment of the revolutionary program. The Party was established in an inflexible and perfect hierarchy obedient to the intentions of its Leader, and was rendered an instrument of government action, ready, with spirit, to face the test. The Italy of Giolitti[3] was finally overcome, at least in the realm of armed politics. Between Giolitti and the new Italy—the Italy of the combat veterans, of the Fascists, and believing Mazzinians[4]—flowed a river of blood. That torrent barred the way to anyone who advocated turning back. The crisis was transcended, and the war began to bear fruit.

9: The Totalitarian Character of the Doctrine of Fascism

The history of the Italian spiritual and political crisis and its solution was immanent in the concept of Fascism. How the legislative and administrative actions of the revolutionary government dealt with that crisis is not the present object of discussion. Rather, the present account is intended to illuminate the spirit which the government brought to its activities—which, in five years, profoundly transformed the nation's laws, orders, and institutions—thereby revealing the essence of Fascism.

It has already been said that before the complexity of the movement, nothing is more instructive for understanding it than, as we have already indicated, to consider Mazzini. His conception was a political conception—a conception of integral politics, a notion of politics which

---

1 *March on Rome* The threat of this march sparked the invitation of King Victor Emmanuel III to Mussolini to take control of the Italian government. The event took place during a general strike and widespread fear of a socialist revolution; Mussolini was supported by the military, the business class, and by many right-wing liberals. The "march" itself never occurred and was used by the fascists as propaganda; nothing occurred other than a Blackshirt (Italian fascist) parade.

2 *Duce of Fascism … Head of the Government* Refers to Mussolini. *Duce* is Italian for commander; *Il Duce* is translated "The Commander," Mussolini's title.

3 *Giolitti* Giovanni Giolitti (1842–1928), Italian Prime Minisiter five times between 1892 and 1921.

4 *Mazzinians* Followers of Giuseppe Mazzini (1805–72), Italian patriot, philosopher, and politician. He fought for the unification of the states of the Italian Pennisula under a single republican government.

does not distinguish itself from morality, from religion, or from every conception of life that does not conceive itself distinct and abstracted from all other fundamental interests of the human spirit. In Mazzini, the political man is he who possesses a moral, religious, and philosophical doctrine. Should one endeavor to separate, in Mazzini's creed and in his propaganda, that which is merely political from that which is his religious, his ethical intuition, moral enjoinments, his metaphysical convictions, one can no longer account for the great historical importance of his belief system and his propaganda. One can no longer understand the reasons why Mazzini attracted so many to himself—and proceeded to disturb the sleep of so many men of State and of the police. The analysis that does not always presuppose a unity [at the base of Mazzini's thought], does not lead to a clarification, but rather to a destruction of those ideas that exercised such historic consequences. It is evidence that human beings do not deal with life in slices, but rather as an indivisible unity.

The first point, therefore, that must be established in a definition of Fascism, is the totalitarian character of its doctrine, which concerns itself not only with political order and direction of the nation, but with its will, thought and sentiment.

10. *Thought and Action*

The second point. The doctrine of Fascism is not a philosophy in the ordinary sense of the term, and still less is it a religion. It is also not an explicated and definitive political doctrine, articulated in a series of formulae. The truth is that the significance of Fascism is not to be measured in the special theoretical or practical theses that it takes up at one or another time. As has been said at its very commencement, it did not arise with a precise and determinate program. Often, having settled on an immediate goal to be attained, a concept to be realized, a course to be followed, it has not hesitated, when put to the test, to change direction and reject as inadequate, or violative of principle, just that goal or that concept. Fascism sought not to bind the future. It has often announced reforms that were politically opportune, but the announcement itself did not bind the regime to their execution. The real commitments of the Duce are always those that are formulated and undertaken at one and the same time. For that reason Mussolini has always considered himself a "tempist," that is to say a person who undertakes a solu-

tion and acts at that proper moment in which action finds all the conditions and reasons mature that render the action possible and opportune. Fascism draws out of the Mazzinian truth, *thought and action*, its most rigorous significance, identifying the two terms in order to have them perfectly coincide, no longer to attribute any value to thought that is not translated or expressed in action. That is the source of all the expressions of "anti-intellectualist" polemics that constitutes one of Fascism's most recurrent themes. It is a polemic that is eminently Mazzinian, because "intellectualism" [as "intellectualism" is understood by Fascists] divorces thought from action, science from life, the brain from the heart, and theory from practice. It is the posture of the talker and the skeptic, of the person who entrenches himself behind the maxim that it is one thing to say something and another thing to do it; it is the utopian who is the fabricator of systems that will never face concrete reality; it is the talk of the poet, the scientist, the philosopher, who confine themselves to fantasy and to speculation and are ill-disposed to look around themselves and see the earth on which they tread and on which are to be found those fundamental human interests that feed their very fantasy and intelligence. "Intellectuals" are all those who represent that old Italy. They were the enemy of Mazzini's heated preachments.

...

11. *The Center of the System*

The third point. The Fascist system is not a system, but has in politics, and in the interest of politics, its center of gravity. Born as a conception of the State, intended to resolve the political problems exacerbated in Italy by the release of the passions of the unthinking masses of the post-World War I period, Fascism took the field as a political method. But in the act of confronting and resolving political problems, Fascism, in accordance with its very nature, by its very method, posed for itself moral, religious, and philosophical problems—and, in so doing, developed and demonstrated its specific totalitarian character. That provided the occasion for putting the political form of its principle to the fore. In manifesting that principle, Fascism revealed its specific content—without immediately revealing its ideal origins in a more profound intuition of life, from which the political principle arises. This allows us to outline a rapid synthesis of the political doctrine of Fascism, which does not exhaust its content, but which constitutes that part, or better that preeminent, and generally most interesting, expression.

12. The Fascist Doctrine of the State

Fascist politics turns entirely on the concept of the national State—a concept which has many points of contact with the doctrine of Nationalism—so many points in fact, that it permitted the fusion of the Nationalist Party with that of Fascism in a single program. Nonetheless, the Fascist concept has its proper character. That cannot be overlooked. Without recognizing that, one would neglect that which is peculiar and characteristic of Fascism. Comparisons are never very generous—still less the one here proposed. Nonetheless, the effort will be undertaken to bring to light the essence of Fascism.

Both Nationalism and Fascism place the State at the very foundation of every individual value and right. For both, the State is not a consequence, but a beginning. The relationship between the individual and the State proposed by Nationalism was the direct antithesis of that advanced by individualistic liberalism and socialism. For Nationalists, the State is conceived as prior to the individual. For liberals and socialists, on the other hand, the individual is understood to be something that precedes the State, who finds in the State something external, something that limits and controls, that suppresses liberty, and that condemns him to those circumstances into which he is born, circumstances within which he must live and die. For Fascism, on the other hand, the State and the individual are one, or better, perhaps, "State" and "individual" are terms that are inseparable in a necessary synthesis.

…

13. The Fascist State as a Democratic State

The Fascist State, therefore, as distinct from the Nationalist State, is an entirely spiritual creation. It is a national State, because from the point of view of Fascism, it is the result of spiritual action rather than a presupposition. The nation is never complete—nor is the State simply the nation in its concrete political form. The State is always *in fieri*.[1] It

---

1   *in fieri*   Latin: pending.

is all always in our hands. It is therefore our own immense responsibility.

But this State that realizes itself in the consciousness and will of the individual, rather than being imposed from on high, cannot have the same relationship with the people imagined by Nationalism. They imagined that the State corresponded with the nation, and conceived both as an already existing entity that it was not necessary to create, but which it was only necessary to come to know. That preexisting entity required a ruling class, characteristically intellectual, that sensed that entity, that first required to be known, understood, appraised, and exalted. The authority of the State was not a product, but a presupposition. It could not depend on the people, in fact, the people depended on the State. The authority that the people were required to recognize was the very precondition of life. Without that authority, sooner or later, one would have to acknowledge that survival was not possible. The Nationalist state was aristocratic state, that constructed itself out of the force it inherited from its origin, that made it valued by the masses. The Fascist State, on the other hand, is a popular state, and, in that sense, a democratic State par excellence. The relationship between the State and the individual is not that between it and one or the other citizen, but with every citizen. Every citizen shares a relationship with the State that is so intimate that the State exists only in so far as it is made to exist by the citizen. Thus, its formation is a product of the consciousness of each individual, and thus of the masses, in which the power of the State consists. That explains the necessity of the Fascist Party and of all the institutions of propaganda and education that foster the political and moral ideals of Fascism, so that the thought and the will of the solitary person, the Duce, becomes the thought and the will of the masses. Out of that arises the enormous difficulty in which it is involved, to bring into the Party, and into the institutions created by the Party, all the people—commencing from their most tender years. It is a formidable problem, the solution of which creates infinite difficulty, because it is almost impossible to conform the masses to the demands of an elite Party of vanguard morality. Such a conformity could only happen slowly, through education and reform. Equally difficult is the duality between governmental action and the action of the Party. As the Party's organization expands almost to the full extent of the State—whatever the effort to consolidate then efforts through the force and unity of discipline, discrepancies remain. The two, however much the effort is made to make their action one through discipline, the danger remained that there would be difficulty, with every initiative and progress—given that all individuals were bound together in a mechanism that, even though encouraged by a single spirit that emanated from the center and proceeded to the periphery, the freedom of movement and autonomy would only slowly languish and disappear.

14. The Corporative State

The great social and constitutional reform that Fascism is accomplishing, instituting the corporative syndicalist regime as a substitute for the liberal State, arose out of the very character of the Fascist State. Fascism accepted from Syndicalism the idea of the educative and moral function of the syndicate. But since the intention was to overcome the antithesis between the State and the syndicate, the effort was made to enter the system of syndicates harmoniously into corporations subject to discipline by the State and to thereby give expression to the organic character of the State. In order to give expression to the will of the individual, the organic State must reach him, not as an abstract political individual that the old liberalism supposed—as a featureless atom. The organic State sought to reach the individual as it could only find him, as he in fact is: as a specialized producer whose tasks moved him to associate himself with others of the same category, all belonging to the same unitary economic organism that is the nation. The syndicate, conforming as much as possible to the concrete reality of the individual, renders him valued for what he is in reality—be it in terms of self-consciousness that he gradually achieves, or from the right he has earned as a consequence of a contribution, through the syndicate, to the general interests of the nation.

This major reform remains in process. Nationalism and syndicalism—together with liberalism, itself—had criticized the old representative form of the liberal State and appealed to a system of organic representation to better capture the reality in which citizens are lodged, and would better represent their psychology and provide support for the development of their personality.

The corporative State seeks to approximate itself to the notion of immanence of the State in the individual. That immanence provides for both the strength of the State [because it is identified with the individual] and the liberty of the individual [because the liberty of the individual is found in the liberty of the State]. That concept provides [the rationale] for the ethical and religious values that Fascism has made its own and which the Duce has regularly invoked in his speeches in the most solemn manner.

HANNAH ARENDT
(1906–1975)

Hannah Arendt was born in 1906 into a German-Jewish family in Königsburg, then part of Germany. She studied philosophy at the University of Marburg with the Lutheran theologian Rudolf Bultmann and philosopher Martin Heidegger. After a year, she went to Freiburg University for one term, where she attended lectures by the phenomenologist Edmund Husserl, then on to Heidelberg University to study with the existentialist Karl Jaspers, under whose supervision she completed her doctoral dissertation on St. Augustine in 1929. Hitler's rise to power in 1933 forced her to leave Germany, and she went briefly to Prague, then to Paris for several years, finally settling in 1941 in New York. In the United States, she taught at Princeton, Berkeley, Chicago, and finally the New School in New York, where she was professor of political philosophy until her death in 1975.

Arendt's political philosophy is deeply marked by her experience with Nazi totalitarianism; much of her work is directly or indirectly a response to it. In her first major work, *The Origins of Totalitarianism* (1951), she not only explored totalitarianism, but also conducted a penetrating analysis of anti-Semitism, imperialism, and racism. Arendt regarded totalitarianism as a new form of government based on ideology and terror, understood as the systematic, institutionalized use of physical and psychological violence. The expansion of capitalism and bureaucratic administration (developed during colonial regimes' suppression of native populations) left people vulnerable to totalitarian ideologies—racism, in the case of Nazism, historical materialism in the case of Stalinism. In totalitarian states, the masses mobilized behind a single party that brutally exercised control over all aspects of life, stamping out all forms of pluralism and difference.

The Human Condition (1958) invoked the Aristotelian distinction between the *vita activa* (active life) and the *vita contemplativa* (contemplative life), and argued that the Western philosophical tradition had wrongly privileged the latter. Again drawing on Aristotle, Arendt saw humankind as a *zoon politikon*—a political animal. Following the civic republican tradition of Aristotle, the Stoics, Machiavelli, Montesquieu and others, she endorsed the ideals of active citizenship and civic engagement, reviving the Greek term *praxis*, understood primarily as political practice. Political deliberation, for Arendt, was not simply a means of achieving consensus, but was an end in itself, in which people exercise their rationality and achieve freedom through deliberation and the mutual setting of ends. It is through *praxis* that we can overcome the isolation, egotism and bureaucratization that characterizes much of modern life. Arendt posited an opposition between participatory democracy and bureaucratic and elitist conceptions of democracy.

In 1961, Arendt reported on the Nazi war criminal Adolf Eichmann's trial in Jerusalem, publishing her account of the events in the *New Yorker* magazine, then in book form as *Eichmann in Jerusalem: A Report on the Banality of Evil* in 1963. Here she controversially described Eichmann—who supervised the murder of hundreds of thousands of Jews—not as evil, mad, or even particularly anti-Semitic, but rather as a thoughtless bureaucrat incapable of exercising his imagination vigorously enough to comprehend his moral atrocities.

Arendt has influenced political thought in many ways. *The Origins of Totalitarianism* is one of the canonical works on totalitarianism, on anti-Semitism, and on post-colonialism. Arendt's criticisms of modernity have influenced postmodern thinkers such as Jean-François Lyotard. Her conception of *praxis*, developed in public communication, is a key predecessor to Jürgen Habermas's theory of communicative action, as well as Seyla Benhabib's version of discourse ethics. It also anticipates the recent revival of republican thought in the work of theorists such as Quentin Skinner and Philip Pettit.

from *The Human Condition* (1958)

Chapter 28: Power and the Space of Appearance

The space of appearance[1] comes into being wherever men are together in the manner of speech and action, and therefore predates and precedes all formal constitution of the public realm and the various forms of government, that is, the various forms in which the public realm can be organized. Its peculiarity is that, unlike the spaces which are the work of our hands, it does not survive the actuality of the movement which brought it into being, but disappears not only with the dispersal of men—as in the case of great catastrophes when the body politic of a people is destroyed—but with the disappearance or arrest of the activities themselves. Wherever people gather together, it is potentially there, but only potentially, not necessarily and not forever. That civilizations can rise and fall, that mighty empires and great cultures can decline and pass away without external catastrophes—and more often than not such external "causes" are preceded by a less visible internal decay that invites disaster—is due to this peculiarity of the public realm, which, because it ultimately resides on action and speech, never altogether loses its potential character. What first undermines and then kills political communities is loss of power[2] and final impotence; and power cannot be stored up and kept in reserve for emergencies, like the instruments of violence, but exists only in its actualization. Where power is not actualized, it passes away, and history is full of examples that the greatest material riches cannot compensate for this loss. Power is actualized only where word and deed have not parted company, where words are not empty and deeds not brutal, where words are not used to veil intentions but to disclose realities, and deeds are not used to violate and destroy but to establish relations and create new realities.

Power is what keeps the public realm, the potential space of appearance between acting and speaking men, in existence. The word itself, its Greek equivalent *dynamis*, like the Latin *potentia* with its various modern derivatives or the German *Macht* (which derives from *mögen* and *möglich*,[3] not from *machen*[4]), indicates its "potential" character. Power is always, as we would say, a power potential and not an unchangeable, measurable, and reliable entity like force or strength. While strength is the natural quality of an individual seen in isolation, power springs up between men when they act together and vanishes the moment they disperse. Because of this peculiarity, which power shares with all potentialities that can only be actualized but never fully materialized, power is to an astonishing degree independent of material factors, either of numbers or means. A comparatively small but well-organized group of men can rule almost indefinitely over large and populous empires, and it is not infrequent in history that small and poor countries get the better of great and rich nations. (The story of David and Goliath is only metaphorically true; the power of a few can be greater than the power of many, but in a contest between two men not power but strength decides, and cleverness, that is, brain power, contributes materially to the outcome on the same level as muscular force.) Popular revolt against materially strong rulers, on the other hand, may engender an almost irresistible power even if it foregoes the use of violence in the face of materially vastly superior forces. To call this "passive resistance" is certainly an ironic idea; it is one of the most active and efficient ways of action ever devised, because it cannot be countered by fighting, where there may be defeat or victory, but only by mass slaughter in which even the victor is defeated, cheated of his prize, since nobody can rule over dead men.

The only indispensable material factor in the generation of power is the living together of people. Only where men live so close together that the potentialities of action are always present can power remain with them, and the foundation of cities, which as city-states have remained paradigmatic for all Western political organization, is therefore indeed the most important material prerequisite for power. What keeps people together after the fleeting moment of action has passed (what we today call "organization") and

---

1   *The space of appearance*   [Unless otherwise indicated, all notes to this selection are by the author rather than the editors of this anthology.] [editors' note] Arendt describes this as that space "where I appear to others as others appear to me, where men exist not merely like other living or inanimate things, but to make their appearance explicitly." It might be thought of as public space—the framework or system of presuppositions and expectations we exist in as a consequence of our *social* existence, our undertaking of joint projects.

2   *power*   [editors' note] Arendt uses this term to refer especially to the capacity for action in the public sphere—for political action, action done by people organized as a group.

---

3   *mögen* and *möglich*   [editors' note] German: "may" and "possible."

4   *machen*   [editors' note] German: "to make."

what, at the same time, they keep alive through remaining together is power. And whoever, for whatever reasons, isolates himself and does not partake in such being together, forfeits power and becomes impotent, no matter how great his strength and how valid his reasons.

If power were more than this potentiality in being together, if it could be possessed like strength or applied like force instead of being dependent upon the unreliable and only temporary agreement of many wills and intentions, omnipotence would be a concrete human possibility. For power, like action, is boundless; it has no physical limitation in human nature, in the bodily existence of man, like strength. Its only limitation is the existence of other people, but this limitation is not accidental, because human power corresponds to the condition of plurality to begin with. For the same reason, power can be divided without decreasing it, and the interplay of powers with their checks and balances is even liable to generate more power, so long, at least, as the interplay is alive and has not resulted in a stalemate. Strength, on the contrary, is indivisible, and while it, too, is checked and balanced by the presence of others, the interplay of plurality in this case spells a definite limitation on the strength of the individual, which is kept in bounds and may be overpowered by the power potential of the many. An identification of the strength necessary for the production of things with the power necessary for action is conceivable only as the divine attribute of one god. Omnipotence therefore is never an attribute of gods in polytheism, no matter how superior the strength of the gods may be to the forces of men. Conversely, aspiration toward omnipotence always implies—apart from its utopian *hubris*—the destruction of plurality.

Under the conditions of human life, the only alternative to power is not strength—which is helpless against power—but force, which indeed one man alone can exert against his fellow men and of which one or a few can possess a monopoly by acquiring the means of violence. But while violence can destroy power, it can never become a substitute for it. From this results the by no means infrequent political combination of force and powerlessness, an array of impotent forces that spend themselves, often spectacularly and vehemently but in utter futility, leaving behind neither monuments nor stories, hardly enough memory to enter into history at all. In historical experience and traditional theory, this combination, even if it is not recognized as such, is known as tyranny, and the time-honored fear of this form of government is not exclusively inspired by its cruelty, which—as the long series of benevolent tyrants

and enlightened despots attests—is not among its inevitable features, but by the impotence and futility to which it condemns the rulers as well as the ruled.

More important is a discovery made, as far as I know, only by Montesquieu, the last political thinker to concern himself seriously with the problem of forms of government. Montesquieu realized that the outstanding characteristic of tyranny was that it rested on isolation—on the isolation of the tyrant from his subjects and the isolation of the subjects from each other through mutual fear and suspicion—and hence that tyranny was not one form of government among others but contradicted the essential human condition of plurality, the acting and speaking together, which is the condition of all forms of political organization. Tyranny prevents the development of power, not only in a particular segment of the public realm but in its entirety; it generates, in other words, impotence as naturally as other bodies politic generate power. This, in Montesquieu's interpretation, makes it necessary to assign it a special position in the theory of political bodies: it alone is unable to develop enough power to remain at all in the space of appearance, the public realm; on the contrary, it develops the germs of its own destruction the moment it comes into existence.[1]

Violence, curiously enough, can destroy power more easily than it can destroy strength, and while a tyranny is always characterized by the impotence of its subjects, who have lost their human capacity to act and speak together, it is not necessarily characterized by weakness and sterility; on the contrary, the crafts and arts may flourish under these conditions if the ruler is "benevolent" enough to leave his subjects alone in their isolation. Strength, on the other hand, nature's gift to the individual which cannot be shared with others, can cope with violence more successfully than with power—either heroically, by consenting to fight and die, or stoically, by accepting suffering and challenging all

---

1   *in Montesquieu's interpretation … comes into existence* In the words of Montesquieu, who ignores the difference between tyranny and despotism: "Le principe du gouvernement despotique se corrompt sans cesse, parcequ'il est corrompu par sa nature. Les autres gouvernements périssent, parceque des accidents particuliers en violent le principe: celui-ci périt par son vice intérieur, lorsque quelques causes accidentelles n'empêchent point son principe de se corrompre" ["The constitution of despotic government entails ceaseless corruption, because it is corrupt by nature. Other forms of government perish because of particular accidental perils; this one perishes of its own internal faults unless some accidental cause prevents the corruption of its constitution."] (*The Spirit of Laws*, Book 8, chapter 10).

affliction through self-sufficiency and withdrawal from the world; in either case, the integrity of the individual and his strength remain intact. Strength can actually be ruined only by power and is therefore always in danger from the combined force of the many. Power corrupts indeed when the weak band together in order to ruin the strong, but not before. The will to power, as the modern age from Hobbes to Nietzsche understood it in glorification or denunciation, far from being a characteristic of the strong, is, like envy and greed, among the vices of the weak, and possibly even their most dangerous one.

If tyranny can be described as the always abortive attempt to substitute violence for power, ochlocracy, or mob rule, which is its exact counterpart, can be characterized by the much more promising attempt to substitute power for strength. Power indeed can ruin all strength and we know that where the main public realm is society, there is always the danger that, through a perverted form of "acting together"—by pull and pressure and the tricks of cliques—those are brought to the fore who know nothing and can do nothing. The vehement yearning for violence, so characteristic of some of the best modern creative artists, thinkers, scholars, and craftsmen, is a natural reaction of those whom society has tried to cheat of their strength.[1]

Power preserves the public realm and the space of appearance, and as such it is also the lifeblood of the human artifice, which, unless it is the scene of action and speech, of the web of human affairs and relationships and the stories engendered by them, lacks its ultimate *raison d'être*. Without being talked about by men and without housing them, the world would not be a human artifice but a heap of unrelated things to which each isolated individual was at liberty to add one more object; without the human artifice to house them, human affairs would be as floating, as futile and vain, as the wanderings of nomad tribes. The melancholy wisdom of *Ecclesiastes*—"Vanity of vanities; all is vanity…. There is no new thing under the sun,… there is no remembrance of former things; neither shall there be any remembrance of things that are to come with those that

shall come after"[2]—does not necessarily arise from specifically religious experience; but it is certainly unavoidable wherever and whenever trust in the world as a place fit for human appearance, for action and speech, is gone. Without action to bring into the play of the world the new beginning of which each man is capable by virtue of being born, "there is no new thing under the sun"; without speech to materialize and memorialize, however tentatively, the "new things" that appear and shine forth, "there is no remembrance"; without the enduring permanence of a human artifact, there cannot "be any remembrance of things that are to come with those that shall come after." And without power, the space of appearance brought forth through action and speech in public will fade away as rapidly as the living deed and the living word.

Perhaps nothing in our history has been so short-lived as trust in power, nothing more lasting than the Platonic and Christian distrust of the splendor attending its space of appearance, nothing—finally in the modern age—more common than the conviction that "power corrupts." The words of Pericles, as Thucydides reports them,[3] are perhaps unique in their supreme confidence that men can enact *and* save their greatness at the same time and, as it were, by one and the same gesture, and that the performance as such will be enough to generate *dynamis* and not need the transforming reification of *homo faber*[4] to keep it in reality.[5] Pericles' speech, though it certainly corresponded to and articulated the innermost convictions of the people of Athens, has always been read with the sad wisdom of hindsight by men who knew that his words were spoken at the beginning of the end. Yet short-lived as this faith in *dynamis* (and consequently in politics) may have been—and it had already come to an end when the first political philosophies were formulated—its bare existence has sufficed to elevate action

---

1   *vehement yearning … their strength* The extent to which Nietzsche's glorification of the will to power was inspired by such experiences of the modern intellectual may be surmised from the following side remark: "Denn die Ohnmacht gegen Menschen, nicht die Ohnmacht gegen die Natur, erzeugt die desperateste Verbitterung gegen das Dasein" [For it is powerlessness against man, not against nature, that generates the most desperate bitterness against existence.] (*Wille zur Macht*, [*The Will to Power*] No. 55).

2   *Vanity of vanities … come after* [editors' note] Ecclesiastes 1.2, 9, 11.

3   *The words of Pericles … reports them* [editors' note] Thucydides, *History of the Peloponnesian War* 2.40, "Pericles's Funeral Oration."

4   *homo faber* [editors' note] Latin: "man the maker." This concept, associated with Arendt, contrasts with the biological name for our species, *homo sapiens*, "man the wise." Arendt's name emphasizes the human capacity for controlling the environment through tools.

5   *will be enough … in reality* In the above-mentioned paragraph [not included in this selection] in the Funeral Oration, Pericles deliberately contrasts the *dynamis* of the *polis* with the craftsmanship of the poets.

to the highest rank in the hierarchy of the *vita activa*[1] and to single out speech as the decisive distinction between human and animal life, both of which bestowed upon politics a dignity which even today has not altogether disappeared.

What is outstandingly clear in Pericles' formulations—and, incidentally, no less transparent in Homer's poems—is that the innermost meaning of the acted deed and the spoken word is independent of victory and defeat and must remain untouched by any eventual outcome, by their consequences for better or worse. Unlike human behavior—which the Greeks, like all civilized people, judged according to "moral standards," taking into account motives and intentions on the one hand and aims and consequences on the other—action can be judged only by the criterion of greatness because it is in its nature to break through the commonly accepted and reach into the extraordinary, where whatever is true in common and everyday life no longer applies because everything that exists is unique and *sui generis*.[2] Thucydides, or Pericles, knew full well that he had broken with the normal standards for everyday behavior when he found the glory of Athens in having left behind "everywhere everlasting remembrance [*mnēmeia aidia*] of their good and their evil deeds." The art of politics teaches men how to bring forth what is great and radiant—*ta megala kai lampra*, in the words of Democritus; as long as the *polis* is there to inspire men to dare the extraordinary, all things are safe; if it perishes, everything is lost.[3] Motives and aims, no matter how pure or how grandiose, are never unique; like psychological qualities, they are typical, characteristic of different types of persons. Greatness, therefore, or the specific meaning of each deed, can lie only in the performance itself and neither in its motivation nor its achievement.

It is this insistence on the living deed and the spoken word as the greatest achievements of which human beings are capable that was conceptualized in Aristotle's notion of *energeia* ("actuality"), with which he designated all activities that do not pursue an end (are *ateleis*) and leave no work behind (no *par' autas erga*), but exhaust their full meaning in the performance itself.[4] It is from the experience of this full actuality that the paradoxical "end in itself" derives its original meaning; for in these instances of action and speech[5] the end (*telos*) is not pursued but lies in the activity itself which therefore becomes an *entelecheia*, and the work is not what follows and extinguishes the process but is imbedded in it; the performance is the work, is *energeia*.[6] Aristotle, in his political philosophy, is still well aware of what is at stake in politics, namely, no less than the *ergon tou anthrōpou*[7] (the "work of man" *qua* man), and if he defined this "work" as "to live well" (*eu zēn*), he clearly meant that "work" here is no work product but exists only in sheer actuality. This specifically human achievement lies altogether outside the category of means and ends; the "work of man" is no end because the means to achieve it—the virtues, or *aretai*—are not qualities which may or may not be actualized, but are themselves "actualities." In other words, the means to achieve the end would already be the end; and this "end," conversely, cannot be considered a means in some other respect, because there is nothing higher to attain than this actuality itself.

It is like a feeble echo of the prephilosophical Greek experience of action and speech as sheer actuality to read time and again in political philosophy since Democritus and Plato that politics is a *technē*, belongs among the arts, and can be likened to such activities as healing or navigation, where, as in the performance of the dancer or play-actor, the "product" is identical with the performing act itself. But we may gauge what has happened to action and speech, which are only in actuality, and therefore the highest ac-

---

1 *vita activa* [editors' note] Latin: active life. Arendt refers to those fundamental conditions for human life, labor (life-support activities), work (production of "unnatural" artifacts), and action (intentional human interaction).

2 *Unlike human behavior … sui generis* The reason why Aristotle in his *Poetics* finds that greatness (*megethos*) is a prerequisite of the dramatic plot is that the drama imitates acting and acting is judged by greatness, by its distinction from the commonplace (1450b25). The same, incidentally, is true for the beautiful, which resides in greatness and *taxis*, the joining together of the parts (1450b34 ff.).

3 *The words of Democritus … everything is lost* See fragment B157 of Democritus in Hermann Diels and Walther Kranz. *Die Fragmente der Vorsokratiker* (Zurich: Weidmann, 1985).

4 *Aristotle's notion … performance itself* For the concept of *energeia* see *Nicomachean Ethics* 1094a1–5; *Physics* 201b31; *On the Soul* 417a16, 431a6. The examples most frequently used are seeing and flute-playing.

5 *action and speech* It is of no importance in our context that Aristotle saw the highest possibility of "actuality" not in action and speech, but in contemplation and thought, in *theōria* and *nous*.

6 *the end (telos) … is energeia* The two Aristotelian concepts, *energeia* and *entelecheia*, are closely interrelated (*energeia …synteinei pros tēn entelecheian* ["(the term) 'actuality' points to (the term) 'complete reality'"]): full actuality (*energeia*) effects and produces nothing besides itself, and full reality (*entelecheia*) has no other end besides itself (see *Metaphysics* 1050a22–35).

7 *ergon tou anthrōpou* Aristotle, *Nicomachean Ethics* 1097b22.

tivities in the political realm, when we hear what modern society, with the peculiar and uncompromising consistency that characterized it in its early stages, had to say about them. For this all-important degradation of action and speech is implied when Adam Smith classifies all occupations which rest essentially on performance—such as the military profession, "churchmen, lawyers, physicians and opera-singers"—together with "menial services," the lowest and most unproductive "labor."[1] It was precisely these occupations—healing, flute-playing, play-acting—which furnished ancient thinking with examples for the highest and greatest activities of man.

◆ ◆ ◆ ◆ ◆

On the Nature of Totalitarianism: An Essay in Understanding (1954)

In order to fight totalitarianism, one need understand only one thing: Totalitarianism is the most radical denial of freedom. Yet this denial of freedom is common to all tyrannies and is of no primary importance for understanding the peculiar nature of totalitarianism. Nonetheless, whoever cannot be mobilized when freedom is threatened will not be mobilized at all. Even moral admonitions, the outcry against crimes unprecedented in history and not foreseen in the Ten Commandments will remain of little avail. The very existence of totalitarian movements in the non-totalitarian world, that is, the appeal totalitarianism exerts on those who have all the information before them and who are warned against it day in and day out, bears eloquent witness to the breakdown of the whole structure of morality, the whole body of commands and prohibitions which had traditionally translated and embodied the fundamental ideas of freedom and justice into terms of social relationships and political institutions.

Still, many people doubt that this breakdown is a reality. They are inclined to think some accident has happened after which one's duty is to restore the old order, appeal to the old knowledge of right and wrong, mobilize the old instincts for order and safety. They label anyone who thinks

and speaks otherwise a "prophet of doom" whose gloominess threatens to darken the sun rising over good and evil for all of eternity.

The fact of the matter is that the "prophets of doom," the historical pessimists of the late nineteenth and early twentieth centuries, from Burckhard[2] to Spengler,[3] were put out of business by the actuality of catastrophes the size and horror of which no one ever foresaw. Certain developments, however, apparently could have been and were predicted. Though these predictions hardly ever occurred in the nineteenth century, they can be found in the eighteenth century, and were overlooked because nothing seemed to justify them. It is worthwhile, for instance, to learn what Kant, in 1793, had to say about the "balance of power" as a solution to the conflicts rising from the European nation-state system: "The so-called balance of powers in Europe is like Swift's house which was built in such perfect harmony with all laws of equilibrium that, when a bird sat down on it, it immediately collapsed—a mere phantasm."[4] The balance achieved by the system of nation-states was not a mere phantasm, but it did collapse exactly as Kant predicted. In the words of a modern historian: "The iron test of the balance of power lies in the very thing it is designed to stave off—war".[5]

More sweeping in outlook and yet closer to reality is another eighteenth-century author, who is usually not counted among the "prophets of doom" and who is as serene, as sober, and even less disturbed (the French Revolution had not yet taken place) than Kant. There is hardly an event of any importance in our recent history that would not fit into the scheme of Montesquieu's[6] apprehensions.

---

1 *Adam Smith ... most unproductive "labor"* Adam Smith, *Wealth of Nations*.

2 *Burckhard* [Unless otherwise noted, all notes to this section are by the editors of this anthology.] Jacob Burckhard (1818-97), Swiss historian, best known for his studies of the Renaissance, which went beyond the study of texts and great works to incorporate all aspects of the culture. For this reason, he is often considered the father of cultural history.

3 *Spengler* Oswald Arnold Gottfried Spengler (1888-1936) was a German historian and philosopher. In his book *The Decline of the West* (1923), he put forward a cyclical theory of civilization and held that in his own time it was at its ebb (the book was written during World War I).

4 *The so-called balance ... a mere phantasm* Immanuel Kant, *On the Common Saying: That may be true in theory but does not apply to practice.*

5 *The iron test ... war* [Arendt's note] Hajo Holborn, *The Political Collapse of Europe*, 1951.

6 *Montesquieu's* Charles-Louis de Secondat, baron de La Brède et de Montesquieu (1689-1755), author of *The Spirit of Laws* (1748)

Montesquieu was the last to inquire into the nature of government; that is, to ask what makes it what it is.[1] But Montesquieu added to this a second and entirely original question: What makes a government act as it acts? He thus discovered that each government has not only its "particular structure" but also a particular "principle" which sets it in motion. Political science has now discarded both questions because they are, in a way, pre-scientific. They refer to preliminary understanding which expresses itself only in giving names: this is a republic, this is a monarchy, this is a tyranny. Still, they start the dialogue of true understanding by asking, What is it that makes a state recognizable as a republic, a monarchy, or a tyranny? After giving the traditional answer to the traditional question—affirming that a republic is a constitutional government with the sovereign power in the hands of the people; a monarchy, a lawful government with sovereign power in the hands of one man; and a tyranny, a lawless government where power is exercised by one man according to his arbitrary will—Montesquieu adds that in a republic the principle of action is virtue, which, psychologically, he equates with love of equality; in a monarchy, the principle of action is honor, whose psychological expression is a passion for distinction; and in a tyranny, the principle of action is fear.

It is striking and strange that Montesquieu, who is famous chiefly for his discovery and articulation of the division of powers into the executive, legislative, and judiciary, defines governments as though power is necessarily sovereign and indivisible. Curiously enough, it was Kant, and not Montesquieu, who redefined the structure of governments according to Montesquieu's own principles.

In his *Perpetual Peace*, Kant introduces a distinction between "forms of domination" (*Formen der Beherrschung*) and forms of government. The forms of domination are distinguished solely according to the locus of power: All states in which the prince has undivided sovereign power are called autocracies; if the power is in the hands of the nobility, the form of domination is aristocracy; and if the people wield absolute power, domination comes about in the form of democracy. Kant's point is that all these forms of domination (as the word "domination" itself indicates) are, strictly

speaking, illegal. Constitutional or lawful government is established through the division of power so that the same body (or man) does not make the laws, execute them, and then sit in judgment on itself. According to this new principle, which comes from Montesquieu and which found unequivocal expression in the Constitution of the United States, Kant indicated two basic structures of government: republican government, based on the division of powers, even if a prince is at the head of the state; and despotic government, where the powers of legislation, execution, and judgment are not separated. In the concrete political sense, power is needed and incorporated in the possession of the means of violence for the execution of laws. Where, therefore, the executive power is not separated from and controlled by legislative and judicial powers, the source of law can no longer be reason and consideration, but becomes power itself. That form of government for which the dictum "Might Is Right" rings true is despotic—and this holds regardless of all other circumstances: a democracy ruled by majority decisions but unchecked by law is just as despotic as an autocracy.

It is true that even Kant's distinction is no longer quite satisfactory. Its chief weakness is that behind the relationship of law and power lies the assumption that the source of law is human reason (still in the sense of the *lumen naturale*[2]) and the source of power is human will. Both assumptions are questionable on historical as well as philosophical grounds. We cannot discuss these difficulties here, nor do we need to. For our purpose, which is to isolate the nature of a new and unprecedented form of government, it may be wise to appeal first to the traditional—though no longer traditionally accepted—criteria. In searching for the nature of totalitarian government, its "structure," in Montesquieu's words, we shall also use Kant's distinction between forms of domination and forms of government, as well as between constitutional (in his words, "republican") and despotic government.

Montesquieu's discovery that each form of government has its own innate principle which sets it into motion and guides all its actions is of great relevance. Not only was this motivating principle closely connected to historical experience (honor obviously being the principle of medieval monarchy, based on nobility, as virtue was the principle of the Roman Republic), but as a principle of motion it introduced history and historical process into structures of

---

in which he put forth one of the earliest developed conceptions of the separation of political powers into executive, legislative, and judicial branches to avoid the abuse of power by any one branch.

1   *that is, to ask what makes it what it is*   [Arendt's note] "sa nature est ce qui le fait être tel" (its nature is what makes it what it is), *Spirit of Laws*, Book 3, ch. 1.

---

2   *lumen naturale*   Latin: natural light.

government which, as the Greeks had originally discovered and defined them, were conceived as unmoved and unmovable. Before Montesquieu's discovery, the only principle of change connected with forms of government was change for the worse, the perversion that would transform an aristocracy (the government of the best) into an oligarchy (the government of a clique for the interest of the clique), or overturn a democracy that had degenerated into ochlocracy (mob rule) into tyranny.

Montesquieu's moving and guiding principles—virtue, honor, fear—are principles insofar as they rule both the actions of the government and the actions of the governed. Fear in a tyranny is not only the subjects' fear of the tyrant, but the tyrant's fear of his subjects as well. Fear, honor, and virtue are not merely psychological motives, but the very criteria according to which all public life is led and judged. Just as it is the pride of a citizen in a republic not to dominate his fellow-citizens in public matters, so it is the pride of a subject in a monarchy to distinguish himself and be publicly honored. In establishing these principles, Montesquieu was not suggesting that all people behave at all times according to the principles of the government under which they happen to live, or that people in republics do not know what honor is, or people in a monarchy what virtue is. Nor does he speak of "ideal types."[1] He analyzes the public life of citizens, not people's private lives, and discovers that in this public life—that is, in the sphere where all men act together concerning things that are of equal concern to each—action is determined by certain principles. If these principles are no longer heeded and the specific criteria of behavior are no longer held valid, the political institutions themselves are jeopardized.

Beneath Montesquieu's distinction between the nature of government (that which makes it what it is) and its moving or guiding principle (that which sets it into motion through actions) lies another difference, a problem which has plagued political thought since its beginning, and which Montesquieu indicates, but does not solve, by his distinction between man as a citizen (a member of a public order) and man insofar as he is an individual. In case of conquest,

for instance, "the citizen may perish and the man survive."[2] This problem is usually dealt with in modern political thought as the distinction between public and private life, or the sphere of politics and the sphere of society; and its troublesome aspect is conventionally found in a pretended double standard of morality.

In modern political thought—insofar as its central predicaments are dictated by Machiavelli's discovery of power as the center of all political life, and of power-relations as the supreme laws of political action—the problem of the individual and the citizen has been complicated and overshadowed by the dilemma between legality as the center of domestic constitutional government and arbitrary sovereignty as the natural condition in the field of international relations. It seems, then, that we are confronted with two sets of duplicity in judging right or wrong in actions—the double standard originating in the simultaneous status of man as both citizen and individual, and the double standard originating in the differentiation between foreign and domestic politics. Both problems are pertinent to our effort to understand the nature of totalitarianism, since totalitarian governments claim to have solved them both. The distinction between and the dilemma of foreign and domestic politics are solved by the claim to global rule. This claim is then substantiated by treating each conquered country, in complete disregard of its own law, as an erstwhile transgressor of totalitarian law and by punishing its inhabitants according to laws administered retroactively. In other words, the claim to global rule is identical to the claim establishing a new and universally valid law on earth. In consequence, all foreign politics are, to the totalitarian mind, disguised domestic politics, and all foreign wars are, in fact, civil wars. The distinction between and the dilemma of citizen and individual, meanwhile, with the concomitant perplexities of the dichotomy between public and personal life, are eliminated by the totalitarian claim to the total domination of man.

To Montesquieu, only the dilemma of the citizen and the individual was a real political problem. The conflict between domestic and foreign politics, as a conflict between law and power, exists only so long as one maintains that power is indivisible and sovereign. Montesquieu as well as Kant held that only division of powers can guarantee the rule of law, and that a world federation would eventually solve

---

1   *ideal types*   Heuristic devices most closely associated with Max Weber (1864-1920). For Weber, ideal types were theoretical abstractions that identified a series of central characteristics of a phenomenon. They neither corresponded perfectly to reality (there is no ideal type of "democracy" in the world) nor provide normative standards, but rather guide our interpretation and understanding.

2   *the citizen ... man survive*   [Arendt's note] "*le citoyen peut périr, et l'homme rester,*" *Spirit of Laws*, Book 10, ch. 3.

the conflicts of sovereignty. An eminently practical step toward the identification of foreign and domestic politics was taken in Article 6 of the United States Constitution, which, in perfect spiritual agreement with Montesquieu, provides that, together with the Constitution and constitutionally enacted laws, "all treaties made ... under authority of the United States, shall be the supreme law of the land."

The distinction between the citizen and the individual becomes a problem as soon as we become aware of the discrepancy between public life, in which I am a citizen like all other citizens, and personal life, in which I am an individual unlike anybody else. Equality before the law is not only the distinguishing feature of modern republics, but also, in a deeper sense, prevails in constitutional governments as such, in that all people living under a constitution must equally receive from it what is rightfully theirs. The law in all constitutional forms of government determines and provides *suum cuique*:[1] through it everybody comes into his own.

The rule of *suum cuique*, however, never extends to all spheres of life. There is no *suum cuique* which could be determined and handed to individuals in their personal lives. The very fact that in all free societies everything is permitted which is not explicitly prohibited reveals the situation clearly: The law defines the boundaries of personal life but cannot touch what goes on within them. In this respect, the law fulfills two functions: it regulates the public-political sphere in which men act in concert as equals and where they have a common destiny, while, at the same time, it circumscribes the space in which our individual destinies unfold—destinies which are so dissimilar that no two biographies will ever read alike. The law in its sublime generality can never foresee and provide the *suum* which everybody receives in his irrevocable uniqueness. Laws, once they are established, are always applied according to precedents; the trouble with the deeds and events of personal life is that this life is destroyed in its very essence as soon as it is judged by standards of comparison or in light of precedents. One could define philistinism, and explain its deadening effect upon the creativity of human life, as the attempt, through a moralizing transformation of customs into general "laws" of behavior equally valid for all, to judge by precedents what by definition defies all precedent.

The trouble, obviously, with this discrepancy between public and personal life, between man as citizen and man as individual, is not only that laws can never be used to guide and judge actions in personal life, but also that the very standards of right and wrong in the two spheres are not the same and are often even in conflict. That such conflicts—ranging from the man who breaks traffic laws because his wife is dying to the central theme of *Antigone*[2]—are always regarded as insoluble, and that such "lawbreakers" are almost invariably depicted by the great tragedians[3] as acting according to a "higher law," reveals the depth of Western man's experience of the calamity of citizenship even in the best body politic. Strangely enough, even his philosophers have deserted him in this particular experience and done their best to evade the issue by elevating civil law to a level of unambiguous universality which it never in fact possesses. Kant's famous categorical imperative[4]—"Act in such a way that the maxim of your action could become a universal law"—indeed strikes to the root of the matter in that it is the quintessence of the claim that the law makes upon us. This rigid morality, however, disregards sympathy and inclination; moreover, it becomes a real source for wrongdoing in all cases where no universal law, not even the imagined law of pure reason, can determine what is right in a particular case.

Even in the personal sphere, where no universal laws can ever determine unequivocally what is right and what is wrong, man's actions are not completely arbitrary. Here he is guided not by laws, under which cases can be subsumed, but by principles—such as loyalty, honor, virtue, faith—which, as it were, map out certain directions. Montesquieu never asked himself if these principles might not have, in themselves, some cognitive power of judging or even creating what is right and wrong. But what he discovered when he added to the traditionally defined structure of govern-

---

1   *suum cuique*   Latin: let each have his own.

2   *central theme of Antigone*   In Sophocles' play *Antigone*, Antigone, daughter of Oedipus, struggles against her uncle Creon to bury her brother Polynices according to the proper rites. (Creon denies Polynices his burial rites because he fought on the losing side of Thebes' civil war.) The central theme of *Antigone* is the conflict between natural or divine law and positive or humanly constructed law.

3   *great tragedians*   The three great Greek tragedians are Aeschylus (c.525-c.456 BCE), Sophocles (496-406 BCE), Euripides (480-406 BCE).

4   *categorical imperative*   The central notion in Immanuel Kant's moral philosophy. The categorical imperative is an imperative that is unconditional—a command that must be obeyed in all circumstances. Kant contrasts it with hypothetical imperatives, which need only be followed under certain circumstances.

ment a moving principle which alone makes men act, rulers and ruled alike, was that law and power-relations in any given form of polity can define only the boundaries within which an entirely different, non-public, sphere of life exists. And it is this non-public sphere from which the sources of action and motion, as distinguished from the stabilizing, structural forces of law and power, spring. Hedged in by law and power, and occasionally overwhelming them, lie the origins of motion and action.

Montesquieu saw, as others had before him, that these principles of action and their standards of right and wrong varied widely in different countries at different times. More important, he discovered that each structure of government, manifesting itself in law and power, had its own correlative principle according to which men living within that structure would act. Only this, incidentally, gave him, and those historians who came after him, the tools to describe the peculiar unity of each culture. Since there was an obvious, historically patent correspondence between the principle of honor and the structure of monarchy, between virtue and republicanism, and between fear (understood not as a psychological emotion but as a principle of action) and tyranny, then there must be some underlying ground from which both man as an individual and man as a citizen sprang. In other words, Montesquieu found that there was more to the dilemma of the personal and the public spheres than discrepancy and conflict, even though they might conflict.

The phenomenon of correspondence between the different spheres of life and the miracle of the unities of cultures and periods despite discrepancies and contingencies indicates that at the bottom of each cultural or historical entity lies a common ground which is both fundament and source, basis and origin. Montesquieu defines the common ground in which the laws of a monarchy are rooted, and from which the actions of its subjects spring, as distinction; and he identifies honor, the supreme guiding principle in a monarchy, with a corresponding love of distinction. The fundamental experience upon which monarchies and, we may add, all hierarchical forms of government are founded is the experience, inherent in the human condition, that men are distinguished, that is, different from each other by birth. Yet we all know that directly opposing this and with no less insistent validity rises the opposite experience, the experience of the inherent equality of all men, "born equal" and distinguished only by social status. This equality—insofar as it is not an equality before God, an infinitely superior

Being before whom all distinctions and differences become negligible—has always meant not only that all men, regardless of their differences, are equally valuable, but also that nature has granted to each an equal amount of power. The fundamental experience upon which republican laws are founded and from which the action of its citizens springs is the experience of living together with and belonging to a group of equally powerful men. The laws which regulate the lives of republican citizens do not serve distinction, but, rather, restrict the power of each that room may remain for the power of his fellow. The common ground of republican law and action is thus the insight that human power is not primarily limited by some superior power, God or Nature, but by the powers of one's equals. And the joy that springs from that insight, the "love of equality" which is virtue, comes from the experience that only because this is so, only because there is equality of power, is man not alone. For to be alone means to be without equals: "One is one and all alone and ever more shall be so," runs the old English nursery rhyme, daring to suggest what to the human mind can only be the supreme tragedy of God.

Montesquieu failed to indicate the common ground of structure and action in tyrannies; we may therefore be permitted to fill in this gap in light of his own discoveries. Fear, the inspiring principle of action in tyranny, is fundamentally connected to that anxiety which we experience in situations of complete loneliness. This anxiety reveals the other side of equality and corresponds to the joy of sharing the world with our equals. The dependence and interdependence which we need in order to realize our power (the amount of strength which is strictly our own) becomes a source of despair whenever, in complete loneliness, we realize that one man alone has no power at all but is always overwhelmed and defeated by superior power. If one man alone had sufficient strength to match his power with the power of nature and circumstance, he would not be in need of company. Virtue is happy to pay the price of limited power for the blessing of being together with other men; fear is the despair over the individual impotence of those who, for whatever reason, have refused to "act in concert." There is no virtue, no love of equality of power, which has not to overcome this anxiety of helplessness, for there is no human life which is not vulnerable to utter helplessness, without recourse to action, if only in the face of death. Fear as a principle of action is in some sense a contradiction in terms, because fear is precisely despair over the impossibility of action. Fear, as distinct from the principles of virtue and honor, has no self-transcending power and is therefore truly anti-political. Fear as a principle of action can only be destructive or, in the words of Montesquieu, "self-corrupting." Tyranny is therefore the only form of government which bears germs of its destruction within itself. External circumstances cause the decline of other forms of government; tyrannies, on the contrary, owe their existence and survival to such external circumstances as prevent their self-corruption.[1]

Thus the common ground upon which lawlessness can be erected and from which fear springs is the impotence all men feel who are radically isolated. One man against all others does not experience equality of power among men, but only the overwhelming, combined power of all others against his own. It is the great advantage of monarchy, or of any hierarchical government, that individuals whose "distinction" defines their social and political status never confront an undistinguished and undistinguishable "all others" against whom they can only summon their own absolute minority of one. It is the specific danger of all forms of government based on equality that the moment the structure of lawfulness—within whose framework the experience of equal power receives its meaning and direction—breaks down or is transformed, the powers among equal men cancel each other out and what is left is the experience of absolute impotence. Out of the conviction of one's own impotence and the fear of the power of all others comes the will to dominate, which is the will of the tyrant. Just as virtue is love of the equality of power, so fear is actually the will to, or, in its perverted form, lust for, power. Concretely and politically speaking, there is no other will to power but the will to dominate. For power itself in its true sense can never be possessed by one man alone; power comes, as it were, mysteriously into being whenever men act "in concert" and disappears, not less mysteriously, whenever one man is all by himself. Tyranny, based on the essential impotence of all men who are alone, is the hubristic attempt to be like God, invested with power individually, in complete solitude.

These three forms of government—monarchy, republicanism, and tyranny—are authentic because the grounds on which their structures are built (the distinction of each, equality of all, and impotence) and from which their principles of motion spring are authentic elements of the human condition and are reflected in primary human experiences.

The question with which we shall now approach totalitarianism is whether or not this unprecedented form of government can lay claim to an equally authentic, albeit until now hidden, ground of the human condition on earth, a ground which may reveal itself only under circumstances of a global unity of humanity—circumstances certainly as unprecedented as totalitarianism itself.

2

Before we proceed, it may be well to admit that we are at least aware of a basic difficulty in this approach. To the modern mind there is perhaps nothing more baffling in Montesquieu's definitions than that he takes at face value the self-interpretations and self-understandings of the governments themselves. That he does not seek ulterior motives behind the confirmations of virtue in a republic, honor in a monarchy, or fear in a tyranny seems all the more surprising in an author who admittedly was the first to observe the great influence of "objective" factors, such as climatic, social, and other circumstances, on the formation of strictly political institutions.

However, in this as in other matters, true understanding has hardly any choice. The sources talk and what they reveal is the self-understanding as well as the self-interpretation of people who act and who believe they know what they are doing. If we deny them this capacity and pretend that we know better and can tell them what their real "motives" are or which real "trends" they objectively represent—no matter what they themselves think—we have robbed them of the very faculty of speech, insofar as speech makes sense. If, for instance, Hitler time and again called Jews the negative center of world history, and in support of his opinion designed factories to liquidate all people of Jewish origin, it is nonsensical to declare that anti-Semitism was not greatly relevant to the construction of his totalitarian regime, or that he merely suffered an unfortunate prejudice. The task of the social scientist is to find the historical and political background of anti-Semitism, but under no circumstances to conclude that Jews are only stand-ins for the petite bourgeoisie or that anti-Semitism is a surrogate for an Oedipus complex, or whatnot. Cases in which people consciously tell lies and, to remain with our example, pretend to hate Jews while in fact they want to murder the bourgeoisie, are very rare and easily detectable. In all other cases, self-understanding and self-interpretation are the very foundation of all analysis and understanding.

---

1   *external circumstances … self-corruption*   [Arendt's note] *Spirit of Laws*, Book 8, ch.10.

Therefore, in trying to understand the nature of totalitarianism, we shall ask in good faith the traditional questions regarding the nature of this form of government and the principle which sets it in motion. Since the rise of the scientific approach in the humanities, that is, with the development of modern historicism, sociology, and economics, such questions have no longer been considered likely to further understanding; Kant, in fact, was the last to think along these lines of traditional political philosophy. Yet while our standards for scientific accuracy have constantly grown and are higher today than at any previous time, our standards and criteria for true understanding seem to have no less constantly declined. With the introduction of completely alien and frequently nonsensical categories of evaluation into the social sciences, they have reached an all-time low. Scientific accuracy does not permit any understanding which goes beyond the narrow limits of sheer factuality, and it has paid a heavy price for this arrogance, since the wild superstitions of the twentieth century, clothed in humbug scientism,[1] began to supplement its deficiencies. Today the need to understand has grown desperate and plays havoc with the standards not only of understanding, but of pure scientific accuracy and intellectual honesty as well.

Totalitarian government is unprecedented because it defies comparison. It has exploded the very alternative on which definitions of the nature of government have relied since the beginning of Western political thought—the alternative between lawful, constitutional or republican government, on the one hand, and lawless, arbitrary, or tyrannical government on the other. Totalitarian rule is "lawless" insofar as it defies positive law; yet it is not arbitrary insofar as it obeys with strict logic and executes with precise compulsion the laws of History or Nature. It is the monstrous, yet seemingly unanswerable claim of totalitarian rule that, far from being "lawless," it goes straight to the sources of authority from which all positive laws—based on "natural law," or on customs and tradition, or on the historical event of divine revelation—receive their ultimate legitimation. What appears lawless to the non-totalitarian world would, on the strength of being inspired by the sources themselves, constitute a higher form of legitimacy, one that can do away with the petty legality of positive laws which can never produce justice in any single, concrete, and

therefore unpredictable case, but can only prevent injustice. Totalitarian lawfulness, executing the laws of Nature or History, does not bother to translate them into standards of right and wrong for individual human beings, but applies them directly to the "species," to mankind. The laws of Nature or History, if properly executed, are expected to produce as their end a single "Mankind," and it is this expectation that lies behind the claim to global rule of all totalitarian governments. Humanity, or, rather, the human species, is regarded as the active carrier of these laws while the rest of the universe is only passively determined by them.

At this point a fundamental difference between the totalitarian and all other conceptions of law comes to light. It is true that Nature or History, as the source of authority for positive laws, could traditionally reveal itself to man, be it as the *lumen naturale* in natural law or as the voice of conscience in historically revealed religious law. This, however, hardly made human beings walking embodiments of these laws. On the contrary, these laws remained distinct—as the authority which demanded obedience—from the actions of men. Compared to the sources of authority, the positive laws of men were considered to be changing and changeable in accordance with circumstance. Nonetheless, these laws were more permanent than the ever and rapidly changing actions of men, and they received this relative permanence from what was, in mortal terms, the timeless presence of their authoritative sources.

In the totalitarian interpretation, all laws become, instead, laws of movement. Nature and History are no longer stabilizing sources of authority for laws governing the actions of mortal men, but are themselves movements. Their laws, therefore, though one might need intelligence to perceive or understand them, have nothing to do with reason or permanence. At the base of the Nazis' belief in race laws lies Darwin's idea of man as a more or less accidental product of natural development—a development which does not necessarily stop with the species of human beings such as we know it. At the base of the Bolsheviks' belief in class lies the Marxian notion of men as the product of a gigantic historical process racing toward the end of historical time—that is, a process that tends to abolish itself. The very term "law" has changed in meaning; from denoting the framework of stability within which human actions were supposed to, and were permitted to, take place, it has become the very expression of these motions themselves.

The ideologies of racism and dialectical materialism that transformed Nature and History from the firm soil

---

1   *scientism*   A pejorative term used to refer to the use of science in domains in which it does not apply, or to the belief that scientific methodology is the only means of attaining knowledge.

supporting human life and action into supra-gigantic forces whose movements race through humanity, dragging every individual willy-nilly with them—either riding atop their triumphant car or crushed under its wheels—may be various and complicated: still, it is surprising to see how, for all practical political purposes, these ideologies always result in the same "law" of elimination of individuals for the sake of the process or progress of the species. From the elimination of harmful or superfluous individuals, the result of natural or historical movement rises like the phoenix from its own ashes; but unlike the fabulous bird, this mankind which is the end and at the same time the embodiment of the movement of either History or Nature requires permanent sacrifices, the permanent elimination of hostile or parasitic or unhealthy classes or races in order to enter upon its bloody eternity.

Just as positive laws in constitutional government are needed to translate and realize the immutable *ius naturale*[1] or the eternal Commandments of God or sempiternal customs and traditions of history, so terror is needed to realize, to translate into living reality, the laws of movement of History or Nature. And just as positive laws[2] that define transgressions in any given society are independent of them, such that their absence does not render the laws superfluous but on the contrary constitutes their most perfect rule, so, too, terror in totalitarian government, ceasing to be a means for the suppression of political opposition, becomes independent of it and rules supreme when opposition no longer stands in its way.

If law, therefore, is the essence of constitutional or republican government, then terror is the essence of totalitarian government. Laws were established to be boundaries (to follow one of the oldest images, Plato's invocation of Zeus as the God of boundaries, at *Laws*, 843a) and to remain static, enabling men to move within them; under totalitarian conditions, on the contrary, every means is taken to "stabilize" men, to make *them* static, in order to prevent any unforeseen, free, or spontaneous acts that might hinder freely racing terror. The law of movement itself, Nature or History, singles out the foes of mankind and no free action of mere men is permitted to interfere with it. Guilt and innocence become meaningless categories; "guilty" is he who stands in the path of terror, that is, who willingly or unwillingly hinders the movement of Nature or History. The

rulers, consequently, do not apply laws, but execute such movement in accordance with its inherent law; they claim to be neither just nor wise, but to know "scientifically."

Terror freezes men in order to clear the way for the movement of Nature or History. It eliminates individuals for the sake of the species; it sacrifices men for the sake of mankind—not only those who eventually become the victims of terror, but in fact all men insofar as this movement, with its own beginning and its own end, can only be hindered by the new beginning and the individual end which the life of each man actually is. With each new birth, a new beginning is born into the world, and a new world has potentially come into being. The stability of laws, erecting the boundaries and the channels of communication between men who live together and act in concert, hedges in this new beginning and assures, at the same time, its freedom; laws assure the potentiality of something entirely new *and* the pre-existence of a common world, the reality of some transcending continuity which absorbs all origins and is nourished by them. Terror first razes these boundaries of man-made law, but not for the sake of some arbitrary tyrannical will, nor for the sake of the despotic power of one man against all, nor, least of all, for the sake of a war of all against all. Terror substitutes for the boundaries and channels of communication between individual men an iron band which presses them all so tightly together that it is as though they were melded into each other, as though they were only one man. Terror, the obedient servant of Nature or History and the omnipresent executor of their predestined movement, fabricates the oneness of all men by abolishing the boundaries of law which provide the living space for the freedom of each individual. Totalitarian terror does not curtail all liberties or abolish certain essential freedoms, nor does it, at least to our limited knowledge, succeed in eradicating the love of freedom from the hearts of men; it simply and mercilessly presses men, such as they are, against each other so that the very space of free action—and this is the reality of freedom—disappears.

Terror exists neither for nor against men; it exists to provide the movement of Nature or History with an incomparable instrument of acceleration. If the undeniable automatism of historical or natural happenings is understood as the stream of necessity, whose meaning is identical to its law of movement and therefore quite independent of any event—which, on the contrary, can only be considered as a superficial and transitory outburst of the deep, permanent law—then the equally undeniable freedom of

---

1   *ius naturale*   Latin: natural law.
2   *positive laws*   Laws created by human beings.

men, which is identical with the fact that each man *is* a new beginning and in that sense begins the world anew, can only be regarded as an irrelevant and arbitrary interference with higher forces. These forces, to be sure, could not be definitively deflected by such ridiculous powerlessness, yet they might still be hindered and prevented from reaching full realization. Mankind, when organized in such a way that it marches with the movement of Nature or History, as if all men were only one man, accelerates the automatic movement of Nature or History to a speed which it could never reach alone. Practically speaking, this means that terror in all cases executes on the spot the death sentences which Nature has already pronounced on unfit races and individuals or which History has declared for dying classes and institutions, without waiting for the slower and less efficient elimination which would presumably be brought about anyhow.

In a perfect totalitarian government, where all individuals have become exemplars of the species, where all action has been transformed into acceleration, and every deed into the execution of death sentences—that is, under conditions in which terror as the essence of government is perfectly sheltered from the disturbing and irrelevant interference of human wishes and needs—no principle of action in Montesquieu's sense is necessary. Montesquieu needed principles of action because for him the essence of constitutional government, lawfulness and distribution of power, was basically stable: It could only negatively set up limitations on actions, not positively establish their principles. Since the greatness, but also the perplexity, of all laws in free societies is that they only indicate what one should not do, and never what one should do, political action and historical movement in constitutional government remain free and unpredictable, conforming to, but never inspired by, its essence.

Under totalitarian conditions, this essence has itself become movement—totalitarian government *is* only insofar as it is kept in constant motion. As long as totalitarian rule has not conquered the whole earth and, with the iron band of terror, melded all individual men into one mankind, terror in its double function as the essence of the government and the principle—not of action, but of motion—cannot be fully realized. To add to this a principle of action, such as fear, would be contradictory. For even fear is still (according to Montesquieu) a principle of action and as such unpredictable in its consequences. Fear is always connected with isolation—which can be either its result or its origin—and the concomitant experiences of impotence and

helplessness. The space freedom needs for its realization is transformed into a desert when the arbitrariness of tyrants destroys the boundaries of laws that hedge in and guarantee to each the realm of freedom. Fear is the principle of human movements in this desert of neighborlessness and loneliness; as such, however, it is still a principle which guides the actions of individual men, who therefore retain a minimal, fearful contact with other men. The desert in which these individual, fearfully atomized men move retains an image, though a distorted one, of that space which human freedom needs.

The close relationship of totalitarian governments to despotic rule is very obvious indeed and extends to almost all areas of government. The totalitarian abolition of classes and of those groups in the population out of which true distinction, as opposed to the arbitrarily created distinctions of orders and stripes, could emerge cannot but remind us of the ancient tale of the Greek tyrant who, in order to introduce a fellow-tyrant to the arts of tyranny, led him out of town to a wheat field and there cut all halms[1] down to equal size.[2] The fact, indeed, that a travesty of equality prevails under all despotic governments has led many good people into the error of believing that from equality springs tyranny or dictatorship, just as the neo-conservativism of our time stems from the radical abolition of all hierarchical and traditional authoritarian factors occurring in all forms of despotism. If we read about the economic despoliation policies so characteristic of short-term efficiency and long-term inefficiency in totalitarian economics, we cannot but remember the old anecdote with which Montesquieu characterized despotic government: The savages of Louisiana, wanting to harvest ripe fruits, simply cut the fruit trees down, because that was quicker and easier.[3] Moreover, terror, torture, and the spy system which hunts for secret and dangerous thoughts have always been mainstays of tyrannies; and it is not surprising that some tyrants even knew the terrifying use that can be made of the human inclination to forget and the human horror of being forgotten. Prisons under despotic rulers, in Asia as well as in Europe, were frequently called places of

---

1   *halms* Stalks.

2   *Greek tyrant … down to equal size* The story comes from Herodotus' *Histories*, 5.92. Periander of Corinth sought advice from the tyrant Thrasybulus of Miletus. After Thrasybulus' demonstration of cutting all the stalks down to size, Periander murdered or exiled all the leading citizens.

3   *The savages of Louisiana … quicker and easier* [Arendt's note] *Spirit of Laws*, Book 1, ch. 13.

oblivion, and frequently the family and friends of the man condemned to a living death in oblivion were warned that they would be punished for even mentioning his name.

The twentieth century has made us forget many horrors of the past, but there is no doubt that totalitarian dictators could attend, if they needed instruction, a long-established school where all means of violence and slyness for the purpose of the domination of man by man have been taught and evaluated. Totalitarian use of violence and especially of terror, however, is distinct from this, not because it so far transcends past limits, and not merely because one cannot very well call the organized and mechanized regular extermination of whole groups or whole peoples "murder" or even "mass murder," but because its chief characteristic is the very opposite of all police and spy terror of the past. All the similarities between totalitarian and traditional forms of tyranny, however striking they may be, are similarities of technique, and apply only to the initial stages of totalitarian rule. Regimes become truly totalitarian only when they have left behind their revolutionary phase and the techniques needed for the seizure and the consolidation of power—without of course ever abandoning them, should the need arise again.

A much more tempting reason for the student of totalitarianism to equate this form of government with tyranny pure and simple—and the only similarity which has a direct bearing on the specific content of each—is that totalitarian and tyrannical rule both concentrate all power in the hands of one man, who uses this power in such a way that he makes all other men absolutely and radically impotent. If, moreover, we remember the insane desire of the Roman emperor Nero, who is reported by ancient legend to have wished that the whole of mankind might have only one head, we cannot help being reminded of our present-day experiences with the so-called Führer principle, which is used by Stalin to the same, or perhaps even greater, extent as by Hitler, and which operates on the assumption not just that only one will survives among a dominated population but also that only one mind suffices to take care of all human activities in general. Yet it is also at this point of closest resemblance between totalitarian and tyrannical rule that the decisive difference emerges most clearly. In his insanity, Nero wished to be confronted with only one head so that the tranquillity of his rule would never be threatened again by any new opposition: he wanted to behead mankind, as it were, once and for all, though he knew that this was impossible. The totalitarian dictator, on the contrary, feels himself the one and only head of the whole human race; he is concerned with opposition only insofar as it must be wiped out before he can even begin his rule of total domination. His ultimate purpose is not the tranquillity of his own rule, but the imitation—in the case of Hitler—or the interpretation—in the case of Stalin—of the laws of Nature or of History. But these are laws of movement, as we have seen, which require constant motion, making the mere leisurely enjoyment of the fruits of domination, the time-honored joys of tyrannical rule (which at the same time were the limits beyond which the tyrant had no interest in exerting his power), impossible by definition. The totalitarian dictator, in sharp distinction from the tyrant, does not believe that he is a free agent with the power to execute his arbitrary will, but, instead, the executioner of laws higher than himself. The Hegelian definition of Freedom as insight into and conforming to "necessity" has here found a new and terrifying realization. For the imitation or interpretation of these laws, the totalitarian ruler feels that only one man is required and that all other persons, all other minds as well as wills, are strictly superfluous. This conviction would be utterly absurd if we were to assume that in some fit of megalomania totalitarian rulers believed they had accumulated and monopolized all possible capacities of the human mind and the human will, i.e., if we were to believe that they actually think themselves infallible. The totalitarian ruler, in short, is not a tyrant and can be understood only by first understanding the nature of totalitarianism.

Still, if totalitarian rule has little in common with the tyrannies of the past, it has even less to do with certain modern forms of dictatorship out of which it developed and with which it has been frequently confused. One-party dictatorships, of either the fascist or communist type, are not totalitarian. Neither Lenin nor Mussolini was a totalitarian dictator, nor even knew what totalitarianism really meant. Lenin's was a revolutionary one-party dictatorship whose power lay chiefly in the party bureaucracy, which Tito[1] tries to replicate today. Mussolini was chiefly a nationalist and, in contrast to the Nazis, a true worshiper of the State, with strong imperialist inclinations; if the Italian army had been better, he probably would have ended as an ordinary military dictator, just as Franco,[2] who emerged from the military hierarchy, tries to be in Spain, with the help given and the

---

1   *Tito*   Josip Broz Tito (1892-1980), leader of the Socialist Republic of Yugoslavia from 1945 until his death.
2   *Franco*   Francisco Franco (1892-1975), dictator of Spain from 1947 until his death.

constraint imposed by the Catholic Church. In totalitarian states, neither army nor church nor bureaucracy was ever in a position to wield or to restrain power; all executive power is in the hands of the secret police (or the élite formations which, as the instance of Nazi Germany and the history of the Bolshevik party show, are sooner or later incorporated into the police). No group or institution in the country is left intact, not just because they have to "co-ordinate" with the regime in power and outwardly support it—which of course is bad enough—but because in the long run they are literally not supposed to survive. The chess players in the Soviet Union who one beautiful day were informed that chess for chess's sake was a thing of the past are a case in point. It was in the same spirit that Himmler[1] emphasized to the SS[2] that no task existed which a real Nazi could perform for its own sake.

In addition to equating totalitarian rule with tyranny, and confusing it with other modern forms of dictatorship and, particularly, of one-party dictatorship, there remains a third way to try to make totalitarianism seem more harmless and less unprecedented or less relevant for modern political problems: the explanation of totalitarian rule in either Germany or Russia by historical or other causes relevant only to that specific country. Against this kind of argumentation stands, of course, the truly terrifying propaganda success both movements have had outside their home countries in spite of very powerful and very informative counter-propaganda from the most respectable and respected sources. No information on concentration camps in Soviet Russia or death factories in Auschwitz deterred the numerous fellow-travelers which both regimes knew how to attract. Yet even if we leave this aspect of attraction undiscussed, there is a more serious argument against this explanation: the curious fact that Nazi Germany and Soviet Russia started from historical, economic, ideological, and cultural circumstances in many respects almost diametrically opposed, yet still arrived at certain results which are structurally identical. This is easily overlooked because these identical structures reveal themselves only in fully developed totalitarian rule. Not only was this point reached at different times in Germany and in Russia, but different fields of political and other activity were

seized at different moments as well. To this difficulty must be added another historical circumstance. Soviet Russia embarked upon the road to totalitarianism only around 1930 and Germany only after 1938. Up to those points, both countries, though already containing a great number of totalitarian elements, could still be regarded as one-party dictatorships. Russia became fully totalitarian only after the Moscow Trials,[3] i.e., shortly before the war, and Germany only during the first years of the war. Nazi Germany in particular never had time to realize completely its evil potential, which can nevertheless be inferred by studying minutes from Hitler's headquarters and other such documents. The picture is further confused by the fact that very few people in the Nazi hierarchy were entirely aware of Hitler's and Bormann's[4] plans. Soviet Russia, though much more advanced in its totalitarian rule, offers very little documentary source material, so that each concrete point always and necessarily remains disputable even though we know enough to arrive at correct over-all estimates and conclusions.

Totalitarianism as we know it today in its Bolshevik and Nazi versions developed out of one-party dictatorships which, like other tyrannies, used terror as a means to establish a desert of neighborlessness and loneliness. Yet when the well-known tranquillity of the cemetery had been obtained, totalitarianism was not satisfied, but turned the instrument of terror at once and with increased vigor into an objective law of movement. Fear, moreover, becomes pointless when the selection of victims is completely free from all reference to an individual's actions or thoughts. Fear, though certainly the all-pervasive mood in totalitarian countries, is no longer a principle of action and can no longer serve as a guide to specific deeds. Totalitarian tyranny is unprecedented in that it melds people together in the desert of isolation and atomization and then introduces a gigantic motion into the tranquillity of the cemetery.

No guiding principle of action taken from the realm of human action—such as virtue, honor, fear—is needed or could be used to set into motion a body politic whose essence is motion implemented by terror. In its stead, totalitarianism relies upon a new principle, which, as such,

---

1 *Himmler* Heinrich Luitpold Himmler (1900-45) oversaw the concentration camps and extermination camps in Nazi Germany.
2 *SS* The *Schutzstaffel*, the Nazi military organization most responsible for the crimes against humanity perpetrated under Hitler and Himmler.

3 *Moscow Trials* A series of show trials between 1936 and 1938 which Stalin used to eliminate his rivals and enemies—many of whom confessed to treason, often after enduring months of torture.
4 *Bormann* Martin Bormann (1900-45), Hitler's private secretary.

dispenses with human action as free deeds altogether and substitutes for the very desire and will to action a craving and need for insight into the laws of movement according to which the terror functions. Human beings, caught or thrown into the process of Nature or History for the sake of accelerating its movement, can become only the executioners or the victims of its inherent law. According to this law, they may today be those who eliminate the "unfit races and individuals" or the "dying classes and decadent peoples" and tomorrow be those who, for the same reasons, must themselves be sacrificed. What totalitarian rule therefore needs, instead of a principle of action, is a means to prepare individuals equally well for the role of executioner and the role of victim. This two-sided preparation, the substitute for a principle of action, is ideology.

3

Ideologies by themselves are as little totalitarian and their use as little restricted to totalitarian propaganda as terror by itself is restricted to totalitarian rule. As we have all learned to our sorrow, it does not matter whether this ideology is as stupid and barren of authentic spiritual content as racism or whether it is as saturated with the best of our tradition as socialism. Only in the hands of the new type of totalitarian governments do ideologies become the driving motor of political action, and this in the double sense that ideologies determine the political actions of the ruler and make these actions tolerable to the ruled population. I call all ideologies in this context *isms* that pretend to have found the key explanation for all the mysteries of life and the world. Thus racism or anti-Semitism is not an ideology, but merely an irresponsible opinion, as long as it restricts itself to praising Aryans and hating Jews; it becomes an ideology only when it pretends to explain the whole course of history as being secretly maneuvered by the Jews, or covertly subject to an eternal race struggle, race mixture, or whatnot. Socialism, similarly, is not an ideology properly speaking as long as it describes class struggles, preaches justice for the underprivileged, and fights for an improvement or revolutionary change of society. Socialism—or communism—becomes an ideology only when it pretends that all history is a struggle of classes, that the proletariat is bound by eternal laws to win this struggle, that a classless society will then come about, and that the state, finally, will wither away. In other words, ideologies are systems of explanation of life and world that claim to explain everything, past and future, without further concurrence with actual experience.

This last point is crucial. This arrogant emancipation from reality and experience, more than any actual content, foreshadows the connection between ideology and terror. This connection not only makes terror an all-embracing characteristic of totalitarian rule, in the sense that it is directed equally against all members of the population, regardless of their guilt or innocence, but also is the very condition for its permanence. Insofar as ideological thinking is independent of existing reality, it looks upon all factuality as fabricated, and therefore no longer knows any reliable criterion for distinguishing truth from falsehood. If it is untrue, said *Das Schwarze Korps*,[1] for instance, that all Jews are beggars without passports, we shall change facts in such a way as to make this statement true. That a man by the name of Trotsky was ever the head of the Red Army[2] will cease to be true when the Bolsheviks have the global power to change all history texts—and so forth. The point here is that the ideological consistency reducing everything to one all-dominating factor is always in conflict with the inconsistency of the world, on the one hand, and the unpredictability of human actions, on the other. Terror is needed in order to make the world consistent and keep it that way; to dominate human beings to the point where they lose, with their spontaneity, the specifically human unpredictability of thought and action.

Such ideologies were fully developed before anybody ever heard the word or conceived the notion of totalitarianism. That their very claim to totality made them almost predestined to play a role in totalitarianism is easy to see. What is less easy to understand, partly because their tenets have been the subject of dreary discussions for centuries in the case of racism, and for many decades in the case of socialism, is what made them such supreme principles and motors of action. As a matter of fact, the only new device the totalitarian rulers invented or discovered in using these ideologies was translating a general outlook into a singular principle ruling over all activities. Neither Stalin nor Hitler

---

1 *Das Schwarze Korps* German: The Black Corps. It was the official newspaper of the *Schutzstaffen* (SS).

2 *That a man by the name … Red Army* Leon Trotsky (1879-1940) was a leader of the Russian revolution and head of the Red Army. He was sentenced to death *in absentia* during the Moscow trials for having plotted to murder Stalin. The charges were refuted in an independent inquiry in Mexico chaired by the American philosopher John Dewey.

added a single new thought, respectively, to socialism or racism; yet only in their hands did these ideologies become deadly serious.

It is at this point that the problem of the role of ideologies in totalitarianism receives its full meaning. What is novel in the ideological propaganda of totalitarian movements even before they seize power is the immediate transformation of ideological content into living reality through instruments of totalitarian organization. The Nazi movement, far from organizing people who happened to believe in racism, organized them according to objective race criteria, so that race ideology was no longer a matter of mere opinion or argument or even fanaticism, but constituted the actual living reality, first of the Nazi movement, and then of Nazi Germany, where the amount of one's food, the choice of one's profession, and the woman one married depended upon one's racial physiognomy and ancestry. The Nazis, as distinguished from other racists, did not so much believe in the truth of racism as desire to change the world into a race reality.

A similar change in the role of ideology took place when Stalin replaced the revolutionary socialist dictatorship in the Soviet Union with a full-fledged totalitarian regime. Socialist ideology shared with all other isms the claim to have found the solution to all the riddles of the universe and to be able to introduce the best system into the political affairs of mankind. The fact that new classes sprang up in Soviet Russia after the October Revolution was of course a blow to socialist theory, according to which the violent upheaval should have been followed by a gradual dying out of class structures. When Stalin embarked upon his murderous purge policies to establish a classless society through the regular extermination of all social layers that might develop into classes, he realized, albeit in an unexpected form, the ideological socialist belief about dying classes. The result is the same: Soviet Russia is as much a classless society as Nazi Germany was a racially determined society. What had been mere ideological opinion before became the lived content of reality. The connection between totalitarianism and all other isms is that totalitarianism can use any of the others as an organizational principle and try to change the whole texture of reality according to its tenets.

The two great obstacles on the road to such transformation are the unpredictability, the fundamental unreliability, of man, on the one hand, and the curious inconsistency of the human world, on the other. Precisely because ideologies by themselves are matters of opinion rather than of truth, the human freedom to change one's mind is a great and pertinent danger. No mere oppression, therefore, but the total and reliable domination of man is necessary if he is to fit into the ideologically determined, factitious world of totalitarianism. Total domination as such is quite independent of the actual content of any given ideology; no matter which ideology one may choose, no matter if one decides to transform the world and man according to the tenets of racism or socialism or any other ism, total domination will always be required. This is why two systems so different from each other in actual content, in origins and objective circumstances, could in the end build almost identical administrative and terror machineries.

For the totalitarian experiment of changing the world according to an ideology, total domination of the inhabitants of one country is not enough. The existence, and not so much the hostility, of any non-totalitarian country is a direct threat to the consistency of the ideological claim. If it is true that the socialist or communist system of the Soviet Union is superior to all other systems, then it follows that under no other system can such a fine thing as a subway really be built. For a time, therefore, Soviet schools used to teach their children that there is no other subway in the world except the subway in Moscow. The Second World War put a halt to such obvious absurdities, but this will only be temporary. For the consistency of the claim demands that in the end no other subway survive except a subway under totalitarian rule: either all others have to be destroyed or the countries where they operate have to be brought under totalitarian domination. The claim to global conquest, inherent in the Communist concept of World Revolution, as it was in the Nazi concept of a master race, is no mere threat born of lust for power or mad overestimation of one's own forces. The real danger is the fact that the factitious, topsy-turvy world of a totalitarian regime cannot survive for any length of time if the entire outside world does not adopt a similar system, allowing all of reality to become a consistent whole, threatened neither by the subjective unpredictability of man nor by the contingent quality of the human world which always leaves some space open for accident.

It is an open and sometimes hotly debated question whether the totalitarian ruler himself or his immediate subordinates believe, along with his mass of adherents and subjects, in the superstitions of the respective ideologies. Since the tenets in question are so obviously stupid and vulgar, those who tend to answer this question affirmatively are also inclined to deny the almost unquestionable qualities and gifts of men like Hitler and Stalin. On the other hand, those who tend to answer this question negatively, believing that the phenomenal deceptiveness of both men is sufficient proof of their cold and detached cynicism, are also inclined to deny the curious incalculability of totalitarian politics, which so obviously violates all rules of self-interest and common sense. In a world used to calculating actions and reactions by these yardsticks, such incalculability becomes a public danger.

Why should lust for power, which from the beginning of recorded history has been considered the political and social sin par excellence, suddenly transcend all previously known limitations of self-interest and utility and attempt not simply to dominate men as they are, but also to change their very nature; not only to kill innocent and harmless bystanders, but to do this even when such murder is an obstacle, rather than an advantage, to the accumulation of power? If we refuse to be caught by mere phrases and their associations and look behind them at the actual phenomena, it appears that total domination, as practiced every day by a totalitarian regime, is separated from all other forms of domination by an abyss which no psychological explanation such as "lust for power" is able to bridge.

This curious neglect of obvious self-interest in totalitarian rule has frequently impressed people as a kind of mistaken idealism. And this impression has some kernel of truth, if we understand by idealism only absence of selfishness and common-sense motives. The selflessness of totalitarian rulers perhaps characterizes itself best through the curious fact that none was ever particularly eager to find a successor among his own children. (It is a noteworthy experience for the student of tyrannies to come across a variation which is not plagued by the ever-present worry of the classical usurper.)

Total domination for totalitarian regimes is never an end in itself. In this respect the totalitarian ruler is more "enlightened" and closer to the wishes and desires of the masses who support him—frequently even in the face of patent disaster—than his predecessors, the power politicians who no longer played the game for the sake of national interest but as a game of power for power's sake. Total domination, despite its frightful attack on the physical existence of people as well as on the nature of man, can play the seemingly old game of tyranny with such unprecedented murderous efficiency because it is used only as a means to an end.

I think that Hitler believed as unquestioningly in race struggle and racial superiority (though not necessarily in the racial superiority of the German people) as Stalin believes in class struggle and the classless society (though not necessarily in world revolution). However, in view of the particular qualities of totalitarian regimes, which might be established according to any arbitrary opinion enlarged into a *Weltanschauung*,[1] it would be quite possible for totalitarian rulers or the men immediately surrounding them not to believe in the actual content of their preaching; it sometimes seems as though the new generation, educated under conditions of totalitarian rule, somehow has lost even the ability to distinguish between such believing and non-believing. If that were the case, the actual aim of totalitarian rule would have to a large extent been achieved: the abolition of convictions as a too unreliable support for the system; and the demonstration that this system, in distinction from all others, has made man, insofar as he is a being of spontaneous thought and action, superfluous.

Underlying these beliefs or non-beliefs, these "idealistic" convictions or cynical calculations, is another belief, of an entirely different quality, which, indeed, is shared by all totalitarian rulers, as well as by people thinking and acting along totalitarian lines, whether or not they know it. This is the belief in the omnipotence of *man* and at the same time of the superfluity of *men*; it is the belief that everything is permitted and, much more terrible, that everything is possible. Under this condition, the question of the original truth or falsehood of the ideologies loses its relevance. If Western philosophy has maintained that reality is truth—for this is of course the ontological basis of the *aequatio rei et intellectus*[2]—then totalitarianism has concluded from this that we can fabricate truth insofar as we can fabricate reality; that we do not have to wait until reality unveils itself and shows us its true face, but can bring into being a reality whose structures will be known to us from the beginning because the whole thing is our product. In other words, it is the underlying conviction of any totalitarian transformation of ideology into reality that it will become true whether it is true or not. Because of this totalitarian relationship to reality, the very concept of truth has lost its meaning. The lies of totalitarian movements, invented for the moment, as well as the forgeries

---

1   *Weltanschauung*   German: world view.
2   *aequatio rei et intellectus*   Latin: correspondence of the mind and body.

committed by totalitarian regimes, are secondary to this fundamental attitude that excludes the very distinction between truth and falsehood.

It is for this end, that is, for the consistency of a lying world order, rather than for the sake of power or any other humanly understandable sinfulness, that totalitarianism requires total domination and global rule and is prepared to commit crimes which are unprecedented in the long and sinful history of mankind.

The operation Hitler and Stalin performed on their respective ideologies was simply to take them dead seriously, and that meant driving their pretentious implications to that extreme of logical consequence where they would look, to the normal eye, preposterously absurd. If you believe in earnest that the bourgeoisie is not simply antagonistic to the interests of the worker, but is dying, then evidently you are permitted to kill all bourgeois. If you take literally the dictum that the Jews, far from merely being the enemies of other people, are actually vermin, created as vermin by nature and therefore predestined to suffer the same fate as lice and bedbugs, then you have established a perfect argument for their extermination. This stringent logicality as an inspiration of action permeates the whole structure of totalitarian movements and totalitarian governments. The most persuasive argument, of which Hitler and Stalin were equally fond, is to insist that whoever says A must necessarily also say B and C and finally end with the last letter of the alphabet. Everything which stands in the way of this kind of reasoning—reality, experience, and the daily network of human relationships and interdependence—is overruled. Even the advice of common self-interest shares this fate in extreme cases, as was proved over and over again by the way Hitler conducted his war. Mere logic, which starts from one single accepted premise—what Hitler used to call his supreme gift of "ice-cold reasoning"—remains always the ultimate guiding principle.

We may say, then, that in totalitarian governments, Montesquieu's principle of action is replaced by ideology. Though up till now we have been confronted with only two types of totalitarianism, each started from an ideological belief whose appeal to large masses of people had already been demonstrated and both of which were therefore thought to be highly appropriate to inspire action, to set the masses in motion. Yet, if we look closer at what is really happening, or has been happening during the last thirty years, to these masses and their individual members, we shall discover the disconcerting ease with which so many changed from a red shirt into a brown,[1] and if that did not work out, into a red shirt again, only to take on the brown again after a little while. These changes—and they are more numerous than we usually admit in our eagerness and hope to see people, after one bad experience, give up shirt-wearing altogether—seem to indicate that it is not even the ideologies, with their demonstrable content, which set people into action, but the logicality of their reasoning all by itself and almost independent of content. This would mean that after ideologies have taught people to emancipate themselves from real experience and the shock of reality by luring them into a fool's paradise where everything is known *a priori*,[2] the next step will lead them, if it has not already done so, away from the content of their paradise; not to make them any wiser, but to mislead them further into the wilderness of mere abstract logical deductions and conclusions. It is no longer race or the establishment of a society based on race that is the "ideal" which appeals, nor class or the establishment of a classless society, but the murderous network of pure logical operations in which one is caught once one accepts either of them. It is as though these shirt-changers console themselves with the thought that no matter what content they accept—no matter which kind of eternal law they decide to believe in—once they have taken this initial step, nothing can ever happen to them anymore, and they are saved.

Saved from what? Maybe we can find the answer if we look once more at the nature of totalitarianism, that is, at its essence of terror and at its principle of logicality, which in combination add up to its nature. It has been frequently said, and it is perfectly true, that the most horrible aspect of terror is that it has the power to bind together completely isolated individuals and that by so doing it isolates these individuals even further. Hitler as well as Stalin may have learned from all the historical examples of tyranny that any group of people joined together by some common interest is the supreme threat to total domination. Only isolated individuals can be dominated totally. Hitler was able to build his organization on the firm ground of an already atomized society which he then artificially atomized even further; Stalin needed the bloody extermination of the peasants, the uprooting of the workers, the repeated purges of the administrative machinery and the party bureaucracy in

---

1   *red shirt into brown* Members of the Nazi paramilitary group the SA (*Sturmabteilung* or stormtroopers) are often referred to as "brown shirts." "Red shirt" may refer to communist sympathies.

2   *a priori* Latin: before experience.

order to achieve the same results. By the terms "atomized society" and "isolated individuals" we mean a state of affairs where people live together without having anything in common, without sharing some visible tangible realm of the world. Just as the inhabitants of an apartment house form a group on the basis of their sharing this particular building, so we, on the strength of the political and legal institutions that provide our general living together with all the normal channels of communication, become a social group, a society, a people, a nation and so forth. And just as the apartment dwellers will become isolated from each other if for some reason their building is taken away from them, so the collapse of our institutions—the ever-increasing political and physical homelessness and spiritual and social rootlessness—is the one gigantic mass destiny of our time in which we all participate, though to very differing degrees of intensity and misery.

Terror, in the sense we were speaking of it, is not so much something which people may fear, but a way of life which takes the utter impotence of the individual for granted and provides for him either victory or death, a career or an end in a concentration camp, completely independent of his own actions or merits. Terror fits the situation of these ever-growing masses to perfection, no matter if these masses are the result of decaying societies or of calculated policies.

But terror by itself is not enough—it fits but it does not inspire. If we observe from this perspective the curious logicality of the ideologies in totalitarian movements, we understand better why this combination can be so supremely valuable. If it were true that there are eternal laws ruling supreme over all things human and demanding of each human being only total conformity, then freedom would be only a mockery, some snare luring one away from the right path; then homelessness would be only a fantasy, an imagined thing, which could be cured by the decision to conform to some recognizable universal law. And then—last not least—not the concert of human minds, but only one man would be needed to understand these laws and to build humanity in such a way as to conform to them under all changing circumstances. The "knowledge" of one alone would suffice, and the plurality of human gifts or insights or initiatives would be simply superfluous. Human contact would not matter; only the preservation of a perfect functionality within the framework established by the one initiated into the "wisdom" of the law would matter.

Logicality is what appeals to isolated human beings, for man—in complete solitude, without any contact with his fellow-men and therefore without any real possibility of experience—has nothing else he can fall back on but the most abstract rules of reasoning. The intimate connection between logicality and isolation was stressed in Martin Luther's little-known interpretation of the biblical passage that says that God created Man, male and female, because "it is not good for man to be alone." Luther says: "A lonely man always deduces one thing from another and carries everything to its worst conclusion"[1]

Logicality, mere reasoning without regard for facts and experience, is the true vice of solitude. But the vices of solitude grow only out of the despair of loneliness. Now, when human contacts have been severed—either through the collapse of our common home, or through the growing expansion of mere functionality whereby the substance, the real matter of human relationships, is slowly eaten away, or through the catastrophic developments of revolutions that themselves resulted from previous collapses—loneliness in such a world is no longer a psychological matter to be handled with such beautiful and meaningless terms as "introvert" or "extrovert." Loneliness, as the concomitant of homelessness and uprootedness, is, humanly speaking, the very disease of our time. To be sure, you may still see people—but they get to be fewer and fewer—who cling to each other as if in midair, without the help of established channels of communication provided by a commonly inhabited world, in order to escape together the curse of becoming inhuman in a society where everybody seems to be superfluous and is so perceived by their fellow-men. But what do these acrobatic performances prove against the despair growing all around us, which we ignore whenever we merely denounce or call people who fall for totalitarian propaganda stupid or wicked or ill informed? These people are nothing of the sort. They have only escaped the despair of loneliness by becoming addicted to the vices of solitude.

Solitude and loneliness are not the same. In solitude we are never alone, but are together with ourselves. In solitude we are always two-in-one; we become one whole individual, in the richness as well as the limitations of definite characteristics, through and only through the company of others. For our individuality, insofar as it is one—unchangeable and unmistakable—we depend entirely on other people. Solitude in which one has the company of oneself need not give up contact with others, and is not outside human com-

---

1   *A lonely man … worst conclusion*   [Arendt's note] "Warum die Einsamkeit zu fliehen?" in *Erbauliche Schriften*.

pany altogether; on the contrary, it prepares us for certain outstanding forms of human rapport, such as friendship and love, that is, for all rapport which transcends the established channels of human communication. If one can endure solitude, bear one's own company, then chances are that one can bear and be prepared for the companionship of others; whoever cannot bear any other person usually will not be able to endure his own self.

The great grace of companionship is that it redeems the two-in-one by making it individual. As individuals we need each other and become lonely if through some physical or some political accident we are robbed of company or companionship. Loneliness develops when man does not find companionship to save him from the dual nature of his solitude, or when man as an individual, in constant need of others for his individuality, is deserted or separated from others. In the latter case, he is all alone, forsaken even by the company of himself.

The great metaphysical questions—the quest for God, freedom, and immortality (as in Kant) or about man and world, being and nothingness, life and death—are always asked in solitude, when man is alone with himself and therefore potentially together with everybody. The very fact that man, for the time being, is deflected from his individuality enables him to ask timeless questions that transcend the questions asked, in different ways, by every individual. But no such questions are asked in loneliness, when man as an individual is deserted even by his own self and lost in the chaos of people. The despair of loneliness is its very dumbness, admitting no dialogue.

Solitude is not loneliness, but can easily become loneliness and can even more easily be confused with it. Nothing is more difficult and rarer than people who, out of the desperate need of loneliness, find the strength to escape into solitude, into company with themselves, thereby mending the broken ties which link them to other men. This is what happened in one happy moment to Nietzsche, when he concluded his great and desperate poem of loneliness with the words: "*Mittags war, da wurde eins zu zwei, und Zarathustra ging an mir vorbei*".[1]

The danger in solitude is of losing one's own self, so that, instead of being together with everybody, one is literally deserted by everybody. This has been the professional risk of the philosopher, who, because of his quest for truth and his concern with questions we call metaphysical (which are actually the only questions of concern to everybody), needs solitude, the being together with his own self and therefore with everybody, as a kind of working condition. As the inherent risk of solitude, loneliness is, therefore, a professional danger for philosophers, which, incidentally, seems to be one of the reasons that philosophers cannot be trusted with politics or a political philosophy. Not only do they have one supreme interest which they seldom divulge—to be left alone, to have their solitude guaranteed and freed from all possible disturbances, such as the disturbance of the fulfillment of one's duty as a citizen—but this interest has naturally led them to sympathize with tyrannies where action is not expected of citizens. Their experience in solitude has given them extraordinary insight into all those relationships which cannot be realized without this being alone with one's own self, but has led them to forget the perhaps even more primary relationships between men and the realm they constitute, springing simply from the fact of human plurality.

We said at the beginning of these reflections that we shall be satisfied with having understood the essence or nature of political phenomena which determine the whole innermost structure of entire eras only if we succeed in analyzing them as signs of the danger of general trends that concern and eventually may threaten all societies—not just those countries where they have already been victorious or are on the point of becoming victorious. The danger totalitarianism lays bare before our eyes—and this danger, by definition, will not be overcome merely by victory over totalitarian governments—springs from rootlessness and homelessness and could be called the danger of loneliness and superfluity. Both loneliness and superfluity are, of course, symptoms of mass society, but their true significance is not thereby exhausted. Dehumanization is implied in both and, though reaching its most horrible consequences in concentration camps, exists prior to their establishment. Loneliness as we know it in an atomized society is indeed, as I tried to show by the quotation from the Bible and its interpretation by Luther, contrary to the basic requirements of the human condition. Even the experience of the merely materially and sensually given world depends, in the last analysis, upon the fact that not one man but men in the plural inhabit the earth....

---

1 *Mittags war ... mir vorbei* German: It was noon, one became two, and I was done with Zarathustra ("Sils-Maria," *Die Fröhliche Wissenschaft*). Arendt quotes from memory.

MICHEL FOUCAULT
(1926–1984)

Michel Foucault was one of the most influential intellectuals of the second half of the twentieth century. Defying easy classification, he undertook highly original studies of madness, medicine, the human sciences, the prison system, and sexuality. His most important books include *The History of Madness, The Birth of the Clinic, The Order of Things, The Archaeology of Knowledge, Discipline and Punish*, and the three-volume *History of Sexuality*. His influence extends across many academic disciplines including history, literary studies, and sociology as well as philosophy and political theory.

Foucault was born in Poitiers, France, in 1926. In 1946 he entered the École Normale Supérieure, where he studied with the existentialist philosopher Jean Hyppolite and with the Marxist philosopher Louis Althusser. Perhaps even more importantly, he came under the influence of the historian of science Georges Canguilhem, who sponsored him throughout his career. In 1961, Foucault submitted *The History of Madness* for his doctoral thesis, along with a translation of Kant's *Anthropology from a Pragmatic Point of View*. After a stint at the University of Tunis and a brief period as head of the philosophy department at the experimental university of Vincennes, he was elected in 1969 to the prestigious Collège de France. Taking the title of Professor of the History of Systems of Thought, he remained there until the end of his life.

Foucault was politically engaged throughout most of his life, founding the *Groupe d'information sur les prisons* in France and reporting on the Iranian revolution. Though he eventually distanced himself from Marxism, he briefly associated with the radical Maoist group the *Gauche Proletarienne* (GP). Typically, he separated his political convictions from his intellectual views. His major works have a somewhat paradoxical style: potentially highly charged examinations of oppression, confinement, normalization, and other morally problematic practices are set out in almost clinical language.

Commentators typically divide Foucault's work into three stages (though continuities extend throughout). His early work is "archaeological," examining the epistemological structures underlying the disciplines of psychiatry, medicine, and the human sciences in different periods. According to Foucault, these structures limit the possibilities for practice and inquiry and differ sharply from era to era. Foucault is critical of standard histories that emphasize progress, and instead, in his own historical approach, emphasizes discontinuity and contingency.

Social and political philosophers are usually most interested in his second (or "genealogical") period, inaugurated by *Discipline and Punish: The Birth of the Prison*. Foucault rejects universal, totalizing theories provided by the Marxists and the liberals, instead turning his attention to local struggles and "subjugated knowledges" that have been obscured by systematic theories. Instead of criticizing society from above with the aid of a materialist theory or a liberal theory of rights, Foucault focuses on particular struggles. Foucault does not provide an absolute normative standard for his investigations and, indeed, rarely takes an explicit moral stance (though the implications are often evident). In fact, Foucault is skeptical about the Marxist or liberal project, believing that the tendency to universalize or totalize often obscures power relations. For liberals, the language of rights reflects progress and liberation; Foucault thought it could also be used to repress and injure.

This general outlook is inspired by Nietzsche, leading Foucault to focus on power and its relationship to knowledge. Standard histories of punishment stress the move from torture and public executions toward more humane approaches. Foucault instead suggests that punishment shifts from the body to the mind through confinement, surveillance, and other disciplinary techniques. These techniques are aided by the development of academic and professional disciplines, such as psychiatry, criminology, jurisprudence, medicine, and education.

In much of his work Foucault develops a dynamic, complex notion of power. Unlike many accounts that identify power with large-scale repression (e.g., state or class power), Foucault focuses on micro-power structures that interact on different levels in often surprising ways. For Foucault, power is not simply repressive, but also creative. In fact, power produces knowledge. In an interview with Alessandro Fontana and Pasquale Pasquino, Foucault put it this way: "If power were never anything but repressive, if it never did anything but to say no, do you really think one would be brought to obey it? What makes power hold good, what makes it accepted, is simply the fact that it doesn't only weigh on us as a force that says no, but that it also traverses and produces things, it induces pleasure, forms knowledge, produces discourse" (*Power/Knowledge*).

Foucault applies this analysis to schools, hospitals, and other institutions, showing how techniques of observation and classification apply timetables, collective training, and forced exercise to create subtle, often invisible forms of control. Of particular interest is his discussion of Jeremy Bentham's proposal for a "panopticon," a prison built around a tower allowing a single observer to watch the cells below. As Foucault points out, its effect would be "to induce in the inmate a state of conscious and permanent visibility that assures the automatic functioning of power" (DP 201). Foucault goes so far as to suggest that the potential for psychological conditioning of such techniques is so powerful that eventually the watcher could abandon the post and the inmates would continue to act as if observed.

Many philosophers, including Jürgen Habermas in an influential critique *The Philosophical Discourse of Modernity*, criticize Foucault's account of power as incapable of providing a normative justification for criticizing problematic power relations. This is a difficult criticism to evaluate, given Foucault's complex and sometimes ambiguous development. Foucault displays considerable ambivalence towards the tradition of providing critical standards (as is evident in his lifelong preoccupation with Kant), but it is by no means clear that he rejects it, as evidenced by his dialogue with Habermas and his essay on Kant's "What is Enlightenment?" His advocacy for prison reform, gay rights and numerous other causes provides an example of localized struggle without—arguably—systematic appeal to universal rights.

Toward the end of his life, Foucault worked on his history of sexuality and continued his discussion of power in *The Will to Knowledge*, before turning to what was to have been a six-volume investigation of different ways of constituting the self in Greek and Roman society, beginning with *The Use of Pleasure* and *The Care of the Self*. He died in 1984 before completing that major project.

◆ ◆ ◆ ◆ ◆

from *Discipline and Punish* (1975)

Panopticism

The following, according to an order published at the end of the seventeenth century, were the measures to be taken when the plague appeared in a town.[1]

First, a strict spatial partitioning: the closing of the town and its outlying districts, a prohibition to leave the town on pain of death, the killing of all stray animals; the division of the town into distinct quarters, each governed by an intendant. Each street is placed under the authority of a syndic,[2] who keeps it under surveillance; if he leaves the street, he will be condemned to death. On the appointed day, everyone is ordered to stay indoors: it is forbidden to leave on pain of death. The syndic himself comes to lock the door of each house from the outside; he takes the key with him and hands it over to the intendant of the quarter; the intendant keeps it until the end of the quarantine. Each family will have made its own provisions; but, for bread and wine, small wooden canals are set up between the street and the interior of the houses, thus allowing each person to receive his ration without communicating with the suppliers and other residents; meat, fish and herbs will be hoisted up into the houses with pulleys and baskets. If it is absolutely necessary to leave the house, it will be done in turn, avoiding any meeting. Only the intendants, syndics and guards will move about the streets and also, be-

---

1   *the measures ... in a town*   [Unless otherwise indicated, all notes to this section are by the author rather than the editors of this anthology.] Archives militaires de Vincennes, A 1,516 sc. Pièce. This regulation is broadly similar to a whole series of others that date from the same period and earlier.
2   *intendant ... syndic*   [editors' note] Both were civil servants.

tween the infected houses, from one corpse to another, the "crows," who can be left to die: these are "people of little substance who carry the sick, bury the dead, clean and do many vile and abject offices." It is a segmented, immobile, frozen space. Each individual is fixed in his place. And, if he moves, he does so at the risk of his life, contagion or punishment.

Inspection functions ceaselessly. The gaze is alert everywhere: "A considerable body of militia, commanded by good officers and men of substance," guards at the gates, at the town hall and in every quarter to ensure the prompt obedience of the people and the most absolute authority of the magistrates, "as also to observe all disorder, theft and extortion." At each of the town gates there will be an observation post; at the end of each street sentinels. Every day, the intendant visits the quarter in his charge, inquires whether the syndics have carried out their tasks, whether the inhabitants have anything to complain of; they "observe their actions." Every day, too, the syndic goes into the street for which he is responsible; stops before each house: gets all the inhabitants to appear at the windows (those who live overlooking the courtyard will be allocated a window looking onto the street at which no one but they may show themselves); he calls each of them by name; informs himself as to the state of each and every one of them—"in which respect the inhabitants will be compelled to speak the truth under pain of death"; if someone does not appear at the window, the syndic must ask why: "In this way he will find out easily enough whether dead or sick are being concealed." Everyone locked up in his cage, everyone at his window, answering to his name and showing himself when asked—it is the great review of the living and the dead.

This surveillance is based on a system of permanent registration: reports from the syndics to the intendants, from the intendants to the magistrates or mayor. At the beginning of the "lock up," the role of each of the inhabitants present in the town is laid down, one by one; this document bears "the name, age, sex of everyone, notwithstanding his condition": a copy is sent to the intendant of the quarter, another to the office of the town hall, another to enable the syndic to make his daily roll call. Everything that may be observed during the course of the visits—deaths, illnesses, complaints, irregularities—is noted down and transmitted to the intendants and magistrates. The magistrates have complete control over medical treatment; they have appointed a physician in charge; no other practitioner may treat, no apothecary prepare medicine, no

confessor visit a sick person without having received from him a written note "to prevent anyone from concealing and dealing with those sick of the contagion, unknown to the magistrates." The registration of the pathological must be constantly centralized. The relation of each individual to his disease and to his death passes through the representatives of power, the registration they make of it, the decisions they take on it.

Five or six days after the beginning of the quarantine, the process of purifying the houses one by one is begun. All the inhabitants are made to leave; in each room "the furniture and goods" are raised from the ground or suspended from the air; perfume is poured around the room; after carefully sealing the windows, doors and even the keyholes with wax, the perfume is set alight. Finally, the entire house is closed while the perfume is consumed; those who have carried out the work are searched, as they were on entry, "in the presence of the residents of the house, to see that they did not have something on their persons as they left that they did not have on entering." Four hours later, the residents are allowed to re-enter their homes.

This enclosed, segmented space, observed at every point, in which the individuals are inserted in a fixed place, in which the slightest movements are supervised, in which all events are recorded, in which an uninterrupted work of writing links the centre and periphery, in which power is exercised without division, according to a continuous hierarchical figure, in which each individual is constantly located, examined and distributed among the living beings, the sick and the dead—all this constitutes a compact model of the disciplinary mechanism. The plague is met by order; its function is to sort out every possible confusion: that of the disease, which is transmitted when bodies are mixed together; that of the evil, which is increased when fear and death overcome prohibitions. It lays down for each individual his place, his body, his disease and his death, his well-being, by means of an omnipresent and omniscient power that subdivides itself in a regular, uninterrupted way even to the ultimate determination of the individual, of what characterizes him, of what belongs to him, of what happens to him. Against the plague, which is a mixture, discipline brings into play its power, which is one of analysis. A whole literary fiction of the festival grew up around the plague: suspended laws, lifted prohibitions, the frenzy of passing time, bodies mingling together without respect, individuals unmasked, abandoning their statutory identity and the figure under which they had been recognized, allowing a quite different truth to appear. But there was also a political dream of the plague, which was exactly its reverse: not the collective festival, but strict divisions; not laws transgressed, but the penetration of regulation into even the smallest details of everyday life through the mediation of the complete hierarchy that assured the capillary functioning of power; not masks that were put on and taken off, but the assignment to each individual of his "true" name, his "true" place, his "true" body, his "true" disease. The plague as a form, at once real and imaginary, of disorder had as its medical and political correlative discipline. Behind the disciplinary mechanisms can be read the haunting memory of "contagions," of the plague, of rebellions, crimes, vagabondage, desertions, people who appear and disappear, live and die in disorder.

If it is true that the leper gave rise to rituals of exclusion, which to a certain extent provided the model for and general form of the great Confinement,[1] then the plague gave rise to disciplinary projects. Rather than the massive, binary division between one set of people and another, it called for multiple separations, individualizing distributions, an organization in depth of surveillance and control, an intensification and a ramification of power. The leper was caught up in a practice of rejection, of exile-enclosure; he was left to his doom in a mass among which it was useless to differentiate; those sick of the plague were caught up in a meticulous tactical partitioning in which individual differentiations were the constricting effects of a power that multiplied, articulated and subdivided itself; the great confinement on the one hand; the correct training on the other. The leper and his separation; the plague and its segmentations. The first is marked; the second analyzed and distributed. The exile of the leper and the arrest of the plague do not bring with them the same political dream. The first is that of a pure community, the second that of a disciplined society. Two ways of exercising power over men, of controlling their relations, of separating out their dangerous mixtures. The plague-stricken town, traversed throughout with hierarchy, surveillance, observation, writing; the town immobilized by the functioning of an extensive power that bears in a distinct way over all individual

bodies—this is the utopia of the perfectly governed city. The plague (envisaged as a possibility at least) is the trial in the course of which one may define ideally the exercise of disciplinary power. In order to make rights and laws function according to pure theory, the jurists place themselves in imagination in the state of nature; in order to see perfect disciplines functioning, rulers dreamt of the state of plague. Underlying disciplinary projects the image of the plague stands for all forms of confusion and disorder; just as the image of the leper, cut off from all human contact, underlies projects of exclusion.

They are different projects, then, but not incompatible ones. We see them coming slowly together, and it is the peculiarity of the nineteenth century that it applied to the space of exclusion of which the leper was the symbolic inhabitant (beggars, vagabonds, madmen and the disorderly formed the real population) the technique of power proper to disciplinary partitioning. Treat "lepers" as "plague victims," project the subtle segmentations of discipline onto the confused space of internment, combine it with the methods of analytical distribution proper to power, individualize the excluded, but use procedures of individualization to mark exclusion—this is what was operated regularly by disciplinary power from the beginning of the nineteenth century in the psychiatric asylum, the penitentiary, the reformatory, the approved school and, to some extent, the hospital. Generally speaking, all the authorities exercising individual control function according to a double mode; that of binary division and branding (mad/sane; dangerous/harmless; normal/abnormal); and that of coercive assignment, of differential distribution (who he is; where he must be; how he is to be characterized; how he is to be recognized; how a constant surveillance is to be exercised over him in an individual way, etc.). On the one hand, the lepers are treated as plague victims; the tactics of individualizing disciplines are imposed on the excluded; and, on the other hand, the universality of disciplinary controls makes it possible to brand the "leper" and to bring into play against him the dualistic mechanisms of exclusion. The constant division between the normal and the abnormal, to which every individual is subjected, brings us back to our own time, by applying the binary branding and exile of the leper to quite different objects; the existence of a whole set of techniques and institutions for measuring, supervising and correcting the abnormal brings into play the disciplinary mechanisms to which the fear of the plague gave rise. All the mechanisms of power which, even today, are disposed around the abnormal individual, to brand him

---

1   *the great Confinement*   [editors' note] Foucault's name for a movement he claims occurred during the seventeenth century in which people judged to be mad were (for the first time) systematically locked away and institutionalized. This historical claim—questioned by some authorities—is found in Foucault's *Madness and Civilization: A History of Insanity in the Age of Reason.*

and to alter him, are composed of those two forms from which they distantly derive.

Bentham's *Panopticon*[1] is the architectural figure of this composition. We know the principle on which it was based: at the periphery, an annular building; at the centre, a tower; this tower is pierced with wide windows that open onto the inner side of the ring; the peripheric building is divided into cells, each of which extends the whole width of the building; they have two windows, one on the inside, corresponding to the windows of the tower; the other, on the outside, allows the light to cross the cell from one end to the other. All that is needed, then, is to place a supervisor in a central tower and to shut up in each cell a madman, a patient, a condemned man, a worker or a schoolboy. By the effect of backlighting, one can observe from the tower, standing out precisely against the light, the small captive shadows in the cells of the periphery. They are like so many cages, so many small theatres, in which each actor is alone, perfectly individualized and constantly visible. The panoptic mechanism arranges spatial unities that make it possible to see constantly and to recognize immediately. In short, it reverses the principle of the dungeon; or rather of its three functions—to enclose, to deprive of light and to hide—it preserves only the first and eliminates the other two. Full lighting and the eye of a supervisor capture better than darkness, which ultimately protected. Visibility is a trap.

To begin with, this made it possible—as a negative effect—to avoid those compact, swarming, howling masses that were to be found in places of confinement, those painted by Goya or described by Howard.[2] Each individual, in his place, is securely confined to a cell from which he is seen from the front by the supervisor; but the side walls prevent him from coming into contact with his companions. He is seen, but he does not see; he is the object of information, never a subject in communication. The arrangement of his room, opposite the central tower, imposes on him an axial visibility; but the divisions of the ring, those separated cells, imply a lateral invisibility. And this invisibility is a guarantee of order. If the inmates are convicts, there is no danger of a plot, an attempt at collective escape, the planning of new crimes for the future, bad reciprocal influences; if they are patients, there is no danger of contagion; if they are madmen there is no risk of their committing violence upon one another; if they are schoolchildren, there is no copying, no noise, no chatter, no waste of time; if they are workers, there are no disorders, no theft, no coalitions, none of those distractions that slow down the rate of work, make it less perfect or cause accidents. The crowd, a compact mass, a locus of multiple exchanges, individualities merging together, a collective effect, is abolished and replaced by a collection of separated individualities. From the point of view of the guardian, it is replaced by a multiplicity that can be numbered and supervised; from the point of view of the inmates, by a sequestered and observed solitude.[3]

Hence the major effect of the Panopticon: to induce in the inmate a state of conscious and permanent visibility that assures the automatic functioning of power. So to arrange things that the surveillance is permanent in its effects, even if it is discontinuous in its action; that the perfection of power should tend to render its actual exercise unnecessary; that this architectural apparatus should be a machine for creating and sustaining a power relation independent of the person who exercises it; in short, that the inmates should be caught up in a power situation of which they are themselves the bearers. To achieve this, it is at once too much and too little that the prisoner should be constantly observed by an inspector: too little, for what matters is that he knows himself to be observed; too much, because he has no need in fact of being so. In view of this, Bentham laid down the principle that power should be visible and unverifiable. Visible: the inmate will constantly have before his eyes the tall outline of the central tower from which he is spied upon. Unverifiable: the inmate must never know whether he is being looked at at any one moment; but he must be sure that he may always be so. In order to make the presence or absence of the inspector unverifiable, so that the prisoners, in their cells, cannot even see a shadow, Bentham envisaged not only venetian blinds on the windows of the central observation hall, but, on the inside, partitions that intersected the hall at right angles and, in order to pass from one quarter to the other, not doors but zig-zag openings; for the slightest noise, a gleam of light, a brightness in a half-opened door would betray the presence of the guardian.[4]

---

1 *Bentham's Panopticon* A model for a prison designed by the utilitarian philosopher Jeremy Bentham that allowed the guards to observe the prisoners at all times. The name comes from the Latin: *pan* (all) and *opticon* (observe).

2 *Howard* John Howard [editors' note] (1726–90), English prison reformer.

3 *Each individual ... observed solitude* Bentham, *Panopticon*, 60–64.

4 *In order to ... the guardian* In the *Postscript* to the *Panopticon*, 1791, Bentham adds dark inspection galleries painted in black

The Panopticon is a machine for dissociating the see/being seen dyad: in the peripheric ring, one is totally seen, without ever seeing; in the central tower, one sees everything without ever being seen.[1]

It is an important mechanism, for it automatizes and disindividualizes power. Power has its principle not so much in a person as in a certain concerted distribution of bodies, surfaces, lights, gazes; in an arrangement whose internal mechanisms produce the relation in which individuals are caught up. The ceremonies, the rituals, the marks by which the sovereign's surplus power was manifested are useless. There is a machinery that assures dissymmetry, disequilibrium, difference. Consequently, it does not matter who exercises power. Any individual, taken almost at random, can operate the machine: in the absence of the director, his family, his friends, his visitors, even his servants.[2] Similarly, it does not matter what motive animates him: the curiosity of the indiscreet, the malice of a child, the thirst for knowledge of a philosopher who wishes to visit this museum of human nature, or the perversity of those who take pleasure in spying and punishing. The more numerous those anonymous and temporary observers are, the greater the risk for the inmate of being surprised and the greater his anxious awareness of being observed. The Panopticon is a marvelous machine which, whatever use one may wish to put it to, produces homogeneous effects of power.

A real subjection is born mechanically from a fictitious relation. So it is not necessary to use force to constrain the convict to good behavior, the madman to calm, the worker to work, the schoolboy to application, the patient to the observation of the regulations. Bentham was surprised that panoptic institutions could be so light: there were no more bars, no more chains, no more heavy locks; all that was needed was that the separations should be clear and the openings well arranged. The heaviness of the old "houses of security," with their fortress-like architecture, could be replaced by the simple, economic geometry of a "house of certainty." The efficiency of power, its constraining force have, in a sense, passed over to the other side—to the side of its surface of application. He who is subjected to a field of visibility, and who knows it, assumes responsibility for the constraints of power; he makes them play spontaneously upon himself; he inscribes in himself the power relation in which he simultaneously plays both roles; he becomes the principle of his own subjection. By this very fact, the external power may throw off its physical weight; it tends to the non-corporal; and, the more it approaches this limit, the more constant, profound and permanent are its effects: it is a perpetual victory that avoids any physical confrontation and which is always decided in advance.

Bentham does not say whether he was inspired, in his project, by Le Vaux's menagerie at Versailles: the first menagerie in which the different elements are not, as they traditionally were, distributed in a park.[3] At the center was an octagonal pavilion which, on the first floor, consisted of only a single room, the king's *salon*; on every side large windows looked out onto seven cages (the eighth side was reserved for the entrance), containing different species of animals. By Bentham's time, this menagerie had disappeared. But one finds in the program of the Panopticon a similar concern with individualizing observation, with characterization and classification, with the analytical arrangement of space. The Panopticon is a royal menagerie; the animal is replaced by man, individual distribution by specific grouping and the king by the machinery of a furtive power. With this exception, the Panopticon also does the work of a naturalist. It makes it possible to draw up differences: among patients, to observe the symptoms of each individual, without the proximity of beds, the circulation of miasmas, the effects of contagion confusing the clinical tables; among schoolchildren, it makes it possible to observe performances (without there being any imitation or copying), to map aptitudes, to assess characters, to draw up rigorous classifications and, in relation to normal development, to distinguish "laziness and stubbornness" from "incurable imbecility"; among workers, it makes it possible to note the aptitudes of each worker, compare the time he takes to perform a task, and if they are paid by the day, to calculate their wages.[4]

---

around the inspector's lodge, each making it possible to observe two stories of cells.

1 *The Panopticon ... without ever being seen*   In his first version of the *Panopticon*, Bentham had also imagined an acoustic surveillance, operated by means of pipes leading from the cells to the central tower. In the *Postscript* he abandoned the idea, perhaps because he could not introduce into it the principle of dissymmetry and prevent the prisoners from hearing the inspector as well as the inspector hearing them. Julius tried to develop a system of dissymmetrical listening (Nikolaus H. Julius [(1783–1862)], *Leçons sur les prisons*, I [(Paris: F.G. Levrault 1831)], 18).

2 *Any individual ... his servants*   Bentham, *Panopticon*, 45.

3 *Le Vaux's menagerie ... in a park*   Gustave Loisel, *Histoire des ménageries de l'antiquité à nos jours* Vol 2 (Paris: Octave Doin et fils & Henri Laurens, 1912), 104–7. [editors' note] The name of the zoo's architect was in fact Louis Le Vau (1612–70).

4 *It makes ... their wages*   Bentham, *Panopticon*, 60–64.

So much for the question of observation. But the Panopticon was also a laboratory; it could be used as a machine to carry out experiments, to alter behavior, to train or correct individuals. To experiment with medicines and monitor their effects. To try out different punishments on prisoners, according to their crimes and character, and to seek the most effective ones. To teach different techniques simultaneously to the workers, to decide which is the best. To try out pedagogical experiments—and in particular to take up once again the well-debated problem of secluded education, by using orphans. One would see what would happen when, in their sixteenth or eighteenth year, they were presented with other boys or girls; one could verify whether, as Helvetius[1] thought, anyone could learn anything; one would follow "the genealogy of every observable idea"; one could bring up different children according to different systems of thought, making certain children believe that two and two do not make four or that the moon is a cheese, then put them together when they are twenty or twenty-five years old; one would then have discussions that would be worth a great deal more than the sermons or lectures on which so much money is spent; one would have at least an opportunity of making discoveries in the domain of metaphysics. The Panopticon is a privileged place for experiments on men, and for analyzing with complete certainty the transformations that may be obtained from them. The Panopticon may even provide an apparatus for supervising its own mechanisms. In this central tower, the director may spy on all the employees that he has under his orders: nurses, doctors, foremen, teachers, warders; he will be able to judge them continuously, alter their behavior, impose upon them the methods he thinks best; and it will even be possible to observe the director himself. An inspector arriving unexpectedly at the centre of the Panopticon will be able to judge at a glance, without anything being concealed from him, how the entire establishment is functioning. And, in any case, enclosed as he is in the middle of this architectural mechanism, is not the director's own fate entirely bound up with it? The incompetent physician who has allowed contagion to spread, the incompetent prison governor or workshop manager will be the first victims of an epidemic or a revolt. "'By every tie I could devise', said the master of the Panopticon, 'my own fate had been bound up by

me with theirs.'"[2] The Panopticon functions as a kind of laboratory of power. Thanks to its mechanisms of observation, it gains in efficiency and in the ability to penetrate into men's behavior; knowledge follows the advances of power, discovering new objects of knowledge over all the surfaces on which power is exercised.

The plague-stricken town, the panoptic establishment—the differences are important. They mark, at a distance of a century and a half, the transformations of the disciplinary program. In the first case, there is an exceptional situation: against an extraordinary evil, power is mobilized; it makes itself everywhere present and visible; it invents new mechanisms; it separates, it immobilizes, it partitions; it constructs for a time what is both a counter-city and the perfect society; it imposes an ideal functioning, but one that is reduced, in the final analysis, like the evil that it combats, to a simple dualism of life and death: that which moves brings death, and one kills that which moves. The Panopticon, on the other hand, must be understood as a generalizable model of functioning; a way of defining power relations in terms of the everyday life of men. No doubt Bentham presents it as a particular institution, closed in upon itself. Utopias, perfectly closed in upon themselves, are common enough. As opposed to the ruined prisons, littered with mechanisms of torture, to be seen in Piranese's engravings, the Panopticon presents a cruel, ingenious cage. The fact that it should have given rise, even in our own time, to so many variations, projected or realized, is evidence of the imaginary intensity that it has possessed for almost two hundred years. But the Panopticon must not be understood as a dream building: it is the diagram of a mechanism of power reduced to its ideal form; its functioning, abstracted from any obstacle, resistance or friction, must be represented as a pure architectural and optical system: it is in fact a figure of political technology that may and must be detached from any specific use.

It is polyvalent in its applications; it serves to reform prisoners, but also to treat patients, to instruct schoolchildren, to confine the insane, to supervise workers, to put beggars and idlers to work. It is a type of location of bodies in space, of distribution of individuals in relation to one another, of hierarchical organization, of disposition of centers and channels of power, of definition of the instruments and modes of intervention of power, which can be implemented in hospitals, workshops, schools, prisons. Whenever one is

---

1 *Helvetius* [editors' note] Claude Helvétius (1715–71) was a French philosopher and literary writer. Among his positions were the views that all human intellects are equal in potential power, and differences arise solely through different education.

2 *By every tie ... with theirs* Bentham, *Panopticon*, 177.

dealing with a multiplicity of individuals on whom a task or a particular form of behavior must be imposed, the panoptic schema may be used. It is—necessary modifications apart—applicable "to all establishments whatsoever, in which, within a space not too large to be covered or commanded by buildings, a number of persons are meant to be kept under inspection"[1] (although Bentham takes the penitentiary house as his prime example, it is because it has many different functions to fulfill—safe custody, confinement, solitude, forced labor and instruction).

In each of its applications, it makes it possible to perfect the exercise of power. It does this in several ways: because it can reduce the number of those who exercise it, while increasing the number of those on whom it is exercised. Because it is possible to intervene at any moment and because the constant pressure acts even before the offences, mistakes or crimes have been committed. Because, in these conditions, its strength is that it never intervenes, it is exercised spontaneously and without noise, it constitutes a mechanism whose effects follow from one another. Because, without any physical instrument other than architecture and geometry, it acts directly on individuals; it gives "power of mind over mind." The panoptic schema makes any apparatus of power more intense: it assures its economy (in material, in personnel, in time); it assures its efficacy by its preventative character, its continuous functioning and its automatic mechanisms. It is a way of obtaining from power "in hitherto unexampled quantity," "a great and new instrument of government...; its great excellence consists in the great strength it is capable of giving to any institution it may be thought proper to apply it to."[2]

It's a case of "it's easy once you've thought of it" in the political sphere. It can in fact be integrated into any function (education, medical treatment, production, punishment); it can increase the effect of this function, by being linked closely with it; it can constitute a mixed mechanism in which relations of power (and of knowledge) may be precisely adjusted, in the smallest detail, to the processes that are to be supervised; it can establish a direct proportion between "surplus power" and "surplus production." In short, it arranges things in such a way that the exercise of power is not added on from the outside, like a rigid, heavy constraint, to the functions it invests, but is so subtly present in them as to increase their efficiency by itself increasing its own points of contact. The panoptic mechanism is not simply a hinge, a point of exchange between a mechanism of power and a function; it is a way of making power relations function in a function, and of making a function function through these power relations. Bentham's Preface to Panopticon opens with a list of the benefits to be obtained from his "inspection-house": "Morals reformed—health preserved—industry invigorated—instruction diffused—public burthens[3] lightened—Economy seated, as it were, upon a rock—the gordian knot of the Poor-Laws not cut, but untied[4]—all by a simple idea in architecture!"[5]

Furthermore, the arrangement of this machine is such that its enclosed nature does not preclude a permanent presence from the outside: we have seen that anyone may come and exercise in the central tower the functions of surveillance, and that, this being the case, he can gain a clear idea of the way in which the surveillance is practiced. In fact, any panoptic institution, even if it is as rigorously closed as a penitentiary, may without difficulty be subjected to such irregular and constant inspections: and not only by the appointed inspectors, but also by the public; any member of society will have the right to come and see with his own eyes how the schools, hospitals, factories, prisons function. There is no risk, therefore, that the increase of power created by the panoptic machine may degenerate into tyranny; the disciplinary mechanism will be democratically controlled, since it will be constantly accessible "to the great tribunal committee of the world."[6] This Panopticon, subtly arranged

---

1   *to all ... under inspection* Bentham, *Panopticon*, 40.

2   *It is a way ... apply it to* Bentham, *Panopticon*, 66.

3   *burthens* [editors' note] Burdens.

4   *gordian knot ... but untied* [editors' note] The "Gordian knot" of Greek tradition was an intricate knot tied by King Gordius of Phrygia and cut by Alexander the Great with his sword. Figuratively, then, it is a very difficult problem that cannot be solved in its own terms; "cutting" the knot solves it with a bold stroke from an unexpected source. The Poor Laws were a legal system set up in the late sixteenth and early seventeenth century in England, establishing government payments or employment for those distinguished as the "deserving poor." Critics argued that it was too costly and encouraged the underlying problems. Bentham proposed an alternative program of punishment and discipline.

5   *Bentham's Preface ... idea in architecture!* Bentham, *Panopticon*, 39.

6   *There is ... the world* Imagining this continuous flow of visitors entering the central tower by an underground passage and then observing the circular landscape of the Panopticon, was Bentham aware of the Panoramas that Barker was constructing at exactly the same period (the first seems to have dated from 1787) and in which the visitors, occupying the central place, saw unfolding around them a landscape, a city or a battle? The visitors occupied exactly the place of the sovereign gaze.

so that an observer may observe, at a glance, so many different individuals, also enables everyone to come and observe any of the observers. The seeing machine was once a sort of dark room into which individuals spied; it has become a transparent building in which the exercise of power may be supervised by society as a whole.

The panoptic schema, without disappearing as such or losing any of its properties, was destined to spread throughout the social body; its vocation was to become a generalized function. The plague-stricken town provided an exceptional disciplinary model: perfect, but absolutely violent; to the disease that brought death, power opposed its perpetual threat of death; life inside it was reduced to its simplest expression; it was, against the power of death, the meticulous exercise of the right of the sword. The Panopticon, on the other hand, has a role of amplification; although it arranges power, although it is intended to make it more economic and more effective, it does so not for power itself, nor for the immediate salvation of a threatened society: its aim is to strengthen the social forces—to increase production, to develop the economy, spread education, raise the level of public morality; to increase and multiply.

How is power to be strengthened in such a way that, far from impeding progress, far from weighing upon it with its rules and regulations, it actually facilitates such progress? What intensificator of power will be able at the same time to be a multiplicator of production? How will power, by increasing its forces, be able to increase those of society instead of confiscating them or impeding them? The Panopticon's solution to this problem is that the productive increase of power can be assured only if, on the one hand, it can be exercised continuously in the very foundations of society, in the subtlest possible way, and if, on the other hand, it functions outside these sudden, violent, discontinuous forms that are bound up with the exercise of sovereignty. The body of the king, with its strange material and physical presence, with the force that he himself deploys or transmits to some few others, is at the opposite extreme of this new physics of power represented by panopticism; the domain of panopticism is, on the contrary, that whole lower region, that region of irregular bodies, with their details, their multiple movements, their heterogeneous forces, their spatial relations; what are required are mechanisms that analyze distributions, gaps, series, combinations, and which use instruments that render visible, record, differentiate and compare: a physics of a relational and multiple power, which has its maximum intensity not in the person of the king, but in the bodies that can be individualized by these relations. At the theoretical level, Bentham defines another way of analyzing the social body and the power relations that traverse it; in terms of practice, he defines a procedure of subordination of bodies and forces that must increase the utility of power while practicing the economy of the prince. Panopticism is the general principle of a new "political anatomy" whose object and end are not the relations of sovereignty but the relations of discipline.

The celebrated, transparent, circular cage, with its high tower, powerful and knowing, may have been for Bentham a project of a perfect disciplinary institution; but he also set out to show how one may "unlock" the disciplines and get them to function in a diffused, multiple, polyvalent way throughout the whole social body. These disciplines, which the classical age had elaborated in specific, relatively enclosed places—barracks, schools, workshops—and whose total implementation had been imagined only at the limited and temporary scale of a plague-stricken town, Bentham dreamt of transforming into a network of mechanisms that would be everywhere and always alert, running through society without interruption in space or in time. The panoptic arrangement provides the formula for this generalization. It program, at the level of an elementary and easily transferable mechanism, the basic functioning of a society penetrated through and through with disciplinary mechanisms.

There are two images, then, of discipline. At one extreme, the discipline-blockade, the enclosed institution, established on the edges of society, turned inwards towards negative functions: arresting evil, breaking communications, suspending time. At the other extreme, with panopticism, is the discipline-mechanism: a functional mechanism that must improve the exercise of power by making it lighter, more rapid, more effective, a design of subtle coercion for a society to come. The movement from one project to the other, from a schema of exceptional discipline to one of a generalized surveillance, rests on a historical transformation: the gradual extension of the mechanisms of discipline throughout the seventeenth and eighteenth centuries, their spread throughout the whole social body, the formation of what might be called in general the disciplinary society.

A whole disciplinary generalization—the Benthamite physics of power represents an acknowledgement of this—had operated throughout the classical age. The spread of disciplinary institutions, whose network was beginning to cover an ever larger surface and occupying above all a less and less marginal position, testifies to this: what was an islet, a privileged place, a circumstantial measure, or a singular model, became a general formula; the regulations characteristic of the Protestant and pious armies of William of Orange or of Gustavus Adolphus[1] were transformed into regulations for all the armies of Europe; the model colleges of the Jesuits, or the schools of Batencour or Démia, following the example set by Sturm,[2] provided the outlines for the general forms of educational discipline; the ordering of the naval and military hospitals provided the model for the entire reorganization of hospitals in the eighteenth century.

But this extension of the disciplinary institutions was no doubt only the most visible aspect of various, more profound processes.

1. *The functional inversion of the disciplines.* At first, they were expected to neutralize dangers, to fix useless or disturbed populations, to avoid the inconveniences of over-large assemblies; now they were being asked to play a positive role, for they were becoming able to do so, to increase the possible utility of individuals. Military discipline is no longer a mere means of preventing looting, desertion or failure to obey orders among the troops; it has become a basic technique to enable the army to exist, not as an assembled crowd, but as a unity that derives from this very unity an increase in its forces; discipline increases the skill of each individual, coordinates these skills, accelerates movements, increases fire power, broadens the fronts of attack without reducing their vigor, increases the capacity for resistance, etc. The discipline of the workshop, while remaining a way of enforcing respect for the regulations and authorities, of preventing thefts or losses, tends to increase aptitudes, speeds, output and therefore profits; it still exerts a moral influence over behavior, but more and more it treats actions in terms of their results, introduces bodies into a machinery, forces into an economy. When, in the seventeenth century,

the provincial schools or the Christian elementary schools were founded, the justifications given for them were above all negative: those poor who were unable to bring up their children left them "in ignorance of their obligations: given the difficulties they have in earning a living, and themselves having been badly brought up, they are unable to communicate a sound upbringing that they themselves never had"; this involves three major inconveniences: ignorance of God, idleness (with its consequent drunkenness, impurity, larceny, brigandage); and the formation of those gangs of beggars, always ready to stir up public disorder and "virtually to exhaust the funds of the Hôtel-Dieu."[3] Now, at the beginning of the Revolution, the end laid down for primary education was to be, among other things, to "fortify," to "develop the body," to prepare the child "for a future in some mechanical work," to give him "an observant eye, a sure hand and prompt habits."[4] The disciplines function increasingly as techniques for making useful individuals. Hence their emergence from a marginal position on the confines of society, and detachment from the forms of exclusion or expiation, confinement or retreat. Hence the slow loosening of their kinship with religious regularities and enclosures. Hence also their rooting in the most important, most central and most productive sectors of society. They become attached to some of the great essential functions: factory production, the transmission of knowledge, the diffusion of aptitudes and skills, the war-machine. Hence, too, the double tendency one sees developing throughout the eighteenth century to increase the number of disciplinary institutions and to discipline the existing apparatuses.

2. *The swarming of disciplinary mechanisms.* While, on the one hand, the disciplinary establishments increase, their mechanisms have a certain tendency to become "de-institutionalized," to emerge from the closed fortresses in which they once functioned and to circulate in a "free" state; the massive, compact disciplines are broken down into flexible methods of control, which may be transferred and adapted. Sometimes the closed apparatuses add to their internal and specific function a role of external surveillance, developing

---

1   *William of Orange or of Gustavus Adolphus* [editors' note] William of Orange (1650–1702) brought his Protestant forces into England in 1688, and in the "Glorious Revolution" of 1689, the Catholic king James II was deposed and he, as William III, and his wife Mary became sovereigns. Gustav II Adolph, called Gustavus Adolphus (1594–1632), king of Sweden (1611–32), was a leader of the Protestant forces in the Thirty Years' War (1618–48).

2   *the schools ... set by Sturm* [editors' note] At the end of the seventeenth century, charity schools using innovative educational methods for education of the poor were established in Lyons by Charles Démia (1637-89) and in Paris by Jacques de Batencour. Johannes Sturm (1507-89) founded the Protestant grammar school at Strasburg in 1538, a school noted for its progressive humanistic methods.

3   *the justifications ... the Hôtel-Dieu* Charles Démia, *Règlement pour les écoles de la ville [et diocèse] de Lyon* (Lyon: André Olyer, no date). [editors' note] The "*Hôtel-Dieu*" ("hostel of God") is the principal hospital in a French town.

4   *the end ... prompt habits* Talleyrand's Report to the Constituent Assembly, 10 September 1791, quoted by Antoine Léon, *La Révolution française et l'éducation technique* (Paris: Société des Études Robespierristes, 1968), 106.

around themselves a whole margin of lateral controls. Thus the Christian School must not simply train docile children; it must also make it possible to supervise the parents, to gain information as to their way of life, their resources, their piety, their morals. The school tends to constitute minute social observatories that penetrate even to the adults and exercise regular supervision over them: the bad behavior of the child, or his absence, is a legitimate pretext, according to Démia, for one to go and question the neighbors, especially if there is any reason to believe that the family will not tell the truth; one can then go and question the parents themselves, to find out whether they know their catechism and the prayers, whether they are determined to root out the vices of their children, how many beds there are in the house and what the sleeping arrangements are; the visit may end with the giving of alms, the present of a religious picture, or the provision of additional beds.[1] Similarly, the hospital is increasingly conceived of as a base for the medical observation of the population outside; after the burning down of the Hôtel-Dieu in 1772,[2] there were several demands that the large buildings, so heavy and so disordered, should be replaced by a series of smaller hospitals; their function would be to take in the sick of the quarter, but also to gather information, to be alert to any endemic or epidemic phenomena, to open dispensaries, to give advice to the inhabitants and to keep the authorities informed of the sanitary state of the region.[3]

One also sees the spread of disciplinary procedures, not in the form of enclosed institutions, but as centers of observation disseminated throughout society. Religious groups and charity organizations had long played this role of "disciplining" the population. From the Counter-Reformation to the philanthropy of the July monarchy,[4] initiatives of this type continued to increase; their aims were religious (conversion and moralization), economic (aid and encouragement to work) or political (the struggle against discontent or agitation). One has only to cite by way of example the regulations for the charity associations in the Paris parishes. The territory to be covered was divided into quarters and cantons and the members of the associations divided themselves up along the same lines. These members had to visit their respective areas regularly. "They will strive to eradicate places of ill-repute, tobacco shops, life-classes, gaming house, public scandals, blasphemy, impiety, and any other disorders that may come to their knowledge." They will also have to make individual visits to the poor; and the information to be obtained is laid down in regulations: the stability of the lodging, knowledge of prayers, attendance at the sacraments, knowledge of a trade, morality (and "whether they have not fallen into poverty through their own fault"); lastly, "one must learn by skilful questioning in what way they behave at home. Whether there is peace between them and their neighbors, whether they are careful to bring up their children in the fear of God ... whether they do not have their older children of different sexes sleeping together and with them, whether they do not allow licentiousness and cajolery in their families, especially in their older daughters. If one has any doubts as to whether they are married, one must ask to see their marriage certificate."[5]

3. *The state-control of the mechanisms of discipline.* In England, it was private religious groups that carried out, for a long time, the functions of social discipline;[6] in France, although a part of this role remained in the hands of parish guilds or charity associations, another—and no doubt the most important part—was very soon taken over by the police apparatus.

The organization of a centralized police had long been regarded, even by contemporaries, as the most direct expression of royal absolutism; the sovereign had wished to have "his own magistrate to whom he might directly entrust his orders, his commissions, intentions, and who was entrusted with the execution of orders and orders under the King's

---

1   *The school ... additional beds*   Démia, *Règlement*, 39–40.

2   *the burning down of the Hôtel-Dieu in 1772*   [editors' note] A fire that destroyed most of the biggest Parisian hospital in the center of the city brought attention to its horribly unsanitary deteriorated conditions; this led to debate and conflict about hospital reforms.

3   *the hospital ... the region*   In the second half of the eighteenth century, it was often suggested that the army should be used for the surveillance and general partitioning of the population. The army, as yet to undergo discipline in the seventeenth century, was regarded as a force capable of instilling it. Cf., for example, Joseph Servan (1741–1808), *Le Soldat citoyen, ou Vues patriotiques sur la manière la plus avantageuse de pourvoir à la défense du royaume* (Neufchâtel: No publisher listed, 1780).

4   *the July monarchy*   A period of liberal, moderate, constitutional monarchy in France; Louis-Phillipe ruled from after the "July

Revolution" of 1830 till he was overthrown during the "February Revolution" in 1848.

5   *the charity associations ... marriage certificate*   Paris, Bibliothèque de l'Arsenal, MS. 2565. Under this number, one also finds regulations for charity associations of the seventeenth and eighteenth centuries.

6   *private religious groups ... social discipline*   (cf. L. Radzinovitz, *The English Criminal Law*, II, 1956, 203–14).

private seal."[1] In effect, in taking over a number of pre-existing functions—the search for criminals, urban surveillance, economic and political supervision—the police magistratures and the magistrature-general that presided over them in Paris transposed them into a single, strict, administrative machine: "All the radiations of force and information that spread from the circumference culminate in the magistrate-general.... It is he who operates all the wheels that together produce order and harmony. The effects of his administration cannot be better compared than to the movement of the celestial bodies."[2]

But, although the police as an institution were certainly organized in the form of a state apparatus, and although this was certainly linked directly to the centre of political sovereignty, the type of power that it exercises, the mechanisms it operates and the elements to which it applies them are specific. It is an apparatus that must be coextensive with the entire social body and not only by the extreme limits that it embraces, but by the minuteness of the details it is concerned with. Police power must bear "over everything": it is not however the totality of the state nor of the kingdom as visible and invisible body of the monarch; it is the dust of events, actions, behavior, opinions—"everything that happens,"[3] the police are concerned with "those things of every moment," those "unimportant things," of which Catherine II spoke in her Great Instruction.[4] With the police, one is in the indefinite world of a supervision that seeks ideally to reach the most elementary particle, the most passing phenomenon of the social body: "The ministry of the magistrates and police officers is of the greatest importance; the objects that it embraces are in a sense definite, one may perceive them only by a sufficiently detailed examination":[5] the infinitely small of political power.

And, in order to be exercised, this power had to be given the instrument of permanent, exhaustive, omnipresent surveillance, capable of making all visible, as long as it could itself remain invisible. It had to be like a faceless gaze that transformed the whole social body into a field of perception: thousands of eyes posted everywhere, mobile attentions ever on the alert, a long, hierarchized network which, according to Le Maire,[6] comprised for Paris the forty-eight *commissaires*, the twenty *inspecteurs*, then the "observers," who were paid regularly, the "*basses mouches*," or secret agents, who were paid by the day, then the informers, paid according to the job done, and finally the prostitutes. And this unceasing observation had to be accumulated in a series of reports and registers; throughout the eighteenth century, an immense police text increasingly covered society by means of a complex documentary organization.[7] And, unlike the methods of judicial or administrative writing, what was registered in this way were forms of behavior, attitudes, possibilities, suspicions—a permanent account of individuals' behavior.

Now, it should be noted that, although this police supervision was entirely "in the hands of the king," it did not function in a single direction. It was in fact a double-entry system: it had to correspond, by manipulating the machinery of justice, to the immediate wishes of the king, but it was also capable of responding to solicitations from below; the celebrated *lettres de cachet*, or orders under the king's private seal, which were long the symbol of arbitrary royal rule and which brought detention into disrepute on political grounds, were in fact demanded by families, masters, local notables, neighbors, parish priests; and their function was to punish by confinement a whole infra-penality, that of disorder, agitation, disobedience, bad conduct; those things that Ledoux[8] wanted to exclude from his architecturally perfect city and which he called "offences of non-surveillance." In short, the eighteenth-century police added a disciplinary function to its role as the auxiliary of justice in the pursuit of criminals and as an instrument for the political supervision of plots, opposition movements or revolts.

---

1   *his own magistrate ... private seal*   A note by Duval, first secretary at the police magistrature, quoted in F. Funck-Brentano, *Catalogue des manuscripts de la bibliothèque de l'Arsenal*, IX, (Paris: E. Plon Nourrit et cie., 1885), 1.

2   *All the radiations ... celestial bodies*   Toussaint Lemoyne Des Essarts, *Dictionnaire universel de police* (Paris, 1786–89), 344 and 528.

3   *Police power ... everything that happens*   Le Maire in a memorandum written at the request of Sartine, in answer to sixteen questions posed by Joseph II on the Parisian police. This memorandum was published by Gazier in 1879.

4   *those unimportant ... Great Instruction*   Supplement to the "*Instruction for the Drawing Up of a New Code*," 1769, article 535.

5   *The ministry ... detailed examination*   Nicolas Delamare (1639–1725), *Traité de police* (1705; Second Edition: Paris: Chez Michel Brunet, 1722) unnumbered Preface.

6   *Le Maire*   [editors' note] Foucault does not give any identification for this authority.

7   *an immense police ... documentary organization*   On the police registers in the eighteenth century, cf. M. Chassaigne, *La Lieutenance générale de police* (1906; reedited at Geneva: Slatkine-Megariotis, 1975).

8   *Ledoux*   [editors' note] Claude Nicholas Ledoux (1736–1806), French architect, identified with the "*Ancien Régime*" and known for his exaggerated neoclassical style and his town planning for the "ideal city."

It was a complex function since it linked the absolute power of the monarch to the lowest levels of power disseminated in society; since, between these different, enclosed institutions of discipline (workshops, armies, schools), it extended an intermediary network, acting where they could not intervene, disciplining the non-disciplinary spaces; but it filled in the gaps, linked them together, guaranteed with its armed force an interstitial discipline and a meta-discipline. "By means of a wise police, the sovereign accustoms the people to order and obedience."[1]

The organization of the police apparatus in the eighteenth century sanctioned a generalization of the disciplines that became co-extensive with the state itself. Although it was linked in the most explicit way with everything in the royal power that exceeded the exercise of regular justice, it is understandable why the police offered such slight resistance to the rearrangement of the judicial power; and why it has not ceased to impose its prerogatives upon it, with ever-increasing weight, right up to the present day; this is no doubt because it is the secular arm of the judiciary; but it is also because, to a far greater degree than the judicial institution, it is identified, by reason of its extent and mechanisms, with a society of the disciplinary type. Yet it would be wrong to believe that the disciplinary functions were confiscated and absorbed once and for all by a state apparatus.

"Discipline" may be identified neither with an institution nor with an apparatus; it is a type of power, a modality for its exercise, comprising a whole set of instruments, techniques, procedures, levels of application, targets; it is a "physics" or an "anatomy" of power, a technology. And it may be taken over either by "specialized" institutions (the penitentiaries or "houses of correction" of the nineteenth century), or by institutions that use it as an essential instrument for a particular end (schools, hospitals), or by pre-existing authorities that find in it a means of reinforcing or reorganizing their internal mechanisms of power (one day we should show how intra-familial relations, essentially in the parents–children cell, have become "disciplined," absorbing since the classical age external schemata, first educational and military, then medical, psychiatric, psychological, which have made the family the privileged locus of emergence for the disciplinary question of the normal and the abnormal); or by apparatuses that have made discipline

their principle of internal functioning (the disciplinarization of the administrative apparatus from the Napoleonic period), or finally by state apparatuses whose major, if not exclusive, function is to assure that discipline reigns over society as a whole (the police).

On the whole, therefore, one can speak of the formation of a disciplinary society in this movement that stretches from the enclosed disciplines, a sort of social "quarantine," to an indefinitely generalizable mechanism of "panopticism." Not because the disciplinary modality of power has replaced all the others; but because it has infiltrated the others, sometimes undermining them, but serving as an intermediary between them, linking them together, extending them and above all making it possible to bring the effects of power to the most minute and distant elements. It assures an infinitesimal distribution of the power relations.

A few years after Bentham, Julius gave this society its birth certificate.[2] Speaking of the panoptic principle, he said that there was much more there than architectural ingenuity: it was an event in the "history of the human mind." In appearance, it is merely the solution of a technical problem; but, through it, a whole type of society emerges. Antiquity had been a civilization of spectacle. "To render accessible to a multitude of men the inspection of a small number of objects": this was the problem to which the architecture of temples, theatres and circuses responded. With spectacle, there was a predominance of public life, the intensity of festivals, sensual proximity. In these rituals in which blood flowed, society found new vigor and formed for a moment a single great body. The modern age poses the opposite problem: "To procure for a small number, or even for a single individual, the instantaneous view of a great multitude." In a society in which the principal elements are no longer the community and public life, but, on the one hand, private individuals and, on the other, the state, relations can be regulated only in a form that is the exact reverse of the spectacle: "It was to the modern age, to the ever-growing influence of the state, to its ever more profound intervention in all the details and all the relations of social life, that was reserved the task of increasing and perfecting its guarantees, by using and directing towards that great aim the building and distribution of buildings intended to observe a great multitude of men at the same time."

1   *By means ... order and obedience*   Emerich de Vattel (1714–67), *Le Droit des gens, ou Principes de la Loi Naturelle Appliqués à la Conduite et aux affaires des Nations et des Souverains* (1758), 162.

2   *Julius gave ... birth certificate*   Julius, *Leçons*, 384–86.

Julius saw as a fulfilled historical process that which Bentham had described as a technical program. Our society is one not of spectacle, but of surveillance; under the surface of images, one invests bodies in depth; behind the great abstraction of exchange, there continues the meticulous, concrete training of useful forces; the circuits of communication are the supports of an accumulation and a centralization of knowledge; the play of signs defines the anchorages of power; it is not that the beautiful totality of the individual is amputated, repressed, altered by our social order, it is rather that the individual is carefully fabricated in it, according to a whole technique of forces and bodies. We are much less Greeks than we believe. We are neither in the amphitheatre, nor on the stage, but in the panoptic machine, invested by its effects of power, which we bring to ourselves since we are part of its mechanism. The importance, in historical mythology, of the Napoleonic character probably derives from the fact that it is at the point of junction of the monarchical, ritual exercise of sovereignty and the hierarchical, permanent exercise of indefinite discipline. He is the individual who looms over everything with a single gaze which no detail, however minute, can escape: "You may consider that no part of the Empire is without surveillance, no crime, no offence, no contravention that remains unpunished, and that the eye of the genius who can enlighten all embraces the whole of this vast machine, without, however, the slightest detail escaping his attention."[1] At the moment of its full blossoming, the disciplinary society still assumes with the Emperor the old aspect of the power of spectacle. As a monarch who is at one and the same time a usurper of the ancient throne and the organizer of the new state, he combined into a single symbolic, ultimate figure the whole of the long process by which the pomp of sovereignty, the necessarily spectacular manifestations of power, were extinguished one by one in the daily exercise of surveillance, in a panopticism in which the vigilance of intersecting gazes was soon to render useless both the eagle and the sun.[2]

The formation of the disciplinary society is connected with a number of broad historical processes—economic, juridico-political and, lastly, scientific—of which it forms part.

1. Generally speaking, it might be said that the disciplines are techniques for assuring the ordering of human multiplicities. It is true that there is nothing exceptional or even characteristic in this: every system of power is presented with the same problem. But the peculiarity of the disciplines is that they try to define in relation to the multiplicities a tactics of power that fulfils three criteria: firstly, to obtain the exercise of power at the lowest possible cost (economically, by the low expenditure it involves; politically, by its discretion, its low exteriorization, its relative invisibility, the little resistance it arouses); secondly, to bring the effects of this social power to their maximum intensity and to extend them as far as possible, without either failure or interval; thirdly, to link this "economic" growth of power with the output of the apparatuses (educational, military, industrial or medical) within which it is exercised; in short, to increase both the docility and the utility of all the elements of the system. This triple objective of the disciplines corresponds to a well-known historical conjuncture. One aspect of this conjuncture was the large demographic thrust of the eighteenth century; an increase in the floating population (one of the primary objects of discipline is to fix; it is an anti-nomadic technique); a change of quantitative scale in the groups to be supervised or manipulated (from the beginning of the seventeenth century to the eve of the French Revolution, the school population had been increasing rapidly, as had no doubt the hospital population; by the end of the eighteenth century, the peace-time army exceeded 200,000 men). The other aspect of the conjuncture was the growth in the apparatus of production, which was becoming more and more extended and complex; it was also becoming more costly and its profitability had to be increased. The development of the disciplinary methods corresponded to these two processes, or rather, no doubt, to the new need to adjust their correlation. Neither the residual forms of feudal power nor the structures of the administrative monarchy, nor the local mechanisms of supervision, nor the unstable, tangled mass they all formed together could carry out this role: they were hindered from doing so by the irregular and inadequate extension of their network, by their often conflicting functioning, but above all by the "costly" nature of the power that was exercised in them. It was costly in several senses: because directly it cost a great deal to the Treasury; because the system of corrupt offices and farmed-out taxes weighed indirectly, but very heavily, on the population; because the resistance it encountered forced it into a cycle of perpetual reinforcement; because it

---

1   *You may consider ... his attention*   Jean-Baptiste Treilhard (1742–1810), *Motifs du code d'instruction criminelle* (1808), 14.

2   *the eagle and the sun*   [editors' note] Foucault may be referring here to the eagle as the symbol of the power of ancient Rome and many other states, and the sun as the symbol of the French king Louis XIV, "The Sun King."

proceeded essentially by levying (levying on money or products by royal, seigniorial, ecclesiastical taxation; levying on men or time by *corvées*[1] of press-ganging,[2] by locking up or banishing vagabonds). The development of the disciplines marks the appearance of elementary techniques belonging to a quite different economy: mechanisms of power which, instead of proceeding by deduction, are integrated into the productive efficiency of the apparatuses from within, into the growth of this efficiency and into the use of what it produces. For the old principle of "levying-violence," which governed the economy of power, the disciplines substitute the principle of "mildness-production-profit." These are the techniques that make it possible to adjust the multiplicity of men and the multiplication of the apparatuses of production (and this means not only "production" in the strict sense, but also the production of knowledge and skills in the school, the production of health in the hospitals, the production of destructive force in the army).

In this task of adjustment, discipline had to solve a number of problems for which the old economy of power was not sufficiently equipped. It could reduce the inefficiency of mass phenomena: reduce what, in a multiplicity, makes it much less manageable than a unity; reduce what is opposed to the use of each of its elements and of their sum; reduce everything that may counter the advantages of number. That is why discipline fixes; it arrests or regulates movements; it clears up confusion; it dissipates compact groupings of individuals wandering about the country in unpredictable ways; it establishes calculated distributions. It must also master all the forces that are formed from the very constitution of an organized multiplicity; it must neutralize the effects of counter-power that spring from them and which form a resistance to the power that wishes to dominate it: agitations, revolts, spontaneous organizations, coalitions—anything that may establish horizontal conjunctions. Hence the fact that the disciplines use procedures of partitioning and verticality, that they introduce, between the different elements at the same level, as solid separations as possible, that they define compact hierarchical networks, in short, that they oppose to the intrinsic, adverse force of multiplicity the technique of the continuous, individualizing pyramid. They must also increase the particular utility of each element of the multiplicity, but by means that

---

1   *corvées*   [editors' note] Days of labor unpaid, or replacing taxes, required by local government authority.

2   *press-ganging*   [editors' note] Forcing men into service (primarily military).

are the most rapid and the least costly, that is to say, by using the multiplicity itself as an instrument of this growth. Hence, in order to extract from bodies the maximum time and force, the use of those overall methods known as time-tables, collective training, exercises, total and detailed surveillance. Furthermore, the disciplines must increase the effect of utility proper to the multiplicities, so that each is made more useful than the simple sum of its elements: it is in order to increase the utilizable effects of the multiple that the disciplines define tactics of distribution, reciprocal adjustment of bodies, gestures and rhythms, differentiation of capacities, reciprocal coordination in relation to apparatuses or tasks. Lastly, the disciplines have to bring into play the power relations, not above but inside the very texture of the multiplicity, as discreetly as possible, as well articulated on the other functions of these multiplicities and also in the least expensive way possible: to this correspond anonymous instruments of power, coextensive with the multiplicity that they regiment, such as hierarchical surveillance, continuous registration, perpetual assessment and classification. In short, to substitute for a power that is manifested through the brilliance of those who exercise it, a power that insidiously objectifies those on whom it is applied; to form a body of knowledge about these individuals, rather than to deploy the ostentatious signs of sovereignty. In a word, the disciplines are the ensemble of minute technical inventions that made it possible to increase the useful size of multiplicities by decreasing the inconveniences of the power which, in order to make them useful, must control them. A multiplicity, whether in a workshop or a nation, an army or a school, reaches the threshold of a discipline when the relation of the one to the other becomes favorable.

If the economic take-off of the West began with the techniques that made possible the accumulation of capital, it might perhaps be said that the methods for administering the accumulation of men made possible a political take-off in relation to the traditional, ritual, costly, violent forms of power, which soon fell into disuse and were superseded by a subtle, calculated technology of subjection. In fact, the two processes—the accumulation of men and the accumulation of capital—cannot be separated; it would not have been possible to solve the problem of the accumulation of men without the growth of an apparatus of production capable of both sustaining them and using them; conversely, the techniques that made the cumulative multiplicity of men useful accelerated the accumulation of capital. At a less general level, the technological mutations of the apparatus of production, the division of labor and the elaboration of the disciplinary techniques sustained an ensemble of very close relations.[1] Each makes the other possible and necessary; each provides a model for the other. The disciplinary pyramid constituted the small cell of power within which the separation, coordination and supervision of tasks was imposed and made efficient; and analytical partitioning of time, gestures and bodily forces constituted an operational schema that could easily be transferred from the groups to be subjected to the mechanisms of production; the massive projection of military methods onto industrial organization was an example of this modeling of the division of labor following the model laid down by the schemata of power. But, on the other hand, the technical analysis of the process of production, its "mechanical" breaking-down, were projected onto the labor force whose task it was to implement it: the constitution of those disciplinary machines in which the individual forces that they bring together are composed into a whole and therefore increased is the effect of this projection. Let us say that discipline is the unitary technique by which the body is reduced as a "political" force at the least cost and maximized as a useful force. The growth of a capitalist economy gave rise to the specific modality of disciplinary power, whose general formulas, techniques of submitting forces and bodies, in short, "political anatomy," could be operated in the most diverse political regimes, apparatuses or institutions.

2. The panoptic modality of power—at the elementary, technical, merely physical level at which it is situated—is not under the immediate dependence or a direct extension of the great juridico-political structures of a society; it is nonetheless not absolutely independent. Historically, the process by which the bourgeoisie became in the course of the eighteenth century the politically dominant class was masked by the establishment of an explicit, coded and formally egalitarian juridical framework, made possible by the organization of a parliamentary, representative regime. But the development and generalization of disciplinary mechanisms constituted the other, dark side of these processes. The general juridical form that guaranteed a system of rights that were egalitarian in principle was supported by these tiny, everyday, physical mechanisms, by all those systems of micro-power that are essentially non-egalitarian and

asymmetrical that we call the disciplines. And although, in a formal way, the representative regime makes it possible, directly or indirectly, with or without relays, for the will of all to form the fundamental authority of sovereignty, the disciplines provide, at the base, a guarantee of the submission of forces and bodies. The real, corporal disciplines constituted the foundation of the formal, juridical liberties. The contract may have been regarded as the ideal foundation of law and political power; panopticism constituted the technique, universally widespread, of coercion. It continued to work in depth on the juridical structures of society, in order to make the effective mechanisms of power function in opposition to the formal framework that is had acquired. The "Enlightenment," which discovered the liberties, also invented the disciplines.

In appearance, the disciplines constitute nothing more than an infra-law. They seem to extend the general forms defined by law to the infinitesimal level of individual lives; or they appear as methods of training that enable individuals to become integrated into these general demands. They seem to constitute the same type of law on a different scale, thereby making it more meticulous and more indulgent. The disciplines should be regarded as a sort of counter-law. They have the precise role of introducing insuperable asymmetries and excluding reciprocities. First, because discipline creates between individuals a "private" link, which is a relation of constraints entirely different from contractual obligation; the acceptance of a discipline may be underwritten by contract; the way in which it is imposed, the mechanisms it brings into play, the non-reversible subordination of one group of people by another, the "surplus" power that is always fixed on the same side, the inequality of position of the different "partners" in relation to the common regulation, all these distinguish the disciplinary link from the contractual link, and make it possible to distort the contractual link systematically from the moment it has as its content a mechanism of discipline. We know, for example, how many real procedures undermine the legal fiction of the work contract: workshop discipline is not the least important. Moreover, whereas the juridical systems define juridical subjects according to universal norms, the disciplines characterize, classify, specialize; they distribute along a scale, around a norm, hierarchize individuals in relation to one another and, if necessary, disqualify and invalidate. In any case, in the space and during the time in which they exercise their control and bring into play the asymmetries of their power, they effect a suspension of the law that is never total, but is

---

1   *the technological mutations ... close relations*   Cf. Marx, *Capital*, vol. 1, chapter XIII and the very interesting analysis in François Guery and Didier Deleule, *Le Corps productif* (Paris: Mame, 1973).

never annulled either. Regular and institutional as it may be, the discipline, in its mechanism, is a "counter-law." And, although the universal juridicism of modern society seems to fix limits on the exercise of power, its universally widespread panopticism enables it to operate, on the underside of the law, a machinery that is both immense and minute, which supports, reinforces, multiplies the asymmetry of power and undermines the limits that are traced around the law. The minute disciplines, the panopticisms of every day may well be below the level of emergence of the great apparatuses and the great political struggles. But, in the genealogy of modern society, they have been, with the class domination that traverses it, the political counterpart of the juridical norms according to which power was redistributed. Hence, no doubt, the importance that has been given for so long to the small techniques of discipline, to those apparently insignificant tricks that it has invented, and even to those "sciences" that give it a respectable face; hence the fear of abandoning them if one cannot find any substitute; hence the affirmation that they are at the very foundation of society, and an element in its equilibrium, whereas they are a series of mechanisms for unbalancing power relations definitively and everywhere; hence the persistence in regarding them as the humble, but concrete form of every morality, whereas they are a set of physico-political techniques.

To return to the problem of legal punishments, the prison with all the corrective technology at its disposal is to be resituated at the point where the codified power to punish turns into a disciplinary power to observe; at the point where the universal punishments of the law are applied selectively to certain individuals and always the same ones; at the point where the redefinition of the juridical subject by the penalty becomes a useful training of the criminal; at the point where the law is inverted and passes outside itself, and where the counter-law becomes the effective and institutionalized content of the juridical forms. What generalizes the power to punish, then, is not the universal consciousness of the law in each juridical subject; it is the regular extension, the infinitely minute web of panoptic techniques.

3. Taken one by one, most of these techniques have a long history behind them. But what was new, in the eighteenth century, was that, by being combined and generalized, they attained a level at which the formation of knowledge and the increase of power regularly reinforce one another in a circular process. At this point, the disciplines crossed the "technological" threshold. First the hospital, then the school,

then, later, the workshop were not simply "reordered" by the disciplines; they became, thanks to them, apparatuses such that any mechanism of objectification could be used in them as an instrument of subjection, and any growth of power could give rise in them to possible branches of knowledge; it was this link, proper to the technological systems, that made possible within the disciplinary element the formation of clinical medicine, psychiatry, child psychology, educational psychology, the rationalization of labor. It is a double process, then: an epistemological "thaw" through a refinement of power relations; a multiplication of the effects of power through the formation and accumulation of new forms of knowledge.

The extension of the disciplinary methods is inscribed in a broad historical process: the development at about the same time of many other technologies—agronomical, industrial, economic. But it must be recognized that, compared with the mining industries, the emerging chemical industries or methods of national accountancy, compared with the blast furnaces or the steam engine, panopticism has received little attention. It is regarded as not much more than a bizarre little utopia, a perverse dream—rather as though Bentham had been the Fourier of a police society, and the Phalanstery[1] had taken on the form of the Panopticon. And yet this represented the abstract formula of a very real technology, that of individuals. There were many reasons why it received little praise; the most obvious is that the discourses to which it gave rise rarely acquired, except in the academic classifications, the status of sciences; but the real reason is no doubt that the power that it operates and which it augments is a direct, physical power that men exercise upon one another. An inglorious culmination had an origin that could be only grudgingly acknowledged. But it would be unjust to compare the disciplinary techniques with such inventions as the steam engine or Amici's microscope.[2] They are much less; and yet, in a way, they are much more. If a historical equivalent or as least a point of comparison had to be found for them, it would be rather in the "inquisitorial" technique.

---

1   *Fourier ... Phalanstery* [editors' note] Charles Fourier (1772–1837), was a French philosopher and socialist, known for his social theories and his proposals for utopian communes which he called Phalansteries.

2   *Amici's microscope* [editors' note] Giovanni Battista Amici, (1786–1868), Italian astronomer and optical instrument designer who built some innovative microscopes c. 1850.

The eighteenth century invented the techniques of discipline and the examination, rather as the Middle Ages invented the judicial investigation. But it did so by quite different means. The investigation procedure, an old fiscal and administrative technique, had developed above all with the reorganization of the Church and the increase of the princely states in the twelfth and thirteenth centuries. At this time it permeated to a very large degree the jurisprudence first of the ecclesiastical courts, then of the lay courts. The investigation as an authoritarian search for a truth observed or attested was thus opposed to the old procedures of the oath, the ordeal,[1] the judicial duel, the judgment of God or even of the transaction between private individuals. The investigation was the sovereign power arrogating to itself the right to establish the truth by a number of regulated techniques. Now, although the investigation has since then been an integral part of western justice (even up to our own day), one must not forget either its political origin, its link with the birth of the states and of monarchical sovereignty, or its later extension and its role in the formation of knowledge. In fact, the investigation has been the no doubt crude, but fundamental element in the constitution of the empirical sciences; it has been the juridico-political matrix of this experimental knowledge, which, as we know, was very rapidly released as the end of the Middle Ages. It is perhaps true to say that, in Greece, mathematics were born from techniques of measurement; the sciences of nature, in any case, were born, to some extent, at the end of the Middle Ages, from the practices of investigation. The great empirical knowledge that covered the things of the world and transcribed them into the ordering of an indefinite discourse that observes, describes and establishes the "facts" (at a time when the western world was beginning the economic and political conquest of this same world) had its operating model no doubt in the Inquisition—that immense invention that our recent mildness has placed in the dark recesses of our memory. Bus what this politico-juridical, administrative and criminal, religious and lay, investigation was to the sciences of nature, disciplinary analysis has been to the sciences of man. These sciences, which have so delighted our "humanity" for over a century, have their technical matrix in the petty, malicious minutiae of the disciplines and their investigations. These investigations are perhaps to psychology, psychiatry, pedagogy, criminology, and so many other strange sciences, what the terrible power of investigation was to the calm knowledge of the animals, the plants or the earth. Another power, another knowledge. On the threshold of the classical age, Bacon,[2] lawyer and statesman, tried to develop a methodology of investigation for the empirical sciences. What Great Observer will produce the methodology of examination for the human sciences? Unless, of course, such a thing is not possible. For, although it is true that, in becoming a technique for the empirical sciences, the investigation has detached itself from the inquisitorial procedure, in which is was historically rooted, the examination has remained extremely close to the disciplinary power that shaped it. It has always been and still is an intrinsic element of the disciplines. Of course it seems to have undergone a speculative purification by integrating itself with such sciences as psychology and psychiatry. And, in effect, its appearance in the form of tests, interviews, interrogations and consultations is apparently in order to rectify the mechanisms of discipline: educational psychology is supposed to correct the rigors of the school, just as the medical or psychiatric interview is supposed to rectify the effects of the discipline of work. But we must not be misled; these techniques merely refer individuals from one disciplinary authority to another, and they reproduce, in a concentrated or formalized form, the schema of power-knowledge proper to each discipline.[3] The great investigation that gave rise to the sciences of nature has become detached from its politico-juridical model; the examination, on the other hand, is still caught up in disciplinary technology.

In the Middle Ages, the procedure of investigation gradually superseded the old accusatory justice, by a process initiated from above; the disciplinary technique, on the other hand, insidiously and as if from below, has invaded a penal justice that is still, in principle, inquisitorial. All the great movements of extension that characterize modern penality—the problematization of the criminal behind his crime, the concern with a punishment that is a correction, a therapy, a normalization, the division of the act of judgment between various authorities that are supposed to

---

1   *the ordeal*   Trial by ordeal was a judicial procedure which subjected the suspect to a difficult task or painful procedure—often burning or near-drowning. Suspects who emerged unscathed were judged innocent. This procedure has ancient roots; its use declined during the late middle ages, largely replaced by torture to extract confessions.

2   *Bacon*   [editors' note] Francis Bacon (1561–1626) was an English statesman and philosopher whose ideas are associated with the growth of empiricism marking the scientific revolution.

3   *these techniques ... each discipline*   [editors' note] On this subject, cf. Michel Tort, *Le quotient intellectual* (Paris: F. Maspero, 1974).

measure, assess, diagnose, cure, transform individuals—all this betrays the penetration of the disciplinary examination into the judicial inquisition.

What is now imposed on penal justice as its point of application, its "useful" object, will no longer be the body of the guilty man set up against the body of the king; nor will it be the juridical subject of an ideal contract; it will be the disciplinary individual. The extreme point of penal justice under the *Ancien Régime* was the infinite segmentation of the body of the regicide: a manifestation of the strongest power over the body of the greatest criminal, whose total destruction made the crime explode into its truth. The ideal point of penality today would be an indefinite discipline: an interrogation without end, an investigation that would be extended without limit to a meticulous and ever more analytical observation, a judgment that would at the same time be the constitution of a file that was never closed, the calculated leniency of a penalty that would be interlaced with the ruthless curiosity of an examination, a procedure that would be at the same time the permanent measure of a gap in relation to an inaccessible norm and the asymptotic movement that strives to meet in infinity. The public execution was the logical culmination of a procedure governed by the Inquisition. The practice of placing individuals under "observation" is a natural extension of a justice imbued with disciplinary methods and examination procedures. Is it surprising that the cellular prison, with its regular chronologies, forced labor, its authorities of surveillance and registration, its experts in normality, who continue and multiply the functions of the judge, should have become the modern instrument of penality? Is it surprising that prisons resemble factories, schools, barracks, hospitals, which all resemble prisons?

◆ ◆ ◆ ◆ ◆

Two Lectures (1976)

Lecture One: 7 January 1976

I have wanted to speak to you of my desire to be finished with, and to somehow terminate a series of researches that have been our concern for some four or five years now, in effect, from the date of my arrival here, and which, I am well aware, have met with increasing difficulties, both for you and for myself. Though these researches were very closely related to each other, they have failed to develop into any continuous or coherent whole. They are fragmentary researches, none of which in the last analysis can be said to have proved definitive, nor even to have led anywhere. Diffused and at the same time repetitive, they have continually re-trod the same ground, invoked the same themes, the same concepts, etc.

You will recall my work here, such as it has been: some brief notes on the history of penal procedure, a chapter or so on the evolution and institutionalization of psychiatry in the nineteenth century, some observations on sophistry, on Greek money, on the medieval Inquisition. I have sketched a history of sexuality or at least a history of knowledge of sexuality on the basis of the confessional practice of the seventeenth century or the forms of control of infantile sexuality in the eighteenth to nineteenth century. I have sketched a genealogical history of the origins of a theory and a knowledge of anomaly and of the various techniques that relate to it. None of it does more than mark time. Repetitive and disconnected, it advances nowhere. Since indeed it never ceases to say the same thing, it perhaps says nothing. It is tangled up into an indecipherable, disorganized muddle. In a nutshell, it is inconclusive.

Still, I could claim that after all these were only trails to be followed, it mattered little where they led; indeed, it was important that they did not have a predetermined starting point and destination. They were merely lines laid down for you to pursue or to divert elsewhere, for me to extend upon or re-design as the case might be. They are, in the final analysis, just fragments, and it is up to you or me to see what we can make of them. For my part, it has struck me that I might have seemed a bit like a whale that leaps to the surface of the water disturbing it momentarily with a tiny jet of spray and lets it be believed, or pretends to believe, or wants to believe, or himself does in fact indeed believe, that down in the depths where no one sees him any more, where he is no longer witnessed nor controlled by anyone, he follows a more profound, coherent and reasoned trajectory. Well, anyway, that was more or less how I at least conceived the situation; it could be that you perceived it differently.

After all, the fact that the character of the work I have presented to you has been at the same time fragmentary, repetitive and discontinuous could well be a reflection of something one might describe as a febrile indolence—a typical affliction of those enamored of libraries, documents, reference works, dusty tomes, texts that are never read, books that are no sooner printed than they are consigned to the shelves of libraries where they thereafter lie dormant to be taken up only some centuries later. It would accord all too well with the busy inertia of those who profess an idle knowledge, a species of luxuriant sagacity, the rich hoard of the *parvenus* whose only outward signs are displayed in footnotes at the bottom of the page. It would accord with all those who feel themselves to be associates of one of the more ancient or more typical secret societies of the West, those oddly indestructible societies unknown it would seem to Antiquity, which came into being with Christianity, most likely at the time of the first monasteries, at the periphery of the invasions, the fires and the forests: I mean to speak of the great warm and tender Freemasonry[1] of useless erudition.

However, it is not simply a taste for such Freemasonry that has inspired my course of action. It seems to me that the work we have done could be justified by the claim that it is adequate to a restricted period, that of the last ten, fifteen, at most twenty years, a period notable for two events which for all they may not be really important are nonetheless to my mind quite interesting.

On the one hand, it has been a period characterized by what one might term the efficacy of dispersed and discontinuous offensives. There are a number of things I have in mind here. I am thinking, for example, where it was a case of undermining the function of psychiatric institutions, of that curious efficacy of localized anti-psychiatric discourses. These are discourses which you are well aware lacked and still lack any systematic principles of coordination of the kind that would have provided or might today provide a system of reference for them. I am thinking of the original reference towards existential analysis or of certain directions inspired in a general way by Marxism, such as Reichian theory.[2] Again, I have in mind that strange efficacy of the attacks that have been directed against traditional morality and hierarchy, attacks which again have no reference except perhaps in a vague and fairly distant way to Reich and Mar-

cuse.[3] On the other hand there is also the efficacy of the attacks upon the legal and penal system, some of which had a very tenuous connection with the general and in any case pretty dubious notion of class justice, while others had a rather more precisely defined affinity with anarchist themes. Equally, I am thinking of the efficacy of a book such as *L'Anti-Oedipe*,[4] which really has no other source of reference than its own prodigious theoretical inventiveness: a book, or rather a thing, an event, which has managed, even at the most mundane level of psychoanalytic practice, to introduce a note of shrillness into that murmured exchange that has for so long continued uninterrupted between couch and armchair.

I would say, then, that what has emerged in the course of the last ten or fifteen years is a sense of the increasing vulnerability to criticism of things, institutions, practices, discourses. A certain fragility has been discovered in the very bedrock of existence—even, and perhaps above all, in those aspects of it that are most familiar, most solid and most intimately related to our bodies and to our everyday behavior. But together with this sense of instability and this amazing efficacy of discontinuous, particular and local criticism, one in fact also discovers something that perhaps was not initially foreseen, something one might describe as precisely the inhibiting effect of global, *totalitarian theories*. It is not that these global theories have not provided nor continue to provide in a fairly consistent fashion useful tools for local research: Marxism and psychoanalysis are proofs of this. But I believe these tools have only been provided on the condition that the theoretical unity of these discourses was in some sense put in abeyance, or at least curtailed, divided, overthrown, caricatured, theatrical zed, or what you will. In each case, the attempt to think in terms of a totality has in fact proved a hindrance to research.

So, the main point to be gleaned from these events of the last fifteen years, their predominant feature, is the *local* character of criticism. That should not, I believe, be taken to mean that its qualities are those of an obtuse, naive or

---

1   *Freemasonry*   [Unless otherwise indicated, all notes to this section are by the editors of this anthology.] The Freemasons (usually known simply as "Masons") are a fraternal organization dating back perhaps to the sixteenth century, with millions of members, and secret rites and symbols. Foucault is using the term figuratively.

2   *Reichian theory*   Psychoanalytic theory based on Freud, developed by Wilhelm Reich (1897–1957), an Austrian-American psychiatrist. At one point, influenced by Marx, Reich argued that the root cause of neurosis was the morality—the result of the economic structure—of bourgeois society.

3   *Marcuse*   Herbert Marcuse (1898–1979), German-American philosopher, a leading radical leftist critic of the social order and friend of the "new left" student rebellions of the 1960s.

4   *L'Anti-Oedipe*   (English title: *Anti-Œdipus: Capitalism and Schizophrenia*), 1972 book by the French philosopher Gilles Deleuze and psychoanalyst Félix Guattari. Influenced by Freud, Marx, and Nietzsche, it combines psychological, economic, and historical analysis, giving an economic/political analysis of desire as expressed or repressed under western capitalism.

primitive empiricism; nor is it a soggy eclecticism, an opportunism that laps up any and every kind of theoretical approach; nor does it mean a self-imposed ascetism which taken by itself would reduce to the worst kind of theoretical impoverishment. I believe that what this essentially local character of criticism indicates in reality is an autonomous, non-centralized kind of theoretical production, one that is to say whose validity is not dependent on the approval of the established regimes of thought.

It is here that we touch upon another feature of these events that has been manifest for some time now: it seems to me that this local criticism has proceeded by means of what one might term "a return of knowledge." What I mean by that phrase is this: it is a fact that we have repeatedly encountered, at least at a superficial level, in the course of most recent times, an entire thematic to the effect that it is not theory but life that matters, not knowledge but reality, not books but money etc.; but it also seems to me that over and above, and arising out of this thematic, there is something else to which we are witness, and which we might describe as an *insurrection of subjugated knowledges*.

By subjugated knowledges I mean two things: on the one hand, I am referring to the historical contents that have been buried and disguised in a functionalist coherence or formal systemization. Concretely, it is not a semiology[1] of the life of the asylum, it is not even a sociology of delinquency, that has made it possible to produce an effective criticism of the asylum and likewise of the prison, but rather the immediate emergence of historical contents. And this is simply because only the historical contents allow us to rediscover the ruptural effects of conflict and struggle that the order imposed by functionalist or systematizing thought is designed to mask. Subjugated knowledges are thus those blocs of historical knowledge which were present but disguised within the body of functionalist and systematizing theory and which criticism—which obviously draws upon scholarship—has been able to reveal.

On the other hand, I believe that by subjugated knowledges one should understand something else, something which in a sense is altogether different, namely, a whole set of knowledges that have been disqualified as inadequate to their task or insufficiently elaborated: naive knowledges, located low down on the hierarchy, beneath the required level of cognition or scientificity. I also believe that it is through the re-emergence of these low-ranking knowledges, these

unqualified, even directly disqualified knowledges (such as that of the psychiatric patient, of the ill person, of the nurse, of the doctor—parallel and marginal as they are to the knowledge of medicine—that of the delinquent etc.), and which involve what I would call a popular knowledge (*le savoir des gens*) though it is far from being a general commonsense knowledge, but is on the contrary a particular, local, regional knowledge, a differential knowledge incapable of unanimity and which owes its force only to the harshness with which it is opposed by everything surrounding it—that it is through the re-appearance of this knowledge, of these local popular knowledges, these disqualified knowledges, that criticism performs its work.

However, there is a strange kind of paradox in the desire to assign to this same category of subjugated knowledges what are on the one hand the products of meticulous, erudite, exact historical knowledge, and on the other hand local and specific knowledges which have no common meaning and which are in some fashion allowed to fall into disuse whenever they are not effectively and explicitly maintained in themselves. Well, it seems to me that our critical discourses of the last fifteen years have in effect discovered their essential force in this association between the buried knowledges of erudition and those disqualified from the hierarchy of knowledges and sciences.

In the two cases—in the case of the erudite as in that of the disqualified knowledges—with what in fact were these buried, subjugated knowledges really concerned? They were concerned with a *historical knowledge of struggles*. In the specialized areas of erudition as in the disqualified, popular knowledge there lay the memory of hostile encounters which even up to this day have been confined to the margins of knowledge.

What emerges out of this is something one might call a genealogy, or rather a multiplicity of genealogical researches, a painstaking rediscovery of struggles together with the rude memory of their conflicts. And these genealogies, that are the combined product of an erudite knowledge and a popular knowledge, were not possible and could not even have been attempted except on one condition, namely that the tyranny of globalizing discourses with their hierarchy and all their privileges of a theoretical *avant-garde* was eliminated.

Let us give the term *genealogy* to the union of erudite knowledge and local memories which allows us to establish a historical knowledge of struggles and to make use of this knowledge tactically today. This then will be a provisional

---

1   *semiology* The science of signs.

definition of the genealogies which I have attempted to compile with you over the last few years.

You are well aware that this research activity, which one can thus call genealogical, has nothing at all to do with an opposition between the abstract unity of theory and the concrete multiplicity of facts. It has nothing at all to do with a disqualification of the speculative dimension which opposes to it, in the name of some kind of scientism, the rigor of well established knowledges. It is not therefore via an empiricism that the genealogical project unfolds, nor even via a positivism[1] in the ordinary sense of that term. What it really does is to entertain the claims to attention of local, discontinuous, disqualified, illegitimate knowledges against the claims of a unitary body of theory which would filter, hierarchize and order them in the name of some true knowledge and some arbitrary idea of what constitutes a science and its objects. Genealogies are therefore not positivistic returns to a more careful or exact form of science. They are precisely anti-sciences. Not that they vindicate a lyrical right to ignorance or non-knowledge: it is not that they are concerned to deny knowledge or that they esteem the virtues of direct cognition and base their practice upon an immediate experience that escapes encapsulation in knowledge. It is not that with which we are concerned. We are concerned, rather, with the insurrection of knowledges that are opposed primarily not to the contents, methods or concepts of a science, but to the effects of the centralizing powers which are linked to the institution and functioning of an organized scientific discourse within a society such as ours. Nor does it basically matter all that much that this institutionalization of scientific discourse is embodied in a university, or, more generally, in an educational apparatus, in a theoretical-commercial institution such as psychoanalysis or within the framework of reference that is provided by a political system such as Marxism; for it is really against the effects of the power of a discourse that is considered to be scientific that the genealogy must wage its struggle.

To be more precise, I would remind you how numerous have been those who for many years now, probably for more than half a century, have questioned whether Marxism was, or was not, a science. One might say that the same issue has been posed, and continues to be posed, in the case of psychoanalysis, or even worse, in that of the semiology of literary texts. But to all these demands of: "Is it or is it not a science?" the genealogies or the genealogists would reply: "If you really want to know, the fault lies in your very determination to make a science out of Marxism or psychoanalysis or this or that study." If we have any objection against Marxism, it lies in the fact that it could effectively be a science. In more detailed terms, I would say that even before we can know the extent to which something such as Marxism or psychoanalysis can be compared to a scientific practice in its everyday functioning, its rules of construction, its working concepts, that even before we can pose the question of a formal and structural analogy between Marxist or psychoanalytic discourse, it is surely necessary to question ourselves about our aspirations to the kind of power that is presumed to accompany such a science. It is surely the following kinds of question that would need to be posed: What types of knowledge do you want to disqualify in the very instant of your demand: "Is it a science"? Which speaking, discoursing subjects—which subjects of experience and knowledge—do you then want to "diminish" when you say: "I who conduct this discourse am conducting a scientific discourse, and I am a scientist"? Which theoretical-political *avant garde* do you want to enthrone in order to isolate it from all the discontinuous forms of knowledge that circulate about it? When I see you straining to establish the scientificity of Marxism I do not really think that you are demonstrating once and for all that Marxism has a rational structure and that therefore its propositions are the outcome of verifiable procedures; for me you are doing something altogether different, you are investing Marxist discourses and those who uphold them with the effects of a power which the West since Medieval times has attributed to science and has reserved for those engaged in scientific discourse.

By comparison, then, and in contrast to the various projects which aim to inscribe knowledges in the hierarchical order of power associated with science, a genealogy should be seen as a kind of attempt to emancipate historical knowledges from that subjection, to render them, that is, capable of opposition and of struggle against the coercion of a theoretical, unitary, formal and scientific discourse. It is based on a reactivation of local knowledges—of minor knowledges, as Deleuze might call them—in opposition to the scientific hierarchization of knowledges and the effects intrinsic to their power: this, then, is the project of these disordered and fragmentary genealogies. If we were

---

1   *empiricism ... positivism*   Empiricism is the position that all genuine knowledge derives from sense-experience. The word "positivism" is used in a variety of ways, but in the most basic one, the one Foucault probably intends to here, it means the position that the only genuine source of knowledge is science.

to characterize it in two terms, then "archaeology" would be the appropriate methodology of this analysis of local discursivities, and "genealogy" would be the tactics whereby, on the basis of the descriptions of these local discursivities, the subjected knowledges which were thus released would be brought into play.

So much can be said by way of establishing the nature of the project as a whole. I would have you consider all these fragments of research, all these discourses, which are simultaneously both superimposed and discontinuous, which I have continued obstinately to pursue for some four or five years now, as elements of these genealogies which have been composed—and by no means by myself alone—in the course of the last fifteen years. At this point, however, a problem arises, and a question: why not continue to pursue a theory which in its discontinuity is so attractive and plausible, albeit so little verifiable? Why not continue to settle upon some aspect of psychiatry or of the theory of sexuality etc.? It is true, one could continue (and in a certain sense I shall try to do so) if it were not for a certain number of changes in the current situation. By this I mean that it could be that in the course of the last five, ten or even fifteen years, things have assumed a different complexion—the contest could be said to present a different physiognomy. Is the relation of forces today still such as to allow these disinterred knowledges some kind of autonomous life? Can they be isolated by these means from every subjugating relationship? What force do they have taken in themselves? And, after all, is it not perhaps the case that these fragments of genealogies are no sooner brought to light, that the particular elements of the knowledge that one seeks to disinter are no sooner accredited and put into circulation, than they run the risk of re-codification, re-colonization? In fact, those unitary discourses, which first disqualified and then ignored them when they made their appearance, are, it seems, quite ready now to annex them, to take them back within the fold of their own discourse and to invest them with everything this implies in terms of their effects of knowledge and power. And if we want to protect these only lately liberated fragments are we not in danger of ourselves constructing, with our own hands, that unitary discourse to which we are invited, perhaps to lure us into a trap, by those who say to us: "All this is fine, but where are you heading? What kind of unity are you after?" The temptation, up to a certain point, is to reply: "Well, we just go on, in a cumulative fashion; after all, the moment at which we risk colonization has not yet arrived."

One could even attempt to throw out a challenge: "Just try to colonize us then!" Or one might say, for example, "Has there been, from the time when anti-psychiatry or the genealogy of psychiatric institutions were launched—and it is now a good fifteen years ago—a single Marxist, or a single psychiatrist, who has gone over the same ground in his own terms and shown that these genealogies that we produced were false, inadequately elaborated, poorly articulated and ill-founded?" In fact, as things stand in reality, these collected fragments of a genealogy remain as they have always been, surrounded by a prudent silence. At most, the only arguments that we have heard against them have been of the kind I believe were voiced by Monsieur Juquin:[1] "All this is all very well, but Soviet psychiatry nonetheless remains the foremost in the world." To which I would reply: "How right you are; Soviet psychiatry is indeed the foremost in the world and it is precisely that which one would hold against it."

The silence, or rather the prudence, with which the unitary theories avoid the genealogy of knowledges might therefore be a good reason to continue to pursue it. Then at least one could proceed to multiply the genealogical fragments in the form of so many traps, demands, challenges, what you will. But in the long run, it is probably over-optimistic, if we are thinking in terms of a contest—that of knowledge against the effects of the power of scientific discourse—to regard the silence of one's adversaries as indicative of a fear we have inspired in them. For perhaps the silence of the enemy—and here at the very least we have a methodological or tactical principle that it is always useful to bear in mind—can also be the index of our failure to produce any such fear at all. At all events, we must proceed just as if we had not alarmed them at all, in which case it will be no part of our concern to provide a solid and homogeneous theoretical terrain for all these dispersed genealogies, nor to descend upon them from on high with some kind of halo of theory that would unite them. Our task, on the contrary, will be to expose and specify the issue at stake in this opposition, this struggle, this insurrection of knowledges against the institutions and against effects of the knowledge and power that invests scientific discourse.

What is at stake in all these genealogies is the nature of this power which has surged into view in all its violence, aggression and absurdity in the course of the last forty years,

---

1   *Monsieur Juquin*   Pierre Juquin (1930–), a deputy of the French Communist Party.

contemporaneously, that is, with the collapse of Fascism and the decline of Stalinism. What, we must ask, is this power—or rather, since that is to give a formulation to the question that invites the kind of theoretical coronation of the whole which I am so keen to avoid—what are these various contrivances of power, whose operations extend to such differing levels and sectors of society and are possessed of such manifold ramifications? What are their mechanisms, their effects and their relations? The issue here can, I believe, be crystallized essentially in the following question: is the analysis of power or of powers to be deduced in one way or another from the economy? Let me make this question and my reasons for posing it somewhat clearer. It is not at all my intention to abstract from what are innumerable and enormous differences; yet despite, and even because of these differences, I consider there to be a certain point in common between the juridical, and let us call it, liberal, conception of political power (found in the *philosophes*[1] of the eighteenth century) and the Marxist conception, or at any rate a certain conception currently held to be Marxist. I would call this common point an economism in the theory of power. By that I mean that in the case of the classic, juridical theory, power is taken to be a right, which one is able to possess like a commodity, and which one can in consequence transfer or alienate, either wholly or partially, through a legal act or through some act that establishes a right, such as takes place through cession or contract. Power is that concrete power which every individual holds, and whose partial or total cession enables political power or sovereignty to be established. This theoretical construction is essentially based on the idea that the constitution of political power obeys the model of a legal transaction involving a contractual type of exchange (hence the clear analogy that runs through all these theories between power and commodities, power and wealth). In the other case—I am thinking here of the general Marxist conception of power—one finds none of all that. Nonetheless, there is something else inherent in this latter conception, something which one might term an eco-

nomic functionality of power. This economic functionality is present to the extent that power is conceived primarily in terms of the role it plays in the maintenance simultaneously of the relations of production and of a class domination which the development and specific forms of the forces of production have rendered possible. On this view, then, the historical *raison d'être* of political power is to be found in the economy. Broadly speaking, in the first case we have a political power whose formal model is discoverable in the process of exchange, the economic circulation of commodities; in the second case, the historical *raison d'être* of political power and the principle of its concrete forms and actual functioning, is located in the economy. Well then, the problem involved in the researches to which I refer can, I believe, be broken down in the following manner: in the first place, is power always in a subordinate position relative to the economy? Is it always in the service of, and ultimately answerable to, the economy? Is its essential end and purpose to serve the economy? Is it destined to realize, consolidate, maintain and reproduce the relations appropriate to the economy and essential to its functioning? In the second place, is power modeled upon the commodity? Is it something that one possesses, acquires, cedes through force or contract, that one alienates or recovers, that circulates, that voids this or that region? Or, on the contrary, do we need to employ varying tools in its analysis—even, that is, when we allow that it effectively remains the case that the relations of power do indeed remain profoundly enmeshed in and with economic relations and participate with them in a common circuit? If that is the case, it is not the models of functional subordination or formal isomorphism that will characterize the interconnection between politics and the economy. Their indissolubility will be of a different order, one that it will be our task to determine.

What means are available to us today if we seek to conduct a non-economic analysis of power? Very few, I believe. We have in the first place the assertion that power is neither given, nor exchanged, nor recovered, but rather exercised, and that it only exists in action. Again, we have at our disposal another assertion to the effect that power is not primarily the maintenance and reproduction of economic relations, but is above all a relation of force. The questions to be posed would then be these: if power is exercised, what sort of exercise does it involve? In what does it consist? What is its mechanism? There is an immediate answer that many contemporary analyses would appear to offer: power is essentially that which represses. Power represses nature,

1 *philosophes* A group of intellectuals that flourished during the mid-eighteenth century associated with the French Enlightenment (notably Diderot, Voltaire, Rousseau, and Montesquieu)—thus the explicit use of the French word to name them—but more loosely including thinkers in other countries, e.g., David Hume and Adam Smith in England. The central ideas for these thinkers were the ideas of progress: the perfectibility of humans and of systematized knowledge, and the rooting out of erroneous belief—often the tenets of organized religion.

the instincts, a class, individuals. Though one finds this definition of power as repression endlessly repeated in present day discourse, it is not that discourse which invented it—Hegel first spoke of it, then Freud and later Reich. In any case, it has become almost automatic in the parlance of the times to define power as an organ of repression. So should not the analysis of power be first and foremost an analysis of the mechanisms of repression?

Then again, there is a second reply we might make: if power is properly speaking the way in which relations of forces are deployed and given concrete expression, rather than analyzing it in terms of cession, contract or alienation, or functionally in terms of its maintenance of the relations of production, should we not analyze it primarily in terms of *struggle, conflict* and *war*? One would then confront the original hypothesis, according to which power is essentially repression, with a second hypothesis to the effect that power is war, a war continued by other means. This reversal of Clausewitz's[1] assertion that war is politics continued by other means has a triple significance: in the first place, it implies that the relations of power that function in a society such as ours essentially rest upon a definite relation of forces that is established at a determinate, historically specifiable moment, in war and by war. Furthermore, if it is true that political power puts an end to war, that it installs, or tries to install, the reign of peace in civil society, this by no means implies that it suspends the effects of war or neutralizes the disequilibrium revealed in the final battle. The role of political power, on this hypothesis, is perpetually to reinscribe this relation through a form of unspoken warfare; to re-inscribe it in social institutions, in economic inequalities, in language, in the bodies themselves of each and everyone of us.

So this would be the first meaning to assign to the inversion of Clausewitz's aphorism that war is politics continued by other means. It consists in seeing politics as sanctioning and upholding the disequilibrium of forces that was displayed in war. But there is also something else that the inversion signifies, namely, that none of the political struggles, the conflicts waged over power, with power, for power, the alterations in the relations of forces, the favoring of certain tendencies, the reinforcements etc., etc., that come about within this "civil peace"—that none of these phenomena in a political system should be interpreted ex-

cept as the continuation of war. They should, that is to say, be understood as episodes, factions and displacements in that same war. Even when one writes the history of peace and its institutions, it is always the history of this war that one is writing. The third, and final, meaning to be assigned to the inversion of Clausewitz's aphorism, is that the end result can only be the outcome of war, that is, of a contest of strength, to be decided in the last analyses by recourse to arms. The political battle would cease with this final battle. Only a final battle of that kind would put an end, once and for all, to the exercise of power as continual war.

So, no sooner do we attempt to liberate ourselves from economistic analyses of power, than two solid hypotheses offer themselves: the one argues that the mechanisms of power are those of repression. For convenience sake, I shall term this Reich's hypothesis. The other argues that the basis of the relationship of power lies in the hostile engagement of forces. Again for convenience, I shall call this Nietzsche's hypothesis.

These two hypotheses are not irreconcilable; they even seem to be linked in a fairly convincing manner. After all, repression could be seen as the political consequence of war, somewhat as oppression, in the classic theory of political right, was seen as the abuse of sovereignty in the juridical order.

One might thus contrast two major systems of approach to the analysis of power: in the first place, there is the old system as found in the *philosophes* of the eighteenth century. The conception of power as an original right that is given up in the establishment of sovereignty, and the contract, as matrix of political power, provide its points of articulation. A power so constituted risks becoming oppression whenever it over-extends itself, whenever—that is—it goes beyond the terms of the contract. Thus we have contract-power, with oppression as its limit, or rather as the transgression of this limit. In contrast, the other system of approach no longer tries to analyze political power according to the schema of contract-oppression, but in accordance with that of war-repression, and, at this point, repression no longer occupies the place that oppression occupies in relation to the contract, that is, it is not abuse, but is, on the contrary, the mere effect and continuation of a relation of domination. On this view, repression is none other than the realization, within the continual warfare of this pseudo-peace, of a perpetual relationship of force.

Thus we have two schemes for the analysis of power. The contract–oppression schema, which is the juridical one,

1   *Clausewitz's*   Carl von Clausewitz (1780–1831), Prussian soldier, military historian and theorist, famous for his work *Vom Kriege* (*On War*), (Berlin: Dummlers Verlag, 1832), containing the famous quotation Foucault mentions.

and the domination–repression or war–repression schema for which the pertinent opposition is not between the legitimate and illegitimate, as in the first schema, but between struggle and submission.

It is obvious that all my work in recent years has been couched in the schema of struggle–repression, and it is this—which I have hitherto been attempting to apply—which I have now been forced to reconsider, both because it is still insufficiently elaborated at a whole number of points, and because I believe that these two notions of repression and war must themselves be considerably modified if not ultimately abandoned. In any case, I believe that they must be submitted to closer scrutiny.

I have always been especially diffident of this notion of repression: it is precisely with reference to those genealogies of which I was speaking just now—of the history of penal right, of psychiatric power, of the control of infantile sexuality etc.—that I have tried to demonstrate to you the extent to which the mechanisms that were brought into operation in these power formations were something quite other, or in any case something much more, than repression. The need to investigate this notion of repression more thoroughly springs therefore from the impression I have that it is wholly inadequate to the analysis of the mechanisms and effects of power that it is so pervasively used to characterize today.

Lecture Two: 14 January 1976

The course of study that I have been following until now—roughly since 1970/71—has been concerned with the *how* of power. I have tried, that is, to relate its mechanisms to two points of reference, two limits: on the one hand, to the rules of right that provide a formal delimitation of power; on the other, to the effects of truth that this power produces and transmits, and which in their turn reproduce this power. Hence we have a triangle: power, right, truth.

Schematically, we can formulate the traditional question of political philosophy in the following terms: how is the discourse of truth, or quite simply, philosophy as that discourse which *par excellence* is concerned with truth, able to fix limits to the rights of power? That is the traditional question. The one I would prefer to pose is rather different. Compared to the traditional, noble and philosophic question it is much more down to earth and concrete. My problem is rather this: what rules of right are implemented by the relations of power in the production of discourses of truth? Or alternatively, what type of power is susceptible of producing discourses of truth that in a society such as ours are endowed with such potent effects? What I mean is this: in a society such as ours, but basically in any society, there are manifold relations of power which permeate, characterize and constitute the social body, and these relations of power cannot themselves be established, consolidated nor implemented without the production, accumulation, circulation and functioning of a discourse. There can be no possible exercise of power without a certain economy of discourses of truth which operates through and on the basis of this association. We are subjected to the production of truth through power and we cannot exercise power except through the production of truth. This is the case for every society, but I believe that in ours the relationship between power, right and truth is organized in a highly specific fashion. If I were to characterize, not its mechanism itself, but its intensity and constancy, I would say that we are forced to produce the truth of power that our society demands, of which it has need, in order to function: we *must* speak the truth; we are constrained or condemned to confess or to discover the truth. Power never ceases its interrogation, its inquisition, its registration of truth: it institutionalizes, professionalizes and rewards its pursuit. In the last analysis, we must produce truth as we must produce wealth, indeed we must produce truth in order to produce wealth in the first place. In another way, we are also subjected to truth in the sense in which it is truth that makes the laws, that produces the true discourse which, at least partially, decides, transmits and itself extends upon the effects of power. In the end, we are judged, condemned, classified, determined in our undertakings, destined to a certain mode of living or dying, as a function of the true discourses which are the bearers of the specific effects of power.

So, it is the rules of right, the mechanisms of power, the effects of truth or if you like, the rules of power and the powers of true discourses, that can be said more or less to have formed the general terrain of my concern, even if, as I know full well, I have traversed it only partially and in a very zig-zag fashion. I should like to speak briefly about this course of research, about what I have considered as being its guiding principle and about the methodological imperatives and precautions which I have sought to adopt. As regards the general principle involved in a study of the relations between right and power, it seems to me that in Western societies since Medieval times it has been royal power that has provided the essential focus around which legal thought has been elaborated. It is in response to the demands of royal power, for its profit and to serve as its instrument or justification, that the juridical edifice of our own society has been developed. Right in the West is the King's right. Naturally everyone is familiar with the famous, celebrated, repeatedly emphasized role of the jurists in the organization of royal power. We must not forget that the re-vitalization of Roman Law in the twelfth century was the major event around which, and on whose basis, the juridical edifice which had collapsed after the fall of the Roman Empire was reconstructed. This resurrection of Roman Law had in effect a technical and constitutive role to play in the establishment of the authoritarian, administrative, and, in the final analysis, absolute power of the monarchy. And when this legal edifice escapes in later centuries from the control of the monarch, when, more accurately, it is turned against that control, it is always the limits of this sovereign power that are put in question, its prerogatives that are challenged. In other words, I believe that the King remains the central personage in the whole legal edifice of the West. When it comes to the general organization of the legal system in the West, it is essentially with the King, his rights, his power and its eventual limitations, that one is dealing. Whether the jurists were the King's henchmen or his adversaries, it is of royal power that we are speaking in every case when we speak of these grandiose edifices of legal thought and knowledge.

There are two ways in which we do so speak. Either we do so in order to show the nature of the juridical armory that invested royal power, to reveal the monarch as the effective embodiment of sovereignty, to demonstrate that his power, for all that it was absolute, was exactly that which befitted his fundamental right. Or, by contrast, we do so in order to show the necessity of imposing limits upon this sovereign power, of submitting it to certain rules of right, within whose confines it had to be exercised in order for it to remain legitimate. The essential role of the theory of right, from medieval times onwards, was to fix the legitimacy of power; that is the major problem around which the whole theory of right and sovereignty is organized.

When we say that sovereignty is the central problem of right in Western societies, what we mean basically is that the essential function of the discourse and techniques of right has been to efface the domination intrinsic to power in order to present the latter at the level of appearance under two different aspects: on the one hand, as the legitimate rights of sovereignty, and on the other, as the legal obligation to obey it. The system of right is centered entirely upon the King, and it is therefore designed to eliminate the fact of domination and its consequences.

My general project over the past few years has been, in essence, to reverse the mode of analysis followed by the entire discourse of right from the time of the Middle Ages. My aim, therefore, was to invert it, to give due weight, that is, to the fact of domination, to expose both its latent nature and its brutality. I then wanted to show not only how right is, in a general way, the instrument of this domination—which scarcely needs saying—but also to show the extent to which, and the forms in which, right (not simply the laws but the whole complex of apparatuses, institutions and regulations responsible for their application) transmits and puts in motion relations that are not relations of sovereignty, but of domination. Moreover, in speaking of domination I do not have in mind that solid and global kind of domination that one person exercises over others, or one group over another, but the manifold forms of domination that can be exercised within society. Not the domination of the King in his central position, therefore, but that of his subjects in their mutual relations: not the uniform edifice of sovereignty, but the multiple forms of subjugation that have a place and function within the social organism.

The system of right, the domain of the law, are permanent agents of these relations of domination, these polymorphous techniques of subjugation. Right should be viewed, I believe, not in terms of a legitimacy to be established, but in terms of the methods of subjugation that it instigates.

The problem for me is how to avoid this question, central to the theme of right, regarding sovereignty and the obedience of individual subjects in order that I may substitute the problem of domination and subjugation for that of sovereignty and obedience. Given that this was to be the general line of my analysis, there were a certain number of methodological precautions that seemed requisite to its pursuit. In the very first place, it seemed important to accept that the analysis in question should not concern itself with the regulated and legitimate forms of power in their central locations, with the general mechanisms through which they operate, and the continual effects of these. On the contrary, it should be concerned with power at its extremities, in its ultimate destinations, with those points where it becomes capillary, that is, in its more regional and local forms and institutions. Its paramount concern, in fact, should be with the point where power surmounts the rules of right which organize and delimit it and extends itself beyond them, invests itself in institutions, becomes embodied in techniques, and equips itself with instruments and eventually even violent means of material intervention. To give an example: rather than try to discover where and how the right of punishment is founded on sovereignty, how it is presented in the theory of monarchical right or in that of democratic right, I have tried to see in what ways punishment and the power of punishment are effectively embodied in a certain number of local, regional, material institutions, which are concerned with torture or imprisonment, and to place these in the climate—at once institutional and physical, regulated and violent—of the effective apparatuses of punishment. In other words, one should try to locate power at the extreme points of its exercise, where it is always less legal in character.

A second methodological precaution urged that the analysis should not concern itself with power at the level of conscious intention or decision; that it should not attempt to consider power from its internal point of view and that it should refrain from posing the labyrinthine and unanswerable question: "Who then has power and what has he in mind? What is the aim of someone who possesses power?" Instead, it is a case of studying power at the point where its intention, if it has one, is completely invested in its real and effective practices. What is needed is a study of power in its external visage, at the point where it is in direct and immediate relationship with that which we can provisionally call its object, its target, its field of application, there—that is to say—where it installs itself and produces its real effects.

Let us not, therefore, ask why certain people want to dominate, what they seek, what is their overall strategy. Let us ask, instead, how things work at the level of on-going subjugation, at the level of those continuous and uninterrupted processes which subject our bodies, govern our gestures, dictate our behaviors, etc. In other words, rather than ask ourselves how the sovereign appears to us in his lofty isolation, we should try to discover how it is that subjects are gradually, progressively, really and materially constituted through a multiplicity of organisms, forces, energies, materials, desires, thoughts etc. We should try to grasp subjection in its material instance as a constitution of subjects. This would be the exact opposite of Hobbes' project in *Leviathan*, and of that, I believe, of all jurists for whom the problem is the distillation of a single will—or rather, the constitution of a unitary, singular body animated by the spirit of sovereignty—from the particular wills of a multiplicity of individuals. Think of the scheme of Leviathan:[1] insofar as he is a fabricated man, Leviathan is no other than the amalgamation of a certain number of separate individualities, who find themselves reunited by the complex of elements that go to compose the State; but at the heart of the State, or rather, at its head, there exists something which constitutes it as such, and this is sovereignty, which Hobbes says is precisely the spirit of Leviathan. Well, rather than worry about the problem of the central spirit, I believe that we must attempt to study the myriad of bodies which are constituted as peripheral *subjects* as a result of the effects of power.

A third methodological precaution relates to the fact that power is not to be taken to be a phenomenon of one individual's consolidated and homogeneous domination over others, or that of one group or class over others. What, by contrast, should always be kept in mind is that power, if we do not take too distant a view of it, is not that which makes the difference between those who exclusively possess and retain it, and those who do not have it and submit to it. Power must by analyzed as something which circulates, or rather as something which only functions in the form of a chain. It is never localized here or there, never in anybody's hands, never appropriated as a commodity or piece of wealth. Power is employed and exercised through a net-like organization. And not only do individuals circulate between its threads; they are always in the position of simultaneously undergoing and exercising this power. They are not only its inert or consenting target; they are always also the elements of its articulation. In other words, individuals are the vehicles of power, not its points of application.

The individual is not to be conceived as a sort of elementary nucleus, a primitive atom, a multiple and inert material on which power comes to fasten or against which it happens to strike, and in so doing subdues or crushes individuals. In fact, it is already one of the prime effects of power that certain bodies, certain gestures, certain discourses, certain desires, come to be identified and constituted as individuals. The individual, that is, is not the *vis-à-vis*[2] of power; it is, I believe, one of its prime effects. The individual is an effect of power, and at the same time, or precisely to the extent to which it is that effect, it is the element of its articulation. The individual which power has constituted is at the same time its vehicle.

---

1   *Leviathan* The Leviathan, a biblical sea-monster, was taken by Hobbes in his book of that name to represent the state.

2   *vis-à-vis* Counterpart.

There is a fourth methodological precaution that follows from this: when I say that power establishes a network through which it freely circulates, this is true only up to a certain point. In much the same fashion we could say that therefore we all have a fascism in our heads, or, more profoundly, that we all have a power in our bodies. But I do not believe that one should conclude from that that power is the best distributed thing in the world, although in some sense that is indeed so. We are not dealing with a sort of democratic or anarchic distribution of power through bodies. That is to say, it seems to me—and this then would be the fourth methodological precaution—that the important thing is not to attempt some kind of deduction of power starting from its centre and aimed at the discovery of the extent to which it permeates into the base, of the degree to which it reproduces itself down to and including the most molecular elements of society. One must rather conduct an *ascending* analysis of power, starting, that is, from its infinitesimal mechanisms, which each have their own history, their own trajectory, their own techniques and tactics, and then see how these mechanisms of power have been—and continue to be—invested, colonized, utilized, involuted, transformed, displaced, extended etc., by ever more general mechanisms and by forms of global domination. It is not that this global domination extends itself right to the base in a plurality of repercussions: I believe that the manner in which the phenomena, the techniques and the procedures of power enter into play at the most basic levels must be analyzed, that the way in which these procedures are displaced, extended and altered must certainly be demonstrated; but above all what must be shown is the manner in which they are invested and annexed by more global phenomena and the subtle fashion in which more general powers or economic interests are able to engage with these technologies that are at once both relatively autonomous of power and act as its infinitesimal elements. In order to make this clearer, one might cite the example of madness. The descending type of analysis, the one of which I believe one ought to be wary, will say that the bourgeoisie has, since the sixteenth or seventeenth century, been the dominant class; from this premise, it will then set out to deduce the internment of the insane. One can always make this deduction, it is always easily done and that is precisely what I would hold against it. It is in fact a simple matter to show that since lunatics are precisely those persons who are useless to industrial production, one is obliged to dispense with them. One could argue similarly in regard to infantile sexuality—and several thinkers, including Wilhelm Reich have indeed sought to do so up to a certain point. Given the domination of the bourgeois class, how can one understand the repression of infantile sexuality? Well, very simply—given that the human body had become essentially a force of production from the time of the seventeenth and eighteenth century, all the forms of its expenditure which did not lend themselves to the constitution of the productive forces—and were therefore exposed as redundant—were banned, excluded and repressed. These kinds of deduction are always possible. They are simultaneously correct and false. Above all they are too glib, because one can always do exactly the opposite and show, precisely by appeal to the principle of the dominance of the bourgeois class, that the forms of control of infantile sexuality could in no way have been predicted. On the contrary, it is equally plausible to suggest that what was needed was sexual training, the encouragement of a sexual precociousness, given that what was fundamentally at stake was the constitution of a labor force whose optimal state, as we well know, at least at the beginning of the nineteenth century, was to be infinite: the greater the labor force, the better able would the system of capitalist production have been to fulfill and improve its functions.

I believe that anything can be deduced from the general phenomenon of the domination of the bourgeois class. What needs to be done is something quite different. One needs to investigate historically, and beginning from the lowest level, how mechanisms of power have been able to function. In regard to the confinement of the insane, for example, or the repression and interdiction of sexuality, we need to see the manner in which, at the effective level of the family, of the immediate environment, of the cells and most basic units of society, these phenomena of repression or exclusion possessed their instruments and their logic, in response to a certain number of needs. We need to identify the agents responsible for them, their real agents (those which constituted the immediate social *entourage*, the family, parents, doctors, etc.), and not be content to lump them under the formula of a generalized bourgeoisie. We need to see how these mechanisms of power, at a given moment, in a precise conjuncture and by means of a certain number of transformations, have begun to become economically advantageous and politically useful. I think that in this way one could easily manage to demonstrate that what the bourgeoisie needed, or that in which its system discovered its real interests, was not the exclusion of the mad or the surveillance and prohibition of infantile masturbation (for, to repeat, such a system can perfectly well tolerate quite opposite practices), but rather, the techniques and procedures themselves of such an exclusion. It is the mechanisms of that exclusion that are necessary, the apparatuses of surveillance, the medicalization of sexuality, of madness, of delinquency, all the micro-mechanisms of power, that came, from a certain moment in time, to represent the interests of the bourgeoisie. Or even better, we could say that to the extent to which this view of the bourgeoisie and of its interests appears to lack content, at least in regard to the problems with which we are here concerned, it reflects the fact that it was not the bourgeoisie itself which thought that madness had to be excluded or infantile sexuality repressed. What in fact happened instead was that the mechanisms of the exclusion of madness, and of the surveillance of infantile sexuality, began from a particular point in time, and for reasons which need to be studied, to reveal their political usefulness and to lend themselves to economic profit, and that as a natural consequence, all of a sudden, they came to be colonized and maintained by global mechanisms and the entire State system. It is only if we grasp these techniques of power and demonstrate the economic advantages or political utility that derives from them in a given context for specific reasons, that we can understand how these mechanisms come to be effectively incorporated into the social whole.

To put this somewhat differently: the bourgeoisie has never had any use for the insane; but the procedures it has employed to exclude them have revealed and realized—from the nineteenth century onwards, and again on the basis of certain transformations—a political advantage, on occasion even a certain economic utility, which have consolidated the system and contributed to its overall functioning. The bourgeoisie is interested in power, not in madness, in the system of control of infantile sexuality, not in that phenomenon itself. The bourgeoisie could not care less about delinquents, about their punishment and rehabilitation, which economically have little importance, but it is concerned about the complex of mechanisms with which delinquency is controlled, pursued, punished and reformed, etc.

As for our fifth methodological precaution: it is quite possible that the major mechanisms of power have been accompanied by ideological productions. There has, for example, probably been an ideology of education, an ideology of the monarchy, an ideology of parliamentary democracy, etc.; but basically I do not believe that what has taken place can be said to be ideological. It is both much more and much less than ideology. It is the production of effective instruments for the formation and accumulation of knowledge—methods of observation, techniques of registration, procedures for investigation and research, apparatuses of control. All this means that power, when it is exercised through these subtle mechanisms, cannot but evolve, organize and put into circulation a knowledge, or rather apparatuses of knowledge, which are not ideological constructs.

By way of summarizing these five methodological precautions, I would say that we should direct our researches on the nature of power not towards the juridical edifice of sovereignty, the State apparatuses and the ideologies which accompany them, but towards domination and the material operators of power, towards forms of subjection and the inflections and utilizations of their localized systems, and towards strategic apparatuses. We must eschew the model of Leviathan in the study of power. We must escape from the limited field of juridical sovereignty and State institutions, and instead base our analysis of power on the study of the techniques and tactics of domination.

This, in its general outline, is the methodological course that I believe must be followed, and which I have tried to pursue in the various researches that we have conducted over recent years on psychiatric power, on infantile sexuality, on political systems, etc. Now as one explores these fields of investigation, observing the methodological precautions I have mentioned, I believe that what then comes into view is a solid body of historical fact, which will ultimately bring us into confrontation with the problems of which I want to speak this year.

This solid, historical body of fact is the juridical-political theory of sovereignty of which I spoke a moment ago, a theory which has had four roles to play. In the first place, it has been used to refer to a mechanism of power that was effective under the feudal monarchy. In the second place, it has served as instrument and even as justification for the construction of the large scale administrative monarchies. Again, from the time of the sixteenth century and more than ever from the seventeenth century onwards, but already at the time of the wars of religion, the theory of sovereignty has been a weapon which has circulated from one camp to another, which has been utilized in one sense or another, either to limit or else to re-enforce royal power: we find it among Catholic monarchists and Protestant anti-monarchists, among Protestant and more-or-less liberal monarchists, but also among Catholic partisans of regicide or dynastic transformation. It functions both in the hands of aristocrats and in the hands of parliamentarians. It is found among the representatives of royal power and among the last feudatories. In short, it was the major instrument of political and theoretical struggle around systems of power of the sixteenth and seventeenth centuries. Finally, in the eighteenth century, it is again this same theory of sovereignty, re-activated through the doctrine of Roman Law, that we find in its essentials in Rousseau and his contemporaries, but now with a fourth role to play: now it is concerned with the construction, in opposition to the administrative, authoritarian and absolutist monarchies, of an alternative model, that of parliamentary democracy. And it is still this role that it plays at the moment of the Revolution.

Well, it seems to me that if we investigate these four roles there is a definite conclusion to be drawn: as long as a feudal type of society survived, the problems to which the theory of sovereignty was addressed were in effect confined to the general mechanisms of power, to the way in which its forms of existence at the higher level of society influenced its exercise at the lowest levels. In other words, the relationship of sovereignty, whether interpreted in a wider or a narrower sense, encompasses the totality of the social body. In effect, the mode in which power was exercised could be defined in its essentials in terms of the relationship sovereign–subject. But in the seventeenth and eighteenth centuries, we have the production of an important phenomenon, the emergence, or rather the invention, of a new mechanism of power possessed of highly specific procedural techniques, completely novel instruments, quite different apparatuses, and which is also, I believe, absolutely incompatible with the relations of sovereignty.

This new mechanism of power is more dependent upon bodies and what they do than upon the Earth and its products. It is a mechanism of power which permits time and labor, rather than wealth and commodities, to be extracted from bodies. It is a type of power which is constantly exercised by means of surveillance rather than in a discontinuous manner by means of a system of levies or obligations distributed over time. It presupposes a tightly knit grid of material coercions rather than the physical existence of a sovereign. It is ultimately dependent upon the principle, which introduces a genuinely new economy of power, that one must be able simultaneously both to increase the subjected forces and to improve the force and efficacy of that which subjects them.

This type of power is in every aspect the antithesis of that mechanism of power which the theory of sovereignty described or sought to transcribe. The latter is linked to a form of power that is exercised over the Earth and its products, much more than over human bodies and their operations. The theory of sovereignty is something which refers to the displacement and appropriation on the part of power, not of time and labor, but of goods and wealth. It allows discontinuous obligations distributed over time to be given legal expression but it does not allow for the codification of a continuous surveillance. It enables power to be founded in the physical existence of the sovereign, but not in continuous and permanent systems of surveillance. The theory of sovereignty permits the foundation of an absolute power in the absolute expenditure of power. It does not allow for a calculation of power in terms of the minimum expenditure for the maximum return.

This new type of power, which can no longer be formulated in terms of sovereignty, is, I believe, one of the great inventions of bourgeois society. It has been a fundamental instrument in the constitution of industrial capitalism and of the type of society that is its accompaniment. This non-sovereign power, which lies outside the form of sovereignty, is disciplinary power. Impossible to describe in the terminology of the theory of sovereignty from which it differs so radically, this disciplinary power ought by rights to have led to the disappearance of the grand juridical edifice created by that theory. But in reality, the theory of sovereignty has continued not only to exist as an ideology of right, but also to provide the organizing principle of the legal codes which Europe acquired in the nineteenth century, beginning with the Napoleonic Code.[1]

Why has the theory of sovereignty persisted in this fashion as an ideology and an organizing principle of these major legal codes? For two reasons, I believe. On the one hand, it has been, in the eighteenth and again in the nineteenth century, a permanent instrument of criticism of the monarchy and of all the obstacles that can thwart the development of disciplinary society. But at the same time, the theory of sovereignty, and the organization of a legal code centered upon it, have allowed a system of right to be superimposed upon the mechanisms of discipline

---

1   *Napoleonic Code*   Large-scale code of French civil law, put in force under Napoleon I in 1804; the first lasting and successful non-monarchical civil code in Europe, it exerted a powerful influence in establishing the rule of law, and on the content of other legal codifications.

in such a way as to conceal its actual procedures, the element of domination inherent in its techniques, and to guarantee to everyone, by virtue of the sovereignty of the State, the exercise of his proper sovereign rights. The juridical systems—and this applies both to their codification and to their theorization—have enabled sovereignty to be democratized through the constitution of a public right articulated upon collective sovereignty, while at the same time this democratization of sovereignty was fundamentally determined by and grounded in mechanisms of disciplinary coercion.

To put this in more rigorous terms, one might say that once it became necessary for disciplinary constraints to be exercised through mechanisms of domination and yet at the same time for their effective exercise of power to be disguised, a theory of sovereignty was required to make an appearance at the level of the legal apparatus, and to re-emerge in its codes. Modern society, then, from the nineteenth century up to our own day, has been characterized on the one hand, by a legislation, a discourse, an organization based on public right, whose principle of articulation is the social body and the delegative status of each citizen; and, on the other hand, by a closely linked grid of disciplinary coercions whose purpose is in fact to assure the cohesion of this same social body. Though a theory of right is a necessary companion to this grid, it cannot in any event provide the terms of its endorsement. Hence these two limits, a right of sovereignty and a mechanism of discipline, which define, I believe, the arena in which power is exercised. But these two limits are so heterogeneous that they cannot possibly be reduced to each other. The powers of modern society are exercised through, on the basis of, and by virtue of, this very heterogeneity between a public right of sovereignty and a polymorphous disciplinary mechanism. This is not to suggest that there is on the one hand an explicit and scholarly system of right which is that of sovereignty, and, on the other hand, obscure and unspoken disciplines which carry out their shadowy operations in the depths, and thus constitute the bedrock of the great mechanism of power. In reality, the disciplines have their own discourse. They engender, for the reasons of which we spoke earlier, apparatuses of knowledge (*savoir*) and a multiplicity of new domains of understanding. They are extraordinarily inventive participants in the order of these knowledge-producing apparatuses. Disciplines are the bearers of a discourse, but this cannot be the discourse of right. The discourse of discipline has nothing in common with that of law, rule, or sovereign will. The disciplines may well be the carriers of a discourse that speaks of a rule, but this is not the juridical rule deriving from sovereignty, but a natural rule, a norm. The code they come to define is not that of law but that of normalization. Their reference is to a theoretical horizon which of necessity has nothing in common with the edifice of right. It is human science which constitutes their domain, and clinical knowledge their jurisprudence.

In short, what I have wanted to demonstrate in the course of the last few years is not the manner in which at the advance front of the exact sciences the uncertain, recalcitrant, confused dominion of human behavior has little by little been annexed to science: it is not through some advancement in the rationality of the exact sciences that the human sciences are gradually constituted. I believe that the process which has really rendered the discourse of the human sciences possible is the juxtaposition, the encounter between two lines of approach, two mechanisms, two absolutely heterogeneous types of discourse: on the one hand there is the re-organization of right that invests sovereignty, and on the other, the mechanics of the coercive forces whose exercise takes a disciplinary form. And I believe that in our own times power is exercised simultaneously through this right and these techniques and that these techniques and these discourses, to which the disciplines give rise invade the area of right so that the procedures of normalization come to be ever more constantly engaged in the colonization of those of law. I believe that all this can explain the global functioning of what I would call a *society of normalization*. I mean, more precisely, that disciplinary normalizations come into ever greater conflict with the juridical systems of sovereignty: their incompatibility with each other is ever more acutely felt and apparent; some kind of arbitrating discourse is made ever more necessary, a type of power and of knowledge that the sanctity of science would render neutral. It is precisely in the extension of medicine that we see, in some sense, not so much the linking as the perpetual exchange or encounter of mechanisms of discipline with the principle of right. The developments of medicine, the general medicalization of behaviors, conducts, discourses, desires, etc., take place at the point of intersection between the two heterogeneous levels of discipline and sovereignty. For this reason, against these usurpations by the disciplinary mechanisms, against this ascent of a power that is tied to scientific knowledge, we find that there is no solid recourse available to us today, such being our situation, except that which lies precisely in the return to a theory of right organized around sovereignty and articulated upon its ancient principle. When today one wants to object in some way to the disciplines and all the effects of power and knowledge that are linked to them, what is it that one does, concretely, in real life, what do the Magistrates Union[1] or other similar institutions do, if not precisely appeal to this canon of right, this famous, formal right, that is said to be bourgeois, and which in reality is the right of sovereignty? But I believe that we find ourselves here in a kind of blind alley: it is not through recourse to sovereignty against discipline that the effects of disciplinary power can be limited, because sovereignty and disciplinary mechanisms are two absolutely integral constituents of the general mechanism of power in our society.

If one wants to look for a non-disciplinary form of power, or rather, to struggle against disciplines and disciplinary power, it is not towards the ancient right of sovereignty that one should turn, but towards the possibility of a new form of right, one which must indeed be anti-disciplinarian, but at the same time liberated from the principle of sovereignty. It is at this point that we once more come up against the notion of repression, whose use in this context I believe to be doubly unfortunate. On the one hand, it contains an obscure reference to a certain theory of sovereignty, the sovereignty of the sovereign rights of the individual, and on the other hand, its usage introduces a system of psychological reference points borrowed from the human sciences, that is to say, from discourses and practices that belong to the disciplinary realm. I believe that the notion of repression remains a juridical-disciplinary notion whatever the critical use one would make of it. To this extent the critical application of the notion of repression is found to be vitiated and nullified from the outset by the two-fold juridical and disciplinary reference it contains to sovereignty on the one hand and to normalization on the other.

---

1   *Magistrates Union*   This Union, established after 1968, has adopted a radical line on civil rights, the law, and the prisons.

PART 2

Race, Gender, and Colonialism

INTRODUCTION TO
RACE, GENDER, AND COLONIALISM
Victoria Kamsler

By the time of the French Revolution of 1789, ideas of liberty and equality had come to prominence in Western political philosophy. But even the most liberal and democratic European societies still applied such ideals in a very partial way, according freedom and equality to some, while subjecting others to very illiberal and undemocratic rule. For example, men (or at least men of property) were seen as capable of exercising liberal-democratic citizenship, women were not, no matter how wealthy or well educated they might be. Similarly, non-European peoples were not seen as capable or worthy of freedom and equality, and so were subject to discrimination domestically, and to colonialism overseas. In due course, powerful social movements arose to contest these exclusions, and to fight for gender and racial equality, and decolonization. To some extent, these movements were simply asking for a more consistent application of long-standing ideals of liberal rights and democratic citizenship. But they also raised new questions about the adequacy of these ideals, and about how best to implement them. Ideologies of sexism and racism had not only shaped particular laws and public institutions, they had also shaped people's consciousness and social identities—these ideologies were "internalized." Fighting racism and sexism, therefore, required tackling issues of identity, consciousness, and habit. Indeed, for some theorists, these struggles to reshape consciousness were more important than struggles over political institutions; they were seen as necessary preconditions for the latter. Struggles over identity and consciousness were not easily contained within a liberal discourse of rights and tolerance, or a liberal divide between the public and private sphere. Indeed, as we will see, some theorists came to believe that achieving gender and racial equality required abandoning liberalism, or at least dramatically reconceiving its principles. It is this commitment to combining practice and theory, public and private, and to conceptual innovation, which has come to characterize theoretical approaches to gender equality.

Contemporary political theories of gender, race, and colonialism emerged with the great democratic social movements of the nineteenth and twentieth centuries. It is useful to compare this practical orientation of the social movements with the theoretical impetus of contemporary liberal theory. The prevalence of rights-based liberal theory owes much to the imposing influence of Rawlsian political philosophy.[1] By contrast, theories of race, gender and colonialism were immersed from the outset in practical necessities, and in the desire for transformation of self and culture. The immediacy and impact of these theories owe much to their blending of private self-reflection and public action. In each instance, the point was to change the world, by redefining it in light of how it was seen through the eyes of "others." While it is hard to generalize about any such large and diverse collection of works, the development of existentialist influence of existentialist philosophy and Marxist theory during the second half of the twentieth century initiated a rich vein of highly abstract thinking that subsequently influenced the much more concrete application to issues of equality. One thing that all these theories and movements share is a practice of conceptual innovation: an attempt to change our shared social and political world by changing how we see and understand it. Our discussion will begin with an historical overview of gender, race and colonial theories, and an analysis of central features of some key texts.

Theoretical Influences

In the Introduction to "Rights-Based Liberalism and its Critics" we observe that

> rights talk has come to dominate social movements. Women's struggle for equality is largely framed in terms of rights, as are the claims of gays and lesbians, the disabled, indigenous people, and immigrant groups.

Although these modern movements for equality and inclusion grew up in tandem with contemporary liberalism, and

---

1   Though Rawls's work has had some role in shaping legal discourse, it has had slight practical influence on the analysis and formation of public policy, which characteristically employs variants of utilitarian cost-benefit analysis.

are now frequently expressed in the language of rights and justice, they contain elements of social and cultural radicalism that often overstep the bounds of the liberal tradition. They draw upon utopian, existential, and Marxist thought and often employ ideas developed by the national liberation movements that swept much of the colonial world. Equally importantly, these movements also embody an attempt to go directly to the roots of lived experience, to articulate a point of view, and create a language for personal and social transformation.

In the case of liberalism, we observe a diverse body of theoretical views built around certain core commitments to principles of individual rights, the rule of law, and constitutional democracy. By contrast, theories of race, gender, and colonialism tend to disagree over certain core assumptions. Yet they all aim at equity and the end of subordination for historically marginalized and disadvantaged groups and peoples. Which of these many roads actually leads to that goal is a matter that may be illuminated by theory, but is best tested by experience.

Roots Intertwined

As focal points of modern social movements and as points of theoretical debate, race, gender, and colonialism may be considered separately. But these movements did not arise in a vacuum, and from the beginning they have influenced, criticized, and supported each other. The complex interactions of the theories connected to these broad categories are illustrated in the works of each of our authors in this section, and embodied in the rich history of their intellectual friendships and rivalries. Although vociferous disputes arose within and among theorists in each domain, each has played a part in the great twentieth- and twenty-first-century movement toward social and political inclusion and democratization.

In order to get some sense of the confluence of these ideas, it may be helpful to consider the life and work of W.E.B. Du Bois. His many and varied contributions to the politics of race and intellectual culture clearly illustrate the themes of 1) the practical roots of critical race theory, 2) the historical influence of modern political ideologies on democratic social movements, and 3) the intertwining sources of theories of race, gender, and colonialism.

With the publication of *The Souls of Black Folk*, Du Bois created the intellectual framework that would become home to an emerging African American intelligentsia. In this work, he describes the phenomenon of double consciousness, which refers both to the sense of seeing oneself from the outside, through the distorting lens of a racist culture, and to the internal struggle to come to terms with two sides of oneself. Du Bois described this psychic division as being "an American, a Negro; two warring ideals in one dark body, whose dogged strength alone keeps it from being torn asunder." The idea of double consciousness has roots in the work of the American transcendentalist thinkers Ralph Waldo Emerson and William James, but Du Bois's use of the concept to describe racial self-awareness is distinctive. As Henry Louis Gates and Cornel West have observed, "this metaphor would prove to be the governing trope of African American literature from the publication of James Weldon Johnson's *The Autobiography of an Ex-Colored Man* (1913) through Ralph Ellison's *Invisible Man* (1952) to Toni Morrison's *Beloved* (1988)."[1] Although best known as a theorist of racial inequality and black identity, Du Bois is an important influence in the history of all three of our subjects: race, gender, and colonialism. Widely regarded as the greatest black public intellectual of his time, he stands at the forefront of the civil rights movement.[2] Du Bois frequently wrote and spoke out against the subordination of women, and black women in particular. To cite only one example, one of his most popular books, *Darkwater*, included an essay ("The Damnation of Women") that argued for the rights of women and the special dignity of black women against a history of abuse. He argued not only for women's equal economic rights, but also for the right of women to determine their own procreative destiny. Du Bois argued

---

1   Henry Louis Gates and Cornel West, *The African-American Century*. New York: The Free Press, (2000) p. 5.

2   However, he was never entirely comfortable with Martin Luther King as a political leader. A lifelong atheist who eventually became a Marxist, Du Bois "observed somewhere that he had expected to live to see anything but a militant Baptist preacher" leading the movement to better the lives of African Americans. David Levering Lewis, *W.E.B. du Bois: The Fight for Equality and the American Century*. (New York: Henry Holt, 2000) p. 557. Lewis notes that "In the Indian journal Gandhi Marg, Du Bois drew obvious parallels between Gandhi's liberation of India and King's successes in Alabama and went on to speculate that the gifted, committed preacher might be the American Gandhi. King wrote a graceful note in response to Du Bois's letter supporting the Montgomery boycott. But nonviolent passive resistance devoid of an economic agenda increasingly disappointed Du Bois, and he finally decided in late 1959 that King was not Gandhi. 'Gandhi submitted,' Du Bois asserted, 'but he also followed a positive (economic) program to offset his negative refusal to use violence'" (p. 557).

that a woman should have the right of motherhood "at her own discretion."[1]

Finally, Du Bois was one of the founding influences on Black Nationalism, Pan-Africanism, and Négritude. These closely related movements differ mainly in focus.

Black Nationalism is primarily concerned with the social, cultural, and political autonomy of African Americans, and their relationships to members of the African diaspora through a shared history of slavery and oppression. Black Nationalists emphasize racial solidarity and a sense of common identity and destiny. After Du Bois, significant Black nationalist figures include Marcus Garvey, Audley "Queen Mother" Moore, Malcolm X, and Louis Farrakhan.

Pan-Africanism seeks the unity of post-colonial African states and peoples emerging from the conditions of colonial rule. Though radical in substance, its concerns are more conventionally political, dealing with statecraft and national identity, and the transnational unity of the African diaspora. Some tension arose within the Pan Africanist movement as to whether African unity should be based upon geography, uniting all peoples of the African continent (a view supported by Kwame Nkrumah of Ghana and Gamal Abdel Nasser of Egypt). Alternatively, African identity could be based on an idea of a people unified by race, or by that of the culture that emerged from Africans' experiences of slavery, which created a sense of shared black identity out of the ordeals of previously distinct linguistic and cultural groups.

Du Bois played a crucial role in the international Pan-Africanist movement. At the end of World War I, when the Armistice was signed, Du Bois attended the Peace Conference in Paris as an observer for the National Association for the Advancement of Colored People (NAACP), and there decided to organize the world's second Pan-African Conference, held in 1923. He was also an associate delegate to the founding conference of the United Nations at San Francisco in 1945; in the wake of that gathering, his concerns about imperialism and colonialism prompted him to convene a fifth Pan-African conference, attended by Kwame Nkrumah, Jomo Kenyatta, and other African nationalist leaders. The conference elected Du Bois president and named him "Father of Pan-Africanism."

Négritude constitutes a body of theory and literature influenced by existentialist thought, with a focus on the distinctive experience of blacks in the context of francophone African and Caribbean cultures. Crucial contributions to the theory of Négritude have been made by Frantz Fanon, Aimé Césaire, Richard Wright, Jean-Paul Sartre, and Léopold Senghor of Senegal. Aimé Césaire conceived the source of African unity in the contingent arising of a shared historical experience, whereas Senghor advocated the idea of an essence of black identity. Their work owes much to the pioneering efforts of Du Bois in the revalorization of black cultural values and the destigmatization of black identity.

The term *négritude* was coined by Aimé Césaire in his 1939 poem, "Cahier d'un retour au pays natal" ("Notebook of a Return to my Native Land"). In this work, Césaire attempts to illuminate and overcome the objectification and self-alienation of the black subject in confrontation with a racist culture. Césaire writes, "ma négritude n'est pas une pierre" (my negritude is not a stone), and challenges the objectification of black identity in a series of tropes of deafness and blindness. When he comes to state positively what negritude consists of, his metaphors describe black agency using the grammatically correct feminine pronoun but with strongly masculine connotations: "elle plonge dans la chair rouge du sol/ elle plonge dans la chair ardente du ciel" (It [feminine] plunges into the red flesh of the earth/ It [feminine] plunges into the burning flesh of the sky).

Theorists of Négritude made use of Hegelian and existentialist accounts of the struggle for recognition, and of the identity of the "Other" to describe and critique black colonial experience. The distinctive universalism and uniformity of French colonial policy, and its strongly assimilationist ideal of citizenship, created a different experience of racial identity and colonial subordination for members of the francophone African diaspora. Colonial France's uniquely homogenizing institutions of culture and language provided a shared, characteristic backdrop in French colonial settings.[2] In particular, there seemed no space for the expression of difference within the French colonial regime.

Fanon's anti-colonial violence

This opposition between colonizer and colonized explodes across the pages of the works of Frantz Fanon in images of incendiary revolt. Among theorists of Négritude, the work

---

1   Ibid., pp. 11–12.

2   However, African culture had made its presence strongly felt in Paris at least since the 1920s; artists such as Matisse and Picasso, and writers such as Jean Cocteau and André Gide referenced a certain generalized anthropological idea of "African Art" in some of their greatest works.

of Fanon has been in equal measure renowned and hard to pin down. Henry Louis Gates observes:

> Fanon's current fascination for us has something to do with the convergence of the problematic of colonialism with that of subject-formation. As a psychoanalyst of culture, as a champion of the wretched of the earth, he is an almost irresistible figure for a criticism that sees itself as both op-positional and postmodern. And yet there's something Rashomon-like about his contemporary guises. It may be a matter of judgement whether his writings are rife with contradiction or richly dialectical, polyvocal, and multivalent; they are in any event highly porous, that is, wide open to interpretation, and the readings they elicit are, as a result, of unfailing *symptomatic* interest: Frantz Fanon, not to put too fine a point on it, is a Ror-schach blot with legs.[1]

A significant feature of Fanon's work is his endorsement of the use of violence in overthrowing colonial regimes, which in any event he took to be inevitable:

> decolonization is always a violent event. At what-ever level we study it—individual encounters, a change of name for a sports club, the guest list at a cocktail party, members of a police force or the board of directors of a state or private bank—de-colonization is quite simply the substitution of one "species" of mankind by another.

This sense of stasis and impasse, of blunt opposition be-tween warring counterparts, required nothing less than the total overthrow and displacement of the colonizers by the colonized. No recognition, no mutuality, no compromise or dialogue were possible between a subject people and their oppressors. When revolution came, it would be total. Fanon writes:

> Challenging the colonial world is not a rational confrontation of viewpoints. It is not a discourse on the universal, but the impassioned claim by the colonized that their world is fundamentally different. The colonial world is a Manichaean world.[2]

Fanon's rejection of the possibility of dialogue, his embrace of violence, his apocalyptic vision of the negation and overthrow of the power and values of the colonizer by the colonized, find their antithesis in the powerful message of non-violence conveyed to the world by a gentler, but more effective anti-colonial leader, India's Mahatma Gandhi.

Non-violence, Racism and Colonialism: Gandhi and King

Mohandas K. Gandhi was the central figure of the move-ment for Indian independence. He is more widely known by the honorary name Mahatma Gandhi, "Mahatma" meaning "great soul." He developed his concepts of ahimsa (non-violence) and satyagraha (meaning both "soul force" and "truth force," Gandhi's unique formulation of the idea of civil disobedience) from his distinctive interpretation of Hindu philosophy and ethics. His religious beliefs simi-larly informed his ascetic commitments to vegetarianism, chastity, self-sufficiency, and simplicity. Gandhi's belief in the positive force of love and truth, and in its capacity ultimately to defeat violence and oppression, draw upon a metaphysical faith in "the principle of non-violence, which is the essence of all religions."

Gandhi's idea of satyagraha was strongly influenced by the American tradition of civil disobedience. In 1942, he wrote to President Franklin D. Roosevelt: "I have profited greatly by the writings of Henry David Thoreau and Ralph Waldo Emerson." And his description of satyagraha contains some elements immediately recognizable from Thoreau's *Civil Disobedience*, as for instance when Gandhi writes: "We can ... free ourselves of the unjust rule of the Government by defying the unjust rule and accepting the punishments that go with it." For Gandhi, acceptance and defiance were not opposed, but combined together in a form of power that was uniquely human, distinguishing the strength of the human spirit from the forces of brute nature.

> Non-violence in its dynamic condition means conscious suffering. It does not mean meek sub-mission to the will of the evildoer, but it means the putting of one's whole soul against the will of the tyrant.

---

1   Henry Louis Gates, Jr., "Critical Fanonism," *Critical Inquiry*, Vol. 17, No. 3. (Spring, 1991), p.458.

2   Manicheanism is an ancient religious doctrine (and Christian heresy) which sees reality as dualistic, containing basic opposite

principles: spirit/matter, good/evil; thus to call an approach "Manichean" is to accuse it of unjustifiable dualistic thinking, di-viding the world into basic, intrinsic, and ineradicable good and evil.

Gandhi objected to the term "passive resistance" because his form of power-in-yielding was not inert, but active in the face of injustice. Up to a point, satyagraha resembled the skill of a martial artist, who gives way before an opponent's force in order to defeat him. But only up to a point. The objective of satyagraha was not to use the opponent's own force and violence to defeat him, but rather to transform the circumstances of domination into circumstances of dialogue.[1] In order to accomplish this, a profound change must take place between the colonizer and the colonized. Only a persistent, firm, but loving attention could accomplish this, breaking the pattern of domination and subordination and replacing it with equal regard and equal standing. What was the source of the effectiveness of satyagraha? To put it in existentialist terms, where satyagraha worked, it broke through the dynamics of the master/slave dialectic, not by a conventional victory, in which the slaves become the new masters, but by a radical reshaping of the terms of engagement, now embodied in a dialogue of equals. Satyagraha is effective because it draws upon a force for change that is more powerful than the force of arms. As Gandhi put it,

> In English there is a saying, "Might is Right." Then there is the doctrine of the survival of the fittest. Both these ideas are contradictory to the above principle. Neither is wholly true. If ill-will were the chief motive-force, the world would have been destroyed long ago.... We are alive solely because of love. We are all ourselves the proof of this.

Gandhi intended satyagraha not simply as a method to attain independence for the state of India, but as a universal technique applicable to non-Hindu peoples the world over. Any circumstance of racial or colonial oppression was supposed to be solvable by this political application of spiritual purity. Not surprisingly, one of the greatest challenges to his ideas came over the fate of the Jews. Gandhi applied his advice to the Jews in Nazi Germany.

> "Can the Jews resist this organized and shameless persecution? Is there a way to preserve their self-respect and not to feel helpless, neglected and forlorn? ... I submit there is," and his answer is

"civil resistance." He argued for its adoption by the Jews in Hitlerite Germany. Gandhi believed that "voluntary suffering" of the Jews would ultimately prevail over the "calculated violence" of Nazism.[2]

Martin Buber, the great Austrian-Israeli Jewish philosopher, eagerly read Gandhi's discussion of the German Jews, and found it deeply disappointing. Buber's most important work, *I and Thou* (1923), had elucidated the idea of dialogue, a mode of open and unlimited communication. Dialogue is the characteristic interaction between "I and Thou," a mutually transforming relationship between two subjects. Buber contrasted this with "I and It," an orientation of a subject toward an object that it may use or seek to know. In a letter that Buber wrote to Gandhi, he claimed that Gandhi had simply failed to grasp the futility of passive resistance in confronting the Nazi threat. Indeed, the context of colonial subordination was significantly unlike the totalitarian project of racial extermination enacted by the Nazis. With such a foe, dialogue is not possible.[3]

Although Gandhi's account of the transformative power of satyagraha could not be generalized to every instance of oppression, his work did have a critical influence on other liberation movements. As mentioned above, Gandhi was

---

1 This discussion of Gandhi and the conception of "dialogue" in satyagraha is drawn from V.V. Ramana Murti, "Buber's Dialogue and Gandhi's Satyagraha," *Journal of the History of Ideas*, Vol. 29, No. 4. (Oct.–Dec., 1968), pp. 605–13.

2 "If Gandhi was able to carry on dialogue with England, it was only because of satyagraha. The very basis of a non-violent struggle between India and England, as Gandhi conceived it, was clearly designed to achieve this rare objective. The old relationship between master and slave was changed thereby into a new partnership between equals in a 'dialogue.' That this took place between two great nations was not the least noteworthy aspect of it." V.V. Ramana Murti, "Buber's Dialogue and Gandhi's Satyagraha" *Journal of the History of Ideas*, Vol. 29, No. 4. (Oct.–Dec., 1968), p. 594 Quoting M.K. Gandhi, *Non-Violence in Peace and War* (Ahmedabad, 1948), I, 159–61.

3 "Martin Buber made a public reply to Gandhi in an open letter addressed to the *Mahatma* on Feb. 24, 1939, from Jerusalem. He took exception to Gandhi's assessment of the real condition of the Jews. While Gandhi's intentions in this case could not be doubted, his appraisal of the Jewish question might not have taken full account of all the factors that were involved. Buber argued that the Jews were unlike the Indians in South Africa. He similarly questioned Gandhi's recommendation of 'non-violence' for the Jews in Germany to resist the 'violence' of Nazism. In defense of his viewpoint against Gandhi's idea of non-violence, Buber asked: 'Now ... Mahatma, ... do you think perhaps that a Jew in Germany could pronounce in public one single sentence of a speech such as yours without being knocked down? ... It does not seem to me convincing when you base your advice to us on the practice of *Satyagraha* in Germany.'" Ramana Murti, p. 606.

influenced by an American conception of civil disobedience,[1] and that influence came full circle when Gandhi's practice of satyagraha was consciously adopted by the American civil rights movement in the 1960s. The similarity between the tactics of the Indian independence movement and the American movement for racial justice and legal equality have often been noted, and their resemblance is no coincidence. King was a profound admirer of Gandhi, and his views about the practice of non-violence were directly influenced by him. Although Gandhi had been assassinated in 1948, King made a pilgrimage to India in 1959 to meet Gandhi's family. When he arrived at the airport in New Delhi, he told the waiting reporters: "To other countries I may go as a tourist, but to India I come as a pilgrim."[2] The profound impact of this trip upon King's understanding of satyagraha and commitment to non-violence was evident in a radio address he made on his final night in India:

> Since being in India, I am more convinced than ever before that the method of nonviolent resistance is the most potent weapon available to oppressed people in their struggle for justice and human dignity. In a real sense, Mahatma Gandhi embodied in his life certain universal principles that are inherent in the moral structure of the universe, and these principles are as inescapable as the law of gravitation.[3]

---

1 "During this first incarceration, Gandhi read Tolstoy, Ruskin, Socrates, Huxley, Bacon, and the *Gita—the* work which greatly influenced him, as it did Thoreau, according to Arthur Christy in his *The Orient in American Transcendentalism.* Since his days in London when he had first studied the *Gita,* Gandhi had rejected the fundamentalist interpretation that this Hindu Bible was a historical work justifying violence. Gandhi felt that 'under the guise of physical warfare, it described the duel that perpetually went on in the hearts of mankind, and that physical warfare was brought in merely to make the description of the internal duel more alluring.' Thoreau, in his criticism of the *Gita* in *A Week on the Concord and Merrimack Rivers,* had protested the seeming justification of violence; Gandhi undoubtedly knew of Thoreau's interest in Oriental literature through reading of *Walden* and Salt's *Life of Henry David Thoreau,* although Gandhi seemingly never saw *A Week* with its extended comments on the *Gita.*" George Hendrick, "The Influence of Thoreau's 'Civil Disobedience' on Gandhi's Satyagraha," *The New England Quarterly,* Vol. 29, No. 4. (Dec., 1956), pp. 462–71. p. 468.

2 The Martin Luther King, Jr., Research and Education Institute, "King's Trip to India." Available: <http://www.stanford.edu/group/King/encyclopedia/index.htm>.

3 Ibid.

In addition to King's own Gandhian influence, two key pacifist organizations served as a direct conduit of Gandhi's ideas into the heart of civil rights movement strategy: the Fellowship of Reconciliation (FOR) and the Congress of Racial Equality (CORE).

So Gandhi's project of satyagraha and non-violence was carried forward in the new context of the struggle for civil rights in the United States—and later, in the context of non-violent resistance to oppression in the Philippines (the overthrow of dictator Ferdinand Marcos) and eastern Europe (the overthrow of a succession of communist dictatorships in 1989-90). But Fanon's approach also had its advocates among anti-colonial leaders, most notably Che Guevara. From a philosophical point of view, a core difference between the adherents of non-violence and of violence centered upon the way they understood the relationship between oppressor and oppressed: should the struggle be seen as a dialectic of master and slave, and a struggle to the death; or was there hope of transcending the opposition between the colonizer and the colonized, by creating the conditions for dialogue and mutual recognition? As we shall see in our discussion of Simone de Beauvoir, existentialism provided a philosophical framework within which these competing views could be articulated and addressed.

De Beauvoir and Gender

De Beauvoir is best known as the author of the *Second Sex,* arguably the most important work of feminist theory of the twentieth century. In this work, de Beauvoir develops an existentialist account of the contingent nature of women's subordination. Like her late medieval predecessor Christine de Pisan, to whose work she refers, de Beauvoir evokes a compendious and erudite picture of misogyny in history, religion, myth, culture, and sexuality. de Beauvoir deploys existentialism's account of the subject as self-creating and transcendent, responsible for its own emergence from immanence and the stasis of mere existence.

> Every subject plays his part as such specifically through exploits or projects that serve as a mode of transcendence; he achieves liberty only through a continual reaching out toward other liberties. There is no justification for the present existence other than its expansion into an indefinitely open future. Every time transcendence falls back into immanence, stagnation, there is a degradation of existence into the *en-soi* (in itself)—the brutish life

of subjection to given conditions—and of liberty into constraint and contingence. This downfall represents a moral fault if the subject consents to it; if it is inflicted upon him, it spells frustration and oppression. In both cases it is an absolute evil[1]

De Beauvoir's famous remark, that "one is not born a woman, but becomes one" marks a cornerstone of the theory of gender. De Beauvoir distinguished between the given, physiological facts of sex, and the cultural and psychological practices of the feminine. By arguing that women's subordination was not a necessary outcome of physical and (purported) intellectual differences between the sexes, but subject to choice and change, she revolutionized the classic "nature versus nurture" debate about the sources of women's subordination. A lifelong companion of the existentialist philosopher, Jean-Paul Sartre, de Beauvoir helped set the tone for much of post World War II intellectual life in France, and in those parts of the intellectual world influenced by Paris. But for the cosmopolitan de Beauvoir, a crucial part of that world was the emergence of voices for black liberation and identity. In *The Second Sex*, de Beauvoir repeatedly emphasizes the similarities between the situation of women and of African Americans. In both cases, racists and anti-feminists invoke science to "prove" the inferiority of blacks and women. She claims that

> ... there are deep similarities between the situation of woman and that of the Negro. Both are being emancipated today from a like paternalism, and the former master class wishes to "keep them in their place"— that is, the place chosen for them.... In both cases the dominant class bases its argument on a state of affairs that it has itself created.

Later feminist and critical race theorists would object to the generalization of "woman" and "the Negro" as uniform subject positions. They would come to emphasize the complexity of personal identity, with cross-cutting allegiances and experiences of class, culture, sexuality, and many other fine-grained features of personal experience. And black feminist or womanist theorists would contest the idea that "woman" and "the Negro" could represent distinct, unique categories, thus blurring the experiences of black women and obscuring their own complex senses of identity. In her novel, *Their Eyes Were Watching God*, Zora Neal Hurston wrote that the black woman is "the mule of the world." De Beauvoir might have agreed, but the simple dualities of her dialectic of the male subject and the female object, the self and the other, the master and the slave, did not lend themselves to any more pluralist analysis. Instead, and in keeping with her existentialist perspective, she argued that "no group ever sets itself up as the One without at once setting up the Other over against itself."

In another example of the confluence of influences, Sartre and de Beauvoir had complicated friendships with the authors James Baldwin and Richard Wright, both black American expatriates who formed part of a shared intellectual circle in Paris. Baldwin was an openly gay African American, and his novels *Giovanni's Room* (1956) and *Another Country* (1962) depict characters at the crossroads of race, gender, and national identity. Wright was the famous and controversial author of *Native Son* (1940) whose central character, Bigger Thomas, embodies the explosive violence that erupts from within life under racism.[2] Wright's existentialist novel *The Outsider* clearly shows the influence of his friendship with Sartre and de Beauvoir, and bears comparison to the famous French existentialist novel, *The Stranger* (*L'Étranger*) (1942), written by their mutual friend, Albert Camus. In *The Outsider* (1953), Wright's black intellectual protagonist is influenced by proto-existentialist works by Kierkegaard, Nietzsche and Dostoevsky and develops a distinctively pro-active American existentialist stance that is unlike Camus's fatalism.

Despite his friendship with Sartre and de Beauvoir, Baldwin disapproved of their influence on Richard Wright, his sometime mentor and rival.

Baldwin wrote about Wright:

> "... I distrusted his association with the French intellectuals, Sartre, de Beauvoir and company. I am not being vindictive toward them or condescending toward Richard Wright when I say that it seemed to me that there was very little they could give him which he could use. It has always seemed to me that ideas were somewhat more real to them than people ..."[3]

This observation of Baldwin's draws us to a conclusion about de Beauvoir and the influence of existentialist thought on

---

1 Simone de Beauvoir, *The Second Sex* (trans. H.M. Parshley) (New York: Penguin, 1972) pp. 28–29.

2 From 1941 to 1943 Orson Welles directed a successful Broadway adaptation of this work on the underlying violence of racial inequality.

3 Quoted in Nina Kressner Cobb: "Richard Wright: Exile and Existentialism" *Phylon (1960)*, Vol. 40, No. 4 (1979) pp. 362–74.

feminist and critical race theory. The existentialist turn marks a mode of thinking about race and gender that is distinctly "theory driven," more concerned with abstraction and generalization. It constitutes a significant exception to our general claim that theories of gender, race, and colonialism owe more to immediate practical concerns than to philosophical theorizing. Existentialism gives a distinctive intellectualizing flavor to works of Négritude, in its preoccupation with the dialectic of transcendent agents and immanent, objectified others.

In democratic theory, the problem of difference and the "other" are illuminated in the work of Iris Young, whose graduate work in existentialism and phenomenology informed her thinking about social justice. Young argues that the dominant paradigm of distributive justice, best known from the work of John Rawls, cannot adequately address the justice claims of marginalized groups. This is because distributive justice, in Young's view, being concerned with the distribution of benefits and burdens of social cooperation to individuals, fails to register the kinds of oppression that go along with membership in historically disadvantaged groups. And in radical feminist theory, the problem of objectification and alienation finds its apotheosis in the work of Catharine MacKinnon.

Catharine MacKinnon's work may be seen as an elaboration of de Beauvoir's view of the pervasiveness of male dominance. For MacKinnon, masculinity subtends the structure and institutions of society to such an extent that it is seen as neutral and the norm. Men's desires, men's perspective, the male gaze, shape the external world of culture and the internal mental landscape of men and women.

Political Theory and Beyond

Beyond their basic commitment to the end of subordination based on race, sex or nationality, movement writings often share a similar approach or method. They characteristically develop an account of a shared experience of oppression based upon a narrative of personal sufferings and strivings. This enterprise typically takes one or both of the following two forms. The first is a kind of representative thinking that starts with introspection about the experience of subordination and generalizes from this to a shared social problem. Here is an example from W.E.B. Du Bois's *The Souls of Black Folk*:

> To the real question, How does it feel to be a problem? I answer seldom a word.... And yet, being a

problem is a strange experience,—peculiar even for one who has never been anything else.... One ever feels his two-ness,—an American, a Negro; two souls, two thoughts, two unreconciled strivings; two warring ideals in one dark body, whose dogged strength alone keeps it from being torn asunder.

Another form is what we might call "consciousness-raising." This more collaborative approach involves different individuals sharing accounts of their own experiences of inequality, and in the process developing new ways to describe and understand their experience. As the practice took hold among Western feminists, it often attained a distinctive democratic character. Instead of the intellectual coercion of Maoist doctrinal correctness, feminist consciousness raising began with the articulation and sharing of individual women's experiences of social, economic and sexual inequality. In practice this worked to provide evidence of patterns of subordination, and was reflected back in a sense of validity and the authority to trust and articulate one's own experience. [1]

Literary Influences

As we have seen, gender, race, and colonial theory all arose out of practical reflection on particular experiences of subordination. A significant feature of these theories lies in the creation of ways of seeing and speaking about the world and one's place in it. So perhaps it is not surprising that significant and influential expressions of thought on these issues are found not only in the realm of political theory but also in psychology, sociology, history, literature, and autobiography. In fact, many of these works respect no clear limits of genre, but cross the boundary of personal and political, combining the felt sense of experience with both polemics and rational argumentation. Among the most important and

---

1   There is an interesting parallel with the evidentiary basis of class-action lawsuits. For example, an individual applying for a job may feel that they have been discriminated against. Perhaps subtle verbal cues lead them to suspect that they are not being assessed on their merits. Having no periscope with which to see inside their interviewer's head, they can prove nothing about an individual's intent to discriminate. However, if we compare evidence from a large number of such experiences and detect a pattern of unequal hiring among qualified applicants, this shared information can confirm the existence of unjust practices, without the burden of proving that particular employers consciously intended to discriminate.

influential thinkers on these subjects are literary artists, some of whom occasionally delve into the realms of theory. The story of racial equality cannot be told without considering the crucial insight and inspiration gleaned from such literary giants as Zora Neal Hurston, Ralph Ellison, and Toni Morrison. This influence is evident in the works of contemporary race theorists such as Kwame Anthony Appiah, Henry Louis Gates, and Cornel West, who often devote as much space to reflections upon literature as they do to social and political theory. The importance of literature in movements for equality reflects the importance of conceptual transformation at the heart of these movements. By re-telling the (un)official story of a race, sex, or people, these works have re-made the concepts that they undertook to describe.

Where did these new literary voices come from? An astonishing wealth of recent scholarship has uncovered early sources of these political narratives of personal identity. The year 1760 saw the publication of the first known slave narrative in the American colonies, *A Narrative of the Uncommon Sufferings and Surprizing* (sic) *Deliverance of Britton Hammon, a Negro Man* by Britton Hammon. Classic slave narratives such as those of Olaudah Equiano, Frederick Douglass, and Harriet Jacobs established a literary convention that wove autobiographical accounts of freedom and oppression into a larger public political narrative. At about the same time, the poet Phyllis Wheatley, a Ghanaian-born slave in Boston, published her first poem in the *Newport Mercury* in 1767. In 1773, she became the second American woman to publish a book, *Poems on Various Subjects, Religious and Moral*. Her poetry caused an international sensation, because it had been widely believed that Negroes were incapable of writing poetry. Wheatley was made to defend her authorship in court, where she successfully proved that the work was her own.[1]

Another significant contribution to the political history of personal narrative came when Sojourner Truth delivered two famous speeches, in Akron, Ohio, in 1851 and in Silver Lake, Indiana, in 1858. She was illiterate, and these speeches are known only through accounts of those who attended. In Akron, a friend took these notes as she was speaking:

> I am a woman's rights. I have as much muscle as any man, and can do as much work as any man. I have plowed and reaped and husked and chopped and mowed, and can any man do more than that? I have heard much about the sexes being equal; I can carry as much as any man, and can eat as much too, if I can get it. As for intellect, all I can say is, if a woman have a pint and a man a quart—why can't she have her little pint full? You need not be afraid to give us our rights for fear we will take too much—for we can't take more than our pint'll hold. The poor men seem to be all in confusion, and don't know what to do. Why children, if you have woman's rights, give it to her and you will feel better. You will have your own rights and they won't be so much trouble. I can't read, but I can hear. I have read the bible and have learned that Eve caused man to sin. Well, if woman upset the world, do give her a chance to set it right side up again ...[2]

Conceptual Innovation

Critical theories of race, gender and colonialism seek inclusion, equity and justice for peoples and groups whose claims are not heard, in part because they do not fit into existing understandings of rights, equal citizenship, or civil liberty. In order for those claims to be recognized, and their validity accepted, basic political and legal concepts and ways of thinking have to be challenged and changed. Conceptual innovation is a key feature of the transformative power of modern social movements, but how does it work? Let us consider a range of possibilities, moving from the least conceptually demanding to the most.

A first possibility involves finding a new way to work out latent features of already existing concepts. This case presupposes some conception of *implicit concepts*[3] according to which there is more to a concept than the way it is actually used. Immanent critique relies on an account of implicit concepts, directing our attention to emancipatory possibilities latent in the practices or beliefs of a shared culture. One example of this kind of conceptual transformation is found in the political and legal strategies of the Civil Rights Movement. Martin Luther King's strategy of non-violent protest was an extension of his own conception of immanent critique: that the rights of the citizen as guar-

---

1   See Henry Louis Gates and Anthony Appiah, eds. *Africana: The Encyclopedia of the African and African American Experience* (New York: Basic Civitas Books, 1999) p. 1171

2   Nell Irvin Painter, *Sojourner Truth: A Life, A Symbol* (New York: Norton, 1996) pp. 125–26.

3   I borrow this phrase from Christopher Peacocke.

anteed by the US Constitution, when properly understood, guaranteed equality under the law for black citizens. Such an appeal to implicit constitutional concepts was possible for King in a way that it was not for Nelson Mandela, in his fight against South African apartheid. Because the basic apparatus of citizen equality was available in the US Constitution as it existed, King believed that a strategy of inclusion was appropriate and likely to be effective. King held a mirror up to the basic values of the constitution, and required the country to engage in self-reflection on the inconsistency of central values with actual beliefs and practices of racial inequality. In contrast, Mandela, confronted a situation in which the regime of apartheid was written into the constitution itself. Hence the more radical politics of Mandela's speech, "I Am Prepared to Die" at the Rivonia trial. In confronting the apartheid regime, Mandela endorsed the use of violence as a last resort.[1]

A second possibility involves a yet stronger element of conceptual innovation. These cases require us to change basic features of the concept itself. The citizenship of women provides a historically significant example of this form of conceptual change. This is so because central features of the idea of citizenship itself were understood as having explicitly masculine connotations, and were clearly meant to apply to men only. Precedents for such views may be traced back at least to Aristotle's *Politics*, in which women, children and slaves were excluded from citizenship precisely on the grounds of a natural and insuperable deficiency of the deliberative capacity that was the *sine qua non* of citizenly participation. Subsequent accounts of citizenship involved criteria such as the property qualification, in circumstances under which male heads of household were the holders of property, or made the availability for military service central to the concept of citizenly duties. In these and other ways, the concept of citizenship was often developed in ways that explicitly excluded women, by making reference to distinctive features of women's social and economic position, their supposed inferior virtues and intellect, and their biological nature. To admit women into the domain of citizenship required a fundamental revision of what had previously been central requirements of the concept of citizenship itself.

A third possibility concerning the nature of conceptual innovation arises under two kinds of circumstances: a) when none of our existing concepts provides an adequate basis for the resolution of our cultural and political discontents, even in some imaginable modified version, or b) we are unable to imagine how our concepts could serve us in this regard. This kind of dilemma confronted contemporary feminists, who through practices of consciousness raising sought to put into words what Betty Freidan once called "the problem that has no name." Anne Phillips captures some sense of the phenomenology of wordlessness that describes this condition:

> One of the defining characteristics of contemporary feminism has been its emphasis on the ways in which women get trapped into a culture of passivity and self-denial. One of the most direct conclusions from this is that women have to "learn" what they want, learn to challenge the silent privileging of the male.... The language through which we think our needs, interests, or rights continually subverts the impulse to liberation, drawing us back into the either/or dichotomies of being like men, or else "naturally" different.... Women themselves are as much at the mercy of these dichotomies as men; it is not that we "know" what we want but have not been able to make ourselves heard.[2]

The practice of consciousness raising did not characteristically appeal to a set of shared or established concepts. Rather, through a dialogic practice, it sought to bring to light, and find words for, elements of shared experience concerning which women found themselves inarticulate. Their lack of adequate conceptual resources was due, at least in part, to the conceptual organization of experience established by their cultures, which provided no outlet for the expression of their experience. The development of the legal concept of sexual harassment (in large part due to Catharine MacKinnon's work as a lawyer and scholar) is one example of this kind of conceptual innovation.

The differences between these three possibilities are not always clear in practice. Actual cases of conceptual innovation in politics may involve all three, and perhaps other forms of conceptual change, in the course of a complex process of innovation and revision of cultural and political ideas. Yet all of these processes lead to a changed understanding of basic political and social ideas, and a challenge to the dominant culture of the time.

---

1   Nelson Mandela, "I Am Prepared to Die" available: <http://www.anc.org.za/ancdocs/history/rivonia.html>.

2   Anne Phillips, *Engendering Democracy*. (University Park, PA, 1991).

W.E.B. DU BOIS
(1868–1963)

William Edward Burghardt Du Bois (pronounced de-BOYS) was a pioneer historian of African Americans, a sociologist, historian, orator, novelist, playwright, and cultural critic. He was also a militant radical leader in the struggle against oppression, in the cause of black pride and social justice.

Du Bois was born in Great Barrington, Massachusetts, a small and almost entirely white town. Intellectually precocious, he became a local correspondent for a New York newspaper at fifteen. He received a bachelor's degree from Fisk, a black college in Nashville, Tennessee; then a second bachelors' degree (*cum laude*) from Harvard, which refused to recognize his first BA. He then completed his MA from Harvard, and, after some work at the University of Berlin, became Harvard's first African American PhD. He then spent a few years teaching, doing groundbreaking sociological research, and writing on black culture and history.

Starting around 1895, Du Bois became involved in a bitter extended controversy with Booker T. Washington, then the most powerful black voice in the US. Washington argued that black people ought not (for the moment) to push for civil rights, political power, or higher education, but should instead better themselves by training for skilled trades. Du Bois advocated instead that the black intellectual elite—the "talented tenth"—should strive to take its place among the intellectual and political leaders in the US, and from there work to improve the lot of the rest of the African American community.

But Du Bois was gradually becoming convinced that the knowledge gained by social science and higher education for black people was not in itself sufficient to combat racism and ameliorate the desperate condition of black Americans; agitation and protest were necessary. In 1906, he organized a movement that soon became the National Association for the Advancement of Colored People (NAACP). As editor for twenty-five years of the Association's *Crisis* magazine, he led protests against racist institutions and practices.

After World War I, Du Bois undertook several projects intended to unite black Americans both with each other and with African blacks; his efforts brought him into competition and conflict with Marcus Garvey, another American black with similar interests but a more popular, less intellectual approach. Despite his limited organizational success, Du Bois is often considered, along with the Liberian politician, educator and author Edward Wilmot Blyden, the father of Pan-Africanism (the movement to unite all of Africa, as well as the African diaspora). During the 1930s, pessimistic about the effectiveness of political activity against US racism, he left the NAACP for a teaching position at Atlanta University, where he wrote his two major books, *Black Reconstruction* (1935), on the post-Civil War socio-economic development of the United States; and *Dusk of Dawn* (1940), which laid out his views on both Africa's and African America's quest for freedom.

A tireless critic of imperialism, Du Bois was long associated with the Communist Party (he became a member of the USA Communist party in 1961, at the age of 93). His call for the outlawing of nuclear weapons (when he was the chairman of the Peace Information Center) led to his prosecution under the Foreign Agents Registration Act. He was acquitted for lack of evidence. Over time, he became increasingly frustrated with attempts at integration and he became increasingly sympathetic to black separatist-nationalist goals. Invited by Ghanaian president Kwame Nkrumah to direct the *Encyclopedia Africana*, he traveled to Ghana in 1961. After being refused a US passport, he became a citizen of Ghana, where he died on the eve of the 1963 March on Washington.

❖ ❖ ❖ ❖ ❖

from *The Souls of Black Folk* (*1903*)

Chapter 1: Of Our Spiritual Strivings

Between me and the other world there is ever an unasked question: unasked by some through feelings of delicacy; by others through the difficulty of rightly framing it. All, nevertheless, flutter round it. They approach me in a half-hesitant sort of way, eye me curiously or compassionately, and then, instead of saying directly, How does it feel to be a problem? they say, I know an excellent colored man in my town; or, I fought at Mechanicsville; or, Do not these Southern outrages make your blood boil? At these I smile, or am interested, or reduce the boiling to a simmer, as the occasion may require. To the real question, How does it feel to be a problem? I answer seldom a word.

And yet, being a problem is a strange experience,—peculiar even for one who has never been anything else, save perhaps in babyhood and in Europe. It is in the early days of rollicking boyhood that the revelation first bursts upon one, all in a day, as it were. I remember well when the shadow swept across me. I was a little thing, away up in the hills of New England, where the dark Housatonic winds between Hoosac and Taghkanic to the sea. In a wee wooden schoolhouse, something put it into the boys' and girls' heads to buy gorgeous visiting-cards—ten cents a package—and exchange. The exchange was merry, till one girl, a tall newcomer, refused my card,—refused it peremptorily, with a glance. Then it dawned upon me with a certain suddenness that I was different from the others; or like, mayhap, in heart and life and longing, but shut out from their world by a vast veil. I had thereafter no desire to tear down that veil, to creep through; I held all beyond it in common contempt, and lived above it in a region of blue sky and great wandering shadows. That sky was bluest when I could beat my mates at examination-time, or beat them at a foot-race, or even beat their stringy heads. Alas, with the years all this fine contempt began to fade; for the worlds I longed for, and all their dazzling opportunities, were theirs, not mine. But they should not keep these prizes, I said; some, all, I would wrest from them. Just how I would do it I could never decide: by reading law, by healing the sick, by telling the wonderful tales that swam in my head,—some way. With other

black boys the strife was not so fiercely sunny: their youth shrunk into tasteless sycophancy, or into silent hatred of the pale world about them and mocking distrust of everything white; or wasted itself in a bitter cry, Why did God make me an outcast and a stranger in mine own house? The shades of the prison-house closed round about us all: walls strait and stubborn to the whitest, but relentlessly narrow, tall, and unscalable to sons of night who must plod darkly on in resignation, or beat unavailing palms against the stone, or steadily, half hopelessly, watch the streak of blue above.

The history of the American Negro is the history of this strife,—this longing to attain self-conscious manhood, to merge his double self into a better and truer self. In this merging he wishes neither of the older selves to be lost. He would not Africanize America, for America has too much to teach the world and Africa. He would not bleach his Negro soul in a flood of white Americanism, for he knows that Negro blood has a message for the world. He simply wishes to make it possible for a man to be both a Negro and an American, without being cursed and spit upon by his fellows, without having the doors of Opportunity closed roughly in his face.

This, then, is the end of his striving: to be a co-worker in the kingdom of culture, to escape both death and isolation, to husband and use his best powers and his latent genius. These powers of body and mind have in the past been strangely wasted, dispersed, or forgotten. The shadow of a mighty Negro past flits through the tale of Ethiopia the Shadowy and of Egypt the Sphinx. Throughout history, the powers of single black men flash here and there like falling stars, and die sometimes before the world has rightly gauged their brightness. Here in America, in the few days since Emancipation, the black man's turning hither and thither in hesitant and doubtful striving has often made his very strength to lose effectiveness, to seem like absence of power, like weakness. And yet it is not weakness,—it is the contradiction of double aims. The double-aimed struggle of the black artisan—on the one hand to escape white contempt for a nation of mere hewers of wood and drawers of water, and on the other hand to plough and nail and dig for a poverty-stricken horde—could only result in making him a poor craftsman, for he had but half a heart in either cause. By the poverty and ignorance of his people, the Negro minister or doctor was tempted toward quackery and demagogy; and by the criticism of the other world, toward ideals that made him ashamed of his lowly tasks. The would-be black savant was confronted by the paradox that the knowledge his people needed was a twice-told tale to his white neighbors, while the knowledge which would teach the white world was Greek to his own flesh and blood. The innate love of harmony and beauty that set the ruder souls of his people a-dancing and a-singing raised but confusion and doubt in the soul of the black artist; for the beauty revealed to him was the soul-beauty of a race which his larger audience despised, and he could not articulate the message of another people. This waste of double aims, this seeking to satisfy two unreconciled ideals, has wrought sad havoc with the courage and faith and deeds of ten thousand thousand people,—has sent them often wooing false gods and invoking false means of salvation, and at times has even seemed about to make them ashamed of themselves.

Away back in the days of bondage they thought to see in one divine event the end of all doubt and disappointment; few men ever worshipped Freedom with half such unquestioning faith as did the American Negro for two centuries. To him, so far as he thought and dreamed, slavery was indeed the sum of all villainies, the cause of all sorrow, the root of all prejudice; Emancipation was the key to a promised land of sweeter beauty than ever stretched before the eyes of wearied Israelites. In song and exhortation swelled one refrain—Liberty; in his tears and curses the God he implored had Freedom in his right hand. At last it came,—suddenly, fearfully, like a dream. With one wild carnival of blood and passion came the message in his own plaintive cadences:—

"Shout, O children!
Shout, you're free!
For God has bought your liberty!"

Years have passed away since then,—ten, twenty, forty; forty years of national life, forty years of renewal and development, and yet the swarthy spectre sits in its accustomed seat at the Nation's feast. In vain do we cry to this our vastest social problem:—

"Take any shape but that, and my firm nerves
Shall never tremble!"

The Nation has not yet found peace from its sins; the freedman has not yet found in freedom his promised land. Whatever of good may have come in these years of change, the shadow of a deep disappointment rests upon the Negro people,—a disappointment all the more bitter because the unattained ideal was unbounded save by the simple ignorance of a lowly people.

The first decade was merely a prolongation of the vain search for freedom, the boon that seemed ever barely to elude their grasp,—like a tantalizing will-o'-the-wisp, maddening and misleading the headless host. The holocaust of war, the terrors of the Ku-Klux Klan, the lies of carpet-baggers, the disorganization of industry, and the contradictory advice of friends and foes, left the bewildered serf with no new watchword beyond the old cry for freedom. As the time flew, however, he began to grasp a new idea. The ideal of liberty demanded for its attainment powerful means, and these the Fifteenth Amendment gave him. The ballot, which before he had looked upon as a visible sign of freedom, he now regarded as the chief means of gaining and perfecting the liberty with which war had partially endowed him. And why not? Had not votes made war and emancipated millions? Had not votes enfranchised the freedmen? Was anything impossible to a power that had done all this? A million black men started with renewed zeal to vote themselves into the kingdom. So the decade flew away, the revolution of 1876 came, and left the half-free serf weary, wondering, but still inspired. Slowly but steadily, in the following years, a new vision began gradually to replace the dream of political power,—a powerful movement, the rise of another ideal to guide the unguided, another pillar of fire by night after a clouded day. It was the ideal of "book-learning"; the curiosity, born of compulsory ignorance, to know and test the power of the cabalistic letters of the white man, the longing to know. Here at last seemed to have been discovered the mountain path to Canaan; longer than the highway of Emancipation and law, steep and rugged, but straight, leading to heights high enough to overlook life.

Up the new path the advance guard toiled, slowly, heavily, doggedly; only those who have watched and guided the faltering feet, the misty minds, the dull understandings, of the dark pupils of these schools know how faithfully, how piteously, this people strove to learn. It was weary work. The cold statistician wrote down the inches of progress here and there, noted also where here and there a foot had slipped or some one had fallen. To the tired climbers, the horizon was ever dark, the mists were often cold, the Canaan was always dim and far away. If, however, the vistas disclosed as yet no goal, no resting-place, little but flattery and criticism, the journey at least gave leisure for reflection and self-examination; it changed the child of

Emancipation to the youth with dawning self-consciousness, self-realization, self-respect. In those sombre forests of his striving his own soul rose before him, and he saw himself,—darkly as through a veil; and yet he saw in himself some faint revelation of his power, of his mission. He began to have a dim feeling that, to attain his place in the world, he must be himself, and not another. For the first time he sought to analyze the burden he bore upon his back, that dead-weight of social degradation partially masked behind a half-named Negro problem. He felt his poverty; without a cent, without a home, without land, tools, or savings, he had entered into competition with rich, landed, skilled neighbors. To be a poor man is hard, but to be a poor race in a land of dollars is the very bottom of hardships. He felt the weight of his ignorance,—not simply of letters, but of life, of business, of the humanities; the accumulated sloth and shirking and awkwardness of decades and centuries shackled his hands and feet. Nor was his burden all poverty and ignorance. The red stain of bastardy, which two centuries of systematic legal defilement of Negro women had stamped upon his race, meant not only the loss of ancient African chastity, but also the hereditary weight of a mass of corruption from white adulterers, threatening almost the obliteration of the Negro home.

A people thus handicapped ought not to be asked to race with the world, but rather allowed to give all its time and thought to its own social problems. But alas! while sociologists gleefully count his bastards and his prostitutes, the very soul of the toiling, sweating black man is darkened by the shadow of a vast despair. Men call the shadow prejudice, and learnedly explain it as the natural defence of culture against barbarism, learning against ignorance, purity against crime, the "higher" against the "lower" races. To which the Negro cries Amen! and swears that to so much of this strange prejudice as is founded on just homage to civilization, culture, righteousness, and progress, he humbly bows and meekly does obeisance. But before that nameless prejudice that leaps beyond all this he stands helpless, dismayed, and well-nigh speechless; before that personal disrespect and mockery, the ridicule and systematic humiliation, the distortion of fact and wanton license of fancy, the cynical ignoring of the better and the boisterous welcoming of the worse, the all-pervading desire to inculcate disdain for everything black, from Toussaint to the devil,—before this there rises a sickening despair that would disarm and discourage any nation save that black host to whom "discouragement" is an unwritten word.

But the facing of so vast a prejudice could not but bring the inevitable self-questioning, self-disparagement, and lowering of ideals which ever accompany repression and breed in an atmosphere of contempt and hate. Whisperings and portents came borne upon the four winds: Lo! we are diseased and dying, cried the dark hosts; we cannot write, our voting is vain; what need of education, since we must always cook and serve? And the Nation echoed and enforced this self-criticism, saying: Be content to be servants, and nothing more; what need of higher culture for half-men? Away with the black man's ballot, by force or fraud,—and behold the suicide of a race! Nevertheless, out of the evil came something of good,—the more careful adjustment of education to real life, the clearer perception of the Negroes' social responsibilities, and the sobering realization of the meaning of progress.

So dawned the time of *Sturm und Drang*: storm and stress to-day rocks our little boat on the mad waters of the world-sea; there is within and without the sound of conflict, the burning of body and rending of soul; inspiration strives with doubt, and faith with vain questionings. The bright ideals of the past,—physical freedom, political power, the training of brains and the training of hands,—all these in turn have waxed and waned, until even the last grows dim and overcast. Are they all wrong,—all false? No, not that, but each alone was over-simple and incomplete,—the dreams of a credulous race-childhood, or the fond imaginings of the other world which does not know and does not want to know our power. To be really true, all these ideals must be melted and welded into one. The training of the schools we need to-day more than ever,—the training of deft hands, quick eyes and ears, and above all the broader, deeper, higher culture of gifted minds and pure hearts. The power of the ballot we need in sheer self-defence,—else what shall save us from a second slavery? Freedom, too, the long-sought, we still seek,—the freedom of life and limb, the freedom to work and think, the freedom to love and aspire. Work, culture, liberty,—all these we need, not singly but together, not successively but together, each growing and aiding each, and all striving toward that vaster ideal that swims before the Negro people, the ideal of human brotherhood, gained through the unifying ideal of Race; the ideal of fostering and developing the traits and talents of the Negro, not in opposition to or contempt for other races, but rather in large conformity to the greater ideals of the American Republic, in order that some day on American soil two world-races may give each to each those characteristics both so sadly lack. We the darker ones come even now not altogether empty-handed: there are to-day no truer exponents of the pure human spirit of the Declaration of Independence than the American Negroes; there is no true American music but the wild sweet melodies of the Negro slave; the American fairy tales and folk-lore are Indian and African; and, all in all, we black men seem the sole oasis of simple faith and reverence in a dusty desert of dollars and smartness. Will America be poorer if she replace her brutal dyspeptic blundering with light-hearted but determined Negro humility? or her coarse and cruel wit with loving jovial good-humor? or her vulgar music with the soul of the Sorrow Songs?

Merely a concrete test of the underlying principles of the great republic is the Negro Problem, and the spiritual striving of the freedmen's sons is the travail of souls whose burden is almost beyond the measure of their strength, but who bear it in the name of an historic race, in the name of this the land of their fathers' fathers, and in the name of human opportunity.

SIMONE DE BEAUVOIR
(1908–1986)

Who Was Simone de Beauvoir?

Born in Paris in 1908, Simone de Beauvoir had become such an important figure in France by the time of her death in 1986 that her funeral was attended by 5,000 people, including four former ministers of the government of President François Mitterrand. A headline announcing her death read "Women, you owe her everything!"

De Beauvoir was the eldest of two daughters in a respectable, conservative bourgeois family, and she spent her formative years heatedly reacting against her parents and their values. She became an atheist while still a teenager, and decided early on to devote her life to writing and studying "rather than" becoming a wife and mother. She studied philosophy at the ancient Parisian university of the Sorbonne and was the youngest person ever to obtain the *agrégation* (the elite French graduate

degree) in philosophy, in 1929. She was 21. In that same year she met the famous existentialist philosopher Jean-Paul Sartre and began an intense relationship with him—the most important of her life—that lasted until his death in 1980.[1]

De Beauvoir and Sartre became notorious throughout France as lovers and soul-mates who maintained an open relationship; both considered themselves sexually "liberated," and de Beauvoir was openly bisexual. Sartre made what he called a "pact" with de Beauvoir—they could have affairs with other people, but they were required to tell each other everything—and he proceeded to match his actions to this rule. As he put it to de Beauvoir: "What *we* have is an *essential* love; but it is a good idea for us also

to experience *contingent* love affairs." Despite the rotating cast of lovers, de Beauvoir remained devoted to Sartre all her life and always maintained that he was the most brilliant man she had ever known. Indeed, she once declared that, her many books, literary prizes, and social influence notwithstanding, her greatest achievement in life was her relationship with Sartre. During her lifetime Sartre, a central figure of existentialism, was regarded as a philosopher of considerably greater stature than de Beauvoir. In recent years, however, as interest in existentialism has waned while feminist thought (together with concepts such as the social construction of gender) has become more prominent, de Beauvoir has been accorded increased attention as a philosopher—to the point where she is now sometimes seen to have made a more lasting contribution to philosophy than her famous companion.

Between 1932 and 1943 de Beauvoir was a high school teacher of philosophy in Rouen, in northwestern France. There, she was subject to official reprimands for her protests about male chauvinism and for her pacifism; finally, a parental complaint made against her for "corrupting" one of her female students caused her dismissal. For the rest of her life, de Beauvoir lived in Paris and made her living from her writing. At the end of World War II, de Beauvoir became an editor at *Les Temps Modernes*, a new political journal founded by Sartre and other French intellectuals. She used this journal to promote her own work, and several excerpts from *The Second Sex* were first published in it.

Interestingly, part of the impetus to write *The Second Sex* came to her as she gradually realized that, unlike some of her female friends, she did *not* at first feel any sense that she was disadvantaged as a woman, but that this feeling of personal satisfaction and of independence resulted primarily from her relationship with a well-known, influential man—Sartre. When she reflected on this relationship, she

---

1   When the university *agrégation* results came out, Sartre was ranked first in the year and de Beauvoir second. Also, incidentally, 1929 was the year de Beauvoir acquired her lifelong nickname, *le Castor* (the French for beaver, because of the resemblance of her surname to "beaver").

realized with astonishment that she was fundamentally different from Sartre "because he was a man and I was only a woman." As she put it, "In writing *The Second Sex* I became aware, for the first time, that I myself was leading a false life, or rather, that I was profiting from this male-oriented society without even knowing it."

She was also influenced by what she saw in America, during a visit in 1947, of the experience of blacks in a segregated society. For example, she was friends with the black American short story writer and novelist, Richard Wright, who, with his white wife Ellen, was a tireless advocate for black equality. For de Beauvoir, feminism was part of a larger project of social justice and human rights. From the late 1940s until the 1960s she was a very public left-wing political activist and a vocal supporter of communism (and critic of American-style capitalism).

The Second Sex is an extended examination of the problems women have encountered throughout history, and of the possibilities left open to them. After the Introduction (reprinted here), the book is broken into two halves: Book One is a historical overview of "Facts and Myths" about women, and Book Two deals with "Women's Life Today." Book One is divided into sections describing the "Destiny" of women according to theories of biology, psychoanalysis and Marxist historical materialism; the "History" of women from prehistoric times to the granting of the vote to women in France in 1947; and "Myths" about women in literature. Book Two is more personal, and talks about women in childhood, adolescence, sexual initiation, various forms of mature loving and sexual relationships, and old age. The conclusion of the book is positive and optimistic, as de Beauvoir tries to set out a model of life and action for future generations of women.

Some Useful Background Information

i) The first words of Book Two of *The Second Sex* are "One is not born, but rather becomes, a woman.[1] No biological, psychological or economic fate determines the figure that the human female presents in society; it is civilisation as a whole that determines this creature." This is how de Beauvoir most famously expresses an influential central thesis of the book: that "woman," as a biological category, is separable from "feminine," as a social construction—or

more generally, that sex is not the same thing as gender. Thus, woman's status under the patriarchy as the Other is a contingent, socially constructed fact rather than an essential truth about the female gender.

It is important to appreciate that de Beauvoir is not denying that there are biological differences between men and women, nor does she insist that these biological differences must be simply ignored in a properly constituted society. Rather, she is arguing that our *biological* constitutions do not determine our *gender* characteristics: such things as 'femininity' or 'masculinity,' being 'nurturing' or 'modest' or 'emotional' or 'delicate'—these things are constructed and constrained purely by *social* influences. Under different social conditions women and men might naturally and freely behave in ways radically different from contemporary social norms.

Thus, according to de Beauvoir, gender is more something we *do*—a way we live—than something we *are*. Gender is constrained by social pressures in large part because social pressures constrain how we can legitimately behave. A woman in, say, Canada in the 1950s could not just decide as an individual to behave like a man—or like someone who is neither masculine nor feminine—and in this way change her gender unilaterally. Even if she were brave enough to attempt the experiment, according to de Beauvoir—and the other existentialists—one cannot possess a certain trait, such as being masculine, unless others recognize one as doing so.

ii) This emphasis on the social construction of gender, race, and other aspects of the reality we experience in our day-to-day lives is related to de Beauvoir's commitment to *existentialism*. Central to existentialism is the doctrine that *existence precedes essence*: humans have no pre-given purpose or essence determined for them by God or by biology. According to existentialism, each consciousness faces the world as an isolated individual, and inevitably creates itself—gives itself determinate form—by making choices. These choices are forced by the need to respond to the things around us, including both passive natural objects and other consciousnesses.

De Beauvoir sees the meeting of one consciousness with another as profoundly disturbing: faced with the gaze of an Other, we recognize a point of view which is necessarily different from our own and so we are required to concede our own incompleteness; furthermore, the opposing consciousness must treat *us* as an Other, which we feel as a threat to destroy us by turning us into an object.

---

1   In the original French this famous phrase reads "On ne naît pas femme, on le devient."

De Beauvoir's feminism can be seen as a development of this idea: in response to the threat posed by other consciousnesses, according to existentialism, one might retaliate by objectifying and dominating the Other, to be able to control it without destroying it and thus be able to withstand its gaze. Thus, according to de Beauvoir, men have objectified and dominated women as the Other, and, succumbing to all-pervasive social pressures, women have allowed themselves to be dominated.

iii) Towards the end of this essay, de Beauvoir mentions the contrast between being *en-soi* (in-itself) and being *pour-soi* (for-itself). Being for-itself is a mode of existence that is purposive and, as it were, constituted by its own activity; being in-itself, by contrast, is a less fully human kind of existence that is more like being a 'thing'—self-sufficient, non-purposive, driven by merely contingent current conditions.

How Important and Influential is This Passage?

The Second Sex is often considered the founding work of twentieth-century feminism. It has been called "one of the most important and far-reaching books on women ever published" (Terry Keefe) and "the best book about women ever written" (*The Guardian*, 1999). From the day it was published it was both popular and controversial: twenty-two thousand copies of the first volume were sold in France in the first week, and de Beauvoir received large quantities of hate mail including some from "very active members of the First Sex." "How courageous you are.... You're going to lose a lot of friends!" one of her friends wrote to her. She was accused of writing a pornographic book (because of *The Second Sex*'s discussion of female sexuality), and the Vatican put it on the Index of prohibited books. "Once," de Beauvoir reported in her autobiography, "during an entire dinner at Nos Provinces on the Boulevard Montparnasse, a table of people nearby stared at me and giggled; I didn't like dragging [her lover, Nelson] Algren into a scene, but as I left I gave them a piece of my mind." On the other hand, some of the contemporary reviews were glowing: *The New Yorker* called it "more than a work of scholarship; it is a work of art, with the salt of recklessness that makes art sting."

After the initial furor died down, the book was criticized by some scholars and critics as being distorted by a middle-class viewpoint—having been written by someone who had no cause to actually feel the pressures that give life

to feminism. The poet Stevie Smith wrote, in 1953: "She has written an enormous book about women and it is soon clear that she does not like them, nor does she like being a woman." This debate continues today, and arguably it is only recently that *The Second Sex* has come to be appreciated seriously as a work of philosophy that stands on its own merits, rather than read solely in terms of de Beauvoir's "biography, relationship with … Sartre, psyche, or feminist credentials" (*TLS*, 2005).

De Beauvoir is a pivotal figure in the history of feminist thought from the Renaissance to the twenty-first century. In the Renaissance and early modern period, writers that we would today think of as feminist (represented by intellectuals such as Christine de Pisan [1365–c. 1430] and Mary Astell [1666–1731]) tended to focus on the social asymmetries between women and men. They argued that women have similar innate abilities to men and should be granted opportunities equivalent to those their male counterparts enjoyed in certain key areas, especially education, the family, and sometimes work and politics. The eighteenth and nineteenth centuries (represented by figures such as Olympe de Gouges [1745–93], Mary Wollstonecraft [1759–97], Sojourner Truth [1797–1883], John Stuart Mill [1806–73], and Harriet Taylor [1807–58]) saw a greater accumulation of forceful writings against the oppression of women, combined with more explicit (but only gradually successful) political campaigns to have women's equal status with men enshrined in law. It was at the end of the nineteenth century—in France, during the 1890s—that the term 'feminism' first appeared.

Up to this point, feminism can be usefully—albeit simplistically—understood as characterized by a demand for equal rights with men. Once women are educated as extensively as men, are given the opportunity to vote, are not forbidden from joining certain professions, and so on, then it was assumed that their innate capacities—in many (though perhaps not all) respects equal to, or even superior to, those of the male sex—would flourish free from oppression. That is, pre–twentieth-century feminism tended to focus on the suppression and distortion of woman's nature by contingent social structures such as laws and institutions. De Beauvoir's writings marked a significant shift and deepening in the nature of feminist thought. She denied that there is an inborn 'female nature' that just awaits the opportunity to break free from male oppression, and insisted that women are dominated by men in *all* aspects of their lives—that their very consciousness, the very shape of their minds, is formed by the patriarchal society of which they are a part. Feminism cannot aspire simply to change the laws and institutions of a country; this will leave the subordinate position of women essentially untouched. Feminists must fight for much more thoroughgoing change to the basic practices and assumptions of the whole society.

Later twentieth-century feminism, often known as *second-wave feminism* (represented here by Susan Moller Okin [1946–2004], Catharine MacKinnon [1946–], Martha Nussbaum [1947–], and Iris Young [1949–2006]), took up this emphasis on the deep and subtle nature of patriarchal dominance (though often without a very self-conscious sense of the debt to de Beauvoir). The distinction between sex and gender—the notion of gender as a social construct—proved especially significant in making this case. For many feminists, this has evolved into a critique of standards that are taken to have an objective and universal status—such as 'rational,' 'true,' and 'right'—but which, feminists argue, in fact reflect particular gender interests. Thus, for example, to argue—as Wollstonecraft did—that women are 'equally rational' as men is to succumb to, rather than combat, one of the hidden patriarchal structures that oppress women.

The so-called *third-wave* (or sometimes, *postmodern*) feminism that began in the 1980s can also be seen as having roots in the work of de Beauvoir. Third-wave feminism emphasizes the claim that gender is a social, contingent, rather than a natural category, and adopts an 'anti-essentialist' stance about women: that is, there is nothing that can be usefully said about woman 'as such,' and instead we must focus in an explicitly un-integrated way on different conceptions of femininity in particular ethnic, religious and social groups.

◆ ◆ ◆ ◆ ◆

from *The Second Sex* Introduction (1949)

For a long time I have hesitated to write a book on woman. The subject is irritating, especially to women; and it is not new. Enough ink has been spilled in the quarreling over feminism, now practically over, and perhaps we should say no more about it. It is still talked about, however, for the voluminous nonsense uttered during the last century seems to have done little to illuminate the problem. After all, is

there a problem? And if so, what is it? Are there women, really? Most assuredly the theory of the eternal feminine still has its adherents who will whisper in your ear: "Even in Russia women still are *women*"; and other erudite persons—sometimes the very same—say with a sigh: "Woman is losing her way, woman is lost." One wonders if women still exist, if they will always exist, whether or not it is desirable that they should, what place they occupy in this world, what their place should be. "What has become of women?" was asked recently in an ephemeral magazine.[1]

But first we must ask: what is a woman? *"Tota mulier in utero,"* says one, "woman is a womb." But in speaking of certain women, connoisseurs declare that they are not women, although they are equipped with a uterus like the rest. All agree in recognizing the fact that females exist in the human species; today as always they make up about one half of humanity. And yet we are told that femininity is in danger; we are exhorted to be women, remain women, become women. It would appear, then, that every female human being is not necessarily a woman; to be so considered she must share in that mysterious and threatened reality known as femininity. Is this attribute something secreted by the ovaries? Or is it a Platonic essence,[2] a product of the philosophic imagination? Is a rustling petticoat enough to bring it down to earth? Although some women try zealously to incarnate this essence, it is hardly patentable. It is frequently described in vague and dazzling terms that seem to have been borrowed from the vocabulary of the seers, and indeed in the times of St. Thomas it was considered an essence as certainly defined as the somniferous virtue of the poppy.[3]

But conceptualism has lost ground. The biological and social sciences no longer admit the existence of unchange-

---

1 *ephemeral magazine* [Unless otherwise indicated, all notes to this section are by the editors of this anthology.] [de Beauvoir's note] *Franchise,* dead today.

2 *Platonic essence* For Plato and a number of other philosophers, each individual object has certain characteristics that are necessarily true of it, and of all other objects of its kind—essences. Citing these was supposed to provide explanations of how things worked. De Beauvoir and the existentialists reject the notion of explanation by essences for people.

3 *somniferous virtue of the poppy* This is the often-quoted case of an empty pseudo-explanation by essences or virtues supposedly given by Scholastic philosophers. In answer to a request for an explanation of why extract of poppies (opium) puts one to sleep, it is "explained" that they have a "soporific" virtue or essence—"soporific" means nothing but *capable of putting one to sleep.*

ably fixed entities that determine given characteristics, such as those ascribed to woman, the Jew, or the Negro. Science regards any characteristic as a reaction dependent in part upon a *situation*. If today femininity no longer exists, then it never existed. But does the word *woman*, then, have no specific content? This is stoutly affirmed by those who hold to the philosophy of the enlightenment, of rationalism;[1] women, to them, are merely the human beings arbitrarily designated by the word *woman*. Many American women particularly are prepared to think that there is no longer any place for woman as such; if a backward individual still takes herself for a woman, her friends advise her to be psychoanalyzed and thus get rid of this obsession. In regard to a work, *Modern Woman: The Lost Sex*, which in other respects has its irritating features, Dorothy Parker[2] has written: ... I cannot be just to books which treat of woman as woman.... My idea is that all of us, men as well as women, should be regarded as human beings." But nominalism is a rather inadequate doctrine, and the antifemininists have had no trouble in showing that women simply *are not* men. Surely woman is, like man, a human being; but such a declaration is abstract. The fact is that every concrete human being is always a singular, separate individual. To decline to accept such notions as the eternal feminine, the black soul, the Jewish character, is not to deny that Jews, Negroes, women exist today—this denial does not represent a liberation for those concerned, but rather a flight from reality. Some years ago a well-known

woman writer refused to permit her portrait to appear in a series of photographs especially devoted to women writers; she wished to be counted among the men. But in order to gain this privilege she made use of her husband's influence! Women who assert that they are men lay claim none the less to masculine consideration and respect. I recall also a young Trotskyite standing on a platform at a boisterous meeting and getting ready to use her fists, in spite of her evident fragility. She was denying her feminine weakness; but it was for love of a militant male whose equal she wished to be. The attitude of defiance of many American women proves that they are haunted by a sense of their femininity. In truth, to go for a walk with one's eyes open is enough to demonstrate that humanity is divided into two classes of individuals whose clothes, faces, bodies, smiles, gaits, interests, and occupations are manifestly different. Perhaps these differences are superficial, perhaps they are destined to disappear. What is certain is that right now they do most obviously exist.

If her functioning as a female is not enough to define woman, if we decline also to explain her through "the eternal feminine," and if nevertheless we admit, provisionally, that women do exist, then we must face the question: what is a woman?

To state the question is, to me, to suggest, at once, a preliminary answer. The fact that I ask it is in itself significant. A man would never get the notion of writing a book on the peculiar situation of the human male.[3] But if I wish to define myself, I must first of all say: "I am a woman"; on this truth must be based all further discussion. A man never begins by presenting himself as an individual of a certain sex; it goes without saying that he is a man. The terms *masculine* and *feminine* are used symmetrically only as a matter of form, as on legal papers. In actuality the relation of the two sexes is not quite like that of two electrical poles, for man represents both the positive and the neutral, as is indicated by the common use of *man* to designate human beings in general; whereas woman represents only the negative, defined by limiting criteria, without reciprocity. In the midst of an abstract discussion it is vexing to hear a man say: "You think thus and so because you are a woman"; but I know that my only defense is to reply: "I think thus and so because it is true," thereby removing my subjective self

---

1　*enlightenment ... nominalism* Enlightenment philosophy is associated with the Scientific Revolution of the seventeenth and eighteenth centuries, rejecting explanation by essences, and preferring instead science done by observation; "rationalism" is a term applied to the approach of a variety of philosophical schools. The central core is reliance on reason, but this surely applies to Plato's theories of explanation (in contrast to the observational core of science since the Enlightenment). De Beauvoir is probably referring here to the emphasis placed in the work of Descartes, Leibniz, and Spinoza (the "continental rationalists") on mathematical reasoning in science; "nominalism" is the position that categories of things do not exist in nature, but are a result of our categorization and naming; thus it too would reject explanations of how something works that appeal to the real essence it supposedly shares with other things of its natural kind.

2　*Dorothy Parker* (1893–1967), American poet and writer, best known for her witty commentaries on contemporary life and her wisecracks. She was an energetic civil libertarian, civil-rights advocate, and left-wing critic, and was persecuted as an alleged communist during the 1950s anti-communist hysteria in the United States.

3　*A man would ... human male* [de Beauvoir's note] The Kinsey Report [Alfred C. Kinsey and others: *Sexual Behavior in the Human Male* (W.B. Saunders Co., 1948)] is no exception, for it is limited to describing the sexual characteristics of American men, which is quite a different matter.

from the argument. It would be out of the question to reply: "And you think the contrary because you are a man," for it is understood that the fact of being a man is no peculiarity. A man is in the right in being a man; it is the woman who is in the wrong. It amounts to this: just as for the ancients there was an absolute vertical with reference to which the oblique was defined, so there is an absolute human type, the masculine. Woman has ovaries, a uterus; these peculiarities imprison her in her subjectivity, circumscribe her within the limits of her own nature. It is often said that she thinks with her glands. Man superbly ignores the fact that his anatomy also includes glands, such as the testicles, and that they secrete hormones. He thinks of his body as a direct and normal connection with the world, which he believes he apprehends objectively, whereas he regards the body of woman as a hindrance, a prison, weighed down by everything peculiar to it. "The female is a female by virtue of a certain *lack* of qualities," said Aristotle; "we should regard the female nature as afflicted with a natural defectiveness." And St. Thomas for his part pronounced woman to be an "imperfect man," an "incidental" being. This is symbolized in Genesis where Eve is depicted as made from what Bossuet[1] called "a supernumerary bone" of Adam.

Thus humanity is male and man defines woman not in herself but as relative to him; she is not regarded as an autonomous being. Michelet[2] writes: "Woman, the relative being...." And Benda[3] is most positive in his *Rapport d'Uriel:* "The body of man makes sense in itself quite apart from that of woman, whereas the latter seems wanting in significance by itself.... Man can think of himself without woman. She cannot think of herself without man." And she is simply what man decrees; thus she is called "the sex," by which is meant that she appears essentially to the male as a sexual being. For him she is sex—absolute sex, no less. She is defined and differentiated with reference to man and not he with reference to her; she is the incidental, the inessential as opposed to the essential. He is the Subject, he is the Absolute—she is the Other.[4]

The category of the *Other* is as primordial as consciousness itself. In the most primitive societies, in the most ancient mythologies, one finds the expression of a duality-that of the Self and the Other. This duality was not originally attached to the division of the sexes; it was not dependent upon any empirical facts. It is revealed in such works as that of Granet on Chinese thought[5] and those of Dumézil on the East Indies and Rome.[6] The feminine element was at first no more involved in such pairs as Varuna-Mitra, Uranus-Zeus,[7] Sun-Moon, and Day-Night than it was in the contrasts between Good and Evil, lucky and unlucky auspices, right and left, God and Lucifer. Otherness is a fundamental category of human thought.

Thus it is that no group ever sets itself up as the One without at once setting up the Other over against itself. If three travelers chance to occupy the same compartment, that is enough to make vaguely hostile "others" out of all the rest of the passengers on the train. In small-town eyes all persons not belonging to the village are "strangers" and suspect; to the native of a country all who inhabit other countries are "foreigners"; Jews are "different" for the anti-Semite, Negroes are "inferior" for American racists, aborig-

a case in which otherness, alterity [altérité], unquestionably marks the nature of a being as its essence, an instance of otherness not consisting purely and simply in the opposition of two species of the same genus? I think that the feminine represents the contrary in its absolute sense, this contrariness being in no wise affected by any relation between it and its correlative and thus remaining absolutely other. Sex is not a certain specific difference ... no more is the sexual difference a mere contradiction.... Nor does this difference lie in the duality of two complementary terms, for two complementary terms imply a pre-existing whole.... Otherness reaches its full flowering in the feminine, a term of the same rank as consciousness but of opposite meaning."

I suppose that Lévinas does not forget that woman, too, is aware of her own consciousness, or ego. But it is striking that he deliberately takes a man's point of view, disregarding the reciprocity of subject and object. When he writes that woman is mystery, he implies that she is mystery for man. Thus his description, which is intended to be objective, is in fact an assertion of masculine privilege.

1   *Bossuet*   Jacques-Benigne Bossuet (1627–1704), French cleric and theologian.

2   *Michelet*   Jules Michelet (1798–1874), French historian.

3   *Benda*   Julien Benda (1867–1956), French philosopher and novelist. *Le rapport d'Uriel* was published in 1946.

4   *she is the Other*   [de Beauvoir's note] Emmanuel Lévinas [French philosopher, 1906–95] expresses this idea most explicitly in his essay *[Le] Temps et L'Autre* [*Time and the Other*, 1948]. "Is there not

5   *Granet on Chinese thought*   Marcel Granet (1884–1940), French sociologist, wrote a large number of works applying sociological methods to the study of China.

6   *Dumézil on the East Indies and Rome*   Georges Dumézil (1898–1986), French comparative philologist known for his theories of myth and social structure.

7   *Varuna-Mitra, Uranus-Zeus*   Varuna and Mitra are gods in ancient Indian mythology, closely associated with each other. Uranus in Greek mythology was the grandfather of Zeus.

ines are "natives" for colonists, proletarians are the "lower class" for the privileged.

Levi-Strauss, at the end of a profound work on the various forms of primitive societies, reaches the following conclusion; "Passage from the state of Nature to the state of Culture is marked by man's ability to view biological relations as a series of contrasts; duality, alternation, opposition, and symmetry, whether under definite or vague forms, constitute not so much phenomena to be explained as fundamental and immediately given data of social reality."[1] These phenomena would be incomprehensible if in fact human society were simply a *Mitsein*[2] or fellowship based on solidarity and friendliness. Things become clear, on the contrary, if, following Hegel,[3] we find in consciousness itself a fundamental hostility toward every other consciousness; the subject can be posed only in being opposed—he sets himself up as the essential, as opposed to the other, the inessential, the object.

But the other consciousness, the other ego, sets up a reciprocal claim. The native traveling abroad is shocked to find himself in turn regarded as a "stranger" by the natives of neighboring countries, As a matter of fact, wars, festivals, trading, treaties, and contests among tribes, nations, and classes tend to deprive the concept *Other* of its absolute sense and to make manifest its relativity; willy-nilly, individuals and groups are forced to realize the reciprocity of their relations. How is it, then, that this reciprocity has not been recognized between the sexes, that one of the contrasting terms is set up as the sole essential, denying any relativity in regard to its correlative and defining the latter as pure otherness? Why is it that women do not dispute male sovereignty? No subject will readily volunteer to become the object, the inessential; it is not the Other who, in defining himself as the Other, establishes the One. The Other is posed as such by the One in defining himself as the One. But if the Other is not to regain the status of being the One, he must be submissive enough to accept this alien point of view. Whence comes this submission in the case of woman?

There are, to be sure, other cases in which a certain category has been able to dominate another completely for a time. Very often this privilege depends upon inequality of numbers-the majority imposes its rule upon the minority or persecutes it. But women are not a minority, like the American Negroes or the Jews; there are as many women as men on earth. Again, the two groups concerned have often been originally independent; they may have been formerly unaware of each other's existence, or perhaps they recognized each other's autonomy. But a historical event has resulted in the subjugation of the weaker by the stronger. The scattering of the Jews, the introduction of slavery into America, the conquests of imperialism are examples in point. In these cases the oppressed retained at least the memory of former days; they possessed in common a past, a tradition, sometimes a religion or a culture.

The parallel drawn by Bebel[4] between women and the proletariat is valid in that neither ever formed a minority or a separate collective unit of mankind. And instead of a single historical event it is in both cases a historical development that explains their status as a class and accounts for the membership of *particular individuals* in that class. But proletarians have not always existed, whereas there have always been women. They are women in virtue of their anatomy and physiology. Throughout history they have always been subordinated to men, and hence their dependency is not the result of a historical event or a social change—it was not something that *occurred.* The reason why otherness in this case seems to be an absolute is in part that it lacks the contingent or incidental nature of historical facts. A condition brought about at a certain time can be abolished at some other time, as the Negroes of Haiti and others have proved; but it might seem that a natural condition is beyond the possibility of change. In truth, however, the nature of things is no more immutably given, once for all, than is historical reality. If woman seems to be the inessential which never becomes the essential, it is because she herself fails to bring about this change. Proletarians say "We"; Negroes also. Regarding themselves as subjects, they transform the bourgeois, the whites, into "others." But women do not

---

1   *Passage from ... social reality*   [de Beauvoir's note] See Claude Lévi-Strauss [b.1908, French structuralist anthropologist]: *Les Structures élémentaires de la parenté* [*The Elementary Structures of Kinship*, 1949]. My thanks are due to C. Levi-Strauss for his kindness in furnishing me with the proofs of his work, which, among others, I have used liberally in Part 2.

2   *Mitsein*   Term associated with the German philosopher Martin Heidegger; it is translated as *being-with-others.*

3   *Hegel*   Georg Wilhelm Friedrich Hegel (1770–1831), central nineteenth-century German idealist philosopher.

4   *Bebel*   August Ferdinand Bebel (1840–1913), German social democrat, organizer, and theoretician; author of *Women and Socialism* (1879).

say "We," except at some congress of feminists or similar formal demonstration; men say "women," and women use the same word in referring to themselves. They do not authentically assume a subjective attitude. The proletarians have accomplished the revolution in Russia, the Negroes in Haiti, the Indo-Chinese are battling for it in Indo-China; but the women's effort has never been anything more than a symbolic agitation. They have gained only what men have been willing to grant; they have taken nothing, they have only received.

The reason for this is that women lack concrete means for organizing themselves into a unit which can stand face to face with the correlative unit. They have no past, no history, no religion of their own; and they have no such solidarity of work and interest as that of the proletariat. They are not even promiscuously herded together in the way that creates community feeling among the American Negroes, the ghetto Jews, the workers of Saint-Denis, or the factory hands of Renault. They live dispersed among the males, attached through residence, housework, economic condition, and social standing to certain men-fathers or husbands-more firmly than they are to other women. If they belong to the bourgeoisie, they feel solidarity with men of that class, not with proletarian women; if they are white, their allegiance is to white men, not to Negro women. The proletariat can propose to massacre the ruling class, and a sufficiently fanatical Jew or Negro might dream of getting sole possession of the atomic bomb and making humanity wholly Jewish or black; but woman cannot even dream of exterminating the males. The bond that unites her to her oppressors is not comparable to any other. The division of the sexes is a biological fact, not an event in human history. Male and female stand opposed within a primordial *Mitsein*, and woman has not broken it. The couple is a fundamental unity with its two halves riveted together, and the cleavage of society along the line of sex is impossible. Here is to be found the basic trait of woman: she is the Other in a totality of which the two components are necessary to one another.

One could suppose that this reciprocity might have facilitated the liberation of woman. When Hercules sat at the feet of Omphale and helped with her spinning, his desire for her held him captive; but why did she fail to gain a lasting power? To revenge herself on Jason, Medea killed their children; and this grim legend would seem to suggest that she might have obtained a formidable influence over him through his love for his offspring. In *Lysistrata* Aristophanes gaily depicts a band of women who joined forces to gain

social ends through the sexual needs of their men; but this is only a play. In the legend of the Sabine women, the latter soon abandoned their plan of remaining *sterile* to punish their ravishers. In truth woman has not been socially emancipated through man's need—sexual desire and the desire for offspring-which makes the male dependent for satisfaction upon the female.

Master and slave, also, are united by a reciprocal need, in this case economic, which does not liberate the slave. In the relation of master to slave the master does not make a point of the need that he has for the other; he has in his grasp the power of satisfying this need through his own action; whereas the slave, in his dependent condition, his hope and fear, is quite conscious of the need he has for his master. Even if the need is at bottom equally urgent for both, it always works in favor of the oppressor and against the oppressed. That is why the liberation of the working class, for example, has been slow.

Now, woman has always been man's dependent, if not his slave; the two sexes have never shared the world in equality. And even today woman is heavily handicapped, though her situation is beginning to change. Almost nowhere is her legal status the same as man's, and frequently it is much to her disadvantage. Even when her rights are legally recognized in the abstract, long-standing custom prevents their full expression in the mores. In the economic sphere men and women can almost be said to make up two castes; other things being equal, the former hold the better jobs, get higher wages, and have more opportunity for success than their new competitors. In industry and politics men have a great many more positions and they monopolize the most important posts. In addition to all this, they enjoy a traditional prestige that the education of children tends in every way to support, for the present enshrines the past—and in the past all history has been made by men. At the present time, when women are beginning to take part in the affairs of the world, it is still a world that belongs to men—they have no doubt of it at all and women have scarcely any. To decline to be the Other, to refuse to be a party to the deal—this would be for women to renounce all the advantages conferred upon them by their alliance with the superior caste. Man-the-sovereign will provide woman-the-liege with material protection and, will undertake the moral justification of her existence; thus she can evade at once both economic risk and the metaphysical risk of a liberty in which ends and aims must be contrived without assistance. Indeed, along with the ethical urge of each individual to affirm his subjective existence, there is also the temptation to forgo liberty and become a thing. This is an inauspicious road, for he who takes it—passive, lost, ruined—becomes henceforth the creature of another's will, frustrated in his transcendence and deprived of every value. But it is an easy road; on it one avoids the strain involved in undertaking an authentic existence. When man makes of woman the *Other*, he may, then, expect her to manifest deep-seated tendencies toward complicity. Thus, woman may fail to lay claim to the status of subject because she lacks definite resources, because she feels the necessary bond that ties her to man regardless of reciprocity, and because she is often very well pleased with her role as the *Other*.

But it will be asked at once: how did all this begin? It is easy to see that the duality of the sexes, like any duality, gives rise to conflict. And doubtless the winner will assume the status of absolute. But why should man have won from the start? It seems possible that women could have won the victory; or that the outcome of the conflict might never have been decided. How is it that this world has always belonged to the men and that things have begun to change only recently? Is this change a good thing? Will it bring about an equal sharing of the world between men and women?

These questions are not new, and they have often been answered. But the very fact that woman *is the Other* tends to cast suspicion upon all the justifications that men have ever been able to provide for it. These have all too evidently been dictated by men's interest. A little known feminist of the seventeenth century, Poulain de la Barre,[1] put it this way: "All that has been written about women by men should be suspect, for the men are at once judge and party to the lawsuit." Everywhere, at all times, the males have displayed their satisfaction in feeling that they are the lords of creation. "Blessed be God ... that He did not make me a woman," say the Jews in their morning prayers, while their wives pray on a note of resignation: "Blessed be the Lord, who created me according to His will." The first among the blessings for which Plato thanked the gods was that he had been created free, not enslaved; the second, a man, not a woman. But the males could not enjoy this privilege fully unless they believed it to be founded on the absolute and the eternal; they sought to make the fact of their supremacy into a right. "Being men, those who have made and com-

piled the laws have favored their own sex, and jurists have elevated these laws into principles," to quote Poulain de la Barre once more.

Legislators, priests, philosophers, writers, and scientists have striven to show that the subordinate position of woman is willed in heaven and advantageous on earth. The religions invented by men reflect this wish for domination. In the legends of Eve and Pandora men have taken up arms against women. They have made use of philosophy and theology, as the quotations from Aristotle and St. Thomas have shown. Since ancient times satirists and moralists have delighted in showing up the weaknesses of women. We are familiar with the savage indictments hurled against women throughout French literature. Montherlant, for example, follows the tradition of Jean de Meung,[2] though with less gusto. This hostility may at times be well founded, often it is gratuitous; but in truth it more or less successfully conceals a desire for self-justification. As Montaigne[3] says, "It is easier to accuse one sex than to excuse the other." Sometimes what is going on is clear enough. For instance, the Roman law limiting the rights of woman cited "the imbecility, the instability of the sex" just when the weakening of family ties seemed to threaten the interests of male heirs. And in the effort to keep the married woman under guardianship, appeal was made in the sixteenth century to the authority of St. Augustine, who declared that "woman is a creature neither decisive nor constant," at a time when the single woman was thought capable of managing her property. Montaigne understood clearly how arbitrary and unjust was woman's appointed lot: "Women are not in the wrong when they decline to accept the rules laid down for them, since the men make these rules without consulting them. No wonder intrigue and strife abound." But he did not go so far as to champion their cause.

It was only later, in the eighteenth century, that genuinely democratic men began to view the matter objectively.

---

1 *Poulain de la Barre* François Poulain de la Barre (1647–1723). A disciple of Descartes, he wrote three works between 1673 and 1675 arguing for the equality of the sexes; the best-known of these is *De L'Égalité Des Deux Sexes* (*Equality of the Two Sexes*).

2 *Montherlant ... Jean de Meung* Henry de Montherlant (1896–1972), French writer whose decadent and eccentric novels glorify masculinity and violence, and decry "feminization." *Jean de Meung* (c. 1250–c. 1305) is sometimes considered the greatest of the French medieval poets. His best-known work is a massive continuation of the earlier *Roman de la Rose* of Guillaume de Lorris; in it, he satirizes many aspects of medieval society, and is especially critical of women.

3 *Montaigne* Michel Eyquem de Montaigne-Delecroix (1533–92), influential French philosopher and essayist.

Diderot,[1] among others, strove to show that woman is, like man, a human being. Later John Stuart Mill[2] came fervently to her defense. But these philosophers displayed unusual impartiality. In the nineteenth century the feminist quarrel became again a quarrel of partisans. One of the consequences of the industrial revolution was the entrance of women into productive labor, and it was just here that the claims of the feminists emerged from the realm of theory and acquired an economic basis, while their opponents became the more aggressive. Although landed property lost power to some extent, the bourgeoisie clung to the old morality that found the guarantee of private property in the solidity of the family. Woman was ordered back into the home the more harshly as her emancipation became a real menace. Even within the working class the men endeavored to restrain woman's liberation, because they began to see the women as dangerous competitors—the more so because they were accustomed to work for lower wages.

In proving woman's inferiority, the antifeminists then began to draw not only upon religion, philosophy, and theology, as before, but also upon science—biology, experimental psychology, etc. At most they were willing to grant "equality in difference" to the *other* sex. That profitable formula is most significant; it is precisely like the "equal but separate" formula of the Jim Crow laws[3] aimed at the North American Negroes. As is well known, this so-called equalitarian segregation has resulted only in the most extreme discrimination. The similarity just noted is in no way due to chance, for whether it is a race, a caste, a class, or a sex that is reduced to a position of inferiority, the methods of justification are the same. "The eternal feminine" corresponds to "the black soul" and to "the Jewish character."

---

1   *Diderot*   Denis Diderot (1713–84), French Enlightenment philosopher best known as the editor of the *Encyclopédie*. In his essay "Sur Les Femmes" (1772) he spoke sympathetically of women's difficult plight, but claimed that their inferior mental capacity made them incapable of real understanding.

2   *John Stuart Mill*   John Stuart Mill (1806–73) was perhaps the leading British nineteenth-century liberal philosopher and political economist. De Beauvoir refers to his work favoring equality of the sexes such as *The Subjection of Women* (1869) (possibly jointly authored with Harriet Taylor Mill).

3   *Jim Crow laws*   State and local laws in the southern US between 1876 and 1965 forbidding interracial marriage and mandating "separate but equal" treatment and facilities for blacks; in fact, these almost always were unequal, with those for blacks being far inferior. "Jim Crow" was the name of a black character in minstrel shows.

True, the Jewish problem is on the whole very different from the other two—to the anti-Semite the Jew is not so much an inferior as he is an enemy for whom there is to be granted no place on earth, for whom annihilation is the fate desired. But there are deep similarities between the situation of woman and that of the Negro. Both are being emancipated today from a like paternalism, and the former master class wishes to "keep them in their place"—that is, the place chosen for them. In both cases the former masters lavish more or less sincere eulogies, either on the virtues of "the good Negro" with his dormant, childish, merry soul—the submissive Negro—or on the merits of the woman who is "truly feminine"—that is, frivolous, infantile, irresponsible-the submissive woman. In both cases the dominant class bases its argument on a state of affairs that it has itself created. As George Bernard Shaw puts it, in substance, "The American white relegates the black to the rank of shoeshine boy; and he concludes from this that the black is good for nothing but shining shoes." This vicious circle is met with in all analogous circumstances; when an individual (or a group of individuals) is kept in a situation of inferiority, the fact is that he *is* inferior. But the significance of the verb to *be* must be rightly understood here; it is in bad faith to give it a static value when it really has the dynamic Hegelian sense of "to have become." Yes, women on the whole *are* today inferior to men; that is, their situation affords them fewer possibilities. The question is: should that state of affairs continue?

Many men hope that it will continue; not all have given up the battle. The conservative bourgeoisie still see in the emancipation of women a menace to their morality and their interests. Some men dread feminine competition. Recently a male student wrote in the *Hebdo-Latin:* "Every woman student who goes into medicine or law robs us of a job." He never questioned his rights in this world. And economic interests are not the only ones concerned. One of the benefits that oppression confers upon the oppressors is that the most humble among them is made to *feel* superior; thus, a "poor white" in the South can console himself with the thought that he is not a "dirty nigger"—and the more prosperous whites cleverly exploit this pride. Similarly, the most mediocre of males feels himself a demigod as compared with women. It was much easier for M. de Montherlant to think himself a hero when he faced women (and women chosen for his purpose) than when he was obliged to act the man among men—something many women have done better than he, for that matter. And in September 1948, in one of his articles in the *Figaro littéraire*, Claude Mauriac[1]—whose great originality is admired by all—could write regarding woman (or at least he thought he *could*): "*We* listen on a tone [*sic!*] of polite indifference ... to the most brilliant among them, well knowing that her wit reflects more or less luminously ideas that come from *us.*" Evidently the speaker referred to is not reflecting the ideas of Mauriac himself, for no one knows of his having any. It may be that she reflects ideas originating with men, but then, even among men there are those who have been known to appropriate ideas not their own; and one can well ask whether Claude Mauriac might not find more interesting a conversation reflecting Descartes, Marx, or Gide rather than himself. What is really remarkable is that by using the questionable *we* he identifies himself with St. Paul, Hegel, Lenin, and Nietzsche, and from the lofty eminence of their grandeur looks down disdainfully upon the bevy of women who make bold to converse with him on a footing of equality. In truth, I know of more than one woman who would refuse to suffer with patience Mauriac's "tone of polite indifference."

I have lingered on this example because the masculine attitude is here displayed with disarming ingenuousness. But men profit in many more subtle ways from the otherness, the alterity[2] of woman. Here is miraculous balm for those afflicted with an inferiority complex, and indeed no one is more arrogant toward women, more aggressive or scornful, than the man who is anxious about his virility. Those who are not fear-ridden in the presence of their fellow men are much more disposed to recognize a fellow creature in woman; but even to these the myth of Woman, the Other, is precious for many reasons.[3] They cannot be blamed for not cheerfully relinquishing all the benefits they derive from the myth, for they realize what they would lose in relinquishing woman as they fancy her to be, while they

fail to realize what they have to gain from the woman of tomorrow. Refusal to pose oneself as the Subject, unique and absolute, requires great self-denial. Furthermore, the vast majority of men make no such claim explicitly. They do not *postulate* woman as inferior, for today they are too thoroughly imbued with the ideal of democracy not to recognize all human beings as equals.

In the bosom of the family, woman seems in the eyes of childhood and youth to be clothed in the same social dignity as the adult males. Later on, the young man, desiring and loving, experiences the resistance, the independence of the woman desired and loved; in marriage, he respects woman as wife and mother, and in the concrete events of conjugal life she stands there before him as a free being. He can therefore feel that social subordination as between the sexes no longer exists and that on the whole, in spite of differences, woman is an equal. As, however, he observes some points of inferiority-the most important being unfitness for the professions-he attributes these to natural causes. When he is in a co-operative and benevolent relation with woman, his theme is the principle of abstract equality, and he does not base his attitude upon such inequality as may exist. But when he is in conflict with her, the situation is reversed: his theme will be the existing inequality, and he will even take it as justification for denying abstract equality.[4]

So it is that many men will affirm as if in good faith that women *are* the equals of man and that they have nothing to clamor for, while *at the same time* they will say that women can never be the equals of man and that their demands are in vain. It is, in point of fact, a difficult matter for man to realize the extreme importance of social discriminations which seem outwardly insignificant but which produce in woman moral and intellectual effects so profound that they appear to spring from her original nature. The most sympathetic of men never fully comprehend woman's concrete situation. And there is no reason to put much trust in the men when they rush to the defense of privileges whose full extent they can hardly measure. We shall not, then, permit ourselves to be intimidated by the number and violence of the attacks launched against women, nor to be entrapped by the self-seeking eulogies bestowed on the "true woman", nor

---

1   *Claude Mauriac* (1914–96) French novelist, considered avant-garde during the 1950s and 1960s.

2   *alterity* Otherness.

3   *even to these ... many reasons* [de Beauvoir's note] A significant article on this theme by Michel Carrouges appeared in No. 292 of the *Cahiers du Sud*. He writes indignantly: "Would that there were no woman myth at all but only a cohort of cooks, matrons, prostitutes, and bluestockings serving functions of pleasure or usefulness!" That is to say, in his view woman has no existence in and for herself; he thinks only of her *function* in the male world. Her reason for existence lies in man. But then, in fact, her poetic "function" as a myth might be more valued than any other. The real problem is precisely to find out why woman should be defined with relation to man.

---

4   *when he is ... abstract equality* [de Beauvoir's note] For example, a man will say that he considers his wife in no wise degraded because she has no gainful occupation. The profession of housewife is just as lofty, and so on. But when the first quarrel comes, he will exclaim: "Why, you couldn't make your living without me!"

to profit by the enthusiasm for woman's destiny manifested by men who would not for the world have any part of it.

We should consider the arguments of the feminists with no less suspicion, however, for very often their controversial aim deprives them of all real value. If the "woman question" seems trivial, it is because masculine arrogance has made of it a "quarrel"; and when quarreling one no longer reasons well. People have tirelessly sought to prove that woman is superior, inferior, or equal to man. Some say that, having been created after Adam, she is evidently a secondary being; others say on the contrary that Adam was only a rough draft and that God succeeded in producing the human being in perfection when He created Eve. Woman's brain is smaller; yes, but it is relatively larger. Christ was made a man; yes, but perhaps for his greater humility. Each argument at once suggests its opposite, and both are often fallacious. If we are to gain understanding, we must get out of these ruts; we must discard the vague notions of superiority, inferiority, equality which have hitherto corrupted every discussion of the subject and start afresh.

Very well, but just how shall we pose the question? And, to begin with, who are we to propound it at all? Man is at once judge and party to the case; but so is woman. What we need is an angel—neither man nor woman—but where shall we find one? Still, the angel would be poorly qualified to speak, for an angel is ignorant of all the basic facts involved in the problem. With a hermaphrodite we should be no better off, for here the situation is most peculiar; the hermaphrodite is not really the combination of a whole man and a whole woman, but consists of parts of each and thus is neither. It looks to me as if there are, after all, certain women who are best qualified to elucidate the situation of woman. Let us not be misled by the sophism that because Epimenides was a Cretan he was necessarily a liar;[1] it is not a mysterious essence that compels men and women to act in good or in bad faith, it is their situation that inclines them more or less toward the search for truth. Many of today's women, fortunate in the restoration of all the privileges pertaining to the estate of the human being, can afford the luxury of impartiality—we even recognize its necessity. We are no longer like our partisan elders; by and large we have won the game. In recent debates on the status

of women the United Nations has persistently maintained that the equality of the sexes is now becoming a reality, and already some of us have never had to sense in our femininity an inconvenience or an obstacle. Many problems appear to us to be more pressing than those which concern us in particular, and this detachment even allows us to hope that our attitude will be objective. Still, we know the feminine world more intimately than do the men because we have our roots in it, we grasp more immediately than do men what it means to a human being to be feminine; and we are more concerned with such knowledge. I have said that there are more pressing problems, but this does not prevent us from seeing some importance in asking how the fact of being women will affect our lives. What opportunities precisely have been given us and what withheld? What fate awaits our younger sisters, and what directions should they take? It is significant that books by women on women are in general animated in our day less by a wish to demand our rights than by an effort toward clarity and understanding. As we emerge from an era of excessive controversy, this book is offered as one attempt among others to confirm that statement.

But it is doubtless impossible to approach any human problem with a mind free from bias. The way in which questions are put, the points of view assumed, presuppose a relativity of interest; all characteristics imply values, and every objective description, so called, implies an ethical background. Rather than attempt to conceal principles more or less definitely implied, it is better to state them openly at the beginning. This will make it unnecessary to specify on every page in just what sense one uses such words as *superior, inferior, better, worse, progress, reaction*, and the like. If we survey some of the works on woman, we note that one of the points of view most frequently adopted is that of the public good, the general interest; and one always means by this the benefit of society as one wishes it to be maintained or established. For our part, we hold that the only public good is that which assures the private good of the citizens; we shall pass judgment on institutions according to their effectiveness in giving concrete opportunities to individuals. But we do not confuse the idea of private interest with that of happiness, although that is another common point of view. Are not women of the harem more happy than women voters? Is not the housekeeper happier than the working woman? It is not too clear just what the word *happy* really means and still less what true values it may mask. There is no possibility of measuring the happi-

---

1   *because Epimenides ... a liar* A reference to a classical logical puzzle: Epimenides of Knossos (Crete), sixth century BCE philosopher and poet, wrote this line in a poem: "The Cretans, always liars, evil beasts, idle bellies!" (But if what he said is true, then there is one time when a Cretan does not lie; so it is false.)

ness of others, and it is always easy to describe as happy the situation in which one wishes to place them.

In particular those who are condemned to stagnation are often pronounced happy on the pretext that happiness consists in being at rest. This notion we reject, for our perspective is that of existentialist ethics. Every subject plays his part as such specifically through exploits or projects that serve as a mode of transcendence; he achieves liberty only through a continual reaching out toward other liberties. There is no justification for present existence other than its expansion into an indefinitely open future. Every time transcendence falls back into immanence, stagnation, there is a degradation of existence into the *"en-soi"*[1]—the brutish life of subjection to given conditions—and of liberty into constraint and contingence. This downfall represents a moral fault if the subject consents to it; if it is inflicted upon him, it spells frustration and oppression. In both cases it is an absolute evil. Every individual concerned to justify his existence feels that his existence involves an undefined need to transcend himself, to engage in freely chosen projects.

Now, what peculiarly signalizes the situation of woman is that she—a free and autonomous being like all human creatures—nevertheless finds herself living in a world where men compel her to assume the status of the Other. They propose to stabilize her as object and to doom her to immanence since her transcendence is to be overshadowed and forever transcended by another ego *(conscience)* which is essential and sovereign. The drama of woman lies in this conflict between the fundamental aspirations of every subject (ego)—who always regards the self as the essential—and the compulsions of a situation in which she is the inessential. How can a human being in woman's situation attain fulfillment? What roads are open to her? Which are blocked? How can independence be recovered in a state of dependency? What circumstances limit woman's liberty and how can they be overcome? These are the fundamental questions on which I would fain throw some light. This means that

I am interested in the fortunes of the individual as defined not in terms of happiness but in terms of liberty.

Quite evidently this problem would be without significance if we were to believe that woman's destiny is inevitably determined by physiological, psychological, or economic forces. Hence I shall discuss first of all the light in which woman is viewed by biology, psychoanalysis, and historical materialism. Next I shall try to show exactly how the concept of the "truly feminine" has been fashioned—why woman has been defined as the Other—and what have been the consequences from man's point of view. Then from woman's point of view I shall describe the world in which women must live; and thus we shall be able to envisage the difficulties in their way as, endeavoring to make their escape from the sphere hitherto assigned them, they aspire to full membership in the human race.

◆ ◆ ◆ ◆ ◆

Introduction to Book 2

The women of today are in a fair way to dethrone the myth of femininity; they are beginning to affirm their independence in concrete ways; but they do not easily succeed in living completely the life of a human being. Reared by women within a feminine world, their normal destiny is marriage, which still means practically subordination to man; for masculine prestige is far from extinction, resting still upon solid economic and social foundations. We must therefore study the traditional destiny of woman with some care. In Book II I shall seek to describe how woman undergoes her apprenticeship, how she experiences her situation, in what kind of universe she is confined, what modes of escape are vouchsafed her. Then only—with so much understood—shall we be able to comprehend the problems of women, the heirs of a burdensome past, who are striving to build a new future. When I use the words woman or *feminine* I evidently refer to no archetype, no changeless essence whatever; the reader must understand the phrase "in the present state of education and custom" after most of my statements. It is not our concern here to proclaim eternal verities, but rather to describe the common basis that underlies every individual feminine existence.

◆ ◆ ◆ ◆ ◆

---

1 *en-soi* (French: in-itself) A term associated with Sartre's existentialism. He divides the universe into two categories: the *en-soi* and the *pour-soi* (*for-itself*). The former is the world of things, each with a nature and essence given by the kind of thing it is, each causally determined; the latter is only self-conscious humans, free of nature, essence, or any constraint or determination except self-cause. De Beauvoir speaks of the "brutish life of subjection" that comes when one is thought of (and treated) as an object—a thing *en-soi*—by others and by oneself.

Part 4: The Formative Years

Chapter 12: Childhood

One is not born, but rather becomes, a woman. No biological, psychological, or economic fate determines the figure that the human female presents in society; it is civilization as a whole that produces this creature, intermediate between male and eunuch, which is described as feminine. Only the intervention of someone else can establish as individual as an *Other*. In so far as he exists in and for himself, the child would hardly be able to think of himself as sexually differentiated. In girls as in boys the body is first of all the radiation of a subjectivity, the instrument that makes possible the comprehension of the world: it is through the eyes, the hands, that children apprehend the universe, and not through the sexual parts. The dramas of birth and of weaning unfold after the same fashion for nurslings of both sexes; these have the same interests and the same pleasures; sucking is at first the source of their most agreeable sensations; then they go through an anal phase in which they get their greatest factions from the excretory functions, which they have in common. Their genital development is analogous; they explore their bodies with the same curiosity and the same indifference; form clitoris and penis they derive the same vague pleasure. As their sensibility comes to require an object, it is turned toward the mother: the soft, smooth, resilient feminine flesh is what arouses sexual desires, and these desires are prehensile; the girl, like the boy, kisses, handles and caresses her mother in an aggressive way; they feel the same jealousy if a new child is born, and they show it in similar behavior patterns: rage, sulkiness, urinary difficulties; and they resort to the same coquettish tricks to gain the love of adults. Up to the age of twelve the little girl is as strong as her brothers, and she shows the same mental powers; there is no field where she is debarred from engaging in rivalry with them. If, well before puberty and sometimes even from early infancy, she seems to us to be already sexually determined, this is not because mysterious instincts directly doom her to passivity, coquetry, maternity; it is because the influence of others upon the child is a factor almost from the start, and thus she is indoctrinated with her vocation from her earliest years.

MARTIN LUTHER KING, JR.
(1929-1968)

Rev. Dr. Martin Luther King Jr., the revered—even venerated—African American civil rights leader, was a hugely influential leader of black America, and he exerted a profound influence on the attitudes of whites. Symbol of the great struggle for human rights in the US, he was the youngest person ever to win the Nobel Peace Prize, and the only non-president to have a national holiday in the US named for him.

King did not discover new forms of social injustice, or offer an original analysis of their causes or possible cures. But he did bring a philosophical perspective to the civil rights movement—a Ghandian reliance on non-violent protest—that was widely adopted. His approach resulted in considerable national sympathy for his cause, and under his leadership the movement achieved considerable success. His writing often reflects his enormously effective rhetorical style, rallying and inspiring blacks and whites alike.

King was born into a family with a strong religious background: his father and grandfather were both Baptist preachers. Intellectually gifted, King began attending Morehouse College at the age of fifteen; during his last year, his plans turned from law and medicine to the clergy, and after graduation he went to Crozier Theological Seminary in Pennsylvania, where he was elected president of his largely white class; he was at the top of his class at graduation. He received his PhD from Boston University in 1955. In Boston he met and married Coretta Scott, and the two moved to Montgomery, Alabama, where he became pastor at a Baptist church. Already active in the civil rights movement, he was chosen to lead the boycott of the bus system in Montgomery (which, like other southern American cities at the time, forced blacks to sit at the back of the bus). The boycott, lasting over a year, was the first major non-violent anti-segregation protest in the US; it succeeded at last when a US Supreme Court decision ruled Mongomery's bus law unconstitutional.

In 1957, King organized and was chosen leader of the Southern Christian Leadership Conference, a coordinating group for the growing protest movement all over the South. As the most visible symbol of the movement, King was subject to massive harassment. He was jailed over forty times, assaulted, threatened with death, and made the target of a vendetta by the notorious J. Edgar Hoover, long-time head of the FBI, who accused him of communist affiliation and attempted in various ways to destroy him politically and personally.

A 1963 protest led by King against segregated lunch-counters in Birmingham, Alabama, received international attention when the police turned dogs and fire hoses on the demonstrators. His well-known letter from the Birmingham jail eloquently expressed his philosophy of non-violence. In that same year, King joined with others to organize a 200,000 person March on Washington, where he delivered his famous "I have a dream" speech.

With King as its widely respected leader, the civil rights movement was at its peak, and many counted the Civil Rights Act of 1964, aimed at eliminating segregation and discrimination, and the Voting Rights Act of 1965, as signs of its substantial progress. But tensions were growing within the movement. King's strategy of non-violent protest, relying on an appeal to the conscience of whites, seemed to some to be inadquate as a means of dealing with the root causes of American racism, especially in its subtler and more complex manifestations in the North. Young radicals criticized King for being too cautious; advocates of black power and pride argued that King's tactic of coalition with white liberals was a mistake, and that segregation was not the core of the problem for African Americans. If his support was dwindling among more radical African Americans it was broadened elsewhere, as he began to play a leading role in anti-poverty activism and in protesting the Vietnam War. But these new efforts were cut short when he was assassinated by a sniper's bullet on April 4, 1968. The date marked, for many liberal blacks and whites, the end of an era of hope for interracial cooperation and progress for human rights.

♦ ♦ ♦ ♦ ♦

Letter From Birmingham Jail
(April 16, 1963)

My Dear Fellow Clergymen:

While confined here in the Birmingham City Jail, I came across your recent statement calling our present activities "unwise and untimely." Seldom, if ever, do I pause to answer criticism of my work and ideas. If I sought to answer all the criticisms that cross my desk, my secretaries would be engaged in little else in the course of the day, and I would have no time for constructive work. But since I feel that you are men of genuine goodwill and your criticisms are sincerely set forth, I would like to answer your statement in what I hope will be patient and reasonable terms.

I think I should give the reason for my being in Birmingham, since you have been influenced by the argument of "outsiders coming in." I have the honor of serving as president of the Southern Christian Leadership Conference, an organization operating in every Southern state, with headquarters in Atlanta, Georgia. We have some eighty-five affiliate organizations all across the South—one being the Alabama Christian Movement for Human Rights. Whenever necessary and possible we share staff, educational and financial resources with our affiliates. Several months ago our local affiliate here in Birmingham invited us to be on call to engage in a nonviolent direct action program if such were deemed necessary. We readily consented and when the hour came we lived up to our promises. So I am here, along with several members of my staff, because I have basic organizational ties here.

Beyond this, I am in Birmingham because injustice is here. Just as the eighth century prophets left their little villages and carried their "thus saith the Lord" far beyond the boundaries of their home towns; and just as the Apostle Paul left his little village of Tarsus and carried the gospel of Jesus Christ to practically every hamlet and city of the Graeco-Roman world, I too am compelled to carry the gospel of freedom beyond my particular home town. Like Paul, I must constantly respond to the Macedonian call for aid.[1]

Moreover, I am cognizant of the interrelatedness of all communities and states. I cannot sit idly by in Atlanta and not be concerned about what happens in Birmingham. Injustice anywhere is a threat to justice everywhere. We are caught in an inescapable network of mutuality, tied in a single garment of destiny. Whatever affects one directly affects all indirectly. Never again can we afford to live with the narrow, provincial "outside agitator" idea. Anyone who lives inside the United States can never be considered an outsider anywhere in this country.

You deplore the demonstrations that are presently taking place in Birmingham. But I am sorry that your statement did not express a similar concern for the conditions that brought the demonstrations into being. I am sure that each of you would want to go beyond the superficial social analyst who looks merely at effects, and does not grapple with underlying causes. I would not hesitate to say that it is unfortunate that so-called demonstrations are taking place in Birmingham at this time, but I would say in more emphatic terms that it is even more unfortunate that the white power structure of this city left the Negro community with no other alternative.

In any nonviolent campaign there are four basic steps: 1) Collection of the facts to determine whether injustices are alive. 2) Negotiation. 3) Self-purification and 4) Direct action. We have gone through all of these steps in Birmingham. There can be no gainsaying of the fact that racial injustice engulfs this community.

Birmingham is probably the most thoroughly segregated city in the United States. Its ugly record of police brutality is known in every section of this country. Its unjust treatment of Negroes in the courts is a notorious reality. There have been more unsolved bombings of Negro homes and churches in Birmingham than any city in this nation. These are the hard, brutal and unbelievable facts. On the basis of these conditions, Negro leaders sought to negotiate with the city fathers. But the political leaders consistently refused to engage in good faith negotiation.

Then came the opportunity last September to talk with some of the leaders of the economic community. In these negotiating sessions certain promises were made by the merchants—such as the promise to remove the humiliating racial signs from the stores. On the basis of these promises

---

1   *the Apostle Paul ... the Macedonian call for aid* [Unless otherwise indicated, all notes in this selection are by the editors of this anthology.] Saint Paul of Tarsus (c. 3–62 CE). King refers to Acts 16.9–10: "And a vision appeared to Paul in the night; There stood

a man of Macedonia, and prayed him, saying, Come over into Macedonia, and help us. And after he had seen the vision, immediately we endeavored to go into Macedonia, assuredly gathering that the Lord had called us to preach the gospel unto them."

Rev. Shuttlesworth and the leaders of the Alabama Christian Movement for Human Rights agreed to call a moratorium on any type of demonstrations. As the weeks and months unfolded we realized that we were the victims of a broken promise. The signs remained. Like so many experiences of the past we were confronted with blasted hopes, and the dark shadow of a deep disappointment settled upon us. So we had no alternative except that of preparing for direct action, whereby we would present our very bodies as a means of laying our case before the conscience of the local and national community. We were not unmindful of the difficulties involved. So we decided to go through a process of self-purification. We started having workshops on nonviolence and repeatedly asked ourselves the questions: "Are you able to accept blows without retaliating?" "Are you able to endure the ordeals of jail?" We decided to set our direct-action program around the Easter season, realizing that with the exception of Christmas, this was the largest shopping period of the year. Knowing that a strong economic withdrawal program would be the by-product of direct action, we felt that this was the best time to bring pressure on the merchants for the needed changes. Then it occurred to us that the March election was ahead and so we speedily decided to postpone action until after election day. When we discovered that Mr. Connor was in the run-off, we decided again to postpone action so that the demonstrations could not be used to cloud the issues. At this time we agreed to begin our nonviolent witness the day after the run-off.

This reveals that we did not move irresponsibly into direct action. We too wanted to see Mr. Connor defeated; so we went through postponement after postponement to aid in this community need. After this we felt that direct action could be delayed no longer.

You may well ask: "Why direct action? Why sit-ins, marches, etc.? Isn't negotiation a better path?" You are exactly right in your call for negotiation. Indeed, this is the purpose of direct action. Nonviolent direct action seeks to create such a crisis and establish such creative tension that a community that has constantly refused to negotiate is forced to confront the issue. It seeks so to dramatize the issue that it can no longer be ignored. I just referred to the creation of tension as a part of the work of the nonviolent resister. This may sound rather shocking. But I must confess that I am not afraid of the word tension. I have earnestly worked and preached against violent tension, but there is a type of constructive nonviolent tension that is necessary for growth. Just as Socrates felt that it was necessary to create a

tension in the mind so that individuals could rise from the bondage of myths and half-truths to the unfettered realm of creative analysis and objective appraisal, we must see the need of having nonviolent gadflies to create the kind of tension in society that will help men to rise from the dark depths of prejudice and racism to the majestic heights of understanding and brotherhood. So the purpose of the direct action is to create a situation so crisis-packed that it will inevitably open the door to negotiation. We, therefore, concur with you in your call for negotiation. Too long has our beloved Southland been bogged down in the tragic attempt to live in monologue rather than dialogue.

One of the basic points in your statement is that our acts are untimely. Some have asked, "Why didn't you give the new administration time to act?" The only answer that I can give to this inquiry is that the new Birmingham administration must be prodded about as much as the outgoing one before it acts. We will be sadly mistaken if we feel that the election of Mr. Boutwell will bring the millennium to Birmingham. While Mr. Boutwell is much more articulate and gentle than Mr. Connor, they are both segregationists, dedicated to the task of maintaining the status quo. The hope I see in Mr. Boutwell is that he will be reasonable enough to see the futility of massive resistance to desegregation. But he will not see this without pressure from the devotees of civil rights. My friends, I must say to you that we have not made a single gain in civil rights without determined legal and nonviolent pressure. History is the long and tragic story of the fact that privileged groups seldom give up their privileges voluntarily. Individuals may see the moral light and voluntarily give up their unjust posture; but as Reinhold Niebuhr[1] has reminded us, groups are more immoral than individuals.

We know through painful experience that freedom is never voluntarily given by the oppressor; it must be demanded by the oppressed. Frankly, I have never yet engaged in a direct action movement that was "well timed," according to the timetable of those who have not suffered unduly from the disease of segregation. For years now I have heard the words [sic] "Wait!" It rings in the ear of every Negro with a piercing familiarity. This "Wait" has almost always meant "Never." We must come to see with

---

1   *Reinhold Niebuhr*   (1892–1971) Influential Protestant clergyman and theologian with a special interest in the connection between religion and political matters; author of *Moral Man and Immoral Society* (1932).

the distinguished jurist of yesterday that "justice too long delayed is justice denied."[1]

We have waited for more than three hundred and forty years for our constitutional and God-given rights. The nations of Asia and Africa are moving with jet-like speed toward the goal of political independence, and we still creep at horse and buggy pace toward the gaining of a cup of coffee at a lunch counter. I guess it is easy for those who have never felt the stinging darts of segregation to say, "Wait." But when you have seen vicious mobs lynch your mothers and fathers at will and drown your sisters and brothers at whim; when you have seen hate filled policemen curse, kick, brutalize and even kill your black brothers and sisters with impunity; when you see the vast majority of your twenty million Negro brothers smothering in an airtight cage of poverty in the midst of an affluent society; when you suddenly find your tongue twisted and your speech stammering as you seek to explain to your six-year-old daughter why she can't go to the public amusement park that has just been advertised on television, and see tears welling up in her eyes when she is told that Funtown is closed to colored children, and see the depressing clouds of inferiority begin to form in her little mental sky, and see her begin to distort her little personality by unconsciously developing a bitterness toward white people; when you have to concoct an answer for a five-year-old son asking in agonizing pathos: "Daddy, why do white people treat colored people so mean?"; when you take a cross-country drive and find it necessary to sleep night after night in the uncomfortable corners of your automobile because no motel will accept you; when you are humiliated day in and day out by nagging signs reading "white" and "colored"; when your first name becomes "nigger," your middle name becomes "boy" (however old you are) and your last name becomes "John," and your wife and mother are never given the respected title "Mrs."; when you are harried by day and haunted by night by the fact that you are a Negro, living constantly at tiptoe stance never quite knowing what to expect next, and plagued with inner fears and outer resentments; when you are forever fighting a degenerating sense of "nobodiness"; then you will understand why we find it difficult to wait.

There comes a time when the cup of endurance runs over, and men are no longer willing to be plunged into an abyss of despair. I hope, sirs, you can understand our legitimate and unavoidable impatience.

You express a great deal of anxiety over our willingness to break laws. This is certainly a legitimate concern. Since we so diligently urge people to obey the Supreme Court's decision of 1954 outlawing segregation in the public schools, it is rather strange and paradoxical to find us consciously breaking laws. One may well ask: "How can you advocate breaking some laws and obeying others?" The answer is found in the fact that there are two types of laws: There are *just* and there are *unjust* laws. I would agree with Saint Augustine that "An unjust law is no law at all."[2]

Now, what is the difference between the two? How does one determine when a law is just or unjust? A just law is a man-made code that squares with the moral law or the law of God. An unjust law is a code that is out of harmony with the moral law. To put it in the terms of Saint Thomas Aquinas, an unjust law is a human law that is not rooted in eternal and natural law. Any law that uplifts human personality is just. Any law that degrades human personality is unjust. All segregation statutes are unjust because segregation distorts the soul and damages the personality. It gives the segregator a false sense of superiority, and the segregated a false sense of inferiority. To use the words of Martin Buber,[3] the Jewish philosopher, segregation substitutes and "I-it" relationship for an "I-thou" relationship, and ends up relegating persons to the status of things. So segregation is not only politically, economically and sociologically unsound, but it is morally wrong and sinful. Paul Tillich[4] has said that sin is separation. Isn't segregation an existential expression of man's tragic separation, an expression of his awful estrangement, his terrible sinfulness? So I can urge men to disobey segregation ordinances because they are morally wrong.

Let us turn to a more concrete example of just and unjust laws. An unjust law is a code that a majority inflicts on

1   *justice too long delayed is justice denied* This quotation is attributed to Thurgood Marshall (1908–93), American civil rights lawyer, the first black justice on the Supreme Court of the United States. It is a version of a familiar legal slogan; William E. Gladstone, (1809–98), British statesman and Prime Minister said "Justice delayed is justice denied."

2   *St. Augustine … "an unjust law is no law at all."* In Latin, *lex iniusta non est lex;* Augustine of Hippo is generally credited with this famous dictum (*De Libero Arbitrio* [*Of Free Choice*], 1, 5).

3   *Martin Buber* (1878–1965), Austrian Jewish theologian-philosopher; his best-known idea was that valuable relations are not based on utility (the "I-it" relation) but instead on mutual affirmation (the "I-thou" relation).

4   *Paul Tillich* (1886–1965), German-American theologian and Protestant existentialist philosopher.

a minority that is not binding on itself. This is difference made legal. On the other hand a just law is a code that a majority compels a minority to follow that it is willing to follow itself. This is sameness made legal.

Let me give another explanation. An unjust law is a code inflicted upon a minority which that minority had no part in enacting or creating because they did not have the unhampered right to vote. Who can say that the legislature of Alabama which set up the segregation laws was democratically elected? Throughout the state of Alabama all types of conniving methods are used to prevent Negroes from becoming registered voters and there are some counties without a single Negro registered to vote despite the fact that the Negro constitutes a majority of the population. Can any law set up in such a state be considered democratically structured?

These are just a few examples of unjust and just laws. There are some instances when a law is just on its face and unjust in its application. For instance, I was arrested Friday on a charge of parading without a permit. Now there is nothing wrong with an ordinance which requires a permit for a parade, but when the ordinance is used to preserve segregation and to deny citizens the First-Amendment[1] privilege of peaceful assembly and peaceful protest, then it becomes unjust.

I hope you can see the distinction I am trying to point out. In no sense do I advocate evading or defying the law as the rabid segregationist would do. This would lead to anarchy. One who breaks an unjust law must do it *openly, lovingly,* (not hatefully as the white mothers did in New Orleans when they were seen on television screaming "nigger, nigger, nigger") and with a willingness to accept the penalty. I submit that an individual who breaks a law that conscience tells him is unjust, and willingly accepts the penalty by staying in jail to arouse the conscience of the community over its injustice, is in reality expressing the very highest respect for law.

Of course, there is nothing new about this kind of civil disobedience. It was seen sublimely in the refusal of Shadrach, Meshach and Abednego to obey the laws of Nebuchadnezzar[2] because a higher moral law was involved. It was practiced superbly by the early Christians who were willing to face hungry lions and the excruciating pain of chopping blocks, before submitting to certain unjust laws of the Roman empire. To a degree academic freedom is a reality today because Socrates practiced civil disobedience.

We can never forget that everything Hitler did in Germany was "legal" and everything the Hungarian freedom fighters did in Hungary was "illegal." It was "illegal" to aid and comfort a Jew in Hitler's Germany. But I am sure that if I had lived in Germany during that time I would have aided and comforted my Jewish brothers even though it was illegal. If I lived in a Communist country today where certain principles dear to the Christian faith are suppressed, I believe I would openly advocate disobeying these anti-religious laws. I must make two honest confessions to you, my Christian and Jewish brothers. First, I must confess that over the last few years I have been gravely disappointed with the white moderate. I have almost reached the regrettable conclusion that the Negro's great stumbling block in the stride toward freedom is not the White Citizen's Counciler or the Ku Klux Klanner,[3] but the white moderate who is more devoted to "order" than to justice; who prefers a negative peace which is the absence of tension to a positive peace which is the presence of justice; who constantly says "I agree with you in the goal you seek, but I can't agree with your methods of direct action;" who paternalistically feels he can set the timetable for another man's freedom; who lives by the myth of time and who constantly advises the Negro to wait until a "more convenient season." Shallow understanding from people of goodwill is more frustrating than absolute misunderstanding from people of ill will.

---

1 *First Amendment* The First Amendment to the US Constitution (part of the Bill of Rights—the first ten amendments) is: "Congress shall make no law respecting an establishment of religion, or prohibiting the free exercise thereof; or abridging the freedom of speech, or of the press; or the right of the people peaceably to assemble, and to petition the Government for a redress of grievances."

2 *Shadrach, Meshach and Abednego to obey the laws of Nebuchadnezzar* This story is in the Bible, Daniel 3.

3 *White Citizen's Councilor or the Ku Klux Klanner* Branches of the White Citizens' Council spread widely across the American South beginning in 1954. Their object was to resist the black equal-rights movement and to perpetuate white supremacy—aims shared with the Ku Klux Klan, which had existed on and off since 1866. Both organizations resorted sometimes to threats and violence against blacks who attempted to exercise their rights, and against workers in the civil rights movement; the difference was that the Klan had largely a working-class membership, and operated secretly and contrary, in many cases, to the law. The White Citizen's Council, on the other hand, was made up of middle-class whites, often in positions of local political power, and its actions were not secret—sometimes it managed to legalize its activities, or to act within local laws.

Lukewarm acceptance is much more bewildering than outright rejection.

I had hoped that the white moderate would understand that law and order exist for the purpose of establishing justice, and that when they fail to do this they become dangerously structured dams that block the flow of social progress. I had hoped that the white moderate would understand that the present tension in the South is merely a necessary phase of the transition from an obnoxious negative peace, where the Negro passively accepted his unjust plight, to a substance-filled positive peace, where all men will respect the dignity and worth of human personality. Actually, we who engage in nonviolent direct action are not the creators of tension. We merely bring to the surface the hidden tension that is already alive. We bring it out in the open where it can be seen and dealt with. Like a boil that can never be cured as long as it is covered up but must be opened with all its pus-flowing ugliness to the natural medicines of air and light, injustice must likewise be exposed, with all of the tension its exposing creates, to the light of human conscience and the air of national opinion before it can be cured.

In your statement you asserted that our actions, even though peaceful, must be condemned because they precipitate violence. But can this assertion be logically made? Isn't this like condemning the robbed man because his possession of money precipitated the evil act of robbery? Isn't this like condemning Socrates because his unswerving commitment to truth and his philosophical delvings precipitated the misguided popular mind to make him drink the hemlock?[1] Isn't this like condemning Jesus because His unique God-Consciousness and never-ceasing devotion to His will precipitated the evil act of crucifixion? We must come to see, as the federal courts have consistently affirmed, that it is immoral to urge an individual to withdraw his efforts to gain his basic constitutional rights because the quest precipitates violence. Society must protect the robbed and punish the robber.

I had also hoped that the white moderate would reject the myth of time. I received a letter this morning from a white brother in Texas which said: "All Christians know that the colored people will receive equal rights eventually, but it is possible that you are in too great of a religious hurry. It has taken Christianity almost 2000 years to accomplish what it has. The teachings of Christ take time to come to earth."

All that is said here grows out of a tragic misconception of time. It is the the strangely irrational notion that there is something in the very flow of time that will inevitably cure all ills. Actually time is neutral. It can be used either destructively or constructively. I am coming to feel that the people of ill-will have used time much more effectively than the people of good will. We will have to repent in this generation not merely for the vitriolic words and actions of the bad people, but for the appalling silence of the good people. We must come to see that human progress never rolls in on wheels of inevitability. It comes through the tireless efforts and persistent work of men willing to be co-workers with God, and without this hard work time itself becomes an ally of the forces of social stagnation. We must use time creatively, and forever realize that the time is always ripe to do right. Now is the time to make real the promise of democracy, and transform our pending national elegy into a creative psalm of brotherhood. Now is the time to lift our national policy from the quicksand of racial injustice to the solid rock of human dignity.

You spoke of our activity in Birmingham as extreme. At first I was rather disappointed that fellow clergymen would see my nonviolent efforts as those of the extremist. I started thinking about the fact that I stand in the middle of two opposing forces in the Negro community. One is a force of complacency made up of Negroes who, as a result of long years of oppression, have been so completely drained of self-respect and a sense of "somebodiness" that they have adjusted to segregation, and, of a few Negroes in the middle class who, because of a degree of academic and economic security, and because at points they profit by segregation, have unconsciously become insensitive to the problems of the masses. The other force is one of bitterness, and hatred comes perilously close to advocating violence. It is expressed in the various black nationalist groups that are springing up over the nation, the largest and best-known being Elijah Muhammad's Muslim movement.[2] This movement is nour-

---

1 *Socrates ... drink hemlock?* See Plato's dialogues *Apology, Crito,* and *Phaedo.*

2 *Elijah Muhammad's Muslim movement* Elijah Muhammad (1897–1975) was the leader of the US black separatist movement officially known as the Nation of Islam, popularly known as the Black Muslims. Founded in 1930, this organization combined traditional Islamic beliefs and practices with advocacy of black separatism and nationalism. It worked to promote black unity and self-help, insisting on a rigid code of discipline among its members. In the 1960s it became increasingly associated with violence, both in the cause of black nationalism and against its apostate former members including Malcolm X, who, it is thought, was murdered by members of the Nation.

ished by the contemporary frustration over the continued existence of racial discrimination. It is made up of people who have lost faith in America, who have absolutely repudiated Christianity, and who have concluded that the white man is an incurable "devil." I have tried to stand between these two forces saying that we need not follow the "do-nothingism" of the complacent or the hatred and despair of the black nationalist. There is the more excellent way of love and nonviolent protest. I'm grateful to God that, through the Negro church, the dimension of nonviolence entered our struggle. If this philosophy had not emerged, I am convinced that by now many streets of the South would be flowing with floods of blood. And I am further convinced that if our white brothers dismiss as "rabble rousers" and "outside agitators" those of us who are working through the channels of nonviolent direct action and refuse to support our nonviolent efforts, millions of Negroes, out of frustration and despair, will seek solace and security in black-nationalist ideologies, a development that will lead inevitably to a frightening racial nightmare.

Oppressed people cannot remain oppressed forever. The urge for freedom will eventually come. This is what happened to the American Negro. Something within has reminded him of his birthright of freedom; something without has reminded him that he can gain it. Consciously and unconsciously, he has been swept in by what the Germans call the *Zeitgeist*, and with his black brothers of Africa, and his brown and yellow brothers of Asia, South America and the Caribbean, he is moving with a sense of cosmic urgency toward the promised land of racial justice. Recognizing this vital urge that has engulfed the Negro community, one should readily understand public demonstrations. The Negro has many pent up resentments and latent frustrations. He has to get them out. So let him march sometime; let him have his prayer pilgrimages to the city hall; understand why he must have sit-ins and freedom rides. If his repressed emotions do not come out in these nonviolent ways, they will come out in ominous expressions of violence. This is not a threat; it is a fact of history. So I have not said to my people "get rid of your discontent." But I have tried to say that this normal and healthy discontent can be channelized through the creative outlet of nonviolent direct action. Now this approach is being dismissed as extremist. I must admit that I was initially disappointed in being so categorized.

But as I continued to think about the matter I gradually gained a bit of satisfaction from being considered an extremist. Was not Jesus an extremist for love—"Love your enemies, bless them that curse you, pray for them that despitefully use you." Was not Amos[1] an extremist for justice—"Let justice roll down like waters and righteousness like a mighty stream." Was not Paul an extremist for the gospel of Jesus Christ—"I bear in my body the marks of the Lord Jesus."[2] Was not Martin Luther an extremist—"Here I stand; I can do none other so help me God." Was not John Bunyan[3] an extremist—"I will stay in jail to the end of my days before I make a butchery of my conscience." Was not Abraham Lincoln an extremist—"This nation cannot survive half slave and half free."[4] Was not Thomas Jefferson[5] an extremist—"We hold these truths to be self-evident, that all men are created equal." So the question is not whether we will be extremist but what kind of extremist will we be. Will we be extremists for hate or will we be extremists for love? Will we be extremists for the preservation of injustice—or will we be extremists for the cause of justice? In that dramatic scene on Calvary's hill, three men were crucified.[6] We must not forget that all three were crucified for the same crime—the crime of extremism. Two were extremists for immorality, and thusly fell below their environment. The other, Jesus Christ, was an extremist for love, truth and goodness, and thereby rose above his environment. So, after all, maybe the South, the nation and the world are in dire need of creative extremists.

I had hoped that the white moderate would see this. Maybe I was too optimistic. Maybe I expected too much. I guess I should have realized that few members of a race that has oppressed another race can understand or appreci-

---

1   *Amos*   In the biblical Book of Amos, the prophet by that name, at God's bidding, castigates the people of Israel and threatens them with doom for having fallen away from God and for having devoted themselves to the pursuit of wealth. This quotation is from Amos 5.24.

2   *I bear ... Lord Jesus*   Galatians 6.17: "From henceforth let no man trouble me: for I bear in my body the marks of the Lord Jesus."

3   *John Bunyan*   (1628–88), English writer and Puritan minister, author of *The Pilgrim's Progress* (1678), which became one of the most widely read books in English after the Bible. Persecuted because of his Puritan beliefs, he refused to cease preaching, and spent years in jail.

4   *This nation ... half free*   Lincoln said "I believe this government cannot endure, permanently half slave and half free," in his "House Divided" Speech, Springfield, Illinois, June 16, 1858.

5   *Thomas Jefferson*   (1743–1826) Third President of the US, author of the Declaration of Independence, from which this quotation is taken.

6   *three men were crucified*   The Bible reports that Jesus was crucified along with two thieves.

ate the deep groans and passionate yearnings of those that have been oppressed and still fewer have the vision to see that injustice must be rooted out by strong, persistent and determined action. I am thankful, however, that some of our white brothers have grasped the meaning of this social revolution and committed themselves to it. They are still all too small in quantity, but they are big in quality. Some like Ralph McGill, Lillian Smith, Harry Golden and James Dabbs[1] have written about our struggle in eloquent, prophetic and understanding terms. Others have marched with us down nameless streets of the South. They have languished in filthy roach-infested jails, suffering the abuse and brutality of angry policemen who see them as "dirty nigger lovers." They, unlike so many of their moderate brothers and sisters, have recognized the urgency of the moment and sensed the need for powerful "action" antidotes to combat the disease of segregation.

Let me rush on to mention my other disappointment. I have been so greatly disappointed with the white church and its leadership. Of course, there are some notable exceptions. I am not unmindful of the fact that each of you has taken some significant stands on this issue. I commend you, Rev. Stallings, for your Christian stand on this past Sunday, in welcoming Negroes to your worship service on a non-segregated basis. I commend the Catholic leaders of this state for integrating Spring Hill College several years ago.

But despite these notable exceptions I must honestly reiterate that I have been disappointed with the church. I do not say that as one of those negative critics who can always find something wrong with the church. I say it as a minister of the gospel, who loves the church; who was nurtured in its bosom; who has been sustained by its spiritual blessings and who will remain true to it as long as the cord of life shall lengthen.

I had the strange feeling when I was suddenly catapulted into the leadership of the bus protest in Montgomery sev-

eral years ago, that we would have the support of the white church. I felt that the white ministers, priests and rabbis of the South would be some of our strongest allies. Instead, some have been outright opponents, refusing to understand the freedom movement and misrepresenting its leaders; all too many others have been more cautious than courageous and have remained silent behind the anesthetizing security of the stained-glass windows.

In spite of my shattered dreams of the past, I came to Birmingham with the hope that the white religious leadership of this community would see the justice of our cause, and with deep moral concern, serve as the channel through which our just grievances would get to the power structure. I had hoped that each of you would understand. But again I have been disappointed. I have heard numerous religious leaders of the South call upon their worshippers to comply with a desegregation decision because it is the *law*, but I have longed to hear white ministers say, "follow this decree because integration is morally *right* and the Negro is your brother." In the midst of blatant injustices inflicted upon the Negro, I have watched white churches stand on the sideline and merely mouth pious irrelevancies and sanctimonious trivialities. In the midst of a mighty struggle to rid our nation of racial and economic injustice, I have heard so many ministers say, "Those are social issues with which the gospel has no real concern." And I have watched so many churches commit themselves to a completely other-worldly religion which made a strange distinction between body and soul, the sacred and the secular.

So here we are moving toward the exit of the twentieth century with a religious community largely adjusted to the status quo, standing as a tail-light behind other community agencies rather than a headlight leading men to higher levels of justice.

I have traveled the length and breadth of Alabama, Mississippi and all the other southern states. On sweltering summer days and crisp autumn mornings I have looked at her beautiful churches with their lofty spires pointing heavenward. I have beheld the impressive outlay of her massive religious education buildings. Over and over again I have found myself asking: "What kind of people worship here? Who is their God? Where were their voices when the lips of Governor Barnett dripped with words of interposition and nullification? Where were they when Governor Wallace[2]

---

1 *Ralph McGill ... James Dabbs* Ralph McGill's (1898–1969) daily column in *Atlanta Constitution* was an important voice for racial tolerance in the South. Lillian Smith (1897–1966) toured the South, speaking against Jim Crow; she wrote *Strange Fruit* (1944) and *Killers of the Dream* (1949). Harry Golden (1902–81), born in Ukraine, was the publisher of *The Carolina Israelite*; his widely read satirical columns mocked Jim Crow laws and racial segregation. James McBride Dabbs (1896–1970), a farmer-writer, was an eloquent spokesman for social justice and racial equity; he wrote *The Southern Heritage* (1958), *The Road Home* (1960), *Who Speaks for the South?* (1964) *and Haunted by God* (1972). All four were white.

2 *Governor Barnett ... Governor Wallace* Ross R. Barnett (1898–1987), Governor of Mississippi 1960–64. An unapologetic racist,

gave the clarion call for defiance and hatred? Where were their voices of support when tired, bruised and weary Negro men and women decided to rise from the dark dungeons of complacency to the bright hills of creative protest?"

Yes, these questions are still in my mind. In deep disappointment, I have wept over the laxity of the church. But be assured that my tears have been tears of love. There can be no deep disappointment where there is not deep love. Yes, I love the church; I love her sacred walls. How could I do otherwise? I am in the rather unique position of being the son, the grandson and the great-grandson of preachers. Yes, I see the church as the body of Christ. But, oh! How we have blemished and scarred that body through social neglect and fear of being nonconformists.

There was a time when the church was very powerful. It was during that period when the early Christians rejoiced when they were deemed worthy to suffer for what they believed. In those days the church was not merely a thermometer that recorded the ideas and principles of popular opinion; it was a thermostat that transformed the mores of society. Whenever the early Christians entered a town the power structure got disturbed and immediately sought to convict them for being "disturbers of the peace" and "outside agitators." But they went on with the conviction that they were "a colony of heaven," and had to obey God rather than man. They were small in number but big in commitment. They were too God-intoxicated to be "astronomically intimidated." They brought an end to such ancient evils as infanticide and gladiatorial contest.

Things are different now. The contemporary church is often a weak, ineffectual voice with an uncertain sound. It is so often the arch supporter of the status quo. Far from being disturbed by the presence of the church, the power structure of the average community is consoled by the church's silent and often vocal sanction of things as they are.

But the judgment of God is upon the church as never before. If the church of today does not recapture the sacrificial spirit of the early church, it will lose its authentic ring, forfeit the loyalty of millions, and be dismissed as an irrelevant social club with no meaning for the twentieth century. I am meeting young people every day whose disappointment with the church has risen to outright disgust.

Maybe again, I have been too optimistic. Is organized religion too inextricably bound to status-quo to save our nation and the world? Maybe I must turn my faith to the inner spiritual church, the church within the church, as the true *ecclesia*[1] and the hope of the world. But again I am thankful to God that some noble souls from the ranks of organized religion have broken loose from the paralyzing chains of conformity and joined us as active partners in the struggle for freedom. They have left their secure congregations and walked the streets of Albany, Georgia, with us. They have gone through the highways of the South on tortuous rides for freedom. Yes, they have gone to jail with us. Some have been kicked out of their churches, and lost support of their bishops and fellow ministers. But they have gone with the faith that right defeated is stronger than evil triumphant. These men have been the leaven in the lump of the race. Their witness has been the spiritual salt that has preserved the true meaning of the Gospel in these troubled times. They have carved a tunnel of hope though the dark mountain of disappointment.

I hope the church as a whole will meet the challenge of this decisive hour. But even if the church does not come to the aid of justice, I have no despair about the future. I have no fear about the outcome of our struggle in Birmingham, even if our motives are presently misunderstood. We will reach the goal of freedom in Birmingham and all over the nation, because the goal of America is freedom. Abused and scorned though we may be, our destiny is tied up with the destiny of America. Before the pilgrims landed at Plymouth we were here. Before the pen of Jefferson etched across the pages of history the majestic words of the Declaration of Independence, we were here. For more than two centuries our fore-parents labored in this country without wages; they made cotton king; and they built the homes of their masters in the midst of brutal injustice and shameful humiliation—and yet out of a bottomless vitality they continued to

he vowed to maintain segregation in the state's public schools, even pledging to go to jail before he would allow integration. But in 1962, directed by the US Supreme Court ruling, the University of Mississippi admitted James H. Meredith, a black applicant. For Barnett's resistance he was fined and sentenced to jail (though both punishments were annulled by the Circuit Court). George Wallace (1919–98) was the hard-line segregationist governor of Alabama. In the inaugural speech for the first of his four terms he said, "In the name of the greatest people that have ever trod this earth, I draw the line in the dust and toss the gauntlet before the feet of tyranny, and I say segregation now, segregation tomorrow, segregation forever." In 1963 he stood in front of a building at the University of Alabama, attempting to prevent the school's integration.

1   *ecclesia* The Church, seen as the convocation of the faithful.

thrive and develop. If the inexpressible cruelties of slavery could not stop us, the opposition we now face will surely fail. We will win our freedom because the sacred heritage of our nation and the eternal will of God are embodied in our echoing demands.

I must close now. But before closing I am impelled to mention one other point in your statement that troubled me profoundly. You warmly commended the Birmingham police force for keeping "order" and "preventing violence." I don't believe you would have so warmly commended the police force if you had seen its angry violent dogs literally biting six unarmed, nonviolent Negroes. I don't believe you would so quickly commend the policemen if you would observe their ugly and inhuman treatment of Negroes here in the city jail; if you would watch them push and curse old Negro women and young Negro girls; if you would see them slap and kick old Negro men and young boys; if you will observe them, as they did on two occasions, refuse to give us food because we wanted to sing our grace together. I'm sorry that I can't join you in your praise for the police department.

It is true that they have been rather disciplined in their public handling of the demonstrators. In this sense they have been rather publicly "nonviolent". But for what purpose? To preserve the evil system of segregation. Over the last few years I have consistently preached that nonviolence demands that the means we use must be as pure as the ends we seek. So I have tried to make it clear that it is wrong to use immoral means to attain moral ends. But now I must affirm that it is just as wrong, or even more so, to use moral means to preserve immoral ends. Maybe Mr. Connor and his policemen have been rather publicly nonviolent, as Chief Pritchett was in Albany, Georgia, but they have used the moral means of nonviolence to maintain the immoral end of flagrant racial injustice. T.S. Eliot[1] as said that there is no greater treason than to do the right deed for the wrong reason.

I wish you had commended the Negro sit-inners and demonstrators of Birmingham for their sublime courage, their willingness to suffer and their amazing discipline in the midst of the most inhuman provocation. One day the South will recognize its real heroes. They will be the James Merediths, courageously and with a majestic sense of pur-

pose, facing jeering and hostile mobs and with the agonizing loneliness that characterizes the life of the pioneer. They will be old oppressed, battered Negro women, symbolized in a seventy-two year old woman of Montgomery, Alabama, who rose up with a sense of dignity and with her people decided not to ride the segregated buses, and responded to one who inquired about her tiredness with ungrammatical profundity; "my feet is tired, but my soul is rested." They will be the young high school and college students, young ministers of the gospel and a host of their elders courageously and nonviolently sitting-in at lunch counters and willingly going to jail for conscience's sake. One day the South will know that when these disinherited children of God sat down at lunch counters they were in reality standing up for the best in the American dream and the most sacred values in our Judaeo-Christian heritage, and thusly, carrying our whole nation back to those great wells of democracy which were dug deep by the founding fathers in the formulation of the Constitution and the Declaration of Independence.

Never before have I written a letter this long, (or should I say a book?). I'm afraid it is much too long to take your precious time. I can assure you that it would have been much shorter if I had been writing from a comfortable desk, but what else is there to do when you are alone for days in the dull monotony of a narrow jail cell other than write long letters, think strange thoughts, and pray long prayers?

If I have said anything in this letter that is an overstatement of the truth and is indicative of an unreasonable impatience, I beg you to forgive me. If I have said anything in this letter that is an understatement of the truth and is indicative of my having a patience that makes me patient with anything less than brotherhood, I beg God to forgive me.

I hope this letter finds you strong in the faith. I also hope that circumstances will soon make it possible for me to meet each of you, not as an integrationist or a civil rights leader, but as a fellow clergyman and a Christian brother. Let us all hope that the dark clouds of racial prejudice will soon pass away and the deep fog of misunderstanding will be lifted from our fear-drenched communities and in some not too distant tomorrow the radiant stars of love and brotherhood will shine over our great nation with all their scintillating beauty.

Yours for the cause of Peace and Brotherhood,
Martin Luther King, Jr.

---

1   *T.S. Eliot*   (1888–1965), British/American poet. "The last temptation is the greatest treason: / To do the right deed for the wrong reason" *Murder in the Cathedral* (1935).

MAHATMA GANDHI
(1869–1948)

One of the most influential leaders of the twentieth century, Mahatma Gandhi was in many respects a paradox. A saintly figure who came to be widely revered, he was an eccentric who stubbornly maintained an allegiance to a wide range of notions that seemed obviously impractical. Yet he became one of the most effective social activists of modern times; he was largely responsible for the success of the independence movement in India, and for the development of ideas of non-violent resistance to oppressive authority that have been influential throughout the world. Einstein said of him, "Generations to come will scarcely believe that such a one as this walked the earth in flesh and blood."

Born in what is now the westernmost state of India, Mohandas Karamchand Gandhi married at 13, and left for England at 18, where he enrolled in a law course at University College, London. Ironically, it was in London that he developed an interest in the Indian tradition of vegetarianism and in various other Indian spiritual traditions. He practiced law, without much success, in London and then for a year in India, before taking a job as legal advisor to a businessman in South Africa. It was there that he first became aware of European racism; a turning point came when he was expelled from a first-class railway carriage despite holding the proper ticket. He conducted several campaigns against racist laws, with limited success, and began to develop a theory for opposition to European dominance, using the Sanskrit term *satyāgraha* ("truth and firmness") to refer to his concept of passive, non-violent resistance, crediting Jesus, Tolstoy, and Thoreau as influences. His short book *Hind Swaraj* ("Indian Home Rule"), written in 1909, was pointedly critical not merely of colonialism but of industrial society and modernity in general.

Returning to India in 1915, Gandhi became increasingly involved in escalating demonstrations resisting British rule and its institutions. In 1919, in response to new repressive laws imposed by the British authority, *satyāgraha* gained millions of followers around India. Gandhi had become the clear leader of the independence movement, with a widespread reputation for saintliness—the title "Mahatma" ("great soul") was given to him by the Indian writer Rabindranath Tagore. While serving a jail term for sedition in 1922, he undertook the first of several widely publicized protest fasts. On his release, he continued to agitate against British rule, leading demonstrations and writing newspaper articles. In 1930 Gandhi led a protest march against the British salt tax, encouraging widespread civil disobedience throughout India; he and several thousand other Indians were arrested. In 1931, he went to London to attempt to negotiate some sort of home rule. No progress was made, however, and when he returned to India Gandhi was arrested again.

Retiring to a remote village, he sought to provide an example of a simpler, more self-sufficient lifestyle, without dependence on western industrial amenities, for example, by spinning and weaving the cloth for his own clothes. In his view, independence alone was useless: what was needed for his country was a complete moral and spiritual regeneration. Striving for personal perfection, he attempted to bring all desires under control—including sleeping naked with women to test the strength of his commitment to celibacy.

Gandhi was again jailed during World War II after he had called on the British to "Quit India now" rather than waiting to negotiate independence upon the conclusion of the war. The post-war British government did finally agree to grant independence, but decided to divide India and create separate Hindu- and Muslim-dominated states. Gandhi's efforts to prevent this partition, and to achieve Muslim-Hindu reconciliation in a time of growing friction, were in vain. In 1947, separate statehood was granted to Hindu India and Muslim Pakistan; Gandhi, despite being hailed as the father of his country, was deeply dismayed by this division. In the ensuing chaos as many as eleven million people were dislocated, and as many as one million lives were lost. In 1948, a Hindu nationalist fanatic, furious at Gandhi's attempts at Hindu-Muslim reconciliation, shot and killed him at a prayer meeting.

Many authorities credit him with providing much of the basis for the relative success of the India of today. Outside India, his political ideal, a sort of anarchistic confederation of self-sufficient independent villages, governed minimally by consensus of the residents, has not been widely shared, but his influence on non-violent anti-racist and anti-imperialist movements has been profound. The model of non-violent mass resistance as a means of achieving political change has been followed by the civil rights movement in the United States in the 1950s and 1960s; by the forces that overthrew the Philippine tyrant Ferdinand Marcos in 1986; and by those that overthrew totalitarian communist regimes throughout Eastern Europe in 1989-91. At the end of 1999, *Time Magazine* named him runner-up to Albert Einstein as "person of the century," and described the Dalai Lama, Lech Wałęsa, Martin Luther King Jr., and Nelson Mandela as "children of Gandhi."

◆ ◆ ◆ ◆ ◆

Satyagraha: Not Passive Resistance [2 September 1917]

The force denoted by the term "passive resistance" and translated into Hindi as *nishkriya pratirodha* is not very accurately described either by the original English phrase or by its Hindi rendering. Its correct description is "satyagraha."[1] Satyagraha was born in South Africa in 1908.[2] There was no word in any Indian language denoting the power which our countrymen in South Africa invoked for the redress of their grievances. There was an English equivalent, namely,

"passive resistance," and we carried on with it. However, the need for a word to describe this unique power came to be increasingly felt, and it was decided to award a prize to anyone who could think of an appropriate term. A Gujarati-speaking gentleman submitted the word "satyagraha," and it was adjudged the best.

"Passive resistance" conveyed the idea of the Suffragette Movement in England. Burning of houses by these women was called "passive resistance" and so also their fasting in prison. All such acts might very well be "passive resistance" but they were no "satyagraha." It is said of "passive resistance" that it is the weapon of the weak, but the power which is the subject of the article can be used only by the strong. This power is not "passive" resistance; indeed it calls for intense activity. The movement in South Africa was not passive but active. The Indians of South Africa believed that Truth was their object, that Truth ever triumphs, and with this definiteness of purpose they persistently held on to Truth. They put up with all the suffering that this persistence implied. With the conviction that Truth is not to be renounced even unto death, they shed the fear of death. In the cause of Truth, the prison was a palace to them and its doors the gateway to freedom.

Satyagraha is not physical force. A satyagrahi[3] does not inflict pain on the adversary; he does not seek his destruction. A satyagrahi never resorts to firearms. In the use of satyagraha, there is no ill-will whatever.

Satyagraha is pure soul-force. Truth is the very substance of the soul. That is why this force is called satyagraha. The soul is informed with knowledge. In it burns the flame of love. If someone gives us pain through ignorance, we shall win him through love. "Non-violence is the supreme *dharma*"[4] is the proof of this power of love. Non-violence is a dormant state. In the waking state, it is love. Ruled by love, the world goes on. In English there is a saying, "Might is Right." Then there is the doctrine of the survival of the fittest. Both these ideas are contradictory to the above principle. Neither is wholly true. If ill-will were the chief motive-force, the world would have been destroyed long ago; and neither would I have had the opportunity to write this article nor would the hopes of the readers be fulfilled. We are alive solely because of love. We are all ourselves the proof of this. Deluded by modern Western civilization, we

---

1   *satyagraha* [Unless otherwise indicated, all notes to this selection are by the editors of this anthology.] Pronounced (roughly) *suh-TYAH-gruh-huh* or *SUH-tyuh-GRA-huh*. The Sanskrit roots of this term give it an association with *determined clinging to the truth*.

2   *South Africa in 1908* The date of the first protest Gandhi led, against discriminatory practices imposed on the Indian community by the government of South Africa, requiring them to hold certificates of registration.

3   *satyagrahi* One who practices satyagraha.

4   *dharma* Sacred law; basic principle that orders the universe; conduct in accord with such a principle.

have forgotten our ancient civilization and worship the might of arms.

We forget the principle of non-violence, which is the essence of all religions. The doctrine of arms stands for ir-religion. It is due to the sway of that doctrine that a san-guinary war is raging in Europe.

In India also we find worship of arms. We see it even in that great work of Tulsidas.[1] But it is seen in all the books that soul-force is the supreme power.

Rama stands for the soul and Ravana[2] for the non-soul. The immense physical might of Ravana is as nothing com-pared to the soul-force of Rama. Ravana's ten heads are as straw to Rama. Rama is a *yogi*, he has conquered self and pride. He is "placid equally in affluence and adversity," he has "neither attachment, nor the intoxication of status." This represents the ultimate in satyagraha. The banner of *satyagraha* can again fly in the Indian sky and it is our duty to raise it. If we take recourse to satyagraha, we can conquer our conquerors the English, make them bow before our tremendous soul-force, and the issue will be of benefit to the whole world.

It is certain that India cannot rival Britain or Europe in force of arms. The British worship the war-god and they can all of them become, as they are becoming, bearers of arms. The hundreds of millions in India can never carry arms. They have made the religion of non-violence their own. It is impossible for the *varnashrama* system[3] to disappear from India.

The way of *varnashrama* is a necessary law of nature. India, by making a judicious use of it, derives much bene-fit. Even the Muslims and the English in India observe this system to some extent. Outside of India, too, people follow it without being aware of it. So long as this institu-tion of *vamashrama* exists in India, everyone cannot bear arms here. The highest place in India is assigned to the *brahmana dhanna*—which is soul-force. Even the armed warrior does obeisance to the Brahmin.[4] So long as this

custom prevails, it is vain for us to aspire for equality with the West in force of arms.

It is our Kamadhenu.[5] It brings good both to the sat-yagrahi and his adversary. It is ever victorious. For instance, Harishchandra was a satyagrahi, Prahlad was a satyagrahi, Mirabai was a satyagrahi. Daniel, Socrates and those Arabs who hurled themselves on the fire of the French artillery were all satyagrahis. We see from these examples that a sat-yagrahi does not fear for his body, he does not give up what he thinks is Truth; the word "defeat" is not to be found in his dictionary, he does not wish for the destruction of his antagonist, he does not vent anger on him; but has only compassion for him.

A satyagrahi does not wait for others, but throws him-self into the fray, relying entirely on his own resources. He trusts that when the time comes, others will do likewise. His practice is his precept. Like air, satyagraha is all-pervad-ing. It is infectious, which means that all people-big and small, men and women—can become satyagrahis. No one is kept out from the army of satyagrahis. A satyagrahi cannot perpetrate tyranny on anyone; he is not subdued through application of physical force; he does not strike at anyone. Just as anyone can resort to satyagraha, it can be resorted to in almost any situation.

People demand historical evidence in support of sat-yagraha. History is for the most part a record of armed activities. Natural activities find very little mention in it. Only uncommon activities strike us with wonder. Satya-graha has been used always and in all situations. The father and the son, the man and the wife are perpetually resorting to satyagraha, one towards the other. When a father gets angry and punishes the son, the son does not hit back with a weapon, he conquers his father's anger by submitting to him. The son refuses to be subdued by the unjust rule of his father but he puts up with the punishment that he may incur through disobeying the unjust father. We can simi-larly free ourselves of the unjust rule of the Government by defying the unjust rule and accepting the punishments that go with it. We do not bear malice towards the Government When we set its fears at rest, when we do not desire to make armed assaults on the administrators, nor to unseat them from power, but only to get rid of their injustice, they will at once be subdued to our will.

---

1 *Tulsidas* Gosvāmī Tulsīdās (1532–1623). Tulsīdās is considered the greatest Hindi poet. He composed a version in his own lan-guage (Awadhi) of the original ancient Sanskrit epic poem about Lord Rama.

2 *Rama ... Ravana* In Hindu mythology, Rama, an incarnation of the god Vishnu, led an army of monkeys in an invasion of the island of Lanka to destroy Ravana and his army of demons.

3 *the varnashrama system* The Indian caste system of rigid social classes. Traditionally, it was taken to be established by sacred law.

4 *Brahmin* A member of the highest of the four major traditional Hindu classes—the "scholarly" caste, including teachers and doc-

tors, and those who officiate at sacred ceremonies.

5 *Kamadhenu* In Hindu mythology, this was the divine cow, mother of all earthly cows, who can grant all wishes.

The question is asked why we should call any rule unjust. In saying so, we ourselves assume the function of a judge. It is true. But in this world, we always have to act as judges for ourselves. That is why the satyagrahi does not strike his adversary with arms. If he has Truth on his side, he will win, and if his thought is faulty, he will suffer the consequences of his fault.

What is the good, they ask, of only one person opposing injustice; for he will be punished and destroyed, he will languish in prison or meet an untimely end through hanging. The objection is not valid. History shows that all reforms have begun with one person. Fruit is hard to come by without tapasya.[1] The suffering that has to be undergone in satyagraha is tapasya in its purest form. Only when the tapasya is capable of bearing fruit do we have the fruit. This establishes the fact that when there is insufficient tapasya, the fruit is delayed. The tapasya of Jesus Christ, boundless though it was, was not sufficient for Europe's need. Europe has disapproved Christ. Through ignorance, it has disregarded Christ's pure way of life. Many Christs will have to offer themselves as sacrifice at the terrible altar of Europe, and only then will realization dawn on that continent. But Jesus will always be the first among these. He has been the sower of the seed and his will therefore be the credit for raising the harvest.

It is said that it is a very difficult, if not an altogether impossible, task to educate ignorant peasants in satyagraha and that it is full of perils, for it is a very arduous business to transform unlettered ignorant people from one condition into another. Both the arguments are just silly. The people of India are perfectly fit to receive the training of satyagraha. India has knowledge of *dharma*, and where there is knowledge of *dharma*. Satyagraha is a very simple matter. The people of India have drunk of the nectar of devotion. This great people overflows with faith. It is no difficult matter to lead such a people on to the right path of satyagraha. Some have a fear that once people get involved in satyagraha, they may at a later stage take to arms. This fear is illusory. From the path of satyagraha, a transition to the path of asatyagraha[2] is impossible. It is possible of course that some people who believe in armed activity may mislead the satyagrahis by infiltrating into their ranks and later making

them take to arms. This is possible in all enterprises. But as compared to other activities, it is less likely to happen in satyagraha, for their motives soon get exposed and when the people are not ready to take up arms, it becomes almost impossible to lead them on to that terrible path. The might of arms is directly opposed to the might of satyagraha. Just as darkness does not abide in light, soulless armed activity cannot enter the sunlike radiance of soul-force. Many Pathans[3] took part in satyagraha in South Africa abiding by all the rules of satyagraha.

Then it is said that much suffering is involved in being a satyagrahi and that the entire people will not be willing to put up with this suffering. The objection is not valid. People in general always follow in the footsteps of the noble. There is no doubt that it is difficult to produce a satyagrahi leader. Our experience is that a satyagrahi needs many more virtues like self-control, fearlessness, etc., than are requisite for one who believes in armed action. The greatness of the man bearing arms does not lie in the superiority of the arms, nor does it lie in his physical prowess. It lies in his determination and fearlessness in face of death. General Gordon[4] was a mighty warrior of the British Empire. In the statue that has been erected in his memory he has only a small baton in his hand. It goes to show that the strength of a warrior is not measured by reference to his weapons but by his firmness of mind. A satyagrahi needs millions of times more of such firmness than does a bearer of arms. The birth of such a man can bring about the salvation of India in no time. Not only India but the whole world awaits the advent of such a man. We may in the meanwhile prepare the ground as much as we can through satyagraha.

How can we make use of satyagraha in the present conditions? Why should we take to satyagraha in the fight for freedom? We are all guilty of killing manliness. So long as our learned Annie Besant[5] is in detention, it is an insult

---

1 *tapasya* The practice of physical and psychological self-denial, and concentration on a goal, for the sake of purification and spiritual growth.

2 *asatyagraha* As the word "satyagraha" implies *clinging to the truth*, the word "asatyagraha" implies *clinging to untruth*.

3 *Pathans* A people indigenous to today's eastern Afghanistan and northwest Pakistan.

4 *General Gordon* Major-General Charles George Gordon, (1833–85), British army officer and administrator. Gordon played an important role in ending the slave trade in the Sudan in the 1870s, but is best known for his death; he had been sent to the Sudan in 1884 on a mission to rescue British troops that had been cut off after a rebellion, but Gordon's forces were themselves besieged in Khartoum for ten months and finally overwhelmed, with Gordon himself killed during the battle.

5 *Annie Besant* (1847–1933) British social reformer, campaigner for women's rights and a supporter of Indian nationalism. She organized the Home Rule League in India in 1916, and was ar-

to our manhood. How can we secure her release through satyagraha? It may be that the Government has acted in good faith, that it has sufficient grounds for keeping her under detention. But, at any rate, the people are unhappy at her being deprived of her freedom. Annie Besant cannot be freed through armed action. No Indian will approve of such an action. We cannot secure her freedom by submitting petitions and the like. Much time has passed. We can all humbly inform the Government that if Mrs. Annie Besant is not released within the time limit prescribed by us, we will all be compelled to follow her path. It is possible that all of us do not like all her actions; but we find nothing in her actions which threatens the "established Government" or the vested interests. Therefore we too by participating in her activities will ask for her lot, that is, we shall all court imprisonment. The members of our Legislative Assembly also can petition the Government and when the petition is not accepted, they can resign their membership. For swaraj[1] also, satyagraha is the unfailing weapon. Satyagraha means that what we want is truth, that we deserve it and that we will work for it even unto death.

Nothing more need be said. Truth alone triumphs. There is no *dharma* higher than Truth. Truth always wins. We pray to God that in this sacred land we may bring about the reign of *dharma* by following satyagraha and that this our country may become an example for all to follow.

◆ ◆ ◆ ◆ ◆

The Doctrine of the Sword
[11 August 1920]

In this age of the rule of brute-force, it is almost impossible for anyone to believe that anyone else could possibly reject the law of the final supremacy of brute-force. And so I receive anonymous letters advising me that I must not interfere with the progress of non-cooperation even though popular violence may break out. Others come to me and assuming that secretly I must be plotting violence, enquire when the happy moment for declaring open violence will arrive. They assure me that the English will never yield to

anything but violence secret or open. Yet others, I am informed, believe that I am the most rascally person living in India because I never give out my real intention and that they have not a shadow of a doubt that I believe in violence just as much as most people do.

Such being the hold that the doctrine of the sword has on the majority of mankind, and as success of non-co-operation depends principally on absence of violence during its pendency[2] and as my views in this matter affect the conduct of a large number of people, I am anxious to state them as clearly as possible.

I do believe that where there is only a choice between cowardice and violence I would advise violence. Thus when my eldest son asked me what he should have done, had he been present when I was almost fatally assaulted in 1908, whether he should have run away and seen me killed or whether he should have used his physical force which he could and wanted to use, and defended me, I told him that it was his duty to defend me even by using violence. Hence it was that I took part in the Boer War, the so called Zulu rebellion and the late War.[3] Hence also do I advocate training in arms for those who believe in the method of violence. I would rather have India resort to arms in order to defend her honor than that she should in a cowardly manner become or remain a helpless witness to her own dishonor.

But I believe that non-violence is infinitely superior to violence, forgiveness is more manly than punishment. *Kshama virasya bhushanam.* 'Forgiveness adorns a soldier.' But abstinence is forgiveness only when there is the power to punish; it is meaningless when it pretends to proceed from a helpless creature. A mouse hardly forgives a cat when

---

rested in 1917; protest against her internment provided a focus for the growing Indian nationalist movement.

1   *swaraj*   Self-government; home rule in general; this term was especially associated with Gandhi's aims for Indian independence.

2   *pendency*   State of awaiting.

3   *Boer War, the so called Zulu rebellion and the late War*   Gandhi lived in South Africa between 1893 and 1914. During the (Second) Boer War (1899–1902), between the British rulers of South Africa and two independent Boer (Dutch origin) provinces, Gandhi organized an ambulance corps for the British army. During the "Zulu Rebellion" (more properly known as The Bambatha Uprising), a Zulu revolt against British rule and taxation, Gandhi led a stretcher-bearer corps. Gandhi had already been active in the struggle against British treatment of colonialized people, and his sympathies were with the Boers and the Zulu; but he wanted to demonstrate that Indians could be responsible citizens in times of crisis. When World War I broke out in 1914, Gandhi was at sea, traveling back to Britain. When he arrived, he gathered his Indian friends to organize an ambulance unit. "If we wished to improve our status through the help and cooperation of the British," he explained, "it was our duty to win their help by standing by them in their hour of need."

it allows itself to be torn to pieces by her. I, therefore, appreciate the sentiment of those who cry out for the condign punishment of General Dyer[1] and his ilk. They would tear him to pieces if they could. But I do not believe India to be helpless. I do not believe myself to be a helpless creature. Only I want to use India's and my strength for a better purpose.

Let me not be misunderstood. Strength does not come from physical capacity. It comes from an indomitable will. An average Zulu is any way more than a match for an average Englishman in bodily capacity. But he flees from an English boy, because he fears the boy's revolver or those who will use it for him. He fears death and is nerveless in spite of his burly figure. We in India may in a moment realize that one hundred thousand Englishmen need not frighten three hundred million human beings. A definite forgiveness would therefore mean a definite recognition of our strength. With enlightened forgiveness must come a mighty wave of strength in us, which would make it impossible for a Dyer and a Frank Johnson[2] to heap affront upon India's devoted head. It matters little to me that for the moment I do not drive my point home. We feel too downtrodden not to be angry and revengeful. But I must not refrain from saying that India can gain more by waiving the right of punishment. We have better work to do, a better mission to deliver to the world.

I am not a visionary. I claim to be a practical idealist. The religion of non-violence is not meant merely for the rishis[3] and saints. It is meant for the common people as well. Non-violence is the law of our species as violence is the law of the brute. The spirit lies dormant in the brute and he knows no law but that of physical might. The dignity of man requires obedience to a higher law—to the strength of the spirit.

I have therefore ventured to place before India the ancient law of self-sacrifice. For satyagraha and its off-shoots, non-co-operation and civil resistance, are nothing but new names for the law of suffering. The rishis, who discovered the law of non-violence in the midst of violence, were greater geniuses than Newton. They were themselves greater warriors than Wellington. Having themselves known the use of arms, they realized their uselessness and taught a weary world that its salvation lay not through violence but through non-violence.

Non-violence in its dynamic condition means conscious suffering. It does not mean meek submission to the will of the evildoer, but it means the putting of one's whole soul against the will of the tyrant. Working under this law of our being, it is possible for a single individual to defy the whole might of an unjust empire to save his honor, his religion, his soul and lay the foundation for that empire's fall or its regeneration.

And so I am not pleading for India to practice non-violence because it is weak. I want her to practice non-violence being conscious of her strength and power. No training in arms is required for realization of her strength. We seem to need it because we seem to think that we are but a lump of flesh. I want India to recognize that she has a soul that cannot perish and that can rise triumphant above every physical weakness and defy the physical combination of a whole world. What is the meaning of Rama, a mere human being, with his host of monkeys, pitting himself against the insolent strength of ten-headed Ravana surrounded in supposed safety by the raging waters on all sides of Lanka?[4] Does it not mean the conquest of physical might by spiritual strength? However, being a practical man, I do not wait till India recognizes the practicability of the spiritual life in the political world. India considers herself to be powerless and paralyzed before the machine-guns, the tanks and the airplanes of the English. And she takes up non-co-operation out of her weakness. It must still serve the same purpose, namely, bring her delivery from the crushing weight of British injustice if a sufficient number of people practice it.

I isolate this non-co-operation from Sinn Feinism,[5] for, it is so conceived as to be incapable of being offered side by side with violence. But I invite even the school of violence

---

1   *General Dyer*   British Brigadier-General Reginald Edward Harry Dyer (1864–1927) was responsible for the Amritsar Massacre (1919); he ordered his troops to fire on unarmed peaceful civilians, more than 1000 of whom may have been killed.

2   *Frank Johnson*   See Gandhi "Freedom's Battle (The Punjab Wrongs)" (1922): "Who ever talks of Col. Frank Johnson who was by far the worst offender? He terrorised guiltless Lahore, and by his merciless orders set the tone to the whole of the Martial Law officers."

3   *rishis*   Hindu saints/sages.

4   *Rama ... all sides of Lanka*   In Hindu mythology, Rama, an incarnation of the god Vishnu, led an army of monkeys in an invasion of the island of Lanka to destroy Ravana and his army of demons.

5   *Sinn Feinism*   Sinn Fein is an Irish nationalist society, founded in the early twentieth century to promote independence from England, unification of Ireland, and Irish culture. Gandhi disassociates himself from its advocacy of violence.

to give this peaceful non-co-operation a trial. It will not fail through its inherent weakness. It may fail because of poverty of response. Then will be the time for real danger. The high-souled men, who are unable to suffer national humiliation any longer, will want to vent their wrath. They will take to violence. So far as I know, they must perish without delivering themselves or their country from the wrong. If India takes up the doctrine of the sword, she may gain momentary victory. Then India will cease to be the pride of my heart. I am wedded to India because I owe my all to her. I believe absolutely that she has a mission for the world. She is not to copy Europe blindly. India's acceptance of the doctrine of the sword will be the hour of my trial. I hope I shall not be found wanting.

◆ ◆ ◆ ◆ ◆

Problems of Non-violence [9 August 1925]

People keep asking me which acts may be termed violent and which non-violent. and what is one's duty at a particular time. While some of these queries reveal the ignorance of the enquirers, others serve to bring out the difficult dilemmas involved. A Punjabi gentleman has put a question the answer to which is worth giving here. It is as follows:

> What should be done when tigers, wolves and other wild beasts come and carry away other animals or human beings? Or, what should be done about germs in water?

In my humble opinion the simple answer is that where there is danger from tigers, wolves and so on, then killing them becomes inevitable. The germs that water contains must also be inevitably destroyed. Violence which is inevitable does not therefore cease to be so and become non-violence. It has to be recognized as violence. I have no doubt that it would be best if we could contrive to survive without destroying tigers, wolves, etc. However, who could do so? Only he who is not afraid of these animals and can regard them as friends, he alone could do so. Anyone who refrains from violence because he is afraid, is nevertheless guilty of violence. The mouse is not non-violent towards the cat. At heart, he always has a feeling of violence towards the cat. He cannot kill the latter because he is weak. He alone has

the power to practice the dharma[1] of ahimsa[2] who although fully capable of inflicting violence does not inflict it. He alone practices the ahimsa dharma who voluntarily and with love refrains from inflicting violence on anyone.

Non-violence implies love, compassion, forgiveness. The Shastras[3] describe these as the virtues of the brave. This courage is not physical but mental. There have been instances of physically frail men having indulged in grave acts of violence with the help of others. There have also been cases where those as physically strong as Yudhishthira have granted pardon to such persons as King Virata.[4] Hence, so long as one has not developed inner strength, one can never practice the dharma of ahimsa. The non-violence practiced by the Banias[5] today does not deserve the name; one finds in it cruelty sometimes and ignorance all the time.

It was because I know this weakness of ours that during the War I went all out to recruit soldiers in Khedra.[6] And, it was for this very reason that I said at that time that perhaps the most brutal act of the British Government was to have disarmed and thus emasculated the Indian people. I hold the same view even today. If anyone afraid at heart cannot, while remaining unarmed, rid himself of that fear, he should certainly arm himself with a stick or an even more deadly weapon.

---

1 *dharma* Sanskrit: good moral practice.
2 *ahimsa* Sanskrit: non-violence.
3 *Shastras* Sanskrit: scriptures.
4 *Yudhishthira ... King Virata* The great ancient Hindu epic *Mahābhārata* includes the story of King Virata and the emperor Yudhishthira, known for his strength in warfare and for his piety.
5 *Banias* Members of a caste of moneylenders and merchants, chiefly in northern and western India. Gandhi was born into this caste.
6 *during the War ... in Khedra* During World War I, Gandhi was actively involved in recruiting soldiers in Khedra for the British Army.

FRANTZ FANON
(1925-1961)

Frantz Fanon is one of the central figures in post-colonial thought. His two major books *Black Skin, White Masks* (1952) and *The Wretched of the Earth* (1961), are acknowledged classics of colonialism and its consequences. In these works and other writings, Fanon contributed to psychiatry, developed a subtle analysis of racism and racial identity, pioneered the field of cultural studies, and developed insightful—if contested—positions on revolution, violence, and nationalism.

Born in 1925, in the French colony of Martinique, Fanon joined the Free French forces in 1943. He served in Morocco during World War II, earning the Croix de Guerre. His war experience left him disillusioned with France, however, as a result of his first-hand experience of French colonialism in North Africa. After the war, he enrolled in the psychiatry program in Lyon's Medical School, defending his thesis in 1951. Two years later, he moved to Algeria as medical chief at the Blida-Joinville psychiatric hospital.

Life in Algeria, where the brutal French-Algeria war was beginning, transformed Fanon's life. In his work, he increasingly came into contact with victims of torture, while also treating the French police who tortured them. He soon joined the FLN (National Liberal Front), editing and writing extensively for the newspaper El Moudjahid; many of these articles are collected in *A Dying Colonialism* (1959). Besides his journalism, Fanon provided medical care to rebels and negotiated with African leaders. The Algerian Provisional Government appointed him ambassador to Ghana in 1960. The next year, Fanon died in hospital in the United States.

Black Skin, White Masks provides a classic, though sometimes obscure analysis of race. The book draws on Fanon's psychiatric training for many of its insights, but its ideas also connect to those of Jean-Paul Sartre's existentialism and the negritude movement. The negritude movement affirmed African identity in a way that presented a flip side of the then-common white supremacist value judgments, praising "black" nature as intuitive, emotional, creative and communal. (One of Fanon's high school teachers was Aimé Césaire, the Martinique poet, politician, and pioneer of the negritude movement.) Fanon recognized the importance of the movement, but his relationship to it was ambivalent.

From Sartre, Fanon draws on the notion that "existence precedes essence" in order to diagnose the core of racism. Sartre's idea is that authentic identity is not something imposed upon us by our biology, history or society, but rather something we create through our choices. Sartre held that not to choose, to allow outside forces to impose our identity, is to act in "bad faith." The notion of identity being determined through the stance one takes towards others fits well with Fanon's claim that black identity forms through its contact with racist white society. In Fanon's view, racism depends on the belief that race is an objective category, rather than something formed by subjective perceptions and prejudices. This view leads him to reject the claim that there is a black "essence," as had been affirmed by racists and by some negritude writers.

In establishing the importance of race within political theory, Fanon moved beyond Marxist analysis. The basic dynamic in Marxism is class struggle, with the dominant class controlling the means of production; Marxists argue that economic structures are the "base" of society, determining the nature of social and cultural institutions. As Fanon argued, however, the Marxist framework does not fit the reality of colonial societies, where class is often ambiguous and complicated by race. Fanon writes, "Looking at the immediacies of the colonial context, it becomes clear that what divides this world is first and foremost what species, what race one belongs to. In the colonies the economic infrastructure is also a superstructure. The cause is effect: you are rich because you are white, you are white because you are rich."

Fanon develops this line of thought in his most influential book, *The Wretched of the Earth*, a sustained reflection on violence, revolution, nationalism and mental illness in a colonial setting. Fanon writes of the basic "Manichaeism" in the colonial world, referring to what he regarded as the irreconcilable dichotomy between colonizers and colonized, and showing how this dichotomy pervades the physical environment in ways that sustain systems of power. Classification, Fanon realized, is a means of control, a tool for maintaining racial lines and dehumanizing the natives.

Unlike the Marxists, who believed that the working class would carry out the revolution, Fanon placed his faith in the peasants, the dispossessed whom he described as making up the "wretched of the earth." Only a revolution from the bottom up could reform society, since the native tradespeople, intellectuals, civil servants and even industrial workers benefit from colonization; Fanon trenchantly criticized the tendency of many recently liberated African nations to succumb to dictatorships and corruption.

Fanon's conviction that change could come only "from the bottom up" provided much of the foundation for the endorsement of violence. Violence, for him, was part of the process of liberation, beginning as a reaction to the violence of colonization; in Fanon's view, "the colonized man finds his freedom in and through violence." He goes further, adding, "at the level of individuals, violence is a cleansing force. It frees the native from his inferiority complex and from his despair and inaction; it makes him fearless and restores his self respect."

Fanon's prose here is in some ways reminiscent of Nietzsche's more inflammatory passages, especially in *The Twilight of the Idols*. But unlike Nietzsche, who had little interest in political or social causes, Fanon argued that violence could unite the colonized under a common cause. Fanon rejected the prospect of peaceful negotiations with colonizers, believing that this would simply fill existing institutions and hierarchies with new elites drawn from the colonized. Fanon's vision was of a nation that would transcend Manichaeism, racism, tribalism and unite the masses in a common cause, collective history and national destiny. In his view the struggle against oppression translates to a struggle against poverty, illiteracy and underdevelopment.

Fanon has left an ambiguous legacy. Fanon inspired many key figures in anti-colonial and liberation movements, including South African activist Steve Biko, Iranian sociologist Ali Shariati, Cuban revolutionary Che Guevara and the American radical activists, the Black Panthers.

Academically, he became a major figure in Edward Said's studies of Orientalism and imperialism and an important reference point within cultural studies. Still, many of his views today seem misplaced or naïve; though his critical remarks on nationalism remain insightful and often accurate, his more positive contribution appears utopian. Similarly, his writing on violence is problematic and disturbing. But his thought remains a vital source for political philosophers who want to think seriously about topics like racism, global inequality, and terrorism.

◆ ◆ ◆ ◆ ◆

from *The Wretched of the Earth* (1961)

On Violence

National liberation, national reawakening, restoration of the nation to the people or Commonwealth, whatever the name used, whatever the latest expression, decolonization is always a violent event. At whatever level we study it—individual encounters, a change of name for a sports club, the guest list at a cocktail party, members of a police force or the board of directors of a state or private bank—decolonization is quite simply the substitution of one "species" of mankind by another. The substitution is unconditional, absolute, total, and seamless. We could go on to portray the rise of a new nation, the establishment of a new state, its diplomatic relations and its economic and political orientation. But instead we have decided to describe the kind of tabula rasa[1] which from the outset defines any decolonization. What is singularly important is that it starts from the very first day with the basic claims of the colonized. In actual fact, proof of success lies in a social fabric that has been changed inside out. This change is extraordinarily important because it is desired, clamored for, and demanded. The need for this change exists in a raw, repressed, and reckless state in the lives and consciousness of colonized men and women. But the eventuality of such a change is also experienced as a

---

1 *tabula rasa* [Unless otherwise indicated, all notes to this selection are by the editors of this anthology.] Latin: blank slate. A starting point without any pre-existing institutions, assumptions, etc.

terrifying future in the consciousness of another "species" of men and women: the *colons*, the colonists.

Decolonization, which sets out to change the order of the world, is clearly an agenda for total disorder. But it cannot be accomplished by the wave of a magic wand, a natural cataclysm, or a gentleman's agreement. Decolonization, we know, is an historical process: In other words, it can only be understood, it can only find its significance and become self coherent insofar as we can discern the history-making movement which gives it form and substance. Decolonization is the encounter between two congenitally antagonistic forces that in fact owe their singularity to the kind of reification[1] secreted and nurtured by the colonial situation. Their first confrontation was colored by violence and their cohabitation—or rather the exploitation of the colonized by the colonizer—continued at the point of the bayonet and under cannon fire. The colonist and the colonized are old acquaintances. And consequently, the colonist is right when he says he "knows" them. It is the colonist who *fabricated* and *continues to fabricate* the colonized subject. The colonist derives his validity, i.e., his wealth, from the colonial system.

Decolonization never goes unnoticed, for it focuses on and fundamentally alters being, and transforms the spectator crushed to a nonessential state into a privileged actor, captured in a virtually grandiose fashion by the spotlight of History. It infuses a new rhythm, specific to a new generation of men, with a new language and a new humanity. Decolonization is truly the creation of new men. But such a creation cannot be attributed to a supernatural power: The "thing" colonized becomes a man through the very process of liberation.

Decolonization, therefore, implies the urgent need to thoroughly challenge the colonial situation. Its definition can, if we want to describe it accurately, be summed up in the well-known words: "The last shall be first."[2] Decolonization is verification of this. At a descriptive level, therefore, any decolonization is a success.

---

1   *reification* To treat something that is merely a concept as if it had an independent reality.
2   *The last shall be first* Mark 29–31: "And Jesus answered and said, Verily I say unto you, There is no man that hath left house, or brethren, or sisters, or father, or mother, or wife, or children, or lands, for my sake, and the gospel's, But he shall receive an hundredfold now in this time, houses, and brethren, and sisters, and mothers, and children, and lands, with persecutions; and in the world to come eternal life. But many that are first shall be last; and the last first."

In its bare reality, decolonization reeks of red-hot cannonballs and bloody knives. For the last can be the first only after a murderous and decisive confrontation between the two protagonists. This determination to have the last move up to the front, to have them clamber up (too quickly, say some) the famous echelons of an organized society, can only succeed by resorting to every means, including, of course, violence.

You do not disorganize a society, however primitive it may be, with such an agenda if you are not determined from the very start to smash every obstacle encountered. The colonized, who have made up their mind to make such an agenda into a driving force, have been prepared for violence from time immemorial. As soon as they are born it is obvious to them that their cramped world, riddled with taboos, can only be challenged by out and out violence.

The colonial world is a compartmentalized world. It is obviously as superfluous to recall the existence of "native" towns and European towns, of schools for "natives" and schools for Europeans, as it is to recall apartheid in South Africa. Yet if we penetrate inside this compartmentalization we shall at least bring to light some of its key aspects. By penetrating its geographical configuration and classification we shall be able to delineate the backbone on which the decolonized society is reorganized.

The colonized world is a world divided in two. The dividing line, the border, is represented by the barracks and the police stations. In the colonies, the official, legitimate agent, the spokesperson for the colonizer and the regime of oppression, is the police officer or the soldier. In capitalist societies, education, whether secular or religious, the teaching of moral reflexes handed down from father to son, the exemplary integrity of workers decorated after fifty years of loyal and faithful service, the fostering of love for harmony and wisdom, those aesthetic forms of respect for the status quo, instill in the exploited a mood of submission and inhibition which considerably eases the task of the agents of law and order. In capitalist countries a multitude of sermonizers, counselors, and "confusion-mongers" intervene between the exploited and the authorities. In colonial regions, however, the proximity and frequent, direct intervention by the police and the military ensure the colonized are kept under close scrutiny, and contained by rifle butts and napalm. We have seen how the government's agent uses a language of pure violence. The agent does not alleviate oppression or mask domination. He displays and demonstrates them with the clear conscience of the law enforcer, and brings violence into the homes and minds of the colonized subject.

The "native" sector is not complementary to the European sector. The two confront each other, but not in the service of a higher unity. Governed by a purely Aristotelian logic,[1] they follow the dictates of mutual exclusion: There is no conciliation possible, one of them is superfluous. The colonist's sector is a sector built to last, all stone and steel. It's a sector of lights and paved roads, where the trash cans constantly overflow with strange and wonderful garbage, undreamed-of leftovers. The colonist's feet can never be glimpsed, except perhaps in the sea, but then you can never get close enough. They are protected by solid shoes in a sector where the streets are clean and smooth, without a pothole, without a stone. The colonist's sector is a sated, sluggish sector, its belly is permanently full of good things. The colonist's sector is a white folks' sector, a sector of foreigners.

The colonized's sector, or at least the "native" quarters, the shanty town, the Medina,[2] the reservation, is a disreputable place inhabited by disreputable people. You are born anywhere, anyhow. You die anywhere, from anything. It's a world with no space, people are piled one on top of the other, the shacks squeezed tightly together. The colonized's sector is a famished sector, hungry for bread, meat, shoes, coal, and light. The colonized's sector is a sector that crouches and cowers, a sector on its knees, a sector that is prostrate. It's a sector of niggers, a sector of towelheads.[3] The gaze that the colonized subject casts at the colonist's sector is a look of lust, a look of envy. Dreams of possession. Every type of possession: of sitting at the colonist's table and sleeping in his bed, preferably with his wife. The colonized man is an envious man. The colonist is aware of this as he catches the furtive glance, and constantly on his guard, realizes bitterly that: "They want to take our place." And it's true there is not one colonized subject who at least once a day does not dream of taking the place of the colonist.

This compartmentalized world, this world divided in two, is inhabited by different species. The singularity of the colonial context lies in the fact that economic reality, inequality, and enormous disparities in lifestyles never manage to mask the human reality. Looking at the immediacies of the colonial context, it is clear that what divides this world is first and foremost what species, what race one belongs to. In the colonies the economic infrastructure is also a superstructure. The cause is effect: You are rich because you are white, you are white because you are rich. This is why a Marxist analysis should always be slightly stretched when it comes to addressing the colonial issue. It is not just the concept of the precapitalist society, so effectively studied by Marx, which needs to be reexamined here. The serf is essentially different from the knight, but a reference to divine right is needed to justify this difference in status. In the colonies the foreigner imposed himself using his cannons and machines. Despite the success of his pacification, in spite of his appropriation, the colonist always remains a foreigner. It is not the factories, the estates, or the bank account which primarily characterize the "ruling class." The ruling species is first and foremost the outsider from elsewhere, different from the indigenous population, "the others."

The violence which governed the ordering of the colonial world, which tirelessly punctuated the destruction of the indigenous social fabric, and demolished unchecked the systems of reference of the country's economy, lifestyles, and modes of dress, this same violence will be vindicated and appropriated when, taking history into their own hands, the colonized swarm into the forbidden cities. To blow the colonial world to smithereens is henceforth a clear image within the grasp and imagination of every colonized subject. To dislocate the colonial world does not mean that once the borders have been eliminated there will be a right of way between the two sectors. To destroy the colonial world means nothing less than demolishing the colonist's sector, burying it deep within the earth or banishing it from the territory.

Challenging the colonial world is not a rational confrontation of viewpoints. It is not a discourse on the universal, but the impassioned claim by the colonized that their world is fundamentally different. The colonial world is a Mani-

---

1   *a purely Aristotelian logic*   Basic principles of Aristotle's logic are (1) Law of Identity: Each existence is identical with itself; (2) Law of Noncontradiction: Each existence is not different from itself; and (3) Law of Excluded Middle: No existence can be both itself and different from itself. These principles are sometimes seen to imply a static and changeless view of reality, as opposed to a view associated with (Hegelian/Marxist) "dialectical" logic in which everything contains contradictions within itself, and thus the principles for change.

2   *the Medina*   The name for the oldest part of North African cities.

3   *towelheads*   Derogatory name sometimes applied to Arabs, in the mistaken belief that they wear turbans—or to Sikhs, who do in fact wear them.

chaean[1] world. The colonist is not content with physically limiting the space of the colonized, i.e., with the help of his agents of law and order. As if to illustrate the totalitarian nature of colonial exploitation, the colonist turns the colonized into a kind of quintessence of evil.[2] Colonized society is not merely portrayed as a society without values. The colonist is not content with stating that the colonized world has lost its values or worse never possessed any. The "native" is declared impervious to ethics, representing not only the absence of values but also the negation of values. He is, dare we say it, the enemy of values. In other words, absolute evil. A corrosive element, destroying everything within his reach, a corrupting element, distorting everything which involves aesthetics or morals, an agent of malevolent powers, an unconscious and incurable instrument of blind forces. And Monsieur Meyer could say in all seriousness in the French National Assembly that we should not let the Republic be defiled by the penetration of the Algerian people. Values are, in fact, irreversibly poisoned and infected as soon as they come into contact with the colonized. The customs of the colonized, their traditions, their myths, especially their myths, are the very mark of this indigence and innate depravity. This is why we should place DDT, which destroys parasites, carriers of disease, on the same level as Christianity, which roots out heresy, natural impulses, and evil. The decline of yellow fever and the advances made by evangelizing form part of the same balance sheet. But triumphant reports by the missions in fact tell us how deep the seeds of alienation have been sown among the colonized. I am talking of Christianity and this should come as no surprise to anybody. The Church in the colonies is a white man's Church, a foreigners' Church. It does not call the colonized to the ways of God, but to the ways of the white man, to the ways of the master, the ways of the oppressor. And as we know, in this story many are called but few are chosen.

Sometimes this Manichaeanism reaches its logical conclusion and dehumanizes the colonized subject. In plain talk, he is reduced to the state of an animal. And consequently, when the colonist speaks of the colonized he uses zoological terms. Allusion is made to the slithery movements of the yellow race, the odors from the "native" quarters, to the hordes, the stink, the swarming, the seething, and the gesticulations. In his endeavors at description and finding the right word, the colonist refers constantly to the bestiary. The European seldom has a problem with figures of speech. But the colonized, who immediately grasp the intention of the colonist and the exact case being made against them, know instantly what he is thinking. This explosive population growth, those hysterical masses, those blank faces, those shapeless, obese bodies, this headless, tailless cohort, these children who seem not to belong to anyone, this indolence sprawling under the sun, this vegetating existence, all this is part of the colonial vocabulary. General de Gaulle[3] speaks of "yellow multitudes," and Monsieur Mauriac[4] of the black, brown, and yellow hordes that will soon invade our shores. The colonized know all that and roar with laughter every time they hear themselves called an animal by the other. For they know they are not animals. And at the very moment when they discover their humanity, they begin to sharpen their weapons to secure its victory.

As soon as the colonized begin to strain at the leash and to pose a threat to the colonist, they are assigned a series of good souls who in the "Symposiums on Culture" spell out the specificity and richness of Western values. But every time the issue of Western values crops up, the colonized grow tense and their muscles seize up. During the period of decolonization the colonized are called upon to be reasonable. They are offered rock-solid values, they are told in great detail that decolonization should not mean regression, and that they must rely on values which have proved to be reliable and worthwhile. Now it so happens that when the colonized hear a speech on Western culture they draw their machetes or at least check to see they are close to hand. The supremacy of white values is stated with such violence, the victorious confrontation of these values with the lifestyle and beliefs of the colonized is so impregnated with aggressiveness, that as a counter measure the colonized rightly make a mockery of them whenever they are mentioned. In the colonial context the colonist only quits undermin-

---

1   *Manichaean*   Manicheanism is an ancient religious doctrine (and Christian heresy) which sees reality as dualistic, containing basic opposite principles: spirit/matter, good/evil; thus to call an approach "Manichean" is to accuse it of unjustifiable dualistic thinking, dividing the world into intrinsic ineradicable good and evil.

2   *The colonial world ... quintessence of evil*   [author's note] We have demonstrated in *Black Skin, White Masks* (New York: Grove Press, 1967) the mechanism of this Manichaean world.

3   *General de Gaulle*   Charles de Gaulle (1890–1970), leader of the Free French during the German World War II occupation of France; head of the interim government following the war; President of France 1959–69. De Gaulle gave all French colonies independence in 1962.

4   *Monsieur Mauriac*   François Mauriac (1885–1970), French novelist, winner of the Nobel Prize for literature, 1958.

ing the colonized once the latter have proclaimed loud and clear that white values reign supreme. In the period of decolonization the colonized masses thumb their noses at these very values, shower them with insults and vomit them up.

[...]

The colonized subject thus discovers that his life, his breathing and his heartbeats are the same as the colonist's. He discovers that the skin of a colonist is not worth more than the "native's." In other words, his world receives a fundamental jolt. The colonized's revolutionary new assurance stems from this. If, in fact, my life is worth as much as the colonist's, his look can no longer strike fear into me or nail me to the spot and his voice can no longer petrify me. I am no longer uneasy in his presence. In reality, to hell with him. Not only does his presence no longer bother me, but I am already preparing to waylay him in such a way that soon he will have no other solution but to flee.

The colonial context, as we have said, is characterized by the dichotomy it inflicts on the world. Decolonization unifies this world by a radical decision to remove its heterogeneity, by unifying it on the grounds of nation and sometimes race. To quote the biting words of Senegalese patriots on the maneuvers of their president, Senghor:[1] "We asked for the Africanization of the top jobs and all Senghor does is Africanize the Europeans." Meaning that the colonized can see right away if decolonization is taking place or not: The minimum demand is that the last become the first.

[....]

We have seen that this violence throughout the colonial period, although constantly on edge, runs on empty. We have seen it channeled through the emotional release of dance or possession. We have seen it exhaust itself in fratricidal struggles. The challenge now is to seize this violence as it realigns itself. Whereas it once reveled in myths and contrived ways to commit collective suicide, a fresh set of circumstances will now enable it to change directions.

From the point of view of political tactics and History, the liberation of the colonies poses a theoretical problem of crucial importance at the current time: When can it be said that the situation is ripe for a national liberation movement? What should be the first line of action? Because decolonization comes in many shapes, reason wavers and abstains from declaring what is a true decolonization and what is not. We shall see that for the politically committed, urgent decisions are needed on means and tactics, i.e., direction and organization. Anything else is but blind voluntarism with the terribly reactionary risks this implies.

What are the forces in the colonial period which offer new channels, new agents of empowerment for the violence of the colonized? First and foremost, the political parties and the intellectual and business elite. However, what is characteristic of certain political groups is that they are strong on principles but abstain from issuing marching orders. During the colonial period the activities of these nationalist political parties are purely for electioneering purposes and amount to no more than a series of philosophic-political discourses on the subject of the rights of peoples to self-determination, the human rights of dignity and freedom from hunger, and the countless declarations of the principle "one man, one vote." The nationalist political parties never insist on the need for confrontation precisely because their aim is not the radical overthrow of the system. Pacifist and law-abiding, partisans, in fact, of order, the new order, these political groups bluntly ask of the colonialist bourgeoisie what to them is essential: "Give us more power." On the specific issue of violence, the elite are ambiguous. They are violent in their words and reformist in their attitudes. While the bourgeois nationalist political leaders say one thing, they make it quite clear it is not what they are really thinking.

This characteristic of the nationalist political parties must be attributed to the nature of their leaders and their supporters. The supporters of the nationalist parties are urban voters. These workers, elementary school teachers, small tradesmen, and shopkeepers who have begun to profit from the colonial situation—in a pitiful sort of way of course—have their own interests in mind. What these supporters are demanding is a better life and improved wages. The dialogue between these political parties and colonialism has continued uninterrupted. Discussions focus on improvements, electoral representation, freedom of the press, and freedom of association. Reforms are discussed. It should come as no surprise therefore that a good many colonial subjects are active members in branches of metro-

---

1   *Senghor* Leopold Senghor (1906–2001), leader of the movement for independence of Senegal from France; first president of Senegal (1960–81); poet, philosopher, and theoretician, known for his advocacy of *négritude,* an influential movement for recognition of, and pride in, French-language African culture.

politan political parties. These colonial subjects are militant activists under the abstract slogan: "Power to the proletariat," forgetting that in their part of the world slogans of national liberation should come first. The colonized intellectual has invested his aggression in his barely veiled wish to be assimilated to the colonizer's world. He has placed his aggression at the service of his own interests, his interests as an individual. The result is the ready emergence of a kind of class of individually liberated slaves, of freed slaves. The intellectual calls for ways of freeing more and more slaves and ways of organizing a genuine class of the emancipated. The masses, however, have no intention of looking on as the chances of individual success improve. What they demand is not the status of the colonist, but his place. In their immense majority the colonized want the colonist's farm. There is no question for them of competing with the colonist. They want to take his place.

The peasantry is systematically left out of most of the nationalist parties' propaganda. But it is obvious that in colonial countries only the peasantry is revolutionary. It has nothing to lose and everything to gain. The underprivileged and starving peasant is the exploited who very soon discovers that only violence pays. For him there is no compromise, no possibility of concession. Colonization or decolonization: it is simply a power struggle. The exploited realize that their liberation implies using every means available, and force is the first. When Monsieur Guy Mollet capitulated to the French settlers in Algeria in 1956,[1] the Front de la Libération Nationale (FLN) in a famous tract stated that colonialism only loosens its hold when the knife is at its throat. No Algerian really thought these terms too violent. The tract merely expressed what every Algerian felt deep down: colonialism is not a machine capable of thinking, a body endowed with reason. It is naked violence and only gives in when confronted with greater violence.

At the critical, deciding moment the colonialist bourgeoisie, which had remained silent up till then, enters the fray. They introduce a new notion, in actual fact a creation of the colonial situation: nonviolence. In its raw state this nonviolence conveys to the colonized intellectual and business elite that their interests are identical to those of the colonialist bourgeoisie and it is therefore indispensable, a matter of urgency, to reach an agreement for the common good. Nonviolence is an attempt to settle the colonial problem around the negotiating table before the irreparable is done, before any bloodshed or regrettable act is committed. But if the masses, without waiting for the chairs to be placed around the negotiating table, take matters into their own hands and start burning and killing, it is not long before we see the "elite" and the leaders of the bourgeois nationalist parties turn to the colonial authorities and tell them: "This is terribly serious! Goodness knows how it will all end. We must find an answer, we must find a compromise."

This notion of compromise is very important in the case of decolonization, for it is far from being a simple matter. Compromise, in fact, involves both the colonial system and the burgeoning national bourgeoisie. The adherents of the colonial system discover that the masses might very well destroy everything. The sabotage of bridges, the destruction of farms, repression and war can severely disrupt the economy. Compromise is also on the agenda for the national bourgeoisie who, unable to foresee the possible consequences of such a whirlwind, fear in fact they will be swept away, and hasten to reassure the colonists: "We are still capable of stopping the slaughter, the masses still trust us, act quickly if you do not want to jeopardize everything." If events go one step further, the leader of the nationalist party distances himself from the violence. He loudly claims he has nothing to do with these Mau-Mau,[2] with these terrorists, these butchers. In the best of cases, he barricades himself in a *no-man's-land* between the terrorists and the colonists and offers his services as "mediator"; which means that since the colonists cannot negotiate with the Mau-Mau, he himself is prepared to begin negotiations. Thus the rear guard of the national struggle, that section of the people who have always been on the other side, now find themselves catapulted to the forefront of negotiations and compromise—precisely because they have always been careful not to break ties with colonialism.

[...]

---

1   *When Monsieur Guy Mollet ... Algeria in 1956* Guy Mollet (1905–75), French socialist politician, was originally opposed to French colonial rule, but when he was Prime Minister in 1956 he acted in defense of the approximately one million French settlers in Algeria, first negotiating with the FLN (the revolutionary body leading the resistance to French rule), then ordering a strong military action against them.

2   *Mau-Mau* Name (given by the British) to the Kenyans who rebelled against British colonial rule, 1952–60. Fanon is using this term figuratively and ironically, to refer to any violent anti-colonial resistance group, seen from the colonial perspective.

In the armed struggle there is what we could call the point of no return. It is almost always attributable to the sweeping repression which encompasses every sector of the colonized population. This point was reached in Algeria in 1955 with the 12,000 victims of Philippeville and in 1956 by Lacoste's creation of rural and urban militias.[1] It then becomes evident for everyone and even for the colonists that "things cannot go on as they are and have to change." The colonized, however, do not keep accounts. They register the enormous gaps left in their ranks as a kind of necessary evil. Since they have decided to respond with violence, they admit the consequences. Their one demand is that they are not asked to keep accounts for others as well. To the expression: "All natives are the same," the colonized reply: "All colonists are the same."[2] When the colonized subject is tortured, when his wife is killed or raped, he complains to no one. The authorities of oppression can appoint as many commissions of inquiry and investigation as they like. In the eyes of the colonized, these commissions do not exist. And in fact, soon it will be seven years of crimes committed in Algeria and not a single Frenchman has been brought before a French court of justice for the murder of an Algerian. In Indochina, Madagascar, and the colonies, the "native" has always known he can expect nothing from the other side. The work of the colonist is to make even dreams of liberty impossible for the colonized. The work of the colonized

is to imagine every possible method for annihilating the colonist. On the logical plane, the Manichaeanism of the colonist produces a Manichaeanism of the colonized. The theory of the "absolute evil of the colonist" is in response to the theory of the "absolute evil of the native."

The arrival of the colonist signified syncretically the death of indigenous society, cultural lethargy, and petrifaction of the individual. For the colonized, life can only materialize from the rotting cadaver of the colonist. Such then is the term-for-term correspondence between the two arguments.

But it so happens that for the colonized this violence is invested with positive, formative features because it constitutes their only work. This violent praxis is totalizing since each individual represents a violent link in the great chain, in the almighty body of violence rearing up in reaction to the primary violence of the colonizer. Factions recognize each other and the future nation is already indivisible. The armed struggle mobilizes the people, i.e., it pitches them in a single direction, from which there is no turning back.

When it is achieved during a war of liberation the mobilization of the masses introduces the notion of common cause, national destiny, and collective history into every consciousness. Consequently, the second phase, i.e., nation building, is facilitated by the existence of this mortar kneaded with blood and rage. This then gives us a better understanding of the originality of the vocabulary used in underdeveloped countries. During the colonial period the people were called upon to fight against oppression. Following national liberation they are urged to fight against poverty, illiteracy, and underdevelopment. The struggle, they say, goes on. The people realize that life is an unending struggle.

The violence of the colonized, we have said, unifies the people. By its very structure colonialism is separatist and regionalist. Colonialism is not merely content to note the existence of tribes, it reinforces and differentiates them. The colonial system nurtures the chieftainships and revives the old *marabout* confraternities.[3] Violence in its practice is totalizing and national. As a result, it harbors in its depths the elimination of regionalism and tribalism. The nationalist parties, therefore, show no pity at all toward the *kaids*[4]

---

1   *This point ... urban militias* Philippeville is a city in Algeria, renamed Skikda after Algerian independence, where an anti-French uprising in 1955 left around 125 dead, and French army reprisal killed many more: 1200 according to French sources, but as many as 12,000, according to others. Robert Lacoste (1898–1989) was installed as governor of Algeria in 1956. He is remembered for instigating "Algerianization" and other administrative reforms, but also for strong military opposition to the liberation forces. [Fanon's note] In order to gauge the importance of this decision by the French government in Algeria we need to return to this period. [An extended quotation from issue no. 4 of *Résistance Algérienne* dated March 28, 1957 follows.]

2   *To the expression ... are the same* [author's note] This is the reason why at the outbreak of hostilities, no prisoners are taken. It is only through politicizing the *cadres* that the leaders manage to get the masses to accept (1) that the recruits dispatched from the *métropole* are not always sent of their own free will and in some cases even are sickened by this war; (2) that it is in the current interest of the movement to wage a struggle abiding by certain international conventions; (3) that an army which takes prisoners is an army, and ceases to be considered a gang of outlaws; (4) in any case, the possession of prisoners constitutes a significant means of applying pressure for protecting our militants held by the enemy.

3   *marabout confraternities* *Marabouts* are North African professional Muslim holy men holding sway over mystical confraternities—brotherhoods of believers.

4   *kaids* A *kaid* (usually spelled *caid*, sometimes *qaid*) is a North African Muslim tribal chief, judge, or senior official.

and the traditional chiefs. The elimination of the *kaids* and the chiefs is a prerequisite to the unification of the people.

At the individual level, violence is a cleansing force. It rids the colonized of their inferiority complex, of their passive and despairing attitude. It emboldens them, and restores their self-confidence. Even if the armed struggle has been symbolic, and even if they have been demobilized by rapid decolonization, the people have time to realize that liberation was the achievement of each and every one and no special merit should go to the leader. Violence hoists the people up to the level of the leader. Hence their aggressive tendency to distrust the system of protocol that young governments are quick to establish. When they have used violence to achieve national liberation, the masses allow nobody to come forward as "liberator." They prove themselves to be jealous of their achievements and take care not to place their future, their destiny, and the fate of their homeland into the hands of a living god. Totally irresponsible yesterday, today they are bent on understanding everything and determining everything. Enlightened by violence, the people's consciousness rebels against any pacification. The demagogues, the opportunists and the magicians now have a difficult task. The praxis which pitched them into a desperate man-to-man struggle has given the masses a ravenous taste for the tangible. Any attempt at mystification in the long term becomes virtually impossible.

[...]

Mutual Foundations for National, Culture, and Liberation Struggles

The sweeping, leveling nature of colonial domination was quick to dislocate in spectacular fashion the cultural life of a conquered people. The denial of a national reality, the new legal system imposed by the occupying power, the marginalization of the indigenous population and their customs by colonial society, expropriation, and the systematic enslavement of men and women, all contributed to this cultural obliteration.

Three years ago at our first congress I demonstrated that in a colonial situation any dynamism is fairly rapidly replaced by a reification of attitudes. The cultural sphere is marked out by safety railings and signposts, every single one of them defense mechanisms of the most elementary type,

comparable in more ways than one to the simple instinct of self-preservation. This period is interesting because the oppressor is no longer content with the objective nonexistence of the conquered nation and culture. Every effort is made to make the colonized confess the inferiority of their culture, now reduced to a set of instinctive responses, to acknowledge the unreality of their nation and, in the last extreme, to admit the disorganized, half-finished nature of their own biological makeup.

The reactions of the colonized to this situation vary. Whereas the masses maintain intact traditions totally incongruous with the colonial situation, whereas the style of artisanship ossifies into an increasingly stereotyped formalism, the intellectual hurls himself frantically into the frenzied acquisition of the occupier's culture, making sure he denigrates his national culture, or else confines himself to making a detailed, methodical, zealous, and rapidly sterile inventory of it.

What both reactions have in common is that they both result in unacceptable contradictions. Renegade or substantialist,[1] the colonized subject is ineffectual precisely because the colonial situation has not been rigorously analyzed. The colonial situation brings national culture virtually to a halt. There is no such thing as national culture, national cultural events, innovations, or reforms within the context of colonial domination, and there never will be. There are scattered instances of a bold attempt to revive a cultural dynamism, and reshape themes, forms, and tones. The immediate, tangible, and visible effects of these minor convulsions is nil. But if we follow the consequences to their very limit there are signs that the veil is being lifted from the national consciousness, oppression is being challenged and there is hope for the liberation struggle.

National culture under colonial domination is a culture under interrogation whose destruction is sought systematically. Very quickly it becomes a culture condemned to clandestinity. This notion of clandestinity can immediately be perceived in the reactions of the occupier who interprets this complacent attachment to traditions as a sign of loyalty to the national spirit and a refusal to submit. This persistence of cultural expression condemned by colonial society is already a demonstration of nationhood. But such a dem-

---

1   *substantialist* "Substantialism" is a term of sociology, referring to the doctrine that human beings are of fundamentally different sorts—for example, that the upper and lower classes have fundamental biological differences, perhaps innate differences in intelligence or morality.

onstration refers us back to the laws of inertia. No offensive has been launched, no relations redefined. There is merely a desperate clinging to a nucleus that is increasingly shriveled, increasingly inert, and increasingly hollow.

After one or two centuries of exploitation the national cultural landscape has radically shriveled. It has become an inventory of behavioral patterns, traditional costumes, and miscellaneous customs. Little movement can be seen. There is no real creativity, no ebullience. Poverty, national oppression, and cultural repression are one and the same. After a century of colonial domination culture becomes rigid in the extreme, congealed, and petrified. The atrophy of national reality and the death throes of national culture feed on one another. This is why it becomes vital to monitor the development of this relationship during the liberation struggle. Cultural denial, the contempt for any national demonstration of emotion or dynamism and the banning of any type of organization help spur aggressive behavior in the colonized. But this pattern of behavior is a defensive reaction, nonspecific, anarchic, and ineffective. Colonial exploitation, poverty, and endemic famine increasingly force the colonized into open, organized rebellion. Gradually, imperceptibly, the need for a decisive confrontation imposes itself and is eventually felt by the great majority of the people. Tensions emerge where previously there were none. International events, the collapse of whole sections of colonial empires and the inherent contradictions of the colonial system stimulate and strengthen combativity, motivating and invigorating the national consciousness.

These new tensions, which are present at every level of the colonial system, have repercussions on the cultural front. In literature, for example, there is relative overproduction. Once a pale imitation of the colonizer's literature, indigenous production now shows greater diversity and a will to particularize. Mainly consumer during the period of oppression, the intelligentsia turns productive. This literature is at first confined to the genre of poetry and tragedy. Then novels, short stories, and essays are tackled. There seems to be a kind of internal organization, a law of expression, according to which poetic creativity fades as the objectives and methods of the liberation struggle become clearer. There is a fundamental change of theme. In fact, less and less do we find those bitter, desperate recriminations, those loud, violent outbursts that, after all, reassure the occupier. In the previous period, the colonialists encouraged such endeavors and facilitated their publication. The occupier, in fact, likened these scathing denunciations, outpourings of misery,

and heated words to an act of catharsis. Encouraging these acts would, in a certain way, avoid dramatization and clear the atmosphere.

But such a situation cannot last. In fact the advances made by national consciousness among the people modify and clarify the literary creation of the colonized intellectual. The people's staying power stimulates the intellectual to transcend the lament. Complaints followed by indictments give way to appeals. Then comes the call for revolt. The crystallization of the national consciousness will not only radically change the literary genres and themes but also create a completely new audience. Whereas the colonized intellectual started out by producing work exclusively with the oppressor in mind—either in order to charm him or to denounce him by using ethnic or subjectivist categories—he gradually switches over to addressing himself to his people.

It is only from this point onward that one can speak of a national literature. Literary creation addresses and clarifies typically nationalist themes. This is combat literature in the true sense of the word, in the sense that it calls upon a whole people to join in the struggle for the existence of the nation. Combat literature, because it informs the national consciousness, gives it shape and contours, and opens up new, unlimited horizons. Combat literature, because it takes charge, because it is resolve situated in historical time.

At another level, oral literature, tales, epics, and popular songs, previously classified and frozen in time, begin to change. The storytellers who recited inert episodes revive them and introduce increasingly fundamental changes. There are attempts to update battles and modernize the types of struggle, the heroes' names, and the weapons used. The method of allusion is increasingly used. Instead of "a long time ago," they substitute the more ambiguous expression "What I am going to tell you happened somewhere else, but it could happen here today or perhaps tomorrow." In this respect the case of Algeria is significant. From 1952–53 on, its storytellers, grown stale and dull, radically changed both their methods of narration and the content of their stories. Once scarce, the public returned in droves. The epic, with its standardized forms, reemerged. It has become an authentic form of entertainment that once again has taken on a cultural value. Colonialism knew full well what it was doing when it began systematically arresting these storytellers after 1955.

The people's encounter with this new song of heroic deeds brings an urgent breath of excitement, arouses forgotten muscular tensions and develops the imagination. Every time the storyteller narrates a new episode, the public is treated to a real invocation. The existence of a new type of man is revealed to the public. The present is no longer turned inward but channeled in every direction. The storyteller once again gives free rein to his imagination, innovates, and turns creator. It even happens that unlikely characters for such a transformation, social misfits such as outlaws or drifters, are rediscovered and rehabilitated. Close attention should be paid to the emergence of the imagination and the inventiveness of songs and folk tales in a colonized country. The storyteller responds to the expectations of the people by trial and error and searches for new models, national models, apparently on his own, but in fact with the support of his audience. Comedy and farce disappear or else lose their appeal. As for drama, it is no longer the domain of the intellectual's tormented conscience. No longer characterized by despair and revolt, it has become the people's daily lot, it has become part of an action in the making or already in progress.

In artisanship, the congealed, petrified forms loosen up. Wood carving, for example, which turned out set faces and poses by the thousands, starts to diversify. The expressionless or tormented mask comes to life, and the arms are raised upwards in a gesture of action. Compositions with two, three, or five figures emerge. An avalanche of amateurs and dissidents encourages the traditional schools to innovate. This new stimulus in this particular cultural sector very often goes unnoticed. Yet its contribution to the national struggle is vital. By bringing faces and bodies to life, by taking the group set on a single socle[1] as creative subject, the artist inspires concerted action.

The awakening national consciousness has had a somewhat similar effect in the sphere of ceramics and pottery. Formalism is abandoned. Jugs, jars, and trays are reshaped, at first only slightly and then quite radically. Colors, once restricted in number, governed by laws of traditional harmony, flood back, reflecting the effects of the revolutionary upsurge. Certain ochers, certain blues that were apparently banned for eternity in a given cultural context, emerge unscathed. Likewise, the taboo of representing the human face, typical of certain clearly defined regions according to sociologists, is suddenly lifted. The metropolitan anthropologists and experts are quick to note these changes and denounce them all, referring rather to a codified artistic

style and culture developing in tune with the colonial situation. The colonialist experts do not recognize these new forms and rush to the rescue of indigenous traditions. It is the colonialists who become the defenders of indigenous style. A memorable example, and one that takes on particular significance because it does not quite involve a colonial reality, was the reaction of white jazz fans when after the Second World War new styles such as bebop established themselves. For them jazz could only be the broken, desperate yearning of an old "Negro," five whiskeys under his belt, bemoaning his own misfortune and the racism of the whites. As soon as he understands himself and apprehends the world differently, as soon as he elicits a glimmer of hope and forces the racist world to retreat, it is obvious he will blow his horn to his heart's content and his husky voice will ring out loud and clear. The new jazz styles are not only born out of economic competition. They are one of the definite consequences of the inevitable, though gradual, defeat of the Southern universe in the USA. And it is not unrealistic to think that in fifty years or so the type of jazz lament hiccupped by a poor, miserable "Negro" will be defended by only those whites believing in a frozen image of a certain type of relationship and a certain form of negritude.

We would also uncover the same transformations, the same progress and the same eagerness if we enquired into the fields of dance, song, rituals, and traditional ceremonies. Well before the political or armed struggle, a careful observer could sense and feel in these arts the pulse of a fresh stimulus and the coming combat. Unusual forms of expression, original themes no longer invested with the power of invocation but the power to rally and mobilize with the approaching conflict in mind. Everything conspires to stimulate the colonized's sensibility, and to rule out and reject attitudes of inertia or defeat. By imparting new meaning and dynamism to artisanship, dance, music, literature, and the oral epic, the colonized subject restructures his own perception. The world no longer seems doomed. Conditions are ripe for the inevitable confrontation.

We have witnessed the emergence of a new energy in the cultural sphere. We have seen that this energy, these new forms, are linked to the maturing of the national consciousness, and now become increasingly objectivized and institutionalized. Hence the need for nationhood at all costs.

A common mistake, hardly defensible, moreover, is to attempt cultural innovations and reassert the value of indigenous culture within the context of colonial domina-

---

1   *socle*   French: pedestal; base for a sculpture.

tion. Hence we arrive at a seemingly paradoxical proposition: In a colonized country, nationalism in its most basic, most rudimentary, and undifferentiated form is the most forceful and effective way of defending national culture. A culture is first and foremost the expression of a nation, its preferences, its taboos, and its models. Other taboos, other values, other models are formed at every level of the entire society. National culture is the sum of all these considerations, the outcome of tensions internal and external to society as a whole and its multiple layers. In the colonial context, culture, when deprived of the twin supports of the nation and the state, perishes and dies. National liberation and the resurrection of the state are the preconditions for the very existence of a culture.

The nation is not only a precondition for culture, its ebullition, its perpetual renewal and maturation. It is a necessity. First of all it is the struggle for nationhood that unlocks culture and opens the doors of creation. Later on it is the nation that will provide culture with the conditions and framework for expression. The nation satisfies all those indispensable requirements for culture which alone can give it credibility, validity, dynamism, and creativity. It is also the national character that makes culture permeable to other cultures and enables it to influence and penetrate them. That which does not exist can hardly have an effect on reality or even influence it. The restoration of the nation must therefore give life in the most biological sense of the term to national culture.

We have thus traced the increasingly essential fissuring of the old cultural strata, and on the eve of the decisive struggle for national liberation, grasped the new forms of expression and the flight of the imagination.

There now remains one fundamental question. What is the relationship between the struggle, the political or armed conflict, and culture? During the conflict is culture put on hold? Is the national struggle a cultural manifestation? Must we conclude that the liberation struggle, though beneficial for culture a posteriori,[1] is in itself a negation of culture? In other words, is the liberation struggle a cultural phenomenon?

We believe the conscious, organized struggle undertaken by a colonized people in order to restore national sovereignty constitutes the greatest cultural manifestation that exists. It is not solely the success of the struggle that consequently validates and energizes culture; culture does

not go into hibernation during the conflict. The development and internal progression of the actual struggle expand the number of directions in which culture can go and hint at new possibilities. The liberation struggle does not restore to national culture its former values and configurations. This struggle, which aims at a fundamental redistribution of relations between men, cannot leave intact either the form or substance of the people's culture. After the struggle is over, there is not only the demise of colonialism, but also the demise of the colonized.

This new humanity, for itself and for others, inevitably defines a new humanism. This new humanism is written into the objectives and methods of the struggle. A struggle, which mobilizes every level of society, which expresses the intentions and expectations of the people, and which is not afraid to rely on their support almost entirely, will invariably triumph. The merit of this type of struggle is that it achieves the optimal conditions for cultural development and innovation. Once national liberation has been accomplished under these conditions, there is none of that tiresome cultural indecisiveness we find in certain newly independent countries, because the way a nation is born and functions exerts a fundamental influence on culture. A nation born of the concerted action of the people, which embodies the actual aspirations of the people and transforms the state, depends on exceptionally inventive cultural manifestations for its very existence.

The colonized who are concerned for their country's culture and wish to give it a universal dimension should not place their trust in a single principle—that independence is inevitable and automatically inscribed in the people's consciousness—in order to achieve this aim. National liberation as objective is one thing, the methods and popular components of the struggle are another. We believe that the future of culture and the richness of a national culture are also based on the values that inspired the struggle for freedom.

And now the moment has come to denounce certain pharisees. Humanity, some say, has got past the stage of nationalist claims. The time has come to build larger political unions, and consequently the old-fashioned nationalists should correct their mistakes. We believe on the contrary that the mistake, heavy with consequences, would be to miss out on the national stage. If culture is the expression of the national consciousness, I shall have no hesitation in saying, in the case in point, that national consciousness is the highest form of culture.

---

1   *a posteriori* Afterwards.

Self-awareness does not mean closing the door on communication. Philosophy teaches us on the contrary that it is its guarantee. National consciousness, which is not nationalism, is alone capable of giving us an international dimension. This question of national consciousness and national culture takes on a special dimension in Africa. The birth of national consciousness in Africa strictly correlates with an African consciousness. The responsibility of the African toward his national culture is also a responsibility toward "Negro-African" culture. This joint responsibility does not rest upon a metaphysical principle but mindfulness of a simple rule which stipulates that any independent nation in an Africa where colonialism still lingers is a nation surrounded, vulnerable, and in permanent danger.

If man is judged by his acts, then I would say that the most urgent thing today for the African intellectual is the building of his nation. If this act is true, i.e., if it expresses the manifest will of the people, if it reflects the restlessness of the African peoples, then it will necessarily lead to the discovery and advancement of universalizing values. Far then from distancing it from other nations, it is the national liberation that puts the nation on the stage of history. It is at the heart of national consciousness that international consciousness establishes itself and thrives. And this dual emergence, in fact, is the unique focus of all culture.

IRIS YOUNG
(1949-2006)

Iris Marion Young was one of the leading feminist political theorists of her time. Born in 1949 in New York City, Young was educated at Queen's College and the University of Pennsylvania. After receiving her PhD in 1974, she taught at Worcester Polytechnic Institute, the University of Pittsburg, and the University of Chicago, where she was a professor of political science. Her books include *Justice and the Politics of Difference* (1990), *Throwing Like a Girl and Other Essays in Feminist Philosophy* (1990), *Intersecting Voices: Dilemmas of Gender, Political Philosophy, and Policy* (1997), and *Inclusion and Democracy* (2000).

Unlike many American philosophers, Young did her graduate work mainly in existentialism, phenomenology, and the history of philosophy. That work allowed her to draw on a broad range of sources; these included the work of the feminist and psychoanalyst Julia Kristeva, the Frankfurt School, and French poststructuralism, as well as the liberal philosophy of John Rawls. She frequently approached diverse topics from surprising angles. Her work on gender and embodied experience; on democratic theory; on globalization; and on international justice questions many of the basic assumptions of liberal theory. So too does her work on race, equality, and poverty. And her *Justice and the Politics of Difference* (1990) established her in the forefront of feminist ethics and political theory. In it she called attention to the liberal universalist assumption that citizens are homogenous, with the same concerns and needs. As she pointed out, this assumption ignores the reality that justice for women, for racial and ethnic minorities, for gays and lesbians, and for the disabled may not require simply equal treatment; it may require recognition of their differences. Young also criticized conceptions of justice that emphasize the distribution of benefits and burdens. According to her, conceptions that prioritize distributive justice overlook or underestimate social and institutional factors that determine people's lives, such as the sexual division of labor, cultural practices, and the power-relations that enable people to make decisions.

Inclusion and Democracy (2000) raised important issues for deliberative democracy. Democratic theorists have often criticized vote-centered representative democracy for being insufficiently democratic. Citizens are reduced to simply electing officials and removing them from office, without any substantial input into policy. Many people thus feel alienated from democratic politics, which in turn breeds apathy, cynicism, and ignorance of current events. Theorists of deliberative democracy argue that democracy must encourage substantial input on public policy, through citizen dialogue in which people debate their views in a non-hierarchical setting.

Any theory of deliberative democracy raises questions of who should be included in the democratic process. Liberal political theorists have typically remarked on the expanding circle of inclusion, with the sphere of justice gradually widening to include women, minorities, people outside one's own community, and, perhaps, animals. Young recognized that even if attempts were made to formally include previously marginalized groups, the unstated expectations, and norms that dominate majority discourse might very well still prevent their genuine participation. Thus, deliberative democracy, according to Young, suffers from a rationalist bias.

Young died in 2006 at the age of 56, after an eighteen-month struggle with esophageal cancer. Her loss was mourned by many who regarded her as one of the most important political theorists of the late twentieth and early twenty-first centuries, and among the most innovative and brilliant contributors to feminist and socialist thought.

◆ ◆ ◆ ◆ ◆

Impartiality and the Civic Public: Some Implications of Feminist Critiques of Moral and Political Theory (1986)

Many writers seeking emancipatory frameworks for challenging both liberal individualist political theory and the continuing encroachment of bureaucracy on everyday life claim to find a starting point in unrealized ideals of modern political theory. John Keane, for example, suggests that recent political movements of women, oppressed sexual and ethnic minorities, environmentalists, and so on return to the contract tradition of legitimacy against the legalistic authority of contemporary state and private bureaucracies. Like many others, Keane looks specifically to Rousseau's unrealized ideals of freedom and cooperative politics.

> According to Rousseau, individualism could no longer be seen as consisting in emancipation through mere competitive opposition to others; its authentic and legitimate form could be constituted only through the communicative intersubjective enrichment of each bodily individual's qualities and achievements to the point of uniqueness and incomparability. Only through political life could the individual become this specific, irreplaceable individual "called" or destined to realize its own incomparable capacities.[1]

There are plausible reasons for claiming that emancipatory politics should define itself as realizing the potential of modern political ideals that have been suppressed by capitalism and bureaucratic institutions. No contemporary emancipatory politics wishes to reject the rule of law as opposed to whim or custom, or fails to embrace a commitment to preserving and deepening civil liberties. A commitment to a democratic society, moreover, can plausibly look upon modern political theory and practice as beginning the democratization of political institutions, which we can deepen and extend to economic and other nonlegislative and nongovernmental institutions.

Nevertheless, in this chapter I urge proponents of contemporary emancipatory politics to break with modernism rather than recover suppressed possibilities of modern political ideals. Whether we consider ourselves continuous or discontinuous with modern political theory and practice, of course, can only be a choice, more or less reasonable given certain presumptions and interests. Since political theory and practice from the eighteenth to the twentieth centuries are hardly unified, making even the phrase "modern political theory" problematic, contemporary political theory and practice both continue and break with aspects of the political past of the West. From the point of view of a feminist interest, nevertheless, emancipatory politics entails a rejection of modern traditions of moral and political life.

Feminists did not always think this, of course. Since Mary Wollstonecraft, generations of women and some men wove painstaking arguments to demonstrate that excluding women from modern public and political life contradicts the liberal democratic promise of universal emancipation and equality. They identified the liberation of women with expanding civil and political rights to include women on the same terms as men, and with the entrance of women into the public life dominated by men on an equal basis with them.

After two centuries of faith that the ideal of equality and fraternity included women have still not brought emancipation for women, contemporary feminists have begun to question the faith itself.[2] Recent feminist analyses of modern political theory and practice increasingly argue that ideals of liberalism and contract theory, such as formal equality and universal rationality, are deeply marred by masculine biases about what it means to be human and the nature of society.[3] If modern culture in the West has been

---

1   *According to Rousseau ... incomparable capacities* [Unless otherwise indicated, all notes to this selection are by the author rather than the editors of this anthology.] John Keane, "Liberalism Under Siege: Power, Legitimation, and the Fate of Modern Contract Theory," in *Public Life in Late Capitalism* (Cambridge, MA: Cambridge University Press, 1984), p. 253. Andrew Levine is another writer who finds in Rousseau an emancipatory alternative to liberalism. See "Beyond Justice: Rousseau Against Rawls," *Journal of Chinese Philosophy*, vol. 4 (1977), pp. 123–42.

2   *contemporary feminists ... the faith itself* I develop the contrast between commitment to a feminist humanism, on the one hand, and reaction against belief in women's liberation as the attainment of equality with men in formerly male-dominated institutions, on the other, in my paper "Humanism, Gynocentrism and Feminist Politics," in *Hypatia: A Journal of Feminist Philosophy*, no. 3, special issue of *Women's Studies International Forum*, vol. 8, no. 5 (1985).

3   *Recent feminist analyses ... nature of society* The literature on these issues has become vast. My own understanding of them is derived from reading, among others, Susan Okin, *Women in Western Political Thought* (Princeton, NJ: Princeton University Press; 1978); Zillah Eisenstein, *The Radical Future of Liberal Feminism* (New York: Longman, 1979); Lynda Lange and Lorrenne Clark, *The Sexism of Social and Political Theory* (Toronto: University of Toronto Press, 1979); Jean Elshtain, *Public Man, Private Woman* (Princeton, NJ: Princeton University Press, 1981); Alison Jaggar, *Feminist Politics and Human Nature* (Totowa, NJ: Rowman and Allenheld, 1983); Carole Pateman, "Feminist Critiques of the Public/Private Dichotomy," in S.I. Benn and G.F. Gaus, ed., *Public and Private in Social Life* (New York: St. Martin's Press, 1983), pp. 281–303; Hannah Pitkin, *Fortune is a Woman* (Berkeley: University of California Press, 1984); Nancy Hartsock, *Money, Sex and Power* (New York: Longman Press, 1983); and Linda Nicholson, *Gender and History* (New York: Columbia University Press, 1986).

thoroughly male dominated, these analyses suggest, there is little hope of laundering some of its ideals to make it possible to include women.

Women are by no means the only group, moreover, that has been excluded from the promise of modern liberalism and republicanism.[1] Many nonwhite people of the world wonder at the hubris of a handful of Western nations to have claimed liberation for humanity at the very same time that they enslaved or subjugated most of the rest of the world. Just as feminists see in male domination no mere aberration in modern politics, so many others have come to regard racism as endemic to modernity as well.[2]

In this chapter I draw out the consequences of two strands of recent feminist responses to modern moral and political theory and weave them together. Part 1 is inspired by Gilligan's critique of the assumption that a Kantian-like "ethic of rights" describes the highest stage of moral development, for women as well as men.[3] Gilligan's work suggests that the deontological tradition of moral theory excludes and devalues women's specific, more particularist and affective experience[4] of moral life. In her classification, however, Gilligan retains an opposition between universal and particular, justice and care, reason and affectivity, which I think her insights clearly challenge.

Thus in part 1, I argue that an emancipatory ethics must develop a conception of normative reason that does not oppose reason to desire and affectivity. I pose this issue by questioning the deontological tradition's assumption of normative reason as impartial and universal. I argue that the ideal of impartiality expresses what Theodor Adorno[5] calls a logic of identity that denies and represses difference. The will to unity expressed by this ideal of impartial and universal reason generates an oppressive opposition between reason and desire or affectivity.

In part 2, I seek to connect this critique of the way modern normative reason generates opposition with feminist critiques of modern political theory, particularly as exhibited in Rousseau and Hegel. Their theories make the public realm of the state express the impartial and universal point of view of normative reason. Their expressions of this ideal of the civic public of citizenship rely on an opposition between public and private dimensions of human life, which corresponds to an opposition between reason, on the one hand, and to the body, affectivity, and desire on the other.

Feminists have shown that the theoretical and practical exclusion of women from the universalist public is no mere accident or aberration. The ideal of the civic public exhibits a will to unity and necessitates the exclusion of aspects of human existence that threaten to disperse the brotherly unity of straight and upright forms, especially the exclusion of women. Since man as citizen expresses the universal and impartial point of view of reason, moreover, someone has to care for his particular desires and feelings. The analysis in part 2 suggests that an emancipatory conception of public life can best ensure the inclusion of all persons and groups not by claiming a unified universality, but by explicitly promoting heterogeneity in public.

In part 3, I suggest that Habermas's theory of communicative action offers the best direction for developing a conception of normative reason that does not seek the unity of a transcendent impartiality and thereby does not oppose reason to desire and affectivity. I argue, however, that despite the potential of his communicative ethics, Habermas remains too committed to the ideals of impartiality and universality. In his conception of communication, more-

---

1   *republicanism*   Classical republicanism, a historical alternative to Lockeian liberalism, replaces the latter's emphasis on individuals and their natural rights with the centrality of democracy and community, stressing the common good—what is best for society as a whole—and advocating that individuals be taught to value civic virtues such as generosity and fairness. This position is so-called because of its historical origin in connection with the Roman Republic, and has no connection whatever with the Republican Party in the US.

2   *many others ... to modernity as well*   See Cornel West, *Prophesy Deliverance!* (Philadelphia: Westminster Press, 1983); and "The Genealogy of Racism: On the Underside of Discourse," *The Journal*, The Society for the Study of Black Philosophy, vol. 1, no. 1 (Winter–Spring 1984), pp. 42–60.

3   *Gilligan's critique ... as well as men*   Carol Gilligan, *In a Different Voice* (Cambridge, MA: Harvard University Press, 1982).

4   *deontological ... particularist and affective experience*   [editors' note] The deontological tradition in ethics focuses on the rightness or wrongness of an action itself, and on duties and obligations. The usual contrast is with another tradition, consequentialism, which understands the morality of actions in terms of the goodness or badness of their consequences. But the contrast here is with an approach which concentrates on "particularist and affective" moral experience—that is, one that concentrates on a particular individual case, rather than on general principles, and which considers "affect"—feelings and emotions—in contrast to the rationalistic deontological approach.

5   *Theodor Adorno*   [editors' note] Adorno (1903–69) was a German sociologist and philosopher, a member, along with Horkheimer, Marcuse, and Habermas, of the Frankfurt School.

over, he reproduces the opposition between reason and affectivity that characterizes modern deontological reason.

Finally, in part 4, I sketch some directions for an alternative conception of public life. The feminist slogan "the personal is political" suggests that no persons, actions, or attributes of persons should be excluded from public discussion and decision-making, although the self-determination of privacy must nevertheless remain. From new ideals of contemporary radical political movements in the United States, I derive the image of a heterogeneous public with aesthetic and affective, as well as discursive, dimensions.

1. The Opposition Between Reason and Affectivity

Modern ethics defines impartiality as the hallmark of moral reason. As a characteristic of reason, impartiality means something different from the pragmatic attitude of being fair, considering other people's needs and desires as well as one's own. Impartiality names a point of view of reason that stands apart from any interests and desires. Not to be partial means being able to see the whole, how all the particular perspectives and interests in a given moral situation relate to one another in a way that, because of its partiality, each perspective cannot see itself. The impartial moral reasoner thus stands outside and above the situation about which he or she reasons, with no stake in it, or is supposed to adopt an attitude toward a situation as though he or she were outside and above it. For contemporary philosophy, calling into question the ideal of impartiality amounts to questioning the possibility of moral theory itself. I will argue, however, that the ideal of normative reason as standing at a point transcending all perspectives is both illusory and oppressive.

Both the utilitarian and deontological traditions of modern ethical theory stress the definition of moral reason as impartial.[1] Here I restrict my discussion to deontological reason for two reasons. Utilitarianism, unlike deontology,

does not assume that there is a specifically normative reason. Utilitarianism defines reason in ethics in the same way as in any other activity: determining the most efficient means for achieving an end (in the case of ethics, the happiness of the greatest number). I am interested here in modern efforts to define a specifically normative reason. Second, I am interested in examining the way a commitment to impartiality results in an opposition between reason and desire, and this opposition is most apparent in deontological reason.

The ideal of an impartial normative reason continues to be asserted by philosophers as "the moral point of view." From the ideal observer to the original position to a spaceship on another planet,[2] moral and political philosophers begin reasoning from a point of view that they claim is impartial. This point of view is usually a counterfactual construct, a situation of reasoning that removes people from their actual contexts of living moral decisions to a situation in which they could not exist. As Michael Sandel argues, the ideal of impartiality requires constructing the ideal of a self abstracted from the context of any real persons: the deontological self is not committed to any particular ends, has no particular history, is a member of no communities, has no body.[3]

Why should normative rationality require the construction of a fictional self in a fictional situation of reasoning? Because this reason, like the scientific reason from which deontology claims to distinguish itself, is impelled by what Adorno calls the logic of identity.[4] In this logic of identity reason does not merely mean having reasons or an account, or intelligently reflecting on and considering a situation. For the logic of identity reason is *ratio*, the principled reduction of the objects of thought to a common measure, to universal laws.

---

1   *Both the utilitarian and deontological ... moral reason as impartial*   Bentham's utilitarianism, for example, assumes something like an "ideal observer" that sees and calculates each individual's happiness and weighs it in relation to all other individuals' happiness, calculating the overall amount of utility. This stance of an impartial calculator is like that of the warden in the panopticon that Foucault takes as expressive of modern normative reason. The moral observer towers over and is able to see individual persons in relation to one another, while remaining itself outside their obser-

vation. See Foucault, *Discipline and Punish* (New York: Vintage, 1977).

2   *a spaceship on another planet*   Bruce Ackerman, *Social Justice in the Liberal State* (New Haven, Conn.: Yale University Press, 1980).

3   *As Michael Sandel argues ... no body*   Michael Sandel, *Liberalism and the Limits of Justice* (Cambridge, MA: Cambridge University Press, 1982); cf. Seyla Benhabib, "The Generalized and the Concrete Other," in Benhabib and Cornell, ed., *Feminism as Critique* (London: Polity Press, 1987), chapter 4; see also Theodore Adorno, *Negative Dialectics* (New York: Continuum Publishing Co., 1973), pp. 238–39.

4   *what Adorno calls the logic of identity*   Adorno, introduction. [editors' note] Adorno argues that the Enlightenment views both the self and nature as unified and homogeneous—denying the multiplicity, diversity, and chaos in each.

The logic of identity consists of an unrelenting urge to think things together, in a unity, to formulate a representation of the whole, a totality. This desire itself is a least as old as Parmenides,[1] and the logic of identity begins with the ancient philosophical notion of universals. Through the notion of an essence, thought brings concrete particulars into unity. As long as qualitative difference defines essence, however, the pure program of identifying thought remains incomplete. Concrete particulars are brought into unity under the universal form, but the forms themselves cannot be reduced to unity.

The Cartesian ego[2] founding modern philosophy realizes the totalizing project. This *cogito* itself expresses the idea of pure identity as the reflective self-presence of consciousness to itself. Launched from this point of transcendental subjectivity, thought now more boldly than ever seeks to comprehend all entities in unity with itself and in a unified system with one another.

But any conceptualization brings the impressions and flux of experience into an order that unifies and compares. It is not the unifying force of concepts per se that Adorno finds dangerous. The logic of identity goes beyond such an attempt to order and describe the particulars of experience. It constructs total systems that seek to engulf the alterity[3] of things in the unity of thought. The problem with the logic of identity is that through it thought seeks to have everything under control, to eliminate all uncertainty and unpredictability, to idealize the bodily fact of sensuous immersion in a world that outruns the subject, to eliminate otherness. Deontological reason expresses this logic of identity by eliminating otherness in at least two ways: the irreducible specificity of situations and the difference among moral subjects.

Normative reason's requirement of impartiality entails a requirement of universality. The impartial reasoner treats all situations according to the same rules, and the more rules can be reduced to the unity of one rule or principle, the more this impartiality and universality will be guaranteed. For Kantian morality, to test the rightness of a judgment the impartial reasoner need not look outside thought, but only seek the consistency and universalizability of a maxim. If reason knows the moral rules that apply universally to action and choice, there will be no reason for one's feelings, interests, or inclinations to enter into the making of moral judgments. This deontological reason cannot eliminate the specificity and variability of concrete situations to which the rules must be applied; by insisting on the impartiality and universality of moral reason, however, it renders itself unable rationally to understand and evaluate particular moral contexts in their particularity.[4]

The ideal of an impartial moral reason also seeks to eliminate otherness in the form of differentiated moral subject. Impartial reason must judge from a point of view outside the particular perspectives of persons involved in interaction, able to totalize these perspectives into a whole, or general will. This is the point of view of a solitary transcendent God.[5] The impartial subject need acknowledge no other subjects whose perspectives should be taken into account and with whom discussion might occur.[6] Thus the claim to be impartial often results in authoritarianism. By asserting oneself as impartial, one claims authority to decide an issue, in place of those whose interests and desires are manifest. From this impartial point of view one need not consult with any other, because the impartial point of view already takes into account all possible perspectives.[7]

In modern moral discourse, being impartial means especially being dispassionate: being entirely unaffected by feelings in one's judgment. The idea of impartiality thus

---

1   *Parmenides*   [editors' note] Parmenides of Elea, early fifth century BCE philosopher, is associated with the view that the universe is unified, eternal, and changeless. His thought had considerable influence on Plato and on the subsequent history of Western philosophy.

2   *Cartesian ego*   [editors' note] The self, seen as rational, self-aware, detached from the physical body and the external world, a pure "I" capable of existence without body, simple and unique. The reference is to Descartes, who held an influential version of this idea.

3   *alterity*   [editors' note] Otherness, differentness.

4   *by insisting on ... in their particularity*   Roberto Unger identifies this problem of applying universals to particulars in modern normative theory. See *Knowledge and Politics* (New York: The Free Press, 1974), pp. 133–44.

5   *This is ... transcendent God*   Thomas A. Spragens, Jr., *The Irony of Liberal Reason* (Chicago: University of Chicago Press, 1981), p. 109.

6   *The impartial subject ... discussion might occur*   Rawls's original position is intended to overcome his monologism of Kantian deontology. Since by definition in the original position everyone reasons from the same perspective, however, abstracted from all particularities of history, place, and situation, the original position is monological in the same sense as Kantian reason. I have argued this in my article "Toward a Critical Theory of Justice," *Social Theory and Practice*, vol. 7, no. 3 (Fall 1981), pp. 279–301; see also Sandel, op. cit., pp. 59–64, and Benhabib, op. cit.

7   *Thus the claim ... all possible perspectives*   Adorno, op. cit., p. 242, p. 295.

seeks to eliminate alterity in a different sense, in the sense of the sensuous, desiring, and emotional experiences that tie me to the concreteness of things, which I apprehend in their particular relation to me. Why does the idea of impartiality require the separation of moral reason from desire, affectivity, and a bodily sensuous relation with things, people, and situations? Because only by expelling desire, affectivity, and the body from reason can impartiality achieve its unity.

The logic of identity typically generates dichotomy instead of unity. The move to bring particulars under a universal category creates a distinction between inside and outside. Since each particular entity or situation has both similarities with and differences from other particular entities and situations, and since they are neither completely identical nor absolutely other, the urge to bring them into unity under a category or principle necessarily entails expelling some of the properties of the entities or situations. Because the totalizing movement always leaves a remainder, the project of reducing particulars to a unity must fail. Not satisfied then to admit defeat in the face of difference, the logic of identity shoves difference into dichotomous normative oppositions: essence–accident, good–bad, normal–deviant. The dichotomies are not symmetrical, however, but stand in a hierarchy. The first term designates the positive unity on the inside; the second, less-valued term designates the leftover outside.[1]

For deontological reason, the movement of expulsion that generates dichotomy happens this way. As I have already discussed, the construct of an impartial point of view is arrived at by abstracting from the concrete particularity of the person in situation. This requires abstracting from the particularity of bodily being, its needs and inclinations, and from the feelings that attach to the experienced particularity of things and events. Normative reason is defined as impartial, and reason defines the unity of the moral subject, both in the sense of knowing the universal principles of morality and in the sense of what all moral subjects have in common

in the same way. This reason thus stands opposed to desire and affectivity as what differentiates and particularizes persons. In the next section I will discuss a similar movement of the expulsion of persons from the civic public in order to maintain its unity.

Several problems follow from the expulsion of desire and feeling from moral reason. Because all feeling, inclinations, needs, desires become thereby equally irrational, they are all equally inferior.[2] By contrast, pre-modern[3] moral philosophy sought standards for distinguishing among good and bad interests, noble and base sentiments. The point of ethics in Aristotle, for example, was precisely to distinguish good desires from bad and to cultivate good desires. Contemporary moral intuitions, moreover, still distinguish good and bad feelings, rational and irrational desires. As Lawrence Blum argues, deontological reason's opposition of moral duty to feeling fails to recognize the role of sentiments of sympathy, compassion, and concern in providing reasons for and motivating moral action.[4] Our experience of moral life teaches us, moreover, that without the impulse of deprivation or anger, for example, many moral choices would not be made.

Thus as a consequence of the opposition between reason and desire, moral decisions grounded in considerations of sympathy, caring, and an assessment of differentiated need are defined as not rational, not "objective," merely sentimental. To the degree that women exemplify or are identified with such styles of moral decision-making, then, women are excluded from moral rationality.[5] The moral rationality of any other groups whose experience or stereotypes associate them with desire, need, and affectivity, moreover, is suspect.

By simply expelling desire, affectivity, and need, deontological reason finally represses them and sets morality in opposition to happiness. The function of duty is to master inner nature, not to form it in the best directions. Since all

1 *The logic of identity ... the leftover outside* I am relying on a reading of Derrida's *Of Grammatology* (Baltimore: Johns Hopkins University Press, 1976), in addition to Adorno's *Negative Dialectics*, for this account. Several writers have noted similarities between Adorno and Derrida in this regard. See Fred Dallmayr, *Twilight of Subjectivity: Contributions to a Post-Structuralist Theory of Politics* (Amherst: University of Massachusetts Press, 1981), pp. 107–14, pp. 127–36; and Michael Ryan, *Marxism and Domination* (Baltimore: Johns Hopkins University Press, 1982), pp. 73–81.

2 *Because all feeling ... equally inferior* Spragens, op. cit., pp. 250–56.

3 *pre-modern* [editors' note] Roughly speaking, the pre-modern era ends at the end of the sixteenth century.

4 *As Lawrence Blum argues ... motivating moral action* Lawrence A. Blum, *Friendship, Altruism and Morality* (London: Routledge and Kegan Paul, 1980).

5 *To the degree ... moral rationality* This is one of Gilligan's points in claiming that there is a "different voice" that has been suppressed; see Benhabib, op. cit.; see also Lawrence Blum, "Kant's and Hegel's Moral Rationalism: A Feminist Perspective," *Canadian Journal of Philosophy*, vol. 12 (June 1982), pp. 287–302.

desiring is equally suspect, we have no way of distinguishing which desires are good and which bad, which will expand the person's capacities and relations with others, and which stunt the person and foster violence. In being excluded from understanding, all desiring, feeling, and needs become unconscious, but certainly do not thereby cease to motivate action and behavior. Reason's task thereby is to control and censure desire.

2. The Unity of the Civic Public

The dichotomy between reason and desire appears in modern political theory in the distinction between the universal, public realm of sovereignty and the state, on the one hand, and the particular private realm of needs and desires, on the other. Modern normative political theory and political practice aim to embody impartiality in the public realm of the state. Like the impartiality of moral reason, this public realm of the state attains its generality by the exclusion of particularity, desire, feeling, and those aspects of life associated with the body. In modern political theory and practice, this public achieves a unity in particular by the exclusion of women and others associated with nature and the body.

As Richard Sennett and others have written, the developing urban centers of the eighteenth century engendered a unique public life.[1] As commerce increased and more people came into the city, the space of the city itself was changed to make for more openness, vast boulevards where people from different classes mingled in the same spaces.[2] As Habermas has argued, one of the functions of this public life of the mid-nineteenth century was to provide a critical space where people discussed and criticized the affairs of the state in a multiplicity of newspapers, coffeehouses, and other forums.[3] While dominated by bourgeois men, public discussion in the coffeehouses admitted men of any class on equal terms.[4] Through the institution of the salons, moreover, as well as by attending the theater and being members of reading societies, aristocratic and bourgeois women participated, and sometimes took the lead in such public discussion.[5]

Public life in this period appears to have been wild, playful, and sexy. The theater was a social center, a forum where wit and satire criticized the state and predominant mores. This wild public to some degree mixed sexes and classes, mixed serious discourse with play, and mixed the aesthetic with the political. It did not survive republican philosophy. The idea of the universalist state that expresses an impartial point of view transcending any particular interest is in part a reaction to this differentiated public. The republicans grounded this universalist state in the idea of the civic public, which political theory and practice institutionalized by the end of the eighteenth century in Europe and the United States to suppress the popular and linguistic heterogeneity of the urban public. This institutionalization reordered social life on a strict division of public and private.

Rousseau's political philosophy is the paradigm of this ideal of the civic public. He develops his conception of politics precisely in reaction to his experience of the urban public of the eighteenth century,[6] as well as in reaction to the premises and conclusions of the atomistic and individualist theory of the state expressed by Hobbes. The civic public expresses the universal and impartial point of view of reason, standing opposed to and expelling desire, sentiment, and the particularity of needs and interests. From the premises of individual desire and want we cannot arrive at a strong enough normative conception of social relations. The difference between atomistic egoism and civil society does not consist simply of the fact that the infinity of individual appetite has been curbed by laws enforced by threat of punishment. Rather, reason brings people together to recognize common interests and a general will.

The sovereign people embody the universal point of view of the collective interest and equal citizenship. In the pursuit of their individual interests people have a particularist orientation. Normative reason reveals an impartial point

---

1   *As Richard Sennett ... public life*   Richard Sennett, *The Fall of Public Man* (New York: Random House, 1974).

2   *As commerce increased ... same spaces*   See Marshall Berman, *All That is Solid Melts Into Air* (New York: Simon and Schuster, 1982).

3   *As Habermas has argued ... . other forums*   Jurgen Habermas, "The Public Sphere: An Encyclopedia Article," *New German Critique*, vol. 1, no. 3 (Fall 1974), pp. 49–55.

4   *While dominated ... equal terms*   Sennett, chapter 4.

5   *Through the institution ... public discussion*   See Joan Landes, "Women and the Public Sphere: The Challenge of Feminist Discourse," paper presented as part of the Bunting Institute Colloquium, April 1983.

6   *He develops ... the eighteenth century*   Charles Ellison, "Rousseau and the Modern City: The Politics of Speech and Dress," *Political Theory*, vol. 13 (1985), pp. 497–534.

of view, however, that all rational persons can adopt, which expresses a general will not reducible to an aggregate of particular interests. Participation in the general will as a citizen is an expression of human nobility and genuine freedom. Such rational commitment to collectivity is not compatible with personal satisfaction, however, and for Rousseau this is the tragedy of the human condition.[1]

Rousseau conceived that this public realm ought to be unified and homogeneous, and indeed suggested methods of fostering among citizens commitment to such unity through civic celebrations. While the purity, unity, and generality of this public realm require transcending and repressing the partiality and differentiation of need, desire, and affectivity, Rousseau hardly believed that human life can or should be without emotion and the satisfaction of need and desire. Man's particular nature as a feeling, needful being is enacted in the private realm of domestic life, over which women are the proper moral guardians.

Hegel's political philosophy developed this conception of the public realm of the state as expressing impartiality and universality as against the partiality and substance of desire. For Hegel the liberal account of social relations, as based on the liberty of self-defining individuals to pursue their own ends, properly describes only one aspect of social life: the sphere of civil society. As a member of civil society, the person pursues private ends for himself and his family. These ends may conflict with those of others, but exchange transactions produce much harmony and satisfaction. Conceived as a member of the state, on the other hand, the person is not a locus of particular desire but the bearer of universally articulated rights and responsibilities. The point of view of the state and law transcends all particular interests to express the universal and rational spirit of humanity. State laws and action express the general will, the interests of the whole society. Since maintaining this universal point of view while engaged in the pursuit of one's own particular interests is difficult, if not impossible, a class of persons is necessary whose sole job is to maintain the public good and the universal point of view of the state. For Hegel, these government officials are the universal class.[2]

Marx, of course, was the first to deny the state's claim to impartiality and universality. The split between the public realm of citizenship and the private realm of individual desire and greed leaves the competition and inequality of that private realm untouched. In capitalist society application of a principle of impartiality reproduces the position of the ruling class, because the interests of the substantially more powerful are considered in the same manner as those without power.[3] Despite this critique, as powerful as it ever was, Marx stops short of questioning the ideal of a public that expresses an impartial and universal normative perspective; he merely asserts that such a public is not realizable within capitalist society.

I think that recent feminist analyses of the dichotomy of public and private in modern political theory imply that the ideal of the civic public as impartial and universal is itself suspect. Modern political theorists and politicians proclaimed the impartiality and generality of the public and at the same time quite consciously found it fitting that some persons—namely women, nonwhites, and sometimes those without property—be excluded from participation in that public. If this was not just a mistake, it suggests that the ideal of the civic public as expressing the general interest, the impartial point of view of reason, itself results in exclusion. By assuming that reason stands opposed to desire, affectivity, and the body, the civic public must exclude bodily and affective aspects of human existence. In practice this assumption forces a homogeneity of citizens upon the civic public. It excludes from the public those individuals and groups that do not fit the model of the rational citizen who can transcend body and sentiment. This exclusion is based on two tendencies that feminists stress: the opposition between reason and desire, and the association of these traits with kinds of persons.

In the social scheme expressed by Rousseau and Hegel, women must be excluded from the public realm of citizenship because they are the caretakers of affectivity, desire, and the body. Allowing appeals to desires and bodily needs to

---

1   *Participation in the general will ... the human condition*   Judith Shklar, *Men and Citizens* (Cambridge, MA: Cambridge University Press, 1969).

2   *For Hegel ... the universal class*   See Z.A. Pelczynski, "The Hegelian Conception of the State," in Pelczynski, ed., *Hegel's Political Philosophy: Problems and Perspectives* (Cambridge, MA: Cambridge University Press, 1971), pp. 1–29; and Anthony S.

Walton, "Public and Private Interests: Hegel on Civil Society and the State," in S. Benn and G. Gaus, ed., *Public and Private in Social Life* (London: St. Martin's Press, 1983), pp. 249–66.

3   *The split between ... those without power*   There are many texts in which Marx makes these sorts of claims, including "On the Jewish Question" and "Critique of the Gotha Program." For some discussion of these points, see Shlomo Avineri, *The Social and Political Thought of Karl Marx* (Cambridge, MA: Cambridge University Press, 1968), pp. 41–48.

move public debates would undermine public deliberation by fragmenting its unity. Even within the domestic realm, moreover, women must be dominated. Their dangerous, heterogeneous sexuality must be kept chaste and confined to marriage. Enforcing chastity on women will keep each family a separated unity, preventing the chaos and blood-mingling that would be produced by illegitimate children. These chaste, enclosed women can then be the proper care-takers of men's desire by tempering its potentially disruptive impulses through moral education. Men's desire for women itself threatens to shatter and disperse the universal rational realm of the public, as well as to disrupt the neat distinction between the public and private. As guardians of the private realm of need, desire, and affectivity, women must ensure that men's impulses do not remove them from the univer-sality of reason. The moral neatness of the female-tended hearth, moreover, will temper the possessively individual-istic impulses of the particularistic realm of business and commerce, which, like sexuality, constantly threatens to explode the unity of society under the umbrella of universal reason.[1]

The bourgeois world instituted a moral division of labor between reason and sentiment, identifying masculinity with reason and femininity with sentiment and desire.[2] As Linda Nicholson has argued, the modern sphere of family and personal life is as much a modern creation as is the modern realm of state and law, and is part of the same process.[3] The impartiality and rationality of the state depend on con-taining need and desire in the private realm of the family.[4] While the realm of personal life and sentiment has been thoroughly devalued because it has been excluded from rationality, it has nevertheless been the focus of increasingly expanded commitment. Modernity developed a concept of "inner nature" that needs nurturance and within which is to be found the authenticity and individuality of the self, rather than in the conformity, regularity, and universality of

the public. The civic public excludes sentiment and desire, then, partly in order to protect its "natural" character.

Not only in Europe, but in the early decades of the United States as well, the white male bourgeoisie conceived republican virtue as rational, restrained, and chaste, not yielding to passion or desire for luxury. The designers of the American Constitution specifically restricted the access of the laboring class to this rational public because they feared disruption of commitment to the general interests. Some, like Jefferson, even feared developing an urban proletariat. These early American republicans were also quite explicit about the need for the homogeneity of citizens, which from the earliest days in the republic involved the relationship of the white republicans to the Black and American Indian people. These republican fathers, such as Jefferson, identi-fied the Red and Black people in their territories with wild nature and passion, just as they feared that women outside the domestic realm were wanton and avaricious. They de-fined moral, civilized republican life in opposition to this backward-looking uncultivated desire, which they identi-fied with women and nonwhites.[5]

To summarize, the ideal of normative reason, moral sense, stands opposed to desire and affectivity. Impartial civilized reason characterizes the virtue of the republican man who rises above passion and desire. Instead of cutting bourgeois man entirely off from the body and affectivity, however, this culture of the rational public confines them to the domestic sphere, which also confines women's passions and provides emotional solace to men and children. Indeed, within this domestic realm sentiments can flower, and each individual can recognize and affirm his particularity. Because virtues of impartiality and universality define the public realm, it precisely ought not to attend to our particularity. Modern normative reason and its political expression in the idea of the civic public, then, have unity and coherence by their expulsion and confinement of everything that would threaten to invade the polity with differentiation: the speci-ficity of women's bodies and desire, the difference of race and culture, the variability of heterogeneity of the needs, the goals and desires of each individual, the ambiguity and changeability of feeling.

---

1   *In the social scheme ... universal reason*   For feminists' analyses of Rousseau and Hegel, see op. cit. Okin, Elshtain, Eisenstein, Lange and Clark, footnote 3 [p. 96]. See also Joel Schwartz, *The Sexual Politics of Jean-Jacques Rousseau* (Chicago: University of Chicago Press, 1984).

2   *The bourgeois world ... sentiment and desire*   See Genevieve Lloyd, *The Man of Reason: "Male" and "Female" in Western Philosophy* (Minneapolis: University of Minnesota Press, 1984); Lynda Glen-non, *Women and Dualism* (New York: Longman, 1979).

3   *As Linda Nicholson ... same process*   Nicholson, op. cit.

4   *The impartiality ... the family*   Zillah Eisenstein claims that the modern state depends on the patriarchal family. Op. cit.

5   *These republican fathers ... women and nonwhites*   Ronald Takaki, *Iron Cages: Race and Culture in 19th Century America* (New York: Knopf, 1979).

3. Habermas As Opposing Reason and Affectivity

I have argued that the modern conception of normative reason derived from the deontological tradition of moral and political theory aims for a unity that expels particularity and desire and sets feeling in opposition to reason. To express that impartiality and universality, a point of view of reasoning must be constructed that transcends all situations, contexts, and perspectives. The identification of such a point of view with reason, however, devalues and represses the concrete needs, feelings, and interests that people have in their practical moral lives and thus imposes an impossible burden on reason itself. Deontological reason generates an opposition between normative reason, on the one hand, and desire and affectivity, on the other. These latter cannot be entirely suppressed and reduced to the unity of impartial and universal reason, however. They sprout out again, menacing because they have been expelled from reason.

Because the ideal of impartiality is illusory, and because claims to assert normative reason as impartial and universal issue practically in the political exclusion of persons associated with affectivity and the body, we need a conception of normative reason that does not hold this ideal and does not oppose reason to affectivity and desire. I think that Habermas's idea of a communicative ethics provides the most promising starting point for such an alternative conception of normative reason. Much about the way he formulates his theory of communicative action, however, retains several problems that characterize deontological reason.

In his theory of communicative action Habermas seeks to develop a conception of rationality with a pragmatic starting point in the experience of discussion that aims to reach an understanding. Reason in such a model does not mean universal principles dominating particulars, but more concretely means giving reasons, the practical stance of being reasonable, willing to talk and listen. Truth and rightness are not something known by intuition or through tests of consistency, but achieved only from a process of discussion. This communicative ethics eliminates the authoritarian monologism[1] of deontological reason. The dialogic model of reason supplants the transcendental ego sitting at a height from which it can comprehend everything by reducing it to synthetic unity.

In the theory of communicative action Habermas also seeks directly to confront the tendency in modern philosophy to reduce reason to instrumental reason, a tendency that follows from its assumption of a solitary reasoning consciousness. He insists that normative, aesthetic, and expressive utterances can be just as rational as factual or strategic ones, but differ from the latter in the manner of evaluating their rationality. For all these reasons Habermas's theory of communicative action has much more to offer a feminist ethics than do modern ethical and political theories. Habermas's communicative ethics remains inadequate, however, from the point of view of the critique of deontological reason I have made, for he retains a commitment to impartiality and reproduces in his theory of communication an opposition between reason and desire.

A dialogic conception of normative reason promises a critique and abandonment of the assumption that normative reason is impartial and universal. Precisely because there is no impartial point of view in which a subject stands detached and dispassionate to assess all perspectives, to arrive at an objective and complete understanding of an issue or experience, all perspectives and participants must contribute to its discussion. Thus dialogic reason ought to imply reason as contextualized, where answers are the outcome of a plurality of perspectives that cannot be reduced to unity. In discussion speakers need not abandon their particular perspective or bracket their motives and feelings. As long as the dialogue allows all perspectives to speak freely and be heard and taken into account, the expression of need, motive, and feelings will not have merely private significance, and will not bias or distort the conclusions because they will interact with other needs, motives, and feelings.

Habermas reneges on this promise to define normative reason contextually and perspectivally, however, because he retains a commitment to the ideal of normative reason as expressing an impartial point of view. Rather than arbitrarily presuppose a transcendental ego as the impartial reasoner, as does the deontological tradition; he claims that an impartial point of view is actually presupposed by a normative discussion that seeks to reach agreement. A faith in the possibility of consensus is a condition of beginning dialogue, and the possibility of such consensus presupposes that people engage in discussion "under conditions that neutralize all motives except that of cooperatively seeking

---

1   *monologism*   [editors' note] This term has its home in literary theory. A monological text is one that depends on the centrality of a single authoritative voice. The contrast is with a dialogical text, which allows for a plurality of independent, equally valid, voices.

truth."[1] Habermas claims here theoretically to reconstruct a presumption of impartiality implicitly carried by any discussion of norms that aims to reach consensus. I take this to be a transcendental argument,[2] inasmuch as he poses this abstraction from motives and desires as a condition of the possibility of consensus. Through this argument Habermas reproduces the opposition between universal and particular, reason and desire characteristic of deontological reason. A more thoroughly pragmatic interpretation of dialogic reason would not have to suppose that participants must abstract from all motives in aiming to reach agreement.[3]

Communicative ethics also promises to break down the opposition between normative reason and desire that deontological reason generates. Individual needs, desires, and feelings can be rationally articulated and understood, no less than can facts about the world or norms.[4] A possible interpretation of communicative ethics then can be that normative claims are the outcome of the expression of needs, feelings, and desires which individuals claim to have met and recognized by others under conditions where all have an equal voice in the expression of their needs and desires. Habermas stops short of interpreting normative reason as the dialogue about meeting needs and recognizing feelings, however. As Seyla Benhabib argues, because Habermas retains a universalistic understanding of normative reason, he finds that norms must express shared interests.[5] In his scheme discussion about individual need and feeling is separate from discussion about norms.

I suggest that Habermas implicitly reproduces an opposition between reason and desire and feeling in his conception of communication itself, moreover, because he devalues and ignores the expressive and bodily aspects of communication. The model of linguistic activity Habermas takes for his conception of communicative action is discourse, or argumentation. In argumentation we find the implicit rules underlying all linguistic action, whether teleological, normative, or dramaturgical. In discourse people make their shared activity the subject of discussion in order to come to agreement about it. People make assertions for which they claim validity, give reasons for their assertions, and require reasons of others. In the ideal model of discourse, no force compels agreement against that of the better argument. This model of the communication situation, which any attempts to reach understanding presuppose, defines the meaning of utterances: the meaning of an utterance consists of the reasons that can be offered for it. To understand the meaning of an utterance is to know the conditions of its validity.[6]

In Habermas's model of communication, understanding consists of participants in discussion understanding the same meaning by an utterance, which means that they agree that the utterance refers to something in the objective, social, or subjective world. The actors

> seek consensus and measure it against truth, rightness and sincerity, that is, against the "fit" or "misfit" between the speech act, on the one hand, and the three worlds to which the actor takes up relations with his utterances, on the other.[7]

> The term "reaching understanding" means, at the minimum, that at least two speaking and acting subjects understand a linguistic expression in the same way.... In communicative action a speaker selects a comprehensible linguistic expression only in order to come to an understanding *with* a hearer *about* something and thereby to make *himself* understandable.[8]

Behind this apparently innocent way of talking about discourse lies the presumption of several unities: the unity of the speaking subject, who knows himself or herself and seeks faithfully to represent his or her feelings; the unity of subjects with one another, which makes it possible for them

---

1   *"under conditions ... cooperatively seeking truth"* Jurgen Habermas, *Reason and the Rationalization of Society* (Boston: Beacon Press, 1983), p. 19. In the footnote to this passage Habermas explicitly connects this presumption with the tradition of moral theory seeking to articulate the impartial "moral point of view."

2   *transcendental argument* [editors' note] An argument for some principle based on its supposed status as a necessary enabling precondition (for experience or knowledge or something of the sort). Kant made systematic use of this sort of argument.

3   *Habermas claims here ... aiming to reach agreement* Richard Bernstein suggests that Habermas vacillates between a transcendental and empirical interpretation of his project in many respects. See *Beyond Objectivism and Relativism* (Philadelphia: University of Pennsylvania Press, 1983), pp. 182–96.

4   *Individual needs ... the world or norms* Habermas, op. cit., pp. 91–93.

5   *As Seyla Benhabib argues ... shared interests* Benhabib, "Communicative Ethics and Moral Autonomy," presented to the American Philosophical Association, December 1982.

6   *The model ... conditions of its validity* Habermas, op. cit., p. 115, pp. 285–300.

7   *seek consensus ... on the other* Habermas, p. 100.

8   *The term ... make himself understandable* Habermas, p. 307.

to have the same meaning; and the unity, in the sense of fit or correspondence, between an utterance and the aspects of one or more of the "worlds" to which it refers. By this manner of theorizing language Habermas exhibits the logic of identity I discussed in part 1, or also what Derrida calls the metaphysics of presence.[1] This model of communication presumes implicitly that speakers can be present to themselves and to one another and that signification consists in the representation by a sign of objects. To be sure, Habermas denies a realist interpretation of the function of utterances; it is not as though there are worlds of things apart from situated human and social linguistic life. Nevertheless he presumes that utterances can have a single meaning understood in the same way by speakers because they affirm that it expresses the same relation to a world. As writers such as Michael Ryan and Dominick LaCapra have argued, such a conception of meaning ignores the manner in which meaning arises from the unique relationship of utterances to one another, and thereby ignores the multiple meaning that any movement of signification expresses.[2]

I suggest, moreover, that this model of communication reproduces the opposition between reason and desire because, like modern normative reason, it expels and devalues difference: the concreteness of the body, the affective aspects of speech, the musical and figurative aspects of all utterances, which all contribute to the formation and understanding of their meaning. John Keane argues that Habermas's model of discourse abstracts from the specifically bodily aspects of speech—gesture, facial expression, tone of voice, rhythm. One can add to this that it abstracts from the material aspects of written language, such as punctuation, sentence construction, and so on. This model of communication also abstracts from the rhetorical dimensions of communication, that is, the evocative terms, metaphors, dramatic elements of the speaking, by which a speaker ad-

dresses himself or herself to this particular audience.[3] When people converse in concrete speaking situations, when they give and receive reasons from one another with the aim of reaching understanding, gesture, facial expression, tone of voice (or, in writing, punctuation, sentence structure, etc.), as well as evocative metaphors and dramatic emphasis, are crucial aspects of their communication.

In the model of ideal discourse that Habermas holds, moreover, there appears to be no role for metaphor, jokes, irony, and other forms of communication that use surprise and duplicity. The model of communication Habermas operates with holds an implicit distinction between "literal" and "figurative" meaning and between a meaning and its manner of expression. Implicitly this model of communication supposes a purity of the meaning of utterances by separating them from their expressive and metaphorical aspects.

He considers irony, paradox, allusion, metaphor, and so on as derivative, even deceptive, modes of linguistic practice, thus assuming the rational literal meaning in opposition to these more playful, multiple, and affective modes of speaking.[4] In the practical context of communication, however, such ambiguous and playful forms of expression usually weave in and out of assertive modes, together providing the communicative act.

Julia Kristeva's conception of speech provides a more embodied alternative to that proposed by Habermas, which might better open a conception of communicative ethics. Any utterance has a dual movement, in her conception, which she refers to as the "symbolic" and "semiotic" moments. The symbolic names the referential function of the utterance, the way it situates the speaker in relation to a reality outside him or her. The semiotic names the unconscious, bodily aspects of the utterance, such as rhythm, tone of voice, metaphor, word play, and gesture.[5] Different kinds of utterances have differing relations of the symbolic and the semiotic. Scientific language, for example, seeks to suppress the semiotic elements, while poetic language emphasizes them. No utterance is without the duality of a relation

---

1   *what Derrida calls the metaphysics of presence*   I am thinking here particularly of Derrida's discussion of Rousseau in *Of Grammatology*. I have dealt with these issues in much more detail in my paper "The Ideal of Community and the Politics of Difference," *Social Theory and Practice*, vol. 12, no. 1 (Spring 1986), pp. 1–26.

2   *such a conception ... signification expresses*   For critiques of Habermas's assumptions about language from a Derridian point of view, which argue that he does not attend the difference and spacing in signification that generates undecidability and ambiguity, see Michael Ryan, *Marxism and Deconstruction* (Baltimore: Johns Hopkins University Press, 1982); Dominick LaCapra, "Habermas and the Grounding of Critical Theory," *History and Theory* (1977), pp. 237–64.

3   *This model ... this particular audience*   Keane, "Elements of a Socialist Theory of Public Life," in op. cit., pp. 169–72.

4   *He considers ... modes of speaking*   Habermas, op. cit., p. 331.

5   *Julia Kristeva's conception ... word play, and gesture*   Kristeva, *Revolution in Poetic Language* (New York: Columbia University Press, 1984), pp. 21–37; "From One Identity to an Other," in *Desire in Language* (New York: Columbia University Press, 1980), pp. 124–47.

of the symbolic and semiotic, however, and it is through their relationship that meaning is generated.

This understanding of language bursts open the unity of the subject that Habermas presupposes, as the sender and receiver and negotiator of meaning. The subject is in process, positioned by the slipping and moving levels of signification, which is always in excess of what is grasped or understood discursively. The heterogeneous semiotic aspects of utterances influence both speakers and hearers in unconscious, bodily, and affective ways that support and move the expressing and understanding of referential meaning. Kristeva is quite clear in rejecting an irrationalist conception that would hold that all utterances are equally sensible and simply reduce any speech to play. The point is not to reverse the privileging of reason over emotion and body that it excludes, but to expose the process of the generation of referential meaning from the supporting valences of semiotic relations.

> Though absolutely necessary, the thetic [i.e., proposition or judgment] is not exclusive: the semiotic, which also precedes it, constantly tears it open, and this transgression brings about all the various transformations of the signifying practice that are called "creation." Whether in the realm of metalanguage (mathematics, for example) or literature, what remodels the symbolic order is always the influx of the semiotic.[1]

What difference does such a theory of language make for a conception of normative reason grounded in a theory of communicative action? As I understand the implications of Kristeva's approach to language, it entails that communication is not only motivated by the aim to reach consensus, a shared understanding of the world, but also and even more basically by a desire to love and be loved. Modulations of eros operate in the semiotic elements of communication, putting the subject's identity in question in relation to itself, to its own past and imagination, and to others in the heterogeneity of their identity. People do not merely hear, take in, and argue about the validity of utterances. Rather we are affected, in an immediate and felt fashion, by the other's expression and its manner of being addressed to us.

Habermas has a place in his model of communication for making feelings the subject of discourse. Such feeling discourse, however, is carefully marked off in his theory from factual or normative discourse. There is no place in his conception of linguistic interaction for the feeling that accompanies and motivates all utterances. In actual situations of discussion, tone of voice, facial expression, gesture, the use of irony, understatement, or hyperbole all serve to carry with the propositional message of the utterance another level of expression relating the participants in terms of attraction or withdrawal, confrontation or affirmation. Speakers not only say what they mean, but also say it excitedly, angrily, in a hurt or offended fashion, and so on, and such emotional qualities of communication contexts should not be thought of as non- or prelinguistic. Recognizing such an aspect of utterances, however, involves acknowledging the irreducible multiplicity and ambiguity of meaning. I am suggesting that only a conception of normative reason that includes these affective and bodily dimensions of meaning can be adequate for a feminist ethics.

4. Toward a Heterogeneous Public Life

I have argued that the distinction between public and private as it appears in modern political theory expresses a will for homogeneity that necessitates the exclusion of many persons and groups, particularly women and racialized groups culturally identified with the body, wildness, and irrationality. In conformity with the modern idea of normative reason, the idea of the public in modern political theory and practice designates a sphere of human existence in which citizens express their rationality and universality, abstracted from their particular situations and needs and opposed to feeling. This feminist critique of the exclusionary public does not imply, as Jean Elshtain suggests, a collapse of the distinction between public and private.[2] Indeed, I agree with those writers, including Elshtain, Habermas, Wolin, and many others, who claim that contemporary social life itself has collapsed the public and that emancipatory politics requires generating a renewed sense of public life. Examination of the exclusionary and homogeneous ideal of the public in modern political theory, however, shows that we cannot envision such renewal of public life as a recovery of Enlightenment ideals. Instead, we need to transform the distinction between public and private that does not correl-

---

1   *Though absolutely necessary ... the semiotic*   Kristeva, *Revolution in Poetic Language*, p. 291.

2   *This feminist critique ... public and private*   Jean Elshtain, *Public Man, Private Woman* (Princeton, NJ: Princeton University Press, 1981), part two.

ate with an opposition between reason and affectivity and desire, or universal and particular.

The primary meaning of public is what is open and accessible. For democratic politics this means two things: there must be public spaces and public expression. A public space is any indoor or outdoor space to which anyone has access. Expression is public when third parties may witness it within institutions that give these others opportunity to respond to the expression and enter a discussion, and through media that allow anyone in principle to enter the discussion. Expression and discussion are political when they raise and address issues of the moral value or human desirability of an institution or practice whose decisions affect a large number of people. This concept of a public, which indeed is derived from aspects of modern urban experience, expresses a conception of social relations in principle not exclusionary.

The traditional notion of the private realm, as Hannah Arendt points out, is etymologically related to deprivation. The private, in her conception, is what should be hidden from view or what cannot be brought to view. The private, in this traditional notion, is connected with shame and incompleteness, and, as Arendt points out, implies excluding bodily and personally affective aspects of human life from the public.[1]

Instead of defining privacy as what the public excludes, privacy should be defined, as an aspect of liberal theory does, as that aspect of his or her life and activity that any individual has a right to exclude others from. I mean here to emphasize the direction of agency, as the individual withdrawing rather than being kept out. With the growth of both state and nonstate bureaucracies, defense of privacy in this sense has become not merely a matter of keeping the state out of certain affairs, but also of asking for positive state action to ensure that the activities of nonstate organizations, such as corporations, respect the claims of individuals to privacy.

The feminist slogan "the personal is political" does not deny a distinction between public and private, but it does deny a social division between public and private spheres, with different kinds of institutions, activities, and human attributes. Two principles follow from this slogan: (a) no social institutions or practices should be excluded a priori as being the proper subject for public discussion and expression; and (b) no persons, actions, or aspects of a person's life should be forced into privacy.

1. The contemporary women's movement has made public issues out of many practices claimed to be too trivial or private for public discussion: the meaning of pronouns, domestic violence against women, the practice of men's opening doors for women, the sexual assault on women and children, the sexual division of housework, and so on. Radical politics in contemporary life consists of taking many actions and activities deemed properly private, such as how individuals and enterprises invest their money, and making public issues out of them.

2. The second principle says that no person or aspects of persons should be forced into privacy. The modern conception of the public, I have argued, creates a conception of citizenship that excludes from public attention most particular aspects of a person. Public life is supposed to be "blind" to sex, race, age, and so on, and all are supposed to enter the public and its discussion on identical terms. Such a conception of a public has resulted in the exclusion of persons and aspects of persons from public life.

Ours is still a society that forces persons or aspects of persons into privacy. Repression of homosexuality is perhaps the most striking example. In the United States today most people seem to hold the liberal view that persons have a right to be gay as long as they remain private about their activities. Calling attention in public to the fact that one is gay, making public displays of gay affection, or even publicly asserting needs and rights for gay people provokes ridicule and fear in many people. Making a public issue out of heterosexuality, moreover, by suggesting that the dominance of heterosexual assumptions is one-dimensional and oppressive can rarely get a public hearing even among feminists and radicals. In general, contemporary politics grants to all persons entrance into the public on condition that they do not claim special rights or needs, or call attention to their particular history or culture, and that they keep their passions private.

The new social movements of the 1960s, 1970s, and 1980s in the United States have begun to create an image of a more differentiated public that directly confronts the

---

1   *The traditional notion ... from the public*   Hannah Arendt, *The Human Condition* (Chicago: University of Chicago Press, 1958).

allegedly impartial and universalist state. Movements of racially oppressed groups, including Black, Chicano and American Indian liberation, tend to reject the assimilationist ideal and assert the right to nurture and celebrate in public their distinctive cultures and forms of life, as well as asserting special claims of justice deriving from suppression or devaluation of their cultures, or compensating for the disadvantage in which the dominant society puts them. The women's movement too has claimed to develop and foster a distinctively women's culture and that both women's specific bodily needs and women's situation in male-dominated society require attending in public to special needs and unique contributions of women. Movements of the disabled, the aged, and gay and lesbian liberation—all have produced an image of public life in which persons stand forth in their differences and make public claims to have specific needs met.

The street demonstrations that in recent years have included most of these groups, as well as traditional labor groups and advocates of environmentalism and nuclear disarmament, sometimes create heterogeneous publics of passion, play, and aesthetic interest. Such demonstrations always focus on issues they seek to promote for public discussion, and these issues are discussed: claims are made and supported. The style of politics of such events, however, has many less discursive elements: gaily decorated banners with ironic or funny slogans, guerilla theater or costumes serving to make political points, giant puppets standing for people or ideas towering over the crowd, chants, music, song, dancing. Liberating public expression means not only lifting formerly privatized issues into the open of public and rational discussion that considers the good of ends as well as means, but also affirming in the practice of such discussion the proper place of passion and play in public.

As the 1970s progressed, and the particular interests and experience expressed by these differing social movements matured in their confidence, coherence, and understanding of the world from the point of view of these interests, a new kind of public became possible that might persist beyond a single demonstration. This public is expressed in the idea of a "Rainbow Coalition." Realized to some degree only for sporadic months during the 1983 Mel King campaign in Boston[1] and the 1984 Jesse Jackson campaign in

certain cities, this is an idea of a political public that goes beyond the ideal of civic friendship in which persons unite for a common purpose on terms of equality and mutual respect.[2] While it includes commitment to equality and mutual respect among participants, the idea of the Rainbow Coalition[3] specifically preserves and institutionalizes in its form of organizational discussion the heterogeneous groups that make it up. In this way it is quite unlike the Enlightenment ideal of the civil public (which might have its practical analogue here in the idea of the "united front"). As a general principle, this heterogeneous public asserts that the only way to ensure that public life will not exclude persons and groups that it has excluded in the past is to give specific recognition to the disadvantage of those groups and bring their specific histories into the public.[4]

I have been suggesting that the Enlightenment ideal of the civic public, where citizens meet in terms of equality and mutual respect, is too rounded and tame an ideal of public. This idea of equal citizenship attains unity because it excludes bodily and affective particularity, as well as the concrete histories of individuals that make groups unable to understand one another. Emancipatory politics should foster a conception of public that in principle excludes no persons, aspects of persons' lives, or topic of discussion and that encourages aesthetic as well as discursive expression. In such a public, consensus and sharing may not always be the goal, but the recognition and appreciation of differences, in the context of confrontation with power.[5]

◆ ◆ ◆ ◆ ◆

---

2   *this is an idea ... mutual respect*   See Drucilla Cornell, "Toward A Modern/Postmodern Reconstruction of Ethics," *University of Pennsylvania Law Review*, vol. 133, no. 2 (1985), pp. 291–380.

3   *1984 Jesse Jackson campaign ... Rainbow Coalition*   [editors' note] In 1984, black civil rights leader Jesse Jackson ran in the primaries for the Democratic nomination for US president, and founded the Rainbow Coalition, a national organization agitating for justice.

4   *As a general principle ... into the public*   Thomas Bender promotes a conception of a heterogeneous public as important for an urban political history that would not be dominated by the perspective of the then- and now-privileged; "The History of Culture and the Culture of Cities," paper presented at meeting of the International Association of Philosophy and Literature, New York City, May 1985.

5   I am grateful to David Alexander for all the time and thought he gave to this paper.

---

1   *the 1983 Mel King campaign in Boston*   [editors' note] Mel King is an educator, community worker, and radical activist who came close to winning a campaign for the office of mayor of Boston.

from *Justice and the Politics of Difference* (1990)

Chapter 1: Displacing the Distributive Paradigm

> It was in general a mistake to make a fuss about so-called *distribution* and put the principal stress on it. Any distribution whatever of the means of consumption is only a consequence of the distribution of the conditions of production themselves. The latter distribution, however, is a feature of the mode of production itself.
>
> -Karl Marx

Thousands of buses converge on the city, and tens of thousands of people of diverse colors, ages, occupations, and life styles swarm onto the mall around the Washington Monument until the march begins. At midday people move into the streets, chanting, singing, waving wild papier-mâché missiles or effigies of government officials. Many carry signs or banners on which a simple slogan is inscribed: "Peace, Jobs, and Justice."

This scene has occurred many times in Washington, D.C., in the last decade, and many more times in other U.S. cities. What does "justice" mean in this slogan? In this context, as in many other political contexts today, I suggest that social justice means the elimination of institutionalized domination and oppression. Any aspect of social organization and practice relevant to domination and oppression is in principle subject to evaluation by ideals of justice.

Contemporary philosophical theories of justice, however, do not conceive justice so broadly. Instead, philosophical theories of justice tend to restrict the meaning of social justice to the morally proper distribution of benefits and burdens among society's members. In this chapter I define and assess this distributive paradigm. While distributive issues are crucial to a satisfactory conception of justice, it is a mistake to reduce social justice to distribution.

I find two problems with the distributive paradigm. First, it tends to focus thinking about social justice on the allocation of material goods such as things, resources, income, and wealth, or on the distribution of social positions, especially jobs. This focus tends to ignore the social structure and institutional context that often help determine distributive patterns. Of particular importance to the analyses that follow are issues of decision making power and procedures, division of labor, and culture.

One might agree that defining justice in terms of distribution tends to bias thinking about justice toward issues concerning wealth, income, and other material goods, and that other issues such as decision making power or the structure of the division of labor are as important, and yet argue that distribution need not be restricted to material goods and resources. Theorists frequently consider issues of the distribution of such nonmaterial goods as power, opportunity, or self-respect. But this widening of the concept of distribution exhibits the second problem with the distributive paradigm. When metaphorically extended to nonmaterial social goods, the concept of distribution represents them as though they were static things, instead of a function of social relations and processes.

In criticizing distributively oriented theories I wish neither to reject distribution as unimportant nor to offer a new positive theory to replace the distributive theories. I wish rather to displace talk of justice that regards persons as primarily possessors and consumers of goods to a wider context that also includes action, decisions about action, and provision of the means to develop and exercise capacities. The concept of social justice includes all aspects of institutional rules and relations insofar as they are subject to potential collective decision. The concepts of domination and oppression, rather than the concept of distribution, should be the starting point for a conception of social justice.

The Distributive Paradigm

A distributive paradigm runs through contemporary discourse about justice, spanning diverse ideological positions. By "paradigm" I mean a configuration of elements and practices which define an inquiry: metaphysical presuppositions, unquestioned terminology, characteristic questions, lines of reasoning, specific theories and their typical scope and mode of application. The distributive paradigm defines social justice as the morally proper distribution of social benefits and burdens among society's members. Paramount among these are wealth, income, and other material resources. The distributive definition of justice often includes, however, nonmaterial social goods such as rights, opportunity, power, and self respect. What marks the distributive paradigm is a tendency to conceive social justice and distribution as coextensive concepts.

A review of how some major theorists define justice makes apparent the prevalence of this conceptual identification of justice with distribution. Rawls defines a "conception of justice as providing in the first instance a standard whereby the distributive aspects of the basic structure of society are to be assessed."[1] W.G. Runciman defines the problem of justice as "the problem of arriving at an ethical criterion by reference to which the distribution of social goods in societies may be assessed."[2] Bruce Ackerman defines the problem of justice initially as that of determining initial entitlements of a scarce resource, manna, which is convertible into any social good.[3]

William Galston makes more explicit than most theorists the logic of a distributive understanding of justice. Justice, he says, involves an ensemble of possessive relations. In a possessive relation the individual is distinct from the object possessed. Justice, he says, may be defined as rightful possession.[4] In such a possessive model the nature of the possessing subject is prior to and independent of the goods possessed; the self underlies and is unchanged by alternative distributions.[5] Justice concerns the proper pattern of the allocation of entities among such antecedently existing individuals. Or as Galston puts it, justice is

> the appropriate assignment of entities to individuals; appropriateness encompasses both the relation between some feature of entities and individuals under consideration and the relation between those entities and possible modes of assignment. The domain of entities may include objects, qualities, positions within a system, or even human beings.[6]

The distributive paradigm of justice so ensnares philosophical thinking that even critics of the dominant liberal framework continue to formulate the focus of justice in exclusively distributive terms. David Miller, for example, claims that liberal conceptions of justice tend to reflect the prevailing social relations, and argues for a more egalitarian conception of justice than traditional theories propose. Yet he also defines the subject matter of justice as "the manner in which benefits and burdens are distributed among persons, where such qualities and relationships can be investigated."[7] Even explicitly socialist or Marxist discussions of justice often fall under the distributive paradigm. In their discussion of justice under socialism, for example, Edward Nell and Onora O'Neill assume that the primary difference between socialist justice and capitalist liberal justice is in their principles of distribution.[8] Similarly, Kai Nielsen elaborates socialist principles of a radical egalitarian justice which have a primarily distributional focus.[9]

Michael Walzer is interestingly ambiguous in relation to the distributive paradigm.[10] Walzer asserts that philosophers' criticisms of the injustice of a social system usually amount to claims that a dominant good should be more widely distributed, that is, that monopoly is unjust. It is more appropriate, he says, to criticize the structure of dominance itself, rather than merely the distribution of the dominant good. Having one sort of social good—say, money—should not give one automatic access to other social goods. If the dominance of some goods over access to other goods is broken, then the monopoly of some group over a particular good may not be unjust. Walzer's analysis here has resonances with my concern to focus primarily on the social structures and processes that produce distributions rather than on the distributions. At the same time, however, Walzer repeatedly and unambiguously uses the language of distribution to discuss social justice, in sometimes reifying and strange ways. In his chapter on the family, for example, he speaks of the just distribution of love and affection.

Most theorists take it as given, then, that justice is about distributions. The paradigm assumes a single model for all analyses of justice: all situations in which justice is at issue

---

1   *"conception of justice ... to be assessed"*   [Unless otherwise noted, all notes are by the author of this selection.] John Rawls, *A Theory of Justice* (1971), p. 9.

2   *"the problem ... may be assessed"*   W.G. Runciman, "Processes, End States and Social Justice." *Philosophical Quarterly* 28 (January, 1978), p. 37.

3   *Bruce Ackerman ... any social good*   Bruce Ackerman, *Social Justice and the Liberal State* (1980), p. 25.

4   *William Galston ... rightful possession*   William Galston, *Justice and the Human Good* (1976), p. 5.

5   *In such ... alternative distributions*   cf. Michael Sandel, *Liberalism and the Limits of Justice* (1982).

6   *the appropriate assignment ... human beings*   Galston, *Justice and the Human Good*, p. 112.

7   *"the manner ... be investigated"*   David Miller, *Social Justice*. (1976), p. 19.

8   *Edward Nell and Onora O'Neill ... principles of distribution*   Edward Nell and Onora O'Neill, "Justice under Socialism," in James Sterba, ed., *Justice: Alternative Political Perspectives* (1980).

9   *Kai Nielsen ... distributional focus*   Kai Nielsen, in "Radical Egalitarian Justice: Justice as Equality." *Social Theory and Practice* 5 (Spring, 1979), pp. 209–26; and in *Liberty and Equality* (1985).

10   *Michael Walzer ... distributive paradigm*   See Michael Walzer, *Spheres of Justice* (1983), pp. 10–13.

are analogous to the situation of persons dividing a stock of goods and comparing the size of the portions individuals have. Such a model implicitly assumes that individuals or other agents lie as nodes, points in the social field, among whom larger or smaller bundles of social goods are assigned. The individuals are externally related to the goods they possess, and their only relation to one another that matters from the point of view of the paradigm is a comparison of the amount of goods they possess. The distributive paradigm thus implicitly assumes a social atomism,[1] inasmuch as there is no internal relation among persons in society relevant to considerations of justice.

The distributive paradigm is also pattern oriented. It evaluates justice according to the end-state pattern of persons and goods that appear on the social field. Evaluation of social justice involves comparing alternative patterns and determining which is the most just. Such a pattern-oriented conceptualization implicitly assumes a static conception of society.

I find two problems with this distributive paradigm, which I elaborate in the next two sections. First, it tends to ignore, at the same time that it often presupposes, the institutional context that determines material distributions. Second, when extended to nonmaterial goods and resources, the logic of distribution misrepresents them.

The Distributive Paradigm Presuppose and Obscures Institutional Context

Most theorizing about social justice focuses on the distribution of material resources, income, or positions of reward and prestige. Contemporary debates among theorists of justice, as Charles Taylor points out,[2] are inspired largely by two practical issues. First, is the distribution of wealth and income in advanced capitalist countries just, and if not, does justice permit or even require the provision of welfare services and other redistributive measures? Second, is the pattern of the distribution of positions of high income and prestige just, and if not, are affirmative action policies just means to rectify that injustice? Nearly all of the writers I cited earlier who define justice in distributive terms identify questions of the equality or inequality of wealth and income as the primary questions of social justice.[3] They usually subsume the second set of questions, about the justice of the distribution of social positions, under the question of economic distribution, since "more desirable" positions usually correspond to those that yield higher income or greater access to resources.

Applied discussions of justice too usually focus on the distribution of material goods and resources. Discussions of justice in medical care, for example, usually focus on the allocation of medical resources such as treatment, sophisticated equipment, expensive procedures, and so on.[4] Similarly, issues of justice enter discussion in environmental ethics largely through consideration of the impact that alternative policies might have on the distribution of natural and social resources among individuals and groups.[5]

As we shall see in detail in Chapter 3, the social context of welfare capitalist society helps account for this tendency to focus on the distribution of income and other resources. Public political dispute in welfare corporate society is largely restricted to issues of taxation, and the allocation of public funds among competing social interests. Public discussions of social injustice tend to revolve around inequalities of wealth and income, and the extent to which the state can or should mitigate the suffering of the poor.

There are certainly pressing reasons for philosophers to attend to these issues of the distribution of wealth and resources. In a society and world with vast differences in the amount of material goods to which individuals have access, where millions starve while others can have anything they want, any conception of justice must address the distribution of material goods. The immediate provision of basic material goods for people now suffering severe deprivation must be a first priority for any program that seeks to make the world more just. Such a call obviously entails considerations of distribution and redistribution.

---

1   *social atomism*   [editors' note] The approach that views social phenomena as arising, at core, from the actions and characteristics of individual people, seen as the basic "atoms"; this contrasts with theories that take relational properties of individuals—how they are connected to one another and to groups—and properties of groups, as basic, unanalyzed, unexplained by individual characteristics.

2   *Charles Taylor points out*   Charles Taylor, "The Nature and Scope of Distributive Justice," in *Philosophy and the Human Sciences* (1985).

3   *Nearly all ... social justice*   See also John Arthur and William Shaw, eds., *Justice and Economic Distribution* (1978).

4   *Discussions of justice ... and so on*   See, e.g., Norman Daniels, *Just Health Care* (1985), especially chapters 3 and 4.

5   *issues of justice ... individuals and groups*   See, e.g., Robert Simon, "Troubled Waters: Global Justice and Ocean Resources," in Tom Regan, ed., *Earthbound* (1984).

But in contemporary American society, many public appeals to justice do not concern primarily the distribution of material goods. Citizens in a rural Massachusetts town organize against a decision to site a huge hazardous waste treatment plant in their town. Their leaflets convince people that state law has treated the community unjustly by denying them the option of rejecting the plant.[1] Citizens in an Ohio city are outraged at the announcement that a major employer is closing down its plant. They question the legitimacy of the power of private corporate decision makers to throw half the city out of work without warning, and without any negotiation and consultation with the community. Discussion of possible compensation makes them snicker; the point is not simply that we are out of jobs and thus lack money, they claim, but that no private party should have the right to decide to decimate the local economy. Justice may require that former workers and other members of the community have the option of taking over and operating the plant themselves.[2] These two cases concern not so much the justice of material distributions as the justice of decisionmaking power and procedures.

Black critics claim that the television industry is guilty of gross injustice in its depictions of Blacks. More often than not, Blacks are represented as criminals, hookers, maids, scheming dealers, or jiving connivers. Blacks rarely appear in roles of authority, glamour, or virtue. Arab Americans are outraged at the degree to which television and film present recognizable Arabs only as sinister terrorists or gaudy princes, and conversely that terrorists are almost always Arab. Such outrage at media stereotyping issues in claims about the injustice not of material distribution, but of cultural imagery and symbols.

In an age of burgeoning computer technology, organizations of clerical workers argue that no person should have to spend the entirety of her working day in front of a computer terminal typing in a set of mindless numbers at monitored high speeds. This claim about injustice concerns not the distribution of goods, for the claim would still be made if VDT operators earned $30,000 annually. Here the primary issues of justice concern the structure of the division of labor and a right to meaningful work.

There are many such claims about justice and injustice in our society which are not primarily about the distribution of income, resources, or positions. A focus on the distribution of material goods and resources inappropriately restricts the scope of justice, because it fails to bring social structures and institutional contexts under evaluation. Several writers make this claim about distributive theories specifically with regard to their inability to bring capitalist institutions and class relations under evaluation. In his classic paper, for example, Allen Wood argues that for Marx justice refers only to superstructural juridical[3] relations of distribution, which are constrained by the underlying mode of production. Because they are confined to distribution, principles of justice cannot be used to evaluate the social relations of production themselves.[4]

Other writers criticize distributive theories of justice, especially Rawls's, for presupposing at the same time that they obscure the context of class inequality that the theories are unable to evaluate.[5] A distributive conception of justice is unable to bring class relations into view and evaluate them, Evan Simpson suggests, because its individualism prevents an understanding of structural phenomena, the "macroscopic transfer emerging from a complicated set of individual actions"[6] which cannot be understood in terms of any particular individual actions or acquisitions.

Many who make this Marxist criticism of the distributive focus of theories of justice conclude that justice is a concept of bourgeois ideology and thus not useful for a socialist normative analysis. Others disagree, and this dispute has occupied much of the Marxist literature on justice. I will argue later that a criticism of the distributive paradigm does not entail abandoning or transcending the concept of justice. For the moment I wish to focus on the point on

---

1   *Citizens in a rural ... the plant*   Iris Young, "Justice and Hazardous Waste," in Michael Bradie, ed., *The Applied Turn in Contemporary Philosophy* (1983).

2   *Citizens in an Ohio ... the plant themselves*   David Schweickart, "Plant Relocations: A Philosophical Reflection," *Review of Radical Political Economics* 16 (Winter, 1984), pp. 32–51.

3   *superstructural juridical*   [editors' note] "Superstructural" means having to do with what Marx called the superstructure—the social institutions—in this case, the juridical ones (having to do with laws and their enforcement) which are determined by the productive forces of the economic base.

4   *Allen Wood ... production themselves*   Allen Wood, "The Marxian Critique of Justice," *Philosophy and Public Affairs* 1 (Spring, 1972): 244–82. Cf. Robert Paul Wolff, *Understanding Rawls*, Princeton: Princeton University Press, 1977, pp. 199–208.

5   *Other writers ... unable to evaluate*   C.B. Macpherson, *Democratic Theory: Essays in Retrieval* (1973); and Kai Nielsen, "Class and Justice," in John Arthur and William Shaw, eds., *Justice and Economic Distribution* (1978).

6   *Evan Simpson ... individual actions*   Evan Simpson, "The Subject of Justice," *Ethics* 90 (July, 1980): p. 497.

which both sides in this dispute agree, namely, that predominant approaches to justice tend to presuppose and uncritically accept the relations of production that define an economic system.

The Marxist analysis of the distributive paradigm provides a fruitful starting point, but it is both too narrow and too general. On the one hand, capitalist class relations are not the only phenomena of social structure or institutional context that the distributive paradigm fails to evaluate. Some feminists point out, for example, that contemporary theories of justice presuppose family structure, without asking how social relations involving sexuality, intimacy, childrearing, and household labor ought best to be organized.[1] Like their forebears, contemporary liberal theorists of justice tend to presume that the units among which basic distributions take place are families, and that it is as family members, often heads of families, that individuals enter the public realm where justice operates.[2] Thus they neglect issues of justice within families—for example, the issue of whether the traditional sexual division of labor still presupposed by much law and employment policy is just.

While the Marxist criticism is too narrow, it is also too vague. The claim that the distributive paradigm fails to bring class relations under evaluation is too general to make clear what specific nondistributive issues are at stake. While property is something distributed, for example, in the form of goods, land, buildings, or shares of stock, the legal relations that define entitlement, possible forms of title, and so on are not goods to be distributed. The legal framework consists of rules defining practices and rights to make decisions about the disposition of goods. Class domination is certainly enacted by agents deciding where to invest their capital—a distributive decision; but the social rules, rights, procedures, and influences that structure capitalist decision making are not distributed goods. In order to understand and evaluate the institutional framework within which distributive issues arise, the ideas of "class" and "mode of production" must be concretized in terms of specific social processes and relations. In Chapter 7 I provide some concretization by addressing issues of the social division of labor.

The general criticism I am making of the predominant focus on the distribution of wealth, income, and positions is that such a focus ignores and tends to obscure the institutional context within which those distributions take place, and which is often at least partly the cause of patterns of distribution of jobs or wealth. Institutional context should be understood in a broader sense than "mode of production." It includes any structures or practices, the rules and norms that guide them, and the language and symbols that mediate social interactions within them, in institutions of state, family, and civil society, as well as the workplace. These are relevant to judgments of justice and injustice insofar as they condition people's ability to participate in determining their actions and their ability to develop and exercise their capacities.

Many discussions of social justice not only ignore the institutional contexts within which distributions occur, but often presuppose specific institutional structures whose justice they fail to bring under evaluation. Some political theories, for example, tend to assume centralized legislative and executive institutions separated from the day-to-day lives of most people in the society, and state officials with the authority to make and enforce policy decisions. They take for granted such institutions of the modern state as bureaucracies and welfare agencies for implementing and enforcing tax schemes and administering services.[3] Issues of the just organization of government institutions, and just methods of political decisionmaking, rarely get raised.

To take a different kind of example, to which I will return in Chapter 7, when philosophers ask about the just principles for allocating jobs and offices among persons, they typically assume a stratification of such positions. They assume a hierarchical division of labor in which some jobs and offices carry significant autonomy, decisionmaking power, authority, income, and access to resources, while others lack most of these attributes. Rarely do theorists explicitly ask whether such a definition and organization of social positions is just.

Many other examples of ways in which theorizing about justice frequently presupposes specific structural and institutional background conditions could be cited. In every case a clear understanding of these background conditions can reveal how they affect distribution—what there is to distribute, how it gets distributed, who distributes, and

---

1   *Some feminists ... to be organized*   See Susan Okin, "Are Our Theories of Justice Gender-neutral?" in Robert Fullinwider and Claudia Mills, eds., *The Moral Foundations of Civil Rights* (1986); and Carole Pateman, *The Sexual Contract* (1988), pp. 41–43.

2   *Like their forebears ... where justice operates*   Linda Nicholson, *Gender and History* (1986), chapter 4.

3   *They take ... administering services*   See, e.g., Rawls, *A Theory of Justice*, pp. 274–84.

what the distributive outcome is. With Michael Walzer, my intention here is "to shift our attention from distribution itself to conception and creation: the naming of the goods, the giving of meaning, and the collective making."[1] I shall focus most of my discussion on three primary categories of nondistributive issues that distributive theories tend to ignore: decisionmaking structure and procedures, division of labor, and culture.

Decisionmaking issues include not only questions of who by virtue of their positions have the effective freedom or authority to make what sorts of decisions, but also the rules and procedures according to which decisions are made. Discussion of economic justice, for example, often deemphasizes the decisionmaking structures which are crucial determinants of economic relations. Economic domination in our society occurs not simply or primarily because some persons have more wealth and income than others, as important as this is. Economic domination derives at least as much from the corporate and legal structures and procedures that give some persons the power to make decisions about investment, production, marketing, employment, interest rates, and wages that affect millions of other people. Not all who make these decisions are wealthy or even privileged, but the decisionmaking structure operates to reproduce distributive inequality and the unjust constraints on people's lives that in Chapter 2 I name exploitation and marginalization. As Carol Gould points out, rarely do theories of justice take such structures as an explicit focus.[2] In the chapters that follow I raise several specific issues of decisionmaking structure, and argue for democratic decisionmaking procedures as an element and condition of social justice.

Division of labor can be understood both distributively and nondistributively. As a distributive issue, division of labor refers to how pregiven occupations, jobs, or tasks are allocated among individuals or groups. As a nondistributive issue, on the other hand, division of labor concerns the definition of the occupations themselves. Division of labor as an institutional structure involves the range of tasks performed in a given position, the definition of the nature, meaning, and value of those tasks, and the relations of cooperation, conflict, and authority among positions. Feminist claims about the justice of a sexual division of labor, for example, have been posed both distributively and non

distributively. On the one hand, feminists have questioned the justice of a pattern of distribution of positions that finds a small proportion of women in the most prestigious jobs. On the other hand, they have also questioned the conscious or unconscious association of many occupations or jobs with masculine or feminine characteristics, such as instrumentality or affectivity, and this is not itself a distributive issue. In Chapter 2 I will discuss the justice of the division of labor in the context of exploitation. In Chapter 7 I consider the most important division of labor in advanced industrial societies, that between task definition and task execution.

Culture is the most general of the three categories of non distributive issues I focus on. It includes the symbols, images, meanings, habitual comportments, stories, and so on through which people express their experience and communicate with one another. Culture is ubiquitous, but nevertheless deserves distinct consideration in discussions of social justice. The symbolic meanings that people attach to other kinds of people and to actions, gestures, or institutions often significantly affect the social standing of persons and their opportunities. In Chapters 2, 4, 5, and 6 I explore the injustice of the cultural imperialism which marks and stereotypes some groups at the same time that it silences their self-expression.

Overextending the Concept of Distribution

The following objection might be made to my argument thus far. It may be true that philosophical discussions of justice tend to emphasize the distribution of goods and to ignore institutional issues of decision-making structure and culture. But this is not a necessary consequence of the distributive definition of justice. Theories of distributive justice can and should be applied to issues of social organization beyond the allocation of wealth, income, and resources. Indeed, this objection insists, many theorists explicitly extend the scope of distributive justice to such nonmaterial goods.

Rawls, for example, regards the subject of justice as "the way in which the major social institutions distribute fundamental rights and duties,"[3] and for him this clearly includes rights and duties related to decision-making, social positions, power, and so on, as well as wealth or income. Similarly, David Miller specifies that "the 'benefits' the distribution of which a conception of justice evaluates should

1   "to shift ... collective making"   Walzer, *Spheres of Justice*, p. 7.
2   *As Carol Gould ... explicit focus*   Carol Gould, *Rethinking Democracy: Freedom and Political Cooperation in Politics, Economics, and Society* (1988), pp. 133–34.

3   "the way ... rights and duties"   Rawls, *A Theory of Justice*, p. 7.

be taken to include intangible benefits such as prestige and self-respect."[1] William Galston, finally, insists that "issues of justice involve not only the distribution of property or income, but also such non-material goods as productive tasks, opportunities for development, citizenship, authority, honor, and so on."[2]

The distributive paradigm of justice may have a bias toward focusing on easily identifiable distributions, such as distributions of things, income, and jobs. Its beauty and simplicity, however, consists in its ability to accommodate any issue of justice, including those concerning culture, decisionmaking structures, and the division of labor. To do so the paradigm simply formulates the issue in terms of the distribution of some material or nonmaterial good among various agents. Any social value can be treated as some thing or aggregate of things that some specific agents possess in certain amounts, and alternative end-state patterns of distribution of that good among those agents can be compared. For example, neoclassical economists have developed sophisticated schemes for reducing all intentional action to a matter of maximizing a utility function in which the utility of all conceivable goods can be quantified and compared.

But this, in my view, is the main problem with the distributive paradigm: it does not recognize the limits to the application of a logic of distribution. Distributive theorists of justice agree that justice is the primary normative concept for evaluating all aspects of social institutions, but at the same time they identify the scope of justice with distribution. This entails applying a logic of distribution to social goods which are not material things or measurable quantities. Applying a logic of distribution to such goods produces a misleading conception of the issues of justice involved. It reifies aspects of social life that are better understood as a function of rules and relations than as things. And it conceptualizes social justice primarily in terms of end-state patterns, rather than focusing on social processes. This distributive paradigm implies a misleading or incomplete social ontology.[3]

But why should issues of social ontology matter for normative theorizing about justice? Any normative claims about society make assumptions about the nature of society, often only implicitly. Normative judgments of justice

are about something, and without a social ontology we do not know what they are about. The distributive paradigm implicitly assumes that social judgments are about what individual persons have, how much they have, and how that amount compares with what other persons have. This focus on possession tends to preclude thinking about what people are doing, according to what institutionalized rules, how their doings and havings are structured by institutionalized relations that constitute their positions, and how the combined effect of their doings has recursive[4] effects on their lives. Before developing this argument further, let us look at some examples of the application of the distributive paradigm to three nonmaterial goods frequently discussed by theorists of justice: rights, opportunity, and self-respect.

I quoted Rawls earlier to the effect that justice concerns the distribution of "rights and duties," and talk of distributing rights is by no means limited to him. But what does distributing a right mean? One may talk about having a right to a distributive share of material things, resources, or income. But in such cases it is the good that is distributed, not the right. What can it mean to distribute rights that do not refer to resources or things, like the right of free speech, or the right of trial by jury? We can conceive of a society in which some persons are granted these rights while others are not, but this does not mean that some people have a certain "amount" or "portion" of a good while others have less. Altering the situation so that everyone has these rights, moreover, would not entail that the formerly privileged group gives over some of its right of free speech or trial by jury to the rest of society's members, on analogy with a redistribuion of income.

Rights are not fruitfully conceived as possessions. Rights are relationships, not things; they are institutionally defined rules specifying what people can do in relation to one another. Rights refer to doing more than having, to social relationships that enable or constrain action.

Talk of distributing opportunities involves a similar confusion. If by opportunity we mean "chance," we can meaningfully talk of distributing opportunities, of some people having more opportunities than others, while some have none at all. When I go to the carnival I can buy three chances to knock over the kewpie doll, and my friend can buy six, and she will have more chances than I. Matters are rather different, however, with other opportunities. James

---

1   *David Miller ... and self-respect"*   Miller, *Social Justice*, p. 22.

2   *William Galston ... and so on"*   Galston, *Justice and the Human Good*, p. 6; cf. p. 116.

3   *ontology*   [editors' note] In philosophy, the branch of metaphysics dealing with the study of being or existence.

4   *recursive*   [editors' note] A "recursive" process is one that is applied to the previous product of its application, over and over.

Nickel defines opportunities as "states of affairs that combine the absence of insuperable obstacles with the presences of means—internal or external—that give one a chance of overcoming the obstacles that remain."[1] Opportunity in this sense is a condition of enablement, which usually involves a configuration of social rules and social relations, as well as an individual's self-conception and skills.

We may mislead ourselves by the fact that in ordinary language we talk about some people having "fewer" opportunities than others. When we talk that way, the opportunities sound like separable goods that can be increased or decreased by being given out or withheld, even though we know that opportunities are not allocated. Opportunity is a concept of enablement rather than possession; it refers to doing more than having. A person has opportunities if he or she is not constrained from doing things, and lives under the enabling conditions for doing them. Having opportunities in this sense certainly does often entail having material possessions, such as food, clothing, tools, land, or machines. Being enabled or constrained refers more directly, however, to the rules and practices that govern one's action, the way other people treat one in the context of specific social relations, and the broader structural possibilities produced by the confluence of a multitude of actions and practices. It makes no sense to speak of opportunities as themselves things possessed. Evaluating social justice according to whether persons have opportunities, therefore, must involve evaluating not a distributive outcome but the social structures that enable or constrain the individuals in relevant situations.[2]

Consider educational opportunity, for example. Providing educational opportunity certainly entails allocating specific material resources—money, buildings, books, computers, and so on—and there are reasons to think that the more resources, the wider the opportunities offered to children in an educational system. But education is primarily a process taking place in a complex context of social relations. In the cultural context of the United States, male children and female children, working-class children and middle-class children, Black children and white children often do not have equally enabling educational opportunities even when an equivalent amount of resources has been devoted to their education. This does not show that distribution is irrelevant to educational opportunity, only that opportunity has a wider scope than distribution.

Many writers on justice, to take a final example, not only regard self-respect as a primary good that all persons in a society must have if the society is to be just, but also talk of distributing self-respect. But what can it mean to distribute self-respect? Self-respect is not an entity or measurable aggregate, it cannot be parceled out of some stash, and above all it cannot be detached from persons as a separable attribute adhering to an otherwise unchanged substance. Self-respect names not some possession or attribute a person has, but her or his attitude toward her or his entire situation and life prospects. While Rawls does not speak of self-respect as something itself distributed, he does suggest that distributive arrangements provide the background conditions for self-respect.[3] It is certainly true that in many circumstances the possession of certain distributable material goods may be a condition of self-respect. Self-respect, however, also involves many nonmaterial conditions that cannot be reduced to distributive arrangements.[4]

People have or lack self-respect because of how they define themselves and how others regard them, because of how they spend their time, because of the amount of autonomy and decisionmaking power they have in their activities, and so on. Some of these factors can be conceptualized in distributive terms, but others cannot. Self-respect is at least as much a function of culture as it is of goods, for example, and in later chapters I shall discuss some elements of cultural imperialism that undermine the self-respect of many persons in our society. The point here is that none of the forms and not all of the conditions of self-respect can meaningfully be conceived as goods that individuals possess; they are rather relations and processes in which the actions of individuals are embedded.

These, then, are the general problems with extending the concept of distribution beyond material goods or measurable quantities to nonmaterial values. First, doing

---

1   *"states of affairs ... obstacles that remain."*   James Nickel, "Equal Opportunity in a Pluralistic Society," in Ellen Frankel Paul, Fred D. Miller, Jeffrey Paul, and John Ahrens, eds., *Equal Opportunity* (1988), p. 110.

2   *Evaluating social justice ... relevant situations*   See Evan Simpson, "The Subject of Justice," and Jeffrey Reiman, "Exploitation, Force, and the Moral Assessment of Capitalism: thoughts on Roemer and Cohen," *Philosophy and Public Affairs* 16 (Winter, 1987): pp. 3–41.

3   *Rawls does not ... for self-respect*   Rawls, *A Theory of Justice*, pp. 148–50.

4   *Self-respect ... distributive arrangements*   See Michael Howard, "Worker Control, Self-Respect, and Self-Esteem," *Philosophy Research Archives* 10 (1985): pp. 455–72.

so reifies social relations and institutional rules. Something identifiable and assignable must be distributed. In accord with its implicit social ontology that gives primacy to substance over relations, moreover, the distributive paradigm tends to conceive of individuals as social atoms, logically prior to social relations and institutions. As Galston makes clear in the passage I quoted earlier,[1] conceiving justice as a distribution of goods among individuals involves analytically separating the individuals from those goods. Such an atomistic conception of the individual as a substance to which attributes adhere fails to appreciate that individual identities and capacities are in many respects themselves the products of social processes and relations. Societies do not simply distribute goods to persons who are what they are apart from society, but rather constitute individuals in their identities and capacities.[2] In the distributive logic, however, there is little room for conceiving persons' enablement or constraint as a function of their relations to one another. As we shall see in Chapter 2, such an atomistic social ontology ignores or obscures the importance of social groups for understanding issues of justice.

Second, the distributive paradigm must conceptualize all issues of justice in terms of patterns. It implies a static social ontology that ignores processes. In the distributive paradigm individuals or other agents lie as points in the social field, among whom larger or smaller packets of goods are assigned. One evaluates the justice of the pattern by comparing the size of the packages individuals have and comparing the total pattern to other possible patterns of assignment.

Robert Nozick argues that such a static or end-state approach to justice is inappropriately ahistorical.[3] End-state approaches to justice, he argues, operate as though social goods magically appear and get distributed. They ignore the processes that create the goods and produce distributive patterns, which they find irrelevant for evaluating justice. For Nozick, only the process is relevant to evaluating distributions. If individuals begin with holdings they are justly entitled to, and undertake free exchanges, then the distributive outcomes are just, no matter what they are. This entitlement theory shares with other theories a possessively individualist social ontology. Society consists only of individuals with "holdings" of social goods which they augment or reduce through individual production and contractual exchange. The theory does not take into account structural effects of the actions of individuals that they cannot foresee or intend, and to which they might not agree if they could. Nevertheless, Nozick's criticism of end-state theories for ignoring social processes is apt.

Important and complex consequences ensue when a theory of justice adopts a narrowly static social ontology. Anthony Giddens claims that social theory in general has lacked a temporal conceptualization of social relations.[4] Action theorists have developed sophisticated accounts of social relations from the point of view of acting subjects with intentions, purposes, and reasons, but they have tended to abstract from the temporal flow of everyday life, and instead talk about isolated acts of isolated individuals. For a theory of justice, this means ignoring the relevance of institutions to justice. Structuralism and functionalist social theories, on the other hand, provide conceptual tools for identifying and explaining social regularities and large-scale institutional patterns. Because they also abstract from the temporal flow of everyday interaction, however, they tend to hypostatize these regularities and patterns and often fail to connect them with accounts of individual action. For a theory of justice, this means separating institutions from choice and normative judgment. Only a social theory that takes process seriously, Giddens suggests, can understand the relation between social structures and action. Individuals are not primarily receivers of goods or carriers of properties, but actors with meanings and purposes, who act with, against, or in relation to one another. We act with knowledge of existing institutions, rules, and the structural consequences of a multiplicity of actions, and those structures are enacted and reproduced through the confluence of our actions. Social theory should conceptualize action as a producer and reproducer of structures, which only exist in action; social action, on the other hand, has those structures and relationships as background, medium, or purpose.

This identification of a weakness in traditional social theory can be applied to the distributive paradigm of justice.

---

1   *Galston makes ... quoted earlier*   Galston, *Justice and the Human Good*, p. 112.

2   *Societies do not ... identities and capacities*   See Sandel, *Liberalism and the Limits of Justice*; and Charles Taylor, "The Nature and Scope of Distributive Justice."

3   *Robert Nozick ... inappropriately ahistorical*   Robert Nozick, *Anarchy, State, and Utopia* (1974), chapter 7.

4   *Anthony Giddens ... social relations*   Anthony Giddens, *Central Problems of Social Theory* (1976), chapter 2; and Giddens, *The Constitution of Society* (1984), chapters 3 and 4.

I disagree with Nozick that end-state patterns are irrelevant to questions of justice. Because they inhibit the ability of some people to live and be healthy, or grant some people resources that allow them to coerce others, some distributions must come into question no matter how they came about. Evaluating patterns of distribution is often an important starting point for questioning about justice. For many issues of social justice, however, what is important is not the particular pattern of distribution at a particular moment, but rather the reproduction of a regular distributive pattern over time.

For example, unless one begins with the assumption that all positions of high status, income, and decisionmaking power ought to be distributed in comparable numbers to women and men, finding that very few top corporate managers are women might not involve any question of injustice. It is in the context of a social change involving more acceptance of women in corporate management, and a considerable increase in the number of women who obtain degrees in business, that a question of injustice becomes most apparent here. Even though more women earn degrees in business, and in-house policies of some companies aim to encourage women's careers, a pattern of distribution of managerial positions that clusters women at the bottom and men at the top persists. Assuming that justice ultimately means equality for women, this pattern is puzzling, disturbing. We are inclined to ask: what's going on here? why is this general pattern reproduced even in the face of conscious efforts to change it? Answering that question entails evaluation of a matrix of rules, attitudes, interactions, and policies as a social process that produces and reproduces that pattern. An adequate conception of justice must be able to understand and evaluate the processes as well as the patterns.

One might object that this account confuses the empirical issue of what causes a particular distribution with the normative issue of whether the distribution is just. As will be apparent in the chapters that follow, however, in the spirit of critical social theory I do not accept this division between empirical and normative social theory. While there is a distinction between empirical and normative statements and the kinds of reasons required for each, no normative theory meant to evaluate existing societies can avoid empirical inquiry, and no empirical investigation of social structures and relations can avoid normative judgments. Inquiry about social justice must consider the context and causes of actual distributions in order to make normative judgments about institutional rules and relations.

The pattern orientation of the distributive paradigm, then, tends to lead to abstraction from institutional rules and relations and a consequent failure to bring them into evaluation. For many aspects of social structure and institutional context cannot be brought into view without examining social processes and the unintended cumulative consequences of individual actions. Without a more temporal approach to social reality, for example, as we shall see in Chapter 2, a theory of justice cannot conceptualize exploitation, as a social process by which the labor of some unreciprocally supports the privilege of others.

Problems with Talk of Distributing Power

I have argued that regarding such social values as rights, opportunities, and self-respect as distributable obscures the institutional and social bases of these values. Some theorists of justice might respond to my criticism of the distributive paradigm as follows: What is in question is indeed not goods, but social power; the distributive paradigm, however, can accommodate these issues by giving more attention to the distribution of power. Certainly I agree that many of the issues I have said are confused or obscured by the distributive paradigm concern social power. While talk of the distribution of power is common, however, I think this is a particularly clear case of the misleading and undesirable implications of extending the concept of distribution beyond material goods.

Distributional theorists of justice disagree on how to approach power. Some explicitly exclude power from the scope of their theories. David Miller, for example, claims that questions of power are not questions of social justice per se, but concern the causes of justice and injustice.[1] Ronald Dworkin explicitly brackets issues of power in his discussion of equality, and chooses to consider only issues of welfare, the distribution of goods, services, income, and so on.[2]

Other philosophers and political theorists, however, clearly include questions of power within the scope of the concept of justice. Many would agree that a theory of justice must be concerned not only with end-state patterns,

1   *David Miller ... justice and injustice*   David Miller, *Social Justice*, p. 22.

2   *Ronald Dworkin ... income, and so on*   Ronald Dworkin, "What Is Equality? Part 1," *Philosophy and Public Affairs* 10 (Summer, 1981): pp. 185–246.

but also with the institutional relations that produce distributions. Their approach to such questions takes the form of assessing the distribution of power in a society or a specific institutional context.

Talk about power in terms of distribution is so common that it does not warrant special notice. The following passage from William Connolly's *Terms of Political Discourse* is typical:

> When one speaks of a power structure one conveys, first, the idea that power in at least some domains is distributed unequally; second, that those with more power in one domain are likely to have it in several important domains as well; third, that such a distribution is relatively persistent; and fourth (but not necessarily), that there is more than a random connection between the distribution of power and the distribution of income, status, privilege, and wealth in the system under scrutiny.[1]

Common though it is, bringing power under the logic of distribution, I suggest, misconstrues the meaning of power. Conceptualizing power in distributive terms means implicitly or explicitly conceiving power as a kind of stuff possessed by individual agents in greater or lesser amounts. From this perspective a power structure or power relations will be described as a pattern of the distribution of this stuff. There are a number of problems with such a model of power.

First, regarding power as a possession or attribute of individuals tends to obscure the fact that power is a relation rather than a thing.[2] While the exercise of power may sometimes depend on the possession of certain resources—money, military equipment, and so on—such resources should not be confused with power itself. The power consists in a relationship between the exerciser and others through which he or she communicates intentions and meets with their acquiescence.

Second, the atomistic bias of distributive paradigms of power leads to a focus on particular agents or roles that have power, and on agents over whom these powerful agents or roles have power. Even when they recognize its relational character, theorists often treat power as a dyadic relation, on the model of ruler and subject. This dyadic modeling of power misses the larger structure of agents and actions that mediates between two agents in a power relation.[3] One agent can have institutionalized power over another only if the actions of many third agents support and execute the will of the powerful. A judge may be said to have power over a prisoner, but only in the context of a network of practices executed by prison wardens, guards, recordkeepers, administrators, parole officers, lawyers, and so on. Many people must do their jobs for the judge's power to be realized, and many of these people will never directly interact with either the judge or the prisoner. A distributive understanding of power as a possession of particular individuals or groups misses this supporting and mediating function of third parties.

A distributive understanding of power, which treats power as some kind of stuff that can be traded, exchanged, and distributed, misses the structural phenomena of domination.[4] By domination I mean structural or systemic phenomena which exclude people from participating in determining their actions or the conditions of their actions.[5] Domination must be understood as structural precisely because the constraints that people experience are usually the intended or unintended product of the actions of many people, like the actions which enable the judge's power. In saying that power and domination have a structural basis, I do not deny that it is individuals who are powerful and who dominate. Within a system of domination some people can be identified as more powerful and others as relatively powerless. Nevertheless a distributive understanding misses the way in which the powerful enact and reproduce their power.

The structured operation of domination whose resources the powerful draw upon must be understood as a process. A distributive conceptualization of power, however, can construct power relations only as patterns. As Thomas Wartenburg argues, conceptualizing power as relational rather than substantive, as produced and reproduced through many people outside the immediate power dyad, brings out the dynamic nature of power relations as an ongoing process.[6]

---

1   *When one ... under scrutiny.*   William Connolly, *The Terms of Political Discourse*, 2d ed. (1983), p. 117.

2   *regarding power ... a thing*   Peter Bachrach and Morton Baratz, "Two Faces of Power," in Roderick Bell, David Edwards, and Harrison Wagner, eds., *Political Power*, New York: Free Press, 1969.

3   *This dyadic modeling ... power relation*   Thomas E. Wartenburg, *The Forms of Power: An Essay in Social Ontology* (1989), chap. 7.

4   *A distributive understanding ... phenomena of domination*   Nancy Hartsock, *Money, Sex and Power* (1983).

5   *By domination ... of their actions*   See Wartenburg, *The Forms of Power*, chapter 6.

6   *Thomas Wartenburg ... an ongoing process*   See Wartenburg, *The Forms of Power*, chapter 9.

A distributive understanding of power obscures the fact that, as Foucault puts it, power exists only in action:[1]

> What, by contrast, should always be kept in mind is that power, if we do not take too distant a view of it, is not that which makes the difference between those who exclusively possess and retain it, and those who do not have it and submit to it. Power must be analyzed as something that circulates, or rather something which only functions in the form of a chain. It is never localized here or there, never in anybody's hands, never appropriated as a commodity or piece of wealth. Power is employed and exercised through a net-like organization. And not only do individuals circulate between its threads; they are always in the position of simultaneously undergoing and exercising their power.[2]

The logic of distribution, in contrast, makes power a machine or instrument, held in ready and turned on at will, independently of social processes.

Finally, a distributive understanding of power tends to conceive a system of domination as one in which power, like wealth, is concentrated in the hands of a few. Assuming such a condition is unjust, a redistribution of power is called for, which will disperse and decentralize power so that a few individuals or groups no longer have all or most of the power. For some systems of domination such a model may be appropriate. As I will argue in the next two chapters, however, it is not appropriate for understanding the operation of domination and oppression in contemporary welfare corporate societies. For these societies witness the ironic situation in which power is widely dispersed and diffused, yet social relations are tightly defined by domination and oppression. When power is understood as "productive," as a function of dynamic processes of interaction within regulated cultural and decisionmaking situations, then it is possible to say that many widely dispersed persons are agents of power without "having" it, or even being privileged. Without a structural understanding of power and domination as processes rather than patterns of distribution, the existence and nature of domination and oppression in these societies cannot be identified.

Defining Injustice as Domination and Oppression

Because distributive models of power, rights, opportunity, and self-respect work so badly, justice should not be conceived primarily on the model of the distribution of wealth, income, and other material goods. Theorizing about justice should explicitly limit the concept of distribution to material goods, like things, natural resources, or money. The scope of justice is wider than distributive issues. Though there may be additional nondistributive issues of justice, my concerns in this book focus on issues of decisionmaking, division of labor, and culture.

Political thought of the modern period greatly narrowed the scope of justice as it had been conceived by ancient and medieval thought. Ancient thought regarded justice as the virtue of society as a whole, the wellorderedness of institutions that foster individual virtue and promote happiness and harmony among citizens. Modern political thought abandoned the notion that there is a natural order to society that corresponds to the proper ends of human nature. Seeking to liberate the individual to define "his" own ends, modern political theory also restricted the scope of justice to issues of distribution and the minimal regulation of action among such self-defining individuals.[3]

While I hardly intend to revert to a full-bodied Platonic conception of justice, I nevertheless think it is important to broaden the understanding of justice beyond its usual limits in contemporary philosophical discourse. Agnes Heller proposes one such broader conception in what she calls an incomplete ethico-political concept of justice.[4] According to her conception, justice names not principles of distribution, much less some particular distributive pattern. This represents too narrow and substantive a way of reflecting on justice. Instead, justice names the perspectives, principles, and procedures for evaluating institutional norms

1   *A distributive understanding ... only in action*   Michel Foucault *Power/Knowledge* (1980), p. 89. See Barry Smart, *Foucault, Marxism, and Critique* (1983), chap. 5; and Jana Sawicki, "Foucault and Feminism: Toward a Politics of Difference," *Hypatia: A Journal of Feminist Philosophy* 1 (Summer, 1986): pp. 23–36.

2   *What, by contrast ... exercising their power*   Foucault, *Power/Knowledge*, p. 98.

3   *Seeking to liberate ... self-defining individuals*   Agnes Heller, *Beyond Justice* (1987), chapter 2; and see Alasdair MacIntyre, *After Virtue* (1981), chapter 17.

4   *Agnes Heller ... concept of justice*   Agnes Heller, *Beyond Justice*, chapter 5.

and rules. Developing Habermas's communicative ethics,[1] Heller suggests that justice is primarily the virtue of citizenship, of persons deliberating about problems and issues that confront them collectively in their institutions and actions, under conditions without domination or oppression, with reciprocity and mutual tolerance of difference. She proposes the following test of the justice of social or political norms:

> Every valid social and political norm and rule (every law) must meet the condition that the foreseeable consequences and side effects the general observance of that law (norm) exacts on the satisfaction of the needs of each and every individual would be accepted by everyone concerned, and that the claim of the norm to actualize the universal values of freedom and/or life could be accepted by each and every individual, regardless of the values to which they are committed.[2]

In the course of this book I shall raise some critical questions about the ideas of citizenship, agreement, and universality embedded in the radically democratic ideal which Habermas and Heller, along with others, express. Nevertheless, I endorse and follow this general conception of justice derived from a conception of communicative ethics. The idea of justice here shifts from a focus on distributive patterns to procedural issues of participation in deliberation and decision making. For a norm to be just, everyone who follows it must in principle have an effective voice in its consideration and be able to agree to it without coercion. For a social condition to be just, it must enable all to meet their needs and exercise their freedom; thus justice requires that all be able to express their needs.

As I understand it, the concept of justice coincides with the concept of the political. Politics as I defined it in the Introduction includes all aspects of institutional organization, public action, social practices and habits, and cultural meanings insofar as they are potentially subject to collective evaluation and decisionmaking. Politics in this inclusive sense certainly concerns the policies and actions of government and the state, but in principle can also concern rules, practices, and actions in any other institutional context.[3]

The scope of justice, I have suggested, is much wider than distribution, and covers everything political in this sense. This coheres with the meaning of justice claims of the sort mentioned at the outset of this chapter. When people claim that a particular rule, practice, or cultural meaning is wrong and should be changed, they are often making a claim about social injustice. Some of these claims involve distributions, but many also refer to other ways in which social institutions inhibit or liberate persons.

Some writers concur that distribution is too narrow a focus for normative evaluation of social institutions, but claim that going beyond this distributive focus entails going beyond the norms of justice per se. Charles Taylor, for example, distinguishes questions of distributive justice from normative questions about the institutional framework of society.[4] Norms of justice help resolve disputes about entitlements and deserts within a particular institutional context. They cannot evaluate that institutional context itself, however, because it embodies a certain conception of human nature and the human good. According to Taylor, confusions arise in theoretical and political discussion when norms of distributive justice are applied across social structures and used to evaluate basic structures. For example, both right and left critics of our society charge it with perpetrating injustices, but according to Taylor the normative perspective from which each side speaks involves a project to construct different institutional forms corresponding to specific conceptions of the human good, a project beyond merely articulating principles of justice.

From a somewhat different perspective, Seyla Benhabib suggests that a normative social theory which evaluates institutions according to whether they are free from domination, meet needs, and provide conditions of emancipation entails going beyond justice as understood by the modern tradition.[5] Because this broader normative social theory entails a critique of culture and socialization in addition to critiques of formal rights and patterns of distribution, it merges questions of justice with questions of the good life.

---

1 *Habermas's communicative ethics* [editors' note] Jürgen Habermas (1929–), German social philosopher and sociologist, associated with the "Frankfurt School." His discourse ethics is based on a theory of communicative action in which the validity of moral norms is determined by the intersubjective, uncoerced agreement of participants in public debate. See the introduction to his work in this anthology.

2 *Every valid ... they are committed.* Agnes Heller, *Beyond Justice*, pp. 240–41.

3 *Politics in this ... institutional context* See Ronald Mason, *Participatory and Workplace Democracy* (1982), pp. 11–24.

4 *Charles Taylor ... framework of society* Charles Taylor, "The Nature and Scope of Distributive Justice."

5 *Seyla Benhabib ... the modern tradition* Seyla Benhabib, *Critique, Norm and Utopia* (1986), pp. 330–36.

I am sympathetic with both these discussions, as well as with Michael Sandel's related argument for recognizing the "limits" of justice and the importance of conceptualizing normative aspects of the self in social contexts that lie beyond those limits.[1] But while I share these writers' general critique of liberal theories of distributive justice, I see no reason to conclude with Taylor and Sandel that this critique reveals the limits of the concept of justice which a normative social philosophy must transcend. I disagree to some extent, moreover, with Taylor's and Benhabib's suggestion that such a wider normative social philosophy merges questions of justice with questions of the good life.

Like many other writers cited earlier in this chapter, Taylor assumes that justice and distribution are coextensive, and therefore that broader issues of institutional context require other normative concepts. Many Marxist theorists who argue that justice is a merely bourgeois concept take a similar position. Whether normative theorists who focus attention on issues of decisionmaking, division of labor, culture, and social organization beyond the distribution of goods call these issues of justice or not is clearly a matter of choice. I can give only pragmatic reasons for my own choice.

Since Plato "justice" has evoked the well-ordered society, and it continues to carry those resonances in contemporary political discussion. Appeals to justice still have the power to awaken a moral imagination and motivate people to look at their society critically, and ask how it can be made more liberating and enabling. Philosophers interested in nurturing this emancipatory imagination and extending it beyond questions of distribution should, I suggest, lay claim to the term justice rather than abandon it.

To a certain extent Heller, Taylor, and Benhabib are right that a postmodern turn to an enlarged conception of justice, reminiscent of the scope of justice in Plato and Aristotle, entails more attention to the definition of ends than the liberal conception of justice allows. Nevertheless, questions of justice do not merge with questions of the good life. The liberal commitment to individual freedom, and the consequent plurality of definitions of the good, must be preserved in any reenlarged conception of justice. The modern restriction of the concept of justice to formal and instrumental principles was meant to promote the value of individual self-definition of ends, or "plans of life," as Rawls calls them. In displacing reflection about justice from a primary focus on distribution to include all institutional and social relations insofar as they are subject to collective decision, I do not mean to suggest that justice should include all moral norms in its scope. Social justice in the sense I intend continues to refer only to institutional conditions, and not to the preferences and ways of life of individuals or groups.

Any normative theorist in the postmodern world is faced with a dilemma. On the one hand, we express and justify norms by appealing to certain values derived from a conception of the good human life. In some sense, then, any normative theory implicitly or explicitly relies on a conception of human nature.[2] On the other hand, it would seem that we should reject the very idea of a human nature as misleading or oppressive.

Any definition of a human nature is dangerous because it threatens to devalue or exclude some acceptable individual desires, cultural characteristics, or ways of life. Normative social theory, however, can rarely avoid making implicit or explicit assumptions about human beings in the formulation of its vision of just institutions. Even though the distributive paradigm carries an individualist conception of society, which considers individual desires and preferences private matters outside the sphere of rational discourse, it assumes a quite specific conception of human nature. It implicitly defines human beings as primarily consumers, desirers, and possessors of goods.[3] C.B. Macpherson argues that in presupposing such a possessively individualist view of human nature the original liberal theorists hypostatized the acquisitive values of emergent capitalist social relations.[4] Contemporary capitalism, which depends more upon widespread indulgent consumption than its penny-pinching Protestant ancestor, continues to presuppose an understanding of human beings as primarily utility maximizers.[5]

The idea of human beings that guides normative social theorizing under the distributive paradigm is an image, rather than an explicit theory of human nature. It makes plausible to the imagination both the static picture of social relations entailed by this distributive paradigm and the notion of separate individuals already formed apart from social goods.

1   *Michael Sandel's ... beyond those limits*   Sandel, *Liberalism and the Limits of Justice*.

2   *any normative theory ... human nature*   See Alison Jaggar, *Feminist Politics and Human Nature* (1983), pp. 18–22.

3   *It implicitly ... possessors of goods*   Agnes Heller, *Beyond Justice*, pp. 180–82.

4   *C.B. Macpherson ... social relations*   C.B. Macpherson, *The Political Theory of Possessive Individualism* (1962).

5   *Contemporary capitalism ... utility maximizers*   Charles Taylor, "The Nature and Scope of Distributive Justice."

Displacing the distributive paradigm in favor of a wider, process-oriented understanding of society, which focuses on power, decisionmaking structures, and so on, likewise shifts the imagination to different assumptions about human beings. Such an imaginative shift could be as oppressive as consumerist images if it is made too concrete. As long as the values we appeal to are abstract enough, however, they will not devalue or exclude any particular culture or way of life.

Persons certainly are possessors and consumers, and any conception of justice should presume the value of meeting material needs, living in a comfortable environment, and experiencing pleasures. Adding an image of people as doers and actors[1] helps to displace the distributive paradigm. As doers and actors, we seek to promote many values of social justice in addition to fairness in the distribution of goods: learning and using satisfying and expansive skills in socially recognized settings; participating in forming and running institutions, and receiving recognition for such participation; playing and, communicating with others, and expressing our experience, feelings, and perspective on social life in contexts where others can listen. Certainly many distributive theorists of justice would recognize and affirm these values. The framework of distribution, however, leads to a deemphasizing of these values and a failure to inquire about the institutional conditions that promote them.

This, then, is how I understand the connection between justice and the values that constitute the good life. Justice is not identical with the concrete realization of these values in individual lives; justice, that is, is not identical with the good life as such. Rather, social justice concerns the degree to which a society contains and supports the institutional conditions necessary for the realization of these values. The values comprised in the good life can be reduced to two very general ones: (1) developing and exercising one's capacities and expressing one's experience,[2] and (2) participating in determining one's action and the conditions of one's action.[3] These are universalist values, in the sense that they assume the equal moral worth of all persons, and thus justice requires their promotion for everyone. To these two general values correspond two social conditions that define injustice: oppression, the institutional constraint on self-development, and domination, the institutional constraint on self-determination.

Oppression consists in systematic institutional processes which prevent some people from learning and using satisfying and expansive skills in socially recognized settings, or institutionalized social processes which inhibit people's ability to play and communicate with others or to express their feelings and perspective on social life in contexts where others can listen. While the social conditions of oppression often include material deprivation or maldistribution, they also involve issues beyond distribution, as I shall show in Chapter 2.

Domination consists in institutional conditions which inhibit or prevent people from participating in determining their actions or the conditions of their actions. Persons live within structures of domination if other persons or groups can determine without reciprocation the conditions of their action, either directly or by virtue of the structural consequences of their actions. Thorough social and political democracy is the opposite of domination. In Chapter 3 I discuss some of the issues of decisionmaking that contemporary welfare state politics ignores, and show how insurgent social movements frequently address issues of domination rather than distribution.

As will become clear in the chapters that follow, I think the concepts of oppression and domination overlap, but there is nevertheless reason to distinguish them. Oppression usually includes or entails domination, that is, constraints upon oppressed people to follow rules set by others. But each face of oppression that I shall discuss in Chapter 2 also involves inhibitions not directly produced by relations of domination. As should become clear in that chapter, moreover, not everyone subject to domination is also oppressed. Hierarchical decision-making structures subject most people in our society to domination in some important aspect of their lives. Many of those people nevertheless enjoy significant institutionalized support for the development and exercise of their capacities and their ability to express themselves and be heard.

---

1   *Adding an image ... doers and actors*   C.B. Macpherson, *Democratic Theory: Essays in Retrieval*; and Samuel Bowles and Herbert Gintis, "Crisis of Liberal Democratic Capitalism: The Case of the United States," *Politics and Society* 11 (1986): pp. 51–94.

2   *developing and exercising ... one's experience*   See Gould, *Rethinking Democracy*, chapter 2; and Galston, *Justice and the Human Good*, pp. 61–69.

3   *participating in determining ... one's action*   See Iris Young, "Self-Determination as a Principle of Justice," *Philosophical Forum* 11 (Fall, 1979): pp. 172–82.

CATHARINE MACKINNON
(1946–)

Catharine MacKinnon offers a feminist analysis of gender as social power—a concept whose key feature is the subordination of women's sexuality. According to MacKinnon, femininity is socially constructed as sexual subordination, and masculinity as sexual dominance. Thus the very existence of men and women as social categories presumes women's inferiority. MacKinnon applies her analysis to issues such as abortion, rape, sexual harrassment, abuse, domestic battery, and pornography.

MacKinnon's work has been highly influential in shaping public policy. With Andrea Dworkin, she wrote an ordinance for the City Council of Indianapolis that addressed pornography as a civil rights issue and that would allow women who had been harmed by pornography to bring lawsuits in federal civil court. The ordinance was passed by the Indianapolis City Council (1984) but was found unconstitutional by an Indiana federal court (*American Booksellers v. Hudnut* 1984). Her analysis of pornography influenced the Canadian Supreme Court's interpretation of obscenity (*R v. Butler*, 1992) and her analysis of sexual harrassment as a form of sex discrimination had a significant impact on the US Supreme Court's approach to sexual harrassment. She is a practicing lawyer who defended Bosnian women survivors of Serb rape, successfully winning damages for rape as genocide (*Kadic v. Karazdic*, 2000).

MacKinnon holds a BA from Smith College (1968) a JD from Yale (1977) and a PhD in Political Science from Yale (1987). She has taught at many universities including Yale, Harvard, Stanford, UCLA, Chicago, and Michigan. Her scholarly works include *Feminism Unmodified* (1987), *Towards a Feminist Theory of the State (1989), Only Words* (1993), *Women's Lives, Men's Laws* (2005), and *Are Women Human?: And Other International Dialogues* (2006).

MacKinnon's main theoretical contribution to feminism is her dominance approach to equality. According to MacKinnon, gender is created by the eroticization of dominance and submission. Women are defined in terms of male sexual desire, which in turn is defined as dominance. Thus women's social role, according to MacKinnon, is sexual availability to men. MacKinnon has been sometimes crticized for focusing too narrowly on sex and sexuality but her approach has been remarkably fruitful for critiquing standard approaches to equality and consequently for rethinking a number of feminist issues.

The standard liberal approach to equality requires that people be treated equally in the absence of relevant differences. What MacKinnon's dominance/subordination thesis implies is that women's very existence consists in their difference, defined as inequality; hence women's equality on the standard view appears as a kind of oxymoron. The liberal view does not allow issues such as pornography, rape, and sexual harrassment to become visible as forms of social inequality. But once we understand that women are socially constructed as dominated we can relocate a variety of feminist issues. Pornography can be reformulated as part of the structure that creates women as subordinate (rather than protected as a matter of free speech); sexual harrassment can be reformulated as a kind of sex discrimination (not treated merely as a matter of individual intimidation); and the issue of abortion can be reformulated in relation to the conditions of subordination under which women become pregnant and raise children (not dealt with merely as a matter of the respective rights of mothers and fetuses).

MacKinnon, in short, has stimulated a wide-ranging rethinking of the connections between gender and power—a rethinking that has profound social and political implications.

◆ ◆ ◆ ◆ ◆

Abortion: On Public and Private (1989)

In a society where women entered sexual intercourse willingly, where adequate contraception was a genuine social priority, there would be no "abortion issue" ... Abortion is violence ... It is the offspring, and will continue to be the accuser of a more pervasive and prevalent violence, the violence of rapism.

—Adrienne Rich, *Of Woman Born*
(New York: Norton, 1976)

Most women who seek abortions became pregnant while having sexual intercourse with men. Most did not mean or wish to conceive. In women's experience, sexuality and reproduction are inseparable from each other and from gender. The abortion debate, by contrast, has centered on separating control over sexuality from control over reproduction, and on separating both from gender. Liberals have supported the availability of the abortion choice as if the woman just happened on the fetus,[1] usually on the implicit view that reproductive control is essential to sexual freedom and economic independence. The political right imagines that the intercourse that precedes conception is usually voluntary, only to urge abstinence, as if sex were up to women. At the same time, the right defends male authority, specifically including a wife's duty to submit to sex. Continuing this logic, many opponents of state funding of abortions would permit funding of abortions when pregnancy results from rape or incest.[2] They make exceptions for those special occasions on which they presume women did not control sex. Abortion's proponents and opponents share a tacit assumption that women significantly control sex.

Feminist investigations suggest otherwise. Sexual intercourse, still the most common cause of pregnancy, cannot simply be presumed coequally determined. Women feel compelled to preserve the appearance—which, acted upon, becomes the reality—of male direction of sexual expression, as if it were male initiative itself that women want, as if it were that which women find arousing. Men enforce this. It is much of what men want in a woman, what pornography eroticizes and prostitutes provide. Rape—that is, intercourse with force that is recognized as force—is adjudicated not according to the power or force that the man wields, but according to indices of intimacy between the parties. The more intimate one is with one's accused rapist, the less likely a court is to find that what happened was rape. Often indices of intimacy include intercourse itself. If "no" can be taken as "yes," how free can "yes" be?

Under these conditions, women often do not use birth control because of its social meaning, a meaning women did not create. Using contraception means acknowledging and planning the possibility of intercourse, accepting one's sexual availability, and appearing non-spontaneous. It means appearing available to male incursions. It also means that one must want to have sex. A good user of contraception can be presumed sexually available and, among other consequences, raped with relative impunity. (Doubters should consider rape cases in which the fact that a woman had a diaphragm in is taken as an indication that what happened to her was intercourse, not rape.) Studies of abortion clinics show that women who repeatedly seek abortions, especially the repeat offenders high on the list of the right's villains—their best case for opposing abortion as female sexual irresponsibility—when asked why, say something like the sex just happened. Every night for two and a half years.[3] Can a woman be presumed to control access to her sexuality if she feels unable to interrupt intercourse to insert a diaphragm? Or worse, cannot even want to, aware that she risks a pregnancy she knows she does not want? Would she stop the man for any other reason, such as, for instance, the real taboo—lack of desire? If not, how is sex, hence its consequences, meaningfully voluntary for women? Norms of sexual rhythm and romance which are felt to be interrupted by women's needs are constructed against women's interests. Sex does not look a lot like free-

---

1   *Liberals have supported ... the fetus*   [Unless otherwise indicated, all notes are by the author of this selection.] See, e.g., D.H. Regan, "Rewriting Roe v. Wade," 77 *Michigan Law Review* (1979): 1569 in which the Good Samaritan happens upon the fetus.

2   *many opponents ... rape or incest*   As of 1973, ten states that had made abortion a crime had exceptions for rape and incest; at least three had exceptions for rape only. Many of these exceptions were based on Model Penal Code 230.3 (Proposed Official Draft 1962), quoted in Doe v. Bolton, 410 U.S. 179, 205–207, App. B (1973). References to states with incest and rape exceptions can be found in Roe v. Wade, 410 U.S. 113 n. 37 (1973). Some versions of the Hyde Amendment, which prohibits use of public money to fund abortions, have contained exceptions for cases of rape or incest. All require immediate reporting of the incident.

3   *Studies of abortion ... two and a half years*   See Kristin Luker, *Taking Chances: Abortion and the Decision Not to Contracept* (Berkeley: University of California Press, 1975).

dom when it appears normatively less costly for women to risk an undesired, often painful, traumatic, dangerous, sometimes illegal, and potentially life-threatening procedure than to protect oneself in advance. Yet abortion policy has never been explicitly approached in the context of how women get pregnant; that is, as a consequence of intercourse under conditions of gender inequality; that is, as an issue of forced sex.

Several important explorations are bracketed by this approach. The first is, what are babies to men? On one level, men respond to women's right to abort as if confronting the possibility of their own potential nonexistence—at women's hands, no less. On another level, men's issues of potency, of continuity as a compensation for mortality, of the thrust to embody themselves or their own image in the world, underlie their relation to babies (and much else). The second bracketed issue is one that, unlike the first, has been discussed extensively in the abortion debate: the moral rightness of abortion. The abortion choice should be available and must be women's, but not because the fetus is not a form of life. Why should women not make life-or-death decisions? The problem has been that if the fetus has *any* standing in the debate, it has more weight than women do. Women's embattled need to survive in a world hostile to their survival has largely precluded exploration of these issues. That is, the perspective from which feminists have addressed abortion has been shaped and constrained by the very conditions of sex inequality which have made abortion access the problem it is. Women have not been able to risk thinking about these issues on their own terms because the terms have not been theirs—in sex, in social life, or in court.

In 1973 the Supreme Court found that a statute that made criminal all abortions except those to save the life of the mother violated the constitutional right to privacy.[1] The privacy right had been previously created as a constitutional principle in a case that decriminalized the prescription and use of contraceptives.[2] In other words, courts use the privacy rubric to connect contraception with abortion through privacy in the same way that feminism does through sexuality. In *Roe*, the right to privacy was found "broad enough to encompass a woman's decision whether or not to terminate her pregnancy." In 1981 three justices observed in a dissent: "In the abortion context, we have held that the right to

privacy shields the woman from undue state intrusion in and external scrutiny of her very personal choice."[3]

In 1981 the Supreme Court decided that this right to privacy did not mean that federal Medicaid programs had to cover medically necessary abortions. Privacy, the Court had said, was guaranteed for "a woman's decision whether or not to terminate her pregnancy." The government was then permitted to support one decision and not another: to fund continuing conceptions and not to fund discontinuing them. Asserting that decisional privacy was nevertheless constitutionally intact, the Court stated that "although the government may not place obstacles in the path of a woman's exercise of her freedom of choice, it need not remove those not of its own creation."[4] It is apparently a very short step from that in which the government has a duty *not* to intervene, to that in which it has *no* duty to intervene. Citing *Harris v. McRae*, the Court found this was no step at all in a case that held state child protection officials were not, absent discrimination, legally responsible for a child who was permanently injured through an abusive situation of which they were aware: "while the State may have been aware of the dangers that Joshua faced in the free world, it played no part in their creation, nor did it do anything to render him any more vulnerable to them."[5] The world without state intervention, the world of state inaction, the private world of Joshua's abuse and poor women's unfunded abortions, is "the free world." For those who use and abuse women and children, it is.

Regarded as the outer edge of the limitations on government, the idea of privacy embodies a tension between precluding public exposure or governmental intrusion on the one hand, and autonomy in the sense of protecting personal self-action on the other. This is a tension, not just two facets of one right. The liberal state resolves this tension by identifying the threshold of the state at its permissible extent of penetration into a domain that is considered free by defin-

1 *In 1973 ... right to privacy* Roe v. Wade, 410 U.S. 113 (1973).
2 *a case ... use of contraceptives* Griswold v. Connecticut, 381 U.S. 479 (1965).

3 *In 1981 ... personal choice* H.L. v. Matheson, 450 U.S. 398, 435 (1981) (Marshall, J., dissenting).
4 *although the government ... own creation* Roe. v. Wade, 410 U.S. 113, 153 (1973) ("a woman's decision whether or not to terminate her pregnancy"); Harris v. McRae, 448 U.S. 297 (1980) (referring to Maher v. Roe, 432 U.S. 464, 474 [1976], on no state responsibility to remove non-state-controlled obstacles).
5 *while the State ... vulnerable to them* Deshaney v. Winnebago County Dept of Social Services, 109 S. Ct. 988 (1989) (no due process "liberty" interest created by state child protection statutes and enforcement, in case of permanent injury to abused child of which agency was aware).

ition: the private sphere. By this move the state secures "an inviolable personality" by ensuring "autonomy of control over the intimacies of personal identity."[1] The state does this by centering its self-restraint on body and home, especially bedroom. By staying out of marriage and the family—essentially meaning sexuality, that is, heterosexuality—from contraception through pornography to the abortion decision, the law of privacy proposes to guarantee individual bodily integrity, personal exercise of moral intelligence, and freedom of intimacy.[2] But have women's rights to access to those values been guaranteed? The law of privacy instead translates traditional liberal values into the rhetoric of individual rights as a means of subordinating those rights to specific social imperatives.[3] In particular, the logic of the grant of the abortion right is consummated in the funding decision, enforcing male supremacy with capitalism, translating the ideology of the private sphere into the individual woman's legal right to privacy as a means of subordinating women's collective needs to the imperatives of male supremacy.

Here, as in other areas of law, the way the male point of view constructs a social event or legal need will be the way that social event or legal need is framed by state policy. To the extent possession is the point of sex, illegal rape will be sex with a woman who is not yours unless the act makes her yours. If part of the thrill of pornography involves eroticizing the putatively prohibited, illegal pornography—obscenity—will be prohibited enough to keep pornography desirable without ever making it truly illegitimate or unavailable. If, from the male standpoint, male is the implicit definition of human, maleness will be the implicit standard by which sex equality is measured in discrimination law. In parallel terms, reproduction is sexual. Men control sexuality. The state supports the interest of men as a group. So

why was abortion legalized? Why were women given even that much control? It is not an accusation of bad faith to answer that the interests of men as a social group converge with the definition of justice embodied in law through the male point of view. The abortion right frames the ways men arrange among themselves to control the reproductive consequences of intercourse. The availability of abortion enhances the availability of intercourse.

Since Freud, the social problem posed by sexuality has been understood as the problem of the innate desire for sexual pleasure being repressed by the constraints of civilization. In this context, inequality arises as an issue only in women's repressive socialization to passivity and coolness (so-called frigidity or desexualization) and in the disparate consequences of biology, pregnancy. Who defines what is sexual, what sexuality therefore is, to whom what stimuli are erotic and why, and who defines the conditions under which sexuality is expressed—these issues have not even been available for consideration. Civilization's answer to these questions has fused women's reproductivity with their attributed sexuality in its definition of what a woman is. Women are defined as women by the uses, sexual and reproductive, to which men wish to put them.

In this context it becomes clear why the struggle for reproductive freedom has never included a woman's right to refuse sex. In the concept of sexual liberation which has undergirded the politics of choice, sexual equality has been a struggle for women to have sex with men on the same terms as men: "without consequences." Meaning, no children. In this sense the abortion right has been sought as freedom from the unequal reproductive consequences of sexual expression, with sexuality centered on heterosexual genital intercourse. It has been as if biological organisms, rather than social relations, reproduced the species. But if one's concern is not how more people can get more sex, but who defines sexuality—both pleasure and violation—and therefore who defines women, the abortion right is situated within a very different problematic: the social and political inequality of the sexes. This repositioning of the issue requires reformulating the problem of sexuality from the repression of drives by civilization to the oppression of women by men.

Even before Roe v. Wade, arguments for abortion under the rubric of feminism have rested upon the right to control one's own body, gender neutral.[4] This argument has been ap-

---

1   *By this move ... personal identity*   T. Gerety, "Redefining Privacy," *Harvard Civil Rights–Civil Liberties Law Review* 12 (1977): 233, 236.

2   *By staying out ... freedom of intimacy*   Kenneth I. Karst, "The Freedom of Intimate Association," *Yale Law Journal* 89 (1980): 624; "Developments—The Family," *Harvard Law Review* 93 (1980): 1157; Doe v. Commonwealth Att'y, 403 F. Supp. 1199 (E.D. Va. 1975) *aff'd without opinion*, 425 U.S. 901 (1976); but cf. People v. Onofre, 51 N.Y. 2d 476 (1980), *cert. denied*, 451 U.S. 987 (1981). The issue was finally decided, for the time, in Bowers v. Hardwick, 478 U.S. 186 (1986) (statute criminalizing consensual sodomy does not violate right to privacy).

3   *The law of privacy ... social imperatives*   Tom Grey, "Eros, Civilization, and the Burger Court," *Law and Contemporary Problems* 43 (1980): 83 was helpful to me in developing this analysis.

4   *Even before ... gender neutral*   *Abele v. Markle* originally included an allegation that prohibiting abortion discriminated against

pealing for the same reasons it is inadequate: socially, women's bodies have not been theirs; women have not controlled their meanings and destinies. Feminists have tried to assert that control without risking pursuit of the idea that something more than women's bodies might be at stake, something closer to a net of relations in which women are gendered and unequal.[1] Some feminists have noticed that women's right to decide has become merged with an overwhelmingly male professional's right not to have his judgment second-guessed by the government.[2] But whatever their underlying politics, most abortion advocates, at least since 1971, have argued in rigidly and rigorously gender-neutral terms.

For instance, Judith Jarvis Thomson's argument that an abducted woman had no obligation to be a celebrated violinist's life support system was to mean that women have no obligation to support a fetus.[3] No woman who needs an abortion—no woman, period—is valued, no potential a woman's life might hold is cherished, like a gender-neutral famous violinist's unencumbered possibilities. The problems of gender are underlined in this analogy rather than solved or even addressed. The origin of the hypothetical in force gives the conclusion much of its moral weight. But the parallel would begin the abortion problem in rape, perhaps confining abortions to instances in which force is recognized as force, like rape or incest. The applicability of the origin

in force to the normal abortion is neither embraced nor disavowed, although the argument was intended to justify the normal abortion. The parable is constructed to begin the debate after sex occurred but requires discussion of the relation of intercourse to rape to make sense of its application. Because this issue has been studiously avoided in the abortion context, the unequal and liberal basis on which woman's private personhood is constructed has been obscured.

Abortion promises women sex with men on the same terms on which men have sex with women. So long as women do not control access to their sexuality, this facilitates women's heterosexual availability. In other words, under conditions of gender inequality, sexual liberation in this sense does not so much free women sexually as it frees male sexual aggression. The availability of abortion removes the one real consequence men could not easily ignore, the one remaining legitimated reason that women have had for refusing sex besides the headache. As Andrea Dworkin puts it, analyzing male ideology on abortion: "Getting laid was at stake."[4]

Privacy doctrine is an ideal vehicle for this process. The liberal ideal of the private holds that, so long as the public does not interfere, autonomous individuals interact freely and equally. Privacy is the ultimate value of the negative state. Conceptually, this private is hermetic. It means that which is inaccessible to, unaccountable to, unconstructed by, anything beyond itself. By definition, it is not part of or conditioned by anything systematic outside it. It is personal, intimate, autonomous, particular, individual, the original source and final outpost of the self, gender neutral. It is defined by everything that feminism reveals women have never been allowed to be or to have, and by everything that women have been equated with and defined in terms of men's ability to have. To complain in public of inequality within the private contradicts the liberal definition of the private. In the liberal view, no act of the state contributes to shaping its internal alignments or distributing its internal forces, so no act of the state should participate in changing it. Its inviolability by the state, framed as an individual right, presupposes that the private is not already an arm of the state. In this scheme, intimacy is implicitly

women in the basis of sex. 452 F. 2d 1121, 1123 (1971). The Second Circuit held instead that prohibiting all abortions was unconstitutional under the Ninth Amendment and the due process clause of the Fourteenth Amendment. Schulman v. N.Y. City Health and Hospitals Corporation, 70 Misc. 2d 1093 (1st Dept. 1973), held that a requirement of identifying women who have abortions publicly discriminates against married and single women by denying them equal protection of the laws as to their right to privacy. This gives women rights but not on the basis of sex. Klein v. Nassau County Medical Center, 347 F. Supp. 496 (1972), won state Medicaid funding for indigent women for medically necessary abortions on grounds that its denial "subjected [indigent women] to coercion to bear children which they do not wish to bear and no other women similarly situated are so coerced" (at 500). This equal protection ruling was thus based on class, not on sex.

1   *Feminists have tried ... gendered and unequal*   See Adrienne Rich, *Of Woman Born: Motherhood as Experience and Institution* (New York: Norton, 1976), chap. 3: "The child that I carry for nine months can be defined *neither* as me nor as not-me" (p. 64).

2   *Some feminists ... by the government*   Kristen Booth Glen, "Abortion in the Courts: A Lay Woman's Historical Guide to the New Disaster Area," *Feminist Studies* 4 (February 1978): 1.

3   *Judith Jarvis Thomson's argument ... support a fetus*   Judith Jarvis Thomson, "A Defense of Abortion," *Philosophy and Public Affairs* 1 (1971): 47.

4   *Getting laid was at stake*   Andrea Dworkin, *Right Wing Women* (New York: Perigee, 1983). See also Friedrich Engels on the benefits of removing private housekeeping into social industry, Chapter 2. Note that the Playboy Foundation has supported abortion rights from day one and continues to, even with shrinking disposable funds, on a level of priority comparable to its opposition to censorship.

thought to guarantee symmetry of power. Injuries arise through violation of the private sphere, not within and by and because of it.

In private, consent tends to be presumed. Showing coercion is supposed to avoid this presumption. But the problem is getting anything private to be perceived as coercive. This is an epistemic problem of major dimensions and explains why privacy doctrine is most at home at home, the place women experience the most force, in the family, and why it centers on sex. Why a person would "allow" force in private (the "why doesn't she leave" question raised to battered women) is a question given its insult by the social meaning of the private as a sphere of choice. For women the measure of the intimacy has been the measure of the oppression. This is why feminism has had to explode the private. This is why feminism has seen the personal as the political. The private is public for those for whom the personal is political. In this sense, for women there is no private, either normatively or empirically. Feminism confronts the fact that women have no privacy to lose or to guarantee. Women are not inviolable. Women's sexuality is not only violable, it is—hence, women are—seen in and as their violation. To confront the fact that women have no privacy is to confront the intimate degradation of women as the public order. The doctrinal choice of privacy in the abortion context thus reaffirms and reinforces what the feminist critique of sexuality criticizes: the public/private split. The political and ideological meaning of privacy as a legal doctrine is continuous with the concrete consequences of the public/private split for the lives of women. In this light, the abortion funding ruling appears consistent with the larger meaning of the original granting of the abortion right.

The right to privacy looks like an injury presented as a gift, a sword in men's hands presented as a shield in women's. Freedom from public intervention coexists uneasily with any right that requires social preconditions to be meaningfully delivered. For example, if inequality is socially pervasive and enforced, equality will require intervention, not abdication, to be meaningful. But the right to privacy is not thought to require social change. It is not even thought to require any social preconditions, other than nonintervention by the public. The point for the abortion cases is not that indigency—which was the specific barrier to effective choice in *Harris v. McRae*—is well within the public power to remedy, nor that the state is hardly exempt in issues of the distribution of wealth. The point is that *Roe v. Wade* presumes that government nonintervention in the private

sphere promotes a woman's freedom of choice. When the alternative is jail, there is much to be said for this presumption. But the *McRae* result sustains the meaning of privacy in *Roe*: women are guaranteed by the public no more than what they can get in private—what they can extract through their intimate associations with men. Women with privileges, including class privileges, get rights.

Women were granted the abortion right as a private privilege, not as a public right over reproduction which is controlled by "a man or The Man,"[1] an individual man or the doctors or the government. Abortion was not so much decriminalized as it was legalized. In *Roe v. Wade*, the government set the stage for the conditions under which women got this right. Most of the control that women won out of legalization has gone directly into the hands of men—husbands, doctors, or fathers—and what remains in women's hands is now subject to attempted reclamation through regulation.[2] This, surely, must be what is meant by reform.

It is not inconsistent, then, that, framed as a privacy right, a woman's decision to abort would have no claim on public support and would genuinely not be seen as burdened by that deprivation.[3] State intervention would have

---

1 *Women were granted ... or The Man* Johnnie Tillmon, "Welfare Is a Women's Issue," *Liberation News Service*, February 26, 1972; reprinted in Rosalyn Baxandall, Linda Gordon, and Susan Reverby, eds., *America's Working Women: A Documentary History, 1600 to the Present* (New York: Random House, 1976), pp. 355–58.

2 *Most of the control ... reclamation through regulation* See H.L. v. Matheson, 450 U.S. 398 (1981); Bellotti v. Baird, 443 U.S. 622 (1979); but see Planned Parenthood of Central Missouri v. Danforth, 428 U.S. 52 (1976). Most attempts to regulate the right out of existence have been defeated; City of Akron v. Akron Reproductive Health Center, 462 U.S. 416 (1983). More recently, see Reproductive Health Service v. Webster, 851 F.2d 1071 (8th Cir. 1988), U.S. app. pndg.

3 *It is not inconsistent ... by that deprivation* A more affirmative vision of the possibilities of *Roe v. Wade* was held by litigators after the decision. See J. Goodman, R.C. Schoenbrod, and N. Stearns, "Doe and Roe: Where Do We Go from Here?" *Women's Rights Law Reporter* 1 (1973): 20, 27. Stearns remarks that "the right to privacy is a passive right. The right to privacy says that the state can't interfere. The right to liberty, particularly founded as it was in the Court's opinion on all of the grave things that happen to a woman's life if she doesn't get an abortion, would seem to imply that the state has some kind of affirmative obligation to ensure that a woman can exercise that right to liberty. That presumably will have very important implications for access questions like Medicaid, for example." Unfortunately, their view that *Roe* guaranteed women a right to abortion as a protected liberty, which is affirmative, rather than as protected privacy, which is passive, did not prevail in later cases.

provided a choice women did not have in private, would have contradicted the male-supremacist structure of the private; this result confirmed that structure. Privacy conceived as a right from public intervention and disclosure is the opposite of the relief that *McRae* sought for welfare women. The women in *McRae*, women whose sexual refusal has counted for particularly little, needed something positive, not abdication, to make their privacy effective. The logic of the Court's response resembles the logic by which women are supposed to consent to sex: preclude the alternatives, then call the one remaining option "her choice." Women's alternatives are precluded prior to the reach of the legal doctrine by conditions of sex, race, and class—the very conditions the privacy frame leaves tacit and guarantees.

Liberalism converges with the left at this edge of the feminist critique of male power. Herbert Marcuse speaks of "philosophies which are 'political' in the widest sense—affecting society as a whole, demonstrably transcending the sphere of privacy."[1] This formulation does and does not describe the feminist political, because "women both have and have not had a common world."[2] Women share isolation in the home and degradation in intimacy. The private sphere, which confines and separates women, is therefore a political sphere, a common ground of women's inequality. Rather than transcending the private as a predicate to politics, feminism politicizes it. For women, the private necessarily transcends the private. If the most private also most "affects society as a whole," the separation between public and private collapses as anything other than potent ideology in life and in law. If marxists treated sex the way they treat class, this analysis would be understood. For example, Schlomo Avineri observes that a person's private status is determined in modern society by property relations (that is, by "civil society"), which relations are no longer private but determine politics. Politics remains a rationalization of property relations, as it was for Marx, but what was private is nonetheless political.[3] The failure of marxism adequately to address intimacy on the one hand, government on the other, is the same failure as the indistinguishability of marxism from liberalism on questions of sexual politics.

When the law of privacy restricts intrusions into intimacy, it bars changes in control over that intimacy through law. The existing distribution of power and resources within the private sphere are precisely what the law of privacy exists to protect. In one remarkable if subliminal admission that male power by men in the family is coextensive with state power, the Supreme Court held that a state could not grant biological fathers the right to veto abortions in the first trimester because, given *Roe*, the state did not have this power.[4] It is probably not a coincidence that the very things feminism regards as central to the subjection of women— the very place, the body; the very relations, heterosexual; the very activities, intercourse and reproduction; and the very feelings, intimate—form the core of privacy doctrine's coverage. Privacy law assumes women are equal to men in there. Through this perspective, the legal concept of privacy can and has shielded the place of battery, marital rape, and women's exploited domestic labor. It has preserved the central institutions whereby women are deprived of identity, autonomy, control, and self-definition. It has protected a primary activity through which male supremacy is expressed and enforced. Just as pornography is legally protected as individual freedom of expression—without any questions about whose freedom and whose expression and at whose expense—abstract privacy protects abstract autonomy, without inquiring into whose freedom of action is being sanctioned, at whose expense.

To fail to recognize the meaning of the private in the ideology and reality of women's subordination by seeking protection behind a right to that privacy is to cut women off from collective verification and state support in the same act. When women are segregated in private, separated from each other one at a time, a right to that privacy isolates women at once from each other and from public recourse. This right to privacy is a right of men "to be let alone"[5] to oppress women

---

1   *Herbert Marcuse ... sphere of privacy* Herbert Marcuse, "Repressive Tolerance," in *A Critique of Pure Tolerance*, ed. Robert Paul Wolff, J. Barrington Moore, and Herbert Marcuse (Boston: Beacon Press, 1965), 91.

2   *women both have ... common world* Adrienne Rich, "Conditions for Work: The Common World of Women," in *Working It Out: Twenty-three Women Writers, Artists, Scientists, and Scholars Talk Out Their Lives and Work*, ed. Sara Ruddick and Pamela Daniels (New York: Pantheon Books, 1977), xiv.

3   *Schlomo Avineri observes ... nonetheless political* Schlomo Avineri, *The Social and Political Thought of Karl Marx* (London: Cambridge

University Press, 1969).

4   *the Supreme Court ... this power* Planned Parenthood of Central Missouri v. Danforth, 428 U.S. 52, 69 (1975) ("The state cannot delegate to a spouse a veto power which the state itself is absolutely and totally prohibited from exercising during the first trimester of pregnancy").

5   *This right ... let alone* S. Warren and L. Brandeis, "The Right to Privacy," *Harvard Law Review* 4 (1980): 205. But note that the right of privacy under some state constitutions has been held to include funding for abortions: Committee to Defend Reproduc-

one at a time. It embodies and reflects the private sphere's existing definition of womanhood. This instance of liberalism—applied to women as if they were persons, gender neutral[1]—reinforces the division between public and private which is not gender neutral. It is an ideological division that lies about women's shared experience and mystifies the unity among the spheres of women's violation. It polices the division between public and private, a very material division that keeps the private beyond public redress and depoliticizes women's subjection within it. Privacy law keeps some men out of the bedrooms of other men.

◆ ◆ ◆ ◆ ◆

Toward a New Theory of Equality (2005)

Equality is valued nearly everywhere but practiced almost nowhere. As an idea, it can be fiercely loved, passionately sought, widely vaunted, legally guaranteed, sentimentally assumed, or complacently taken for granted. As a reality, in lives lived or institutions run, it hardly exists anywhere.

This is true among men but it is nowhere more true than between women and men. Sex equality is fairly common as a legal guarantee, its application varying widely in meaning and meaningfulness, as a principle ranging in acceptance from obvious to anathema, with the inequality of the sexes thriving alongside it. Sex inequality is diverse empirically, ideologically, and legally, varying in extent, form, and degree,[2] with some places far worse for women than others, but nowhere is sex equality achieved. Equality between women and men, in realms from the institutional to the intimate, remains more dream than fact.

The goal of legal equality is to end discrimination and produce social equality. After about thirty years of trying, very hard in some places, it has yet to succeed. There is no equality between women and men, and there is little among men either, certainly not on an ethnic or racial basis. Eco-

---

tive Rights v. Meyers, 29 Cal. 3d 252 (1981); Moe v. Secretary of Admin. and Finance, 417 N.E.2d 387 (Mass. 1981).

1   *This instance ... gender neutral*   Examination of the legal record in *Roe v. Wade* and *Harris v. McRae* reveals that little legal attempt was made to get beyond the gender neutrality of privacy doctrine to frame the abortion issue directly as one of inequality of the sexes—that is, as an issue of sex discrimination. The original complaint in *Roe v. Wade* contained a cause of action for denial of equal protection of the laws, First Amended Complaint CA-3-3690-B (N.D. Tex., Apr. 22, 1970) IV, 5. But the inequality complained of did not, as it developed, refer to inequality on the basis of sex. Oral argument in the district court appears to have been confined largely to the right to privacy. Opinion of the District Court, Civil Action No. CA-3-3690-B and 3-3691-C (June 17, 1970) 116 n.7. In the U.S. Supreme Court, the Center for Constitutional Rights filed an amicus brief arguing that criminal abortion statutes like those of Texas and Georgia "violate the most basic Constitutional rights of women." "[It] is the woman who bears the disproportionate share of the de jure and de facto burdens and penalties of pregnancy, child birth and child rearing. Thus any statute which denies a woman the right to determine whether she will bear those burdens denies her the equal protection of the laws." *Brief Amicus Curiae* on behalf of New Women Lawyers, Women's Health and Abortion Project, Inc., National Abortion Action Coalition 6 (Aug. 2, 1971). The brief assumes that sex is equal and voluntary, even if pregnancy may not be: "Man and woman have equal responsibility for the act of sexual intercourse. Should the woman accidentally become pregnant, against her will, however, she endures in many instances the entire burden or 'punishment'" (p. 26); "And it is not sufficient to say that the woman 'chose' to have sexual intercourse, for she did not choose to become pregnant" (p. 31).

The complaint in *Harris v. McRae* alleged discrimination "based on poverty, race and minority status, which deprives and punishes the plaintiff class of women in violation of due process and equal protection of the law." Plaintiffs' and Proposed Intervenors' Amended Complaint, McRae v. Califano, 74 Civ. 1804 (JFD) Jan. 5, 1977, para. 74. It does not allege discrimination on the basis of sex. Only one brief argues sex discrimination, and that to argue that since women are *socially* discriminated against on the basis of sex, denying them abortions is an additional hardship, is not to make the *legal* argument that not paying for abortions, a state act that hurts only women, is sex discrimination. As framed by NOW, "the plight of indigent women denied medically necessary abortions is exacerbated by the pervasive sex discrimination that impacts especially hard on women in poverty." Brief *Amicus Curiae* for NOW et. al., No. 79–1268 (U.S. Supreme Court, Mar. 18, 1980) 44.

Every social basis for discrimination against women other than the sexual, and every legal basis for discrimination against women other than gender has been used to attempt to support the abortion right. In the United States, with the partial exception of the CCR brief—an effort at once made audacious and impressive and weakened by the fact that sex discrimination by law had just been recognized as unconstitutional—burdens on abortion seem virtually never to have been legally argued as simple sex discrimination.

2   *Sex inequality ... and degree*   [Unless otherwise indicated, all notes to this selection are by the author rather than the editors of this anthology.] United Nations, *The World's Women 1970–1990, Trends and Statistics* (1991).

nomic measures document this failure particularly clearly; discrimination on combined grounds illustrate it especially vividly. Of the many possible explanations, legal equality theory itself needs to be considered. On the view that the existing approach is consistent with the outcomes it has produced—that it is determinately connected with its results or lack of them—I will examine the dominant legal equality theory, its assumptions and consequences, and offer and explore a responsive alternative.

I

Equality animates law both implicitly and explicitly. Implicitly, the whole idea of "the rule of law" embodies one idea of equality. Law as law means the kind of equalization that comes from elevating rules over force and status, a leveling principle that treats everyone the same, no favorites and no exceptions, except when distinctions can be justified. Legal method involves reasoning through analogy and distinction,[1] that is, treating things alike based on their similarities and unalike based on their differences. Most elaborately in common law systems that proceed through cases, but also in systems that reason from authoritative principles, law itself works through treating the same that which is the same and treating differently that which is different.

On the more explicit level, equality is often guaranteed positively as a right. International treaties and conventions, constitutions, and statutes provide for it in governments' relations with each other, in government's relation to the governed, and in citizens' relations among themselves. Constitutional and treaty-based equality favors prohibiting inequalities imposed by official action and centers on unequal laws, although there are exceptions and many attempts to expand it beyond that. Statutory equality treats selected spheres of civil society, typically employment and education.

In an unbroken line, mainstream equality thinking, systemic and doctrinal, flows from Aristotle's analysis in the *Ethica Nichomachea* that equality means treating likes alike and unlikes unalike.[2] To be the same is to be entitled to the same; to be different is to be treated differently. At any rate, this concept is the meaning universally attributed to his sometimes obscure discussion. Aristotle's distributive justice, from which legal mainstream equality primarily flows, is "a species of the proportionate."[3]

Less important for present purposes than what Aristotle actually thought is what has been made of the equality concept drawn from him, as applied in law over time. In the United States, bedrock to Fourteenth Amendment equality is that one must be the same as a relevant comparator to be entitled to equality of treatment. Equality was not part of the original Constitution; it was added after the Civil War to help eliminate official racism and was not applied to sex until 1971.[4] Its threshold requirement is that equality claimants must be "similarly situated" to those not treated unequally before an equality claim can be made. This language was used under the Fourteenth Amendment for the first time in 1884: "Class legislation, discriminating against some and favoring others, is prohibited, but legislation which ... within the sphere of its operation ... affects alike all persons similarly situated, is not within the amendment."[5] Another case soon after formulated the concept concisely in the form in which it has been used since. In its terms, under the Fourteenth Amendment, "the classification must be reasonable, not arbitrary, and must rest upon some ground of difference having a fair and substantial relation to the object of the legislation, so that all persons similarly circumstanced shall be treated alike."[6] The reasonable relation came from earlier due process cases; treating likes alike derived from Aristotle, his translators and transliterators. One hundred years later, when civil equality for African Americans still had not even remotely been achieved, Congress passed the Civil Rights Act of 1964, prohibiting discrimination based on race, color, national origin, religion, and sex in accommodation and employment.[7] That act has been interpreted through an analytically parallel requirement of comparability.

Termed "formal equality," this principle has become the familiar equality calculus of sameness and difference,

---

1   *Legal method ... analogy and distinction*   See Edward H. Levi, *An Introduction to Legal Reasoning* (Chicago: University of Chicago Press, 1949), 2–3.

2   *Aristotle's analysis ... unlikes unalike*   Aristotle, *Nicomachean Ethics*, Book 5 Chapter 3 1131^a, 1131^b (W.D. Ross, trans. and ed., *The Works of Aristotle, Vol. IX: Ethica Nicomachea* [Oxford: Clarendon Press, 1925]: 112–16.)

3   *a species of the proportionate*   Aristotle, *Nicomachean Ethics*, 1131^a.

4   *was not applied to sex until 1971*   Reed v. Reed, 404 U.S. 71 (1971).

5   *Class legislation ... the amendment*   Barbier v. Connolly, 113 U.S. 27, 30–32 (1885).

6   *the classification ... treated alike*   Royster Guano Co. v. Virginia, 253 U.S. 412, 415 (1920). See also Hayes v. Missouri, 120 U.S. 68, 71 (1887).

7   *the Civil Rights Act ... accommodation and employment*   42 U.S.C. §2000e-2.

of identity and distinction, requiring same treatment if one is the same, different treatment if one is different. Inequality means different treatment for likes, same treatment for unlikes. This approach, which tracks Aristotle's concept but is not usually cited to him, has been embraced as obvious by legal institutions worldwide, defining the core and ambit of legal equality in constitutions, statutes, and international law. It is the ruling approach to equality in the United States and, if anything, tends to be adhered to more strictly in Europe. An exception is Canada's interpretation of its new Charter of Rights and Freedoms since 1989.

While some progress has been made using this sameness/difference equality concept—most of it for small elites of men and a few privileged women, which is more than nothing—some of the historical uses of this approach—applications, not misapplications—give one pause. Aristotle, his concept of equality apparently undisturbed, defended slavery and lived in a society in which prostitution (sexual slavery) thrived and no women were citizens.[1] This approach readily supported official racial segregation by law in the United States, African Americans being construed as different from whites; equality under the Fourteenth Amendment meant legally imposed segregation of Black from white in the schools, courthouses, parks, pools, prisons, hospitals, restaurants, trains, and cemeteries of civil society.[2]

The same equality reasoning and language was used under the Third Reich to justify hierarchy of so-called Aryans over Jews.[3] In a discussion that explicitly embraces this same equality model, respected German constitutional scholar Ulrich Scheuner said, "From the racial foundation of today's German laws follows inevitably the cutting off of foreign elements, especially the Jews, from the German body politic, and their differential treatment."[4] One sign over a Nazi extermination camp—these signs specialized in vicious twists on homely phrases—stated "*Jedem Das Seine*," an eerie echo of Aristotle's formulation that equality means "each has one's own."[5]

This is not to hold Aristotle responsible for the Nazi atrocities, nor to say that a proper concept of equality in law alone could necessarily have stopped them. However, the ease with which this equality logic, which by then had taken on a life of its own, rationalized these extremes of social inequality, at just the points at which law was most needed to stand against them, encourages deeper scrutiny. Combined with the fact that legal equality guarantees promise and aim for a social equality they have yet to produce, even under less cataclysmic circumstances, while at the same time producing perverse outcomes with perfect logical consistency—the invalidation of affirmative action programs designed to reverse decades of racial exclusion are another example[6]—it is as ominous as it is curious that the same equality logic that was used to legalize apartheid and genocide remains legally fundamental in an American law that has repudiated segregation and a European law that has rejected fascism. Germany rejected all Nazi law by applying its current constitutional equality approach,[7] while continuing to use the same approach to equality itself that the Nazis used. At least as remarkable is the fact that the identical sameness/difference approach remains the equality concept in use in international human rights law, which arose largely to make sure that nothing like the Holocaust ever happened again.

Equality law and its results have not gone entirely unquestioned. Some of its conceptual absurdities and human costs have been sharply contested, largely in the racial context.[8] But the critique has stopped well short of questioning

1   *Aristotle, his concept ... no women were citizens* See Elizabeth V. Spelman, *Inessential Woman: Problems of Exclusion in Feminist Thought* (Boston: Beacon Press, 1988), 37–56.

2   *equality under ... civil society* Plessy v. Ferguson, 163 U.S. 537 (1896).

3   *The same equality ... Aryans over Jews* Georg Weippert, *Das Prinzip der Hierarchie*, (Hamburg: Hanseatische Verlag, 1932), 29.

4   *From the racial ... differential treatment* "Der Gleichheitsgedanke in der volkischen Verfassungsordnung," 99 *Zeitschrift für die Gesamte Staatswissenschaft* 245 (1939): 260–67 ("Aus der volkischen Grundlage des heutigen deutschen Rechts folgt notwendig die Absonderung der artfremden Elemente, insbesondere der Juden, aus dem deutschen Volkskorper und ihre.... differentielle Behandlung," p. 267).

5   *One sign ... one's own* Annedore Prengel, "Gleichheit versus Differenz—eine falsche Alternative im feministischen Diskurs" in Ute Gerhard et al., eds., *Differenz und Gleichheit* (Frankfurt: Helmer, 1990), 120, 121.

6   *the invalidation ... are another example* Regents of the University of California v. Bakke, 438 U.S. 265 (1978).

7   *Germany rejected ... equality approach* BVerfGe 23, 98, at 99.

8   *Some of its ... racial context* Owen Fiss, "Groups and the Equal Protection Clause," *Philosophy and Public Affairs* 5 (1976): 107; Alan Freeman, "Legitimizing Racial Discrimination Through Antidiscrimination Law: A Critical Review of Supreme Court Doctrine," *Minnesota Law Review* 62 (1978): 1049; Kimberlé Crenshaw, "Race, Reform and Retrenchment: Transformation and Legitimation in Antidiscrimination Law," *Harvard Law Review* 101 (1988): 1331.

this standard approach to equality itself. No political theorist has argued that Aristotle was wrong: that treating likes alike and unlikes unalike is not what equality is all about, nor is treating likes unalike or unalikes alike what the problem of inequality really looks like. In over thirty years of progressive litigation on race and sex in the United States, no court of law has squarely been asked to assess whether requiring the parties to be alike—in doctrinal language "similarly situated," the threshold for equal protection scrutiny—perpetuates social inequality, as was argued in Canada in 1989. Unchallenged, the approach's underlying assumptions have been submerged from view.

These assumptions include the reference points for sameness (the same as whom?), the social creation and definition of differences (how is difference created and perceived?), and the comparative empirical approach itself (why not measure treatment and status against a principle or a standard or an outcome rather than measuring people's attributes against each other?). Aristotle says that "if they are not equal, they will not have what is equal."[1] But how do we know or measure who "are" equal? What defines who is equal, so we know inequality when we see it? Moreover, why can differences justify inequalities? Because some people cannot walk up stairs, thus are "different" from those who can, are buildings constructed so they cannot enter them not unequal? What is "one's own" anyway? What if the goods of societies are systematically maldistributed as far back as the eye can see, or merely today from cradle to grave? Relative to what is maintaining a certain distribution "equality"?

Further, why should unequal groups have to be "like" groups who have not had this problem before their inequality can be complained of? Socially dominant groups never have to meet any comparative test to acquire or retain the privileges and advantages they have. How can a subordinate group be seen as, or be, "like" dominant groups if society has organized inequalities along the lines of the group's socially perceived "unalikeness"? The worse conditions of inequality are, the more disparate are the circumstances in which people are placed—circumstances that at once reflect inequality and create and define difference. In any case, what does sameness have to do with entitlement to equal treatment? And who is the relevant comparator? Should the best athletic facilities go to the most athletically

talented, those who need the most help, those who have had the worst facilities to date, those who can improve the most from using them, or should everyone have the same facilities, despite their differences? Why shouldn't people be treated alike, say admitted to schools, on the basis of their unalikeness from each other? On all these questions, the Aristotelian theory offers no guidance.

The result has been that so long as Blacks are socially constructed as different from whites, or Jews from "Aryans," or women from men, they can be treated differently, even if that "difference" has meant systematic disadvantage from indignity to apartheid to liquidation—and this equality principle has been satisfied. Treating members of disadvantaged groups as well or better based on their unalikeness, the value of diversity, is contrary to the theory, making affirmative action squarely contrary to it, even as treating disadvantaged groups less well never seems to be seen as treating advantaged groups better based on their unalikeness. These are outcomes to which this reasoning has demonstrably led and to which it is conceptually open. In this light, the historical examples of the applications of this principle are not isolated excesses. The principle is consistent with its practice. Nothing in it defines all human beings as being equal. Nothing in it requires that the definition of human be equally comprised of the defining qualities of all groups of people. Judgments like this—what does merit look like? who is deemed human?—Aristotle left to individual character. Political systems since have left these same kinds of judgments to the political realm—to power and force. At the same time, this equality principle has been presented as equality-producing, a counterbalance to, rather than a vehicle for, the power politics that forcefully shape the unequal status quo.

If socially unequal groups, in order to demand equal treatment, must first be situated the same as groups not afflicted by inequality, many of the worst injuries of inequality will be obscured and few will be corrected. It seems you have to first have equality before you can get it, expanding the implications of Anatole France's trenchant irony that "law, in its majestic equality, forbids the rich as well as the poor to sleep under bridges, to beg in the streets, and to steal bread."[2] Only the already disadvantaged will be made worse off by laws that are equal in this sense, because the ad-

1   *if they are ... is equal* Aristotle, *Nichomachean Ethics*, trans. by W.D. Ross and revised by J.L. Ackrill and J.O. Urmson (Oxford: Oxford World Classics, 1980), 112.

2   *Anatole France's ... steal bread* John Cournos, *A Modern Plutarch* (Indianapolis: Bobbs-Merrill Co., 1928), 27 (quoting Anatole France).

vantaged ipso facto will never be in a position to run afoul of them. By the same token, the disadvantaged will never be made better off by this equality because they will never be in a position to take advantage of it. Who that needs this equality can get it? Under it, just as those who can least afford it can continue to be treated worse, those who most need it can continue not to receive its help. If situated differences must be elided to gain access to equal benefits, how will the consequences of inequality be exposed in order to rectify them? If equal treatment requires the same treatment for those who have and those who have not, for those who need and those who are not in need, how will their status relative to one another ever change?

Whatever Aristotle intended, those who see the way out of these traps as different treatment for differences should first notice that same treatment for sameness has been the fundamental equality rule in every legal equality regime. Equality in this approach has meant, first, same treatment based on relevant empirical sameness, equivalence, symmetry with a relevant comparator. To get what we have, be like us. Different treatment for differences, treating unalikes unalike, in Aristotle's formulation on a par with the main rule, as applied in legal systems, has been in some tension with the main rule, indeed is widely regarded as second-class equality. In reality, experience with it has not, in the main, been good. Different treatment, from the Nazi's "special treatment,"[1] a euphemism for extermination, to arguments that women's weakness and incapacity require "special protection,"[2] have mostly operated as the opposite of equality, to put it mildly. U.S. sex discrimination law's "special benefits" rule has often been seen to be in tension with, not complementary to, the fundamental rule of equal treatment, called "gender neutrality." Affirmative action, cast as "different treatment" for differences, is seen by its critics to be in tension with the fundamental equality principle of same treatment (whether in fact it is or not). Different treatment is thought to be where the double standard lives. Affirming differences sometimes has, in any case, not overcome the imposed homogeneity and affirmation of privilege of the sameness model. If "same treatment" for sameness has offered an illusory equality, "different treatment" for differences has been demeaning and dangerous, at times catastrophically so.

2

So far, the analysis here has considered social inequality in general, including among men, focusing on the way this mainstream equality approach has limited the pursuit of equality through law. As to issues of sex in particular, Aristotle thought of the sexes as different. Perhaps his abstract equality formulation took sex as an underlying concrete template for an unlikeness that could, consistent with equality, be treated unalike. He believed that "the excellence of character ... the temperance of a man and of a woman, or the courage and justice of a man and a woman, are not, as Socrates maintained, the same: the courage of a man is shown in commanding, of a woman in obeying. And this holds of all other excellences...."[3] The sexes are different: men tell women what to do, women do it, and so on. Gender is defined as a difference, the sex difference. This has been as much social construct, imposed social fact, as philosophical argument. Human societies have tended to define women as such in terms of just such differences from men, whether real or imagined, generally enforced to women's detriment in resources, roles, respect, and rights.

If equality is a sameness and gender a difference; if first-order equality is defined in terms of sameness, and women as such are "not the same" as men, women cannot be equal to men until they are no longer women. This is neither to affirm women's sameness to men, the usual approach, nor to affirm women as "different," a currently fashionable strategy in some circles (although conservatives beat the fashion by a couple of centuries). This is to point out the collision between the existing equality paradigm and the social definition of women and men as such. How sex equality can be produced if sex is a difference and first-class equality is predicated on sameness is problematic. Sex equality becomes something of an oxymoron, a contradiction in terms.

In practice, legal systems attempting to be progressive try to get around the drawbacks of this equality approach by carving out what are seen as exceptions to it. Predominantly allowed is different treatment where differences are seen to be real but valuable—such as pregnancy and maternity leaves even though no man needs one, or affirmative action although members of dominant groups do not qualify for it. The problem with this kind of exceptionalism, however

---

1   the Nazi's special treatment The Nazi term was *Sonderbehandlung*.

2   *Arguments that ... special protection* See, e.g., Mulier v. Oregon, 208 U.S. 412 (1908).

3   *the excellence of character ... all other excellences* Aristotle, *The Politics*, trans. Benjamin Jowett, ed. Steven Everson (London: Cambridge Univ. Press, 1988) 19.

practically helpful in cushioning the impact of the standard equality approach, is that the same principle—different treatment for real differences—has not only squarely rationalized the worst human rights abuses in history; it continues to be used to justify systematic forms of disadvantage like paying women in the most sex-segregated jobs less money. Women do different jobs, so they can be paid differently, meaning less. Nothing in Aristotle's approach prevents treating someone less well who is "differently situated" or "different" by virtue of being already less well off. That tautology is precisely equality under this approach, and precisely inequality, worse and more of it, in the real world.

A system-level consequence of this mainstream approach, rectified nowhere, is the failure to see as inequality issues many that are, especially those that are sexual or reproductive. Sexual violence, because of the overwhelming predominance of male perpetrators and female victims, and its rootedness in normative images of sexuality seen as naturally gendered, has tacitly been construed as an expression of the sex difference, therefore not an issue of sex inequality at all. Because overwhelmingly one sex is the perpetrators and the other is the victims, sexual violence is not sex discrimination, it is sex, that is, a "difference." The law of sexual harassment, which recognizes one form of sexual aggression as sex discrimination, is a bit of a miracle in this light, and in some tension with the mainstream structure, which hives off sexual abuse into the criminal law, ignoring its inequality dimensions. Similarly, because women and men contribute differently to reproduction, women's needs for reproductive rights have been brought under equality law only partially, as exceptions, with severe doctrinal strain, or, in the case of the right to abortion, not at all.

Women had no voice in contesting Aristotle's formulation in his day and have had little institutional power in shaping its legal applications since. Despite this lack of representation, including in democracies, women have in the last twenty years begun to articulate their condition in public. The facts that have emerged in this way, taken together, have revealed a grim system of unequal pay, allocation to disrespected work, sexual stigmatization, sexual violation as children and adults, and domestic battering. Women are attributed demeaned physical characteristics, used in denigrating entertainment, depersonalized as objects, deprived of reproductive control, and forced into prostitution[1]—all

this in the civilized West. Elsewhere, if women are permitted gainful employment at all, it can be all that and chattel status, early and forced marriage, inability to divorce, compulsory veiling, genital mutilation, honor killings, ritual murder as in suttee,[2] and more.

These abuses have occurred, in varying forms, for a very long time in a context characterized by disenfranchisement, preclusion from property ownership, possession and use as object, exclusion from public life, sex-based poverty, degraded sexuality, and devaluation of worth and contributions throughout society. Like other inequalities, but in its own way, the subjection of women is institutionalized, including in law, cumulatively and systematically shaping access to human dignity, respect, resources, physical security, credibility, membership in community, speech, and power. Composed of all its variations, the group women has a collective social history of disempowerment, exploitation, and subordination extending to the present, such that, in the words of the philosopher Richard Rorty, to be a woman "is not yet the name of a way of being human."[3]

This is not all there is to every woman's life, any more than racism is all there is to every Black American's life or class oppression is all there is to every working person's life under capitalism. Too, oppressive social systems legitimate themselves by individual exceptions. Many people enjoy the illusion that they, and most everyone they know, live their lives in freedom, in their minds anyway, or in exceptionality, in circumscribed areas at least. Thus can women have a feeling of freedom and dignity, and men a sense of nonparticipation in sex inequality, even as women's unequal status relative to men goes largely unchallenged.

We can choose to call this reality "the sex difference"—as, in their way, many sociobiologists, conservatives, postmodernists, and members of the religious right, consistent with the deep structure of conventional equality theory, do. It can be represented as Aristotle's level line disproportionately divided, which so long as each has their own, is equality. In this equality tradition, to describe something

---

1 *Women are attributed ... forced into prostitution* See Catharine A. MacKinnon, "Reflections on Sex Equality Under Law," *Yale Law Journal* 100 (1991): 1281; Catharine A. MacKinnon, *Toward a Feminist Theory of the State* (Cambridge: Harvard University Press, 1989).

2 *suttee* [editors' note] The (now illegal) traditional Hindu ritual in which a woman throws herself on her husband's funeral pyre.

3 *is not yet ... being human* Richard Rorty, "Feminism and Pragmatism," in *The Tanner Lectures on Human Values: 1992*, Grethe B. Peterson, ed. (Salt Lake City: University of Utah Press, 1992), 1, 7.

as a difference means it does not need to be changed, cannot be changed, is not produced by inequality, and is not unequal. So, although few openly defend mass rape in war or husbands slaughtering their wives in so-called peacetime as "just the sex difference," this is the reigning default conceptualization of such occurrences, insofar as they are not conceived as violations of sex equality rights. If the reality of women's status and treatment described merely refers to sex differences, equality already exists and the existing legal approach is in no need of change. Alternatively, these facts can be represented as a hierarchy, a top-down arrangement of imposed superiority and inferiority, of better off and worse off, advantaged and disadvantaged. To this, difference is relatively indifferent. For instance, the sexes could be "different" to the degree they are hierarchically (i.e., differently), situated and treated, without making that hierarchy equal in any sense except as so deemed under the mainstream model. To describe the facts as representing a hierarchy also means to see them as changeable, as overwhelmingly produced by inequality, as unequal, and as in need of change.

Once women are seen as men's human equals—an assumption presumably made when a legal sex equality standard is adopted, at the same time making it more possible to notice that the sexes are social unequals—systematically fewer material resources and life chances and more sex-specific victimization for one sex become difficult to justify. In addition, although equality is not only a second-order right to other rights, entitlements to life, liberty, property, security, dignity, and self-determination are thereby violated, to mention a few. And if the sexes are different, they are equally different. Once the hierarchy of social outcomes is noticed, it becomes difficult to explain why men are not paid less and assaulted by women more for *their* "differences." Measuring the equality approach created in women's silence and exclusion against the realities of women's lives, as women have begun to articulate them, the analytical and practical shortcomings of the existing approach thus emerge, revealing the need for a reconstructed equality theory to remedy them. The new paradigm moves behind and beyond sameness and difference to the subordination and dominance that has been the real problem of inequality all along.

Take Aristotle's "difference" between commanding and obeying, tracking sex. Giving and taking orders is one of the most universally recognized hierarchies known, including among men. In other words, his "difference" is a hierarchy. The embedding of hierarchy in relations that do not attract equality scrutiny makes predictable what has happened when this approach is applied in legal systems. Sex equality for the "similarly situated" best provides equality for whoever is "the same as men." Actually, these people have *been* men: white men have brought most of the leading Supreme Court sex discrimination cases.[1] Next in line are women whose biographies most closely approximate those men, elite women with privileges (white skin, money, education, and so on). Unrecognized here is that it is hierarchy, not difference as such, that is the opposite of equality. The inequality that is hierarchy, existing theory builds in as difference, meaning something that can be treated differently—that is, less well, hierarchically as lower—thus making the theory systematically unable to identify the one thing it needs to be able to identify and eliminate, in order to do what it has to do.

3

The implications of this critique are far-reaching and transformative. In politics and law, they range from state theory to doctrine, from jurisprudential theory to positive law, from epistemology to constitutional interpretation. Once the reality of gender is faced, it becomes clear the extent to which the laws, the legal system, the state as such, and relations between states have built in the experiences of the dominant and have been built from the perspective of those who created them. In the sociology of knowledge, this is a common kind of observation. Those who have created these systems have been the dominant gender group, the naming of which—men—becomes what is considered an extreme position, particularly when it is noted that the result has been their systematic hegemony over half the human race. To be clear: this equality theory is not a conspiracy theory; it relies on no conscious invidious motivation. It assumes, as other political theories do, only that people act in their own interest, as they see it, when they can. Why they see their interest as they do, and why they are permitted to act on it unchecked, is a separate question. The present analysis merely observes a political system of institutionalized interest supported by social facts of patterned behaviors and its embodiment in legal doctrine and philosophy. Nor is it a moral theory of who should do what. It is a political analysis of who gets what, how, and why, when that is dramatically differentially distributed, it is also a critique of terming

---

1   *white men ... discrimination cases*   David Cole, "Strategies of Difference: Litigating for Women's Rights in a Man's World," *Law and Inequality* 2 (1982): 33, 34, n.4.

"equality" the maintenance of that system and embodying it in legal equality doctrine. It should be noted that the conflict between ranks in a hierarchy need not be intractable. The sex hierarchy is merely big, old, pervasive, tenacious, denied, and a good many people are in love with it. Once it is faced as posing a certain division of interest enforced by force, like other serious inequalities such as race and class (and inextricably interconnected with them), it can be faced as in need of change through its own solutions.

The Supreme Court of Canada expressly adopted this alternate theory of equality in its first equality decision under the new Charter of Rights and Freedoms in 1985, in Law Society v. Andrews, a case adjudicating whether non-citizens could be made to wait longer than citizens before becoming lawyers.[1] Interpreting the Charter to effectuate its purposes, the Court determined that the purpose of an equality provision is to "promote equality." This does not sound like much, but it is everything: given social inequality, it requires that law has to move the world to be legal. It no longer leaves equality law standing neutrally in the face of an unequal world, sorting sameness from difference, reinforcing social inequalities by law. It requires courts to interpret laws so as *actually to produce* social equality. One might have thought this was obvious. The point of equality law is to produce equality. What else is it for—to produce inequality? That this stance is regarded as a major departure supports the indictment of the prior theory as status quo—reinforcing.

The Andrews Court explicitly repudiated the "similarly situated" test for equality, noting that this approach had justified racial segregation in the United States and could have supported the Nuremberg laws.[2] Aristotle and 2,000 years of equality abstractions based on him, including the Enlightenment's elevation of universality over particularity, came tumbling down, at least in Canada. That Court rejected the logic of the mainstream approach for having treated pregnancy less well than other nonwork reasons for not working because pregnancy is a difference, for treating First Nations women worse than men because Canadian Indians were a special class, and for treating all Native Peoples worse than non-Native Peoples because all Indians were treated alike. In its place was put a concrete, substantive, openly social-context–sensitive test of "historical disadvantage." The

sky did not fall. At last report, women and men continued to go on dates, babies continued to be born, and so forth.

This decision is a tectonic shift, a fundamental movement in the ground. One effect is to expose hierarchy where it has not been seen before, as in the areas of sexual assault and reproductive rights. Canada's new equality principle has been used to extend statutes of limitations in incest cases,[3] to sue a city for failing to warn women of a known serial rapist,[4] and to give credibility to battered women.[5] Less explicitly, but no less potently, it has influenced outcomes that include preventing men from vetoing abortions,[6] keeping a midwife who delivered a baby that died from being convicted of negligent murder,[7] and keeping raped women's names and identities out of the media.[8] It may also provide real rights for gay men and lesbian women.

If equality theory had been written to end women's inequality to men, it would certainly have included employment and education, but it would not have left out the street and the family, as the existing equality approach has. Sexual coercion (including sexual abuse of children, sexual harassment, rape, prostitution, and pornography) and deprivation of reproductive control (including forced sterilization, lack of sex education and contraception, misogynist gynecology, female infanticide, forced sex, and criminalization of abortion) are arguably central to the ways in which women, as a group, have been historically disadvantaged. In this light, the laws of rape and abortion are equality laws in disguise—deep disguise. More precisely, they are unequal laws that have never been held to an equality standard on social problems where group-based inequality is enacted. If rape is really a practice of sex discrimination, existing positive law and patterns of nonprosecution for sexual assault must meet constitutional sex equality standards. If reproductive control is a sex equality issue, deprivation of reproductive control is a sex equality violation, and prohibitions on abortion must sustain sex equality scrutiny or be found illegal under existing constitutions and international conventions.

---

1   *Law Society ... becoming lawyers*   Andrews v. Law Society of B.C., [1989] 1 S.C.R 143.

2   *The Andrews Court ... Nuremberg laws*   1 S.C.R. 143 at ¶10.

3   *Canada's new ... incest cases*   M. (K.) v. M. (H.), [1992] 3 S.C.R. 6.

4   *to sue ... serial rapist*   Jane Doe v. Board of Commissioners, 126 C.C.C.3d 12 (1998).

5   *to give ... battered women*   R. v. Lavallée, 1 S.C.R. 852 (1990).

6   *it has influenced ... vetoing abortions*   Daigle v. Tremblay, 2 S.C.R. 530 (1989).

7   *keeping a midwife ... negligent murder*   Queen v. Sullivan and Lemay, [1991] 1 S.C.R. 489.

8   *keeping raped ... the media*   Queen v. Canadian Newspapers Co. [1988] 2 S.C.R. 122.

This same new equality theory can be discerned beneath the U.S. Congress's law against gender-motivated violence, which makes rape and battering federal sex discrimination claims,[1] as well as in proposals to make pornography civilly actionable as sex discrimination.[2] The jurisprudence of the approach observes that sex inequality occurs in civil society, between women and men, and is then backed up and enforced through law. In many areas of its application, it names equality as the issue there for the first time. This is changing not only the content of law but potentially law's relation to unequal social life. Given that the state form has traditionally embodied male authority, a jurisprudence of equality cannot simply rely upon further empowering the state. It cannot rest with rules with different content, as big an improvement as that could be. It must also work structurally to redistribute the state power, by enabling women, with institutional support, to confront and remedy inequalities they encounter, including in intimate settings. Recognizing women's human rights on this level has major implications for the law of family, contract, and crime, as well as for constitutional and international law. As to equality as legal method, this substantive approach to equality reveals that the "rule of law" has not meant the same equalization for women that it has meant among men, at least for some of them. Assessment of the logic and outcomes of formal equality suggests that its "rule of law" form will never produce real positive equality either.

Effectively addressing the realities of social inequality between women and men requires addressing all inequalities. Indeed, much gender inequality is inextricable from inequalities women share with some men. On this point, consider two Canadian milestones: cases holding that hate propaganda and pornography threaten equality rights. One case involves a man who taught Holocaust denial to high school students;[3] the other involves a pornographer.[4] The

Supreme Court of Canada found that the equality of Jews and women, recognized as historically disadvantaged groups, was more important than the speech interests restricted by criminalizing expression that promoted their inequality. It found that racist and anti-Semitic hate propaganda produces and reinforces social subordination from segregation to genocide. Parliament, it held, may justifiably conclude that pornography, in its making and through its use, contributes to violation of and discrimination against women individually and as a group, harming the community's interest in equality. Thus both can be restricted. The United States, firmly in the grip of the traditional equality approach and blind to the hierarchy of systematic group-based disadvantage, remains unable to see that inequality is involved in issues of hate speech and pornography at all.[5]

The point of the new equality jurisprudence is to institutionalize social equality, rather than inequality, through legal equality initiatives. It begins by articulating the systematic, pervasive, and cumulative absence of equality throughout society, including in democracies, and by moving to put legal power to redress it into the hands of affected groups through law. In this vision, law can be something people do, not just something states do to people. This democratic shift in legal form as well as content—called civil rights as pioneered by the Black movement in the United States, with echoes in the human rights of transnational law—is appropriate to an aspiration to transform social hierarchy from the bottom up. Beyond clarifying unnoticed dynamics in law and history, and stimulating needed scholarship and analysis, the goal of this theory is to close the gap between legal promise and social reality in the equality area. This approach could be adopted anywhere. A legal regime capable of producing equality of women to men—half the human race to the other—made up as they are of all existing inequalities, might learn what it needs to know to produce equality among men as well.

---

1   *the U.S. Congress's ... discrimination claims*   The Violence Against Women Act, Pub. L. No. 103–122, Title IV, 108 Stat. 1902 (1994).

2   *proposals to make ... sex discrimination*   Catharine A. MacKinnon, *Only Words* (Cambridge: Harvard University Press, 1993).

3   *One case ... high school students*   R. v. Keegstra, [1990] 3 S.C.R. 697.

4   *the other involves a pornographer*   R. v. Butler, [1992] 1 S.C.R. 452. Elsewhere, German law opposes *Völksverhetzung* (hatred of peoples, or racial hatred), but more in reference to the value of dignity than equality. Eastern Europe and other emerging democracies define the systematic violation of women's equality through pornography as an emblem and spoil of long-sought

freedom, revealing a one-sided notion of freedom predicated on the subordination of women. The European Parliament has recognized pornography as a systematic practice of sex discrimination, Comm. Civil Liberties and Intern. Aff. Res. 83–0121/93 at 4–7, U.N. Doc. A30259/93 (24 September 1993), but this insight has not been enacted as law anywhere nor yet reached the European legal system.

5   *The United States ... pornography at all*   American Booksellers Ass'n Inc. v. Hudnut, 771 F.2d 323 (7th Cir. 1985); R.A.V. v. City of St. Paul, Minn., 505 U.S. 377 (1992); Collin v. Smith, 578 F.2d 1197 (7th Cir. 1978).

PART 3

Rights-Based Liberalism and Its Critics

INTRODUCTION TO *RIGHTS-BASED LIBERALISM AND ITS CRITICS*
Alex Sager and Will Kymlicka

Rights-based liberalism arguably enjoys a hegemonic position in social and political thought today—largely as a result of the influence of John Rawls. A high percentage of the major social and political theorists of the past two generations can be viewed either as rights-based liberals developing and refining the tradition or as critics responding to what they consider to be the tradition's inadequacies.

Despite the dominance of rights-based liberalism over this period, it is not easy to offer a simple definition of its principal tenets. Liberalism covers a great deal of territory, and holds varying meanings for different theorists. A short list of important twentieth- and twenty-first-century liberal thinkers includes such diverse figures as T.H. Green, John Dewey, Isaiah Berlin, Friedrich August von Hayek, Robert Nozick, Ronald Dworkin, John Rawls, Susan Moller Okin, and Martha Nussbaum. The differences between these thinkers are arguably at least as significant as their points of agreement. Liberalism may thus very well be best thought of as a family of doctrines, rather than a unified whole.

As a term in political philosophy,[1] liberalism is typically used to refer to an approach that upholds institutions such as constitutional democracy, rule of law, toleration of diverse lifestyles, separation of church and state, freedom of speech and expression, and individual rights and freedoms. A state run on liberal principles requires a large private sphere free from state interference so as to allow individuals to choose their particular lifestyles and values. Liberalism also often endorses the institution of private property—though liberal egalitarians advocate placing very significant limits on the inequalities generated by private ownership in capitalist societies, and socialist liberals argue for the public ownership of the major means of production.

By definition, liberalism is a doctrine concerned with liberty, but there is considerable disagreement as to how liberty ought to be understood. Though taxonomies differ, it is common to distinguish between classical and modern liberalism. Classical liberalism emphasizes negative rights and private property with limited government interference. Modern liberalism does not deny the importance of negative rights, but advocates government action to enable citizens to exercise their freedom. Part of the reason for this is that the liberal tradition has evolved differently in England, America, France, and Germany, with their different systems of government and law. But the ambiguity of liberalism also reflects theorists' moral and political commitments: their views on the proper role of the state, the balance they strike between their commitment to individualism and commitment to community, and the convictions they hold about the institution of private property.

The first section of this overview sets out many of the sources for two broad conceptions of liberty, the first emphasizing freedom and negative rights, the other stressing the importance of democratic participation. Second, we list some of the major institutions and values endorsed by liberal thought and put into place in liberal societies. Third, we shift from liberalism founded on utilitarian principles to liberalism based on inviolable rights, characterized most prominently by the work of John Rawls. Finally, we examine well-known criticisms of rights-based liberalism. Particularly, we address those put forth by Marxists, communitarians, feminists, and multiculturalists, and explore some ways in which liberals might reply to these criticisms. To what extent do these criticisms deepen liberal thought? To what extent do they require that liberalism be fundamentally modified or rejected? In closing, we also briefly explore some of the challenges raised by globalization for liberal thought.

Two Conceptions of Liberty

Isaiah Berlin famously (and controversially) distinguished between negative and positive liberties in his essay "Two Concepts of Liberty." For Berlin, negative liberty is *freedom from* coercion; you are free in a negative sense if no one is

---

1   *As a term in political philosophy*   The term has a variety of overlapping uses; *economic liberalism*, for example, is a concept largely focused on freedom in trade. Some liberals hold that private property and liberty are closely connected and that the freedom to dispose of one's wealth without government interference is basic. This view is by no means undisputed.

preventing you from achieving your goals. Of course, simply because no one is preventing you from achieving goals does not mean you will attain them. As Berlin points out, it is questionable how "free" someone is who lacks food, money, or an adequate education. Positive liberty requires *freedom to* achieve one's ends or real freedom of opportunity (as opposed to formal freedom of opportunity) which may require substantial resources to achieve. Berlin also identified positive liberty with agents' autonomy or capacity for self-rule, especially as developed in the work of Rousseau (more on this below).

Berlin identified negative liberty with classical liberalism, which has its roots in seventeenth-century England, most prominently in Thomas Hobbes's *Leviathan* (1651) and John Locke's *Two Treatises of Government* (1689). Though Hobbes has an uneasy relationship with the liberal tradition—his theory of government was strongly authoritarian, granting the state virtually absolute power over its subjects—his concept of a social contract established the notion of the state originating in the consent of its subjects. According to Hobbes, individuals in the state of nature are in a state of war of all-against-all in which life is "solitary, poor, nasty, brutish, and short." It is therefore rational for individuals to submit to the authority of the state.

Later writers such as Locke and David Hume took up Hobbes's definition of liberty as freedom from constraint. In his *Second Treatise*, Locke developed two central devices for political theory, a liberal version of the social contract and a theory of natural law that was radical for his time.[1] Locke viewed the state of nature more benignly than had Hobbes. Whereas Hobbes argued that people must transfer *all* of their rights to the sovereign (except the right to self-preservation) for the sake of stability, Locke held that they only transferred *some* of their rights. The Lockean sovereign is bound to uphold the natural law and its subjects are justified in rebelling if it fails to meet his obligation. Despite their differences, Locke, like Hobbes, based the legitimacy of government on consent (or tacit consent[2]).

Locke is often held to have limited the state's role to protecting "life, liberty and property."[3] There is some truth to this claim, but Locke also writes in his *First Treatise*:

> We know God hath not left one man so to the mercy of another that he may starve him if he please ... As justice gives every man a title to the product of his honest industry, and the fair acquisitions of his ancestors descended to him; so charity gives every man a title to so much of another's plenty, as will keep him from extreme want, where he has no means to subsist otherwise.

Of course, a right to be free from "extreme want" hardly anticipates the modern welfare state. Those who focus on such minimal rights tend to be highly skeptical about paternalistic state measures to promote liberty, on the ground that individuals are typically the best judges of their own interests, and also best equipped to realize them. State interference can become tyrannical and its dictates may represent the views of dominant groups, resulting in the oppression of minorities or unpopular points of view. States also typically lack the information necessary to dictate social policy for complex societies. In the twentieth century, this classical liberal view of liberty as freedom from coercion has been endorsed by libertarian writers such as Hayek and Nozick.

What classical liberalism tended to overlook was the way in which vast inequalities of wealth generated by laissez-faire capitalism placed enormous power in the hands of a small minority, leading to non-governmental forms of oppression. John Stuart Mill, under the influence of Harriett Taylor Mill, came to realize that freedom of self-development—a central goal of his brand of liberalism—requires economic security and opportunity. In Britain, the social philosophers and "new" liberals, L.T. Hobhouse and T.H. Green, stressed the social circumstances needed for achieving individual liberty, and endorsed collective action for economic reform, as well as state intervention in social and cultural life.[4] Such

---

1 The social contract and natural law tradition have a long history going back to ancient times. Plato sets out a form of the social contract in the *Crito* and the *Republic*. Natural law is prominent in the writings of Stoic philosophers, as well as in the Christian tradition (perhaps most importantly in the work of St. Thomas Aquinas).

2 Contemporary liberals generally do not believe that society is the product of an actual contract. Rather, those working in the social contract tradition find versions of the concept of a social contract to be useful tools for reflecting on norms of justice, legitimacy,

and other phenomena. On this line of thought, it is damning if a society imposes restrictions or burdens on people that they would not have agreed to if they had been given a choice.

3 See below for more discussion on liberalism and private property.

4 Green also contributed to the analysis of freedom, arguing that a person is free if her actions are in some sense her own. Thus, we are unfree if we're overcome by cravings beyond our control—Green had alcoholism in mind—or if we have not critically reflected on our ends and considered the long-term consequences. This conception of freedom is also evident in John Stuart Mill's *On Liberty*.

measures for promoting positive liberty were first carried out on a large scale in Western democracies in the 1930s and 1940s (notably, by Franklin Roosevelt's New Deal between 1933 and 1938), and continue in some form in most liberal states today.

As mentioned above, positive freedom is not simply concerned with providing means for people to achieve their ends. It also involves the concept of autonomy or self-rule. The concept is elaborated in the work of the early nineteenth-century French-Swiss political theorist, Benjamin Constant, whose distinction between the "liberties of the ancients" and the "liberties of the moderns" influenced Berlin's essay. Constant argued that there were two distinct conceptions of liberty in political thought. The liberties of the ancients were connected to democratic participation in the state, permitting citizens to influence decision-making through public deliberation and voting; the liberties of the moderns provided protection from the state.

Though Constant traced the liberties of the ancients to classical Greece and Rome, the most important proponent of such liberties was arguably the French philosopher Jean-Jacques Rousseau, who developed a quite different version of liberalism. Rousseau viewed freedom not as absence of coercion, but rather as the ability to exercise control over one's life. Citizens achieved freedom by participating in the democratic process of forming the "general will." This raised an apparent paradox: since freedom for Rousseau could only be achieved by submitting one's individual will to the general will, there were occasions in which people could be forced to be free.

Though Rousseau's conception of liberty has been roundly criticized by classical liberals—Benjamin Constant referred to Rousseau's *Social Contract* as "the most formidable ally of all despotism"—it does provide a distinct perspective, sometimes referred to as the *étatiste* conception of liberalism, and highlights the importance of democracy for political theory. As the social contract theorists realized, society is very much a system of cooperation, and democratic citizen-control over its policies is one means of expanding people's freedom, by allowing them to work together to achieve shared ends.

Some Major Characteristics of Liberalism

We have briefly discussed two major conceptions of liberalism and their historical origins, as well as stressed the diversity of views internal to liberal thought. The diversity, however, is not so great that we cannot make some general remarks on the nature of liberalism; we must simply keep in mind in doing so that most individual theorists would qualify these generalizations or, indeed, reject some of them altogether.

Though liberalism has important precursors in the ancient philosophy of Greece and Rome, and the Italian city-states of the Renaissance, modern liberalism began in the seventeenth century in opposition to monarchy, theocracy, and other forms of authoritarian rule. Liberals typically view society as made up of diverse social, cultural, religious, and political groups, and hold that individuals typically differ significantly in their life plans and conception of the good. This view of individuals and societies supports particular institutions and values that can fairly be said to be typical of liberal thought.

Some of the central liberal institutions are:

1) Constitutionalism—Liberal government is limited by constitutional rules that protect individual rights and set political values that check governmental power. Liberal societies are governed by the rule of law, which protects citizens from the abuse of public officials and private powers.

2) Separation of powers—Liberals typically hold that power should be divided between different branches of government. The best-known version follows Montesquieu's view—incorporated into the US Constitution by James Madison—that government should be divided between the executive, legislative, and judiciary branch.

3) Democracy—Liberal societies subscribe to democracy, the rule by the many; the legitimacy of government rests on the consent of the people. Most liberals advocate some form of representative democracy with open and fair elections, though some liberals also call for more direct representation, perhaps through citizen assemblies or referenda.

4) Private sphere—Citizens in liberal societies live significant parts of their lives away from public affairs. Liberal societies permit a private sphere where people can pursue their individual goals free from governmental interference.

5) Private property—Most liberals advocate some sort of private property rights, though they differ as to their extent and their sanctity. Many liberals have also linked

liberal freedom to free markets, though this does not rule out the possibility and perhaps necessity of some form of government intervention.

Beyond these institutions, most liberals endorse some form of these central values:

1) Individualism—Liberals view people primarily as individuals, rather than members of families, villages, classes, religions, or nations. Particularly important is *moral individualism*: larger groups have moral value only insofar as they have moral value for the individuals who compose them.

2) Moral equality—Liberalism extends equal rights to all citizens. Nowadays that principle is generally understood to imply that such rights are extended irrespective of gender, race, class, religion, or sexual origin.

3) Rights and liberties—Support for individual rights and liberties are basic to any liberal account (though as we see below, precisely how to understand these rights and liberties is contested within the liberal tradition). These typically include (but are not limited to):
   a. Freedom of thought and speech.
   b. Freedom of religion.
   c. *Habeas corpus* or freedom from unlawful and arbitrary detention.
   d. Rights to life, liberty, and security of person.
   e. Freedom from torture or cruel and unusual punishment.

4) Equality of opportunity—Classical liberals reject class distinctions and stress the importance of social mobility; modern liberals often add that equality of opportunity also requires government intervention to ensure that all citizens are actually able to effectively enjoy their freedom.

5) Toleration—Liberals stress the need to tolerate, and perhaps even celebrate cultural, religious, and political diversity.

6) Neutral government—In liberal societies, the government is expected to refrain from promoting, any more than necessary, a single conception of the good.

7) Progressivism—Liberals look toward the future, rather than the status quo or the past. They are generally cautiously optimistic that rational thought and reasonable discussion can resolve the most pressing social and economic problems (though they are also aware of the pitfalls of utopian thinking).

From Utilitarianism to Rights-Based Liberalism

In the decades prior to the publication of John Rawls's *A Theory of Justice* in 1971, utilitarianism dominated liberal thought. Since utilitarianism was the only systematic theory that could be used to evaluate public policy, most theorists either endorsed utilitarianism or relied on "intuitionism," which attempts to balance competing intuitions or values in a non-systematic way.

Utilitarians hold that social and political institutions should be judged by their utility and that they should aim at maximizing utility—in Bentham's phrase, producing "the greatest happiness for the greatest number."[1] The systematization of utilitarian insights in economics using individual preference rankings and Pareto efficiency[2] also added to the attraction of utilitarianism, providing the welcome rigor of social choice theory and game theory.

Jeremy Bentham famously called natural rights "nonsense on stilts" and wrote that "the indestructible prerogatives of mankind have no need to be supported upon the sandy foundations of a fiction."[3] There is a place for rights in utilitarian theories, but they are ultimately a means to the end of promoting happiness. Bentham considered rights to be purely legal notions; they were justified only insofar as they promoted the greatest happiness for the great number.

This deflationary account of rights has struck many as misguided. During the 1960s civil rights movement in the US, protestors did not hold that segregation was wrong because it made people unhappy or led to less happiness overall. In a society where the majority of people support and benefit from segregation, it is quite possible that more

---

1   Bentham attributed the phrase to the Unitarian clergyman, scientist, chemist, and political reformer Joseph Priestley or the Italian jurist Cesare Beccaria's *Essays on Crimes and Punishments* (1764). The latter may have derived the phrase from the French-Swiss philosopher Claude Adrien Helvetius's *De l'ésprit* (1758). It also has an antecedent in Francis Hutcheson's (1694–1746) *Inquiry into the Origins of our Ideas of Beauty and Virtue*, though Bentham was probably unaware of this.

2   Pareto efficiency or optimality is a notion in neo-classical economics in which an economic system is "efficient" if no one can be made better off without at least one person being made worse off. The fact that a distribution is "Pareto efficient" says little about the actual distribution of resources—social systems that permit great inequalities can be Pareto efficient.

3   Jeremy Bentham (1748–1832), *Anarchical Fallacies; being an examination of the Declaration of Rights issued during the French Revolution*.

overall happiness is created at the expense of the oppressed minority. Protestors argued against segregation not on utilitarian grounds, but because it systematically violated people's rights, including the right to equal treatment and respect, and the right to equality of opportunity.[1] It was also an unacceptable infringement on the liberty of segregated groups.

In fact, many would agree that segregation would be wrong even in a world in which people happily accepted segregation (perhaps as the result of early childhood indoctrination and adaptive preferences[2]). Even if utilitarians were to agree with rights-based theorists that segregation could not be morally justified, they seem to those advocating rights-based liberalism to reach this conclusion for the wrong *type* of reason. The importance of rights is that they provide a counter-majoritarian recourse against social injustice.

Though there were well-known criticisms of utilitarianism before the 1970s, there was a dearth of systematic alternatives to it. That changed with the publication in 1971 of Rawls's *A Theory of Justice*. In this major work, Rawls revived and reinvented a Kantian version of the social contract, in which parties choose principles of justice in the "original position," a hypothetical state of nature for determining the just distribution of rights and duties. In Rawls's model, free, rational, and self-interested parties choose the principles of justice behind a "veil of ignorance" which prevents them from knowing their own place in society, their social status, social class, gender, natural abilities, or psychological traits. Behind the veil of ignorance they are even prevented from knowing their own conception of the good. They are, however, aware of what Rawls calls the "circumstances of justice" in which individuals with different life goals have roughly equal physical and mental powers and needs in a world of moderate scarcity, as well as the competing theories of justice. On Rawls's account, all of the excluded information is morally irrelevant for the purposes of justice. The veil of

ignorance thus simulates a fair agreement between moral persons, since it reflects what people would choose if they were not self-interested, biased, or influenced (consciously or unconsciously) by their role or position. This intuitive test of fairness works in a similar way to how a fair division of a cake could be ensured by preventing the person cutting it from knowing which piece she will receive.

Rawls claimed that parties under the veil of ignorance would choose "justice as fairness" over utilitarianism and other competing accounts of justice. Justice as fairness endorses two principles, with the first principle taking priority over the second:

> First Principle: Each person is to have an equal right to the most extensive total system of equal basic liberties compatible with a similar system of liberty for all.
>
> Second Principle: Social and economic inequalities are to be arranged so that they are both: (a) to the greatest benefit of the least advantaged, consistent with the just savings principle,[3] and (b) attached to offices and positions open to all under conditions of fair equality of opportunity.

The First Principle guarantees a set of basic rights that are safeguarded from utilitarian calculus. These rights can only be abridged to protect the basic rights of others, not to advance overall happiness. The Second Principle says that inequalities in economic resources should be designed not to the greatest benefit of society as a whole (as in utilitarianism), but rather to the greatest benefit of the least advantaged—i.e., inequalities are only permitted if they benefit those who are thereby less well off. Both are anti-utilitarian provisions that limit the extent to which the weak or disadvantaged can be sacrificed for the greater good of others. Rawls argues that parties under the veil of ignorance would also choose what he calls "primary goods": basic rights, liberties, and opportunities, income, wealth, and the "social-basis for self-respect."

A Theory of Justice also contains a trenchant criticism of utilitarianism. Though the precise content of Rawls's criticisms is sometimes hard to decipher, he seems to identify three problems with utilitarianism. First, there is the issue raised above: utilitarianism permits, under some circum-

---

1 Thus, in the famous 1954 US Supreme Court case *Brown v Board of Education*, it was determined that segregation in education deprived black children of the equal protection of the laws guaranteed by the Fourteenth Amendment of the US constitution: "segregation of children in public schools solely on the basis of race deprives children of the minority group of equal educational opportunities, even though the physical facilities and other 'tangible' factors may be equal."

2 Adaptive preferences refer to the well-known psychological propensity of people to come to accept adverse circumstances and forms of deprivation despite the fact that they do not appear to reflect what they would choose under more favorable conditions.

3 The just savings principle is a principle of intergenerational justice that puts away funds to guarantee the realization and preservation of a just society across generations.

stances, the violation of people's rights. Second, utilitarianism—at least in its cruder forms—counts every source of utility equally. Thus, it is argued that utilitarians appear committed to balancing the pleasure of the white supremacist's sadistic satisfaction with the anguish of her victim's humiliation. But surely sadistic preferences shouldn't count at all.

Rawls's third and most original argument is that utilitarianism fails to respect the "separateness of persons." It is common for people to sacrifice happiness during one period of their life for future benefits. Individuals may work long hours to better prepare for retirement or suffer the rigors of medical school for a lucrative and rewarding career. This is fairly uncontroversial since the trade-off is *within* a single life: people anticipate future benefits for their present sacrifice.[1] But utilitarianism, since it is committed to maximizing utility, seems to allow these sorts of trade-offs *between* lives. This violates what Rawls refers to as the "inviolability of persons."

A Theory of Justice, together with Rawls's later articles and books such as *Political Liberalism* (1993) and *The Law of Peoples* (1999), has triggered an avalanche of secondary literature. Virtually all social and political theory written today is informed by Rawls, at least indirectly. Theorists holding alternative or opposing positions have felt the need to respond to Rawls. Thus, Robert Nozick's libertarian manifesto *Anarchy, State, and Utopia* (1974) provides detailed criticisms of Rawls, as does Michael Sandel's communitarian classic *Liberalism and the Limits of Justice* (1982).

"Rights-talk" has also come to dominate social movements. Women's struggle for equality is largely framed in terms of rights, as are the claims of gays and lesbians, the disabled, indigenous people, and immigrant groups. The influence of social and political philosophy on these movements is diffuse, and lines of influence may run in both directions; the Universal Declaration of Human Rights and the many later national and international treaties and convenants on human rights no doubt contribute to, as well as reflect, the increasing role of rights in our cultural environment. Still, there is no doubt that rights-based liberalism in some form has come to inform debate throughout the public sphere, as well as the academic world.

---

1 That said, the issue of personal identity raises fascinating questions about the rationality of trade-offs between our present and future (selves). See Derek Parfit, *Reasons and Persons* (Oxford University Press, 1984) for the classic discussion. David Shoemaker provides an excellent introduction to these issues in *Personal Identity and Ethics* (Broadview Press, 2008).

Criticisms of Rights-Based Liberalism

The prominence of rights-based liberalism has made it the target of powerful criticisms. Marxists have drawn attention to the exploitation and alienation of wage-laborers in liberal capitalist societies; some feminists have pointed to the seeming indifference of liberal principles to the special concerns raised by gender; communitarians have condemned what they have seen as the excessive individualism of liberal theory and its neglect of shared communal values; multiculturalists have sometimes portrayed liberal universalism as a tool for domination that pays insufficient attention to difference and to the unique values of aboriginal and ethnic groups.

Though some theorists urge that the model of rights-based liberalism be replaced altogether, others argue that in many cases liberalism has learned from its critics and as a result, is now much better equipped to address the many concerns of today's world.

Marxist Criticisms of Liberalism

Marxism largely fell out of favor after the collapse of the Soviet Union in 1991. "Analytic Marxism," which enjoyed some prominence in the 1980s as it applied the tools of analytic philosophy and neo-classical economics to Marxist theory, has been largely eclipsed by left-wing liberalism. Even prominent advocates such as G.A. Cohen now in many cases produce work that is recognizably liberal in nature (though *radically* liberal).

Nonetheless, liberal theory owes a great deal to Marxism and its critiques. Marxists have often pointed out that liberal justice, viewed in terms of civil and political rights and formal equality of opportunity, ignores material inequalities. It is hard to disagree with Marx that nineteenth-century capitalism (with its subsistence wages, debilitating work week, extensive use of child labor, and dangerous, noxious work sites) was exploitative, alienating, and, in general, intolerable. And similar criticisms also apply to the capitalist institutions that have recently taken shape in much of the developing world. But it is less clear to what extent Marxist criticisms apply to the modern welfare state with its minimum wage, forty hour (or shorter) work week, unemployment insurance, and other social assistance and regulatory measures.

The charge that liberalism ignores material inequalities is an important challenge to classical liberalism or libertarianism, but it has less force against liberal egalitarian theories such as that put forward by Rawls. Marxists and socialists argue that Rawls is not egalitarian enough, but such disagreements may still be disputed on a liberal playing field. The question, then, becomes an issue of the type and extent of material equality necessary for a just society and whether extensive egalitarianism can and should be justified within a liberal framework.

Marxists have more radical arguments against liberalism. Orthodox Marxism rejects liberal accounts of rights for a number of reasons. It frequently holds that rights are "ideological," serving to justify current practices such as the private ownership of the means of production. There is something to this claim, but it is unclear that it undermines liberalism. If it can be shown that some rights are ideological in a pejorative sense—i.e., part of a system of beliefs that always serves to legitimize the currently dominant interests of a society—liberals might use this information to modify the list of rights they endorse.

Many Marxists would not be satisfied with this response, holding instead that *all* liberal rights are ideological.[1] In *On the Jewish Question*, Marx takes liberal rights to task for presupposing conflict between people. Rights isolate people, presupposing that we need protection from each other. But this, according to Marx, is because of the nature of capitalist society—divided between those who own the means of production and those forced to work for wages, and driven by competition, acquisitiveness, and the pursuit of self-interest. Thus, in his 1875 *Critique of the Gotha Program*, Marx wrote:

> In a higher phase of communist society, after the enslaving subordination of the individual to the division of labor, and therewith also the antithesis between mental and physical labor, has vanished; after labor has become not only a means of life but life's prime want; after the productive forces have also increased with the all-around development of the individual, and all the springs of co-operative wealth flow more abundantly—only then can the narrow horizon of bourgeois right be crossed in its entirety and society inscribe on its banners: From each according to his ability, to each according to his needs!

---

1   In fact, Marx and many of his followers often claim that morality itself is ideological, reflecting and reinforcing the economic relations of society. An approach deriving from this view, known as scientific historical materialism, purports to show that society would inevitably progress towards a communist revolution, thus eliminating the need for moral reflection. The rejection of morality by Marxism is deeply puzzling, given that much of its attraction is moral disgust at the ruthless exploitation and alienation in capitalist societies.

Marx's conception of freedom is based on our mutual relations in a human community. In a classless communist society, in his view, the state will become superfluous and "wither away." This way of thinking attacks what Rawls called the conditions of justice (following Hume in *An Enquiry Concerning the Principles of Morals* [1751]). Liberals view justice as characterized by moderate scarcity and limited benevolence. Resources are not infinite and human beings are not angels. Unlike conservatives, liberals are generally optimistic, believing in the possibility of social progress, but they reject Marxist and anarchist visions of a stateless society as utopian. Liberals believe that the world can be much better than it is, but that there will always be a need for institutions to mediate potential conflicts.

How large a role should such institutions play? That question has prompted an important debate in recent liberal theory. A central tenet of *A Theory of Justice* and many other works in liberal social and political theory is John Rawls's claim that "justice is the first virtue of social institutions." For Rawls and many other liberals, principles of justice apply to the major social, political, and economic institutions of a society, *not* to individual actions. Thus, distributive justice is accomplished through measures such as progressive taxation, not by individual acts of charity. Individuals have a duty to support just institutions, but beyond that are free to pursue their personal projects and relationships without undue concern for justice (on the grounds that their society's institutions are sufficiently just).

G.A. Cohen has criticized this approach, arguing that its focus on institutions neglects the way in which individual attitudes can undermine the realization of principles of justice. A society with institutions committed to an egalitarian principle, for example, is unlikely to fully realize this principle if many people's choices conflict with it. But while there are reasons for thinking that liberalism cannot limit itself exclusively or even mainly to the major social, political, and economic institutions, few people seriously consider the possibility that these institutions could be eliminated altogether. Even in a socialist society, there would still be a role for justice to mediate conflict.

Communitarian Criticisms of Liberalism

Communitarian critics of liberalism call attention to what they view as liberalism's neglect of community in favor of individualism. Community plays an important role in the history of social and political thought, in the work of Aristotle, Rousseau, Hegel, Marx and others. The French

Revolution called for "liberté, égalité, et fraternité" (liberty, equality, and solidarity), but solidarity has been somewhat neglected in the liberal tradition. Communitarians address this neglect. The more radical communitarian critics of liberal theory suggest that abstract, universal, liberal principles be replaced altogether with "thick" principles drawn from communities' shared practices and mutual understandings; other less radical communitarian thinkers see their contribution more narrowly, as drawing attention to some of the inadequacies of liberalism as it is commonly understood.

The most important communitarian works are generally thought to be Alasdair MacIntyre's *After Virtue: A Study in Moral Theory* (1981), Michael Sandel's *Liberalism and the Limits of Justice* (1982), Michael Walzer's *Spheres of Justice: A Defence of Pluralism and Equality* (1983), along with many of the articles collected in Charles Taylor's *Philosophy and the Human Sciences: Philosophical Papers, Volume 2* (1985). Notably, none of the major communitarian writers actually accepts the label "communitarian," which has been adopted largely by their commentators and critics.

What communitarians take issue with is the degree to which liberals privilege a conception of individuals as autonomous and capable of rationally reflecting on their ends and way of life. This idea is prominent in Immanuel Kant's claim that persons are "ends in themselves," able to choose their own ends and act upon them.[1] John Stuart Mill prized freedom of conscience, opinion, and pursuit, setting out powerful arguments for freedom of speech. He also criticized the tendency of democracy to suppress individuality by enforcing homogeneity. John Dewey's experimentalism emphasized the importance of the freedom to explore diverse ways of life in which one's choices allow a form of "self-creation." John Rawls held that individuals have a conception of the good and the ability to choose a rational life plan. Even if liberalism does not require self-creation or development as a perfectionist end that all individuals should freely strive towards, all liberals place value on the ability to critically evaluate one's own culture and way of life. Of course, individuals may decide to live traditional lives, even surrendering their autonomy to religious or other authorities, but this, in itself, is a choice. Private associations must also be voluntary, and liberal societies must guarantee individuals' freedom to leave them.

Communitarians have criticized this set of ideas on a number of grounds. First, communitarians have criticized liberal individualism for presupposing an "atomistic" (Charles Taylor) or "unencumbered" (Michael Sandel) theory of the self that fails to take account of how the self is formed by its role in the community. Liberals endorse personal freedom and individual rights, but ignore how the very existence of such rights presupposes social relationships. Thus, according to communitarians, liberals should reject the "atomistic" conception of human beings and commit themselves to sustaining the social practices that make individual liberty possible. Solidarity, then, has at least as much importance as individual liberty.

One difficulty with this communitarian critique is that it sometimes conflates an *ontological* account of individualism with a *moral* account. No liberal denies that people develop their identities through their interaction with other human beings, or that such development takes place within a particular culture and community (or set of cultures and communities, as is often the case today). Nor do liberals reject the claim that community is deeply important for most people, or that most worthwhile freedoms presuppose a human community in which they can be exercised.[2] The communitarian critique of the liberal conception of the self may call for a reevaluation of liberal values, perhaps giving more weight to the importance of sustaining communal goods, but this may be seen as refining and developing liberalism, rather than overturning it.[3]

A second claim, developed by Michael Sandel, is that justice is only a "remedial" virtue that corrects flaws in social life—justice is needed only when the social virtues of benevolence and solidarity fall short. Sandel refers to the family as a social institution that, in ideal circumstances, does not require justice, since love and solidarity are sufficient to achieve morally praiseworthy familial relations. Sandel goes as far as to argue that claims of justice may in some cases actually undermine harmonious familial relations.

---

1   Kant writes in his essay "What is Enlightenment?" that "Enlightenment is man's emergence from his self-imposed immaturity. Immaturity is the inability to use one's understanding without guidance from another. This immaturity is self-imposed when its cause lies not in lack of understanding, but in lack of resolve and courage to use it without guidance from another."

2   Liberals do hold that communities only have moral worth insofar as individuals value these communities, which may conflict with some communitarian claims that communities are good independent of how individuals value them.

3   A radical liberal individualist might not even accept this. She might acknowledge that liberty presupposes community, but then claim that liberty alone has moral worth—communal goods are only valuable insofar as they contribute to individual liberty.

Sandel's claim evokes Marxist criticisms of liberalism, but from a different perspective. The Marxist vision of communism is progressive, looking forward to a society of equals; communitarians insist, instead, on a conservative or even reactionary view of community,[1] which exists in current social practices or shared social understandings—or, as may be the case, existed before liberal individualism and mass market commercialism undermined them. So while some communitarians echo the Marxist accusation that justice is unnecessary in a genuine community, Marxists would respond that the exploitative and alienated relationships they criticize are entrenched in the communities these communitarians praise.

Liberals have rejected the communitarian account of justice as a remedial virtue for two reasons. First, as feminists have clearly shown, the family is often a setting for dominance and oppression for women. The problem doesn't stem from a lack of love or solidarity, but rather from unequal power relations that decisively affect the sexual division of labor (among other things). In other words, it is a matter of justice. This criticism can easily be extended to other institutions, from schools and places of work to political forums. Liberals do not claim that justice is the only virtue, but that there is a strong case it is a necessary one, not merely to spur remedial measures, but also to provide a standard set of requirements for morally adequate social interaction. Second, it is not obvious why justice need interfere with love and solidarity. If anything, liberal theorists argue, placing people in a relationship of equality and non-domination ought to contribute to genuinely virtuous relationships, not detract from them.

Third, communitarians accuse liberals of failing to take seriously the value of political participation, treating it as merely instrumental; communitarians typically hold that political participation is valuable in itself, an essential part of the human good (a claim that goes back to Aristotle[2]). While there is some truth to this accusation for some types of liberalism, liberals have attempted to reply in two ways. First, they may deny that political participation is intrinsically valuable; the claim that such participation has intrinsic value is notoriously hard to justify to those who do not share this conception of the good. Second, they may suggest that this accusation ignores the Rousseauian conception of liberalism, in which autonomy is gained through democratically forming the general will. In this case, communitarianism can be seen as drawing attention to an often-neglected aspect of liberalism, reestablishing its importance for political theory.

Fourth, Michael Walzer has argued in *Spheres of Justice* against liberal universalism, urging a particularist account of "complex equality" grounded in groups' shared understandings. The meanings that people attach to social goods are irreducibly communal. Walzer thus views political philosophy largely as the task of interpreting norms already implicit in actual communities, rather than proposing and defending universal abstract principles.

Communitarians in general have come down on the "particularist" side of the universalist/particularist debate. They accuse liberals of excessive abstraction and insufficient attention to what people actually value. Liberals, it is claimed, presuppose a neutral Archimedean point or, to use Thomas Nagel's phrase, "a view from nowhere" from which social structures can be criticized. Instead, communitarians contend, everyone—including the social and political theorist—is embedded in a system of shared understandings and values; the liberals' pretense that their principles are universal merely disguises their own particular biases. Attention to actual communities, by contrast, may reveal particularlist "thick" values guiding people's lives—values which may be more satisfying than universal "thin" liberal principles.[3]

No doubt there is much to be said for the careful examination of social practices, but liberals often claim that communitarian critiques provide simply another corrective to liberal universalism. Liberals do not have to reject thick values, as long as they do not conflict with liberal principles. While there are certainly cases in which liberal universal principles *do* conflict with particularlist values—for example, many cultures endorse the subordination of women—liberals have argued that in these cases liberal universalist theory points to deep-set problems with communal values.

---

1   Unlike the commentators of the 1960s who invoked Marx in criticizing individualism, the two major figures most frequently invoked in the 1980s work of communitarians such as Alisdair MacIntyre, Charles Taylor, and Michael Sandel are arguably Aristotle (MacIntyre) and Hegel (Charles Taylor and Michael Sandel).

2   This objection has also been taken up by advocates of civic republics such as Quentin Skinner and Philip Pettit.

3   Notably, Rawls's later work is informed by these communitarian criticisms of liberal universalism. In *Political Liberalism* (1993), Rawls makes the more modest claim that he is simply trying to provide the best *liberal* account of justice. He does not try to argue that a non-liberal society would accept his two principles. In *The Law of Peoples*, Rawls allows for the possibility of "decent, hierarchical societies," that eschew liberal principles. Needless to say, Rawls's retreat from universality has been controversial, especially among fans of *A Theory of Justice*.

Some Marxists and communitarians have argued that there is a sinister side to rights-based liberalism; liberalism has often been accused as a tool of dominance over traditional, non-liberal groups. Even an avowed critic of colonialism such as John Stuart Mill justified despotic rule of "uncivilized" groups in terms of the *mission civilisatrice*—the European imperative to bring civilization to the non-Western world. More recently, critics have accused politicians of using the language of liberal rights to justify foreign interventions. According to these critics, humanitarian language has disguised crass pecuniary and neo-imperialist interests.

It is almost beyond argument that such behavior has occurred, but once again it is unclear whether this is a problem with liberalism itself or reflects a misapplication of its principles. Imperialism conflicts directly with liberal values such as the importance of self-determination, freedom, tolerance, and equality—in fact, many criticisms of imperialism (including those of Mill) are made on explicitly liberal grounds.

There may also be deep problems with giving too much credence to people's shared values. Familiar criticisms of relativism have led many liberals in the late twentieth and early twenty-first centuries to be dubious of communitarian accounts. To some liberals Walzer's arguments could be taken as justification for the Indian caste system (an example he refers to), the infibulation of female children, the execution of homosexuals, infanticide, and many other objectionable practices, so long as they reflect a community's shared meanings and values.[1] Also, Walzer may not sufficiently take into account the fact that most communities are internally pluralistic, and that the supposedly shared values are often imposed by the more powerful members of society.

Communitarianism has been mostly critical. So far no one has developed a systematic communitarian theory on a par with *A Theory of Justice* or other classic liberal works. This is partly due to its nature: attention to particular communal practices is unlikely to contribute straightforwardly to the type of generalizations necessary for systematic theorizing. As a result, liberals have learned a great deal from

their communitarian critics, but liberal theory retains its hegemonic position.

Feminism

Perhaps even more so than liberalism, feminism is a complex, sometimes even contradictory, intellectual and political movement. Liberal feminists, radical feminists, postmodern feminists—to list only three of the multiple feminist hybrids—differ on a wide range of substantial matters; what they hold in common is their commitment to the elimination of the subordination of women.

With a few notable exceptions, women were largely invisible in social and political thought until the late nineteenth century. Most of the leading theorists had deeply misogynist views about women. Aristotle held women to be defective males and that men's "courage" lies in commanding, while women's lies in obeying. Rousseau's *Émile* is a textbook on educating girls to serve their husbands. Thomas Jefferson's famous Locke-inspired opening to the second paragraph of the Declaration of Independence (1776) reads:

> We hold these truths to be self-evident, that all men are created equal, that they are endowed by their Creator with certain unalienable Rights, that among these are Life, Liberty, and the Pursuit of Happiness.

"All men" here is not intended as an inclusive term; Jefferson excluded women just as he excluded slaves and wrote:

> Were our state a pure democracy there would still be excluded from our deliberations women, who, to prevent depravation of morals and ambiguity of issue, should not mix promiscuously in gatherings of men.

Misogynistic examples from the philosophical canon can be easily multiplied. It is not surprising, then, that many early feminist writings aimed at correcting false dogmas about the inferiority of women, and at extending basic rights to women. Historically, this concurred with many of the goals of rights-based liberalism. Eighteenth-and-nineteenth-century thinkers such as Mary Wollstonecraft, Harriet Taylor Mill and John Stuart Mill advanced liberal arguments for the rights of women. This was also the goal of the "first wave" of twentieth-century feminism that achieved universal suffrage, access to education, and the abolition of discriminatory statutes in much of the world.

---

1   Walzer's account of justice involves "complex equality" in which a society is just if no sphere of justice—politics, business, education, religion, etc., which have their own distributive norms determined by social meanings—is permitted to dominate the others. This arguably provides a universal criterion for equality—non-dominance—though it is unclear to what extent this would meet the objection of relativism. In later work, Walzer admits that there are some thin values that admit universal acceptance.

The first wave feminists accomplished much on the assumption that the elimination of discriminatory barriers would suffice for gender equality. Once the formal obstacles to equality were removed, it was widely believed, women would gradually achieve parity with men in the workplace and in the political sphere.

This proved to be wrong. Women still systematically occupy lower-paid positions at work, perform a disproportionate share of domestic labor and childcare—often returning home from work for their "second shift"—and suffer from domestic violence. The position of women as the primary caregivers for young children places them in relationships of dependence with their partners; single women with children are often forced to subsist on low-wage work in order to make ends meet.

The legal scholar and feminist theorist, Catharine MacKinnon, and other scholars have shown how gender inequality is built into many of society's major social institutions. "Gender-neutral" rules systematically favor men in many of the most highly respected and lucrative positions. For example, many professional careers require long hours and single-minded devotion to the job; this effectively excludes many talented women wishing to have a family, simply because women are the primary caregivers and there is in most areas a dearth of affordable childcare.

MacKinnon shifts the debate from discrimination to domination: what is needed is an analysis of male domination which structures the distribution of benefits and burdens in patriarchal societies. Men have created a society in which, intentionally or not, gender has become relevant for success. Even apparently non-discriminatory practices will then systematically favor men. It is necessary, then, to examine the power relations between men and women and the way that "normality" has been defined in terms of masculinity.

The feminist criticism of liberal neutrality is immensely important, and has prompted a fundamental shift for modern liberalism. But not all feminists would hold that it has required an abandoning of the central tenants of liberalism; liberal feminists, certainly, hold that an adequate liberalism will address feminist concerns. If institutions systematically and arbitrarily enforce relations of domination of men over women, liberal feminists have argued, institutional reform may be employed to address issues of discrimination and an imbalance in power relations.

Another central feminist criticism of liberalism focuses on the distinction between the public and private spheres. To use John Rawls's phrase, liberalism is not a "comprehensive doctrine"; it is compatible with a wide variety of life plans and conceptions of the good. Liberals can be Muslims, Catholics, Hindus, or secular humanists; the liberal state has limited scope, allowing people to pursue their personal lives largely free from state interference. Traditionally, liberals have considered the family a voluntary association largely to be governed by love and affection, not coercive laws. Is such an approach adequate, many feminists have asked, to deal with systemic gender inequality that pervades private as well as public spheres?

Until relatively recently, family law in most jurisdictions explicitly disadvantaged women with laws that denied women property rights, laws that ruled out the possibility of marital rape, laws that made divorce impossible or disproportionately burdensome on women (e.g., by leaving them financially destitute or denying child custody). But even if all explicitly sexist laws were abolished—it is by no means clear that such is currently the case, even in progressive liberal states—the family would continue to generate gender inequality. The sexual division of labor in family life continues to burden women; girls are socialized into sexist roles, developing adaptive preferences for lives of female subordination; domestic abuse is shielded from the public eye.

These criticisms are surely accurate, but to what degree do they necessarily entail an objection to liberalism? Do revisions to the distinctions liberals have traditionally made between public and private spheres necessitate a rejection of liberal theory itself? It is doubtful that feminists have problems with privacy *per se*. Feminists generally do not want the state to unduly interfere in their personal decisions or relationships. Many liberals would also agree that choices made according to adaptive preferences are not free choices, and would support means of dispelling them. Similarly, state measures to help women exit the family if they so choose and be assured of adequate financial support, or to provide compensation for domestic labor seem congenial to liberal equality. Defenders of liberalism have argued that many feminist proposals may be compatible with liberalism—at least, with a liberalism that has profited from feminist interrogation and that has been suitably modified to address gender-related concerns.

A very different sort of feminist objection to liberalism has come from the psychologist, Carol Gilligan. Gilligan has argued that liberalism's emphasis on individuality, rights, fairness, and formal and abstract rules is gender biased; in her view it obscures the importance of responsibility, narrative, and attention to context that characterize women's moral judgments. Gilligan distinguishes between a feminine "ethic of care" and a masculine "ethic of justice," which she claims are fundamentally incompatible.

Gilligan's view that on average women tend to reason morally in a fundamentally different way than men is highly controversial, and has been rejected by, among others, many feminist scholars. Even those who sympathize with her position have generally concluded that both men and women apply a combination of the two strategies, even if they may tend to favor one over the other. Gilligan's critics have also cast doubt on her suggestion that liberals entirely overlook responsibility, narrative, and—especially—context; if this were the case, it is unclear how liberal principles could be applied at all. Nor does the empirical claim that the moral reasoning of men and women is different imply the normative claim that liberalism is defective—after all, the difference might be explained by sexist socialization.

Still, it is plausible to suggest that the liberal emphasis on individuality and autonomy often fails to pay sufficient attention to human vulnerability and interdependence—as we have seen, this is also a Marxist and communitarian complaint. The debate regarding to what extent feminist criticisms supplement or supplant liberal thought is ongoing.

Multiculturalism

In *Considerations on Representative Government*, John Stuart Mill could confidently state, "Free institutions are next to impossible in a country made up of different nationalities. Among a people without fellow-feeling, especially if they read and speak different languages, the united public opinion, necessary to the working of representative government, cannot exist." Though Mill refers specifically to the challenges of dual or multinational states, he expresses a common assumption that liberalism relies on a relatively homogenous population, unified by a common language, history, culture, and customs. The rise of the nation-state in the late eighteenth and the nineteenth centuries was accompanied by nation-building, in which a common national identity, culture, and language were forged through the spread of universal education, the suppression of minority cultural and linguistic groups, and other, sometimes coercive, measures.

Thus, T.H. Marshall in his classic essay "Citizenship and Social Class" traces the development of rights in relationship to citizenship. In the eighteenth century, according to Marshall's taxonomy, civil rights came into play, protecting people from the abuses of state power. These included the right to own property, the right to make and enforce contracts, the right to receive due process of law, and the right to practice one's religion. Civil rights were followed in the nineteenth century by political rights such as the right to vote (universal male suffrage) and the right to hold office; social rights such as the right to health care or to education arose only in the twentieth century. The granting of social rights, in particular, had as one of its goals the aim of integrating excluded groups into the national culture—Marshall had in mind the working classes—securing "loyalty to a civilization that is a common possession." The evolution of rights, on this account, reflects progress towards an inclusive norm of universal citizenship, which is actively created through social programs aimed at assimilation.

The homogeneity of the modern state has often been exaggerated. For all that relatively homogeneous countries such as France have often been seen as paradigms of the nation-state, it has long been common for states to accommodate multiple languages, religions, and cultures.[1] In recent times it has become even more common; most modern societies are deeply pluralistic. People in a given state cannot be assumed to share the same culture or religion, speak the same language at home, or endorse the same values or way of life. Moreover, a variety of labels—"multiculturalism," "the politics of difference," "identity politics," "the politics of recognition"—make it clear that minority groups are increasingly demanding recognition and acknowledgement of their rights—rights that often demand differentiation from the dominant population. National minorities such as the Québécois, Catalans, Scots, and Flemish have demanded self-governing rights in order to preserve their distinct way of life within multinational states; indigenous peoples often reject integration and call for measures such as land claims, treaty rights, and some form of self-government in order to preserve their traditional cultures. Ethnic groups, racial or religious minorities, gays and lesbians, and many within the disability-rights movement call for what Iris Marion Young calls "differentiated citizenship" to address their particular needs and concerns.

Many of the concerns raised by multiculturalism arguably derive from liberal values such as equality. The explosion of "rights-talk" fits very much into a liberal framework—what is often at issue is the interpretation of rights and an understanding of the social and historical

---

1   The nation of France, following the Revolution, was built by an explicit and often coercive nation-building movement that wiped out many regional languages and assimilated many of its ethnic groups.

context of minority groups. Feminists, critical race theorists, and multicultural scholars have shown how Western democracies are structured in a hierarchy around the norm of the white, heterosexual, able-bodied male. Similarly, there is increasing awareness of historical injustices towards minority groups, as well as of the way that state "neutrality" is now understood to mask an (often implicit) official policy on language, culture, and religion. Whether such awareness requires abandoning liberalism is a debated question.

Thus, some liberals claim that the call for affirmative action is a call to extend liberal notions of liberal equality in the face of systematic discrimination. Arguments for the right of Muslims to take prayer-break during working hours; for measures allowing Jews to respect the Sabbath; or for measures allowing Sikhs to wear the turban as part of a public uniform can all be seen as an extension of freedom of religion. The demand for self-government rights for national and aboriginal groups is arguably an application of the liberal commitment to democracy.

There is, of course, considerable controversy about these issues, but the controversy has been seen as a struggle *within* liberal thought, not a threat to it. Scholars such as Will Kymlicka and Joseph Raz have drawn on and transformed communitarian criticisms of liberalism in arguing that liberal autonomy relies crucially on access to one's culture, since shared cultural meanings, practices, and language determine individuals' meaningful choices. If this is correct, there are *liberal* reasons for granting the cultural rights demanded by national, aboriginal, ethnic and other groups. Language rights too can be defended on liberal grounds as responding to state policies that may endanger linguistic minorities by favoring a dominant language.

Some multicultural claims, however, do appear to conflict with general liberal principles. The repeal of racist laws preventing Asian, Middle Eastern, and African immigration in the developed world has led to a large number of migrants to Western democracies from states with very different cultural and political practices.[1] Such

migration—and attitudes often unfairly associated with it—has given rise to heated debates around the world over the degree to which it may represent a threat to liberal societies. Many of these debates are best understood as a product of racism, xenophobia, Islamophobia, ethnic nationalism, or the scapegoating of immigrants for the rapid and often alienating change of societies under economic globalization. Some issues, though, do pose a direct challenge to liberal thought. Does liberal toleration require permitting illiberal minorities to carry out practices that appear to conflict with liberal precepts? Does freedom of religion provide grounds for permitting practices such as polygamy or for allowing ethnic groups to employ a conception of Sharia, Halakha, or Canon law within their own communities? Can parents practice infibulation on their daughters? Should arranged marriages be honored in liberal democracies? Do traditional cultures that enforce the subordination of women violate liberal equality? If so, what measures, if any, should be taken in response?

Liberalism provides considerable scope for personal choice. The liberal right to freedom of association has traditionally allowed for illiberal organizations to a large degree. At the same time, liberal states enforce the individual right of exit. Women in a liberal society are free to join organizations such as fundamentalist Christian churches that deny gender equality, but these churches cannot compel women to remain members. Liberals debate how freedom of exit should be understood, but they generally reject more radical claims that group rights should exclude minorities from state interference. These groups sometimes appeal to the communitarian argument for respecting their way of life, grounded in longstanding cultural practices or religious traditions.

To what extent are group rights justifiable in a liberal society? Liberals are able to accommodate group rights insofar as these rights reflect the interests or further the autonomy of the individuals who compose the group. Thus aboriginal land rights, or rights that help linguistic minorities preserve their heritage can likely be justified on liberal grounds. However, group rights that better allow groups to control their members' behavior or to harm their members would appear to be impermissible on liberal grounds. In such areas there may indeed be real conflict between multiculturalism and liberalism. Liberalism is, after all, a substantial doctrine committed to individual rights, freedom, and to moral equality. Liberalism may support the toleration of illiberal groups, but it has serious difficulties accommodating groups that coerce their members so that membership is no longer

---

1 Roughly 191 million people now live outside of the country of their birth, around 3% of the world population. According to the 2005 United Nations Populations Division statistics, migrants make up 9.1% of the population of the United Kingdom, 10.7% of France and 22.9% of Switzerland. In the United States, 12.9% of the population was born abroad, compared to 18.9% in Canada, 20.3% in Australia and 39.6% in Israel. Over 38 million people born abroad live in the United States, over 10 million in Germany, and around 6 million in Canada.

voluntary.[1] Liberalism's advantage, it may fairly be argued, is its flexibility, its ability to grow in response to criticism, and its ability to accommodate individuals and groups with diverse views about what they value and how they wish to live their lives.

Conclusion

Rights-based liberalism remains a rich field of scholarship, and contributions continue to be made in all of the areas discussed above. Recently, social and economic globalization has led to an explosion of debate about the future of liberalism. Commentators have pointed to apparent tensions in liberal doctrine. Liberalism co-evolved with the nation-state and is, in many ways, ideally suited to the institutions of the nation-state. At the same time, liberalism's commitment to universality, equality, and rights extends to every member of the human population.

According to the United Nations Development Program, 1 billion people live on 1 dollar a day Purchasing Power Parity (PPP); 2 billion live on no more than 2 dollars a day PPP.[2] One billion people do not have access to clean drinking water, 2.6 billion lack basic sanitation and nearly 5,000 children die every day from preventable causes. This reality raises questions about what responsibility—if any—privileged developed states may have to combat extreme poverty. Are there duties that extend across borders? Are these duties mainly negative, such as a duty to refrain from actively harming people in other states, or are there positive duties to ensure that everyone receives what are sometimes referred to as subsistence rights?

Other international issues are pressing. How should humanity deal with environmental problems that pay no heed to national boundaries? How should the international community address human rights abuses such as genocide, whether carried out by state actors or other groups? How should global migration be managed in a way that adequately balances the rights and interests of migrants, particularly refugees, and those of states? What should liberals make of the international democracy deficit that results when global bodies such as the UN, the G7, the IMF, the World Bank and others make decisions without consulting the people affected? Many of these questions are currently being addressed in an essentially rights-based liberal framework. They will no

doubt continue to lead theorists to refine and modify their liberalism, but many would hold that rights-based liberalism has the tools to critically evaluate global issues from a moral point of view.

Since the end of the Cold War, liberal democracy has become the hegemonic ideology around the world, without any serious competitors. Indeed some commentators at the time declared "the end of history,"[3] asserting that liberal democracy had now become the only legitimate form of political order. Moreover, the sort of liberal democracy that has triumphed is arguably a "rights-based" model, one that recognizes counter-majoritarian rights for individuals and minorities, and protects them from being sacrificed for the greater good of the majority. It is a form of liberal democracy that increasingly is committed to protecting the rights of vulnerable and historically disadvantaged groups, such as racial minorities, indigenous peoples or homosexuals, against the prejudices (and votes) of the majority. The commitment to such a rights-based liberalism is arguably stronger today than ever before, and is increasingly affirmed by international human rights norms.

However, this hegemony of rights-based liberalism has not meant the end of political debate. On the contrary, as we have seen, liberal democracies face a number of difficult challenges which remain unresolved. For example, we see growing income inequality, both within and between countries, which raises questions about the ability of liberal-democratic welfare states to ensure justice. We also see growing levels of political apathy in the Western democracies, which raises questions about the ability of liberal democracy to sustain the loyalty and participation of citizens. And we see ongoing forms of exclusion of historically disadvantaged groups, such as women, African Americans, gays, immigrants or people with disabilities, which raises questions about the ability of a "rights-based" liberalism to truly address the sources of inequality. These are the sorts of issues that have motivated socialist, communitarian, feminist and multiculturalist critiques of liberalism, and they remain as important today as they ever have. While there are no longer clear ideological competitors to liberal democracy, there are no shortage of internal stresses that are straining the capacity of liberal democracies to live up to their ideals of freedom and equality.

---

1   Of course, what makes a decision voluntary is contested.
2   Purchasing Power Parity (PPP) is a way of comparing the relative value of two currencies by measuring what can actually be purchased with each currency.

---

3   See Francis Fukuyama's essay "The End of History" in the summer 1989 issue of *The National Interest*.

JOHN RAWLS
(1921-2002)

Who is John Rawls?

John Borden Rawls, who died in 2002, was perhaps the most important political philosopher of recent decades, and his 1971 book *A Theory of Justice* is widely regarded as the most significant work of political theory published in the twentieth century. Rawls was born in 1921 in Baltimore to a wealthy southern family; his father was a successful tax lawyer and constitutional expert, while his mother was the feminist president of the local League of Women Voters. As a boy Rawls was sent to Kent, a renowned Episcopalian preparatory school in Connecticut, to be educated, and then went on to Princeton for his undergraduate degree. In 1943 he joined the US infantry and served in New Guinea, the Philippines and Japan (where he witnessed first-hand the aftermath of the atomic bombing of Hiroshima). He turned down the opportunity to become an officer, left the army as a private in 1946, and returned to Princeton to pursue a PhD in philosophy.

After completing his doctorate he taught at Princeton for two years, visited Oxford University for a year on a Fulbright Fellowship, and was then employed as a professor at Cornell. In 1962, after two years at MIT, Rawls moved to Harvard University, where he was appointed James Bryant Conant Professor of Philosophy in 1979. Throughout the eighties and early nineties Rawls was an omnipresent figure in the field of political philosophy, and he exerted a great influence on the discipline through his teaching and mentoring of younger academics as well as his writings. Unfortunately, in 1995, Rawls suffered the first of several strokes, which eventually left him unable to work; however he was able to complete one final book—*The Law of Peoples* (1999), dealing with the topic of international relations—before his death.

Though Rawls was always much more a reclusive academic than a campaigning public figure, his work was nevertheless guided by a very deep personal commitment to combating injustice. Because of his family's origins in the American south, one of Rawls's earliest moral concerns was the injustice of black slavery: he was interested in formulating a moral theory that not only showed slavery to be unjust, but that described its injustice *in the right way*. Unlike utilitarian theorists who argue that the institution of slavery is wrong because its good consequences are outweighed by its harmful consequences, Rawls held that slavery is the kind of thing that should *never* be imposed on another human being, no matter what overall benefits or efficiencies it might bring about. Thus Rawls found himself in opposition to the then-dominant political morality of utilitarianism. This led him to seek a new foundation for social justice in the work of Immanuel Kant and social contract theorists such as John Locke and Jean-Jacques Rousseau.

A guiding assumption behind Rawls's neo-Kantian project (he called it "Kantian constructivism") was that "the right" is separate from and prior to "the good." This latter claim is the idea (which is found in Kant) that the morally right thing to do cannot be defined in terms of some moral good, such as happiness or equality. Certain constraints on how people can be treated always take precedence over the general welfare.

The central doctrine which has informed Rawls's political morality is what he calls "justice as fairness." This is the view that social institutions should not confer morally arbitrary long-term advantages on some persons at the expense of others. Rawls stresses how one's prospects and opportunities in life are strongly influenced by the circumstances of one's birth—one's place in the social, political and economic structure defined by the basic institutions of one's society. For example, one might have been born the child of slaveowners or of slaves or to a wealthy political dynasty in New England or to a poor family in a Philadelphia ghetto. But these important differences are morally arbitrary: they are a mere matter of luck, and not something for which people deserve to be either rewarded or punished. According to Rawls, therefore, the fundamental problem of social justice is to ensure that the basic institutions of our society are set up in such a way that they do not generate and perpetuate morally arbitrary inequalities.

For Rawls, this implies the radical conclusion that inequalities in wealth, income and other "primary social goods" are justified *only* if they are to the advantage of the least well off in society. Rawls's work has thus been widely taken as a philosophical foundation for a highly egalitarian version of the modern welfare state (though Rawls himself takes issue with welfare-state capitalism, instead endorsing either what he calls a "property-owning democracy" or liberal socialism). And because of his emphasis on a set of universal, indefeasible basic rights and liberties, it has been accorded an important place in the rich tradition of liberal political thought.

What is the Structure of these Readings?

The first selections reprinted here come from the revised edition of Rawls's seminal 1971 book *A Theory of Justice*. This book has three parts. The first deals with the theory of justice as fairness, laying out the two principles of justice and the argument for them from the "original position"; the second part illustrates the content of the principles of justice by describing the basic structure the institutions of a democratic society must have if they are to be just. The third part of the book gives more detail about the theory of the good at play in Rawls's account of justice, and argues that in a well-ordered society various values will be congruent in such a way that they contribute to social stability.

The readings given here come from Part One of *A Theory of Justice*. In the first, Rawls contrasts his own theory with the classical doctrine of utilitarianism, and in doing so discusses the relative priority between two key ethical concepts: the right and the good. The second reading begins with a section entitled "The Main Idea of the Theory of Justice," in which Rawls presents his theory of justice as fairness as a development of the social contract tradition in political theory. The central idea is that "the principles of justice are thought of as arising from an original agreement in a situation of equality," and thus Rawls's most immediate task is to characterize this "original position" and consider what principles would be agreed in it. Rawls develops and defends his two principles of justice which he states in *Justice as Fairness: A Restatement* as:

1) Each person has the same indefeasible claim to a fully adequate scheme of equal basic liberties, which scheme is compatible with the same scheme of liberties for all; and

2) Social and economic inequalities are to satisfy two conditions: first, they are to be attached to offices and positions open to all under conditions of fair equality of opportunity; and second, they are to be to the greatest benefit of the least-advantaged members of society.

The first principle is prior to the second, and the requirement of fair equality of opportunity is prior to the "difference principle" (the principle that inequalities are to the greatest benefit of the least advantaged members of society). This means that equal basic liberties must be guaranteed before fair equality of opportunity is addressed and that fair equality of opportunity must be reached before applying the difference principle.

Sections laying out Rawls's initial positions on both these topics are included here, and then a series of passages where Rawls—enlarging on his two principles—argues that morally arbitrary inequalities should not be allowed to influence the distribution of social shares.

The second selection included here is the article "The Idea of an Overlapping Consensus." Rawls came to believe that *A Theory of Justice* did not sufficiently distinguish between comprehensive moral doctrines that cover all aspects of life and political doctrines, which are limited to the political domain and do not (for the most part) intrude on people's private lives. In *Political Liberalism* (1993), Rawls's major work after *A Theory of Justice*, Rawls identifies the central question as: "How is it possible that there exist over time a stable and just society of free and equal citizens profoundly divided by reasonable though incompatible religious, philosophical, and moral doctrines?" Liberal, democratic societies value freedom of conscience and tolerance. This leads to a wide variety of religious and secular views about how one should lead one's life. "The Idea of an Overlapping Consensus" reflects a growing concern in Rawls's later work about the question of stability in societies characterized by a "pluralism of incompatible yet reasonable comprehensive doctrines."

In "The Idea of an Overlapping Consensus" Rawls argues that people divided by reasonable comprehensive doctrines can still agree upon a set of political principles. This agreement is rooted not in mutual self-interest or compromise, but rather in a commitment to the basic institutions and political principles which are endorsed from within each person's reasonable comprehensive view.

Some Useful Background Information

i) Rawls believes that democratic societies are always characterised by what he calls "the fact of reasonable pluralism." By this he means "the fact of profound and irreconcilable differences in citizens' reasonable comprehensive religious and philosophical conceptions of the world, and in their views of the moral and aesthetic values to be sought in human life." A consequence of this reasonable pluralism, Rawls believes, is that a democratic society can never genuinely be a *community*—it can never be a collection of persons united in affirming and pursuing the same conception of a good life. Rawls therefore proposes that we adopt—in fact, tacitly already have adopted—a different view of contemporary society: one that sees it as *a fair system of cooperation between free and equal citizens*. The task of a theory of justice then becomes that of specifying the fair terms of cooperation (and doing so in a way that is acceptable—that seems fair—even to citizens who have widely divergent conceptions of the good).

ii) Rawls assumes that the primary subject of this kind of theory of justice will be what he calls the *basic structure* of society. "[T]he basic structure of society is the way in which the main political and social institutions of society fit together into one system of social cooperation, and the way they assign basic rights and duties and regulate the division of advantages that arises from social cooperation over time. ... The basic structure is the background social framework within which the activities of associations and individuals take place." Examples of components of the basic structure include the political constitution, the relationship between the judiciary and the government, the structure of the economic system, and the social institution of the family. The kinds of things *not* included in the basic structure—and thus affected only indirectly by Rawls's theory of justice—are the internal arrangements of associations such as churches and universities, particular pieces of non-constitutional legislation or legal decisions, and social relationships between individual citizens.

iii) If justice consists in the fair terms of cooperation for society viewed as a system of cooperation, then the question becomes: how are these fair terms of cooperation arrived at? Since the fact of reasonable pluralism precludes appeal to any kind of shared moral authority or outlook, Rawls concludes that the free terms of cooperation must be "settled by an agreement reached by free and equal citizens engaged in cooperation, and made in view of what they regard as their reciprocal advantage." Furthermore this contract, like any agreement, must be made under conditions which are fair to all the parties involved. Rawls's attempt to specify the circumstances in which agreement on the basic structure of society would be fair is called the *original position*.

In the original position, the parties to the contract are placed behind what Rawls calls a *veil of ignorance*: they are not allowed to know their social positions, or their particular comprehensive doctrines of the good, or their race, sex, or ethnic group, or their genetic endowments in such things as strength and intelligence. In other words, knowledge of all the contingent or arbitrary aspects of one's place in actual society are removed; on the other hand, the parties in the original position are assumed to be well-informed about such things as economic and political theory and human psychology, and to be rational. In this way, all information which would, in Rawls's view, introduce unfair distortions into the social contract is excluded from the original position, and only the data needed to make a fair decision is allowed in. Thus, for example, there could be no question of rich people trying to establish a basic social structure which protects their wealth by disadvantaging the poor, since nobody in the original position knows whether they are rich or poor.

Rawls's idea is that whatever contract would be agreed to by representatives in the original position must be a fair one—one that any reasonable citizen could accept, no matter what their place in society or conception of the good. This contract is, of course, merely hypothetical (that is, there was never actually any such situation as the original position): Rawls's point is not that citizens are actually bound by a historical social contract, but that the thought-experiment of making a contract in the original position is a device for showing what principles of justice *we should accept if we are reasonable*. And, Rawls argues, the principles which would be rationally arrived at in the original position will not be, say, utilitarian, or non-egalitarian, but will be something very much like his two principles of justice.

◆ ◆ ◆ ◆ ◆

from *A Theory of Justice* (Revised Edition [1999])

3. *The Main Idea of the Theory of Justice*

My aim is to present a conception of justice which generalizes and carries to a higher level of abstraction the familiar theory of the social contract as found, say, in Locke, Rousseau, and Kant.[1] In order to do this we are not to think of the original contract as one to enter a particular society or to set up a particular form of government. Rather, the guiding idea is that the principles of justice for the basic structure of society are the object of the original agreement. They are the principles that free and rational persons concerned to further their own interests would accept in an initial position of equality as defining the fundamental terms of their association. These principles are to regulate all further agreements; they specify the kinds of social cooperation that can be entered into and the forms of government that can be established. This way of regarding the principles of justice I shall call justice as fairness.

Thus we are to imagine that those who engage in social cooperation choose together, in one joint act, the principles which are to assign basic rights and duties and to determine the division of social benefits. Men are to decide in advance how they are to regulate their claims against one another and what is to be the foundation charter of their society. Just as each person must decide by rational reflection what

constitutes his good, that is, the system of ends which it is rational for him to pursue, so a group of persons must decide once and for all what is to count among them as just and unjust. The choice which rational men would make in this hypothetical situation of equal liberty, assuming for the present that this choice problem has a solution, determines the principles of justice.

In justice as fairness the original position of equality corresponds to the state of nature in the traditional theory of the social contract. This original position is not, of course, thought of as an actual historical state of affairs, much less as a primitive condition of culture. It is understood as a purely hypothetical situation characterized so as to lead to a certain conception of justice.[2] Among the essential features of this situation is that no one knows his place in society, his class position or social status, nor does anyone know his fortune in the distribution of natural assets and abilities, his intelligence, strength, and the like. I shall even assume that the parties do not know their conceptions of the good or their special psychological propensities. The principles of justice are chosen behind a veil of ignorance. This ensures that no one is advantaged or disadvantaged in the choice of principles by the outcome of natural chance or the contingency of social circumstances. Since all are similarly situated and no one is able to design principles to favor his particular condition, the principles of justice are the result of a fair agreement or bargain. For given the circumstances of the original position, the symmetry of everyone's relations to each other, this initial situation is fair between individuals as moral persons, that is, as rational beings with their own ends and capable, I shall assume, of a sense of justice. The original position is, one might say, the appropriate initial status quo, and thus the fundamental agreements reached in it are fair. This explains the propriety of the name "justice as fairness": it conveys the idea that the principles of justice are agreed to in an initial situation that is fair. The name does not mean that the

---

1   *the familiar theory ... Locke, Rousseau, and Kant* [Unless otherwise indicated, all notes to this selection are by the author.] As the text suggests, I shall regard Locke's *Second Treatise of Government*, Rousseau's *The Social Contract*, and Kant's ethical works beginning with *The Foundations of the Metaphysics of Morals* as definitive of the contract tradition. For all of its greatness, Hobbes's *Leviathan* raises special problems. A general historical survey is provided by J.W. Gough, *The Social Contract*, 2nd ed. (Oxford: The Clarendon Press, 1957), and Otto Gierke, *Natural Law and the Theory of Society*, trans. with an introduction by Ernest Barker (Cambridge: The University Press, 1934). A presentation of the contract view as primarily an ethical theory is to be found in G.R. Grice, *The Grounds of Moral Judgment* (Cambridge: The University Press, 1967). See also §19, note 30. [Editors' note] The references Rawls gives using the '§' symbol are to other sections of the book (*A Theory of Justice: Revised Edition*) from which the excerpts printed here are taken. Here we reprint §§3, 4, 5, 6, 11, 13, 14, 15, 17, and 27, but we have not omitted Rawls's references to other sections not included, for readers who wish to find the other relevant passages he mentions.

---

2   *a purely hypothetical situation ... conception of justice* Kant is clear that the original agreement is hypothetical. See *The Metaphysics of Morals*, pt. I (*Rechtslehre*), especially §§47, 52; and pt. II of the essay "Concerning the Common Saying: This May Be True in Theory but It Does Not Apply in Practice," in *Kant's Political Writings*, ed. Hans Reiss and trans. by H.B. Nisbet (Cambridge: The University Press, 1970), pp. 73–87. See Georges Vlachos, *La Pensée politique de Kant* (Paris: Presses Universitaires de France, 1962), pp. 326–35; and J.G. Murphy, *Kant: The Philosophy of Right* (London: Macmillan, 1970), pp. 109–12, 133–36, for a further discussion.

concepts of justice and fairness are the same, any more than the phrase "poetry as metaphor" means that the concepts of poetry and metaphor are the same.

Justice as fairness begins, as I have said, with one of the most general of all choices which persons might make together, namely, with the choice of the first principles of a conception of justice which is to regulate all subsequent criticism and reform of institutions. Then, having chosen a conception of justice, we can suppose that they are to choose a constitution and a legislature to enact laws, and so on, all in accordance with the principles of justice initially agreed upon. Our social situation is just if it is such that by this sequence of hypothetical agreements we would have contracted into the general system of rules which defines it. Moreover, assuming that the original position does determine a set of principles (that is, that a particular conception of justice would be chosen), it will then be true that whenever social institutions satisfy these principles those engaged in them can say to one another that they are cooperating on terms to which they would agree if they were free and equal persons whose relations with respect to one another were fair. They could all view their arrangements as meeting the stipulations which they would acknowledge in an initial situation that embodies widely accepted and reasonable constraints on the choice of principles. The general recognition of this fact would provide the basis for a public acceptance of the corresponding principles of justice. No society can, of course, be a scheme of cooperation which men enter voluntarily in a literal sense; each person finds himself placed at birth in some particular position in some particular society, and the nature of this position materially affects his life prospects. Yet a society satisfying the principles of justice as fairness comes as close as a society can to being a voluntary scheme, for it meets the principles which free and equal persons would assent to under circumstances that are fair. In this sense its members are autonomous and the obligations they recognize self-imposed.

One feature of justice as fairness is to think of the parties in the initial situation as rational and mutually disinterested. This does not mean that the parties are egoists, that is, individuals with only certain kinds of interests, say in wealth, prestige, and domination. But they are conceived as not taking an interest in one another's interests. They are to presume that even their spiritual aims may be opposed, in the way that the aims of those of different religions may be opposed. Moreover, the concept of rationality must be interpreted as far as possible in the narrow sense, standard

in economic theory, of taking the most effective means to given ends. I shall modify this concept to some extent, as explained later (§25), but one must try to avoid introducing into it any controversial ethical elements. The initial situation must be characterized by stipulations that are widely accepted.

In working out the conception of justice as fairness one main task clearly is to determine which principles of justice would be chosen in the original position. To do this we must describe this situation in some detail and formulate with care the problem of choice which it presents. These matters I shall take up in the immediately succeeding chapters. It may be observed, however, that once the principles of justice are thought of as arising from an original agreement in a situation of equality, it is an open question whether the principle of utility[1] would be acknowledged. Offhand it hardly seems likely that persons who view themselves as equals, entitled to press their claims upon one another, would agree to a principle which may require lesser life prospects for some simply for the sake of a greater sum of advantages enjoyed by others. Since each desires to protect his interests, his capacity to advance his conception of the good, no one has a reason to acquiesce in an enduring loss for himself in order to bring about a greater net balance of satisfaction. In the absence of strong and lasting benevolent impulses, a rational man would not accept a basic structure merely because it maximized the algebraic sum of advantages irrespective of its permanent effects on his own basic rights and interests. Thus it seems that the principle of utility is incompatible with the conception of social cooperation among equals for mutual advantage. It appears to be inconsistent with the idea of reciprocity implicit in the notion of a well-ordered society. Or, at any rate, so I shall argue.

I shall maintain instead that the persons in the initial situation would choose two rather different principles: the first requires equality in the assignment of basic rights and duties, while the second holds that social and economic inequalities, for example inequalities of wealth and authority, are just only if they result in compensating benefits for everyone, and in particular for the least advantaged members of society. These principles rule out justifying institutions on the grounds that the hardships of some are offset

---

1   *principle of utility* [editors' note] This is the central principle of utilitarianism; roughly speaking, it understands the best society as the one which maximizes the total of some good such as pleasure, happiness, or, in some contemporary versions, preference-satisfaction.

by a greater good in the aggregate. It may be expedient but it is not just that some should have less in order that others may prosper. But there is no injustice in the greater benefits earned by a few provided that the situation of persons not so fortunate is thereby improved. The intuitive idea is that since everyone's well-being depends upon a scheme of cooperation without which no one could have a satisfactory life, the division of advantages should be such as to draw forth the willing cooperation of everyone taking part in it, including those less well situated. The two principles mentioned seem to be a fair basis on which those better endowed, or more fortunate in their social position, neither of which we can be said to deserve, could expect the willing cooperation of others when some workable scheme is a necessary condition of the welfare of all.[1] Once we decide to look for a conception of justice that prevents the use of the accidents of natural endowment and the contingencies of social circumstance as counters in a quest for political and economic advantage, we are led to these principles. They express the result of leaving aside those aspects of the social world that seem arbitrary from a moral point of view.

The problem of the choice of principles, however, is extremely difficult. I do not expect the answer I shall suggest to be convincing to everyone. It is, therefore, worth noting from the outset that justice as fairness, like other contract views, consists of two parts: (1) an interpretation of the initial situation and of the problem of choice posed there, and (2) a set of principles which, it is argued, would be agreed to. One may accept the first part of the theory (or some variant thereof), but not the other, and conversely. The concept of the initial contractual situation may seem reasonable although the particular principles proposed are rejected. To be sure, I want to maintain that the most appropriate conception of this situation does lead to principles of justice contrary to utilitarianism and perfectionism,[2] and therefore that the contract doctrine provides an alternative to these views. Still, one may dispute this contention even though one grants that the contractarian method is a useful way of studying ethical theories and of setting forth their underlying assumptions.

Justice as fairness is an example of what I have called a contract theory. Now there may be an objection to the term "contract" and related expressions, but I think it will serve reasonably well. Many words have misleading connotations which at first are likely to confuse. The terms "utility" and "utilitarianism" are surely no exception. They too have unfortunate suggestions which hostile critics have been willing to exploit; yet they are clear enough for those prepared to study utilitarian doctrine. The same should be true of the term "contract" applied to moral theories. As I have mentioned, to understand it one has to keep in mind that it implies a certain level of abstraction. In particular, the content of the relevant agreement is not to enter a given society or to adopt a given form of government, but to accept certain moral principles. Moreover, the undertakings referred to are purely hypothetical: a contract view holds that certain principles would be accepted in a well-defined initial situation.

The merit of the contract terminology is that it conveys the idea that principles of justice may be conceived as principles that would be chosen by rational persons, and that in this way conceptions of justice may be explained and justified. The theory of justice is a part, perhaps the most significant part, of the theory of rational choice. Furthermore, principles of justice deal with conflicting claims upon the advantages won by social cooperation; they apply to the relations among several persons or groups. The word "contract" suggests this plurality as well as the condition that the appropriate division of advantages must be in accordance with principles acceptable to all parties. The condition of publicity for principles of justice is also connoted by the contract phraseology. Thus, if these principles are the outcome of an agreement, citizens have a knowledge of the principles that others follow. It is characteristic of contract theories to stress the public nature of political principles. Finally there is the long tradition of the contract doctrine. Expressing the tie with this line of thought helps to define ideas and accords with natural piety. There are then several advantages in the use of the term "contract." With due precautions taken, it should not be misleading.

A final remark. Justice as fairness is not a complete contract theory. For it is clear that the contractarian idea can be extended to the choice of more or less an entire ethical system, that is, to a system including principles for all the virtues[3] and not only for justice. Now for the most part I shall consider only principles of justice and others closely

---

1   *The two principles ... welfare of all*   For the formulation of this intuitive idea I am indebted to Allan Gibbard.

2   *perfectionism*   [editors' note] Rawls defines perfectionism as a moral view that aims at the maximum achievement of human excellence in art, science, and culture.

3   *virtues*   [editors' note] Virtues are typically understood as stable character dispositions that consistently guide an agent's actions.

related to them; I make no attempt to discuss the virtues in a systematic way. Obviously if justice as fairness succeeds reasonably well, a next step would be to study the more general view suggested by the name "rightness as fairness." But even this wider theory fails to embrace all moral relationships, since it would seem to include only our relations with other persons and to leave out of account how we are to conduct ourselves toward animals and the rest of nature. I do not contend that the contract notion offers a way to approach these questions which are certainly of the first importance; and I shall have to put them aside. We must recognize the limited scope of justice as fairness and of the general type of view that it exemplifies. How far its conclusions must be revised once these other matters are understood cannot be decided in advance.

4. The Original Position and Justification

I have said that the original position is the appropriate initial status quo which insures that the fundamental agreements reached in it are fair. This fact yields the name "justice as fairness." It is clear, then, that I want to say that one conception of justice is more reasonable than another, or justifiable with respect to it, if rational persons in the initial situation would choose its principles over those of the other for the role of justice. Conceptions of justice are to be ranked by their acceptability to persons so circumstanced. Understood in this way the question of justification is settled by working out a problem of deliberation: we have to ascertain which principles it would be rational to adopt given the contractual situation. This connects the theory of justice with the theory of rational choice.

If this view of the problem of justification is to succeed, we must, of course, describe in some detail the nature of this choice problem. A problem of rational decision has a definite answer only if we know the beliefs and interests of the parties, their relations with respect to one another, the alternatives between which they are to choose, the procedure whereby they make up their minds, and so on. As the circumstances are presented in different ways, correspondingly different principles are accepted. The concept of the original position, as I shall refer to it, is that of the most philosophically favored interpretation of this initial choice situation for the purposes of a theory of justice.

But how are we to decide what is the most favored interpretation? I assume, for one thing, that there is a broad measure of agreement that principles of justice should be chosen under certain conditions. To justify a particular description of the initial situation one shows that it incorporates these commonly shared presumptions. One argues from widely accepted but weak premises to more specific conclusions. Each of the presumptions should by itself be natural and plausible; some of them may seem innocuous or even trivial. The aim of the contract approach is to establish that taken together they impose significant bounds on acceptable principles of justice. The ideal outcome would be that these conditions determine a unique set of principles; but I shall be satisfied if they suffice to rank the main traditional conceptions of social justice.

One should not be misled, then, by the somewhat unusual conditions which characterize the original position. The idea here is simply to make vivid to ourselves the restrictions that it seems reasonable to impose on arguments for principles of justice, and therefore on these principles themselves. Thus it seems reasonable and generally acceptable that no one should be advantaged or disadvantaged by natural fortune or social circumstances in the choice of principles. It also seems widely agreed that it should be impossible to tailor principles to the circumstances of one's own case. We should insure further that particular inclinations and aspirations, and persons' conceptions of their good do not affect the principles adopted. The aim is to rule out those principles that it would be rational to propose for acceptance, however little the chance of success, only if one knew certain things that are irrelevant from the standpoint of justice. For example, if a man knew that he was wealthy, he might find it rational to advance the principle that various taxes for welfare measures be counted unjust; if he knew that he was poor, he would most likely propose the contrary principle. To represent the desired restrictions one imagines a situation in which everyone is deprived of this sort of information. One excludes the knowledge of those contingencies which sets men at odds and allows them to be guided by their prejudices. In this manner the veil of ignorance is arrived at in a natural way. This concept should cause no difficulty if we keep in mind the constraints on arguments that it is meant to express. At any time we can enter the original position, so to speak, simply by following a certain procedure, namely, by arguing for principles of justice in accordance with these restrictions.

It seems reasonable to suppose that the parties in the original position are equal. That is, all have the same rights in the procedure for choosing principles; each can make proposals, submit reasons for their acceptance, and so on. Obviously the purpose of these conditions is to represent equality between human beings as moral persons, as creatures having a conception of their good and capable of a sense of justice. The basis of equality is taken to be similarity in these two respects. Systems of ends are not ranked in value; and each man is presumed to have the requisite ability to understand and to act upon whatever principles are adopted. Together with the veil of ignorance, these conditions define the principles of justice as those which rational persons concerned to advance their interests would consent to as equals when none are known to be advantaged or disadvantaged by social and natural contingencies.

There is, however, another side to justifying a particular description of the original position. This is to see if the principles which would be chosen match our considered convictions of justice or extend them in an acceptable way. We can note whether applying these principles would lead us to make the same judgments about the basic structure of society which we now make intuitively and in which we have the greatest confidence; or whether, in cases where our present judgments are in doubt and given with hesitation, these principles offer a resolution which we can affirm on reflection. There are questions which we feel sure must be answered in a certain way. For example, we are confident that religious intolerance and racial discrimination are unjust. We think that we have examined these things with care and have reached what we believe is an impartial judgment not likely to be distorted by an excessive attention to our own interests. These convictions are provisional fixed points which we presume any conception of justice must fit. But we have much less assurance as to what is the correct distribution of wealth and authority. Here we may be looking for a way to remove our doubts. We can check an interpretation of the initial situation, then, by the capacity of its principles to accommodate our firmest convictions and to provide guidance where guidance is needed.

In searching for the most favored description of this situation we work from both ends. We begin by describing it so that it represents generally shared and preferably weak conditions. We then see if these conditions are strong enough to yield a significant set of principles. If not, we look for further premises equally reasonable. But if so, and these principles match our considered convictions of justice, then so far well and good. But presumably there will be discrepancies. In this case we have a choice. We can either modify the account of the initial situation or we can revise our existing judgments, for even the judgments we take provisionally as fixed points are liable to revision. By going back and forth, sometimes altering the conditions of the contractual circumstances, at others withdrawing our judgments and conforming them to principle, I assume that eventually we shall find a description of the initial situation that both expresses reasonable conditions and yields principles which match our considered judgments duly pruned and adjusted. This state of affairs I refer to as reflective equilibrium.[1] It is an equilibrium because at last our principles and judgments coincide; and it is reflective since we know to what principles our judgments conform and the premises of their derivation. At the moment everything is in order. But this equilibrium is not necessarily stable. It is liable to be upset by further examination of the conditions which should be imposed on the contractual situation and by particular cases which may lead us to revise our judgments. Yet for the time being we have done what we can to render coherent and to justify our convictions of social justice. We have reached a conception of the original position.

I shall not, of course, actually work through this process. Still, we may think of the interpretation of the original position that I shall present as the result of such a hypothetical course of reflection. It represents the attempt to accommodate within one scheme both reasonable philosophical conditions on principles as well as our considered judgments of justice. In arriving at the favored interpretation of the initial situation there is no point at which an appeal is made to self-evidence in the traditional sense either of general conceptions or particular convictions. I do not claim for the principles of justice proposed that they are necessary truths or derivable from such truths. A conception of justice cannot be deduced from self-evident premises or conditions on principles; instead, its justification is a matter of the mutual support of many considerations, of everything fitting together into one coherent view.

A final comment. We shall want to say that certain principles of justice are justified because they would be agreed to in an initial situation of equality. I have emphasized that this original position is purely hypothetical. It is natural to ask why, if this agreement is never actually entered into,

---

1   *reflective equilibrium* The process of mutual adjustment of principles and considered judgments is not peculiar to moral philosophy. See Nelson Goodman, *Fact, Fiction, and Forecast* (Cambridge, MA: Harvard University Press, 1955), pp. 65–68, for parallel remarks concerning the justification of the principles of deductive and inductive inference.

we should take any interest in these principles, moral or otherwise. The answer is that the conditions embodied in the description of the original position are ones that we do in fact accept. Or if we do not, then perhaps we can be persuaded to do so by philosophical reflection. Each aspect of the contractual situation can be given supporting grounds. Thus what we shall do is to collect together into one conception a number of conditions on principles that we are ready upon due consideration to recognize as reasonable. These constraints express what we are prepared to regard as limits on fair terms of social cooperation. One way to look at the idea of the original position, therefore, is to see it as an expository device which sums up the meaning of these conditions and helps us to extract their consequences. On the other hand, this conception is also an intuitive notion that suggests its own elaboration, so that led on by it we are drawn to define more clearly the standpoint from which we can best interpret moral relationships. We need a conception that enables us to envision our objective from afar: the intuitive notion of the original position is to do this for us.[1]

5. Classical Utilitarianism

There are many forms of utilitarianism, and the development of the theory has continued in recent years. I shall not survey these forms here, nor take account of the numerous refinements found in contemporary discussions. My aim is to work out a theory of justice that represents an alternative to utilitarian thought generally and so to all of these different versions of it. I believe that the contrast between the contract view and utilitarianism remains essentially the same in all these cases. Therefore I shall compare justice as fairness with familiar variants of intuitionism,[2] perfectionism, and utilitarianism in order to bring out the underlying

differences in the simplest way. With this end in mind, the kind of utilitarianism I shall describe here is the strict classical doctrine which receives perhaps its clearest and most accessible formulation in Sidgwick. The main idea is that society is rightly ordered, and therefore just, when its major institutions are arranged so as to achieve the greatest net balance of satisfaction summed over all the individuals belonging to it.[3]

---

3   *the strict classical doctrine ... belonging to it*   I shall take Henry Sidgwick's *The Methods of Ethics*, 7th ed. (London, 1907), as summarizing the development of utilitarian moral theory. Book III of his *Principles of Political Economy* (London, 1883) applies this doctrine to questions of economic and social justice, and is a precursor of A.C. Pigou, *The Economics of Welfare* (London: Macmillan, 1920). Sidgwick's *Outlines of the History of Ethics*, 5th ed. (London, 1902), contains a brief history of the utilitarian tradition. We may follow him in assuming, somewhat arbitrarily, that it begins with Shaftesbury's *An Inquiry Concerning Virtue and Merit* (1711) and Hutcheson's *An Inquiry Concerning Moral Good and Evil* (1725). Hutcheson seems to have been the first to state clearly the principle of utility. He says in *Inquiry*, sec. III, §8, that "that action is best, which procures the greatest happiness for the greatest numbers; and that, worst, which, in like manner, occasions misery." Other major eighteenth century works are Hume's *A Treatise of Human Nature* (1739), and *An Enquiry Concerning the Principles of Morals* (1751); Adam Smith's *A Theory of the Moral Sentiments* (1759); and Bentham's *The Principles of Morals and Legislation* (1789). To these we must add the writings of J.S. Mill represented by *Utilitarianism* (1863) and Frances Y. Edgeworth's *Mathematical Psychics* (London, 1888).

The discussion of utilitarianism has taken a different turn in recent years by focusing on what we may call the coordination problem and related questions of publicity. This development stems from the essays of R.F. Harrod, "Utilitarianism Revised," *Mind* 45 (1936); J.D. Mabbott, "Punishment," *Mind* 48 (1939); Jonathan Harrison, "Utilitarianism, Universalisation, and Our Duty to Be Just," *Proceedings of the Aristotelian Society* 53 (1952–53); and J.O. Urmson, "The Interpretation of the Philosophy of J.S. Mill's Utilitarianism," *Philosophical Quarterly* 3 (1953). See also J.J.C. Smart, "Extreme and Restricted Utilitarianism," *Philosophical Quarterly* 6 (1956), and his *An Outline of a System of Utilitarian Ethics* (Cambridge: The University Press, 1961). For an account of these matters, see David Lyons, *Forms and Limits of Utilitarianism* (Oxford: The Clarendon Press, 1965); and Allan Gibbard, "Utilitarianisms and Coordination" (dissertation, Harvard University, 1971). The problems raised by these works, as important as they are, I shall leave aside as not bearing directly on the more elementary question of distribution which I wish to discuss.

Finally, we should note here the essays of J.C. Harsanyi, in particular, "Cardinal Utility in Welfare Economics and in the Theory of Risk-Taking," *Journal of Political Economy*, 1953, and "Cardinal Welfare, Individualistic Ethics, and Interpersonal Comparisons of Utility," *Journal of Political Economy*, 1955; and R.B. Brandt,

---

1   *a conception ... for us*   Henri Poincaré remarks: "Il nous faut une faculté qui nous fasse voir le but de loin; et cette faculté, c'est l'intuition." ["We need a faculty which makes us see the good from afar; and this faculty is intuition.] *La Valeur de la science* (Paris: Flammarion, 1909), p. 27.

2   *intuitionism*   [editors' note] A variety of ethical views, roughly those that hold that the ethical properties cannot be reduced to non-normative properties and can be known by "intuition." Intuitionists often claim that we know certain actions or states of affairs are right or wrong by directly observing their normative properties. Thus, we know the wrongness of senselessly torturing an innocent being through intuition—there is nothing more to be said of the matter.

We may note first that there is, indeed, a way of thinking of society which makes it easy to suppose that the most rational conception of justice is utilitarian. For consider: each man in realizing his own interests is certainly free to balance his own losses against his own gains. We may impose a sacrifice on ourselves now for the sake of a greater advantage later. A person quite properly acts, at least when others are not affected, to achieve his own greatest good, to advance his rational ends as far as possible. Now why should not a society act on precisely the same principle applied to the group and therefore regard that which is rational for one man as right for an association of men? Just as the well-being of a person is constructed from the series of satisfactions that are experienced at different moments in the course of his life, so in very much the same way the well-being of society is to be constructed from the fulfillment of the systems of desires of the many individuals who belong to it. Since the principle for an individual is to advance as far as possible his own welfare, his own system of desires, the principle for society is to advance as far as possible the welfare of the group, to realize to the greatest extent the comprehensive system of desire arrived at from the desires of its members. Just as an individual balances present and future gains against present and future losses, so a society may balance satisfactions and dissatisfactions between different individuals. And so by these reflections one reaches the principle of utility in a natural way: a society is properly arranged when its institutions maximize the net balance of satisfaction. The principle of choice for an association of men is interpreted as an extension of the principle of choice for one man. Social justice is the principle of rational prudence applied to an aggregative conception of the welfare of the group (§30).[1]

"Some Merits of One Form of Rule-Utilitarianism," *University of Colorado Studies* (1967). See below §§27-28.

1 *Social justice ... of the group (§30)* On this point see also D.P. Gauthier, *Practical Reasoning* (Oxford: Clarendon Press, 1963), 126f. The text elaborates the suggestion found in "Constitutional Liberty and the Concept of Justice," *Nomos VI: Justice.* ed. C.J. Friedrich and J.W. Chapman (New York: Atherton Press, 1963), 124f, which in turn is related to the idea of justice as a higher-order administrative decision. See [Rawls,] "Justice as Fairness," *Philosophical Review* 67 (April 1958):164–94. For references to utilitarians who explicitly affirm this extension, see §30, note 37. That the principle of social integration is distinct from the principle of personal integration is stated by R.B. Perry, *General Theory of Value* (New York: Longmans, Green, and Company, 1926), pp. 674–77. He attributes the error of overlooking this fact to Emile Durkheim and others with similar views. Perry's conception of

This idea is made all the more attractive by a further consideration. The two main concepts of ethics are those of the right and the good; the concept of a morally worthy person is, I believe, derived from them. The structure of an ethical theory is, then, largely determined by how it defines and connects these two basic notions. Now it seems that the simplest way of relating them is taken by teleological theories: the good is defined independently from the right, and then the right is defined as that which maximizes the good.[2] More precisely, those institutions and acts are right which of the available alternatives produce the most good, or at least as much good as any of the other institutions and acts open as real possibilities (a rider needed when the maximal class is not a singleton[3]). Teleological theories have a deep intuitive appeal since they seem to embody the idea of rationality. It is natural to think that rationality is maximizing something and that in morals it must be maximizing the good. Indeed, it is tempting to suppose that it is self-evident that things should be arranged so as to lead to the most good.

It is essential to keep in mind that in a teleological theory the good is defined independently from the right. This means two things. First, the theory accounts for our considered judgments as to which things are good (our judgments of value) as a separate class of judgments intuitively distinguishable by common sense, and then proposes the hypothesis that the right is maximizing the good as already specified. Second, the theory enables one to judge the goodness of things without referring to what is right. For example, if pleasure is said to be the sole good, then presumably pleasures can be recognized and ranked in value by criteria that do not presuppose any standards of right, or what we would normally think of as such. Whereas if the distribution of goods is also counted as a good, perhaps a higher order one, and the theory directs us to produce the most good (including the good of distribution among others), we no longer have a teleological view in the classical sense. The problem of distribution falls under the concept of right as one intuitively understands it, and so the theory lacks an independent definition of the good. The clarity and

---

social integration is that brought about by a shared and dominant benevolent purpose. See below, §24.

2 *teleological theories: ... the good* Here I adopt W.K. Frankena's definition of teleological theories in *Ethics* (Englewood Cliffs, NJ: Prentice Hall, Inc., 1963), p. 13.

3 *when the maximal class is not a singleton* [editors' note] When there is more than one action which provides equal, maximum-good outcomes.

simplicity of classical teleological theories derives largely from the fact that they factor our moral judgments into two classes, the one being characterized separately while the other is then connected with it by a maximizing principle.

Teleological doctrines differ, pretty clearly, according to how the conception of the good is specified. If it is taken as the realization of human excellence in the various forms of culture, we have what may be called perfectionism. This notion is found in Aristotle and Nietzsche, among others. If the good is defined as pleasure, we have hedonism; if as happiness, eudaimonism, and so on. I shall understand the principle of utility in its classical form as defining the good as the satisfaction of desire, or perhaps better, as the satisfaction of rational desire. This accords with the view in all essentials and provides, I believe, a fair interpretation of it. The appropriate terms of social cooperation are settled by whatever in the circumstances will achieve the greatest sum of satisfaction of the rational desires of individuals. It is impossible to deny the initial plausibility and attractiveness of this conception.

The striking feature of the utilitarian view of justice is that it does not matter, except indirectly, how this sum of satisfactions is distributed among individuals any more than it matters, except indirectly, how one man distributes his satisfactions over time. The correct distribution in either case is that which yields the maximum fulfillment. Society must allocate its means of satisfaction whatever these are, rights and duties, opportunities and privileges, and various forms of wealth, so as to achieve this maximum if it can. But in itself no distribution of satisfaction is better than another except that the more equal distribution is to be preferred to break ties.[1] It is true that certain common sense precepts of justice, particularly those which concern the protection of liberties and rights, or which express the claims of desert, seem to contradict this contention. But from a utilitarian standpoint the explanation of these precepts and of their seemingly stringent character is that they are those precepts which experience shows should be strictly respected and departed from only under exceptional circumstances if the sum of advantages is to be maximized.[2] Yet, as with all other precepts, those of justice are derivative from the one end of attaining the greatest balance of satisfaction. Thus there is no reason in principle why the greater gains of some should not compensate for the lesser losses of others; or more im-

portantly, why the violation of the liberty of a few might not be made right by the greater good shared by many. It simply happens that under most conditions, at least in a reasonably advanced stage of civilization, the greatest sum of advantages is not attained in this way. No doubt the strictness of common sense precepts of justice has a certain usefulness in limiting men's propensities to injustice and to socially injurious actions, but the utilitarian believes that to affirm this strictness as a first principle of morals is a mistake. For just as it is rational for one man to maximize the fulfillment of his system of desires, it is right for a society to maximize the net balance of satisfaction taken over all of its members.

The most natural way, then, of arriving at utilitarianism (although not, of course, the only way of doing so) is to adopt for society as a whole the principle of rational choice for one man. Once this is recognized, the place of the impartial spectator and the emphasis on sympathy in the history of utilitarian thought is readily understood. For it is by the conception of the impartial spectator and the use of sympathetic identification in guiding our imagination that the principle for one man is applied to society. It is this spectator who is conceived as carrying out the required organization of the desires of all persons into one coherent system of desire; it is by this construction that many persons are fused into one. Endowed with ideal powers of sympathy and imagination, the impartial spectator is the perfectly rational individual who identifies with and experiences the desires of others as if these desires were his own. In this way he ascertains the intensity of these desires and assigns them their appropriate weight in the one system of desire the satisfaction of which the ideal legislator then tries to maximize by adjusting the rules of the social system. On this conception of society separate individuals are thought of as so many different lines along which rights and duties are to be assigned and scarce means of satisfaction allocated in accordance with rules so as to give the greatest fulfillment of wants. The nature of the decision made by the ideal legislator is not, therefore, materially different from that of an entrepreneur deciding how to maximize his profit by producing this or that commodity, or that of a consumer deciding how to maximize his satisfaction by the purchase of this or that collection of goods. In each case there is a single person whose system of desires determines the best allocation of limited means. The correct decision is essentially a question of efficient administration. This view of social cooperation is the consequence of extending to society the principle of choice for one man, and then, to make this extension work,

---

1   *in itself ... break ties*   On this point see Sidgwick, *The Methods of Ethics*, 416f.

2   *from a utilitarian standpoint ... is to be maximized*   See J.S. Mill, *Utilitarianism*, ch. 5, last two parts.

conflating all persons into one through the imaginative acts of the impartial sympathetic spectator. Utilitarianism does not take seriously the distinction between persons.

6. *Some Related Contrasts*

It has seemed to many philosophers, and it appears to be supported by the convictions of common sense, that we distinguish as a matter of principle between the claims of liberty and right on the one hand and the desirability of increasing aggregate social welfare on the other; and that we give a certain priority, if not absolute weight, to the former. Each member of society is thought to have an inviolability founded on justice or, as some say, on natural right, which even the welfare of every one else cannot override. Justice denies that the loss of freedom for some is made right by a greater good shared by others. The reasoning which balances the gains and losses of different persons as if they were one person is excluded. Therefore in a just society the basic liberties are taken for granted and the rights secured by justice are not subject to political bargaining or to the calculus of social interests.

Justice as fairness attempts to account for these common sense convictions concerning the priority of justice by showing that they are the consequence of principles which would be chosen in the original position. These judgments reflect the rational preferences and the initial equality of the contracting parties. Although the utilitarian recognizes that, strictly speaking, his doctrine conflicts with these sentiments of justice, he maintains that common sense precepts of justice and notions of natural right have but a subordinate validity as secondary rules; they arise from the fact that under the conditions of civilized society there is great social utility in following them for the most part and in permitting violations only under exceptional circumstances. Even the excessive zeal with which we are apt to affirm these precepts and to appeal to these rights is itself granted a certain usefulness, since it counterbalances a natural human tendency to violate them in ways not sanctioned by utility. Once we understand this, the apparent disparity between the utilitarian principle and the strength of these persuasions of justice is no longer a philosophical difficulty. Thus while the contract doctrine accepts our convictions about the priority of justice as on the whole sound, utilitarianism seeks to account for them as a socially useful illusion.

A second contrast is that whereas the utilitarian extends to society the principle of choice for one man, justice as fair-

ness, being a contract view, assumes that the principles of social choice, and so the principles of justice, are themselves the object of an original agreement. There is no reason to suppose that the principles which should regulate an association of men is simply an extension of the principle of choice for one man. On the contrary: if we assume that the correct regulative principle for anything depends on the nature of that thing, and that the plurality of distinct persons with separate systems of ends is an essential feature of human societies, we should not expect the principles of social choice to be utilitarian. To be sure, it has not been shown by anything said so far that the parties in the original position would not choose the principle of utility to define the terms of social cooperation. This is a difficult question which I shall examine later on. It is perfectly possible, from all that one knows at this point, that some form of the principle of utility would be adopted, and therefore that contract theory leads eventually to a deeper and more roundabout justification of utilitarianism. In fact a derivation of this kind is sometimes suggested by Bentham and Edgeworth, although it is not developed by them in any systematic way and to my knowledge it is not found in Sidgwick.[1] For the present I shall simply assume that the persons in the original position would reject the utility principle and that they would adopt instead, for the kinds of reasons previously sketched, the two principles of justice already mentioned. In any case, from the standpoint of contract theory one cannot arrive at a principle of social choice merely by extending the principle of rational prudence to the system of desires constructed by the impartial spectator. To do this is not to take seriously the plurality and distinctness of individuals, nor to recognize as the basis of justice that to which men would consent. Here we may note a curious anomaly. It is customary to think of utilitarianism as individualistic, and certainly there are good reasons for this. The utilitarians were strong defenders of liberty and freedom of thought, and they held that the good of society is constituted by the advantages enjoyed by individuals. Yet utilitarianism is not individualistic, at least when arrived at by the more natural course of reflection, in that, by conflating all systems of desires, it applies to society the principle of choice for one

---

1   *a derivation ... in Sidgwick*   For Bentham see *The Principles of International Law.* Essay 1, in *The Works of Jeremy Bentham*, ed. John Bowring (Edinburgh, 1838–43), vol. II, p. 537; for Edgeworth see *Mathematical Psychics*, pp. 52–56, and also the first pages of "The Pure Theory of Taxation," *Economic Journal* 7 (1897), where the same argument is presented more briefly. See below, §28.

man. And thus we see that the second contrast is related to the first, since it is this conflation, and the principle based upon it, which subjects the rights secured by justice to the calculus of social interests.

The last contrast that I shall mention now is that utilitarianism is a teleological theory whereas justice as fairness is not. By definition, then, the latter is a deontological theory, one that either does not specify the good independently from the right, or does not interpret the right as maximizing the good. (It should be noted that deontological theories are defined as non-teleological ones, not as views that characterize the rightness of institutions and acts independently from their consequences. All ethical doctrines worth our attention take consequences into account in judging rightness. One which did not would simply be irrational, crazy.) Justice as fairness is a deontological theory in the second way. For if it is assumed that the persons in the original position would choose a principle of equal liberty and restrict economic and social inequalities to those in everyone's interests, there is no reason to think that just institutions will maximize the good. (Here I suppose with utilitarianism that the good is defined as the satisfaction of rational desire.) Of course, it is not impossible that the most good is produced but it would be a coincidence. The question of attaining the greatest net balance of satisfaction never arises in justice as fairness; this maximum principle is not used at all.

There is a further point in this connection. In utilitarianism the satisfaction of any desire has some value in itself which must be taken into account in deciding what is right. In calculating the greatest balance of satisfaction it does not matter, except indirectly, what the desires are for.[1] We are to arrange institutions so as to obtain the greatest sum of satisfactions; we ask no questions about their source or quality but only how their satisfaction would affect the total of well-being. Social welfare depends directly and solely upon the levels of satisfaction or dissatisfaction of individuals. Thus if men take a certain pleasure in discriminating against one another, in subjecting others to a lesser liberty as a means of enhancing their self-respect, then the satisfaction of these desires must be weighed in our deliberations according to their intensity, or whatever, along with other desires. If society decides to deny them fulfillment, or to suppress them, it is because they tend to be socially destructive and a greater welfare can be achieved in other ways.

In justice as fairness, on the other hand, persons accept in advance a principle of equal liberty and they do this without a knowledge of their more particular ends. They implicitly agree, therefore, to conform their conceptions of their good to what the principles of justice require, or at least not to press claims which directly violate them. An individual who finds that he enjoys seeing others in positions of lesser liberty understands that he has no claim whatever to this enjoyment. The pleasure he takes in others' deprivations is wrong in itself: it is a satisfaction which requires the violation of a principle to which he would agree in the original position. The principles of right, and so of justice, put limits on which satisfactions have value; they impose restrictions on what are reasonable conceptions of one's good. In drawing up plans and in deciding on aspirations men are to take these constraints into account. Hence in justice as fairness one does not take men's propensities and inclinations as given, whatever they are, and then seek the best way to fulfill them. Rather, their desires and aspirations are restricted from the outset by the principles of justice which specify the boundaries that men's systems of ends must respect. We can express this by saying that in justice as fairness the concept of right is prior to that of the good. A just social system defines the scope within which individuals must develop their aims, and it provides a framework of rights and opportunities and the means of satisfaction within and by the use of which these ends may be equitably pursued. The priority of justice is accounted for, in part, by holding that the interests requiring the violation of justice have no value. Having no merit in the first place, they cannot override its claims.[2]

This priority of the right over the good in justice as fairness turns out to be a central feature of the conception. It imposes certain criteria on the design of the basic structure as a whole; these arrangements must not tend to generate propensities and attitudes contrary to the two principles of justice (that is, to certain principles which are given from the first a definite content) and they must insure that just institutions are stable. Thus certain initial bounds are placed upon what is good and what forms of character are morally worthy, and so upon what kinds of persons men should be. Now any theory of justice will set up some limits of this

---

1   *In calculating ... desires are for*   Bentham, *The Principles of Morals and Legislation*, ch. I, sec. IV.

2   *The priority of justice ... its claims*   The priority of right is a central feature of Kant's ethics. See, for example, *The Critique of Practical Reason*. ch. II, bk. I of *pt. I*, esp. 62–65 of vol. 5 of *Kants Gesammelte Schriften. Preussische Akademie der Wissenschaften* (Berlin, 1913). A clear statement is to be found in "Theory and Practice" (to abbreviate the title), *Political Writings*, p. 67f.

kind, namely, those that are required if its first principles are to be satisfied given the circumstances. Utilitarianism excludes those desires and propensities which if encouraged or permitted would, in view of the situation, lead to a lesser net balance of satisfaction. But this restriction is largely formal, and in the absence of fairly detailed knowledge of the circumstances it does not give much indication of what these desires and propensities are. This is not, by itself, an objection to utilitarianism. It is simply a feature of utilitarian doctrine that it relies very heavily upon the natural facts and contingencies of human life in determining what forms of moral character are to be encouraged in a just society. The moral ideal of justice as fairness is more deeply embedded in the first principles of the ethical theory. This is characteristic of natural rights views (the contractarian tradition) in comparison with the theory of utility.

In setting forth these contrasts between justice as fairness and utilitarianism, I have had in mind only the classical doctrine. This is the view of Bentham and Sidgwick and of the utilitarian economists Edgeworth and Pigou. The kind of utilitarianism espoused by Hume would not serve my purpose; indeed, it is not strictly speaking utilitarian. In his well-known arguments against Locke's contract theory, for example, Hume maintains that the principles of fidelity and allegiance both have the same foundation in utility, and therefore that nothing is gained from basing political obligation on an original contract. Locke's doctrine represents, for Hume, an unnecessary shuffle: one might as well appeal directly to utility.[1] But all Hume seems to mean by utility is the general interests and necessities of society. The principles of fidelity and allegiance derive from utility in the sense that the maintenance of the social order is impossible unless these principles are generally respected. But then Hume assumes that each man stands to gain, as judged by his long-term advantage, when law and government conform to the precepts founded on utility. No mention is made of the gains of some outweighing the disadvantages of others. For Hume, then, utility seems to be identical with some form of the common good; institutions satisfy its demands when they are to everyone's interests, at least in the long run. Now if this interpretation of Hume is correct, there is offhand no conflict with the priority of justice and no incompatibility with Locke's contract doctrine. For the role

of equal rights in Locke is precisely to ensure that the only permissible departures from the state of nature are those which respect these rights and serve the common interest. It is clear that all the transformations from the state of nature which Locke approves of satisfy this condition and are such that rational men concerned to advance their ends could consent to them in a state of equality. Hume nowhere disputes the propriety of these constraints. His critique of Locke's contract doctrine never denies, or even seems to recognize, its fundamental contention.

The merit of the classical view as formulated by Bentham, Edgeworth, and Sidgwick is that it clearly recognizes what is at stake, namely, the relative priority of the principles of justice and of the rights derived from these principles. The question is whether the imposition of disadvantages on a few can be outweighed by a greater sum of advantages enjoyed by others; or whether the weight of justice requires an equal liberty for all and permits only those economic and social inequalities which are to each person's interests. Implicit in the contrasts between classical utilitarianism and justice as fairness is a difference in the underlying conceptions of society. In the one we think of a well-ordered society as a scheme of cooperation for reciprocal advantage regulated by principles which persons would choose in an initial situation that is fair, in the other as the efficient administration of social resources to maximize the satisfaction of the system of desire constructed by the impartial spectator from the many individual systems of desires accepted as given. The comparison with classical utilitarianism in its more natural derivation brings out this contrast.

11. Two Principles of Justice

I shall now state in a provisional form the two principles of justice that I believe would be agreed to in the original position. The first formulation of these principles is tentative. As we go on I shall consider several formulations and approximate step by step the final statement to be given much later. I believe that doing this allows the exposition to proceed in a natural way.

The first statement of the two principles reads as follows.

> First: each person is to have an equal right to the most extensive scheme of equal basic liberties compatible with a similar scheme of liberties for others.

---

1   *Locke's doctrine ... directly to utility*   "Of the Original Contract," *Essays: Moral, Political, and Literary,* ed. T.H. Green and T.H. Grose, vol 1 (London, 1875), 454f.

Second: social and economic inequalities are to be arranged so that they are both (a) reasonably expected to be to everyone's advantage, and (b) attached to positions and offices open to all.

There are two ambiguous phrases in the second principle, namely "everyone's advantage" and "open to all." Determining their sense more exactly will lead to a second formulation of the principle in §13. The final version of the two principles is given in §46; §39 considers the rendering of the first principle.

These principles primarily apply, as I have said, to the basic structure of society and govern the assignment of rights and duties and regulate the distribution of social and economic advantages. Their formulation presupposes that, for the purposes of a theory of justice, the social structure may be viewed as having two more or less distinct parts, the first principle applying to the one, the second principle to the other. Thus we distinguish between the aspects of the social system that define and secure the equal basic liberties and the aspects that specify and establish social and economic inequalities. Now it is essential to observe that the basic liberties are given by a list of such liberties. Important among these are political liberty (the right to vote and to hold public office) and freedom of speech and assembly; liberty of conscience and freedom of thought; freedom of the person, which includes freedom from psychological oppression and physical assault and dismemberment (integrity of the person); the right to hold personal property and freedom from arbitrary arrest and seizure as defined by the concept of the rule of law. These liberties are to be equal by the first principle.

The second principle applies, in the first approximation, to the distribution of income and wealth and to the design of organizations that make use of differences in authority and responsibility. While the distribution of wealth and income need not be equal, it must be to everyone's advantage, and at the same time, positions of authority and responsibility must be accessible to all. One applies the second principle by holding positions open, and then, subject to this constraint, arranges social and economic inequalities so that everyone benefits.

These principles are to be arranged in a serial order with the first principle prior to the second. This ordering means that infringements of the basic equal liberties protected by the first principle cannot be justified, or compensated for, by greater social and economic advantages. These liberties have a central range of application within which they can be limited and compromised only when they conflict with other basic liberties. Since they may be limited when they clash with one another, none of these liberties is absolute; but however they are adjusted to form one system, this system is to be the same for all. It is difficult, and perhaps impossible, to give a complete specification of these liberties independently from the particular circumstances—social, economic, and technological—of a given society. The hypothesis is that the general form of such a list could be devised with sufficient exactness to sustain this conception of justice. Of course, liberties not on the list, for example, the right to own certain kinds of property (e.g., means of production) and freedom of contract as understood by the doctrine of laissez-faire[1] are not basic; and so they are not protected by the priority of the first principle. Finally, in regard to the second principle, the distribution of wealth and income, and positions of authority and responsibility, are to be consistent with both the basic liberties and equality of opportunity.

The two principles are rather specific in their content, and their acceptance rests on certain assumptions that I must eventually try to explain and justify. For the present, it should be observed that these principles are a special case of a more general conception of justice that can be expressed as follows.

All social values—liberty and opportunity, income and wealth, and the social bases of self-respect—are to be distributed equally unless an unequal distribution of any, or all, of these values is to everyone's advantage.

Injustice, then, is simply inequalities that are not to the benefit of all. Of course, this conception is extremely vague and requires interpretation.

As a first step, suppose that the basic structure of society distributes certain primary goods, that is, things that every rational man is presumed to want. These goods normally have a use whatever a person's rational plan of life. For simplicity, assume that the chief primary goods at the disposition of society are rights, liberties, and opportunities, and income and wealth. (Later on in Part Three the primary good of self-respect has a central place.) These are the social primary goods. Other primary goods such as health and

---

1   *doctrine of laissez-faire*   [editor's note] "*Laissez-faire*" is French, meaning "leave alone." The doctrine maintains that private initiative and ownership are to be allowed free rein, unconstrained by governmental intervention other than what is absolutely necessary for markets to function.

vigor, intelligence and imagination, are natural goods; although their possession is influenced by the basic structure, they are not so directly under its control. Imagine, then, a hypothetical initial arrangement in which all the social primary goods are equally distributed: everyone has similar rights and duties, and income and wealth are evenly shared. This state of affairs provides a benchmark for judging improvements. If certain inequalities of wealth and differences in authority would make everyone better off than in this hypothetical starting situation, then they accord with the general conception.

Now it is possible, at least theoretically, that by giving up some of their fundamental liberties men are sufficiently compensated by the resulting social and economic gains. The general conception of justice imposes no restrictions on what sort of inequalities are permissible; it only requires that everyone's position be improved. We need not suppose anything so drastic as consenting to a condition of slavery. Imagine instead that people seem willing to forego certain political rights when the economic returns are significant. It is this kind of exchange which the two principles rule out; being arranged in serial order they do not permit exchanges between basic liberties and economic and social gains except under extenuating circumstances (§§26, 39).

For the most part, I shall leave aside the general conception of justice and examine instead the two principles in serial order. The advantage of this procedure is that from the first the matter of priorities is recognized and an effort made to find principles to deal with it. One is led to attend throughout to the conditions under which the absolute weight of liberty with respect to social and economic advantages, as defined by the lexical order of the two principles,[1] would be reasonable. Offhand, this ranking appears extreme and too special a case to be of much interest; but there is more justification for it than would appear at first sight. Or at any rate, so I shall maintain

---

1   *the lexical order of the two principles*   [editors' note] Strictly speaking, this means sorting a group of items in the order they would appear if they were listed in a dictionary (i.e., roughly, alphabetically), but listing first all words made up of only *one* letter, then all the words made up of *two* letters, and so on. (The main idea here is to impose a useful order on an infinite sequence of formulae.) In the philosophical literature on justice, however, the phrase is generally used to mean a strict prioritizing of principles: first principle A must be satisfied, and only then should we worry about principle B; only when both A and B are satisfied can we apply principle C; and so on.

(§82). Furthermore, the distinction between fundamental rights and liberties and economic and social benefits marks a difference among primary social goods that suggests an important division in the social system. Of course, the distinctions drawn and the ordering proposed are at best only approximations. There are surely circumstances in which they fail. But it is essential to depict clearly the main lines of a reasonable conception of justice; and under many conditions anyway, the two principles in serial order may serve well enough.

The fact that the two principles apply to institutions has certain consequences. First of all, the rights and basic liberties referred to by these principles are those which are defined by the public rules of the basic structure. Whether men are free is determined by the rights and duties established by the major institutions of society. Liberty is a certain pattern of social forms. The first principle simply requires that certain sorts of rules, those defining basic liberties, apply to everyone equally and that they allow the most extensive liberty compatible with a like liberty for all. The only reason for circumscribing basic liberties and making them less extensive is that otherwise they would interfere with one another.

Further, when principles mention persons, or require that everyone gain from an inequality, the reference is to representative persons holding the various social positions, or offices established by the basic structure. Thus in applying the second principle I assume that it is possible to assign an expectation of well-being to representative individuals holding these positions. This expectation indicates their life prospects as viewed from their social station. In general, the expectations of representative persons depend upon the distribution of rights and duties throughout the basic structure. Expectations are connected: by raising the prospects of the representative man in one position we presumably increase or decrease the prospects of representative men in other positions. Since it applies to institutional forms, the second principle (or rather the first part of it) refers to the expectations of representative individuals. As I shall discuss below (§14), neither principle applies to distributions of particular goods to particular individuals who may be identified by their proper names. The situation where someone is considering how to allocate certain commodities to needy persons who are known to him is not within the scope of the principles. They are meant to regulate basic institutional arrangements. We must not assume that there is much similarity from the standpoint of justice between an administrative allotment of goods to specific persons and the appropriate design of society. Our common sense intuitions for the former may be a poor guide to the latter.

Now the second principle insists that each person benefit from permissible inequalities in the basic structure. This means that it must be reasonable for each relevant representative man defined by this structure, when he views it as a going concern, to prefer his prospects with the inequality to his prospects without it. One is not allowed to justify differences in income or in positions of authority and responsibility on the ground that the disadvantages of those in one position are outweighed by the greater advantages of those in another. Much less can infringements of liberty be counterbalanced in this way. It is obvious, however, that there are indefinitely many ways in which all may be advantaged when the initial arrangement of equality is taken as a benchmark. How then are we to choose among these possibilities? The principles must be specified so that they yield a determinate conclusion. I now turn to this problem.

13. Democratic Equality and the Difference Principle

The democratic interpretation, as the table suggests,[1] is arrived at by combining the principle of fair equality of opportunity with the difference principle. This principle removes the indeterminateness of the principle of efficiency by singling out a particular position from which the social and economic inequalities of the basic structure are to be judged. Assuming the framework of institutions required by equal liberty and fair equality of opportunity, the higher expectations of those better situated are just if and only if they work as part of a scheme which improves the expectations of the least advantaged members of society. The intuitive idea is that the social order is not to establish and secure the more attractive prospects of those better off unless doing so is to the advantage of those less fortunate. (See the discussion of the difference principle that follows.)

The Difference Principle

Assume that indifference curves now represent distributions that are judged equally just. Then the difference principle is a

strongly egalitarian conception in the sense that unless there is a distribution that makes both persons better off (limiting ourselves to the two-person case for simplicity), an equal distribution is to be preferred. The indifference curves take the form depicted in figure 5. These curves are actually made up of vertical and horizontal lines that intersect at right angles at the 45° line (again supposing an interpersonal and cardinal interpretation of the axes). No matter how much either person's situation is improved, there is no gain from the standpoint of the difference principle unless the other gains also.

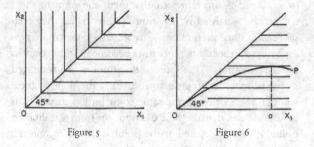

Figure 5   Figure 6

Suppose that x_1 is the most favored representative man in the basic structure. As his expectations are increased so are the prospects of x_2, the least advantaged man. In figure 6 let the curve OP represent the contribution to x_2's expectations made by the greater expectations of x_1. The point O, the origin, represents the hypothetical state in which all social primary goods are distributed equally. Now the OP curve is always below the 45° line, since x_1 is always better off. Thus the only relevant parts of the indifference curves are those below this line, and for this reason the upper left-hand part of figure 6 is not drawn in. Clearly the difference principle is perfectly satisfied only when the OP curve is just tangent to the highest indifference curve that it touches. In figure 6 this is at the point a.

Note that the contribution curve, the curve OP, rises upward to the right because it is assumed that the social cooperation defined by the basic structure is mutually advantageous. It is no longer a matter of shuffling about a fixed stock of goods. Also, nothing is lost if an accurate interpersonal comparison of benefits is impossible. It suffices that the least favored person can be identified and his rational preference determined.

A view less egalitarian than the difference principle, and perhaps more plausible at first sight, is one in which the indifference lines for just distributions (or for all things considered) are smooth curves convex to the origin, as in figure 7. The indifference curves for social welfare functions

---

1   *as the table suggests*   [editors' note] This table is in §12, not included in our selection.

are often depicted in this fashion. This shape of the curves expresses the fact that as either person gains relative to the other, further benefits to him become less valuable from a social point of view.

A classical utilitarian, on the other hand, is indifferent as to how a constant sum of benefits is distributed. He appeals to equality only to break ties. If there are but two persons, then assuming an interpersonal cardinal interpretation of the axes, the utilitarian's indifference lines for distributions are straight lines perpendicular to the 45° line. Since, however, x_1 and x_2 are representative men, the gains to them have to be weighted by the number of persons they each represent. Since presumably x_2 represents rather more persons than x_1, the indifference lines become more horizontal, as seen in figure 8. The ratio of the number of advantaged to the number of disadvantaged defines the slope of these straight lines. Drawing the same contribution curve OP as before, we see that the best distribution from a utilitarian point of view is reached at the point which is beyond the point b where the OP curve reaches its maximum. Since the difference principle selects the point b and b is always to the left of a, utilitarianism allows, other things equal, larger inequalities.

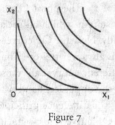

Figure 7

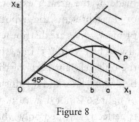

Figure 8

To illustrate the difference principle, consider the distribution of income among social classes. Let us suppose that the various income groups correlate with representative individuals by reference to whose expectations we can judge the distribution. Now those starting out as members of the entrepreneurial class in property-owning democracy, say, have a better prospect than those who begin in the class of unskilled laborers. It seems likely that this will be true even when the social injustices which now exist are removed. What, then, can possibly justify this kind of initial inequality in life prospects? According to the difference principle, it is justifiable only if the difference in expectation is to the advantage of the representative man who is worse off, in this case the representative unskilled worker.

The inequality in expectation is permissible only if lowering it would make the working class even more worse off. Supposedly, given the rider in the second principle concerning open positions, and the principle of liberty generally, the greater expectations allowed to entrepreneurs encourages them to do things which raise the prospects of laboring class. Their better prospects act as incentives so that the economic process is more efficient, innovation proceeds at a faster pace, and so on. I shall not consider how far these things are true. The point is that something of this kind must be argued if these inequalities are to satisfy by the difference principle.

I shall now make a few remarks about this principle. First of all, in applying it, one should distinguish between two cases. The first case is that in which the expectations of the least advantaged are indeed maximized (subject, of course, to the mentioned constraints). No changes in the expectations of those better off can improve the situation of those worst off. The best arrangement obtains, what I shall call a perfectly just scheme. The second case is that in which the expectations of all those better off at least contribute to the welfare of the more unfortunate. That is, if their expectations were decreased, the prospects of the least advantaged would likewise fall. Yet the maximum is not yet achieved. Even higher expectations for the more advantaged would raise the expectations of those in the lowest position. Such a scheme is, I shall say, just throughout, but not the best just arrangement. A scheme is unjust when the higher expectations, one or more of them, are excessive. If these expectations were decreased, the situation of the least favored would be improved. How unjust an arrangement is depends on how excessive the higher expectations are and to what extent they depend upon the violation of the other principles of justice, for example, fair equality of opportunity; but I shall not attempt to measure the degrees of injustice. The point to note here is that while the difference principle is, strictly speaking, a maximizing principle, there is a significant distinction between the cases that fall short of the best arrangement. A society should try to avoid situations where the marginal contributions of those better off are negative, since, other things equal, this seems a greater fault than falling short of the best scheme when these contributions are positive. The even larger difference between classes violates the principle of mutual advantage as well as democratic equality (§17).

A further point is this. We saw that the system of natural liberty and the liberal conception go beyond the principle of efficiency[1] by setting up certain background institutions and leaving the rest to pure procedural justice. The democratic conception holds that while pure procedural justice may be invoked to some extent at least, the way previous interpretations do this still leaves too much to social and natural contingency. But it should be noted that the difference principle is compatible with the principle of efficiency. For when the former is fully satisfied, it is indeed impossible to make any one representative man better off without making another worse off, namely, the least advantaged representative man whose expectations we are to maximize. Thus justice is defined so that it is consistent with efficiency, at least when the two principles are perfectly fulfilled. Of course, if the basic structure is unjust, these principles will authorize changes that may lower the expectations of some of those better off; and therefore the democratic conception is not consistent with the principle of efficiency if this principle is taken to mean that only changes which improve everyone's prospects are allowed. Justice is prior to efficiency and requires some changes that are not efficient in this sense. Consistency obtains only in the sense that a perfectly just scheme is also efficient.

Next, we may consider a certain complication regarding the meaning of the difference principle. It has been taken for granted that if the principle is satisfied, everyone is benefited. One obvious sense in which this is so is that each man's position is improved with respect to the initial arrangement of equality. But it is clear that nothing depends upon being able to identify this initial arrangement; indeed, how well off men are in this situation plays no essential role in applying the difference principle. We simply maximize the expectations of the least favored position subject to the required constraints. As long as doing this is an improvement for everyone, as so far I have assumed it is, the estimated gains from the situation of hypothetical equality are irrelevant, if not largely impossible to ascertain anyway. There may be, however, a further sense in which everyone is advantaged when the difference principle is satisfied, at least if we make certain assumptions. Let us suppose that inequalities in expectations are chain-connected: that is, if an advantage has the effect of raising the expectations of the lowest position, it raises the expectations of all positions in between. For example, if the greater expectations for entrepreneurs benefit the unskilled worker, they also benefit the semi-skilled. Notice that chain connection says nothing about the case where the least advantaged do not gain, so that it does not mean that all effects move together. Assume further that expectations are close-knit: that is, it is impossible to raise or lower the expectation of any representative man without raising or lowering the expectation of every other representative man, especially that of the least advantaged. There is no loose-jointed-ness, so to speak, in the way expectations hang together. Now with these assumptions there is a sense in which everyone benefits when the difference principle is satisfied. For the representative man who is better off in any two-way comparison gains by the advantages offered him, and the man who is worse off gains from the contributions which these inequalities make. Of course, these conditions may not hold. But in this case those who are better off should not have a veto over the benefits available for the least favored. We are still to maximize the expectations of those most disadvantaged. (See the accompanying discussion of chain connection.)

Chain Connection

For simplicity assume that there are three representative men. Let x_1 be the most favored and x_3 the least favored with x_2 in between. Let the expectations of x_1 be marked off along the horizontal axis, the expectations of x_2 and x_3 along the vertical axis. The curves showing the contribution of the most favored to the other groups begin at the origin as the hypothetical position of equality. Moreover, there is a maximum gain permitted to the most favored on the assumption that, even if the difference principle would allow it, there would be unjust effects on the political system and the like excluded by the priority of liberty.

The difference principle selects the point where the curve for x_3 reaches its maximum, for example, the point a in figure 9.

Chain connection means that at any point where the x_3 curve is rising to the right, the x_2 curve is also rising, as in the intervals left of the points a and b in figures 9 and 10. Chain connection says nothing about the case where the x_3 curve is falling to the right, as in the interval to the right of the point a in figure 9. The x_2 curve may be either rising or falling (as indicated by the dashed line x_2). Chain connection does not hold to the right of b in figure 10.

---

1   *principle of efficiency*   [editors' note] Rawls defines this (in §12) as follows: "The principle holds that a configuration is efficient whenever it is impossible to change it so as to make some persons (at least one) better off without at the same time making other persons (at least one) worse off."

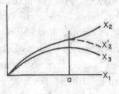

Figure 9

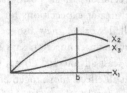

Figure 10

Intervals in which both the x_2 and the x_3 curves are rising define the intervals of positive contributions. Any more to the right increases the average expectation (average utility if utility is measured by expectations) and also satisfies the principle of efficiency as a criterion of change, that is, points to the right improve everyone's situation.

In figure 9 the average expectations may be rising beyond the point a, although the expectations of the least favored are falling. (This depends on the weights of the several groups.) The difference principle excludes this and selects the point a.

Close-knitness means that there are no flat stretches on the curves for x_2 and x_3. At each point both curves are either rising or falling. All the curves illustrated are close-knit.

I shall not examine how likely it is that chain connection and close-knit-ness hold. The difference principle is not contingent on these relations being satisfied. However, when the contributions of the more favored positions spread generally throughout society and are not confined to particular sectors, it seems plausible that if the least advantaged benefit so do others in between. Moreover, a wide diffusion of benefits is favored by two features of institutions both exemplified by the basic structure: first, they are set up to advance certain fundamental interests which everyone has in common, and second, offices and positions are open. Thus it seems probable that if the authority and powers of legislators and judges, say, improve the situation of the less favored, they improve that of citizens generally. Chain connection may often be true, provided the other principles of justice are fulfilled. If this is so, then we may observe that within the region of positive contributions (the region where the advantages of all those in favored positions raise the prospects of the least fortunate), any movement toward the perfectly just arrangement improves everyone's expectation. Under these circumstances the difference principle has somewhat similar practical consequences for the principles of efficiency and average utility (if utility is measured by primary goods). Of course, if chain connection rarely holds,

this similarity is unimportant. But it seems likely that within a just social scheme a general diffusion of benefits often takes place.

There is a further complication. Close-knitness is assumed in order to simplify the statement of the difference principle. It is clearly conceivable, however likely or important in practice, that the least advantaged are not affected one way or the other by some changes in expectations of the best off although these changes benefit others. In this sort of case close-knitness fails, and to cover the situation we can express a more general principle as follows: in a basic structure with n relevant representatives, first maximize the welfare of the worst off representative man; second, for equal welfare of the worst-off representative, maximize the welfare of the second worst-off representative man, and so on until the last case which is, for equal welfare of all the preceding n-1 representatives, maximize the welfare of the best-off representative man. We may think of this as the lexical difference principle.[1] I think, however, that in actual cases this principle is unlikely to be relevant, for when the greater potential benefits to the more advantaged are significant, there will surely be some way to improve the situation of the less advantaged as well. The general laws governing the institutions of the basic structure insure that cases requiring the lexical principle will not arise. Thus I shall always use the difference principle in the simpler form, and so the outcome of the last several sections is that the second principle reads as follows:

> Social and economic inequalities are to be arranged so that they are both (a) to the greatest expected benefit of the least advantaged and (b) attached to offices and positions open to all under conditions of fair equality of opportunity.

Finally, a comment about terminology. Economics may wish to refer to the difference principle as the maximin criterion,[2] but I have carefully avoided this name for several reasons. The maximin criterion is generally understood as a rule for choice under great uncertainty (§26), whereas the

---

1   *the lexical difference principle*   On this point, see A.K. Sen, *Collective Choice and Social Welfare* (San Francisco: Holden-Day, 1970), 138n.

2   *maximin criterion*   [editors' note] This is one rule for choice, given uncertainty about outcomes. Given more than one possible choice, and more than one possible result from each choice, the maximin criterion advises maximizing the minimum outcome— that is, picking the alternative whose worst possible outcome is better than the worst possible outcome for any other alternative.

difference principle is a principle of justice. It is undesirable to use the same name for two things that are so distinct. The difference principle is a very special criterion: it applies primarily to the basic structure of society via representative individuals whose expectations are to be estimated by an index of primary goods (§15). In addition, calling the difference principle the maximin criterion might wrongly suggest that the main argument for this principle from the original position derives from an assumption of very high risk aversion. There is indeed a relation between the difference principle and such an assumption, but extreme attitudes to risk are not postulated (§28); and in any case, there are many considerations in favor of the difference principle in which the aversion to risk plays no role at all. Thus it is best to use the term "maximin criterion" solely for the rule of choice under uncertainty.

14. Fair Equality of Opportunity and Pure Procedural Justice

I should now like to comment upon the second part of the second principle, henceforth to be understood as the liberal principle of fair equality of opportunity. It must not then be confused with the notion of careers open to talents; nor must one forget that since it is tied in with the difference principle its consequences are quite distinct from the liberal interpretation of the two principles taken together. In particular, I shall try to show further on (§17) that this principle is not subject to the objection that it leads to a meritocratic society.[1] Here I wish to consider a few other points, especially its relation to the idea of pure procedural justice.

First, though, I should note that the reasons for requiring open positions are not solely, or even primarily, those of efficiency. I have not maintained that offices must be open if in fact everyone is to benefit from an arrangement. For it may be possible to improve everyone's situation by assigning certain powers and benefits to positions despite the fact that certain groups are excluded from them. Although access is restricted, perhaps these offices can still attract superior talent and encourage better performance. But the principle of open positions forbids this. It expresses the conviction that if some places were not open on a basis fair to all, those kept out would be right in feeling unjustly treated even though

they benefited from the greater efforts of those who were allowed to hold them. They would be justified in their complaint not only because they were excluded from certain external rewards of office but because they were debarred from experiencing the realization of self which comes from a skillful and devoted exercise of social duties. They would be deprived of one of the main forms of human good.

Now I have said that the basic structure is the primary subject of justice. Of course, any ethical theory recognizes the importance of the basic structure as a subject of justice, but not all theories regard its importance in the same way. In justice as fairness society is interpreted as a cooperative venture for mutual advantage. The basic structure is a public system of rules defining a scheme of activities that leads men to act together so as to produce a greater sum of benefits and assigns to each certain recognized claims to a share in the proceeds. What a person does depends upon what the public rules say he will be entitled to, and what a person is entitled to depends on what he does. The distribution which results is arrived at by honoring the claims determined by what persons undertake to do in the light of these legitimate expectations.

These considerations suggest the idea of treating the question of distributive shares as a matter of pure procedural justice.[2] The intuitive idea is to design the social system so that the outcome is just whatever it happens to be, at least so long as it is within a certain range. The notion of pure procedural justice is best understood by a comparison with perfect and imperfect procedural justice. To illustrate the former, consider the simplest case of fair division. A number of men are to divide a cake: assuming that the fair division is an equal one, which procedure, if any, will give this outcome? Technicalities aside, the obvious solution is to have one man divide the cake and get the last piece, the others being allowed their pick before him. He will divide the cake equally, since in this way he assures for himself the largest share possible. This example illustrates the two characteristic features of perfect procedural justice. First, there is an independent criterion for what is a fair division, a criterion defined separately from and prior to the procedure which is to be followed. And second, it is possible to devise a pro-

---

1. *meritocratic society* [editors' note] A system of government in which positions are filled based on merit—ability and talent—rather than on wealth, class, popularity, family or political connections, etc.

2. *procedural justice* For a general discussion of procedural justice, see Brian Barry, *Political Argument* (London: Routledge and Kegan Paul, 1965), ch. VI. On the problem of fair division, see R.D. Luce and Howard Raiffa, *Games and Decisions* (New York: John Wiley and Sons, Inc., 1957), pp. 363–68: and Hugo Steinhaus, "The Problem of Fair Division," *Econometrica* 16 (1948).

cedure that is sure to give the desired outcome. Of course, certain assumptions are made here, such as that the man selected can divide the cake equally, wants as large a piece as he can get, and so on. But we can ignore these details. The essential thing is that there is an independent standard for deciding which outcome is just and a procedure guaranteed to lead to it. Pretty clearly, perfect procedural justice is rare, if not impossible, in cases of much practical interest.

Imperfect procedural justice is exemplified by a criminal trial. The desired outcome is that the defendant should be declared guilty if and only if he has committed the offense with which he is charged. The trial procedure is framed to search for and to establish the truth in this regard. But it seems impossible to design the legal rules so that they always lead to the correct result. The theory of trials examines which procedures and rules of evidence, and the like, are best calculated to advance this purpose consistent with the other ends of the law. Different arrangements for hearing cases may reasonably be expected in different circumstances to yield the right results, not always but at least most of the time. A trial, then, is an instance of imperfect procedural justice. Even though the law is carefully followed, and the proceedings fairly and properly conducted, it may reach the wrong outcome. An innocent man may be found guilty, a guilty man may be set free. In such cases we speak of a miscarriage of justice: the injustice springs from no human fault but from a fortuitous combination of circumstances which defeats the purpose of the legal rules. The characteristic mark of imperfect procedural justice is that while there is an independent criterion for the correct outcome, there is no feasible procedure which is sure to lead to it.

By contrast, pure procedural justice obtains when there is no independent criterion for the right result: instead there is a correct or fair procedure such that the outcome is likewise correct or fair, whatever it is, provided that the procedure has been properly followed. This situation is illustrated by gambling. If a number of persons engage in a series of fair bets, the distribution of cash after the last bet is fair, or at least not unfair, whatever this distribution is. I assume here that fair bets are those having a zero expectation of gain, that the bets are made voluntarily, that no one cheats, and so on. The betting procedure is fair and freely entered into under conditions that are fair. Thus the background circumstances define a fair procedure. Now any distribution of cash summing to the initial stock held by all individuals could result from a series of fair bets. In this sense all of these particular distributions are equally fair. A distinctive

feature of pure procedural justice is that the procedure for determining the just result must actually be carried out; for in these cases there is no independent criterion by reference to which a definite outcome can be known to be just. Clearly we cannot say that a particular state of affairs is just because it could have been reached by following a fair procedure. This would permit far too much. It would allow one to say that almost any distribution of goods is just, or fair, since it could have come about as a result of fair gambles. What makes the final outcome of betting fair, or not unfair, is that it is the one which has arisen after a series of fair gambles. A fair procedure translates its fairness to the outcome only when it is actually carried out.

In order, therefore, to apply the notion of pure procedural justice to distributive shares it is necessary to set up and to administer impartially a just system of institutions. Only against the background of a just basic structure, including a just political constitution and a just arrangement of economic and social institutions, can one say that the requisite just procedure exists. In Part Two I shall describe a basic structure that has the necessary features (§43). Its various institutions are explained and connected with the two principles of justice.

The role of the principle of fair opportunity is to insure that the system of cooperation is one of pure procedural justice. Unless it is satisfied, distributive justice could not be left to take care of itself, even within a restricted range. Now the practical advantage of pure procedural justice is that it is no longer necessary to keep track of the endless variety of circumstances and the changing relative positions of particular persons. One avoids the problem of defining principles to cope with the enormous complexities which would arise if such details were relevant. It is a mistake to focus attention on the varying relative positions of individuals and to require that every change, considered as a single transaction viewed in isolation, be in itself just. It is the arrangement of the basic structure which is to be judged, and judged from a general point of view. Unless we are prepared to criticize it from the standpoint of a relevant representative man in some particular position, we have no complaint against it. Thus the acceptance of the two principles constitutes an understanding to discard as irrelevant as a matter of social justice much of the information and many of the complications of everyday life.

In pure procedural justice, then, distributions of advantages are not appraised in the first instance by confronting a stock of benefits available with given desires and needs of known individuals. The allotment of the items produced takes place in accordance with the public system of rules, and this system determines what is produced, how much is produced, and by what means. It also determines legitimate claims the honoring of which yields the resulting distribution. Thus in this kind of procedural justice the correctness of the distribution is founded on the justice of the scheme of cooperation from which it arises and on answering the claims of individuals engaged in it. A distribution cannot be judged in isolation from the system of which it is the outcome or from what individuals have done in good faith in the light of established expectations. If it is asked in the abstract whether one distribution of a given stock of things to definite individuals with known desires and preferences is better than another, then there is simply no answer to this question. The conception of the two principles does not interpret the primary problem of distributive justice as one of allocative justice.

By contrast allocative justice applies when a given collection of goods is to be divided among definite individuals with known desires and needs. The collection to be allotted is not the product of these individuals, nor do they stand in any existing cooperative relations. Since there are no prior claims on the things to be distributed, it is natural to share them out according to desires and needs, or even to maximize the net balance of satisfaction. Justice becomes a kind of efficiency, unless equality is preferred. Suitably generalized, the allocative conception leads to the classical utilitarian view. For as we have seen, this doctrine assimilates justice to the benevolence of the impartial spectator and the latter in turn to the most efficient design of institutions to promote the greatest balance of satisfaction. The point to note here is that utilitarianism does not interpret the basic structure as a scheme of pure procedural justice. For the utilitarian has, in principle anyway, an independent standard for judging all distributions, namely, whether they produce the greatest net balance of satisfaction. In his theory, institutions are more or less imperfect arrangements for bringing about this end. Thus given existing desires and preferences, and the developments into the future which they allow, the statesman's aim is to set up those social schemes that will best approximate an already specified goal. Since these arrangements are subject to the unavoidable constraints and hindrances of everyday life, the basic structure is a case of imperfect procedural justice.

For the time being I shall suppose that the two parts of the second principle are lexically ordered. Thus we have

one lexical ordering within another. The advantage of the special conception is that it has a definite shape and suggests certain questions for investigation, for example, under what assumptions if any would the lexical ordering be chosen? Our inquiry is given a particular direction and is no longer confined to generalities. Of course, this conception of distributive shares is obviously a great simplification. It is designed to characterize in a clear way a basic structure that makes use of the idea of pure procedural justice. But all the same we should attempt to find simple concepts that can be assembled to give a reasonable conception of justice. The notions of the basic structure, of the veil of ignorance, of a lexical order, of the least favored position. as well as of pure procedural justice are all examples of this. By themselves none of these could be expected to work, but properly put together they may serve well enough. It is too much to suppose that there exists for all or even most moral problems a reasonable solution. Perhaps only a few can be satisfactorily answered. In any case social wisdom consists in framing institutions so that intractable difficulties do not often arise and in accepting the need for clear and simple principles.

15. Primary Social Goods as the Basis of Expectations

So much, then, for a brief statement and explanation of the two principles of justice and of the procedural conception which they express. In later chapters I shall present further details by describing an arrangement of institutions that realizes this conception. At the moment, however, there are several preliminary matters that must be faced. I begin with a discussion of expectations and how they are to be estimated.

The significance of this question can be brought out by a comparison with utilitarianism. When applied to the basic structure this view requires us to maximize the algebraic sum of expected utilities taken over all relevant positions. (The classical principle weights these expectations by the number of persons in these positions, the average principle by the fraction of persons.) Leaving aside for the next section the question as to what defines a relevant position, it is clear that utilitarianism assumes some fairly accurate measure of utility. Not only is it necessary to have a cardinal measure[1] for each representative individual but

---

1   *cardinal measure* [editors' note] A cardinal measure for utility assigns a numerical value to each good for a person (e.g., 1, 2, 5, 8 utiles, etc.). Another form of measurement is *ordinal*: here one merely ranks things in order, from more to less of a certain fac-

some method of correlating the scales of different persons is presupposed if we are to say that the gains of some are to outweigh the losses of others. It is unreasonable to demand great precision, yet these estimates cannot be left to our unguided intuition. Moreover, they may be based on ethical and other notions, not to mention bias and self-interest, which puts their validity in question. Simply because we do in fact make what we call interpersonal comparisons of well-being does not mean that we understand the basis of these comparisons or that we should accept them as sound. To settle these matters we need to give an account of these judgments, to set out the criteria that underlie them (§49). For questions of social justice we should try to find some objective grounds for these comparisons, ones that men can recognize and agree to. I believe that the real objection to utilitarianism lies elsewhere. Even if interpersonal comparisons can be made, these comparisons must reflect values which it makes sense to pursue. The controversy about interpersonal comparisons tends to obscure the real question, namely, whether the total (or average) happiness is to be maximized in the first place.

The difference principle tries to establish objective grounds for interpersonal comparisons in two ways. First of all, as long as we can identify the least advantaged representative man, only ordinal judgments of well-being are required from then on. We know from what position the social system is to be judged. It does not matter how much worse off this representative individual is than the others. The further difficulties of cardinal measurement do not arise since no other interpersonal comparisons are necessary. The difference principle, then, asks less of our judgments of welfare. We never have to calculate a sum of advantages involving a cardinal measure. While qualitative interpersonal comparisons are made in finding the bottom position, for the rest the ordinal judgments of one representative man suffice.

Second, the difference principle introduces a simplification for the basis of interpersonal comparisons. These comparisons are made in terms of expectations of primary social goods. In fact, I define these expectations simply as the index[1] of these goods which a representative individual can

look forward to. One man's expectations are greater than another's if this index for some one in his position is greater. Now primary goods, as I have already remarked, are things which it is supposed a rational man wants whatever else he wants. Regardless of what an individual's rational plans are in detail, it is assumed that there are various things which he would prefer more of rather than less. With more of these goods men can generally be assured of greater success in carrying out their intentions and in advancing their ends, whatever these ends may be. The primary social goods, to give them in broad categories, are rights, liberties, and opportunities, and income and wealth. (A very important primary good is a sense of one's own worth; but for simplicity I leave this aside until much later, §67.) It seems evident that in general these things fit the description of primary goods. They are social goods in view of their connection with the basic structure; liberties and opportunities are defined by the rules of major institutions and the distribution of income and wealth is regulated by them.

The theory of the good adopted to account for primary goods will be presented more fully in Chapter VII. It is a familiar one going back to Aristotle, and something like it is accepted by philosophers so different in other respects as Kant and Sidgwick. It is not in dispute between the contract doctrine and utilitarianism. The main idea is that a person's good is determined by what is for him the most rational long-term plan of life given reasonably favorable circumstances. A man is happy when he is more or less successful in the way of carrying out this plan. To put it briefly, the good is the satisfaction of rational desire. We are to suppose, then, that each individual has a rational plan of life drawn up subject to the conditions that confront him. This plan is designed to permit the harmonious satisfaction of his interests. It schedules activities so that various desires can be fulfilled without interference. It is arrived at by rejecting other plans that are either less likely to succeed or do not provide for such an inclusive attainment of aims. Given the alternatives available, a rational plan is one which cannot be improved upon; there is no other plan which, taking everything into account, would be preferable.

Let us consider several difficulties. One problem clearly is the construction of the index of primary social goods. Assuming that the two principles of justice are serially ordered, this problem is greatly simplified. The basic liberties are always equal, and there is fair equality of opportunity; one does not need to balance these liberties and rights against other values. The primary social goods that vary in

---

tor; the prospects for a sensible ranking of this sort seem brighter, though interpersonal comparisons are often seen still to be a problem.

1   *index* [editors' note] A number assigned to an item giving its relevant magnitude—calculated, perhaps, as an aggregation of a variety of factors.

their distribution are the rights and prerogatives of authority, and income and wealth. But the difficulties are not so great as they might seem at first because of the nature of the difference principle. The only index problem that concerns us is that for the least advantaged group. The primary goods enjoyed by other representative individuals are adjusted to raise this index, subject of course to the usual constraints. It is unnecessary to define weights for the more favored positions in any detail, as long as we are sure that they are more favored. But often this is easy since they frequently have more of each primary good that is distributed unequally. If we know how the distribution of goods to the more favored affects the expectations of the most disfavored, this is sufficient. The index problem largely reduces, then, to that of weighting primary goods for the least advantaged. We try to do this by taking up the standpoint of the representative individual from this group and asking which combination of primary social goods it would be rational for him to prefer. In doing this we admittedly rely upon intuitive estimates. But this cannot be avoided entirely.

Another difficulty is this. It may be objected that expectations should not be defined as an index of primary goods anyway but rather as the satisfactions to be expected when plans are executed using these goods. After all, it is in the fulfillment of these plans that men gain happiness, and therefore the estimate of expectations should not be founded on the available means. Justice as fairness, however, takes a different view. For it does not look behind the use which persons make of the rights and opportunities available to them in order to measure, much less to maximize, the satisfactions they achieve. Nor does it try to evaluate the relative merits of different conceptions of the good. Instead, it is assumed that the members of society are rational persons able to adjust their conceptions of the good to their situation. There is no necessity to compare the worth of the conceptions of different persons once it is supposed they are compatible with the principles of justice. Everyone is assured an equal liberty to pursue whatever plan of life he pleases as long as it does not violate what justice demands. Men share in primary goods on the principle that some can have more if they are acquired in ways which improve the situation of those who have less. Once the whole arrangement is set up and going no questions are asked about the totals of satisfaction or perfection.

It is worth noting that this interpretation of expectations represents, in effect, an agreement to compare men's situations solely by reference to things which it is assumed they all normally need to carry out their plans. This seems the most feasible way to establish a publicly recognized objective and common measure that reasonable persons can accept. Whereas there cannot be a similar agreement on how to estimate happiness as defined, say, by men's success in executing their rational plans, much less on the intrinsic value of these plans. Now founding expectations on primary goods is another simplifying device. I should like to comment in passing that this and other simplifications are accompanied by some sort of philosophical explanation, though this is not strictly necessary. Theoretical assumptions must, of course, do more than simplify; they must identify essential elements that explain the facts we want to understand. Similarly, the parts of a theory of justice must represent basic moral features of the social structure, and if it appears that some of these are being left aside, it is desirable to assure ourselves that such is not the case. I shall try to follow this rule. But even so, the soundness of the theory of justice is shown as much in its consequences as in the prima facie acceptability of its premises. Indeed, these cannot be usefully separated and therefore the discussion of institutional questions, particularly in Part Two, which may seem at first unphilosophical, is in fact unavoidable.

17. The Tendency to Equality

I wish to conclude this discussion of the two principles by explaining the sense in which they express an egalitarian conception of justice. Also I should like to forestall the objection to the principle of fair opportunity that it leads to a meritocratic society. In order to prepare the way for doing this, I note several aspects of the conception of justice that I have set out.

First we may observe that the difference principle gives some weight to the considerations singled out by the principle of redress. This is the principle that undeserved inequalities call for redress; and since inequalities of birth and natural endowment are undeserved, these inequalities are to be somehow compensated for.[1] Thus the principle holds that in order to treat all persons equally, to provide genuine equality of opportunity, society must give more attention to those with fewer native assets and to those born into the less favorable social positions. The idea is to redress the bias of

1 *the principle ... compensated for* See Herbert Spiegelberg, "A Defense of Human Equality," *Philosophical Review* 53 (1944), 101, 113–23; and D.D. Raphael, "Justice and Liberty," *Proceedings of the Aristotelian Society* 51 (1950–51), 187f.

contingencies in the direction of equality. In pursuit of this principle greater resources might be spent on the education of the less rather than the more intelligent, at least over a certain time of life, say the earlier years of school.

Now the principle of redress has not to my knowledge been proposed as the sole criterion of justice, as the single aim of the social order. It is plausible as most such principles are only as a prima facie principle, one that is to be weighed in the balance with others. For example, we are to weigh it against the principle to improve the average standard of life, or to advance the common good.[1] But whatever other principles we hold, the claims of redress are to be taken into account. It is thought to represent one of the elements in our conception of justice. Now the difference principle is not of course the principle of redress. It does not require society to try to even out handicaps as if all were expected to compete on a fair basis in the same race. But the difference principle would allocate resources in education, say, so as to improve the long-term expectation of the least favored. If this end is attained by giving more attention to the better endowed, it is permissible; otherwise not. And in making this decision, the value of education should not be assessed solely in terms of economic efficiency and social welfare. Equally if not more important is the role of education in enabling a person to enjoy the culture of his society and to take part in its affairs, and in this way to provide for each individual a secure sense of his own worth.

Thus although the difference principle is not the same as that of redress, it does achieve some of the intent of the latter principle. It transforms the aims of the basic structure so that the total scheme of institutions no longer emphasizes social efficiency and technocratic values. The difference principle represents, in effect, an agreement to regard the distribution of natural talents as in some respects a common asset and to share in the greater social and economic benefits made possible by the complementarities of this distribution. Those who have been favored by nature, whoever they are, may gain from their good fortune only on terms that improve the situation of those who have lost out. The naturally advantaged are not to gain merely because they are more gifted, but only to cover the costs of training and education and for using their endowments in ways that help the less fortunate as well. No one deserves his greater natural capacity nor merits a more favorable starting place in society. But, of course, this is no reason to ignore, much less

to eliminate these distinctions. Instead, the basic structure can be arranged so that these contingencies work for the good of the least fortunate. Thus we are led to the difference principle if we wish to set up the social system so that no one gains or loses from his arbitrary place in the distribution of natural assets or his initial position in society without giving or receiving compensating advantages in return.

In view of these remarks we may reject the contention that the ordering of institutions is always defective because the distribution of natural talents and the contingencies of social circumstance are unjust, and this injustice must inevitably carry over to human arrangements. Occasionally this reflection is offered as an excuse for ignoring injustice, as if the refusal to acquiesce in injustice is on a par with being unable to accept death. The natural distribution is neither just nor unjust; nor is it unjust that persons are born into society at some particular position. These are simply natural facts. What is just and unjust is the way that institutions deal with these facts. Aristocratic and caste societies are unjust because they make these contingencies the ascriptive basis for belonging to more or less enclosed and privileged social classes. The basic structure of these societies incorporates the arbitrariness found in nature. But there is no necessity for men to resign themselves to these contingencies. The social system is not an unchangeable order beyond human control but a pattern of human action. In justice as fairness men agree to avail themselves of the accidents of nature and social circumstance only when doing so is for the common benefit. The two principles are a fair way of meeting the arbitrariness of fortune; and while no doubt imperfect in other ways, the institutions which satisfy these principles are just.

A further point is that the difference principle expresses a conception of reciprocity. It is a principle of mutual benefit. At first sight, however, it may appear unfairly biased towards the least favored. To consider this question in an intuitive way, suppose for simplicity that there are only two groups in society, one noticeably more fortunate than the other. Subject to the usual constraints (defined by the priority of the first principle and fair equality of opportunity), society could maximize the expectations of either group but not both, since we can maximize with respect to only one aim at a time. It seems clear that society should not do the best it can for those initially more advantaged; so if we reject the difference principle, we must prefer maximizing some weighted mean of the two expectations. But if we give any weight to the more fortunate, we are valuing for their

---

1   *we are to ... common good*   See, for example, Spiegelberg, 120f.

own sake the gains to those already more favored by natural and social contingencies. No one had an antecedent claim to be benefited in this way, and so to maximize a weighted mean is, so to speak, to favor the more fortunate twice over. Thus the more advantaged, when they view the matter from a general perspective, recognize that the well-being of each depends on a scheme of social cooperation without which no one could have a satisfactory life; they recognize also that they can expect the willing cooperation of all only if the terms of the scheme are reasonable. So they regard themselves as already compensated, as it were, by the advantages to which no one (including themselves) had a prior claim. They forego the idea of maximizing a weighted mean and regard the difference principle as a fair basis for regulating the basic structure.

One may object that those better situated deserve the greater advantages they could acquire for themselves under other schemes of cooperation whether or not these advantages are gained in ways that benefit others. Now it is true that given a just system of cooperation as a framework of public rules, and the expectations set up by it, those who, with the prospect of improving their condition, have done what the system announces it will reward are entitled to have their expectations met. In this sense the more fortunate have title to their better situation; their claims are legitimate expectations established by social institutions and the community is obligated to fulfill them. But this sense of desert is that of entitlement. It presupposes the existence of an ongoing cooperative scheme and is irrelevant to the question whether this scheme itself is to be designed in accordance with the difference principle or some other criterion (§48).

Thus it is incorrect that individuals with greater natural endowments and the superior character that has made their development possible have a right to a cooperative scheme that enables them to obtain even further benefits in ways that do not contribute to the advantages of others. We do not deserve our place in the distribution of native endowments, any more than we deserve our initial starting place in society. That we deserve the superior character that enables us to make the effort to cultivate our abilities is also problematic; for such character depends in good part upon fortunate family and social circumstances in early life for which we can claim no credit. The notion of desert does not apply here. To be sure, the more advantaged have a right to their natural assets, as does everyone else; this right is covered by the first principle under the basic liberty protecting the integrity of the person. And so the more advantaged are

entitled to whatever they can acquire in accordance with the rules of a fair system of social cooperation. Our problem is how this scheme, the basic structure of society, is to be designed. From a suitably general standpoint, the difference principle appears acceptable to both the more advantaged and the less advantaged individual. Of course, none of this is strictly speaking an argument for the principle, since in a contract theory arguments are made from the point of view of the original position. But these intuitive considerations help to clarify the principle and the sense in which it is egalitarian.

I noted earlier (§13) that a society should try to avoid the region where the marginal contributions of those better off to the well-being of the less favored are negative. It should operate only on the upward rising part of the contribution curve (including of course the maximum). On this segment of the curve the criterion of mutual benefit is always fulfilled. Moreover, there is a natural sense in which the harmony of social interests is achieved; representative men do not gain at one another's expense since only reciprocal advantages are allowed. To be sure, the shape and slope of the contribution curve is determined in part at least by the natural lottery in native assets, and as such it is neither just nor unjust. But suppose we think of the forty-five degree line as representing the ideal of a perfect harmony of interests; it is the contribution curve (a straight line in this case) along which everyone gains equally. Then it seems that the consistent realization of the two principles of justice tends to raise the curve closer to the ideal of a perfect harmony of interests. Once a society goes beyond the maximum it operates along the downward sloping part of the curve and a harmony of interests no longer exists. As the more favored gain the less advantaged lose, and vice versa. Thus it is to realize the ideal of the harmony of interests on terms that nature has given us, and to meet the criterion of mutual benefit, that we should stay in the region of positive contributions.

A further merit of the difference principle is that it provides an interpretation of the principle of fraternity. In comparison with liberty and equality, the idea of fraternity[1] has had a lesser place in democratic theory. It is thought to be less specifically a political concept, not in itself defining any of the democratic rights but conveying instead certain

---

1   *liberty and equality, the idea of fraternity*   [editors' note] Rawls alludes here to the slogan associated with the French Revolution: "*Liberté, égalité, fraternité!*" (liberty, equality, solidarity).

attitudes of mind and forms of conduct without which we would lose sight of the values expressed by these rights.[1] Or closely related to this, fraternity is held to represent a certain equality of social esteem manifest in various public conventions and in the absence of manners of deference and servility.[2] No doubt fraternity does imply these things, as well as a sense of civic friendship and social solidarity, but so understood it expresses no definite requirement. We have yet to find a principle of justice that matches the underlying idea. The difference principle, however, does seem to correspond to a natural meaning of fraternity: namely, to the idea of not wanting to have greater advantages unless this is to the benefit of others who are less well off. The family, in its ideal conception and often in practice, is one place where the principle of maximizing the sum of advantages is rejected. Members of a family commonly do not wish to gain unless they can do so in ways that further the interests of the rest. Now wanting to act on the difference principle has precisely this consequence. Those better circumstanced are willing to have their greater advantages only under a scheme in which this works out for the benefit of the less fortunate.

The ideal of fraternity is sometimes thought to involve ties of sentiment and feeling which it is unrealistic to expect between members of the wider society. And this is surely a further reason for its relative neglect in democratic theory. Many have felt that it has no proper place in political affairs. But if it is interpreted as incorporating the requirements of the difference principle, it is not an impracticable conception. It does seem that the institutions and policies which we most confidently think to be just satisfy its demands, at least in the sense that the inequalities permitted by them contribute to the well-being of the less favored. Or at any rate, so I shall try to make plausible in Chapter V. On this interpretation, then, the principle of fraternity is a perfectly feasible standard. Once we accept it we can associate the traditional ideas of liberty, equality, and fraternity with the democratic interpretation of the two principles of justice as follows: liberty corresponds to the first principle, equality to the idea of equality in the first principle together with equality of fair opportunity, and fraternity to the difference principle. In this way we have found a place for the concep-

tion of fraternity in the democratic interpretation of the two principles, and we see that it imposes a definite requirement on the basic structure of society. The other aspects of fraternity should not be forgotten, but the difference principle expresses its fundamental meaning from the standpoint of social justice.

Now it seems evident in the light of these observations that the democratic interpretation of the two principles will not lead to a meritocratic society.[3] This form of social order follows the principle of careers open to talents and uses equality of opportunity as a way of releasing men's energies in the pursuit of economic prosperity and political dominion. There exists a marked disparity between the upper and lower classes in both means of life and the rights and privileges of organizational authority. The culture of the poorer strata is impoverished while that of the governing and technocratic elite is securely based on the service of the national ends of power and wealth. Equality of opportunity means an equal chance to leave the less fortunate behind in the personal quest for influence and social position.[4] Thus a meritocratic society is a danger for the other interpretations of the principles of justice but not for the democratic conception. For, as we have just seen, the difference principle transforms the aims of society in fundamental respects. This consequence is even more obvious once we note that we must when necessary take into account the essential primary good of self-respect and the fact that a well-ordered society is a social union of social unions (§79). It follows that the confident sense of their own worth should be sought for the least favored and this limits the forms of hierarchy and the degrees of inequality that justice permits. Thus, for example, resources for education are not to be allotted solely or necessarily mainly according to their return as estimated in productive trained abilities, but also according to their worth in enriching the personal and social life of citizens, including here the less favored. As a society progresses the latter consideration becomes increasingly more important.

---

1 *It is thought ... these rights* See J.R. Pennock, *Liberal Democracy: Its Merits and Prospects* (New York: Rinehart, 1950), p. 94f.

2 *fraternity is held ... deference and servility* See R.B. Perry, *Puritanism and Democracy* (New York: The Vanguard Press, 1944), ch. 19, sec. 8.

3 *the democratic interpretation ... meritocratic society* The problem of a meritocratic society is the subject of Michael Young's fantasy, *The Rise of the Meritocracy* (London: Thames and Hudson, 1958).

4 *Equality of opportunity ... social position* For elaborations of this point to which I am indebted, see John Schaar, "Equality of Opportunity and Beyond," *Nomos IX: Equality*, ed. by J.R. Pennock and J.W. Chapman (New York: Atherton Press, 1967); and B.A.O. Williams, "The Idea of Equality," in *Philosophy, Politics, and Society*, ed. Peter Laslett and W.G. Runciman (Oxford: Basil Blackwell, 1962), 125–29.

These remarks must suffice to sketch the conception of social justice expressed by the two principles for institutions. Before taking up the principles for individuals I should mention one further question. I have assumed so far that the distribution of natural assets is a fact of nature and that no attempt is made to change it, or even to take it into account. But to some extent this distribution is bound to be affected by the social system. A caste system, for example, tends to divide society into separate biological populations, while an open society encourages the widest genetic diversity.[1] In addition, it is possible to adopt eugenic policies, more or less explicit. I shall not consider questions of eugenics, confining myself throughout to the traditional concerns of social justice. We should note, though, that it is not in general to the advantage of the less fortunate to propose policies which reduce the talents of others. Instead, by accepting the difference principle, they view the greater abilities as a social asset to be used for the common advantage. But it is also in the interest of each to have greater natural assets. This enables him to pursue a preferred plan of life. In the original position, then, the parties want to insure for their descendants the best genetic endowment (assuming their own to be fixed). The pursuit of reasonable policies in this regard is something that earlier generations owe to later ones, this being a question that arises between generations. Thus over time a society is to take steps at least to preserve the general level of natural abilities and to prevent the diffusion of serious defects. These measures are to be guided by principles that the parties would be willing to consent to for the sake of their successors. I mention this speculative and difficult matter to indicate once again the manner in which the difference principle is likely to transform problems of social justice. We might conjecture that in the long run, if there is an upper bound on ability, we would eventually reach a society with the greatest equal liberty the members of which enjoy the greatest equal talent. But I shall not pursue this thought further.

[...]

24. The Veil of Ignorance

The idea of the original position is to set up a fair procedure so that any principles agreed to will be just. The aim is to use the notion of pure procedural justice as a basis of theory.

Somehow we must nullify the effects of specific contingencies which put men at odds and tempt them to exploit social and natural circumstances to their own advantage. Now in order to do this I assume that the parties are situated behind a veil of ignorance. They do not know how the various alternatives will affect their own particular case and they are obliged to evaluate principles solely on the basis of general considerations.[2]

It is assumed, then, that the parties do not know certain kinds of particular facts. First of all, no one knows his place in society, his class position or social status; nor does he know his fortune in the distribution of natural assets and abilities, his intelligence and strength, and the like. Nor, again, does anyone know his conception of the good, the particulars of his rational plan of life, or even the special features of his psychology such as his aversion to risk or liability to optimism or pessimism. More than this, I assume that the parties do not know the particular circumstances of their own society. That is, they do not know its economic or political situation, or the level of civilization and culture it has been able to achieve. The persons in the original position have no information as to which generation they belong. These broader restrictions on knowledge are appropriate in part because questions of social justice arise between generations as well as within them, for example, the question of the appropriate rate of capital saving and of the conservation of natural resources and the environment of nature. There is also, theoretically anyway, the question of a reasonable genetic policy. In these cases too, in order to carry through the idea of the original position, the parties must not know the contingencies that set them in opposition. They must choose principles the consequences of

---

1   *A caste system ... genetic diversity*   See Theodosius Dobzhansky, *Mankind Evolving* (New Haven: Yale University Press, 1962), pp. 242–52, for a discussion of this question.

2   *the parties are situated ... general considerations*   The veil of ignorance is so natural a condition that something like it must have occurred to many. The formulation in the text is implicit, I believe, in Kant's doctrine of the categorical imperative, both in the way this procedural criterion is defined and the use Kant makes of it. Thus when Kant tells us to test our maxim by considering what would be the case were it a universal law of nature, he must suppose that we do not know our place within this imagined system of nature. See, for example, his discussion of the topic of practical judgment in *The Critique of Practical Reason*, Academy Edition, vol. 5, pp. 68–72. A similar restriction on information is found in J.C. Harsanyi, "Cardinal Utility in Welfare Economics and in the Theory of Risk-taking," *Journal of Political Economy* 61 (1953). However, other aspects of Harsanyi's view are quite different, and he uses the restriction to develop a utilitarian theory. See the last paragraph of §27.

which they are prepared to live with whatever generation they turn out to belong to.

As far as possible, then, the only particular facts which the parties know is that their society is subject to the circumstances of justice and whatever this implies. It is taken for granted, however, that they know the general facts about human society. They understand political affairs and the principles of economic theory; they know the basis of social organization and the laws of human psychology. Indeed, the parties are presumed to know whatever general facts affect the choice of the principles of justice. There are no limitations on general information, that is, on general laws and theories, since conceptions of justice must be adjusted to the characteristics of the systems of social cooperation which they are to regulate, and there is no reason to rule out these facts. It is, for example, a consideration against a conception of justice that, in view of the laws of moral psychology, men would not acquire a desire to act upon it even when the institutions of their society satisfied it. For in this case there would be difficulty in securing the stability of social cooperation. An important feature of a conception of justice is that it should generate its own support. Its principles should be such that when they are embodied in the basic structure of society men tend to acquire the corresponding sense of justice and develop a desire to act in accordance with its principles. In this case a conception of justice is stable. This kind of general information is admissible in the original position.

The notion of the veil of ignorance raises several difficulties. Some may object that the exclusion of nearly all particular information makes it difficult to grasp what is meant by the original position. Thus it may be helpful to observe that one or more persons can at any time enter this position, or perhaps better, simulate the deliberations of this hypothetical situation, simply by reasoning in accordance with the appropriate restrictions. In arguing for a conception of justice we must be sure that it is among the permitted alternatives and satisfies the stipulated formal constraints. No considerations can be advanced in its favor unless they would be rational ones for us to urge were we to lack the kind of knowledge that is excluded. The evaluation of principles must proceed in terms of the general consequences of their public recognition and universal application, it being assumed that they will be complied with by everyone. To say that a certain conception of justice would be chosen in the original position is equivalent to saying that rational deliberation satisfying certain conditions and

restrictions would reach a certain conclusion. If necessary, the argument to this result could be set out more formally. I shall, however, speak throughout in terms of the notion of the original position. It is more economical and suggestive, and brings out certain essential features that otherwise one might easily overlook.

These remarks show that the original position is not to be thought of as a general assembly which includes at one moment everyone who will live at some time; or, much less, as an assembly of everyone who could live at some time. It is not a gathering of all actual or possible persons. If we conceived of the original position in either of these ways, the conception would cease to be a natural guide to intuition and would lack a clear sense. In any case, the original position must be interpreted so that one can at any time adopt its perspective. It must make no difference when one takes up this viewpoint, or who does so: the restrictions must be such that the same principles are always chosen. The veil of ignorance is a key condition in meeting this requirement. It insures not only that the information available is relevant, but that it is at all times the same.

It may be protested that the condition of the veil of ignorance is irrational. Surely, some may object, principles should be chosen in the light of all the knowledge available. There are various replies to this contention. Here I shall sketch those which emphasize the simplifications that need to be made if one is to have any theory at all. (Those based on the Kantian interpretation of the original position are given later, §40.) To begin with, it is clear that since the differences among the parties are unknown to them, and everyone is equally rational and similarly situated, each is convinced by the same arguments. Therefore, we can view the agreement in the original position from the standpoint of one person selected at random. If anyone after due reflection prefers a conception of justice to another, then they all do, and a unanimous agreement can be reached. We can, to make the circumstances more vivid, imagine that the parties are required to communicate with each other through a referee as intermediary, and that he is to announce which alternatives have been suggested and the reasons offered in their support. He forbids the attempt to form coalitions, and he informs the parties when they have come to an understanding. But such a referee is actually superfluous, assuming that the deliberations of the parties must be similar.

Thus there follows the very important consequence that the parties have no basis for bargaining in the usual sense.

No one knows his situation in society nor his natural assets, and therefore no one is in a position to tailor principles to his advantage. We might imagine that one of the contractees threatens to hold out unless the others agree to principles favorable to him. But how does he know which principles are especially in his interests? The same holds for the formation of coalitions: if a group were to decide to band together to the disadvantage of the others, they would not know how to favor themselves in the choice of principles. Even if they could get everyone to agree to their proposal, they would have no assurance that it was to their advantage, since they cannot identify themselves either by name or description. The one case where this conclusion fails is that of saving. Since the persons in the original position know that they are contemporaries (taking the present time of entry interpretation), they can favor their generation by refusing to make any sacrifices at all for their successors; they simply acknowledge the principle that no one has a duty to save for posterity. Previous generations have saved or they have not; there is nothing the parties can now do to affect that. So in this instance the veil of ignorance fails to secure the desired result. Therefore, to handle the question of justice between generations, I modify the motivation assumption and add a further constraint (§22). With these adjustments, no generation is able to formulate principles especially designed to advance its own cause and some significant limits on savings principles can be derived (§44). Whatever a person's temporal position, each is forced to choose for all.[1]

The restrictions on particular information in the original position are, then, of fundamental importance. Without them we would not be able to work out any definite theory of justice at all. We would have to be content with a vague formula stating that justice is what would be agreed to without being able to say much, if anything, about the substance of the agreement itself. The formal constraints of the concept of right, those applying to principles directly, are not sufficient for our purpose. The veil of ignorance makes possible a unanimous choice of a particular conception of justice. Without these limitations on knowledge the bargaining problem of the original position would be hopelessly complicated. Even if theoretically a solution were to exist, we would not, at present anyway, be able to determine it.

The notion of the veil of ignorance is implicit, I think, in Kant's ethics (§40). Nevertheless the problem of defining the knowledge of the parties and of characterizing the alternatives open to them has often been passed over, even by contract theories. Sometimes the situation definitive of moral deliberation is presented in such an indeterminate way that one cannot ascertain how it will turn out. Thus Perry's doctrine is essentially contractarian: he holds that social and personal integration must proceed by entirely different principles, the latter by rational prudence, the former by the concurrence of persons of good will. He would appear to reject utilitarianism on much the same grounds suggested earlier: namely, that it improperly extends the principle of choice for one person to choices facing society. The right course of action is characterized as that which best advances social aims as these would be formulated by reflective agreement, given that the parties have full knowledge of the circumstances and are moved by a benevolent concern for one another's interests. No effort is made, however, to specify in any precise way the possible outcomes of this sort of agreement. Indeed, without a far more elaborate account, no conclusions can be drawn.[2] I do not wish here to criticize others; rather, I want to explain the necessity for what may seem at times like so many irrelevant details.

Now the reasons for the veil of ignorance go beyond mere simplicity. We want to define the original position so that we get the desired solution. If a knowledge of particulars is allowed, then the outcome is biased by arbitrary contingencies. As already observed, to each according to his threat advantage is not a principle of justice. If the original position is to yield agreements that are just, the parties must be fairly situated and treated equally as moral persons. The arbitrariness of the world must be corrected for by adjusting the circumstances of the initial contractual situation. Moreover, if in choosing principles we required unanimity even when there is full information, only a few rather obvious cases could be decided. A conception of justice based on unanimity in these circumstances would indeed be weak and trivial. But once knowledge is excluded, the requirement of unanimity is not out of place and the fact that it can be satisfied is of great importance. It enables us to say of the preferred conception of justice that it represents a genuine reconciliation of interests.

A final comment. For the most part I shall suppose that the parties possess all general information. No general

---

1   *Whatever a person's ... choose for all*   Rousseau, *The Social Contract*, bk. 2, ch. 4, par. 5.

2   *No effort ... can be drawn*   See R.B. Perry, *The General Theory of Value* (New York: Longmans, Green and Company, 1926), pp. 674–82.

facts are closed to them. I do this mainly to avoid complications. Nevertheless a conception of justice is to be the public basis of the terms of social cooperation. Since common understanding necessitates certain bounds on the complexity of principles, there may likewise be limits on the use of theoretical knowledge in the original position. Now clearly it would be very difficult to classify and to grade the complexity of the various sorts of general facts. I shall make no attempt to do this. We do however recognize an intricate theoretical construction when we meet one. Thus it seems reasonable to say that other things equal one conception of justice is to be preferred to another when it is founded upon markedly simpler general facts, and its choice does not depend upon elaborate calculations in the light of a vast array of theoretically defined possibilities. It is desirable that the grounds for a public conception of justice should be evident to everyone when circumstances permit. This consideration favors, I believe, the two principles of justice over the criterion of utility.

◆ ◆ ◆ ◆ ◆

The Idea of an Overlapping Consensus (1987)

The aims of political philosophy depend on the society it addresses. In a constitutional democracy one of its most important aims is presenting a political conception of justice that can not only provide a shared public basis for the justification of political and social institutions but also helps ensure stability from one generation to the next. Now a basis of justification that rests on self- or group-interests alone cannot be stable; such a basis must be, I think, even when moderated by skilful constitutional design, a mere *modus vivendi*,[1] dependent on a fortuitous conjunction of contingencies. What is needed is a regulative political conception of justice that can articulate and order in a principled way the political ideals and values of a democratic regime, thereby specifying the aims the constitution is to achieve and the limits it must respect. In addition, this political conception needs to be such that there is some hope of its gaining the support of an overlapping consensus, that is, a consensus in

which it is affirmed by the opposing religious, philosophical and moral doctrines likely to thrive over generations in a more or less just constitutional democracy, where the criterion of justice is that political conception itself.

In the first part of my discussion (Secs 1–2) I review three features of a political conception of justice and note why a conception with these features is appropriate given the historical and social conditions of a modern democratic society, and in particular, the condition I shall refer to as the fact of pluralism. The second part (Secs 3–7) takes up four illustrative—but I think misplaced—objections we are likely to have to the idea of an overlapping consensus, and to its corollary that social unity in a democracy cannot rest on a shared conception of the meaning, value and purpose of human life. This corollary does not imply, as one might think, that therefore social unity must rest solely on a convergence of self- and group-interests, or on the fortunate outcome of political bargaining. It allows for the possibility of stable social unity secured by an overlapping consensus on a reasonable political conception of justice. It is this conception of social unity for a democratic society I want to explain and defend.

By way of background, several comments. When Hobbes addressed the contentious divisions of his day between religious sects, and between the Crown, aristocracy and middle-classes, the basis of his appeal was self-interest:[2] men's fear of death and their desire for the means of a commodious life. On this basis he sought to justify obedience to an existing effective (even if need be absolute) sovereign. Hobbes did not think this form of psychological egoism was true; but he thought it was accurate enough for his purposes. The assumption was a political one, adopted to give his views practical effect. In a society fragmented by sectarian divisions and warring interests, he saw no other common foothold for political argument.

How far Hobbes's perception of the situation was accurate we need not consider, for in our case matters are different. We are the beneficiaries of three centuries of

---

1 *modus vivendi* [Unless otherwise indicated, all notes to this selection are by the author.] [editors' note] Latin: way of living. In politics, a *modus vivendi* refers to a (usually) temporary and informal arrangement between disputing parties.

2 *when Hobbes addressed ... self-interest* [editors' note] The political philosopher Thomas Hobbes (1588–1679) lived through the three English Civil Wars which took place from 1642 to 1651. England at the time was divided politically in its support of the king or parliament. It was also divided over religion, with disputes both among Protestants and between Protestants and Catholics. What Rawls later refers to as the "Hobbesian strand of liberalism" refers to an agreement to abide by principles based on mutual self-interest, rather than on commitment to shared moral ideals.

democratic thought and developing constitutional practice; and we can presume not only some public understanding of, but also some allegiance to, democratic ideals and values as realized in existing political institutions. This opens the way to elaborate the idea of an overlapping consensus on a political conception of justice: such a consensus, as we shall see, is moral both in its object and grounds, and so is distinct from a consensus, inevitably fragile, founded solely on self- or group-interest, even when ordered by a well-framed constitution.[1] The idea of an overlapping consensus enables us to understand how a constitutional regime characterized by the fact of pluralism might, despite its deep divisions, achieve stability and social unity by the public recognition of a reasonable political conception of justice.

I

The thesis of the first part of my discussion is that the historical and social conditions of a modern democratic society require us to regard a conception of justice for its political institutions in a certain way. Or rather, they require us to do so, if such a conception is to be both practicable and consistent with the limits of democratic politics. What these conditions are, and how they affect the features of a practicable conception, I note in connection with three features of a political conception of justice, two of which I now describe, leaving the third for the next section.

The first feature of a political conception of justice is that, while such a conception is, of course, a moral conception, it is a moral conception worked out for a specific kind of subject, namely, for political, social and economic institutions.[2] In particular, it is worked out to apply to what we may call the "basic structure" of a modern constitutional democracy. (I shall use "constitutional democracy," and "democratic regime," and similar phrases interchangeably.) By this structure I mean a society's main political, social and economic institutions, and how they fit together into one unified scheme of social cooperation. The focus of a political conception of justice is the framework of basic institutions and the principles, standards and precepts that apply to them, as well as how those norms are expressed in the character and attitudes of the members of society who realize its ideals. One might suppose that this first feature is already implied by the meaning of a political conception of justice: for if a conception does not apply to the basic structure of society, it would not be a political conception at all. But I mean more than this, for I think of a political conception of justice as a conception framed in the first instance[3] solely for the special case of the basic structure.

The second feature complements the first: a political conception is not to be understood as a general and comprehensive moral conception that applies to the political order, as if this order was only another subject, another kind of case, falling under that conception.[4] Thus, a political conception of justice is different from many familiar moral doctrines, for these are widely understood as general and comprehensive views. Perfectionism[5] and utilitarianism are

---

1 *such a consensus ... well-framed constitution* Occasionally I refer to the Hobbesian strand in liberalism, by which I mean the idea that ordered liberty is best achieved by skilful constitutional design framed to guide self- (family-) and group-interests to work for social purposes by the use of various devices such as balance of powers and the like; it can be found in Montesquieu's *Spirit of Laws* (1748), Hume's essay "That Politics may be reduced to a Science" (1741), in Madison's *Federalist*, Number 10 (1788), and in Kant's "Perpetual Peace" (1796). This strand becomes purely Hobbesian to the extent that it sees self- (family-) and group-interests as the only available, or the only politically relevant, kind of motivation; of course, Montesquieu, Hume, Madison and Kant did not hold this view.

2 *The first feature ... political, social and economic institutions* In saying that a conception is moral I mean, among other things, that its content is given by certain ideals, principles, and standards: and that these norms articulate certain values, in this case political values.

3 *But I mean ... first instance* The phrase "in the first instance" indicates that we are to focus first on the basic structure. Should we find a reasonably satisfactory conception of justice for this case, we can then try to extend it to further cases, of which one of the most important is the relations between states and the system of cooperation between them. I accept Kant's view in "Perpetual Peace" that a world state would be either an oppressive autocracy, or continually disturbed by open or latent civil wars between regions and peoples. Hence we would look for principles to regulate a confederation of states and to specify the powers of its several members. We also need to clarify how the principles of justice apply to associations within the state. On this, see the remarks in "The Basic Structure as Subject," Secs 2 and 9, in *Values and Morals*, ed. A.I. Goldman and Jaegwon Kim (Reidel, 1978).

4 I think of a moral conception as general when it applies to a wide range of subjects of appraisal (in the limit of all subjects universally), and as comprehensive when it includes conceptions of what is of value in human life, ideals of personal virtue and character, and the like, that are to inform much of our conduct (in the limit of our life as a whole). Many religious and philosophical doctrines tend to be general and fully comprehensive. See also footnote 23 on p 14.

5 *Perfectionism* [editors' note] A wide range of moral views which aim at promoting human excellence.

clear examples, since the principles of perfection and utility are thought to apply to all kinds of subjects ranging from the conduct of individuals and personal relations to the organization of society as a whole, and even to the law of nations. Their content as political doctrines is specified by their application to political institutions and questions of social policy. Idealism[1] and Marxism in their various forms are also general and comprehensive. By contrast, a political conception of justice involves, so far as possible, no prior commitment to any wider doctrine. It looks initially to the basic structure and tries to elaborate a reasonable conception for that structure alone.

Now one reason for focusing directly on a political conception for the basic structure is that, as a practical political matter, no general and comprehensive view can provide a publicly acceptable basis for a political conception of justice.[2] The social and historical conditions of modern democratic regimes have their origins in the Wars of Religion[3] following the Reformation[4] and the subsequent development of the principle of toleration, and in the growth of constitutional government and of large industrial market economies. These conditions profoundly affect the requirements of a workable conception of justice: among other things, such a conception must allow for a diversity of general and comprehensive doctrines, and for the plurality of conflicting, and indeed incommensurable, conceptions

of the meaning, value and purpose of human life (or what I shall call for short 'conceptions of the good') affirmed by the citizens of democratic societies.[5]

This diversity of doctrines—the fact of pluralism—is not a mere historical condition that will soon pass away; it is, I believe, a permanent feature of the public culture of modern democracies. Under the political and social conditions secured by the basic rights and liberties historically associated with these regimes, the diversity of views will persist and may increase. A public and workable agreement on a single general and comprehensive conception could be maintained only by the oppressive use of state power.[6] Since we are concerned with securing the stability of a constitutional regime, and wish to achieve free and willing agreement on a political conception of justice that establishes at least the constitutional essentials, we must find another basis of agreement than that of a general and comprehen-

---

1 *Idealism* [editors' note] *Idealism* refers to a range of philosophical views that hold that important aspects of reality are, in some sense, mind-dependent.

2 *Now one reason ... political conception of justice* By a publicly acceptable basis I mean a basis that includes ideals, principles and standards that all members of society can not only affirm but also mutually recognize before one another. A public basis involves, then, the public recognition of certain principles as regulative of political institutions, and as expressing political values that the constitution is to be framed to realize.

3 *Wars of Religion* [editors' note] Rawls refers to the wars that ravaged Europe during the sixteenth and seventeenth centuries. They included the French wars of religion from 1562–98, the sixteenth-century wars between Spain, the Netherlands, and England, the English Civil War, and the brutal Thirty Years War which involved most of Europe from 1618 until its end in 1648 with the Peace of Westphalia, in which rulers accepted the principle of the Peace of Augsburg of 1555, giving each prince the right to determine the state religion.

4 *the Reformation* [editors' note] The Protestant reformation is typically dated from 1517, when Martin Luther nailed his Ninety-Five Theses to the door of the Wittenberg Castle Church, leading to the splintering of the Roman Catholic Church and the sixteenth- and seventeenth-century religious wars.

5 *among other things ... democratic societies* It is a disputed question whether and in what sense conceptions of the good are incommensurable. For our purposes here, incommensurability is to be understood as a political fact, an aspect of the fact of pluralism: namely, the fact that there is no available political understanding as to how to commensurate these conceptions for settling questions of political justice.

6 *A public and workable agreement ... state power* For convenience, I give a fuller list of these social and historical conditions, beginning with the three already mentioned above: (1) the fact of pluralism; (2) the fact of the permanence of pluralism, given democratic institutions; (3) the fact that agreement on a single comprehensive doctrine presupposes the oppressive use of state power. Four additional ones are: (4) the fact that an enduring and stable democratic regime, one not divided into contending factions and hostile classes, must be willingly and freely supported by a substantial majority of at least its politically active citizens; (5) the fact that a comprehensive doctrine, whenever widely, if not universally, shared in society, tends to become oppressive and stifling; (6) the fact that reasonably favourable conditions (administrative, economic, technological and the like), which make democracy possible, exist; and finally, (7) the fact that the political culture of a society with a democratic tradition implicitly contains certain fundamental intuitive ideas from which it is possible to work up a political conception of justice suitable for a constitutional regime. (This last is important when we characterize a political conception of justice in the next section.) We may think of the first six of these seven conditions as known by common sense, that is, as known from our shared history and the evident features and aspects of our political culture and present circumstances. They belong to what we might refer to as the common sense political sociology of democratic societies. When elaborating a political conception of justice, we must bear in mind that it must be workable and practicable in a society in which the first six conditions obtain.

sive doctrine.[1] And so, as this alternative basis, we look for a political conception of justice that might be supported by an overlapping consensus.

We do not, of course, assume that an overlapping consensus is always possible, given the doctrines currently existing in any democratic society. It is often obvious that it is not, not at least until firmly held beliefs change in fundamental ways.[2] But the point of the idea of an overlapping consensus on a political conception is to show how, despite a diversity of doctrines, convergence on a political conception of justice may be achieved and social unity sustained in long-run equilibrium, that is, over time from one generation to the next.

2

So far I have noted two features of a political conception of justice: first, that it is expressly framed to apply to the basic structure of society: and second, that it is not to be seen as derived from any general and comprehensive doctrine.

Perhaps the consequences of these features are clear. Yet it may be useful to survey them. For while no one any longer supposes that a practicable political conception for a constitutional regime can rest on a shared devotion to the Catholic or the Protestant Faith, or to any other religious view, it may still be thought that general and comprehensive philosophical and moral doctrines might serve in this role. The second feature denies this not only for Hegel's idealism and Marxism, and for teleological moral views, as I have said, but also for many forms of liberalism as well. While I believe that in fact any workable conception of political justice for a democratic regime must indeed be in an appropriate sense liberal—I come back to this question later—its liberalism will not be the liberalism of Kant or of J. S. Mill, to take two prominent examples.

Consider why: the public role of a mutually recognized political conception of justice is to specify a point of view from which all citizens can examine before one another whether or not their political institutions are just. It enables them to do this by citing what are recognized among them

as valid and sufficient reasons singled out by that conception itself.[3] Questions of political justice can be discussed on the same basis by all citizens, whatever their social position, or more particular aims and interests, or their religious, philosophical or moral views. Justification in matters of political justice is addressed to others who disagree with us, and therefore it proceeds from some consensus: from premises that we and others recognize as true, or as reasonable for the purpose of reaching a working agreement on the fundamentals of political justice. Given the fact of pluralism, and given that justification begins from some consensus, no general and comprehensive doctrine can assume the role of a publicly acceptable basis of political justice.

From this conclusion it is clear what is problematic with the liberalisms of Kant and Mill. They are both general and comprehensive moral doctrines: general in that they apply to a wide range of subjects, and comprehensive in that they include conceptions of what is of value in human life, ideals of personal virtue and character that are to inform our thought and conduct as a whole. Here I have in mind Kant's ideal of autonomy and his connecting it with the values of the Enlightenment, and Mill's ideal of individuality and his connecting it with the values of modernity. These two liberalisms both comprehend far more than the political.[4] Their doctrines of free institutions rest in large part on ideals and values that are not generally, or perhaps even widely, shared in a democratic society. They are not a practicable public basis of a political conception of justice, and I suspect the same is true of many liberalisms besides those of Kant and Mill.

Thus we come to a third feature of a political conception of justice, namely, it is not formulated in terms of a general and comprehensive religious, philosophical or moral doctrine but rather in terms of certain fundamental intuitive ideas viewed as latent in the public political culture of a democratic society. These ideas are used to articulate and or-

---

1   *Since we are concerned ... general and comprehensive doctrine*   Here I assume that free and willing agreement is agreement endorsed by our considered convictions on due reflection, or in what I have elsewhere called "reflective equilibrium." See *A Theory of Justice*, pp 19ff, 48ff.

2   *It is often obvious ... fundamental ways*   How these beliefs might change is discussed later in Secs VI–VII.

3   *It enables them ... conception itself*   I suppose these reasons to be specified by the ideals, principles and standards of the mutually acknowledged political conception, which is, as noted earlier, a moral conception. Thus political institutions are not thought of as justified to all citizens simply in terms of a happy convergence of self- or group-interest, and the like. This conception of justification is in contrast with the Hobbesian strand in the tradition of liberal thought; it is found in Rousseau's *Social Contract* (1762) and plays a central role in Hegel's *Philosophy of Right* (1821).

4   *These two liberalism ... far more than the political*   For Kant again see "What is Enlightenment?" and for Mill see especially "On Liberty" (1859), Ch III, pars 1–9.

der in a principled way its basic political values. We assume that in any such society there exists a tradition of democratic thought, the content of which is at least intuitively familiar to citizens generally. Society's main institutions, together with the accepted forms of their interpretation, are seen as a fund of implicitly shared fundamental ideas and principles. We suppose that these ideas and principles can be elaborated into a political conception of justice, which we hope can gain the support of an overlapping consensus. Of course, that this can be done can be verified only by actually elaborating a political conception of justice and exhibiting the way in which it could be thus supported. It's also likely that more than one political conception may be worked up from the fund of shared political ideas; indeed, this is desirable, as these rival conceptions will then compete for citizens' allegiance and be gradually modified and deepened by the contest between them.

Here I cannot, of course, even sketch the development of a political conception. But in order to convey what is meant, I might say that the conception I have elsewhere called "justice as fairness" is a political conception of this kind.[1] It can be seen as starting with the fundamental intuitive idea of political society as a fair system of social cooperation between citizens regarded as free and equal persons, and as born into the society in which they are assumed to lead a complete life. Citizens are further described as having certain moral powers that would enable them to take part in social cooperation. The problem of justice is then understood as that of specifying the fair terms of social cooperation between citizens so conceived. The conjecture is that by working out such ideas, which I view as implicit in the public political culture, we can in due course arrive at widely acceptable principles of political justice.[2]

The details are not important here. What is important is that, so far as possible, these fundamental intuitive ideas are not taken for religious, philosophical, or metaphysical ideas. For example, when it is said that citizens are regarded as free and equal persons, their freedom and equality are to be understood in ways congenial to the public political culture and explicable in terms of the design and requirements of its basic institutions. The conception of citizens as free and equal is, therefore, a political conception, the content of which is specified in connection with such things as the basic rights and liberties of democratic citizens.[3] The hope is that the conception of justice to which this conception of citizens belongs will be acceptable to a wide range of comprehensive doctrines and hence supported by an overlapping consensus.

But, as I have indicated and should emphasize, success in achieving consensus requires that political philosophy try to be, so far as possible, independent and autonomous from other parts of philosophy, especially from philosophy's long-standing problems and controversies. For given the aim of consensus, to proceed otherwise would be self-defeating. But as we shall see (in Sec 4) we may not be able to do this entirely when we attempt to answer the objection that claims that aiming for consensus implies scepticism or indifference to religious, philosophical or moral truth. Nevertheless, the reason for avoiding deeper questions remains. For as I have said above, we can present a political view either by starting explicitly from within a general and comprehensive doctrine, or we can start from fundamental intuitive ideas regarded as latent in the public political culture. These two ways of proceeding are very different, and this difference is significant even though we may sometimes be forced to as-

---

1   *But in order to convey ... political conception of this kind*   For the fullest discussion, see *A Theory of Justice* (1971). I have discussed justice as fairness as a political conception in "Justice as Fairness: Political not Metaphysical," *Philosophy and Public Affairs*, Summer 1985. Ronald Dworkin's liberal conception of equality is, I think, another example of a political conception of justice. See his *A Matter of Principle* (Cambridge, Harvard University Press, 1986), the essays in Part Three on liberalism and justice.

2   *principles of political justice*   These principles will express and give certain weights to familiar political values such as liberty and equality, fair equality of opportunity, and the efficient design of institutions to serve the common good, and the like. But we can arrive at a political conception of justice in a very different way, namely, by balancing these competing values directly against one another and eventually adjusting them to one another in the light of the overall balance, or pattern, of values that seems best to us.

A procedure of this kind is suggested by Sir Isaiah Berlin; see for example his essay "Equality," in *Concepts and Categories* (Oxford, 1980), p 100. The advantage of starting with the fundamental intuitive idea of society as a fair system of social cooperation may be that we do not simply balance values directly in the light of an overall pattern, but see how the values and their weights are arrived at in the way they are specified by the deliberations of the parties in the original position. Here I refer to the details of how justice as fairness is worked out. The thought here is that these details provide a clearer conception of how weights may be determined than the idea of balancing in the light of an overall pattern. But perhaps the idea of society as a fair system of social cooperation might itself be regarded as such a pattern, in which case the two procedures could coincide.

3   *The conception of citizens as free and equal ... basic rights and liberties of democratic citizens*   On this, see "Political not Metaphysical." Sec V.

sert certain aspects of our own comprehensive doctrine. So while we may not be able to avoid comprehensive doctrines entirely, we do what we can to reduce relying on their more specific details, or their more disputed features. The question is: what is the least that must be asserted; and if it must be asserted, what is its least controversial form?

Finally, connected with a political conception of justice is an essential companion conception of free public reason. This conception involves various elements. A crucial one is this: just as a political conception of justice needs certain principles of justice for the basic structure to specify its content, it also needs certain guidelines of enquiry and publicly recognized rules of assessing evidence to govern its application. Otherwise, there is no agreed way for determining whether those principles are satisfied, and for settling what they require of particular institutions, or in particular situations. Agreement on a conception of justice is worthless—not an effective agreement at all—without agreement on these further matters. And given the fact of pluralism, there is, I think, no better practicable alternative than to limit ourselves to the shared methods of, and the public knowledge available to, common sense, and the procedures and conclusions of science when these are not controversial. It is these shared methods and this common knowledge that allows us to speak of *public* reason.[1] As I shall stress later on, the acceptance of this limit is not motivated by scepticism or indifference to the claims of comprehensive doctrines; rather, it springs from the fact of pluralism, for this fact means that in a pluralist society free public reason can be effectively established in no other way.[2]

3

I now turn to the second part of my discussion (Secs 3-7) and take up four objections likely to be raised against the idea of social unity founded on an overlapping consensus on a political conception of justice. These objections I want to rebut, for they can prevent our accepting what I believe is the most reasonable basis of social unity available to us. I begin with perhaps the most obvious objection, namely, that an overlapping consensus is a mere *modus vivendi*. But first several explanatory comments.

Earlier I noted what it means to say that a conception of justice is supported by an overlapping consensus. It means that it is supported by a consensus including the opposing religious, philosophical and moral doctrines likely to thrive over generations in the society effectively regulated by that conception of justice. These opposing doctrines we assume to involve conflicting and indeed incommensurable comprehensive conceptions of the meaning, value and purpose of human life (or conceptions of the good), and there are no resources within the political view to judge those conflicting conceptions. They are equally permissible provided they respect the limits imposed by the principles of political justice. Yet despite the fact that there are opposing comprehensive conceptions affirmed in society, there is no difficulty as to how an overlapping consensus may exist. Since different premises may lead to the same conclusions, we simply suppose that the essential elements of the political conception, its principles, standards and ideals, are theorems, as it were, at which the comprehensive doctrines in the consensus intersect or converge.

To fix ideas I shall use a model case of an overlapping consensus to indicate what is meant; and I shall return to this example from time to time. It contains three views: one view affirms the political conception because its religious doctrine and account of faith lead to a principle of toleration and underwrite the fundamental liberties of a constitutional regime; the second view affirms the political

---

1   *public reason*   For a fuller discussion, see *A Theory of Justice*, Sec 34, and "Kantian Constructivism," Lect II, pp 535–43. [editors' note] Public reason plays a crucial role in Rawls's *Political Liberation* and later work. Essentially, public reason is the mode of reasoning designed to address the public as a whole—as opposed to reasoning within private associations such as churches. Public reasoning involves assumptions all people can accept, and is based in common sense and established science, rather than controversial metaphysical claims. Rawls limits public reason to constitutional essentials of claims of basic justice. Rawls's conception of public reason is inspired by Kant's essay "What Is Enlightenment" and other works. The concept is developed in the chapter "Public Reason" in *Political Liberalism* and in the essay "Public Reason Revisted," published in the book version of *The Law of Peoples*.

2   *As I shall stress later on, the acceptance of this limit ... effectively established in no other way*   Two other elements of the idea of free public reason in justice as fairness are these: the first is a publicly recognized conception of everyone's (rational) advantage, or good, to be used as an agreed basis of interpersonal comparisons

in matters of political justice. This leads to an account of primary goods. See "Social Unity and Primary Goods," in A.K. Sen and B. Williams, eds. *Utilitarianism and Beyond* (Cambridge University Press, 1982), Secs I–V. The second further element is the idea of publicity, which requires that the principles of political justice and their justification (in their own terms) be publicly available to all citizens, along with the knowledge of whether their political institutions are just or unjust. See "Kantian Constructivism," Lect II, pp 535–43.

conception on the basis of a comprehensive liberal moral doctrine such as those of Kant and Mill; while the third supports the political conception not as founded on any wider doctrine but rather as in itself sufficient to express political values that, under the reasonably favourable conditions that make a more or less just constitutional democracy possible, normally outweigh whatever other values may oppose them. Observe about this example that only the first two views—the religious doctrine and the liberalism of Kant or Mill—are general and comprehensive. The political conception of justice itself is not; although it does hold that under reasonably favourable conditions, it is normally adequate for questions of political justice. Observe also that the example assumes that the two comprehensive views agree with the judgments of the political conception in this respect.

To begin with the objection: some will think that even if an overlapping consensus should be sufficiently stable, the idea of political unity founded on an overlapping consensus must still be rejected, since it abandons the hope of political community and settles instead for a public understanding that is at bottom a mere *modus vivendi*. To this objection, we say that the hope of political community must indeed be abandoned, if by such a community we mean a political society united in affirming a general and comprehensive doctrine. This possibility is excluded by the fact of pluralism together with the rejection of the oppressive use of state power to overcome it. I believe there is no practicable alternative superior to the stable political unity secured by an overlapping consensus on a reasonable political conception of justice. Hence the substantive question concerns the significant features of such a consensus and how these features affect social concord and the moral quality of public life. I turn to why an overlapping consensus is not a mere *modus vivendi*.[1]

A typical use of the phrase "*modus vivendi*" is to characterize a treaty between two states whose national aims and interests put them at odds. In negotiating a treaty each state would be wise and prudent to make sure that the agreement proposed represents an equilibrium point: that is, that the terms and conditions of the treaty are drawn up in such a way that it is public knowledge that it is not advantageous for either state to violate it. The treaty will then be adhered to because doing so is regarded by each as in its national interest, including its interest in its reputation as a state that honours treaties. But in general both states are ready to pursue their goals at the expense of the other, and should conditions change they may do so. This background highlights the way in which a treaty is a mere *modus vivendi*. A similar background is present when we think of social consensus founded on self- or group-interests, or on the outcome of political bargaining: social unity is only apparent as its stability is contingent on circumstances remaining such as not to upset the fortunate convergence of interests.

Now, that an overlapping consensus is quite different from a *modus vivendi* is clear from our model case. In that example, note two aspects: first, the object of consensus, the political conception of justice, is itself a moral conception. And second, it is affirmed on moral grounds, that is, it includes conceptions of society and of citizens as persons, as well as principles of justice, and an account of the cooperative virtues through which those principles are embodied in human character and expressed in public life. An overlapping consensus, therefore, is not merely a consensus on accepting certain authorities, or on complying with certain institutional arrangements, founded on a convergence of self- or group-interests. All three views in the example affirm the political conception: as I have said, each recognizes

---

1   *modus vivendi*   Note that what is impracticable is not *all* values of community (recall that a community is understood as an association or society whose unity rests on a comprehensive conception of the good) but only *political* community and its values. Justice as fairness assumes, as other liberal political views do also, that the values of community are not only essential but realizable, first in the various associations that carry on their life within the framework of the basic structure, and second in those associations that extend across the boundaries of nation-states, such as churches and scientific societies. Liberalism rejects the state as a community because, among other things, it leads to the systematic denial of basic liberties and to the oppressive use of the state's monopoly of (legal) force. I should add that in the well-ordered society of justice as fairness citizens share a common aim, and one that has high priority: namely, the aim of political justice, that is, the aim of ensuring that political and social institutions are just, and of giving justice to persons generally, as what citizens need for themselves and want for one another. It is not true, then, that on a liberal view citizens have no fundamental common aims. Nor is it true that the aim of political justice is not an important part of their identity (using the term "identity," as is now often done, to include the basic aims and projects by reference to which we characterize the kind of person we very much want to be). But this common aim of political justice must not be mistaken for (what I have called) a conception of the good. For a discussion of this last point, see Amy Gutmann, "Communitarian Critics of Liberalism," *Philosophy and Public Affairs*, Summer 1985, p 311, footnote 14.

its concepts, principles and virtues as the shared content at which their several views coincide. The fact that those who affirm the political conception start from within their own comprehensive view, and hence begin from different premises and grounds, does not make their affirmation any less religious, philosophical or moral, as the case may be.

The preceding two aspects (moral object and moral grounds) of an overlapping consensus connect with a third aspect, that of stability: that is, those who affirm the various views supporting the political conception will not withdraw their support of it should the relative strength of their view in society increase and eventually become dominant. So long as the three views are affirmed and not revised, the political conception will still be supported regardless of shifts in the distribution of political power. We might say: each view supports the political conception for its own sake, or on its own merits; and the test for this is whether the consensus is stable with respect to changes in the distribution of power among views. This feature of stability highlights a basic contrast between an overlapping consensus and a *modus vivendi*, the stability of which does depend on happenstance and a balance of relative forces.

This becomes clear once we change our example and include the views of Catholics and Protestants in the sixteenth century. We no longer have an overlapping consensus on the principle of toleration. At that time both faiths held that it was the duty of the ruler to uphold the true religion and to repress the spread of heresy and false doctrine. In this case the acceptance of the principle of toleration would indeed be a mere *modus vivendi*, because if either faith becomes dominant, the principle of toleration will no longer be followed. Stability with respect to the distribution of power no longer holds. So long as views held by Catholics and Protestants in the sixteenth century are very much in the minority, and are likely to remain so, they do not significantly affect the moral quality of public life and the basis of social concord. For the vast majority in society are confident that the distribution of power will range over and be widely shared by views in the consensus that affirm the political conception of justice for its own sake. But should this situation change, the moral quality of political life will also change in ways I assume to be obvious and to require no comment.

The preceding remarks prompt us to ask which familiar conceptions of justice can belong to a consensus stable with respect to the distribution of power. It seems that while some teleological conceptions can so belong, others quite possibly cannot, for example, utilitarianism.[1] Or at least this seems to be the case unless certain assumptions are made limiting the content of citizens' desires, preferences, or interests.[2] Otherwise there appears to be no assurance that restricting or suppressing the basic liberties of some may not be the best way to maximize the total (or average) social welfare. Since utilitarianism in its various forms is a historically prominent and continuing part of the tradition of democratic thought, we may hope there are ways of construing or revising utilitarian doctrine so that it can support a conception of justice appropriate for a constitutional regime, even if it can do so only indirectly[3] as a means to the greatest welfare. Insofar as utilitarianism is likely to persist in a well-ordered society, the overlapping consensus is in that case all the more stable and secure.

4

I turn to the second objection to the idea of an overlapping consensus on a political conception of justice: namely, that the avoidance of general and comprehensive doctrines implies indifference or scepticism as to whether a political conception of justice is true. This avoidance may appear to suggest that such a conception might be the most reasonable one for us even when it is known not to be true, as if truth were simply beside the point. In reply, it would be fatal to the point of a political conception to see it as sceptical about, or indifferent to, truth, much less as in conflict with it. Such scepticism or indifference would put political philosophy in conflict with numerous comprehensive doctrines, and thus defeat from the outset its aim of achieving an overlapping consensus. In following the method of avoidance, as we may call it, we try, so far as we can, neither

---

1   *utilitarianism*   Here I mean the view of Bentham, Edgeworth, and Sidgwick, and of such contemporary writers as R.B. Brandt in *A Theory of the Good and the Right* (Oxford: Clarendon Press, 1979), R.M. Hare in *Moral Thinking* (Oxford: Clarendon Press, 1981), and J.J.C. Smart in *Utilitarianism: For and Against* (Cambridge: The University Press, 1973).

2   *desires, preferences, or interests*   Desires, preferences, and interests are not the same but have distinct features; and these differences play an important part in different versions of utilitarianism espoused by the writers mentioned in the previous footnote. I believe, however, that the general point in the text holds against all these versions.

3   *indirectly*   The adverb 'indirectly' here refers to indirect utilitarianism so-called. For a clear account of J.S. Mill's view as exemplifying this doctrine, see John Gray, *Mill on Liberty: A Defence* (London: Routledge, 1983).

to assert nor to deny any religious, philosophical or moral views, or their associated philosophical accounts of truth and the status of values. Since we assume each citizen to affirm some such view or other, we hope to make it possible for all to accept the political conception as true, or as reasonable, from the standpoint of their own comprehensive view, whatever it may be.[1]

Properly understood, then, a political conception of justice need be no more indifferent, say, to truth in morals than the principle of toleration, suitably understood, need be indifferent to truth in religion. We simply apply the principle of toleration to philosophy itself. In this way we hope to avoid philosophy's long-standing controversies, among them controversies about the nature of truth and the status of values as expressed by realism and subjectivism. Since we seek an agreed basis of public justification in matters of justice, and since no political agreement on those disputed questions can reasonably be expected, we turn instead to the fundamental intuitive ideas we seem to share through the public political culture. We try to develop from these ideas a political conception of justice congruent with our considered convictions on due reflection. Just as with religion, citizens situated in thought and belief within their comprehensive doctrines, regard the political conception of justice as true, or as reasonable, whatever the case may be.

Some may not be satisfied with this: they may reply that, despite these protests, a political conception of justice must express indifference or scepticism. Otherwise it could not lay aside fundamental religious, philosophical and moral questions because they are politically difficult to settle, or

may prove intractable. Certain truths, it may be said, concern things so important that differences about them have to be fought out, even should this mean civil war. To this we say first, that questions are not removed from the political agenda, so to speak, solely because they are a source of conflict. Rather, we appeal to a political conception of justice to distinguish between those questions that can be reasonably removed from the political agenda and those that cannot, all the while aiming for an overlapping consensus. Some questions still on the agenda will be controversial, at least to some degree; this is normal with political issues.

To illustrate: from within a political conception of justice let's suppose we can account both for equal liberty of conscience, which takes the truths of religion off the political agenda, and the equal political and civil liberties, which by ruling out serfdom and slavery takes the possibility of those institutions off the agenda.[2] But controversial issues inevitably remain: for example, how more exactly to draw the boundaries of the basic liberties when they conflict (where to set 'the wall between church and state'); how to interpret the requirements of distributive justice even when there is considerable agreement on general principles for the basic structure; and finally, questions of policy such as the use of nuclear weapons. These cannot be removed from politics. But by avoiding comprehensive doctrines we try to bypass religion and philosophy's profoundest controversies so as to have some hope of uncovering a basis of a stable overlapping consensus.

Nevertheless in affirming a political conception of justice we may eventually have to assert at least certain aspects of our own comprehensive (by no means necessarily fully

---

1   *Since we assume ... whatever it may be*   It is important to see that the view that philosophy in the classical sense as the search for truth about a prior and independent moral order cannot provide the shared basis for a political conception of justice (asserted in "Political not Metaphysical," p 230) does not presuppose the controversial metaphysical claim that there is no such order. The above paragraph makes clear why it does not. The reasons I give for that view are historical and sociological, and have nothing to do with metaphysical doctrines about the status of values. What I hold is that we must draw the obvious lessons of our political history since the Reformation and the Wars of Religion, and the development of modern constitutional democracies. As I say in Sec 1 above, it is no longer reasonable to expect us to reach *political* agreement on a general and comprehensive doctrine as a way of reaching political agreement on constitutional essentials, unless, of course, we are prepared to use the apparatus of the state as an instrument of oppression. If we are not prepared to do that, we must, as a practical matter, look for what I have called a political conception of justice.

2   *takes the possibility of those institutions off the agenda*   To explain: when certain matters are taken off the political agenda, they are no longer regarded as proper subjects for political decision by majority or other plurality voting. In regard to equal liberty of conscience and rejection of slavery and serfdom, this means that the equal basic liberties in the constitution that cover these matters are taken as fixed, settled once and for all. They are part of the public charter of a constitutional regime and not a suitable topic for on-going public debate and legislation, as if they can be changed at any time, one way or the other. Moreover, the more established political parties likewise acknowledge these matters as settled. Of course, that certain matters are taken off the political agenda does not mean that a political conception of justice should not explain why this is done. Indeed, as I note above, a political conception should do precisely this. For thinking of basic rights and liberties as taking certain questions off the political agenda I am indebted to Stephen Holmes.

comprehensive[1]) religious or philosophical doctrine. This happens whenever someone insists, for example, that certain questions are so fundamental that to ensure their being rightly settled justifies civil strife. The religious salvation of those holding a particular religion, or indeed the salvation of a whole people, may be said to depend on it. At this point we may have no alternative but to deny this, and to assert the kind of thing we had hoped to avoid. But the aspects of our view that we assert should not go beyond what is necessary for the political aim of consensus. Thus, for example, we may assert in some form the doctrine of free religious faith that supports equal liberty of conscience; and given the existence of a just constitutional regime, we deny that the concern for salvation requires anything incompatible with that liberty. We do not state more of our comprehensive view than we think would advance the quest for consensus.

The reason for this restraint is to respect, as best we can, the limits of free public reason (mentioned earlier at the end of Sec 2). Let's suppose that by respecting these limits we succeed in reaching an overlapping consensus on a conception of political justice. Some might say that reaching this reflective agreement is itself sufficient grounds for regarding that conception as true, or at any rate highly probable. But we refrain from this further step: it is unnecessary and may interfere with the practical aim of finding an agreed public basis of justification. The idea of an overlapping consensus leaves this step to be taken by citizens individually in accordance with their own general and comprehensive views.

In doing this a political conception of justice completes and extends the movement of thought that began three centuries ago with the gradual acceptance of the principle of toleration and led to the non-confessional state and equal liberty of conscience. This extension is required for an agreement on a political conception of justice given the historical and social circumstances of a democratic society. In this way the full autonomy of democratic citizens connects with a conception of political philosophy as itself autonomous and independent of general and comprehensive doctrines. In applying the principles of toleration to philosophy itself it is left to citizens individually to resolve for themselves the questions of religion, philosophy and morals in accordance with the views they freely affirm.

5

A third objection is the following: even if we grant that an overlapping consensus is not a *modus vivendi*, it may be said that a workable political conception must be general and comprehensive. Without such a doctrine on hand, there is no way to order the many conflicts of justice that arise in public life. The idea is that the deeper the conceptual and philosophical bases of those conflicts, the more general and comprehensive the level of philosophical reflection must be if their roots are to be laid bare and an appropriate ordering found. It is useless, the objection concludes, to try to work out a political conception of justice expressly for the basic structure apart from any comprehensive doctrine. And as we have just seen, we may be forced to refer, at least in some way, to such a view.[2]

This objection is perfectly natural: we are indeed tempted to ask how else could these conflicting claims be adjudicated. Yet part of the answer is found in the third view in our model case: namely, a political conception of justice regarded not as a consequence of a comprehensive doctrine but as in itself sufficient to express values that normally outweigh whatever other values oppose them, at least under the reasonably favourable conditions that make a constitutional democracy possible. Here the criterion of a just regime is specified by that political conception; and the values in question are seen from its principles and standards, and from its account of the cooperative virtues of political justice, and the like. Those who hold this conception have, of course, other views as well, views that specify values and

---

1   *(by no means necessarily fully comprehensive)*   I think of a doctrine as fully comprehensive if it covers all recognized values and virtues within one rather precisely articulated system; whereas a doctrine is only partially comprehensive when it comprises a number of non-political values and virtues and is rather loosely articulated. This limited scope and looseness turns out to be important with regard to stability in Sec VI–VII below.

2   *And as we have just seen ... such a view*   It is essential to distinguish between general and comprehensive views and views we think of as abstract. Thus, when justice as fairness begins from the fundamental intuitive idea of society as a fair system of cooperation and proceeds to elaborate that idea, the resulting conception of political justice may be said to be abstract. It is abstract in the same way that the conception of a perfectly competitive market, or of general economic equilibrium, is abstract: that is, it singles out, or focuses on, certain aspects of society as especially significant from the standpoint of political justice and leaves others aside. But whether the conception that results itself is general and comprehensive, as I have used those terms, is a separate question. I believe the conflicts implicit in the fact of pluralism force political philosophy to present conceptions of justice that are abstract, if it is to achieve its aims; but the same conflicts prevent those conceptions from being general and comprehensive.

306 RIGHTS-BASED LIBERALISM AND ITS CRITICS

virtues belonging to other parts of life; they differ from citizens holding the two other views in our example of an overlapping consensus in having no fully (as opposed to partially[1]) comprehensive doctrine within which they see all values and virtues as being ordered. They don't say such a doctrine is impossible, but rather practically speaking unnecessary. Their conviction is that, within the scope allowed by the basic liberties and the other provisions of a just constitution, all citizens can pursue their way of life on fair terms and properly respect its (non-public) values. So long as those constitutional guarantees are secure, they think no conflict of values is likely to arise that would justify their opposing the political conception as a whole, or on such fundamental matters as liberty of conscience, or equal political liberties, or basic civil rights, and the like.

Those holding this partially comprehensive view might explain it as follows. We should not assume that there exist reasonable and generally acceptable answers for all or even for many questions of political justice that might be asked. Rather, we must be prepared to accept the fact that only a few such questions can be satisfactorily resolved. Political wisdom consists in identifying those few, and among them the most urgent. That done, we must frame the institutions of the basic structure so that intractable conflicts are unlikely to arise; we must also accept the need for clear and simple principles, the general form and content of which we hope can be publicly understood. A political conception is at best but a guiding framework of deliberation and reflection which helps us reach political agreement on at least the constitutional essentials. If it seems to have cleared our view and made our considered convictions more coherent; if it has narrowed the gap between the conscientious convictions of those who accept the basic ideas of a constitutional regime, then it has served its practical political purpose. And this remains true even though we can't fully explain our agreement: we know only that citizens who affirm the political conception, and who have been raised in and are familiar with the fundamental ideas of the public political culture, find that, when they adopt its framework of deliberation, their judgments converge sufficiently so that political cooperation on the basis of mutual respect can be maintained. They view the political conception as itself normally sufficient and may not expect, or think they need, greater political understanding than that.

But here we are bound to ask: how can a political conception of justice express values that, under the reasonably favourable conditions that make democracy possible, normally outweigh whatever other values conflict with them? One way is this. As I have said, the most reasonable political conception of justice for a democratic regime will be, broadly speaking, liberal. But this means, as I will explain in the next section, that it protects the familiar basic rights and assigns them a special priority; it also includes measures to ensure that all persons in society have sufficient material means to make effective use of those basic rights. Faced with the fact of pluralism, a liberal view removes from the political agenda the most divisive issues, pervasive uncertainty and serious contention about which must undermine the bases of social cooperation.

The virtues of political cooperation that make a constitutional regime possible are, then, *very great* virtues. I mean, for example, the virtues of tolerance and being ready to meet others halfway, and the virtue of reasonableness and the sense of fairness. When these virtues (together with the modes of thought and sentiments they involve) are widespread in society and sustain its political conception of justice, they constitute a very great public good, part of society's political capital.[2] Thus, the values that conflict with the political conception of justice and its sustaining virtues may be normally outweighed because they come into conflict with the very conditions that make fair social cooperation possible on a footing of mutual respect.

Moreover, conflicts with political values are much reduced when the political conception is supported by an overlapping consensus, the more so the more inclusive the consensus. For in this case the political conception is not viewed as incompatible with basic religious, philosophical and moral values. We avoid having to consider the claims of the political conception of justice against those of this or that comprehensive view; nor need we say that political values are intrinsically more important than other values and that's why the latter are overridden. Indeed, saying that is the kind of thing we hope to avoid, and achieving an overlapping consensus enables us to avoid it.

---

1   (*as opposed to partially*)   For the distinction between a doctrine's being fully vs partially comprehensive, see Sec 4.

2   *society's political capital*   The term "capital" is appropriate and familiar in this connection because these virtues are built up slowly over time and depend not only on existing political and social institutions (themselves slowly built up), but also on citizens' experience as a whole and their knowledge of the past. Again, like capital, these virtues depreciate, as it were, and must be constantly renewed by being reaffirmed and acted from in the present.

To conclude: given the fact of pluralism, what does the work of reconciliation by free public reason, and thus enables us to avoid reliance on general and comprehensive doctrines, is two things: first, identifying the fundamental role of political values in expressing the terms of fair social cooperation consistent with mutual respect between citizens regarded as free and equal; and second, uncovering a sufficiently inclusive concordant fit among political and other values as displayed in an overlapping consensus.

6

The last difficulty I shall consider is that the idea of an overlapping consensus is utopian; that is, there are not sufficient political, social, or psychological forces either to bring about an overlapping consensus (when one does not exist), or to render one stable (should one exist). Here I can only touch on this intricate question and I merely outline one way in which such a consensus might come about and its stability made secure. For this purpose I use the idea of a liberal conception of political justice, the content of which I stipulate to have three main elements (noted previously): first, a specification of certain basic rights, liberties, and opportunities (of the kind familiar from constitutional democratic regimes); second, an assignment of a special priority to those rights, liberties, and opportunities, especially with respect to the claims of the general good and of perfectionist values; and third, measures assuring to all citizens adequate all-purpose means to make effective use of their basic liberties and opportunities.[1]

---

1   *For this purpose ... basic liberties and opportunities*   A fuller idea of the content of a liberal conception of justice is this: (1) political authority must respect the rule of law and a conception of the common good that includes the good of every citizen; (2) liberty of conscience and freedom of thought is to be guaranteed, and this extends to the liberty to follow one's conception of the good, provided it does not violate the principles of justice; (3) equal political rights are to be assured, and in addition freedom of the press and assembly, the right to form political parties, including the idea of a loyal opposition; (4) fair equality of opportunity and free choice of occupation are to be maintained against a background of diverse opportunities; and (5) all citizens are to be assured a fair share of material means so that they are suitably independent and can take advantage of their equal basic rights, liberties and fair opportunities. Plainly each of these elements can be understood in different ways, and so there are many liberalisms. However, I think of them all as sharing at least the three mentioned in the text.

Now let's suppose that at a certain time, as a result of various historical events and contingencies, the principles of a liberal conception have come to be accepted as a mere *modus vivendi*, and that existing political institutions meet their requirements. This acceptance has come about, we may assume, in much the same way as the acceptance of the principle of toleration as a *modus vivendi* came about following the Reformation: at first reluctantly, but nevertheless as providing the only alternative to endless and destructive civil strife. Our question, then, is this: how might it happen that over generations the initial acquiescence in a liberal conception of justice as a *modus vivendi* develops into a stable and enduring overlapping consensus? In this connection I think a certain looseness in our comprehensive views, as well as their not being fully comprehensive, may be particularly significant. To see this, let's return to our model case.

One way in which that example is atypical is that two of the three doctrines were described as fully general and comprehensive, a religious doctrine of free faith and the comprehensive liberalism of Kant or Mill. In these cases the acceptance of the political conception was said to be derived from and to depend solely on the comprehensive doctrine. But how far in practice does the allegiance to a political conception actually depend on its derivation from a comprehensive view? There are several possibilities. For simplicity distinguish three cases: the political conception is derived from the comprehensive doctrine; it is not derived from but is compatible with that doctrine; and last, the political conception is incompatible with it. In everyday life we have not usually decided, or even thought much about, which of these cases hold. To decide among them would raise highly complicated issues; and it is not clear that we need to decide among them. Most people's religious, philosophical and moral doctrines are not seen by them as fully general and comprehensive, and these aspects admit of variations of degree. There is lots of slippage, so to speak, many ways for the political conception to cohere loosely with those (partially) comprehensive views, and many ways within the limits of a political conception of justice to allow for the pursuit of different (partially) comprehensive doctrines. This suggests that many if not most citizens come to affirm their common political conception without seeing any particular connection, one way or the other, between it and their other views. Hence it is possible for them first to affirm the political conception and to appreciate the public good it accomplishes in a democratic society. Should an incompatibility later be recognized between the political conception and their wider doctrines, then they might very well adjust or revise these doctrines rather than reject the political conception.[1]

At this point we ask: in virtue of what political values might a liberal conception of justice gain an allegiance to itself? An allegiance to institutions and to the conception that regulates them may, of course, be based in part on long-term self- and group-interests, custom, and traditional attitudes, or simply on the desire to conform to what is expected and normally done. Widespread allegiance may also be encouraged by institutions securing for all citizens the political values included under what Hart calls the minimum content of natural law. But here we are concerned with the further bases of allegiance generated by a liberal conception of justice.[2]

Now when a liberal conception effectively regulates basic political institutions, it meets three essential requirements of a stable constitutional regime. First, given the fact of pluralism—the fact that necessitates a liberal regime as a *modus vivendi* in the first place—a liberal conception meets the urgent political requirement to fix, once and for all, the content of basic rights and liberties, and to assign them special priority. Doing this takes those guarantees off the political agenda and puts them beyond the calculus of social interests, thereby establishing clearly and firmly the terms of social cooperation on a footing of mutual respect. To regard that calculus as relevant in these matters leaves the status and content of those rights and liberties still unsettled; it subjects them to the shifting circumstances of time and place, and by greatly raising the stakes of political controversy, dangerously increases the insecurity and hostility of public life. Thus, the unwillingness to take these

matters off the agenda perpetuates the deep divisions latent in society; it betrays a readiness to revive those antagonisms in the hope of gaining a more favourable position should later circumstances prove propitious. So, by contrast, securing the basic liberties and recognizing their priority achieves the work of reconciliation and seals mutual acceptance on a footing of equality.

The second requirement is connected with a liberal conception's idea of free public reason. It is highly desirable that the form of reasoning a conception specifies should be, and can publicly be seen to be, correct and reasonably reliable in its own terms.[3] A liberal conception tries to meet these desiderata in several ways. As we have seen, in working out a political conception of justice it starts from fundamental intuitive ideas latent in the shared public culture; it detaches political values from any particular comprehensive and sectarian (non-public) doctrine; and it tries to limit that conception's scope to matters of political justice (the basic structure and its social policies). Further, (as we saw in Sec 2) it recognizes that an agreement on a political conception of justice is to no effect without a companion agreement on guidelines of public enquiry and rules for assessing evidence. Given the fact of pluralism, these guidelines and rules must be specified by reference to the forms of reasoning available to common sense, and by the procedures and conclusions of science when not controversial. The role of these shared methods and this common knowledge in applying the political conception makes reason *public*; the protection given to freedom of speech and thought makes it *free*. The claims of religion and philosophy (as previously emphasized) are not excluded out of scepticism or indifference, but as a condition of establishing a shared basis for free public reason.

A liberal conception's idea of public reason also has a certain simplicity. To illustrate: even if general and comprehensive teleological conceptions were acceptable as political conceptions of justice, the form of public reasoning they specify would be politically unworkable. For if the elaborate theoretical calculations involved in applying their principles are publicly admitted in questions of political justice (consider, for example, what is involved in applying the principle of utility to the basic structure), the highly speculative

---

1   *Should an incompatibility ... rather than reject the political conception*   Note that here we distinguish between the initial allegiance to, or appreciation of, the political conception and the later adjustment or revision of comprehensive doctrines to which that allegiance or appreciation leads when inconsistencies arise. These adjustments or revisions we may suppose to take place slowly over time as the political conception shapes comprehensive views to cohere with it. For much of this approach I am indebted to Samuel Scheffler.

2   *liberal conception of justice*   See *The Concept of Law*, (Oxford, 1961), pp 189–95, for what Hart calls the minimum content of natural law. I assume that a liberal conception (as do many other familiar conceptions) includes this minimum content; and so in the text I focus on the basis of the allegiance such a conception generates in virtue of the distinctive content of its principles.

3   *its own terms*   Here the phrase "in its own terms" means that we are not at present concerned with whether the conception in question is true, or reasonable (as the case may be), but with how easily its principles and standards can be correctly understood and reliably applied in public discussion.

nature and enormous complexity of these calculations are bound to make citizens with conflicting interests highly suspicious of one another's arguments. The information they presuppose is very hard if not impossible to obtain, and often there are insuperable problems in reaching an objective and agreed assessment. Moreover, even though we think our arguments sincere and not self-serving when we present them, we must consider what it is reasonable to expect others to think who stand to lose when our reasoning prevails. Arguments supporting political judgments should, if possible, not only be sound but such that they can be publicly seen to be sound. The maxim that justice must not only be done, but be seen to be done, holds good not only in law but in free public reason.

The third requirement met by a liberal conception is related to the preceding ones. The basic institutions enjoined by such a conception, and its conception of free public reason—when effectively working over time—encourage the cooperative virtues of political life: the virtue of reasonableness and a sense of fairness, a spirit of compromise and a readiness to meet others halfway, all of which are connected with the willingness if not the desire to cooperate with others on political terms that everyone can publicly accept consistent with mutual respect. Political liberalism tests principles and orders institutions with an eye to their influence on the moral quality of public life, on the civic virtues and habits of mind their public recognition tends to foster, and which are needed to sustain a stable constitutional regime. This requirement is related to the preceding two in this way. When the terms of social cooperation are settled on a footing of mutual respect by fixing once and for all the basic liberties and opportunities with their priority, and when this fact itself is publicly recognized, there is a tendency for the essential cooperative virtues to develop. And this tendency is further strengthened by successful conduct of free public reason in arriving at what are regarded as just policies and fair understandings.

The three requirements met by a liberal conception are evident in the fundamental structural features of the public world it realizes, and in its effects on citizens' political character, a character that takes the basic rights and liberties for granted and disciplines its deliberations in accordance with the guidelines of free public reason. A political conception of justice (liberal or otherwise) specifies the form of a social world—a background framework within which the life of associations, groups, and individual citizens proceeds. Inside that framework a working consensus may often be secured by a convergence of self- or group-interests; but to secure stability that framework must be honoured and seen as fixed by the political conception, itself affirmed on moral grounds.

The conjecture, then, is that as citizens come to appreciate what a liberal conception does, they acquire an allegiance to it, an allegiance that becomes stronger over time. They come to think it both reasonable and wise for them to confirm their allegiance to its principles of justice as expressing values that, under the reasonably favourable conditions that make democracy possible, normally counterbalance whatever values may oppose them. With this an overlapping consensus is achieved.

7

I have just outlined how it may happen that an initial acquiescence in a liberal conception of justice as a mere *modus vivendi* changes over time into a stable overlapping consensus. Thus the conclusion just reached is all we need to say in reply to the objection that the idea of such a consensus is utopian. Yet to make this conclusion more plausible, I shall indicate, necessarily only briefly, some of the main assumptions underlying the preceding account of how political allegiance is generated.

First, there are the assumptions contained in what I shall call a reasonable moral psychology, that is, a psychology of human beings as capable of being reasonable and engaging in fair social cooperation. Here I include the following: (1) besides a capacity for a conception of the good, people have a capacity to acquire conceptions of justice and fairness (which specify fair terms of cooperation) and to act as these conceptions require; (2) when they believe that institutions or social practices are just, or fair (as these conceptions specify), they are ready and willing to do their part in those arrangements provided they have reasonable assurance that others will also do their part; (3) if other persons with evident intention strive to do their part in just or fair arrangements, people tend to develop trust and confidence in them; (4) this trust and confidence becomes stronger and more complete as the success of shared cooperative arrangements is sustained over a longer time; and also (5) as the basic institutions framed to secure our fundamental interests (the basic rights and liberties) are more firmly and willingly recognized.

We may also suppose that everyone recognizes what I have called the historical and social conditions of modern democratic societies: (i) the fact of pluralism and (ii) the fact of its permanence, as well as (iii) the fact that this pluralism can be overcome only by the oppressive use of state power (which presupposes a control of the state no group possesses). These conditions constitute a common predicament. But also seen as part of this common predicament is (iv) the fact of moderate scarcity and (v) the fact of there being numerous possibilities of gains from well-organized social cooperation, if only cooperation can be established on fair terms. All these conditions and assumptions characterize the circumstances of political justice.

Now we are ready to draw on the preceding assumptions to answer once again the question: how might an overlapping consensus on a liberal conception of justice develop from its acceptance as a mere *modus vivendi*? Recall our assumption that the comprehensive doctrines of most people are not fully comprehensive, and how this allows scope for the development of an independent allegiance to a liberal conception once how it works is appreciated. This independent allegiance in turn leads people to act with evident intention in accordance with liberal arrangements, since they have reasonable assurance (founded on past experience) that others will also comply with them. So gradually over time, as the success of political cooperation continues, citizens come to have increasing trust and confidence in one another.

Note also that the success of liberal institutions may come as a discovery of a new social possibility: the possibility of a reasonably harmonious and stable pluralist society. Before the successful and peaceful practice of toleration in societies with liberal political institutions there was no way of knowing of that possibility. It can easily seem more natural to believe, as the centuries' long practice of intolerance appeared to confirm, that social unity and concord requires agreement on a general and comprehensive religious, philosophical or moral doctrine. Intolerance was accepted as a condition of social order and stability.[1] The weakening of that belief helps to clear the way for liberal institutions. And if we ask how the doctrine of free faith might develop, perhaps it is connected with the fact that it is difficult, if not impossible, to believe in the damnation of those with whom we have long cooperated on fair terms with trust and confidence.

To conclude: the third view of our model case, seen as a liberal conception of justice, may encourage a mere *modus vivendi* to develop eventually into an overlapping consensus precisely because it is not general and comprehensive. The conception's limited scope together with the looseness of our comprehensive doctrines allows leeway for it to gain an initial allegiance to itself and thereby to shape those doctrines accordingly as conflicts arise, a process that takes place gradually over generations (assuming a reasonable moral psychology). Religions that once rejected toleration may come to accept it and to affirm a doctrine of free faith; the comprehensive liberalisms of Kant and Mill, while viewed as suitable for non-public life and as possible bases for affirming a constitutional regime, are no longer proposed as political conceptions of justice. On this account an overlapping consensus is not a happy coincidence, even if aided as it no doubt must be by historical good fortune, but is rather in part the work of society's public tradition of political thought.

8

I conclude by commenting briefly on what I have called political liberalism. We have seen that this view steers a course between the Hobbesian strand in liberalism—liberalism as a *modus vivendi* secured by a convergence of self- and group-interests as coordinated and balanced by well-designed constitutional arrangements—and a liberalism founded on a comprehensive moral doctrine such as that of Kant or Mill. By itself, the former cannot secure an enduring social unity, the latter cannot gain sufficient agreement. Political liberalism is represented in our model case of an overlapping consensus by the third view once we take the political conception in question as liberal. So understood political liberalism is the view that under the reasonably favourable conditions that make constitutional democracy possible, political institutions satisfying the principles of a liberal conception of justice realize political values and ideals that normally outweigh whatever other values oppose them.

Political liberalism must deal with two basic objections: one is the charge of scepticism and indifference, the other that it cannot gain sufficient support to assure compliance with its principles of justice. Both of these objections are answered by finding a reasonable liberal conception of justice that can be supported by an overlapping consensus. For such a consensus achieves compliance by a concordant fit

---

1   *Intolerance was accepted ... stability*   Hume remarks on this in part 6 of "Liberty of the Press" (1741).

between the political conception and general and comprehensive doctrines together with the public recognition of the very great value of the political virtues. But as we saw, success in finding an overlapping consensus forces political philosophy to be, so far as possible, independent of and autonomous from other parts of philosophy, especially from philosophy's long-standing problems and controversies. And this in turn gives rise to the objection that political liberalism is sceptical of religious and philosophical truth, or indifferent to their values. But if we relate the nature of a political conception to the fact of pluralism and with what is essential for a shared basis of free public reason, this objection is seen to be mistaken. We can also note (see the end of Sec 4) how political philosophy's independence and autonomy from other parts of philosophy connects with the freedom and autonomy of democratic citizenship.

Some may think that to secure stable social unity in a constitutional regime by looking for an overlapping consensus detaches political philosophy from philosophy and makes it into politics. Yes and no: the politician, we say, looks to the next election, the statesman to the next generation, and philosophy to the indefinite future. Philosophy sees the political world as an on-going system of cooperation over time, in perpetuity practically speaking. Political philosophy is related to politics because it must be concerned, as moral philosophy need not be, with practical political possibilities.[1] This has led us to outline, for example, how it is possible for the deep divisions present in a pluralistic society to be reconciled through a political conception of justice that gradually over generations becomes the focus of an overlapping consensus. Moreover, this concern with practical possibility compels political philosophy to consider fundamental institutional questions and the assumptions of a reasonable moral psychology.

Thus political philosophy is not mere politics: in addressing the public culture it takes the longest view, looks to society's permanent historical and social conditions, and tries to mediate society's deepest conflicts. It hopes to uncover, and to help to articulate, a shared basis of consensus on a political conception of justice drawing upon citizens' fundamental intuitive ideas about their society and their place in it. In exhibiting the possibility of an overlapping consensus in a society with a democratic tradition confronted by the fact of pluralism, political philosophy assumes the role Kant gave to philosophy generally: the defence of reasonable faith. In our case this becomes the defence of reasonable faith in the real possibility of a just constitutional regime.

---

1 *Philosophy sees the political world ... practical political possibilities* On this point, see the instructive remarks by Joshua Cohen, "Reflections on Rousseau: Autonomy and Democracy," *Philosophy and Public Affairs*, Summer 1986, pp 296f.

ROBERT NOZICK
(1938-2002)

Biographical Information

Robert Nozick was born in 1938 and grew up in Brooklyn, New York; he took his undergraduate degree at Columbia College and his PhD, on theories of rational decision-making, at Princeton. He taught at Princeton from 1962 until 1965, Harvard University from 1965 to 1967, Rockefeller University from 1967 until 1969, and then returned to Harvard, a full professor of philosophy, at the tender age of 30. Nozick was already well-known in philosophical circles when his first book, *Anarchy, State, and Utopia* (1974) propelled him into the public eye with its controversial but intellectually dazzling defense of political libertarianism. It won the National Book Award and was later named by *The Times Literary Supplement* as one of "The Hundred Most Influential Books Since the War." In 1998 Nozick was made Joseph Pellegrino University Professor. He died of stomach cancer in 2002 at the age of 63.

As a young man, Nozick was a radical left-winger; he was converted to libertarianism—the view that individual rights should be maximized and the role of the state minimized—as a graduate student, largely through his reading of *laissez-faire* economists such as F.A. Hayek and Milton Friedman. However, he was never fully comfortable with his public reputation as a right-wing ideologue: in a 1978 article in *The New York Times Magazine*, he said that "right-wing people like the pro-free-market argument, but don't like the arguments for individual liberty in cases like gay rights—although I view them as an interconnecting whole."

In the same article, Nozick also described his fresh and lively approach to philosophical writing, noting that "[i]t is as though what philosophers want is a way of saying something that will leave the person they're talking to no escape. Well, why should they be bludgeoning people like that? It's not a nice way to behave."

Nozick's philosophical interests were notably broad. Though best known for his work in political philosophy,

he also made important contributions to epistemology (especially his notion of knowledge as a kind of "truth tracking"), metaphysics (with his "closest continuer" theory of personal identity) and decision theory (particularly through his introduction of Newcomb's problem to the philosophical literature).

The Structure of *Anarchy, State, and Utopia*

In Part 1 of *Anarchy, State, and Utopia*, Nozick argues that a minimal state is justified; then, in Part 2, he argues that no state more powerful or extensive than a minimal state is morally justified. In Part 3 he argues that this is not an unfortunate result: rather, the minimal state is "a framework for utopia" and "inspiring as well as right." The section reprinted here comes from the first section of the first chapter of Part 2, where Nozick argues that considerations of distributive justice do not require going beyond the minimal state. On the contrary, a proper account of distributive justice shows that state interference in distributive patterns must violate the rights of individuals.

Nozick begins by describing, in outline, what he considers the correct theory of distributive justice: he calls this the *entitlement theory of justice in holdings*, and presents it as made up of exactly three principles of justice. Nozick goes on to contrast what he calls *historical* theories of justice with *end-state* principles, and explains that the entitlement theory belongs to the former—in his view more plausible—type. He then distinguishes between two possible varieties of historical principles of justice—*patterned* or *non-patterned*—and claims that his entitlement theory belongs to the latter class. In the next section, Nozick argues that all end-state or patterned theories of distributive justice are inconsistent with liberty—that is, they are committed to the repeated violation of the rights of individuals. Indeed, he argues, "[t]axation of earnings from labor is on a par with forced labor."

The final two sections in this selection deal with what Nozick calls the principle of justice in acquisition. He begins by criticizing John Locke's seventeenth-century theory of just acquisition, but preserves a version of the Lockean proviso that an acquisition is just only if it leaves "enough and as good left in common for others"; he then goes on to spell out some of the details and implications of such a proviso, including some of the constraints its "historical shadow" places on just transfers of holdings.

Useful Background Information

Nozick argues in *Anarchy, State, and Utopia* that only a minimal or "night-watchman" state is consistent with individual liberty. A minimal state has a monopoly on the use of force within its boundaries (except for force used in immediate self-defense), and it uses this monopoly to guard its citizens against violence, theft, and fraud, and to enforce compliance with legally made contracts. Beyond this, however, the minimal state has no other legitimate function. For example, in the minimal state there will be no central bank or other forms of economic regulation, no department of public works, no public education system, no welfare provisions or state pensions, no social healthcare system, no environmental protection regulations or agencies, and so on.

A Common Misconception

Nozick does not believe it is actually *immoral* to help the poor (or preserve the environment, or provide universal healthcare, or foster the arts, etc.). He argues that it is immoral to *force* people to do these things—in other words, that we have no legally enforceable *duty* to do them—but it is perfectly consistent with this to believe that it would be *morally good* if we were (voluntarily) to contribute to these ends.

◆ ◆ ◆ ◆ ◆

from *Anarchy, State, and Utopia* (1974)

from *Chapter 7: Distributive Justice*

The minimal state is the most extensive state that can be justified. Any state more extensive violates people's rights. Yet many persons have put forth reasons purporting to justify a more extensive state. It is impossible within the compass of this book to examine all the reasons that have been put forth. Therefore, I shall focus upon those generally acknowledged to be most weighty and influential, to see precisely wherein they fail. In this chapter we consider the claim that a more extensive state is justified, because necessary (or the best instrument) to achieve distributive justice; in the next chapter we shall take up diverse other claims.

The term "distributive justice" is not a neutral one. Hearing the term "distribution," most people presume that some thing or mechanism uses some principle or criterion to give out a supply of things. Into this process of distributing shares some error may have crept. So it is an open question, at least, whether redistribution should take place; whether we should do again what has already been done once, though poorly. However, we are not in the position of children who have been given portions of pie by someone who now makes last minute adjustments to rectify careless cutting. There is no *central* distribution, no person or group entitled to control all the resources, jointly deciding how they are to be doled out. What each person gets, he gets from others who give to him in exchange for something, or as a gift. In a free society, diverse persons control different resources, and new holdings arise out of the voluntary exchanges and actions of persons. There is no more a distributing or distribution of shares than there is a distributing of mates in a society in which persons choose whom they shall marry. The total result is the product of many individual decisions which the different individuals involved are entitled to make. Some uses of the term "distribution," it is true, do not imply a previous distributing appropriately judged by some criterion (for example, "probability distribution"); nevertheless, despite the title of this chapter, it would be best to use a terminology that clearly is neutral. We shall speak of people's holdings; a principle of justice in holdings describes (part of) what justice tells us (requires) about holdings. I shall state first what I take to be the correct view about justice in holdings, and then turn to the discussion of alternate views.[1]

Section 1

The Entitlement Theory

The subject of justice in holdings consists of three major topics. The first is the *original acquisition of holdings*, the appropriation of unheld things. This includes the issues of how unheld things may come to be held, the process, or processes, by which unheld things may come to be held, the things that may come to be held by these processes, the extent of what comes to be held by a particular process, and so on. We shall refer to the complicated truth about this topic, which we shall not formulate here, as the principle of justice in acquisition. The second topic concerns the *transfer of holdings* from one person to another. By what processes may a person transfer holdings to another? How may a person acquire a holding from another who holds it? Under this topic come general, descriptions of voluntary exchange, and gift and (on the other hand) fraud, as well as reference to particular conventional details fixed upon in a given society. The complicated truth about this subject (with placeholders for conventional details) we shall call their principle of justice in transfer. And we shall suppose it also includes principles governing how a person may divest himself of a holding, passing it into an unheld state.)

If the world were wholly just, the following inductive definition would exhaustively cover the subject of justice in holdings.

1. A person who acquires a holding in accordance with the principle of justice in acquisition is entitled to that holding.
2. A person who acquires a holding in accordance with the principle of justice in transfer, from someone else entitled to the holding, is entitled to the holding.

3. No one is entitled to a holding except by (repeated) applications of 1 and 2.

The complete principle of distributive justice would say simply that a distribution is just if everyone is entitled to the holdings they possess under the distribution.

A distribution is just if it arises from another just distribution by legitimate means. The legitimate means of moving from one distribution to another are specified by the principle of justice in transfer. The legitimate first "moves" are specified by the principle of justice in acquisition.[2] Whatever arises from a just situation by just steps is itself just. The means of change specified by the principle of justice in transfer preserve justice. As correct rules of inference are truth-preserving, and any conclusion deduced via repeated application of such rules from only true premises is itself true, so the means of transition from one situation to another specified by the principle of justice in transfer are justice-preserving, and any situation actually arising from repeated transitions in accordance with the principle from a just situation is itself just. The parallel between justice-preserving transformations and truth-preserving transformations illuminates where it fails as well as where it holds. That a conclusion could have been deduced by truth-preserving means from premises that are true suffices to show its truth. That from a just situation a situation *could* have arisen via justice-preserving means does *not* suffice to show its justice. The fact that a thief's victims voluntarily *could* have presented him with gifts does not entitle the thief to his ill-gotten gains. Justice in holdings is historical; it depends upon what actually has happened: We shall return to this point later.

Not all actual situations are generated in accordance with the two principles of justice in holdings: the principle of justice in acquisition and the principle of justice in transfer. Some people steal from others, or defraud them, or enslave them, seizing their product and preventing them from living as they choose, or forcibly exclude others from competing in exchanges. None of these are permissible modes of transition from one situation to another. And some persons acquire holdings by means not sanctioned by

---

1   *I shall state ... alternate views*   [Unless otherwise indicated, all notes to this selection are by the author rather than the editors of this anthology.] The reader who has looked ahead and seen that the second part of this chapter [not included in the selection here] discusses Rawls's theory mistakenly may think that every remark or argument in the first part against alternative theories of justice is meant to apply to, or anticipate, a criticism of Rawls's theory. This is not so; there are other theories also worth criticizing.

2   *The legitimate ... justice in acquisition*   Applications of the principle of justice in acquisition may also occur as part of the move from one distribution to another. You may find an unheld thing now and appropriate it. Acquisitions also are to be understood as included when, to simplify, I speak only of transitions by transfers.

the principle of justice in acquisition. The existence of past injustice (previous violations of the first two principles of justice in holdings) raises the third major topic under justice in holding: the rectification of injustice in holdings. If past injustice has shaped present holdings in various ways, some identifiable and some not, what now, if anything, ought to be done to rectify these injustices? What obligations do the performers of injustice have toward those whose position is worse than it would have been had the injustice not been done? Or, than it would have been had compensation been paid promptly? How, if at all, do things change if the beneficiaries and those made worse off are not the direct parties in the act of injustice, but, for example, their descendants? Is an injustice done to someone whose holding was itself based upon an unrectified injustice? How far back must one go in wiping clean the historical slate of injustices? What may victims of injustice permissibly do in order to rectify the injustices being done to them, including the many injustices done by persons acting through their government? I do not know of a thorough or theoretically sophisticated treatment of such issues.[1] Idealizing greatly, let us suppose theoretical investigation will produce a principle of rectification. This principle uses historical information about previous situations and injustices done in them (as defined by the first two principles of justice and rights against interference), and information about the actual course of events that flowed from these injustices, until the present, and it yields a description (or descriptions) of holdings in the society. The principle of rectification presumably will make use of its best estimate of subjunctive information about what would have occurred (or a probability distribution over what might have occurred, using the expected value) if the injustice had not taken place. If the actual description of holdings turns out not to be one of the descriptions yielded by the principle, then one of the descriptions yielded must be realized.[2]

---

1   *I do not know ... such issues*   See, however, the useful book by Boris Bittker, *The Case for Black Reparations* (New York: Random House, 1973).

2   *If the actual description ... must be realized*   If the principle of rectification of violations of the first two principles yields more than one description of holdings, then some choice must be made as to which of these is to be realized. Perhaps the sort of considerations about distributive justice and equality that I argue against play a legitimate role in *this* subsidiary choice. Similarly, there may be room for such considerations in deciding which otherwise arbitrary features a statute will embody when such features are

The general outlines of the theory of justice in holdings are that the holdings of a person are just if he is entitled to them by the principles of justice in acquisition and transfer, or by the principle of rectification of injustice (as specified by the first two principles). If each person's holdings are just, then the total set (distribution) of holdings is just. To turn these general outlines into a specific theory we would have to specify the details of each of the three principles of justice in holdings: the principle of acquisition of holdings, the principle of transfer of holdings, and the principle of rectification of violations of the first two principles. I shall not attempt that task here. (Locke's principle of justice in acquisition is discussed below.)

Historical Principles and End-Result Principles

The general outlines of the entitlement theory illuminate the nature and defects of other conceptions of distributive justice. The entitlement theory of justice in distribution is *historical;* whether a distribution is just depends upon how it came about. In contrast, *current time-slice principles* of justice hold that the justice of a distribution is determined by how things are distributed (who has what) as judged by some *structural* principle(s) of just distribution. A utilitarian who judges between any two distributions by seeing which has the greater sum of utility and, if the sums tie, applies some fixed equality criterion to choose the more equal distribution, would hold a current time-slice principle of justice. As would someone who had a fixed schedule of trade-offs between the sum of happiness and equality. According to a current time-slice principle, all that needs to be looked at, in judging the justice of a distribution, is who ends up with what; in comparing any two distributions one need look only at the matrix presenting the distributions. No further information need be fed into a principle of justice. It is a consequence of such principles of justice that any two structurally identical distributions are equally just. (Two distributions are structurally identical if they present the same profile, but perhaps have different persons occupying the particular slots. My having ten and your having five, and my having five and your having ten are structurally identical distributions.) Welfare economics is the theory of current time-slice principles of justice. The subject is conceived as operating on matrices representing only current

---

unavoidable because other considerations do not specify a precise line; yet a line must be drawn.

information about distribution. This, as well as some of the usual conditions (for example, the choice of distribution is invariant under relabeling of columns), guarantees that welfare economics will be a current time-slice theory, with all of its inadequacies.

Most persons do not accept current time-slice principles as constituting the whole story about distributive shares. They think it relevant in assessing the justice of a situation to consider not only the distribution it embodies, but also how that distribution came about. If some persons are in prison for murder or war crimes, we do not say that to assess the justice of the distribution in the society we must look only at what this person has, and that person has, and that person has,...at the current time. We think it relevant to ask whether someone did something so that he *deserved* to be punished, deserved to have a lower share. Most will agree to the relevance of further information with regard to punishments and penalties. Consider also desired things. One traditional socialist view is that workers are entitled to the product and full fruits of their labor; they have earned it; a distribution is unjust if it does not give the workers what they are entitled to. Such entitlements are based upon some past history. No socialist holding this view would find it comforting to be told that because the actual distribution *A* happens to coincide structurally with the one he desires *D*, *A* therefore is no less just than *D*; it differs only in that the "parasitic" owners of capital receive under *A* what the workers are entitled to under *D*, and the workers receive under *A* what the owners are entitled to under *D*, namely very little. This socialist rightly, in my view, holds onto the notions of earning, producing, entitlement, desert, and so forth, and he rejects current time-slice principles that look only to the structure of the resulting set of holdings. (The set of holdings resulting from what? Isn't it implausible that how holdings are produced and come to exist has no effect at all on who should hold what?) His mistake lies in his view of what entitlements arise out of what sorts of productive processes.

We construe the position we discuss too narrowly by speaking of *current* time-slice principles. Nothing is changed if structural principles operate upon a time sequence of current time-slice profiles and, for example, give someone more now to counterbalance the less he has had earlier. A utilitarian or an egalitarian or any mixture of the two over time will inherit the difficulties of his more myopic comrades. He is not helped by the fact that *some* of the information others consider relevant in assessing a distribution is reflected, unrecoverably, in past matrices. Henceforth, we

shall refer to such unhistorical principles of distributive justice, including the current time-slice principles, as *end-result principles* or *end-state principles*.

In contrast to end-result principles of justice, *historical principles* of justice hold that past circumstances or actions of people can create differential entitlements or differential deserts to things. An injustice can be worked by moving from one distribution to another structurally identical one, for the second, in profile the same, may violate people's entitlements or deserts; it may not fit the actual history.

Patterning

The entitlement principles of justice in holdings that we have sketched are historical principles of justice. To better understand their precise character, we shall distinguish them from another subclass of the historical principles. Consider, as an example, the principle of distribution according to moral merit. This principle requires that total distributive shares vary directly with moral merit; no person should have a greater share than anyone whose moral merit is greater. (If moral merit could be not merely ordered but measured on an interval or ratio scale, stronger principles could be formulated.) Or consider the principle that results by substituting "usefulness to society" for "moral merit" in the previous principle. Or instead of "distribute according to moral merit," or "distribute according to usefulness to society," we might consider "distribute according to the weighted sum of moral merit, usefulness to society, and need," with the weights of the different dimensions equal. Let us call a principle of distribution *patterned* if it specifies that a distribution is to vary along with some natural dimension, weighted sum[1] of natural dimensions, or lexicographic ordering[2] of natural dimensions. And let us say

---

1 *weighted sum* [editors' note] A weighted sum is obtained by adding terms, each of which is given a certain value (weight) by using a multiplier which reflects their relative importance.

2 *lexicographic ordering* [editors' note] Strictly speaking, this means sorting a group of items in the order they would appear if they were listed in a dictionary (i.e., roughly, alphabetically), but listing first all words made up of only *one* letter, then all the words made up of *two* letters, and so on. (The main idea here is to impose a useful order on an infinite sequence of formulae.) In the philosophical literature on justice, however, the phrase is generally used to mean a strict prioritizing of principles: first principle A must be satisfied, and only then should we worry about principle B; only when both A and B are satisfied can we apply principle C; and so on.

a distribution is patterned if it accords with some patterned principle. (I speak of natural dimensions, admittedly without a general criterion for them, because for any set of holdings some artificial dimensions can be gimmicked up to vary along with the distribution of the set.) The principle of distribution in accordance with moral merit is a patterned historical principle, which specifies a patterned distribution. "Distribute according to I.Q." is a patterned principle that looks to information not contained in distributional matrices. It is not historical, however, in that it does not look to any past actions creating differential entitlements to evaluate a distribution; it requires only distributional matrices whose columns are labeled by I.Q. scores. The distribution in a society, however, may be composed of such simple patterned distributions, without itself being simply patterned. Different sectors may operate different patterns, or some combination of patterns may operate in different proportions, across a society. A distribution composed in this manner, from a small number of patterned distributions, we also shall term "patterned." And we extend the use of "pattern" to include the overall designs put forth by combinations of end-state principles.

Almost every suggested principle of distributive justice is patterned: to each according to his moral merit, or needs, or marginal product,[1] or how hard he tries, or the weighted sum of the foregoing, and so on. The principle of entitlement we have sketched is not patterned.[2] There is no one natural dimension or weighted sum or combination of a small number of natural dimensions that yields the distributions generated in accordance with the principle of entitlement. The set of holdings that results when some persons receive their marginal products, others win at gambling, others receive a share of their mate's income, others receive gifts from foundations, others receive interest on loans, others receive gifts from admirers, others receive returns on investment, others make for themselves much of what they have, others find things, and so on, will not be patterned. Heavy strands of patterns will run through it; significant portions of the variance in holdings will be accounted for by pattern-variables. If most people most of the time choose to transfer some of their entitlements to others only in exchange for something from them, then a large part of what many people hold will vary with what they held that others wanted. More details are provided by the theory of marginal productivity. But gifts to relatives, charitable donations, bequests to children, and the like, are not best conceived, in the first instance, in this manner. Ignoring the strands of pattern, let us suppose for the moment that a distribution actually arrived at by the operation of the principle of entitlement is random with respect to any pattern. Though the resulting set of holdings will be unpatterned, it will not be incomprehensible, for it can be seen as arising from the operation of a small number of principles. These principles specify how an initial distribution may arise (the principle of acquisition of holdings) and how distributions may be transformed into others (the principle of transfer of holdings). The process whereby the set of holdings is generated will be intelligible, though the set of holdings itself that results from this process will be unpatterned.

The writings of F.A. Hayek[3] focus less than is usually done upon what patterning distributive justice requires. Hayek argues that we cannot know enough about each person's situation to distribute to each according to his moral merit (but would justice demand we do so if we did have this knowledge?); and he goes on to say, "our objection is against all attempts to impress upon society a deliberately chosen pattern of distribution, whether it be an order of equality or of inequality."[4] However, Hayek concludes that in a free society there will be distribution

---

1 *marginal product* [editors' note] The contribution that each additional worker makes to total output. Thus, to be rewarded according to one's marginal product is to be paid in proportion to the amount that your contribution has increased output over what it would have been if you hadn't been employed.

2 *The principle ... is not patterned* One might try to squeeze a patterned conception of distributive justice into the framework of the entitlement conception, by formulating a gimmicky obligatory "principle of transfer" that would lead to the pattern. For example, the principle that if one has more than the mean income one must transfer everything one holds above the mean to persons below the mean so as to bring them up to (but not over) the mean. We can formulate a criterion for a "principle of transfer" to rule out such obligatory transfers, or we can say that no correct principle of transfer, no principle of transfer in a free society will be like this. The former is probably the better course, though the latter also is true.

Alternatively, one might think to make the entitlement conception instantiate a pattern, by using matrix entries that express the relative strength of a person's entitlements as measured by some real-valued function. But even if the limitation to natural dimensions failed to exclude this function, the resulting edifice would *not* capture our system of entitlements to *particular* things.

3 *F.A. Hayek* [editors' note] Friedrich August Hayek (1899–1992) was an Austrian-British economist and political philosopher best known for his critique of socialism and the welfare state, and defense of *laissez-faire* economic individualism.

4 *our objection ... or of inequality* F.A. Hayek, *The Constitution of Liberty* (Chicago: University of Chicago Press, 1960), p. 87.

in accordance with value rather than moral merit; that is, in accordance with the perceived value of a person's actions and services to others. Despite his rejection of a patterned conception of distributive justice, Hayek himself suggests a pattern he thinks justifiable: distribution in accordance with the perceived benefits given to others, leaving room for the complaint that a free society does not realize exactly this pattern. Stating this patterned strand of a free capitalist society more precisely, we get "To each according to how much he benefits others who have the resources for benefiting those who benefit them." This will seem arbitrary unless some acceptable initial set of holdings is specified, or unless it is held that the operation of the system over time washes out any significant effects from the initial set of holdings. As an example of the latter, if almost anyone would have bought a car from Henry Ford, the supposition that it was an arbitrary matter who held the money then (and so bought) would not place Henry Ford's earnings under a cloud. In any event, *his* coming to hold it is not arbitrary. Distribution according to benefits to others *is* a major patterned strand in a free capitalist society, as Hayek correctly points out, but it is only a strand and does not constitute the whole pattern of a system of entitlements (namely, inheritance, gifts for arbitrary reasons, charity, and so on) or a standard that one should insist a society fit. Will people tolerate for long a system yielding distributions that they believe are unpatterned?[1] No doubt people will not long accept a distribution they believe is *unjust*. People want their society to be and to look just. But must the look of justice reside in a resulting pattern rather than in the underlying generating principles? We are in no position to conclude that the inhabitants of a society embodying an entitlement conception of justice in holdings will find it unacceptable. Still, it must be granted that were people's reasons for transferring some of their holdings to others always irrational or arbitrary, we would find this disturbing. (Suppose people

always determined what holdings they would transfer, and to whom, by using a random device.) We feel more comfortable upholding the justice of an entitlement system if most of the transfers under it are done for reasons. This does not mean necessarily that all deserve what holdings they receive. It means only that there is a purpose or point to someone's transferring a holding to one person rather than to another; that usually we can see what the transferrer thinks he's gaining, what cause he thinks he's serving, what goals he thinks he's helping to achieve, and so forth.

Since in a capitalist society people often transfer holdings to others in accordance with how much they perceive these others benefiting them, the fabric constituted by the individual transactions and transfers is largely reasonable and intelligible.[2] (Gifts to loved ones, bequests to children, charity to the needy also are nonarbitrary components of the fabric.) In stressing the large strand of distribution in accordance with benefit to others, Hayek shows the point of many transfers, and so shows that the system of transfer of entitlements is not just spinning its gears aimlessly. The system of entitlements is defensible when constituted by the individual aims of individual transactions. No overarching aim is needed, no distributional pattern is required.

To think that the task of a theory of distributive justice is to fill in the blank in "to each according to his _____" is to be predisposed to search for a pattern; and the separate treatment of from each according to his _____" treats production and distribution as two separate and independent issues. On an entitlement view these are *not* two separate questions. Whoever makes something, having bought or contracted for all other held resources used in the process (transferring some of his holdings for these cooperating factors), is entitled to it. The situation is *not* one of something's getting made, and there being an open question of who is to get it. Things come into the world already attached to

1   *Will people ... are unpatterned* This question does not imply that they will tolerate any and every patterned distribution. In discussing Hayek's views, Irving Kristol has recently speculated that people will not long tolerate a system that yields distributions patterned in accordance with value rather than merit. ("'When Virtue Loses All Her Loveliness'—Some Reflections on Capitalism and 'The Free Society,'" *The Public Interest* 17 [Fall 1970]: 3–15.) Kristol, following some remarks of Hayek's, equates the merit system with justice. Since some case can be made for the external standard of distribution in accordance with benefit to others, we ask about a weaker (and therefore more plausible) hypothesis.

2   *Since in a capitalist society ... reasonable and intelligible* We certainly benefit because great economic incentives operate to get others to spend much time and energy to figure out how to serve us by providing things we will want to pay for. It is not mere paradox mongering to wonder whether capitalism should be criticized for most rewarding and hence encouraging, not individualists like Thoreau who go about their own lives, but people who are occupied with serving others and winning them as customers. But to defend capitalism one need not think businessmen are the finest human types. (I do not mean to join here the general maligning of businessmen, either.) Those who think the finest should acquire the most can try to convince their fellows to transfer resources in accordance with *that* principle.

people having entitlements over them. From the point of view of the historical entitlement conception of justice in holdings, those who start afresh to complete "to each according to his _____" treat objects as if they appeared from nowhere, out of nothing. A complete theory of justice might cover this limit case as well; perhaps here is a use for the usual conceptions of distributive justice.[1]

So entrenched are maxims of the usual form that perhaps we should present the entitlement conception as a competitor. Ignoring acquisition and rectification, we might say:

> From each according to what he chooses to do, to each according to what he makes for himself (perhaps with the contracted aid of others) and what others choose to do for him and choose to give him of what they've been given previously (under this maxim) and haven't yet expended or transferred.

This, the discerning reader will have noticed, has its defects as a slogan. So as a summary and great simplification (and not as a maxim with any independent meaning) we have:

> *From each as they choose, to each as they are chosen.*

How Liberty Upsets Patterns

It is not clear how those holding alternative conceptions of distributive justice can reject the entitlement conception of justice in holdings. For suppose a distribution favored by one of these non-entitlement conceptions is realized. Let us suppose it is your favorite one and let us call this distribution D_1; perhaps everyone has an equal share, perhaps shares vary in accordance with some dimension you treasure. Now suppose that Wilt Chamberlain[2] is greatly in demand by basketball teams, being a great gate attraction. (Also sup-

pose contracts run only for a year, with players being free agents.) He signs the following sort of contract with a team: In each home game, twenty-five cents from the price of each ticket of admission goes to him. (We ignore the question of whether he is "gouging" the owners, letting them look out for themselves.) The season starts, and people cheerfully attend his team's games; they buy their tickets, each time dropping a separate twenty-five cents of their admission price into a special box with Chamberlain's name on it. They are excited about seeing him play; it is worth the total admission price to them. Let us suppose that in one season one million persons attend his home games, and Wilt Chamberlain winds up with $250,000, a much larger sum than the average income and larger even than anyone else has.[3] Is he entitled to this income? Is this new distribution D_2, unjust? If so, why? There is no question about whether each of the people was entitled to the control over the resources they held in D_1; because that was the distribution (your favorite) that (for the purposes of argument) we assumed was acceptable. Each of these persons chose to give twenty-five cents of their, money to Chamberlain. They could have spent it on going to the movies, or on candy bars, or on copies of *Dissent* magazine, or of *Monthly Review*. But they all, at least one million of them, converged on giving it to Wilt Chamberlain in exchange for watching him play basketball. If D_1 was a just distribution, and people voluntarily moved from it to D_2, transferring parts of their shares they were given under D_1 (what was it for if not to do something with?), isn't D_2 also just? If the people were entitled to dispose of the resources to which they were entitled (under D_1), didn't this include their being entitled to give it to, or exchange it with, Wilt Chamberlain? Can anyone else complain on grounds of justice? Each other person already has his legitimate share under D_1. Under D_1, there is nothing that anyone has that anyone else has a claim of justice against. After someone transfers something to Wilt Chamberlain, third parties *still* have their legitimate shares; *their* shares are not changed. By what process could such a transfer among two persons give rise to a legitimate claim of distributive justice on a portion of what was transferred, by a third party who had no claim of justice on any holding of the others *before* the transfer?[4] To cut off objections irrelevant

1 *A complete theory ... distributive justice* Varying situations continuously from that limit situation to our own would force us to make explicit the underlying rationale of entitlements and to consider whether entitlement considerations lexicographically precede the considerations of the usual theories of distributive justice, so that *the slightest* strand of entitlement outweighs the considerations of the usual theories of distributive justice.

2 *Wilt Chamberlain* [editors' note] Wilt Chamberlain (1936–99) was the best known American basketball player during the 1960s. He was seven-time consecutive winner of the National Basketball Association scoring title from 1960 to 1966, and in 1962 he scored a record 100 points in a single game.

3 *Let us suppose ... anyone else has* [editors' note] In 1974, the US average (mean) income was $5,762.

4 *By what process ... the transfer?* Might not a transfer have instrumental effects on a third party, changing his feasible options? (But what if the two parties to the transfer independently had used their holdings in this fashion?) I discuss this question below, but

here, we might imagine the exchanges occurring in a socialist society, after hours. After playing whatever basketball he does in his daily work, or doing whatever other daily work he does, Wilt Chamberlain decides to put in *overtime* to earn additional money. (First his work quota is set; he works time over that.) Or imagine it is a skilled juggler people like to see, who puts on shows after hours.

Why might someone work overtime in a society in which it is assumed their needs are satisfied? Perhaps because they care about things other than needs. I like to write in books that I read, and to have easy access to books for browsing at odd hours. It would be very pleasant and convenient to have the resources of Widener Library[1] in my back yard. No society, I assume, will provide such resources close to each person who would like them as part of his regular allotment (under D_1). Thus, persons either must do without some extra things that they want, or be allowed to do something extra to get some of these things. On what basis could the inequalities that would eventuate be forbidden? Notice also that small factories would spring up in a socialist society, unless forbidden. I melt down some of my personal possessions (under D_1) and build a machine out of the material. I offer you, and others, a philosophy lecture once a week in exchange for your cranking the handle on my machine, whose products I exchange for yet other things, and so on. (The raw materials used by the machine are given to me by others who possess them under D_1, in exchange for hearing lectures.) Each person might participate to gain things over and above their allotment under D_1. Some persons even might want to leave their job in socialist industry and work full time in

this private sector. I shall say something more about these issues in the next chapter. Here I wish merely to note how private property even in means of production would occur in a socialist society that did not forbid people to use as they wished some of the resources they are given under the socialist distribution D_1.[2] The socialist society would have to forbid capitalist acts between consenting adults.

The general point illustrated by the Wilt Chamberlain example and the example of the entrepreneur in a socialist society is that no end-state principle or distributional patterned principle of justice can be continuously realized without continuous interference with people's lives. Any favored pattern would be transformed into one unfavored by the principle, by people choosing to act in various ways; for example, by people exchanging goods and services with other people, or giving things to other people, things the transferrers are entitled to under the favored distributional pattern. To maintain a pattern one must either continually interfere to stop people from transferring resources as they wish to, or continually (or periodically) interfere to take from some persons resources that others for some reason chose to

---

note here that this question concedes the point for distributions of ultimate intrinsic noninstrumental goods (pure utility experiences, so to speak) that are transferable. It also might be objected that the transfer might make a third party more envious because it worsens his position relative to someone else. I find it incomprehensible how this can be thought to involve a claim of justice. On envy, see Chapter 8.

Here and elsewhere in this chapter, a theory which incorporates elements of pure procedural justice might find what I say acceptable, *if* kept in its proper place; that is, if background institutions exist to ensure the satisfaction of certain conditions on distributive shares. But if these institutions are not themselves the sum or invisible-hand result of people's voluntary (nonaggressive) actions, the constraints they impose require justification. At no point does *our* argument assume any background institutions more extensive than those of the minimal night-watchman state, a state limited to *protecting* persons against murder, assault, theft, fraud, and so forth.

1   *Widener Library*   [editors' note] Harvard University's library.

2   *Here I wish … distribution D_1*   See the selection from John Henry MacKay's novel, *The Anarchists* (Boston: Benjamin R. Tucker, Publisher, 1891), reprinted in Leonard Krimmerman and Lewis Perry, eds., *Patterns of Anarchy* (New York: Doubleday Anchor Books, 1966), in which an individualist anarchist presses upon a communist anarchist the following question: "Would you, in the system of society which you call 'free Communism' prevent individuals from exchanging their labor among themselves by means of their own medium of exchange? And further: Would you prevent them from occupying land for the purpose of personal use?" The novel continues: "[the] question was not to be escaped. If he answered 'Yes!' he admitted that society had the right of control over the individual and threw overboard the autonomy of the individual which he had always zealously defended; if on the other hand, he answered 'No!' he admitted the right of private property which he had just denied so emphatically…. Then he answered 'In Anarchy any number of men must have the right of forming a voluntary association, and so realizing their ideas in practice. Nor can I understand how any one could justly be driven from the land and house which he uses and occupies … every serious man must declare himself: for Socialism, and thereby for force and against liberty, or for Anarchism, and thereby for liberty and against force.'" In contrast, we find Noam Chomsky writing, "Any consistent anarchist must oppose private ownership of the means of production," "the consistent anarchist then … will be a socialist … of a particular sort." Introduction to Daniel Guerin, *Anarchism: From Theory to Practice* (New York: Monthly Review Press, 1970), pages xiii, xv.

transfer to them. (But if some time limit is to be set on how long people may keep resources others voluntarily transfer to them, why let them keep these resources for *any* period of time? Why not have immediate confiscation?) It might be objected that all persons voluntarily will choose to refrain from actions which would upset the pattern. This presupposes unrealistically (1) that all will most want to maintain the pattern (are those who don't, to be "reeducated" or forced to undergo "self-criticism"?), (2) that each can gather enough information about his own actions and the ongoing activities of others to discover which of his actions will upset the pattern, and (3) that diverse and far-flung persons can coordinate their actions to dovetail into the pattern. Compare the manner in which the market is neutral among persons' desires, as it reflects and transmits widely scattered information via prices, and coordinates persons' activities.

It puts things perhaps a bit too strongly to say that every patterned (or end-state) principle is liable to be thwarted by the voluntary actions of the individual parties transferring some of their shares they receive under the principle. For perhaps some *very* weak patterns are not so thwarted.[1] Any distributional pattern with any egalitarian component is overturnable by the voluntary actions of individual persons over time; as is every patterned condition with sufficient content so as actually to have been proposed as presenting the central core of distributive justice. Still, given the possibility that some weak conditions or patterns may not

be unstable in this way, it would be better to formulate an explicit description of the kind of interesting and contentful patterns under discussion, and to prove a theorem about their instability. Since the weaker the patterning, the more likely it is that the entitlement system itself satisfies it, a plausible conjecture is that any patterning either is unstable or is satisfied by the entitlement system.

Sen's Argument

Our conclusions are reinforced by considering a recent general argument of Amartya K. Sen.[2] Suppose individual rights are interpreted as the right to choose which of two alternatives is to be more highly ranked in a social ordering of the alternatives. Add the weak condition that if one alternative unanimously is preferred to another then it is ranked higher by the social ordering. If there are two different individuals each with individual rights, interpreted as above, over different pairs of alternatives (having no members in common), then for some possible preference rankings of the alternatives by the individuals, there is no linear social ordering. For suppose that person A has the right to decide among (X, Y) and person B has the right to decide among (Z, W); and suppose their individual preferences are as follows (and that there are no other individuals). Person A prefers W to X to Y to Z, and person B prefers Y to Z to W to X. By the unanimity condition, in the social ordering W is preferred to X (since each individual prefers it to X), and Y is preferred to Z (since each individual prefers it to Z). Also in the social ordering, X is preferred to Y, by person A's right of choice among these two alternatives. Combining these three binary rankings, we get W preferred to X preferred to Y preferred to Z, in the social ordering. However, by person B's right of choice, Z must be preferred to W in the social ordering. There is no transitive social ordering satisfying all these conditions, and the social ordering, therefore, is nonlinear. Thus far, Sen.

The trouble stems from treating an individual's right to choose among alternatives as the right to determine the relative ordering of these alternatives within a social ordering. The alternative which has individuals rank *pairs* of alternatives, and separately rank the individual alternatives is no better; their ranking of pairs feeds into some method of amalgamating preferences to yield a social ordering of

---

1   *For perhaps ... so thwarted*   Is the patterned principle stable that requires merely that a distribution be Pareto-optimal? [A distribution is *Pareto-optimal* if no one can be made better off without making someone else worse off.] One person might give another a gift or bequest that the second could exchange with a third to their mutual benefit. Before the second makes this exchange, there is not Pareto-optimality. Is a stable pattern presented by a principle choosing that among the Pareto-optimal positions that satisfies some further condition *C*? It may seem that there cannot be a counterexample, for won't any voluntary exchange made away from a situation show that the first situation wasn't Pareto-optimal? (Ignore the implausibility of this last claim for the case of bequests.) But principles are to be satisfied over time, during which new possibilities arise. A distribution that at one time satisfies the criterion of Pareto-optimality might not do so when some new possibilities arise (Wilt Chamberlain grows up and starts playing basketball); and though people's activities will tend to move then to a new Pareto-optimal position, *this* new one need not satisfy the contentful condition *C*. Continual interference will be needed to insure the continual satisfaction of *C*. (The theoretical possibility of a pattern's being maintained by some invisible-hand process that brings it back to an equilibrium that fits the pattern when deviations occur should be investigated.)

2   *Our conclusions... Amartya K. Sen*   Sen, *Collective Choice and Social Welfare* (San Francisco: Holden-Day, Inc., 1970), chaps. 6 and 6*.

pairs; and the choice among the alternatives in the highest ranked pair in the social ordering is made by the individual with the right to decide between this pair. This system also has the result that an alternative may be selected although everyone prefers some other alternative; for example, *A* selects *X* over *Y*, where (*X, Y*) somehow is the highest ranked *pair* in the social ordering of pairs, although everyone, including *A*, prefers *W* to *X*. (But the choice person *A* was given, however, was only between *X* and *Y*.)

A more appropriate view of individual rights is as follows. Individual rights are co-possible; each person may exercise his rights as he chooses. The exercise of these rights fixes some features of the world. Within the constraints of these fixed features, a choice may be made by a social choice mechanism based upon a social ordering; if there are any choices left to make! Rights do not determine a social ordering but instead set the constraints within which a social choice is to be made, by excluding certain alternatives, fixing others, and so on. (If I have a right to choose to live in New York or in Massachusetts, and I choose Massachusetts, then alternatives involving my living in New York are not appropriate objects to be entered in a social ordering.) Even if all possible alternatives are ordered first, apart from anyone's rights, the situation is not changed: for then the highest ranked alternative *that is not excluded by anyone's exercise of his rights* is instituted. Rights do not determine the position of an alternative or the relative position of two alternatives in a social ordering; they *operate upon* a social ordering to constrain the choice it can yield.

If entitlements to holdings are rights to dispose of them, then social choice must take place *within* the constraints of how people choose to exercise these rights. If any patterning is legitimate, it falls within the domain of social choice, and hence is constrained by people's rights. *How else can one cope with Sen's result?* The alternative of first having a social ranking with rights exercised within *its* constraints is no alternative at all. Why not just select the top-ranked alternative and forget about rights? If that top-ranked alternative itself leaves some room for individual choice (and here is where "rights" of choice is supposed to enter in) there must be something to stop these choices from transforming it into another alternative. Thus Sen's argument leads us again to the result that patterning requires continuous interference with individuals' actions and choices.[1]

Redistribution and Property Rights

Apparently, patterned principles allow people to choose to expend upon themselves, but not upon others, those resources they are entitled to (or rather, receive) under some favored distributional pattern D_1. For if each of several persons chooses to expend some of his D_1 resources upon one other person, then that other person will receive more than his D_1 share, disturbing the favored distributional pattern. Maintaining a distributional pattern is individualism with a vengeance! Patterned distributional principles do not give people what entitlement principles do, only better distributed. For they do not give the right to choose what to do with what one has; they do not give the right to choose to pursue an end involving (intrinsically, or as a means) the enhancement of another's position. To such views, families are disturbing; for within a family occur transfers that upset the favored distributional pattern. Either families themselves become units to which distribution takes place, the column occupiers (on what rationale?), or loving behavior is forbidden. We should note in passing the ambivalent position of radicals toward the family. Its loving relationships are seen as a model to be emulated and extended across the whole society, at the same time that it is denounced as a suffocating institution to be broken and condemned as a focus of parochial concerns that interfere with achieving radical goals. Need we say that it is not appropriate to enforce across the wider society the relationships of love and care appropriate within a family, relationships which are voluntarily undertaken?[2] Incidentally, love is an interesting instance of another relationship that is historical, in that (like justice) it depends upon what actually occurred. An adult may come to love another because of the other's characteristics; but it is

---

1   *Thus Sen's argument ... actions and choices*   Oppression will be less noticeable if the background institutions do not prohibit certain

actions that upset the patterning (various exchanges or transfers of entitlement), but rather prevent them from being done, by nullifying them.

2   *Need we say ... voluntarily undertaken?*   One indication of the stringency of Rawls's difference principle, which we attend to in the second part of this chapter, is its inappropriateness as a governing principle even within a family of individuals who love one another. Should a family devote its resources to maximizing the position of its least well off and least talented child, holding back the other children or using resources for their education and development only if they will follow a policy through their lifetimes of maximizing the position of their least fortunate sibling? Surely not. How then can this even be considered as the appropriate policy for enforcement in the wider society? (I discuss below what I think would be Rawls's reply: that some principles apply at the macro level which do not apply to microsituations.)

the other person, and not the characteristics, that is loved.[1] The love is not transferable to someone else with the same characteristics, even to one who "scores" higher for these characteristics. And the love endures through changes of the characteristics that gave rise to it. One loves the particular person one actually encountered. Why love is historical, attaching to persons in this way and not to characteristics, is an interesting and puzzling question.

Proponents of patterned principles of distributive justice focus upon criteria for determining who is to receive holdings; they consider the reasons for which someone should have something, and also the total picture of holdings. Whether or not it is better to give than to receive, proponents of patterned principles ignore giving altogether. In considering the distribution of goods, income, and so forth, their theories are theories of recipient justice; they completely ignore any right a person might have to give something to someone. Even in exchanges where each party is simultaneously giver and recipient, patterned principles of justice focus only upon the recipient role and its supposed rights. Thus discussions tend to focus on whether people (should) have a right to inherit, rather than on whether people (should) have a right to bequeath or on whether persons who have a right to hold also have a right to choose that others hold in their place. I lack a good explanation of why the usual theories of distributive justice are so recipient oriented; ignoring givers and transferrers and their rights is of a piece with ignoring producers and their entitlements. But why is it *all* ignored?

Patterned principles of distributive justice necessitate redistributive activities. The likelihood is small that any actual freely-arrived-at set of holdings fits a given pattern; and the likelihood is nil that it will continue to fit the pattern as people exchange and give. From the point of view of an entitlement theory, redistribution is a serious matter indeed, involving, as it does, the violation of people's rights. (An exception is those takings that fall under the principle of the rectification of injustices.) From other points of view, also, it is serious.

Taxation of earnings from labor is on a par with forced labor.[2] Some persons find this claim obviously true: taking the earnings of *n* hours labor is like taking *n* hours from the person; it is like forcing the person to work *n* hours for another's purpose. Others find the claim absurd. But even these, *if* they object to forced labor, would oppose forcing unemployed hippies to work for the benefit of the needy.[3] And they would also object to forcing each person to work five extra hours each week for the benefit of the needy. But a system that takes five hours' wages in taxes does not seem to them like one that forces someone to work five hours, since it offers the person forced a wider range of choice in activities than does taxation in kind with the particular labor specified. (But we can imagine a gradation of systems of forced labor, from one that specifies a particular activity, to one that gives a choice among two activities, to...; and so on up.) Furthermore, people envisage a system with something like a proportional tax on everything above the amount necessary for basic needs. Some think this does not force someone to work extra hours, since there is no fixed number of extra hours he is forced to work, and since he can avoid the tax entirely by earning only enough to cover his basic needs. This is a very uncharacteristic view of forcing for those who *also* think people are forced to do something *whenever* the alternatives they face are considerably worse. However, *neither* view is correct. The fact that others intentionally intervene, in violation of a side constraint against aggression, to threaten force to limit the alternatives, in this case to paying taxes or (presumably the worse alternative) bare subsistence, makes the taxation system one of forced labor and distinguishes it from other cases of limited choices which are not forcings.[4]

The man who chooses to work longer to gain an income more than sufficient for his basic needs prefers some extra goods or services to the leisure and activities he could per-

---

alternatively, whether the arguments emphasize the great similarities between such taxation and forced labor, to show it is plausible and illuminating to view such taxation in the light of forced labor. This latter approach would remind one of how John Wisdom conceives of the claims of metaphysicians.

3   *But even these ... the needy*   Nothing hangs on the fact that here and elsewhere I speak loosely of needs, since I go on, each time, to reject the criterion of justice which includes it. If, however, something did depend upon the notion, one would want to examine it more carefully. For a skeptical view, see Kenneth Minogue, *The Liberal Mind* (New York: Random House, 1963), 103–12.

4   *The fact that ... not forcings*   Further details which this statement should include are contained in my essay "Coercion," in *Philosophy, Science, and Method*, ed. S. Morgenbesser, P. Suppes, and M. White (New York: St. Martin's Press, 1969).

---

1   *An adult ... that is loved*   See Gregory Vlastos, "The Individual as an Object of Love in Plato" in his *Platonic Studies* (Princeton: Princeton University Press, 1973), pp. 3–34.

2   *Taxation of earnings ... forced labor*   I am unsure as to whether the arguments I present below show that such taxation merely *is* forced labor; so that "is on a par with" means "is one kind of." Or

form during the possible nonworking hours; whereas the man who chooses not to work the extra time prefers the leisure activities to the extra goods or services he could acquire by working more. Given this, if it would be illegitimate for a tax system to seize some of a man's leisure (forced labor) for the purpose of serving the needy, how can it be legitimate for a tax system to seize some of a man's goods for that purpose? Why should we treat the man whose happiness requires certain material goods or services differently from the man whose preferences and desires make such goods unnecessary for his happiness? Why should the man who prefers seeing a movie (and who has to earn money for a ticket) be open to the required call to aid the needy, while the person who prefers looking at a sunset (and hence need earn no extra money) is not? Indeed, isn't it surprising that redistributionists choose to ignore the man whose pleasures are so easily attainable without extra labor, while adding yet another burden to the poor unfortunate who must work for his pleasures? If anything, one would have expected the reverse. Why is the person with the nonmaterial or nonconsumption desire allowed to proceed unimpeded to his most favored feasible alternative, whereas the man whose pleasures or desires involve material things and who must work for extra money (thereby serving whomever considers his activities valuable enough to pay him) is constrained in what he can realize? Perhaps there is no difference in principle. And perhaps some think the answer concerns merely administrative convenience. (These questions and issues will not disturb those who think that forced labor to serve the needy or to realize some favored end-state pattern is acceptable.) In a fuller discussion we would have (and want) to extend our argument to include interest, entrepreneurial profits, and so on. Those who doubt that this extension can be carried through, and who draw the line here at taxation of income from labor, will have to state rather complicated patterned *historical* principles of distributive justice, since end-state principles would not distinguish *sources* of income in any way. It is enough for now to get away from end-state principles and to make clear how various patterned principles are dependent upon particular views about the sources or the illegitimacy or the lesser legitimacy of profits, interest, and so on; which particular views may well be mistaken.

What sort of right over others does a legally institutionalized end-state pattern give one? The central core of the notion of a property right in *X*, relative to which other parts of the notion are to be explained, is the right to determine what shall be done with *X*; the right to choose which of the constrained set of options concerning *X* shall be realized or attempted.[1] The constraints are set by other principles or laws operating in the society; in our theory, by the Lockean rights people possess (under the minimal state). My property rights in my knife allow me to leave it where I will, but not in your chest. I may choose which of the acceptable options involving the knife is to be realized. This notion of property helps us to understand why earlier theorists spoke of people as having property in themselves and their labor. They viewed each person as having a right to decide what would become of himself and what he would do, and as having a right to reap the benefits of what he did.

This right of selecting the alternative to be realized from the constrained set of alternatives may be held by an *individual* or by a *group* with some procedure for reaching a joint decision; or the right may be passed back and forth, so that one year I decide what's to become of *X*, and the next year you do (with the alternative of destruction, perhaps, being excluded). Or, during the same time period, some types of decisions about *X* may be made by me, and others by you. And so on. We lack an adequate, fruitful, analytical apparatus for classifying the *types* of constraints on the set of options among which choices are to be made, and the *types* of ways decision powers can be held, divided, and amalgamated. A *theory* of property would, among other things, contain such a classification of constraints and decision modes, and from a small number of principles would follow a host of interesting statements about the *consequences* and effects of certain combinations of constraints and modes of decision.

When end-result principles of distributive justice are built into the legal structure of a society, they (as do most patterned principles) give each citizen an enforceable claim to some portion of the total social product; that is, to some portion of the sum total of the individually and jointly made products. This total product is produced by individuals laboring, using means of production others have saved to bring into existence, by people organizing production or

---

1   *The central core ... realized or attempted* On the themes in this and the next paragraph, see the writings of Armen Alchian ["Uncertainty, evolution, and Economic Theory," *Journal of Political Economy* 58 (1950): 211–21; Alchian and W.A. Allen, *University Economics*, 2nd ed. (Belmont, CA: Wadsworth, 1971); Alchian and Harold Demsetz, "Production, Information Costs, and Economic Organization," *American Economic Review* 62 (1972): 777–95.]

creating means to produce new things or things in a new way. It is on this batch of individual activities that patterned distributional principles give each individual an enforceable claim. Each person has a claim to the activities and the products of other persons, independently of whether the other persons enter into particular relationships that give rise to these claims, and independently of whether they voluntarily take these claims upon themselves, in charity or in exchange for something.

Whether it is done through taxation on wages or on wages over a certain amount, or through seizure of profits, or through there being a big *social pot* so that it's not clear what's coming from where and what's going where, patterned principles of distributive justice involve appropriating the actions of other persons. Seizing the results of someone's labor is equivalent to seizing hours from him and directing him to carry on various activities. If people force you to do certain work, or unrewarded work, for a certain period of time, they decide what you are to do and what purposes your work is to serve apart from your decisions. This process whereby they take this decision from you makes them a *part-owner* of you; it gives them a property right in you. Just as having such partial control and power of decision, by right, over an animal or inanimate object would be to have a property right in it.

End-state and most patterned principles of distributive justice institute (partial) ownership by others of people and their actions and labor. These principles involve a shift from the classical liberals' notion of self-ownership to a notion of (partial) property, rights in *other* people.

Considerations such as these confront end-state and other patterned conceptions of justice with the question of whether the actions necessary to achieve the selected pattern don't themselves violate moral side constraints. Any view holding that there are moral side constraints on actions, that not all moral considerations can be built into end states that are to be achieved (see Chapter 3, pp. 28-30), must face the possibility that some of its goals are not achievable by any morally permissible available means. An entitlement theorist will face such conflicts in a society that deviates from the principles of justice for the generation of holdings, if and only if the only actions available to realize the principles themselves violate some moral constraints. Since deviation from the first two principles of justice (in acquisition and transfer) will involve other persons' direct and aggressive intervention to violate rights, and since moral constraints will not exclude defensive or retributive

action in such cases, the entitlement theorist's problem rarely will be pressing. And whatever difficulties he has in applying the principle of rectification to persons who did not themselves violate the first two principles are difficulties in balancing the conflicting considerations so as correctly to formulate the complex principle of rectification itself; he will not violate moral side constraints by applying the principle. Proponents of patterned conceptions of justice, however, often will face head-on clashes (and poignant ones if they cherish each party to the clash) between moral side constraints on how individuals may be treated and their patterned conception of justice that presents an end state or other pattern that *must* be realized.

May a person emigrate from a nation that has institutionalized some end-state or patterned distributional principle? For some principles (for example, Hayek's) emigration presents no theoretical problem. But for others it is a tricky matter. Consider a nation having a compulsory scheme of minimal social provision to aid the neediest (or one organized so as to maximize the position of the worst-off group); no one may opt out of participating in it. (None may say, "Don't compel me to contribute to others and don't provide for me via this compulsory mechanism if I am in need.") Everyone above a certain level is forced to contribute to aid the needy. But if emigration from the country were allowed, anyone could choose to move to another country that did not have compulsory social provision but otherwise was (as much as possible) identical. In such a case, the person's *only* motive for leaving would be to avoid participating in the compulsory scheme of social provision. And if he does leave, the needy in his initial country will receive no (compelled) help from him. What rationale yields the result that the person be permitted to emigrate, yet forbidden to stay and opt out of the compulsory scheme of social provision? If providing for the needy is of overriding importance, this does militate against allowing internal opting out; but it also speaks against allowing external emigration. (Would it also support, to some extent, the kidnapping of persons living in a place without compulsory social provision, who could be forced to make a contribution to the needy in your community?) Perhaps the crucial component of the position that allows emigration solely to avoid certain arrangements, while not allowing anyone internally to opt out of them, is a concern for fraternal feelings within the country. "We don't want anyone here who doesn't contribute, who doesn't care enough about the others to contribute." That concern, in this case, would have to be tied to the view that forced aiding tends to produce fraternal feelings between the aided and the aider (or perhaps merely to the view that the knowledge that someone or other voluntarily is not aiding produces unfraternal feelings).

Locke's Theory of Acquisition

Before we turn to consider other theories of justice in detail, we must introduce an additional bit of complexity into the structure of the entitlement theory. This is best approached by considering Locke's attempt to specify a principle of justice in acquisition. Locke views property rights in an unowned object as originating through someone's mixing his labor with it. This gives rise to many questions. What are the boundaries of what labor is mixed with? If a private astronaut clears a place on Mars, has he mixed his labor with (so that he comes to own) the whole planet, the whole uninhabited universe, or just a particular plot? Which plot does an act bring under ownership? The minimal (possibly disconnected) area such that an act decreases entropy in that area, and not elsewhere? Can virgin land (for the purposes of ecological investigation by high-flying airplane) come under ownership by a Lockean process? Building a fence around a territory presumably would make one the owner of only the fence (and the land immediately underneath it).

Why does mixing one's labor with something make one the owner of it? Perhaps because one owns one's labor, and so one comes to own a previously unowned thing that becomes permeated with what one owns. Ownership seeps over into the rest. But why isn't mixing what I own with what I don't own a way of losing what I own rather than a way of gaining what I don't? If I own a can of tomato juice and spill it in the sea so that its molecules (made radioactive, so I can check this) mingle evenly throughout the sea, do I thereby come to own the sea, or have I foolishly dissipated my tomato juice? Perhaps the idea, instead, is that laboring on something improves it and makes it more valuable; and anyone is entitled to own a thing whose value he has created. (Reinforcing this, perhaps, is the view that laboring is unpleasant. If some people made things effortlessly, as the cartoon characters in *The Yellow Submarine* trail flowers in their wake, would they have lesser claim to their own products whose making didn't *cost* them anything?) Ignore the fact that laboring on something may make it less valuable (spraying pink enamel paint on a piece of driftwood that you have found). Why should one's entitlement extend to the whole object rather than just to the *added value* one's labor has produced? (Such reference to value might also serve to delimit the extent of ownership; for example, substitute "increases the value of" for "decreases entropy in" in the above entropy criterion.) No workable or coherent value-added property scheme has yet been devised, and any such scheme presumably would fall to objections (similar to those) that fell the theory of Henry George.[1]

It will be implausible to view improving an object as giving full ownership to it, if the stock of unowned objects that might be improved is limited. For an object's coming under one person's ownership changes the situation of all others. Whereas previously they were at liberty (in Hohfeld's sense[2]) to use the object, they now no longer are. This change in the siuation of others (by removing their liberty to act on a previously unowned object) need not worsen their situation. If I appropriate a grain of sand from Coney Island, no one else may now do as they will with *that* grain of sand. But there are plenty of other grains of sand left for them to do the same with. Or if not grains of sand, then other things. Alternatively, the things I do with the grain of sand I appropriate might improve the position of others, counterbalancing their loss of the liberty to use that grain. The crucial point is whether appropriation of an unowned object worsens the situation of others.

Locke's proviso that there be "enough and as good left in common for others" (sect. 27[3]) is meant to ensure that the situation of others is not worsened. (If this proviso is met is there any motivation for his further condition of nonwaste?) It is often said that this proviso once held but now no longer does. But there appears to be an argument for the conclusion that if the proviso no longer holds, then it cannot ever have held so as to yield permanent and inheritable property rights. Consider the first person Z for

---

1   *the theory of Henry George* [editors' note] Henry George (1839–97), American economist, is known for his "Single Tax" theory: that the only tax should be on the natural value of the land one owned (not of the value added to the land by human labor). Taxing the income from productive labor, he argued, is unfair and discourages production, but income from land holdings was unearned and unjustly distributed.

2   *liberty (in Hohfeld's sense)* [editors' note] Wesley Hohfeld (1879–1918), American jurist, clarified the notion of *liberty* by associating it with the concepts of *rights* and *duties*: A has the liberty to do X if A has no duty not to do X and if nobody else has the right to interfere with A's doing X.

3   *(sect. 27)* [editors' note] Of John Locke's *Second Treatise of Government.*

whom there is not enough and as good left to appropriate. The last person Y to appropriate left Z without his previous liberty to act on an object, and so worsened Z's situation. So Y's appropriation is not allowed under Locke's proviso. Therefore the next to last person X to appropriate left Y in a worse position, for X's act ended permissible appropriation. Therefore X's appropriation wasn't permissible. But then the appropriator two from last, W, ended permissible appropriation and so, since it worsened X's position, W's appropriation wasn't permissible. And so on back to the first person A to appropriate a permanent property right.

This argument, however, proceeds too quickly. Someone may be made worse off by another's appropriation in two ways: first, by losing the opportunity to improve his situation by a particular appropriation or anyone; and second, by no longer being able to use freely (without appropriation) what he previously could. A *stringent* requirement that another not be made worse off by an appropriation would exclude the first way if nothing else counterbalances the diminution in opportunity, as well as the second. A *weaker* requirement would exclude the second way, though not the first. With the weaker requirement, we cannot zip back so quickly from Z to A, as in the above argument; for though person Z can no longer *appropriate*, there may remain some for him to *use* as before. In this case Y's appropriation would not violate the weaker Lockean condition. (With less remaining that people are at liberty to use, users might face more inconvenience, crowding, and so on; in that way the situation of others might be worsened, unless appropriation stopped far short of such a point.) It is arguable that no one legitimately can complain if the weaker provision is satisfied. However, since this is less clear than in the case of the more stringent proviso, Locke may have intended this stringent proviso by "enough and as good" remaining, and perhaps he meant the non-waste condition to delay the end point from which the argument zips back.

Is the situation of persons who are unable to appropriate (there being no more accessible and useful unowned objects) worsened by a system allowing appropriation and permanent property? Here enter the various familiar social considerations favoring private property: it increases the social product by putting means of production in the hands of those who can use them most efficiently (profitably); experimentation is encouraged, because with separate persons controlling resources, there is no one person or small group whom someone with a new idea must convince to try it out; private property enables people to decide on the pattern and

types of risks they wish to bear, leading to specialized types of risk bearing; private property protects future persons by leading some to hold back resources from current consumption for future markets; it provides alternate sources of employment for unpopular persons who don't have to convince any one person or small group to hire them, and so on. These considerations enter a Lockean theory to support the claim that appropriation of private property satisfies the intent behind the "enough and as good left over" proviso, *not* as a utilitarian justification of property. They enter to rebut the claim that because the proviso is violated no natural right to private property can arise by a Lockean process. The difficulty in working such an argument to show that the proviso is satisfied is in fixing the appropriate base line for comparison. Lockean appropriation makes people no worse off than they would be *how?*[1] This question of fixing the baseline needs more detailed investigation than we are able to give it here. It would be desirable to have an estimate of the general economic importance of original appropriation in order to see how much leeway there is for differing theories of appropriation and of the location of the baseline. Perhaps this importance can be measured by the percentage of all income that is based upon untransformed raw materials and given resources (rather than upon human actions), mainly rental income representing the unimproved value of land, and the price of raw material *in situ*, and by the percentage of current wealth which represents such income in the past.[2]

We should note that it is not only persons favoring *private* property who need a theory of how property rights legitimately originate. Those believing in collective property, for example those believing that a group of persons living in an area jointly own the territory, or its mineral resources, also must provide a theory of how such property rights arise; they must show why the persons living there

---

1   *Lockean appropriation ... would be how?*   Compare this with Robert Paul Wolff's "A Refutation of Rawls' Theorem on Justice," *Journal of Philosophy* 63, no. 7 (March 31, 1966), sect. 2. Wolff's criticism does not apply to Rawls's conception under which the baseline is fixed by the difference principle.

2   *Perhaps this importance ... in the past*   I have not seen a precise estimate. David Friedman, *The Machinery of Freedom* (New York: Harper & Row, 1973), pp. xiv, xv, discusses this issue and suggests 5 percent of U.S. national income as an upper limit for the first two factors mentioned. However he does not attempt to estimate the percentage of current wealth which is based upon such income in the past. (The vague notion of "based upon" merely indicates a topic needing investigation.)

have rights to determine what is done with the land and resources there that persons living elsewhere don't have (with regard to the same land and resources).

The Proviso

Whether or not Locke's particular theory of appropriation can be spelled out so as to handle various difficulties, I assume that any adequate theory of justice in acquisition will contain a proviso similar to the weaker of the ones we have attributed to Locke. A process normally giving rise to a permanent bequeathable property right in a previously unowned thing will not do so if the position of others no longer at liberty to use the thing is thereby worsened. It is important to specify *this* particular mode of worsening the situation of others, for the proviso does not encompass other modes. It does not include the worsening due to more limited opportunities to appropriate (the first way above, corresponding to the more stringent condition), and it does not include how I "worsen" a seller's position if I appropriate materials to make some of what he is selling, and then enter into competition with him. Someone whose appropriation otherwise would violate the proviso still may appropriate provided he compensates the others so that their situation is not thereby worsened; unless he does compensate these others, his appropriation will violate the proviso of the principle of justice in acquisition and will be an illegitimate one.[1] A theory of appropriation incorporating this Lockean proviso will handle correctly the cases (objections to the theory lacking the proviso) where someone appropriates the total supply of something necessary for life.[2]

A theory which includes this proviso in its principle of justice in acquisition must also contain a more complex principle of justice in transfer. Some reflection of the proviso about appropriation constrains later actions. If my appropriating all of a certain substance violates the Lockean proviso, then so does my appropriating some and purchasing all the rest from others who obtained it without otherwise violating the Lockean proviso. If the proviso excludes someone's appropriating all the drinkable water in the world, it also excludes his purchasing it all. (More weakly, and messily, it may exclude his charging certain prices for some of his supply.) This proviso (almost?) never will come into effect; the more someone acquires of a scarce substance which others want, the higher the price of the rest will go, and the more difficult it will become for him to acquire it all. But still, we can imagine, at least, that something like this occurs: someone makes simultaneous secret bids to the separate owners of a substance, each of whom sells assuming he can easily purchase more from the other owners; or some natural catastrophe destroys all of the supply of something except that in one person's possession. The total supply could not be permissibly appropriated by one person at the beginning. His later acquisition of it all does not show that the original appropriation violated the proviso (even by a reverse argument similar to the one above that tried to zip back from Z to A). Rather, it is the combination of the original appropriation *plus* all the later transfers and actions that violates the Lockean proviso.

Each owner's title to his holding includes the historical shadow of the Lockean proviso on appropriation. This excludes his transferring it into an agglomeration that does violate the Lockean proviso and excludes his using it in a way, in coordination with others or independently of them,

---

1 *Someone whose appropriation ... illegitimate one* Fourier held that since the process of civilization had deprived the members of society of certain liberties (to gather, pasture, engage in the chase), a socially guaranteed minimum provision for persons was justified as compensation for the loss (Alexander Gray, *The Socialist Tradition* [New York: Harper & Row, 1968], 188). But this puts the point too strongly. This compensation would be due those persons, if any, for whom the process of civilization was a *net loss*, for whom the benefits of civilization did not counterbalance being deprived of these particular liberties.

2 *A theory of appropriation ... necessary for life* For example, Rashdall's case of someone who comes upon the only water in the desert several miles ahead of others who also will come to it and appropriates it all. Hastings Rashdall, "The Philosophical Theory of Property," in *Property, its Duties and Rights* (London: Macmillan, 1915).

We should note Ayn Rand's theory of property rights ["Man's Rights" in *The Virtue of Selfishness* (New York: New American

Library, 1964], p. 94], wherein these follow from the right to life, since people need physical things to live. But a right to life is not a right to whatever one needs to live; other people may have rights over these other things (see Chapter 3 of this book). At most, a right to life would be a right to have or strive for whatever one needs to live, provided that having it does not violate anyone else's rights. With regard to material things, the question is whether having it does violate any right of others. (Would appropriation of all unowned things do so? Would appropriating the water hole in Rashdall's example?) Since special considerations (such as the Lockean proviso) may enter with regard to material property, one *first* needs a theory of property rights before one can apply any supposed right to life (as amended above). Therefore the right to life cannot provide the foundation for a theory of property rights.

so as to violate the proviso by making the situation of others worse than their baseline situation. Once it is known that someone's ownership runs afoul of the Lockean proviso, there are stringent limits on what he may do with (what it is difficult any longer unreservedly to call) "his property." Thus a person may not appropriate the only water hole in a desert and charge what he will. Nor may he charge what he will if he possesses one, and unfortunately it happens that all the water holes in the desert dry up, except for his. This unfortunate circumstance, admittedly no fault of his, brings into operation the Lockean proviso and limits his property rights.[1] Similarly, an owner's property right in the only island in an area does not allow him to order a castaway from a shipwreck off his island as a trespasser, for this would violate the Lockean proviso.

Notice that the theory does not say that owners do have these rights, but that the rights are overridden to avoid some catastrophe. (Overridden rights do not disappear; they leave a trace of a sort absent in the cases under discussion[2].) There is no such external (and *ad hoc*?) overriding. Considerations internal to the theory of property itself, to its theory of acquisition and appropriation, provide the means for handling such cases. The results, however, may be coextensive with some condition about catastrophe, since the baseline for comparison is so low as compared to the productiveness of a society with private appropriation that the question of the Lockean proviso being violated arises only in the case of catastrophe (or a desert-island situation).

The fact that someone owns the total supply of something necessary for others to stay alive does *not* entail that his (or anyone's) appropriation of anything left some people (immediately or later) in a situation worse than the baseline one. A medical researcher who synthesizes a new substance that effectively treats a certain disease and who refuses to sell except on his terms does not worsen the situation of others by depriving them of whatever he has appropriated. The others easily can possess the same materials he appropriated; the researcher's appropriation or purchase of chemicals didn't make those chemicals scarce in a way so as to violate the Lockean proviso. Nor would someone else's purchasing the total supply of the synthesized substance from the medical researcher. The fact that the medical researcher uses easily available chemicals to synthesize the drug no more violates the Lockean proviso than does the fact that the only surgeon able to perform a particular operation eats easily obtainable food in order to stay alive and to have the energy to work. This shows that the Lockean proviso is not an "end-state principle"; it focuses on a particular way that appropriative actions affect others, and not on the structure of the situation that results.[3]

Intermediate between someone who takes all of the public supply and someone who makes the total supply out of easily obtainable substances is someone who appropriates the total supply of something in a way that does not deprive the others of it. For example, someone finds a new substance in an out-of-the-way place. He discovers that it effectively treats a certain disease and appropriates the total supply. He does not worsen the situation of others; if he did not stumble upon the substance no one else would have, and the others would remain without it. However, as time passes, the likelihood increases that others would have come across the substance; upon this fact might be based a limit to his property right in the substance so that others are not below their baseline position; for example, its bequest might be limited. The theme of someone worsening another's situation by depriving him of something he otherwise would possess may also illuminate the example of patents. An inventor's patent does not deprive others of an object which would not exist if not for the inventor. Yet patents would have this effect on others who independently invent the object. Therefore, these independent inventors, upon whom the burden of proving independent discovery may rest, should not be excluded from utilizing their own invention as they wish (including selling it to others). Furthermore, a known inventor drastically lessens the chances of actual

1   *This unfortunate circumstance ... his property rights*   The situation would be different if his water hole didn't dry up, due to special precautions he took to prevent this. Compare our discussion of the case in the text with Hayek, *The Constitution of Liberty*, 136; and also with Ronald Hamowy, "Hayek's Concept of Freedom; A Critique," *New Individualist Review* (April 1961), pp. 28–31.

2   *(Overridden rights ... under discussion.)*   I discuss overriding and its moral traces in "Moral Complications and Moral Structures," *Natural Law Forum* 13 (1968), 1–50.

3   *This shows ... situation that results*   Does the principle of compensation (Chapter 4) introduce patterning considerations? Though it requires compensation for the disadvantages imposed by those seeking security from risks, it is not a patterned principle. For it seeks to remove only those disadvantages which prohibitions inflict on those who might present risks to others, not all disadvantages. It specifies an obligation on those who impose the prohibition, which stems from their own particular acts, to remove a particular complaint those prohibited may make against them.

independent invention. For persons who know of an invention usually will not try to reinvent it, and the notion of independent discovery here would be murky at best. Yet we may assume that in the absence of the original invention, sometime later someone else would have come up with it. This suggests placing a time limit on patents, as a rough rule of thumb to approximate how long it would have taken, in the absence of knowledge of the invention, for independent discovery.

I believe that the free operation of a market system will not actually run afoul of the Lockean proviso. (Recall that crucial to our story in Part I of how a protective agency becomes dominant and a *de facto* monopoly is the fact that it wields force in situations of conflict, and is not merely in competition, with other agencies. A similar tale cannot be told about other businesses.) If this is correct, the proviso will not play a very important role in the activities of protective agencies and will not provide a significant opportunity for future state action. Indeed, were it not for the effects of previous *illegitimate* state action, people would not think the possibility of the proviso's being violated as of more interest than any other logical possibility. (Here I make an empirical historical claim; as does someone who disagrees with this.) This completes our indication of the complication in the entitlement theory introduced by the Lockean proviso.

G.A. COHEN
(1941–)

G.A. Cohen is the leading exponent of radical egalitarianism in contemporary political philosophy. Besides acting as one of the central torchbearers of Marx's legacy, he has made major contributions to liberal political philosophy, presenting powerful criticisms of Robert Nozick's libertarianism and John Rawls's liberal egalitarianism, as well as playing a key role in discussions regarding the justification for egalitarianism principles, and the form that they should take.

Cohen grew up in a Jewish Communist family in Montreal and attended the radical Jewish Communist Morris Winchewsky School, until the Quebec "Red Squad" closed it when he was eleven. He received his BA from McGill University and his BPhil from Oxford, where he studied under Isaiah Berlin and Gilbert Ryle, and fell under the spell of analytic philosophy. From 1963 until 1984 he taught at University College London, later taking up the position of Chichele Professor of Social and Political Theory at All Souls College, Oxford, formerly held by Sir Isaiah Berlin.

Cohen's work during the first part of his career centered on Marx's theory of history, culminating in his Isaac Deutscher Memorial Prize-winning 1978 work *Karl Marx's Theory of History: A Defense*, often considered the first major work in "analytic" Marxism. Analytic Marxism, which attracted intellectuals from philosophy, economics, political science and sociology, applies the techniques of analytic philosophy and neoclassical economics to Marxist texts and themes. In *Karl Marx's Theory of History*, Cohen reconstructs Marx's arguments and presents a broad-ranging defense of historical materialism, the view that history can be largely explained in terms of the growth and transformation of productive power.

Later, Cohen came to reject the inevitability of a socialist revolution. Marxists had traditionally relied on a view of the working class which held that this group made up a majority of the population that produced societies' wealth but were nevertheless exploited and impoverished. Under these conditions, the working class would not only have little to lose by revolution, but would also possess the power necessary to transform society. These conditions are no longer met in advanced capitalist societies. In these societies, the working class is no longer the worst off and fails to form a majority given the rise of the service and other sectors. Instead, the needy and exploited have fragmented into many groups.

By the 1990s, analytic Marxism was largely in decline, with most of its prominent practitioners adopting liberal or social-democratic political positions. In *If You're an Egalitarian, Why Are You So Rich?* (2000), Cohen recounts his journey from Marxism to radical liberal egalitarianism. Traditionally, Marxists were suspicious of morality, viewing it as an ideology for justifying economic inequalities and reinforcing class domination. Furthermore, since they viewed class revolution as inevitable and the injustice of capitalism as straightforward, they saw no need for detailed moral reflection. At the same time, as Cohen points out, the attraction of Marxism depends on moral convictions, including disgust at exploitation, dominance and inequality, and empathy with human suffering. Liberalism, which rejects historical materialism and searches for distributional principles in conditions of relative scarcity, provides, in his view, a rich tradition for addressing questions of social and economic justice.

Self-Ownership, Freedom, and Equality (1995) contains, in a revised form, many of Cohen's major papers on liberalism, many of them focused on Robert Nozick's libertarianism which roused him from his "dogmatic socialist slumber." Nozick is renowned—some would say notorious—for his entitlement theory of justice, which strongly rejects the view (held by Rawls, among many other liberals) that justice requires a redistribution of goods from the better to the least well-off members of society. In "Robert Nozick and Wilt Chamberlain: how patterns preserve liberty" (included here) and other essays in *Self-Ownership, Freedom, and Equality*, Cohen draws attention to some surprising parallels between socialist and libertarian thought, particularly the concept of "self-ownership," which he identifies as Nozick's central thesis. As Cohen puts it, self-ownership entails that "each person is the morally rightful owner of his own person and powers, and, consequently, that each is free (morally speaking) to use those powers as he wishes, provided that he does not deploy them aggressively against others."

Recently, Cohen has criticized John Rawls's claim that the subject of justice is the basic structure of the society's major social and economic institutions. Rawls's focus on institutions is partly motivated by a desire to relieve individuals of a duty to promote justice whenever possible: if our society's institutions are fairly just, we can go about our daily lives without having to give larger issues of justice too much thought. Cohen rejects this, claiming that Rawls's difference principle—roughly stated, the principle that any inequalities should be for the benefit of the worst off—is insufficiently egalitarian. Rawls permits a modest amount of inequality because he believes that allowing some people to acquire more provides an incentive that ultimately benefits the worst-off members of society. Drawing inspiration from feminist criticisms of Rawls (such as those of Susan Moller Okin, included in this volume), Cohen argues for the inherent importance of individual attitudes and convictions to the formation and maintenance of appropriate notions of justice. If most people truly endorsed egalitarianism, incentives would be unnecessary, and would result in a more thorough and radical egalitarianism.

◆ ◆ ◆ ◆ ◆

Robert Nozick and Wilt Chamberlain: How Patterns Preserve Liberty (1977)

Let us now suppose that I have sold the product of my own labor for money, and have used the money to hire a laborer, i.e., I have bought somebody else's labor power. Having taken advantage of this labor-power of another, I turn out to be the owner of value which is considerably higher than the value I spent on its purchase. This, *from one point of view*, is very just, because it has already been recognized, after all, that I can use what I have secured by exchange as is best and most ad-

vantageous to myself.... (George Plekhanov, *The Development of the Monist View of History*[1])

1. Robert Nozick occupies the point of view Plekhanov describes, and his *Anarchy, State, and Utopia*[2] is in good measure an ingenious elaboration of the argument for capitalism that Plekhanov adumbrates. The capitalism Nozick advocates is more pure than the one we have today. It lacks taxation for social welfare, and it permits degrees of poverty and of inequality far greater than most apologists for contemporary bourgeois society would now countenance.

This chapter is only indirectly a critique of Nozick's defense of capitalism. Its immediate aim is to refute Nozick's major argument against a rival of capitalism, socialism. The refutation vindicates socialism against that argument, but no one opposed to socialism on other grounds should expect to be converted by what is said here.

Nozick's case against socialism can be taken in two ways. He proposes a definition of justice in terms of liberty, and on that basis he argues that what socialists[3] consider just is not in fact just. But even if his definition of justice is wrong, so that the basis of his critique, taken in this first way, is faulty, he would still press a claim against socialism, namely, that, however *just* it may or may not be, it is incompatible with *liberty*. Even if Nozick is mistaken about what justice is, he might still be right that the cost in loss of liberty imposed by what socialists regard as just is intolerably high. (Hence the title of the section of the book on which we shall focus: "How Liberty Upsets Patterns"—patterns being distributions answering to, for example, a socialist principle of justice.) So it is not enough, in defending socialism against Nozick, to prove that he has not shown that it is unjust. It must also be proved that he has not shown that it frustrates liberty.

2. A full definition of socialism is not required for our purposes. All we need suppose is that a socialist society upholds

---

1. *George Plekhanov* [Unless otherwise indicated, all notes to this selection are by the author rather than the editors of this anthology.] [editors' note] George Plekhanov (1856–1918) was a Russian revolutionary and Marxist theorist. This quotation is from *The Development of the Monist View of History*, written 1895; published in English, London: Lawrence & Wishart, 1947.

2. *Anarchy, State, and Utopia* [editors' note] References to this book are indicated by page numbers in square brackets in this selection.

3. *socialists* And others, such as American liberals, but my concern is with the application of the argument to socialism.

some principle of equality in the distribution of benefits enjoyed and burdens borne by its members. The principle need not be specified further, since Nozick's argument is against the institution of *any* such principle.

Let us now imagine that such an egalitarian principle is instituted, and that it leads to a distribution of goods and bads which, following Nozick, we shall call D_1. Then Nozick argues by example that D_1 can be maintained only at the price of tyranny and injustice. The example concerns the best basketball player in the imagined society.

> ... suppose that Wilt Chamberlain is greatly in demand by basketball teams, being a great gate attraction.... He signs the following sort of contract with a team: In each home game, twenty-five cents from the price of each ticket of admission goes to him.... The season starts, and people cheerfully attend his team's games; they buy their tickets, each time dropping a separate twenty-five cents of their admission price into a special box with Chamberlain's name on it. They are excited about seeing him play; it is worth the total admission price to them. Let us suppose that in one season one million persons attend his home games, and Wilt Chamberlain winds up with $250,000, a much larger sum than the average income.... Is he entitled to this income? Is this new distribution D_2, unjust? If so, why? There is *no* question about whether each of the people was entitled to the control over the resources they held in D_1; because that was the distribution... that (for the purposes of argument) we assumed was acceptable. Each of these persons *chose* to give twenty-five cents of their money to Chamberlain. They could have spent it on going to the movies, or on candy bars, or on copies of *Dissent* magazine, or of *Monthly Review*. But they all, at least one million of them, converged on giving it to Wilt Chamberlain in exchange for watching him play basketball. If D_1 was a just distribution, and people voluntarily moved from it to D_2, transfer parts of their shares they were given under D_1 (what was it for if not to do something with?), isn't D_2 also just? If the people were entitled to dispose of the resources to which they were entitled (under D_1), didn't this include their being entitled to give it to, or exchange it

with, Wilt Chamberlain? Can anyone else complain on grounds of justice? Each other person already has his legitimate share under D_1. Under D_1, there is nothing that anyone has that anyone else has a claim of justice against.

> After someone transfers something to Wilt Chamberlain, third parties *still* have their legitimate shares; *their* shares are not changed. By what process could such a transfer among two persons give rise to a legitimate claim of distributive justice on a portion of what was transferred, by a third party who had no claim of justice on any holding of the others *before* the transfer? [161-62]

According to Nozick

> (1) "Whatever arises from a just situation by just steps is itself just" [151].

Nozick holds that *steps* are just if they are free of injustice, and that they are free of injustice if they are fully voluntary on the part of all the agents who take them. We can therefore spell (1) out as follows:

> (2) Whatever arises from a just situation as a result of fully voluntary transactions on the part of all the transacting agents is itself just.

So convinced is Nozick that (2) is true that he thinks that it must be accepted by people attached to a doctrine of justice which in other respects differs from his own. That is why he feels able to rely on (2) in the Chamberlain parable, despite having granted, for the sake of argument, the justice of an initial situation patterned by an egalitarian principle.

Even if (2) is true, it does not follow that pattern D_1 can be maintained only at the price of injustice, for people might simply *fail* to use their liberty in a pattern-subverting manner. But that is not an interesting possibility. A more interesting one is that they deliberately *refuse* to use their liberty subversively. Reasons for refusing will be adduced shortly. But is (2) true? Does liberty always preserve justice?

A standard way of testing the claim would be to look for states of affairs which would be accounted unjust but which might be generated by the route (2) endorses. Perhaps the strongest counter-example of this form would be slavery. We might then say: voluntary self-enslavement is possible. But slavery is unjust. Therefore (2) is false. Yet whatever may be the merits of that argument, we know that Nozick is not moved by it. For he thinks that there is no injustice in a slavery that arises out of the approved process.[1]

Though Nozick accepts slavery with an appropriate genesis, there is a restriction, derived from (2) itself, on the kind of slavery he accepts: (2) does not allow slave status to be inherited by offspring of the self-enslaved, for then a concerned party's situation would be decided for him, independently of his will. "Some things individuals may choose for themselves no one may choose for another" [331]. Let us remember this when we come to scrutinize the Wilt Chamberlain transaction, for widespread contracting of the kind which occurs in the parable might have the effect of seriously modifying, for the worse, the situation of members of future generations.

Should we say that in Nozick's conception of justice a slave society need be no less just than one where people are free? That would be a tendentious formulation. For Nozick can claim that rational persons in an initially just situation are unlikely to contract into slavery, except, indeed, where circumstances are so special that it would be wrong to forbid them to do so. This diminishes the danger that (2) can be used to stamp approval on morally repellent social arrangements.

I attribute some such response to Nozick on the basis, *inter alia*, of this passage:

> it must be granted that were people's reasons for transferring some of their holdings to others always irrational or arbitrary, we would find this *disturbing....* We feel more comfortable upholding the justice of an entitlement system if most of the transfers under it are done for reasons. This does not mean necessarily that all deserve what holdings they receive. It means only that there is a purpose or point to someone's transferring a holding to one person rather than to another; that usually we can see what the transferrer thinks he's gaining, what cause he *thinks* he's serving, what goals he *thinks* he's helping to achieve, and so forth.

Since in a capitalist society people often transfer holdings to others in accordance with how much they *perceive* these others benefiting them, the fabric constituted by the individual transactions and transfers is largely reasonable and intelligible [159, my emphases].

Accordingly, Nozick emphasizes the motives people have when they pay to watch Chamberlain, instead of stipulating that they do so freely and leaving us to guess why. It is important to the persuasive allure of the example that we should consider what the fans are doing not only voluntary but sensible: transactions are disturbing (even though they are entirely just?[2]) when we cannot see what the (or some of the) contracting parties *think* they are gaining by them.

Yet we should surely also be disturbed if we can indeed see what the agent *thinks* he is gaining, but we know that what he *will* gain is not that, but something he thinks less valuable; or that what results is not only the gain he expects but also unforeseen consequences which render negative the net value, according to his preferences and standards, of the transaction. We should not be content if what he *thinks* he is getting is good, but what he actually gets is bad, by his own lights. I shall assume that Nozick would accept this plausible extension of his concession. It is hard to see how he could resist it.

Accordingly, if we can show that Chamberlain's fans get not only the pleasure of watching him minus twenty-five cents, but also uncontemplated disbenefits of a significant order, then, even if, for Nozick, the outcome remains just, it should, even to Nozick, be disturbing. We shall need to ask whether we do not find Chamberlain's fans insufficiently reflective, when we think through, as they do not, the *full* consequences of what they are doing.

But now we can go further. For, in the light of the considerations just reviewed, (2) appears very probably false. Nozick says that a transaction is free of injustice if every transacting agent agrees to it. Perhaps that is so. But transactional justice, so characterized, is supposed—given an initially just situation—to confer justice on what results from it. (That is why (2) is supposed to follow from (1).) And that is questionable. Of each person who agrees to a transaction we may ask: *would he have agreed to it had he known what its outcome would be?* Since the answer may be

---

1   *slavery that arises out of the approved process*   A putative example of justly generated slavery: *A* and *B* are identical in talents and tastes. Each would so like to own a slave that he is willing to risk becoming one in exchange for the same chance of getting one. So they toss a coin, *B* loses, and *A* clamps chains on him. For penetrating remarks on Nozick's toleration of slavery, see Attracta Ingram's *Political Theory of Rights* (New York: Oxford University Press, 1994), pp. 38–39. For a reply to Ingram, see Hillel Steiner, *An Essay on Rights* (Oxford: Blackwell, 1994), pp. 232–33.

2   *transactions are disturbing ... entirely just?)*   Nozick does not say whether or not our finding a transaction "disturbing" should affect our judgment of its justice.

negative, it is far from evident that transactional justice, as described, transmits justice to its results.

Perhaps the desired transmission occurs when the answer to the italicized question is positive. Perhaps, in other words, we can accept (3), which increases the requirements for steps to be justice-preserving:

> (3) Whatever arises from a just situation as a result of fully voluntary transactions which all transacting agents would still have agreed to if they had known what the results of so transacting were to be is itself just.

(3) looks plausible, but its power to endorse market-generated states of affairs is, while not nil, very weak. Stronger[1] principles may also be plausible,[2] but (2), Nozick's principle, is certainly too strong to be accepted without much more defense than he provides.

3. Let us now apply this critique of Nozick's principles to the parable which is supposed to secure (or reveal) our allegiance to them.

Before describing the Chamberlain transaction, Nozick says: "It is not clear how those holding alternative conceptions of distributive justice can reject the entitlement conception of justice in holdings" [160]. There follows the Chamberlain story, where we assume that D_1 is just, and are then, supposedly, constrained to admit that D_2, into which it is converted, must also be just; an admission, according to Nozick, which is tantamount to accepting the entitlement conception. But how much of it must we accept if we endorse D_2 as just? At most that there is *a* role for the entitlement principle. For what the transaction subverts is the original pattern, not the principle governing it, *taken as a principle conjoinable with others to form a total theory of just or legitimate holdings*. The example, even if successful, does not defeat the initial assumption that D_1 is just.

Rather, it exploits that assumption to argue that D_2, though it breaks D_1's pattern, must also be just. The Chamberlain story, even when we take it at its face value, impugns not the original distribution, but the *exclusive* rightness of the principle mandating it.

Now Nozick is certainly right to this extent, even if we do not accept everything he says about the Chamberlain story: there must be *a* role for entitlement in determining acceptable holdings.[3] For unless the just society forbids gifts, it must allow transfers which do not answer to a patterning principle. This is compatible with placing restraints on the scope of gift, and we shall shortly see why an egalitarian society might be justified in doing so. But the present point is that assigning a certain role to unregulated transactions in the determination of holdings is compatible with using an egalitarian principle to decide the major distribution of goods and to limit, for example by taxation, how much more or less than what he would get under that principle alone a person may come to have in virtue of transactions which escape its writ. I think socialists do well to concede that an egalitarian principle should not be the only guide to the justice of holdings, or that, if it is, then justice should not be the only guide to policy with respect to holdings.[4]

Among the reasons for limiting how much an individual may hold, regardless of how he came to hold it, is to prevent him from acquiring, through his holdings, an unacceptable amount of power over others: the Chamberlain transaction looks less harmless when we focus on that consideration.[5]

---

1   *Stronger*   In the sense that they endorse a larger set of market-generated states of affairs. Notice that the weaker the conditions for justice in steps are in a principle of the form of (2) and (3), the stronger, in the specified sense, that principle is.

2   *Stronger principles ... be plausible*   Some might say that this is one of them, but I would disagree:

> (4) Whatever arises from a just situation as a result of fully voluntary transactions where the transacting agents know in advance the probabilities of all significantly different possible outcomes is itself just.

  I raise doubts about (4) in subsection 1e of Chapter 2 below [not included in this excerpt—eds.].

3   *there must be ... acceptable holdings*   For an investigation of the concept of entitlement that is deeper and more general than Nozick's own, see Robert J. van der Veen and Philippe Van Parijs, "Entitlement Theories of Justice," *Economics and Philosophy* 1/1 (1985): 69–81. Pages 70–74 of that article are particularly instructive in the present connection: the authors show both that all theories of justice have an entitlement component and that no theory of justice is a pure entitlement theory.

4   *an egalitarian principle ... respect to holdings*   I prefer the second formulation, being persuaded that distributive justice, roughly speaking, is equality. (See Christopher Ake, "Justice as Equality," *Philosophy and Public Affairs* 5, no. 1 (Fall 1975): 69–89.) For more on the trade-off between equality (be it justice or not) and other desiderata, see section 2 of my "On the Currency of Egalitarian Justice," *Ethics* 99 (1989): 906–44.

5   *Among the reasons ... that consideration*   My near-exclusive emphasis on this consideration in the sequel does not mean that I think that there are no other important ones, including the sheer unfairness of substantial differences in people's purchasing power. But swollen purchasing power, as such, which is not immediately the same thing as power *over* others, is less likely than the latter to worry those who are not already principled egalitarians.

The fans "are excited about seeing him play; it is worth the total admission price to them." The idea is that they see him play if and only if they pay, and seeing him play is worth more to them than anything else they can get for twenty-five cents. So it may be, but this fails to cover everything in the outcome which is relevant. For, once Chamberlain has received the payments, he is in a very special position of power in what was previously an egalitarian society. The fans' access to resources might now be prejudiced by the disproportionate access Chamberlain's wealth gives him, and the consequent power over others that he now has. *For all that Nozick shows*, a socialist may claim that this is not a bargain informed people in an egalitarian society will be apt to make: they will refrain from so contracting as to upset the equality they prize, and they will be especially averse to doing so because the resulting changes would profoundly affect their children. (This may seem an hysterical projection of the effect of the Chamberlain transaction, but I take it that we have to consider the upshot of general performance of transactions of that kind, and then the projection is entirely realistic.)

It is easy to think carelessly about the example. How we feel about people like Chamberlain getting a lot of money *as things are* is a poor index of how people would feel in the imagined situation. Among us the ranks of the rich and the powerful exist, and it can be pleasing, given that they do, when a figure like Chamberlain joins them. Who better and more innocently deserves to be among them? But the case before us is a society of equality in danger of losing its essential character. Reflective people would have to consider not only the joy of watching Chamberlain and its immediate money price but also the fact, which socialists say that they would deplore, that their society would be set on the road to class division. In presenting the Chamberlain fable Nozick ignores the commitment people may have to living in a society of a particular kind, and the rhetorical power of the illustration depends on that omission. At a later stage, Nozick takes up this point, but, so I argue in section 4 below, he says nothing interesting about it.

Nozick tacitly supposes that a person willing to pay twenty-five cents to watch Wilt play, is *ipso facto* a person willing to pay *Wilt* twenty-five cents to watch him play. It is no doubt true that in our society people rarely care who gets the money they forgo to obtain goods. But the tacit supposition is false, and the common unconcern is irrational. Nozick exploits our familiarity with this unconcern. Yet a person might welcome a world in which he and a million others watch Wilt play, at a cost of twenty-five cents to each, and consistently disfavor one in which, in addition, Wilt rakes in a cool quarter million.

Accordingly, if a citizen of the D1 society joins with others in paying twenty-five cents to Wilt to watch Wilt play, without thinking about the effect on Wilt's power, then the result may be deemed "disturbing" in the sense of [159] (see above). Of course a single person's paying a quarter makes no appreciable difference if the rest are anyway going to do so. But a convention might evolve not to make such payments, or, more simply, there could be a democratically authorized taxation system which maintains wealth differentials within acceptable limits. Whether Wilt would then still play is a further question on which I shall not comment, except to say that anyone who thinks it obvious that he would not play misunderstands human nature, or basketball, or both.

4. In defending the justice of the Chamberlain transaction, Nozick glances at the position of persons not directly party to it: "After someone transfers something to Wilt Chamberlain, third parties *still* have their legitimate shares; *their* shares are not changed" [161]. That is false, in one relevant sense. For a person's effective share depends on what he can do with what he has, and that depends not only on how much he has but on what others have and on how what others have is distributed. If it is distributed equally among them he will often be better placed than if some have especially large shares. Third parties, including the as yet unborn, may therefore have an interest against the contract. It is roughly the same interest as the fans themselves may have in not making it. (But, unlike third parties, a fan gets the compensation of watching Wilt play, which—I have not ruled this out—might be worth a whole lot of inequality, as far as a particular individual fan is concerned.)

Nozick addresses this issue in a footnote:

> Might not a transfer have instrumental effects on a third party, changing his feasible options? (But what if the two parties to a transfer independently had used their holdings in this fashion?) [162]

He promises further treatment of the problem later, and, although he does not say where it will come, he presumably has in mind his section on "Voluntary Exchange," which I shall address in section 7 below. Here I respond to Nozick's parenthetical rhetorical question.

First, there are some upshots of transfers of holdings, some effects on the options of the other parties, which will not occur as effects of the unconcerted use of dispersed holdings by individuals, because those individuals could not, or would not, use them in that way. The Chamberlain fans, acting independently, are less likely than Chamberlain is to buy a set of houses and leave them unoccupied, with speculative intent. Sometimes, though, a set of fans, acting independently, could indeed bring about effects inimical to the interests of others, of just the kind one may fear Chamberlain might cause. But whoever worries about Chamberlain doing so will probably also be concerned about the case where it results from the independent action of many. The rhetorical second question in the Nozick passage should not silence those who ask the first one.[1]

As an argument about *justice*[2] the Chamberlain story is either question-begging or uncompelling. Nozick asks:

> If the people were entitled to dispose of the resources to which they were entitled (under D_1), didn't this include their being entitled to give it to, or exchange it with, Wilt Chamberlain? [161]

If this interrogative is intended as a vivid way of asserting the corresponding indicative, then Nozick is telling us that the rights in shares with which people were vested are violated unless they are allowed to contract as described. If so, he begs the question. For it will be clear that their rights are violated only if the entitlement they received was of the absolute Nozickian sort, and this cannot be assumed. Whatever principles underlie D_1 will generate restrictions on the use of what is distributed in accordance with them.[3]

The other way of taking the quoted question is not as an assertion but as an appeal. Nozick is then asking us whether we do not agree that any restrictions which would forbid the Chamberlain transaction must be unjustified. So construed the argument is not question-begging, but it is inconclusive. For considerations which might justify restrictions on transactions are not canvassed. It is easy to think that what happens afterwards is that Chamberlain eats lots of chocolate, sees lots of movies and buys lots of subscriptions to expensive socialist journals. But, as I have insisted, we must remember the considerable power that he can now exercise over others.[4] In general, holdings are not only sources of enjoyment but, in certain distributions, sources of power. Transfers which look unexceptionable come to seem otherwise when we bring into relief the aspect neglected in "libertarian" apologetic.

5. Let us turn, now, from justice to liberty: is it true that a "socialist society would have to forbid capitalist acts between consenting adults" [163]? Socialism perishes if there are too many such acts, but it does not follow that it must forbid them. In traditional socialist doctrine capitalist action wanes not primarily because it is illegal, but because the impulse behind it atrophies, or, less Utopianly, because other impulses become stronger, or because people believe that capitalistic exchange is unfair. *Such expectation rests on a conception of human nature, and so does its denial.* Nozick has a different conception, for which he does not argue, one that fits many twentieth-century Americans, which is no reason for concluding that it is universally true. The people in Nozick's state of nature are intelligible only as well-socialized products of a market society. In the contrary socialist conception, human beings have and may develop further a (non-instrumental) desire for community, a relish of cooperation, and an aversion to being on either side of a master/servant relationship. No one should assume without argument, or take it on trust from the socialist tradition, that this conception is sound. But *if* it is sound, then there will be no need for incessant invigilation against "capitalist acts," and Nozick does not *argue* that it is unsound. Hence he has not shown that socialism conflicts with freedom, even if his unargued premise that its citizens will want to

---

1 *The rhetorical ... first one* The purpose of the second question, so I take it, is to suggest this argument:
   1. The fans might have so used their several quarters with the same effect on third parties that one who asks the first question fears Wilt's use of his quarter million might have.
   2. No one could object to the fans so using their quarters.
   ∴ 3. No one can object to what Wilt does with his quarter million.
   Whether or not the stated premises imply that argument's conclusion, the present point is that an alert rejecter of its conclusion will also reject its second premise.

2 *an argument about justice* Recall the two ways of taking Nozick, distinguished at section 1 above.

3 *Whatever principles ... accordance with them* Thomas Nagel construes Nozick as I do in the paragraph above, and my reply to Nozick, so construed, follows Nagel. See his "Libertarianism Without Foundations," *Yale Law Journal* 85 (1975), pp. 201–02.

4 *But, as I have insisted ... exercise over others* Once again—see above—this assessment will seem hysterical only if we fail to take the Chamberlain transaction as we must for it to pose a serious challenge, namely as an example of something which occurs regularly, or will occur regularly in the future.

perform capitalist acts attracts the assent of the majority of his readers.

How much equality would conflict with liberty in given circumstances depends on how much people would value equality in those circumstances. If life in a cooperative commonwealth appeals to them, they do not have to sacrifice liberty to belong to it.

This banal point relates to the first of what Nozick says are the three "unrealistic" presuppositions of the moral and practical possibility of socialism:

> (5) that all will most want to maintain the [socialist] pattern
> (6) that each can gather enough information about his own actions and the ongoing activities of others to discover which of his actions will upset the pattern
> (7) that diverse and far-flung persons can coordinate their actions to dovetail into the pattern [163].

Something like the first presupposition is made by socialists in the light of the idea of human nature which informs their tradition. It is, of course, controversial, but its dismissal as "unrealistic" contributes nothing to the controversy.

Socialists presuppose only something *like* (5), because they need not think that everyone will have socialist sentiments, but only a preponderant majority, especially in the nascency of socialism. If (5) itself is unrealistic, three possibilities present themselves: very few would lack enthusiasm for socialism; very many would; some intermediate proportion would. What I mean by these magnitudes emerges immediately.

In the first possibility, there remain a few capitalistically minded persons, meaning by "a few" that their capitalist acts would not undermine the basic socialist structure. No sane socialist should commit himself to the suppression of capitalist activity on the stated scale. (It might even be desirable to allocate to capitalistophiles a territory in which they can bargain with and hire one another.)

Suppose, though, that the disposition to perform capitalist acts is strong and widespread, so that socialism[1] is possible only with tyranny. What socialist favors socialism in such circumstances? What socialist denies that there are such circumstances? Certainly Marx insisted that it would be folly to attempt an institution of socialism except under the propitious conditions he was confident capitalism would create.[2] A socialist believes that propitious conditions are accessible. He need not proclaim the superiority of socialism regardless of circumstances.

Could a socialist society contain an amount of inclination to capitalism of such a size that unless it were coercively checked socialism would be subverted, yet sufficiently small that, in socialist judgment, socialism, with the required coercion, would still be worthwhile? Marxian socialists believe so, and that does commit them to prohibiting capitalist acts between consenting adults in certain circumstances, notably those which follow a successful revolution. But why should they flinch from that prohibition? They can defend it by reference to the social good and widened freedom that it promotes. Nozick would object that the prohibition violates moral "side constraints": certain freedoms, for example of contract, ought never to be infringed, whatever the consequences of allowing their exercise may be. We shall look at side constraints in the next section.

But first we must treat presuppositions (6) and (7) (see above). Unlike (5), these are red herrings. At most, they are preconditions of realizing socialist justice *perfectly*.[3] But justice is not the only virtue of social orders (and it is not even "the first virtue" of socialism, for most socialists). Even if we identify justice with equality, as socialists, broadly speaking, do, we may tolerate deviations from equality consequent on

---

1   *socialism* Or "socialism": scare-quotes would be added by those who think that socialism is, by definition, incompatible with tyranny; but, contrary to what some socialists seem to think, such a definition, even if it is correct, provides no argument against those who say that the (extensively non-market) form of economy that many socialists favor required tyranny.

2   *he was confident capitalism would create* According to Marx, socialist revolution will not succeed unless and until "capitalist production has already developed the productive forces of labor in general to a sufficiently high level" (*Theories of Surplus Value*, Vol. 2, p. 580), failing which "all the old filthy business would necessarily be restored" (*The German Ideology*, p. 49) in the aftermath of revolution. See sections (6) and (7) of Chapter 7 of my *Karl Marx's Theory of History: A Defense* (Oxford: Clarendon Press, 1978). See also Chapter 5, section 6, below [not included in this selection.—eds.].

3   *At most ... socialist justice perfectly* I say "at most" because even that is probably false. Given the truth of (5), people could form a Pattern Maintenance Association and appoint experts to watch over and correct the pattern. With popular willingness to do what the experts said, and a properly sophisticated technology for detecting deviations, (6) and (7) would be unnecessary to pattern maintenance without coercion (unless doing what the experts say counts as a way of coordinating action, in which case (7) is required in the above fantasy—but it is easily satisfied).

perturbations caused by gift, small-scale market transactions, and so on. Considerations of privacy, acquired expectations, the moral and economic costs of surveillance, etc. declare against attempting a realization of justice in the high degree that would be possible if (6) and (7) were satisfied. We let justice remain rough, in deference to other values.

Accordingly, socialism tolerates gift-giving, and "loving behavior" is not "forbidden" [167]. Gift is possible under a system which limits how much anyone may have and what he may do with it. Relatively well-endowed persons will sometimes not be fit recipients of gifts, but we are assuming a socialist psychology whose natural tendency is not to give to them that hath. And the notion that the institutions we are contemplating fetter the expression of love is too multiply bizarre to require comment.

6. Any but the most utopian socialist must be willing under certain conditions to restrict the liberty of a few for the sake of the liberty of many.[1] But, so Nozick would charge, such a socialist would thereby violate "moral side constraints" that apply to all human action. For Nozick thinks that we may never restrict one person's freedom in order to enhance the welfare or the freedom of very many others, or even of everyone, that person included (where we know that the restriction will redound to his benefit).

If children are undernourished in our society, we are not allowed to tax millionaires in order to finance a subsidy on the price of milk to poor families, for we would be violating the rights, and the "dignity" of the millionaires [334].[2] We cannot appeal that the effective liberty of the children (and the adults they will become) would be greatly enhanced at little expense to the millionaires' freedom, for Nozick forbids any act which restricts freedom: he does not

call for its maximization. (This means that if it were true that certain exercises of freedom would lead to totalitarianism, Nozick would still protect them. Market freedom itself would be sacrificed by Nozick if the only way to preserve it were by limiting it[3].)

If Nozick argues for this position, he does so in the section called "Why Side Constraints?" which begins as follows:

> Isn't it *irrational* to accept a side constraint C, rather than a view that directs minimizing the violations of C? ... If nonviolation of C is so important, shouldn't that be the goal? How can a concern for the nonviolation of C lead to the refusal to violate C even when this would prevent other more extensive violations of C? What is the rationale for placing the nonviolation of rights as a side constraint upon action instead of including it solely as a goal of one's actions?
>
> Side constraints upon action reflect the underlying Kantian principle that individuals are ends and not merely means; they may not be sacrificed or used for the achieving of other ends without their consent. Individuals are inviolable [30-31].

The second paragraph is lame as a response to the questions of the first, for they obviously reassert themselves: if such sacrifice and violation are so horrendous, why should we not be concerned to minimize their occurrence?[4] There is more appearance of argument[5] in the final paragraph of the section:

---

1   *Any but the most utopian socialist ... liberty of many*   See Chapter 2, subsection 2c [not included in this selection—eds.], on how socialist restriction on private property rights may enhance general freedom.

2   *If children are undernourished ... "dignity" of the millionaires*   "'But isn't justice to be tempered with compassion?' Not by the guns of the state. When private persons choose to transfer resources to help others, this fits within the entitlement conception of justice" [348]. "Fits within" is evasive. The choice "fits" because it is a choice, not because of its content. For Nozick there is no more justice in a millionaire's giving a five dollar bill to a starving child than in his using it to light his cigar while the child dies in front of him.

For subtle comments on Nozick's falsely exclusive and exhaustive distinction between compulsory and voluntary donation, see Nagel, "Libertarianism Without Foundations," 199–200.

3   *Market freedom ... by limiting it*   It is, indeed, a reasonable conjecture that market freedom is less than it was, partly because, had the bourgeois state not imposed restrictions on it, its survival would have been jeopardized.

4   *if such sacrifice ... minimize their occurrence*   Since 1977 (when what is substantially the text of this chapter was first published), many philosophers have offered challenging answers to this question, especially in response to Samuel Scheffler's relentless pressing of it in his *Rejection of Consequentialism* (Oxford: Clarendon Press, 1982). I cannot address those answers here. (For an attempt to show that Nozick's invocation of Kant is unjustified, see section 4 of Chapter 10 below [not included in this excerpt—eds.].)

5   *There is more appearance of argument*   Note, though, that what Nozick initially contends against is *violating rights in order to reduce the violation of rights*, whereas in what follows his target is *violating rights to expand aggregate welfare*. He is unconvincing on both counts, but one who agrees with him about "overall social good" could still press the questions. [editors' note] In the paragraph quoted from Nozick above: "But why may not .... Why not, similarly, hold...."

Side constraints express the inviolability of other persons. But why may not one violate persons for the greater social good? Individually, we each sometimes choose to undergo some pain or sacrifice for a greater benefit or to avoid a greater harm…. Why not, *similarly*, hold that some persons have to bear some costs that benefit other persons more, for the sake of the overall social good? But there is no *social entity* with a good that undergoes some sacrifice for its own good. There are only individual people, different individual people, with their own individual lives. Using one of these people for the benefit of others, uses him and benefits the others. Nothing more. What happens is that something is done to him for the sake of others. Talk of an overall social good covers this up…. [32-33].

This passage is hard to construe. In one interpretation what is says is correct but ineffectual, in the other what is says is pertinent, but wrong, and anyone who is impressed has probably failed to spot the ambiguity. For it is unclear whether Nozick is only arguing *against* one who puts redistribution across lives on a moral par with a person's sacrificing something for his own greater benefit, or arguing *for* the moral impermissibility of redistribution. In other words, is Nozick simply rejecting argument *A*, or is he (also) propounding argument *B*?

> *A* since persons compose a social entity relevantly akin to the entity a single person is *(p)*, redistribution across persons is morally permissible *(q)*.
>
> *B* since it is false that *p*, it is false that *q*.

If Nozick is just rejecting argument *A*, then I agree with him, but side constraints remain unjustified. Unless we take Nozick to be propounding argument *B*, there is no case to answer. And then the answer is that the truth of *p* is not a necessary condition of the truth of *q*. A redistributor does not have to believe in a social entity.[1]

According to Nozick, the redistributive attitude ignores the separateness of persons. But what does it mean to say in

a normative tone of voice (for it is uncontroversial, descriptively speaking) that persons are separate? Either it means that who gets what is morally relevant, or it means that it is morally forbidden to redistribute across persons. If the first (moral relevance) is what is meant, then all patterned principles (as opposed to, for example, the unpatterned end-state principle of utilitarianism[2]) embody the requirement, and even an unpatterned egalitarianism manifestly presupposes the moral separateness of persons. If the second (prohibition on redistribution) is what is meant, then the separateness of persons is no *argument* against redistribution.

Side constraints remain unjustified, and socialists need not apologize for being willing to restrict freedom in order to expand it.

7. I now examine Nozick's section on "Voluntary Exchange," which I presumed (see above) to be his more extended treatment of the problem of the effect of market transactions on persons not party to them, including the as yet unborn. Nozick allows that agreed exchanges between *A* and *B* may reduce *C*'s *options*, but he implies that they do not thereby reduce *C*'s *freedom*. He explicitly says that they do not render involuntary anything that *C* does. And since what *C* is forced to do he does involuntarily, it follows that, for Nozick, the actions of *A* and *B*, though reducing *C*'s options, cannot have the result that *C* is *forced* to do something that he might not otherwise have done.

The last claim entails a denial of a thesis central to the socialist critique of capitalism, which may usefully be expressed in the terms of Nozick's doctrine of natural rights, without commitment to the truth of the latter.

For Nozick, every person has a natural right not to work for any other. If one is a slave, then, unless one contracted freely into slavery (see above), one's rights were violated, as they are in slave states, which do not confer on everyone as a matter of civil right the rights that he enjoys naturally. And natural rights would remain violated if the law permitted slaves to choose for which master they should labor, as long as it forbade them to withhold their services from all masters whatsoever.

One difference between a modern capitalist state and a slave state is that the natural right not to be subordinate in the manner of a slave is a civil right in modern capital-

---

1   *A redistributor … social entity*   For elaboration of this point, see Nagel ("Libertarianism Without Foundations," pp. 197-98), who takes Nozick to be propounding *B*.

2   *as opposed to … unpatterned end-state principle of utilitarianism*   For the differences among non-entitlement principles between ones that are and ones that are not patterned, see pp. 153ff. of *Anarchy*. (Nozick is not careful in his application of this distinction.)

ism. The law excludes formation of a set of persons who are legally obliged to work for other persons. That status being forbidden, everyone is entitled to work for no one. But the power matching this right[1] is differentially enjoyed. Some *can* live without subordinating themselves, but most cannot. The latter face a structure generated by a history of market transactions in which, it is reasonable to say, they are *forced* to work for some or other person or group. Their natural rights are not matched by corresponding effective powers.

This division between the powerful and the powerless with respect to the alienation of labor power is the heart of the socialist objection to claims on behalf of the justice and freedom of capitalist arrangements. The rights Nozick says we have by nature we also have civilly under capitalism, but the matching powers are widely lacking. That lack is softened in contemporary rich capitalist countries, because of a hard-won institutionalization of a measure of protection for working-class people. In Nozick's capitalism such institutionalization would be forbidden on the ground that it was coercive, and the lack would be greater.

But Nozick, in the course of his full reply to the problem of "third parties," denies that even the most abject proletarian is *forced* to work for some capitalist or other. Addressing himself to "market exchanges between workers and owners of capital," he invites us to reflect on the situation of a certain Z (so-called because he is at the bottom of the heap in a twenty-six-person economy) who is "faced with working [for a capitalist] or starving":

> the choices and actions of all other persons do not add up to providing Z with some other option. (He may have various options about what job to take.) Does Z choose to work voluntarily?... Z does choose voluntarily if the other individuals A through Y each acted voluntarily and within their rights... A person's choice among differing degrees of unpalatable alternatives is not rendered nonvoluntary by the fact that others voluntarily chose and acted within their rights in a way that did not provide him with a more palatable alternative....

[Whether other people's option-closing actions] makes one's resulting action non-voluntary depends on whether these others had the right to act as they did. [262, 263-64.]

One might think that people of necessity lack the right so to act that someone ends up in Z's position, a view that I put forward later (see below). But here we suppose, with Nozick, that all of A through Y acted as impeccably upright marketeers and therefore did nothing wrong. If so, says Nozick, Z is not *forced* to work for a capitalist. If he chooses to, the choice is voluntary.

Notice that Nozick is not saying that Z, although forced to work or starve, is not forced to *work*, since he may choose to starve. Rather, he would deny that Z is forced to work-or-starve, even though Z has no other alternative, and would accept that Z is indeed forced to work, if, contrary to what Nozick holds, he is forced to work or starve. For Nozick believes that

> (8) if Z is forced to do A or B, and A is the only thing it would be reasonable for him to do, and Z does A for this reason, then Z is forced to do A.[2]

Nozick holds that

> (9) Z is forced to choose between working and starving only if human actions caused his alternatives to be restricted in that way,

and that

> (10) Z is forced so to choose only if the actions bringing about the restriction on his alternatives were illegitimate.

Both claims are false, but we need not discuss (9) here.[3] For we are concerned with choice restriction which Nozick himself attributes to the actions of person, *viz.*, some or all of A through Y. We need therefore only reject his claim that

---

1   *But the power matching this right*   The concept of a *power which matches a right* is explicated in section (2) of Chapter 8 of my *Karl Marx's Theory of History*. The basic idea: power p matches right r if and only if what X is *de jure* able to do when X has r is what X is *de facto* able to do when X has p. [editors' note] *de jure*: by law; *de facto*: in fact.

2   See Nozick "Coercion" in Sidney Morgenbesser, Patrick Suppes, and Morton White, eds., *Philosophy, Science, and Method: Essays in Honor of Ernest Nagel* (New York: St. Martin's Press, 1969), p. 446. I derive (8) above from principle (7) of the "Coercion" essay on the basis of Nozick's commitment to: Z is forced to do A if and only if there is a person P who forces Z to do A. See (9) in the next sentence of the text above.

3   *Both claims are false ... here*   For criticism of (9), see Harry Frankfurt, "Coercion and Moral Responsibility," in Ted Honderich, ed., *Essays on Freedom of Action* (London: Routledge & Kegan Paul, 1973), pp. 83–84.

if someone is forced to do something, then someone acted *illegitimately:* we need to refute (10) only.

Let me once again display the text in which (10) is affirmed:

> Other people's actions may place limits on one's available opportunities. Whether this makes one's resulting action non-voluntary depends upon whether these others had the right to act as they did [262].

But there is no such dependence, as the following pair of examples shows.

Suppose farmer Fred owns a tract of land across which villager Victor has a right of way. Then, if Fred erects an insurmountable fence around the land, Victor is forced to use another route, as Nozick will agree, since Fred, in erecting the fence, acted illegitimately. Now consider farmer Giles, whose similar tract is regularly traversed by villager William, not as of right, but because Giles is a tolerant soul. But then Giles erects an insurmountable fence around his land for reasons which justify him in doing so. According to Nozick, William may not truly say that, like Victor, he is now forced to use another route. But the examples, though different, do not so contrast as to make such a statement false. William is no less forced to change his route than Victor is. (10) is false even if—what I also deny—(9) is true, and the thesis that Z is forced to place his labor power at the disposal of some or other member of the capitalist class is sustained.

8. Nozick's claim about Z is so implausible that it may seem puzzling, coming as it does from an extremely acute thinker. Can it be that he is driven to it because it occupies a strategic place in his defense of libertarian capitalism? How is libertarian capitalism *libertarian* if it erodes the liberty of a large class of people?

Still, we can imagine Nozick granting that Z is forced to work for a capitalist, and attempting to recoup his position by saying this: Z is indeed so forced, but, since what brings it about that he is forced is a sequence of legitimate transactions, there is no moral case against his being so forced, no injustice in it. (Cf. (1) and (2) above.)

That would be less impressive than the original claim. Nozick is in a stronger position—could he but defend it—when he holds that capitalism does not deprive workers of freedom than if he grants that the worker is forced to subordinate himself yet insists that, even so, his situation, being justly generated, is, however otherwise regrettable, unexceptionable from the standpoint of justice. For the original claim, if true, entitles Nozick to say, given his other theses, that capitalism is not only a just but also a free society; while the revised claim makes him say that capitalism is just, but not entirely free. When Z is accurately described capitalism is less attractive, whatever we may say about it from the standpoint of justice.

Turning to that standpoint, and bearing Z in mind, what should we say about Nozick's important thesis (1)? It seems reasonable to add to the constraints on just acquisition a provision that no one may so acquire goods that others suffer severe loss of liberty as a result. We might, that is, *accept* thesis (1) but extend the conditions steps must meet to be just, and thus reject capitalism.[1]

Alternatively, we might grant, in concessive spirit, that there is no transactional injustice (no unjust step) in the generation of Z's position, but *reject* (1), and contend that the generative process must be regulated, even, perhaps, at the cost of some injustice, to prevent its issuing in very unjust results. Nozick would invoke side constraints against that, but they lack authority (see section 6 above).

Whatever option we take—and there are others—it should now be clear that "libertarian" capitalism sacrifices liberty to capitalism, a truth its advocates are able to deny only because they are prepared to abuse the language of freedom.[2]

---

1   *but extend the conditions ... thus reject capitalism*   It is immaterial here if this yields what Nozick would call a "gimmicky" (see [157]) reading of (1).

2   *Whatever option we take ... language of freedom*   For an extended defense of that charge of abuse, see sections 2 and 3 of Chapter 2 below [not included in this selection—eds.].

ISAIAH BERLIN
(1909–1997)

Berlin was born in 1909 in Riga, Latvia, the son of a successful Jewish merchant who moved the family to St. Petersburg, and then, in 1921 to London. At Oxford he studied classics, philosophy, and economics. In 1932, he was elected to a Prize Fellowship at All Souls and taught there until his retirement in 1975, surrounded by many of the leading analytic philosophers of the day, including J.L. Austin, A.J. Ayer, and Stuart Hampshire. During World War II he was posted to New York and then Washington, with the job of sending back information about the wartime mood of Americans. Sent to the British Embassy in Moscow, he talked to several Soviet writers, including the poet Anna Akhmatova and the poet and novelist Boris Pasternak. They deeply impressed him with their courage, living under what he called a "miserable regime," and his conversations with them left their mark on his future political views. After the war he returned to university life in Britain, but discovered he was no longer interested in analytic philosophy, which he now found sterile; he turned instead to the study of history and of social and political ideas. Associated with Oxford for the rest of his career, he nevertheless visited and lectured widely around the world. He died in Oxford in 1997, aged 88.

In what is perhaps his best known essay, "The Hedgehog and The Fox" (1953), Berlin cites a line from the seventh-century BCE Greek poet Archilochus: "The fox knows many things, but the hedgehog knows one big thing." The essay distinguishes two sorts of people: "foxes" who have a variety of aims and approaches, and "hedgehogs," who have a single dominating organizing aim or principle. Berlin was very much a fox. Besides his works on political philosophy, he was an astute literary critic and historian, writing on Romanticism, the Enlightenment, and nationalism, as well as on Russian social and political thought, and on liberalism. His first major work, the intellectual biography *Karl Marx* (1939), is still widely read.

Berlin's most influential social and political ideas are his distinction between positive and negative liberty, and his account of value pluralism. His essay "Two Concepts of Liberty" (1958) came at a time in which political theory was thought to be in decline in the English-speaking world, and contributed to its revival. Negative liberty, as Berlin sees it, is freedom from coercion, understood as the deliberate interference of other human beings. One has negative liberty to act in a certain way when there are no laws or other external obstacles preventing that action. Positive liberty, on the other hand, might be thought of as empowerment: the real ability to do something, to control one's destiny and to achieve one's basic aims. So, for example, everyone has the negative liberty to become wealthy—there are no laws against it—but almost nobody in poverty has the power—the positive liberty—to do so. Berlin argued that sometimes the two sorts of liberty are contraries, in that to grant some people positive liberty, legal restrictions on others might be required, reducing their negative liberty. Though Berlin's distinction has been criticized (for example by Charles Taylor), it remains a central text in any discussion of liberty.

Berlin's account of value pluralism is equally influential, though there is some controversy about its details (and, indeed, its coherence). Berlin claimed that values are incommensurable, that values often conflict, and there is often no principled metric for deciding between them. According to Berlin, we have to choose between many ends, each valuable in itself, and there is no single right answer about what to choose. Liberty may conflict with equality, social justice with the private pursuit of truth or beauty, and so on. He thus rejects utilitarian accounts that hold that all values can be reduced to a single standard (e.g., pleasure) so that they can be compared. Value pluralism is related to his defense of negative liberty, since the absence of a right standard provides grounds for minimizing interference with individuals' decisions about which values to embrace.

Berlin has left a substantial legacy. His value pluralism is evident in Michael Walzer's *Spheres of Justice* (1983), as well as in John Rawls's *Political Liberalism* (1993). His work on nationalism anticipates formulations of liberal nationalism in the work of theorists such as David Miller and Yael Tamir; his interest in the politics of culture resonates with movements in identity politics and multiculturalism. He remains a major source of inspiration within liberal, pluralist thought.

◆ ◆ ◆ ◆ ◆

Two Concepts of Liberty (1958)

If men never disagreed about the ends of life, if our ancestors had remained undisturbed in the Garden of Eden, the studies to which the Chichele Chair of Social and Political Theory[1] is dedicated could scarcely have been conceived. For these studies spring from, and thrive on, discord. Someone may question this on the ground that even in a society of saintly anarchists, where no conflicts about ultimate purposes can take place, political problems, for example constitutional or legislative issues, might still arise. But this objection rests on a mistake. Where ends are agreed, the only questions left are those of means, and these are not political but technical, that is to say, capable of being settled by experts or machines, like arguments between engineers or doctors. That is why those who put their faith in some immense, world-transforming phenomenon, like the final triumph of reason or the proletarian revolution, must believe that all political and moral problems can thereby be turned into technological ones. That is the meaning of Engels's famous phrase (paraphrasing Saint-Simon) about "replacing the government of persons by the administration of things,"[2] and the Marxist prophecies about the withering

away of the State and the beginning of the true history of humanity. This outlook is called Utopian by those for whom speculation about this condition of perfect social harmony is the play of idle fancy. Nevertheless, a visitor from Mars to any British—or American—university today might perhaps be forgiven if he sustained the impression that its members lived in something very like this innocent and idyllic state, for all the serious attention that is paid to fundamental problems of politics by professional philosophers.

Yet this is both surprising and dangerous. Surprising because there has, perhaps, been no time in modern history when so large a number of human beings, in both the East and the West, have had their notions, and indeed their lives, so deeply altered, and in some cases violently upset, by fanatically held social and political doctrines. Dangerous, because when ideas are neglected by those who ought to attend to them—that is to say, those who have been trained to think critically about ideas—they sometimes acquire an unchecked momentum and an irresistible power over multitudes of men that may grow too violent to be affected by rational criticism. Over a hundred years ago, the German poet Heine[3] warned the French not to underestimate the power of ideas: philosophical concepts nurtured in the stillness of a professor's study could destroy a civilization. He spoke of Kant's *Critique of Pure Reason* as the sword with which German deism[4] had been decapitated, and described the works of Rousseau as the blood-stained weapon which, in the hands of Robespierre,[5] had destroyed the old regime; and prophesied that the romantic faith of Fichte and Schel-

---

1   *Chichele Chair of Social and Political Theory* [Unless otherwise indicated, all notes to this selection are by the author.] [editors' note] This essay is based on Berlin's Inaugural Lecture when he was appointed to Chichele Chair of Social and Political Theory at Oxford, named in honor of Henry Chichele (c. 1364–1443), Archbishop of Canterbury and founder of All Souls College.

2   *replacing the government of persons by the administration of things* Engels, *Herrn Eugen Dührings Umwälzung der Wissenschaft*, 7th ed. (Stuttgart, 1910), p. 302. [*Herr Eugen Dühring's*

Revolution in Science, tr. E. Burns (New York, 1935), pp. 291–92.] [editors' note] Friedrich Engels (1820–95), German social scientist and philosopher, collaborated with Marx on the development of communist theory; and was co-author of *The Communist Manifesto*. Henri de Saint-Simon (1760–1825) was a French utopian thinker, considered an important founder of modern socialism.

3   *Heine* [editors' note] Christian Johann Heinrich Heine (1797–1856), one of the greatest German romantic poets, best known for his lyric poetry which was set to music by Schumann, Schubert, Brahms and other composers.

4   *German deism* [editors' note] Deism is a religious philosophy (especially popular with Enlightenment philosophers) that holds that God does not interfere with the course of the world and that religious truths can be discovered through the use of reason.

5   *Robespierre* [editors' note] Maximilien François Marie Isidore de Robespierre (1758–94), a disciple of Rousseau, was one of the leaders of the French revolution and an instrumental force in the Reign of Terror.

ling[1] would one day be turned, with terrible effect, by their fanatical German followers, against the liberal culture of the West. The facts have not wholly belied this prediction; but if professors can truly wield this fatal power, may it not be that only other professors, or, at least, other thinkers (and not governments or congressional committees), can alone disarm them?

Our philosophers seem oddly unaware of these devastating effects of their activities. It may be that, intoxicated by their magnificent achievements in more abstract realms, the best among them look with disdain upon a field in which radical discoveries are less likely to be made, and talent for minute analysis is less likely to be rewarded. Yet, despite every effort to separate them, conducted by a blind scholastic pedantry, politics has remained indissolubly intertwined with every other form of philosophical enquiry. To neglect the field of political thought, because its unstable subject-matter, with its blurred edges, is not to be caught by the fixed concepts, abstract models and fine instruments suitable to logic or to linguistic analysis—to demand a unity of method in philosophy, and reject whatever the method cannot successfully manage—is merely to allow oneself to remain at the mercy of primitive and uncriticized political beliefs. It is only a very vulgar historical materialism that denies the power of ideas, and says that ideals are mere material interests in disguise. It may be that, without the pressure of social forces, political ideas are stillborn: what is certain is that these forces, unless they clothe themselves in ideas, remain blind and undirected.

Political theory is a branch of moral philosophy, which starts from the discovery, or application, of moral notions in the sphere of political relations. I do not mean, as I think some Idealist philosophers may have believed, that all historical movements or conflicts between human beings are reducible to movements or conflicts of ideas or spiritual forces, nor even that they are effects (or aspects) of them. But I do mean that to understand such movements or conflicts is, above all, to understand the ideas or attitudes to life involved in them, which alone make such movements a part of human history, and not mere natural events. Political words and notions and acts are not intelligible save in the context of the issues that divide the men who use them. Consequently our own attitudes and activities are likely to

---

1   *Fichte and Schelling* [editors' note] Johann Gottlieb Fichte (1762–1814) and Friedrich Wilhelm Joseph Schelling (1775–1854) were German idealist philosophers who played important roles in the development of German Romanticism.

remain obscure to us, unless we understand the dominant issues of our own world. The greatest of these is the open war that is being fought between two systems of ideas which return different and conflicting answers to what has long been the central question of politics—the question of obedience and coercion. "Why should I (or anyone) obey anyone else?" "Why should I not live as I like?" "Must I obey?" "If I disobey, may I be coerced?" "By whom, and to what degree, and in the name of what, and for the sake of what?"

Upon the answers to the question of the permissible limits of coercion opposed views are held in the world today, each claiming the allegiance of very large numbers of men. It seems to me, therefore, that any aspect of this issue is worthy of examination.

I

To coerce a man is to deprive him of freedom—freedom from what? Almost every moralist in human history has praised freedom. Like happiness and goodness, like nature and reality, it is a term whose meaning is so porous that there is little interpretation that it seems able to resist. I do not propose to discuss either the history of this protean word or the more than two hundred senses of it recorded by historians of ideas. I propose to examine no more than two of these senses—but they are central ones, with a great deal of human history behind them, and, I dare say, still to come. The first of these political senses of freedom or liberty (I shall use both words to mean the same), which (following much precedent) I shall call the "negative" sense, is involved in the answer to the question "What is the area within which the subject—a person or group of persons—is or should be left to do or be what he is able to do or be, without interference by other persons?" The second, which I shall call the "positive" sense, is involved in the answer to the question "What, or who, is the source of control or interference that can determine someone to do, or be, this rather than that?" The two questions are clearly different, even though the answers to them may overlap.

The notion of negative freedom

I am normally said to be free to the degree to which no man or body of men interferes with my activity. Political liberty in this sense is simply the area within which a man can act unobstructed by others. If I am prevented by others from doing what I could otherwise do, I am to that degree unfree; and if this area is contracted by other men beyond a certain minimum, I can be described as being coerced, or, it may be, enslaved. Coercion is not, however, a term that covers every form of inability. If I say that I am unable to jump more than ten feet in the air, or cannot read because I am blind, or cannot understand the darker pages of Hegel,[1] it would be eccentric to say that I am to that degree enslaved or coerced. Coercion implies the deliberate interference of other human beings within the area in which I could otherwise act. You lack political liberty or freedom only if you are prevented from attaining a goal by human beings.[2] Mere incapacity to attain a goal is not lack of political freedom.[3] This is brought out by the use of such modern expressions as "economic freedom" and its counterpart, "economic slavery." It is argued, very plausibly, that if a man is too poor to afford something on which there is no legal ban—a loaf of bread, a journey round the world, recourse to the law courts—he is as little free to have it as he would be if it were forbidden him by law. If my poverty were a kind of disease which prevented me from buying bread, or paying for the journey round the world or getting my case heard, as lameness prevents me from running, this inability would not naturally be described as a lack of freedom, least of all political freedom. It is only because I believe that my inability to get a given thing is due to the fact that other human beings have made arrangements whereby I am, whereas others are not, prevented from having enough money with which to pay for it, that I think myself a victim of coercion or slavery. In other words, this use of the term depends on a particular social and economic theory about the causes of my poverty or weakness. If my lack of material means is due to my lack of mental or physical capacity, then I begin to speak of being deprived of freedom (and not simply about poverty) only if I accept the theory.[4] If, in addition, I believe that I am being kept in want by a specific arrangement which

I consider unjust or unfair, I speak of economic slavery or oppression. The nature of things does not madden us, only ill will does, said Rousseau.[5] The criterion of oppression is the part that I believe to be played by other human beings, directly or indirectly, with or without the intention of doing so, in frustrating my wishes. By being free in this sense I mean not being interfered with by others. The wider the area of non-interference the wider my freedom.

This is what the classical English political philosophers meant when they used this word.[6] They disagreed about how wide the area could or should be. They supposed that it could not, as things were, be unlimited, because if it were, it would entail a state in which all men could boundlessly interfere with all other men; and this kind of "natural" freedom would lead to social chaos in which men's minimum needs would not be satisfied; or else the liberties of the weak would be suppressed by the strong. Because they perceived that human purposes and activities do not automatically harmonize with one another, and because (whatever their official doctrines) they put high value on other goals, such as justice, or happiness, or culture, or security, or varying degrees of equality, they were prepared to curtail freedom in the interests of other values and, indeed, of freedom itself. For, without this, it was impossible to create the kind of association that they thought desirable. Consequently, it is assumed by these thinkers that the area of men's free action must be limited by law. But equally it is assumed, especially by such libertarians as Locke and Mill in England, and Constant and Tocqueville in France, that there ought to exist a certain minimum area of personal freedom which must on no account be violated; for if it is overstepped, the individual will find himself in an area too narrow for even that minimum development of his natural faculties which alone makes it possible to pursue, and even to conceive, the various ends which men hold good or right or sacred. It follows that a frontier must be drawn between the area of private life and that of public authority. Where it is to be drawn is a matter of argument, indeed of haggling.

---

1   *Hegel* [editors' note] G.W.F. Hegel (1770–1831), central German idealist philosopher.

2   *You lack ... human beings* I do not, of course, mean to imply the truth of the converse.

3   *Mere incapacity ... political freedom* Helvétius [Claude Adrien Helvétius (1715–71), French enlightenment poet and philosopher] made this point very clearly: "The free man is the man who is not in irons, not imprisoned in a gaol, nor terrorized like a slave by the fear of punishment." It is not lack of freedom not to fly like an eagle or swim like a whale. *De l'esprit*, First Discourse, Chapter 4.

4   *only if I accept the theory* The Marxist conception of social laws is, of course, the best-known version of this theory, but it forms a

large element in some Christian and utilitarian, and all socialist, doctrines.

5   *The nature of things ... said Rousseau* Rousseau, *Émile*, book 2, volume 4.

6   *This is what ... they used this word* "A free man," said Hobbes, "is he that ... is not hindered to do what he has a will to." *Leviathan*, chapter 21. Law is always a fetter, even if it protects you from being bound in chains that are heavier than those of law, say some more repressive law or custom, or arbitrary despotism or chaos. Bentham says much the same.

Men are largely interdependent, and no man's activity is so completely private as never to obstruct the lives of others in any way. "Freedom for the pike is death for the minnows";[1] the liberty of some must depend on the restraint of others. Freedom for an Oxford don, others have been known to add, is a very different thing from freedom for an Egyptian peasant.

This proposition derives its force from something that is both true and important, but the phrase itself remains a piece of political claptrap. It is true that to offer political rights, or safeguards against intervention by the State, to men who are half-naked, illiterate, underfed and diseased is to mock their condition; they need medical help or education before they can understand, or make use of, an increase in their freedom. What is freedom to those who cannot make use of it? Without adequate conditions for the use of freedom, what is the value of freedom? First things come first: there are situations in which—to use a saying satirically attributed to the nihilists by Dostoevsky—boots are superior to Pushkin;[2] individual freedom is not everyone's primary need. For freedom is not the mere absence of frustration of whatever kind; this would inflate the meaning of the word until it meant too much or too little. The Egyptian peasant needs clothes or medicine before, and more than, personal liberty, but the minimum freedom that he needs today, and the greater degree of freedom that he may need tomorrow, is not some species of freedom peculiar to him, but identical with that of professors, artists and millionaires.

What troubles the consciences of Western liberals is, I think, the belief, not that the freedom that men seek differs according to their social or economic conditions, but that the minority who possess it have gained it by exploiting, or, at least, averting their gaze from, the vast majority who do not. They believe, with good reason, that if individual liberty is an ultimate end for human beings, none should be deprived of it by others; least of all that some should enjoy it at the expense of others. Equality of liberty; not to treat others as I should not wish them to treat me; repayment of my debt to those who alone have made possible my liberty or prosperity or enlightenment; justice, in its simplest and most universal sense—these are the foundations of liberal morality: Liberty is not the only goal of men. I can, like the Russian critic Belinsky,[3] say that if others are to be deprived of it—if my brothers are to remain in poverty, squalor and chains—then I do not want it for myself, I reject it with both hands and infinitely prefer to share their fate. But nothing is gained by a confusion of terms. To avoid glaring inequality or widespread misery I am ready to sacrifice some, or all, of my freedom: I may do so willingly and freely; but it is freedom that I am giving up for the sake of justice or equality or the love of my fellow men. I should be guilt-stricken, and rightly so, if I were not, in some circumstances, ready to make this sacrifice. But a sacrifice is not an increase in what is being sacrificed, namely freedom, however great the moral need or the compensation for it. Everything is what it is: liberty is liberty, not equality or fairness or justice or culture, or human happiness or a quiet conscience. If the liberty of myself or my class or nation depends on the misery of a number of other human beings, the system which promotes this is unjust and immoral. But if I curtail or lose my freedom in order to lessen the shame of such inequality, and do not thereby materially increase the individual liberty of others, an absolute loss of liberty occurs. This may be compensated for by a gain in justice or in happiness or in peace, but the loss remains, and it is a confusion of values to say that although my "liberal" individual freedom may go by the board, some other kind of freedom—"social" or "economic"—is increased. Yet it remains true that the freedom of some must at times be curtailed to secure the freedom of others. Upon what principle should this be done? If freedom is a sacred, untouchable value, there can be no such principle. One or other of these conflicting rules or principles must, at any rate in practice, yield: not always for reasons which can be clearly stated, let alone generalized into rules or universal maxims. Still, a practical compromise has to be found.

Philosophers with an optimistic view of human nature and a belief in the possibility of harmonizing human interests, such as Locke or Adam Smith or, in some moods, Mill, believed that social harmony and progress were compatible with reserving a large area for private life over which neither the State nor any other authority must be allowed to tres-

1   *Freedom for the pike ... the minnows* R.H. Tawney, *Equality* (1938), 3rd ed. chapter 5, section 2, "Equality and Liberty."

2   *Dostoevsky ... Pushkin* [editors' note] Fyodor Mikhailovich Dostoevsky (1821–81) is, along with Leo Tolstoy, one of the two most important Russian novelists. The quotation that "boots are superior to Pushkin" comes from his piece "Mr. Shchedrin, or the Schism Among the Nihilists." Alexander Sergeyevich Pushkin (1799–1837), widely regarded as the greatest Russian poet, was largely responsible for inventing modern Russian literature.

3   *Belinsky* [editors' note] Vissarion Grigoryevich Belinsky (1811–48), Russian literary critic and radical political activist.

pass. Hobbes, and those who agreed with him, especially conservative or reactionary thinkers, argued that if men were to be prevented from destroying one another and making social life a jungle or a wilderness, greater safeguards must be instituted to keep them in their places; he wished correspondingly to increase the area of centralized control and decrease that of the individual. But both sides agreed that some portion of human existence must remain independent of the sphere of social control. To invade that preserve, however small, would be despotism. The most eloquent of all defenders of freedom and privacy, Benjamin Constant, who had not forgotten the Jacobin dictatorship,[1] declared that at the very least the liberty of religion, opinion, expression, property must be guaranteed against arbitrary invasion. Jefferson, Burke, Paine,[2] Mill compiled different catalogs of individual liberties, but the argument for keeping authority at bay is always substantially the same. We must preserve a minimum area of personal freedom if we are not to "degrade or deny our nature."[3] We cannot remain absolutely free, and must give up some of our liberty to preserve the rest. But total self-surrender is self-defeating. What then must the minimum be? That which a man cannot give up without offending against the essence of his human nature. What is this essence? What are the standards which it entails? This has been, and perhaps always will be, a matter of infinite debate. But whatever the principle in terms of which the area of noninterference is to be drawn, whether it is that of natural law or natural rights, or of utility, or the pronouncements of a categorical imperative, or the sanctity of the social contract, or any other concept with which men have sought to clarify and justify their convictions, liberty in this sense means liberty *from*; absence of interference beyond the shifting, but always recognizable, frontier. "The only freedom which deserves the name, is that of pursuing our own good in our own way,"[4] said the most celebrated of its champions. If this is so, is compulsion ever justified?

Mill had no doubt that it was. Since justice demands that all individuals be entitled to a minimum of freedom, all other individuals were of necessity to be restrained, if need be by force, from depriving anyone of it. Indeed, the whole function of law was the prevention of just such collisions: the State was reduced to what Lassalle[5] contemptuously described as the functions of a night-watchman or traffic policeman.

What made the protection of individual liberty so sacred to Mill? In his famous essay he declares that, unless the individual is left to live as he wishes in "the part [of his conduct] which merely concerns himself,"[6] civilization cannot advance; the truth will not, for lack of a free market in ideas, come to light; there will be no scope for spontaneity, originality, genius, for mental energy, for moral courage. Society will be crushed by the weight of "collective mediocrity."[7] Whatever is rich and diversified will be crushed by the weight of custom, by men's constant tendency to conformity; which breeds only "withered" capacities, "pinched and hidebound," "cramped and dwarfed" human beings. "Pagan self-assertion" is as worthy as "Christian self-denial."[8] "All errors which [a man] is likely to commit against advice and warning, are far outweighed by the evil of allowing others to constrain him to what they deem his good."[9] The defense of liberty consists in the "negative" goal of warding off interference. To threaten a man with persecution unless he submits to a life in which he exercises no choices of his goals; to block before him every door but one, no matter how noble the prospect upon which it opens, or how benevolent the motives of those who arrange this, is to sin against the truth that he is a man, a being with a life of his own to live. This is liberty as it has been conceived by liberals in the modern world from the days of Erasmus (some would say of Ockham[10]) to our own. Every plea for civil liberties and individual rights, every protest against exploitation and

---

1   *Jacobin dictatorship* [editors' note] Over the period 1792–95 the Jacobins took power in post-revolutionary France, instituting the Reign of Terror and violently suppressing all opposition both from monarchists and from other revolutionaries.

2   *Jefferson, Burke, Paine* Thomas Jefferson (American statesman and author, 1743–1826); Edmund Burke (British statesman and orator, 1729–97); and Thomas Paine (American political leader and writer, 1737–1809).

3   *degrade or deny our nature* Constant, *Principes de politique* [*Principles of Politics*] (1806–10), Chapter 1.

4   *The only freedom ... in our own way* J.S. Mill, *On Liberty* (1869), Chapter 1.

5   *Lassalle* [editors' note] Ferdinand Lassalle (1825–64), German jurist and socialist.

6   *in the part ... concerns himself* *On Liberty*, chapter 1.

7   *collective mediocrity* Ibid.

8   *Pagan self-assertion ... Christian self-denial* The last two phrases are from John Sterling's essay on Simonides: vol 1, in his *Essays and Tales*, ed. Julius Charles Hare, 1848.

9   *All errors ... deem his good* Ibid., chapter 4.

10 *Erasmus ... Ockham* [editors' note] Desiderius Erasmus (1466?– 1536), Dutch Christian humanist, was a leading northern European Renaissance thinker. William of Ockham (1285?–1349?), innovative English philosopher and theologian.

humiliation, against the encroachment of public authority, or the mass hypnosis of custom or organized propaganda, springs from this individualistic, and much disputed, conception of man.

Three facts about this position may be noted. In the first place Mill confuses two distinct notions. One is that all coercion is, in so far as it frustrates human desires, bad as such, although it may have to be applied to prevent other, greater evils; while non-interference, which is the opposite of coercion, is good as such, although it is not the only good. This is the "negative" conception of liberty in its classical form. The other is that men should seek to discover the truth, or to develop a certain type of character of which Mill approved—critical, original, imaginative, independent, nonconforming to the point of eccentricity, and so on—and that truth can be found, and such character can be bred, only in conditions of freedom. Both these are liberal views, but they are not identical, and the connection between them is, at best, empirical. No one would argue that truth or freedom of self-expression could flourish where dogma crushes all thought. But the evidence of history tends to show (as, indeed, was argued by James Stephen in his formidable attack on Mill in his Liberty, Equality, Fraternity[1]) that integrity, love of truth, and fiery individualism grow at least as often in severely disciplined communities, among, for example, the puritan Calvinists of Scotland or New England, or under military discipline, as in more tolerant or indifferent societies; and if this is so, Mill's argument for liberty as a necessary condition for the growth of human genius falls to the ground. If his two goals proved incompatible, Mill would be faced with a cruel dilemma, quite apart from the further difficulties created by the inconsistency of his doctrines with strict utilitarianism, even in his own humane version of it.[2]

In the second place, the doctrine is comparatively modern. There seems to be scarcely any discussion of individual liberty as a conscious political ideal (as opposed to its actual existence) in the ancient world. Condorcet[3] had already remarked that the notion of individual rights was absent from the legal conceptions of the Romans and Greeks; this seems to hold equally of the Jewish, Chinese, and all other ancient civilizations that have since come to light.[4] The domination of this ideal has been the exception rather than the rule, even in the recent history of the West. Nor has liberty in this sense often formed a rallying cry for the great masses of mankind. The desire not to be impinged upon, to be left to oneself, has been a mark of high civilization on the part of both individuals and communities. The sense of privacy itself, of the area of personal relationships as something sacred in its own right, derives from a conception of freedom which, for all its religious roots, is scarcely older, in its developed state, than the Renaissance or the Reformation.[5] Yet its decline would mark the death of a civilization, of an entire moral outlook.

The third characteristic of this notion of liberty is of greater importance. It is that liberty in this sense is not incompatible with some kinds of autocracy, or at any rate with the absence of self-government. Liberty in this sense is principally concerned with the area of control, not with its source. Just as a democracy may, in fact, deprive the individual citizen of a great many liberties which he might have in some other form of society, so it is perfectly conceivable that a liberal-minded despot would allow his subjects a large measure of personal freedom. The despot who leaves his subjects a wide area of liberty may be unjust, or encourage the wildest inequalities, care little for order, or virtue, or knowledge; but provided he does not curb their liberty, or at least curbs it less than many other regimes, he meets with Mill's specification.[6]

---

1   *James Stephen ... Liberty Equality, Fraternity* James Fitzjames Stephen published this well-known treatise in London, 1873. In it he accused Mill of turning the ideals of the French Revolution into a religion.

2   *If his two goals ... humane version of it* This is but another illustration of the natural tendency of all but a very few thinkers to believe that all the things they hold good must be intimately connected, or at least compatible, with one another. The history of thought, like the history of nations, is strewn with examples of inconsistent, or at least disparate, elements artificially yoked together in a despotic system, or held together by the danger of some common enemy. In due course the danger passes, and conflicts between the allies arise, which often disrupt the system, sometimes to the great benefit of mankind.

3   *Condorcet* [editors' note] The Marquis de Condorcet (1743–94) was a French philosopher and political scientist known for his progressive, typically Enlightenment, views.

4   *this seems to hold equally ... come to light* See the valuable discussion of this in Michel Villey, *Leçons d'histoire de la philosophie du droit* (Paris, 1957), chapter 14, which traces the embryo of the notion of subjective rights to Ockham (see p. 272).

5   *The sense of privacy itself ... Reformation* Christian (and Jewish or Muslim) belief in the absolute authority of divine or natural laws, or in the equality of all men in the sight of God, is very different from belief in freedom to live as one prefers.

6   *but provided he does not curb ... Mill's specification* Indeed, it is arguable that in the Prussia of Frederick the Great or in the

Freedom in this sense is not, at any rate logically, connected with democracy or self-government. Self-government may, on the whole, provide a better guarantee of the preservation of civil liberties than other regimes, and has been defended as such by libertarians. But there is no necessary connection between individual liberty and democratic rule. The answer to the question "Who governs me?" is logically distinct from the question "How far does government interfere with me?" It is in this difference that the great contrast between the two concepts of negative and positive liberty, in the end, consists.[1] For the "positive"

Austria of Joseph II men of imagination, originality and creative genius, and, indeed, minorities of all kinds, were less persecuted and felt the pressure, both of institutions and custom, less heavy upon them than in many an earlier or later democracy.

1   *It is in this difference ... consists*   "Negative liberty" is something the extent of which, in a given case, it is difficult to estimate. It might, *prima facie*, seem to depend simply on the power to choose between at any rate two alternatives. Nevertheless, not all choices are equally free, or free at all. If in a totalitarian State I betray my friend under threat of torture, perhaps even if I act from fear of losing my job, I can reasonably say that I did not act freely. Nevertheless, I did, of course, make a choice, and could, at any rate in theory, have chosen to be killed or tortured or imprisoned. The mere existence of alternatives is not, therefore, enough to make my action free (although it may be voluntary) in the normal sense of the word. The extent of my freedom seems to depend on *(a)* how many possibilities are open to me (although the method of counting these can never be more than impressionistic; possibilities of action are not discrete entities like apples, which can be exhaustively enumerated); *(b)* how easy or difficult each of these possibilities is to actualize; *(c)* how important in my plan of life, given my character and circumstances, these possibilities are when compared with each other; *(d)* how far they are closed and opened by deliberate human acts; *(e)* what value not merely the agent, but the general sentiment of the society in which he lives, puts on the various possibilities. All these magnitudes must be "integrated," and a conclusion, necessarily never precise, or indisputable, drawn from this process. It may well be that there are many incommensurable kinds and degrees of freedom, and that they cannot be drawn up on any single scale of magnitude. Moreover, in the case of societies, we are faced by such (logically absurd) questions as "Would arrangement X increase the liberty of Mr. A more than it would that of Messrs B, C and D between them, added together?" The same difficulties arise in applying utilitarian criteria. Nevertheless, provided we do not demand precise measurement, we can give valid reasons for saying that the average subject of the King of Sweden is, on the whole, a good deal freer today [1958] than the average citizen of Spain or Albania. Total patterns of life must be compared directly as wholes, although the method by which we make the comparison, and the truth of the conclusions, are difficult or impossible to demonstrate. But the vagueness of the concepts, and the multiplicity of the criteria involved, are at-

---

sense of liberty comes to light if we try to answer the question, not "What am I free to do or be?", but "By whom am I ruled?" or "Who is to say what I am, and what I am not, to be or do?" The connection between democracy and individual liberty is a good deal more tenuous than it seemed to many advocates of both. The desire to be governed by myself, or at any rate to participate in the process by which my life is to be controlled, may be as deep a wish as that for a free area for action, and perhaps historically older. But it is not a desire for the same thing. So different is it, indeed, as to have led in the end to the great clash of ideologies that dominates our world. For it is this, the "positive" conception of liberty, not freedom from, but freedom to—to lead one prescribed form of life—which the adherents of the "negative" notion represent as being, at times, no better than a specious disguise for brutal tyranny:

2: The notion of positive freedom

The "positive" sense of the word "liberty" derives from the wish on the part of the individual to be his own master. I wish my life and decisions to depend on myself, not on external forces of whatever kind. I wish to be the instrument of my own, not of other men's, acts of will. I wish to be a subject, not an object; to be moved by reasons, by conscious purposes, which are my own, not by causes which affect me, as it were, from outside. I wish to be somebody, not nobody; a doer—deciding, not being decided for, self-directed and not acted upon by external nature or by other men as if I were a thing, or an animal, or a slave incapable of playing a human role, that is, of conceiving goals and policies of my own and realizing them. This is at least part of what I mean when I say that I am rational, and that it is my reason that distinguishes me as a human being from the rest of the world. I wish, above all, to be conscious of myself as a thinking, willing, active being, bearing responsibility for my choices and able to explain them by reference to my own ideas and purposes. I feel free to the degree that I believe this to be true, and enslaved to the degree that I am made to realize that it is not.

The freedom which consists in being one's own master, and the freedom which consists in not being prevented from choosing as I do by other men, may, on the face of it, seem concepts at no great logical distance from each other—no

---

tributes of the subject-matter itself, not of our imperfect methods of measurement, or of incapacity for precise thought.

more than negative and positive ways of saying much the same thing. Yet the "positive" and "negative" notions of freedom historically developed in divergent directions, not always by logically reputable steps, until, in the end, they came into direct conflict with each other.

One way of making this clear is in terms of the independent momentum which the, initially perhaps quite harmless, metaphor of self-mastery acquired. "I am my own master"; "I am slave to no man"; but may I not (as Platonists or Hegelians tend to say) be a slave to nature? Or to my own "unbridled" passions? Are these not so many species of the identical genus "slave"—some political or legal, others moral or spiritual? Have not men had the experience of liberating themselves from spiritual slavery, or slavery to nature, and do they not in the course of it become aware, on the one hand, of a self which dominates, and, on the other, of something in them which is brought to heel? This dominant self is then variously identified with reason, with my "higher nature," with the self which calculates and aims at what will satisfy it in the long run, with my "real," or "ideal," or "autonomous" self, or with my self "at its best"; which is then contrasted with irrational impulse, uncontrolled desires, my "lower" nature, the pursuit of immediate pleasures, my "empirical" or "heteronomous" self, swept by every gust of desire and passion, needing to be rigidly disciplined if it is ever to rise to the full height of its "real" nature. Presently the two selves may be represented as divided by an even larger gap; the real self may be conceived as something wider than the individual (as the term is normally understood), as a social "whole" of which the individual is an element or aspect: a tribe, a race, a Church, a State, the great society of the living and the dead and the yet unborn. This entity is then identified as being the "true" self which, by imposing its collective, or "organic," single will upon its recalcitrant "members," achieves its own, and therefore their, "higher" freedom. The perils of using organic metaphors to justify the coercion of some men by others in order to raise them to a "higher" level of freedom have often been pointed out. But what gives such plausibility as it has to this kind of language is that we recognize that it is possible, and at times justifiable, to coerce men in the name of some goal (let us say, justice or public health) which they would, if they were more enlightened, themselves pursue, but do not, because they are blind or ignorant or corrupt. This renders it easy for me to conceive of myself as coercing others for their own sake, in their, not my, interest. I am then claiming that I know what they truly need better than

they know it themselves. What, at most, this entails is that they would not resist me if they were rational and as wise as I and understood their interests as I do. But I may go on to claim a good deal more than this. I may declare that they are actually aiming at what in their benighted state they consciously resist, because there exists within them an occult entity—their latent rational will, or their "true" purpose—and that this entity, although it is belied by all that they overtly feel and do and say, is their "real" self, of which the poor empirical self in space and time may know nothing or little; and that this inner spirit is the only self that deserves to have its wishes taken into account.[1] Once I take this view, I am in a position to ignore the actual wishes of men or societies, to bully, oppress, torture them in the name, and on behalf, of their "real" selves, in the secure knowledge that whatever is the true goal of man (happiness, performance of duty, wisdom, a just society, self-fulfillment) must be identical with his freedom—the free choice of his "true," albeit often submerged and inarticulate, self.

This paradox has been often exposed. It is one thing to say that I know what is good for X, while he himself does not; and even to ignore his wishes for its—and his—sake; and a very different one to say that he has *eo ipso*[2] chosen it, not indeed consciously, not as he seems in everyday life, but in his role as a rational self which his empirical self may not know—the "real" self which discerns the good, and cannot help choosing it once it is revealed. This monstrous impersonation, which consists in equating what X would choose if he were something he is not, or at least not yet, with what X actually seeks and chooses, is at the heart of all political theories of self-realization. It is one thing to say that I may be coerced for my own good, which I am too blind to see: this may, on occasion, be for my benefit; indeed it may enlarge the scope of my liberty. It is another to say that if it is my good, then I am not being coerced, for I have willed

---

1 *I may declare ... into account* "[T]he ideal of true freedom is the maximum of power for all members of human society alike to make the best of themselves," said T.H. Green in 1881: [*Lectures on the Principles of Political Obligation and Other Writings*, ed. Paul Harris and John Morrow (Cambridge etc., 1986)], p. 200. Apart from the confusion of freedom with equality, this entails that if a man chose some immediate pleasure—which (in whose view?) would not enable him to make the best of himself (what self?)—what he was exercising was not "true" freedom: and if deprived of it, he would not lose anything that mattered. Green was a genuine liberal: but many a tyrant could use this formula to justify his worst acts of oppression.

2 *eo ipso* [editors' note] Latin: by that very fact.

it, whether I know this or not, and am free (or "truly" free) even while my poor earthly body and foolish mind bitterly reject it, and struggle with the greatest desperation against those who seek, however benevolently, to impose it.

This magical transformation, or sleight of hand (for which William James so justly mocked the Hegelians[1]), can no doubt be perpetrated just as easily with the "negative" concept of freedom, where the self that should not be interfered with is no longer the individual with his actual wishes and needs as they are normally conceived, but the "real" man within, identified with the pursuit of some ideal purpose not dreamed of by his empirical self. And, as in the case of the "positively" free self, this entity may be inflated into some super-personal entity—a State, a class, a nation, or the march of history itself, regarded as a more "real" subject of attributes than the empirical self. But the "positive" conception of freedom as self-mastery, with its suggestion of a man divided against himself, has in fact, and as a matter of history, of doctrine and of practice, lent itself more easily to this splitting of personality into two: the transcendent, dominant controller, and the empirical bundle of desires and passions to be disciplined and brought to heel. It is this historical fact that has been influential. This demonstrates (if demonstration of so obvious a truth is needed) that conceptions of freedom directly derive from views of what constitutes a self, a person, a man. Enough manipulation of the definition of man, and freedom can be made to mean whatever the manipulator wishes. Recent history has made it only too clear that the issue is not merely academic.

The consequences of distinguishing between two selves will become even clearer if one considers the two major forms which the desire to be self-directed—directed by one's "true" self—has historically taken: the first, that of self-abnegation in order to attain independence; the second, that of self-realization, or total self-identification with a specific principle or ideal in order to attain the selfsame end.

3: The retreat to the inner citadel

I am the possessor of reason and will; I conceive ends and I desire to pursue them; but if I am prevented from attaining them I no longer feel master of the situation. I may be prevented by the laws of nature, or by accidents, or the activities of men, or the effect, often undesigned, of human institutions. These forces may be too much for me. What am I to do to avoid being crushed by them? I must liberate myself from desires that I know I cannot realize. I wish to be master of my kingdom, but my frontiers are long and insecure, therefore I contract them in order to reduce or eliminate the vulnerable area. I begin by desiring happiness, or power, or knowledge, or the attainment of some specific object. But I cannot command them. I choose to avoid defeat and waste, and therefore decide to strive for nothing that I cannot be sure to obtain. I determine myself not to desire what is unattainable. The tyrant threatens me with the destruction of my property, with imprisonment, with the exile or death of those I love. But if I no longer feel attached to property, no longer care whether or not I am in prison, if I have killed within myself my natural affections, then he cannot bend me to his will, for all that is left of myself is no longer subject to empirical fears or desires. It is as if I had performed a strategic retreat into an inner citadel—my reason, my soul, my "noumenal" self [2]—which, do what they may, neither external blind force, nor human malice, can touch. I have withdrawn into myself; there, and there alone, I am secure. It is as if I were to say: "I have a wound in my leg. There are two methods of freeing myself from pain. One is to heal the wound. But if the cure is too difficult or uncertain, there is another method. I can get rid of the wound by cutting off my leg. If I train myself to want nothing to which the possession of my leg is indispensable, I shall not feel the lack of it." This is the traditional self-emancipation of ascetics and quietists, of stoics or Buddhist sages, men of various religions or of none, who have fled the world, and escaped the yoke of society or public opinion, by some process of deliberate self-transformation that enables them to care no longer for any of its values, to remain, isolated and independent, on its edges, no longer vulnerable to its weapons.[3] All political isolationism, all

---

1   *William James so justly mocked the Hegelians* [editors' note] William James (1842–1910), American philosopher and psychologist, who developed the philosophy of pragmatism. Scornful comments on the Hegelians are scattered throughout his work.

2   *"noumenal" self* [editors' note] The distinction is employed by Kant. A "noumenal" object is one that is supposed to be part of objective mind-independent reality, by contrast with "phenomenal" objects—things as they appear to us, which are thus dependent for their nature partly on our perceptual and conceptual apparatus. There is a problem, of course, about how noumenal objects may be known—if at all. For Kant, the noumenal self is free and not subject to the laws of causality.

3   *This is the tradition self-emancipation ... its weapons* "A wise man, though he be a slave, is at liberty, and from this it follows that though a fool rule, he is in slavery," said St. Ambrose (c. 338–397), Frankish bishop of Milan, influential "doctor of the Church."] It

economic autarky, every form of autonomy, has in it some element of this attitude. I eliminate the obstacles in my path by abandoning the path; I retreat into my own sect, my own planned economy, my own deliberately insulated territory, where no voices from outside need be listened to and no external forces can have effect. This is a form of the search for security; but it has also been called the search for personal or national freedom or independence.

From this doctrine, as it applies to individuals, it is no very great distance to the conceptions of those who, like Kant, identify freedom not indeed with the elimination of desires, but with resistance to them, and control over them. I identify myself with the controller and escape the slavery of the controlled. I am free because, and in so far as, I am autonomous. I obey laws, but I have imposed them on, or found them in, my own uncoerced self.

Freedom is obedience, but, in Rousseau's words, "obedience to a law which we prescribe to ourselves,"[1] and no man can enslave himself. Heteronomy is dependence on outside factors, liability to be a plaything of the external world that I cannot myself fully control, and which *pro tanto*[2] controls and "enslaves" me. I am free only to the degree to which my person is "fettered" by nothing that obeys forces over which I have no control; I cannot control the laws of nature; my free activity must therefore, *ex hypothesi*,[3] be lifted above the empirical world of causality. This is not the place in which to discuss the validity of this ancient and famous doctrine; I only wish to remark that the related notions of freedom as resistance to (or escape from) unrealizable desire, and as independence of the sphere of causality, have played a central role in politics no less than in ethics.

For if the essence of men is that they are autonomous beings authors of values, of ends in themselves, the ultimate authority of which consists precisely in the fact that they are willed freely—then nothing is worse than to treat them as if they were not autonomous, but natural objects, played on by causal influences, creatures at the mercy of external stimuli, whose choices can be manipulated by their rulers, whether by threats of force or offers of rewards. To treat men in this way is to treat them as if they were not self-determined. "Nobody may compel me to be happy in his own way," said Kant. Paternalism is "the greatest despotism imaginable."[4] This is so because it is to treat men as if they were not free, but human material for me, the benevolent reformer, to mold in accordance with my own, not their, freely adopted purpose. This is, of course, precisely the policy that the early utilitarians recommended. Helvétius (and Bentham) believed not in resisting, but in using, men's tendency to be slaves to their passions; they wished to dangle rewards and punishments before men—the acutest possible form of heteronomy—if by this means the "slaves" might be made happier.[5] But to manipulate men, to propel them towards goals which you—the social reformer—see, but they may not, is to deny their human essence, to treat them as objects without wills of their own, and therefore to degrade them. That is why to lie to men, or to deceive them, that is, to use them as means for my, not their own, independently conceived ends, even if it is for their own benefit, is, in effect, to treat them as subhuman, to behave as if their ends are less ultimate and sacred than my own. In the name of what can I ever be justified in forcing men to do what they have not willed or consented to? Only in the name of some value higher than themselves. But if, as Kant held, all values are made so by the free acts of men, and called values only so far as they are this, there is no value higher than the individual. Therefore to do this is to coerce men in the name of something less ultimate than themselves—to bend them to my will, or to someone else's particular craving for (his or their) happiness or expediency or security or convenience. I am aiming at something desired (from whatever motive, no matter how noble) by me or my group, to which I am using

might equally well have been said by Epictetus (c. 55–c. 135), Greek Stoic philosopher] or Kant. *Corpus scriptorum ecclesiasticorum latinorum*, vol. 82, part I, ed. Otto Faller (Vienna, 1968), letter 7, §24 (p. 55).

1   *obedience to a law ... prescribe to ourselves*   Rousseau, *Social Contract*, book 1, chapter 8: vol. 3, p. 365 in *Oeuvres completes* [ed. Bernard Gagnebin and others (Paris, 1959–95)].

2   *pro tanto*   [editors' note] Latin: to that extent.

3   *ex hypothesi*   [editors' note] Latin: by hypothesis—that is, according to what has been assumed.

4   *Nobody may compel ... despotism imaginable*   [Unless otherwise indicated, references to Kant's work below give volume and page numbers from *Kant's Gesammelte Schriften* (Berlin, 1900–); this is the standard way to refer to his work used in many translations.] vol. 8, p. 290, line 27, and p. 291, line 3.

5   *Helvétius (and Bentham) ... might be made happier*   "Proletarian coercion, in all its forms, from executions to forced labor, is, paradoxical as it may sound, the method of molding communist humanity out of the human material of the capitalist period." These lines by the Bolshevik leader Nikolay Bukharin, especially the term "human material," vividly convey this attitude. Nikolay Bukharin, *Ekonomika perekhodnogo perioda* ["Economics in the Transitional Period"] (Moscow, 1920), chapter 10, p. 146. [editors' note] Claude Adrien Helvétius (1715–71), was a French philosopher notorious for his advocacy of hedonism.

other men as means. But this is a contradiction of what I know men to be, namely ends in themselves. All forms of tampering with human beings, getting at them, shaping them against their will to your own pattern, all thought-control and conditioning,[1] is, therefore, a denial of that in men which makes them men and their values ultimate.

Kant's free individual is a transcendent being, beyond the realm of natural causality. But in its empirical form—in which the notion of man is that of ordinary life—this doctrine was the heart of liberal humanism, both moral and political, that was deeply influenced both by Kant and by Rousseau in the eighteenth century. In its a priori version it is a form of secularized Protestant individualism, in which the place of God is taken by the conception of the rational life, and the place of the individual soul which strains towards union with him is replaced by the conception of the individual, endowed with reason, straining to be governed by reason and reason alone, and to depend upon nothing that might deflect or delude him by engaging his irrational nature. Autonomy, not heteronomy: to act and not to be acted upon. The notion of slavery to the passions is—for those who think in these terms more than a metaphor. To rid myself of fear, or love, or the desire to conform is to liberate myself from the despotism of something which I cannot control. Sophocles, whom Plato reports as saying that old age alone has liberated him from the passion of love[2]—the yoke of a cruel master—is reporting an experience as real as that of liberation from a human tyrant or slave owner. The psychological experience of observing myself yielding to some "lower" impulse, acting from a motive that I dislike, or of doing something which at the very moment of doing I may detest, and reflecting later that I was "not myself," or "not in control of myself," when I did it, belongs

to this way of thinking and speaking. I identify myself with my critical and rational moments. The consequences of my acts cannot matter, for they are not in my control; only my motives are. This is the creed of the solitary thinker who has defied the world and emancipated himself from the chains of men and things. In this form the doctrine may seem primarily an ethical creed, and scarcely political at all; nevertheless its political implications are clear, and it enters into the tradition of liberal individualism at least as deeply as the "negative" concept of freedom.

It is perhaps worth remarking that in its individualistic form the concept of the rational sage who has escaped into the inner fortress of his true self seems to arise when the external world has proved exceptionally arid, cruel or unjust. "He is truly free," said Rousseau, "who desires what he can perform, and does what he desires."[3] In a world where a man seeking happiness or justice or freedom (in whatever sense) can do little, because he finds too many avenues of action blocked to him, the temptation to withdraw into himself may become irresistible. It may have been so in Greece, where the Stoic ideal cannot be wholly unconnected with the fall of the independent democracies before centralized Macedonian autocracy. It was so in Rome, for analogous reasons, after the end of the Republic.[4] It arose in Germany in the seventeenth century, during the period of the deepest national degradation of the German States that followed the Thirty Years War, when the character of public life, particularly in the small principalities, forced those who prized the dignity of human life, not for the first or last time, into a kind of inner emigration. The doctrine that maintains that what I cannot have I must teach myself not to desire, that a desire eliminated, or successfully resisted, is as good as a desire satisfied, is a sublime, but, it seems to me, unmistakable, form of the doctrine of sour grapes:[5] what I cannot be sure of, I cannot truly want.

This makes it clear why the definition of negative liberty as the ability to do what one wishes—which is, in effect,

---

1   *all thought-control and conditioning*   Kant's psychology, and that of the Stoics and Christians too, assumed that some element in man—the "inner fastness of his mind"—could be made secure against conditioning. The development of the techniques of hypnosis, "brainwashing," subliminal suggestion and the like has made this a priori assumption, at least as an empirical hypothesis, less plausible.

2   *Sophocles, whom Plato reports ... passion of love*   [editors' note] In Book 1 of Plato's *Republic*, Cephalus says: "How well I remember the aged poet Sophocles, when in answer to the question, How does love suit with age, Sophocles,—are you still the man you were? Peace, he replied; most gladly have I escaped the thing of which you speak; I feel as if I had escaped from a mad and furious master." Sophocles (496?–406? BCE), was one of the three great tragic dramatists of ancient Athens.

3   *He is truly free ... does what he desires*   [Rousseau, *Émile*], p. 309.

4   *It was so in Rome ... end of the Republic*   It is not perhaps far-fetched to assume that the quietism of the Eastern sages was, similarly, a response to the despotism of the great autocracies, and flourished at periods when individuals were apt to be humiliated, or at any rate ignored or ruthlessly managed, by those possessed of the instruments of physical coercion.

5   *sour grapes*   [editors' note] Disparagement of what one is unable to attain. The term alludes to Aesop's fable of the fox who, unable to reach the grapes hanging high on the vine, dismissed them as sour in an effort to save face.

the definition adopted by Mill—will not do. If I find that I am able to do little or nothing of what I wish, I need only contract or extinguish my wishes, and I am made free. If the tyrant (or "hidden persuader") manages to condition his subjects (or customers) into losing their original wishes and embracing ("internalizing") the form of life he has invented for them, he will, on this definition, have succeeded in liberating them. He will, no doubt, have made them *feel* free—as Epictetus feels freer than his master[1] (and the proverbial good man is said to feel happy on the rack[2]). But what he has created is the very antithesis of political freedom.

Ascetic self-denial may be a source of integrity or serenity and spiritual strength, but it is difficult to see how it can be called an enlargement of liberty. If I save myself from an adversary by retreating indoors and locking every entrance and exit, I may remain freer than if I had been captured by him, but am I freer than if I had defeated or captured him? If I go too far, contract myself into too small a space, I shall suffocate and die. The logical culmination of the process of destroying everything through which I can possibly be wounded is suicide. While I exist in the natural world, I can never be wholly secure. Total liberation in this sense (as Schopenhauer[3] correctly perceived) is conferred only by death.[4]

I find myself in a world in which I meet with obstacles to my will. Those who are wedded to the "negative" concept of freedom may perhaps be forgiven if they think that self-abnegation is not the only method of overcoming obstacles;

that it is also possible to do so by removing them: in the case of non-human objects, by physical action; in the case of human resistance, by force or persuasion, as when I induce somebody to make room for me in his carriage, or conquer a country which threatens the interests of my own. Such acts may be unjust, they may involve violence, cruelty, the enslavement of others, but it can scarcely be denied that thereby the agent is able in the most literal sense to increase his own freedom. It is an irony of history that this truth is repudiated by some of those who practice it most forcibly, men who, even while they conquer power and freedom of action, reject the "negative" concept of it in favor of its "positive" counterpart. Their view rules over half our world; let us see upon what metaphysical foundation it rests.

4: Self-realization

The only true method of attaining freedom, we are told, is by the use of critical reason, the understanding of what is necessary and what is contingent. If I am a schoolboy, all but the simplest truths of mathematics obtrude themselves as obstacles to the free functioning of my mind, as theorems whose necessity I do not understand; they are pronounced to be true by some external authority, and present themselves to me as foreign bodies which I am expected mechanically to absorb into my system. But when I understand the functions of the symbols, the axioms, the formation and transformation rules—the logic whereby the conclusions are obtained—and grasp that these things cannot be otherwise, because they appear to follow from the laws that govern the processes of my own reason,[5] then mathematical truths no longer obtrude themselves as external entities forced upon me which I must receive whether I want to or not, but as something which I now freely will in the course of the natural functioning of my own rational activity. For the mathematician, the proof of these theorems is part of the free exercise of his natural reasoning capacity. For the musician, after he has assimilated the pattern of the composer's score, and has made the composer's ends his own, the playing the music is not obedience to external laws, a compulsion and a barrier to liberty, but a free, unimpeded exercise. The player is bound to the score as an ox to the plow, or a factory worker to the machine. He has absorbed the score

---

1   *Epictetus feels freer than his master*   [editors' note] This Ancient Roman Stoic philosopher (55?–135? CE), was born a slave. He advocated a calm acceptance of one's fate, over which one had no control; this state, he said, constituted freedom, and was possible even for a slave.

2   *the proverbial good man is said to feel happy on the rack*   [editors' note] Aristotle quotes this variously attributed proverb (*Nicomachean Ethics*, pp. 7, 13), but disagrees.

3   *Schopenhauer*   [editors' note] Arthur Schopenhauer (1788–1860), German philosopher, known for his philosophy of pessimism.

4   *Total liberation ... conferred only by death*   It is worth remarking that those who demanded—and fought for—liberty for the individual or for the nation in France during this period of German quietism did not fall into this attitude. Might this not be precisely because, despite the despotism of the French monarchy and the arrogance and arbitrary behavior of privileged groups in the French State, France was a proud and powerful nation, where the reality of political power was not beyond the grasp of men of talent, so that withdrawal from battle into some untroubled heaven above it, whence it could be surveyed dispassionately by the self-sufficient philosopher, was not the only way out? The same holds for England in the nineteenth century and well after it, and for the United States today.

---

5   *the logic ... my own reason*   Or, as some modern theorists maintain, because I have, or could have, invented them for myself, since the rules are man-made.

into his own system, has, by understanding it, identified it with himself, has changed it from an impediment to free activity into an element in that activity itself.

What applies to music or mathematics must, we are told, in principle apply to all other obstacles which present themselves as so many lumps of external stuff blocking free self-development. That is the program of enlightened rationalism from Spinoza[1] to the latest (at times unconscious) disciples of Hegel. *Sapere aude.*[2] What you know, that of which you understand the necessity—the rational necessity—you cannot, while remaining rational, want to be otherwise. For to want something to be other than what it must be is, given the premises—the necessities that govern the world to be *pro tanto*[3] either ignorant or irrational. Passions, prejudices, fears, neuroses spring from ignorance, and take the form of myths and illusions. To be ruled by myths, whether they spring from the vivid imaginations of unscrupulous charlatans who deceive us in order to exploit us, or from psychological or sociological causes, is a form of heteronomy, of being dominated by outside factors in a direction not necessarily willed by the agent. The scientific determinists of the eighteenth century supposed that the study of the sciences of nature, and the creation of sciences of society on the same model, would make the operation of such causes transparently clear, and thus enable individuals to recognize their own part in the working of a rational world, frustrating only when misunderstood. Knowledge liberates, as Epicurus[4] taught long ago, by automatically eliminating irrational fears and desires.

Herder,[5] Hegel, and Marx substituted their own vitalistic models of social life[6] for the older, mechanical, ones, but believed, no less than their opponents, that to understand the world is to be freed. They merely differed from them in stressing the part played by change and growth in what made human beings human. Social life could not be understood by an analogy drawn from mathematics or physics. One must also understand history, that is, the peculiar laws of continuous growth, whether by "dialectical" conflict or otherwise, that govern individuals and groups in their interplay with each other and with nature. Not to grasp this is, according to these thinkers, to fall into a particular kind of error, namely the belief that human nature is static, that its essential properties are the same everywhere and at all times, that it is governed by unvarying natural laws, whether they are conceived in theological or materialistic terms, which entails the fallacious corollary that a wise lawgiver can, in principle, create a perfectly harmonious society at any time by appropriate education and legislation, because rational men, in all ages and countries, must always demand the same unaltering satisfactions of the same unaltering basic needs. Hegel believed that his contemporaries (and indeed all his predecessors) misunderstood the nature of institutions because they did not understand the laws—the rationally intelligible laws, since they spring from the operation of reason—that create and alter institutions and transform human character and human action. Marx and his disciples maintained that the path of human beings was obstructed not only by natural forces, or the imperfections of their own characters, but, even more, by the workings of their own social institutions, which they had originally created (not always consciously) for certain purposes, but whose functioning they systematically came to misconceive, in practice even more than in theory, and which thereupon became obstacles to their creators' progress. Marx offered social and economic hypotheses to account for the inevitability of such misunderstanding, in particular of the illusion that such man-made arrangements were independent forces, as inescapable as the laws of nature. As instances of such pseudo-objective forces, he pointed to the laws of supply and demand, or the institution of prop-

---

1   *rationalism from Spinoza* [editors' note] Rationalism is the position that basic necessary self-evident truths can be known by the reason alone, unaided by perception. It also tends to emphasize the importance of rationality in living the right sort of life. The Dutch philosopher Baruch Spinoza (1632–77) was one of the leading seventeenth-century rationalists.

2   *Sapere aude* [editors' note] Latin: Dare to know—that is, dare to use your own intelligence. One source for this slogan is Immanuel Kant's essay *Was Ist Aufklärung?* ("What is Enlightenment?" 1784): "Enlightenment is man's emergence from his self-imposed immaturity. Immaturity is the inability to use one's intelligence without direction from another. This immaturity is self-imposed when its cause lies not in lack of intelligence, but in lack of resolve and courage to use it without direction from another. *Sapere Aude!* Have courage to use your own intelligence! That is the motto of enlightenment."

3   *pro tanto* [editors' note] Latin: Only to that extent.

4   *Epicurus* [editors' note] Born a slave, his doctrine was that real happiness, as possible for a slave as for the master, is freedom from fear—of the gods, of death, of the afterlife.

5   *Herder* [editors' note] Johann Gottfried von Herder (1744–1803), German philosopher and literary critic, associated with the beginnings of German Romanticism.

6   *vitalistic models of social life* [editors' note] Vitalism is the view that living organisms function according to a vital force, rather than by mechanistic principles. In this application, a society is seen as strongly analogous to a living organism.

erty, or the eternal division of society into rich and poor, or owners and workers, as so many unaltering human categories. Not until we had reached a stage at which the spells of these illusions could be broken, that is, until enough men reached a social stage that alone enabled them to understand that these laws and institutions were themselves the work of human minds and hands, historically needed in their day, and later mistaken for inexorable, objective powers, could the old world be destroyed, and more adequate and liberating social machinery substituted.

We are enslaved by despots—institutions or beliefs or neuroses which can be removed only by being analyzed and understood. We are imprisoned by evil spirits which we have ourselves—albeit not consciously—created, and can exorcise them only by becoming conscious and acting appropriately: indeed, for Marx understanding is appropriate action. I am free if, and only if, I plan my life in accordance with my own will; plans entail rules; a rule does not oppress me or enslave me if I impose it on myself consciously, or accept it freely, having understood it, whether it was invented by me or by others, provided that it is rational, that is to say, conforms to the necessities of things. To understand why things must be as they must be is to will them to be so. Knowledge liberates not by offering us more open possibilities amongst which we can make our choice, but by preserving us from the frustration of attempting the impossible. To want necessary laws to be other than they are is to be prey to an irrational desire—a desire that what must be X should also be not-X. To go further, and believe these laws to be other than what they necessarily are, is to be insane. That is the metaphysical heart of rationalism. The notion of liberty contained in it is not the "negative" conception of a field (ideally) without obstacles, a vacuum in which nothing obstructs me, but the notion of self-direction or self-control. I can do what I will with my own. I am a rational being; whatever I can demonstrate to myself as being necessary, as incapable of being otherwise, in a rational society—that is, in a society directed by rational minds, towards goals such as a rational being would have—cannot, being rational, wish to sweep out of my way. I assimilate it into my substance as I do the laws of logic, of mathematics, of physics, the rules of art, the principles that govern everything of which I understand, and therefore will, the rational purpose, by which I can never be thwarted, since I cannot want it to be other than it is.

This is the positive doctrine of liberation by reason. Socialized forms of it, widely disparate and opposed to each other as they are, are at the heart of many of the nationalist, Communist, authoritarian and totalitarian creeds of our day. It may, in the course of its evolution, have wandered far from its rationalist moorings. Nevertheless, it is this freedom that, in democracies and in dictatorships, is argued about, and fought for, in many parts of the earth today. Without attempting to trace the historical evolution of this idea, I should like to comment on some of its vicissitudes.

5: The Temple of Sarastro[1]

Those who believed in freedom as rational self-direction were bound, sooner or later, to consider how this was to be applied not merely to a man's inner life, but to his relations with other members of his society. Even the most individualistic among them—and Rousseau, Kant and Fichte certainly began as individualists—came at some point to ask themselves whether a rational life not only for the individual, but also for society, was possible, and if so, how it was to be achieved. I wish to be free to live as my rational will (my "real self") commands, but so must others be. How am I to avoid collisions with their wills? Where is the frontier that lies between my (rationally determined) rights and the identical rights of others? For if I am rational, I cannot deny that what is right for me, must, for the same reasons, be right for others who are rational like me. A rational (or free) State would be a State governed by such laws as all rational men would freely accept; that is to say, such laws as they would themselves have enacted had they been asked what, as rational beings, they demanded; hence the frontiers would be such as all rational men would consider to be the right frontiers for rational beings.

But who, in fact, was to determine what these frontiers were? Thinkers of this type argued that if moral and political problems were genuine—as surely they were—they must in principle be soluble; that is to say, there must exist one and only one true solution to any problem. All truths could in principle be discovered by any rational thinker, and demonstrated so clearly that all other rational men could not but accept them; indeed, this was already to a large extent the case in the new natural sciences. On this assumption the problem of political liberty was soluble by establishing a just order that would give to each man all the freedom to which a rational being was entitled. My claim to unfettered

---

1   *Sarastro's temple in The Magic Flute*   [editors' note] The character of Sarastro in Mozart's opera *The Magic Flute* represents enlightened rational absolutist rule—for the sake of good, but despotic nevertheless.

freedom can prima facie at times not be reconciled with your equally unqualified claim; but the rational solution of one problem cannot collide with the equally true solution of another, for two truths cannot logically be incompatible; therefore a just order must in principle be discoverable—an order of which the rules make possible correct solutions to all possible problems that could arise in it. This ideal, harmonious state of affairs was sometimes imagined as a Garden of Eden before the Fall of Man, an Eden from which we were expelled, but for which we were still filled with longing; or as a golden age still before us, in which men, having become rational, will no longer be "other-directed," nor "alienate" or frustrate one another. In existing societies justice and equality are ideals which still call for some measure of coercion, because the premature lifting of social controls might lead to the oppression of the weaker and the stupider by the stronger or abler or more energetic and unscrupulous. But it is only irrationality on the part of men (according to this doctrine) that leads them to wish to oppress or exploit or humiliate one another. Rational men will respect the principle of reason in each other, and lack all desire to fight or dominate one another. The desire to dominate is itself a symptom of irrationality, and can be explained and cured by rational methods. Spinoza offers one kind of explanation and remedy, Hegel another, Marx a third. Some of these theories may perhaps, to some degree, supplement each other, others are not combinable. But they all assume that in a society of perfectly rational beings the lust for domination over men will be absent or ineffective. The existence of, or cravings for, oppression will be the first symptom that the true solution to the problems of social life has not been reached.

This can be put in another way. Freedom is self-mastery, the elimination of obstacles to my will, whatever these obstacles may be—the resistance of nature, of my ungoverned passions, of irrational institutions, of the opposing wills or behavior of others. Nature I can, at least in principle, always mold by technical means, and shape to my will. But how am I to treat recalcitrant human beings? I must, if I can, impose my will on them too, "mold" them to my pattern, cast parts for them in my play. But will this not mean that I alone am free, while they are slaves? They will be so if my plan has nothing to do with their wishes or values, only with my own. But if my plan is fully rational, it will allow for the full development of their "true" natures, the realization of their capacities for rational decisions, for "making the best of themselves"—as a part of the realization of my

own "true" self. All true solutions to all genuine problems must be compatible: more than this, they must fit into a single whole; for this is what is meant by calling them all rational and the universe harmonious. Each man has his specific character, abilities, aspirations, ends. If I grasp both what these ends and natures are, and how they all relate to one another, I can, at least in principle, if I have the knowledge and the strength, satisfy them all, so long as the nature and the purposes in question are rational. Rationality is knowing things and people for what *they* are: I must not use stones to make violins, nor try to make born violin-players play flutes. If the universe is governed by reason, then there will be no need for coercion; a correctly planned life for all will coincide with full freedom—the freedom of rational self-direction—for all. This will be so if, and only if, the plan is the true plan—the one unique pattern which alone fulfills the claims of reason. Its laws will be the rules which reason prescribes: they will only seem irksome to those whose reason is dormant, who do not understand the true "needs" of their own "real" selves. So long as each player recognizes and plays the part set him by reason—the faculty that understands his true nature and discerns his true ends there can be no conflict. Each man will be a liberated, self-directed actor in the cosmic drama. Thus Spinoza tells us that children, although they are coerced, are not slaves, because they obey orders given in their own interests, and that the subject of a true commonwealth is no slave, because the common interests must include his own.[1] Similarly, Locke says "Where there is no law there is no freedom," because rational law is a direction to a man's "proper interests" or "general good"; and adds that since law of this kind is what "hedges us in only from bogs and precipices" it "ill deserves the name of confinement,"[2]: and speaks of desires to escape from it as being irrational, forms of "license," as "brutish,"[3]: and so on. Montesquieu, forgetting his liberal moments, speaks of political liberty as being not permission to do what we want, or even what the law allows, but only "the power of doing what we ought to will,"[4] which Kant

---

1   *Thus Spinoza ... include his own*   *Tractatus Theologico-Politicus*, chapter 16: p. 137 in Benedict de Spinoza, *The Political Works*, ed. A. G. Wernham (Oxford, 1958).

2   *ill deserves confinement*   Locke, *Two Treatises of Government*, second treatise, § 57.

3   *brutish*   Ibid., §§ 6, 163.

4   *the power of doing ... ought to will*   De l'esprit des lois, book 2, chapter 3: p. 205 in *Oeuvres completes de Montesquieu*, ed. A. Masson (Paris, 1950–1955), vol. 1 A. [Baron de Montesquieu (1689–1755), French writer and legal theorist.]

virtually repeats. Burke proclaims the individual's "right" to be restrained in his own interest, because "the presumed consent of every rational creature is in unison with the pre-disposed order of things."[1]

The common assumption of these thinkers (and of many a schoolman before them and Jacobin and Communist after them) is that the rational ends of our "true" natures must coincide, or be made to coincide, however violently our poor, ignorant, desire-ridden, passionate, empirical selves may cry out against this process. Freedom is not freedom to do what is irrational, or stupid, or wrong. To force empirical selves into the right pattern is no tyranny, but liberation.[2] Rousseau tells me that if I freely surrender all the parts of my life to society, I create an entity which, because it has been built by an equality of sacrifice of all its members, can-not wish to hurt anyone of them; in such a society, we are informed, it can be in nobody's interest to damage anyone else. "In giving myself to all, I give myself to none,"[3] and get back as much as I lose, with enough new force to pre-serve my new gains. Kant tells us that when "the individual has entirely abandoned his wild, lawless freedom, to find it again, unimpaired, in a state of dependence according to law," that alone is true freedom, "for this dependence is the work of my own will acting as a lawgiver."[4] Liberty, so far from being incompatible with authority, becomes virtu-ally identical with it. This is the thought and language of all the declarations of the rights of man in the eighteenth century, and of all those who look upon society as a design constructed according to the rational laws of the wise law-giver, or of nature, or of history, or of the Supreme Being. Bentham, almost alone, doggedly went on repeating that

the business of laws was not to liberate but to restrain: every law is an infraction of liberty[5]—even if such infraction leads to an increase of the sum of liberty.

If the underlying assumptions had been correct—if the method of solving social problems resembled the way in which solutions to the problems of the natural sciences are found, and if reason were what rationalists said that it was—all this would perhaps follow. In the ideal case, lib-erty coincides with law: autonomy with authority. A law which forbids me to do what I could not, as a sane being, conceivably wish to do is not a restraint of my freedom. In the ideal society, composed of wholly responsible beings, rules, because I should scarcely be conscious of them, would gradually wither away. Only one social movement was bold enough to render this assumption quite explicit and accept its consequences—that of the Anarchists. But all forms of liberalism founded on a rationalist metaphysics are less or more watered-down versions of this creed.

In due course, the thinkers who bent their energies to the solution of the problem on these lines came to be faced with the question of how in practice men were to be made rational in this way. Clearly they must be educated. For the uneducated are irrational, heteronomous, and need to be coerced, if only to make life tolerable for the rational if they are to live in the same society and not be compelled to withdraw to a desert or some Olympian height. But the uneducated cannot be expected to understand or co-operate with the purposes of their educators. Education, says Fichte, must inevitably work in such a way that "you will later recog-nize the reasons for what I am doing now."[6] Children cannot be expected to understand why they are compelled to go to school, nor the ignorant—that is, for the moment, the majority of mankind—why they are made to obey the laws that will presently make them rational. "Compulsion is also a kind of education."[7] You learn the great virtue of obedi-ence to superior persons. If you cannot understand your own interests as a rational being, I cannot be expected to consult you, or abide by your wishes, in the course of making you rational. I must, in the end, force you to be protected against smallpox, even though you may not wish it. Even Mill is prepared to say that I may forcibly prevent a man from cross-ing a bridge if there is not time to warn him that it is about

1 *the presumed consent ... things* *Appeal from the Old to the New Whigs* (1791): pp. 93–94 in *The Works of the Right Honourable Edmund Burke* (World's Classics edition), vol. 5 (London, 1907).

2 *To force empirical selves ... but liberation* On this Bentham seems to me to have said the last word: "The liberty of doing evil, is it not liberty? If it is not liberty, what is it then? ... Do we not say that liberty should be taken away from fools, and wicked persons, because they abuse it?" *The Works of Jeremy Bentham*, ed. John Bowring (Edinburgh, 1843), vol. I, p. 301. Compare with this the view of the Jacobins in the same period, discussed by Crane Brinton in "Political Ideas in the Jacobin Clubs," *Political Science Quarterly* 43 (1928), pp. 249–64, esp. 257: "no man is free in doing evil. To prevent him is to free him." This view is echoed in almost identical terms by British Idealists at the end of the fol-lowing century.

3 *In giving myself ... myself to none* *Social Contract*, book 1, chapter 6: vol. 3, p. 361 in *Oeuvres completes* op. cit.

4 *for this dependence ... acting as a lawgiver* Vol. 6, p. 316, line 2.

5 *every law is an infraction of liberty* [*The Works of Jeremy Bentham*, vol. 1, p. 301]; Ibid.: "every law is contrary to liberty."

6 *you will later ... I am doing now* Johann Gottlieb Fichte's *Säm-mtliche Werke*, ed. I.H. Fichte (Berlin, 1845–6), vol. 7, p. 576.

7 *Compulsion is also a kind of education* Ibid., p. 574.

to collapse, for I know, or am justified in assuming, that he cannot wish to fall into the water. Fichte knows what the uneducated German of his time wishes to be or do better than he can possibly know this for himself. The sage knows you better than you know yourself, for you are the victim of your passions, a slave living a heteronomous life, purblind, unable to understand your true goals. You want to be a human being. It is the aim of the State to satisfy your wish. "Compulsion is justified by education for future insight."[1] The reason within me, if it is to triumph, must eliminate and suppress my "lower" instincts, my passions and desires, which render me a slave; similarly (the fatal transition from individual to social concepts is almost imperceptible) the higher elements in society—the better educated, the more rational, those who "possess the highest insight of their time and people"[2]—may exercise compulsion to rationalize the irrational section of society. For—so Hegel, Bradley, Bosanquet[3] have often assured us—by obeying the rational man we obey ourselves: not indeed as we are, sunk in our ignorance and our passions, weak creatures afflicted by diseases that need a healer, wards who require a guardian, but as we could be if we were rational; as we could be even now, if only we would listen to the rational element which is, *ex hypothesi*, within every human being who deserves the name.

The philosophers of "Objective Reason," from the tough, rigidly centralized, "organic" State of Fichte, to the mild and humane liberalism of T.H. Green,[4] certainly supposed themselves to be fulfilling, and not resisting, the rational demands which, however inchoate, were to be found in the breast of every sentient being.

But I may reject such democratic optimism, and turning away from the teleological determinism of the Hegelians towards some more voluntarist philosophy, conceive the idea of imposing on my society—for its own betterment—a plan of my own, which in my rational wisdom I have elaborated; and which, unless I act on my own, perhaps against the permanent wishes of the vast majority of my fellow citizens, may never come to fruition at all. Or, abandoning the concept of reason altogether, I may conceive myself as an inspired artist, who molds men into patterns in the light of his unique vision, as painters combine colors or composers sounds; humanity is the raw material upon which I impose my creative will; even though men suffer and die in the process, they are lifted by it to a height to which they could never have risen without my coercive—but creative—violation of their lives. This is the argument used by every dictator, inquisitor and bully who seeks some moral, or even aesthetic, justification for his conduct. I must do for men (or with them) what they cannot do for themselves, and I cannot ask their permission or consent, because they are in no condition to know what is best for them; indeed, what they will permit and accept may mean a life of contemptible mediocrity, or perhaps even their ruin and suicide. Let me quote from the true progenitor of the heroic doctrine, Fichte, once again: "No one has ... rights against reason." "Man is afraid of subordinating his subjectivity to the laws of reason. He prefers tradition or arbitrariness."[5] Nevertheless, subordinated he must be.[6] Fichte puts forward the claims of what he called reason; Napoleon, or Carlyle,[7] or romantic authoritarians may worship other values, and see in their establishment by force the only path to "true" freedom.

The same attitude was pointedly expressed by August Comte,[8] who asked why, if we do not allow free thinking in chemistry or biology, we should allow it in morals or politics. Why indeed? If it makes sense to speak of political truths—assertions of social ends which all men, because they are men, must, once they are discovered, agree to be such; and if, as Comte believed, scientific method will in due course reveal them; then what case is there for freedom of opinion or action—at least as an end in itself, and not merely as a stimulating intellectual climate—either for individuals or for groups? Why should any conduct be tolerated that is not authorized by appropriate experts? Comte put bluntly what had been implicit in the rationalist theory of politics from its ancient Greek beginnings. There can, in principle, be only one correct way of life; the wise lead it

---

1 *Compulsion is justified ... future insight* Ibid., p. 578.

2 *possess the highest insight ... time and people* Ibid., p. 576.

3 *Bradley, Bosanquet* [editors' note] F.H. Bradley (1846–1924) and Bernard Bosanquet (1848–1923), were leading British Idealists; this movement, which rejected the influence of Hume and Mill in favor of Kant and Hegel, dominated British philosophy at the end of the nineteenth century.

4 *T.H. Green* [editors' note] Thomas Hill Green (1836–82), political philosopher and reformer, another British Idealist.

5 *Man is afraid ... tradition or arbitrariness* Ibid., pp. 578, 580.

6 *Nevertheless, subordinated he must be* "To compel men to adopt the right form of government, to impose Right on them by force, is not only the right, but the sacred duty of every man who has both the insight and the power to do so." Ibid., vol. 4, p. 436.

7 *Carlyle* [editors' note] Thomas Carlyle (1795–1881) was a Scottish essayist and historian, and an influential Victorian social critic.

8 *August Comte* [editors' note] Auguste Comte (1798–1857), French positivist philosopher, who was a founder of sociology.

spontaneously, that is why they are called wise. The unwise must be dragged towards it by all the social means in the power of the wise; for why should demonstrable error be suffered to survive and breed? The immature and untutored must be made to say to themselves: "Only the truth liberates, and the only way in which I can learn the truth is by doing blindly today what you, who know it, order me, or coerce me, to do, in the certain knowledge that only thus will I arrive at your clear vision; and be free like you."

We have wandered indeed from our liberal beginnings. This argument, employed by Fichte in his latest phase, and after him by other defenders of authority, from Victorian schoolmasters and colonial administrators to the latest nationalist or Communist dictator, is precisely what the Stoic and Kantian morality protests against most bitterly in the name of the reason of the free individual following his own inner light. In this way the rationalist argument, with its assumption of the single true solution, has led by steps which, if not logically valid, are historically and psychologically intelligible from an ethical doctrine of individual responsibility and individual self-perfection to an authoritarian State obedient to the directives of an elite of Platonic guardians.

What can have led to so strange a reversal—the transformation of Kant's severe individualism into something close to a pure totalitarian doctrine on the part of thinkers some of whom claimed to be his disciples? This question is not of merely historical interest, for not a few contemporary liberals have gone through the same peculiar evolution. It is true that Kant insisted, following Rousseau, that a capacity for rational self-direction belonged to all men; that there could be no experts in moral matters, since morality was a matter not of specialized knowledge (as the Utilitarians and *philosophes*[1] had maintained), but of the correct use of a universal human faculty; and consequently that what made men free was not acting in certain self-improving ways, which they could be coerced to do, but knowing why they ought to do so, which nobody could do for, or on behalf of, anyone else. But even Kant, when he came to deal with political issues, conceded that no law, provided that it was such that I should, if I were asked, approve it as a rational being, could possibly deprive me of any portion of my rational freedom. With this the door was opened wide to the rule of experts. I cannot consult all men about all enactments all the time. The government cannot be a continuous plebiscite. Moreover, some men are not as well attuned to the voice of their own reason as others: some seem singularly deaf. If I am a legislator or a ruler, I must assume that if the law I impose is rational (and I can consult only my own reason) it will automatically be approved by all the members of my society so far as they are rational beings. For if they disapprove, they must, *pro tanto*, be irrational; then they will need to be repressed by reason: whether their own or mine cannot matter, for the pronouncements of reason must be the same in all minds. I issue my orders and, if you resist, take it upon myself to repress the irrational element in you which opposes reason. My task would be easier if you repressed it in yourself; I try to educate you to do so. But I am responsible for public welfare, I cannot wait until all men are wholly rational. Kant may protest that the essence of the subject's freedom is that he, and he alone, has given himself the order to obey. But this is a counsel of perfection. If you fail to discipline yourself, I must do so for you; and you cannot complain of lack of freedom, for the fact that Kant's rational judge has sent you to prison is evidence that you have not listened to your own inner reason, that, like a child, a savage, an idiot, you are either not ripe for self-direction, or permanently incapable of it.[2]

---

1   *philosophes*   [editors' note] (French: philosophers) Thinkers and writers of eighteenth-century France who shared a faith in human reason; in science; in open-minded secular thought; and in the ideals of the Enlightenment. These included Voltaire, Montesquieu, Diderot, d'Alembert, and Rousseau.

2   *If you fail ... incapable of it*   Kant came nearest to asserting the "negative" ideal of liberty when (in one of his political treatises) he declared that "The greatest problem of the human race, to the solution of which it is compelled by nature, is the establishment of a civil society universally administering right according to law. It is only in a society which possesses the greatest liberty ... and also the most exact determination and guarantee of the limits of [the] liberty [of each individual] in order that it may co-exist with the liberty of others—that the highest purpose of nature, which is the development of all her capacities, can be attained in the case of mankind." "Idee zu einer allgemeinen Geschichte in weltburgerlicher Absicht" [Idea for a Universal History from a Cosmopolitan Point of View] (1784), in vol. 8, p. 22, line 6. Apart from the teleological implications, this formulation does not at first appear very different from orthodox liberalism. The crucial point, however, is how to determine the criterion for the "exact determination and guarantee of the limits" of individual liberty. Most modern liberals, at their most consistent, want a situation in which as many individuals as possible can realize as many of their ends as possible, without assessment of the value of these ends as such, save in so far as they may frustrate the purposes of others. They wish the frontiers between individuals or groups of men to be drawn solely with a view to preventing collisions between human purposes, all of which must be considered to be equally ultimate, uncriticizable ends in themselves. Kant, and the

If this leads to despotism, albeit by the best or the wisest—to Sarastro's temple in The Magic Flute—but still despotism, which turns out to be identical with freedom, can it be that there is something amiss in the premises of the argument? That the basic assumptions are themselves somewhere at fault? Let me state them once more: first, that all men have one true purpose, and one only; that of rational self-direction; second, that the ends of all rational beings must of necessity fit into single universal, harmonious pattern, which some men may be able to discern more clearly than others; third, that all conflict, and consequently all tragedy, is due solely to the clash of reason with the rational or the insufficiently rational—the immature and undeveloped elements in life, whether individual or communal—and that such clashes are, in principle, avoidable, and for wholly rational beings impossible; finally, that when all men have been made rational, they will obey the rational laws of their own natures, which are one and the same in them all; and so be at once wholly law-abiding and wholly free. Can it be that Socrates and the creators of the central Western tradition in ethics and politics who followed him have been mistaken, for more than two millennia, that virtue is not knowledge, nor freedom identical with either? That despite the fact that it rules the lives of more men than ever before in its long history, not one of the basic assumptions of this famous view is demonstrable, or, perhaps, even true?

6: The search for status

There is yet another historically important approach to this topic, which, by confounding liberty with her sisters, equality and fraternity, leads to similarly illiberal conclusions. Ever since the issue was raised towards the end of the eighteenth century, the question of what is meant by "an individual" has been asked persistently, and with increasing effect. In so far as I live in society, everything that I do inevitably affects, and is affected by, what others do. Even Mill's strenuous effort to mark the distinction between the spheres of private and social life breaks down under examination. Virtually all Mill's critics have pointed out that everything that I do may have results which will harm other human beings. Moreover, I am a social being in a deeper sense than that of interaction with others. For am I not what I am, to some degree, in virtue of what others think and feel me to be? When I ask myself what I am, and answer: an Englishman, a Chinese, a merchant, a man of no importance, a millionaire, a convict—I find upon analysis that to possess these attributes entails being recognized as belonging to a particular group or class by other persons in my society, and that this recognition is part of the meaning of most of the terms that denote some of my most personal and permanent characteristics. I am not disembodied reason. Nor am I Robinson Crusoe,[1] alone upon his island. It is not only that my material life depends upon interaction with other men, or that I am what I am, as a result of social forces, but that some, perhaps all, of my ideas about myself, in particular my sense of my own moral and social identity, are intelligible only in terms of the social network in which I am (the metaphor must not be pressed too far) an element.

The lack of freedom about which men or groups complain amounts, as often as not, to the lack of proper recognition. I may be seeking not for what Mill would wish me to seek, namely security from coercion, arbitrary arrest, tyranny, deprivation of certain opportunities of action, or for room within which I am legally accountable to no one for my movements. Equally, I may not be seeking for a rational plan of social life, or the self-perfection of a dispassionate sage. What I may seek to avoid is simply being ignored, or patronized, or despised, or being taken too much for granted—in short, not being treated as an individual, having my uniqueness insufficiently recognized, being classed as a member of some featureless amalgam, a statistical unit

---

rationalists of his type, do not regard all ends as of equal value. For them the limits of liberty are determined by applying the rules of "reason," which is much more than the mere generality of rules as such, and is a faculty that creates or reveals a purpose identical in, and for, all men. In the name of reason anything that is non-rational may be condemned, so that the various personal aims which their individual imaginations and idiosyncrasies lead men to pursue —for example, aesthetic and other non-rational kinds of self-fulfillment—may, at least in theory, be ruthlessly suppressed to make way for the demands of reason. The authority of reason and of the duties it lays upon men is identified with individual freedom, on the assumption that only rational ends can be the "true" objects of a "free" man's "real" nature.

I have never, I must own, understood what "reason" means in this context; and here merely wish to point out that the a priori assumptions of this philosophical psychology are not compatible with empiricism: that is to say, with any doctrine founded on knowledge derived from experience of what men are and seek.

1   *Robinson Crusoe*   [editors' note] In the novel of that title, written by Daniel Defoe, and first published in 1719, the title character is cast away on a tropical island. His traveling companions are all dead, and he is initially alone on the island; this is the image most people have of this story. But in fact he encounters many other characters as the novel progresses.

without identifiable, specifically human features and purposes of my own. This is the degradation that I am fighting against—I am not seeking equality of legal rights, nor liberty to do as I wish (although I may want these too), but a condition in which I can feel that I am, because I am taken to be, a responsible agent, whose will is taken into consideration because I am entitled to it, even if I am attacked and persecuted for being what I am or choosing as I do.

This is a hankering after status and recognition: "The poorest he that is in England hath a life to live as the greatest he."[1] I desire to be understood and recognized, even if this means to be unpopular and disliked. And the only persons who can so recognize me, and thereby give me the sense of being someone, are the members of the society to which, historically, morally, economically, and perhaps ethnically, I feel that I belong.[2] My individual self is not something which I can detach from my relationship with others, or from those attributes of myself which consist in their attitude towards me. Consequently, when I demand to be liberated from, let us say, the status of political or social dependence, what I demand is an alteration of the attitude towards me of those whose opinions and behavior help to determine my own image of myself.

And what is true of the individual is true of groups, social, political, economic, religious, that is, of men conscious of needs and purposes which they have as members of such groups. What oppressed classes or nationalities, as a rule, demand is neither simply unhampered liberty of action for their members, nor, above everything, equality of social or economic opportunity, still less assignment of a place in a frictionless, organic State devised by the rational lawgiver. What they want, as often as not, is simply recognition (of their class or nation, or color or race) as an independent source of human activity, as an entity with a will of its own, intending to act in accordance with it (whether it is good or legitimate, or not), and not to be ruled, educated, guided, with however light a hand, as being not quite fully human, and therefore not quite fully free.

This gives a far wider than a purely rationalist sense to Kant's remark that paternalism is "the greatest despotism imaginable."[3] Paternalism is despotic, not because it is more oppressive than naked, brutal, unenlightened tyranny, nor merely because it ignores the transcendental reason embodied in me, but because it is an insult to my conception of myself as a human being, determined to make my own life in accordance with my own (not necessarily rational or benevolent) purposes, and, above all, entitled to be recognized as such by others. For if I am not so recognized, then I may fail to recognize, I may doubt, my own claim to be a fully independent human being. For what I am is, in large part, determined by what I feel and think; and what I feel and think is determined by the feeling and thought prevailing in the society to which I belong, of which, in Burke's sense, I form not an isolable atom, but an ingredient (to use a perilous but indispensable metaphor) in a social pattern. I may feel unfree in the sense of not being recognized as a self-governing individual human being; but I may feel it also as a member of an unrecognized or insufficiently respected group: then I wish for the emancipation of my entire class, or community, or nation, or race, or profession. So much can I desire this, that I may, in my bitter longing for status, prefer to be bullied and misgoverned by some member of my own race or social class, by whom I am, nevertheless, recognized as a man and a rival—that is, as an equal—to being well and tolerantly treated by someone from some higher and remoter group, someone who does not recognize me for what I wish to feel myself to be.

This is the heart of the great cry for recognition on the part of both individuals and groups, and, in our own day, of professions and classes, nations and races. Although I may not get "negative" liberty at the hands of the members of my own society, yet they are members of my own

---

1   *The poorest ... the greatest he*   [editors' note] Thomas Rainborow, speaking at Putney in 1647: p. 301 in *The Clarke Papers: Selections from the Papers of William Clarke*, ed. C.H. Firth, vol. 1 (London, 1891).

2   *And the only persons ... belong*   This has an obvious affinity with Kant's doctrine of human freedom; but it is a socialized and empirical version of it, and therefore almost its opposite. Kant's free man needs no public recognition for his inner freedom. If he is treated as a means to some external purpose, that is a wrong action on the part of his exploiters, but his own "noumenal" status is untouched, and he is fully free, and fully a man, however he may be treated. The need spoken of here is bound up wholly with the relation that I have with others; I am nothing if I am unrecognized. I cannot ignore the attitude of others with Byronic disdain, fully conscious of my own intrinsic worth and vocation, or escape into my inner life, for I am in my own eyes as others see me. I identify myself with the point of view of my milieu: I feel myself to be somebody or nobody in terms of my position and function in the social whole; this is the most "heteronomous" condition imaginable.

3   *Kant's remark that paternalism is "the greatest despotism imaginable."*   Found in his essay "On the common saying: That may be correct in theory, but it is of no use in practice" [8:290–1].

group; they understand me, as I understand them; and this understanding creates within me the sense of being somebody in the world. It is this desire for reciprocal recognition that leads the most authoritarian democracies to be, at times, consciously preferred by their members to the most enlightened oligarchies, or sometimes causes a member of some newly liberated Asian or African State to complain less today, when he is rudely treated by members of his own race or nation, than when he was governed by some cautious, just, gentle, well-meaning administrator from outside. Unless this phenomenon is grasped, the ideals and behavior of entire peoples who, in Mill's sense of the word, suffer deprivation of elementary human rights, and who, with every appearance of sincerity, speak of enjoying more freedom than when they possessed a wider measure of these rights, become an unintelligible paradox.

Yet it is not with individual liberty, in either the "negative" or the "positive" sense of the word, that this desire for status and recognition can easily be identified. It is something no less profoundly needed and passionately fought for by human beings—it is something akin to, but not itself, freedom; although it entails negative freedom for the entire group, it is more closely related to solidarity, fraternity, mutual understanding, need for association on equal terms, all of which are sometimes—but misleadingly—called social freedom. Social and political terms are necessarily vague. The attempt to make the vocabulary of politics too precise may render it useless. But it is no service to the truth to loosen usage beyond necessity. The essence of the notion of liberty, in both the "positive" and the "negative" senses, is the holding off of something or someone—of others who trespass on my field or assert their authority over me, or of obsessions, fears, neuroses, irrational forces—intruders and despots of one kind or another. The desire for recognition is a desire for something different: for union, closer understanding, integration of interests, a life of common dependence and common sacrifice. It is only the confusion of desire for liberty with this profound and universal craving for status and understanding, further confounded by being identified with the notion of social self-direction, where the self to be liberated is no longer the individual but the "social whole," that makes it possible for men, while submitting to the authority of oligarchs or dictators, to claim that this in some sense liberates them.

Much has been written on the fallacy of regarding social groups as being literally persons or selves, whose control and discipline of their members is no more than self-discipline, voluntary self-control which leaves the individual agent free. But even on the "organic" view, would it be natural or desirable to call the demand for recognition and status a demand for liberty in some third sense? It is true that the group from which recognition is sought must itself have a sufficient measure of "negative" freedom—from control by any outside authority—otherwise recognition by it will not give the claimant the status he seeks. But is the struggle for higher status, the wish to escape from an inferior position, to be called a struggle for liberty? Is it mere pedantry to confine this word to the main senses discussed above, or are we, as I suspect, in danger of calling any improvement of his social situation favored by a human being an increase of his liberty, and will this not render this term so vague and distended as to make it virtually useless? And yet we cannot simply dismiss this case as a mere confusion of the notion of freedom with that of status, or solidarity, or fraternity, or equality, or some combination of these. For the craving for status is, in certain respects, very close to the desire to be an independent agent.

We may refuse this goal the title of liberty; yet it would be a shallow view that assumed that analogies between individuals and groups, or organic metaphors, or several senses of the word "liberty," are mere fallacies, due either to assertions of likeness between entities in respects in which they are unlike, or simple semantic confusion. What is wanted by those who are prepared to barter their own and others' liberty of individual action for the status of their group, and their own status within the group, is not simply a surrender of liberty for the sake of security, of some assured place in a harmonious hierarchy in which all men and all classes know their place, and are prepared to exchange the painful privilege of choosing—"the burden of freedom"—for the peace and comfort and relative mindlessness of an authoritarian or totalitarian structure. No doubt there are such men and such desires, and no doubt such surrenders of individual liberty can occur, and, indeed, have often occurred. But it is a profound misunderstanding of the temper of our times to assume that this is what makes nationalism or Marxism attractive to nations which have been ruled by alien masters, or to classes whose lives were directed by other classes in a semi-feudal, or some other hierarchically organized regime. What they seek is more akin to what Mill called "Pagan self-assertion,"[1] but in a collective, socialized form. Indeed, much of what he says about his own reasons for desiring liberty—the value that he puts on boldness and non-con-

---

1   *Pagan self-assertion*   Following Sterling.

formity, on the assertion of the individual's own values in the face of the prevailing opinion, on strong and self-reliant personalities free from the leading-strings of the official lawgivers and instructors of society—has little enough to do with his conception of freedom as non-interference, but a great deal with the desire of men not to have their personalities set at too low a value, assumed to be incapable of autonomous, original, "authentic" behavior, even if such behavior is to be met with opprobrium, or social restrictions, or inhibitive legislation.

This wish to assert the "personality" of my class, or group or nation, is connected both with the answer to the question "What is to be the area of authority?" (for the group must not be interfered with by outside masters), and, even more closely, with the answer to the question "Who is to govern us?"—govern well or badly, liberally or oppressively, but above all "Who?" And such answers as "Representatives elected by my own and others' untrammeled choice," or "All of us gathered together in regular assemblies," or "The best," or "The wisest," or "The nation as embodied in these or those persons or institutions," or "The divine leader" are answers that are logically, and at times also politically and socially, independent of what extent of "negative" liberty I demand for my own or my group's activities. Provided the answer to "Who shall govern me?" is somebody or something which I can represent as "my own," as something which belongs to me, or to whom I belong, I can, by using words which convey fraternity and solidarity, as well as some part of the connotation of the "positive" sense of the word "freedom" (which it is difficult to specify more precisely), describe it as a hybrid form of freedom; at any rate as an ideal which is perhaps more prominent than any other in the world today, yet one which no existing term seems precisely to fit. Those who purchase it at the price of their "negative," Millian freedom certainly claim to be "liberated" by this means, in this confused, but ardently felt, sense. "Whose service is perfect freedom" can in this way be secularized, and the State, or the nation, or the race, or an assembly, or a dictator, or my family or milieu, or I myself, can be substituted for the Deity, without thereby rendering the word "freedom" wholly meaningless.[1]

No doubt every interpretation of the word "liberty," however unusual, must include a minimum of what I have called "negative" liberty. There must be an area within which I am not frustrated. No society literally suppresses all the liberties of its members; a being who is prevented by others from doing anything at all on his own is not a moral agent at all, and could not either legally or morally be regarded as a human being, even if a physiologist or a biologist, or even a psychologist, felt inclined to classify him as a man. But the fathers of liberalism—Mill and Constant—want more than this minimum: they demand a maximum degree of noninterference compatible with the minimum demands of social life. It seems unlikely that this extreme demand for liberty has ever been made by any but a small minority of highly civilized and self-conscious human beings. The bulk of humanity has certainly at most times been prepared to sacrifice this to other goals: security, status, prosperity, power, virtue, rewards in the next world; or justice, equality, fraternity, and many other values which appear wholly, or in part, incompatible with the attainment of the greatest degree of individual liberty, and certainly do not need it as a precondition for their own realization. It is not a demand for *Lebensraum*[2] for each individual that has stimulated the rebellions and wars of liberation for which men have been ready to die in the past, or, indeed, in the present. Men who have fought for freedom have commonly fought for the right to be governed by themselves or their representatives—sternly governed, if need be, like the Spartans, with little individual liberty, but in a manner which allowed

---

1   *Whose service is perfect freedom ... word "freedom" wholly meaningless*   This argument should be distinguished from the traditional approach of some of the disciples of Burke or Hegel, who say that, since I am made what I am by society or history, to escape from them is impossible and to attempt it irrational. No doubt I cannot leap out of my skin, or breathe outside my proper element; it is

a mere tautology to say that I am what I am, and cannot want to be liberated from my essential characteristics, some of which are social. But it does not follow that all my attributes are intrinsic and inalienable, and that I cannot seek to alter my status within the "social network," or "cosmic web," which determines my nature; if this were the case, no meaning could be attached to such words as "choice" or "decision" or "activity." If they are to mean anything, attempts to protect myself against authority, or even to escape from my "station and its duties," cannot be excluded as automatically irrational or suicidal. [editors' note] The quotation "whose service is perfect freedom" is from the Collect for Peace in the Anglican *Book of Common Prayer*; this line from a frequently recited prayer would be familiar to all traditional Anglicans.

2   *Lebensraum*   [editors' note] German: living space. The primary association with this term is its use by Hitler: Lebensraum was a central plank in the Nazi policy, and referred to the German need for land and natural resources, a putative justification for international expansion, taking over territory from neighboring "inferior races." Berlin is using this term more generally, meaning adequate "space" in a broad sense for living, developing, functioning.

them to participate, or at any rate to believe that they were participating, in the legislation and administration of their collective lives. And men who have made revolutions have, as often as not, meant by liberty no more than the conquest of power and authority by a given sect of believers in a doctrine, or by a class, or by some other social group, old or new. Their victories certainly frustrated those whom they ousted, and sometimes repressed, enslaved or exterminated vast numbers of human beings. Yet such revolutionaries have usually felt it necessary to argue that, despite this, they represented the party of liberty, or "true" liberty, by claiming universality for their ideal, which the "real selves" of even those who resisted them were also alleged to be seeking, although they were held to have lost the way to the goal, or to have mistaken the goal itself owing to some moral or spiritual blindness. All this has little to do with Mill's notion of liberty as limited only by the danger of doing harm to others. It is the non-recognition of this psychological and political fact (which lurks behind the apparent ambiguity of the term 'liberty') that has, perhaps, blinded some contemporary liberals to the world in which they live. Their plea is clear, their cause is just. But they do not allow for the variety of basic human needs. Nor yet for the ingenuity with which men can prove to their own satisfaction that the road to one ideal also leads to its contrary.

7: Liberty and sovereignty

The French Revolution, like all great revolutions, was, at least in its Jacobin form, just such an eruption of the desire for "positive" freedom of collective self-direction on the part of a large body of Frenchmen who felt liberated as a nation, even though the result was, for a good many of them, a severe restriction of individual freedoms. Rousseau had spoken exultantly of the fact that the laws of liberty might prove to be more austere than the yoke of tyranny. Tyranny is service to human masters. The law cannot be a tyrant. Rousseau does not mean by liberty the "negative" freedom of the individual not to be interfered with within a defined area, but the possession by all, and not merely by some, of the fully qualified members of a society of a share in the public power which is entitled to interfere with every aspect of every citizen's life. The liberals of the first half of the nineteenth century correctly foresaw that liberty in this "positive" sense could easily destroy too many of the "negative" liberties that they held sacred. They pointed out that the sovereignty of the people could easily destroy that of in-

dividuals. Mill explained, patiently and unanswerably, that government by the people was not, in his sense, necessarily freedom at all. For those who govern are not necessarily the same "people" as those who are governed, and democratic self-government is not the government "of each by himself," but, at best, "of each by all the rest."[1] Mill and his disciples spoke of "the tyranny of the majority" and of the tyranny of "the prevailing opinion and feeling,"[2] and saw no great difference between that and any other kind of tyranny which encroaches upon men's activities beyond the sacred frontiers of private life.

No one saw the conflict between the two types of liberty better, or expressed it more clearly, than Benjamin Constant. He pointed out that the transference by a successful rising of unlimited authority, commonly called sovereignty, from one set of hands to another does not increase liberty, but merely shifts the burden of slavery. He reasonably asked why a man should deeply care whether he is crushed by a popular government or by a monarch, or even by a set of oppressive laws. He saw that the main problem for those who desire "negative," individual freedom is not who wields this authority, but how much authority should be placed in any set of hands. For unlimited authority in anybody's grasp was bound, he believed, sooner or later, to destroy somebody. He maintained that usually men protested against this or that set of governors as oppressive, when the real cause of oppression lay in the mere fact of the accumulation of power itself, wherever it might happen to be, since liberty was endangered by the mere existence of absolute authority as such. "It is not against the arm that one must rail," he wrote, "but against the weapon. Some weights are too heavy for the human hand."[3] Democracy may disarm a given oligarchy, a given privileged individual or set of individuals, but it can still crush individuals as mercilessly as any previous ruler. An equal right to oppress—or interfere—is not equivalent to liberty. Nor does universal consent to loss of liberty somehow miraculously preserve it merely by being universal, or by being consent. If I consent to be oppressed, or acquiesce in my condition with detachment or irony, am I the less oppressed? If I sell myself into slavery, am I the less a slave?

---

1   *of each by all the rest*   John Stuart Mill, *On Liberty*, p. 219.

2   *Mill and his disciples ... opinion and feeling*   Ibid., pp. 219–20.

3   *It is not against the arm ... human hand*   *De l'esprit de conquête et de l'usurpation dans leur rapports avec la civilisation européenne* in Benjamin Constant, *Écrits politiques*, ed. Marcel Gauchet (Paris, 1997), p. 312.

If I commit suicide, am I the less dead because I have taken my own life freely? "Popular government is merely a spasmodic tyranny, monarchy a more centralized despotism."[1] Constant saw in Rousseau the most dangerous enemy of individual liberty, because he had declared that "In giving myself to all, I give myself to none."[2] Constant could not see why, even though the sovereign is "everybody," it should not oppress one of the "members" of its indivisible self, if it so decided. I may, of course, prefer to be deprived of my liberties by an assembly, or a family, or a class in which I am a minority. It may give me an opportunity one day of persuading the others to do for me that to which I feel I am entitled. But to be deprived of my liberty at the hands of my family or friends or fellow citizens is to be deprived of it just as effectively. Hobbes was at any rate more candid: he did not pretend that a sovereign does not enslave; he justified this slavery, but at least did not have the effrontery to call it freedom.

Throughout the nineteenth century liberal thinkers maintained that if liberty involved a limit upon the powers of any man to force me to do what I did not, or might not, wish to do, then, whatever the ideal in the name of which I was coerced, I was not free; that the doctrine of absolute sovereignty was a tyrannical doctrine in itself. If I wish to preserve my liberty it is not enough to say that it must not be violated unless someone or other—the absolute ruler, or the popular assembly, or the King in Parliament, or the judges, or some combination of authorities, or the laws themselves (for the laws may be oppressive)—authorizes its violation. I must establish a society in which there must be some frontiers of freedom which nobody should be permitted to cross. Different names or natures may be given to the rules that determine these frontiers: they may be called natural rights, or the word of God, or natural law, or the demands of utility or of the "permanent interests of man."[3] I may believe them to be valid a priori, or assert them to be my own ultimate ends, or the ends of my society or culture. What these rules or commandments will have in common is that they are accepted so widely, and are grounded so deeply in the actual nature of men as they have developed through history, as to be, by now, an essential part of what we mean by being a normal human being. Genuine belief

in the inviolability of a minimum extent of individual liberty entails some such absolute stand. For it is clear that it has little to hope for from the rule of majorities; democracy as such is logically uncommitted to it, and historically has at times failed to protect it, while remaining faithful to its own principles. Few governments, it has been observed, have found much difficulty in causing their subjects to generate any will that the government wanted. The triumph of despotism is to force the slaves to declare themselves free. It may need no force; the slaves may proclaim their freedom quite sincerely: but they are none the less slaves. Perhaps the chief value for liberals of political —"positive"—rights, of participating in the government, is as a means for protecting what they hold to be an ultimate value, namely individual—"negative"—liberty.

But if democracies can, without ceasing to be democratic, suppress freedom, at least as liberals have used the word, what would make a society truly free? For Constant, Mill, Tocqueville, and the liberal tradition to which they belong, no society is free unless it is governed by at any rate two interrelated principles: first, that no power, but only rights, can be regarded as absolute, so that all men, whatever power governs them, have an absolute right to refuse to behave inhumanly; and, second, that there are frontiers, not artificially drawn, within which men should be inviolable, these frontiers being defined in terms of rules so long and widely accepted that their observance has entered into the very conception of what it is to be a normal human being, and, therefore, also of what it is to act inhumanly or insanely; rules of which it would be absurd to say, for example, that they could be abrogated by some formal procedure on the part of some court or sovereign body. When I speak of a man as being normal, a part of what I mean is that he could not break these rules easily, without a qualm of revulsion. It is such rules as these that are broken when a man is declared guilty without trial, or punished under a retroactive law; when children are ordered to denounce their parents, friends to betray one another, soldiers to use methods of barbarism; when men are tortured or murdered, or minorities are massacred because they irritate a majority or a tyrant. Such acts, even if they are made legal by the sovereign, cause horror even in these days, and this springs from the recognition of the moral validity—irrespective of the laws—of some absolute barriers to the imposition of one man's will on another. The freedom of a society, or a class or a group, in this sense of freedom, is measured by the strength of these barriers, and the number and importance

---

1 *Popular government ... centralized despotism* Ibid., p. 316.
2 *In giving myself ... myself to none* Rousseau, *Social Contract*, book 1, chapter 6: vol 3, p. 361; cf. Constant, *Principes de politique*, p. 313.
3 *permanent interests of man* Mill, [*On Liberty*] p. 224.

of the paths which they keep open for their members—if not for all, for at any rate a great number of them.[1]

This is almost at the opposite pole from the purposes of those who believe in liberty in the "positive"—self-directive—sense. The former want to curb authority as such. The latter want it placed in their own hands. That is a cardinal issue. These are not two different interpretations of a single concept, but two profoundly divergent and irreconcilable attitudes to the ends of life. It is as well to recognize this, even if in practice it is often necessary to strike a compromise between them. For each of them makes absolute claims. These claims cannot both be fully satisfied. But it is a profound lack of social and moral understanding not to recognize that the satisfaction that each of them seeks is an ultimate value which, both historically and morally, has an equal right to be classed among the deepest interests of mankind.

8: The One and the Many

One belief, more than any other, is responsible for the slaughter of individuals on the altars of the great historical ideals—justice or progress or the happiness of future generations, or the sacred mission or emancipation of a nation or race or class, or even liberty itself, which demands the sacrifice of individuals for the freedom of society. This is the belief that somewhere, in the past or in the future, in divine revelation or in the mind of an individual thinker, in the pronouncements of history or science, or in the simple heart of an uncorrupted good man, there is a final solution. This ancient faith rests on the conviction that all the positive values in which men have believed must, in the end, be compatible, and perhaps even entail one another. "Nature binds truth, happiness and virtue together by an indissoluble chain," said one of the best men who ever lived, and spoke in similar terms of liberty, equality, and justice.[2]

But is this true? It is a commonplace that neither political equality nor efficient organization nor social justice is compatible with more than a modicum of individual liberty, and certainly not with unrestricted *laissez-faire*;[3] that justice and generosity, public and private loyalties, the demands of genius and the claims of society can conflict violently with each other. And it is no great way from that to the generalization that not all good things are compatible, still less all the ideals of mankind. But somewhere, we shall be told, and in some way, it must be possible for all these values to live together, for unless this is so, the universe is not a cosmos, not a harmony; unless this is so, conflicts of values may be an intrinsic, irremovable element in human life. To admit that the fulfillment of some of our ideals may in principle make the fulfillment of others impossible is to say that the notion of total human fulfillment is a formal contradiction, a metaphysical chimera. For every rationalist metaphysician, from Plato to the last disciples of Hegel or Marx, this abandonment of the notion of a final harmony in which all riddles are solved, all contradictions reconciled, is a piece of crude empiricism, abdication before brute facts, intolerable bankruptcy of reason before things as they are, failure to explain and to justify, to reduce everything to a system, which "reason" indignantly rejects.

But if we are not armed with an a priori guarantee of the proposition that a total harmony of true values is somewhere to be found—perhaps in some ideal realm the characteristics of which we can, in our finite state, not so much as conceive—we must fall back on the ordinary resources of empirical observation and ordinary human knowledge. And these certainly give us no warrant for supposing (or even understanding what would be meant by saying) that all good things, or all bad things for that matter, are recon-

---

1   *The freedom of a society ... great number of them*   In Great Britain such legal power is, of course, constitutionally vested in the absolute sovereign—the Monarch in Parliament. What makes this country comparatively free, therefore, is the fact that this theoretically omnipotent entity is restrained by Custom or opinion from behaving as such. It is clear that what matters is not the form of these restraints on power—whether they are legal, or moral, or constitutional—but their effectiveness.

2   *Nature binds truth ... equality and justice*   Condorcet, from whose *Esquisse* these words are quoted [*Esquisse d'un tableau historique des progrès de l'esprit humain*, ed. O.H. Prior and Yvon Belaval (Paris, 1970), p. 228], declares that the task of social science is

to show "by what bonds nature has united the progress of enlightenment with that of liberty, virtue and respect for the natural rights of man; how these ideals, which alone are truly good, yet so often separated from each other that they are even believed to be incompatible, should, on the contrary, become inseparable, as soon as enlightenment has reached a certain level simultaneously among a large number of nations." He goes on to say that "Men still preserve the errors of their childhood, of their country and of their age long after having recognized all the truths needed for destroying them." Ibid., pp. 9, 10. Ironically enough, his belief in the need for and possibility of uniting all good things may well be precisely the kind of error he himself so well described.

3   *laissez-faire*   [editors' note] French: allow to act. A principle according to which government should interfere to the minimum degree possible in economic matters, or in the conduct of people in general.

cilable with each other. The world that we encounter in ordinary experience is one in which we are faced with choices between ends equally ultimate, and claims equally absolute, the realization of some of which must inevitably involve the sacrifice of others. Indeed, it is because this is their situation that men place such immense value upon the freedom to choose; for if they had assurance that in some perfect state, realizable by men on earth, no ends pursued by them would ever be in conflict, the necessity and agony of choice would disappear, and with it the central importance of the freedom to choose. Any method of bringing this final state nearer would then seem fully justified, no matter how much freedom were sacrificed to forward its advance.

It is, I have no doubt, some such dogmatic certainty that has been responsible for the deep, serene, unshakable conviction in the minds of some of the most merciless tyrants and persecutors in history that what they did was fully justified by its purpose. I do not say that the ideal of self-perfection—whether for individuals or nations or Churches or classes—is to be condemned in itself, or that the language which was used in its defense was in all cases the result of a confused or fraudulent use of words, or of moral or intellectual perversity. Indeed, I have tried to show that it is the notion of freedom in its "positive" sense that is at the heart of the demands for national or social self-direction which animate the most powerful and morally just public movements of our time, and that not to recognize this is to misunderstand the most vital facts and ideas of our age. But equally it seems to me that the belief that some single formula can in principle be found whereby all the diverse ends of men can be harmoniously realized is demonstrably false. If, as I believe, the ends of men are many, and not all of them are in principle compatible with each other, then the possibility of conflict—and of tragedy—can never wholly be eliminated from human life, either personal or social. The necessity of choosing between absolute claims is then an inescapable characteristic of the human condition. This gives its value to freedom as Acton[1] conceived of it—as an end in itself, and not as a temporary need, arising out of our confused notions and irrational and disordered lives, a predicament which a panacea could one day put right.

I do not wish to say that individual freedom is, even in the most liberal societies, the sole, or even the dominant, criterion of social action. We compel children to be educated, and we forbid public executions. These are certainly curbs to freedom. We justify them on the ground that ignorance, or a barbarian upbringing, or cruel pleasures and excitements are worse for us than the amount of restraint needed to repress them. This judgment in turn depends on how we determine good and evil, that is to say, on our moral, religious, intellectual, economic and aesthetic values; which are, in their turn, bound up with our conception of man, and of the basic demands of his nature. In other words, our solution of such problems is based on our vision, by which we are consciously or unconsciously guided, of what constitutes a fulfilled human life, as contrasted with Mill's "cramped and dwarfed," "pinched and hidebound" natures.[2] To protest against the laws governing censorship or personal morals as intolerable infringements of personal liberty presupposes a belief that the activities which such laws forbid are fundamental needs of men as men, in a good (or, indeed, any) society. To defend such laws is to hold that these needs are not essential, or that they cannot be satisfied without sacrificing other values which come higher—satisfy deeper needs—than individual freedom, determined by some standard that is not merely subjective, a standard for which some objective status—empirical or a priori—is claimed.

The extent of a man's, or a people's, liberty to choose to live as he or they desire must be weighed against the claims of many other values, of which equality, or justice, or happiness, or security, or public order are perhaps the most obvious examples. For this reason, it cannot be unlimited. We are rightly *reminded* by R. H. Tawney[3] that the liberty of the strong, whether their strength is physical or economic, must be restrained. This maxim claims respect, not as a consequence of some a priori rule, whereby the respect for the liberty of one man logically entails respect for the liberty of others like him; but simply because respect for the principles of justice, or shame at gross inequality of treatment, is as basic in men as the desire for liberty. That we cannot have everything is a necessary, not a contingent, truth. Burke's plea for the constant need to compensate, to reconcile, to balance; Mill's plea for novel "experiments in living"[4] with their permanent possibility of error—the knowledge that it is not merely in practice but in principle impossible to reach

---

1   *Acton*   [editors' note] John Emerich Edward Dalberg-Acton, 1st Baron Acton, (1834–1902), usually called simply Lord Acton, was an English historian, famous for the statement, "Power tends to corrupt; absolute power corrupts absolutely."

2   *Mill's "cramped and dwarfed" ... natures*   Mill, *On Liberty*, p. 224.

3   *R.H. Tawney*   Richard Henry Tawney (1880–1962), English economist, historian, social critic.

4   *experiments in living*   Mill, *On Liberty*, Chapters 3 and 4.

clear-cut and certain answers, even in an ideal world of wholly good and rational men and wholly clear ideas—may madden those who seek for final solutions and single, all-embracing systems, guaranteed to be eternal. Nevertheless, it is a conclusion that cannot be escaped by those who, with Kant, have learnt the truth that "Out of the crooked timber of humanity no straight thing was ever made."[1]

There is little need to stress the fact that monism, and faith in a single criterion, has always proved a deep source of satisfaction both to the intellect and to the emotions. Whether the standard of judgment derives from the vision of some future perfection, as in the minds of the *philosophes* in the eighteenth century and their technocratic successors in our own day, or is rooted in the past—*la terre et les morts*[2]—as maintained by German historicists or French theocrats, or neo-Conservatives in English-speaking countries, it is bound, provided it is inflexible enough, to encounter some unforeseen and unforeseeable human development, which it will not fit; and will then be used to justify the a priori barbarities of Procrustes[3]—the vivisection of actual human societies into some fixed pattern dictated by our fallible understanding of a largely imaginary past or a wholly imaginary future. To preserve our absolute categories or ideals at the expense of human lives offends equally against the principles of science and of history; it is an attitude found in equal measure on the right and left wings in our days, and is not reconcilable with the principles accepted by those who respect the facts.

Pluralism, with the measure of "negative" liberty that it entails, seems to me a truer and more humane ideal than the goals of those who seek in the great disciplined, authoritarian structures the ideal of "positive" self-mastery by classes, or peoples, or the whole of mankind. It is truer, because it does, at least, recognize the fact that human goals are many, not all of them commensurable, and in perpetual rivalry with one another. To assume that all values can be graded on one scale, so that it is a mere matter of inspection to determine the highest, seems to me to falsify our knowledge that men are free agents, to represent moral decision as an operation which a slide-rule could, in principle, perform. To say that in some ultimate, all-reconciling yet realizable synthesis duty is interest, or individual freedom is pure democracy or an authoritarian State, is to throw a metaphysical blanket over either self-deceit or deliberate hypocrisy. It is more humane because it does not (as the system-builders do) deprive men, in the name of some remote, or incoherent, ideal, of much that they have found to be indispensable to their life as unpredictably self-transforming human beings.[4] In the end, men choose between ultimate values; they choose as they do because their life and thought are determined by fundamental moral categories and concepts that are, at any rate over large stretches of time and space, and whatever their ultimate origins, a part of their being and thought and sense of their own identity; part of what makes them human.

It may be that the ideal of freedom to choose ends without claiming eternal validity for them, and the pluralism of values connected with this, is only the late fruit of our declining capitalist civilization: an ideal which remote ages and primitive societies have not recognized, and one which posterity will regard with curiosity, even sympathy, but little comprehension. This may be so; but no skeptical conclusions seem to me to follow. Principles are not less sacred because their duration cannot be guaranteed. Indeed, the very desire for guarantees that our values are eternal and secure in some objective heaven is perhaps only a craving for the certainties of childhood or the absolute values of our primitive past. "To realize the relative validity of one's convictions," said an admirable writer of our time, "and yet stand for them unflinchingly is what distinguishes a civilized man from a barbarian."[5] To demand more than this is perhaps a deep and incurable metaphysical need; but to allow such a need to determine one's practice is a symptom of an equally deep, and more dangerous, moral and political immaturity.

---

1 *Out of the crooked timber ... no straight thing was ever made* Vol. 8, p. 23, line 22.

2 *la terre et les morts* [editors' note] French: the earth and the dead. This slogan is associated with the right-wing anti-Semitic romantic nationalism of Maurice Barrès (1862–1923), French novelist, journalist, politician.

3 *Procrustes* [editors' note] This character in Greek mythology stretched or shortened captives to fit his iron bed (having first secretly adjusted the bed to be too long or too short). Reference to him (e.g., by the word *Procrustean*) conveys the idea of production of conformity by ruthless arbitrary means.

4 *It is more humane ... transforming human beings* On this also Bentham seems to me to have spoken well: "Individual interests are the only real interests ... Can it be conceived that there are men so absurd as to ... prefer the man who is not, to him who is; to torment the living, under pretence of promoting the happiness of those who are not born, and who may never be born?" *The Works of Jeremy Bentham*, vol. 1, p. 321. This is one of the infrequent occasions when Burke agrees with Bentham; for this passage is at the heart of the empirical, as against the metaphysical, view of politics.

5 *To realize the relative validity ... from a barbarian* Joseph A. Schumpeter, *Capitalism, Socialism, and Democracy* (London, 1943), p. 243.

CHARLES TAYLOR
(1931–)

Charles Taylor grew up in Montreal in a bilingual family, with a Francophone mother and an Anglophone father. He completed his BA in history at McGill University in 1952 and won a Rhodes Scholarship to Oxford, where he received his DPhil in 1961.

The unusual political, linguistic, and social character of Quebec influenced him philosophically and politically. He ran four times for Parliament as an NDP candidate, in 1965 challenging future Prime Minister Pierre Trudeau. He contributed to the Belanger-Campeau commission on the future of Quebec, served on the Conseil de la Langue Française and has written widely on secession and the place of Quebec in Canada. In the collection, *Reconciling the Solitudes* (1993), he sets out a vision of Quebec as a distinct society within a federalist framework. Quebec awarded him the Prix Léon-Gérin in 1992 for his contributions to Quebec intellectual life.

Taylor has written major papers and books in philosophy of language, philosophy of action, epistemology, philosophy of religion, ethics, and political philosophy. Many of these can be found in the collections *Human Agency and Language: Philosophical Papers 1* (1985), *Philosophy and the Human Sciences: Philosophical Papers 2* (1985) and *Philosophical Arguments* (1995). Taylor has also contributed widely to the history of philosophy, especially German Idealism. His major study *Hegel* was published in 1975. He examines questions of modernity and authenticity in *The Malaise of Modernity* (1991) and *Sources of Self* (1989), in which he traces the development of the modern self from the ancient Greeks to contemporary times.

Taylor's political philosophy is deeply marked by his views about the role of community and language in forming identity. Following Isaiah Berlin, political philosophers commonly distinguish between "positive" and "negative" liberty. Negative liberty involves freedom from external

coercion or obstacles. Positive liberty requires something more, the ability to exercise it.

A common argument for positive freedom is that real freedom requires access to certain goods and opportunities. If we can't make use of negative freedom, we aren't really free at all. In "What's Wrong with Negative Liberty?" Taylor takes another approach, arguing that the normal conception of negative freedom is incoherent. To illustrate this point, Taylor borrows Harry Frankfurt's notion of second order desires—desires about desires. We have some desires we don't identify with (e.g., the desire for a cigarette), while others are crucial for our identity. Second order desires allow us to evaluate our desires.

Taylor's key point is that we are not always in the best position to judge our desires. He argues that freedom necessarily involves some sort of means of discriminating among motivations. It is not enough simply to act free from external restraint. It is also a question of identity: who we are and what most matters to us. We need self-understanding, since "the application even of our negative notion of freedom requires a background conception of what is significant, according to which some restrictions are seen to be without relevance for freedom altogether, and others are judged as being of greater and lesser importance" (*Philosophy and the Human Sciences*, p. 219).

This distinction between positive and negative freedom plays a key role in another debate between a version of procedural, atomistic liberalism and republicanism or communitarianism. Procedural liberals generally argue that in our contemporary, pluralistic society, the state must avoid substantial endorsement of conceptions of the good. Freedom for them is mostly negative. Republicanism and communitarianism instead demand positive liberty. Freedom is set out in terms of participation in public affairs, giving citizens the opportunity to shape democratic practices.

In "Cross-Purposes: The Liberal-Communitarian Debate," Taylor analyzes this debate, arguing that both liberal and communitarians have confused issues of ontology and advocacy. On the ontological side, communitarians argue that liberals adopt a false vision of the isolated, self-interested individual. This neglects the way our identities are formed by our society and ignores how these factors influence what we value. Though Taylor is sympathetic to these concerns, he stresses that issues about the *ontology* of identity or selfhood are distinct from questions *advocating* how our political institutions ought to be organized.

Besides outlining the confusions in this debate, Taylor argues that liberals ignore the vital role that patriotic identification and a shared notion of the common good play in democratic politics. Using the Watergate Scandal as an example, he stresses how it awoke a sense of patriotic identification, involving deeply entrenched ideals that Nixon and his cohorts had violated. According to Taylor, this sense of common identity is necessary to prevent despotism and other abuses. A republican conception is thus necessary for democratic politics, though this still leaves open important questions about the nature and extent of advocacy.

◆ ◆ ◆ ◆ ◆

What's Wrong with Negative Liberty? (1979)

This is an attempt to resolve one of the issues that separate "positive" and "negative" theories of freedom, as these have been distinguished in Isaiah Berlin's seminal essay, "Two concepts of liberty."[1] Although one can discuss almost endlessly the detailed formulation of the distinction, I believe it is undeniable that there are two such families of conceptions of political freedom abroad in our civilization.

Thus there clearly are theories, widely canvassed in liberal society, which want to define freedom exclusively in terms of the independence of the individual from interference by others, be these governments, corporations or private persons; and equally clearly these theories are chal-

lenged by those who believe that freedom resides at least in part in collective control over the common life. We unproblematically recognize theories descended from Rousseau and Marx as fitting in this category.

There is quite a gamut of views in each category. And this is worth bearing in mind, because it is too easy in the course of polemic to fix on the extreme, almost caricatural variants of each family. When people attack positive theories of freedom, they generally have some Left totalitarian theory in mind, according to which freedom resides exclusively in exercising collective control over one's destiny in a classless society, the kind of theory which underlies, for instance, official communism. This view, in its caricaturally extreme form, refuses to recognize the freedoms guaranteed in other societies as genuine. The destruction of "bourgeois freedoms" is no real loss of freedom, and coercion can be justified in the name of freedom if it is needed to bring into existence the classless society in which alone men are properly free. Men can, in short, be forced to be free.

Even as applied to official communism, this portrait is a little extreme, although it undoubtedly expresses the inner logic of this kind of theory. But it is an absurd caricature if applied to the whole family of positive conceptions. This includes all those views of modern political life which owe something to the ancient republican tradition, according to which men's ruling themselves is seen as an activity valuable in itself, and not only for instrumental reasons. It includes in its scope thinkers like Tocqueville, and even arguably the J.S. Mill of *On Representative Government*. It has no necessary connection with the view that freedom consists *purely and simply* in the collective control over the common life, or that there is no freedom worth the name outside a context of collective control. And it does not therefore generate necessarily a doctrine that men can be forced to be free.

On the other side, there is a corresponding caricatural version of negative freedom which tends to come to the fore. This is the tough-minded version, going back to Hobbes, or in another way to Bentham, which sees freedom simply as the absence of external physical or legal obstacles. This view will have no truck with other less immediately obvious obstacles to freedom, for instance, lack of awareness, or false consciousness, or repression, or other inner factors of this kind. It holds firmly to the view that to speak of such inner factors as relevant to the issue about freedom, to speak for instance of someone's being less free because of false consciousness, is to abuse words. The only clear meaning which can be given to freedom is that of the absence of external obstacles.

---

1   *"Two concepts of liberty"*   [Unless otherwise indicated, all notes to this selection are by the author rather than the editors of this anthology.] In *Four Essays on Liberty* (London and New York: Oxford University Press, 1969), 118–72 [reprinted in this volume].

I call this view caricatural as a representative portrait of the negative view, because it rules out of court one of the most powerful motives behind the modern defense of freedom as individual independence, viz., the post-Romantic idea that each person's form of self-realization is original to him/her, and can therefore only be worked out independently. This is one of the reasons for the defense of individual liberty by among others J. S. Mill (this time in his *On Liberty*). But if we think of freedom as including something like the freedom of self-fulfillment, or self-realization according to our own pattern, then we plainly have something which can fail for inner reasons as well as because of external obstacles. We can fail to achieve our own self-realization through inner fears, or false consciousness, as well as because of external coercion. Thus the modern notion of negative freedom which gives weight to the securing of each person's right to realize him/herself in his/her own way cannot make do with the Hobbes/Bentham notion of freedom. The moral psychology of these authors is too simple, or perhaps we should say too crude, for its purposes.

Now there is a strange asymmetry here. The extreme caricatural views tend to come to the fore in the polemic, as I mentioned above. But whereas the extreme "forced-to-be-free" view is one which the opponents of positive liberty try to pin on them, as one would expect in the heat of argument, the proponents of negative liberty themselves often seem anxious to espouse their extreme, Hobbesian view. Thus even Isaiah Berlin, in his eloquent exposition of the two concepts of liberty, seems to quote Bentham[1] approvingly and Hobbes[2] as well. Why is this?

To see this we have to examine more closely what is at stake between the two views. The negative theories, as we saw, want to define freedom in terms of individual independence from others; the positive also want to identify freedom with collective self-government. But behind this lie some deeper differences of doctrines.

Isaiah Berlin points out that negative theories are concerned with the area in which the subject should be left without interference, whereas the positive doctrines are concerned with who or what controls. I should like to put the point behind this in a slightly different way. Doctrines of positive freedom are concerned with a view of freedom which involves essentially the exercising of control over one's life. On this view, one is free only to the extent that one has effectively determined oneself and the shape of one's life. The concept of freedom here is an exercise-concept.

By contrast, negative theories can rely simply on an opportunity-concept, where being free is a matter of what we can do, of what it is open to us to do, whether or not we do anything to exercise these options. This certainly is the case of the crude, original Hobbesian concept. Freedom consists just in there being no obstacle. It is a sufficient condition of one's being free that nothing stand in the way.

But we have to say that negative theories *can* rely on an opportunity-concept, rather than that they necessarily do so rely, for we have to allow for that part of the gamut of negative theories mentioned above which incorporates some notion of self-realization. Plainly this kind of view cannot rely simply on an opportunity-concept. We cannot say that someone is free, on a self-realization view, if he is totally unrealized, if for instance he is totally unaware of his potential, if fulfilling it has never even arisen as a question for him, or if he is paralyzed by the fear of breaking with some norm which he has internalized but which does not authentically reflect him. Within this conceptual scheme, some degree of exercise is necessary for a man to be thought free. Or if we want to think of the internal bars to freedom as obstacles on all fours with the external ones, then being in a position to exercise freedom, having the opportunity, involves removing the internal barriers; and this is not possible without having to some extent realized myself. So that with the freedom of self-realization, having the opportunity to be free requires that I already be exercising freedom. A pure opportunity-concept is impossible here.

But if negative theories can be grounded on either an opportunity- or an exercise-concept, the same is not true of positive theories. The view that freedom involves at least partially collective self-rule is essentially grounded on an exercise-concept. For this view (at least partly) identifies freedom with self-direction, that is, the actual exercise of directing control over one's life.

But this already gives us a hint towards illuminating the above paradox, that while the extreme variant of positive freedom is usually pinned on its protagonists by their opponents, negative theorists seem prone to embrace the crudest versions of their theory themselves. For if an opportunity-concept is not combinable with a positive theory, but either it or its alternative can suit a negative theory, then one way of ruling out positive theories in principle is by firmly espousing an opportunity-concept. One cuts off

---

1   *Berlin, in his ... Bentham*   Berlin quotes Bentham in *Four Essays on Liberty*, 148.

2   *Hobbes*   Berlin quotes Hobbes in *Four Essays on Liberty*, 164.

the positive theories by the root, as it were, even though one may also pay a price in the atrophy of a wide range of negative theories as well. At least by taking one's stand firmly on the crude side of the negative range, where only opportunity concepts are recognized, one leaves no place for a positive theory to grow.

Taking one's stand here has the advantage that one is holding the line around a very simple and basic issue of principle, and one where the negative view seems to have some backing in common sense. The basic intuition here is that freedom is a matter of being able to do something or other, of not having obstacles in one's way, rather than being a capacity that we have to realize. It naturally seems more prudent to fight the Totalitarian Menace at this last-ditch position, digging in behind the natural frontier of this simple issue, rather than engaging the enemy on the open terrain of exercise-concepts, where one will have to fight to discriminate the good from the bad among such concepts; fight, for instance, for a view of individual self-realization against various notions of collective self-realization, of a nation, or a class. It seems easier and safer to cut all the nonsense off at the start by declaring all self-realization views to be metaphysical hog-wash. Freedom should just be tough-mindedly defined as the absence of external obstacles.

Of course, there are independent reasons for wanting to define freedom tough-mindedly. In particular there is the immense influence of the anti-metaphysical, materialist, natural-science-oriented temper of thought in our civilization. Something of this spirit at its inception induced Hobbes to take the line that he did, and the same spirit goes marching on today. Indeed, it is because of the prevalence of this spirit that the line is so easy to defend, forensically speaking, in our society.

Nevertheless, I think that one of the strongest motives for defending the crude Hobbes-Bentham concept, that freedom is the absence of external obstacles, physical or legal, is the strategic one above. For most of those who take this line thereby abandon many of their own intuitions, sharing as they do with the rest of us in a post-Romantic civilization which puts great value on self-realization, and values freedom largely because of this. It is fear of the Totalitarian Menace, I would argue, which has led them to abandon this terrain to the enemy.

I want to argue that this not only robs their eventual forensic victory of much of its value, since they become incapable of defending liberalism in the form we in fact value it, but I want to make the stronger claim that this Maginot Line mentality[1] actually ensures defeat, as is often the case with Maginot Line mentalities. The Hobbes-Bentham view, I want to argue, is indefensible as a view of freedom.

To see this, let us examine the line more closely, and the temptation to stand on it. The advantage of the view that freedom is the absence of external obstacles is its simplicity. It allows us to say that freedom is being able to do what you want, where what you want is unproblematically understood as what the agent can identify as his desires. By contrast an exercise-concept of freedom requires that we discriminate among motivations. If we are free in the exercise of certain capacities, then we are not free, or less free, when these capacities are in some way unfulfilled or blocked. But the obstacles can be internal as well as external. And this must be so, for the capacities relevant to freedom must involve some self-awareness, self-understanding, moral discrimination and self-control, otherwise their exercise could not amount to freedom in the sense of self-direction; and this being so, we can fail to be free because these internal conditions are not realized. But where this happens, where, for example, we are quite self-deceived, or utterly fail to discriminate properly the ends we seek, or have lost self-control, we can quite easily be doing what we want in the sense of what we can identify as our wants, without being free; indeed, we can be further entrenching our unfreedom.

Once one adopts a self-realization view, or indeed any exercise-concept of freedom, then being able to do what one wants can no longer be accepted as a sufficient condition of being free. For this view puts certain conditions on one's motivation. You are not free if you are motivated, through fear, inauthentically internalized standards, or false consciousness, to thwart your self-realization. This is sometimes put by saying that for a self-realization view, you have to be able to do what you really want, or to follow your real will, or to fulfill the desires of your own true self. But these formulae, particularly the last, may mislead, by making us think that exercise-concepts of freedom are tied to some particular metaphysic, in particular that of a higher and lower self. We shall see below that this is far from being

---

1 *Maginot Line mentality* [editors' note] The Maginot Line was a line of concrete fortifications of various sorts erected by France on its border with Germany between World War I and World War II. France mistakenly thought that this would make it immune to attack by Germany, and neglected other possible means of defense. A "Maginot Line mentality" is thus the disposition to put one's faith in a simple and rigid strategy for defense that is, however, a failure.

the case, and that there is a much wider range of bases for discriminating authentic desires.

In any case, the point for our discussion here is that for an exercise-concept of freedom, being free cannot just be a question of doing what you want in the unproblematic sense. It must also be that what you want does not run against the grain of your basic purposes, or your self-realization. Or to put the issue in another way, which converges on the same point, the subject himself cannot be the final authority on the question whether he is free; for he cannot be the final authority on the question whether his desires are authentic, whether they do or do not frustrate his purposes.

To put the issue in this second way is to make more palpable the temptation for defenders of the negative view to hold their Maginot Line. For once we admit that the agent himself is not the final authority on his own freedom, do we not open the way to totalitarian manipulation? Do we not legitimate others, supposedly wiser about his purposes than himself, redirecting his feet on the right path, perhaps even by force, and all this in the name of freedom?

The answer is that of course we don't. Not by this concession alone. For there may also be good reasons for holding that others are not likely to in a better position to understand his real purposes. This indeed plausibly follows from the post-Romantic view above that each person has his own original form of realization. Some others, who know us intimately, and who surpass us in wisdom, are undoubtedly in a position to advise us, but no official body can possess a doctrine or a technique whereby they could know how to put us on the rails, because such a doctrine or technique cannot in principle exist if human beings really differ in their self-realization.

Or again, we may hold a self-realization view of freedom, and hence believe that there are certain conditions on my motivation necessary to my being free, but also believe that there are other necessary conditions which rule out my being forcibly led towards some definition of my self-realization by external authority. Indeed, in these last two paragraphs I have given a portrait of what I think is a very widely held view in liberal society, a view which values self-realization, and accepts that it can fail for internal reasons, but which believes that no valid guidance can be provided in principle by social authority, because of human diversity and originality, and holds that the attempt to impose such guidance will destroy other necessary conditions of freedom.

It is however true that totalitarian theories of positive freedom do build on a conception which involves dis-criminating between motivations. Indeed, one can represent the path from the negative to the positive conceptions of freedom as consisting of two steps: the first moves us from a notion of freedom as doing what one wants to a notion which discriminates motivations and equates freedom with doing what we really want, or obeying our real will, or truly directing our lives. The second step introduces some doctrine purporting to show that we cannot do what we really want, or follow our real will, outside of a society of a certain canonical form, incorporating true self-government. It follows that we can only be free in such a society, and that being free *is* governing ourselves collectively according to this canonical form.

We might see an example of this second step in Rousseau's view that only a social contract society in which all give themselves totally to the whole preserves us from other-dependence and ensures that we obey only ourselves; or in Marx's doctrine of man as a species-being who realizes his potential in a mode of social production, and who must thus take control of this mode collectively.

Faced with this two-step process, it seems safer and easier to stop it at the first step, to insist firmly that freedom is just a matter of the absence of external obstacles, that it therefore involves no discrimination of motivation and permits in principle no second-guessing of the subject by anyone else. This is the essence of the Maginot Line strategy. It is very tempting. But I want to claim that it is wrong. I want to argue that we cannot defend a view of freedom which does not involve at least some qualitative discrimination as to motive, that is which does not put some restrictions on motivation among the necessary conditions of freedom, and hence which could rule out second-guessing in principle.

There are some considerations one can put forward straight off to show that the pure Hobbesian concept will not work, that there are some discriminations among motivations which are essential to the concept of freedom as we use it. Even where we think of freedom as the absence of external obstacles, it is not the absence of such obstacles *simpliciter*.[1] For we make discriminations between obstacles as representing more or less serious infringements of freedom. And we do this, because we deploy the concept against a background understanding that certain goals and activities are more significant than others.

Thus we could say that my freedom is restricted if the local authority puts up a new traffic light at an intersec-

---

1   *simpliciter*   [editors' note] Simply—that is, alone, just in itself.

tion close to my home; so that where previously I could cross as I liked, consistently with avoiding collision with other cars, now I have to wait until the light is green. In a philosophical argument, we might call this a restriction of freedom, but not in a serious political debate. The reason is that it is too trivial, the activity and purposes inhibited here are not really significant. It is not just a matter of our having made a trade-off, and considered that a small loss of liberty was worth fewer traffic accidents, or less danger for the children; we are reluctant to speak here of a loss of liberty at all; what we feel we are trading off is convenience against safety.

By contrast a law which forbids me from worshipping according to the form I believe in is a serious blow to liberty; even a law which tried to restrict this to certain times (as the traffic light restricts my crossing of the intersection to certain times) would be seen as a serious restriction. Why this difference between the two cases? Because we have a background understanding, too obvious to spell out, of some activities and goals as highly significant for human beings and others as less so. One's religious belief is recognized, even by atheists, as supremely important, because it is that by which the believer defines himself as a moral being. By contrast my rhythm of movement through the city traffic is trivial. We do not want to speak of these two in the same breath. We do not even readily admit that liberty is at stake in the traffic light case. For *de minimis non curat libertas.*[1]

But this recourse to significance takes us beyond a Hobbesian scheme. Freedom is no longer just the absence of external obstacle *tout court,*[2] but the absence of external obstacle to significant action, to what is important to man. There are discriminations to be made; some restrictions are more serious than others, some are utterly trivial. About many, there is of course controversy. But what the judgment turns on is some sense of what is significant for human life. Restricting the expression of people's religious and ethical convictions is more significant than restricting their movement around uninhabited parts of the country; and both are more significant than the trivia of traffic control.

But the Hobbesian scheme has no place for the notion of significance. It will allow only for purely quantitative

judgments. On the toughest-minded version of his conception, where Hobbes seems to be about to define liberty in terms of the absence of physical obstacles, one is presented with the vertiginous prospect of human freedom being measurable in the same way as the degrees of freedom of some physical object, say a lever. Later we see that this will not do, because we have to take account of legal obstacles to my action. But in any case, such a quantitative conception of freedom is a non-starter.

Consider the following diabolical defense of Albania as a free country. We recognize that religion has been abolished in Albania, whereas it hasn't been in Britain. But on the other hand there are probably far fewer traffic lights per head in Tirana than in London. (I haven't checked for myself, but this is a very plausible assumption.[3]) Suppose an apologist for Albanian socialism were nevertheless to claim that this country was freer than Britain, because the number of acts restricted was far smaller. After all, only a minority of Londoners practice some religion in public places, but all have to negotiate their way through traffic. Those who do practice a religion generally do so on one day of the week, while they are held up at traffic lights every day. In sheer quantitative terms, the number of acts restricted by traffic lights must be greater than that restricted by a ban on public religious practice. So if Britain is considered a free society, why not Albania?

Thus the application even of our negative notion of freedom requires a background conception of what is significant, according to which some restrictions are seen to be without relevance for freedom altogether, and others are judged as being of greater and lesser importance. So some discrimination among motivations seems essential to our concept of freedom. A minute's reflection shows why this must be so. Freedom is important to us because we are purposive beings. But then there must be distinctions in the significance of different kinds of freedom based on the distinction in the significance of different purposes.

But of course, this still does not involve the kind of discrimination mentioned above, the kind which would allow us to say that someone who was doing what he wanted (in the unproblematic sense) was not really free, the kind of discrimination which allows us to put conditions on people's motivations necessary to their being free, and hence

---

1   *de minimis non curat libertas*   [editors' note] Taylor here plays on the Latin slogan "*De minimis non curat lex*" ("The law does not concern itself with trivialities"). Taylor's version translates as "Liberty does not concern itself with trivialities."

2   *tout court*   [editors' note] Briefly—that is, without qualification.

3   *this is a very plausible assumption*   [editors' note] Taylor is correct. It is reported that the first traffic lights were installed in Albania in January, 1994, nine years after this chapter was published.

to second-guess them. All we have shown is that we make discriminations between more or less significant freedoms, based on discriminations among the purposes people have.

This creates some embarrassment for the crude negative theory, but it can cope with it by simply adding a recognition that we make judgments of significance. Its central claim that freedom just is the absence of external obstacles seems untouched, as also its view of freedom as an opportunity-concept. It is just that we now have to admit that not all opportunities are equal.

But there is more trouble in store for the crude view when we examine further what these qualitative discriminations are based on. What lies behind our judging certain purposes/feelings as more significant than others? One might think that there was room here again for another quantitative theory; that the more significant purposes are those we want more. But this account is either vacuous or false.

It is true but vacuous if we take wanting more just to mean being more significant. It is false as soon as we try to give wanting more an independent criterion, such as, for instance, the urgency or force of a desire, or the prevalence of one desire over another, because it is a matter of the most banal experience that the purposes we know to be more significant are not always those which we desire with the greatest urgency to encompass, nor the ones that actually always win out in cases of conflict of desires.

When we reflect on this kind of significance, we come up against what I have called elsewhere the fact of strong evaluation, the fact that we human subjects are not only subjects of first-order desires, but of second-order desires, desires about desires. We experience our desires and purposes as qualitatively discriminated, as higher or lower, noble or base, integrated or fragmented, significant or trivial, good and bad. This means that we experience some of our desires and goals as intrinsically more significant than others: some passing comfort is less important than the fulfillment of our life-time vocation, our *amour propre*[1] less important than a love relationship; while we experience some others as bad, not just comparatively but absolutely: we desire not to be moved by spite, or some childish desire to impress at all costs. And these judgments of significance are quite independent of the strength of the respective desires: the craving for comfort may be overwhelming at this moment,

we may be obsessed with our *amour propre*, but the judgment of significance stands.

But then the question arises whether this fact of strong evaluation doesn't have other consequences for our notion of freedom, than just that it permits us to rank freedoms in importance. Is freedom not at stake when we find ourselves carried away by a less significant goal to over-ride a highly significant one? Or when we are led to act out of a motive we consider bad or despicable?

The answer is that we sometimes do speak in this way. Suppose I have some irrational fear, which is preventing me from doing something I very much want to do. Say the fear of public speaking is preventing me from taking up a career that I should find very fulfilling, and that I should be quite good at, if I could just get over this "hang-up." It is clear that we experience this fear as an obstacle, and that we feel we are less than we would be if we could overcome it.

Or again, consider the case where I am very attached to comfort. To go on short rations, and to miss my creature comforts for a time, makes me very depressed. I find myself making a big thing of this. Because of this reaction I cannot do certain things that I should like very much to do, such as going on an expedition over the Andes, or a canoe trip in the Yukon. Once again, it is quite understandable if I experience this attachment as an obstacle, and feel that I should be freer without it.

Or I could find that my spiteful feelings and reactions which I almost cannot inhibit are undermining a relationship which is terribly important to me. At times, I feel as though I am almost assisting as a helpless witness at my own destructive behavior, as I lash out again with my unbridled tongue at her. I long to be able not to feel this spite. As long as I feel it, even control is not an option, because it just builds up inside until it either bursts out, or else the feeling somehow communicates itself, and queers things between us. I long to be free of this feeling.

These are quite understandable cases, where we can speak of freedom or its absence without strain. What I have called strong evaluation is essentially involved here. For these are not just cases of conflict, even cases of painful conflict. If the conflict is between two desires with which I have no trouble identifying, there can be no talk of lesser freedom, no matter how painful or fateful. Thus if what is breaking up my relationship is my finding fulfillment in a job which, say, takes me away from home a lot, I have indeed a terrible conflict, but I would have no temptation to speak of myself as less free.

---

1   *amour propre* [editors' note] French: sense of self-importance —vanity.

Even seeing a great difference in the significance of the two terms doesn't seem to be a sufficient condition of my wanting to speak of freedom and its absence. Thus my marriage may be breaking up because I like going to the pub and playing cards on Saturday nights with the boys. I may feel quite unequivocally that my marriage is much more important than the release and comradeship of the Saturday night bash. But nevertheless I would not want to talk of my being freer if I could slough off this desire.

The difference seems to be that in this case, unlike the ones above, I still identify with the less important desire, I still see it as expressive of myself, so that I could not lose it without altering who I am, losing something of my personality. Whereas my irrational fear, my being quite distressed by discomfort, my spite—these are all things which I can easily see myself losing without any loss whatsoever to what I am. This is why I can see them as obstacles to my purposes, and hence to my freedom, even though they are in a sense unquestionably desires and feelings of mine.

Before exploring further what is involved in this, let us go back and keep score. It would seem that these cases make a bigger breach in the crude negative theory. For they seem to be cases in which the obstacles to freedom are internal; and if this is so, then freedom cannot simply be interpreted as the absence of *external* obstacles; and the fact that I am doing what I want, in the sense of following my strongest desire, is not sufficient to establish that I am free. On the contrary, we have to make discriminations among motivations, and accept that acting out of some motivations, for example irrational fear or spite, or this too great need for comfort, is not freedom, is even a negation of freedom.

But although the crude negative theory cannot be sustained in the face of these examples, perhaps something which springs from the same concerns can be reconstructed. For although we have to admit that there are internal, motivational, necessary conditions for freedom, we can perhaps still avoid any legitimation of what I called above the second-guessing of the subject. If our negative theory allows for strong evaluation, allows that some goals are really important to us, and that other desires are seen as not fully ours, then can it not retain the thesis that freedom is being able to do what I want, that is, what I can identify myself as wanting, where this means not just what I identify as my strongest desire, but what I identify as my true, authentic desire or purpose? The subject would still be the final arbiter of his being free/unfree, as indeed he is clearly capable of discerning this in the examples above, where I relied precisely on the subject's own experience of constraint, of motives with which he cannot identify. We should have sloughed off the untenable Hobbesian reductive-materialist metaphysics, according to which only external obstacles count, as though action were just movement, and there could be no internal, motivational obstacles to our deeper purposes. But we would be retaining the basic concern of the negative theory, that the subject is still the final authority as to what his freedom consists in, and cannot be second-guessed by external authority. Freedom would be modified to read: the absence of internal or external obstacles to what I truly or authentically want. But we would still be holding the Maginot Line. Or would we?

I think not, in fact. I think that this hybrid or middle position is untenable, where we are willing to admit that we can speak of what we truly want, as against what we most strongly desire, and of some desires as obstacles to our freedom, while we still will not allow for second-guessing. For to rule this out in principle is to rule out in principle that the subject can ever be wrong about what he truly wants. And how can he never, in principle, be wrong, unless there is nothing to be right or wrong about in this matter?

That in fact is the thesis our negative theorist will have to defend. And it is a plausible one for the same intellectual (reductive-empiricist) tradition from which the crude negative theory springs. On this view, our feelings are brute facts about us; that is, it is a fact about us that we are affected in such and such a way, but our feelings cannot themselves be understood as involving some perception or sense of what they relate to, and hence as potentially veridical or illusory, authentic or inauthentic. On this scheme, the fact that a certain desire represented one of our fundamental purposes, and another a mere force with which we cannot identify, would concern merely the brute quality of the affect in both cases. It would be a matter of the raw feel of these two desires that this was their respective status.

In such circumstances, the subject's own classification would be incorrigible. There is no such thing as an imperceptible raw feel. If the subject failed to experience a certain desire as fundamental, and if what we meant by "fundamental" applied to desire was that the felt experience of it has a certain quality, then the desire could not be fundamental. We can see this if we look at those feelings which we can agree are brute in this sense: for instance, the stab of pain I feel when the dentist jabs into my tooth, or the crawling unease when someone runs his fingernail along the blackboard. There can be no question of misperception here. If I fail to "perceive" the pain, I am not in pain. Might it not be so with our fundamental desires, and those which we repudiate?

The answer is clearly no. For first of all, many of our feelings and desires, including the relevant ones for these kinds of conflicts, are not brute. By contrast with pain and the fingernail-on-blackboard sensation, shame and fear, for instance, are emotions which involve our experiencing the situation as bearing a certain import for us, as being dangerous or shameful. This is why shame and fear can be inappropriate, or even irrational, where pain and a frisson cannot. Thus we can be in error in feeling shame or fear. We can even be consciously aware of the unfounded nature of our feelings, and this is when we castigate them as irrational.

Thus the notion that we can understand all our feelings and desires as brute, in the above sense, is not on. But more, the idea that we could discriminate our fundamental desires, or those which we want to repudiate, by the quality of brute affect is grotesque. When I am convinced that some career, or an expedition in the Andes, or a love relationship, is of fundamental importance to me (to recur to the above examples), it cannot be just because of the throbs, élans[1] or tremors I feel; I must also have some sense that these are of great significance for me, meet important, long-lasting needs, represent a fulfillment of something central to me, will bring me closer to what I really am, or something of the sort. The whole notion of our identity, whereby we recognize that some goals, desires, allegiances are central to what we are, while others are not or are less so, can make sense only against a background of desires and feelings which are not brute, but what I shall call import-attributing, to invent a term of art for the occasion.

Thus we have to see our emotional life as made up largely of import-attributing desires and feelings, that is, desires and feelings which we can experience mistakenly. And not only can we be mistaken in this, we clearly must accept, in cases like the above where we want to repudiate certain desires, that we are mistaken.

For let us consider the distinction mentioned above between conflicts where we feel fettered by one desire, and those where we do not, where, for instance, in the example mentioned above, a man is torn between his career and his marriage. What made the difference was that in the case of genuine conflict both desires are the agent's, whereas in the cases where he feels fettered by one, this desire is one he wants to repudiate.

But what is it to feel that a desire is not truly mine? Presumably, I feel that I should be better off without it, that I do not lose anything in getting rid of it, I remain quite complete without it. What could lie behind this sense?

Well, one could imagine feeling this about a brute desire. I may feel this about my addiction to smoking, for instance—wish I could get rid of it, experience it as a fetter, and believe that I should be well rid of it. But addictions are a special case; we understand them to be unnatural, externally induced desires. We could not say in general that we are ready to envisage losing our brute desires without a sense of diminution. On the contrary, to lose my desire for, and hence delectation in, oysters, mushroom pizza, or Peking duck would be a terrible deprivation. I should fight against such a change with all the strength at my disposal.

So being brute is not what makes desires repudiable. And besides, in the above examples the repudiated desires are not brute. In the first case, I am chained by unreasoning fear, an import-attributing emotion, in which the fact of being mistaken is already recognized when I identify the fear as irrational or unreasoning. Spite, too, which moves me in the third case, is an import-attributing emotion. To feel spite is to see oneself and the target of one's resentment in a certain light; it is to feel in some way wounded, or damaged, by his success or good fortune, and the more hurt the more he is fortunate. To overcome feelings of spite, as against just holding them in, is to come to see self and other in a different light, in particular, to set aside self-pity, and the sense of being personally wounded by what the other does and is.

(I should also like to claim that the obstacle in the third example, the too great attachment to comfort, while not itself import-attributing, is also bound up with the way we see things. The problem is here not just that we dislike discomfort, but that we are too easily depressed by it; and this is something which we overcome only by sensing a different order of priorities, whereby small discomforts matter less. But if this is thought too dubious, we can concentrate on the other two examples.)

Now how can we feel that an import-attributing desire is not truly ours? We can do this only if we see it as mistaken, that is, the import or the good it supposedly gives us a sense of is not a genuine import or good. The irrational fear is a fetter, because it is irrational; spite is a fetter because it is rooted in a self-absorption which distorts our perspec-

---

1   *élans* [editors' note] Enthusiasms.

tive on everything, and the pleasures of venting it preclude any genuine satisfaction. Losing these desires we lose nothing, because their loss deprives us of no genuine good or pleasure or satisfaction. In this they are quite different from my love of oysters, mushroom pizza and Peking duck.

It would appear from this that to see our desires as brute gives us no clue as to why some of them are repudiable. On the contrary it is precisely their not being brute which can explain this. It is because they are import-attributing desires which are mistaken that we can feel that we would lose nothing in sloughing them off. Everything which is truly important to us would be safe-guarded. If they were just brute desires, we could not feel this unequivocally, as we certainly do not when it comes to the pleasures of the palate. True, we also feel that our desire to smoke is repudiable, but there is a special explanation here, which is not available in the case of spite.

Thus we can experience some desires as fetters, because we can experience them as not ours. And we can experience them as not ours because we see them as incorporating a quite erroneous appreciation of our situation and of what matters to us. We can see this again if we contrast the case of spite with that of another emotion which partly overlaps, and which is highly considered in some societies, the desire for revenge. In certain traditional societies this is far from being considered a despicable emotion. On the contrary, it is a duty of honor on a male relative to avenge a man's death. We might imagine that this too might give rise to conflict. It might conflict with the attempts of a new regime to bring some order to the land. The government would have to stop people taking vengeance, in the name of peace.

But short of a conversion to a new ethical outlook, this would be seen as a tradeoff, the sacrifice of one legitimate goal for the sake of another. And it would seem monstrous were one to propose reconditioning people so that they no longer felt the desire to avenge their kin. This would be to unman them.[1]

Why do we feel so different about spite (and for that matter also revenge)? Because the desire for revenge for an ancient Icelander was his sense of a real obligation incumbent on him, something it would be dishonorable to repudiate; while for us, spite is the child of a distorted perspective on things.

We cannot therefore understand our desires and emotions as all brute, and in particular we cannot make sense of our discrimination of some desires as more important and fundamental, or of our repudiation of others, unless we understand our feelings to be import-attributing. This is essential to there being what we have called strong evaluation. Consequently the halfway position which admits strong evaluation, admits that our desires may frustrate our deeper purposes, admits therefore that there may be inner obstacles to freedom, and yet will not admit that the subject may be wrong or mistaken about these purposes—this position does not seem tenable. For the only way to make the subject's assessment incorrigible in principle would be to claim that there was nothing to be right or wrong about here; and that could only be so if experiencing a given feeling were a matter of the qualities of brute feeling. But this it cannot be if we are to make sense of the whole background of strong evaluation, more significant goals, and aims that we repudiate. This whole scheme requires that we understand the emotions concerned as import-attributing, as, indeed, it is clear that we must do on other grounds as well.

But once we admit that our feelings are import-attributing, then we admit the possibility of error, or false appreciation. And indeed, we have to admit a kind of false appreciation which the agent himself detects in order to make sense of the cases where we experience our own desires as fetters. How can we exclude in principle that there may be other false appreciations which the agent does not detect? That he may be profoundly in error, that is, have a very distorted sense of his fundamental purposes? Who can say that such people cannot exist? All cases are, of course, controversial; but I should nominate Charles Manson and Andreas Baader[2] for this category, among others. I pick them out as people with a strong sense of some purposes and goals as incomparably more fundamental than others, or at least with a propensity to act the having such a sense so as to take in even themselves a good part of the time, but whose sense of fundamental purpose was shot through with confusion and error. And once we recognize such extreme cases, how avoid admitting that many of the rest of mankind can suffer to a lesser degree from the same disabilities?

---

1   *This would be to unman them*   Compare the unease we feel at the reconditioning of the hero of Anthony Burgess's *A Clockwork Orange*.

2   *Charles Manson and Andreas Baader*   [editors' note] Manson, born 1934, was leader of a cult "family" convicted of multiple murders in Los Angeles in 1969. Baader (German, 1943–77) was one of the leaders of the Baader-Meinhof Gang, a left-wing West German guerrilla group.

What has this got to do with freedom? Well, to resume what we have seen: our attributions of freedom make sense against a background sense of more and less significant purposes, for the question of freedom/unfreedom is bound up with the frustration/fulfillment of our purposes. Further, our significant purposes can be frustrated by our own desires, and where these are sufficiently based on misappreciation, we consider them as not really ours, and experience them as fetters. A man's freedom can therefore be hemmed in by internal, motivational obstacles, as well as external ones. A man who is driven by spite to jeopardize his most important relationships, in spite of himself, as it were, or who is prevented by unreasoning fear from taking up the career he truly wants, is not really made more free if one lifts the external obstacles to his venting his spite or acting on his fear. Or at best he is liberated into a very impoverished freedom.

If through linguistic/ideological purism one wants to stick to the crude definition, and insist that men are equally freed from whom the same external obstacles are lifted, regardless of their motivational state, then one will just have to introduce some other term to mark the distinction, and say that one man is capable of taking proper advantage of his freedom, and the other (the one in the grip of spite, or fear) is not. This is because in the meaningful sense of "free," that for which we value it, in the sense of being able to act on one's important purposes, the internally fettered man is not free. If we choose to give "free" a special (Hobbesian) sense which avoids this issue, we will just have to introduce another term to deal with it.

Moreover, since we have already seen that we are always making judgments of degrees of freedom, based on the significance of the activities or purposes which are left unfettered, how can we deny that the man, externally free but still stymied by his repudiated desires, is less free than one who has no such inner obstacles?

But if this is so, then can we not say of the man with a highly distorted view of his fundamental purpose, the Manson or Baader of my discussion above, that he may not be significantly freer when we lift even the internal barriers to his doing what is in line with this purpose, or at best may be liberated into a very impoverished freedom? Should a Manson overcome his last remaining compunction against sending his minions to kill on caprice, so that he could act unchecked, would we consider him freer, as we should undoubtedly consider the man who had done away with spite or unreasoning fear? Hardly, and certainly not to the same degree. For what he sees as his purpose here partakes so much of the nature of spite and unreasoning fear in the other cases, that is, it is an aspiration largely shaped by confusion, illusion and distorted perspective.

Once we see that we make distinctions of degree and significance in freedoms depending on the significance of the purpose fettered/enabled, how can we deny that it makes a difference to the degree of freedom not only whether one of my basic purposes is frustrated by my own desires but also whether I have grievously misidentified this purpose? The only way to avoid this would be to hold that there is no such thing as getting it wrong, that your basic purpose is just what you feel it to be. But there is such a thing as getting it wrong, as we have seen, and the very distinctions of significance depend on this fact.

But if this is so, then the crude negative view of freedom, the Hobbesian definition, is untenable. Freedom cannot just be the absence of external obstacles, for there may also be internal ones. And nor may the internal obstacles be just confined to those that the subject identifies as such, that he is the final arbiter; for he may be profoundly mistaken about his purposes and about what he wants to repudiate. And if so, he is less capable of freedom in the meaningful sense of the word. Hence we cannot maintain the incorrigibility of the subject's judgments about his freedom, or rule our second-guessing, as we put it above. And at the same time, we are forced to abandon the pure opportunity-concept of freedom.

For freedom now involves my being able to recognize adequately my more important purposes, and my being able to overcome or at least neutralize my motivational fetters, as well as my way being free of external obstacles. But clearly the first condition (and, I would argue, also the second) require me to have become something, to have achieved a certain condition of self-clairvoyance and self-understanding. I must be actually exercising self-understanding in order to be truly or fully free. I can no longer understand freedom just as an opportunity-concept.

In all these three formulations of the issue—opportunity- versus exercise-concept; whether freedom requires that we discriminate among motivations; whether it allows of second-guessing the subject—the extreme negative view shows up as wrong. The idea of holding the Maginot Line before this Hobbesian concept is misguided not only because it involves abandoning some of the most inspiring terrain of liberalism, which is concerned with individual self-realization, but also because the line turns out to be untenable. The first step from the Hobbesian definition to a positive notion, to a view of freedom as the ability to fulfill my purposes, and as being greater the more significant the purposes, is one we cannot help taking. Whether we must also take the second step, to a view of freedom which sees it as realizable or fully realizable only within a certain form of society; and whether in taking a step of this kind one is ne-cessarily committed to justifying the excesses of totalitarian oppression in the name of liberty; these are questions which must now be addressed. What is certain is that they can-not simply be evaded by a philistine definition of freedom which relegates them by fiat to the limbo of metaphysical pseudo-questions. This is altogether too quick a way with them.

MICHAEL J. SANDEL
(1953–)

Michael Sandel, one of the best-known contemporary critics of liberalism, graduated summa cum laude from Brandeis University in 1975 and traveled to Oxford for his doctorate as a Rhodes Scholar. There he studied with Charles Taylor and graduated in 1981. Since 1980, he has been in the Department of Government at Harvard University where his undergraduate course "Justice" regularly attracts over 1000 students. From 2002 to 2005 he served on the President's Council on Bioethics, an advisory group on the ethics of new medical technology.

Michael Sandel achieved philosophical fame in 1982 with the publication of *Liberalism and the Limits of Justice*, a widely read critique of liberalism and John Rawls. According to Sandel, liberals endorse a "thin" conception of the self which is "given prior to its ends." Liberals typically stress the importance of individuals freely pursuing a life-plan that may or may not reflect the goals society sets for them. Against this conception, Sandel holds that the self is "embedded," i.e., constituted by our communal role and the community's ends. From the beginning we all are inevitably and inextricably related to others and to our communities; our identity and conception of the good flows from these relations.

What follows from this critique of the thin conception of self? Sandel's critics agree that communal relations constitute our identities in significant ways, but have pointed out that this does not necessarily imply these identities or communal relations ought to be celebrated. It is possible to agree with Sandel's account of the self, but argue that people should try to distance their ends from what their communities dictate—after all, many communities are racist, sexist, class-based, and/or homophobic.

Sandel's own views are associated with the communitarian movement in political philosophy (though he has expressed reservations about the application of this category to himself, preferring to align himself with classical republican thought). Throughout his work, Sandel questions the liberal emphasis on individualism, and on rights-based practices that abstract from considerations of the common good. He contests the liberal view that government should be neutral regarding religious and moral views, and rejects Rawls's idea that just societal arrangements are not to be based on a prior idea of the moral good. His own views emphasize the community, stressing the importance of teaching individuals to value civic virtues and the common good—to feel responsible for a larger whole.

◆ ◆ ◆ ◆ ◆

The Procedural Republic and the Unencumbered Self[1] (1984)

Political philosophy seems often to reside at a distance from the world. Principles are one thing, politics another, and even our best efforts to "live up" to our ideals typically founder on the gap between theory and practice.[2]

But if political philosophy is unrealizable in one sense, it is unavoidable in another. This is the sense in which philosophy inhabits the world from the start; our practices and institutions are embodiments of theory. To engage in a political practice is already to stand in relation to theory.[3] For all our uncertainties about ultimate questions of political philosophy—of justice and value and the nature of the good life—the one thing we know is that we live *some* answer all the time.

In this essay I will try to explore the answer we live now, in contemporary America. What is the political philosophy implicit in our practices and institutions? How does it stand, as philosophy? And how do tensions in the philosophy find expression in our present political condition?

It may be objected that it is a mistake to look for a single philosophy, that we live no "answer," only answers. But a plurality of answers is itself a kind of answer. And the political theory that affirms this plurality is the theory I propose to explore.

The Right and the Good

We might begin by considering a certain moral and political vision. It is a liberal vision, and like most liberal visions gives pride of place to justice, fairness, and individual rights. Its core thesis is this: a just society seeks not to promote any particular ends, but enables its citizens to pursue their own ends, consistent with a similar liberty for all; it therefore must govern by principles that do not presuppose any particular conception of the good. What justifies these regulative principles above all is not that they maximize the general welfare, or cultivate virtue, or otherwise promote the good, but rather that they conform to the concept of *right*, a moral category given prior to the good, and independent of it.

This liberalism says, in other words, that what makes the just society just is not the *telos* or purpose or end at which it aims, but precisely its refusal to choose in advance among competing purposes and ends. In its constitution and its laws, the just society seeks to provide a framework within which its citizens can pursue their own values and ends, consistent with a similar liberty for others.

The ideal I've described might be summed up in the claim that the right is prior to the good, and in two senses: The priority of the right means first, that individual rights cannot be sacrificed for the sake of the general good (in this it opposes utilitarianism), and second, that the principles of justice that specify these rights cannot be premised on any particular vision of the good life. (In this it opposes teleological conceptions in general.)

This is the liberalism of much contemporary moral and political philosophy, most fully elaborated by Rawls, and indebted to Kant for its philosophical foundations.[4] But I

---

1   *The Procedural Republic and the Unencumbered Self* [Unless otherwise indicated, all notes are by the author.] An earlier version of this article was presented to the Political Philosophy Colloquium at Princeton University, and to the Legal Theory Workshop at Columbia Law School. I am grateful to the participants, and also to the Editor, William Connolly, for helpful comments and criticisms. I would also like to thank the Ford Foundation for support of a larger project of which this essay is a first installment.

2   *Political philosophy ... theory and practice* An excellent example of this view can be found in Samuel Huntington, *American Politics: The Promise of Disharmony* (Cambridge: Harvard University Press, 1981). See especially his discussion of the "ideals versus institutions" gap, pp. 10–12, 39–41, 61–84, 221–62.

3   *To engage ... to theory* See, for example, the conceptions of a "practice" advanced by Alasdair MacIntyre and Charles Taylor. MacIntyre, *After Virtue* (Notre Dame: University of Notre Dame Press, 1981), 175–209. Taylor, "Interpretation and the Sciences of Man," *Review of Metaphysics* 25 (1971), pp. 3–51.

4   *This is ... philosophical foundations* John Rawls, *A Theory of Justice* (Oxford: Oxford University Press, 1971). Immanuel Kant, *Groundwork of the Metaphysics of Morals*, trans. H.J. Paton. (1785; New York: Harper and Row, 1956). Kant, *Critique of Pure Reason*, trans. Norman Kemp Smith (1781, 1787; London: Macmillan, 1929). Kant, *Critique of Practical Reason*, trans. L.W. Beck (1788; Indianapolis: Bobbs-Merrill, 1956). Kant, "On the Common Saying: 'This May Be True in Theory, But It Does Not Apply in Practice,'" in Hans Reiss, ed., *Kant's Political Writings*. (1793; Cambridge: Cambridge University Press, 1970). Other recent versions of the claim for the priority of the right over good can be found in Robert Nozick, *Anarchy, State and Utopia* (New York: Basic Books, 1974); Ronald Dworkin, *Taking Rights Seriously* (London: Duckworth, 1977); Bruce Ackerman, *Social Justice in the Liberal State* (New Haven: Yale University Press, 1980).

am concerned here less with the lineage of this vision than with what seem to me three striking facts about it.

First, it has a deep and powerful philosophical appeal. Second, despite its philosophical force, the claim for the priority of the right over the good ultimately fails. And third, despite its philosophical failure, this liberal vision is the one by which we live. For us in late twentieth century America, it is our vision, the theory most thoroughly embodied in the practices and institutions most central to our public life. And seeing how it goes wrong as philosophy may help us to diagnose our present political condition. So first, its philosophical power; second, its philosophical failure; and third, however briefly, its uneasy embodiment in the world.

But before taking up these three claims, it is worth pointing out a central theme that connects them. And that is a certain conception of the person, of what it is to be a moral agent. Like all political theories, the liberal theory I have described is something more than a set of regulative principles. It is also a view about the way the world is, and the way we move within it. At the heart of this ethic lies a vision of the person that both inspires and undoes it. As I will try to argue now, what make this ethic so compelling, but also, finally, vulnerable, are the promise and the failure of the unencumbered self.

Kantian Foundations[1]

The liberal ethic asserts the priority of right, and seeks principles of justice that do not presuppose any particular conception of the good. This is what Kant means by the supremacy of the moral law, and what Rawls means when he writes that "justice is the first virtue of social institutions."[2] Justice is more than just another value. It provides the framework that *regulates* the play of competing values and ends; it must therefore have a sanction independent of those ends. But it is not obvious where such a sanction could be found.

Theories of justice, and for that matter, ethics, have typically founded their claims on one or another conception of human purposes and ends. Thus Aristotle said the measure of a *polis* is the good at which it aims, and even J.S. Mill, who in the nineteenth century called "justice the chief part,

and incomparably the most binding part of all morality," made justice an instrument of utilitarian ends.[3]

This is the solution Kant's ethic rejects. Different persons typically have different desires and ends, and so any principle derived from them can only be contingent. But the moral law needs a *categorical* foundation, not a contingent one. Even so universal a desire as happiness will not do. People still differ in what happiness consists of, and to install any particular conception as regulative would impose on some the conceptions of others, and so deny at least to some the freedom to choose their *own* conceptions. In any case, to govern ourselves in conformity with desires and inclinations, given as they are by nature or circumstance, is not really to be *self*-governing at all. It is rather a refusal of freedom, a capitulation to determinations given outside us.

According to Kant, the right is "derived entirely from the concept of freedom in the external relationships of human beings, and has nothing to do with the end which all men have by nature [i.e., the aim of achieving happiness] or with the recognized means of attaining this end."[4] As such, it must have a basis prior to all empirical ends. Only when I am governed by principles that do not presuppose any particular ends am I free to pursue my own ends consistent with a similar freedom for all.

But this still leaves the question of what the basis of the right could possibly be. If it must be a basis prior to all purposes and ends, unconditioned even by what Kant calls "the special circumstances of human nature,"[5] where could such a basis conceivably be found? Given the stringent demands of the Kantian ethic, the moral law would seem almost to require a foundation in nothing, for any empirical precondition would undermine its priority. "Duty!" asks Kant at his most lyrical, "What origin is there worthy of thee, and where is to be found the root of thy noble descent which proudly rejects all kinship with the inclinations?"[6]

His answer is that the basis of the moral law is to be found in the *subject*, not the object of practical reason, a subject capable of an autonomous will. No empirical end, but rather "a subject of ends, namely a rational being him-

---

1 *Kantian Foundations* This section, and the two that follow, summarize arguments developed more fully in Michael Sandel, *Liberalism and the Limits of Justice* (Cambridge: Cambridge University Press, 1982).

2 *what Rawls means ... social institutions* Rawls, *Theory*, 3.

3 *J.S. Mill ... utilitarian ends* John Stuart Mill, *Utilitarianism*, in *The Utilitarians* (1893; Garden City: Doubleday, 1973), p. 465. Mill, *On Liberty*, in *The Utilitarians*, p. 485 (Originally published 1849).

4 *According to Kant ... attaining this end* Kant, "Common Saying," 73.

5 *what Kant calls ... human nature* Kant, *Groundwork*, p. 92.

6 *"Duty!" asks Kant ... the inclinations* Kant, *Critique*, p. 89.

self, must be made the ground for all maxims of action."[1] Nothing other than what Kant calls "the subject of all possible ends himself" can give rise to the right, for only this subject is also the subject of an autonomous will. Only this subject could be that "something which elevates man above himself as part of the world of sense" and enables him to participate in an ideal, unconditioned realm wholly independent of our social and psychological inclinations. And only this thoroughgoing independence can afford us the detachment we need if we are ever freely to choose for ourselves, unconditioned by the vagaries of circumstance.[2]

Who or what exactly *is* this subject? It is, in a certain sense, *us*. The moral law, after all, is a law we give *ourselves;* we don't *find* it, we *will* it. That is how it (and we) escape the reign of nature and circumstance and merely empirical ends. But what is important to see is that the "we" who do the willing are not "we" qua particular persons, you and me, each for ourselves—the moral law is not up to us as individuals—but "we" qua participants in what Kant calls "pure practical reason," "we" qua participants in a transcendental subject.[3]

Now what is to guarantee that I *am* a subject of this kind, capable of exercising pure practical reason? Well, strictly speaking, there *is* no guarantee; the transcendental subject is only a possibility. But it is a possibility I must *presuppose* if I am to think of myself as a free moral agent. Were I wholly an empirical being, I would not be capable of freedom, for every exercise of will would be conditioned by the desire for some object. All choice would be heteronomous[4] choice, governed by the pursuit of some end. My will could never be a first cause, only the effect of some prior cause, the instrument of one or another impulse or inclination. "When we think of ourselves as free," writes Kant, "we transfer ourselves into the intelligible world as members and recognize the autonomy of the will."[5] And so

the notion of a subject prior to and independent of experience, such as the Kantian ethic requires, appears not only possible but indispensable, a necessary presupposition of the possibility of freedom.

How does all of this come back to politics? As the subject is prior to its ends, so the right is prior to the good. Society is best arranged when it is governed by principles that do not presuppose any particular conception of the good, for any other arrangement would fail to respect persons as being capable of choice; it would treat them as objects rather than subjects, as means rather than ends in themselves.

We can see in this way how Kant's notion of the subject is bound up with the claim for the priority of right. But for those in the Anglo-American tradition, the transcendental subject will seem a strange foundation for a familiar ethic. Surely, one may think, we can take rights seriously and affirm the primacy of justice without embracing the *Critique of Pure Reason*. This, in any case, is the project of Rawls.

He wants to save the priority of right from the obscurity of the transcendental subject. Kant's idealist metaphysic, for all its moral and political advantage, cedes too much to the transcendent, and wins for justice its primacy only by denying it its human situation. "To develop a viable Kantian conception of justice," Rawls writes, "the force and content of Kant's doctrine must be detached from its background in transcendental idealism" and recast within the "canons of a reasonable empiricism."[6] And so Rawls's project is to preserve Kant's moral and political teaching by replacing Germanic obscurities with a domesticated metaphysic more congenial to the Anglo-American temper. This is the role of the original position.

From Transcendental Subject to Unencumbered Self

The original position tries to provide what Kant's transcendental argument cannot—a foundation for the right that is prior to the good, but still situated in the world. Sparing all but essentials, the original position works like this: It invites us to imagine the principles we would choose to govern our society if we were to choose them in advance, before we knew the particular persons we would be—whether rich or poor, strong or weak, lucky or unlucky—before we knew even our interests or aims or conceptions of the good. These

---

1   *a subject ... of action* Kant, *Groundwork*, 105.

2   *Only this subject ... vagaries of circumstance* Kant, *Critique*, p. 89.

3   *transcendental subject* [editors' note] This, for Kant, is what constitutes the real person—subjectivity stripped of all its relations to external objects, not knowable through the senses, but rather intelligible only through "transcendental" reasoning—that is, discoverable as the only possible grounding for the unity of all our experience—what makes my experience *mine*.

4   *heteronomous* [editors' note] Subject to external laws or causes and hence for Kant unfree, heteronomous choice is contrasted with *autonomous* or self-governing choice.

5   *When we ... autonomy of the will* Kant, *Groundwork*, 121.

6   *Rawls writes ... reasonable empiricism* Rawls, "The Basic Structure as Subject," *American Philosophical Quarterly* (1977), 165.

principles—the ones we would choose in that imaginary situation—are the principles of justice. What is more, if it works, they are principles that do not presuppose any particular ends.

What they *do* presuppose is a certain picture of the person, of the way we must be if we are beings for whom justice is the first virtue. This is the picture of the unencumbered self, a self understood as prior to and independent of purposes and ends.

Now the unencumbered self describes first of all the way we stand toward the things we have, or want, or seek. It means there is always a distinction between the values I *have* and the person I *am*. To identify any characteristics as *my* aims, ambitions, desires, and so on, is always to imply some subject "me" standing behind them, at a certain distance, and the shape of this "me" must be given prior to any of the aims or attributes I bear. One consequences of this distance is to put the self *itself* beyond the reach of its experience, to secure its identity once and for all. Or to put the point another way, it rules out the possibility of what we might call *constitutive* ends. No role or commitment could define me so completely that I could not understand myself without it. No project could be so essential that turning away from it would call into question the person I am.

For the unencumbered self, what matters above all, what is most essential to our personhood, are not the ends we choose but our capacity to choose them. The original position sums up this central claim about us. "It is not our aims that primarily reveal our nature," writes Rawls, "but rather the principles that we would acknowledge to govern the background conditions under which these aims are to be formed.... We should therefore reverse the relation between the right and the good proposed by teleological doctrines and view the right as prior."[1]

Only if the self is prior to its ends can the right be prior to the good. Only if my identity is never tied to the aims and interests I may have at any moment can I think of myself as a free and independent agent, capable of choice.

This notion of independence carries consequences for the kind of community of which we are capable. Understood as unencumbered selves, we are of course free to join in voluntary association with others, and so are capable of community in the cooperative sense. What is denied to the unencumbered self is the possibility of membership in any community bound by moral ties antecedent to choice; he cannot belong to any community where the self *itself* could be at stake. Such a community—call it constitutive as against merely cooperative—would engage the identity as well as the interests of the participants, and so implicate its members in a citizenship more thoroughgoing than the unencumbered self can know.

For justice to be primary, then, we must be creatures of a certain kind, related to human circumstance in a certain way. We must stand to our circumstance always at a certain distance, whether as transcendental subject in the case of Kant, or as unencumbered selves in the case of Rawls. Only in this way can we view ourselves as subjects as well as objects of experience, as agents and not just instruments of the purposes we pursue.

The unencumbered self and the ethic it inspires, taken together, hold out a liberating vision. Freed from the dictates of nature and the sanction of social roles, the human subject is installed as sovereign, cast as the author of the only moral meanings there are. As participants in pure practical reason, or as parties to the original position, we are free to construct principles of justice unconstrained by an order of value antecedently given. And as actual, individual selves, we are free to choose our purposes and ends unbound by such an order, or by custom or tradition or inherited status. So long as they are not unjust, our conceptions of the good carry weight, whatever they are, simply in virtue of our having chosen them. We are, in Rawls's words, "self-originating sources of valid claims."[2]

This is an exhilarating promise, and the liberalism it animates is perhaps the fullest expression of the Enlightenment's quest for the self-defining subject. But is it true? Can we make sense of our moral and political life by the light of the self-image it requires? I do not think we can, and I will try to show why not by arguing first within the liberal project, then beyond it.

Justice and Community

We have focused so far on the foundations of the liberal vision, on the way it derives the principles it defends. Let us turn briefly now to the substance of those principles, using Rawls as our example. Sparing all but essentials once again, Rawls's two principles of justice are these: first, equal basic

---

1 *It is not ... as prior* Rawls, *Theory*, p. 560.

2 *We are ... valid claims* Rawls, "Kantian Constructivism in Moral Theory," *Journal of Philosophy* 77 (1980), p. 543.

liberties for all, and second, only those social and economic inequalities that benefit the least-advantaged members of society (the difference principle).

In arguing for these principles, Rawls argues against two familiar alternatives—utilitarianism and libertarianism. He argues against utilitarianism that it fails to take seriously the distinction between persons. In seeking to maximize the general welfare, the utilitarian treats society as whole as if it were a single person; it conflates our many, diverse desires into a single system of desires, and tries to maximize. It is indifferent to the distribution of satisfactions among persons, except insofar as this may affect the overall sum. But this fails to respect our plurality and distinctness. It uses some as means to the happiness of all, and so fails to respect each as an end in himself. While utilitarians may sometimes defend individual rights, their defense must rest on the calculation that respecting those rights will serve utility in the long run. But this calculation is contingent and uncertain. So long as utility is what Mill said it is, "the ultimate appeal on all ethical questions,"[1] individual rights can never be secure. To avoid the danger that their life prospects might one day be sacrificed for the greater good of others, the parties to the original position therefore insist on certain basic liberties for all, and make those liberties prior.

If utilitarians fail to take seriously the distinctness of persons, libertarians go wrong by failing to acknowledge the arbitrariness of fortune. They define as just whatever distribution results from an efficient market economy, and oppose all redistribution on the grounds that people are entitled to whatever they get, so long as they do not cheat or steal or otherwise violate someone's rights in getting it. Rawls opposes this principle on the ground that the distribution of talents and assets and even efforts by which some get more and others get less is arbitrary from a moral point of view, a matter of good luck. To distribute the good things in life on the basis of these differences is not to do justice, but simply to carry over into human arrangements the arbitrariness of social and natural contingency. We deserve, as individuals, neither the talents our good fortune may have brought, nor the benefits that flow from them. We should therefore regard these talents as common assets, and regard one another as common beneficiaries of the rewards they bring. "Those who have been favored by nature, whoever they are, may gain from their good fortune only on terms that improve the situation of those who have lost out.... In justice as fairness, men agree to share one another's fate."[2]

This is the reasoning that leads to the difference principle. Notice how it reveals, in yet another guise, the logic of the unencumbered self. I cannot be said to deserve the benefits that flow from, say, my fine physique and good looks, because they are only accidental, not essential facts about me. They describe attributes I *have*, not the person I *am*, and so cannot give rise to a claim of desert. Being an unencumbered self, this is true of *everything* about me. And so I cannot, as an individual, deserve anything at all.

However jarring to our ordinary understandings this argument may be, the picture so far remains intact; the priority of right, the denial of desert, and the unencumbered self all hang impressively together.

But the difference principle requires more, and it is here that the argument comes undone. The difference principle begins with the thought, congenial to the unencumbered self, that the assets I have are only accidentally mine. But it ends by assuming that these assets are therefore *common* assets and that society has a prior claim on the fruits of their exercise. But this assumption is without warrant. Simply because I, as an individual, do not have a privileged claim on the assets accidentally residing "here," it does not follow that everyone in the world collectively does. For there is no reason to think that their location in society's province or, for that matter, within the province of humankind, is any *less* arbitrary from a moral point of view. And if their arbitrariness within *me* makes them ineligible to serve *my* ends, there seems no obvious reason why their arbitrariness within any particular society should not make them ineligible to serve that society's ends as well.

To put the point another way, the difference principle, like utilitarianism, is a principle of sharing. As such, it must presuppose some prior moral tie among those whose assets it would deploy and whose efforts it would enlist in a common endeavor. Otherwise, it is simply a formula for using some as means to others ends, a formula this liberalism is committed to reject.

But on the cooperative vision of community alone, it is unclear what the moral basis for this sharing could be. Short of the constitutive conception, deploying an individual's assets for the sake of the common good would seem an offense against the "plurality and distinctness" of individuals this liberalism seeks above all to secure.

---

1   *So long as ... ethical questions* Mill, *On Liberty*, p. 485.

2   *Those who ... another's fate* Rawls, *Theory*, 101–02.

If those whose fate I am required to share really are, morally speaking, *others*, rather than fellow participants in a way of life with which my identity is bound, the difference principle falls prey to the same objections as utilitarianism. Its claim on me is not the claim of a constitutive community whose attachments I acknowledge, but rather the claim of a concatenated collectivity whose entanglements I confront.

What the difference principle requires, but cannot provide, is some way of identifying those *among* whom the assets I bear are properly regarded as common, some way of seeing ourselves as mutually indebted and morally engaged to begin with. But as we have seen, the constitutive aims and attachments that would save and situate the difference principle are precisely the ones denied to the liberal self; the moral encumbrances and antecedent obligations they imply would undercut the priority of right.

What, then, of those encumbrances? The point so far is that we cannot be persons for whom justice is primary, and also be persons for whom the difference principle is a principle of justice. But which must give way? Can we view ourselves as independent selves, independent in the sense that our identity is never tied to our aims and attachments?

I do not think we can, at least not without cost to those loyalties and convictions whose moral force consists partly in the fact that living by them is inseparable from understanding ourselves as the particular persons we are—as members of this family or community or nation or people, as bearers of that history, as citizens of this republic. Allegiances such as these are more than values I happen to have, and to hold, at a certain distance. They go beyond the obligations I voluntarily incur and the "natural duties" I owe to human beings as such. They allow that to some I owe more than justice requires or even permits, not by reason of agreements I have made but instead in virtue of those more or less enduring attachments and commitments that, taken together, partly define the person I am.

To imagine a person incapable of constitutive attachments such as these is not to conceive an ideally free and rational agent, but to imagine a person wholly without character, without moral depth. For to have character is to know that I move in a history I neither summon nor command, which carries consequences nonetheless for my choices and conduct. It draws me closer to some and more distant from others; it makes some aims more appropriate, others less so. As a self-interpreting being, I am able to reflect on my history and in this sense to distance myself from it, but the distance is always precarious and provisional, the point of reflection never finally secured outside the history itself. But the liberal ethic puts the self beyond the reach of its experience, beyond deliberation and reflection. Denied the expansive self-understandings that could shape a common life, the liberal self is left to lurch between detachment on the one hand, and entanglement on the other. Such is the fate of the unencumbered self, and its liberating promise.

The Procedural Republic

But before my case can be complete, I need to consider one powerful reply. While it comes from a liberal direction, its spirit is more practical than philosophical. It says, in short, that I am asking too much. It is one thing to seek constitutive attachments in our private lives; among families and friends, and certain tightly knit groups, there may be found a common good that makes justice and rights less pressing. But with public life—at least today, and probably always—it is different. So long as the nation-state is the primary form of political association, talk of constitutive community too easily suggests a darker politics rather than a brighter one; amid echoes of the moral majority, the priority of right, for all its philosophical faults, still seems the safer hope.

This is a challenging rejoinder, and no account of political community in the twentieth century can fail to take it seriously. It is challenging not least because it calls into question the status of political philosophy and its relation to the world. For if my argument is correct, if the liberal vision we have considered is not morally self-sufficient but parasitic on a notion of community it officially rejects, then we should expect to find that the political practice that embodies this vision is not *practically* self-sufficient either—that it must draw on a sense of community it cannot supply and may even undermine. But is that so far from the circumstance we face today? Could it be that through the original position darkly, on the far side of the veil of ignorance, we may glimpse an intimation of our predicament, a refracted vision of ourselves?

How does the liberal vision—and its failure—help us make sense of our public life and its predicament? Consider, to begin, the following paradox in the citizen's relation to the modern welfare state. In many ways, we in the 1980s stand near the completion of a liberal project that has run its course from the New Deal through the Great Society and into the present. But notwithstanding the extension of the franchise and the expansion on individual rights and entitlements in recent decades, there is a widespread sense that, individually and collectively, our control over the forces that govern our lives is receding rather than increasing. This sense is deepened by what appear simultaneously as the power and the powerlessness of the nation-state. One the one hand, increasing numbers of citizens view the state as an overly intrusive presence, more likely to frustrate their purposes than advance them. And yet, despite its unprecedented role in the economy and society, the modern state seems itself disempowered, unable effectively to control the domestic economy, to respond to persisting social ills, or to work America's will in the world.

This is a paradox that has fed the appeals of recent politicians (including Carter and Reagan), even as it has frustrated their attempts to govern. To sort it out, we need to identify the public philosophy implicit in our political practice, and to reconstruct its arrival. We need to trace the advent of the procedural republic, by which I mean a public life animated by the liberal vision and self-image we've considered.

The story of the procedural republic goes back in some ways to the founding of the republic, but its central drama begins to unfold around the turn of the century. As national markets and large-scale enterprise displaced a decentralized economy, the decentralized political forms of the early republic became outmoded as well. If democracy was to survive, the concentration of economic power would have to be met by a similar concentration of political power. But the Progressives understood, or some of them did, that the success of democracy required more than the centralization of government; it also required the nationalization of politics. The primary form of political community had to be a recast on a national scale. For Herbert Croly, writing in 1909, the "nationalizing of American political, economic, and social life" was "an essentially formative and enlightening political transformation." We would become more of a democracy only as we became "more of a nation...in ideas, in institutions, and in spirit."[1]

This nationalizing project would be consummated in the New Deal,[2] but for the democratic tradition in America, the embrace of the nation was a decisive departure. From Jefferson to the populists, the party of democracy in American political debate had been, roughly speaking, the party of the provinces, of decentralized power, of small-town and small-scale America. And against them had stood the party of the nation—first Federalists, then Whigs, then the Republicans of Lincoln—a party that spoke for the consolidation of the union. It was thus the historic achievement of the New Deal to unite, in a single party and political program, what Samuel Beer has called "liberalism and the national idea."[3]

What matters for our purpose is that, in the twentieth century, liberalism made its peace with concentrated power. But it was understood at the start that the terms of this peace required a strong sense of national community, morally and politically to underwrite the extended involvements of a modern industrial order. If a virtuous republic of small-scale, democratic communities was no longer a possibility, a national republic seemed democracy's next best hope. This was still, in principle at least, a politics of the common good. It looked to the nation, not as a neutral framework for the play of competing interests, but rather as a formative community, concerned to shape a common life suited to the scale of modern social and economic forms.

But this project failed. By the mid- or late twentieth century, the national republic had run its course. Except for extraordinary moments, such as war, the nation proved too vast a scale across which to cultivate the shared self-understandings necessary to community in the formative, or constitutive sense. And so the gradual shift, in our practices and institutions, from a public philosophy of common purposes to one of fair procedures, from a politics of good to a politics of right, from the national republic to the procedural republic.

Our Present Predicament

A full account of this transition would take a detailed look at the changing shape of political institutions, constitutional interpretation, and the terms of political discourse in the broadest sense. But I suspect we would find in the *practice* of the procedural republic two broad tendencies foreshadowed by its philosophy: first, a tendency to crowd out democratic

---

1   *For Herbert Croly ... in spirit* Croly, *The Promise of American Life* (Indianapolis: Bobbs-Merrill, 1965), pp. 270–73.

2   *the New Deal* [editors' note] Collective name for a wide range of federal policies and agencies created by President Franklin Roosevelt in the US from 1933–38, with the immediate aim of recovery from the Great Depression. The lasting effect was a considerable increase in the involvement of government in the lives of the people.

3   *what Samuel Beer ... national idea* Beer, "Liberalism and the National Idea," *The Public Interest*, Fall (1966), pp. 70–82.

possibilities; second, a tendency to undercut the kind of community on which it nonetheless depends.

Where liberty in the early republic was understood as a function of democratic institutions and dispersed power,[1] liberty in the procedural republic is defined in opposition to democracy, as an individual's guarantee against what the majority might will. I am free insofar as I am the bearer of rights, where rights are trumps.[2] Unlike the liberty of the early republic, the modern version permits—in fact even requires—concentrated power. This has to do with the universalizing logic of rights. Insofar as I have a right, whether to free speech or a minimum income, its provision cannot be left to the vagaries of local preferences but must be assured at the most comprehensive level of political association. It cannot be one thing in New York and another in Alabama. As rights and entitlements expand, politics is therefore displaced from smaller forms of association and relocated at the most universal form—in our case, the nation. And even as politics flows to the nation, power shifts away from democratic institutions (such as legislatures and political parties) and toward institutions designed to be insulated from democratic pressures, and hence better equipped to dispense and defend individual rights (notably the judiciary and bureaucracy).

These institutional developments may begin to account for the sense of powerlessness that the welfare state fails to address and in some ways doubtless deepens. But it seems to me a further clue to our condition recalls even more directly the predicament of the unencumbered self—lurching, as we left it, between detachment on the one hand, the entanglement on the other. For it is a striking feature of the welfare state that it offers a powerful promise of individual rights, and also demands of its citizens a high measure of mutual engagement. But the self-image that attends the rights cannot sustain the engagement.

As bearers of rights, where rights are trumps, we think of ourselves as freely choosing, individual selves, unbound by obligations antecedent to rights, or to the agreements we make. And yet, as citizens of the procedural republic that secures these rights, we find ourselves implicated willy-nilly in a formidable array of dependencies and expectations we did not choose and increasingly reject.

In our public life, we are more entangled, but less attached, than ever before. It is as though the unencumbered self presupposed by the liberal ethic had begun to come true—less liberated than disempowered, entangled in a network of obligations and involvements unassociated with any act of will, and yet unmediated by those common identifications or expansive self-definitions that would make them tolerable. As the scale of social and political organization has become more comprehensive, the terms of our collective identity have become more fragmented, and the forms of political life have outrun the common purpose needed to sustain them.

Something like this, it seems to me, has been unfolding in America for the past half-century or so. I hope I have said at least enough to suggest the shape a fuller story might take. And I hope in any case to have conveyed a certain view about politics and philosophy and the relation between them—that our practices and institutions are themselves embodiments of theory, and to unravel their predicament is, at least in part, to seek after the self-image of the age.

1   *liberty in the early republic ... dispersed power*   See, for example, Laurence Tribe, *American Constitutional Law* (Mineola: The Foundation Press, 1978), pp. 2–3.

2   *I am free ... rights are trumps*   See Ronald Dworkin, "Liberalism," in Stuart Hampshire, ed., *Public and Private Morality* (Cambridge: Cambridge University Press, 1978), p. 136.

MICHAEL WALZER
(1935–)

Michael Walzer is highly regarded both as an academic philosopher and as editor-in-chief of *Dissent*, where he writes issue-based commentaries for a general audience. His philosophical work is distinguished by its attention to real world examples drawn from current events and history. Walzer has published widely on topics in moral and political philosophy including liberalism, globalization, nationalism, toleration, and the history of Jewish political thought, but remains best known for his groundbreaking *Just and Unjust Wars* (1977, second edition 1992) and his theory of "complex equality" set forth in *Spheres of Justice* (1983).

In *Just and Unjust Wars*, Walzer poses the question: When can a war be morally justified? He dismisses pacifism, the view that war is never morally justified, but also rejects realism, the view that denies that—or at least is skeptical that—moral concepts can be applied to war and international relations. He advances moral grounds for when going to war is justified, and proposes rules of conduct during and after war. *Just and Unjust Wars* also addresses topics such as terrorism, humanitarian intervention, war crimes, civilian casualties, and the ethics of reprisals. Throughout, Walzer illustrates his discussion with examples from contemporary and historical wars.

In *Spheres of Justice*, Walzer questions a political philosophical tradition that begins with Plato. On this conception of political philosophy, common in liberal thought, philosophers attempt to provide an independent standard or set of principles enabling us to evaluate actual societies and their institutions. This amounts to a universal theory of justice, defined apart from any particular society. Political philosophers, then, propose an objective normative standard that provides a tool for criticizing actual societies.

Walzer can be understood as reacting against the most prominent recent work in this tradition, John Rawls's *A Theory of Justice*. Rawls draws on the social contract tradition by proposing a hypothetical "original position,"

where rational agents choose principles of justice. In order to ensure that agents choose principles of justice and not simply negotiate their self-interest, he stipulates that they choose beneath a "veil of ignorance." Parties under the veil of ignorance do not know any of their personal information, including their age, sex, social class, religion, natural abilities, etc. Since these parties might be anybody in society, Rawls argues that it would be rational for them to choose principles that guarantee basic liberties, as well as a strong egalitarian principle that distributes resources to the least well-off members of society.

Walzer rejects this general approach, a stance he shares with other philosophers with "communitarian" leanings, including Michael Sandel, Alisdair MacIntyre and Charles Taylor. Communitarians argue that universal accounts of justice fail to pay adequate attention to actual practices and institutions. There is no external standpoint, since we all work within our culture and shared history. Moreover, people value their traditions, so the attempt to impose a universal standard relies on a simplistic and often unrealistic account of justice. Political philosophy, for Walzer, becomes a matter of cultural interpretation, revealing meanings already implicit in the culture.

His theory of justice therefore provides an account of "complex equality." For Walzer, any account of equality needs to address the question of *what* should be distributed, and specify the rules for its distribution (*how* should it be distributed and *to whom*?). Unlike many political philosophers, who give an abstract account of distributive justice independent of any particular society, Walzer adopts what is sometimes called a "conventionalist" account. Justice, for Walzer, is a human construction, something that arises in particular societies over time. What counts as a *just* distribution for any particular good thus varies between groups. The task of the philosopher is the *interpretation* of existing practices and norms, rather than the discovery of universal, objective principles.

If Walzer is sensitive to differences among human societies, he does not reject the existence at some level of universal principles. Here he distinguishes between "thick" and "thin" accounts of justice. A thin account of justice is "minimal and universal," involving basic human rights that apply across societies. Walzer suggests that all (or almost all) moral codes reflect these basic rights and principles in some form or other.

At the same time, every society embeds this thin account of justice in a thicker account that reflects the shared meanings of the particular society. Basic human rights in practice function mainly as constraints, specifying how we must *not* act towards others. But any full account of justice needs to be much richer, providing positive norms for how we ought to live, what things we should value, and how we should distribute goods. It is these that are relative to a particular culture. Walzer argues that this dual approach more accurately captures our actual experience of justice and shared self-understanding than would the lofty aspirations of a more purely universal theory.

◆ ◆ ◆ ◆ ◆

from *Spheres of Justice* (1983)

Chapter 1: Complex Equality

Pluralism

Distributive justice[1] is a large idea. It draws the entire world of goods within the reach of philosophical reflection. Nothing can be omitted; no feature of our common life can escape scrutiny. Human society is a distributive community. That's not all it is, but it is importantly that: we come together to share, divide, and exchange. We also come together to make the things that are shared, divided, and exchanged; but that very making—work itself—is distributed among us in a division of labor. My place in the economy, my standing in the political order, my reputation among my fellows, my

---

1   *Distributive justice* [Unless otherwise specified, all notes are by the author of this selection.] [editors' note] Distributive justice deals with the fair division of goods, benefits or burdens. It is commonly distinguished from retributive justice, which concerns the ethics of punishment.

material holdings: all these come to me from other men and women. It can be said that I have what I have rightly or wrongly, justly or unjustly; but given the range of distributions and the number of participants, such judgments are never easy.

The idea of distributive justice has as much to do with being and doing as with having, as much to do with production as with consumption, as much to do with identity and status as with land, capital, or personal possessions. Different political arrangements enforce, and different ideologies justify, different distributions of membership, power, honor, ritual eminence, divine grace, kinship and love, knowledge, wealth, physical security, work and leisure, rewards and punishments, and a host of goods more narrowly and materially conceived—food, shelter, clothing, transportation, medical care, commodities of every sort, and all the odd things (paintings, rare books, postage stamps) that human beings collect. And this multiplicity of goods is matched by a multiplicity of distributive procedures, agents, and criteria. There are such things as simple distributive systems—slave galleys, monasteries, insane asylums, kindergartens (though each of these, looked at closely, might show unexpected complexities); but no full-fledged human society has ever avoided the multiplicity. We must study it all, the goods and the distributions, in many different times and places.

There is, however, no single point of access to this world of distributive arrangements and ideologies. There has never been a universal medium of exchange. Since the decline of the barter economy, money has been the most common medium. But the old maxim according to which there are some things that money can't buy is not only normatively but also factually true. What should and should not be up for sale is something men and women always have to decide and have decided in many different ways. Throughout history, the market has been one of the most important mechanisms for the distribution of social goods; but it has never been, it nowhere is today, a complete distributive system.

Similarly, there has never been either a single decision point from which all distributions are controlled or a single set of agents making decisions. No state power has ever been so pervasive as to regulate all the patterns of sharing, dividing, and exchanging out of which a society takes shape. Things slip away from the state's grasp; new patterns are worked out—familial networks, black markets, bureaucratic alliances, clandestine political and religious organizations. State officials can tax, conscript, allocate, regulate, appoint, reward, punish, but they cannot capture the full range of goods or substitute themselves for every other agent of distribution. Nor can anyone else do that: there are market coups and cornerings,[1] but there has never been a fully successful distributive conspiracy.

And finally, there has never been a single criterion, or a single set of interconnected criteria, for all distributions. Desert, qualification, birth and blood, friendship, need, free exchange, political loyalty, democratic decision: each has had its place, along with many others, uneasily coexisting, invoked by competing groups, confused with one another.

In the matter of distributive justice, history displays a great variety of arrangements and ideologies. But the first impulse of the philosopher is to resist the displays of history, the world of appearances, and to search for some underlying unity: a short list of basic goods, quickly abstracted to a single good; a single distributive criterion or an interconnected set; and the philosopher himself standing, symbolically at least, at a single decision point. I shall argue that to search for unity is to misunderstand the subject matter of distributive justice. Nevertheless, in some sense the philosophical impulse is unavoidable. Even if we choose pluralism, as I shall do, that choice still requires a coherent defense. There must be principles that justify the choice and set limits to it, for pluralism does not require us to endorse every proposed distributive criteria or to accept every would-be agent. Conceivably, there is a single principle and a single legitimate kind of pluralism. But this would still be a pluralism that encompassed a wide range of distributions. By contrast, the deepest assumption of most of the philosophers who have written about justice, from Plato onward, is that there is one, and only one, distributive system that philosophy can rightly encompass.

Today this system is commonly described as the one that ideally rational men and women would choose if they were forced to choose impartially, knowing nothing of their own situation, barred from making particularist claims, confronting an abstract set of goods.[2] If these constraints on knowing and claiming are suitably shaped, and if the goods are suitably defined, it is probably true that

a singular conclusion can be produced. Rational men and women, constrained this way or that, will choose one, and only one, distributive system. But the force of that singular conclusion is not easy to measure. It is surely doubtful that those same men and women, if they were transformed into ordinary people, with a firm sense of their own identity, with their own goods in their hands, caught up in everyday troubles, would reiterate their hypothetical choice or even recognize it as their own. The problem is not, most importantly, with the particularism of interest, which philosophers have always assumed they could safely—that is, uncontroversially—set aside. Ordinary people can do that too, for the sake, say, of the public interest. The greater problem is with the particularism of history, culture, and membership. Even if they are committed to impartiality, the question most likely to arise in the minds of the members of a political community is not, What would rational individuals choose under universalizing conditions of such-and-such a sort? But rather, What would individuals like us choose, who are situated as we are, who share a culture and are determined to go on sharing it? And this is a question that is readily transformed into, What choices have we already made in the course of our common life? What understandings do we (really) share?

Justice is a human construction, and it is doubtful that it can be made in only one way. At any rate, I shall begin by doubting, and more than doubting, this standard philosophical assumption. The questions posed by the theory of distributive justice admit of a range of answers, and there is room within the range for cultural diversity and political choice. It's not only a matter of implementing some singular principle or set of principles in different historical settings. No one would deny that there is a range of morally permissible implementations. I want to argue for more than this: that the principles of justice are themselves pluralistic in form; that different social goods ought to be distributed for different reasons, in accordance with different procedures, by different agents; and that all these differences derive from different understandings of the social goods themselves-the inevitable product of historical and cultural particularism.

A Theory of Goods

Theories of distributive justice focus on a social process commonly described as if it had this form:

People distribute goods to (other) people.

---

1   *coups and cornerings*   A *coup* is a sudden takeover; a *cornering* of the market happens when someone achieves a monopoly.

2   *Today this system is commonly described ... abstract set of goods*   See John Rawls, *A Theory of Justice* (Cambridge, MA, 1971); Jürgen Habermas, *Legitimation Crisis*, trans. Thomas McCarthy (Boston, 1975), esp. p. 133; Bruce Ackerman, *Social Justice in the Liberal State* (New Haven, 1980).

Here, "distribute" means give, allocate, exchange, and so on, and the focus is on the individuals who stand at either end of these actions: not on producers and consumers, but on distributive agents and recipients of goods. We are as always interested in ourselves, but, in this case, in a special and limited version of ourselves, as people who give and take. What is our nature? What are our rights? What do we need, want, deserve? What are we entitled to? What would we accept under ideal conditions? Answers to these questions are turned into distributive principles, which are supposed to control the movement of goods. The goods, defined by abstraction, are taken to be movable in any direction.

But this is too simple an understanding of what actually happens, and it forces us too quickly to make large assertions about human nature and moral agency—assertions unlikely, ever, to command general agreement. I want to propose a more precise and complex description of the central process:

> *People conceive and create goods, which they then distribute among themselves.*

Here, the conception and creation precede and control the distribution. Goods don't just appear in the hands of distributive agents who do with them as they like or give them out in accordance with some general principle.[1] Rather, goods with their meanings—because of their meanings—are the crucial medium of social relations; they come into people's minds before they come into their hands; distributions are patterned in accordance with shared conceptions of what the goods are and what they are for. Distributive agents are constrained by the goods they hold; one might almost say that goods distribute themselves among people.

> *Things are in the saddle*
> *And ride mankind.*[2]

But these are always particular things and particular groups of men and women. And, of course, we make the things— even the saddle. I don't want to deny the importance of human agency, only to shift our attention from distribution itself to conception and creation: the naming of the goods, and the giving of meaning, and the collective making. What we need to explain and limit the pluralism of distributive possibilities is a theory of goods. For our immediate purposes, that theory can be summed up in six propositions.

1. All the goods with which distributive justice is concerned are social goods. They are not and they cannot be idiosyncratically valued. I am not sure that there are any other kinds of goods; I mean to leave the question open. Some domestic objects are cherished for private and sentimental reasons, but only in cultures where sentiment regularly attaches to such objects. A beautiful sunset, the smell of new-mown hay, the excitement of an urban vista: these perhaps are privately valued goods, though they are also, and more obviously, the objects of cultural assessment. Even new inventions are not valued in accordance with the ideas of their inventors; they are subject to a wider process of conception and creation. God's goods, to be sure, are exempt from this rule—as in the first chapter of Genesis: "and God saw every thing that He had made, and, behold, it was very good" (1:31). That evaluation doesn't require the agreement of mankind (who might be doubtful), or of a majority of men and women, or of any group of men and women meeting under ideal conditions (though Adam and Eve in Eden would probably endorse it). But I can't think of any other exemptions. Goods in the world have shared meanings because conception and creation are social processes. For the same reason, goods have different meanings in different societies. The same "thing" is valued for different reasons, or it is valued here and disvalued there. John Stuart Mill once complained that "people like in crowds," but I know of no other way to like or to dislike social goods.[3] A solitary person could hardly understand the meaning of the goods or figure out the reasons for taking them as likable or dislikable. Once people like in crowds, it becomes possible for individuals to break away, pointing to latent or subversive meanings, aiming at alternative values-including the values, for example, of notoriety and eccentricity. An easy eccentricity has

1   *Goods don't just appear ... some general principle*   Robert Nozick makes a similar argument in *Anarchy, State, and Utopia* (New York, 1974), pp. 149–50, but with radically individualistic conclusions that seem to me to miss the social character of production.

2   *Things are in the saddle/ And ride mankind*   Ralph Waldo Emerson, "Ode," in *The Complete Essays and Other Writings*, ed. Brooks Atkinson (New York, 1940), p. 770.

3   *John Stuart Mill ... dislike social goods*   John Stuart Mill, *On Liberty*, in *The Philosophy of John Stuart Mill*, ed. Marshall Cohen (New York, 1961), p. 255. For an anthropological account of liking and not liking social goods, see Mary Douglas and Baron Isherwood, *The World of Goods* (New York, 1979).

sometimes been one of the privileges of the aristocracy: it is a social good like any other.

2. Men and women take on concrete identities because of the way they conceive and create, and then possess and employ social goods. "The line between what is me and mine," wrote William James, "is very hard to draw."[1] Distributions can not be understood as the acts of men and women who do not yet have particular goods in their minds or in their hands. In fact, people already stand in a relation to a set of goods; they have a history of transactions, not only with one another but also with the moral and material world in which they live. Without such a history, which begins at birth, they wouldn't be men and women in any recognizable sense, and they wouldn't have the first notion of how to go about the business of giving, allocating, and exchanging goods.

3. There is no single set of primary or basic goods conceivable across all moral and material worlds—or, any such set would have to be conceived in terms so abstract that they would be of little use in thinking about particular distributions. Even the range of necessities, if we take into account moral as well as physical necessities, is very wide, and the rank orderings are very different. A single necessary good, and one that is always necessary—food, for example—carries different meanings in different places. Bread is the staff of life, the body of Christ, the symbol of the Sabbath, the means of hospitality, and so on. Conceivably, there is a limited sense in which the first of these is primary, so that if there were twenty people in the world and just enough bread to feed the twenty, the primacy of bread-as-staff-of-life would yield a sufficient distributive principle. But that is the only circumstance in which it would do so; and even there, we can't be sure. If the religious uses of bread were to conflict with its nutritional uses—if the gods demanded that bread be baked and burned rather than eaten—it is by no means clear which use would be primary. How, then, is bread to be incorporated into the universal list? The question is even harder to answer, the conventional answers less plausible, as we pass from necessities to opportunities, powers, reputations, and so on. These can be incorpor-

ated only if they are abstracted from e), very particular meaning—hence, for all practical purposes, rendered meaningless.

4. But it is the meaning of goods that determines their movement. Distributive criteria and arrangements are intrinsic not to the good-in-itself but to the social good. If we understand what it is, what it means to those for whom it is a good, we understand how, by whom, and for what reasons it ought to be distributed. All distributions are just or unjust relative to the social meanings of the goods at stake. This is in obvious ways a principle of legitimation, but it is also a critical principle.[2] When medieval Christians, for example, condemned the sin of simony,[3] they were claiming that the meaning of a particular social good, ecclesiastical office, excluded its sale and purchase. Given the Christian understanding of office, it followed—I am inclined to say, it necessarily followed—that office holders should be chosen for their knowledge and piety and not for their wealth. There are presumably things that money can buy, but not this thing. Similarly, the words prostitution and bribery, like simony, describe the sale and purchase of goods that, given certain understandings of their meaning, ought never to be sold or purchased.

5. Social meanings are historical in character; and so distributions, and just and unjust distributions, change over time. To be sure, certain key goods have what we might think of as characteristic normative structures, reiterated across the lines (but not all the lines) of time

---

1 *"The line between ... is very hard to draw"* William James, quoted in C.R. Snyder and Howard Fromkin, *Uniqueness: The Human Pursuit of Difference* (New York, 1980), p. 108.

2 *This is in obvious ways ... critical principle* Aren't social meanings, as Marx said, nothing other than "the ideas of the ruling class," "the dominant material relationships grasped as ideas?" [Karl Marx, *The German Ideology*, ed. R. Pascal (New York, 1947), p. 89] I don't think that they are ever only that or simply that, though the members of the ruling class and the intellectuals they patronize may well be in a position to exploit and distort social meanings in their own interests. When they do that, however, they are likely to encounter resistance, rooted (intellectually) in those same meanings. A people's culture is always a joint, even if it isn't an entirely cooperative, production; and it is always a complex production. The common understanding of particular goods incorporates principles, procedures, conceptions of agency, that the rulers would not choose if they were choosing right now—and so provides the terms of social criticism. The appeal to what I shall call "internal" principles against the usurpations of powerful men and women is the ordinary form of critical discourse.

3 *Simony* [editors' note] The buying and selling of church-related pardons or offices.

and space. It is because of this reiteration that the British philosopher Bernard Williams is able to argue that goods should always be distributed for "relevant reasons"—where relevance seems to connect to essential rather than to social meanings.[1] The idea that offices, for example, should go to qualified candidates—though not the only idea that has been held about offices—is plainly visible in very different societies where simony and nepotism, under different names, have similarly been thought sinful or unjust. (But there has been a wide divergence of views about what sorts of position and place are properly called "offices.") Again, punishment has been widely understood as a negative good that ought to go to people who are judged to deserve it on the basis of a verdict, not of a political decision. (But what constitutes a verdict? Who is to deliver it? How, in short, is justice to be done to accused men and women? About these questions there has been significant disagreement.) These examples invite empirical investigation. There is no merely intuitive or speculative procedure for seizing upon relevant reasons.

6. When meanings are distinct, distributions must be autonomous. Every social good or set of goods constitutes, as it were, a distributive sphere within which only certain criteria and arrangements are appropriate. Money is inappropriate in the sphere of ecclesiastical office; it is an intrusion from another sphere. And piety should make for no advantage in the marketplace, as the marketplace has commonly been understood. Whatever can rightly be sold ought to be sold to pious men and women and also to profane, heretical, and sinful men and women (else no one would do much business). The market is open to all comers; the church is not. In no society, of course, are social meanings entirely distinct. What happens in one distributive sphere affects what happens in the others; we can look, at most, for relative autonomy. But relative autonomy, like social meaning, is a critical principle-indeed, as I shall be arguing throughout this book, a radical principle. It is radical even though it doesn't point to

a single standard against which all distributions are to be measured. There is no single standard. But there are standards (roughly knowable even when they are also controversial) for every social good and every distributive sphere in every particular society; and these standards are often violated, the goods usurped, the spheres invaded, by powerful men and women.

Dominance and Monopoly

In fact, the violations are systematic. Autonomy is a matter of social meaning and shared values, but it is more likely to make for occasional reformation and rebellion than for everyday enforcement. For all the complexity of their distributive arrangements, most societies are organized on what we might think of as a social version of the gold standard:[2] one good or one set of goods is dominant and determinative of value in all the spheres of distribution. And that good or set of goods is commonly monopolized, its value upheld by the strength and cohesion of its owners. I call a good dominant if the individuals who have it, because they have it, can command a wide range of other goods. It is monopolized whenever a single man or woman, a monarch in the world of value—or a group of men and women, oligarchs—successfully hold it against all rivals. Dominance describes a way of using social goods that isn't limited by their intrinsic meanings or that shapes those meanings in its own image. Monopoly describes a way of owning or controlling social goods in order to exploit their dominance. When goods are scarce and widely needed, like water in the desert, monopoly itself will make them dominant. Mostly, however, dominance is a more elaborate social creation, the work of many hands, mixing reality and symbol. Physical strength, familial reputation, religious or political office, landed wealth, capital, technical knowledge: each of these, in different historical periods, has been dominant; and each of them has been monopolized by some group of men and women. And then all good things come to those who have the one best thing. Possess that one, and the others come in train. Or, to change the metaphor, a dominant good is converted into another good, into many others, in accordance with what often appears to be a natural process but is in fact magical, a kind of social alchemy.

---

1   *It is because of this reiteration ... social meanings*   Bernard Williams, *Problems of the Self: Philosophical Papers, 1956–1972* (Cambridge, England, 1973), pp. 230–49 ("The Idea of Equality"). This essay is one of the starting points of my own thinking about distributive justice. See also the critique of William's argument (and of an earlier essay of my own) in Amy Gutmann, *Liberal Equality* (Cambridge, England, 1980), chap. 4.

2   *gold standard*   [editors' note] The gold standard is a monetary system where the currency is backed by a fixed amount of gold, in part as a guard against inflation. It fell out of use in 1971.

No social good ever entirely dominates the range of goods; no monopoly is ever perfect. I mean to describe tendencies only, but crucial tendencies. For we can characterize whole societies in terms of the patterns of conversion that are established within them. Some characterizations are simple: in a capitalist society, capital is dominant and readily converted into prestige and power; in a technocracy,[1] technical knowledge plays the same part. But it isn't difficult to imagine, or to find, more complex social arrangements. Indeed, capitalism and technocracy are more complex than their names imply, even if the names do convey real information about the most important forms of sharing, dividing, and exchanging. Monopolistic control of a dominant good makes a ruling class, whose members stand atop the distributive system—much as philosophers, claiming to have the wisdom they love,[2] might like to do. But since dominance is always incomplete and monopoly imperfect, the rule of every ruling class is unstable. It is continually challenged by other groups in the name of alternative patterns of conversion.

Distribution is what social conflict is all about. Marx's heavy emphasis on productive processes should not conceal from us the simple truth that the struggle for control of the means of production is a distributive struggle. Land and capital are at stake, and these are goods that can be shared, divided, exchanged, and endlessly converted. But land and capital are not the only dominant goods; it is possible (it has historically been possible) to come to them by way of other goods-military or political power, religious office and charisma, and so on. History reveals no single dominant good and no naturally dominant good, but only different kinds of magic and competing bands of magicians.

The claim to monopolize a dominant good—when worked up for public purposes—constitutes an ideology. Its standard form is to connect legitimate possession with some set of personal qualities through the medium of a philosophical principle. So aristocracy, or the rule of the best, is the principle of those who lay claim to breeding and intelligence: they are commonly the monopolists of landed wealth and familial reputation. Divine supremacy is the principle of those who claim to know the word of God: they are the monopolists of grace and office. Meritocracy, or the career open to talents, is the principle of those who claim to be talented: they are most often the monopolists of education. Free exchange is the principle of those who are ready, or who tell us they are ready, to put their money at risk: they are the monopolists of movable wealth. These groups—and others, too, similarly marked off by their principles and possessions—compete with one another, struggling for supremacy. One group wins, and then a different one; or coalitions are worked out, and supremacy is uneasily shared. There is no final victory, nor should there be. But that is not to say that the claims of the different groups are necessarily wrong, or that the principles they invoke are of no value as distributive criteria; the principles are often exactly right within the limits of a particular sphere. Ideologies are readily corrupted, but their corruption is not the most interesting thing about them.

It is in the study of these struggles that I have sought the guiding thread of my own argument. The struggles have, I think, a paradigmatic form. Some group of men and women—class, caste, strata, estate, alliance, or social formation—comes to enjoy a monopoly or a near monopoly of some dominant good; or, a coalition of groups comes to enjoy, and so on. This dominant good is more or less systematically converted into all sorts of other things—opportunities, powers, and reputations. So wealth is seized by the strong, honor by the wellborn, office by the well educated. Perhaps the ideology that justifies the seizure is widely believed to be true. But resentment and resistance are {almost} as pervasive as belief. There are always some people, and after a time there are a great many, who think the seizure is not justice but usurpation. The ruling group does not possess, or does not uniquely possess, the qualities it claims; the conversion process violates the common understanding of the goods at stake. Social conflict is intermittent, or it is endemic;[3] at some point, counterclaims are put forward. Though these are of many different sorts, three general sorts are especially important:

1. The claim that the dominant good, whatever it is, should be redistributed so that it can be equally or at least more widely shared: this amounts to saying that monopoly is unjust.
2. The claim that the way should be opened for the autonomous distribution of all social goods: this amounts to saying that dominance is unjust.

---

1   *technocracy* [editors' note] A society ruled by technical experts.
2   *wisdom they love* [editors' note] *Philosophy*, translated from the Greek, literally means "love of wisdom." Walzer obliquely refers to Plato's *Republic*, where Plato sets out an educational program to groom philosopher rulers.

---

3   *endemic* [editors' note] Confined to a certain region.

3. The claim that some new good, monopolized by some new group, should replace the currently dominant good: this amounts to saying that the existing pattern of dominance and monopoly is unjust.

The third claim is, in Marx's view, the model of every revolutionary ideology—except, perhaps, the proletarian or last ideology.[1] Thus, the French Revolution in Marxist theory: the dominance of noble birth and blood and of feudal landholding is ended, and bourgeois wealth is established in its stead. The original situation is reproduced with different subjects and objects (this is never unimportant), and then the class war is immediately renewed. It is not my purpose here to endorse or to criticize Marx's view. I suspect, in fact, that there is something of all three claims in every revolutionary ideology, but that, too, is not a position that I shall try to defend here. Whatever its sociological significance, the third claim is not philosophically interesting—unless one believes that there is a naturally dominant good, such that its possessors could legitimately claim to rule the rest of us. In a sense, Marx believed exactly that. The means of production is the dominant good throughout history, and Marxism is a historicist doctrine insofar as it suggests that whoever controls the prevailing means legitimately rules.[2] After the communist revolution, we shall all control the means of production: at that point, the third claim collapses into the first. Meanwhile, Marx's model is a program for ongoing distributive struggle. It will matter, of course, who wins at this or that moment, but we won't know why or how it matters if we attend only to the successive assertions of dominance and monopoly.

Simple Equality

It is with the first two claims that I shall be concerned, and ultimately with the second alone, for that one seems to me to capture best the plurality of social meanings and the real complexity of distributive systems. But the first is the more common among philosophers; it matches their own search for unity and singularity; and I shall need to explain its difficulties at some length.

Men and women who make the first claim challenge the monopoly but not the dominance of a particular social good. This is also a challenge to monopoly in general; for if wealth, for example, is dominant and widely shared, no other good can possibly be monopolized. Imagine a society in which everything is up for sale and every citizen has as much money as every other. I shall call this the "regime of simple equality." Equality is multiplied through the conversion process, until it extends across the full range of social goods. The regime of simple equality won't last for long, because the further progress of conversion, free exchange in the market, is certain to bring inequalities in its train. If one wanted to sustain simple equality over time, one would require a "monetary law" like the agrarian laws of ancient times[3] or the Hebrew sabbatical, providing for a periodic return to the original condition. Only a centralized and activist state would be strong enough to force such a return; and it isn't clear that state officials would actually be able or willing to do that, if money were the dominant good. In any case, the original condition is unstable in another way. It's not only that monopoly will reappear, but also that dominance will disappear.

In practice, breaking the monopoly of money neutralizes its dominance. Other goods come into play, and inequality takes on new forms. Consider again the regime of simple equality. Everything is up for sale, and everyone has the same amount of money. So everyone has, say, an equal ability to buy an education for his children. Some do that, and others don't. It turns out to be a good investment: other social goods are, increasingly, offered for sale only to people with educational certificates. Soon everyone invests in education; or, more likely, the purchase is universalized through the tax system. But then the school is turned into a competitive world within which money is no longer dominant. Natural talent or family upbringing or skill in writing examinations is dominant instead, and educational success and certification are monopolized by some new group. Let's call them (what they call themselves) the "group of the talented." Eventually the members of this group claim

---

1   *in Marx's view ... last ideology*   [editors' note] Marx viewed history in terms of struggle between economic classes. Periodically, there is a revolution driven by the material forces of production, and a new class ascends to power. Marx characterized his time as a struggle between the proletariat (the working class) and the bourgeoisie (factory owners, etc.) which would eventually result in a revolution of the proletariat and the abolition of class.

2   *The means of production ... prevailing means legitimately rules*   See Alan W. Wood, "The Marxian Critique of Justice," *Philosophy and Public Affairs* 1 (1972): 244–82.

3   *agrarian laws of ancient time*   [editors' note] Laws instituted in ancient Rome intended to limit land ownership and redistribute land to small farmers.

that the good they control should be dominant outside the school: offices, titles, prerogatives, wealth too, should all be possessed by themselves. This is the career open to talents, equal opportunity, and so on. This is what fairness requires; talent will out; and in any case, talented men and women will enlarge the resources available to everyone else. So Michael Young's[1] meritocracy is born, with all its attendent inequalities.[2]

What should we do now? It is possible to set limits to the new conversion patterns, to recognize but constrain the monopoly power of the talented. I take this to be the purpose of John Rawls's difference principle, according to which inequalities are justified only if they are designed to bring, and actually do bring, the greatest possible benefit to the least advantaged social class.[3] More specifically, the difference principle is a constraint imposed on talented men and women, once the monopoly of wealth has been broken. It works in this way: Imagine a surgeon who claims more than his equal share of wealth on the basis of the skills he has learned and the certificates he has won in the harsh competitive struggles of college and medical school. We will grant the claim if, and only if, granting it is beneficial in the stipulated ways. At the same time, we will act to limit and regulate the sale of surgery—that is, the direct conversion of surgical skill into wealth.

This regulation will necessarily be the work of the state, just as monetary laws and agrarian laws are the work of the state. Simple equality would require continual state intervention to break up or constrain incipient monopolies and to repress new forms of dominance. But then state power itself will become the central object of competitive struggles. Groups of men and women will seek to monopolize and then to use the state in order to consolidate their control of other social goods. Or, the state will be monopolized by its own agents in accordance with the iron law of oligarchy.[4] Politics is always the most direct path to dominance, and political power (rather than the means of production) is probably the most important, and certainly

the most dangerous, good in human history.[5] Hence the need to constrain the agents of constraint, to establish constitutional checks and balances. These are limits imposed on political monopoly, and they are all the more important once the various social and economic monopolies have been broken.

One way of limiting political power is to distribute it widely. This may not work, given the well-canvassed dangers of majority tyranny; but these dangers are probably less acute than they are often made out to be. The greater danger of democratic government is that it will be weak to cope with re-emerging monopolies in society at large, with the social strength of plutocrats,[6] bureaucrats, technocrats, meritocrats, and so on. In theory, political power is the dominant good in a democracy, and it is convertible in any way the citizens choose. But in practice, again, breaking the monopoly of power neutralizes its dominance. Political power cannot be widely shared without being subjected to the pull of all the other goods that the citizens already have or hope to have. Hence democracy is, as Marx recognized, essentially a reflective system, mirroring the prevailing and emerging distribution of social goods.[7] Democratic decision making will be shaped by the cultural conceptions that determine or underwrite the new monopolies. To prevail against these monopolies, power will have to be

1   *Michael Young*   [editors' note] Michael Young, Baron Young of Dartington (1915–2002), author of the satire *The Rise of the Meritocracy* (1958).

2   *So Michael Young's meritocracy … its attendant inequalities*   Michael Young, *The Rise of the Meritocracy, 1870–2033* (Hammondsworth, England, 1961)—a brilliant piece of social science fiction.

3   *I take this to be the purpose of John Rawls's difference principle … least advantaged social class*   Rawls, *Theory of Justice*, pp.75ff.

4   *oligarchy*   [editors' note] Rule by the few.

5   *Politics … human history*   I should note here what will become more clear as I go along, that political power is a special sort of good. It has a twofold character. First, it is like the other things that men and women make, value, exchange, and share: sometimes dominant, sometimes not; sometimes widely held, sometimes the possession of a very few. And, second, it is unlike all the other things because, however it is had and whoever has it, political power is the regulative agency for social goods generally. It is used to defend the boundaries of all the distributive spheres, including its own, and to enforce the common understandings of what goods are and what they are for. (But it can also be used, obviously, to invade the different spheres and to override those understandings.) In this second sense, we might say, indeed, that political power is always dominant—at the boundaries, but not within them. The central problem of political life is to maintain that crucial distinction between "at" and "in." But this is a problem that cannot be solved given the imperatives of simple equality.

6   *plutocrats*   [editors' note] People who exercise power over others in virtue of their wealth.

7   *Hence democracy … distribution of social goods*   See Marx's comment, in his "Critique of the Gotha Program," that the democratic republic is the "form of state" within which the class struggle will be fought to a conclusion: the struggle is immediately and without distortion reflected in political life (Marx and Engels, *Selected Works* [Moscow, 1951], vol.II, p.31).

centralized, perhaps itself monopolized. Once again, the state must be very powerful if it is to fulfill the purposes assigned to it by the difference principle or by any similarly interventionist rule.

Still, the regime of simple equality might work. One can imagine a more or less stable tension between emerging monopolies and political constraints, between the claim to privilege put forward by the talented, say, and the enforcement of the difference principle, and then between the agents of enforcement and the democratic constitution. But I suspect that difficulties will recur, and that at many points in time the only remedy for private privilege will be statism,[1] and the only escape from statism will be private privilege. We will mobilize power to check monopoly, then look for some way of checking the power we have mobilized. But there is no way that doesn't open opportunities for strategically placed men and women to seize and exploit important social goods.

These problems derive from treating monopoly, and not dominance, as the central issue in distributive justice. It is not difficult, of course, to understand why philosophers (and political activists, too) have focused on monopoly. The distributive struggles of the modern age begin with a war against the aristocracy's singular hold on land, office, and honor. This seems an especially pernicious monopoly because it rests upon birth and blood, with which the individual has nothing to do, rather than upon wealth, or power, or education, all of which—at least in principle—can be earned. And when every man and woman becomes, as it were, a smallholder[2] in the sphere of birth and blood, an important victory is indeed won. Birthright ceases to be a dominant good; henceforth, it purchases very little; wealth, power, and education come to the fore. With regard to these latter goods, however, simple equality cannot be sustained at all, or it can only be sustained subject to the vicissitudes I have just described. Within their own spheres, as they are currently understood, these three tend to generate natural monopolies that can be repressed only if state power is itself dominant and if it is monopolized by officials committed to the repression. But there is, I think, another path to another kind of equality.

Tyranny and Complex Equality

I want to argue that we should focus on the reduction of dominance—not, or not primarily, on the break-up or the constraint of monopoly. We should consider what it might mean to narrow the range within which particular goods are convertible and to vindicate the autonomy of distributive spheres. But this line of argument, though it is not uncommon historically, has never fully emerged in philosophical writing. Philosophers have tended to criticize (or to justify) existing or emerging monopolies of wealth, power, and education. Or, they have criticized (or justified) particular conversions-of wealth into education or of office into wealth. And all this, most often, in the name of some radically simplified distributive system. The critique of dominance will suggest instead a way of reshaping and then living with the actual complexity of distributions.

Imagine now a society in which different social goods are monopolistically held—as they are in fact and always will be, barring continual state intervention—but in which no particular good is generally convertible. As I go along, I shall try to define the precise limits on convertibility, but for now the general description will suffice. This is a complex egalitarian society. Though there will be many small inequalities, inequality will not be multiplied through the conversion process. Nor will it be summed across different goods, because the autonomy of distributions will tend to produce a variety of local monopolies, held by different groups of men and women. I don't want to claim that complex equality would necessarily be more stable than simple equality, but I am inclined to think that it would open the way for more diffused and particularized forms of social conflict. And the resistance to convertibility would be maintained, in large degree, by ordinary men and women within their own spheres of competence and control, without large-scale state action.

This is, I think, an attractive picture, but I have not yet explained just why it is attractive. The argument for complex equality begins from our understanding—I mean, our actual, concrete, positive, and particular understanding—of the various social goods. And then it moves on to an account of the way we relate to one another through those goods. Simple equality is a simple distributive condition, so that if I have fourteen hats and you have fourteen hats, we are equal. And it is all to the good if hats are dominant, for then our equality is extended through all the spheres of social life. On the view that I shall take here, however,

---

1   *statism*   [editors' note] A governmental or economic system that involves considerable state intervention.

2   *smallholder*   [editors' note] Literally, a person who owns or borrows a small piece of land for farming; here it refers to the possessor of a small amount of something.

we simply have the same number of hats, and it is unlikely that hats will be dominant for long. Equality is a complex relation of persons, mediated by the goods we make, share, and divide among ourselves; it is not an identity of possessions. It requires then, a diversity of distributive criteria that mirrors the diversity of social goods.

The argument for complex equality has been beautifully put by Pascal[1] in one of his *Pensées*.

> The nature of tyranny is to desire power over the whole world and outside its own sphere.
>
> There are different companies—the strong, the handsome, the intelligent, the devout—and each man reigns in his own, not elsewhere. But sometimes they meet, and the strong and the handsome fight for mastery—foolishly, for their mastery is of different kinds. They misunderstand one another, and make the mistake of each aiming at universal dominion. Nothing can win this, not even strength, for it is powerless in the kingdom of the wise....
>
> *Tyranny.* The following statements, therefore, are false and tyrannical: "Because I am handsome, so I should command respect." "I am strong, therefore men should love me...." "I am ... et cetera."
>
> Tyranny is the wish to obtain by one means what can only be had by another. We owe different duties to different qualities: love is the proper response to charm, fear to strength, and belief to learning.[2]

Marx made a similar argument in his early manuscripts; perhaps he had this *pensée* in mind:

> Let us assume man to be man, and his relation to the world to be a human one. Then love can only be exchanged for love, trust for trust, etc. If you wish to enjoy art you must be an artistically cultivated person; if you wish to influence other people, you must be a person who really has a stimulating and encouraging effect upon others.... If you love without evoking love in re-

turn, i.e., if you are not able, by the manifestation of yourself as a loving person, to make yourself a beloved person—then your love is impotent and a misfortune.[3]

These are not easy arguments, and most of my book is simply an exposition of their meaning. But here I shall attempt something more simple and schematic: a translation of the arguments into the terms I have already been using.

The first claim of Pascal and Marx is that personal qualities and social goods have their own spheres of operation, where they work their effects freely, spontaneously, and legitimately. There are ready or natural conversions that follow from, and are intuitively plausible because of, the social meaning of particular goods. The appeal is to our ordinary understanding and, at the same time, against our common acquiescence in illegitimate conversion patterns. Or, it is an appeal from our acquiescence to our resentment. There is something wrong, Pascal suggests, with the conversion of strength into belief. In political terms, Pascal means that no ruler can rightly command my opinions merely because of the power he wields. Nor can he, Marx adds, rightly claim to influence my actions: if a ruler wants to do that, he must be persuasive, helpful, encouraging, and so on. These arguments depend for their force on some shared understanding of knowledge, influence, and power. Social goods have social meanings, and we find our way to distributive justice through an interpretation of those meanings. We search for principles internal to each distributive sphere.

The second claim is that the disregard of these principles is tyranny. To convert one good into another, when there is no intrinsic connection between the two, is to invade the sphere where another company of men and women properly rules. Monopoly is not inappropriate within the spheres. There is nothing wrong, for example, with the grip that persuasive and helpful men and women (politicians) establish on political power. But the use of political power to gain access to other goods is a tyrannical use. Thus, an old description of tyranny is generalized: princes become tyrants, according to medieval writers, when they seize the

---

1   *Pascal* [editors' note] Blaise Pascal, seventeenth-century French religious philosopher, mathematician, and physicist.

2   *The nature of tyranny ... belief to learning*   Blaise Pascal, *The Pensées*, trans. J.M. Cohen (Harmondsworth, England, 1961), p. 96 (no.244).

3   *Let us assume man to be man ... your love is impotent and a misfortune*   Karl Marx, *Economic and Philosophical Manuscripts*, in *Early Writings*, ed. T.B. Bottomore (London, 1963), pp. 193–94. It is interesting to note an earlier echo of Pascal's argument in Adam Smith's *Theory of Moral Sentiments* (Edinburgh, 1813), vol. I, pp. 378–79.

property or invade the family of their subjects.[1] In political life—but more widely, too—the dominance of goods makes for the domination of people.

The regime of complex equality is the opposite of tyranny. It establishes a set of relationships such that domination is impossible. In formal terms, complex equality means that no citizen's standing in one sphere or with regard to one social good can be undercut by his standing in some other sphere, with regard to some other good. Thus, citizen X may be chosen over citizen Y for political office, and then the two of them will be unequal in the sphere of politics. But they will not be unequal generally so long as X's office gives him no advantages over Y in any other sphere—superior medical care, access to better schools for his children, entrepreneurial opportunities, and so on. So long as office is not a dominant good, is not generally convertible, office holders will stand, or at least can stand, in a relation of equality to the men and women they govern.

But what if dominance were eliminated, the autonomy of the spheres established—and the same people were successful in one sphere after another, triumphant in every company, piling up goods without the need for illegitimate conversions? This would certainly make for an inegalitarian society, but it would also suggest in the strongest way that a society of equals was not a lively possibility. I doubt that any egalitarian argument could survive in the face of such evidence. Here is a person whom we have freely chosen (without reference to his family ties or personal wealth) as our political representative. He is also a bold and inventive entrepreneur. When he was younger, he studied science, scored amazingly high grades in every exam, and made important discoveries. In war, he is surpassingly brave and wins the highest honors. Himself compassionate and compelling, he is loved by all who know him. Are there such people? Maybe so, but I have my doubts. We tell stories like the one I have just told, but the stories are fictions, the conversion of power or money or academic talent into legendary fame. In any case, there aren't enough such people to constitute a ruling class and dominate the rest of us. Nor can they be successful in every distributive sphere, for there are some spheres to which the idea of success doesn't pertain. Nor are their children likely, under conditions of complex equality, to inherit their success. By and large, the

most accomplished politicians, entrepreneurs, scientists, soldiers, and lovers will be different people; and so long as the goods they possess don't bring other goods in train, we have no reason to fear their accomplishments.

The critique of dominance and domination points toward an open-ended distributive principle. No social good x should be distributed to men and women who possess some other good y merely because they possess y and without regard to the meaning of x. This is a principle that has probably been reiterated, at one time or another, for every y that has ever been dominant. But it has not often been stated in general terms. Pascal and Marx have suggested the application of the principle against all possible y's, and I shall attempt to work out that application. I shall be looking, then, not at the members of Pascal's companies—the strong or the weak, the handsome or the plain—but at the goods they share and divide. The purpose of the principle is to focus our attention; it doesn't determine the shares or the division. The principle directs us to study the meaning of social goods, to examine the different distributive spheres from the inside.

Three Distributive Principles

The theory that results is unlikely to be elegant. No account of the meaning of a social good, or of the boundaries of the sphere within which it legitimately operates, will be uncontroversial. Nor is there any neat procedure for generating or testing different accounts. At best, the arguments will be rough, reflecting the diverse and conflict-ridden character of the social life that we seek simultaneously to understand and to regulate—but not to regulate until we understand. I shall set aside, then, all claims made on behalf of any single distributive criterion, for no such criterion can possibly match the diversity of social goods. Three criteria, however, appear to meet the requirements of the open-ended principle and have often been defended as the beginning and end of distributive justice, so I must say something about each of them. Free exchange, desert, and need: all three have real force, but none of them has force across the range of distributions. They are part of the story, not the whole of it.

Free Exchange

Free exchange is obviously open-ended; it guarantees no particular distributive outcome. At no point in any exchange process plausibly called "free" will it be possible to predict

---

1   *Thus, an old description ... family of their subjects*   See the summary account in Jean Bodin, *Six Books of a Commonweale*, ed. Kenneth Douglas McRae (Cambridge, Mass., 1962), pp. 210–18.

the particular division of social goods that will obtain at some later point.[1] (It may be possible, however, to predict the general structure of the division.) In theory at least, free exchange creates a market within which all goods are convertible into all other goods through the neutral medium of money. There are no dominant goods and no monopolies. Hence the successive divisions that obtain will directly reflect the social meanings of the goods that are divided. For each bargain, trade, sale, and purchase will have been agreed to voluntarily by men and women who know what that meaning is, who are indeed its makers. Every exchange is a revelation of social meaning. By definition, then, no x will ever fall into the hands of someone who possesses y, merely because he possesses y and without regard to what x actually means to some other member of society. The market is radically pluralistic in its operations and its outcomes, infinitely sensitive to the meanings that individuals attach to goods. What possible restraints can be imposed on free exchange, then, in the name of pluralism?

But everyday life in the market, the actual experience of free exchange, is very different from what the theory suggests. Money, supposedly the neutral medium, is in practice a dominant good, and it is monopolized by people who possess a special talent for bargaining and trading—the green thumb of bourgeois society. Then other people demand a redistribution of money and the establishment of the regime of simple equality, and the search begins for some way to sustain that regime. But even if we focus on the first untroubled moment of simple equality-free exchange on the basis of equal shares-we will still need to set limits on what can be exchanged for what. For free exchange leaves distributions entirely in the hands of individuals, and social meanings are not subject, or are not always subject, to the interpretative decisions of individual men and women.

Consider an easy example, the case of political power. We can conceive of political power as a set of goods of varying value, votes, influence, offices, and so on. Any of these can be traded on the market and accumulated by individuals willing to sacrifice other goods. Even if the sacrifices are real, however, the result is a form of tyranny—petty tyranny, given the conditions of simple equality. Because I am willing to do without my hat, I shall vote twice; and you who value the vote less than you value my hat, will not vote at all. I suspect that the result is tyrannical even

with regard to the two of us, who have reached a voluntary agreement. It is certainly tyrannical with regard to all the other citizens who must now submit to my disproportionate power. It is not the case that votes can't be bargained for; on one interpretation, that's what democratic politics is all about. And democratic politicians have certainly been known to buy votes, or to try to buy them, by promising public expenditures that benefit particular groups of voters. But this is done in public, with public funds, and subject to public approval. Private trading is ruled out by virtue of what politics, or democratic politics, is—that is, by virtue of what we did when we constituted the political community and of what we still think about what we did.

Free exchange is not a general criterion, but we will be able to specify the boundaries within which it operates only through a careful analysis of particular social goods. And having worked through such an analysis, we will come up at best with a philosophically authoritative set of boundaries and not necessarily with the set that ought to be politically authoritative. For money seeps across all boundaries—this is the primary form of illegal immigration; and just where one ought to try to stop it is a question of expediency as well as of principle. Failure to stop it at some reasonable point has consequences throughout the range of distributions, but consideration of these belongs in a later chapter.

Desert

Like free exchange, desert seems both open-ended and pluralistic. One might imagine a single neutral agency dispensing rewards and punishments, infinitely sensitive to all the forms of individual desert. Then the distributive process would indeed be centralized, but the results would still be unpredictable and various. There would be no dominant good. No x would ever be distributed without regard to its social meaning; for, without attention to what x is, it is conceptually impossible to say that x is deserved. All the different companies of men and women would receive their appropriate reward. How this would work in practice, however, is not easy to figure out. It might make sense to say of this charming man, for example, that he deserves to be loved. It makes no sense to say that he deserves to be loved by this (or any) particular woman. If he loves her while she remains impervious to his (real) charms, that is his misfortune. I doubt that we would want the situation corrected by some outside agency. The love of particular men and women, on our understanding of it, can only be distributed

---

1   *At no point ... some later point*   See Nozick on "patterning." *Anarchy, State, and Utopia*, pp. 155 ff.

by themselves, and they are rarely guided in these matters by considerations of desert.

The case is exactly the same with influence. Here, let's say, is a woman widely thought to be stimulating and encouraging to others. Perhaps she deserves to be an influential member of our community. But she doesn't deserve that I be influenced by her or that I follow her lead. Nor would we want my followership, as it were, assigned to her by any agency capable of making such assignments. She may go to great lengths to stimulate and encourage me, and do all the things that are commonly called stimulating or encouraging. But if I (perversely) refuse to be stimulated or encouraged, I am not denying her anything that she deserves. The same argument holds by extension for politicians and ordinary citizens. Citizens can't trade their votes for hats; they can't individually decide to cross the boundary that separates the sphere of politics from the marketplace. But within the sphere of politics, they do make individual decisions; and they are rarely guided, again, by considerations of desert. It's not clear that offices can be deserved—another issue that I must postpone; but even if they can be, it would violate our understanding of democratic politics were they simply distributed to deserving men and women by some central agency.

Similarly, however we draw the boundaries of the sphere within which free exchange operates, desert will play no role within those boundaries. I am skillful at bargaining and trading, let's say, and so accumulate a large number of beautiful pictures. If we assume, as painters mostly do, that pictures are appropriately traded in the market, then there is nothing wrong with my having the pictures. My title is legitimate. But it would be odd to say that I deserve to have them simply because I am good at bargaining and trading. Desert seems to require an especially close connection between particular goods and particular persons, whereas justice only sometimes requires a connection of that sort. Still, we might insist that only artistically cultivated people, who deserve to have pictures, should actually have them. It's not difficult to imagine a distributive mechanism. The state could buy all the pictures that were offered for sale (but artists would have to be licensed, so that there wouldn't be an endless number of pictures), evaluate them, and then distribute them to artistically cultivated men and women, the better pictures to the more cultivated. The state does something like this, sometimes, with regard to things that people need-medical care, for example—but not with regard to things that people deserve. There are practical

difficulties here, but I suspect a deeper reason for this difference. Desert does not have the urgency of need, and it does not involve having (owning and consuming) in the same way. Hence, we are willing to tolerate the separation of owners of paintings and artistically cultivated people, or we are unwilling to require the kinds of interference in the market that would be necessary to end the separation. Of course, public provision is always possible alongside the market, and so we might argue that artistically cultivated people deserve not pictures but museums. Perhaps they do, but they don't deserve that the rest of us contribute money or appropriate public funds for the purchase of pictures and the construction of buildings: They will have to persuade us that art is worth the money; they will have to stimulate and encourage our own artistic cultivation. And if they fail to do that, their own love of art may well turn out to be "impotent and a misfortune."[1]

Even if we were to assign the distribution of love, influence, offices, works of art, and so on, to some omnipotent arbiters of desert, how would we select them? How could anyone deserve such a position? Only God, who knows what secrets lurk in the hearts of men, would be able to make the necessary distributions. If human beings had to do the work, the distributive mechanism would be seized early on by some band of aristocrats (so they would call themselves) with a fixed conception of what is best and most deserving, and insensitive to the diverse excellences of their fellow citizens. And then desert would cease to be a pluralist criterion; we would find ourselves face to face with a new set (of an old sort) of tyrants. We do, of course, choose people as arbiters of desert-to serve on juries, for example, or to award prizes; it will be worth considering later what the prerogatives of a juror are. But it is important to stress here that he operates within a narrow range. Desert is a strong claim, but it calls for difficult judgments; and only under very special conditions does it yield specific distributions.

Need

Finally, the criterion of need. "To each according to his needs" is generally taken as the distributive half of Marx's famous maxim: we are to distribute the wealth of the com-

---

1   *impotent and a misfortune*   [editors' note] Walzer refers to Karl Marx's *The Economic and Philosophical Manuscripts*: "If you love without evoking love in return, i.e., if you are not able, by the manifestation of yourself as a loving person, to make yourself a beloved person, then your love is impotent and a misfortune."

munity so as to meet the necessities of its members.[1] A plausible proposal, but a radically incomplete one. In fact, the first half of the maxim is also a distributive proposal, and it doesn't fit the rule of the second half. "From each according to his ability" suggests that jobs should be distributed (or that men and women should be conscripted to work) on the basis of individual qualifications. But individuals don't in any obvious sense need the jobs for which they are qualified. Perhaps such jobs are scarce, and there are a large number of qualified candidates: which candidates need them most? If their material needs are already taken care of, perhaps they don't need to work at all. Or if, in some non-material sense, they all need to work, then that need won't distinguish among them, at least not to the naked eye. It would in any case be odd to ask a search committee looking, say, for a hospital director to make its choice on the basis of the needs of the candidates rather than on those of the staff and the patients of the hospital. But the latter set of needs, even if it isn't the subject of political disagreement, won't yield a single distributive decision.

Nor will need work for many other goods. Marx's maxim doesn't help at all with regard to the distribution of political power, honor and fame, sailboats, rare books, beautiful objects of every sort. These are not things that anyone, strictly speaking, needs. Even if we take a loose view and define the verb to need the way children do, as the strongest form of the verb to want, we still won't have an adequate distributive criterion. The sorts of things that I have listed cannot be distributed equally to those with equal wants because some of them are generally, and some of them are necessarily, scarce, and some of them can't be possessed at all unless other people, for reasons of their own, agree on who is to possess them.

Need generates a particular distributive sphere, within which it is itself the appropriate distributive principle. In a poor society, a high proportion of social wealth will be drawn into this sphere. But given the great variety of goods that arises out of any common life, even when it is lived at a very low material level, other distributive criteria will always be operating alongside of need, and it will always be necessary to worry about the boundaries that mark them off from one another. Within its sphere, certainly, need meets the general distributive rule about x and y. Needed goods distributed to needy people in proportion to their neediness

are obviously not dominated by any other goods. It's not having y, but only lacking x that is relevant. But we can now see, I think, that every criterion that has any force at all meets the general rule within its own sphere, and not elsewhere. This is the effect of the rule: different goods to different companies of men and women for different reasons and in accordance with different procedures. And to get all this right, or to get it roughly right, is to map out the entire social world.

Hierarchies and Caste Societies

Or, rather, it is to map out a particular social world. For the analysis that I propose is imminent and phenomenological in character. It will yield not an ideal map or a master plan but, rather, a map and a plan appropriate to the people for whom it is drawn, whose common life it reflects. The goal, of course, is a reflection of a special kind, which picks up those deeper understandings of social goods which are not necessarily mirrored in the everyday practice of dominance and monopoly. But what if there are no such understandings? I have been assuming all along that social meanings call for the autonomy, or the relative autonomy, of distributive spheres; and so they do much of the time. But it's not impossible to imagine a society where dominance and monopoly are not violations but enactments of meaning, where social goods are conceived in hierarchical terms. In feudal Europe, for example, clothing was not a commodity (as it is today) but a badge of rank. Rank dominated dress. The meaning of clothing was shaped in the image of the feudal order. Dressing in finery to which one wasn't entitled was a kind of lie; it made a false statement about who one was. When a king or a prime minister dressed as a commoner in order to learn something about the opinions of his subjects, this was a kind of politic deceit. On the other hand, the difficulties of enforcing the clothing code (the sumptuary laws[2]) suggests that there was all along an alternative sense of what clothing meant. At some point, at least, one can begin to recognize the boundaries of a distinct sphere within which people dress in accordance with what they can afford or what they are willing to spend or how they want to look. The sumptuary laws may still be enforced, but now one can make—and ordinary men and women do, in fact, make-egalitarian arguments against them.

---

1 *we are to distribute ... necessities of its members* Marx, "Gotha Program" [11], pp. 210–18.

2 *sumptuary laws* [editors' note] Laws dictating what type of clothing could be worn, related especially to rank and class.

Can we imagine a society in which all goods are hierarchically conceived? Perhaps the caste system of ancient India had this form (though that is a far-reaching claim, and it would be prudent to doubt its truth: for one thing, political power seems always to have escaped the laws of caste). We think of castes as rigidly segregated groups, of the caste system as a "plural society," a world of boundaries.[1] But the system is constituted by an extraordinary integration of meanings. Prestige, wealth, knowledge, office, occupation, food, clothing, even the social good of conversation: all are subject to the intellectual as well as to the physical discipline of hierarchy. And the hierarchy is itself determined by the single value of ritual purity. A certain kind of collective mobility is possible, for castes or subcastes can cultivate the outward marks of purity and (within severe limits) raise their position in the social scale. And the system as a whole rests upon a religious doctrine that promises equality of opportunity, not in this life but across the lives of the soul. The individual's status here and now "is the result of his conduct in his last incarnation ... and if unsatisfactory can be remedied by acquiring merit in his present life which will raise his status in the next."[2] We should not assume that men and women are ever entirely content with radical inequality. Nevertheless, distributions here and now are part of a single system, largely unchallenged, in which purity is dominant over other goods—and birth and blood are dominant over purity. Social meanings overlap and cohere.

The more perfect the coherence, the less possible it is even to think about complex equality. All goods are like crowns and thrones in a hereditary monarchy. There is no room, and there are no criteria, for autonomous distributions. In fact, however, even hereditary monarchies are rarely so simply constructed. The social understanding of royal power commonly involves some notion of divine grace, or magical gift, or human insight; and these criteria for office holding are potentially independent of birth and blood. So it is for most social goods: they are only imperfectly integrated into larger systems; they are understood,

at least sometimes, in their own terms. The theory of goods explicates understandings of this sort (where they exist), and the theory of complex equality exploits them. We say, for example, that it is tyrannical for a man without grace or gift or insight to sit upon the throne. And this is only the first and most obvious kind of tyranny. We can search for many other kinds.

Tyranny is always specific in character: a particular boundary crossing, a particular violation of social meaning. Complex equality requires the defense of boundaries; it works by differentiating goods just as hierarchy works by differentiating people. But we can only talk of a regime of complex equality when there are many boundaries to defend; and what the right number is cannot be specified. There is no right number. Simple equality is easier: one dominant good widely distributed makes an egalitarian society. But complexity is hard: how many goods must be autonomously conceived before the relations they mediate can become the relations of equal men and women? There is no certain answer and hence no ideal regime. But as soon as we start to distinguish meanings and mark out distributive spheres, we are launched on an egalitarian enterprise.

The Setting of the Argument

The political community is the appropriate setting for this enterprise. It is not, to be sure, a self-contained distributive world: only the world is a self-contained distributive world, and contemporary science fiction invites us to speculate about a time when even that won't be true. Social goods are shared, divided, and exchanged across political frontiers. Monopoly and dominance operate almost as easily beyond the frontiers as within them. Things are moved, and people move themselves, back and forth across the lines. Nevertheless, the political community is probably the closest we can come to a world of common meanings. Language, history, and culture come together (come more closely together here than anywhere else) to produce a collective consciousness. National character, conceived as a fixed and permanent mental set, is obviously a myth; but the sharing of sensibilities and intuitions among the members of a historical community is a fact of life. Sometimes political and historical communities don't coincide, and there may well be a growing number of states in the world today where sensibilities and intuitions aren't readily shared; the sharing takes place in smaller units. And then, perhaps, we should

1   *We think of castes ... world of boundaries*   J.H. Hutton, *Caste in India: Its Nature, Function, and Origins* (4th ed., Bombay, 1963), pp. 127-28. I have also drawn on Célestin Bouglé, *Essays on the Caste System*, trans. D.F. Pocock (Cambridge, England, 1971), esp. Part III, chaps. 3 and 4; and Louis Dumont, *Homo Hierarchus: The Caste System and Its Implications* (revised English ed., Chicago, 1980).

2   *The individual's status ... raise his status in the next*   Hutton, *Caste in India* [17], p. 125.

look for some way to adjust distributive decisions to the requirements of those units. But this adjustment must itself be worked out politically, and its precise character will depend upon understandings shared among the citizens about the value of cultural diversity, local autonomy, and so on. It is to these understandings that we must appeal when we make our arguments—all of us, not philosophers alone; for in matters of morality, argument simply is the appeal to common meanings.

Politics, moreover, establishes its own bonds of commonality. In a world of independent states, political power is a local monopoly. These men and women, we can say, under whatever constraints, shape their own destiny. Or they struggle as best they can to shape their own destiny. And if their destiny is only partially in their own hands, the struggle is entirely so. They are the ones whose decision it is to tighten or loosen distributive criteria, to centralize or decentralize procedures, to intervene or refuse to intervene in this or that distributive sphere. Probably, some set of leaders make the actual decisions, but the citizens should be able to recognize the leaders as their own. If the leaders are cruel or stupid or endlessly venal, as they often are, the citizens or some of the citizens will try to replace them, fighting over the distribution of political power. The fight will be shaped by the institutional structures of the community—that is, by the outcomes of previous fights. Politics present is the product of politics past. It establishes an unavoidable setting for the consideration of distributive justice.

There is one last reason for adopting the view of the political community as setting, a reason that I shall elaborate on at some length in the next chapter. The community is itself a good—conceivably the most important good—that gets distributed. But it is a good that can only be distributed by taking people in, where all the senses of that latter phrase are relevant: they must be physically admitted and politically received. Hence membership cannot be handed out by some external agency; its value depends upon an internal decision. Were there no communities capable of making such decisions, there would in this case be no good worth distributing.

The only plausible alternative to the political community is humanity itself, the society of nations, the entire globe. But were we to take the globe as our setting, we would have to imagine what does not yet exist: a community that included all men and women everywhere. We would have to invent a set of common meanings for

these people, avoiding if we could the stipulation of our own values. And we would have to ask the members of this hypothetical community (or their hypothetical representatives) to agree among themselves on what distributive arrangements and patterns of conversion are to count as just. Ideal contractualism or undistorted communication, which represents one approach—not my own—to justice in particular communities, may well be the only approach for the globe as a whole.[1] But whatever the hypothetical agreement, it could not be enforced without breaking the political monopolies of existing states and centralizing power at the global level. Hence the agreement (or the enforcement) would make not for complex but for simple equality—if power was dominant and widely shared—or simply foe tyranny—if power was seized, as it probably would be, by a set of international bureaucrats. In the first case, the people of the world would have to live with the difficulties I have described: the continual reappearance of local privilege, the continual reassertion of global statism. In the second case, they would have to live with difficulties that are considerably worse. I will have a little more to say about these difficulties later. For now I take them to be reasons enough to limit myself to cities, countries, and states that have, over long periods of time, shaped their own internal life.

With regard to membership, however, important questions arise between and among such communities, and I shall try to focus on them and to draw into the light all those occasions when ordinary citizens focus on them. In a limited way, the theory of complex equality can be extended from particular communities to the society of nations, and the extension has this advantage: it will not run roughshod over local understandings and decisions. Just for that reason, it also will not yield a uniform system of distributions across the globe, and it will only begin to address the problems raised by mass poverty in many parts of the globe. I don't think the beginning unimportant; in any case, I can't move beyond it. To do that would require a different theory, which would take as its subject not the common life of citizens but the more distanced relations of states: a different theory, a different book, another time.

---

1   *Ideal contractualism ... globe as a whole*   See Charles Beitz, *Political Theory and International Relations* (Princeton, 1979) part III, for an effort to apply Rawlsian ideal contractualism to international society.

WILL KYMLICKA
(1962–)

Will Kymlicka is a leading writer on liberalism, multiculturalism and citizenship, as well as a prominent figure in public debates on these issues; he is best known for his work on minority rights, most fully worked out in *Multicultural Citizenship*. Kymlicka received his BA in philosophy and politics from Queen's University and his DPhil from Oxford in 1987, under the guidance of G.A. Cohen. He is the author of many articles and books, including *Multicultural Odysseys* (2007), *Politics in the Vernacular: Nationalism, Multiculturalism, Citizenship* (2001), *Finding Our Way: Rethinking Ethnocultural Relations in Canada* (1998), *Multicultural Citizenship: A Liberal Theory of Minority Rights* (1995), and *Liberalism, Community and Culture* (1989). His *Contemporary Political Philosophy: An Introduction* (2nd edition 2001) is widely used in political philosophy classes.

In many respects Kymlicka's work may be seen as arising from the liberal/communitarian debate that occupied political philosophy in the 1980s. After World War II, liberals strongly emphasized individual rights over group rights. Liberalism, according to this view, demanded universal moral principles that entailed neutrality among particular groups. Attention to human rights and the rights of individual citizens was sufficient, since principles such as freedom of association, religion, and speech would protect minority groups indirectly.

Though this view gained widespread acceptance, some authors (notable among them Michael Sandel, Michael Walzer, Alasdair MacIntyre, and Charles Taylor) argued that liberalism was neglecting the shared practices and meanings created by social interaction. According to these communitarians, our identities and values are embedded in existing societies or communities. The attempt to abstract them from society distorts reality and neglects the common good. Furthermore, it neglects the fact that all states *do* promote particular cultural values in their language policy, recognized holidays, and national symbols; liberal "neutrality" often masks a bias favoring the dominant culture.

If this is true, then liberal neutrality violates a fundamental *liberal* principle: the right to equal treatment. Kymlicka, using a wide range of evidence to illustrate his points, notes that many governments recognize this, granting special rights or attempting to accommodate national minorities, First Nation groups, and ethnic groups. This allows him to offer a nuanced, liberal nationalist view that incorporates communitarian aspects. Along with the communitarians, he argues that freedom of choice depends on shared cultural meanings, practices, and languages provided by our background culture. At the same time, he acknowledges the need to protect minority cultures.

If liberal neutrality does violate the right to equal treatment, it appears a moral obligation for differential treatment comes directly out of the liberal tradition. Just as providing wheelchair access to handicapped people is morally required in order for them to participate equally in society, granting special rights to allow minority groups access to their societal culture may be necessary for their equal participation.

Kymlicka distinguishes between national minorities and polyethnic groups composed of recent immigrants. Nations involve "a historical community, more or less institutionally complete, occupying a given territory or homeland, sharing a distinct language and culture." Many multinational states include national groups that have become minorities either through conquest and colonization or voluntary affiliation to a federation. These groups typically aspire to some form of self-government and autonomy within the larger state to preserve their distinct culture (some larger groups also pursue secession). Kymlicka refers to provisions granting these groups greater autonomy as *self-government rights*.

Ethnic groups also make up a significant portion of many populations, especially in the United States, Canada, and Australia (and, to a lesser extent, many European and Asian states). Most immigrants want to integrate into their new country, learn the language, and participate in public institutions. At the same time, they want to preserve some aspects of their culture and demand what Kymlicka calls *polyethnic rights*. (These may include public funding for cultural associations and events, language classes in schools, and exemptions from certain laws and regulations.)

Kymlicka also discusses *special representation rights*, which attempt to address issues arising in unrepresentative political systems (e.g., in which minorities, women, and other historically disadvantaged groups are represented in disproportionately low numbers).

Kymlicka remains deeply engaged with current issues in multiculturalism, as well as contemporary political philosophy. He currently teaches at Queen's University, where he holds a Canada Research Chair in Political Philosophy.

◆ ◆ ◆ ◆ ◆

from *Multicultural Citizenship* (1995)

Chapter 6: Justice and Minority Rights

I have argued that access to a societal culture is essential for individual freedom. I have also argued that most people have a deep bond to their own culture, and that they have a legitimate interest in maintaining this bond. But what particular claims are justified by this interest? Not all interests can be satisfied in a world of conflicting interests and scarce resources. Protecting one person's cultural membership has costs for other people and other interests, and we need to determine when these trade-offs are justified.

As I noted in Chapter 1, many liberals believe that people's interest in cultural membership is adequately protected by the common rights of citizenship, and that any further measures to protect this interest are illegitimate. They argue that a system of universal individual rights already accommodates cultural differences, by allowing each person the freedom to associate with others in the pursuit

of shared religious or ethnic practices. Freedom of association enables people from different backgrounds to pursue their distinctive ways of life without interference. Every individual is free to create or join various associations, and to seek new adherents for them, in the "cultural market-place." Every way of life is free to attract adherents, and if some ways of life are unable to maintain or gain the voluntary adherence of people that may be unfortunate, but it is not unfair. On this view, giving political recognition or support to particular cultural practices or associations is unnecessary and unfair. It is unnecessary, because a valuable way of life will have no difficulty attracting adherents. And it is unfair, because it subsidizes some people's choices at the expense of others.

Proponents of this "strict separation of state and ethnicity" view need not deny that people have a deep bond to their own culture (although some do). They may just argue that cultures do not need state assistance to survive. If a societal culture is worth saving, one could argue, the members of the culture will sustain it through their own choices. If the culture is decaying, it must be because some people no longer find it worthy of their allegiance. The state, on this view, should not interfere with the cultural market-place—it should neither promote nor inhibit the maintenance of any particular culture. Rather, it should respond with "benign neglect" to ethnic and national differences.

I think this common view is not only mistaken, but actually incoherent. The idea of responding to cultural differences with "benign neglect" makes no sense. Government decisions on languages, internal boundaries, public holidays, and state symbols unavoidably involve recognizing, accommodating, and supporting the needs and identities of particular ethnic and national groups. The state unavoidably promotes certain cultural identities, and thereby disadvantages others. Once we recognize this, we need to rethink the justice of minority rights claims. In this chapter, I will argue that some self-government rights and polyethnic rights are consistent with, and indeed required by, liberal justice. (I examine the case of group representation rights in Chapter 7.) I will consider three sorts of arguments that attempt to defend these measures within a broadly liberal framework: equality, historical agreement, and diversity. I will argue that each has some merit, although the latter two depend in part on the first. In each case, I will first consider how these arguments apply to the self-government rights of national minorities, and then examine their application to the polyethnic rights of ethnic groups.

1. The Equality Argument

Many defenders of group-specific rights for ethnic and national minorities insist that they are needed to ensure that all citizens are treated with genuine equality. On this view, "the accommodation of differences is the essence of true equality,"[1] and group-specific rights are needed to accommodate our differences. I think this argument is correct, within certain limits.

Proponents of "benign neglect" will respond that individual rights already allow for the accommodation of differences, and that true equality requires equal rights for each individual regardless of race or ethnicity.[2] As I noted in Chapter 4, this assumption that liberal equality precludes group-specific rights is relatively recent, and arose in part as an (over-)generalization of the racial desegregation movement in the United States. It has some superficial plausibility. In many cases, claims for group-specific rights are simply an attempt by one group to dominate and oppress another.

But some minority rights eliminate, rather than create, inequalities. Some groups are unfairly disadvantaged in the cultural market-place, and political recognition and support rectify this disadvantage. I will start with the case of national minorities. The viability of their societal cultures may be undermined by economic and political decisions made by the majority. They could be outbid or outvoted on resources and policies that are crucial to the survival of their societal cultures. The members of majority cultures do not face this problem. Given the importance of cultural membership, this is a significant inequality which, if not addressed, becomes a serious injustice.

Group-differentiated rights—such as territorial autonomy, veto powers, guaranteed representation in central institutions, land claims, and language rights—can help rectify this disadvantage, by alleviating the vulnerability of minority cultures to majority decisions. These external protections ensure that members of the minority have the same opportunity to live and work in their own culture as members of the majority.

As I discussed in Chapter 3, these rights may impose restrictions on the members of the larger society, by making it more costly for them to move into the territory of the minority (e.g. longer residency requirements, fewer government services in their language), or by giving minority members priority in the use of certain land and resources (e.g. indigenous hunting and fishing rights). But the sacrifice required of non-members by the existence of these rights is far less than the sacrifice members would face in the absence of such rights.

Where these rights are recognized, members of the majority who choose to enter the minority's homeland may have to forgo certain benefits they are accustomed to. This is a burden. But without such rights, the members of many minority cultures face the loss of their culture, a loss which we cannot reasonably ask people to accept.

---

1   *the accommodation ... true equality*   [Unless otherwise indicated, all notes to this selection are by the author rather than the editors of this anthology.] This phrase is from the judgment of the Canadian Supreme Court in explaining its interpretation of the equality guarantees under the Canadian Charter of Rights (*Andrews* v. *Law Society of British Columbia* 1 SCR 143; 56 DLR (4th) 1). See also Government of Canada 1991b: 10.

2   *Proponents of ... race or ethnicity*   For examples of this view, see Rainer Knopff, "Language and Culture in the Canadian Debate: The Battle of the White Papers," *Canadian Review of Studies in Nationalism* 6/1 (1979): 66–82; F.L. Morton, "Group Rights versus Individual Rights in the Charter: The Special Cases of Natives and the Québécois," in N. Nevitte and A. Kornberg (eds.), *Minorities and the Canadian State* (Oakville: Mosaic Press, 1985), pp. 71–85; Chandran Kukathas, "Are There any Cultural Rights?" *Political Theory* 20/1 (1992): 105–39; Barry Hindess, "Multiculturalism and Citizenship," in Chandran Kukathas (ed.), *Multicultural Citizens: The Philosophy and Politics of Identity* (St Leonards: Centre for Independent Studies, 1993), pp. 33–45; Gerhard Maré, *Brothers Born of Warrior Blood: Politics and Ethnicity and South Africa* (Johannesburg: Raven Press, 1992), pp. 107–10; John Rawls, "Fairness to Goodness," *Philosophical Review* 84 (1975): 536–54; and the references cited in this work by Waluchow, Ch. 1 n. 4. 4 [as follows:] For liberal endorsements of this position, see Nathan Glazer, *Affirmative Discrimination: Ethnic Inequality and Public Policy* (New York: Basic Books, 1975), p. 220; Glazer, "Individual Rights against Group Rights," in A. Tay and E. Kamenka (eds.), *Human Rights* (London: Edward Arnold, 1978), p. 98; Glazer, *Ethnic Dilemmas: 1964–1982* (Cambridge, MA: Harvard University Press, 1983), p. 124; Milton Gordon, "Toward a General Theory of Racial and Ethnic Group Relations," in N. Glazer and D. Moynihan (eds.), *Ethnicity, Theory and Experience* (Cambridge MA: Harvard University Press, 1975), p. 105; John Porter, "Ethnic Pluralism in Canadian Perspective," in Glazer and Moynihan, p. 295; Pierre van den Berghe "Protection of Ethnic Minorities: A Critical Appraisal," in R. Wirsing (ed.), *Protection of Ethnic Minorities: Comparative Perspectives* (New York: Pergamon, 1981), p. 347; Janet Ajzenstat, "Liberalism and Assimilation: Lord Durham Revisited," in S. Brooks (ed.), *Political Thought in Canada: Contemporary Perspectives* (Toronto: Irwin, 1984), pp. 251–52; Richard Rorty, *Objectivity, Relativism, and Truth: Philo-*

---

sophical Papers I (Cambridge: Cambridge University Press, 1991), p. 209; Chadran Kukathas, *The Fraternal Conceit: Individualist versus Collectivist Ideas of Community* (St Leonard's: Centre for Independent Studies, 1991), p. 22; John Edwards, *Language, Society and Identity* (Oxford: Blackwell, 1985); H. Brotz, "Multiculturalism in Canada: A Muddle," *Canadian Public Policy* 6/1 (1980): 44.

Any plausible theory of justice should recognize the fairness of these external protections for national minorities. They are clearly justified, I believe, within a liberal egalitarian theory, such as Rawls's and Dworkin's, which emphasizes the importance of rectifying unchosen inequalities. Indeed inequalities in cultural membership are just the sort which Rawls says we should be concerned about, since their effects are "profound and pervasive and present from birth."[1]

This equality-based argument will only endorse special rights for national minorities if there actually is a disadvantage with respect to cultural membership, and if the rights actually serve to rectify the disadvantage. Hence the legitimate scope of these rights will vary with the circumstances. In North America, indigenous groups are more vulnerable to majority decisions than the Québécois or Puerto Ricans, and so their external protections will be more extensive. For example, restrictions on the sale of land which are necessary in the context of indigenous peoples are not necessary, and hence not justified, in the case of Québec or Puerto Rico.[2]

At some point, demands for increased powers or resources will not be necessary to ensure the same opportunity to live and work in one's culture. Instead, they will simply be attempts to gain benefits denied to others, to have more resources to pursue one's way of life than others have. This was clearly the case with apartheid, where whites constituting under 20 per cent of the population controlled 87 per cent of the land mass of the country, and monopolized all the important levers of state power.

One could imagine a point where the amount of land reserved for indigenous peoples would not be necessary to provide reasonable external protections, but rather would simply provide unequal opportunities to them. Justice would then require that the holdings of indigenous peoples be subject to the same redistributive taxation as the wealth of other advantaged groups, so as to assist the less well off in society. In the real world, of course, most indigenous peoples are struggling to maintain the bare minimum of land needed to sustain the viability of their communities. But it is possible that their land holdings could exceed what justice allows.[3]

1 *profound and pervasive and present from birth* John Rawls, *A Theory of Justice* (London, Oxford University Press, 1971), p. 96; cf. Ronald Dworkin, "What is Equality? Part II: Equality of Resources," *Philosophy and Public Affairs* 10/4 (1981): 283–345. I explored this relationship between national rights and liberal egalitarian justice in Will Kymlicka, *Liberalism, Community, and Culture* (Oxford: Oxford University Press, 1989), ch. 9. For what it is worth, I continue to endorse the argument in that chapter, but I should have been clearer about its scope. I would now describe the argument in that chapter as an equality-based defense of certain external protections for national minorities. I did not use those terms at the time, in part because I did not have a very clear conception of the variety of rights, groups, and moral justifications that are involved in the debate.

2 *This equality-based argument ... Puerto Rico* I am here disagreeing with Tamir, who argues that the larger a national minority is, the more rights it should have (Yael Tamir, *Liberal Nationalism* (Princeton: Princeton University Press, 1993), p. 75. On my view, if a national group is large enough, it may have little need for group differentiated rights, since it can ensure its survival and development through the usual operation of the economic marketplace and democratic decision-making. (This might be true, for example, if a binational state contained two nations of roughly equal size and wealth.)

3 *In the real ... justice allows* On the role of indigenous land claims in a liberal egalitarian framework, see Will Kymlicka, "Concepts of Community and Social Justice," in Fen O. Hampson and Judith Reppy (eds.), *Earthly Goods: Global Environmental Change and Social Justice* (Ithaca: Cornell University Press, 1996); Peter Penz, "Development Refugees and Distributive Justice: Indigenous Peoples, Land and the Developmentalist State," *Public Affairs Quarterly* 6/1 (1992): 105–31; Penz, "Colonization of Tribal Lands in Bangladesh and Indonesia: State Rationales, Rights to Land, and Environmental Justice," in Michael Howard (ed.), *Asia's Environmental Crisis* (Boulder, CO: Westview Press, 1993), pp. 37–72; John Russell "Nationalistic Minorities and Liberal Traditions," in Philip Bryden et al. (eds.), *Protecting Rights and Liberties: Essays on the Charter and Canada's Political, Legal and Intellectual Life* (Toronto: University of Toronto Press, 1993), pp. 205–41; James Tully, "Aboriginal Property and Western Theory: Recovering a Middle Ground," *Social Philosophy and Policy* 11/2 (1994): 153–80. It is important to note that the equality argument for land claims is not based on notions of compensatory justice. The compensatory argument says that because indigenous peoples were the legal owners of their traditional lands, and because their lands were taken away illegally, they should be compensated for this historical wrong. Since the debate over land claims is often couched in the language of compensatory justice, I should say a word about this. I take it as given that indigenous peoples have suffered terrible wrongs in being dispossessed of their lands, and that they should be compensated for this in some way. Moreover, I believe that indigenous peoples continue to have certain property rights under the common law (in former British colonies), wherever these have not been explicitly extinguished by legislation. (That is to say, the *terra nullius* doctrine is wrong in terms both of morality and the common law.) But it is a mistake, I think, to put too much weight on historical property rights. For one thing, these claims do not, by themselves, explain why indigenous peoples have rights of self-government. Many groups have been wrongfully dispossessed of property and other economic opportunities, including women, blacks, and Japanese immigrants in the United States and Canada during World War II. Each of these groups may be entitled to certain forms of compensatory justice, but this does not by itself explain or justify granting powers of self-government (rather than compensatory programs to promote inte-

The legitimacy of certain measures may also depend on their timing. For example, many people have suggested that a new South African constitution should grant a veto power

gration and equal opportunity within the mainstream). Suffering historical injustice is neither necessary nor sufficient for claiming self-government rights (see this work by Kymlicka, Ch. 2, s. 2).

Moreover, the idea of compensating for historical wrongs, taken to its logical conclusion, implies that all the land which was wrongly taken from indigenous peoples in the Americas or Australia or New Zealand should be returned to them. This would create massive unfairness, given that the original European settlers and later immigrants have now produced hundreds of millions of descendants, and this land is the only home they know. Changing circumstances often make it impossible and undesirable to compensate for certain historical wrongs. As Jeremy Waldron puts it, certain historical wrongs are "superseded" ("Superseding Historic Injustice," *Ethics* 103/1 [1992]: 4–28). Also, the land held by some indigenous groups at the time of contact was itself the result of the conquest or coercion of other indigenous groups (Richard Mulgan, *Maori, Pakeha and Democracy* (Auckland: Oxford University Press, 1989), pp. 30–1; Keith Crowe, *A History of the Original Peoples of Northern Canada* (Montreal: McGill-Queen's University Press, 1974), pp. 65–81. The compensatory argument would presumably require rectifying these pre-contract injustices as well. (For other difficulties with compensatory claims, see Lea Brilmayer, "Groups, Histories, and International Law," *Cornell International Law Journal* 25/3 [1992]: 555–63.)

The equality argument does not try to turn back the historical clock, nor to restore groups to the situation they would have been in the absence of any historical injustice. (These compensatory aims actually fit more comfortably with Nozick's libertarian theory of entitlement than with a liberal egalitarian theory of distributive justice—see David Lyons, "The New Indian Claims and Original Rights to Land," in J. Paul (ed.), *Reading Nozick: Essays on Anarchy, State and Utopia* (Totowa, NJ: Rowman & Littlefield, 1981).) The aim of the equality argument is to provide the sort of land base needed to sustain the viability of self-governing minority communities, and hence to prevent unfair disadvantages with respect to cultural membership now and in the future. In short, the equality argument situates land claims within a theory of distributive justice, rather than compensatory justice. Waldron assumes that indigenous land claims are all based on claims for compensatory justice (Waldron, "Superseding Historic Injustice"). In fact, however, most indigenous groups focus, not on reclaiming all of what they had before European settlement, but on what they need now to sustain themselves as distinct societies (see the declaration of the World Council of Indigenous Peoples, quoted in Garth Nettheim ""Peoples" and "Populations": Indigenous Peoples and the Rights of Peoples," in James Crawford (ed.), *The Rights of Peoples* (Oxford: Oxford University Press, 1988), p. 115; Andrew Sharp, *Justice and the Maori: Maori Claims in New Zealand Political Argument in the 1980s* (Auckland: Oxford University Press, 1990), pp. 150–53). Historical factors are, of course, relevant in other ways. The "historical agreement" argument I discuss below is very much history-based.

over certain important decisions to some or all of the major national groups. This sort of veto power is a familiar feature of various "consociational[1] democracies" in Europe, and, as I discuss in the next chapter, under certain circumstances it can promote justice. But it would probably be unjust to give privileged groups a veto power before there has been a dramatic redistribution of wealth and opportunities.[2] A veto power can promote justice if it helps protect a minority from unjust policies that favor the majority; but it is an obstacle to justice if it allows a privileged group the leverage to maintain its unjust advantages.

So the ideal of "benign neglect" is not in fact benign. It ignores the fact that the members of a national minority face a disadvantage which the members of the majority do not face. In any event, the idea that the government could be neutral with respect to ethnic and national groups is patently false. As I noted in Chapter 5, one of the most important determinants of whether a culture survives is whether its language is the language of government—i.e., the language of public schooling, courts, legislatures, welfare agencies, health services, etc. When the government decides the language of public schooling, it is providing what is probably the most important form of support needed by societal cultures; since it guarantees the passing on of the language and its associated traditions and conventions to the next generation. Refusing to provide public schooling in a minority language, by contrast, is almost inevitably condemning that language to ever-increasing marginalization.

The government therefore cannot avoid deciding which societal cultures will be supported. And if it supports the majority culture, by using the majority's language in schools and public agencies, it cannot refuse official recognition to minority languages on the ground that this violates "the separation of state and ethnicity." This shows that the analogy between religion and culture is mistaken. As I noted earlier, many liberals say that just as the state should not recognize, endorse, or support any particular church, so it should not recognize, endorse, or support any particular cultural group or identity (Ch. 1, s. 1). But the analogy does not work. It is quite possible for a state not to have an established church.

1   *consociational*   [editors' note] A state which has significant divisions along lines of language, religion, or ethnicity. Switzerland and Belgium are European consociational democracies.

2   *But it would ... wealth and opportunities*   Herbert Adam, "The Failure of Political Liberalism," in H. Adam and H. Giliomee (eds.), *Ethnic Power Mobilized: Can South Africa Change?* (New Haven: Yale University Press, 1979), p. 295.

But the state cannot help but give at least partial establishment to a culture when it decides which language is to be used in public schooling, or in the provision of state services. The state can (and should) replace religious oaths in courts with secular oaths, but it cannot replace the use of English in courts with no language.

This is a significant embarrassment for the "benign neglect" view, and it is remarkable how rarely language rights are discussed in contemporary liberal theory.[1] As Brian Weinstein put it, political theorists have had a lot to say about "the language of politics"—that is, the symbols, metaphors, and rhetorical devices of political discourse—but have had virtually nothing to say about "the politics of language"—that is, the decisions about which languages to use in political, legal, and educational forums.[2] Yet language rights are a fundamental cause of political conflict, even violence, throughout the world, including Canada, Belgium, Spain, Sri Lanka, the Baltics, Bulgaria, Turkey, and many other countries.[3]

One could argue that decisions about the language of schooling and public services should be determined, not by officially recognizing the existence of various groups, but simply by allowing each political subunit to make its own language policy on a democratic basis. If a national minority forms a majority in the relevant unit, they can decide to have their mother tongue adopted as an official language in that unit. But this is because they are a local majority, not because the state has officially recognized them as a "nation."

This is sometimes said to be the American approach to language rights, since there is no constitutional definition of language rights in the United States. But in fact the American government has historically tried to make sure that such "local" decisions are always made by political units that have an anglophone majority. As discussed in Chapter 2, decisions about state borders, or about when to admit territories as states, have been explicitly made with the aim of ensuring that there will be an anglophone majority. States in the American south-west and Hawaii were only offered statehood when the national minorities residing in those areas were outnumbered by settlers and immigrants. And some people oppose offering statehood to Puerto Rico precisely on the grounds that it will never have an anglophone majority.[4]

This illustrates a more general point. Leaving decisions about language to political subunits just pushes back the problem. What are the relevant political units—what level of government should make these decisions? Should each neighborhood be able to decide on the language of public schooling and public services in that neighborhood? Or should this decision be left to larger units, such as cities or provinces? And how do we decide on the boundaries of these subunits? If we draw municipal or provincial boundaries in one way, then a national minority will not form even a local majority. But if we draw the boundaries another way, then the national minority will form a local majority. In a multination state, decisions on boundaries and the division of powers are inevitably decisions about which national group will have the ability to use which state powers to sustain its culture.[5]

---

1 *it is remarkable ... liberal theory* The only attempt I know of to reconcile official languages with "benign neglect" is by Rainer Knopff. He argues that language has two functions: it can function as the vehicle for the transmission of a particular culture, but it can also function as "a culturally neutral, or utilitarian, means of communication which allows those of different cultures to participate in the same political community" ("Language and Culture in the Canadian Debate: The Battle of the White Papers," 67). By placing the emphasis on the utilitarian function, governments "can enact official languages without at the same time legislating official cultures" ... [I]n enacting "official languages," one does not necessarily imply that the cultures which these languages transmit and represent thereby become "official cultures" (67). Culture, Knopff argues, "remains a purely private affair" in Canada, for while English and French have official backing as the "utilitarian" languages, all languages compete on equal terms for "cultural" allegiance. It is the "task of the individual members of a culture to show the excellence of their product on the cultural marketplace, as it were. If they succeed, the language of that culture will become attractive to others ... if [a] culture, and hence, language, cannot show itself to be worthy of choice in the light of standards of the good, then it deserves to disappear" (70). This view of language as a "culturally neutral medium" has been thoroughly discredited in the literature. In any event, it is simply not true that teaching in the English language in public schools is totally divorced from the teaching of the history and customs of the anglophone society.

2 *As Brian Weinstein ... educational forums* Brian Weinstein, *The Civic Tongue: Political Consequences of Language Choices* (New York: Longman, 1983), p. 7-13.

3 *Yet language rights ... many other countries* D.L. Horowitz, *Ethnic Groups in Conflict* (Berkeley: University of California Press, 1985), pp. 219–24.

4 *decisions about ... anglophone majority* Alvin Rubinstein, "Is Statehood for Puerto Rico in the National Interest?" *In Depth: A Journal for Values and Public Policy*, Spring (1993): 87–99; Nathan Glazer (1983), *Ethnic Dilemmas: 1964–1982* (Cambridge: Harvard University Press, 1983), p. 280.

5 *In a multination state ... its culture* Some commentators say that governments should draw boundaries and distribute powers so as

For example, as I noted in Chapter 2, the Inuit in Canada wish to divide the Northwest Territories into two,[1] so that they will form the majority in the eastern half. This is seen as essential to the implementation of their right of self-government. Some liberals object that this proposal violates the separation of state and ethnicity by distributing public benefits and state powers so as to make it easier for a specific group to preserve its culture. But all decisions regarding boundaries and the distribution of powers in multination states have this effect. We can draw boundaries and distribute legislative powers so that a national minority has an increased ability within a particular region to protect its societal culture; or we can draw boundaries and distribute legislative powers so that the majority nation controls decisions regarding language, education, immigration, etc. on a country-wide basis.

The whole idea of "benign neglect" is incoherent, and reflects a shallow understanding of the relationship between states and nations. In the areas of official languages, political boundaries, and the division of powers, there is no way to avoid supporting this or that societal culture, or deciding which groups will form a majority in political units that control culture-affecting decisions regarding language, education, and immigration.

So the real question is, what is a fair way to recognize languages, draw boundaries, and distribute powers? And the answer, I think, is that we should aim at ensuring that all national groups have the opportunity to maintain themselves as a distinct culture, if they so choose. This ensures that the good of cultural membership is equally protected for the members of all national groups. In a democratic society, the majority nation will always have its language and societal culture supported, and will have the legislative power to protect its interests in culture-affecting decisions. The question is whether fairness requires that the same benefits and opportunities should be given to national minorities. The answer, I think, is clearly yes.

Hence group-differentiated self-government rights compensate for unequal circumstances which put the members of minority cultures at a systemic disadvantage in the cultural market-place, regardless of their personal choices in life. This is one of many areas in which true equality requires not identical treatment, but rather differential treatment in order to accommodate differential needs.[2]

---

to protect the viability of national minorities, but that they should not state in law that they are doing this. This enables the state to continue claiming that it treats all ethnic and national differences with "benign neglect." For example, van den Berghe argues that deliberately designing or revising federal units to protect minority cultures is consistent with "benign neglect," so long as it does not involve the explicit legal recognition of groups. He thinks it is one thing to define the powers and boundaries of a political subunit so as to ensure the protection of a minority culture (what he calls "indirect consociationalism"), but quite another for the constitution or statute law to cite the existence of that minority as the reason for those arrangements (what he calls "group rights") (Pierre van den Berghe, *The Ethnic Phenomenon* (New York: Elsevier, 1981), p. 348). But surely this is hypocritical. If the agreed purpose of indirect consociationalism is to protect minority cultures, then anyone who values honesty and transparency in government (as liberals claim to do) should want that justification to be clear to everyone. Van den Berghe's solution violates the "publicity condition" which Rawls imposes on liberal theories of justice (*A Theory of Justice*, p. 133). Nonetheless, this attitude seems to be widely shared. While most Canadians accept that the powers and boundaries of Quebec were fixed to accommodate the needs of the francophone minority in Canada, many objected to the government's proposal to state in the constitution that Quebec formed a "distinct society" as the homeland of the French Canadian nation, because they saw this as violating the principle that the constitution should not recognize particular ethnic or national groups. Quebecers, however, are no longer willing to have their special status hidden away. They view it as a matter of basic respect that their separate identity be recognized and affirmed at the level of constitutional principle (Charles Taylor, "Shared and Divergent Values," in Ronald Watts and D. Brown [eds.], *Options for a New Canada* [Toronto: University of Toronto Press, 1991], p. 64).

1   *the Inuit ... into two*   [editors' note] In 1999, a few years after this was published, the eastern three-fifths of the Northwest Territories became a separate territory called Nunavut.

2   *This is one ... differential needs*   This is similar to the debate over affirmative action for women or people with disabilities. Like self-government rights, affirmative action programs asymmetrically distribute rights or opportunities on the basis of group membership. Proponents argue that they are required for genuine equality. Critics respond that the economic market-place (like the cultural market-place) already respects equality, by treating job applicants without regard for their group membership. However, an equality-based argument for group-specific affirmative action can be made if the actual operation of the economic market-place works to the disadvantage of certain groups. As with self-government rights, the equality argument for affirmative action seeks to show how the structure of common individual rights is intended to treat all people equally, but in fact works to the disadvantage of the members of a particular collectivity. Many group-specific claims can be seen in this way—that is, as compensating for the disadvantages and vulnerabilities of certain groups within the structure of common individual rights.

Of course, as I discussed in Ch. 1, affirmative action for women or people with disabilities differs in many ways from self-government rights for national minorities, since they are compensating for very different kinds of injustices. The former is intended to

This does not mean that we should entirely reject the idea of the cultural market-place. Once the societal cultures of national groups are protected, through language rights and territorial autonomy, then the cultural market-place does have an important role to play in determining the character of the culture. Decisions about which particular aspects of one's culture are worth maintaining and developing should be left to the choices of individual members. For the state to intervene at this point to support particular options or customs within the culture, while penalizing or discouraging others, would run the risk of unfairly subsidizing some people's choices.[1] But that is not the aim or effect of many rights for national minorities, which are instead concerned with external protections (see Ch. 3, s. 1).

Let me now turn to polyethnic rights for ethnic groups. I believe there is an equality-based argument for these rights as well, which also invokes the impossibility of separating state from ethnicity, but in a different way. I argued in Chapter 5 that the context of choice for immigrants, unlike national minorities, primarily involves equal access to the mainstream culture(s). Having uprooted themselves from their old culture, they are expected to become members of the national societies which already exist in their new country. Hence promoting the good of cultural membership for immigrants is primarily a matter of enabling integration, by providing language training and fighting patterns of discrimination and prejudice. Generally speaking, this is more a matter of rigorously enforcing the common rights of citizenship than providing group-differentiated rights. In so far as common rights of citizenship in fact create equal access to mainstream culture, then equality with respect to cultural membership is achieved.

But even here equality does justify some group-specific rights. Consider the case of public holidays. Some people object to legislation that exempts Jews and Muslims from Sunday closing legislation, on the ground that this violates the separation of state and ethnicity. But almost any decision on public holidays will do so. In the major immigration countries, public holidays currently reflect the needs of Christians. Hence government offices are closed on Sunday, and on the major religious holidays (Easter, Christmas). This need not be seen as a deliberate decision to promote Christianity and discriminate against other faiths (although this was undoubtedly part of the original motivation). Decisions about government holidays were made when there was far less religious diversity, and people just took it for granted that the government work-week should accommodate Christian beliefs about days of rest and religious celebration.

But these decisions can be a significant disadvantage to the members of other religious faiths. And having established a work-week that favors Christians, one can hardly object to exemptions for Muslims or Jews on the ground that they violate the separation of state and ethnicity. These groups are simply asking that their religious needs be taken into consideration in the same way that the needs of Christians have always been taken into account. Public holidays are another significant embarrassment for the "benign neglect" view, and it is interesting to note how rarely they are discussed in contemporary liberal theory.

Similar issues arise regarding government uniforms. Some people object to the idea that Sikhs or Orthodox Jews should be exempted from requirements regarding headgear in the police or military. But here again it is important to recognize how the existing rules about government uniforms have been adopted to suit Christians. For example, existing dress-codes do not prohibit the wearing of wedding rings, which are an important religious symbol for many Christians (and Jews). And it is virtually inconceivable that designers of government dress-codes would have ever considered designing a uniform that prevented people from wearing wedding rings, unless this was strictly necessary for the job. Again, this should not be seen as a deliberate attempt to promote Christianity. It simply would have been taken for granted that uniforms should not unnecessarily conflict with Christian religious beliefs. Having adopted dress-codes that meet Christian needs, one can hardly object to exemptions for Sikhs and Orthodox Jews on the ground that they violate "benign neglect."

One can multiply the examples. For example, many state symbols such as flags, anthems, and mottoes reflect a particular ethnic or religious background ("In God We Trust"). The demand by ethnic groups for some symbolic affirmation of the value of polyethnicity (e.g. in government declarations and documents) is simply a demand that their identity be given the same recognition as the original Anglo-Saxon settlers.

---

help disadvantaged groups integrate into society, by breaking down unjust barriers to full integration. The latter is intended to help cultural communities maintain their distinctiveness, by protecting against external decisions. This means that the former are (in theory) temporary, whereas the latter are permanent, barring dramatic shifts in population.

1   *For the state ... some people's choices* Will Kymlicka, "Liberal Individualism and Liberal Neutrality," *Ethics* 99/4 (1989): 883–905.

It may be possible to avoid some of these issues by re-designing public holidays, uniforms, and state symbols. It is relatively easy to replace religious oaths with secular ones, and so we should. It would be more difficult, but perhaps not impossible, to replace existing public holidays and work-weeks with more "neutral" schedules for schools and government offices.[1]

But there is no way to have a complete "separation of state and ethnicity." In various ways, the ideal of "benign neglect" is a myth. Government decisions on languages, internal boundaries, public holidays, and state symbols unavoidably involve recognizing, accommodating, and supporting the needs and identities of particular ethnic and national groups. Nor is there any reason to regret this fact. There is no reason to regret the existence of official languages and public holidays, and no one gains by creating unnecessary conflicts between government regulations and religious beliefs. The only question is how to ensure that these unavoidable forms of support for particular ethnic and national groups are provided fairly—that is, how to ensure that they do not privilege some groups and disadvantage others. In so far as existing policies support the language, culture, and identity of dominant nations and ethnic groups, there is an argument of equality for ensuring that some attempts are made to provide similar support for minority groups, through self-government and polyethnic rights.

---

1   *It would be ... government offices*   Imagine that schools and government offices (and presumably private businesses as well) were open seven days a week all year round, including Christmas and Easter, and that each student and employee was allowed to choose two days off per week, two weeks vacation per year, plus, say, five additional holidays per year. This would maximize each individual's ability to adapt their schedule to their religious beliefs. But I do not know whether this is realistic or even desirable, given the extent to which social life is built around common weekends and holidays. As an atheist, I have no commitment to resting on the Sabbath or celebrating religious holidays. But I do like the fact that most of my friends and family, regardless of their religion, language, and ethnicity, do not work on the weekends or on certain public holidays. Maintaining friendships and other voluntary associations would be much more difficult if society (including schools and other government institutions) were not organized in this way. Perhaps a better solution would be to have one major holiday from each of the largest religious groups in the country. We could have one Christian holiday (say, Christmas), but replace Easter and Thanksgiving with a Muslim and Jewish holiday. This would maintain the value of common holidays, and would also encourage people of each faith to learn something about the beliefs of other faiths.

2. *The Role of Historical Agreements*

A second argument in defense of group-differentiated rights for national minorities is that they are the result of historical agreements, such as the treaty rights of indigenous peoples, or the agreement by which two or more peoples agreed to federate.

There are a variety of such agreements in Western democracies, although their provisions have often been ignored or repudiated. For example, the American government has unilaterally abrogated certain treaties with Indian tribes, and the Canadian government proposed in 1969 to extinguish all of its Indian treaties. The language rights guaranteed to Chicanos in the American south-west under the 1848 Treaty of Guadalupe Hidalgo were rescinded by the anglophone settlers as soon as they formed a majority. The language and land rights guaranteed to the Métis under the Manitoba Act of 1870 suffered the same fate in Canada. Yet many treaties and historical agreements between national groups continue to be recognized, and some have considerable legal force. For example, the 1840 Treaty of Waitangi signed by Maori chiefs and British colonists in New Zealand, declared a "simple nullity" in 1877, has re-emerged as a central legal and political document.[2]

The importance of honoring historical agreements is emphasized by proponents of group-differentiated rights, but has had little success convincing opponents. Those people who think that group-differentiated rights are unfair have not been appeased by pointing to agreements that were made by previous generations in different circumstances, often undemocratically and in conditions of substantial inequality in bargaining power. Surely some historical agreements are out of date, while others are patently unfair, signed under duress or ignorance. Why should not governments do what principles of equality require now, rather than what outdated and often unprincipled agreements require?[3]

---

2   *the 1840 Treaty ... political document*   Sharp, *Justice and the Maori*.

3   *Why should not ... agreements require?*   E.g., the Canadian government justified its proposal to eliminate the treaty rights of Indians on the grounds that "we can only be just in our time" (P.E. Trudeau, speech of 8 Aug. 1969, repr. as "Justice in our Time," in Eldon Soifer (ed.), *Ethical Issues: Perspectives for Canadians* (Peterborough: Broadview Press 1992, p. 295). Trudeau was paraphrasing John F. Kennedy's famous quote about justice for blacks in the United States.

One answer is to reconsider an underlying assumption of the equality argument. The equality argument assumes that the state must treat its citizens with equal respect. But there is the prior question of determining which citizens should be governed by which states. For example, how did the American government acquire the legitimate authority to govern Puerto Rico or the Navaho? And how did the Canadian government acquire legitimate authority over the Québécois and the Métis?

As I noted in Chapter 2, United Nations declarations state that all "peoples" are entitled to "self-determination"— i.e., an independent state. Obviously this principle is not reflected in existing boundaries, and it would be destabilizing, and indeed impossible, to fulfill. Moreover, not all peoples want their own state. Hence it is not uncommon for two or more peoples to decide to form a federation. And if the two communities are of unequal size, it is not uncommon for the smaller culture to demand various group-differentiated rights as part of the terms of federation. Forming a federation is one way of exercising a people's right of self-determination, and the historical terms of federation reflect the group's judgment about how best to exercise that right.

For example, the group-differentiated rights accorded French Canadians in the original confederation agreement in 1867, and the group-differentiated rights accorded Indians under various treaties, reflect the terms under which these communities joined Canada. It can be argued that these agreements define the terms under which the Canadian state acquired authority over these groups. These communities could have exercised their self-determination in other ways, but chose to join Canada, because they were given certain promises. If the Canadian government reneges on these promises, then it voids (morally, if not legally) the agreement which made those communities part of Canada.[1] Because these agreements define the terms under which various groups agreed to federate with Canada, the authority of the Canadian state over these groups flows from, but is also limited by, these agreements.[2]

In short, the way in which a national minority was incorporated often gives rise to certain group-differentiated rights. If incorporation occurred through a voluntary federation, certain rights might be spelled out in the terms of federation (e.g. in treaties), and there are legal and moral arguments for respecting these agreements. If incorporation was involuntary (e.g. colonization), then the national minority might have a claim of self-determination under international law which can be exercised by renegotiating the terms of federation so as to make it a more voluntary federation.[3]

This historical argument may justify the same rights as the equality argument. Many of the group-differentiated rights which are the result of historical agreements can be seen as providing the sort of protection required by the equality argument. For example, the right to local autonomy for Indian tribes/bands could be justified on the equality argument, if it helps the larger state show equal concern for the members of Indian communities. Autonomy is also justified on the historical argument, in so far as Indian peoples never gave the federal government jurisdiction over certain issues.

Indeed, it is likely that the equality and historical arguments will yield similar policies. If local autonomy is required to ensure that members of a minority are not disadvantaged, then it is likely that the minority would have demanded autonomy as part of the terms of federation (had the negotiations been fair).

The negotiations between English and French regarding the terms of federation in Canada provide a clear example of this. The Québécois realized that if they agreed to enter the Canadian state in 1867, they would become a permanent minority in the country, and so could be outvoted on decisions made at the federal level. They therefore faced the question whether they should remain outside Confederation, maintaining their status as a separate colony within the British Empire, and hoping one day to become a separate country with a francophone majority.

---

1   *If the Canadian ... part of Canada*   Chartrand argues that this is the current situation with respect to the Métis in Canada, who agreed to join Canada on the basis of promises made to them under the Manitoba Act 1870, which have since been broken (Paul Chartrand "Aboriginal Self-Government: The Two Sides of Legitimacy," in Susan Phillips [ed.], *How Ottawa Spends: 1993–1994* [Ottawa: Carleton University Press, 1993], p. 241).

2   *Because these agreements ... these agreements*   Paul Chartrand, *Manitoba's Métis Settlement Scheme of 1870* (Saskatoon: Univer-

sity of Saskatchewan Native Law Centre, 1991); and "Aboriginal Self-Government: The Two Sides of Legitimacy," in Susan Phillips (ed.), *How Ottawa Spends: 1993–1994* (Ottawa: Carleton University Press, 1993), pp. 240–01.

3   *If incorporation ... voluntary federation*   Patrick Macklem, "Distributing Sovereignty: Indian Nations and Equality of Peoples," *Stanford Law Review*, 45/5 (1993); and John Danley, "Liberalism, Aboriginal Rights and Cultural Minorities," *Philosophy and Public Affairs*, 20/2 (1991): 168–85.

Québécois leaders agreed to join Canada, even though they would be a minority in the federal parliament. But in return they insisted that jurisdiction over language and education be guaranteed to the provinces, not the federal government. This was "the non-negotiable condition in return for which they were prepared to concede the principle of representation by population" in the new parliament, a principle that "would institutionalize their minority position" within the new country.[1] In deciding whether to accept the terms of federation, therefore, Québécois leaders were explicitly concerned about equality—that is, how to ensure that they would not be disadvantaged in the new country. Since they had considerable bargaining power in the negotiations, they were able to ensure their equality in the agreement, through guarantees of language rights and provincial autonomy.

While the equality and historical arguments often lead to the same result, they are none the less quite distinct. On the historical argument, the question is not how should the state treat "its" minorities, but rather what are the terms under which two or more peoples decided to become partners? The question is not how should the state act fairly in governing its minorities, but what are the limits to the state's right to govern them?

For example, the two arguments may generate different answers to the question of federal funding of self-government rights. Under the equality argument, fairness may require positive state support for the measures required to maintain the viability of the national group. If fairness requires recognizing self-government in certain areas of jurisdiction, then presumably fairness will also require providing the resources needed to make self-government meaningful. The historical argument, however, may only generate a negative right to noninterference from the federal state. If the members of the national minority never gave the federal government the authority to govern them in certain areas, the federal government is unlikely to accept responsibility for funding minority self-government (unless this is itself part of the historical agreement). Any federal obligation to support self-government might be seen more as a form of humanitarian foreign aid than as a matter of domestic egalitarian justice.[2]

Contemporary political philosophers have had very little to say about the moral status of such historical agreements. For example, while Rawls recognizes a moral duty to respect treaties between countries,[3] he does not say anything about treaties or other agreements between nations within a country. This is surprising, because such agreements played a vital role in the creation and expansion of many countries, including the United States and Canada.

Respect for such agreements is important, I believe, not only to respect the self-determination of the minority, but also to ensure that citizens have trust in the actions of government. Historical agreements signed in good faith give rise to legitimate expectations on the part of citizens, who come to rely on the agreements made by governments, and it is a serious breach of trust to renege on them.

One difficulty with historical agreements is that they are often hard to interpret. For example, the Canadian government claims Quebec's "right to be different" was implicitly recognized in the original Confederation agreement.[4] But others deny this, and insist that Confederation was a union of provinces, not a compact between two cultures. Similar disputes arise over the interpretation of some Indian treaties. Moreover, some Indian tribes did not sign treaties, or signed them under duress. It seems arbitrary and unfair that some groups signed historical agreements while others, through no fault of their own, did not.

Where historical agreements are absent or disputed, groups are likely to appeal to the equality argument. Indian tribes/bands which have clear treaty rights often rest their claim for group-differentiated status on historical agreement; groups who did not sign treaties are more likely to appeal to the equality argument. It is often quite arbitrary whether a particular group happened to sign a particular agreement. However, the equality argument can help those groups which, for whatever reason, lack historical rights.[5]

---

1   *This was ... new country*   Jennifer Smith, "Canadian Confederation and the Influence of American Federalism," in Marian McKenna (ed.), *The Canadian and American Constitutions in Comparative Perspective* (Calgary: University of Calgary Press, 1993), p. 75.

2   *Any federal obligation ... egalitarian justice*   It is interesting to note that some Aboriginal groups in Canada insist that their demands

for federal funding of self-government are based solely on historical compensation for the wrongful taking of land, not on appeals to distributive justice between citizens (Noel Lyon, *Aboriginal Self-Government: Rights of Citizenship and Access to Government Services* [Kingston: Institute of Intergovernmental Relations, 1984]).

3   *Rawls recognizes ... between countries*   Rawls, *A Theory of Justice*, p. 378.

4   *the Canadian government ... Confederation agreement*   Government of Canada, *Shaping Canada's Future Together: Proposals* (Ottawa: Supply and Services, 1991), vi.

5   *Where historical agreements ... historical rights*   For a subtle discussion of the complex interaction between the equality and treaty

Historical agreements are much less common in the case of ethnic groups, since immigrants are rarely promised any special rights before arriving in their new country. Indeed, opponents of polyethnic rights sometimes say that ethnic groups should not expect any new group-differentiated rights, precisely because they agreed to come knowing full well that such rights did not exist. Yet there are some cases of polyethnic rights based on historical agreement. For example, the Hutterites (a Christian sect) were explicitly promised by Canadian immigration officials that they would be exempted from certain laws regarding education, land ownership, and military service if they settled in western Canada. (The Canadian government was anxious at the time to settle the newly opened up western frontier.)

This now seems like an anomalous case of an immigrant group given privileges denied to other citizens, and attempts have been made to eliminate these historical rights. On the other hand, solemn promises were given to the Hutterites, who would have emigrated elsewhere had these promises not been made. In this sense, they too can claim that the historical agreement defines the terms under which the Canadian government acquired authority over them.

In assessing group-differentiated rights claims, therefore, we need to know whether the rights being claimed are rectifying disadvantages, or recognizing historical agreements arising from the terms of federation. Both of these are legitimate grounds for group-differentiated rights, I believe, but both raise some difficult issues.

For example, how should we respond to agreements that are now unfair, due to changing conditions? The land claims recognized in various treaties may be too much, or too little, given changes in the size and lifestyle of indigenous communities. The powers given to Quebec in 1867 may no longer be appropriate in an age of telecommunications. To stick to the letter of historical agreements when they no longer meet the needs of minorities seems wrong.

Because of these changing circumstances, and because the original agreements are hard to interpret, many minority communities want to renegotiate their historical agreements. They want to make their group-differentiated rights more explicit in the constitution, and often more expansive. This is a major cause of the current constitutional crisis in Canada. For it has given those Canadians who see group-differentiated rights as unfair a chance to restrict, rather than entrench, such rights.

This suggests that, if we wish to defend group-differentiated rights, we should not rely solely on historical agreements. Since historical agreements must always be interpreted, and inevitably need to be updated and revised, we must be able to ground the historical agreements in a deeper theory of justice. The historical and equality arguments must work together.

3. The Value of Cultural Diversity

A third defense of group-differentiated rights for national minorities appeals to the value of cultural diversity. As I have discussed, liberals extol the virtue of having a diversity of lifestyles within a culture, so presumably they also endorse the additional diversity which comes from having two or more cultures in the same country. Surely intercultural diversity contributes to the richness of people's lives, as well as intracultural diversity.[1]

This argument is attractive to many people because it avoids relying solely on the interests of group members, and instead focuses on how the larger society also benefits from group-differentiated rights. As Richard Falk puts it, "societal diversity enhances the quality of life, by enriching our experience, expanding cultural resources." Hence protecting minority cultures "is increasingly recognized to be an expression of overall enlightened self-interest."[2] Whereas the first two arguments appeal to the *obligations* of the majority, this third argument appeals to the *interests* of the majority, and defends rights in terms of self-interest not justice.

Cultural diversity is said to be valuable, both in the quasi-aesthetic sense that it creates a more interesting world, and because other cultures contain alternative models of social organization that may be useful in adapting to new circumstances.[3] This latter point is often made with respect

---

arguments in the New Zealand context, see Sharp, *Justice and the Maori: Maori Claims in New Zealand Political Argument in the 1980s*, pp. 135–36; and Mulgan, *Maori, Pakeha and Democracy*, ch. 4. As Sharp notes, there is a tendency to read principles of equality back into the historical treaties.

1   *Surely intercultural ... intracultural diversity*   Brian Schwartz, *First Principles, Second Thoughts: Aboriginal Peoples, Constitutional Reform and Canadian Statecraft* (Montreal: Institute for Research on Public Policy, 1986), ch. 1.

2   *societal diversity ... enlightened self-interest*   Richard Falk, "The Rights of Peoples (in Particular, Indigenous Peoples)," in James Crawford (ed.), *The Rights of Peoples* (Oxford: Oxford University Press, 1988), p. 23.

3   *Cultural diversity ... new circumstances*   These arguments parallel common arguments for the protection of endangered plant and

to indigenous peoples, whose traditional lifestyles provide a model of a sustainable relationship to the environment. As Western attitudes towards nature are increasingly recognized to be unsustainable and self-destructive, indigenous peoples "may provide models, inspiration, guidance in the essential work of world order redesign."[1]

There is some truth in this argument about the value of cultural diversity. None the less, I think it is a mistake to put much weight on it as a defense of national rights. First, one of the basic reasons for valuing intracultural diversity has less application to intercultural diversity. The value of diversity within a culture is that it creates more options for each individual, and expands her range of choices. But protecting national minorities does not expand the range of choices open to members of the majority in the same way. As I explained last chapter, choosing to leave one's culture is qualitatively different from choosing to move around within one's culture. The former is a difficult and painful prospect for most people, and very few people in the mainstream choose to assimilate into a minority culture. Indeed, measures to protect national minorities may actually reduce diversity within the majority culture, compared with a situation where minorities, unable to maintain their own societal culture, are forced to integrate and add their distinctive contribution to the diversity of the mainstream culture. Having two or more cultures within a state does expand choices for each individual, but only to a limited degree, and it would be implausible to make this the primary justification for minority rights.

There are other aesthetic and educational benefits from cultural diversity, apart from the value of expanding individual choice. But it is not clear that any of these values by themselves can justify minority rights. One problem is that the benefits of diversity to the majority are spread thinly and widely, whereas the costs for particular members of the majority are sometimes quite high. Every one may benefit, in a diffuse way, from having flourishing minority cultures in Quebec and Puerto Rico. But some members of the majority culture are asked to pay a significant price

so that others can gain this diffuse benefit. For example, unilingual anglophones residing in Quebec or Puerto Rico are unlikely to get government employment or publicly funded education in English—benefits which they would take for granted elsewhere. Similarly, non-Indians residing on Indian lands may be discriminated against in terms of their access to natural resources, or their right to vote in local elections. It is not clear that the diffuse benefits of diversity for society as a whole justify imposing these sorts of sacrifices on particular people. It seems to me that these sacrifices are only consistent with justice if they are needed, not to promote benefits to the members of the majority, but to prevent even greater sacrifices to the members of the national minority.

Moreover, there are many ways of promoting diversity, and it seems likely that protecting national minorities involves more cost to the majority than other possible ways. For example, a society could arguably gain more diversity at less cost by increasing immigration from a variety of countries than by protecting national minorities. The diversity argument cannot explain why we have an obligation to sustain the particular sort of diversity created by the presence of a viable, self-governing national minority.

There is one further problem with the diversity argument. Let us say that the aesthetic or educational value of diversity does justify imposing certain costs on people in the majority culture. Why then does the value of diversity not also justify imposing a duty on the members of the minority to maintain their traditional culture? If the benefits of cultural diversity to the larger society can justify restricting individual liberties or opportunities, why does it matter whether these restrictions are imposed on people inside or outside the group? I noted earlier that a liberal theory of minority rights can accept external protections, but not internal restrictions. It is difficult to see how the diversity argument can make this distinction. Because it appeals to the interests of the larger society, it cannot explain why minorities should be able to decide for themselves whether or how to maintain their culture.

So it seems to me that the diversity argument is insufficient, by itself, to justify the rights of national minorities. Protecting national minorities does provide benefits to the majority, and these are worth pointing out. But these diffuse benefits are better seen as a desirable by-product of national rights, rather than their primary justification. To date, most majority cultures have not seen it in their "enlightened self-interest" to maintain minority cultures. No

animal species, which are seen both as enriching the world aesthetically, and as providing potential sources of valuable genetic material or other substances that might be of human benefit.

1   "may provide ... order redesign" Falk, p. 23. Cf. Jason Clay, "Epilogue: The Ethnic Future of Nations," *Third World Quarterly* 11/4 (1989): 233; and Sharon O'Brien, "Cultural Rights in the United States: A Conflict of Values," *Law and Inequality Journal*, p. 5 (1987): 358.

doubt this is due in part to ethnocentric prejudice, but we must recognize the powerful interests that majority nations often have in rejecting self-government rights for national minorities—e.g. increased access to the minority's land and resources, increased individual mobility, political stability, etc. It is unlikely that majorities will accept national rights solely on the basis of self-interest, without some belief that they have an obligation of justice to accept them. Conversely, it is unlikely that majorities will accept their obligations of justice towards national minorities without a belief that they gain something in the process. The diversity argument works best, therefore, when it is combined with arguments of justice.

The diversity argument is more plausible as a defense of polyethnic rights for ethnic groups. Unlike national self-government, these rights do contribute directly to diversity within the majority culture. Moreover, they do not involve the same sort of restrictions on the mobility or economic opportunities of the majority. Indeed, certain polyethnic policies can be seen as natural extensions of state policies regarding the funding of the arts, museums, educational television, etc.[1] Yet here again the problem arises that there are many ways of promoting diversity. Teaching children to be bilingual promotes diversity, but this cannot explain why we should teach immigrant languages in particular. Hence the diversity argument supplements, but cannot replace, justice arguments based on equality or historical agreement.

---

1 *Indeed, certain polyethnic ... educational television, etc.* Many liberals defend state funding of the arts or museums on the ground that the state has a responsibility to ensure an adequate range of options for future generations, which the cultural market-place may fail to protect (Ronald Dworkin, *A Matter of Principle* [London: Harvard University Press, 1985], ch. 11; Joseph Raz, *The Morality of Freedom* [Oxford: Oxford University Press, 1986], p. 162; Samuel Black, "Revisionist Liberalism and the Decline of Culture," *Ethics* 102/2 [1992]: 244–67; Will Kymlicka, "Liberal Individualism and Liberal Neutrality," *Ethics* 99/4 [1989]: 893–95). If we accept that active measures are justified to preserve the richness and diversity of our cultural resources, then programs such as the funding of ethnic festivals or immigrant language classes can be seen as falling under this heading. Indeed, as I noted in Chapter 2, some people defend this funding simply as a way of ensuring that ethnic groups are not discriminated against in state funding of art and culture. (I should note that other liberals view any such state funding as illegitimate [E.g., Rawls, *A Theory of Justice* 331–32; Jeremy Waldron, "Autonomy and Perfectionism in Raz's *Morality of Freedom*," *Southern California Law Review* 62/3–4 (1989): 1097–152].)

4. The Analogy with States

So far, I have been assuming that the burden of proof lies on those who wish to find room for group-differentiated rights within the liberal tradition. But we can and should question this assumption. In many ways, it is opponents of group-differentiated rights who are proposing a revision of liberal theory and practice. As I discussed in Chapter 4, certain group-differentiated rights have been a long-established part of the liberal tradition. Moreover, such rights are logically presupposed by existing liberal practice.

For example, most liberal theorists accept without question that the world is, and will remain, composed of separate states, each of which is assumed to have the right to determine who can enter its borders and acquire citizenship. I believe that this assumption can only be justified in terms of the same sorts of values which ground group-differentiated rights within each state. I believe that the orthodox liberal view about the right of states to determine who has citizenship rests on the same principles which justify group-differentiated citizenship within states, and that accepting the former leads logically to the latter.

This point is worth exploring in some depth. The existence of states, and the right of governments to control entry across state borders, raises a deep paradox for liberals. Most liberal theorists defend their theories in terms of "equal respect for persons," and the "equal rights of individuals." This suggests that all "persons" or "individuals" have an equal right to enter a state, participate in its political life, and share in its natural resources.

In fact, however, these rights are typically reserved for *citizens*. And not everyone can become a citizen, even if they are willing to swear allegiance to liberal principles. On the contrary, there are millions of people who want to gain citizenship in various liberal democracies, but who are refused. Even the most open Western country in terms of immigration accepts only a fraction of the number of people who would come if there were genuinely open borders. Indeed, would-be immigrants are often refused entry, turned back at the border by armed border guards. These people are refused the right to enter and participate in the state because they were not born into the right group.

Citizenship, therefore, is an inherently group-differentiated notion. Unless one is willing to accept either a single world-government or completely open borders between states—and very few liberal theorists have endorsed either of these—then distributing rights and benefits on the basis of citizenship is to treat people differently on the basis of their group membership.[1]

This creates a profound contradiction within most liberal theories. As Samuel Black notes, liberal theorists often begin by talking about the moral equality of "persons," but end up talking about the equality of "citizens," without explaining or even noticing the shift.[2] What can justify restricting the rights of citizenship to members of a particular group, rather than all persons who desire it?

Some critics have argued that liberals cannot justify this restriction, and that the logic of liberalism requires open borders, except perhaps for temporary restrictions in the name of public order.[3] And surely that is right if we cling to the idea that liberalism should be indifferent to people's cultural membership and national identity. Open borders would dramatically increase the mobility and opportunities of individuals, and, if liberalism requires treating people solely "as individuals" without regard for their group membership, then open borders clearly are preferable from a liberal point of view.

I believe, however, that some limits on immigration can be justified if we recognize that liberal states exist, not only to protect standard rights and opportunities of individuals, but also to protect people's cultural membership. Liberals implicitly assume that people are members of societal cultures, that these cultures provide the context for individual choice, and that one of the functions of having separate states is to recognize the fact that people belong to separate cultures. I noted examples of this in the liberal tradition in Chapter 4, and with Rawls's discussion of citizenship and the bonds of culture in Chapter 5. Once we make these assumptions explicit, however, it is clear that, in multination states, some people's cultural membership can only be recognized and protected by endorsing group-differentiated rights within the state.

Liberal theorists invariably limit citizenship to the members of a particular group, rather than all persons who desire it. The most plausible reason for this—namely, to recognize and protect our membership in distinct cultures—is also a reason for allowing group-differentiated citizenship within a state. There may be other reasons for restricting citizenship to a particular group which do not make any reference to the importance of cultural groups. It is difficult to say, since few liberals actually discuss the shift from "equality of persons" to "equality of citizens." But I think it is fair to say this: in so far as liberal theorists accept the principle that citizenship can be restricted to the members of a particular group, the burden of proof lies on them to explain why they are not also committed to accepting group-differentiated rights within a state.[4] So long as liberals believe in separate states with restricted citizenship, the burden of proof lies as much with opponents of group-differentiated rights as with their defenders.

---

1   *Unless one is ... group membership*   Hence the popular contrast between "consociational" and "universal" modes of incorporating individuals into the state is misleading (e.g., Michael Asch, "Consociation and the Resolution of Aboriginal Political Rights," *Culture* 10/1 [1990]: 93–102). There is a distinction between models of citizenship that incorporate citizens on a uniform basis or through membership in some group. But uniform citizenship is not *universal* citizenship. No country allows for universal citizenship.

2   *As Samuel Black ... noticing the shift*   "Individualism at an Impasse," *Canadian Journal of Philosophy*, 21/3 (1991).

3   *Some critics ... public order*   See the references in this work by Kymlicka, Ch. 5 n. 17 [as follows:] Of course, once that national existence is not threatened, then people will favor increased mobility, since being able to move and work in other cultures is a valuable option for some people under some circumstances. For liberal defenders of open borders—all of whom see themselves as criticizing the orthodox liberal view—see Bruce Ackerman, *Social Justice in the Liberal State* (New Haven: Yale University Press, 1980), pp. 89–95; Joseph Carens, "Aliens and Citizens: The Case for Open Borders," *Review of Politics* 49/3 (1987): 251–73; James Hudson, "The Philosophy of Immigration," *Journal of Libertarian Studies* 8/1 (1986): 51–62; Timothy King, "Immigration from Developing Countries: Some Philosophical Issues," *Ethics* 93/3 (1983): 525–36; Veit M. Bader, "Citizenship and Exclusion. Radical Democracy, Community and Justice. What is wrong with communitarianism?" *Political Theory* 23/2 (1995): 211–46.

4   *in so far ... within a state*   One theorist who has attempted to square the circle is Michael Walzer. He argues that restricting citizenship in a state to the members of a particular group is justified in the name of protecting a distinct culture (what he calls a "community of character"). He recognizes that this same argument can be given for group-differentiated rights *within* a state, but rejects such rights because they violate our "shared understandings" (*Spheres of Justice: A Defense of Pluralism and Equality* [Oxford: Blackwell, 1983], ch. 2). I have argued elsewhere that Walzer's argument is unsuccessful (*Liberalism, Community, and Culture* ch. 11). See also Ch. 4 of the present work by Kymlicka. I should emphasize again that my defense of the legitimacy of partially closed borders is not intended to defend the right of national groups to maintain more than their fair share of resources. On the contrary, I would argue that a country forfeits its right to restrict immigration if it has failed to live up to its obligations to share its wealth with the poorer countries of the world. See Bader, "Citizenship and Exclusion: Radical Democracy, Community and Justice"; and Ackerman, *Social Justice in the Liberal State* 256–57.

5. *Conclusion*

In the last two chapters, I have tried to show that liberals can and should accept a wide range of group-differentiated rights for national minorities and ethnic groups, without sacrificing their core commitments to individual freedom and social equality.

It may be useful briefly to summarize my argument. I have tried to show how freedom of choice is dependent on social practices, cultural meanings, and a shared language. Our capacity to form and revise a conception of the good is intimately tied to our membership in a societal culture, since the context of individual choice is the range of options passed down to us by our culture. Deciding how to lead our lives is, in the first instance, a matter of exploring the possibilities made available by our culture.

However, minority cultures in multination states may need protection from the economic or political decisions of the majority culture if they are to provide this context for their members. For example, they may need self-governing powers or veto rights over certain decisions regarding language and culture, and may need to limit the mobility of migrants or immigrants into their homelands.

While these group-differentiated rights for national minorities may seem discriminatory at first glance, since they allocate individual rights and political powers differentially on the basis of group membership, they are in fact consistent with liberal principles of equality. They are indeed required by the view, defended by Rawls and Dworkin, that justice requires removing or compensating for undeserved or "morally arbitrary" disadvantages, particularly if these are "profound and pervasive and present from birth."[1] Were it not for these group-differentiated rights, the members of minority cultures would not have the same ability to live and work in their own language and culture that the members of majority cultures take for granted. This, I argued, can be seen as just as profound and morally arbitrary a disadvantage as the inequalities in race and class that liberals more standardly worry about.

This equality-based argument for group-differentiated rights for national minorities is further strengthened by appeals to historical agreements and the value of cultural diversity. And it is confirmed by the way that liberals implicitly invoke cultural membership to defend existing state borders and restrictions on citizenship. I have also argued that polyethnic rights for ethnic groups can be justified in terms of promoting equality and cultural diversity within the mainstream culture.

These claims are by no means uncontroversial, and there are many places where they could be challenged. One could deny that cultural meanings are dependent on a societal culture, or that individuals are closely tied to their own particular societal culture. One could also deny that minority cultures are vulnerable to the decisions of the larger society; or that this vulnerability constitutes an injustice; or that historical agreements have any moral weight; or that cultural diversity is worth promoting.

Yet I think each of these claims is plausible. Anyone who disputes them would be required to provide some alternative account of what makes meaningful choices available to people, or what justice requires in terms of language rights, public holidays, political boundaries, and the division of powers. Moreover, one would also have to offer an alternative account of the justification for restricting citizenship to the members of a particular group, rather than making it available to anyone who desires it. It is not enough to simply assert that a liberal state should respond to ethnic and national differences with benign neglect. That is an incoherent position that avoids addressing the inevitable connections between state and culture.

The idea that group-differentiated rights for national and ethnic groups can and should be accepted by liberals is hardly a radical suggestion. In fact, many multination liberal democracies already accept such an obligation, and provide public schooling and government services in the language of national minorities. Many have also adopted some form of federalism, so that national minorities will form a majority in one of the federal units (states, provinces, or cantons). And many polyethnic liberal states have adopted various forms of polyethnic policies and group-specific rights or exemptions for immigrant groups. Like Jay Sigler, I believe that providing a liberal defense of minority rights "does not create a mandate for vast change. It merely ratifies and explains changes that have taken place in the absence of theory."[2]

But if there are strong arguments in favor of group-differentiated rights, why have liberals so often rejected them? As I noted in Chapter 4, the explanation cannot be that liberalism is premised on "abstract individualism,"

---

1   *justice requires ... from birth* Rawls, *A Theory of Justice*, p. 96.

2   *does not create ... absence of theory* Jay Sigler, *Minority Rights: A Comparative Analysis* (Westport, CT: Greenwood, 1983), p. 196.

on a conception of the individual as a solitary atom who is independent of her cultural environment. I hope that Chapters 4 and 5 have dispelled any perception that liberals ignore individuals' dependence on society and culture.

But this raises a puzzle. If individual autonomy and self-identity are tied to membership in one's societal culture, developing a theory of the rights of minority cultures would seem to be one of the very first tasks of any liberal theory. Why then have so few contemporary liberal theorists supported measures to protect cultural groups, such as group-specific language rights, land claims, or federal autonomy? I have explored some of the historical reasons in Chapter 4. Another part of the explanation, I think, is that contemporary liberal theorists implicitly assume that countries contain only one nation. They are well aware that modern states are culturally diverse—indeed, the pluralistic nature of modern liberal democracies is a pervasive theme in their writings. But they implicitly assume that this diversity is the sort that comes either from variations in people's conceptions of the good or from immigration—that is, they focus on philosophical, religious, and ethnic diversity within a single culture based on a shared language.[1] They do not recognize or discuss the existence of states that are multinational, with a diversity of societal cultures, languages, and national groups.

For example, Dworkin notes that "in the modern world of immigration and boundary shifts," citizens do not share a racial or ethnic background, and that the communal life of the political community cannot include a single "ethnic allegiance."[2] But, as I noted earlier, he does assume a common "cultural structure" based on a "shared language."[3] Similarly, while Rawls emphasizes the "fact of pluralism"—particular-ly religious pluralism—he equates the political community with a single "complete culture," and with a single "people" who belong to the same "society and culture."[4]

This implicit assumption that states are uninational is rarely explained or defended. It is not as if these theorists explicitly reject the possibility that national minorities have special rights, or directly criticize the arguments of equality or history in defense of these rights. On the contrary, they simply ignore the issue entirely. There is no discussion by contemporary liberal theorists of the differences between nation-states and polyethnic or multination states, or of the arguments for modifying liberal principles in countries which are a "federation of peoples."

This shows, I think, that it is a mistake to subsume the issue of minority rights under one of the more familiar debates in contemporary political philosophy—e.g. the debate between "individualists" and "communitarians," or between "universalists" and "contextualists," or between "impartialists" and "difference theorists," or between "rationalists" and "postmodernists." This is a very common tendency.[5] But it stems from an over-simplified view of the issues involved in minority rights. According to many commentators, the central question in assessing minority rights is whether one accepts in principle the idea of giving political recognition to communities or group differences. Defenders of individualism and universalism are then said

---

1   *they focus ... shared language*   On the tendency of liberals to treat diversity as a matter of variations in individual values and beliefs, see Anne Phillips, *Democracy and Difference* (Philadelphia: Pennsylvania State University Press, 1993); Anna Galeotti, "Citizenship and Equality: The Place for Toleration," *Political Theory* 21/4 (1993): 590. For an example of this "overly cerebral" conception of diversity, see John Rawls, *Political Liberalism* (New York, Columbia University Press, 1993), xxvii–xxix, where he treats modern conflicts of race, ethnicity, and gender as if they were analogous to conflict over religious belief during the Reformation—i.e., as conflicts over individuals' beliefs about "the meaning, value and purposes of human life."

2   *Dworkin notes ... "ethnic allegiance"*   "Liberal Community," *California Law Review* 77/3 (1989), p. 497.

3   *he does assume ... "shared language"*   Dworkin, *A Matter of Principle* (London: Harvard University Press, 1985), pp. 230, 233; and "Liberal Community," 488.

4   *Rawls emphasizes ... society and culture*   "The Basic Structure as Subject," in A. Goldman and J. Kim (eds.), *Values and Morals* (Dordrecht: Reidel, 1978), p. 70 n.8; *Political Liberalism* (New York: Columbia University Press, 1993), pp. 18, 222, 277; "The Law of Peoples," in S. Shute and S. Hurley (eds.), *On Human Rights: The Oxford Amnesty Lectures 1993* (New York: Basic Books, 1993), p. 48.

5   *This is ... common tendency*   See e.g., Iris Marion Young, "Together in Difference: Transforming the Logic of Group Political Conflict," in Judith Squires (ed.), *Principled Positions: Postmodernism and the Rediscovery of Value* (London: Lawrence and Wishart, 1993); Myron Gochnauer, "Philosophical Musings on Persons, Groups, and Rights," *University of New Brunswick Law Journal*, 40/1 (1991); Marlies Galenkamp, *Individualism and Collectivism: The Concept of Collective Rights* (Rotterdam: Rotterdamse Filosofische Studies, 1993); Leon Trakman, "Group Rights: A Canadian Perspective," *New York University Journal of International Law and Politics*, 24/4 (1992); Gerald Torres, "Critical Race Theory: The Decline of the Universalist Ideal and the Hope of Plural Justice," *Minnesota Law Review*, p. 75 (1991); Adeno Addis, "Individualism, Communitarianism, and the Rights of Ethnic Minorities," *Notre Dame Law Review*, 67/3 (1991). Cf. Tzvetan Todorov, *On Human Diversity: Nationalism, Racism and Exoticism in French Thought* (Cambridge: Harvard University Press, 1993).

to be opposed in principle to such recognition, whereas defenders of community and difference are in principle supportive of them. But, as I have emphasized, all political theories must accord recognition to certain forms of group differences and support certain cultural communities. This is inevitable in any theory which confronts issues of language policy, public holidays, political boundaries, and immigration rules. This is as true of liberal individualists and socialist internationalists as of conservatives, communitarians, and postmodernists.

So the debate over minority rights is not about whether it is ever legitimate to support "communities" or to recognize "difference." Rather, the debate is whether to support the particular sort of cultural difference and community exhibited by national minorities. And, as I have noted, some liberals, despite their "individualism" and "universalism," recognize that justice requires extending the same support to national minorities that majority nations receive. Conversely, some communitarians and particularists, despite their commitment to "community" and "difference," have been reluctant to accept the demands of national minorities. They view national minorities in the same way they view ethnic groups or new social movements—that is, as forms of difference and community that can and should be accommodated by group-specific rights within the larger society. They are unwilling to accept that national minorities require recognition as separate and self-governing societies alongside the mainstream society.[1]

As I noted in Chapter 4, the history of minority rights suggests that there is little or no correlation between meta-ethical debates and support for the rights of national minorities. People's views on minority rights are shaped, not only by their foundational moral or philosophical premises, but by more concrete factors, including ethnocentric prejudice, fears about international peace and superpower relations, and concerns about the preconditions of democratic consensus and social harmony. These considerations do not correlate in any simple or consistent way with people's underlying philosophical and moral premises.

These larger philosophical debates are not irrelevant to the policy debate over minority rights. But the connection between the two debates is mediated by many additional assumptions about the nature of ethnic and national differences, and their role in domestic and international politics. It is these additional assumptions that largely account for the actual position endorsed by particular theorists, whatever their deeper philosophical premises.

For this reason, the demands of national minorities and ethnic groups raise a deep challenge to all Western political traditions. All of these traditions have been shaped, implicitly or explicitly, by the same historical influences which have shaped liberal thinking. The task of developing a consistent and principled theory of minority rights is not one that liberals face alone.

[...]

---

1   *some communitarians ... mainstream society*   This is true of Young's postmodernist account of minority rights. According to her view of "relational difference," cultural groups must "understand themselves as participating in the same society," and as "part of a single polity," whose common decision-making procedures are seen as "legitimately binding" on all people equally. Cultural difference within a state should be accommodated by group-differentiated rights within a single society—e.g., by group representation within the mainstream polity—rather than by establishing two or more separate and self-governing societies within a state (Iris Marion Young "Together in Difference: Transforming the Logic of Group Political Conflict," in Judith Squires (ed.), *Principled Positions: Postmodernism and the Rediscovery of Value* [London: Lawrence and Wishart, 1993], pp. 121–50). Like many liberals, she fears the impact of national rights on other political movements or on domestic peace.

JÜRGEN HABERMAS
(1929–)

Jürgen Habermas was born in Düsseldof, Germany in 1929. His experience under the Nazi regime and the Nuremberg trials and documentaries of the concentration camps mark his political philosophy, as well as his work as a public intellectual. Despite the highly technical nature of his philosophical and sociological work, Habermas has always tied his research closely to social issues. He was particularly vocal in the 1980s in opposing German revisionist historians who contested the uniqueness of the Holocaust among twentieth-century atrocities and attempted to minimize the responsibility of the German people. The most important of these essays are collected in *The New Conservatism: Cultural Criticism and the Historian's Debate* (1989).

Habermas's range is extraordinary—Richard Rorty called him the "leading systematic philosopher of our time." Among the disciplines to which he has contributed are social and political philosophy, sociology, theology, and law. A short list of influences on his work include Marx and the Frankfurt school; the sociology of Max Weber, Emile Durkheim, and George Herbert Mead; the philosophy of language of J.L. Austin and John Searle; the developmental psychology of Piaget and Kohlberg; psychoanalysis; the pragmatism of Peirce and John Dewey. Though it is impossible to attempt even a summary of his main contributions to social and political thought, Habermas's work is united by the conviction that social life and human emancipation are possible through our capacity to communicate as equals.

Often considered the leading contemporary representative of the Frankfurt school of critical theory—he became Theodore Adorno's assistant in 1956 and received Max Horkheimer's chair in 1964—Habermas has sharply criticized its rejection of the Enlightenment project. Enlightenment figures such as Voltaire and Kant argue for the emancipatory power of reason to further human progress and liberation; Adorno and Horkheimer in their influential book *Dialect of Enlightenment* (1944, revised edition 1947) instead argue that the development of instrumental reasoning resulted in bureaucratic and economic domination. Stricken by twentieth-century tragedies such as the mass murders perpetrated by totalitarian states, Horkheimer and Adorno came to the pessimistic conviction that rationality itself inevitably leads to the domination of nature and, consequently, of humanity.

The early critical theorists influenced many postmodern thinkers such as Foucault, Derrida, and Lyotard, who reject or express skepticism in the emancipatory power of reason. In writings such as the essays included in *The Philosophical Discourse of Modernity* (1987), Habermas takes issue with these postmodernist theorists and argues that they have a one-sided conception of rationality as means/ends reasoning. Though this idea takes many forms as Habermas's thinking evolves from the 1960s to the present, his basic claim is that not all rationality is instrumental; rather, there is the possibility of communicative rationality which retains emancipatory power.

The importance of communication is an important theme of Habermas's early work *The Structural Transformation of the Public Sphere: an Inquiry into a Category of Bourgeois Society* (1962, English translation 1989), which analyzes the bourgeois public sphere that originated in eighteenth-century European salons and literary journals. Here Habermas finds an ideal of free discussion among equals about matters of the public good, which provides a counterbalance to both government and business. Though Habermas is well aware of the limitations of actual eighteenth-century practice—to begin with, the working class and most women were excluded from the public sphere— he argues that the public sphere still approximates an ideal worth striving for.

Habermas also shows how during the nineteenth century mass communication and media revolutionized the public sphere, transforming ideas into commodities. This analysis is very much in accordance with that of Adorno and Horkheimer, but Habermas draws from it a very different lesson. Rather than pessimism about the nature of rationality, Habermas advocates forums that foster democratic discussion between ordinary citizens.

This basic insight led to the theory of communicative action which underlies Habermas's ethics and political thought. In his monumental two-volume *Theory of Communicative Action* (1981) Habermas holds that unrestrained, uncoerced communication provides for the possibility of achieving intersubjective agreement based on reason. Drawing on Austin and Searle's speech act theory and Chomsky's theory of linguistic competence, Habermas constructs a theory of communicative competence underlying our ability to speak. Language, as he points out, has many functions. We can use language strategically and instrumentally to achieve our goals. For instance, we can threaten to harm our interlocutors if they refuse to do what we order. But we can also use language to communicate and mutually aim at reaching understanding. Habermas argues that the act of speaking necessarily presupposes that the speaker is capable of giving reasons supporting her position. These reasons can be empirical, moral, aesthetic, etc., but are open to public dispute. Speech acts are valid insofar as they can be justified to other interlocutors.

One important aspect of the theory of communicative action is that it provides an alternative account of democracy. Influential views of democracy suggest that democracy is merely the competition of interest groups struggling for political power (pluralist democracy) or the election of elites whose only accountability is the public's ability to remove them from office (elitist democracy). In *Between Facts and Norms* (1996), Habermas sets out his views on the political institutions and legal order of the liberal constitutional state. He distinguishes between two spheres of politics (a distinction already present in a rough form in *The Structural Transformation of the Public Sphere*): a formal political sphere composed of political parties, parliaments, cabinets, and the like (but excluding state bureaucracy); and an informal or "anarchic" sphere of civil society made up of non-governmental associations, the media, activist groups, etc. Habermas thus envisages both a formal legislation that enacts law and an informal arena (a public sphere) in which members of civil society deliberate and form public opinion. Civil society interacts with and counterbalances formal legislative structures.

Law is characterized by the fact that it can be coercively enforced; its coercive nature raises questions about its justifiability. For Habermas, laws are legitimate or valid if they are capable, at least in theory, of meeting with the agreement of all affected. When laws are subject to the criticisms of civil society, they tend to be rational and legitimate. This allows Habermas to claim that basic constitutional rights are both grounded in the exercise of popular sovereignty (which guarantees their justifiability) and serve to protect the conditions under which popular sovereignty can be exercised.

Habermas has been hugely influential, as the many articles and books on his work attest. His popular writings regularly appear in *Die Zeit*, one of Germany's most respected newspapers. He is a key figure in recent debates about deliberative democracy, nationalism, and cosmopolitanism, and the possibility of extending democracy to a global political order. His students include Axel Honneth, Thomas McCarthy, Jeremy Shapiro, and Claus Offe. Social thinkers influenced by him include Seyla Benhabib, Iris Young, James Bohman, and David Held. Finally, he has engaged in debate with dozens of the twentieth century's most important intellectuals, including Foucault, John Rawls, and Cardinal Ratzinger (now Pope Benedict XVI).

◆ ◆ ◆ ◆ ◆

The Public Sphere (1962)

Concept

By "public sphere" we mean first of all a domain of our social life in which such a thing as public opinion can be formed. Access to the public sphere is open in principle to all citizens. A portion of the public sphere is constituted in every conversation in which private persons come together to form a public. They are then acting neither as business or professional people conducting their private affairs, nor as legal consociates subject to the legal regulations of a state bureaucracy and obligated to obedience. Citizens act as a public when they deal with matters of general interest without being subject to coercion; thus with the guarantee that they may assemble and unite freely, and express and publicize their opinions freely. When the public is large, this kind of communication requires certain means of dissemination and influence; today, newspapers and periodicals, radio and television are the media of the public sphere. We speak of a political public sphere (as distinguished from a literary one, for instance) when the public discussions concern objects connected with the practice of the state. The coercive power of the state is the counterpart, as it were, of the political public sphere, but it is not a part of it. State power is, to be sure, considered "public" power, but it owes the attribute of publicness to its task of caring for the public, that is, providing for the common good of all legal consociates. Only when the exercise of public authority has actually been subordinated to the requirement of democratic publicness does the political public sphere acquire an institutionalized influence on the government, by way of the legislative body. The term "public opinion" refers to the functions of criticism and control of organized state authority that the public exercises informally, as well as formally during periodic elections. Regulations concerning the publicness (or publicity [*Publizität*] in its original meaning) of state-related activities, as, for instance, the public accessibility required of legal proceedings, are also connected with this function of public opinion. To the public sphere as a sphere mediating between state and society, a sphere in which the public as the vehicle of public opinion is formed, there corresponds the principle of publicness—the publicness that once had to win out against the secret politics of monarchs and that since then has permitted democratic control of state activity.

It is no accident that these concepts of the public sphere and public opinion were not formed until the eighteenth century. They derive their specific meaning from a concrete historical situation. It was then that one learned to distinguish between opinion and public opinion, or *opinion publique*. Whereas mere opinions (things taken for granted as part of a culture, normative convictions, collective prejudices and judgments) seem to persist unchanged in their quasi-natural structure as a kind of sediment of history, public opinion, in terms of its very idea, can be formed only if a public that engages in rational discussion exists. Public discussions that are institutionally protected and that take, with critical intent, the exercise of political authority as their theme have not existed since time immemorial—they developed only in a specific phase of bourgeois society, and only by virtue of a specific constellation of interests could they be incorporated into the order of the bourgeois constitutional state.

History

It is not possible to demonstrate the existence of a public sphere in its own right, separate from the private sphere, in the European society of the High Middle Ages. At the same time, however, it is not a coincidence that the attributes of authority at that time were called "public." For a public representation of authority existed at that time. At all levels of the pyramid established by feudal law, the status of the feudal lord is neutral with respect to the categories "public" and "private"; but the person possessing that status represents it publicly; he displays himself, represents himself as the embodiment of a "higher" power, in whatever degree.

This concept of representation has survived into recent constitutional history. Even today the power of political authority on its highest level, however much it has become detached from its former basis, requires representation through the head of state. But such elements derive from a pre-bourgeois social structure. Representation in the sense of the bourgeois public sphere, as in "representing" the nation or specific clients, has nothing to do with *representative publicness*, which inheres in the concrete existence of a lord. As long as the prince and the estates of his realm "are" the land, rather than merely "representing" it, they are capable of this kind of representation; they represent their authority "before" the people rather than for the people.

The feudal powers (the church, the prince, and the nobility) to which this representative publicness adheres disintegrated in the course of a long process of polarization; by the end of the eighteenth century they had decomposed into private elements on the one side and public on the other. The position of the church changed in connection with the Reformation; the tie to divine authority that the church represented, that is, religion, became a private matter. Historically, what is called the freedom of religion safeguarded the first domain of private autonomy; the church itself continued its existence as one corporate body under public law among others. The corresponding polarization of princely power acquired visible form in the separation of the public budget from the private household property of the feudal lord. In the bureaucracy and the military (and in part also in the administration of justice), institutions of public power became autonomous vis-à-vis the privatized sphere of the princely court. In terms of the estates, finally, elements from the ruling groups developed into organs of public power, into parliament (and in part also into judicial organs); elements from the occupational status groups, insofar as they had become established in urban corporations and in certain differentiations within the estates of the land, developed into the sphere of bourgeois society, which would confront the state as a genuine domain of private autonomy.

Representative publicness gave way to the new sphere of "public power" that came into being with the national and territorial states. Ongoing state activity (permanent administration, a standing army) had its counterpart in the permanence of relationships that had developed in the meantime with the stock market and the press, through traffic in goods and news. Public power became consolidated as something tangible confronting those who were subject to it and who at first found themselves only negatively defined by it. These are the "private persons" who are excluded from public power because they hold no office. "Public" no longer refers to the representative court of a person vested with authority; instead, it now refers to the competence-regulated activity of an apparatus furnished with a monopoly on the legitimate use of force. As those to whom this public power is addressed, private persons subsumed under the state form the public.

As a private domain, society, which has come to confront the state, as it were, is on the one hand clearly differentiated from public power; on the other hand, society becomes a matter of public interest insofar as with the rise of a market economy the reproduction of life extends beyond the confines of private domestic power. The *bourgeois public sphere* can be understood as the sphere of private persons assembled to form a public. They soon began to make use of the public sphere of informational newspapers, which was officially regulated, against the public power itself, using those papers, along with the morally and critically oriented weeklies, to engage in debate about the general rules governing relations in their own essentially privatized but publicly relevant sphere of commodity exchange and labor.

The Liberal Model of the Public Sphere

The medium in which this debate takes place—public discussion—is unique and without historical prototype. Previously the estates had negotiated contracts with their princes in which claims to power were defined on a case-by-case basis. As we know, this development followed a different course in England, where princely power was relativized through parliament, than on the Continent, where the estates were mediatized by the monarch. The "third estate" then broke with this mode of equalizing power, for it could no longer establish itself as a ruling estate. Given a commercial economy, a division of authority accomplished through differentiation of the rights of those possessing feudal authority (liberties belonging to the estates) was no longer possible—the power under private law of disposition of capitalist property is nonpolitical. The bourgeois are private persons; as such, they do not "rule." Thus their claims to power in opposition to public power are directed not against a concentration of authority that should be "divided" but rather against the principle of established authority. The principle of control, namely publicness, that the bourgeois public opposes to the principle of established authority

aims at a transformation of authority as such, not merely the exchange of one basis of legitimation for another.

In the first modern constitutions the sections listing basic rights provide an image of the liberal model of the public sphere: they guarantee society as a sphere of private autonomy; opposite it stands a public power limited to a few functions; between the two spheres, as it were, stands the domain of private persons who have come together to form a public and who, as citizens of the state, mediate the state with the needs of bourgeois society, in order, as the idea goes, to thus convert political authority to "rational" authority in the medium of this public sphere. Under the presuppositions of a society based on the free exchange of commodities, it seemed that the general interest, which served as the criterion by which this kind of rationality was to be evaluated, would be assured if the dealings of private persons in the marketplace were emancipated from social forces and their dealings in the public sphere were emancipated from political coercion.

The political daily press came to have an important role during this same period. In the second half of the eighteenth century, serious competition to the older form of news writing as the compiling of items of information arose in the form of literary journalism. Karl Bücher[1] describes the main outlines of this development: "From mere institutions for the publication of news, newspapers became the vehicles and guides of public opinion as well, weapons of party politics. The consequence of this for the internal organization of the newspaper enterprise was the insertion of a new function between the gathering of news and its publication: the editorial function. For the newspaper publisher, however, the significance of this development was that from a seller of new information he became a dealer in public opinion." Publishers provided the commercial basis for the newspaper without, however, commercializing it as such. The press remained an institution of the public itself, operating to provide and intensify public discussion, no longer a mere organ for the conveyance of information, but not yet a medium of consumer culture.

This type of press can be observed especially in revolutionary periods, when papers associated with the tiniest political coalitions and groups spring up, as in Paris in 1789.

---

1   *Karl Bücher*   [All notes in the present selection are by the editors of this anthology.] Karl Bücher (1847-1930) was a German economist and founder of the first institute for the academic study of journalism. Habermas gives no information regarding the source for this quotation.

In the Paris of 1848 every halfway prominent politician still formed his own club, and every other one founded his own *journal:* over 450 clubs and more than 200 papers came into being there between February and May alone. Until the permanent legalization of a public sphere that functioned politically, the appearance of a political newspaper was equivalent to engagement in the struggle for a zone of freedom for public opinion, for publicness as a principle. Not until the establishment of the bourgeois constitutional state was a press engaged in the public use of reason relieved of the pressure of ideological viewpoints. Since then it has been able to abandon its polemical stance and take advantage of the earning potential of commercial activity. The ground was cleared for this development from a press of viewpoints to a commercial press at about the same time in England, France, and the United States, during the 1830s. In the course of this transformation from the journalism of writers who were private persons to the consumer services of the mass media, the sphere of publicness was changed by an influx of private interests that achieved privileged representation within it.

The Public Sphere in Mass Welfare-State Democracies

The liberal model of the public sphere remains instructive in regard to the normative claim embodied in institutionalized requirements of publicness; but it is not applicable to actual relationships within a mass democracy that is industrially advanced and constituted as a social-welfare state. In part, the liberal model had always contained ideological aspects; in part, the social presuppositions to which those aspects were linked have undergone fundamental changes. Even the forms in which the public sphere was manifested, forms which made its idea seem to a certain extent obvious, began to change with the Chartist movement[1] in England and the February Revolution[2] in France. With the spread of the press and propaganda, the public expanded beyond the confines of the bourgeoisie. Along with its social exclusivity the public lost the cohesion given it by institutions of convivial social intercourse and by a relatively high standard of education. Accordingly, conflicts which in the past were

---

1 *Chartist movement* Active between 1838 and 1848. Its primary aim was electoral reform; it may have been the first mass workers' movement in history.

2 *February Revolution* In 1848, this revolt replaced the French monarchy with a liberal reformist republic.

pushed off into the private sphere now enter the public sphere. Group needs, which cannot expect satisfaction from a self-regulating market, tend toward state regulation. The public sphere, which must now mediate these demands, becomes a field for competition among interests in the cruder form of forcible confrontation. Laws that have obviously originated under the "pressure of the streets" can scarcely continue to be understood in terms of a consensus achieved by private persons in public discussion; they correspond, in more or less undisguised form, to compromises between conflicting private interests. Today it is social organizations that act in relation to the state in the political public sphere, whether through the mediation of political parties or directly, in interplay with public administration. With the interlocking of the public and private domains, not only do political agencies take over certain functions in the sphere of commodity exchange and social labor; societal powers also take over political functions. This leads to a kind of "refeudalization" of the public sphere. Large-scale organizations strive for political compromises with the state and with one another, behind closed doors if possible; but at the same time they have to secure at least plebiscitarian approval from the mass of the population through the deployment of a staged form of publicity.

The political public sphere in the welfare state is characterized by a singular weakening of its critical functions. Whereas at one time publicness was intended to subject persons or things to the public use of reason and to make political decisions susceptible to revision before the tribunal of public opinion, today it has often enough already been enlisted in the aid of the secret policies of interest groups; in the form of "publicity" it now acquires public prestige for persons or things and renders them capable of acclamation in a climate of nonpublic opinion. The term "public relations" itself indicates how a public sphere that formerly emerged from the structure of society must now be produced circumstantially on a case-by-case basis. The central relationship of the public, political parties, and parliament is also affected by this change in function.

This existing trend toward the weakening of the public sphere, as a principle, is opposed, however, by a welfare-state transformation of the functioning of basic rights: the requirement of publicness is extended by state organs to all organizations acting in relation to the state. To the extent to which this becomes a reality, a no longer intact public of private persons acting as individuals would be replaced by a public of organized private persons. Under current circumstances, only the latter could participate effectively in a process of public communication using the channels of intraparty and intra-organizational public spheres, on the basis of a publicness enforced for the dealings of organizations with the state. It is in this process of public communication that the formation of political compromises would have to achieve legitimation. The idea of the public sphere itself, which signified a rationalization of authority in the medium of public discussions among private persons, and which has been preserved in mass welfare-state democracy, threatens to disintegrate with the structural transformation of the public sphere. Today it could be realized only on a different basis, as a rationalization of the exercise of social and political power under the mutual control of rival organizations committed to publicness in their internal structure as well as in their dealings with the state and with one another.

Three Normative Models of Democracy

In what follows I refer to the idealized distinction between the "liberal" and the "republican" understanding of politics—terms which mark the fronts in the current debate in the United States initiated by the so-called communitarians. Drawing on the work of Frank Michelman, I will begin by describing the two polemically contrasted models of democracy with specific reference to the concept of the citizen, the concept of law, and the nature of processes of political will-formation. In the second part, beginning with a critique of the "ethical overload" of the republican model, I introduce a third, procedural model of democracy for which I propose to reserve the term "deliberative politics."

I

The crucial difference between liberalism and republicanism consists in how the role of the democratic process is understood. According to the "liberal" view, this process accomplishes the task of programming the state in the interest of society, where the state is conceived as an apparatus of public administration, and society is conceived as a system of market-structured interactions of private persons and their labor. Here politics (in the sense of the citizens' political will-formation) has the function of bundling together and bringing to bear private social interests against a state apparatus that specializes in the administrative employment of political power for collective goals.

On the republican view, politics is not exhausted by this mediating function but is constitutive for the socialization process as a whole. Politics is conceived as the reflexive form of substantial ethical life. It constitutes the medium in which the members of quasi-natural solidary communities become aware of their dependence on one another and, acting with full deliberation as citizens, further shape and develop existing relations of reciprocal recognition into an association of free and equal consociates under law. With this, the liberal architectonic of government and society undergoes an important change. In addition to the hierarchical regulatory apparatus of sovereign state authority and the decentralized regulatory mechanism of the market—that is, besides administrative power and self-interest—*solidarity* appears as a third source of social integration.

This horizontal political will-formation aimed at mutual understanding or communicatively achieved consensus is even supposed to enjoy priority, both in a genetic and a normative sense. An autonomous basis in civil society independent of public administration and market-mediated private commerce is assumed as a precondition for the practice of civic self-determination. This basis prevents political communication from being swallowed up by the government apparatus or assimilated to market structures. Thus, on the republican conception, the political public sphere and its base, civil society, acquire a strategic significance. Together they are supposed to secure the integrative power and autonomy of the communicative practice of the citizens.[1] The uncoupling of political communication from the economy has as its counterpart a coupling of administrative power with the communicative power generated by political opinion- and will-formation.

These two competing conceptions of politics have different consequences.

(a) In the first place, their concepts of the citizen differ. According to the liberal view, the citizen's status is determined primarily by the individual rights he or she has vis-à-vis the state and other citizens. As bearers of individual rights citizens enjoy the protection of the government as long as they pursue their private interests within the boundaries drawn by legal statutes—and this includes protection against state interventions that violate the legal prohibition on government interference. Individual rights are negative

---

1   *Together they are ... the citizens* [Unless otherwise indicated, all notes to this selection are by the author.] Cf. H. Arendt, *On Revolution* (New York: Viking, 1965); *On Violence* (New York: Harvest, 1970).

rights[1] that guarantee a domain of freedom of choice within which legal persons are freed from external compulsion. Political rights have the same structure: they afford citizens the opportunity to assert their private interests in such a way that, by means of elections, the composition of parliamentary bodies, and the formation of a government, these interests are finally aggregated into a political will that can affect the administration. In this way the citizens in their political role can determine whether governmental authority is exercised in the interest of the citizens as members of society.[2]

According to the republican view, the status of citizens is not determined by the model of negative liberties to which these citizens can lay claim as private persons. Rather, political rights—preeminently rights of political participation and communication—are positive liberties. They do not guarantee freedom from external compulsion, but guarantee instead the possibility of participating in a common practice, through which the citizens can first make themselves into what they want to be—politically responsible subjects of a community of free and equal citizens.[3] To this extent, the political process does not serve just to

keep government activity under the surveillance of citizens who have already acquired a prior social autonomy through the exercise of their private rights and prepolitical liberties. Nor does it act only as a hinge between state and society, for democratic governmental authority is by no means an original authority. Rather, this authority proceeds from the communicative power generated by the citizens' practice of self-legislation, and it is legitimated by the fact that it protects this practice by institutionalizing public freedom.[4] The state's *raison d'être* does not lie primarily in the protection of equal individual rights but in the guarantee of an inclusive process of opinion- and will-formation in which free and equal citizens reach an understanding on which goals and norms lie in the equal interest of all. In this way the republican citizen is credited with more than an exclusive concern with his or her private interests.

(b) The polemic against the classical concept of the legal person as bearer of individual rights reveals a controversy about the concept of law itself. Whereas on the liberal conception the point of a legal order is to make it possible to determine which individuals in each case are entitled to which rights, on the republican conception these "subjective" rights owe their existence to an "objective" legal order that both enables and guarantees the integrity of an autonomous life in common based on equality and mutual respect. On the one view, the legal order is conceived in terms of individual rights; on the other, their objective legal content is given priority.

To be sure, this conceptual dichotomy does not touch on the *intersubjective* content of rights that demand reciprocal respect for rights and duties in symmetrical relations of recognition. But the republican concept at least points in the direction of a concept of law that accords equal weight to both the integrity of the individual and the integrity of the community in which persons as both individuals and members can first accord one another reciprocal recognition. It ties the legitimacy of the laws to the democratic

---

1   *negative rights* [editors' note] *Negative rights* entail duties not to interfere with the exercise of these rights; in contrast, *positive rights* impose duties on others to help one realize one's rights. For example, a negative right to freedom of speech requires merely that others do not silence speech; a positive right to health care, however, imposes a duty on someone (typically the state) to provide health care.

2   *In this way ... members of society* Cf. F.I. Michelman, "Political Truth and the Rule of Law," *Tel Aviv University Studies in Law* 8 (1988): 283: "The political society envisioned by bumper-sticker republicans is the society of private rights bearers, an association whose first principle is the protection of the lives, liberties, and estates of its individual members. In that society, the state is justified by the protection it gives to those prepolitical interests; the purpose of the constitution is to ensure that the state apparatus, the government, provides such protection for the people at large rather than serves the special interests of the governors or their patrons; the function of citizenship is to operate the constitution and thereby to motivate the governors to act according to that protective purpose; and the value to you of your political franchise—your right to vote and speak, to have your views heard and counted—is the handle it gives you on influencing the system so that it will adequately heed and protect *your* particular, prepolitical rights and other interests."

3   *Rather, political rights ... equal citizens* On the distinction between positive and negative freedom see Charles Taylor, "What is Human Agency?" in *Human Agency and Language: Philosophical Papers 1* (Cambridge: Cambridge University Press, 1985), pp. 15–44.

4   *Rather, this authority ... public freedom* Michelman, "Political Truth and the Rule of Law," p. 284: "In [the] civic constitutional vision, political society is primarily the society not of rights bearers, but of citizens, an association whose first principle is the creation and provision of a public realm within which a people, together, argue and reason about the right terms of social coexistence, terms that they will set together and which they understand as comprising their common good.... Hence, the state is justified by its purpose of establishing and ordering the public sphere within which persons can achieve freedom in the sense of self-government by the exercise of reason in public dialogue."

procedure by which they are generated and thereby pre-serves an internal connection between the citizens' practice of self-legislation and the impersonal sway of the law:

> For republicans, rights ultimately are nothing but determinations of prevailing political will, while for liberals, some rights are always grounded in a "higher law" of transpolitical reason or rev-elation…. In a republican view, a community's objective, common good substantially consists in the success of its political endeavor to define, establish, effectuate, and sustain the set of rights (less tendentiously, laws) best suited to the condi-tions and *mores* of that community. Whereas in a contrasting liberal view, the higher-law rights provide the transactional structures and the curbs on power required so that pluralistic pursuit of diverse and conflicting interests may proceed as satisfactorily as possible.[1]

The right to vote, interpreted as a positive right, be-comes the paradigm of rights as such, not only because it is constitutive for political self-determination, but because it shows how inclusion in a community of equals is connected with the individual right to make autonomous contribu-tions and take personal positions on issues:

> [T]he claim is that we all take an interest in each others' enfranchisement because (i) our choice lies between hanging together and hanging sep-arately; (ii) hanging together depends on recipro-cal assurances to all of having one's vital interests heeded by others; and (iii) in the deeply pluralized conditions of contemporary American society, such assurances are not attainable through virtual representations but only by maintaining at least the semblance of a politics in which everyone is conceded a voice.[2]

This structure, read off from the political rights of participa-tion and communication, is extended to *all* rights via the legislative process constituted by political rights. Even the authorization guaranteed by private law to pursue private,

freely chosen goals simultaneously imposes an obligation to respect the limits of strategic action which are agreed to be in the equal interest of all.

(c) The different ways of conceptualizing the role of citizen and the law express a deeper disagreement about the nature of the political process. On the liberal view, politics is essentially a struggle for positions that grant access to administrative power. The political process of opinion- and will-formation in the public sphere and in parliament is shaped by the competition of strategically acting collectives trying to maintain or acquire positions of power. Success is measured by the citizens' approval of persons and programs, as quantified by votes. In their choices at the polls, voters express their preferences. Their votes have the same struc-ture as the choices of participants in a market, in that their decisions license access to positions of power that political parties fight over with a success-oriented attitude similar to that of players in the market. The input of votes and the output of power conform to the same pattern of strategic action.

According to the republican view, the political opin-ion- and will-formation in the public sphere and in parlia-ment does not obey the structures of market processes but rather the obstinate structures of a public communication oriented to mutual understanding. For politics as the prac-tice of self-determination, the paradigm is not the market but dialogue. From this perspective there is a structural difference between communicative power, which proceeds from political communication in the form of discursively generated majority decisions, and the administrative power possessed by the governmental apparatus. Even the parties that struggle over access to positions of governmental power must bend themselves to the deliberative style and the stub-born character of political discourse:

> Deliberation … refers to a certain attitude toward social cooperation, namely, that of openness to persuasion by reasons referring to the claims of others as well as one's own. The deliberative med-ium is a good faith exchange of views—including participants' reports of their own understanding of their respective vital interests—… in which a vote, if any vote is taken, represents a pooling of judgments.[3]

---

1   *For republicans … satisfactorily as possible* Michelman, "Con-ceptions of Democracy in American Constitutional Argument: Voting Rights," *Florida Law Review* 41 (1989): 446f. (hereafter "Voting Rights").

2   *[T]he claim is … conceded a voice* Michelman, "Voting Rights," 484.

3   *Deliberation … pooling of judgments* Michelman, "Conceptions of Democracy in American Constitutional Argument: The Case

Hence the conflict of opinions conducted in the political arena has legitimating force not just in the sense of an authorization to occupy positions of power; on the contrary, the ongoing political discourse also has binding force for the way in which political authority is exercised. Administrative power can only be exercised on the basis of policies and within the limits laid down by laws generated by the democratic process.

2

So much for the comparison between the two models of democracy that currently dominate the discussion between the so-called communitarians and liberals, above all in the US. The republican model has advantages and disadvantages. In my view it has the advantage that it preserves the radical democratic meaning of a society that organizes itself through the communicatively united citizens and does not trace collective goals back to "deals" made between competing private interests. Its disadvantage, as I see it, is that it its too idealistic in that it makes the democratic process dependent on the virtues of citizens devoted to the public weal. For politics is not concerned in the first place with questions of ethical self-understanding. The mistake of the republican view consists in an ethical foreshortening of political discourse.

To be sure, ethical discourses aimed at achieving a collective self-understanding—discourses in which participants attempt to clarify how they understand themselves as members of a particular nation, as members of a community or a state, as inhabitants of a region, etc., which traditions they wish to cultivate, how they should treat each other, minorities, and marginal groups, in what sort of society they want to live—constitute an important part of politics. But under conditions of cultural and social pluralism, behind politically relevant goals there often lie interests and value-orientations that are by no means constitutive of the identity of the political community as a whole, that is, for the totality of an intersubjectively shared form of life. These interests and value-orientations, which conflict with one another within the same polity without any prospect of consensual resolution, need to be counterbalanced in a way that cannot be effected by ethical discourse, even though the results of this nondiscursive counterbalancing are subject to the proviso that they must not violate the basic values of a culture. The

balancing of interests takes the form or reaching a compromise between parties who rely on their power and ability to sanction. Negotiations of this sort certainly presuppose a readiness to cooperate, that is, a willingness to abide by the rules and to arrive at results that are acceptable to all parties, though for different reasons. But compromise-formation is not conducted in the form of a rational discourse that neutralizes power and excludes strategic action. However, the fairness of compromises is measured by presuppositions and procedures which for their part are in need of rational, indeed normative, justification from the standpoint of justice. In contrast with ethical questions, questions of justice are not by their very nature tied to a particular collectivity. Politically enacted law, if it is to be legitimate, must be at least in harmony with moral principles that claim a general validity that extends beyond the limits of any concrete legal community.

The concept of deliberative politics acquires empirical relevance only when we take into account the multiplicity of forms of communication in which a common will is produced, that is, not just ethical self-clarification but also the balancing of interests and compromise, the purposive choice of means, moral justification, and legal consistency testing. In this process the two types of politics which Michelman distinguishes in an ideal-typical fashion can interweave and complement one another in a rational manner. "Dialogical" and "instrumental" politics can *interpenetrate* in the medium of deliberation if the corresponding forms of communication are sufficiently institutionalized. Everything depends on the conditions of communication and the procedures that lend the institutionalized opinion- and will-formation their legitimating force. The third model of democracy, which I would like to propose, relies precisely on those conditions of communication under which the political process can be presumed to produce rational results because it operates deliberatively at all levels.

Making the proceduralist conception of deliberative politics the cornerstone of the theory of democracy results in differences both from the republican conception of the state as an ethical community and from the liberal conception of the state as the guardian of a market society. In comparing the three models, I take my orientation from that dimension of politics which has been our primary concern, namely, the democratic opinion- and will-formation that issue in popular elections and parliamentary decrees.

According to the liberal view, the democratic process takes place exclusively in the form of compromises between competing interests. Fairness is supposed to be guaranteed

---

of Pornography Regulation," *Tennessee Law Review* 291 (1989): 293.

by rules of compromise-formation that regulate the general and equal right to vote, the representative composition of parliamentary bodies, their order of business, and so on. Such rules are ultimately justified in terms of liberal basic rights. According to the republican view, by contrast, democratic will-formation is supposed to take the form of an ethical discourse of self-understanding; here deliberation can rely for its content on a culturally established background consensus of the citizens, which is rejuvenated through the ritualistic reenactment of a republican founding act. Discourse theory takes elements from both sides and integrates them into the concept of an ideal procedure for deliberation and decision making. Weaving together negotiations and discourses of self-understanding and of justice, this democratic procedure grounds the presumption that under such conditions reasonable or fair results are obtained. According to this proceduralist view, practical reason withdraws from universal human rights or from the concrete ethical life of a specific community into the rules of discourse and forms of argumentation that derive their normative content from the validity-basis of action oriented to reaching understanding, and ultimately from the structure of linguistic communication.[1]

These descriptions of the structures of democratic process set the stage for different normative conceptualizations of state and society. The sole presupposition is a public administration of the kind that emerged in the early modern period together with the European state system and in functional interconnection with a capitalist economic system. According to the republican view, the citizens' political opinion- and will-formation forms the medium through which society constitutes itself as a political whole. Society is centered in the state; for in the citizens' practice of political self-determination the polity becomes conscious of itself as a totality and acts on itself via the collective will of the citizens. Democracy is synonymous with the political self-organization of society. This leads to a polemical understanding of politics as directed against the state apparatus. In Hannah Arendt's political writings one can see the thrust of republican arguments: in opposition to the civic privatism of a depoliticized population and in opposition to the acquisition of legitimation through entrenched parties, the political public sphere should be revitalized to the point where a regenerated citizenry can, in the forms of a decentralized self-governance, (once again) appropriate the governmental authority that has been usurped by a self-regulating bureaucracy.

According to the liberal view, this separation of the state apparatus from society cannot be eliminated but only bridged by the democratic process. However, the weak normative connotations of a regulated balancing of power and interests stands in need of constitutional channeling. The democratic will-formation of self-interested citizens, construed in minimalist terms, constitutes just one element within a constitution that disciplines governmental authority through normative constraints (such as basic rights, separation of powers, and legal regulation of the administration) and forces it, through competition between political panics, on the one hand, and between government and opposition, on the other, to take adequate account of competing interests and value orientations. This state-centered understanding of politics does not have to rely on the unrealistic assumption of a citizenry capable of acting collectively. Its focus is not so much the input of a rational political will-formation but the output of successful administrative accomplishments. The thrust of liberal arguments is directed against the disruptive potential of an administrative power that interferes with the independent social interactions of private persons. The liberal model hinges not on the democratic self-determination of deliberating citizens but on the legal institutionalization of an economic society that is supposed to guarantee an essentially nonpolitical common good through the satisfaction of the private aspirations of productive citizens.

Discourse theory invests the democratic process with normative connotations stronger than those of the liberal model but weaker than those of the republican model. Once again, it takes elements from both sides and fits them together in a new way. In agreement with republicanism, it gives center stage to the process of political opinion- and will-formation, but without understanding the constitution as something secondary; on the contrary, it conceives the basic principles of the constitutional state as a consistent answer to the question of how the demanding communicative presuppositions of a democratic opinion- and will-formation can be institutionalized. Discourse theory does not make the success of deliberative politics depend on a collectively acting citizenry but on the institutionalization of corresponding procedures. It no longer operates with the concept of a social whole centered in the state and conceived as a goal-oriented subject writ large. But neither does

1   *According to this ... linguistic communication* Cf. J. Habermas, "Popular Sovereignty as Procedure," in *Between Facts and Norms: Contributions to a Discourse Theory of Law and Democracy*, trans. W. Rehg (Cambridge MA: MIT Press, 1996), pp. 463–90.

it localize the whole in a system of constitutional norms mechanically regulating the interplay of powers and interests in accordance with the market model. Discourse theory altogether jettisons the assumptions of the philosophy of consciousness, which invite us either to ascribe the citizens' practice of self-determination to one encompassing macro-subject or to apply the anonymous rule of law to competing individuals. The former approach represents the citizenry as a collective actor which reflects the whole and acts for its sake; on the latter, individual actors function as dependent variables in systemic processes that unfold blindly because no consciously executed collective decisions are possible over and above individual acts of choice (except in a purely metaphorical sense).

Discourse theory works instead with the *higher-level intersubjectivity* of communication processes that unfold in the institutionalized deliberations in parliamentary bodies, on the one hand, and in the informal networks of the public sphere, on the other. Both within and outside parliamentary bodies geared to decision making, these subjectless modes of communication form arenas in which a more or less rational opinion- and will-formation concerning issues and problems affecting society as a whole can take place. Informal opinion-formation result in institutionalized election decisions and legislative decrees through which communicatively generated power is transformed into administratively utilizable power. As on the liberal model, the boundary between state and society is respected; but here civil society, which provides the social underpinning of autonomous publics, is as distinct from the economic system as it is from the public administration. This understanding of democracy leads to the normative demand for a new balance between the three resources of money, administrative power, and solidarity from which modern societies meet their need for integration and regulation. The normative implications are obvious: the integrative force of solidarity, which can no longer be drawn solely from sources of communicative action, should develop through widely expanded autonomous public spheres as well as through legally institutionalized procedures of democratic deliberation and decision making and gain sufficient strength to hold its own against the other two social forces—money and administrative power.

3

This view has implications for how one should understand legitimation and popular sovereignty. On the liberal view, democratic will-formation has the exclusive function of *legitimating* the exercise of political power. The outcomes of elections license the assumption of governmental power, though the government must justify the use of power to the public and parliament. On the republican view, democratic will-formation has the significantly stronger function of *constituting* society as a political community and keeping the memory of this founding act alive with each new election. The government is not only empowered by the electorate's choice between teams of leaders to exercise a largely open mandate, but is also bound in a programmatic fashion to carry out certain policies. More a committee than an organ of the state, it is part of a self-governing political community rather than the head of a separate governmental apparatus. Discourse theory, by contrast, brings a third idea into play: the procedures and communicative presuppositions of democratic opinion- and will-formation function as the most important sluices for the discursive rationalization of the decisions of a government and an administration bound by law and statute. On this view, *rationalization* signifies more than mere legitimation but less than the constitution of political power. The power available to the administration changes its general character once it is bound to a process of democratic opinion and will-formation that does not merely retrospectively monitor the exercise of political power but also programs it in a certain way. Notwithstanding this discursive rationalization, only the political system itself can "act." It is a subsystem specialized for collectively binding decisions, whereas the communicative structures of the public sphere comprise a far-flung network of sensors that respond to the pressure of society-wide problems and stimulate influential opinions. The public opinion which is worked up via democratic procedures into communicative power cannot itself "rule" but can only channel the use of administrative power in specific directions.

The concept of *popular sovereignty* stems from the republican appropriation and revaluation of the early modern notion of sovereignty originally associated with absolutist regimes. The state, which monopolizes the means of legitimate violence, is viewed as a concentration of power which can overwhelm all other temporal powers. Rousseau transposed this idea, which goes back to Bodin,[1] to the will of the united people, fused it with the classical idea of the

---

1   *Bodin* [editors' note] Jean Bodin (1530–96), French jurist and natural-law political philosopher, known for his theory of sovereignty.

self-rule of free and equal citizens, and sublimated it into the modern concept of autonomy. Despite this normative sublimation, concept of sovereignty remained bound to the notion of an embodiment in the (at first actually physically assembled) people. According to the republican view, the at least potentially assembled people are the bearers of a sovereignty that cannot in principle be delegated: in their capacity as sovereign, the people cannot let themselves be represented by others. Constitutional power is founded on the citizens' practice of self-determination, not on that of their representatives. Against this, liberalism offers the more realistic view that, in the constitutional state, the authority emanating from the people is exercised only "by means of elections and voting and by specific legislative, executive, and judicial organs."[1]

These two views exhaust the alternatives only on the dubious assumption that state and society must be conceived in terms of a whole and its parts, where the whole is constituted either by a sovereign citizenry or by a constitution. By contrast to the discourse theory of democracy corresponds the image of a *decentered* society, though with the political public sphere it sets apart an arena for the detection, identification, and interpretation of problems affecting society as a whole. If we abandon the conceptual framework of the philosophy of the subject, sovereignty need neither be concentrated in the people in a concretistic manner nor banished into the anonymous agencies established by the constitution. The "self" of the self-organizing legal community disappears in the subjectless forms of communication that regulate the flow of discursive opinion- and will-formation whose fallible results enjoy the presumption of rationality. This is not to repudiate the intuition associated with the idea of popular sovereignty but rather to interpret it in intersubjective terms. Popular sovereignty, even though it has become anonymous, retreats into democratic procedures and the legal implementation of their demanding communicative presuppositions only to be able to make itself felt as communicatively generated

power. Strictly speaking, this communicative power springs from the interactions between legally institutionalized will-formation and culturally mobilized publics. The latter for their part find a basis in the associations of a civil society distinct from the state and the economy alike.

The normative self-understanding of deliberative politics does indeed call for a discursive mode of socialization for the *legal community;* but this mode does not extend to the whole of the society in which the constitutionally established political system is *embedded*. Even on its own proceduralist self-understanding, deliberative politics remains a component of a complex society, which as a whole resists the normative approach of legal theory. In this regard, the discourse-theoretic reading of democracy connects with an objectifying sociological approach that regards the political system neither as the peak nor the center; nor even as the structuring model of society, but as just *one* action system among others. Because it provides a kind of surety for the solution of the social problems that threaten integration, politics must indeed be able to communicate, via the medium of law, with all of the other legitimately ordered spheres of action, however these may be structured and steered. But the political system remains dependent on other functional mechanisms, such as the revenue-production of the economic system, in more than just a trivial sense; on the contrary, deliberative politics, whether realized in the formal procedures of institutionalized opinion- and will-formation or only in the informal networks of the political public sphere, stands in an internal relation to the contexts of a rationalized lifeworld that meets it halfway. Deliberatively filtered political communications are especially dependent on the resources of the lifeworld—on a free and open political culture and an enlightened political socialization, and above all on the initiatives of opinion-shaping associations. These resources emerge and regenerate themselves spontaneously for the most part—at any rate, they can only with difficulty be subjected to political control.

---

1   *by means of ... judicial organs* Cf. *The Basic Law of the Federal Republic of Germany*, article 20, sec. 2. [editors' note] This document, *Grundgesetz für die Bundesrepublik Deutschland*, was drawn up as the constitution of post-WWII West Germany, and came into effect in 1949. This is the full text of Article 20 Section 2: "All state authority is derived from the people. It shall be exercised by the people through elections and other votes and through specific legislative, executive, and judicial bodies."

AMARTYA SEN
(1933–)

In the present era of academic specialization, 1998 Nobel Laureate for Economics Amartya Sen is a rare intellectual who has contributed at the highest level both to philosophy and to economics. Sen's key contributions to social choice theory and developmental economics inform his philosophical views; he has also been instrumental in bringing questions of value into economics, challenging tendencies among economists to rely on models that presuppose self-interest to be always the primary human motivation. In this work, he has raised questions of welfare, individual rights, justice, equality, and democracy.

Born in Calcutta, India, in 1933, Sen graduated from Calcutta University with a BA in economics, then went on to Trinity College, Cambridge, where he completed another BA in pure economics in 1955, followed by a PhD in 1959. He has taught at the University of Calcutta, Jadavpur University, Oxford University, the London School of Economics, Trinity College, Dublin, and Cambridge University. He is currently Lamont University Professor at Harvard.

Sen's early experience in India shaped his abiding interest in inequality as a political and moral question. As a child, Sen witnessed the Bengal famine, where an estimated three million people died. In *Poverty and Famines: An Essay on Entitlement and Deprivation* (1981), Sen demonstrated that the cause of famine was often not lack of food; instead he pointed to the unequal distribution of food, unemployment, declining wages, and rising food prices as contributing causes. Rural laborers who had lost their jobs died simply because they were unable to purchase food.

This research informs Sen's capabilities approach, one of the most influential contributions to the debate over the morally relevant measure of equality. Social and political theorists with a commitment to egalitarianism agree that equality in some respects is important, but differ on how it should best be measured. Some theorists favor the utilitar-

ian view that what counts is individuals' well-being. This approach has been criticized on the grounds that it fails to account adequately for personal responsibility and desert. It also has counter-intuitive consequences such as entailing an obligation to give more to people with "expensive tastes" than those who are satisfied with less. Theorists such as John Rawls and Ronald Dworkin have suggested instead that the relevant metric is resources. Thus John Rawls favors an account of equality based on measures of "primary goods," all-purpose goods that enable individuals to carry out their life plans no matter what they are.

Sen rejects both approaches, arguing that such discussions of the redistribution of resources focus exclusively on means and not on what people can actually do with their resources. In particular, Sen worries that approaches based on resources underestimate the importance of individual difference. Someone in a wheelchair may have exactly the same resources as a person without a disability, but it would be odd to claim that they have been treated equally in the *morally relevant* sense. What is important for Sen is real (as opposed to formal) freedom to achieve one's goals or, as he puts it, "capabilities to achieve functionings."

This view led Sen and the Pakistani economist Mahbub ul Haq to develop the Human Development Index, which is now used by the United Nations Development Programme (UNDP) in its annual Human Development Report. Replacing the crude measure of Gross National Product (GNP) per capita, which fails to take account of inequalities among citizens and basic quality of life, the Human Development Index includes measures of life expectancy at birth, adult literacy rate, and school enrolment, as well as GDP per capita.

◆ ◆ ◆ ◆ ◆

from *Development as Freedom* (1999)

Chapter 1: The Perspective of Freedom

It is not unusual for couples to discuss the possibility of earning more money, but a conversation on this subject from around the eighth century B.C. is of some special interest. As that conversation is recounted in the Sanskrit text *Brihadaranyaka Upanishad*, a woman named Maitreyee and her husband, Yajnavalkya, proceed rapidly to a bigger issue than the ways and means of becoming more wealthy: *How far would wealth go to help them get what they want?*[1] Maitreyee wonders whether it could be the case that if "the whole earth, full of wealth" were to belong just to her, she could achieve immortality through it. "No," responds Yajnavalkya, "like the life of rich people will be your life. But there is no hope of immortality by wealth." Maitreyee remarks, "What should I do with that by which I do not become immortal?"

Maitreyee's rhetorical question has been cited again and again in Indian religious philosophy to illustrate both the nature of the human predicament and the limitations of the material world. I have too much skepticism of otherworldly matters to be led there by Maitreyee's worldly frustration, but there is another aspect of this exchange that is of rather immediate interest to economics and to understanding the nature of development. This concerns the relation between incomes and achievements, between commodities and capabilities, between our economic wealth and our ability to live as we would like. While there is a connection between opulence and achievements, the linkage may or may not be very strong and may well be extremely contingent on other circumstances. The issue is not the ability to live forever on which Maitreyee—bless her soul—happened to concentrate, but the capability to live really long (without being cut off in one's prime) and to have a good life while alive (rather than a life of misery and unfreedom)—things that would be strongly valued and desired by nearly all of us. The gap between the two perspectives (that is, between an exclusive concentration on economic wealth and a broader focus on the lives we can

lead) is a major issue in conceptualizing development. As Aristotle noted at the very beginning of the *Nicomachean Ethics* (resonating well with the conversation between Maitreyee and Yajnavalkya three thousand miles away), "wealth is evidently not the good we are seeking; for it is merely useful and for the sake of something else."[2]

If we have reasons to want more wealth, we have to ask: What precisely are these reasons, how do they work, on what are they contingent and what are the things we can "do" with more wealth? In fact, we generally have excellent reasons for wanting more income or wealth. This is not because income and wealth are desirable for their own sake, but because, typically, they are admirable general-purpose means for having more freedom to lead the kind of lives we have reason to value.

The usefulness of wealth lies in the things that it allows us to do—the substantive freedoms it helps us to achieve. But this relation is neither exclusive (since there are significant influences on our lives other than wealth) nor uniform (since the impact of wealth on our lives varies with other influences). It is as important to recognize the crucial role of wealth in determining living conditions and the quality of life as it is to understand the qualified and contingent nature of this relationship. An adequate conception of development must go much beyond the accumulation of wealth and the growth of gross national product and other income-related variables. Without ignoring the importance of economic growth, we must look well beyond it.

The ends and means of development require examination and scrutiny for a fuller understanding of the development process; it is simply not adequate to take as our basic objective just the maximization of income or wealth, which is, as Aristotle noted, "merely useful and for the sake of something else." For the same reason, economic growth cannot sensibly be treated as an end in itself. Development has to be more concerned with enhancing the lives we lead and the freedoms we enjoy. Expanding the freedoms that we have reason to value not only makes our lives richer and more unfettered, but also allows us to be fuller social persons, exercising our own volitions and interacting with—and influencing—the world in which we live. In chapter 3 this general approach is more fully proposed

---

1   *How far would wealth ... what they want*   [Unless otherwise indicated, all notes to this selection are by the author.] *Brihadaranyaka Upanishad* 2.4, pp. 2–3.

2   *wealth is evidently ... sake of something else*   Aristotle, *The Nicomachean Ethics*, translated by W.D. Ross (Oxford: Oxford University Press, revised edition, 1980), book 1, section 5, p. 7.

and scrutinized, and is evaluatively compared with other approaches that compete for attention.[1]

Forms of Unfreedom

Very many people across the world suffer from varieties of unfreedom. Famines continue to occur in particular regions, denying to millions the basic freedom to survive. Even in those countries which are no longer sporadically devastated by famines, undernutrition may affect very large numbers of vulnerable human beings. Also, a great many people have little access to health care, to sanitary arrangements or to clean water, and spend their lives fighting unnecessary morbidity, often succumbing to premature mortality. The richer countries too often have deeply disadvantaged people, who lack basic opportunities of health care, or functional education, or gainful employment, or economic and social security. Even within very rich countries, sometimes the longevity of substantial groups is no higher than that in much poorer economies of the so-called third world. Further, inequality between women and men afflicts—and sometime prematurely ends—the lives of millions of women, and, in different ways, severely restricts the substantive freedoms that women enjoy.

Moving to other deprivations of freedom, a great many people in different countries of the world are systematically denied political liberty and basic civil rights. It is sometimes claimed that the denial of these rights helps to stimulate economic growth and is "good" for rapid economic development. Some have even championed harsher political systems—with denial of basic civil and political rights—for their alleged advantage in promoting economic development. This thesis (often called "the Lee thesis," attributed in some form to the former prime minister of Singapore, Lee Kuan Yew) is sometimes backed by some fairly rudimentary empirical

evidence. In fact, more comprehensive intercountry comparisons have not provided any confirmation of this thesis, and there is little evidence that authoritarian politics actually helps economic growth. Indeed, the empirical evidence very strongly suggests that economic growth is more a matter of a friendlier economic climate than of a harsher political system. This issue will receive examination in chapter 6.

Furthermore, economic development has other dimensions, including economic security. Quite often economic insecurity can relate to the lack of democratic rights and liberties. Indeed, the working of democracy and of political rights can even help to prevent famines and other economic disasters. Authoritarian rulers, who are themselves rarely affected by famines (or other such economic calamities), tend to lack the incentive to take timely preventive measures. Democratic governments, in contrast, have to win elections and face public criticism, and have strong incentives to undertake measures to avert famines and other such catastrophes. It is not surprising that no famine has ever taken place in the history of the world in a functioning democracy—be it economically rich (as in contemporary Western Europe or North America) or relatively poor (as in postindependence India, or Botswana, or Zimbabwe). Famines have tended to occur in colonial territories governed by rulers from elsewhere (as in British India or in an Ireland administered by alienated English rulers), or in one-party states (as in the Ukraine in the 1930s, or China during 1958-61, or Cambodia in the 1970s), or in military dictatorships (as in Ethiopia, or Somalia, or some of the Sahel countries in the near past). Indeed, as this book goes to press, the two countries that seem to be leading the "famine league" in the world are North Korea and Sudan—both eminent examples of dictatorial rule. While the prevention of famine illustrates the incentive advantages with great clarity and force, the advantages of democratic pluralism do, in fact, have a much wider reach.

But—most fundamentally—political liberty and civil freedoms are directly important on their own, and do not have to be justified indirectly in terms of their effects on the economy. Even when people without political liberty or civil rights do not lack adequate economic security (and happen to enjoy favorable economic circumstances), they are deprived of important freedoms in leading their lives and denied the opportunity to take part in crucial decisions regarding public affairs. These deprivations restrict social and political lives, and must be seen as repressive even

---

1   *In chapter 3 ... compete for attention*   I have discussed, in earlier publications, different aspects of a freedom-centered view of social evaluation; on this see my "Equality of What?" in S. McMurrin, ed., *Tanner Lectures on Human Values*, volume 1 (Cambridge: Cambridge University Press, 1980); *Choice, Welfare and Measurement* (Oxford: Blackwell; Cambridge, MA: MIT Press, 1982; republished, Cambridge, Mass.: Harvard University Press, 1997); *Resources, Values and Development* (Cambridge, Mass.: Harvard University Press, 1984); "Well-Being, Agency and Freedom: The Dewey Lectures 1984," *Journal of Philosophy* 82 (April 1985); *Inequality Reexamined* (Oxford: Clarendon Press; Cambridge, Mass.: Harvard University Press, 1992). See also Martha Nussbaum and Amartya Sen, eds., *The Quality of Life* (Oxford: Clarendon Press, 1993).

without their leading to other afflictions (such as economic disasters). Since political and civil freedoms are constitutive elements of human freedom, their denial is a handicap in itself. In examining the role of human rights in development, we have to take note of the constitutive as well as the instrumental importance of civil rights and political freedoms. These issues are examined in chapter 6.

Processes and Opportunities

It should be clear from the preceding discussion that the view of freedom that is being taken here involves both the *processes* that allow freedom of actions and decisions, and the actual *opportunities* that people have, given their personal and social circumstances. Unfreedom can arise either through inadequate processes (such as the violation of voting privileges or other political or civil rights) or through inadequate opportunities that some people have for achieving what they minimally would like to achieve (including the absence of such elementary opportunities as the capability to escape premature mortality or preventable morbidity or involuntary starvation).

The distinction between the *process aspect* and the *opportunity aspect* of freedom involves quite a substantial contrast. It can be pursued at different levels. I have discussed elsewhere the respective roles and requirements of (as well as mutual connections between) the process aspect and the opportunity aspect of freedom.[1] While this may not be the occasion to go into the complex and subtle issues that relate to this distinction, it is very important to see freedom in a sufficiently broad way. It is necessary to avoid confining attention only to appropriate procedures (as so-called libertarians sometimes do, without worrying at all about whether some disadvantaged people suffer from systematic deprivation of substantive opportunities), or, alternatively, only to adequate opportunities (as so-called consequentialists sometimes do, without worrying about the nature of the processes that bring the opportunities about or the freedom of choice that people have). Both processes and opportunities have importance of their own, and each aspect relates to seeing development as freedom.

Two Roles of Freedom

The analysis of development presented in this book treats the freedoms of individuals as the basic building blocks. Attention is thus paid particularly to the expansion of the "capabilities" of persons to lead the kind of lives they value—and have reason to value. These capabilities can be enhanced by public policy, but also, on the other side, the direction of public policy can be influenced by the effective use of participatory capabilities by the public. The *two-way relationship* is central to the analysis presented here.

There are two distinct reasons for the crucial importance of individual freedom in the concept of development, related respectively to *evaluation* and *effectiveness*.[2] First, in the normative approach used here, substantive individual freedoms are taken to be critical. The success of a society is to be evaluated, in this view, primarily by the substantive freedoms that the members of that society enjoy. This evaluative position differs from the informational focus of more traditional normative approaches, which focus on other variables, such as utility, or procedural liberty, or real income.

Having greater freedom to do the things one has reason to value is (1) significant in itself for the person's overall freedom, and (2) important in fostering the person's opportunity to have valuable outcomes.[3] Both are relevant to the evaluation of freedom of the members of the society and thus crucial to the assessment of the society's development. The reasons for this normative focus (and in particular for seeing justice in terms of individual freedoms and its social correlates) is more fully examined in chapter 3.

The second reason for taking substantive freedom to be so crucial is that freedom is not only the basis of the evaluation of success and failure, but it is also a principal determinant of individual initiative and social effectiveness. Greater freedom enhances the ability of people to help themselves and also to influence the world, and these mat-

---

1 *I have discussed elsewhere ... opportunity aspect of freedom* In my Kenneth Arrow Lectures, included in *Freedom, Rationality and Social Choice: Arrow Lectures and Other Essays* (Oxford: Clarendon Press, 2000). A number of technical issues in the assessment and evaluation of freedom are also examined in that analysis.

2 *There are two distinct reasons ... evaluation and effectiveness* The evaluative and the operational reasons have been explored more fully in my "Rights and Agency," *Philosophy and Public Affairs* 11 (1982), reprinted in Samuel Scheffler, ed., *Consequentialism and Its Critics* (New York: Oxford University Press, 1988); "Well-Being, Agency and Freedom"; *On Ethics and Economics* (Oxford: Blackwell, 1987).

3 *Having greater freedom ... valuable outcomes* The components correspond respectively to (1) the process aspect and (2) the opportunity aspect of freedom, which are analyzed in my Kenneth Arrow Lectures, included in *Freedom, Rationality and Social Choice*, cited earlier.

ters are central to the process of development. The concern here relates to what we may call (at the risk of some over-simplification) the "agency aspect" of the individual.

The use of the term "agency" calls for a little clarification. The expression "agent" is sometimes employed in the literature of economics and game theory to denote a person who is acting on some one else's behalf (perhaps being led on by a "principal"), and whose achievements are to be assessed in the light of someone else's (the principal's) goals. I am using the term "agent" not in this sense, but in its older- -and "grander"—sense as someone who acts and brings about change, and whose achievements can be judged in terms of her own values and objectives, whether or not we assess them in terms of some external criteria as well. This work is particularly concerned with the agency role of the individual as a member of the public and as a participant in economic, social and political actions (varying from taking part in the market to being involved, directly or indirectly, in individual or joint activities in political and other spheres).

This has a bearing on a great many public policy issues, varying from such strategic matters as the widespread temptation of policy bosses to use fine-tuned "targeting" (for "ideal delivery" to a supposedly inert population), to such fundamental subjects as attempts to dissociate the running of governments from the process of democratic scrutiny and rejection (and the participatory exercise of political and civil rights[1]).

Evaluative Systems: Incomes and Capabilities

On the evaluative side, the approach used here concentrates on a factual base that differentiates it from more traditional practical ethics and economic policy analysis, such as the "economic" concentration on the primacy of *income and wealth* (rather than on the characteristics of human lives and substantive freedoms), the "utilitarian" focus on *mental satisfaction* (rather than on creative discontent and constructive dissatisfaction), the "libertarian" preoccupation

with *procedures* for liberty (with deliberate neglect of consequences that derive from those procedures) and so on. The overarching case for a different factual base, which focuses on substantive freedoms that people have reason to enjoy, is examined in chapter 3.

This is not to deny that deprivation of individual capabilities can have close links with the lowness of income, which connects in both directions: (1) low income can be a major reason for illiteracy and ill health as well as hunger and undernourishment, and (2) conversely, better education and health help in the earning of higher incomes. These connections have to be fully seized. But there are also other influences on the basic capabilities and effective freedoms that individuals enjoy, and there are good reasons to study the nature and reach of these interconnections. Indeed, precisely because income deprivations and capability deprivations often have considerable correlational linkages, it is important to avoid being mesmerized into thinking that taking note of the former would somehow tell us enough about the latter. The connections are not that tight, and the departures are often much more important from a policy point of view than the limited concurrence of the two sets of variables. If our attention is shifted from an exclusive concentration on income poverty to the more inclusive idea of capability deprivation, we can better understand the poverty of human lives and freedoms in terms of a different informational base (involving statistics of a kind that the income perspective tends to crowd out as a reference point for policy analysis). The role of income and wealth—important as it is along with other influences—has to be integrated into a broader and fuller picture of success and deprivation.

Poverty and Inequality

The implications of this informational base for the analysis of poverty and inequality are examined in chapter 4. There are good reasons for seeing poverty as a deprivation of basic capabilities, rather than merely as low income. Deprivation of elementary capabilities can be reflected in premature mortality, significant undernourishment (especially of children), persistent morbidity, widespread illiteracy and other failures. For example, the terrible phenomenon of "missing women" (resulting from unusually higher age-specific mortality rates of women in some societies, particularly in South Asia, West Asia, North Africa, and China) has to be analyzed with demographic, medical and social informa-

---

1   *This has a bearing ... civil rights*   I have tried to discuss the issue of "targeting" in "The Political Economy of Targeting," keynote address to the 1992 Annual World Bank Conference on Development Economics, published in Dominique van de Walle and Kimberly Nead, eds., *Public Spending and the Poor: Theory and Evidence* (Baltimore: Johns Hopkins University Press, 1995). The issue of political freedom as a part of development is addressed in my "Freedoms and Needs," *New Republic*, January 10 and 17, 1994.

tion, rather than in terms of low incomes, which sometimes tell us rather little about the phenomenon of gender inequality.[1]

The shift in perspective is important in giving us a different—and more directly relevant—view of poverty not only in the *developing* countries, but also in the more *affluent* societies. The presence of massive unemployment in Europe (10 to 12 percent in many of the major European countries) entails deprivations that are not well reflected in income distribution statistics. These deprivations are often downplayed on the grounds that the European system of social security (including unemployment insurance) tends to make up for the loss of income of the unemployed. But unemployment is not merely a deficiency of income that can be made up through transfers by the state (at heavy fiscal cost that can itself be a very serious burden); it is also a source of far-reaching debilitating effects on individual freedom, initiative, and skills. Among its manifold effects, unemployment contributes to the "social exclusion" of some groups, and it leads to losses of self-reliance, self-confidence and psychological and physical health. Indeed, it is hard to escape a sense of manifest incongruity in contemporary European attempts to move to a more "self-help" social climate without devising adequate policies for reducing the massive and intolerable levels of unemployment that make such self-help extremely difficult.

Income and Mortality

Even in terms of the connection between mortality and income (a subject in which Maitreyee was rather overambitious), it is remarkable that the extent of deprivation for particular groups in very rich countries can be comparable to that in the so-called third world. For example, in the United States, African Americans as a group have no higher—indeed have a lower—chance of reaching advanced ages than do people born in the immensely poorer economies of China or the Indian state of Kerala (or in Sri Lanka, Jamaica or Costa Rica[2]).

This is shown in figures 1.1 and 1.2. Even though the per capita income of African Americans in the United States is considerably lower than that of the white population, African Americans are very many times richer in income terms than the people of China or Kerala (even after correcting for cost-of-living differences). In this context, the comparison of survival prospects of African Americans vis-à-vis those of the very much poorer Chinese, or Indians in Kerala, is of particular interest. African Americans tend to do better in terms of survival at low age groups (especially in terms of infant mortality) vis-à-vis the Chinese or the Indians, but the picture changes over the years.

In fact, it turns out that men in China and in Kerala decisively outlive African American men in terms of surviving to older age groups. Even African American women end up having a survival pattern for the higher ages similar to that of the much poorer Chinese, and decidedly lower survival rates than the even poorer Indians in Kerala. So it is not only the case that American blacks suffer from *relative* deprivation in terms of income per head vis-à-vis American whites, they also are *absolutely* more deprived than the low-income Indians in Kerala (for both women and men), and the Chinese (in the case of men), in terms of living to ripe old ages. The causal influences on these contrasts (that is, between living standards judged by income per head and those judged by the ability to survive to higher ages) include social arrangements and community relations such as medical coverage, public health care, school education, law and order, prevalence of violence and so on.[3]

It is also worth noting that African Americans in the United States as a whole include a great many internal diversities. Indeed, if we look at the black male populations in particular U.S. cities (such as New York City, San Francisco, St. Louis or Washington, D.C.), we find that they are overtaken in terms of survival by people from China or Kerala at much earlier ages.[4] They are also overtaken by many other

---

1   *For example, the terrible phenomenon ... gender inequality*   I have discussed this issue in "Missing Women," *British Medical Journal* 304 (1992).

2   *For example, in the United States ... (or in Sri Lanka, Jamaica or Costa Rica)*   These and other such comparisons are presented in my "The Economics of Life and Death," *Scientific American* 266 (April 1993), and "Demography and Welfare Economics," *Empirica* 22 (1995).

3   *The causal influences ... prevalence of violence and so on*   On this see my "Economics of Life and Death," and also the medical literature cited there. See also Jean Drèze and Amartya Sen, *Hunger and Public Action* (Oxford: Clarendon Press, 1989). On this general issue, see also M.F. Perutz, "Long Live the Queen's Subjects," *Philosophical Transactions of the Royal Society of London* 352 (1997).

4   *Indeed, if we look ... much earlier ages*   This can be worked out from the background data used to make life expectancy calculations (for 1990), as presented in C.J.L. Murray, C.M. Michaud, M.T. McKenna and J.S. Marks, *U.S. Patterns of Mortality by*

Development as Freedom.
Figure 1.1. Variations in Male Survival Rates by Region.

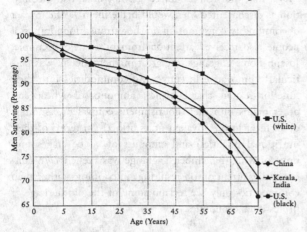

The Perspective of Freedom.
Figure 1.2. Variations in Female Survival Rates by Region.

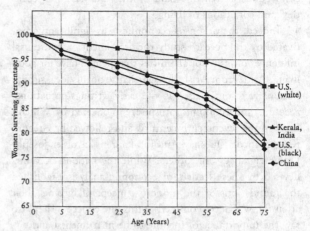

Sources: United States, *1991–93:* U.S. Department of Health and Human Services, *Health United States 1995* (Hyattsville, Md.: National Center for Health Statistics, 1996); Kerala, 1991: Government of India, *Sample Registration Systems: Fertility and Mortality Indicators 1991* (New Delhi: Office of the Registrar General, 1991); China, 1992: World Health Organization, *World Health Statistics Annual 1994* (Geneva: World Health Organization, 1994).

third world populations; for example, Bangladeshi men have a better chance of living to ages beyond forty years than African American men from the Harlem district of the prosperous city of New York.[1] All this is in spite of the fact that African Americans in the United States are very many times richer than the people of comparison groups in the third world.

Freedom, Capability and the Quality of Life

In the foregoing discussion, I have been concentrating on a very elementary freedom: the ability to survive rather than succumb to premature mortality. This is, obviously, a significant freedom, but there are many others that are also important. Indeed, the range of relevant freedoms can be very wide. The extensive coverage of freedoms is sometimes

seen as a problem in getting an "operational" approach to development that is freedom-centered. I think this pessimism is ill-founded, but I shall postpone taking up this issue until chapter 3, when the foundational approaches to valuation will be considered together.

It should, however, be noted here that the freedom-centered perspective has a generic similarity to the common concern with "quality of life," which too concentrates on the way human life goes (perhaps even the choices one has) and not just on the resources or income that a person commands.[2] The focusing on the quality of life and on substantive freedoms, rather than just on income or wealth, may look like something of a departure from the established traditions of economics, and in a sense it is (especially if comparisons are made with some of the more austere income-centered analysis that can be found in contemporary economics). But in fact these broader approaches are in tune with lines of analysis that have been part of professional economics right from the beginning. The Aristotelian connections are obvious enough (Aristotle's focus on "flourishing" and "capacity" clearly relates to the quality of life and to substantive freedoms, as has

County and Race: 1965–1994 (Cambridge, MA: Harvard Center for Population and Development Studies, 1998). See especially table 6d.

1 *for example, Bangladeshi men ... New York* See Colin McCord and Harold P. Freeman, "Excess Mortality in Harlem," *New England Journal of Medicine* 322 (January 18, 1990); see also M.W. Owen, S.M. Teutsch, D.F. Williamson and J.S. Marks, "The Effects of Known Risk Factors on the Excess Mortality of Black Adults in the United States," *Journal of the American Medical Association* 263, no. 6 (February 9, 1990).

2 *It should, however, be noted ... person commands* See Nussbaum and Sen, eds., *The Quality of Life* (1993).

been discussed by Martha Nussbaum[1]). There are strong connections also with Adam Smith's analysis of "necessities" and conditions of living.[2]

Indeed, the origin of economics was significantly motivated by the need to study the assessment of, and causal influences on, the opportunities that people have for good living. Aside from Aristotle's classic use of this idea, similar notions were much used in the early writings on national accounts and economic prosperity, pioneered by William Petty in the seventeenth century, and followed by Gregory King, François Quesnay, Antoine-Laurent Lavoisier, Joseph-Louis Lagrange[3] and others. While the national accounts devised by these leaders of economic analysis established the foundations of the modern concept of income, their attention was never confined to this one concept. They also saw the importance of income to be instrumental and circumstantially contingent.[4]

For example, while William Petty had pioneered both "the income method" and "the expenditure method" of estimating national income (the modern methods of estimation directly follow from these early attempts), he was explicitly concerned with "the Common Safety" and "each Man's particular Happiness." Petty's stated objective for undertaking his study related directly to the assessment of people's living conditions. He managed to combine scientific investigation with a significant dose of seventeenth-century politics ("to show" that "the King's subjects are not in so bad a condition as discontented Men would make them"). The impact of commodity consumption on the various functionings of people also received attention from others. For example, Joseph-Louis Lagrange, the great mathematician, was particularly innovative in converting commodities into their function-related characteristics: amounts of wheat and other grains into their nourishment equivalent, amounts of all meat into equivalent units of beef (in terms of their nutritional qualities) and amounts of all beverages into units of wine (remember, Lagrange was French[5]). In concentrating attention on resulting functionings rather than commodities only, we reclaim some of the old heritage of professional economics.

Markets and Freedoms

The role of the market mechanism is another subject that calls for some reclaiming of old heritage. The relation of the market mechanism to freedom and thus to economic development raises questions of at least two quite distinct types, which need to be clearly distinguished. First, a denial of opportunities of transaction, through arbitrary controls, can be a source of unfreedom in itself. People are then prevented from doing what can be taken to be—in the absence of compelling reasons to the contrary—something that is within their right to do. This point does not depend on the efficiency of the market mechanism or on any extensive analysis of the consequences of having or not having a market system; it turns simply on the importance of freedom of exchange and transaction without let or hindrance.

This argument for the market has to be distinguished from a second argument, which is very popular right now: that markets typically work to expand income and wealth and economic opportunities that people have. Arbitrary restrictions of the market mechanism can lead to a reduction of freedoms because of the consequential effects of the

1   *The Aristotelian connections ... as has been discussed by Martha Nussbaum*   See Martha Nussbaum, "Nature, Function and Capability: Aristotle on Political Distribution," *Oxford Studies in Ancient Philosophy* (1988; supplementary volume); see also Nussbaum and Sen, eds., *The Quality of Life* (1993).

2   *There are strong connections ... conditions of living*   See Adam Smith, *An Inquiry into the Nature and Causes of the Wealth of Nations* (1776), republished, R.H. Campbell and A.S. Skinner, eds. (Oxford: Clarendon Press, 1976), volume 2, book 5, chapter 2 (section on "Taxes upon Consumable Commodities"), pp. 469–71.

3   *William Petty ... Gregory King, François Quesnay, Antoine-Laurent Lavoisier, Joseph-Louis Lagrange*   [editor's note] Sir William Petty, English (1623–87), economist who served Cromwell and his successors; Gregory King, English (1648–1712), pioneered economic statistics; François Quesnay, French (1694–1774), economist associated with the "Physiocrats," early economic scientists who emphasized the importance of agriculture; Antoine-Laurent de Lavoisier (1743–94), better known for his important work in chemistry; Joseph-Louis Lagrange (1736–1813), astronomer and important mathematician.

4   *They also saw the importance ... circumstantially contingent*   These issues are discussed in my Tanner Lectures at Cambridge in 1985, published in Geoffrey Hawthorn, ed., *The Standard of Living*, (Cambridge: Cambridge University Press, 1987).

5   *remember, Lagrange was French*   Lagrange thus presented in the late eighteenth century what was probably the first analysis of what came to be known in our times as "the new view of consumption" (Kevin J. Lancaster, "A New Approach to Consumer Theory," *Journal of Political Economy* 74 [1996], and W.M. Gorman, "A Possible Procedure for Analyzing Quality Differentials in the Egg Market," *Review of Economic Studies* 47 [1980]). These and related matters are discussed in my *The Standard of Living* (1987).

absence of markets. Deprivations can result when people are denied the economic opportunities and favorable consequences that markets offer and support.

These two arguments in favor of the market mechanism, both relevant to the perspective of substantive freedoms, have to be separated out. In the contemporary economic literature, it is the latter argument—based on the effective working and favorable results of the market mechanism—that receives virtually all the attention.[1] That argument is certainly strong, in general, and there is plenty of empirical evidence that the market system can be an engine of fast economic growth and expansion of living standards. Policies that restrict market opportunities can have the effect of restraining the expansion of substantive freedoms that would have been generated through the market system, mainly through overall economic prosperity. This is not to deny that markets can sometimes be counterproductive (as Adam Smith himself pointed out, in supporting in particular the need for control in the financial market[2]). There are serious arguments for regulation in some cases. But by and large the positive effects of the market system are now much more widely recognized than they were even a few decades ago.

However, this case for the use of markets is altogether different from the argument that people have the right to undertake transactions and exchange. Even if such rights are not accepted as being inviolable—and entirely independent of their consequences—it can still be argued that there is some social loss involved in denying people the right to interact economically with each other. If it so happens that the effects of such transactions are so bad for others that

this prima facie presumption in favor of allowing people to transact as they like may be sensibly restricted, there is still something directly lost in imposing this restriction (even if it is outweighed by the alternative loss of the indirect effects of these transactions on *others*).

The discipline of economics has tended to move away from focusing on the value of freedoms to that of utilities, incomes and wealth. This narrowing of focus leads to an underappreciation of the full role of the market mechanism, even though economics as a profession can hardly be accused of not praising the markets enough. The issue, however, is not the amount of praise, but the reasons for it.

Take for example the well-known argument in economics that a competitive market mechanism can achieve a type of efficiency that a centralized system cannot plausibly achieve both because of the economy of information (each person acting in the market does not have to know very much) and the compatibility of incentives (each person's canny actions can merge nicely with those of others). Consider now, contrary to what is generally assumed, a case in which the same economic result is brought about by a fully centralized system with all the decisions of everyone regarding production and allocation being made by a dictator. Would that have been just as good an achievement?

It is not hard to argue that something would be missing in such a scenario, to wit, the freedom of people to act as they like in deciding on where to work, what to produce, what to consume and so on. Even if in both the scenarios (involving, respectively, free choice and compliance to dictatorial order) a person produces the same commodities in the same way and ends up with the same income and buys the same goods, she may still have very good reason to prefer the scenario of free choice over that of submission to order. There is a distinction between "culmination outcomes" (that is, only final outcomes without taking any note of the process of getting there, including the exercise of freedom) and "comprehensive outcomes" (taking note of the processes through which the culmination outcomes come about)—a distinction the central relevance of which I have tried to analyze more fully elsewhere.[3] The merit of the

---

1   *In the contemporary economic literature ... virtually all the attention*   A distinguished exception is Robert Nozick, *Anarchy, State and Utopia* (New York: Basic Books, 1974).

2   *This is not to deny ... control in the financial market*   This was mainly in the context of Adam Smith's support for legislation against "usury," and the need to control the turmoil that follows from the overindulgence of speculative investment by those whom Adam Smith called "prodigals and projectors. " See Smith, *Wealth of Nations*, volume 1, book 2, chapter 4, paragraphs 14–15, in the edition of Campbell and Skinner (1976), pp. 356–57. The term "projector" is used by Smith not in the neutral sense of "one who forms a project," but in the pejorative sense, apparently common from 1616 (according to *The Shorter Oxford English Dictionary*), meaning, among other things, "a promoter of bubble companies; a speculator; a cheat." Giorgio Basevi has drawn my attention to some interesting parallels between Smith's criticism and Jonathan Swift's unflattering portrayal of "projectors" in *Gulliver's Travels*, published in 1726, half a century before *Wealth of Nations*.

3   *There is a distinction ... more fully elsewhere*   The importance of the distinction between "comprehensive outcomes" and "culmination outcomes," in various different contexts, is discussed in my "Maximization and the Act of Choice," *Econometrica* 65 (July 1997). For the relevance of the distinction in the specific case of the market mechanism and its alternatives, see my "Markets and Freedoms," *Oxford Economic Papers* 45 (1993), and "Markets

market system does not lie only in its capacity to generate more efficient culmination outcomes.

The shift in the focus of attention of pro-market economics from freedom to utility has been achieved at some cost: the neglect of the central value of freedom itself. John Hicks, one of the leading economists of this century, who himself was far more utility-oriented than freedom-oriented, did put the issue with admirable clarity in a passage on this subject:

> The liberal, or non-interference, principles of the classical (Smithian or Ricardian) economists were not, in the first place, economic principles; they were an application to economics of principles that were thought to apply to a much wider field. The contention that economic freedom made for economic efficiency was no more than a secondary support.... What I do question is whether we are justified in forgetting, as completely as most of us have done, the other side of the argument.[1]

This point may look somewhat esoteric in the context of economic development in view of the priority that the development literature tends to give to generating high incomes, a bigger basket of consumer goods and other culmination results. But it is far from esoteric. One of the biggest changes in the process of development in many economies involves the replacement of bonded labor and forced work, which characterize parts of many traditional agricultures, with a system of free labor contract and unrestrained physical movement. A freedom-based perspective on development picks up this issue immediately in a way that an evaluative system that focuses only on culmination outcomes may not.

The point can be illustrated with the debates surrounding the nature of slave labor in the southern United States before its abolition. The classic study on this subject by Robert Fogel and Stanley Engerman (*Time on the Cross: The Economics of American Negro Slavery*) includes a remarkable

finding about the relatively high "pecuniary incomes" of the slaves. (Controversies on some issues covered in this book did not seriously undermine this finding.) The commodity baskets of consumption of slaves compared favorably—certainly not unfavorably—with the incomes of free agricultural laborers. And the slaves' life expectancy too was, relatively speaking, not especially low—"nearly identical with the life expectation of countries as advanced as France and Holland," and "much longer [than] life expectations [of] free urban industrial workers in both the United States and Europe."[2] And yet slaves did run away, and there were excellent reasons for presuming that the interest of the slaves was not well served by the system of slavery. In fact, even the attempts, after the abolition of slavery, to get the slaves back, to make them work like slaves (particularly in the form of "gang work"), but at high wages, were not successful.

> After the slaves were freed many planters attempted to reconstruct their work gangs on the basis of wage payments. But such attempts generally foundered, despite the fact that the wages offered to freedmen exceeded the incomes they had received as slaves by more than 100 percent. Even at this premium planters found it impossible to maintain the gang system once they were deprived of the right to apply force.[3]

The importance of freedom of employment and that in working practice is crucial to understanding the valuations involved.[4]

In fact, Karl Marx's favorable remarks on capitalism as against the unfreedom of precapitalist labor arrangements related exactly to this question, which also produced Marx's

---

and the Freedom to Choose," in Horst Siebett, ed., *The Ethical Foundations of the Market Economy* (Tübingen: J.C.B. Mohr, 1994). See also chapter 4 of the present work [not included in this selection—eds.]

1   *What I do question ... other side of the argument*   J.R. Hicks, *Wealth and Welfare* (Oxford: Basil Blackwell, 1981), p. 138. Robert W. Fogel and Stanley L. Engerman, *Time on the Cross: The Economics of American Negro Slavery* (Boston: Little, Brown, 1974), pp. 12.5–6.

2   *much longer [than] life expectations ... United States and Europe*   Robert W. Fogel and Stanley L. Engerman, *Time on the Cross: The Economics of American Negro Slavery* (Boston: Little, Brown, 1974), pp. 125–26.

3   *Even at this premium ... right to apply force*   Fogel and Engerman, *Time on the Cross*, pp. 237-38.

4   *The importance of freedom ... valuations involved*   Different aspects of this momentous issue have been examined in Fernando Henrique Cardoso, *Capitalismo e Escravidão no Brasil Meridional: o negro na sociadade escravocrata do Rio Grande do Sul* (Rio de Janeiro: Paz e Terra, 1977); Robin Blackburn, *The Overthrow of Colonial Slavery, 1776–1848* (London and New York: Verso, 1988); Tom Brass and Marcel van der Linden, eds., *Free and Unfree Labor* (Berne: European Academic Publishers, 1997); Stanley L. Engerman, ed., *Terms of Labor: Slavery, Serfdom and Free Labor* (Stanford, Calif.: Stanford University Press, 1998).

characterization of the American Civil War as "the one great event of contemporary history."[1] Indeed, this issue of market-based freedom is quite central to the analysis of bonded labor—common in many developing countries—and the transition to free-contract labor arrangements. This, in fact, is one of the cases in which Marxian analysis has tended to have an affinity with libertarian concentration on freedom as opposed to utility.

For example, in his major study of transition from bonded labor to wage labor in India, V.K. Ramachandran provides an illuminating picture of the empirical importance of this question in the contemporary agrarian situation in southern India:

> Marx distinguishes between (to use the term used by Jon Elster) the *formal freedom* of the worker under capitalism and the *real unfreedom* of workers in pre-capitalist systems: "the freedom of workers to change employers makes him free in a way not found in earlier modes of production." The study of the development of wage labor in agriculture is important from another perspective as well. The extension of the freedom of workers in a society to sell their labor power is an enhancement of their positive freedom, which is, in turn, an important measure of how well that society is doing.[2]

The linked presence of labor bondage with indebtedness yields a particularly tenacious form of unfreedom in many precapitalist agricultures.[3] Seeing development as freedom permits a direct approach to this issue that is not parasitic on having to show that labor markets also raise productivity of agriculture—a serious issue on its own but quite different from the question of freedom of contract and employment.

Some of the debates surrounding the terrible issue of child labor also relate to this question of freedom of choice. The worst violations of the norm against child labor come typically from the virtual slavery of children in disadvantaged families and from their being forced into exploitative employment (as opposed to being free and possibly going to school[4]). This direct issue of freedom is an integral part of this vexed question.

Values and the Process of Valuation

I return now to *evaluation*. Since our freedoms are diverse, there is room for explicit valuation in determining the relative weights of different types of freedoms in assessing individual advantages and social progress. Valuations are, of course, involved in all such approaches (including utilitarianism, libertarianism, and other approaches, to be discussed in chapter 3), even though they are often made implicitly. Those who prefer a mechanical index, without the need to be explicit about what values are being used and why, have a tendency to grumble that the freedom-based approach requires that valuations be explicitly made. Such complaints have frequently been aired. But explicitness, I shall argue, is an important asset for a valuational exercise, especially for it to be open to public scrutiny and criticism. Indeed, one of the strongest arguments in favor of political freedom lies precisely in the opportunity it gives citizens to discuss and debate—and to participate in the selection of—values in the choice of priorities (to be discussed in chapters 6 through 11).

Individual freedom is quintessentially a social product, and there is a two-way relation between (1) social arrangements to expand individual freedoms and (2) the use of individual freedoms not only to improve the respective lives but also to make the social arrangements more appropriate and effective. Also, individual conceptions of justice and propriety, which influence the specific uses that individuals make of their freedoms, depend on social associations—particularly on the interactive formation of public perceptions and on collaborative comprehension of problems and remedies. The analysis and assessment of public policies have to be sensitive to these diverse connections.

---

1   *the one great event of contemporary history*   Karl Marx, *Capital*, volume 1 (London: Sonnenschein, 1887), chapter 10, section 3, p. 240. See also his *Grundrisse* (Harmondsworth: Penguin Books, 1973).

2   *The extension of the freedom of workers ... society is doing*   V.K. Ramachandran, *Wage Labour and Unfreedom in Agriculture: An Indian Case Study* (Oxford: Clarendon Press, 1990), pp. 1–2.

3   *The linked presence of labor bondage ... precapitalist agricultures*   An important empirical study of this aspect of bondage and unfreedom, among others, can be found in Sudipto Mundle, *Backwardness and Bondage: Agrarian Relations in a South Bihar District* (New Delhi: Indian Institute of Public Administration, 1979).

4   *The worst violations ... possibly going to school*   On this see *Decent Work: The Report of the Director-General of the ILO* (Geneva: ILO, 1999). This is one of the special emphases in the program of the new director-general, Juan Somavia.

Tradition, Culture and Democracy

The issue of participation is also central to some of the foundational questions that have plagued the force and reach of development theory. For example, it has been argued by some that economic development as we know it may actually be harmful for a nation, since it may lead to the elimination of its traditions and cultural heritage.[1] Objections of this kind are often quickly dismissed on the ground that it is better to be rich and happy than to be impoverished and traditional. This may be a persuasive slogan, but it is scarcely an adequate response to the critique under discussion. Nor does it reflect a serious engagement with the critical valuational issue that is being raised by development skeptics.

The more serious issue, rather, concerns the source of authority and legitimacy. There is an inescapable valuational problem involved in deciding what to choose if and when it turns out that some parts of tradition cannot be maintained along with economic or social changes that may be needed for other reasons. It is a choice that the people involved have to face and assess. The choice is neither closed (as many development apologists seem to suggest), nor is it one for the elite "guardians" of tradition to settle (as many development skeptics seem to presume). If a traditional way of life has to be sacrificed to escape grinding poverty or minuscule longevity (as many traditional societies have had for thousands of years), then it is the people directly involved who must have the opportunity to participate in deciding what should be chosen. The real conflict is between

1) the basic value that the people must be allowed to decide freely what traditions they wish or not wish to follow; and

2) the insistence that established traditions be followed (no matter what), or, alternatively, people must obey the decisions by religious or secular authorities who enforce traditions—real or imagined.

The force of the former precept lies in the basic importance of human freedom, and once that is accepted there are strong implications on what can or cannot be done in the name of tradition. The approach of "development as freedom" emphasizes this precept.

Indeed, in the freedom-oriented perspective the liberty of all to participate in deciding what traditions to observe cannot be ruled out by the national or local "guardians"— neither by the ayatollahs (or other religious authorities), nor by political rulers (or governmental dictators), nor by cultural "experts" (domestic or foreign). The pointer to any real conflict between the preservation of tradition and the advantages of modernity calls for a participatory resolution, not for a unilateral rejection of modernity in favor of tradition by political rulers, or religious authorities, or anthropological admirers of the legacy of the past. The question is not only not closed, it must be wide open for people in the society to address and join in deciding. An attempt to choke off participatory freedom on grounds of traditional values (such as religious fundamentalism, or political custom, or the so-called Asian values) simply misses the issue of legitimacy and the need for the people affected to participate in deciding what they want and what they have reason to accept.

This basic recognition has remarkable reach and powerful implications. A pointer to tradition does not provide ground for any general suppression of media freedom, or of the rights of communication between one citizen and another. Even if the oddly distorted view of how authoritarian Confucius really was is accepted as being historically correct (a critique of that interpretation will be taken up in chapter 10), this still does not give anyone an adequate ground for practicing authoritarianism through censorship or political restriction, since the legitimacy of adhering today to the views enunciated in the sixth century B.C. has to be decided by those who live today.

Also, since participation requires knowledge and basic educational skills, denying the opportunity of schooling to any group—say, female children—is immediately contrary to the basic conditions of participatory freedom. While these rights have often been disputed (one of the severest onslaughts coming recently from the leadership of the Taliban in Afghanistan), that elementary requirement cannot be escaped in a freedom-oriented perspective. The approach of development as freedom has far-reaching implications not only for the ultimate objectives of development, but also for processes and procedures that have to be respected.

---

1   *For example, it has been argued ... cultural heritage*   This point of view is forcefully developed in Stephen M. Marglin and Frederique Appfel Marglin, eds., *Dominating Knowledge* (Oxford: Clarendon Press, 1993). On related anthropological insights, see also Veena Das, *Critical Events: An Anthropological Perspective on Contemporary India* (Delhi: Oxford University Press, 1995).

Concluding Remarks

Seeing development in terms of the substantive freedoms of people has far-reaching implications for our understanding of the process of development and also for the ways and means of promoting it. On the evaluative side, this involves the need to assess the requirements of development in terms of removing the unfreedoms from which the members of the society may suffer. The process of development, in this view, is not essentially different from the history of overcoming these unfreedoms. While this history is not by any means unrelated to the process of economic growth and accumulation of physical and human capital, its reach and coverage go much beyond these variables.

In focusing on freedoms in evaluating development, it is not being suggested that there is some unique and precise "criterion" of development in terms of which the different development experiences can always be compared and ranked. Given the heterogeneity of distinct components of freedom as well as the need to take note of different persons' diverse freedoms, there will often be arguments that go in contrary directions. The motivation underlying the approach of "development as freedom" is not so much to order all states—or all alternative scenarios—into one "complete ordering," but to draw attention to important aspects of the process of development, each of which deserves attention. Even after such attention is paid, there will no doubt remain differences in possible overall rankings, but their presence is not embarrassing to the purpose at hand.

What would be damaging would be the neglect—often to be seen in the development literature—of centrally relevant concerns because of a lack of interest in the freedoms of the people involved. An adequately broad view of development is sought in order to focus the evaluative scrutiny on things that really matter, and in particular to avoid the neglect of crucially important subjects. While it may be nice to think that considering the relevant variables will automatically take different people to exactly the same conclusions on how to rank alternative scenarios, the approach requires no such unanimity. Indeed, debates on such matters, which can lead to important political arguments, can be part of the process of democratic participation that characterizes development. There will be occasion, later on in this book, to examine the substantial issue of participation as a part of the process of development.

MARTHA NUSSBAUM
(1947–)

Martha Nussbaum occupies a central place in contemporary philosophy. She has made important contributions to social and political philosophy and she is a major figure in the study of ancient Greek and Roman thought, and in ethics. Her most recent work presents a political theory based on the capabilities approach, which she develops from a feminist and cosmopolitan perspective. The evolution of her thought testifies to a fertile intellectual dialogue with key figures of her generation, to which she lends her sometimes polemical, always inimitable voice.

Martha Craven was born May 6, 1947 in New York and converted to Judaism at the age of twenty, shortly before her marriage to Alan Nussbaum, whose name she kept after their divorce in 1987. After completing her BA in theatre and classics at New York University, she completed her MA and PhD at Harvard. She has taught at Harvard, Brown, and Oxford, and currently holds the post of Ernst Freund Distinguished Service Professor of Law and Ethics at the University of Chicago, which includes appointments in the philosophy department, law faculty, and divinity school. Between 1986 and 1993, she was a research advisor at the World Institute of Developmental Economic Research in Helsinki; there she met Amartya Sen (1998 Noble Laureate in economics), with whom she developed her capability approach. She has won many of the major awards in her field and has been granted twenty-five honorary degrees from universities around the world.

Nussbaum's work may be classified into three branches. First, her work on Aristotle, especially her book *The Fragility of Goodness: Luck and Ethics in Greek Tragedy and Philosophy* (1986) has contributed to scholarship in ancient philosophy, while, at the same time, engaging with contemporary debates in ethics.

Second, in *The Therapy of Desire: Theory and Practice in Hellenistic Ethics* (1994), she has presented a cognitivist

theory of emotions. For Nussbaum, emotions are not blind, irrational impulses, but rather judgments of value that play a central role in moral deliberation. This view is developed in later works, such as *Upheavals of Thought: The Intelligence of Emotions* (2001) and *Cultivating Humanity* (1997). In the latter book, Nussbaum argues for the role of emotions in civic education.

Her book *The Quality of Life* (1993) (co-edited with Amartya Sen) marks the growth of a third branch in her work. Spurred on by her investigations at the United Nations University, she became increasingly concerned with issues of international development, and particularly with the vulnerable circumstances of many women. Standard measures of quality of life fail to capture what goes on in many people's lives; thus gross domestic product (GDP) is an inadequate approach for measuring quality of life, since it fails to account for the distribution of wealth. What is needed, according to Sen and Nussbaum, is an approach that accounts adequately for the capabilities of individuals—what they can actually *do* with the resources at their disposal.

Nussbaum's elaboration of the capability approach in *Women and Human Development: The Capabilities Approach* (2000) develops out of observations about and concern for women's vulnerability. Nussbaum's approach is individualistic and universalistic, based on an Aristotelian conception of human nature. Throughout the book, she opposes the utilitarian perspective of social justice, drawing on arguments put forward by Rawls and Sen that the utilitarian perspective on justice ignores the separateness of persons, among other things.

Nussbaum is a harsh critic of patriarchy, arguing that women are sometimes victims of "adaptive preferences," a well-known psychological phenomenon in which individuals in deprived circumstances come to accept their current situation. (For example, women in a society where they are not permitted to study may lose any desire to pursue education.) At the same time, she is determined, through her moral universalism and radically agnostic feminism, to develop an approach that avoids Western liberal paternalism and provides scope for cultural and religious diversity. She stresses that the capability approach must respect individual autonomy so that individuals—regardless of their heritage—can pursue the culturally diverse "functionings" which they choose to pursue.

Women and Human Development criticized utilitarianism, but left open the possibility that Nussbaum's capability approach might fit largely within a Rawlsian framework. In her 2006 book *Frontiers of Justice: Disability, Nationality, Species Membership*, Nussbaum deepens the capabilities approach by setting it against the social contract tradition, particularly in the work of John Rawls. Drawing on Aristotelian and Kantian sources, she shows how the capabilities approach differs from conceptions of justice based on mutual benefit. In particular, the social contract tradition has difficulty in providing an adequate account of justice beyond national borders, in addressing issues concerning the severely handicapped; and in dealing with issues concerning the ethical treatment of animals. In collaboration with Cass Sunstein, Nussbaum has also broadened the capabilities approach to include other species (in order to incorporate non-human animals into our moral and political consideration). Here she creates a list of capabilities that she considers core social entitlements to which every human being, regardless of their culture, should have access. Notably, this list provides an alternative to John Rawls's theory of primary goods. Besides life, health, and bodily integrity (including protection against sexual assault and domestic violence), Nussbaum argues that social entitlements should include the capacity to use one's senses, imagination and thought; to enjoy a healthy emotional life; to control one's physical and political environment; and to play.

In Nussbaum's hands, the capabilities approach has become a promising perspective in political philosophy, one that holds real potential for addressing many ethical and political questions. It is without doubt a vitally important contribution to contemporary philosophy.

● ● ● ● ●

Human Capabilities, Female Human Beings (1995)

Human beings are not by nature kings, or nobles, or courtiers, or rich. All are born naked and poor. All are subject to the miseries of life, to frustrations, to ills, to needs, to pains of every kind. Finally, all are condemned to death. That is what is really the human being; that is what no mortal can avoid. Begin, then, by studying what is the most inseparable from human nature, that which most constitutes humanness.

—Jean-Jacques Rousseau, *Émile*, Book IV

Women, a majority of the world's population, receive only a small share of developmental opportunities. They are often excluded from education or from the better jobs, from political systems or from adequate health care ... In the countries for which relevant data are available, the female human development index is only 60% that of males.　　—*Human Development Report* 1993, United Nations Development Program

Were our state a pure democracy there would still be excluded from our deliberations women, who, to prevent depravation of morals and ambiguity of issue, should not mix promiscuously in gatherings of men.　　　　　　—Thomas Jefferson

Being a woman is not yet a way of being a human being.　　　　　　—Catharine MacKinnon

1. *Feminism and Common Humanity*[1]

Begin with the human being: with the capacities and needs that join all humans, across barriers of gender and class and

---

[1]　*Feminism and Common Humanity* [Unless otherwise indicated all notes are by the author rather than the editors of this anthology.] The argument of this paper is closely related to that of several other papers of mine, to which I shall refer frequently in what follows: "Nature, Function, and Capability," *Oxford Studies in Ancient Philosophy*, suppl. vol. 1 (1988), pp. 145–84; "Non-Relative Virtues: An Aristotelian Approach," *Midwest Studies in Philosophy* 13 (1988), pp. 32–53, and, in an expanded version, in M. Nussbaum and A. Sen (eds.), *The Quality of Life* (Oxford: Clarendon Press, 1993), pp. 242–76; "Aristotelian Social Democracy," in R.B. Douglass, G. Mara, and H. Richardson (eds.), *Liberalism and the Good* (New York: Routledge, 1990), pp. 203–52; "Aristo-

race and nation. To a person concerned with the equality and dignity of women, this advice should appear in one way promising. For it instructs us to focus on what all human beings share, rather than on the privileges and achievements of a dominant group, and on needs and basic functions, rather than power or status. Women have rarely been kings, or nobles, or courtiers, or rich. They have, on the other hand, frequently been poor and sick and dead.

But this starting point will be regarded with scepticism by many contemporary feminists. For it is all too obvious that throughout the history of political thought, both Western and non-Western, such allegedly-unbiased general concepts have served in various ways to bolster male privilege and to marginalize women. Human beings are not born kings, or nobles, or courtiers. They are, or so it seems,[1] born male and female. The nakedness on which Rousseau places such emphasis reveals a difference that is taken by Rousseau himself to imply profound differences in capability and social role. His remarks about human nature are the prelude to his account of Emile's education. Sophie, Emile's female companion, will be said to have a different "nature" and a different education. Whether, as here, women are held to be bearers of a different "nature" from unmarked "human nature," or whether they are simply said to be degenerate and substandard exemplars of the same "nature," the result is usually the same: a judgement of female inferiority, which can then be used to justify and stabilize oppression.[2]

I shall argue nonetheless that we should in fact begin with a conception of the human being and human functioning in thinking about women's equality in developing countries. This notion can be abused. It can be developed in a gender-biased way. It can be unjustly and prejudicially applied. It can be developed in ways that neglect relevant differences among women of different nationalities, classes, and races. But I shall argue that, articulated in a certain way (and I shall be emphatically distinguishing my approach from others that use an idea of 'human nature') it is our best starting point for reflection. It is our best route to stating correctly what is wrong with the situations that confronted Saleha Begum and Metha Bai,[3] the best basis for claims of justice on their behalf, and on behalf of the huge numbers of women in the world who are currently being deprived of their full "human development."

I note that the concept of the human being has already been central to much of the best feminist and internationalist thinking. Consider, for example, J.S. Mill's remarks on "human improvement" in *The Subjection of Women*; Amartya Sen's use of a notion of "human capability" to confront gender-based inequalities; the Sen-inspired use of a notion of "human development" in the UN Report to describe and criticize gender-based inequalities; Susan Moller Okin's proposal for a "humanist justice" in her recent major work of feminist political theory; Catharine MacKinnon's graphic description of women's current situation, quoted as my epigraph; and, of course, the role that various accounts of "human rights," or even "The Rights of Man" have played in claiming justice for women.[4]

---

tle on Human Nature and the Foundations of Ethics," in *World, Mind, and Ethics: Essays on the Philosophy of Bernard Williams*, R. Harrison and J. Altham (eds.) (Cambridge: Cambridge University Press, 1995); "Human Functioning and Social Justice: In Defense of Aristotelian Essentialism," *Political Theory* 20 (1992), pp. 202–46.

1   *They are, or so it seems*   By this I mean that the difference in external genitalia figures in social life as it is interpreted by human cultures; thus we are never dealing simply with facts given at birth, but always with what has been made of them (see below, section 8 for discussion of the role of culture in biological claims about male/female differences). Thus, even the common distinction between "gender," a cultural concept, and "sex," the allegedly pure biological concept, is inadequate to capture the depth of cultural interpretation in presenting even the biological "facts" to human beings, from the very start of a child's life. See Anne Fausto-Sterling, *Myths of Gender* (2nd edn., New York: Basic Books, 1992). I have discussed these issues further in "Constructing Love, Desire, and Care," forthcoming in D. Estlund and M. Nussbaum (eds.), *Laws and Nature: Shaping Sex, Preference, and Family* (Oxford University Press).

2   *a judgement of female inferiority ... stabilize oppression*   For a historical argument along these lines from the history of Western

scientific thought, see Thomas Laqueur, *Making Sex* (Berkeley and Los Angeles: University of California Press, 1989). The papers in Nussbaum et al., Woman, Culture, and Development: A Study of Human Capabilities (Oxford; Oxford University Press, 1995) by Amartya Sen, Xiaorong Li, and Roop Rekha Verma, show that the use of ideas of nature to convey a false sense of appropriateness, "justifying" unjust practices, is by no means confined to the Western tradition.

3   *It is our best route ... Metha Bai*   See Martha Chen's paper "A Matter of Survival: Women's Employment in Bangladesh," in Martha Nussbaum and Jonathan Glover (eds), *Woman, Culture and Development: A Study of Human Capabilities* (Delhi: Oxford University Press, 1995: 37-60).

4   *J.S. Mill's ... justice for women*   J.S. Mill, *The Subjection of Women* (Indianapolis: Bobbs Merrill, 1988); Amartya Sen, "Gender and Cooperative Conflicts," in I. Tinker (ed.), *Persistent Inequalities* (New York: Oxford University Press, 1990); "Gender Inequality and Theories of Justice" in this volume and "More Than a Million Women are Missing," *New York Review of Books: Human*

Much the same can be said more generally, I think, about internationalist thought.[1]

To cite just one example, I take my proposal to be the feminist analogue of the proposal recently made by Ghanaian philosopher Kwame Anthony Appiah when he wrote, 'We will only solve our problems if we see them as human problems arising out of a special situation, and we shall not solve them if we see them as African problems, generated by our being somehow unlike others.'[2]

My proposal is frankly universalist and "essentialist." That is, it asks us to focus on what is common to all, rather than on differences (although, as we shall see, it does not neglect these), and to see some capabilities and functions as more central, more at the core of human life, than others. Its primary opponents on the contemporary scene will be "anti-essentialists" of various types, thinkers who urge us to begin not with sameness but with difference— both between women and men and across groups of women—and to seek norms defined relatively to a local context and locally held beliefs.[3]

This opposition takes many forms, and I shall be responding to several distinct objections that opponents may bring against my universalist proposal. But I can begin to motivate my enterprise by telling several true stories of conversations that have taken place at WIDER, in which the relativist position[4] seemed to have alarming implications for women's lives. I have in some cases conflated two separate conversations into one; otherwise things happened as I describe them.[5]

1. At a conference on "Value and Technology," an American economist who has long been a left-wing critic of neoclassical economics delivers a paper urging the preservation of traditional ways of life in a rural area of India, now under threat of contamination from Western development projects. As evidence of the excellence of this rural way of life, he points to the fact that, whereas we Westerners experience a sharp split between the values that prevail in the workplace and the values that prevail in the home, here, by contrast, there exists what the economist calls 'the embedded way of life'; the same values obtaining in both places. His example: just as in the home a menstruating woman is thought to pollute the kitchen and therefore may not enter it, so too in the workplace a menstruating woman is taken to pollute the loom and may not enter the room where looms are kept. Amartya Sen objects that this example is repellant, rather than admirable: surely such practices both degrade the women in question and inhibit their freedom. The first economist's collaborator, an elegant French anthropologist

Development Report 1993, for the United Nations Development Programme (UNDP) (New York and Oxford: Oxford University Press, 1993); Susan Moller Okin, *Justice, Gender, and the Family* (New York: Basic Books, 1989), see my review of Okin, "Justice for Women," *New York Review of Books* October 1992; Catharine MacKinnon, remark cited by Richard Rorty in "Feminism and Pragmatism," *Michigan Quarterly Review* 30 (1989), p. 263. MacKinnon has since acknowledged the remark.

1 *Much the same ... internationalist thought* For a compelling argument linking feminism and internationalism, see Onora O'Neill, "Justice, Gender, and International Boundaries," in M. Nussbaum and A. Sen (eds.), *The Quality of Life*, pp. 303–23.

2 *"We will only solve ... somehow unlike others."* Kwame Anthony Appiah, *In My Father's House: Africa in the Philosophy of Culture* (New York and Oxford: Oxford University Press, 1992), p. 136.

3 *seek norms defined relatively to a local context and locally held beliefs* On the other hand, it is closely related to Kantian approaches using the universal notion of personhood. See, for example, Onora O'Neill, "Justice, Gender, and International Boundaries," with my commentary (324–35). In *Woman, Culture, and Development* see the papers of Onora O'Neill, Ruth Anna Putnam, and Roop Rekha Verma. Below I shall be making some criticisms of the concept of "person" in feminist argument, and related criticisms of liberal Kantian approaches (on which see also ASD and my review of Okin). But these differences are subtle and take place against a background of substantial agreement. See also David Crocker, "Functioning and Capability: The Foundation of Sen's and Nussbaum's Development Ethics," *Political Theory* 20 (1992), p. 584 ff.

4 *relativist position* By relativism, I mean the view that the only available criterion of adjudication is some local group or individual. Thus relativism, as I understand it, is a genus of which the brand of reliance on individuals' subjective preferences frequently endorsed in neoclassical economics is one species. (Economists, of course, are relativist only about value, not about what they construe as the domain of scientific "fact.") This affinity will later be relevant to my comments on the Marglin project. My opponents also frequently employ the term "postmodernist" to characterize their position: this is a vaguer term, associated in a very general way with the repudiation of both metaphysical realism (to be defined below) and universalism.

5 *otherwise things happened as I describe them* Much of the material described in these examples is now published in *Dominating Knowledge: Development, Culture, and Resistance*, F.A. Marglin and S.A. Marglin (eds.) (Oxford: Clarendon Press, 1990). The issue of "embeddedness" and menstruation taboos is discussed in S.A. Marglin, "Losing Touch: The Cultural Conditions of Worker Accommodation and Resistance," 217–82, and related issues are discussed in S.A. Marglin, "Toward the Decolonization of the Mind," 1–28. On Sittala Devi, see F.A. Marglin, "Smallpox in Two Systems of Knowledge," 102–44; and for related arguments see Ashis Nandy and Shiv Visvanathan, "Modern Medicine and Its Non-Modern Critics," 144–84.

(who would, I suspect, object violently to a purity check at the seminar room door), replies to Sen. Doesn't he realize that there is, in these matters, no privileged place to stand? This, after all, has been shown by both Derrida and Foucault. Doesn't he know that he is neglecting the otherness of Indian ideas by bringing his Western essentialist values into the picture?[1]

2. The same French anthropologist now delivers her paper. She expresses regret that the introduction of smallpox vaccination to India by the British eradicated the cult of Sittala Devi, the goddess to whom one used to pray in order to avert smallpox. Here, she says, is another example of Western neglect of difference. Someone (it might have been me) objects that it is surely better to be healthy rather than ill, to live rather than to die. The answer comes back: Western essentialist medicine conceives of things in terms of binary oppositions: life is opposed to death, health to disease.[2]

But if we cast away this binary way of thinking, we will begin to comprehend the otherness of Indian traditions.

At this point Eric Hobsbawm, who has been listening to the proceedings in increasingly uneasy silence, rises to deliver a blistering indictment of the traditionalism and relativism that prevail in this group. He lists historical examples of ways in which appeals to tradition have been used to support oppression and violence.[3]

His final example is that of National Socialism in Germany. In the confusion that ensues, most of the relativist social scientists—above all those from far away, who do not know who Hobsbawm is—demand that he be asked to leave the room. The radical American economist, disconcerted by this apparent tension between his relativism and his affiliation with the left, convinces them, with difficulty, to let Hobsbawm remain.

3. We shift now to another conference two years later, a philosophical conference organized by Amartya Sen and me.[4] Sen makes it clear that he holds the perhaps unsophisticated view that life is opposed to death in a very binary way, and that such binary oppositions can and should be used in development analysis. His paper[5] contains much universalist talk of human functioning and capability; he begins to speak of freedom of choice as a basic human good. At this point he is interrupted by the radical economist of my first story, who insists that contemporary anthropology has shown that non-Western people are not especially attached to freedom of choice. His example: a new book on Japan has shown that Japanese males, when they get home from work, do not wish to choose what to eat for dinner, what to wear, etc. They wish all these choices to be taken out of their hands by their wives. A heated exchange follows about what this example really shows. I leave it to your imaginations to reconstruct it. In the end, the confidence of the radical economist is unshaken: Sen and I are both victims of bad universalist thinking, who fail to respect "difference."[6]

---

1 *Doesn't he know ... values into the picture* For Sen's own account of the plurality and internal diversity of Indian values, one that strongly emphasizes the presence of a rationalist and critical strand in Indian traditions, see M. Nussbaum and A. Sen, "Internal Criticism and Indian Relativist Traditions," in M. Krausz (ed.), *Relativism* (Notre Dame, Ind.: Notre Dame University Press, 1989)—a paper originally presented at the same WIDER conference and refused publication by the Marglins in its proceedings; and "India and the West," *The New Republic*, 7 June 1993.

2 *life is opposed to death, health to disease* S.A. Marglin, in "Toward the Decolonization," 22–3, suggests that binary thinking is peculiarly Western. But such oppositions are pervasive in all traditions with which I have any acquaintance: in the *Upanishads*, for example (see the epigraph to "Human Functioning"), in Confucian thought (see, again, the epigraph to "Human Functioning"), in Ibo thought (see, for many examples, Chinua Achebe's *Things Fall Apart* [London: William Heinemann, 1958]). Critics of such oppositions have not explained how one can speak coherently without bouncing off one thing against another. I believe that Aristotle was right to hold that to say anything at all one must rule out something, at the very least the contradictory of what one puts forward. The arguments of Nietzsche, which are frequently put forward as if they undermine all binary oppositions, actually make far more subtle and concrete points about the origins of certain oppositions, and the interests served by them.

3 *He lists historical examples ... oppression and violence* See E. Hobsbawm and T. Ranger (eds.), *The Invention of Tradition* (Cambridge: Cambridge University Press, 1983). In his *New Republic* piece, Sen makes a similar argument about contemporary India: the Western construction of India as mystical and "other" serves the purposes of the fundamentalist BJP, who are busy refashioning history to serve the ends of their own political power. An eloquent critique of the whole notion of the "other," and of the associated "nativism," where Africa is concerned, can be found in Appiah (above n. 7), especially in the essays "The Postcolonial and the Postmodern," 137–57 and "Topologies of Nativism," 47–72.

4 *We shift now ... Amartya Sen and me* The proceedings of this conference are now published as Nussbaum and Sen (eds.), *The Quality of Life* (n. 1 above).

5 *His paper* "Capability and Well-Being," in Nussbaum and Sen, pp. 30–53.

6 *Sen and I ... who fail to respect "difference"* Marglin has since published this point in "Toward the Decolonization." His reference

Here we see the relativist position whose influence in development studies motivated the work that has led to the present volume. The phenomenon is an odd one. For we see here highly intelligent people, people deeply committed to the good of women and men in developing countries, people who think of themselves as progressive and feminist and anti-racist, people who correctly argue that the concept of development is an evaluative concept requiring normative argument[1]—effectively eschewing normative argument and taking up positions that converge, as Hobsbawm correctly saw, with the positions of reaction, oppression, and sexism. Under the banner of their fashionable opposition to "essentialism" march ancient religious taboos, the luxury of the pampered husband, educational deprivation, unequal health care, and premature death. (And in my own universalist Aristotelian way, I say it at the outset, I do hold that death is opposed to life in the most binary way imaginable, and freedom to slavery, and hunger to adequate nutrition, and ignorance to knowledge. Nor do I believe that it is only, or even primarily, in Western thinking that such oppositions are, and should be, important.)

The relativist challenge to a universal notion of the human being and human functioning is not always accompanied by clear and explicit philosophical arguments. This is especially true in the material from development studies to which I have referred, where the philosophical debate concerning relativism in ethics and in science is not confronted, and universalism is simply denounced as the legacy of Western conceptions of 'episteme'[2] that are alleged to be in league with imperialism and oppression.[3] ... Here, then, I shall simply set out rather schematically and briefly, for the purposes of my own argument, several objections to the use of a universal notion of human functioning in development analysis to which I shall later respond.

2. The Assault on Universalism

Many critics of universalism in ethics are really critics of metaphysical realism who assume that realism is a necessary basis for universalism. I shall argue that this assumption is false. By metaphysical realism I mean the view (commonly held in both Western and non-Western philosophical traditions) that there is some determinate way the world is, apart from the interpretive workings of the cognitive faculties of

---

is to Takeo Doi, *The Anatomy of Dependence* (Tokyo: Kedansho, 1971). On women and men in Japan, See *Human Development Report 1993*, p. 26: "Japan, despite some of the world's highest levels of human development, still has marked inequalities in achievement between men and women. The 1993 human development index puts Japan first. But when the HDI is adjusted for gender disparity, Japan slips to number 17 ... Women's average earnings are only 51% those of men, and women are largely excluded from decision-making positions ... Their representation is even lower in the political sphere ... In legal rights in general, Japan's patrilineal society is only gradually changing to offer women greater recognition and independence. Japan now has political and non-governmental organizations pressing for change ..." The question of freedom of choice is thus on the agenda in Japan in a large way, precisely on account of the sort of unequal functioning vividly illustrated in Marglin's example, where menial functions are performed by women, in order that men may be free to perform their managerial and political functions.

1 *For we see here ... requiring normative argument* See S.A. Marglin, "Toward the Decolonization."

2 *'episteme'* See S.A. Marglin, "Losing Touch." I put the term in quotes to indicate that I am alluding to Marglin's use of the term, not to the concept as I understand it.

3 *imperialism and oppression* See S.A. Marglin, "Toward the Decolonization" and "Losing Touch." Similar claims are common in feminist argument. For example, in *The Feminist Theory of the State* (Cambridge, Mass.: Harvard University Press, 1989), Catharine MacKinnon argues that "objectivity" as traditionally conceived in the Western epistemological tradition is causally linked to the objectification and abuse of women. This line of argument is effectively criticized in Louise M. Antony, "Quine as Feminist: The Radical Import of Naturalized Epistemology," in L.M. Antony and C. Witt (eds.), *A Mind of One's Own: Feminist Essays on Reason and Objectivity* (Boulder, Colo.: Westview Press, 1992), pp. 185–225. See also the detailed examination of MacKinnon's argument in the same volume by Sally Haslanger, in "On Being Objective and Being Objectified," 85–125. MacKinnon's fundamental contributions in the areas of sexual harassment and pornography do not depend on this analysis, and are actually undermined by it. The core of her thought actually reveals a strong commitment to a type of ethical universalism, as my epigraph indicates. See, in the Antony volume, the persuasive analysis by Liz Rappaport, "Generalizing Gender: Reason and Essence in the Legal Thought of Catharine MacKinnon," 127–43. Alcoff's contribution in the present volume continues the debate about feminism and reason; and see also L. Alcoff and E. Potter (eds.), *Feminist Epistemologies* (New York: Routledge 1993). For a healthy scepticism about the role of "anti-essentialism" within feminism, see Seyla Benhabib, "Feminism and the Question of Postmodernism," in *Situating the Self: Gender, Community, and Postmodernism in Contemporary Ethics* (New York: Routledge, 1992), pp. 203–42; Sabina Lovibond, "Feminism and Postmodernism," *New Left Review*, p. 178 (November–December 1989), pp. 5–28; Val Moghadam, "Against Eurocentrism and Nativism," *Socialism and Democracy*, fall/winter (1989: 81–104); Moghadam, *Gender, Development, and Policy: Toward Equity and Empowerment*, UNU/WIDER Research for Action series, November (1990).

living beings. Far from requiring technical metaphysics for its articulation, this is a very natural way to view things, and is in fact a very common daily-life view, in both Western and non-Western traditions. We did not make the stars, the earth, the trees: they are what they are there outside of us, waiting to be known. And our activities of knowing do not change what they are.

On such a view, the way the human being essentially and universally is will be part of the independent furniture of the universe, something that can in principle be seen and studied independently of any experience of human life and human history. Frequently it is held that a god or gods have this sort of knowledge, and perhaps some wise humans also. This knowledge is usually understood to have normative force. The heavenly account of who we are constrains what we may legitimately seek to be.[1] It is this conception of inquiry into the nature of the human that the Marglins are attacking in their critique of what they call Western *episteme*. They clearly believe it to be a necessary prop to any ethical universalism.

The common objection to this sort of realism is that such extra-historical and extra-experiential metaphysical truths are not in fact available. Sometimes this is put sceptically: the independent structure may still be there, but we cannot reliably grasp it. More often, today, doubt is cast on the coherence of the whole realist idea that there is some one determinate structure to the way things are, independent of all human interpretation. This is the objection that non-philosophers tend to associate with Jacques Derrida's assault on the "metaphysics of presence,"[2] which he takes to have dominated the entirety of the Western philosophical tradition, and with Richard Rorty's closely related assault on the idea that the knowing mind is, at its best, a "mirror of nature."[3] But it actually has a far longer and more complicated history, even within Western philosophy, beginning at least as early as Kant's assault on transcendent metaphysics, and perhaps far earlier, in some of Aristotle's

criticisms of Platonism.[4] A similar debate was long familiar in classical Indian philosophy, and no doubt it has figured in other philosophical traditions as well.[5] Contemporary arguments about realism are many and complex, involving, frequently, technical issues in the philosophy of science and the philosophy of language.

The debate about realism appears to be far from over. The central issues continue to be debated with vigour and subtlety, and a wide range of views is currently on the table. On the other hand, the attack on realism has been sufficiently deep and sufficiently sustained that it would appear strategically wise for an ethical and political view that seeks broad support not to rely on the truth of metaphysical realism, if it can defend itself in some other way. If, then, all universalist and humanist conceptions in ethics are required to regard the universal conception of the human being as part of the independent furniture of the world, unmediated by human self-interpretation and human history, such conceptions do appear to be in some difficulty, and there may well be good reasons to try to do without them.

But universalism does not require such support.[6] For universal ideas of the human do arise within history and

---

1   *The heavenly account ... seek to be*   For an account of this sort of normative argument, see Alasdair MacIntyre, *After Virtue* (Notre Dame, Ind.: Notre Dame University Press, 1989).

2   *metaphysics of presence*   J. Derrida, *Of Grammatology*, trans. G. Spivak (Baltimore: The Johns Hopkins University Press, 1976). The term is meant to suggest the idea that reality is simply "there" and that knowledge consists in being "present" to it, without any interfering barrier or mediation.

3   *"mirror of nature"*   R. Rorty, *Philosophy and the Mirror of Nature* (Princeton, NJ: Princeton University Press, 1979).

4   *Aristotle's criticisms of Platonism*   See, for example, G.E.L. Owen, *"Tithenai ta Phainomena,"* in *Logic, Science, and Dialectic* (London: Duckworth, 1986), and M. Nussbaum, *The Fragility of Goodness: Luck and Ethics in Greek Tragedy and Philosophy* (Cambridge: Cambridge University Press, 1986). See also Hilary Putnam, *Aristotle After Wittgenstein*, Lindlay Lecture, University of Kansas, 1991.

5   *A similar debate ... other philosophical traditions as well*   See the illuminating discussion in B.K. Matilal, *Perception* (Oxford: Clarendon Press, 1985). It is worth noting that this fundamental work is not cited anywhere in Marglin and Marglin, although Matilal was present at the conference and delivered a paper critical of the Marglins' characterization of Indian traditions. This paper was dropped from the volume. Matilal also described the implications of the realism debate for Indian ethical thought: see "Ethical Relativism and the Confrontation of Cultures," in Krausz (ed.), *Relativism* (Notre Dame, Ind.: Notre Dame University Press, 1989), pp. 339–62.

6   *But universalism does not require such support*   There is a longer version of my criticism of contemporary attacks on universalism in "Human Functioning." See also "Skepticism About Practical Reason in Literature and the Law," *Harvard Law Review* 107 (1994), pp. 714–44. In both of these papers I study the surprising convergence between "left" and "right" in the critique of normative argument, the "postmodern" positions of many thinkers on the left proving, often, difficult to distinguish from claims about the arbitrariness of evaluation in neoclassical economics. In Barbara Herrnstein Smith's *Contingencies of Value* (Durham: Duke University Press, 1988), we even see a fusion of the two positions,

from human experience, and they can ground themselves in experience. Indeed, if, as the critics of realism allege, we are always dealing with our own interpretations anyhow, they must acknowledge that universal conceptions of the human are prominent and pervasive among such interpretations, hardly to be relegated to the dustbin of metaphysical history along with rare and recondite philosophical entities such as the Platonic forms. As Aristotle so simply puts it, 'One may observe in one's travels to distant countries the feelings of recognition and affiliation that link every human being to every other human being.'[1] Or, as Kwame Anthony Appiah eloquently tells the story of his bicultural childhood, a child who visits one set of grandparents in Ghana and another in rural England, who has a Lebanese uncle and who later, as an adult, has nieces and nephews from more than seven different nations, comes to notice not unbridgeable alien "otherness," but a great deal of human commonality, and comes to see the world as a "network of points of affinity."[2] Pursuing those affinities, one may accept the conclusions of the critics of realism, while still believing that a universal conception of the human being is both available to ethics and a valuable starting point. I shall be proposing a version of such an account, attempting to identify a group of especially central and basic human functions that ground these affinities.

But such an experiential and historical universalism[3] is still vulnerable to some, if not all, of the objections standardly brought against universalism. I therefore need to introduce those objections, and later to test my account against them.

2.1. Neglect of Historical and Cultural Differences

The opposition charges that any attempt to pick out some elements of human life as more fundamental than others, even without appeal to a transhistorical reality, is bound to be insufficiently respectful of actual historical and cultural differences. People, it is claimed, understand human life and humanness in widely different ways: and any attempt to produce a list of the most fundamental properties and functions of human beings is bound to enshrine certain understandings of the human and to demote others. Usually, the objector continues, this takes the form of enshrining the understanding of a dominant group at the expense of minority understandings. This type of objection is frequently made by feminists, and can claim support from many historical examples, in which the human has indeed been defined by focusing on the characteristics of males, as manifested in the definer's culture.

It is far from clear what this objection shows. In particular it is far from clear that it supports the idea that we ought to base our ethical norms, instead, on the current preferences and the self-conceptions of people who are living what the objector herself claims to be lives of deprivation and oppression.[4] But it does show at least that the project of

---

a postmodernism concluding that, in the absence of transcendent standards, we should understand value judgements as attempts to maximize expected utility.

1   *One may observe ... every other human being*   Aristotle, *Nicomachean Ethics* VIII.I, 1155a 21–2. I discuss this passage in "Aristotle on Human Nature" and "Non-Relative Virtues."

2   *Or, as Kwame Anthony Appiah ... points of affinity*   K.A. Appiah, *In My Father's House*, pp. vii–viii: "If my sisters and I were 'children of two worlds,' no one bothered to tell us this; we lived in one world, in two 'extended' families divided by several thousand miles and an allegedly insuperable cultural distance that never, so far as I can recall, puzzled or perplexed us much." Appiah's argument does not in any sense neglect distinctive features of concrete histories; indeed, one of its purposes is to demonstrate how varied, when concretely seen, histories really are. But his argument, like mine, seeks a subtle balance between perception of the particular and recognition of the common. In his essay "The Postcolonial and the Postmodern" (137–57), Appiah shows that it is all too often the focus on "otherness" that produces a lack of concrete engagement with individual lives. Speaking of the sculpture "Yoruba Man with Bicycle" that appears on the cover of the book, Appiah comments: "The *Man with a Bicycle* is produced by someone who does not care that the bicycle is the white man's invention—it is not there to be Other to the Yoruba Self; it is there because someone cared for its solidity; it is there because it will take us further than our feet will take us ..." (157).

3   *But such an experiential and historical universalism*   In this category, as closely related to my own view, I would place the "internal–realist" conception of Hilary Putnam articulated in *Reason, Truth, and History* (Cambridge: Cambridge University Press, 1981), *The Many Faces of Realism* (La Salle: Open Court Publishing, 1987), and *Realism With a Human Face* (Cambridge, MA: Harvard University Press, 1990); and also the views of Charles Taylor, for example in *Sources of the Self: The Making of Modern Identity* (Cambridge, Mass.: Harvard University Press, 1989), and "Explanation and Practical Reason," in Nussbaum and Sen (eds.), *The Quality of Life*, pp. 208–31.

4   *deprivation and oppression*   In this sense I am thoroughly in agreement with Susan Okin's reply to the charge of "substitutionalism" that has been made against her book, and in agreement with both Okin and Ruth Anna Putnam that it is a mistake to conceive of the moral point of view as constituted by the actual voices of all disadvantaged parties, see Okin's and Putnam's papers in *Woman, Culture and Development*. See my further comments below, Section 5.

choosing one picture of the human over another is fraught with difficulty, political as well as philosophical.

2.2. Neglect of Autonomy

A different objection is presented by liberal opponents of universalism; my relativist opponents, the Marglins, endorse it as well. (Many such objectors, though not, I believe, the Marglins, are themselves willing to give a universal account of the human in at least some ways, holding freedom of choice to be everywhere of central importance.) The objection is that by determining in advance what elements of human life have most importance, the universalist project fails to respect the right of people to choose a plan of life according to their own lights, determining what is central and what is not.[1] This way of proceeding is "imperialistic." Such evaluative choices must be left to each citizen. For this reason, politics must refuse itself a determinate theory of the human being and the human good.

2.3. Prejudicial Application

If we operate with a determinate conception of the human being that is meant to have some normative moral and political force, we must also, in applying it, ask which beings we shall take to fall under the concept. And here the objector notes that, all too easily—even if the conception itself is equitably and comprehensively designed—the powerless can be excluded. Aristotle himself, it is pointed out, held that women and slaves were not full-fledged human beings; and since his politics were based on his view of human functioning, the failure of these beings (in his view) to exhibit the desired mode of functioning contributed to their political exclusion and oppression.

It is, once again, hard to know what this objection is supposed to show. In particular, it is hard to know how, if at all, it is supposed to show that we would be better off without such determinate universal concepts. For it could be plausibly argued that it would have been even easier to exclude women and slaves on a whim if one did not have such a concept to contend with. Indeed, this is what I shall

be arguing.[2] On the other hand, it does show that we need to think not only about getting the concept right but also about getting the right beings admitted under the concept.

Each of these objections has some merit. Many universal conceptions of the human being have been insular in an arrogant way, and neglectful of differences among cultures and ways of life. Some have been neglectful of choice and autonomy. And many have been prejudicially applied. But none of this shows that all such conceptions must fail in one or more of these ways. But at this point I need to advance a definite example of such a conception, in order both to display its merits and to argue that it can in fact answer these charges.

3. A Conception of the Human Being: The Central Human Capabilities

Here, then, is a sketch for an account of the most important functions and capabilities of the human being in terms of which human life is defined. The basic idea is that we ask ourselves, "What are the characteristic activities[3] of the human being? What does the human being do, characteristically, as such—and not, say, as a member of a particular group, or a particular local community?" To put it another way, what are the forms of activity, of doing and being, that constitute the human form of life and distinguish it from other actual or imaginable forms of life, such as the lives of animals and plants, or, on the other hand, of immortal gods as imagined in myths and legends (which frequently have precisely the function of delimiting the human[4])?

...

---

1   *The objection ... what is central and what is not*   Can the Marglins consistently make this objection while holding that freedom of choice is just a parochial Western value? It would appear not; on the other hand, F.A. Marglin (here differing, I believe, from S.A. Marglin) also held in oral remarks delivered at the 1986 conference that logical consistency is simply a parochial Western value.

2   *Indeed, this is what I shall be arguing*   The politics of the history of Western philosophy have been interpreted this way, with much plausibility though perhaps insufficient historical argumentation, by Noam Chomsky, in *Cartesian Linguistics* (New York: Harper & Row, 1966). Chomsky argues that Cartesian rationalism, with its insistence on innate essences, was politically more progressive, more hostile to slavery and imperialism, than empiricism, with its insistence that people were just what experience had made of them. My analysis of Stoic feminist argument (below Section 7) bears this out.

3   *characteristic activities*   The use of this term does not imply that the functions all involve doing something especially "active." (See here Sen, "Capability and Well-Being," in *The Quality of Life*, pp. 30–53.) In Aristotelian terms, and in mine, being healthy, reflecting, being pleased, are all "activities."

4   *To put it in another way ... delimiting the human*   For further discussion of this point, and examples, see "Aristotle on Human Nature."

3.1. Level One of the Conception of the Human Being: The Shape of the Human Form of Life

3.1.1. Mortality All human beings face death and, after a certain age, know that they face it. This fact shapes more or less every other element of human life. Moreover, all human beings have an aversion to death. Although in many circumstances death will be preferred to the available alternatives, the death of a loved one, or the prospect of one's own death, is an occasion for grief and/or fear. If we encountered an immortal anthropomorphic being, or a mortal being who showed no aversion to death and no tendency at all to avoid death, we would judge, in both of these cases, that the form of life was so different from our own that the being could not be acknowledged as human.

3.1.2. The Human Body We live all our lives in bodies of a certain sort, whose possibilities and vulnerabilities do not as such belong to one human society rather than another. These bodies, similar far more than dissimilar (given the enormous range of possibilities) are our homes, so to speak, opening certain options and denying others, giving us certain needs and also certain possibilities for excellence. The fact that any given human being might have lived anywhere and belonged to any culture is a great part of what grounds our mutual recognitions; this fact, in turn, has a great deal to do with the general humanness of the body, its great distinctness from other bodies. The experience of the body is culturally shaped, to be sure; the importance we ascribe to its various functions is also culturally shaped. But the body itself, not culturally variant in its nutritional and other related requirements, sets limits on what can be experienced and valued, ensuring a great deal of overlap.

There is much disagreement, of course, about how much of human experience is rooted in the body. Here religion and metaphysics enter the picture in a non-trivial way. Therefore, in keeping with the non-metaphysical character of the list, I shall include at this point only those features that would be agreed to be bodily even by determined dualists. The more controversial features, such as thinking, perceiving, and emotion, I shall discuss separately, taking no stand on the question of dualism.

1. *Hunger and thirst: the need for food and drink.* All human beings need food and drink in order to live; all have comparable, though varying, nutritional requirements. Being in one culture rather than another does not make one metabolize food differently. Furthermore, all human beings have appetites that are indices of need. Appetitive experience is to some extent culturally shaped; but we are not surprised to discover much similarity and overlap. Moreover, human beings in general do not wish to be hungry or thirsty (though of course they might choose to fast for some reason). If we discovered someone who really did not experience hunger and thirst at all, or, experiencing them, really did not care about eating and drinking, we would judge that this creature was (in Aristotle's words) "far from being a human being."

2. *Need for shelter.* A recurrent theme in myths of humanness is the nakedness of the human being, its relative unprotectedness in the animal world, its susceptibility to heat, cold, and the ravages of the elements. Stories that explore the difference between our needs and those of furry or scaly or otherwise protected creatures remind us how far our life is constituted by the need to find protection through clothing and housing.

3. *Sexual Desire.* Though less urgent as a need than the needs for food, drink, and shelter (in the sense that one can live without its satisfaction) sexual need and desire are features of more or less every human life, at least beyond a certain age. It is, and has all along been, a most important basis for the recognition of others different from ourselves as human beings.

4. *Mobility.* Human beings are, as the old definition goes, featherless bipeds—that is, creatures whose form of life is in part constituted by the ability to move from place to place in a certain characteristic way, not only through the aid of tools that they have made, but with their very own bodies. Human beings like moving about, and dislike being deprived of mobility. An anthropomorphic being who, without disability, chose never to move from birth to death would be hard to view as human.

3.1.3. Capacity for Pleasure and Pain Experiences of pain and pleasure are common to all human life (though, once again, both their expression and, to some extent, the experience itself may be culturally shaped). Moreover, the aversion to pain as a fundamental evil is a primitive and, it appears, unlearned part of being a human animal. A society whose members altogether lacked that aversion would surely be judged to be beyond the bounds of humanness.

3.1.4. Cognitive Capability: Perceiving, Imagining, Thinking All human beings have sense-perception, the ability to imagine, and the ability to think, making distinctions and "reaching out for understanding." And these abilities are regarded as of central importance. It is an open question what sorts of accidents or impediments to individuals in these areas will be sufficient for us to judge that the life in question is not really human any longer. But it is safe to say that if we imagine a group of beings whose members totally lack sense-perception, or totally lack imagination, or totally lack reasoning and thinking, we are not in any of these cases imagining a group of human beings, no matter what they look like.

3.1.5. *Early Infant Development* All human beings begin as hungry babies, aware of their own helplessness, experiencing their alternating closeness to and distance from that, and those, on whom they depend. This common structure to early life[1]—which is clearly shaped in many different ways by different social arrangements—gives rise to a great deal of overlapping experience that is central in the formation of desires, and of complex emotions such as grief, love, and anger. This, in turn, is a major source of our ability to recognize ourselves in the emotional experiences of those whose lives are very different in other respects from our own. If we encountered a group of apparent humans and then discovered that they never had been babies and had never, in consequence, had those experiences of extreme dependency, need, and affection, we would, I think, have to conclude that their form of life was sufficiently different from our own that they could not be considered part of the same kind.

3.1.6. *Practical Reason* All human beings participate (or try to) in the planning and managing of their own lives, asking and answering questions about what is good and how one should live. Moreover, they wish to enact their thought in their lives—to be able to choose and evaluate, and to function accordingly. This general capability has many concrete forms, and is related in complex ways to the other capabilities, emotional, imaginative, and intellectual. But a being who altogether lacks this would not be likely to be regarded as fully human, in any society.

3.1.7. *Affiliation With Other Human Beings* All human beings recognize and feel some sense of affiliation and concern for other human beings. Moreover, we value the form of life

that is constituted by these recognitions and affiliations. We live with and in relation to others, and regard a life not lived in affiliation with others to be a life not worth the living. (Here I would really wish, with Aristotle, to spell things out further. We define ourselves in terms of at least two types of affiliation: intimate family and/or personal relations, and social or civic relations.)

3.1.8. *Relatedness to Other Species and to Nature* Human beings recognize that they are not the only living things in their world: that they are animals living alongside other animals, and also alongside plants, in a universe that, as a complex interlocking order, both supports and limits them. We are dependent upon that order in countless ways; and we also sense that we owe that order some respect and concern, however much we may differ about exactly what we owe, to whom, and on what basis. Again, a creature who treated animals exactly like stones and could not be brought to see any difference would probably be regarded as too strange to be human. So too would a creature who did not in any way respond to the natural world.

3.1.9. *Humour and Play* Human life, wherever it is lived, makes room for recreation and laughter. The forms play takes are enormously varied—and yet we recognize other humans, across cultural barriers, as the animals who laugh. Laughter and play are frequently among the deepest and also the first modes of our mutual recognition. Inability to play or laugh is taken, correctly, as a sign of deep disturbance in a child; if it proves permanent we will doubt whether the child is capable of leading a fully human life. An entire society that lacked this ability would seem to us both terribly strange and terribly frightening.

3.1.10. *Separateness* However much we live with and for others, we are, each of us, "one in number,"[2] proceeding on a separate path through the world from birth to death. Each person feels only his or her own pain and not anyone else's. Each person dies without entailing logically the death of anyone else. When one person walks across the room, no other person follows automatically. When we count the number of human beings in a room, we have no difficulty figuring out where one begins and the other ends. These obvious facts need stating, since they might have been

---

1   *This common structure to early life*   I discuss this issue in much more detail in Lecture 3 of my 1993 Gifford Lectures, University of Edinburgh, *Upheavals of Thought: The Intelligence of Emotions* (Cambridge: Cambridge University Press, 2001).

2   *one in number* Aristotle, ubiquitously in the accounts of substance.

otherwise. We should bear them in mind when we hear talk about the absence of individualism in certain societies. Even the most intense forms of human interaction, for example sexual experience, are experiences of responsiveness, not of fusion. If fusion is made the goal, the result is bound to be disappointment.

3.1.11. Strong Separateness Because of separateness, each human life has, so to speak, its own peculiar context and surroundings—objects, places, a history, particular friendships, locations, sexual ties—that are not exactly the same as those of anyone else, and in terms of which the person to some extent identifies herself. Though societies vary a great deal in the degree and type of strong separateness that they permit and foster, there is no life yet known that really does (as Plato wished) fail to use the words "mine" and "not mine" in some personal and non-shared way. What I use, live in, respond to, I use, live in, respond to from my own separate existence. And on the whole, human beings recognize one another as beings who wish to have at least some separateness of context, a little space to move around in, some special items to use or love.

This is a working list. It is put out to generate debate. It has done so and will continue to do so, and it will be revised accordingly.

As I have said, the list is composed of two different sorts of items; limits and capabilities. As far as capabilities go, to call them parts of humanness is to make a very basic sort of evaluation. It is to say that a life without this item would be too lacking, too impoverished, to be human at all. Obviously, then, it could not be a good human life. So this list of capabilities is a ground-floor or minimal conception of the good. (In the sense that it does not fully determine the choice of a way of life, but simply regulates the parameters of what can be chosen, it plays, however, the role traditionally played in liberal political theory by a conception of the right[1].)

With the limits, things are more complicated. In selecting the limits for attention, we have, once again, made a basic sort of evaluation, saying that these things are so important that life would not be human without them. But what we have said is that human life, in its general form, consists of the awareness of these limits plus a struggle against them. Humans do not wish to be hungry, to feel pain, to die. (Separateness is highly complex, both a limit

and a capability. Much the same is true of many of the limits implied by the shape and the capacities of the body.) On the other hand, we cannot assume that the correct evaluative conclusion to draw is that we should try as hard as possible to get rid of the limit altogether. It is characteristic of human life to prefer recurrent hunger plus eating to a life with neither hunger nor eating; to prefer sexual desire and its satisfaction to a life with neither desire nor satisfaction. Even where death is concerned, the desire for immortality, which many human beings certainly have, is a peculiar desire: for it is not clear that the wish to lose one's finitude completely is a desire that one can coherently entertain for oneself or for someone one loves. It seems to be a wish for a transition to a way of life so wholly different, with such different values and ends, that it seems that the identity of the individual will not be preserved. So the evaluative conclusion, in mapping out a ground-floor conception of the good (saying what functioning is necessary for a life to be human) will have to be expressed with much caution, clearly, in terms of what would be a humanly good way of countering the limitation.

4. *The Two Thresholds*

Things now get very complicated. For we want to describe two distinct thresholds: a threshold of capability to function beneath which a life will be so impoverished that it will not be human at all; and a somewhat higher threshold, beneath which those characteristic functions are available in such a reduced way that, though we may judge the form of life a human one, we will not think it a *good* human life. The latter threshold is the one that will eventually concern us when we turn to public policy: for we don't want societies to make their citizens capable of the bare minimum. My view holds, with Aristotle, that a good political arrangement is one "in accordance with which anyone whatsoever might do well and live a flourishing life."[2]

These are clearly, in many areas, two distinct thresholds, requiring distinct levels of resource and opportunity. One may be alive without being well nourished. As Marx observed, one may be able to use one's senses without being able to use them in a fully human way. And yet there is need for caution here. For in many cases the move from human life to good human life is supplied by the citizen's own pow-

---

1 *(In the sense ... conception of the right)*   On these issues, see further in "Aristotelian Social Democracy."

2 *in accordance ... a flourishing life*   Aristotle, *Politics* VII.I: see "Nature, Function, and Capability."

ers of choice and self-definition, in such a way that once society places them above the first threshold, moving above the second is more or less up to them. This is especially likely to be so, I think, in areas such as affiliation and practical reasoning, where in many cases once social institutions permit a child to cross the first threshold its own choices will be central in raising it above the second. (This is not always so, however: for certain social conditions, for example certain mindless forms of labour or, we may add, traditional hierarchical gender relations, may impede the flourishing of affiliation and practical reason, while not stamping it out entirely.) On the other hand, it is clear that where bodily health and nutrition, for example, are concerned, there is a considerable difference between the two thresholds, and a difference that is standardly made by resources over which individuals do not have full control. It would then be the concern of quality-of-life assessment to ask whether all citizens are capable, not just of the bare minimum, but of *good life* in these areas. Clearly there is a continuum here. Nor will it in practise be at all easy to say where the upper threshold, especially, should be located.

I shall not say much about the first threshold, but shall illustrate it by a few examples. What is an existence that is so impoverished that it cannot properly be called a human life? Here we should count, I believe, many forms of existence that take place at the end of a human life—all those in which the being that survives has irretrievably lost sensation and consciousness (in what is called a 'permanent vegetative condition'); and also, I would hold, some that fall short of this, but in which the capacity to recognize loved ones, to think and to reason, has irreversibly decayed beyond a certain point. I would include the extreme absence of ability to engage in practical reasoning that is often the outcome of the notorious frontal lobotomy. I would also include an absence of mobility so severe that it makes speech, as well as movement from place to place, impossible.

It follows from this that certain severely damaged infants are not human ever, even if born from two human parents: again, those with global and total sensory incapacity and/or no consciousness or thought; also, I think, those with no ability at all to recognize or relate to others. (This of course tells us nothing about what we owe them morally, it just separates that question from moral questions about human beings[1].)

Again, we notice the evaluative character of these threshold judgements. The fact that a person who has lost her arms cannot play a piano does not make us judge that she no longer lives a human life; had she lost the capacity to think and remember, or to form affectionate relationships, it would have been a different matter.

Many such disasters are not to be blamed on social arrangements, and in those cases the first threshold has no political implications. But many are, where bad nutrition and health care enter in. The role of society is even more evident if we think of a more controversial group of first-threshold cases, in which the non-human outcome was environmentally caused: the rare cases of children who have grown up outside a human community, or in a severely dysfunctional home, and utterly lack language and reason, or lack social abilities in an extreme and irreversible way. We can focus the political question more productively, however, if we now turn from the question of mere human life to the question of good life, the level we would really like to see a human being attain.

Here, as the next level of the conception of the human being, I shall now specify certain basic functional capabilities at which societies should aim for their citizens, and which quality of life measurements should measure. In other words, this will be an account of the second threshold—although in some areas it may coincide, for the reasons I have given, with the first: once one is capable of human functioning in this area one is also capable, with some further effort and care, of good functioning. I introduce this list as a list of capabilities to function, rather than of actual functionings, since I shall argue that capability, not actual functioning, should be the goal of public policy.

---

1 *(This of course ... human beings)* It may support what James Rachels calls "moral individualism" (*Created From Animals* [Oxford and New York: Oxford University Press, 1990]), in which our moral obligations flow from the endowments of the individual creature with whom we are dealing, rather than from its species, and our goal should be to promote—or at least not to impede—the form of flourishing of which the being is basically capable. On this view such an infant should get the same treatment that we would give to an animal of similar endowment. But we may also decide to give the fact that it is an offspring of humans some moral weight; nothing I have said here rules that out.

4.1. Level 2 of the Conception of the Human Being: Basic Human Functional Capabilities

1. Being able to live to the end of a human life of normal length,[1] not dying prematurely, or before one's life is so reduced as to be not worth living.

2. Being able to have good health; to be adequately nourished;[2] to have adequate shelter;[3] having opportunities for sexual satisfaction, and for choice in matters of reproduction;[4] being able to move from place to place.

3. Being able to avoid unnecessary and non-beneficial pain, so far as possible, and to have pleasurable experiences.

4. Being able to use the senses; being able to imagine, to think, and to reason—and to do these things in a way informed and cultivated by an adequate education, including, but by no means limited to, literacy and basic mathematical and scientific training.[5] Being able to use imagination and thought in connection with experiencing and producing spiritually enriching materials and events of one's own choice; religious, literary, musical, and so forth. I believe that the protection of this capability requires not only the provision of education, but also legal guarantees of freedom of expression with respect to both political and artistic speech, and of freedom of religious exercise.

5. Being able to have attachments to things and persons outside ourselves; to love those who love and care for us, to grieve at their absence; in general, to love, to grieve, to experience longing and gratitude.[6] Supporting this capabil-

---

1   *Being able to live ... normal length*   Although "normal length" is clearly relative to current human possibilities, and may need, for practical purposes, to be to some extent relativized to local conditions, it seems important to think of it—at least at a given time in history—in universal and comparative terms, as the *Human Development Report* does, to give rise to complaint in a country that has done well with some indicators of life quality, but badly on life expectancy. And although some degree of relativity may be put down to the differential genetic possibilities of different groups (the "missing women" statistics, for example, allow that on the average women live somewhat longer than men), it is also important not to conclude prematurely that inequalities between groups—for example, the growing inequalities in life expectancy between blacks and whites in the USA—are simply genetic variation, not connected with social injustice.

2   *adequately nourished*   The precise specification of these health rights is not easy, but the work currently being done on them in drafting new constitutions in South Africa and Eastern Europe gives reason for hope that the combination of a general specification of such a right with a tradition of judicial interpretation will yield something practicable. It should be noticed that I speak of health, not just health care: and health itself interacts in complex ways with housing, with education, with dignity. Both health and nutrition are controversial as to whether the relevant level should be specified universally, or relatively to the local community and its traditions: for example, is low height associated with nutritional practices to be thought of as "stunting," or as felicitous adaptation to circumstances of scarcity? For an excellent summary of this debate, see S.R. Osmani (ed.), *Nutrition and Poverty*, WIDER series (Oxford: Clarendon Press, 1990), especially the following papers: on the relativist side, T.N. Srinivasan, "Undernutrition: Concepts, Measurements, and Policy Implications," 97–120; on the universalist side, C. Gopalan, "Undernutrition: Measurement and Implications," 17–48; for a compelling adjudication of the debate, coming out on the universalist side, see Osmani, "On Some Controversies in the Measurement of Undernutrition," 121–61.

3   *shelter*   There is a growing literature on the importance of shelter for health: e.g., that the provision of adequate housing is the single largest determinant of health status for HIV infected persons. Housing rights are increasingly coming to be constitutionalized, at least in a negative form—giving squatters grounds for appeal, for example, against a landlord who would bulldoze their shanties. On this as a constitutional right, see proposed Articles 11, 12, and 17 of the South African Constitution, in a draft put forward by the ANC committee, advisor Albie Sachs, where this is given as an example of a justifiable housing right.

4   *matters of reproduction*   I shall not elaborate here on what I think promoting this capability requires, since there is a future volume in the WIDER series devoted to this topic: J. Glover, M. Nussbaum, and C. Sunstein (eds.), *Women, Equality, and Reproduction*.

5   *basic mathematical and scientific training*   A good example of an education right that I would support is given in the ANC South African Constitution draft, Article 11: "Education shall be free and compulsory up to the age of sixteen, and provision shall be made for facilitating access to secondary, vocational, and tertiary education on an equal basis for all. Education shall be directed towards the development of the human personality and a sense of personal dignity, and shall aim at strengthening respect for human rights and fundamental freedoms and promoting understanding, tolerance, and friendship amongst South Africans and between nations." The public (or otherwise need-blind) provision of higher education will have to be relative to local possibilities, but it is at least clear that the USA lags far behind most other countries of comparable wealth in this area.

6   *in general, to love ... experience longing and gratitude*   On the emotions as basic human capabilities, see, in addition to my other chapter in *Woman, Culture, and Development* my 1993 Gifford Lectures, *Upheavals of Thought: A Theory of the Emotions* (Cambridge: Cambridge University Press, 2001). My omission of anger from this list of basic emotional capabilities reveals an ambivalence about its role that I discuss at length, both in Gifford Lectures 3 and 10, and in *The Therapy of Desire: Theory and Practice in Hellenistic Ethics* (Princeton, NJ: Princeton University Press, 1994)

ity means supporting forms of human association that can be shown to be crucial in their development.[1]

6. Being able to form a conception of the good and to engage in critical reflection about the planning of one's own life. This includes, today, being able to seek employment outside the home and to participate in political life.

7. Being able to live for and to others, to recognize and show concern for other human beings, to engage in various forms of social interaction; to be able to imagine the situation of another and to have compassion for that situation; to have the capability for both justice and friendship. Protecting this capability means, once again, protecting institutions that constitute such forms of affiliation, and also protecting the freedoms of assembly and political speech.

8. Being able to live with concern for and in relation to animals, plants, and the world of nature.

9. Being able to laugh, to play, to enjoy recreational activities.

10. Being able to live one's own life and nobody else's. This means having certain guarantees of non-interference with certain choices that are especially personal and definitive of selfhood, such as choices regarding marriage, childbearing, sexual expression, speech, and employment.

10a. Being able to live one's own life in one's own surroundings and context. This means guarantees of freedom of association and of freedom from unwarranted search and seizure; it also means a certain sort of guarantee of the integrity of personal property, though this guarantee may be limited in various ways by the demands of social equality, and is always up for negotiation in connection with the interpretation of the other capabilities, since personal property, unlike personal liberty, is a tool of human functioning rather than an end in itself.

My claim is that a life that lacks any one of these capabilities, no matter what else it has, will fall short of being a good human life. So it would be reasonable to take these

things as a focus for concern, in assessing the quality of life in a country and asking about the role of public policy in meeting human needs. The list is certainly general—and this is deliberate, in order to leave room for plural specification and also for further negotiation. But I claim that it does, rather like a set of constitutional guarantees, offer real guidance in the ongoing historical process of further refinement and specification, and far more accurate guidance than that offered by the focus on utility, or even on resources.

A few comments are in order about the relationship of this version of the list to other versions I have published previously. First, taking some lessons from the *Human Development Report*, it is considerably more specific about matters such as education and work, so as to give the development theorist something concrete to measure. Secondly, it is far more explicitly concerned with guarantees of personal liberty of expression, reproductive choice, and religion.[2] This was not only called for in general, but called forth by the attempt to articulate the specific requisites of equal female capability.[3] Thirdly, in accordance with its commitment to the distinction between ends and means, it understands "property rights" as instrumental to other human capabilities,[4] and therefore to a certain extent, as up for negotiation in general social planning.

The list is, emphatically, a list of separate components. We cannot satisfy the need for one of them by giving a larger amount of another. All are of central importance and all are distinct in quality. This limits the trade-offs that it will be reasonable to make, and thus limits the applicability of quantitative cost-benefit analysis. At the same time, the items on the list are related to one another in many complex ways. For example our characteristic mode of nutrition, unlike that of sponges, requires moving from here to

---

chs. 7, 11, and 12. See also "Equity and Mercy," *Philosophy and Public Affairs*, spring 1993.

1   *Supporting this capability ... crucial in their development*   In my 1993 Gifford Lectures, I spell out what I think this entails where "the family" is concerned. On the whole, I am in agreement with Susan Okin that some form of intimate family love is of crucial importance in child development, but that this need not be the traditional Western nuclear family. I also agree with Okin that the important educational role of the family makes it all the more crucial that the family should be an institution characterized by justice, as well as love. See Okin, *Justice, Gender, and the Family*.

2   *Secondly, it is far more explicitly concerned ... reproductive choice, and religion*   "Aristotelian Social Democracy" said that a list of such liberties needed to be added to the Aristotelian scheme, but it did not include them in the account of capabilities itself. These issues are further developed in a future WIDER volume on reproductive rights and women's capabilities, based on the papers given at our 1993 conference, and edited by Jonathan Glover and Martha Nussbaum (*Woman, Culture, and Development: A Study of Human Capabilities*, Oxford: Oxford University Press, 1995).

3   *This was not only called for ... requisites of equal female capability*   For reproductive choice as an equality issue, see Sunstein's paper in this volume, and also his "Gender, Reproduction, and Law," in Glover and Nussbaum.

4   *other human capabilities*   On this see also "Aristotelian Social Democracy."

there. And we do whatever we do as separate beings, tracing distinct paths through space and time. Notice that reproductive choices involve both sexual capability and issues of separateness, and bind the two together in a deep and complex way.

A further comment is in order, concerning the relationship of this threshold list to an account of human equality. A commitment to bringing all human beings across a certain threshold of capability to choose represents a certain sort of commitment to equality: for the view treats all persons as equal bearers of human claims, no matter where they are starting from in terms of circumstances, special talents, wealth, gender, or race. On the other hand, I have said nothing so far about how one should regard inequalities that persist once the threshold level has been attained for all persons. To some extent I feel this would be premature, since the threshold level has so rarely been attained for the complete capability set. On the other hand, one can imagine a situation—perhaps it could be that of the USA or Japan, given certain large changes in health support here, or educational distribution there, that would meet threshold conditions and still exhibit inequalities of attainment between the genders or the races. We have two choices here: either to argue that this situation actually contains capability failure after all; or to grant that the capability view needs to be supplemented by an independent theory of equality. I am not yet certain what I want to say about this, but I am inclined to the first alternative, since I think that gender inequality of the sort one sees in a prosperous nation does none the less push the subordinated racial or gender group beneath an acceptable threshold of autonomy, dignity, and emotional well being. Indeed, subordination is itself a kind of capability failure, a failure to attain complete personhood. So I am inclined to say that, properly fleshed out, the second threshold would be incompatible with systematic subordination of one group to another.

5. The Role of the Conception in Development Policy

My claim is that we urgently need a conception of the human being and human functioning in public policy. If we try to do without this sort of guidance when we ask how goods, resources, and opportunities should be distributed, we reject guidance that is, I think, superior to that offered by any of the other guides currently available.

I shall focus here on the area of most concern to our project: the assessment of the quality of life in a developing country, with special attention to the lives of women. For the time being, I shall take the nation state as my basic unit, and the question I shall ask is, "How is the nation doing, with respect to the quality of life of its citizens?" In other words, I shall be asking the sort of question asked by the UN *Human Development Report*. I shall not propose a general theory about how the needs revealed by such an assessment should be met: whether by centralized government planning, for example, or through a system of incentives, and whether through direct subsidies or through the provision of opportunities for employment. Nor shall I ask what responsibilities richer nations have to poorer nations, in ensuring that the needs of all human beings are met the world over. That is an urgent question, and it must at a later date be confronted. For now, however, I shall focus on the correct understanding of the goal, where each separate nation is concerned.

The basic claim I wish to make—concurring with Amartya Sen—is that the central goal of public planning should be the *capabilities* of citizens to perform various important functions. The questions that should be asked when assessing quality of life in a country are (and of course this is a central part of assessing the quality of its political arrangements) "How well have the people of the country been enabled to perform the central human functions?" and, "Have they been put in a position of mere human subsistence with respect to the functions, or have they been enabled to live well?" In other words, we ask where the people are, with respect to the second list. And we focus on getting as many people as possible above the second threshold, with respect to the interlocking set of capabilities enumerated by that list.[1] Naturally, the determination of whether certain individuals and groups are across the threshold is only as precise a matter as the determination of the threshold; and I have left things deliberately somewhat open-ended at this point, in keeping with the procedures of the *Human Development Report*, believing that the best way to work toward a more precise determination is to allow the community of nations

---

1   *And we focus ... enumerated by that list*   With Sen, I hold that the capability set should be treated as an interlocking whole: for my comments on his arguments, see "Nature, Function, and Capability." Tensions will frequently arise among members of the list, and I shall comment on some of those below. But it should be clear by now that the architectonic role of practical reasoning imposes strict limits on the sort of curb on personal autonomy that will be tolerated for the sake of increased nutritional well-being, etc.

to hammer it out after an extended comparative inquiry, of the sort the report makes possible. Again, we will have to answer various questions about the costs we are willing to pay to get all citizens above the threshold, as opposed to leaving a small number below and allowing the rest a considerably above-threshold life quality. Here my claim is that capability-equality, in the sense of moving all above the threshold, should be taken as the central goal. As with Rawls's Difference Principle, so here: inequalities in distribution above the threshold should be tolerated only if they move more people across it;[1] once all are across, societies are to a great extent free to choose the other goals that they wish to pursue.

The basic intuition from which the capability approach starts, in the political arena, is that human capabilities exert a moral claim that they should be developed. Human beings are creatures such that, provided with the right educational and material support, they can become fully capable of the major human functions, can cross the first and second thresholds. That is, they are creatures with certain lower-level capabilities (which I have elsewhere called 'basic capabilities'[2]) to perform the functions in question. When these capabilities are deprived of the nourishment that would transform them into the high-level capabilities that figure on my list, they are fruitless, cut off, in some way but a shadow of themselves. They are like actors who never get to go on the stage, or a musical score that is never performed. Their very being makes forward reference to functioning. Thus if functioning never arrives on the scene they are hardly even what they are. This may sound like a metaphysical idea, and in a sense it is (in that it is an idea discussed in Aristotle's *Metaphysics*). But that does not mean that it is not a basic and pervasive empirical idea, an idea that underwrites many of our daily practises and judgements in many times and places. I claim that just as we hold that a child who dies before getting to maturity has died especially tragically—for her activities of growth and preparation for adult activity now have lost their point—so too with capability and functioning more generally: we believe that certain basic and central human endowments have a claim to be assisted in developing, and exert that claim on others, and especially, as Aristotle saw, on government. We shall see the work this consideration can do in arguments for women's equality. I think it is the underlying basis, in the Western philosophical tradition, for many notions of human rights. I suggest, then, that in thinking of political planning we begin from this notion, thinking of the basic capabilities of human beings as needs for functioning, which give rise to correlated political duties.

There is, then, an empirical basis for the determination that a certain being is one of the ones to which our normative conception and its associated duties applies. It is the gap between potential humanness and its full realization that exerts a moral claim. If the worker described by Marx as not capable of a truly human use of his senses[3] had really been a non-human animal, the fact that he was given a form of life suited to such an animal would not be a tragedy. If women were really turtles, the fact that being a woman is not yet a way of being a human being would not be, as it is, an outrage. There is, of course, enormous potential for abuse in determining who has these basic capabilities. The history of IQ testing is just one chapter in an inglorious saga of prejudiced capability-testing that goes back at least to the Noble Lie of Plato's Republic. Therefore we should, I think, proceed as if every offspring of two human parents has the basic capabilities, unless and until long experience with the individual has convinced us that damage to that individual's condition is so great that it could never in any way arrive at the higher capability level.

The political and economic application of this approach is evident in a variety of areas. Amartya Sen has developed

---

1   *As with Rawls's Difference Principle ... more people across it*   Chris Bobonich, "Internal Realism, Human Nature, and Distributive Justice: A Response to Martha Nussbaum," *Modern Philology*, May 1993 supplement, pp. 74–92, worries that this will impose enormous sacrifices. But I think that this is because he has not imagined things in detail, nor thought about my claim that once people have what they basically need, they can get all sorts of other good things through their own efforts. If I have enough food to be well-nourished, more food will just rot on the shelf or make me fat. If my basic health needs are met, it seems right that I should not be able to claim expensive unnecessary luxuries (say, cosmetic surgery) at the public expense so long as even one person in my country is without support for basic needs. And so forth. One must take seriously the Aristotelian idea, which is basic to both Sen's and my programmes, that resources are just tools for functioning and have a limit given by what is needed for that functioning. Above that limit, they are just a heap of stuff, of no value in themselves.

2   *(which I have elsewhere called 'basic capabilities')*   See "Nature, Function, and Capability," with reference to Aristotle; and below, Section 9.

3   *If the worker ... truly human use of his senses*   Marx, *Economic and Philosophical Manuscripts of 1844*, discussed in "Nature, Function, and Capability" and "Aristotle on Human Nature."

a number of its concrete implications in the areas of welfare and development economics, and has focused particularly on its application to the assessment of women's quality of life.[1] With his advice, the UN *Human Development Reports* have begun to gather information and to rank nations in accordance with the type of plural-valued capability-focused measuring the approach suggests. In a closely related study, Iftekhar Hossein has used the approach to give an account of poverty as capability failure.[2] Independently, a very similar approach has been developed by Finnish and Swedish social scientists, above all Erik Allardt and Robert Erikson.[3] Wishing to develop ways of gathering information about how their people are doing that would be more sensitive and informationally complete than polls based on ideas of utility, they worked out lists of the basic human capabilities for functioning, and then examined the performance of various groups in the population—above all women and minorities—in these terms, thus anticipating the procedures of the *Human Development Report*, which devotes a great deal of attention to gender differences, urban-rural differences, and so forth.

The "capabilities approach" has clear advantages over other current approaches to quality of life assessment. Assessment that uses GNP per capita as its sole measure fails to concern itself with the distribution of resources, and thus can give high marks to countries with enormous inequalities. Nor does this approach examine other human goods that are not reliably correlated with the presence of resources: infant mortality, for example, or access to education, or the quality of racial and gender relations, or the presence or absence of political freedoms. The *Human Development Report* for 1993 informs us, for example, that the United Arab Emirates has Real GNP per capita of $16,753—tenth highest in the world, higher, for example, than Norway or Australia—while overall, in the aggregation of all the indicators of life quality, it ranks only sixty-seventh in the world

(out of 173 nations measured). Its adult literacy rate is 55%, far lower than any of the 66 countries generally ahead of it, and also than many generally below it. (Both Norway and Australia have adult literacy of 99%.) The maternal mortality rate of 130 per 100,000 live births is comparatively high. The proportion of women progressing beyond secondary education is very low, and only 6% of the labour force is female (as opposed, for example, to 42% in Seychelles, 35% in Brazil, 43% in China, 47% in Viet Nam, 26% in India, and 20% in Nigeria). In fact, in all the world only Algeria (4%) has a lower proportion of females in the labour force, only Iraq (6%) ties it, and only Qatar (7%), Saudi Arabia (7%), Libya (9%), Jordan (10%), Pakistan (11%), Bangladesh (7%) and Afghanistan (8%) come close. Evidence links female wage-earning outside the home strongly to female health care and life-expectancy.[4] And in fact, we find that the ratio of females to males in the United Arab Emirates is the amazing 48:100, lowest in all the world. If this is discounted as employment related, we may pursue the other countries in our low external employment comparison class. The ratio of females to males in nations in which there is no reason to suppose sexual discrimination in nourishment and health care is, Sen has shown, about 106:100 in Europe and North America—or, if we focus only on the developing world, taking sub-Saharan Africa as our "norm," 102:100. In Qatar it is 60:100, in Saudi Arabia 84, in Libya 91, in Jordan 95, in Pakistan 92, in Bangladesh 94, in Afghanistan 94.

These are some of the numbers that we start noticing if we focus on capabilities and functioning, rather than simply on GNP. They are essential to the understanding of how women are doing. In fact, they are the numbers from which Sen's graphic statistics regarding "missing women" emerge. (The number of "missing women" is the number of extra women who would be in a given country if that country had the same sex ratio as sub-Saharan Africa.) They strongly support Martha Chen's argument that the right to work is a right basic to the lives of women not only in itself, but for its impact on other basic capabilities and functionings. Saleha Begum's employment led to better nutritional and health status for herself and, indeed, her children and family. Metha Bai may soon become one of the statistics from which the number of missing women is made.

Would other available approaches have done the job as well? The common approach that measures quality of life in

---

1   *Amartya Sen ... women's quality of life*   See especially Sen's paper in *Women, Culture, and Development*; also "More than a Million Women are Missing," *New York Review of Books* 37 (1990) 61–66.

2   *Iftekhar Hossein ... poverty as capability failure*   Iftekhar Hossein, "Poverty as Capability Failure," Ph.D. Dissertation in Economics, Helsinki University, 1990.

3   *above all Erik Allardt and Robert Erikson*   See Allardt, "Having, Loving, Being: An Alternative to the Swedish Model of Welfare Research," and Erikson, "Descriptions of Inequality: The Swedish Approach to Welfare Research," in Nussbaum and Sen, *The Quality of Life*, pp. 88–94 and 67–84.

4   *Evidence links ... life-expectancy*   See Sen, "More than a Million Women."

terms of utility—polling people concerning the satisfaction of their preferences—would have missed the obvious fact that desires and subjective preferences are not always reliable indicators of what a person really needs. Preferences, as Amartya Sen's work has repeatedly shown, are highly malleable.[1] The rich and pampered easily become accustomed to their luxury, and view with pain and frustration a life in which they are treated just like everyone else. Males are a special case of this: we do not need to go abroad to know that males frequently resent a situation in which they are asked to share child care and domestic responsibilities on an equal basis.[2] The poor and deprived frequently adjust their expectations and aspirations to the low level of life they have known. Thus they may not demand more education, better health care. Like the women described in Sen's account of health surveys in India, they may not even know what it is to feel healthy.[3] Like the rural Bangladeshi women so vividly described in Martha Chen's *A Quiet Revolution*,[4] they may not even know what it means to have the advantages of education. We may imagine that many women in the countries I have mentioned would not fight, as Seleha Begum did, for participation in the workforce; nor would they be aware of the high correlation between work outside the home and other advantages. As Sen argues, they may have fully internalized the ideas behind the traditional system of discrimination, and may view their deprivation as "natural." Thus if we rely on utility as our measure of life

quality, we most often will get results that support the *status quo* and oppose radical change.[5]

If these criticisms apply to approaches that focus on utility in general, they apply all the more pointedly to the sort of local-tradition relativism espoused by the Marglins, in which the measure of quality of life will be the satisfaction of a certain group of preferences, namely the traditional ones of a given culture. Indeed, it is illuminating to consider how close, in its renunciation of critical normative argument, the Marglin approach is to the prevailing economic approaches of which it presents itself as a radical critique. A preference-based approach that gives priority to the preferences of traditional culture is likely to be especially subversive of the quality of life of women who have been on the whole badly treated by prevailing traditional norms. And one can see this clearly in the Marglins' own examples. For menstruation taboos impose severe restrictions on women's power to form a plan of life and to execute the plan they have chosen. They are members of the same family of traditional attitudes about women and the workplace that made it difficult for Saleha Begum to support herself and her family, that make it impossible for Metha Bai to sustain the basic functions of life. And the Japanese husband who allegedly renounces freedom of choice actually enhances it, in the ways that matter, by asking the woman to look after the boring details of life. One can sympathize with many of the Marglins' goals—respect for diversity, desire to preserve aspects of traditional life that appear to be rich in spiritual and artistic value—without agreeing that extreme relativism of the sort they endorse is the best way to pursue these concerns.

As for liberal approaches that aim at equality in the distribution of certain basic resources, these have related

1   *Preferences ... highly malleable*   See also Jon Elster, *Sour Grapes* (Cambridge: Cambridge University Press, 1983); Cass R. Sunstein, "Preferences and Politics," *Philosophy and Public Affairs*, 20 (1991), pp. 3–34.

2   *we do not need ... equal basis*   Päivi Setälä, Professor of Women's Studies at the University of Helsinki, informs me that recent studies show that even in Finland, only 40% of the housework is done by males. This, in the second nation in the world (after New Zealand, in 1906) to give females the vote, a nation as committed to sex equality as any in the world. We can assume that the situation is causally related to male preferences.

3   *Like the women ... feel healthy*   On the disparity between externally observed health status and self-reports of satisfaction about health, see Sen, *Commodities and Capabilities* (Amsterdam: North-Holland, 1985).

4   *Like the rural Bangladeshi women ... A Quiet Revolution*   Martha Chen, *A Quiet Revolution: Women in Transition in Rural Bangladesh* (Cambridge, Mass.: Schenkman, 1983). I describe this account of a rural women's literacy project, and its large-scale impact on women's quality of life, in "Non-Relative Virtues," "Aristotelian Social Democracy," and "Human Functioning and Social Justice."

5   *Thus if we rely on utility ... oppose radical change*   This is a criticism of economic utilitarianism, not of sophisticated philosophical forms of utilitarianism that build in means to filter or correct preferences. Nonetheless, the human-functioning approach would still object to the role played by the commensurability of values in utilitarianism, and to the related suggestion that for any two distinct ends we can, without loss of what is relevant for choice, imagine trade-offs in purely quantitative terms. Furthermore, most forms of utilitarianism are committed to aggregating utilities across lives, and thus to neglecting separateness, which I have defended as fundamental. I have addressed some of these questions elsewhere, for example, in "The Discernment of Perception" in *Love's Knowledge*, and in "The Literary Imagination in Public Life," *New Literary History* (fall 1993). Sen's work has addressed them in greater detail. I therefore leave them to one side for the purposes of the present inquiry.

problems, since these, too, refuse to take a stand on the ends to which the resources are means.[1] Wealth and income are not good in their own right; they are good only insofar as they promote human functioning. Secondly, human beings have widely varying needs for resources, and any adequate definition of who is "better off" and "worse off" must reflect that fact.[2] Women who have traditionally not been educated, for example, may well require more of the relevant resources to attain the same capability level: that is why, in the case discussed by Martha Chen, the Bangladesh Rural Advancement Committee created a special female literacy programme, rather than a programme that distributed equal resources to all. Thirdly, by defining being "well-off" in terms of possessions alone, the liberal fails to go deep enough in imagining the impediments to functioning that are actually present in many lives—in their conditions of labour or exclusion from labour, for example, in their frequently unequal family responsibilities, in the obstacles to self-realization imposed by traditional norms and values.[3] The stories of Saleha Begum and Metha Bai are vivid examples of such unequal obstacles. No right-to-work effort, and no expenditure of resources in that connection, were necessary in order to make men capable of working in the fields in Bangladesh. No male of Metha Bai's caste would have to overcome threats of physical violence in order to go out of the house to work for life-sustaining food.

---

1   *As for liberal approaches ... resources are means*   For a detailed consideration of these approaches, see "Aristotelian Social Democracy," "Human Functioning," with references to related arguments of Sen. "Aristotelian Social Democracy" contains a detailed account of the relationship between Rawls's resourcism and my project, which is a particularly subtle one. Rawls is willing to take a stand on certain items: thus liberty and the social conditions of self-respect figure on his list of "primary goods," as well as wealth and income. On the other hand, he has repeatedly denied that his index of primary goods could, or should, be replaced by an index of functionings as in the *Human Development Report*.

2   *Secondly, human beings ... reflect that fact*   This is the central point repeatedly made by Sen against Rawls; for an overview, see "Capability and Well-Being" in *The Quality of Life*, with references.

3   *in their conditions ... traditional norms and values*   In Rawls's liberalism the problem is even more acute, since the parties who are either well or not well off are "heads of households," usually taken to be male, who are alleged to deliberate on behalf of the interests of their family members. But women cannot in fact rely on the altruism of males to guarantee their economic security, or even survival. In addition to Sen's work on this issue, see Susan Moller Okin, *Justice, Gender, and the Family*. In my review of Okin, I offer this as a reason for Okin to be more critical of resource-based liberalism than she is.

6. Answering the Objections: Human Functioning and Pluralism

I have commended the human-function view by contrast to its rivals on the development scene. But I must now try to show how it can answer the objections I described earlier.

Concerning *neglect of historical and cultural difference*, I can begin by insisting that this normative conception of human capability and functioning is general, and in a sense vague, for precisely this reason. The list claims to have identified in a very general way components that are fundamental to any human life. But it allows in its very design for the possibility of multiple specifications of each of the components. This is so in several different ways. First, the constitutive circumstances of human life, while broadly shared, are themselves realized in different forms in different societies. The fear of death, the love of play, relationships of friendship and affiliation with others, even the experience of the bodily appetites never turn up in simply the vague and general form in which we have introduced them here, but always in some specific and historically rich cultural realization, which can profoundly shape not only the conceptions used by the citizens in these areas, but also their experiences themselves. Nonetheless, we do have in these areas of our common humanity sufficient overlap to sustain a general conversation, focusing on our common problems and prospects. And sometimes the common conversation will permit us to criticize some conceptions of the grounding experiences themselves, as at odds with other things human beings want to do and to be.

When we are choosing a conception of good functioning with respect to these circumstances, we can expect an even greater degree of plurality to become evident. Here the approach wants to retain plurality in two significantly different ways: what I may call the way of *plural specification*, and what I may call the way of *local specification*.

Plural specification means what its name implies. Public policy, while using a determinate conception of the good at a high level of generality, leaves a great deal of latitude for citizens to specify each of the components more concretely, and with much variety, in accordance with local traditions, or individual tastes. Many concrete forms of life, in many different places and circumstances, display functioning in accordance with all the major capabilities.

As for local specification: good public reasoning, I believe and have argued, is always done, when well done, with a rich sensitivity to the concrete context, to the characters of the agents and their social situation. This means that in addition to the pluralism I have just described, the Aristotelian needs to consider a different sort of plural specification of the good. For sometimes what is a good way of promoting education in one part of the world will be completely ineffectual in another. Forms of affiliation that flourish in one community may prove impossible to sustain in another. In such cases, the Aristotelian must aim at some concrete specification of the general list that suits, and develops out of, the local conditions. This will always most reasonably be done in a participatory dialogue[1] with those who are most deeply immersed in those conditions. For though Aristotelianism does not hesitate to criticize tradition where tradition perpetrates injustice or oppression, it also does not believe in saying anything at all without rich and full information, gathered not so much from detached study as from the voices of those who live the ways of life in question. Martha Chen's work, both here and in her book, gives an excellent example of how such sensitivity to the local may be combined with a conviction that the central values on the list are worth pursuing even when tradition has not endorsed them.

The liberal charges the capability approach with *neglect of autonomy*, arguing that any such determinate conception removes from the citizens the chance to make their own choices about the good life. This is a complicated issue: three points can be stressed. First, the list is a list of capabilities, not a list of actual functions, precisely because the conception is designed to leave room for choice. Government is not directed to push citizens into acting in certain valued ways; instead, it is directed to make sure that all human beings have the necessary resources and conditions for acting in those ways. It leaves the choice up to them. A person with plenty of food can always choose to fast. A person who has been given the capability for sexual expression can always choose celibacy. The person who has access to subsidized education can always decide to do something else instead. By making opportunities available, government enhances, and does not remove, choice.[2] It will not always be easy to say at what point someone is really capable of making a choice, especially in areas where there are severe traditional obstacles to functioning. Sometimes our best strategy may well be to look at actual functioning and infer negative capability (tentatively) from its absence.[3] But the conceptual distinction remains very important.

Secondly, this respect for choice is built deeply into the list itself, in the architectonic role it gives to practical reasoning. One of the most central capabilities promoted by the conception will be the capability of choice itself.[4] We should note that the major liberal view in this area (that of John Rawls) agrees with our approach in just this area. For Rawls insists that satisfactions that are not the outgrowth of one's very own choices have no moral worth; and he conceives of the two moral powers (analogous to our practical reasoning), and of sociability (corresponding to our affiliation) as built into the definition of the parties in the original position, and thus as necessary constraints on any outcome they will select.[5]

Finally, the capability view insists that choice is not pure spontaneity, flourishing independent of material and social conditions. If one cares about autonomy, then one must care about the rest of the form of life that supports it, and the material conditions that enable one to live that form of life. Thus the approach claims that its own comprehensive concern with flourishing across all areas of life is a better way of promoting choice than is the liberal's narrower concern with spontaneity alone, which sometimes tolerates situations in which individuals are in other ways cut off from the fully human use of their faculties.

I turn now to the objection about application; it raises especially delicate questions where women are concerned.

---

1   *participatory dialogue*   Martha Chen and her fellow development workers, in the project described in *A Quiet Revolution*, were indebted in their practice to Paolo Freire's notion of "participatory dialogue."

2   *By making opportunities ... choice*   Sen has stressed this throughout his writing on the topic. For an overview, see "Capability and Well-Being."

3   *Sometimes our best strategy ... from its absence*   This is the strategy used by Erikson's Swedish team, when studying inequalities in political participation: see "Descriptions of Inequality." The point was well made by Bernard Williams in his response to Sen's Tanner Lectures: see Williams, "The Standard of Living: Interests and Capabilities," in G. Hawthorn (ed.), *The Standard of Living* (Cambridge: Cambridge University Press, 1987). To give just one example of the issue, we will need to ask to what extent laws regulating abortion, sodomy laws, the absence of civil rights laws, etc., restrict the capability for sexual expression of women and homosexuals in a given society. The gay American military officer who chooses celibacy for fear of losing his job has not, in the relevant sense, been given a capability of choosing.

4   *One of the most central capabilities ... choice itself*   See also Sen, *Commodities and Capabilities*.

5   *For Rawls insists ... they will select*   The relevant textual references are gathered and discussed in "Aristotelian Social Democracy."

7. Who Gets Included? Women as Human Beings

In a now well-known remark, which I cite here as an epigraph, the feminist lawyer Catharine MacKinnon claimed that 'being a woman is not yet a way of being a human being.'[1] This means, I think, that most traditional ways of categorizing and valuing women have not accorded them full membership in the human species, as that species is generally defined. MacKinnon is no doubt thinking in particular of the frequent denials to women of the rational nature that is taken to be a central part of what it is to be human. It is sobering to remind oneself that quite a few leading philosophers, including Aristotle and Rousseau, the "fathers" (certainly not mothers) of my idea, did deny women full membership in human functioning as they understood that notion. If this is so, one might well ask, of what use is it really to identify a set of central human capabilities? For the basic (lower-level) capacity to develop these can always be denied to women, even by those who grant their centrality. Does this problem show that the human function idea is either hopelessly in league with patriarchy or, at best, impotent as a tool for justice?

I believe that it does not. For if we examine the history of these denials we see, I believe, the great power of the conception of the human as a source of moral claims. Acknowledging the other person as a member of the very same kind would have generated a sense of affiliation and a set of moral and educational duties. That is why, to those bent on shoring up their own power, the stratagem of splitting the other off from one's own species seems so urgent and so seductive. But to deny humanness to beings with whom one lives in conversation and interaction is a fragile sort of self-deceptive stratagem, vulnerable to sustained and consistent reflection, and also to experiences that cut through self-deceptive rationalization.[2] Any moral conception can be withheld, out of ambition or hatred or shame. But the conception of the human being, spelled out, as here, in a roughly determinate way, in terms of circumstances of life and functions in these circumstances, seems much harder to withhold than other conceptions that have been made the basis for ethics—"rational being," for example, or (as I have suggested) "person."

To illustrate this point, I now turn to the earliest argument known to me in the Western philosophical tradition that uses a conception of the human being for feminist ends. It is not the first feminist argument in the Western tradition: for Plato's *Republic* precedes (and influences) it.[3] But Plato's argument in favour of equal education for women is heavily qualified by his elitism with respect to all functions for all human beings; thus it is able to generate only elitist conclusions for males and females alike. Platonic justice is not the "humanist justice" of Susan Okin's powerful phrase. The argument I have in mind is, instead, the first argument of the Roman Stoic thinker Musonius Rufus in his brief treatise, "That Women Too Should Do Philosophy," written in the first century AD.[4] This argument is all the more interesting in that it, in effect, uses Aristotelian concepts to correct Aristotle's mistake about women—showing, I think, that an Aristotelian who is both internally consistent and honest about the evidence cannot avoid the egalitarian normative conclusion that women, as much as men, should receive a higher education (for that is in effect what is meant by doing philosophy[5]).

---

1   *being a woman ... human being*   The remark was cited by Richard Rorty in "Feminism and Pragmatism," *Michigan Quarterly Review*, 30 (1989), p. 231; it has since been confirmed and repeated by MacKinnon herself.

2   *But to deny humanness ... self-deceptive rationalization*   See n. 37 above on Raoul Hilberg's account, in *The Destruction of the European Jews*, of the Nazi device of categorizing Jews as animals or inanimate objects, and the vulnerability of that stratagem to "breakthroughs," in which the mechanisms of denial were caught off guard.

3   *for Plato's Republic precedes (and influences) it*   The most comprehensive and incisive account of Plato's arguments about women is now in Stephen Halliwell, *Plato: Republic* Book V (Warminster: Aris and Phillips, 1992), Introduction and commentary to the relevant passages. See also Okin, *Women in Western Political Thought*.

4   *The argument I have in mind ... first century AD*   For Musonius's collected works see the edition by O. Hense (Leipzig: Teubner Library, 1905). Other works with radical conclusions for women's issues include "Should Boys and Girls Have the Same Education?" (answering yes to that question); "Should One Raise all the Children Who are Born?" (arguing against infanticide, a particular threat to female offspring); "On the Goal of Marriage" (arguing against the sexual double standard and in favour of equal sexual fidelity for both sexes; arguing as well against the common view that female slaves were available for sexual use).

5   *showing, I think, that an Aristotelian ... doing philosophy*   Stoics are of course highly critical of much that passes for higher education, holding that the traditional "liberal studies" are not "liberal" in the right way, that is, do not truly "free" the mind to take charge of its own reasoning. See Seneca, *Moral Epistle* 88.

The argument has a tacit premise. It is that—at least with respect to certain central functions of the human being—the presence in a creature of a basic (untrained, lower-level) capability to perform the functions in question, given suitable support and education, exerts a claim on society that those capabilities should be developed to the point at which the person is fully capable of choosing the functions in question. This premise needed no argument in the philosophical culture of Greco-Roman antiquity, since that moral claim is more or less taken to be implicit in the notion of capability itself. I have tried to give it intuitive support in the argument of this paper.

The argument itself now follows with a truly radical simplicity. Its second premise consists of an appeal to the experience of the imaginary recalcitrant male interlocutor. Women, he is asked to concede on the basis of experience, do in fact have the basic capabilities to perform a wide variety of the most important human functions. They have the five senses. They have the same number of bodily parts, implying similar functional possibilities in that sphere. They have the ability to think and reason, just as males do. And, finally, they have responsiveness to ethical distinctions, making (whether well or badly) distinctions between the good and the bad. Some time is then spent establishing a third premise: that "higher education" of the sort offered by the Stoic ideal of liberal education, is necessary for the full development of the perceptual, intellectual, and moral capabilities. Conclusion: women, like men, should have this education.

The puzzle, for us, is the second premise. Why does the interlocutor accept it? We see from the surrounding material that the interlocutor is a husband who interacts with his wife in a number of areas of life that are explicitly enumerated: planning and managing a household (where she is the one who manages most of the daily business); having and raising children (where he observes, or imagines, her in labour, enduring risk and pain for the sake of the family and, later, caring for and educating the child); having sexual relations with him, and refusing to have sex with others; having a real friendship with him, based on common contemporary ideas of 'sharing life together';[1] deciding how to treat the people around her; being fair, for example, to the household staff; and, finally, confronting all the dangers and the moral ambiguities of the politics of first century AD Rome—refusing to capitulate, he says, to the unjust demands of a tyrant. In all of these operations of life, the argument seems to be, he tacitly acknowledges, in fact strongly relies upon, his wife's capability to engage in practical reasoning and ethical distinction making. Indeed, he is depicted as someone who would like these things done *well*—for he wants his wife not to reason badly when political life gets tough, or to treat the servants with cruelty, or to botch the education of the children. So in his daily life he acknowledges her humanity, her possession of the basic (lower-level) capabilities for fully human functioning. How, then, Musonius reasonably asks him, can he consistently deny her what would be necessary in order to develop and fulfil that humanity?

This, I believe, is an impressively radical argument. And it led to (or reflected) a social situation that marked a high point for women in the Western tradition for thousands of years since and to come.[2] We do not need to show that the views of Musonius on women were perfect in all respects; in many ways they were not. But his argument shows, I believe, the power of a universal conception of the human being in claims of justice for women. For the interlocutor might have refused to acknowledge that his wife was a 'person': it was to some extent up to him to define that rather refined and elusive concept. He could not fail to acknowledge that she was a human being, with the basic capability for the functions in question. For he had acknowledged that already, in his daily life.

...

♦ ♦ ♦ ♦ ♦

---

1 *sharing life together* See Musonius, "On the Goal of Marriage." Similar conceptions are defended by Seneca and Plutarch. On this shift in thinking about the marital relationship, see the useful discussion in Foucault, *History of Sexuality*, vol. III, trans. R. Hurley (New York: Pantheon, 1985).

2 On the way in which Christianity disrupted the emerging feminist consensus, see G.E. M. de Ste. Croix, *The Class Struggle in the Ancient Greek World* (London: Duckworth, 1987).

Beyond "Compassion and Humanity": *Justice for Nonhuman Animals* (2004)

by Martha Nussbaum and Cass Sunstein

Certainly it is wrong to be cruel to animals.... The capacity for feelings of pleasure and pain and for the forms of life of which animals are capable clearly impose duties of compassion and humanity in their case. I shall not attempt to explain these considered beliefs. They are outside the scope of the theory of justice, and it does not seem possible to extend the contract doctrine so as to include them in a natural way.

—John Rawls, *A Theory of Justice*

In conclusion, we hold that circus animals... are housed in cramped cages, subjected to fear, hunger, pain, not to mention the undignified way of life they have to live, with no respite and the impugned notification has been issued in conformity with the...values of human life, [and] philosophy of the Constitution.... Though not homosapiens [*sic*], they are also beings entitled to dignified existence and humane treatment sans cruelty and torture.... Therefore, it is not only our fundamental duty to show compassion to our animal friends, but also to recognize and protect their rights.... If humans are entitled to fundamental rights, why not animals?

—*Nair v. Union of India*, Kerala High Court, June 2000

"Beings Entitled to Dignified Existence"

In 55 BCE the Roman leader Pompey staged a combat between humans and elephants. Surrounded in the arena, the animals perceived that they had no hope of escape. According to Pliny, they then "entreated the crowd, trying to win their compassion with indescribable gestures, bewailing their plight with a sort of lamentation." The audience, moved to pity and anger by their plight, rose to curse Pom-

pey, feeling, writes Cicero, that the elephants had a relation of commonality (*societas*) with the human race.[1]

We humans share a world and its scarce resources with other intelligent creatures. These creatures are capable of dignified existence, as the Kerala High Court says. It is difficult to know precisely what we mean by that phrase, but it is rather clear what it does not mean: the conditions of the circus animals in the case, squeezed into cramped, filthy cages, starved, terrorized, and beaten, given only the minimal care that would make them presentable in the ring the following day. The fact that humans act in ways that deny animals a dignified existence appears to be an issue of justice, and an urgent one, although we shall have to say more to those who would deny this claim. There is no obvious reason why notions of basic justice, entitlement, and law cannot be extended across the species barrier, as the Indian court boldly does.

Before we can perform this extension with any hope of success, however, we need to get clear about what theoretical approach is likely to prove most adequate. I shall argue that the capabilities approach as I have developed it— an approach to issues of basic justice and entitlement and to the making of fundamental political principles[2]—provides better theoretical guidance in this area than that supplied by contractarian and utilitarian approaches to the question of animal entitlements, because it is capable of recognizing a wide range of types of animal dignity, and of corresponding needs for flourishing.

Kantian Contractarianism: Indirect Duties, Duties of Compassion

Kant's own view about animals is very unpromising. He argues that all duties to animals are merely indirect duties

---

1   *The audience ... the human race*   [Unless otherwise indicated, all notes to this selection are by the author.] The incident is discussed in Pliny *Nat. Hist.* 8.7.20–21, Cicero *Ad Fam.* 7.1.3; see also Dio Cassius *Hist.* 39, 38, 2–4. See the discussion in Richard Sorabji, *Animal Minds and Human Morals: The Origins of the western Debate* (Ithaca, N.Y.: Cornell University Press, 1993), pp. 124–25.

2   *an approach ... political principles*   For this approach, see Martha C. Nussbaum, *Women and Human Development* (Cambridge: Cambridge University Press, 2000), and "Capabilities as Fundamental Entitlements: Sen and Social Justice," *Feminist Economics* 9 (2003): 33–59. The approach was pioneered by Amartya Sen within economics, and is used by him in some rather different ways, without a definite commitment to a normative theory of justice.

to humanity, in that (as he believes) cruel or kind treatment of animals strengthens tendencies to behave in similar fashion to humans. Thus he rests the case for decent treatment of animals on a fragile empirical claim about psychology. He cannot conceive that beings who (in his view) lack self-consciousness and the capacity for moral reciprocity could possibly be objects of moral duty. More generally, he cannot see that such a being can have dignity, an intrinsic worth.

One may, however, be a contractarian—and indeed, in some sense a Kantian—without espousing these narrow views. John Rawls insists that we have direct moral duties to animals, which he calls "duties of compassion and humanity."[1] But for Rawls these are not issues of justice, and he is explicit that the contract doctrine cannot be extended to deal with these issues, because animals lack those properties of human beings "in virtue of which they are to be treated in accordance with the principles of justice" (*TJ* 504). Only moral persons, defined with reference to the "two moral powers," are subjects of justice.

To some extent, Rawls is led to this conclusion by his Kantian conception of the person, which places great emphasis on rationality and the capacity for moral choice. But it is likely that the very structure of his contractarianism would require such a conclusion, even in the absence of that heavy commitment to rationality. The whole idea of a bargain or contract involving both humans and nonhuman animals is fantastic, suggesting no clear scenario that would assist our thinking. Although Rawls's Original Position, like the state of nature in earlier contractarian theories,[2] is not supposed to be an actual historical situation, it is supposed to be a coherent fiction that can help us think well. This means that it has to have realism, at least, concerning the powers and needs of the parties and their basic circumstances. There is no comparable fiction about our decision to make a deal with other animals that would be similarly coherent and helpful. Although we share a world of scarce resources with animals, and although there is in a sense a state of rivalry among species that is comparable to the rivalry in the state of nature, the asymmetry of power between humans and nonhuman animals is too great to imagine the bargain as a real bargain. Nor can we imagine that the bargain would

actually be for mutual advantage, for if we want to protect ourselves from the incursions of wild animals, we can just kill them, as we do. Thus, the Rawlsian condition that no one party to the contract is strong enough to dominate or kill all the others is not met. Thus Rawls's omission of animals from the theory of justice is deeply woven into the very idea of grounding principles of justice on a bargain struck for mutual advantage (on fair terms) out of a situation of rough equality.

To put it another way, all contractualist views conflate two questions, which might have been kept distinct: Who frames the principles? And for whom are the principles framed? That is how rationality ends up being a criterion of membership in the moral community: because the procedure imagines that people are choosing principles *for themselves*. But one might imagine things differently, including in the group for whom principles of justice are included many creatures who do not and could not participate in the framing.

We have not yet shown, however, that Rawls's conclusion is wrong. I have said that the cruel and oppressive treatment of animals raises issues of justice, but I have not really defended that claim against the Rawlsian alternative. What exactly does it mean to say that these are issues of justice, rather than issues of "compassion and humanity"? The emotion of compassion involves the thought that another creature is suffering significantly, and is not (or not mostly) to blame for that suffering.[3] It does not involve the thought that someone is to blame for that suffering. One may have compassion for the victim of a crime, but one may also have compassion for someone who is dying from disease (in a situation where that vulnerability to disease is nobody's fault). "Humanity" I take to be a similar idea. So compassion omits the essential element of blame for wrongdoing. That is the first problem. But suppose we add that element, saying that duties of compassion involve the thought that it is *wrong* to cause animals suffering. That is, a duty of compassion would not be just a duty to have compassion, but a duty, as a result of one's compassion, to refrain from acts that cause the suffering that occasions the compassion. I believe that Rawls would make this addition, although he certainly does not tell us what he takes duties of compassion

---

1   *duties of compassion and humanity*   All references are to John Rawls, *A Theory of Justice* (Cambridge, Mass.: Harvard University Press, 1971), hereafter *TJ*.

2   *the state ... contractarian theories*   Rawls himself makes the comparison at *TJ* 12; his analogue to the state of nature is the equality of the parties in the Original Position.

3   *The emotion ... that suffering*   See the analysis in Martha C. Nussbaum, *Upheavals of Thought: The Intelligence of Emotions* (Cambridge: Cambridge University Press, 2001), ch. 6; thus far the analysis is uncontroversial, recapitulating a long tradition of analysis.

to be. What is at stake, further, in the decision to say that the mistreatment of animals is not just morally wrong, but morally wrong in a special way, raising questions of justice?

This is a hard question to answer, since justice is a much-disputed notion, and there are many types of justice, political, ethical, and so forth. But it seems that what we most typically mean when we call a bad act unjust is that the creature injured by that act has an entitlement not to be treated in that way, and an entitlement of a particularly urgent or basic type (since we do not believe that all instances of unkindness, thoughtlessness, and so forth are instances of injustice, even if we do believe that people have a right to be treated kindly, and so on). The sphere of justice is the sphere of basic entitlements. When I say that the mistreatment of animals is unjust, I mean to say not only that it is wrong *of us* to treat them in that way, but also that they have a right, a moral entitlement, not to be treated in that way. It is unfair *to them*. I believe that thinking of animals as active beings who have a good and who are entitled to pursue it naturally leads us to see important damages done to them as unjust. What is lacking in Rawls's account, as in Kant's (though more subtly) is the sense of the animal itself as an agent and a subject, a creature in interaction with whom we live. As we shall see, the capabilities approach does treat animals as agents seeking a flourishing existence; this basic conception, I believe, is one of its greatest strengths.

Utilitarianism and Animal Flourishing

Utilitarianism has contributed more than any other ethical theory to the recognition of animal entitlements. Both Bentham and Mill[1] in their time and Peter Singer[2] in our own have courageously taken the lead in freeing ethical thought from the shackles of a narrow species-centered conception of worth and entitlement. No doubt this achievement was connected with the founders' general radicalism and their skepticism about conventional morality, their willingness to follow the ethical argument wherever it leads. These remain very great virtues in the utilitarian position. Nor does

utilitarianism make the mistake of running together the question "Who receives justice?" with the question "Who frames the principles of justice?" Justice is sought for all sentient beings, many of whom cannot participate in the framing of principles.

Thus it is in a spirit of alliance that those concerned with animal entitlements might address a few criticisms to the utilitarian view. There are some difficulties with the utilitarian view, in both of its forms. As Bernard Williams and Amartya Sen usefully analyze the utilitarian position, it has three independent elements: consequentialism (the right choice is the one that produces the best overall consequences), sum-ranking (the utilities of different people are combined by adding them together to produce a single total), and hedonism, or some other substantive theory of the good (such as preference satisfaction)[3]. Consequentialism by itself causes the fewest difficulties, since one may always adjust the account of well-being, or the good, in consequentialism so as to admit many important things that utilitarians typically do not make salient: plural and heterogeneous goods, the protection of rights, even personal commitments or agent-centered goods. More or less any moral theory can be consequentialized, that is, put in a form where the matters valued by that theory appear in the account of consequences to be produced.[4] Although I do have some doubts about a comprehensive consequentialism as the best basis for political principles in a pluralistic liberal society, I shall not comment on them at present, but shall turn to the more evidently problematic aspects of the utilitarian view.[5]

Let us next consider the utilitarian commitment to aggregation, or what is called "sum-ranking." Views that

---

1 *Bentham and Mill* [editors' note] Jeremy Bentham (1748–1832), English philosopher, legal and social reformer; early advocate of utilitarianism and animal rights. Bentham influenced the moral philosopher and political economist John Stuart Mill (1806–73) on these matters.

2 *Peter Singer* Singer's *Animal Liberation* (1974) is the best-known twentieth-century statement of the case against "speciesism" (a term coined by Singer).

3 *As Bernard Williams ... preference satisfaction* See Amartya Sen and Bernard Williams, introduction to *Utilitarianism and Beyond* (Cambridge: Cambridge University Press, 1982), pp. 3–4.

4 *More or less ... to be produced* See the comment by Nussbaum in *Goodness and Advice*, Judith Jarvis Thomson's Tanner Lectures (Princeton, NJ: Princeton University Press, 2000), discussing work along these lines by Amartya Sen and others.

5 *Although I do ... utilitarian view* Briefly put, my worries are those of Rawls in *Political Liberalism* (New York: Columbia University Press, 1996), who points out that it is illiberal for political principles to contain any comprehensive account of what is best. Instead, political principles should be committed to a partial set of ethical norms endorsed for political purposes, leaving it to citizens to fill out the rest of the ethical picture in accordance with their own comprehensive conceptions of value, religious or secular. Thus I would be happy with a partial political consequentialism, but not with comprehensive consequentialism, as a basis for political principles.

measure principles of justice by the outcome they produce need not simply add all the relevant goods together. They may weight them in other ways. For example, one may insist that each and every person has an indefeasible[1] entitlement to come up above a threshold on certain key goods. In addition, a view may, like Rawls's view, focus particularly on the situation of the least well off, refusing to permit inequalities that do not raise that person's position. These ways of considering well-being insist on treating people as ends: they refuse to allow some people's extremely high well-being to be purchased, so to speak, through other people's disadvantage. Even the welfare of society as a whole does not lead us to violate an individual, as Rawls says.

Utilitarianism notoriously refuses such insistence on the separateness and inviolability of persons. Because it is committed to the sum-ranking of all relevant pleasures and pains (or preference satisfactions and frustrations), it has no way of ruling out in advance results that are extremely harsh toward a given class or group. Slavery, the lifelong subordination of some to others, the extremely cruel treatment of some humans or of nonhuman animals—none of this is ruled out by the theory's core conception of justice, which treats all satisfactions as fungible[2] in a single system. Such results will be ruled out, if at all, by empirical considerations regarding total or average well-being. These questions are notoriously indeterminate (especially when the number of individuals who will be born is also unclear, a point I shall take up later). Even if they were not, it seems that the best reason to be against slavery, torture, and lifelong subordination is a reason of justice, not an empirical calculation of total or average well-being. Moreover, if we focus on preference satisfaction, we must confront the problem of adaptive preferences. For while some ways of treating people badly always cause pain (torture, starvation), there are ways of subordinating people that creep into their very desires, making allies out of the oppressed. Animals too can learn submissive or fear-induced preferences. Martin Seligman's experiments, for example, show that dogs who have been conditioned into a mental state of learned helplessness have immense difficulty learning to initiate voluntary movement, if they can ever do so.[3]

There are also problems inherent in the views of the good most prevalent within utilitarianism: hedonism (Bentham) and preference satisfaction (Singer). Pleasure is a notoriously elusive notion. Is it a single feeling, varying only in intensity and duration, or are the different pleasures as qualitatively distinct as the activities with which they are associated? Mill, following Aristotle, believed the latter, but if we once grant that point, we are looking at a view that is very different from standard utilitarianism, which is firmly wedded to the homogeneity of good.[4]

Such a commitment looks like an especially grave error when we consider basic political principles. For each basic entitlement is its own thing and is not bought off, so to speak, by even a very large amount of another entitlement. Suppose we say to a citizen: We will take away your free speech on Tuesdays between 3 and 4 p.m., but in return, we will give you, every single day, a double amount of basic welfare and health care support. This is just the wrong picture of basic political entitlements. What is being said when we make a certain entitlement basic is that it is important always and for everyone, as a matter of basic justice. The only way to make that point sufficiently clearly is to preserve the qualitative separateness of each element within our list of basic entitlements.

Once we ask the hedonist to admit plural goods, not commensurable on a single quantitative scale, it is natural to ask, further, whether and pain are the only things we ought to be looking at. Even if one thinks of pleasure as closely linked to activity, and not simply as a passive sensation, making it the sole end leaves out much of the value we attach to activities of various types. There seem to be valuable things in an animal's life other than pleasure, such as free movement and physical achievement, and also altruistic sacrifice for kin and group. The grief of an animal for a dead child or parent, or the suffering of a human friend, also seem to be valuable, a sign of attachments that are intrinsically good. There are also bad pleasures, including some of the pleasures of the circus audience—and it is unclear whether such pleasures should even count positively in the social calculus. Some pleasures of animals in harming other animals may also be bad in this way.

Does preference utilitarianism do better? We have already identified some problems, including the problem of misinformed or malicious preferences and that of adaptive

---

1   *indefeasible*   [editors' note] Not defeatable, i.e., an entitlement that cannot be overruled by other considerations.

2   *fungible*   [editors' note] Interchangeable.

3   *Martin Seligman's ... do so*   Martin Seligman, *Helplessness: On Development, Depression, and Death* (New York: Freeman, 1975).

4   *Mill, following ... homogeneity of good*   Here I agree with Thomson (who is thinking mostly about Moore); see *Goodness and Advice*.

(submissive) preferences. Singer's preference utilitarianism, moreover, defining *preference* in terms of conscious awareness, has no room for deprivations that never register in the animal's consciousness. But of course animals raised under bad conditions can't imagine the better way of life they have never known, and so the fact that they are not living a more flourishing life will not figure in their awareness. They may still feel pain, and this the utilitarian can consider. What the view cannot consider is all the deprivation of valuable life activity that they do not feel.

Finally, all utilitarian views are highly vulnerable on the question of numbers. The meat industry brings countless animals into the world who would never have existed but for that. For Singer, these births of new animals are not by themselves a bad thing: Indeed, we can expect new births to add to the total of social utility, from which we would then subtract the pain such animals suffer. It is unclear where this calculation would come out. Apart from this question of indeterminacy, it seems unclear that we should even say that these births of new animals are a good thing, if the animals are brought into the world only as tools of human rapacity.

So utilitarianism has great merits, but also great problems.

Types of Dignity, Types of Flourishing: Extending the Capabilities Approach

The capabilities approach in its current form starts from the notion of human dignity and a life worthy of it. But I shall now argue that it can be extended to provide a more adequate basis for animal entitlements than the two theories under consideration. The basic moral intuition behind the approach concerns the dignity of a form of life that possesses both deep needs and abilities; its basic goal is to address the need for a rich plurality of life activities. With Aristotle and Marx, the approach has insisted that there is waste and tragedy when a living creature has the innate, or "basic," capability for some functions that are evaluated as important and good, but never gets the opportunity to perform those functions. Failures to educate women, failures to provide adequate health care, failures to extend the freedoms of speech and conscience to all citizens—all these are treated as causing a kind of premature death, the death of a form of flourishing that has been judged to be worthy of respect and wonder. The idea that a human being should have a chance to flourish in its own way, provided it does no harm to others, is thus very deep in the account the capabilities approach gives of the justification of basic political entitlements.

The species norm is evaluative, as I have insisted; it does not simply read off norms from the way nature actually is. The difficult questions this valuational exercise raises for the case of nonhuman animals will be discussed in the following section. But once we have judged that a central human power is one of the good ones, one of the ones whose flourishing defines the good of the creature, we have a strong moral reason for promoting its flourishing and removing obstacles to it.

Dignity and Wonder: The Intuitive Starting Point

The same attitude to natural powers that guides the approach in the case of human beings guides it in the case of all forms of life. For there is a more general attitude behind the respect we have for human powers, and it is very different from the type of respect that animates Kantian ethics. For Kant, only humanity and rationality are worthy of respect and wonder; the rest of nature is just a set of tools. The capabilities approach judges instead, with the biologist Aristotle (who criticized his students' disdain for the study of animals), that there is something wonderful and wonder-inspiring in all the complex forms of animal life.

Aristotle's scientific spirit is not the whole of what the capabilities approach embodies, for we need, in addition, an ethical concern that the functions of life not be impeded, that the dignity of living organisms not be violated. And yet, if we feel wonder looking at a complex organism, that wonder at least suggests the idea that it is good for that being to flourish as the kind of thing it is. And this idea is next door to the ethical judgment that it is wrong when the flourishing of a creature is blocked by the harmful agency of another. That more complex idea lies at the heart of the capabilities approach.

So I believe that the capabilities approach is well placed, intuitively, to go beyond both contractarian and utilitarian views. It goes beyond the contractarian view in its starting point, a basic wonder at living beings, and a wish for their flourishing and for a world in which creatures of many types flourish. It goes beyond the intuitive starting point of utilitarianism because it takes an interest not just in pleasure and pain, but in complex forms of life. It wants to see each thing flourish as the sort of thing it is.

By Whom and for Whom? The Purposes of Social Cooperation

For a contractarian, as we have seen, the question "Who makes the laws and principles?" is treated as having, necessarily, the same answer as the question "For whom are the laws and principles made?" That conflation is dictated by the theory's account of the purposes of social cooperation. But there is obviously no reason at all why these two questions should be put together in this way. The capabilities approach, as so far developed for the human case, looks at the world and asks how to arrange that justice be done in it; Justice is among the intrinsic ends that it pursues. Its parties are imagined looking at all the brutality and misery, the goodness and kindness of the world, and trying to think how to make a world in which a core group of very important entitlements, inherent in the notion of human dignity, will be protected. Because they look at the whole of the human world, not just people roughly equal to themselves, they are able to be concerned directly and non-derivatively, as we saw, with the good of the mentally disabled. This feature makes it easy to extend the approach to include human-animal relations.

Let us now begin the extension. The purpose of social cooperation, by analogy and extension, ought to be to live decently together in a world in which many species try to flourish. (Cooperation itself will now assume multiple and complex forms.) The general aim of the capabilities approach in charting political principles to shape the human-animal relationship would be, following the intuitive ideas of the theory, that no animal should be cut off from the chance at a flourishing life and that all animals should enjoy certain positive opportunities to flourish. With due respect for a world that contains many forms of life, we attend with ethical concern to each characteristic type of flourishing and strive that it not be cut off or fruitless.

Such an approach seems superior to contractarianism because it contains direct obligations of justice to animals; it does not make these derivative from or posterior to the duties we have to fellow humans, and it is able to recognize that animals are subjects who have entitlements to flourishing and who thus are subjects of justice, not just objects of compassion. It is superior to utilitarianism because it respects each individual creature, refusing to aggregate the goods of different lives and types of lives. No creature is being used as a means to the ends of others, or of society as a whole. The capabilities approach also refuses to aggregate across the diverse constituents of each life and type of life. Thus, unlike utilitarianism, it can keep in focus the fact that each species has a different form of life and different ends; moreover, within a given species, each life has multiple and heterogeneous ends.

How Comprehensive?

In the human case, the capabilities approach does not operate with a fully comprehensive conception of the good, because of the respect it has for the diverse ways in which people choose to live their lives in a pluralistic society. It aims at securing some core entitlements that are held to be implicit in the idea of a life with dignity, but it aims at capability, not functioning, and it focuses on a small list. In the case of human-animal relations, the need for restraint is even more acute, since animals will not in fact be participating directly in the framing of political principles, and thus they cannot revise them over time should they prove inadequate.

And yet there is a countervailing consideration: Human beings affect animals' opportunities for flourishing pervasively, and it is hard to think of a species that one could simply leave alone to flourish in its own way. The human species dominates the other species in a way that no human individual or nation has ever dominated other humans. Respect for other species' opportunities for flourishing suggests, then, that human law must include robust, positive political commitments to the protection of animals, even though, had human beings not so pervasively interfered with animals' ways of life, the most respectful course might have been simply to leave them alone, living the lives that they make for themselves.

The Species and the Individual

What should the focus of these commitments be? It seems that here, as in the human case, the focus should be the individual creature. The capabilities approach attaches no importance to increased numbers as such; its focus is on the well-being of existing creatures and the harm that is done to them when their powers are blighted.

As for the continuation of species, this would have little moral weight as a consideration of justice (though it might have aesthetic significance or some other sort of ethical significance), if species were just becoming extinct because of factors having nothing to do with human action that affects individual creatures. But species are becoming extinct because human beings are killing their members and damaging their natural environments. Thus, damage to species occurs through damage to individuals, and this individual damage should be the focus of ethical concern within the capabilities approach.

Do Levels of Complexity Matter?

Almost all ethical views of animal entitlements hold that there are morally relevant distinctions among forms of life. Killing a mosquito is not the same sort of thing as killing a chimpanzee. But the question is: What sort of difference is relevant for basic justice? Singer, following Bentham, puts the issue in terms of sentience. Animals of many kinds can suffer bodily pain, and it is always bad to cause pain to a sentient being. If there are nonsentient or barely sentient animals—and it appears that crustaceans, mollusks, sponges, and the other creatures Aristotle called "stationary animals" are such creatures— there is either no harm or only a trivial harm done in killing them. Among the sentient creatures, moreover, there are some who can suffer additional harms through their cognitive capacity: A few animals can foresee and mind their own deaths, and others will have conscious, sentient interests in continuing to live that are frustrated by death. The painless killing of an animal that does not foresee its own death or take a conscious interest in the continuation of its life is, for Singer and Bentham, not bad, for all badness, for them, consists in the frustration of interests, understood as forms of conscious awareness.[1] Singer is not, then, saying that some animals are inherently more worthy of esteem than others. He is simply saying that, if we agree with him that all harms reside in sentience, the creature's form of life limits the conditions under which it can actually suffer harm.

Similarly, James Rachels, whose view does not focus on sentience alone, holds that the level of complexity of a creature affects what can be a harm for it.[2] What is relevant to the harm of pain is sentience; what is relevant to the harm of a specific type of pain is a specific type of sentience (e.g., the ability to imagine one's own death). What is relevant to

the harm of diminished freedom is a capacity for freedom or autonomy. It would make no sense to complain that a worm is being deprived of autonomy, or a rabbit of the right to vote.

What should the capabilities approach say about this issue? It seems to me that it should not follow Aristotle in saying that there is a natural ranking of forms of life, some being intrinsically more worthy of support and wonder than others. That consideration might have evaluative significance of some other kind, but it seems dubious that it should affect questions of basic justice.

Rachels's view offers good guidance here. Because the capabilities approach finds ethical significance in the flourishing of basic (innate) capabilities—those that are evaluated as both good and central (see the section on evaluating animal capabilities)—it will also find harm in the thwarting or blighting of those capabilities. More complex forms of life have more and more complex capabilities to be blighted, so they can suffer more and different types of harm. Level of life is relevant not because it gives different species differential worth per se, but because the type and degree of harm a creature can suffer varies with its form of life.

At the same time, I believe that the capabilities approach should admit the wisdom in utilitarianism. Sentience is not the only thing that matters for basic justice, but it seems plausible to consider sentience a threshold condition for membership in the community of beings who have entitlements based on justice. Thus, killing a sponge does not seem to be a matter of basic justice.

Does the Species Matter?

For the utilitarians, and for Rachels, the species to which a creature belongs has no moral relevance. All that is morally relevant are the capacities of the individual creature: Rachels calls this view "moral individualism." Utilitarian writers are fond of comparing apes to young children and to mentally disabled humans. The capabilities approach, by contrast, with its talk of characteristic functioning and forms of life, seems to attach some significance to species membership as such. What type of significance is this?

We should admit that there is much to be learned from reflection on the continuum of life. Capacities do crisscross and overlap; a chimpanzee may have more capacity for empathy and perspectival thinking than a very young child or an older autistic child. And capacities that humans sometimes arrogantly claim for themselves alone are found very

---

1   *The painless killing ... conscious awareness*   Peter Singer, "Animals and the Value of Life," in *Matters of Life and Death: New Introductory Essays on Moral Philosophy*, Tom Regan, ed. (New York: Random House, 1980), p. 356.

2   *James Rachels ... harm for it*   James Rachels, *Created from Animals: The Moral Implication of Darwinism* (New York: Oxford University Press, 1990).

widely in nature. But it seems wrong to conclude from such facts that species membership is morally and politically irrelevant. A mentally disabled child is actually very different from a chimpanzee, though in certain respects some of her capacities may be comparable. Such a child's life is tragic in a way that the life of a chimpanzee is not tragic: She is cut off from forms of flourishing that, but for the disability, she might have had, disabilities that it is the job of science to prevent or cure, wherever that is possible. There is something blighted and disharmonious in her life, whereas the life of a chimpanzee may be perfectly flourishing. Her social and political functioning is threatened by these disabilities, in a way that the normal functioning of a chimpanzee in the community of chimpanzees is not threatened by its cognitive endowment.

All this is relevant when we consider issues of basic justice. For a child born with Down syndrome, it is crucial that the political culture in which he lives make a big effort to extend to him the fullest benefits of citizenship he can attain, through health benefits, education, and the reeducation of the public culture. That is so because he can only flourish as a human being. He has no option of flourishing as a happy chimpanzee. For a chimpanzee, on the other hand, it seems to me that expensive efforts to teach language, while interesting and revealing, are not matters of basic justice. A chimpanzee flourishes in its own way, communicating with its own community in a perfectly adequate manner that has gone on for ages.

In short, the species norm (duly evaluated) tells us what the appropriate benchmark is for judging whether a given creature has decent opportunities for flourishing.

Evaluating Animal Capabilities: No Nature Worship

In the human case, the capabilities view does not attempt to extract norms directly from some facts about human nature. We should know what we can about the innate capacities of human beings, and this information is valuable, in telling us what our opportunities are and what our dangers might be. But we must begin by evaluating the innate powers of human beings, asking which ones are the good ones, the ones that are central to the notion of a decently flourishing human life, a life with dignity. Thus not only evaluation but also ethical evaluation is put into the approach from the start. Many things that are found in human life are not on the capabilities list.

There is a danger in any theory that alludes to the characteristic flourishing and form of life of a species: the danger of romanticizing nature, or suggesting that things are in order as they are, if only we would stop interfering. This danger looms large when we turn from the human case, where it seems inevitable that we will need to do some moral evaluating, to the animal case, where evaluating is elusive and difficult. Inherent in at least some environmentalist writing is a picture of nature as harmonious and wise, and of humans as wasteful overreachers who would live better were we to get in tune with this fine harmony. This image of nature was already very sensibly attacked by John Stuart Mill in his great essay "Nature," which pointed out that nature, far from being morally normative, is actually violent, heedless of moral norms, prodigal, full of conflict, harsh to humans and animals both. A similar view lies at the heart of much modern ecological thinking, which now stresses the inconstancy and imbalance of nature,[1] arguing, inter alia, that many of the natural ecosystems that we admire as such actually sustain themselves to the extent that they do only on account of various forms of human intervention.

Thus, a no-evaluation view, which extracts norms directly from observation of animals' characteristic ways of life, is probably not going to be a helpful way of promoting the good of animals. Instead, we need a careful evaluation of both "nature" and possible changes. Respect for nature should not and cannot mean just leaving nature as it is, and must involve careful normative arguments about what plausible goals might be.

In the case of humans, the primary area in which the political conception inhibits or fails to foster tendencies that are pervasive in human life is the area of harm to others. Animals, of course, pervasively cause harm, both to members of their own species and, far more often, to members of other species.

In both of these cases, the capabilities theorist will have a strong inclination to say that the harm-causing capabilities in question are not among those that should be protected by political and social principles. But if we leave these capabilities off the list, how can we claim to be promoting flourishing lives? Even though the capabilities approach is not utilitarian and does not hold that all good is in sentience, it will still be difficult to maintain that a

---

1   *much modern ... of nature*   Daniel B. Botkin, "Adjusting Law to Nature's Discordant Harmonies," *Duke Environmental Law and Policy Forum* 7 (1996): 25–37.

creature who feels frustration at the inhibition of its predatory capacities is living a flourishing life. A human being can be expected to learn to flourish without homicide and, let us hope, even without most killing of animals. But a lion who is given no exercise for its predatory capacity appears to suffer greatly.

Here the capabilities view may, however, distinguish two aspects of the capability in question. The capability to kill small animals, defined as such, is not valuable, and political principles can omit it (and even inhibit it in some cases, to be discussed in the following section). But the capability to exercise one's predatory nature so as to avoid the pain of frustration may well have value, if the pain of frustration is considerable. Zoos have learned how to make this distinction. Noticing that they were giving predatory animals insufficient exercise for their predatory capacities, they had to face the question of the harm done to smaller animals by allowing these capabilities to be exercised. Should they give a tiger a tender gazelle to crunch on? The Bronx Zoo has found that it can give the tiger a large ball on a rope, whose resistance and weight symbolize the gazelle. The tiger seems satisfied. Wherever predatory animals are living under direct human support and control, these solutions seem the most ethically sound.

Positive and Negative, Capability and Functioning

In the human case, there is a traditional distinction between positive and negative duties that it seems important to call into question. Traditional moralities hold that we have a strict duty not to commit aggression and fraud, but we have no correspondingly strict duty to stop hunger or disease, nor to give money to promote their cessation.[1]

The capabilities approach calls this distinction into question. All the human capabilities require affirmative support, usually including state action. This is just as true of protecting property and personal security as it is of health care, just as true of the political and civil liberties as it is of providing adequate shelter.

In the case of animals, unlike the human case, there might appear to be some room for a positive-negative distinction that makes some sense. It seems at least coherent to say that the human community has the obligation to refrain from certain egregious harms toward animals, but that it is not obliged to support the welfare of all animals, in the sense of ensuring them adequate food, shelter, and health care. The animals themselves have the rest of the task of ensuring their own flourishing.

There is much plausibility in this contention. And certainly if our political principles simply ruled out the many egregious forms of harm to animals, they would have done quite a lot. But the contention, and the distinction it suggests, cannot be accepted in full. First of all, large numbers of animals live under humans' direct control: domestic animals, farm animals, and those members of wild species that are in zoos or other forms of captivity. Humans have direct responsibility for the nutrition and health care of these animals, as even our defective current systems of law acknowledge.[2] Animals in the "wild" appear to go their way unaffected by human beings. But of course that can hardly be so in many cases in today's world. Human beings pervasively affect the habitats of animals, determining opportunities for nutrition, free movement, and other aspects of flourishing.

Thus, while we may still maintain that one primary area of human responsibility to animals is that of refraining from a whole range of bad acts (to be discussed shortly), we cannot plausibly stop there. The only questions should be how extensive our duties are, and how to balance them against appropriate respect for the autonomy of a species.

In the human case, one way in which the approach respects autonomy is to focus on capability, and not functioning, as the legitimate political goal. But paternalistic treatment (which aims at functioning rather than capability) is warranted wherever the individual's capacity for choice and autonomy is compromised (thus, for children and the severely mentally disabled). This principle suggests that paternalism is usually appropriate when we are dealing with nonhuman animals. That conclusion, however, should be qualified by our previous endorsement of the idea that species autonomy, in pursuit of flourishing, is part of the good for nonhuman animals. How, then, should the two principles be combined, and can they be coherently combined?

I believe that they can be combined, if we adopt a type of paternalism that is highly sensitive to the different

---

1   *Traditional moralities ... their cessation*   See the critique by Martha Nussbaum in "Duties of Justice, Duties of Material Aid: Cicero's Problematic Legacy," *Journal of Political Philosophy* 7 (1999): 1–31.

2   *Humans have ... law acknowledge*   The laws do not cover all animals, in particular, not animals who are going to be used for food or fur.

forms of flourishing that different species pursue. It is no use saying that we should just let tigers flourish in their own way, given that human activity ubiquitously affects the possibilities for tigers to flourish. This being the case, the only decent alternative to complete neglect of tiger flourishing is a policy that thinks carefully about the flourishing of tigers and what habitat that requires, and then tries hard to create such habitats. In the case of domestic animals, an intelligent paternalism would encourage training, discipline, and even, where appropriate, strenuous training focused on special excellences of a breed (such as the border collie or the hunter-jumper). But the animal, like a child, will retain certain entitlements, which they hold regardless of what their human guardian thinks about it. They are not merely objects for human beings' use and control.

Toward Basic Political Principles: The Capabilities List

It is now time to see whether we can actually use the human basis of the capabilities approach to map out some basic political principles that will guide law and public policy in dealing with animals. The list I have defended as useful in the human case is as follows:

The Central Human Capabilities

1. *Life.* Being able to live to the end of a human life of normal length; not dying prematurely, or before one's life is so reduced as to be not worth living.

2. *Bodily Health.* Being able to have good health, including reproductive health; to be adequately nourished; to have adequate shelter.

3. *Bodily Integrity.* Being able to move freely from place to place; to be secure against violent assault, including sexual assault and domestic violence; having opportunities for sexual satisfaction and for choice in matters of reproduction.

4. *Senses, Imagination, and Thought.* Being able to use the senses, to imagine, think, and reason—and to do these things in a "truly human" way, a way informed and cultivated by an adequate education, including, but by no means limited to, literacy and basic mathematical and scientific training. Being able to use imagination and thought in connection with experiencing and producing works and events of one's own choice, religious, literary, musical, and so forth. Being able to use one's

mind in ways protected by guarantees of freedom of expression with respect to both political and artistic speech, and freedom of religious exercise. Being able to have pleasurable experiences and to avoid non-beneficial pain.

5. *Emotions.* Being able to have attachments to things and people outside ourselves; to love those who love and care for us and to grieve at their absence; in general, to love, to grieve, to experience longing, gratitude and justified anger. Not having one's emotional development blighted by fear and anxiety. (Supporting this capability means supporting forms of human association that can be shown to be crucial to our development.)

6. *Practical Reason.* Being able to form a conception of the good and to, engage in critical reflection about the planning of one's life. (This entails protection for the liberty of conscience and religious observance.)

7. *Affiliation.* (A) Being able to live with and toward others, to recognize and show concern for other human beings, to engage in various forms of social interaction; to be able to imagine the situation of another. (Protecting this capability means protecting institutions that constitute and nourish such forms of affiliation, and also protecting the freedom of assembly and political speech.) (B) Having the social bases of self-respect and nonhumiliation; being able to be treated as a dignified being whose worth is equal to that of others. (This entails provisions of nondiscrimination on the basis of race, sex, sexual orientation, ethnicity, caste, religion, national origin.)

8. *Other Species.* Being able to live with concern for and in relation to animals, plants, and the world of nature.

9. *Play.* Being able to laugh, to play, to enjoy recreational activities.

10. *Control over One's Environment.* (A) Political. Being able to participate effectively in political choices that govern one's life; having the right of political participation; protections of free speech and association. (B) Material. Being able to hold property (both land and movable goods), and having property rights on an equal basis with others; having the right to seek employment on an equal basis with others; having the freedom from unwarranted search and seizure. In work, being able to work as a human being, exercising practical reason and entering into meaningful relationships of mutual recognition with other workers,

Although the entitlements of animals are species specific, the main categories of the existing list, suitably fleshed out, turn out to be a good basis for a sketch of some basic political principles.

1. *Life.* In the capabilities approach, all animals are entitled to continue their lives, whether or not they have such a conscious interest. All sentient animals have a secure entitlement against gratuitous killing for sport. Killing for luxury items such as fur falls in this category, and should be banned. On the other hand, intelligently respectful paternalism supports euthanasia for elderly animals in pain. In the middle are the very difficult cases, such as the question of predation to control populations, and the question of killing for food. The reason these cases are so difficult is that animals will die anyway in nature, and often more painfully. Painless predation might well be preferable to allowing the animal to be torn to bits in the wild or starved through overpopulation. As for food, the capabilities approach agrees with utilitarianism in being most troubled by the torture of living animals. If animals were really killed in a painless fashion, after a healthy and free-ranging life, what then? Killings of extremely young animals would still be problematic, but it seems unclear that the balance of considerations supports a complete ban on killings for food.

2. *Bodily Health.* One of the most central entitlements of animals is the entitlement to a healthy life. Where animals are directly under human control, it is relatively clear what policies this entails: laws banning cruel treatment and neglect; laws banning the confinement and ill treatment of animals in the meat and fur industries; laws forbidding harsh or cruel treatment for working animals, including circus animals; laws regulating zoos and aquariums, mandating adequate nutrition and space. Many of these laws already exist, although they are not well enforced. The striking asymmetry in current practice is that animals being raised for food are not protected in the way other animals are protected. This asymmetry must be eliminated..

3. *Bodily Integrity.* This goes closely with the preceding. Under the capabilities approach, animals have direct entitlements against violations of their bodily integrity by violence, abuse, and other forms of harmful treatment—whether or not the treatment in question is painful. Thus the declawing of cats would probably be banned under this rubric, on the grounds that it prevents the cat from flourishing in its own characteristic way, even though it may be done in a painfree manner and cause no subsequent pain. On the other hand, forms of training that, though involving discipline, equip the animal to manifest excellences that are part of its characteristic capabilities profile would not be eliminated.

4. *Senses, Imagination, and Thought.* For humans, this capability creates a wide range of entitlements: to appropriate education, to free speech and artistic expression, to the freedom of religion. It also includes a more general entitlement to pleasurable experiences and the avoidance of nonbeneficial pain. By now it ought to be rather obvious where the latter point takes us in thinking about animals: toward laws banning harsh, cruel, and abusive treatment and ensuring animals' access to sources of pleasure, such as free movement in an environment that stimulates and pleases the senses. The freedom-related part of this capability has no precise analogue, and yet we can come up with appropriate analogues in the case of each type of animal, by asking what choices and areas of freedom seem most important to each. Clearly this reflection would lead us to reject close confinement and to regulate the places in which animals of all kinds are kept for spaciousness, light and shade, and the variety of opportunities they offer the animals for a range of characteristic activities. Again, the capabilities approach seems superior to utilitarianism in its ability to recognize such entitlements, for few animals will have a conscious interest, as such, in variety and space.

5. *Emotions.* Animals have a wide range of emotions. All or almost all sentient animals have fear. Many animals can experience anger, resentment, gratitude, grief, envy, and joy. A small number—those who are capable of perspectival thinking—can experience compassion.[1] Like human beings, they are entitled to lives in which it is open to them to have attachments to others, to love and care for others, and not to have those attachments warped by enforced isolation or the deliberate infliction of fear. We understand well what this means where our cherished domestic animals are in question. Oddly, we do not extend the same consideration to

---

1   *Animals have ... experience compassion*   On all this, see Nussbaum, *Upheavals of Thought*, ch. 2.

animals we think of as "wild." Until recently, zoos took no thought for the emotional needs of animals, and animals being used for research were often treated with gross carelessness in this regard, being left in isolation and confinement when they might easily have had decent emotional lives.[1]

6. *Practical Reason.* In each case, we need to ask to what extent the creature has a capacity to frame goals and projects and to plan its life. To the extent that this capacity is present, it ought to be supported, and this support requires many of the same policies already suggested by capability 4: plenty of room to move around, opportunities for a variety of activities.

7. *Affiliation.* In the human case, this capability has two parts: an interpersonal part (being able to live with and toward others) and a more public part, focused on self-respect and nonhumiliation. It seems to me that the same two parts are pertinent for nonhuman animals. Animals are entitled to opportunities to form attachments (as in capability 5) and to engage in characteristic forms of bonding and interrelationship. They are also entitled to relations with humans, where humans enter the picture, that are rewarding and reciprocal, rather than tyrannical. At the same time, they are entitled to live in a world public culture that respects them and treats them as dignified beings. This entitlement does not just mean protecting them from instances of humiliation that they will feel as painful. The capabilities approach here extends more broadly than utilitarianism, holding that animals are entitled to world policies that grant them political rights and the legal status of dignified beings, whether they understand that status or not.

8. *Other Species.* If human beings are entitled to "be able to live with concern for and in relation to animals, plants, and the world of nature," so too are other animals, in relation to species not their own, including the human species, and the rest of the natural world. This capability, seen from both the human and the animal side, calls for the gradual formation of an interdependent world in which all species will enjoy cooperative and mutually supportive relations with one another. Nature is not that way and never has been. So it calls,

in a very general way, for the gradual supplanting of the natural by the just.

9. *Play.* This capability is obviously central to the lives of all sentient animals. It calls for many of the same policies we have already discussed: provision of adequate space, light, and sensory stimulation in living places, and, above all, the presence of other species members.

10. *Control over One's Environment.* In the human case, this capability has two prongs, the political and the material. The political is defined in terms of active citizenship and rights of political participation. For nonhuman animals, the important thing is being part of a political conception that is framed so as to respect them and that is committed to treating them justly. It is important, however, that animals have entitlements directly, so that a human guardian has standing to go to court, as with children, to vindicate those entitlements. On the material side, for nonhuman animals, the analogue to property rights is respect for the territorial integrity of their habitats, whether domestic or in the wild.

Are there animal capabilities not covered by this list, suitably specified? It seems to me not, although in the spirit of the capabilities approach we should insist that the list is open-ended, subject to supplementation or deletion.

In general, the capabilities approach suggests that it is appropriate for nations to include in their constitutions or other founding statements of principle a commitment to animals as subjects of political justice and a commitment that animals will be treated with dignity. The constitution might also spell out some of the very general principles suggested by this capabilities list. The rest of the work of protecting animal entitlements might be done by suitable legislation and by court cases demanding the enforcement of the law, where it is not enforced. At the same time, many of the issues covered by this approach cannot be dealt with by nations in isolation, but can only be addressed by international cooperation. So we also need international accords committing the world community to the protection of animal habitats and the eradication of cruel practices.

The Ineliminability of Conflict

In the human case, we often face the question of conflict between one capability and another. But if the capabilities list and its thresholds are suitably designed, we ought to say

---

1   *Until recently ... emotional lives* See Steven Wise, *Rattling the Cage: Toward Legal Rights for Animals* (Cambridge, MA: Perseus, 2000), ch. 1.

that the presence of conflict between one capability and another is a sign that society has gone wrong somewhere.[1] We should focus on long-term planning that will create a world in which all the capabilities can be secured to all citizens.

Our world contains persistent and often tragic conflicts between the well-being of human beings and the well-being of animals. Some bad treatment of animals can be eliminated without serious losses in human wellbeing: Such is the case with the use of animals for fur, and the brutal and confining treatment of animals used for food. The use of animals for food in general is a much more difficult case, since nobody really knows what the impact on the world environment would be of a total switch to vegetarian sources of protein, or the extent to which such a diet could be made compatible with the health of all the world's children. A still more difficult problem is the use of animals in research.

A lot can be done to improve the lives of research animals without stopping useful research. As Steven Wise has shown, primates used in research, often live in squalid, lonely conditions while they are used as medical subjects. This of course is totally unnecessary and morally unacceptable and could be ended without ending the research. Some research that is done is unnecessary and can be terminated, for example, the testing of cosmetics on rabbits, which seems to have been bypassed without loss of quality by some cosmetic firms. But much important research with major consequences for the life and health of human beings and other animals will inflict disease, pain, and death on at least some animals, even under the best conditions.

I do not favor stopping all such research. What I do favor is (a) asking whether the research is really necessary for a major human capability; (b) focusing on the use of less-complex sentient animals where possible, on the grounds that they suffer fewer and lesser harms from such research; (c) improving the conditions of research animals, including palliative terminal care when they have contracted a terminal illness, and supportive interactions with both humans and other animals; (d) removing the psychological brutality that is inherent in so much treatment of animals for research; (e) choosing topics cautiously and seriously, so that no animal is harmed for a frivolous reason; and (f) a constant effort to develop experimental methods (for example, computer simulations) that do not have these bad consequences.

Above all, it means constant public discussion of these issues, together with an acknowledgment that such uses of animals in research are tragic, violating basic entitlements. Such public acknowledgments are far from useless. They state what is morally true, and thus acknowledge the dignity of animals and our own culpability toward them. They reaffirm dispositions to behave well toward them where no such urgent exigencies intervene. Finally, they prompt us to seek a world in which the pertinent research could in fact be done in other ways.

Toward a Truly Global Justice

It has been obvious for a long time that the pursuit of global justice requires the inclusion of many people and groups who were not previously included as fully equal subjects of justice: the poor; members of religious, ethnic, and racial minorities; and more recently women, the disabled, and inhabitants of nations distant from one's own.

But a truly global justice requires not simply that we look across the world for other fellow species members who are entitled to a decent life. It also requires looking around the world at the other sentient beings with whose lives our own are inextricably and complexly intertwined. Traditional contractarian approaches to the theory of justice did not and, in their very form, could not confront these questions as questions of justice. Utilitarian approaches boldly did so, and they deserve high praise. But in the end, I have argued, utilitarianism is too homogenizing—both across lives and with respect to the heterogeneous constituents of each life—to provide us with an adequate theory of animal justice. The capabilities approach, which begins from an ethically attuned wonder before each form of animal life, offers a model that does justice to the complexity of animal lives and their strivings for flourishing. Such a model seems an important part of a fully global theory of justice.

---

1   *But if ... wrong somewhere*   See Martha C. Nussbaum, "The Costs of Tragedy: Some Moral Implications of Cost-Benefit Analysis," in *Cost-Benefit Analysis*, Matthew D. Adler and Eric A. Posner, eds. (Chicago: University of Chicago Press, 2001), pp. 169–200.

SUSAN MOLLER OKIN
(1946–2004)

Susan Moller Okin was one of the most influential feminist political theorists of the late twentieth century. Situating questions of gender and the family at the forefront of her analysis, she reconfigured the terrain of political theory. In her three books and numerous articles, she highlights women's omission from political philosophy and argues for various theoretical and social reforms that would address and remedy women's subordinate social status.

Okin was born in New Zealand in 1946, where she earned a BA in History at the University of Auckland. She went on to earn a Masters in Politics at Oxford and a PhD in Government at Harvard. She taught at a number of institutions, including the University of Auckland, Vassar, Brandeis, and Harvard, before moving in 1990 to Stanford, where she was the Martha Sutton Weeks Professor of Ethics in Society and Professor of Political Science. At the time of her death in 2004, she was a visiting professor at Harvard University's Radcliffe Institute for Advanced Study.

In her first book, *Women in Western Political Thought* (1979), Okin investigates the role of women in ancient, modern, and contemporary political philosophy. She analyzes the assumptions of various historical figures such as Plato, Aristotle, Rousseau, and Mill (paying particular attention to their blind spots over issues of gender), and she considers whether their theories can be reformed to include women on an equal footing. Published at a time when few such studies had been undertaken, Okin's book broke new ground and prompted political philosophers to begin confronting neglected questions about gender.

By the 1980s, the second wave of the women's movement had inspired feminist research in a variety of fields; however, its impact on mainstream philosophy remained limited. While political philosophy blossomed in the 1970s and 80s, the most prominent political philosophers were men who rarely engaged feminist themes. In her second book, *Justice, Gender, and the Family* (1989), Okin examined and sought to remedy this neglect. Here she critically analyzes contemporary communitarianism, libertarianism, and liberalism, paying particular attention to John Rawls's theory of justice. She argues that, in various ways, each theory overlooks the significance of women's contributions in the family, either by assuming that the family is already "just" or by suggesting that power relations within the "private" domestic sphere fall outside the scope of justice. While portraying their work as gender neutral, these theorists make assumptions that reveal their male bias—for instance, envisioning the subject of political theory as a "head of household" who does not take primary responsibility for childrearing or household labor. Okin identifies and criticizes such assumptions; she contends that the sexual division of labor within the family makes women vulnerable, and that inequalities in the workplace exacerbate this disadvantage.

In "Justice as Fairness: For Whom?" the first selection from *Justice, Gender, and the Family* included here, Okin commends Rawls for calling attention to the family's important role as a "school of moral development." Nonetheless, she notes that Rawls does not explain *how* a family becomes just or even *whether* actual families are already just. Critical of this and other omissions, Okin proposes a feminist revision: the family should be understood as part of the basic structure—for Rawls, the primary social and political institutions of the society—and the parties in Rawls's "original position" should be ignorant of their gender. Without knowing whether they represent men or women, they would not endorse principles that disadvantaged women, either in the family or in the larger society. In "Toward a Humanist Justice" (the book's conclusion), Okin elaborates on this alternative theory and proposes specific policy reforms, including high quality, subsidized day care; workplace programs that encourage shared parenting and do not assume that employees have wives at home; and payment arrangements whereby checks are issued both to the earner and to the partner who does not work outside the home. Although these programs have yet to be adopted, Okin's critique of Rawls has been very influential in political theory, prompting a reply from Rawls and encouraging both feminists and liberals to rethink liberal approaches to justice.

Later in her career, Okin examined questions of multiculturalism, international development, and human rights. Her controversial and widely discussed "Is Multiculturalism Bad for Women?" is the subject of a 1999 book featuring her essay, commentaries, and a reply. Although the title suggests a broader focus, Okin centers on Will Kymlicka's liberal argument in favor of group rights for cultural minorities in the West. She notes that the cultural rights at issue often concern matters that directly affect women—such as sexuality, reproduction, and marriage—and worries that granting such rights can reinforce men's control over women. In their commentaries, Okin's critics claim that her work suffers from a variety of problems: paying insufficient attention to the actual voices of minority women; implying that Western societies actually embody liberal ideals of equality; and suggesting that feminism and liberalism are always compatible. Even her critics concede, however, that Okin's work raises important questions about the nature of group rights, multiculturalism, liberalism, and feminism.

Debra Satz of Stanford claimed that Okin, at the time of her death, was "perhaps the best feminist political philosopher in the world," and Jane J. Mansbridge of Harvard remarked, "Her insights on gender and the family shed new light on almost every political theory of major importance."

◆ ◆ ◆ ◆ ◆

from *Justice, Gender, and the Family* (1989)

Chapter 5: Justice as Fairness: For Whom?

John Rawls's *A Theory of Justice* has had the most powerful influence of any work of contemporary moral and political theory. The scope of Rawls's influence is indicated by the fact that all the theorists I have discussed so far make an

issue of their respective disagreements with his method and, in most cases, with his conclusions.[1] Now, I turn to Rawls's theory of justice as fairness, to examine not only what it explicitly says and does not say, but also what it *implies*, on the subjects of gender, women, and the family.

There is strikingly little indication, throughout most of *A Theory of Justice*, that the modern liberal society to which the principles of justice are to be applied is deeply and pervasively gender-structured. Thus an ambiguity runs throughout the work, which is continually noticeable to anyone reading it from a feminist perspective. On the one hand, as I shall argue, a consistent and wholehearted application of Rawls's liberal principles of justice can lead us to challenge fundamentally the gender system of our society. On the other hand, in his own account of his theory, this challenge is barely hinted at, much less developed. After critiquing Rawls's theory for its neglect of gender, I shall ask two related questions: What effects does a feminist reading

---

1 *all the theorists ... his conclusions* [Unless otherwise indicated, notes to this selection are by the author rather than the editors of this anthology.] Bloom, having written an extremely critical analysis of Rawls's *Theory* soon after it appeared ("Justice: John Rawls vs. the Tradition of Political Philosophy," *American Political Science* Review 69, no. 2 [1975]), is still trying to ridicule its defense of a liberal society that respects its members' equal rights to make choices about their modes of life (*The Closing of the American Mind* [New York: Simon & Schuster, 1987]), pp. 30, 229. MacIntyre, in *Whose Justice? Whose Rationality?* (Notre Dame: University of Notre Dame Press, 1988), repeatedly focuses on one brief passage from Rawls, in which, stressing the heterogeneity of human aims, he claims that to subordinate all else to one end "strikes us as irrational, or more likely as mad" (MacIntyre, citing Rawls, pp. 165, 179, 337). It is only by taking the passage out of context that MacIntyre is able to infer that Rawls's critique of "dominant-end views" implies that Aristotle was mad, since Aristotle's conception of "the good life" is itself *quite* heterogeneous, requiring material goods and services, friends and children, as well as virtuous behavior and intellectual activity. Nozick's defense of the rights of individuals to what they acquire by luck and good fortune as well as by effort is primarily directed against the redistributive implications of Rawls's difference principle (*Anarchy, State, and Utopia* [New York: Basic Books, 1974], esp. chap. 7). Sandel's entire argument in *Liberalism and the Limits of Justice* (Cambridge: Cambridge University Press, 1982) is directed against Rawls, and he makes only a few vague gestures toward any alternative theory. Finally, Walzer clearly dissents from (and apologetically caricatures) Rawls's *method* of theorizing about justice, but his own arguments and conclusions about what is just, at least in the context of our society, suggest that he has far fewer disagreements with Rawls's conclusions than these other theorists (*Spheres of Justice* [New York: Basic Books, 1983], esp. pp. 79–82; *Interpretation and Social Criticism* [Cambridge: Harvard University Press, 1987], pp. 11–17).

of Rawls have on some of his fundamental ideas (particularly those most attacked by critics); and what undeveloped potential does the theory have for feminist critique, and in particular for our attempts to answer the question, Can justice co-exist with gender?

Central to Rawls's theory of justice is a construct, or heuristic device, that is both his most important single contribution to moral and political theory and the focus of most of the controversy his theory still attracts, nearly twenty years after its publication. Rawls argues that the principles of justice that should regulate the basic institutions of society are those that would be arrived at by persons reasoning in what is termed "the original position." His specifications for the original position are that "the parties" who deliberate there are rational and mutually disinterested, and that while no limits are placed on the general information available to them, a "veil of ignorance" conceals from them all knowledge of their individual characteristics and their social position. Though the theory is presented as a contract theory, it is so only in an odd and metaphoric sense, since "no one knows his situation in society nor his natural assets, and therefore no one is in a position to tailor principles to his advantage." Thus they have "no basis for bargaining in the usual sense." This is how, Rawls explains, "the arbitrariness of the world ... [is] corrected for." in order that the principles arrived at will be fair. Indeed, since no one knows who he is, all think identically and the standpoint of any one party represents that of all. Thus the principles of justice are arrived at unanimously.[1] Later in this chapter, I shall address some of the criticisms that have been made of Rawls's original position and of the nature of those who deliberate there. I shall show that his theory can be read in a way that either obviates these objections or answers them satisfactorily. But first, let us see how the theory treats women, gender, and the family.

Justice for All?

Rawls, like almost all political theorists until very recently, employs in *A Theory of Justice* supposedly generic male terms of reference.[2] *Men, mankind, he,* and *his* are interspersed with gender-neutral terms of reference such as *individual* and *moral person.* Examples of intergenerational concern are worded in terms of "fathers" and "sons," and the difference principle is said to correspond to "the principle of fraternity."[3] This linguistic usage would perhaps be less significant if it were not for the fact that Rawls self-consciously subscribes to a long tradition of moral and political philosophy that has used in its arguments either such "generic" male terms or more inclusive terms of reference ("human beings," "persons," "all rational beings as such"), only to exclude women from the scope of its conclusions. Kant is a clear example.[4] But when Rawls refers to the generality and universality of Kant's ethics, and when he compares the principles chosen in his own original position to those regulative of Kant's kingdom of ends, "acting from [which] expresses our nature as free and equal rational persons,"[5] he does not mention the fact that women were not included among those persons to whom Kant meant his moral theory to apply. Again, in a brief discussion of Freud's account of moral development, Rawls presents Freud's theory of the formation of the male superego in largely gender-neutral terms, without mentioning the fact that Freud considered women's moral development to be sadly deficient, on account of their incomplete resolution of the Oedipus complex.[6] Thus there is a blindness to the sexism of the tradition in which Rawls is a participant, which tends to render his terms of reference more ambiguous than they might otherwise be. A feminist reader finds it difficult not to keep asking, Does this theory of justice apply to women?

This question is not answered in the important passages listing the characteristics that persons in the original position are not to know about themselves, in order to formulate impartial principles of justice. In a subsequent

---

1   *Thus the principles ... unanimously*   Rawls, *A Theory of Justice* (Boston: Harvard University Press, 1971), pp. 139–41; sec. 24 *passim.*

2   *Rawls ... male terms of reference*   He no longer does this in more recent writings, where the language is gender-neutral. See, for example, "Kantian Constructivism in Moral Theory," *The Journal of Philosophy* 77, no. 9 (1980); "Justice As Fairness: Political Not

Metaphysical," *Philosophy and Public Affairs* 14, no. 3 (1985). As will become apparent, this gender neutrality is to a large extent false, since Rawls does not confront the justice or injustice of gender, and the gendered family in particular.

3   *Men, mankind ... fraternity*   Rawls, *Theory*, pp. 105–6, 208–09, 288–89.

4   *a long tradition ... clear example*   See Susan Moller Okin, "Women and the Making of the Sentimental Family," *Philosophy and Public Affairs* 11, no. 1 (1982): 78–82; Carole Pateman, *The Sexual Contract* (Stanford: Stanford University Press, 1988), pp. 168–73.

5   *Rawls refers ... rational persons*   Rawls, *Theory*, pp. 251, 256. See also "Kantian Constructivism in Moral Theory." *Journal of Philosophy* (September 1980), p. 77(9): 515–72.

6   *Rawls presents Freud's ... Oedipus complex*   Rawls, *Theory*, p. 459.

article, Rawls has made it clear that sex is one of those morally irrelevant contingencies that are hidden by the veil of ignorance.[1] But throughout *A Theory of Justice*, while the list of things unknown by a person in the original position includes "his place in society, his class position or social status,...his fortune in the distribution of natural assets and abilities, his intelligence and strength, and the like,...his conception of the good, the particulars of his rational plan of life, even the special features of his psychology,"[2] "his" sex is not mentioned. Since the parties also "know the general facts about human society,"[3] presumably including the fact that it is gender-structured both by custom and still in some respects by law, one might think that whether or not they knew their sex might matter enough to be mentioned. Perhaps Rawls meant to cover it by his phrase "and the like," but it is also possible that he did not consider it significant.

The ambiguity is exacerbated by the statement that those free and equal moral persons in the original position who formulate the principles of justice are to be thought of not as "single individuals" but as "heads of families" or "representatives of families."[4] Rawls says that it is not necessary to think of the parties as heads of families, but that he will generally do so. The reason he does this, he explains, is to ensure that each person in the original position cares about the well-being of some persons in the next generation. These "ties of sentiment" between generations, which Rawls regards as important for the establishment of inter-generational justice—his just savings principle—, would otherwise constitute a problem because of the general assumption that the parties in the original position are mutually disinterested. In spite of the ties of sentiment *within* families, then, "as representatives of families their interests are opposed as the circumstances of justice imply."[5]

The head of a family need not necessarily, of course, be a man. Certainly in the United States, at least, there has been a striking growth in the proportion of female-headed households during the last several decades. But the very fact that, in common usage, the term "female-headed household" is used *only* in reference to households without resident adult males implies the assumption that any present male takes precedence over a female as the household or family head. Rawls does nothing to contest this impression when he says of those in the original position that "imagining themselves to be fathers, say, they are to ascertain how much they should set aside for their sons by noting what they would believe themselves entitled to claim of their fathers."[6] He makes the "heads of families" assumption only in order to address the problem of justice between generations, and presumably does not intend it to be a sexist assumption. Nevertheless, he is thereby effectively trapped into the public/domestic dichotomy and, with it, the conventional mode of thinking that life within the family and relations between the sexes are not properly regarded as part of the subject matter of a theory of social justice.

Let me here point out that Rawls, for good reason, states at the outset of his theory that the family is part of the subject matter of a theory of social justice. "For *us*" he says, "the primary subject of justice is the basic structure of society, or more exactly, the way in which the major social institutions distribute fundamental rights and duties and determine the division of advantages from social cooperation." The political constitution and the principal economic and social arrangements are basic because "taken together as one scheme, [they] define men's rights and duties and influence their life prospects, what they can expect to be and how well they can hope to do. The basic structure is the primary subject of justice *because its effects are so profound and present from the start*" (emphasis added).[7] Rawls specifies "the monogamous family" as an example of such major social institutions, together with the political constitution, the legal protection of essential freedoms, competitive markets, and private property.[8] Although this initial inclusion of the family as a basic social institution to which the principles of justice should apply is surprising in the light of the history of liberal thought, with its dichotomy between domestic and public spheres, it is necessary, given Rawls's stated criteria for inclusion in the basic structure.

---

1   *sex is ... veil of ignorance* Rawls, "Fairness to Goodness," *Philosophical Review* 84 (1975): 537. He says: "That we have one conception of the good rather than another is not relevant from a moral standpoint. In acquiring it we are influenced by the same sort of contingencies that lead us to rule out a knowledge of our sex and class."

2   *the list ... his psychology* Rawls, *Theory*, p. 137; see also p. 12.

3   *the parties ... human society* Ibid., p. 137. Numerous commentators on *Theory* have made the objection that "the general facts about human society" are often issues of great contention.

4   *those free ... of families* Ibid., pp. 128, 146.

5   *as representatives ... justice imply* Ibid., p. 128; see also p. 292.

6   *imagining themselves ... their fathers* Ibid., p. 289.

7   *"taken together ... the start"* Ibid., p. 7.

8   *the monogamous ... private property* Ibid., pp. 7, 462–63. Later, he takes a more agnostic position about the compatibility of his principles of justice with socialist as well as private property economies (sec. 42).

It would scarcely be possible to deny that different family structures, and different distributions of rights and duties within families, affect men's "life prospects, what they can expect to be and how well they can hope to do," and even more difficult to deny their effects on the life prospects of women. There is no doubt, then, that in Rawls's initial definition of the sphere of social justice, the family is included and the public/domestic dichotomy momentarily cast in doubt. However, the family is to a large extent ignored, though assumed, in the rest of the theory.[1]

The Barely Visible Family

In part 1 of *A Theory of Justice*, Rawls derives and defends the two principles of justice—the principle of equal basic liberty, and the "difference principle" combined with the requirement of fair equality of opportunity. These principles are intended to apply to the basic structure of society. They are "to govern the assignment of rights and duties and to regulate the distribution of social and economic advantages."[2] Whenever the basic institutions have within them differences in authority, in responsibility, or in the distribution of resources such as wealth or leisure, the second principle requires that these differences must be to the greatest benefit of the least advantaged and must be attached to positions accessible to all under conditions of fair equality of opportunity.

In part 2, Rawls discusses at some length the application of his principles of justice to almost all the institutions of the basic social structure that are set out at the beginning of the book. The legal protection of liberty of thought and conscience is defended, as are democratic constitutional institutions and procedures; competitive markets feature prominently in the discussion of the just distribution of income; the issue of the private or public ownership of the means of production is explicitly left open, since Rawls argues that his principles of justice might be compatible with certain versions of either.[3] But throughout all these discussions, the issue of whether the monogamous family, in either its traditional or any other form, is a just social institution, is never raised. When Rawls announces that "the sketch of the system of institutions that satisfy the two principles of justice is now complete,"[4] he has paid no attention at all to the internal justice of the family. In fact, apart from passing references, the family appears in *A Theory of Justice* in only three contexts: as the link between generations necessary for the just savings principle; as an obstacle to fair equality of opportunity (on account of the inequalities among families); and as the first school of moral development. It is in the third of these contexts that Rawls first specifically mentions the family as a just institution—not, however, to consider whether the family "in some form" is a just institution but to assume it.[5]

Clearly, however, by Rawls's own reasoning about the social justice of major social institutions, this assumption is unwarranted. The serious significance of this for the theory as a whole will be addressed shortly. The central tenet of the theory, after all, is that justice as fairness characterizes institutions whose members could hypothetically have agreed to their structure and rules from a position in which they did not know which place in the structure they were to occupy. The argument of the book is designed to show that the two principles of justice are those that individuals in such a hypothetical situation would agree upon. But since those in the original position are the heads or representatives of families, they are not in a position to determine questions of justice within families. As Jane English has pointed out, "By making the parties in the original position heads of families rather than individuals, Rawls makes the family opaque to claims of justice."[6] As far as children are concerned, Rawls makes an argument from paternalism for their temporary inequality and restricted liberty.[7] (This, while it may suffice in basically sound, benevolent families, is of no

Welfare State," in *Democracy and the Welfare State*, ed. Amy Gutmann (Princeton: Princeton University Press, 1988).

4 *the sketch ... now complete* Rawls, *Theory*, p. 303.

5 *Rawls first ... assume it* Ibid., pp. 463, 490. See Deborah Kearns, "A Theory of Justice—and Love; Rawls on the Family," *Politics (Australasian Political Studies Association Journal)* 18, no. 2 (1983): 39–40, for an interesting discussion of the significance for Rawls's theory of moral development on his failure to address the justice of the family.

6 *"By making ... of justice"* English, "Justice Between Generations," *Philosophical Studies* 31, no. 2 (1977): 95.

7 *makes an argument ... restricted liberty* Rawls, *Theory*, pp. 208–09.

1 *However, the family ... the theory* It is noteworthy that in a subsequent paper on the subject of why the basic structure is the primary subject of justice, Rawls does not mention the family as part of the basic structure. See "The Basic Structure As Subject," *American Philosophical Quarterly* 14, no. 2 (1977): 159.

2 *They are ... economic advantages* Rawls, *Theory*, p. 61.

3 *Rawls argues ... of either* For a good recent discussion of Rawls's view of just property institutions, see Richard Krouse and Michael McPherson, "Capitalism, 'Property-Owning Democracy,' and the

use or comfort in abusive or neglectful situations, where Rawls's principles would seem to require that children be protected through the intervention of outside authorities.) But wives (or whichever adult member[s] of a family are *not* its "head") go completely unrepresented in the original position. If families are just, as Rawls later assumes, then they must become just in some different way (unspecified by him) from other institutions, for it is impossible to see how the viewpoint of their less advantaged members ever gets to be heard.

There are two occasions when Rawls seems either to depart from his assumption that those in the original position are "family heads" or to assume that a "head of a family" is equally likely to be a woman as a man. In the assignment of the basic rights of citizenship, he argues, favoring men over women is "justified by the difference principle... only if it is to the advantage of women and acceptable from their standpoint." Later he seems to imply that the injustice and irrationality of racist doctrines are also characteristic of sexist ones.[1] But in spite of these passages, which appear to challenge formal sex discrimination, the discussions of institutions in part 2 implicitly rely, in a number of respects, on the assumption that the parties formulating just institutions are (male) heads of (fairly traditional) families, and are therefore not concerned with issues of just distribution within the family or between the sexes. Thus the "heads of families" assumption, far from being neutral or innocent, has the effect of banishing a large sphere of human life—and a particularly large sphere of most women's lives—from the scope of the theory.

During the discussion of the distribution of wealth, for example, it seems to be assumed that all the parties in the original position expect, once the veil of ignorance is removed, to be participants in the paid labor market. Distributive shares are discussed in terms of household income, but reference to "individuals" is interspersed into this discussion as if there were no difference between the advantage or welfare of a household and that of an individual.[2] This confusion obscures the fact that wages are paid to employed members of the labor force, but that in societies characterized by gender (all current societies) a much larger proportion of women's than men's labor is unpaid and is often not even acknowledged as labor. It also obscures the fact that

the resulting disparities in the earnings of men and women, and the economic dependence of women on men, are likely to affect power relations within the household, as well as access to leisure, prestige, political power, and so on, among its adult members. Any discussion of justice *within* the family would have to address these issues. (In the last two chapters of this book,[3] I shall examine current gendered family structure and practices in the light of standards of justice, including Rawls's, and, finding them wanting, suggest some ways in which the family, and marriage in particular, might be reformed so as to become more just.)

Later, in Rawls's discussion of the obligations of citizens, his assumption that justice is agreed on by heads of families in the original position seems to prevent him from considering another issue of crucial importance: women's exemption from the draft. He concludes that military conscription is justifiable in the case of defense against an unjust attack on liberty, so long as institutions "try to make sure that the risks of suffering from these imposed misfortunes are more or less evenly shared by all members of society over the course of their life, and that there is no avoidable *class* bias in selecting those who are called for duty" (emphasis added).[4] The complete exemption of women from this major interference with the basic liberties of equal citizenship is not even mentioned.

In spite of two explicit rejections of the justice of formal sex discrimination in part 1, then, Rawls seems in part 2 to be heavily influenced by his "family heads" assumption. He does not consider as part of the basic structure of society the greater economic dependence of women and the sexual division of labor within the typical family, or any of the broader social ramifications of this basic gender structure. Moreover, in part 3, where he takes as a given the justice of the family "in some form," he does not discuss any alternative forms. Rather, he sounds very much as though he is thinking in terms of traditional, gendered family structure and roles. The family, he says, is "a small association, normally characterized by a definite hierarchy, in which each member has certain rights and duties." The family's role as moral teacher is achieved partly through parental expectations of the "virtues of a good son or a good daughter." In the family and in other associations such as schools, neighborhoods, and peer groups, Rawls continues, one learns various moral

---

1   *the injustice ... sexist ones*   Ibid., pp. 99, 149.
2   *reference to "individuals" ... an individual*   Ibid., pp. 270–74, 304–09.
3   *the last two chapters of this book*   [editors' note] The last chapter is reprinted below.
4   *try to ... for duty*   Ibid., pp. 380–81.

virtues and ideals, leading to those adopted in the various statuses, occupations, and family positions of later life. "The content of these ideals is given by the various conceptions of a good wife and husband, a good friend and citizen, and so on."[1] Given these unusual departures from the supposedly generic male terms of reference used throughout the book, it seems likely that Rawls means to imply that the goodness of daughters is distinct from the goodness of sons, and that of wives from that of husbands. A fairly traditional gender system seems to be assumed.

Rawls not only assumes that "the basic structure of a well-ordered society includes the family *in some form*" (emphasis added); he adds that "in a broader inquiry the institution of the family might be questioned, and other arrangements might indeed prove to be preferable."[2] But why should it require a broader inquiry than the colossal task in which *A Theory of Justice* is engaged, to raise questions about the institution and the form of the family? Surely Rawls is right in initially naming it as one of those basic social institutions that most affect the life chances of individuals and should therefore be part of the primary subject of justice. The family is not a private association like a church or a university, which vary considerably in the type and degree of commitment each expects from its members, and which one can join and leave voluntarily. For although one has some choice (albeit a highly constrained one) about marrying into a gender-structured family, one has no choice at all about being born into one. Rawls's failure to subject the structure of the family to his principles of justice is particularly serious in the light of his belief that a theory of justice must take account of "how [individuals] get to be what they are" and "cannot take their final aims and interests, their attitudes to themselves and their life, as given."[3] For the gendered family, and female parenting in particular, are clearly critical determinants in the different ways the two sexes are socialized—how men and women "get to be what they are."

If Rawls were to assume throughout the construction of his theory that all human adults are participants in what goes on behind the veil of ignorance, he would have no option but to require that the family, as a major social institution affecting the life chances of individuals, be constructed in accordance with the two principles of justice. I shall begin to develop this positive potential of Rawls's theory in the final section of this chapter, and shall take it further in the concluding chapter of the book. But first I turn to a major problem for the theory that results from its neglect of the issue of justice within the family: its placing in jeopardy Rawls's account of how one develops a sense of justice.

Gender, the Family, and the Development of a Sense of Justice

Apart from being briefly mentioned as the link between generations necessary for Rawls's just savings principle, and as an obstacle to fair equality of opportunity, the family appears in Rawls's theory in only one context—albeit one of considerable importance: as the earliest school of moral development. Rawls argues, in a much-neglected section of part 3 of *A Theory of Justice*, that a just, well-ordered society will be stable only if its members continue to develop a sense of justice, "a strong and normally effective desire to act as the principles of justice require."[4] He turns his attention specifically to childhood moral development, aiming to indicate the major steps by which a sense of justice is acquired.

It is in this context that Rawls *assumes* that families are just. Moreover, these supposedly just families play a fundamental role in his account of moral development. First, the love of parents for their children, which comes to be reciprocated, is important in his account of the development of a sense of self-worth. By loving the child and being "worthy objects of his admiration ... they arouse in him a sense of his own value and the desire to become the sort of person that they are." Rawls argues that healthy moral development in early life depends upon love, trust, affection, example, and guidance.[5]

At a later stage in moral development, which he calls "the morality of association," Rawls perceives the family, though he describes it in gendered and hierarchical terms, as the first of many associations in which, by moving through a sequence of roles and positions, our moral understanding increases. The crucial aspect of the sense of fairness that is learned during this stage is the capacity—which, as I shall argue, is essential for being able to think *as if* in the original

---

1   *in part 3 ... and so on*   Ibid., pp. 467, 468.
2   *the basic structure ... be preferable*   Ibid., pp. 462–63.
3   *how [individuals] get ... as given*   Rawls, "The Basic Structure as Subject," *American Philosophical Quarterly* (April 1977), 14(2): 160.
4   *a just, well-ordered ... principles of justice require*   Rawls, *Theory*, p. 454.
5   *healthy moral ... and guidance*   Ibid., pp. 465, 466.

position—to take up the different points of view of others and to learn "from their speech, conduct, and countenance" to see things from their perspectives. We learn to perceive, from what they say and do, what other people's ends, plans, and motives are. Without this experience, Rawls says, "we cannot put ourselves into another's place and find out what we would do in his position," which we need to be able to do in order "to regulate our own conduct in the appropriate way by reference to it." Building on attachments formed in the family, participation in different roles in the various associations of society leads to the development of a person's "capacity for fellow feeling" and to "ties of friendship and mutual trust." Just as in the first stage "certain natural attitudes develop toward the parents, so here ties of friendship and confidence grow up among associates. In each case certain natural attitudes underlie the corresponding moral feelings: a lack of these feelings would manifest the absence of these attitudes."[1]

This whole account of moral development is strikingly unlike the arid, rationalist account given by Kant, whose ideas are so influential in many respects on Rawls's thinking about justice. For Kant, who claimed that justice must be grounded in reason alone, any feelings that do not follow from independently established moral principles are morally suspect—"mere inclinations."[2] By contrast, Rawls clearly recognizes the importance of feelings, first nurtured within supposedly just families, in the development of the capacity for moral thinking. In accounting for his third and final stage of moral development, where persons are supposed to become attached to the principles of justice themselves, Rawls says that "the sense of justice is continuous with the love of mankind." At the same time, he acknowledges our particularly strong feelings about those to whom we are closely attached, and says that this is rightly reflected in our moral judgments: even though "our moral sentiments display an independence from the accidental circumstances of our world, ... our natural attachments to particular persons and groups still have an appropriate place." He indicates clearly that empathy, or imagining oneself in the circumstances of others, plays a major role in moral development. It is not surprising that he turns away from Kant, and toward moral philosophers such as Adam Smith, Elizabeth Anscombe, Philippa Foot, and Bernard

Williams in developing his ideas about the moral emotions or sentiments.[3]

Rawls's summary of his three psychological laws of moral development emphasizes the fundamental importance of loving parenting for the development of a sense of justice. The three laws, Rawls says, are

> not merely principles of association or of reinforcement ... [but] assert that the active sentiments of love and friendship, and even the sense of justice, arise from the manifest intention of other persons to act for our good. Because we recognize that they wish us well, we care for their well-being in return.[4]

Each of the laws of moral development, as set out by Rawls, depends upon the one before it, and the first assumption of the first law is: "given that family institutions are just,.... " Thus Rawls frankly and for good reason acknowledges that the whole of moral development rests at base upon the loving ministrations of those who raise small children from the earliest stages, and on the moral character—in particular, the *justice*—of the environment in which this takes place. At the foundation of the development of the sense of justice, then, are an activity and a sphere of life that, though by no means necessarily so, have throughout history been predominantly the activity and the sphere of women.

Rawls does not explain the basis of his assumption that family institutions are just. If gendered families are *not* just, but are, rather, a relic of caste or feudal societies in which roles, responsibilities, and resources are distributed not in accordance with the two principles of justice but in accordance with innate differences that are imbued with enormous social significance, then Rawls's whole structure of moral development would seem to be built on shaky ground. Unless the households in which children are first nurtured, and see their first examples of human interaction, are based on equality and reciprocity rather than on dependence and domination—and the latter is too often the case—how can whatever love they receive from their parents make up for the injustice they see before them in the relationship between these same parents? How, in hierarchical families in which sex roles are rigidly assigned,

1   *Without this ... these attitudes*   Ibid., pp. 469–71.
2   *For Kant ... mere inclinations*   See Okin, "Reason and Feeling in Thinking About Justice," *Ethics* 99, no. 2 (1989): 231–35.
3   *Rawls clearly recognizes ... emotions or sentiments*   Rawls, *Theory*, pp. 476, 475, 479ff.
4   *not merely ... in return*   Ibid., p. 494; see also pp. 490–91.

are we to learn, as Rawls's theory of moral development requires us, to "put ourselves into another's place and find out what we would do in his position"? Unless they are parented equally by adults of both sexes, how will children of both sexes come to develop a sufficiently similar and well-rounded moral psychology to enable them to engage in the kind of deliberation about justice that is exemplified in the original position? If both parents do not share in nurturing activities, are they both likely to maintain in adult life the capacity for empathy that underlies a sense of justice?[1] And finally, unless the household is connected by a continuum of just associations to the larger communities within which people are supposed to develop fellow feelings for each other, how will they grow up with the capacity for enlarged sympathies such as are clearly required for the practice of justice? Rawls's neglect of justice within the family is clearly in tension with the requirements of his own theory of moral development. Family justice must be of central importance for social justice.

I have begun to suggest a feminist reading of Rawls, drawing on his theory of moral development and its emphasis on the moral feelings that originate in the family. This reading can, I think, contribute to the strengthening of Rawls's theory against some of the criticisms that have been made of it.[2] For, in contrast with his account of moral development, much of his argument about how persons in the original position arrive at the principles of justice is expressed in terms of mutual disinterest and rationality—the language of rational choice. This, I contend, leaves what he says unnecessarily open to three criticisms: it involves unacceptably egoistic and individualistic assumptions about human nature; taking an "outside" perspective, it is of little or no relevance to actual people thinking about justice; and its aim to create universalistic and impartial principles leads to the neglect of "otherness" or difference.[3] I think all three

criticisms are mistaken, but they result at least in part from Rawls's tendency to use the language of rational choice.

In my view, the original position and what happens there are described far better in other terms. As Rawls himself says, the combination of conditions he imposes on them "forces each person in the original position to take the good of others into account."[4] The parties can be presented as the "rational, mutually disinterested" agents characteristic of rational choice theory only because they do not know *which* self they will turn out to be. The veil of ignorance is such a demanding stipulation that it converts what would, without it, be self-interest into equal concern for others, including others who are very different from ourselves. Those in the original position cannot think from the position of *nobody*, as is suggested by those critics who then conclude that Rawls's theory depends upon a "disembodied" concept of the self. They must, rather, think from the perspective of *everybody*, in the sense of *each in* turn. To do this requires, at the very least, both strong empathy and a preparedness to listen carefully to the very different points of view of others. As I have suggested, these capacities seem more likely to be widely distributed in a society of just families, with no expectations about or reinforcements of gender.

Rawls's Theory of Justice as a Tool for Feminist Criticism

The significance of Rawls's central, brilliant idea, the original position, is that it forces one to question and consider traditions, customs, and institutions from all points of view, and ensures that the principles of justice will be acceptable

---

1 *If both … of justice?* On the connections among nurturing, empathy, and gender, see, for example, Judith Kegan Gardiner, "Self Psychology as Feminist Theory," *Signs* 12, no. 4 (1987), esp. 771 and 778–80; Sara Ruddick, "Maternal Thinking," *Feminist Studies* 6, no. 2 (1980).

2 *This reading … made of it* See Okin, "Reason and Feeling," for the more detailed argument from which this and the following paragraph are summarized.

3 *This, I contend … "otherness" or difference* Thomas Nagel, "Rawls on Justice," in *Reading Rawls*, ed. Norman Daniels (New York: Basic Books, 1974), (reprinted from *Philosophical Review* 72 [1973]), makes the first argument. Michael J. Sandel, *Liberalism and the Limits of Justice* (Cambridge: Cambridge University Press, 1982),

makes the first two arguments. The second argument is made by both Alasdair MacIntyre, in *After Virtue* (Notre Dame: University of Notre Dame Press, 1981), for example, pp. 119 and 233, and Michael Walzer, in *Spheres of Justice* (New York: Basic Books, 1983), pp. xiv and 5, and *Interpretation and Social Criticism* (Cambridge: Harvard University Press, 1987), pp. 11–16. The third argument, though related to some of the objections raised by Sandel and Walzer, is primarily made by feminist critics, notably Seyla Benhabib, in "The Generalized and the Concrete Other," in *Feminism As Critique*, ed. Benhabib and Drucilla Cornell (Minneapolis: University of Minnesota Press, 1987); and Iris Marion Young, in "Toward a Critical Theory of Justice," *Social Theory and Practice* 7 (1981), and "Impartiality and the Civic Public," in *Feminism as Critique*. The second and third objections are combined in Carole Pateman's claim that "Rawls's original position is a logical abstraction of such rigor that nothing happens there" (*The Sexual Contract* [Stanford: Stanford University Press, 1988], p. 43).

4 *forces each person … into account* Rawls, *Theory*, p. 148.

to everyone, regardless of what position "he" ends up in. The critical force of the original position becomes evident when one considers that some of the most creative critiques of Rawls's theory have resulted from more radical or broad interpretations of the original position than his own.[1] The theory, in principle, avoids both the problem of domination that is inherent in theories of justice based on traditions or shared understandings and the partiality of libertarian theory to those who are talented or fortunate. For feminist readers, however, the problem of the theory as stated by Rawls himself is encapsulated in that ambiguous "he." As I have shown, while Rawls briefly rules out formal, legal discrimination on the grounds of sex (as on other grounds that he regards as "morally irrelevant"), he fails entirely to address the justice of the gender system, which, with its roots in the sex roles of the family and its branches extending into virtually every corner of our lives, is one of the fundamental structures of our society. If, however, we read Rawls in such a way as to take seriously both the notion that those behind the veil of ignorance do not know what sex they are and the requirement that the family and the gender system, as basic social institutions, are to be subject to scrutiny, constructive feminist criticism of these contemporary institutions follows. So, also, do hidden difficulties for the application of a Rawlsian theory of justice in a gendered society.

I shall explain each of these points in turn. But first, both the critical perspective and the incipient problems of a feminist reading of Rawls can perhaps be illuminated by a description of a cartoon I saw a few years ago. Three elderly, robed male justices are depicted, looking down with astonishment at their very pregnant bellies. One says to the others, without further elaboration: "Perhaps we'd better reconsider that decision." This illustration graphically demonstrates the importance, in thinking about justice, of a concept like Rawls's original position, which makes us adopt the positions of others—especially positions that we ourselves could never be in. It also suggests that those thinking in such a way might well conclude that more than formal legal equality of the sexes is required if justice is to be done. As we have seen in recent years, it is quite possible to enact and uphold "gender-neutral" laws concerning pregnancy, abortion, childbirth leave, and so on that in effect discriminate against women. The United States Supreme Court decided in 1976, for example, that "an exclusion of pregnancy from a disability-benefits plan providing general coverage is not a gender-based discrimination at all."[2] One of the virtues of the cartoon is its suggestion that one's thinking on such matters is likely to be affected by the knowledge that one might become "a pregnant person." The illustration also points out the limits of what is possible, in terms of thinking ourselves into the original position, as long as we live in a gender-structured society. While the elderly male justices can, in a sense, imagine themselves as pregnant, what is a much more difficult question is whether, in order to construct principles of justice, they can imagine themselves as women. This raises the question of whether, in fact, sex is a morally irrelevant and contingent characteristic in a society structured by gender.

Let us first assume that sex is contingent in this way, though I shall later question this assumption. Let us suppose that it is possible, as Rawls clearly considers it to be, to hypothesize the moral thinking of representative human beings, as ignorant of their sex as of all the other things hidden by the veil of ignorance. It seems clear that, while Rawls does not do this, we must consistently take the relevant positions of both sexes into account in formulating and applying principles of justice. In particular, those in the original position must take special account of the perspective of women, since their knowledge of "the general facts about human society" must include the knowledge that women have been and continue to be the less advantaged sex in a great number of respects. In considering the basic institutions of society, they are more likely to pay special attention to the family than virtually to ignore it. Not only is it potentially the first school of social justice, but its customary unequal assignment of responsibilities and privileges to the two sexes and its socialization of children into sex roles make it, in its current form, an institution of crucial importance for the perpetuation of sex inequality.

In innumerable ways, the principles of justice that Rawls arrives at are inconsistent with a gender-structured society and with traditional family roles. The critical impact of a feminist application of Rawls's theory comes chiefly from his second principle, which requires that inequalities

---

1   *more radical or broad interpretations of the original position than his own*   Charles Beitz, for example, argues that there is no justification for not extending its application to the population of the entire world, which would lead to challenging virtually everything that is currently assumed in the dominant "statist" conception of international relations (*Political Theory and International Relations* [Princeton: Princeton University Press, 1979]).

2   *an exclusion ... at all*   See *General Electric v. Gilbert*, 429 U.S. 125 (1976), p. 136.

be both "to the greatest benefit of the least advantaged" and "attached to offices and positions open to all."[1] This means that if any roles or positions analogous to our current sex roles—including those of husband and wife, mother and father—were to survive the demands of the first requirement, the second requirement would prohibit any linkage between these roles and sex. Gender, with its ascriptive designation of positions and expectations of behavior in accordance with the inborn characteristic of sex, could no longer form a legitimate part of the social structure, whether inside or outside the family. Three illustrations will help to link this conclusion with specific major requirements that Rawls makes of a just or well-ordered society.

First, after the basic political liberties, one of the most essential liberties is "the important liberty of free choice of occupation."[2] It is not difficult to see that this liberty is compromised by the assumption and customary expectation, central to our gender system, that women take far greater responsibility for housework and child care, whether or not they also work for wages outside the home. In fact, both the assignment of these responsibilities to women—resulting in their asymmetric economic dependence on men—and the related responsibility of husbands to support their wives compromise the liberty of choice of occupation of both sexes. But the customary roles of the two sexes inhibit women's choices over the course of a lifetime far more severely than those of men; it is far easier in practice to switch from being a wage worker to occupying a domestic role than to do the reverse. While Rawls has no objection to some aspects of the division of labor, he asserts that, in a well-ordered society, "no one need be servilely dependent on others and made to choose between monotonous and routine occupations which are deadening to human thought and sensibility" and that work will be "meaningful for all."[3] These conditions are far more likely to be met in a society that does not assign family responsibilities in a way that makes women into a marginal sector of the paid work force and renders likely their economic dependence upon men. Rawls's principles of justice, then, would seem to require a radical rethinking not only of the division of labor within families but also of all the nonfamily institutions that assume it.

Second, the abolition of gender seems essential for the fulfillment of Rawls's criterion for political justice. For he argues that not only would equal formal political liberties be espoused by those in the original position, but that any inequalities in the *worth* of these liberties (for example, the effects on them of factors like poverty and ignorance) must be justified by the difference principle. Indeed, "the constitutional process should preserve the equal representation of the original position to the degree that this is practicable."[4] While Rawls discusses this requirement in the context of class differences, stating that those who devote themselves to politics should be "drawn more or less equally from all sectors of society,"[5] it is just as clearly and importantly applicable to sex differences. The equal political representation of women and men, especially if they are parents, is clearly inconsistent with our gender system. The paltry number of women in high political office is an obvious indication of this. Since 1789, over 10,000 men have served in the United States House of Representatives, but only 107 women; some 1,140 men have been senators, compared with 15 women. Only one recent appointee, Sandra Day O'Connor, has ever served on the Supreme Court. These levels of representation of any other class constituting more than a majority of the population would surely be perceived as a sign that something is grievously wrong with the political system. But as British politician Shirley Williams recently said, until there is "a revolution in shared responsibilities for the family, in child care and in child rearing," there will not be "more than a very small number of women ... opting for a job as demanding as politics."[6]

Finally, Rawls argues that the rational moral persons in the original position would place a great deal of emphasis on the securing of self-respect or self-esteem. They "would wish to avoid at almost any cost the social conditions that undermine self-respect," which is "perhaps the most important" of all the primary goods.[7] In the interests of this primary value, if those in the original position did not know

1   *to the greatest ... open to all*   Rawls, *Theory*, p. 302.

2   *the important liberty ... of occupation*   Ibid., p. 274.

3   *no one ... meaningful for all*   Ibid., p. 529.

4   *the constitutional process ... this is practicable*   Ibid., p. 222; see also pp. 202–05, 221–28.

5   *drawn more or less ... sectors of society*   Ibid., p. 228.

6   *a revolution ... as politics*   Elizabeth Holtzman and Shirley Williams, "Women in the Political World: Observations," *Daedalus* 116, no. 4 (Fall 1987). The statistics cited here are also from this article. Despite superficial appearances, the situation is no different in Great Britain. As of 1987, 41 out of the 630 members of the British House of Commons were women, and Margaret Thatcher is far more of an anomaly among British prime ministers than the few reigning queens have been among British monarchs.

7   *"would wish ... primary goods*   Rawls, *Theory*, pp. 440, 396; see also pp. 178–79.

whether they were to be men or women, they would surely be concerned to establish a thoroughgoing social and economic equality between the sexes that would protect either sex from the need to pander to or servilely provide for the pleasures of the other. They would emphasize the importance of girls' and boys' growing up with an equal sense of respect for themselves and equal expectations of self-definition and development. They would be highly motivated, too, to find a means of regulating pornography that did not seriously compromise freedom of speech. In general, they would be unlikely to tolerate basic social institutions that asymmetrically either forced or gave strong incentives to members of one sex to serve as sex objects for the other.

There is, then, implicit in Rawls's theory of justice a potential critique of gender-structured social institutions, which can be developed by taking seriously the fact that those formulating the principles of justice do not know their sex. At the beginning of my brief account of this feminist critique, however, I made an assumption that I said would later be questioned—that a person's sex is, as Rawls at times indicates, a contingent and morally irrelevant characteristic, such that human beings really can hypothesize ignorance of this fact about them. First, I shall explain why, unless this assumption is a reasonable one, there are likely to be further feminist ramifications for a Rawlsian theory of justice, in addition to those I have just sketched out. I shall then argue that the assumption is very probably not plausible in any society that is structured along the lines of gender. I reach the conclusions not only that our current gender structure is incompatible with the attainment of social justice, but also that the disappearance of gender is a prerequisite for the *complete* development of a nonsexist, fully human theory of justice.

Although Rawls is clearly aware of the effects on individuals of their different places in the social system, he regards it as possible to hypothesize free and rational moral persons in the original position who, temporarily freed from the contingencies of actual characteristics and social circumstances, will adopt the viewpoint of the "representative" human being. He is under no illusions about the difficulty of this task: it requires a "great shift in perspective" from the way we think about fairness in everyday life. But with the help of the veil of ignorance, he believes that we can "take up a point of view that everyone can adopt on an equal footing," so that "we share a common standpoint along with others and do not make our judgments from a personal slant." The result of this rational impartiality or objectivity,

Rawls argues, is that, all being convinced by the same arguments, agreement about the basic principles of justice will be unanimous. He does not mean that those in the original position will agree about *all* moral or social issues—"ethical differences are bound to remain"—but that complete agreement will be reached on all basic principles, or "essential understandings." A critical assumption of this argument for unanimity, however, is that all the parties have similar motivations and psychologies (for example, he assumes mutually disinterested rationality and an absence of envy) and have experienced similar patterns of moral development, and are thus presumed capable of a sense of justice. Rawls regards these assumptions as the kind of "weak stipulations" on which a general theory can safely be founded.[1]

The coherence of Rawls's hypothetical original position, with its unanimity of representative human beings, however, is placed in doubt if the kinds of human beings we actually become in society differ not only in respect to interests, superficial opinions, prejudices, and points of view that we can discard for the purpose of formulating principles of justice, but also in their basic psychologies, conceptions of the self in relation to others, and experiences of moral development. A number of feminist theorists have argued in recent years that, in a gender-structured society, the different life experiences of females and males from the start in fact affect their respective psychologies, modes of thinking, and patterns of moral development in significant ways.[2] Special attention has been paid to the effects on the

1   *Rawls regards ... be founded*   Rawls, "Kantian Constructivism," p. 551; *Theory*, pp. 516–17, 139–41, 149.

2   *A number ... significant ways*   Major books contributing to this thesis are Jean Baker Miller, *Toward a New Psychology of Women* (Boston: Beacon Press, 1976); Dorothy Dinnerstein, *The Mermaid and the Minotaur* (New York: Harper & Row, 1977); Nancy Chodorow, *The Reproduction of Mothering* (Berkeley: University of California Press, 1978); Carol Gilligan, *In a Different Voice* (Cambridge: Harvard University Press, 1982); Nancy Hartsock, *Money, Sex, and Power* (New York: Longman, 1983). Some of the more important individual papers are Jane Flax, "The Conflict Between Nurturance and Autonomy in Mother-Daughter Relationships and Within Feminism," *Feminist Studies* 4, no. 2 (Summer 1978); Judith Kegan Gardiner, "Self Psychology"; and Sara Ruddick, "Maternal Thinking." Summaries and/or analyses are presented in Jean Grimshaw, *Philosophy and Feminist Thinking* (Minneapolis: University of Minnesota Press, 1986), chaps. 5–8; Alison Jaggar, *Feminist Politics and Human Nature* (Totowa, N.J.: Rowman and Allanheld, 1983), chap. 11; Susan Moller Okin, "Thinking Like a Woman," in *Theoretical Perspectives on Sexual Difference*, ed. Deborah Rhode (New Haven: Yale University Press, forthcoming);

psychological and moral development of both sexes of the fact, fundamental to our gendered society, that children of both sexes are reared primarily by women. It has been argued that the experience of individuation—of separating oneself from the nurturer with whom one is originally psychologically fused—is a very different experience for girls than for boys, leaving the members of each sex with a different perception of themselves and of their relations with others.[1] In addition, it has been argued that the experience of *being* primary nurturers (and of growing up with this expectation) also affects the psychological and moral perspective of women, as does the experience of growing up in a society in which members of one's sex are in many ways subordinate to the other sex. Feminist theorists have scrutinized and analyzed the different experiences we encounter as we develop, from our actual lived lives to our absorption of their ideological underpinnings, and have filled out in valuable ways Simone de Beauvoir's claim that "one is not born, but rather becomes, a woman."[2]

What seems already to be indicated by these studies, despite their incompleteness so far, is that *in a gender-structured society* there is such a thing as the distinct standpoint of women, and that this standpoint cannot be adequately taken into account by male philosophers doing the theoretical equivalent of the elderly male justices depicted in the cartoon. The formative influence of female parenting on small children, especially, seems to suggest that sex difference is even more likely to affect one's thinking about justice in a gendered society than, for example, racial difference in a society in which race has social significance, or class difference in a class society. The notion of the standpoint of women, while not without its own problems, suggests that a fully human moral or political theory can be developed only with the full participation of both sexes. At the very least, this will require that women take their place with men in the dialogue in approximately equal numbers and in positions of comparable influence. In a society structured along the lines of gender, this cannot happen.

In itself, moreover, it is insufficient for the development of a fully human theory of justice. For if principles of justice are to be adopted unanimously by representative human beings ignorant of their particular characteristics and positions in society, they must be persons whose psychological and moral development is in all essentials identical. This means that the social factors influencing the differences presently found between the sexes—from female parenting to all the manifestations of female subordination and dependence—would have to be replaced by genderless institutions and customs. Only children who are equally mothered and fathered can develop fully the psychological and moral capacities that currently seem to be unevenly distributed between the sexes. Only when men participate equally in what have been principally women's realms of meeting the daily material and psychological needs of those close to them, and when women participate equally in what have been principally men's realms of larger scale production, government, and intellectual and artistic life, will members of both sexes be able to develop a more complete *human* personality than has hitherto been possible. Whereas Rawls and most other philosophers have assumed that human psychology, rationality, moral development, and other capacities are completely represented by the males of the species, this assumption itself has now been exposed as part of the male-dominated ideology of our gendered society.

What effect might consideration of the standpoint of women in gendered society have on Rawls's theory of justice? It would place in doubt some assumptions and conclusions, while reinforcing others. For example, the discussion of rational plans of life and primary goods might be focused more on relationships and less exclusively on the complex activities that he values most highly, if it were to take account of, rather than to take for granted, the traditionally more female contributions to human life.[3] Rawls says that self-respect or self-esteem is "perhaps the most important primary good," and that "the parties in the original position would wish to avoid at almost any cost the social conditions that undermine [it]."[4] Good early physical and especially psychological nur-

---

Joan Tronto, "'Women's Morality': Beyond Gender Difference to a Theory of Care," *Signs* 12, no. 4 (Summer 1987).

1 *It has been argued ... relations with others* This thesis, developed by Nancy Chodorow on the basis of psychoanalytic object-relations theory, is explained in more detail in chapter 6 of *Justice, Gender, and the Family.*

2 *one is ... a woman* Simone de Beauvoir, *The Second Sex,* trans. H.M. Parshley (New York: Vintage Books, 1952), p. 301.

3 *the discussion ... human life* Brian Barry has made a similar, though more general, criticism of Rawls's focus on the value of the complexity of activities (the "Aristotelian principle") in *The Liberal Theory of Justice* (Oxford: Oxford University Press, 1973), pp. 27-30. Rawls leaves room for such criticism and adaptation of his theory of primary goods when he says that it "depends upon psychological premises [that] may prove incorrect" (*Theory,* p. 260).

4 *the parties ... that undermine [it]* Rawls, *Theory,* pp. 396, 440.

turance in a favorable setting is essential for a child to develop self-respect or self-esteem. Yet there is no discussion of this in Rawls's consideration of the primary goods. Since the basis of self-respect is formed in very early childhood, just family structures and practices in which it is fostered and in which parenting itself is esteemed, and high-quality, subsidized child care facilities to supplement them, would surely be fundamental requirements of a just society. On the other hand, as I indicated earlier, those aspects of Rawls's theory, such as the difference principle, that require a considerable capacity to identify with others, can be strengthened by reference to conceptions of relations between self and others that seem in gendered society to be more predominantly female, but that would in a gender-free society be more or less evenly shared by members of both sexes.

The arguments of this chapter have led to mixed conclusions about the potential usefulness of Rawls's theory of justice from a feminist viewpoint, and about its adaptability to a genderless society. Rawls himself neglects gender and, despite his initial statement about the place of the family in the basic structure, does not consider whether or in what form the family is a just institution. It seems significant, too, that whereas at the beginning of *A Theory of Justice* he explicitly distinguishes the institutions of the basic structure (*including* the family) from other "private associations" and "various informal conventions and customs of everyday life," in his most recent work he distinctly reinforces the impression that the family belongs with those "private" and therefore nonpolitical associations, for which he suggests the principles of justice are less appropriate or relevant.[1] He does this, moreover, despite the fact that his own theory of moral development rests centrally on the early experience of persons within a family environment that is both loving and just. Thus the theory as it stands contains an internal paradox. Because of his assumptions about gender, he has not applied the principles of justice to the realm of human nurturance, a realm that is essential to the achievement and the maintenance of justice.

---

1   *in his most ... appropriate or relevant*   Ibid., p. 8. The more recent development is connected with Rawls's endorsement of the public/private dichotomy in Charles Larmore, *Patterns of Moral Complexity* (Cambridge: Cambridge University Press, 1987). Rawls most explicitly indicates that the family belongs in the "private" sphere, to which the principles of justice are not intended to apply, in "Justice As Fairness: Political Not Metaphysical," p. 245 n.27, and in "The Priority of Right and Ideas of the Good," *Philosophy and Public Affairs* 17, no. 4 (1988): esp. 263.

On the other hand, I have argued that the feminist *potential* of Rawls's method of thinking and his conclusions is considerable. The original position, with the veil of ignorance hiding from its participants their sex as well as their other particular characteristics, talents, circumstances, and aims, is a powerful concept for challenging the gender structure. Once we dispense with the traditional liberal assumptions about public versus domestic, political versus nonpolitical spheres of life, we can use Rawls's theory as a tool with which to think about how to achieve justice between the sexes both within the family and in society at large.

Chapter 8: Conclusion: Toward a Humanist Justice

The family is the linchpin of gender, reproducing it from one generation to the next. As we have seen, family life as typically practiced in our society is not just, either to women or to children. Moreover, it is not conducive to the rearing of citizens with a strong sense of justice. In spite of all the rhetoric about equality between the sexes, the traditional or quasi-traditional division of family labor still prevails. Women are made vulnerable by constructing their lives around the expectation that they will be primary parents; they become more vulnerable within marriages in which they fulfill this expectation, whether or not they also work for wages; and they are most vulnerable in the event of separation or divorce, when they usually take over responsibility for children without adequate support from their ex-husbands. Since approximately half of all marriages end in divorce, about half of our children are likely to experience its dislocations, often made far more traumatic by the socioeconomic consequences of both gender-structured marriage and divorce settlements that fail to take account of it. I have suggested that, for very important reasons, the family *needs* to be a just institution, and have shown that contemporary theories of justice neglect women and ignore gender. How can we address this injustice?

This is a complex question. It is particularly so because we place great value on our freedom to live different kinds of lives, there is no current consensus on many aspects of gender, and we have good reason to suspect that many of our beliefs about sexual difference and appropriate sex roles are heavily influenced by the very fact that we grew up in a gender-structured society. All of us have been affected, in our very psychological structures, by the fact of gender in our personal pasts, just as our society has been deeply affected by its strong influence in our collective past. Because of the lack of shared meanings about gender, it constitutes a particularly hard case for those who care deeply about both personal freedom and social justice. The way we divide the labor and responsibilities in our personal lives seems to be one of those things that people should be free to work out for themselves, but because of its vast repercussions it belongs clearly within the scope of things that must be governed by principles of justice. Which is to say, in the language of political and moral theory, that it belongs both to the sphere of "the good" and to that of "the right."

I shall argue here that any just and fair solution to the urgent problem of women's and children's vulnerability must encourage and facilitate the equal sharing by men and women of paid and unpaid work, of productive and reproductive labor. We must work toward a future in which all will be likely to choose this mode of life. A just future would be one without gender. In its social structures and practices, one's sex would have no more relevance than one's eye color or the length of one's toes. No assumptions would be made about "male" and "female" roles; childbearing would be so conceptually separated from child rearing and other family responsibilities that it would be a cause for surprise, and no little concern, if men and women were not equally responsible for domestic life or if children were to spend much more time with one parent than the other. It would be a future in which men and women participated in more or less equal numbers in every sphere of life, from infant care to different kinds of paid work to high-level politics. Thus it would no longer be the case that having no experience of raising children would be the practical prerequisite for attaining positions of the greatest social influence. Decisions about abortion and rape, about divorce settlements and sexual harassment, or about any other crucial social issues would not be made, as they often are now, by legislatures and benches of judges overwhelmingly populated by men whose power is in large part due to their advantaged position in the gender structure. If we are to be at all true to our democratic ideals, moving away from gender is essential. Obviously, the attainment of such a social world requires major changes in a multitude of institutions and social settings outside the home, as well as within it.

Such changes will not happen overnight. Moreover, any present solution to the vulnerability of women and children that is just and respects individual freedom must take into account that most people currently live in ways that are greatly affected by gender, and most still favor many aspects of current, gendered practices. Sociological studies confirm what most of us already infer from our own personal and professional acquaintances: there are no currently shared meanings in this country about the extent to which differences between the sexes are innate or environmental, about the appropriate roles of men and women, and about which family forms and divisions of labor are most beneficial for partners, parents, and children.[1] There are those, at one extreme, for whom the different roles of the two sexes, especially as parents, are deeply held tenets of religious belief. At the other end of the spectrum are those of us for whom the sooner all social differentiation between the sexes vanishes, the better it will be for all of us. And there are a thousand varieties of view in between. Public policies must respect people's views and choices. But they must do so only insofar as it can be ensured that these choices do not result, as they now do, in the vulnerability of women and children. Special protections must be built into our laws and public policies to ensure that, for those who choose it, the division of labor between the sexes does not result in injustice. In the face of these difficulties—balancing freedom and the effects of past choices against the needs of justice—I do not pretend to have arrived at any complete or fully satisfactory answers. But I shall attempt in this final chapter to suggest some social reforms, including changes in public policies and reforms of family law, that may help us work toward a solution to the injustices of gender.

Marriage has become an increasingly peculiar contract, a complex and ambiguous combination of anachronism and present-day reality. There is no longer the kind of agreement that once prevailed about what is expected of the parties to a marriage. Clearly, at least in the United States, it is no longer reasonable to assume that marriage will last a lifetime, since only half of current marriages are expected to. And yet, in spite of the increasing legal equality of men and women and the highly publicized figures about married women's increased participation in the labor force, many couples continue to adhere to more or less traditional patterns of role differentiation. As a recent article put it, women are "out of the house but not out of the kitchen."[2] Consequently, often working part-time or taking time out

---

1   *Sociological studies ... parents, and children*   See Susan Moller Okin, *Justice, Gender, and the Family* (New York: Basic Books, 1989), chap. 3, pp. 67-68.

2   *out of ... the kitchen*   "Women: Out of the House But Not Out of the Kitchen," *New York Times*, February 24, 1988, pp. A1, C10.

from wage work to care for family members, especially children, most wives are in a very different position from their husbands in their ability to be economically self-supporting. This is reflected, as we have seen, in power differentials between the sexes within the family. It means also, in the increasingly common event of divorce, usually by mutual agreement, that it is the mother who in 90 percent of cases will have physical custody of the children. But whereas the greater need for money goes one way, the bulk of the earning power almost always goes the other. This is one of the most important causes of the feminization of poverty, which is affecting the life chances of ever larger numbers of children as well as their mothers. The division of labor within families has always adversely affected women, by making them economically dependent on men. Because of the increasing instability of marriage, its effects on children have now reached crisis proportions.

Some who are critical of the present structure and practices of marriage have suggested that men and women simply be made free to make their own agreements about family life, contracting with each other, much as business contracts are made.[1] But this takes insufficient account of the history of gender in our culture and our own psychologies, of the present substantive inequalities between the sexes, and, most important, of the well-being of the children who result from the relationship. As has long been recognized in the realm of labor relations, justice is by no means always enhanced by the maximization of freedom of contract, if the individuals involved are in unequal positions to start with. Some have even suggested that it is consistent with justice to leave spouses to work out their own divorce settlement.[2] By this time, however, the two people ending a marriage are likely to be far *more* unequal. Such a practice would be even more catastrophic for most women and children than is the present system. Wives in any but the rare cases in which they as individuals have remained their husbands' socioeconomic equals could hardly be expected to reach a just solution if

left "free" to "bargain" the terms of financial support or child custody. What would they have to bargain *with*?

There are many directions that public policy can and should take in order to make relations between men and women more just. In discussing these, I shall look back to some of the contemporary ways of thinking about justice that I find most convincing. I draw particularly on Rawls's idea of the original position and Walzer's conception of the complex equality found in separate spheres of justice, between which I find no inconsistency. I also keep in mind critical legal theorists' critique of contract, and the related idea, suggested earlier, that rights to privacy that are to be valuable to all of us can be enjoyed only insofar as the sphere of life in which we enjoy them ensures the equality of its adult members and protects children. Let us begin by asking what kind of arrangements persons in a Rawlsian original position would agree to regarding marriage, parental and other domestic responsibilities, and divorce. What kinds of policies would they agree to for other aspects of social life, such as the workplace and schools, that affect men, women, and children and relations among them? And let us consider whether these arrangements would satisfy Walzer's separate spheres test—that inequalities in one sphere of life not be allowed to overflow into another. Will they foster equality within the sphere of family life? For the protection of the privacy of a domestic sphere in which inequality exists is the protection of the right of the strong to exploit and abuse the weak.

Let us first try to imagine ourselves, as far as possible, in the original position, knowing neither what our sex nor any other of our personal characteristics will be once the veil of ignorance is lifted.[3] Neither do we know our place in society or our particular conception of the good life. Particularly relevant in this context, of course, is our lack of knowledge of our beliefs about the characteristics of men and women and our related convictions about the appropriate division of labor between the sexes. Thus the positions we represent must include a wide variety of beliefs on these matters. We may, once the veil of ignorance is lifted, find ourselves feminist men or feminist women whose conception of the good life includes the minimization of social differentiation between the sexes. Or we may find ourselves traditional-

1   *Some who ... contracts are made*   See, for example, Marjorie Maguire Schultz, "Contractual Ordering of Marriage: A New Model for State Policy," *California Law Review* 70, no. 2 (1982); Lenore Weitzman, *The Marriage Contract: Spouses, Lovers, and the Law* (New York: The Free Press, 1981), parts 3–4.

2   *Some have ... divorce settlement*   See, for example, David L. Kirp, Mark G. Yudof, and Marlene Strong Franks, *Gender Justice* (Chicago: University of Chicago Press, 1986), pp. 183–85. Robert H. Mnookin takes an only slightly less laissez-faire approach, in "Divorce Bargaining: The Limits on Private Ordering," *University of Michigan Journal of Law Reform* 18, no. 4 (1985).

3   *Let us first ... is lifted*   I say "as far as possible" because of the difficulties already pointed out in chapter 5. Given the deep effects of gender on our psychologies, it is probably more difficult for us, having grown up in a gender-structured society, to imagine not knowing our sex than anything else about ourselves. Nevertheless, this should not prevent us from trying.

ist men or women, whose conception of the good life, for religious or other reasons, is bound up in an adherence to the conventional division of labor between the sexes. The challenge is to arrive at and apply principles of justice having to do with the family and the division of labor between the sexes that can satisfy these vastly disparate points of view and the many that fall between.

There are some traditionalist positions so extreme that they ought not be admitted for consideration, since they violate such fundamentals as equal basic liberty and self-respect. We need not, and should not, that is to say, admit for consideration views based on the notion that women are inherently inferior beings whose function is to fulfill the needs of men. Such a view is no more admissible in the construction of just institutions for a modern pluralist society than is the view, however deeply held, that some are naturally slaves and others naturally and justifiably their masters. We need not, therefore, consider approaches to marriage that view it as an inherently and desirably hierarchical structure of dominance and subordination. Even if it were conceivable that a person who did not know whether he or she would turn out to be a man or a woman in the society being planned would subscribe to such views, they are not admissible. Even if there were no other reasons to refuse to admit such views, they must be excluded for the sake of children, for everyone in the original position has a high personal stake in the quality of childhood. Marriages of dominance and submission are bad for children as well as for their mothers, and the socioeconomic outcome of divorce after such a marriage is very likely to damage their lives and seriously restrict their opportunities.

With this proviso, what social structures and public policies regarding relations between the sexes, and the family in particular, could we agree on in the original position? I think we would arrive at a basic model that would absolutely minimize gender. I shall first give an account of some of what this would consist in. We would also, however, build in carefully protective institutions for those who wished to follow gender-structured modes of life. These too I shall try to spell out in some detail.

Moving Away from Gender

First, public policies and laws should generally assume no social differentiation of the sexes. Shared parental responsibility for child care would be both assumed and facilitated. Few people outside of feminist circles seem willing to

acknowledge that society does not have to choose between a system of female parenting that renders women and children seriously vulnerable and a system of total reliance on day care provided outside the home. While high-quality day care, subsidized so as to be equally available to all children, certainly constitutes an important part of the response that society should make in order to provide justice for women and children, it is only one part.[1] If we start out with the reasonable assumption that women and men are equally parents of their children, and have equal responsibility for both the unpaid effort that goes into caring for them and their economic support, then we must rethink the demands of work life throughout the period in which a worker of either sex is a parent of a small child. We can no longer cling to the by now largely mythical assumption that every worker has "someone else" at home to raise "his" children.

The facilitation and encouragement of equally shared parenting would require substantial changes.[2] It would

1   *While high-quality ... one part*   It seems reasonable to conclude that the effects of day care on children are probably just as variable as the effects of parenting—that is to say, very widely variable depending on the quality of the day care and of the parenting. There is no doubt that good out-of-home day care is expensive—approximately $100 per full-time week in 1987, even though child-care workers are now paid only about two-thirds as much per hour as other comparably educated women workers (Victor Fuchs, *Women's Quest for Economic Equality* [Cambridge: Harvard University Press, 1988], pp. 137–38). However, it is undoubtedly easier to control its quality than that of informal "family day care." In my view, based in part on my experience of the excellent day-care center that our children attended for a total of seven years, good-quality day care must have small-scale "home rooms" and a high staff-to-child ratio, and should pay staff better than most centers now do. For balanced studies of the effects of day care on a poor population, see Sally Provence, Audrey Naylor, and June Patterson, *The Challenge of Daycare* (New Haven: Yale University Press, 1977); and, most recently, Lisbeth B. Schorr (with Daniel Schorr), *Within Our Reach—Breaking the Cycle of Disadvantage* (New York: Anchor Press, Doubleday, 1988), chap. 8.

2   *The facilitation ... substantial changes*   Much of what I suggest here is not new; it has formed part of the feminist agenda for several decades, and I first made some of the suggestions I develop here in the concluding chapter of *Women in Western Political Thought* (Princeton: Princeton University Press, 1979). Three recent books that address some of the policies discussed here are Fuchs, *Women's Quest*, chap. 7; Philip Green, *Retrieving Democracy: In Search of Civic Equality* (Totowa, N.J.: Rowman and Allanheld, 1985), pp. 96–108; and Anita Shreve, *Remaking Motherhood: How Working Mothers Are Shaping Our Children's Future* (New York: Fawcett Columbine, 1987), pp. 173–78. In Fuchs's chapter he carefully analyzes the potential economic and social effects of alternative policies to improve women's economic status, and concludes that "child-cen-

mean major changes in the workplace, all of which could be provided on an entirely (and not falsely) gender-neutral basis. Employers must be required by law not only completely to eradicate sex discrimination, including sexual harassment. They should also be required to make positive provision for the fact that most workers, for differing lengths of time in their working lives, are also parents, and are sometimes required to nurture other family members, such as their own aging parents. Because children are borne by women but can (and, I contend, should) be raised by both parents equally, policies relating to pregnancy and birth should be quite distinct from those relating to parenting. Pregnancy and childbirth, to whatever varying extent they require leave from work, should be regarded as temporarily disabling conditions like any others, and employers should be mandated to provide leave for all such conditions.[1] Of course, pregnancy and childbirth are far *more* than simply "disabling conditions," but they should be treated as such for leave) purposes, in part because their disabling effects vary from one woman to another. It seems unfair to mandate, say, eight or more weeks of leave for a condition that disables many women for less time and some for much longer, while *not* mandating leave for illnesses or other disabling conditions. Surely a society as rich as ours can afford to do both.

Parental leave during the postbirth months must be available to mothers and fathers on the same terms, to facilitate shared parenting; they might take sequential leaves

or each might take half-time leave. All workers should have the right, without prejudice to their jobs, seniority, benefits, and so on, to work less than full-time during the first year of a child's life, and to work flexible or somewhat reduced hours at least until the child reaches the age of seven. Correspondingly greater flexibility of hours must be provided for the parents of a child with any health problem or disabling condition. The professions whose greatest demands (such as tenure in academia or the partnership hurdle in law) coincide with the peak period of child rearing must restructure their demands or provide considerable flexibility for those of their workers who are also participating parents. Large-scale employers should also be required to provide high-quality on-site day care for children from infancy up to school age. And to ensure equal quality of day care for all young children, *direct government subsidies* (not tax credits, which benefit the better-off) should make up the difference between the cost of high-quality day care and what less well paid parents could reasonably be expected to pay.

There are a number of things that schools, too, must do to promote the minimization of gender. As Amy Gutmann has recently noted, in their present authority structures (84 percent of elementary school teachers are female, while 99 percent of school superintendents are male), "schools do not simply reflect, they perpetuate the social reality of gender preferences when they educate children in a system in which men rule women and women rule children." She argues that, since such sex stereotyping is "a formidable obstacle" to children's rational deliberation about the lives they wish to lead, sex should be regarded as a relevant qualification in the hiring of both teachers and administrators, until these proportions have become much more equal.[2]

An equally important role of our schools must be to ensure in the course of children's education that they become fully aware of the politics of gender. This does not only mean ensuring that women's experience and women's writing are included in the curriculum, although this in itself is undoubtedly important.[3] Its political significance

---

tered policies" such as parental leave and subsidized day care are likely to have more of a positive impact on women's economic position than "labor market policies" such as antidiscrimination, comparable pay for comparable worth, and affirmative action have had and are likely to have. Some potentially very effective policies, such as on-site day care and flexible and/or reduced working hours for parents of young or "special needs" children, seem to fall within both of his categories.

1 *Pregnancy and childbirth ... all such conditions* The dilemma faced by feminists in the recent California case *Guerra v. California Federal Savings and Loan Association*, 107 S. Ct. 683 (1987) was due to the fact that state law mandated leave for pregnancy and birth that it did *not* mandate for other disabling conditions. Thus to defend the law seemed to open up the dangers of discrimination that the earlier protection of women in the workplace had resulted in. (For a discussion of this general issue of equality versus difference, see, for example, Wendy W. Williams, "The Equality Crisis: Some Reflections on Culture, Courts, and Feminism," *Women's Rights Law Reporter* 7, no. 3 [1982].) The Supreme Court upheld the California law on the grounds that it treated workers equally in terms of their rights to become parents.

2 *As Amy Gutmann ... more equal* Amy Gutmann, *Democratic Education* (Princeton: Princeton University Press, 1987), pp. 112–15; quotation from pp. 113–14. See also Elisabeth Hansot and David Tyack, "Gender in American Public Schools: Thinking Institutionally," *Signs* 13, no. 4 (1988).

3 *An equally important ... undoubtedly important* A classic text on this subject is Dale Spender, ed., *Men's Studies Modified: The Impact of Feminism on the Academic Disciplines* (Oxford: Pergamon Press, 1981).

has become obvious from the amount of protest that it has provoked. Children need also to be taught about the present inequalities, ambiguities, and uncertainties of marriage, the facts of workplace discrimination and segregation, and the likely consequences of making life choices based on assumptions about gender. They should be discouraged from thinking about their futures as *determined* by the sex to which they happen to belong. For many children, of course, personal experience has already "brought home" the devastating effects of the traditional division of labor between the sexes. But they do not necessarily come away from this experience with positive ideas about how to structure their own future family lives differently. As Anita Shreve has recently suggested, "the old home-economics courses that used to teach girls how to cook and sew might give way to the new home economics: teaching girls and boys how to combine working and parenting."[1] Finally, schools should be required to provide high-quality after-school programs, where children can play safely, do their homework, or participate in creative activities.

The implementation of all these policies would significantly help parents to share the earning and the domestic responsibilities of their families, and children to grow up prepared for a future in which the significance of sex difference is greatly diminished. Men could participate equally in the nurturance of their children, from infancy and throughout childhood, with predictably great effects on themselves, their wives or partners, and their children. And women need not become vulnerable through economic dependence. In addition, such arrangements would alleviate the qualms many people have about the long hours that some children spend in day care. If one parent of a preschooler worked, for example, from eight to four o'clock and the other from ten to six o'clock, a preschool child would be at day care for only six hours (including nap time), and with each one or both of her or his parents the rest of the day. If each parent were able to work a six-hour day, or a four-day week, still less day care would be needed. Moreover, on-site provision of day care would enable mothers to continue to nurse, if they chose, beyond the time of their parental leave.[2]

The situation of single parents and their children is more complicated, but it seems that it too, for a number of reasons, would be much improved in a society in which sex difference was accorded an absolute minimum of social significance. Let us begin by looking at the situation of never-married mothers and their children. First, the occurrence of pregnancy among single teenagers, which is almost entirely unintended, would presumably be reduced if girls grew up more assertive and self-protective, and with less tendency to perceive their futures primarily in terms of motherhood. It could also be significantly reduced by the wide availability of sex education and contraception.[3] Second, the added weight of responsibility given to fatherhood in a gender-free society would surely give young men more incentive than they now have not to incur the results of careless sexual behavior until they were ready to take on the responsibilities of being parents. David Ellwood has outlined a policy for establishing the paternity of all children of single mothers at the time of birth, and for enforcing the requirement that their fathers contribute to their support throughout childhood, with provision for governmental backup support in cases where the father is unable to pay. These proposals seem eminently fair and sensible, although the minimum levels of support suggested ($1,500 to $2,000 per year) are inadequate, especially since the mother is presumed to be

---

409 n34. Given this fact, it seems quite unjustified to argue that lactation *dictates* that mothers be the primary parents, even during infancy.

3   *It could also ... and contraception*   In Sweden, where the liberalization of abortion in the mid-1970s was accompanied by much expanded birth-control education and information and reduced-cost contraceptives, the rates of both teenage abortion and teenage birth decreased significantly. The Swedish teenage birthrate was by 1982 less than half what it had been in the 1970s. Mary Ann Glendon, *Abortion and Divorce in Western Law* (Cambridge: Harvard University Press, 1987), p. 23 and n65. Chapter 3 of Schorr's *Within Our Reach* gives an excellent account of programs in the United States that have proven effective in reducing early and unplanned pregnancies. Noting the strong correlation between emotional and economic deprivation and early pregnancy, she emphasizes the importance, if teenagers are to have the incentive not to become pregnant, of their believing that they have a real stake in their own futures, and developing the aspirations and self-assertiveness that go along with this. As Victor Fuchs points out, approximately two-thirds of unmarried women who give birth are twenty or older (*Women's Quest*, p. 68). However, these women are somewhat more likely to have work skills and experience, and it seems likely that many live in informal "common law marriage" heterosexual or lesbian partnerships, rather than being in *fact* single parents.

---

1   *the old home-economics ... working and parenting*   Shreve, *Remaking Motherhood* (New York: Viking, 1987), p. 237.

2   *on-site provision ... parental leave*   Although 51 percent of infants are breast-fed at birth, only 14 percent are entirely breast-fed at six weeks of age. Cited from P. Leach, *Babyhood* (New York: Alfred A. Knopf, 1983), by Sylvia Ann Hewlett, in A *Lesser Life: The Myth of Women's Liberation in America* (New York: Morrow, 1986), p.

either taking care of the child herself or paying for day care (which often costs far more than this) while she works.[1]

Third, never-married mothers would benefit greatly from a work structure that took parenthood seriously into account, as well as from the subsidization of high-quality day care. Women who grew up with the expectation that their work lives would be as important a part of their futures as the work lives of men would be less likely to enter dead-ended, low-skilled occupations, and would be better able to cope economically with parenthood without marriage.

Most single parenthood results, however, not from single mothers giving birth, but from marital separation and divorce. And this too would be significantly altered in a society not structured along the lines of gender. Even if rates of divorce were to remain unchanged (which is impossible to predict), it seems inconceivable that separated and divorced fathers who had shared equally in the nurturance of their children from the outset would be as likely to neglect them, by not seeing them or not contributing to their support, as many do today. It seems reasonable to expect that children after divorce would still have two actively involved parents, and two working adults economically responsible for them. Because these parents had shared equally the paid work and the family work, their incomes would be much more equal than those of most divorcing parents today. Even if they were quite equal, however, the parent without physical custody should be required to contribute to the child's support, *to the point where the standards of living of the two households were the same.* This would be very different from the situation of many children of divorced parents today, dependent for both their nurturance and their economic support solely on mothers whose wage work has been interrupted by primary parenting.

It is impossible to predict all the effects of moving toward a society without gender. Major current injustices to women and children would end. Men would experience both the joys and the responsibilities of far closer and more sustained contact with their children than many have today.

Many immensely influential spheres of life—notably politics and the professional occupations—would for the first time be populated more or less equally by men and women, most of whom were also actively participating parents. This would be in great contrast to today, when most of those who rise to influential positions are either men who, if fathers, have minimal contact with their children, or women who have either forgone motherhood altogether or hired others as full-time caretakers for their children because of the demands of their careers.

These are the people who make policy at the highest levels—policies not only *about* families and their welfare and about the education of children, but about the foreign policies, the wars and the weapons that will determine the future or the lack of future for all these families and children. Yet they are almost all people who gain the influence they do in part by never having had the day-to-day experience of nurturing a child. This is probably the most significant aspect of our gendered division of labor, though the least possible to grasp. The effects of changing it could be momentous.

Protecting the Vulnerable

The pluralism of beliefs and modes of life is fundamental to our society, and the genderless society I have just outlined would certainly not be agreed upon by all as desirable. Thus when we think about constructing relations between the sexes that could be agreed upon in the original position, and are therefore just from all points of view, we must also design institutions and practices acceptable to those with more traditional beliefs about the characteristics of men and women, and the appropriate division of labor between them. It is essential, if men and women are to be allowed to so divide their labor, as they must be if we are to respect the current pluralism of beliefs, that society protect the vulnerable. Without such protection, the marriage contract seriously exacerbates the initial inequalities of those who entered into it, and too many women and children live perilously close to economic disaster and serious social dislocation; too many also live with violence or the continual threat of it. It should be noted here that the rights and obligations that the law would need to promote and mandate in order to protect the vulnerable need not—and should not—be designated in accordance with sex, but in terms of different functions or roles performed. There are only a minute percentage of "house husbands"

1 *David Ellwood ... she works* David Ellwood, *Poor Support: Poverty in the American Family* (New York: Basic Books, 1988), pp. 163–74. He estimates that full-time day care for each child can be bought for $3,000 per year, and half-time for $1,000. He acknowledges that these estimated costs are "modest." I think they are unrealistic, unless the care is being provided by a relative or close friend. Ellwood reports that, as of 1985, only 18 percent of never-married fathers were ordered to pay child support, and only 11 percent actually paid any (p. 158).

in this country, and a very small number of men whose work lives take second priority after their wives'. But they can quite readily be protected by the same institutional structures that can protect traditional and quasi-traditional wives, so long as these are designed without reference to sex.

Gender-structured marriage, then, needs to be regarded as a currently necessary institution (because still chosen by some) but one that is socially problematic. It should be subjected to a number of legal requirements, at least when there are children.[1] Most important, there is no need for the division of labor between the sexes to involve the economic dependence, either complete or partial, of one partner on the other. Such dependence can be avoided if both partners have *equal legal entitlement* to all earnings coming into the household. The clearest and simplest way of doing this would be to have employers make out wage checks equally divided between the earner and the partner who provides all or most of his or her unpaid domestic services. In many cases, of course, this would not change the way couples actually manage their finances; it would simply codify what they already agree on—that the household income is rightly shared, because in a real sense jointly earned. Such couples recognize the fact that the wage-earning spouse is no more supporting the homemaking and child-rearing spouse than the latter is supporting the former; the form of support each offers the family is simply different. Such couples might well take both checks, deposit them in a joint account, and really share the income, just as they now do with the earnings that come into the household.

In the case of some couples, however, altering the entitlement of spouses to the earned income of the household as I have suggested *would* make a significant difference. It would make a difference in cases where the earning or higher-earning partner now directly exploits this power, by refusing to make significant spending decisions jointly, by failing to share the income, or by psychologically or physically abusing the nonearning or low-earning partner, reinforced by the notion that she (almost always the wife)

has little option but to put up with such abuse or to take herself and her children into a state of destitution. It would make a difference, too, in cases where the higher-earning partner indirectly exploits this earning power in order to perpetuate the existing division of labor in the family. In such instances considerable changes in the balance of power would be likely to result from the legal and societal recognition that the partner who does most of the domestic work of the family contributes to its well-being just as much, and therefore rightly *earns* just as much, as the partner who does most of the workplace work.

What I am suggesting is *not* that the wage-working partner pay the homemaking partner for services rendered. I do not mean to introduce the cash nexus into a personal relationship where it is inappropriate. I have simply suggested that since both partners in a traditional or quasi-traditional marriage work, there is no reason why only one of them should get paid, or why one should be paid far more than the other. The equal splitting of wages would constitute public recognition of the fact that the currently unpaid labor of families is just as important as the paid labor. If we do *not* believe this, then we should insist on the complete and equal sharing of both paid and unpaid labor, as occurs in the genderless model of marriage and parenting described earlier. It is only if we *do* believe it that society can justly allow couples to distribute the two types of labor so unevenly. But in such cases, given the enormous significance our society attaches to money and earnings, we should insist that the earnings be recognized as equally earned by the two persons. To call on Walzer's language, we should do this in order to help prevent the inequality of family members in the sphere of wage work to invade their domestic sphere.

It is also important to point out that this proposal does not constitute unwarranted invasion of privacy or any more state intervention into the life of families than currently exists. It would involve only the same kind of invasion of privacy as is now required by such things as registration of marriages and births, and the filing of tax returns declaring numbers and names of dependents. And it *seems* like intervention in families only because it would alter the existing relations of power within them. If a person's capacity to fulfill the terms of his or her work is dependent on having a spouse at home who raises the children and in other ways sustains that worker's day-to-day life, then it is no more interventionist to pay both equally for their contributions than only to pay one.

---

1   *Gender-structured ... are children*   Mary Ann Glendon has set out a "children first" approach to divorce (Glendon, *Abortion and Divorce*, pp. 94ff.); here I extend the same idea to ongoing marriage, where the arrival of a child is most often the point at which the wife becomes economically dependent. I see no reason why what I propose here should be restricted to couples who are legally married. It should apply equally to "common law" relationships that produce children, and in which a division of labor is practiced.

The same fundamental principle should apply to separation and divorce, to the extent that the division of labor has been practiced within a marriage. Under current divorce laws, as we have seen, the terms of exit from marriage are disadvantageous for almost all women in traditional or quasi-traditional marriages. Regardless of the consensus that existed about the division of the family labor, these women lose most of the income that has supported them *and* the social status that attached to them because of their husband's income and employment, often at the same time as suddenly becoming single parents, and prospective wage workers for the first time in many years. This combination of prospects would seem to be enough to put most traditional wives off the idea of divorcing even if they had good cause to do so. In addition, since divorce in the great majority of states no longer requires the consent of both spouses, it seems likely that wives for whom divorce would spell economic and social catastrophe would be inhibited in voicing their dissatisfactions or needs within marriage. The terms of exit are very likely to affect the use and the power of voice in the ongoing relationship. At worst, these women may be rendered virtually defenseless in the face of physical or psychological abuse. This is not a system of marriage and divorce that could possibly be agreed to by persons in an original position in which they did not know whether they were to be male or female, traditionalist or not. It is a fraudulent contract, presented as beneficial to all but in fact to the benefit only of the more powerful.

For all these reasons, it seems essential that the terms of divorce be redrawn so as to reflect the gendered or nongendered character of the marriage that is ending, to a far greater extent than they do now.[1] The legal system of a society that allows couples to divide the labor of families in a traditional or quasi-traditional manner *must* take responsibility for the vulnerable position in which marital breakdown places the partner who has completely or partially lost the capacity to be economically self-supporting. When such a marriage ends, it seems wholly reasonable to expect a person whose career has been largely unencumbered by domestic responsibilities to support financially the partner who undertook these responsibilities. This support, in the form of combined alimony and child support, should be far more substantial than the token levels often ordered by the courts now. *Both postdivorce households should enjoy the same standard of living.* Alimony should not end after a few years, as the (patronizingly named) "rehabilitative alimony" of today does; it should continue for at least as long as the traditional division of labor in the marriage did and, in the case of short-term marriages that produced children, until the youngest child enters first grade and the custodial parent has a real chance of making his or her own living. After that point, child support should continue at a level that enables the children to enjoy a standard of living equal to that of the noncustodial parent. There can be no reason consistent with principles of justice that some should suffer economically vastly more than others from the breakup of a relationship whose asymmetric division of labor was mutually agreed on.

I have suggested two basic models of family rights and responsibilities, both of which are currently needed because this is a time of great transition for men and women and great disagreement about gender. Families in which roles and responsibilities are equally shared regardless of sex are far more in accord with principles of justice than are typical families today. So are families in which those who undertake more traditional domestic roles are protected from the risks they presently incur. In either case, justice as a whole will benefit from the changes. Of the two, however, I claim that the genderless family is more just, in the three important respects that I spelled out at the beginning of this book: it is more just to women; it is more conducive to equal opportunity both for women and for children of both sexes; and it creates a more favorable environment for the rearing of citizens of a just society. Thus, while protecting those whom gender now makes vulnerable, we must also put our best efforts into promoting the elimination of gender.

The increased justice to women that would result from moving away from gender is readily apparent. Standards for just social institutions could no longer take for granted and exclude from considerations of justice much of what women now do, since men would share in it equally. Such central components of justice as what counts as productive labor, and what count as needs and deserts, would be greatly affected by this change. Standards of justice would become

---

1   *it seems essential ... they do now*   My suggestions for protecting traditional and quasi-traditional wives in the event of divorce are similar to those of Lenore Weitzman in *The Divorce Revolution: The Unexpected Social and Economic Consequences for Women and Children in America* (New York: The Free Press, 1985), chap. 11, and Mary Ann Glendon in *Abortion and Divorce*, chap. 2. Although they would usually in practice protect traditional wives, the laws should be gender-neutral so that they would equally protect divorcing men who had undertaken the primary functions of parenting and homemaking.

humanist, as they have never been before. One of the most important effects of this would be to change radically the situation of women as citizens. With egalitarian families, and with institutions such as workplaces and schools designed to accommodate the needs of parents and children, rather than being based as they now are on the traditional assumption that "someone else" is at home, mothers would not be virtually excluded from positions of influence in politics and the workplace. They would be represented at every level in approximately equal numbers with men.

In a genderless society, children too would benefit. They would not suffer in the ways that they do now because of the injustices done to women. It is undeniable that the family in which each of us grows up has a deeply formative influence on us—on the kind of persons we want to be as well as the kind of persons we are.[1] This is one of the reasons why one *cannot* reasonably leave the family out of "the basic structure of society," to which the principles of justice are to apply. Equality of opportunity to become what we want to be would be enhanced in two important ways by the development of families without gender and by the public policies necessary to support their development. First, the growing gap between the economic well-being of children in single-parent and those in two-parent families would be reduced. Children in single-parent families would benefit significantly if fathers were held equally responsible for supporting their children, whether married to their mothers or not; if more mothers had sustained labor force attachment; if high-quality day care were subsidized; and if the workplace were designed to accommodate parenting. These children would be far less likely to spend their formative years in conditions of poverty, with one parent struggling to fulfill the functions of two. Their life chances would be significantly enhanced.

Second, children of both sexes in gender-free families would have (as some already have) much more opportunity for self-development free from sex-role expectations and sex-typed personalities than most do now. Girls and boys who grow up in highly traditional families, in which sex difference is regarded as a determinant of everything from roles, responsibilities, and privileges to acceptable dress, speech, and modes of behavior, clearly have far less freedom to develop into whatever kind of person they want to be

than do those who are raised without such constraints. It is too early for us to know a lot about the developmental outcomes and life choices of children who are equally parented by mothers and fathers, since the practice is still so recent—and so rare. Persuasive theories such as Chodorow's, however, would lead us to expect much less differentiation between the sexes to result from truly shared parenting.[2] Even now, in most cases without men's equal fathering, both the daughters and the sons of wage-working mothers have been found to have a more positive view of women and less rigid views of sex roles; the daughters (like their mothers) tend to have greater self-esteem and a more positive view of themselves as workers, and the sons, to expect equality and shared roles in their own future marriages.[3] We might well expect that with mothers in the labor force *and* with fathers as equal parents, children's attitudes and psychologies will become even less correlated with their sex. In a very crucial sense, their opportunities to become the persons they want to be will be enlarged.

Finally, it seems undeniable that the enhancement of justice that accompanies the disappearance of gender will make the family a much better place for children to develop a sense of justice. We can no longer deny the importance of the fact that families are where we first learn, by example and by how we are treated, not only how people do relate to each other but also how they *should*. How would families not built on gender be better schools of moral development? First, the example of co-equal parents with shared roles, combining love with justice, would provide a far better example of human relations for children than the domination and dependence that often occur in traditional marriage. The fairness of the distribution of labor, the equal respect, and the interdependence of his or her parents would surely be a powerful first example to a child in a family with equally shared roles. Second, as I have argued, having a sense of justice requires that we be able to empathize, to abstract from

---

1   *the family ... persons we are*   Here I paraphrase Rawls's wording in explaining why the basic structure of society is basic. "The Basic Structure as Subject," *American Philosophical Quarterly* 14, no. 2 (1977): 160.

2   *Persuasive theories ... shared parenting*   Nancy Chodorow, "Family Structure and Feminine Personality," in *Woman, Culture, and Society*, ed. M.X. Rosaldo and Louise Lamphere (Stanford: Stanford University Press, 1974); idem, *The Reproduction of Mothering: Psychoanalysis and the Sociology of Gender* (Berkeley: University of California Press, 1978). For related arguments, see also Isaac Balbus, *Marxism and Domination* (Princeton: Princeton University Press, 1978); Dorothy Dinnerstein, *The Mermaid and the Minotaur: Sexual Arrangements and Human Malaise* (New York: Harper & Row, 1976).

3   *both the daughters ... future marriages*   Shreve, *Remaking Motherhood*, chaps. 3–7.

our own situation and to think about moral and political issues from the points of view of others. We cannot come to either just principles or just specific decisions by thinking, as it were, as if we were nobody, or thinking from nowhere; we must, therefore, learn to think from the point of view of others, including others who are different from ourselves.

To the extent that gender is de-emphasized in our nurturing practices, this capacity would seem to be enhanced, for two reasons. First, if female primary parenting leads, as it seems to, to less distinct ego boundaries and greater capacity for empathy in female children, and to a greater tendency to self-definition and abstraction in males, then might we not expect to find the two capacities better combined in children of both sexes who are reared by parents of both sexes? Second, the experience of being nurturers, throughout a significant portion of our lives, also seems likely to result in an increase in empathy, and in the combination of personal moral capacities, fusing feelings with reason, that just citizens need.[1]

For those whose response to what I have argued here is the practical objection that it is unrealistic and will cost too much, I have some answers and some questions. Some of what I have suggested would not cost anything, in terms of public spending, though it would redistribute the costs and other responsibilities of rearing children more evenly between men and women. Some policies I have endorsed, such as adequate public support for children whose fathers cannot contribute, may cost more than present policies, but may not, depending on how well they work.[2] Some, such as subsidized high-quality day care, would be expensive in themselves, but also might soon be offset by other savings, since they would enable those who would otherwise be full-time child carers to be at least part-time workers.

All in all, it seems highly unlikely that the *long-term* costs of such programs—even if we count only monetary costs, not costs in human terms—would outweigh the long-term benefits. In many cases, the cycle of poverty could be broken—and children enabled to escape from, or to avoid falling into, it—through a much better early start in life.[3] But even if my suggestions would cost, and cost a lot, we have to ask: How much do we care about the injustices of gender? How much do we care that women who have spent the better part of their lives nurturing others can be discarded like used goods? How ashamed are we that one-quarter of our children, in one of the richest countries in the world, live in poverty? How much do we care that those who raise children, *because* of this choice, have restricted opportunities to develop the rest of their potential, and very little influence on society's values and direction? How much do we care that the family, our most intimate social grouping, is often a school of day-to-day injustice? How much do we *want* the just families that will produce the kind of citizens we need if we are ever to achieve a just society?

---

1   *the experience ... citizens need*   See, for example, Sara Ruddick, "Maternal Thinking," *Feminist Studies* 6, no. 2 (1980); Diane Ehrensaft, "When Women and Men Mother," in *Mothering: Essays in Feminist Theory*, ed. Joyce Trebilcot (Totowa, NJ: Rowman and Allanheld, 1984); Judith Kegan Gardiner, "Self Psychology as Feminist Theory," *Signs* 12, no. 4 (1987), esp. 778–80.

2   *Some policies ... they work*   David Ellwood estimates that "if most absent fathers contributed the given percentages, the program would actually save money" (*Poor Support*, p. 169).

3   *In many cases ... start in life*   Schorr's *Within Our Reach* documents the ways in which the cycle of disadvantage can be effectively broken, even for those in the poorest circumstances.

THOMAS POGGE
(1953–)

Thomas Pogge is one of today's leading philosophers writing on global justice. Along with Charles Beitz and Henry Shue, he is one of the first-wave theorists of global justice, largely responsible for bringing issues of world poverty, international development and the implications of rights across borders into mainstream political theory.

After completing his undergraduate studies at Hamburg University in sociology in 1977, Pogge received his PhD from Harvard under the supervision of John Rawls in 1983. Pogge has been associated with Columbia University since 1983; he taught in the philosophy department until 2006, before moving to the political science department (He is now Professor of Philosophy and International Affairs at Yale.) His first major work, *Realizing Rawls* (1989) defended Rawls against criticisms put forward by the libertarian Robert Nozick and the communitarian Michael Sandel and developed further many of Rawls's central claims. The book's most influential contribution, however, was to extend the Rawlsian framework to a global level.

Rawls originally restricted his theory of justice to a closed society leaving to one side issues such as immigration, international trade, and global distributive justice. In his writings about international justice such as *The Law of Peoples* (1999), Rawls envisaged that representatives of "peoples" would negotiate the principles of international justice. Included within the society of peoples are what Rawls called "decent hierarchical peoples." Though these peoples respect fundamental human rights, they are not liberal, democratic societies and may subordinate women, minorities, or other groups. In *The Law of Peoples* Rawls also advocated some redistribution across borders, but proposed limiting such redistribution to what would be necessary to allow peoples to sustain their basic institutions. Rawls did not propose any global application of his famous difference principle, which allows inequalities only insofar as they are to the greatest benefit of the least well-off members of society.

Pogge advocates a form of cosmopolitanism in which individual human beings are the ultimate units of moral concern; each individual matters equally and principles of justice have global force. His claim that individuals are the ultimate units of moral concern and that each individual matters equally is not particularly controversial among liberal theorists, but his suggestion that principles of distributive justice apply globally is widely disputed. In *Realizing Rawls*, Pogge applies a version of Rawls's original position on a global level to determine the basic rights, liberties, and principles of justice that would govern a just global order. Instead of representatives of peoples negotiating the principles of justice, Pogge suggests that individual persons should do so. On Pogge's account, these persons would not know the particular society they are born into and would thus choose substantive principles of global distributive justice. This has also led him to propose different means of gradually decentralizing state sovereignty by allocating power to sub- and supra- state level organizations.

In *Realizing Rawls*, Pogge also sets out a claim he would later develop in the selection of essays published in *World Poverty and Human Rights* (2002): the failure to adequately address the misery of the world's poor does not merely violate a positive duty to mutual aid, but in fact violates a negative duty not to subject the poor to unjust social and economic institutions. It is commonly thought that the duty not to harm others is more stringent than the duty to aid—thus, it is worse to steal someone's bread than to fail to provide the hungry with food. On Pogge's account, the international institutional structure does not merely fail to help the global poor, but actively harms them. In his view the global rich have imposed a global institutional order through international economic institutions such as the World Trade Organization, the World Bank, and the International Monetary Fund; this global order foreseeably and avoidably prevents the global poor from exercising their basic socioeconomic rights.

Pogge continues to publish widely on global justice and poverty. In collaboration with economist Sanjay Reddy he has criticized methods for measuring poverty used in the *World Development Report* published by the World Bank. He has advocated a "global resources dividend," a resource-based tax that would be used to combat global poverty. Recently, he has written on international law and how it affects extreme poverty and the effects of patent law on poorer states.

• • • • •

Cosmopolitanism and Sovereignty (1992)[1]

The human future suddenly seems open. This is an inspiration; we can step back and think more freely. Instead of containment or détente, political scientists are discussing grand pictures: the end of history, or the inevitable proliferation and mutual pacifism of capitalist democracies. And politicians are speaking of a new world order. My inspiration is a little more concrete. After developing a rough, cosmopolitan specification of our task to promote moral progress, I offer an idea for gradual global institutional reform. Dispersing political authority over nested territorial units would decrease the intensity of the struggle for power and wealth within and among states, thereby reducing the incidence of war, poverty, and oppression. In such a multilayered scheme, borders could be redrawn more easily to accord with the aspirations of peoples and communities.

Institutional Cosmopolitanism Based on Human Rights

Three elements are shared by all cosmopolitan positions. First, *individualism*: the ultimate units of concern are hu-

man beings, or persons[2]—rather than, say, family lines, tribes, ethnic, cultural, or religious communities, nations, or states. The latter may be units of concern only indirectly, in virtue of their individual members or citizens. Second, *universality*: the status of ultimate unit of concern attaches to every living human being equally[3]—not merely to some subset, such as men, aristocrats, Aryans, whites, or Muslims. Third, *generality*: this special status has global force. Persons are ultimate units of concern for everyone—not only for their compatriots, fellow religionists, or such like.

Let me separate three cosmopolitan approaches by introducing two distinctions. The first is that between legal and moral cosmopolitanism. *Legal* cosmopolitanism is committed to a concrete political ideal of a global order under which all persons have equivalent legal rights and duties, that is, are fellow citizens of a universal republic.[4] *Moral* cosmopolitanism holds that all persons stand in certain moral relations to one another: we are required to respect one another's status as ultimate units of moral concern—a requirement that imposes limits upon our conduct and, in particular, upon our efforts to construct institutional schemes. This view is more abstract, and in this sense weaker than legal cosmopolitanism: though compatible with the latter, it is also compatible with other patterns of human interaction, for example, with a system of autonomous states and even with a plurality of self-contained communities. Here I present a variant of moral cosmopolitanism, though below I also discuss whether this position mandates efforts to move from our global status quo in the direction of a more cosmopolitan world order (in the sense of legal cosmopolitanism).

The central idea of moral cosmopolitanism is that every human being has a global stature as an ultimate unit of moral concern. Such moral concern can be fleshed out in countless ways. One may focus on subjective goods and ills (human happiness, desire fulfillment, preference satisfac-

---

1   *Cosmopolitanism and Sovereignty*   [Unless otherwise indicated, all notes to this selection are by the author rather than the editors of this anthology.] This essay has benefited from various incisive comments and suggestions by Andreas Føllesdal, Bonnie Kent, Ling Tong, and my fellow participants at the "Ethikon East/West Dialogue Conference on the Restructuring of Political and Economic Systems," held in Berlin in January 1991, with funding provided by the Pew Charitable Trusts.

2   *human beings, or persons*   The differences between the notions of a person and a human being are not essential to the present discussion.

3   *the status ... human being equally*   There is some debate about the extent to which we should give weight to the interests of future persons and also to those of past ones (whose deaths are still recent). I leave this issue aside because it is at right angles to the debate between cosmopolitanism and its alternatives.

4   *universal republic*   One recent argument for a world state is advanced in Kai Nielsen, "World Government, Security, and Global Justice," in *Problems of International Justice*, ed. Steven Luper-Foy (Boulder, CO: Westview, 1988).

tion, or pain avoidance) or on more objective ones (such as human need fulfillment, capabilities, opportunities, or resources). Also, one might relativize these measures, for example, by defining the key ill as being worse off than anyone need be, or as falling below the mean—which is equivalent to replacing straightforward aggregation (sum ranking or averaging) by a version of maximin[1] or egalitarianism, respectively. In order to get to my topic quickly, I do not discuss these matters but simply opt for a variant of moral cosmopolitanism that is formulated in terms of human rights (with straightforward aggregation).[2] In doing so, I capture what most other variants likewise consider essential. And my further reflections can, in any case, easily be generalized to other variants of moral cosmopolitanism.

My second distinction lies within the domain of the moral. It concerns the nature of the moral constraints to be imposed. An *institutional* conception postulates certain fundamental principles of justice. These apply to institutional schemes and are thus second-order principles: standards for assessing the ground rules and practices that regulate human interactions. An *interactional* conception, by contrast, postulates certain fundamental principles of ethics. These principles, like institutional ground rules, are first order in that they apply directly to the conduct of persons and groups.[3]

Interactional cosmopolitanism assigns direct responsibility for the fulfillment of human rights to other (individual and collective) agents, whereas institutional cosmopolitanism assigns such responsibility to institutional schemes. On the latter view, the responsibility of persons is then indirect—a shared responsibility for the justice of any practices one supports: one ought not to participate in an unjust institutional scheme (one that violates human rights) without making reasonable efforts to aid its victims and to promote institutional reform.

Institutional and interactional conceptions are again compatible and thus may be combined.[4] Here I focus, however, on a variant of institutional cosmopolitanism while leaving open the question of its supplementation by a variant of interactional cosmopolitanism. I hope to show that making the institutional view primary leads to a much stronger and more plausible overall morality. Let us begin by examining how our two approaches would yield different accounts of human rights and human rights violations.

On the interactional view, human rights impose constraints on conduct, while on the institutional view they impose constraints upon shared practices. The latter approach has two straightforward limitations. First, its applicability is contingent, in that human rights are activated only through the emergence of social institutions. Where such institutions are lacking, human rights are merely latent and human rights violations cannot exist at all. Thus, if we accept a purely institutional conception of human rights, then we need some additional moral conception if we wish to deny that all is permitted in a very disorganized state of nature.

---

1   *maximin*   [editor's note] In decision theory, a maximin principle chooses the alternative under which the worst outcome is the least harmful. Thus if it were to choose among alternative societies, it would select the one in which the least worst-off person is better off than the least worst-off person in the others. Rawls, in *A Theory of Justice* and other works, argued for a version of maximin called the difference principle in which social and economic inequalities are only justified if "they are to be of the greatest benefit to the least-advantaged members of society."

2   *human rights (with straightforward aggregation)*   I have in mind here a rather minimal conception of human rights, one that rules out truly severe abuses, deprivations, and inequalities while still being compatible with a wide range of political, moral, and religious cultures. The recent development of, and progress within, both governmental and nongovernmental international organizations supports the hope, I believe, that such a conception might, in our world, become the object of a worldwide overlapping consensus. Compare Thomas W. Pogge, *Realizing Rawls* (Ithaca, NY: Cornell University Press, 1989), chap. 5.

3   *These principles ... persons and groups*   Interactional cosmopolitanism has been defended in numerous works. A paradigm example is Henry Shue, *Basic Rights* (Princeton, NJ: Princeton University Press, 1980). Luban, another advocate of this position, puts the point as follows: "A human right, then, will be a right whose beneficiaries are all humans and whose obligors are all humans in a

position to effect the right" (David Luban, "Just War and Human Rights," in *International Ethics*, ed. Charles Beitz et al. [Princeton, NJ: Princeton University Press, 1985], p. 209). Robert Nozick's *Anarchy, State, and Utopia* (New York: Basic, 1974)—however surprising the rights he singles out as fundamental—is also an instance of interactional cosmopolitanism. For institutional cosmopolitanism, see Charles Beitz, *Political Theory and International Relations* (Princeton, NJ: Princeton University Press, 1979), pt. 3, and "Cosmopolitan Ideals and National Sentiment," *Journal of Philosophy* 80 (1983): 591–600; and Pogge, *Realizing Rawls*, chap. 6.

4   *Institutional and interactional ... thus may be combined*   This is done, e.g., by John Rawls, who asserts (i) a natural duty to uphold and promote just institutions and also (ii) various other natural duties that do not presuppose shared institutions, such as duties to avoid injury and cruelty, duties to render mutual aid, and a duty to bring about just institutions where none presently exist. See John Rawls, *A Theory of Justice* (Cambridge, MA: Harvard University Press, 1971), pp. 114–15, 334.

Second, the cosmopolitanism of the institutional approach is contingent as well, in that the global moral force of human rights is activated only through the emergence of a global scheme of social institutions, which triggers obligations to promote any feasible reforms of this scheme that would enhance the fulfillment of human rights. So long as there is a plurality of self-contained cultures, the responsibility for such violations does not extend beyond their boundaries.[1] It is only because all human beings are now participants in a single, global institutional scheme—involving such institutions as the territorial state and a system of international law and diplomacy as well as a world market for capital, goods, and services—that all human rights violations have come to be, at least potentially, everyone's concern.[2]

These two limitations do not violate generality. I have a duty toward every other person not to cooperate in imposing an unjust institutional scheme upon her, even while this duty triggers human-rights-based obligations only to fellow participants in the same institutional scheme. This is analogous to how the duty to keep one's promises is general even while it triggers obligations only vis-à-vis persons to whom one has actually made a promise.

We see here how the institutional approach makes available an appealing intermediate position between two interactional extremes: it goes beyond simple libertarianism, according to which we may ignore harms that we do not directly bring about, without falling into a utilitarianism of rights à la Shue, which commands us to take account of all relevant harms whatsoever, regardless of our causal relation to these harms.[3]

Consider a human right not to be enslaved. On an interactional view, this right would constrain persons, who must not enslave one another. On an institutional view, the right would constrain legal and economic institutions: slavery must not be permitted or enforced. This leads to an important difference regarding the moral role of those who are neither slaves nor slaveholders. On the interactional view, such third parties have no responsibility vis-à-vis existing slaves, unless the human right in question involved, besides the negative duty not to enslave, also a positive duty to protect or rescue others from enslavement. Such positive duties have been notoriously controversial. On the institutional view, by contrast, some third parties may be implicated far more directly in the human rights violation. If they are not making reasonable efforts toward institutional reform, the more privileged participants in an institutional scheme in which slavery is permitted or even enforced—even those who own no slaves themselves—are here seen as cooperating in the enslavement, in violation of a negative duty. The institutional view thus broadens the circle of those who share responsibility for certain deprivations and abuses beyond what a simple libertarianism would justify, and it does so without having to affirm positive duties.

To be sure, working for institutional reform is doing something (positive). But, in the context of practices, this—as even libertarians recognize—does not entail that the duty in question is therefore a positive one: the negative duty not to abuse just practices may also generate positive obligations, as when one must act to keep a promise or contract one has made. Once one is a participant in social practices, it may no longer be true that one's negative duties require merely forbearance.

The move from an interactional to an institutional approach thus blocks one way in which the rich and mighty in today's developed countries like to see themselves as morally disconnected from the fate of the less fortunate denizens of the Third World. It overcomes the claim that one need only refrain from violating human rights directly, that one cannot reasonably be required to become a soldier in the global struggle against human rights violators and a comforter of their victims worldwide. This claim is not refuted but shown to be irrelevant. We are asked to be concerned about human rights violations not simply insofar as they exist at all, but only insofar as they are produced by social institutions in which we are significant participants. Our negative duty not to cooperate in the imposition of unjust practices, together with our continuing participation in an unjust institutional scheme, triggers obligations to promote feasible reforms of this scheme that would enhance the fulfillment of human rights.

---

1   *extend beyond their boundaries*   On the interactional approach, by contrast, any positive human rights would impose duties on persons anywhere to give possible aid and protection in specified cases of need.

2   *that all human rights ... everyone's concern*   These two limitations are compatible with the belief that we have a duty to create a comprehensive institutional scheme. Thus, Kant believed that any persons and groups who cannot avoid influencing one another ought to enter into a juridical state. See Hans Reiss, ed., *Kant's Political Writings* (Cambridge: Cambridge University Press, 1970), p. 73.

3   *it goes beyond ... harms*   The second extreme I am here alluding to is consequentialism in ethics, i.e., any consequentialist view that applies directly to agents—be it of the ideal or real, of the act, rule, or motive variety. There are also noninteractional variants of consequentialism, such as Bentham's utilitarianism, which applies to institutions.

One may think that a shared responsibility for the justice of the social institutions in which we participate cannot plausibly extend beyond our national institutional scheme, in which we participate as citizens, and which we can most immediately affect. But such a limitation is untenable because it treats as natural or God-given the existing global institutional framework, which is in fact imposed by human beings who are collectively quite capable of changing it. Therefore at least we—privileged citizens of powerful and approximately democratic countries—share a collective responsibility for the justice of the existing global order and hence also for any contribution it may make to the incidence of human rights violations.[1]

The practical importance of this conclusion evidently hinges on the extent to which our global institutional scheme is causally responsible for current deprivations. Consider this challenge: "Human rights violations and their distribution have local explanations. In some countries torture is rampant, while it is virtually nonexistent in others. Some regions are embroiled in frequent wars, while others are not. In some countries democratic institutions thrive, while others bring forth a succession of autocrats. And again, some poor countries have developed rapidly, while others are getting poorer year by year. Therefore our global institutional scheme has very little to do with the deplorable state of human rights fulfillment on earth."

This challenge appeals to true premises but draws an invalid inference. Our global institutional scheme can obviously not figure in the explanation of local human rights violations, but only in the macroexplanation of their global incidence. This parallels how Japanese culture may figure in the explanation of the Japanese suicide rate or how the laxity of U.S. handgun legislation may figure in the explanation of the North American homicide rate, without thereby explaining particular suicides/homicides or even intercity differentials in rates. In these parallel cases the need for a macroexplanation is obvious from the fact that there are other societies whose suicide/homicide rates are significantly lower. In the case of global institutions, the need for a macroexplanation of the overall incidence of human rights violations is less obvious because—apart from some rather inconclusive historical comparisons—the contrast to observable alternative global institutional schemes is lacking. Still, it is highly likely that there are feasible (i.e., practicable and accessible) alternative global regimes that would tend to engender lower rates of deprivation. This is clear, for example, in regard to economic institutions, where the centrifugal tendencies of certain free-market schemes are well understood from our experience with various national and regional schemes. This supports a generalization to the global plane, to the conjecture that the current constitution of the world market must figure prominently in the explanation of the fact that our world is one of vast and increasing international inequalities in income and wealth (with consequent huge differentials in national rates of infant mortality, life expectancy, disease, and malnutrition). Such a macroexplanation does not preempt microexplanations of why one poor country is developing rapidly and why another is not. It would explain why so few are while so many are not.

Consider this further challenge to the practical moral importance of our shared responsibility for the justice of our global institutional scheme: "An institutional scheme can be held responsible for only those deprivations it establishes, that is (at least implicitly), calls for. Thus, we cannot count against the current global regime the fact that it tends to engender a high incidence of war, torture, and starvation because nothing in the existing (written or unwritten) international ground rules calls for such deprivations—they actually forbid both torture and the waging of aggressive war. The prevalence of such deprivations therefore indicates no flaw in our global order and, a fortiori, no global duties on our part (though we do of course have some local duties to see to it that our government does not bring about torture, starvation, or an unjust war)."

This position is implausible. First, it would be irrational to assess social institutions without regard to the effects they predictably engender. For an institutional change (e.g., in economic ground rules) might benefit everyone (e.g., by increasing compliance, or through incentive effects). Second, social institutions are human artifacts (produced and abolished, perpetuated and revised by human beings), and it would be unprecedented not to take account of the predictable effects of human artifacts. (We choose between two engineering designs by considering not merely their suitability for their particular purpose but also their incidental effects, e.g., on pollution and the like, insofar as these are predictable.) Third, we consistently take incidental effects into account in debates about the design of domestic institutions (incentive effects of penal and tax codes, etc.).[2]

---

1 *human rights violations* Talk of such a contribution makes implicit reference to alternative feasible global regimes.

2 *Third, we consistently take ... (incentive effects of penal and tax codes, etc.)* The supposed moral significance of the distinction between

These arguments reaffirm my broadly consequentialist assessment of social institutions, which leads us to aim for the feasible global institutional scheme that produces the best pattern of human rights fulfillment, irrespective of the extent to which this pattern is established or engendered. We thus consider the existing global institutional scheme unjust insofar as the pattern of human rights fulfillment it tends to produce is inferior to the pattern that its best feasible alternatives would tend to produce. This broadly consequentialist variant of institutional cosmopolitanism accords with how the concern for human rights is understood within the *Universal Declaration of Human Rights*. Section 28 reads: "Everyone is entitled to a social *and International* order in which the rights and freedoms set forth in this Declaration can be fully realised" (my emphasis).[1]

This result suggests a further difference between the interactional and institutional approaches, concerning the way each counts violations of certain human rights. It cannot reasonably be required of an institutional scheme, for example, that it reduce the incidence of physical assaults to zero. This would be impossible, and approximating such an ideal as closely as possible would require a police state. The institutional approach thus counts a person's human right to physical integrity as fully satisfied if her physical integrity is reasonably secure.[2] This entails that—even in the presence of a shared institutional scheme—some of what count as human rights violations on the interactional view (e.g., certain assaults) do not count as human rights violations on the institutional view (because the persons whose physical integrity was violated were reasonably well protected). Conversely, some of what count as human rights violations on the institutional view (e.g., inadequate protection against assaults) may not register on the interactional view (as when insufficiently protected persons are not actually assaulted).

Let me close this more abstract part of my discussion with a sketch of how my institutional view relates to social and economic human rights and the notion of distributive justice. A man sympathetic to the moral claims of the poor, Michael Walzer, has written: "The idea of distributive justice presupposes a bounded world, a community, within which distributions take place, a group of people committed to dividing, exchanging, and sharing, first of all among themselves."[3] This is precisely the picture of distributive justice that Robert Nozick (among others) has so vigorously attacked. To the notion of dividing he objects that "there is no *central* distribution, no person or group entitled to control all the resources, jointly deciding how they are to be doled out."[4] And as for the rest, he would allow persons to do all the exchanging and sharing they like, but strongly reject any enforced sharing implemented by some redistribution bureaucracy.

The institutional approach involves a conception of distributive justice that differs sharply from the one Walzer supports and Nozick attacks. Here the issue of distributive justice is not how to distribute a given pool of resources or how to improve upon a given distribution but, rather, how to choose or design the economic ground rules, which regulate property, cooperation, and exchange and thereby condition production and distribution. (On the particular view I have defended, e.g., we should aim for a set of economic ground rules under which each participant would be able to meet her basic social and economic needs.) These economic ground rules—the object of distributive justice on the institutional approach—are prior to both production and distribution and therefore involve neither the idea of an already existing pool of stuff to be doled out nor the idea of already owned resources to be redistributed.

The institutional conception of distributive justice also does not presuppose the existence of a community of persons committed first of all to share with one another. Rather, it has a far more minimal rationale: we face a choice of economic ground rules that is partly open—not determined by causal necessity, nor preempted by some God-given or natural or neutral scheme that we must choose irrespective of its effects. This choice has a tremen-

---

the established and the engendered effects of social institutions is extensively discussed in Pogge, *Realizing Rawls*, secs. 2–4.

1   *"Everyone is entitled ... can be fully realised"* (my emphasis). Similarly also Rawls's first principle of justice: "Every person has the same indefeasible claim to a fully adequate scheme of equal basic liberties, which scheme is compatible with the same scheme of liberties for all" (latest version, unpublished). In both cases the postulated entitlement or claim is clearly second order.

2   *The institutional approach ... reasonably secure*   This notion is defined in probabilistic terms, perhaps by taking account of various personal characteristics. Thus it is quite possible that the human right to physical integrity is today fulfilled in the United States for middle-aged whites or suburbanites but not for black youths or inner-city residents.

3   *"The idea of distributive justice ... all among themselves"*   Michael Walzer, "The Distribution of Membership," in *Boundaries*, ed. Peter Brown and Henry Shue (Totowa, N.J.: Rowman & Littlefield, 1981), p. 1. Compare the largely identical chap. 2 of Michael Walzer, *Spheres of Justice* (New York: Basic, 1983), p. 31.

4   *there is no central distribution ... doled out*   Nozick, p. 149.

dous impact on human lives, an impact from which persons cannot be insulated and cannot insulate themselves. Our present global economic regime produces a stable pattern of widespread malnutrition and starvation among the poor (with some 20 million persons dying every year from hunger and trivial diseases), and there are likely to be feasible alternative regimes that would not produce similarly severe deprivations. In such a case of avoidable deprivations, we are confronted not by persons who are merely poor and starving but also by victims of an institutional scheme—impoverished and starved. There is an injustice in this economic scheme, which it would be wrong for its more affluent participants to perpetuate. And that is so quite independently of whether we and the starving are united by a communal bond or committed to sharing resources with one another, just as murdering a person is wrong irrespective of such considerations. This is what the assertion of social and economic human rights comes to within my institutional cosmopolitanism.

This institutional cosmopolitanism does not, as such, entail crisp practical conclusions. One reason for this is that I have not—apart from allusions to Rawls and the *Universal Declaration*—given a full list of precisely defined human rights together with relative weights or priority rules. Another reason is that this institutional cosmopolitanism bears upon the burning issues of the day only in an indirect way, mediated by empirical regularities and correlations. This is so chiefly because of its broadly consequentialist character, that is, its commitment to take the engendered consequences of an institutional scheme as seriously, morally, as its established consequences. Whether an institutional scheme establishes avoidable deprivations or inequalities (such as slavery or male suffrage) can be read off from the (written or unwritten) ground rules characterizing this scheme. With regard to engendered deprivations and inequalities, however, we face far more complex empirical questions about how the existing institutional scheme, compared to feasible modifications thereof, tends to affect the incidence of human rights violations, such as rates of infant mortality, child abuse, crime, war, malnutrition, poverty, personal dependence, and exclusion from education or health care.

The intervention of such empirical matters, and the openness of the notion of human rights, do not mean that no conclusions can be drawn about the burning issues, only that what we can conclude is less precise and less definite than one might have hoped.

The Idea of State Sovereignty

Before discussing how we should think about sovereignty in light of my institutional cosmopolitanism, let me define this term, in a somewhat unusual way, as a two-place relation: A is *sovereign* over B if and only if

1. A is a governmental body or officer ("agency"), and
2. B are persons, and
3. A has unsupervised and irrevocable authority over B
   a) to lay down rules constraining their conduct, or
   b) to judge their compliance with rules, or
   c) to enforce rules against them through preemption, prevention, or punishments, or
   d) to act in their behalf vis-à-vis other agencies (ones that do or do not have authority over them) or persons (ones whom A is sovereign over, or not).

A has *absolute sovereignty* over B if and only if

1. A is sovereign over B, and
2. no other agency has any authority over A or over B which is not supervised and revocable by A.

Any A having (absolute) sovereignty over some B can then be said to be an (absolute) sovereign (the one-place predicate).[1]

Central to contemporary political thought and reality is the idea of the autonomous territorial state as the preeminent mode of political organization. In the vertical dimension, sovereignty is very heavily concentrated at a single level; it is states and only states that merit separate colors on a political map of our world. For nearly every human being, and for almost every piece of territory, there is exactly one government with preeminent authority over, and primary responsibility for, this person or territory. And each person is thought to owe primary political allegiance and loyalty to this government with preeminent authority over him or her. National governments dominate and control the decision making of smaller political units as well as supranational decisions, which tend to be made through intergovernmental bargaining.[2]

---

1   *Any A having (absolute) sovereignty ... (the one-place predicate)*   It is quite possible, and not without historical justification, to define sovereignty the way I have defined absolute sovereignty. In that case the expression "distribution of sovereignty" would be an oxymoron.

2   *intergovernmental bargaining*   One promising exception to this is the European Parliament.

From the standpoint of a cosmopolitan morality—which centers around the fundamental needs and interests of individual human beings, and of all human beings—this concentration of sovereignty at one level is no longer defensible. What I am proposing instead is not the idea of a world state, which is really a variant of the preeminent-state idea. Rather, the proposal is that governmental authority—or sovereignty—be widely dispersed in the vertical dimension. What we need is both centralization and decentralization, a kind of second-order decentralization away from the now dominant level of the state. Thus, persons should be citizens of, and govern themselves through, a number of political units of various sizes, without any one political unit being dominant and thus occupying the traditional role of state. And their political allegiance and loyalties[1] should be widely dispersed over these units: neighborhood, town, county, province, state, region, and world at large. People should be politically at home in all of them, without converging upon any one of them as the lodestar of their political identity.[2]

Before defending and developing this proposal by reference to my institutional cosmopolitanism, let me address two types of objection to any vertical division of sovereignty.

Objections of type 1 dispute that sovereignty can be divided at all. The traditional form of this objection rests on the belief that a juridical state (as distinct from a lawless state of nature) presupposes an absolute sovereign. This dogma of absolute sovereignty arises (e.g., in Hobbes and Kant)

roughly as follows. A juridical state, by definition, involves a recognized decision mechanism that uniquely resolves any dispute. This mechanism requires some agency because a mere written or unwritten code (constitution, holy scripture) cannot settle disputes about its own interpretation. But so long as this agency is limited or divided—whether horizontally (i.e., by territory or by governmental function) or vertically (as in my proposal)—a juridical state has not been achieved because there is no recognized way in which conflicts over the precise location of the limit or division can be authoritatively resolved. A genuine state of peace requires then an agency of last resort—ultimate, supreme, and unconstrained. Such an agency may still be limited by (codified or uncodified) obligations. But these can obligate merely *in foro interno* because to authorize subjects, or some second agency, to determine whether the first agency is overstepping its bounds would enable conflicts about this question for which there would be no legal path of resolution.[3]

This argument, which—strictly construed—would require an absolute world sovereign, has been overtaken by the historical facts of the last two hundred years or so, which show conclusively that what cannot work in theory works quite well in practice. Law-governed coexistence is possible without a supreme and unconstrained agency. There is, it is true, the possibility of ultimate conflicts: of disputes in regard to which even the legally correct method of resolution is contested. To see this, one need only imagine how a constitutional democracy's three branches of government might engage in an all-out power struggle, each going to the very brink of what, on its understanding, it is constitutionally authorized to do. From a theoretical point of view, this possibility shows that we are not insured against, and thus live in permanent danger of, constitutional crises. But this no longer undermines our confidence in a genuine division

---

1   *political allegiance and loyalties*   This includes the sentiments of patriotism, if such there must be. Beitz points out two respects in which patriotic allegiance to political units may be desirable: it supports a sense of shared loyalty ("Cosmopolitan Ideals," p. 599); and it allows one to see oneself as a significant contributor to a common cultural project: "Just as we can see ourselves as striving to realize in our own lives various forms of individual perfection, so we can see our countries as striving for various forms of social and communal perfection" ("Cosmopolitan Ideals," p. 600). Neither of these considerations entail that, say, Britain must be the sole object of your patriotic allegiance rather than some combination of Glasgow, Scotland, Britain, Europe, humankind, and perhaps even such geographically dispersed units as the Anglican church, the World Trade Union Movement, PEN, or Amnesty International.

2   *political identity*   Many individuals might, of course, identify more with one of their citizenships than with the others. But in a multilayered scheme such prominent identifications would be less frequent and, most important, would not converge: even if some residents of Glasgow would see themselves as primarily British, others would identify more with Europe, with Scotland, with Glasgow, or with humankind at large.

3   *no legal path of resolution*   This dogma—prefigured in Aquinas, Dante, Marsilius, and Bodin—is most fully stated in chaps. 14, 26, and 29 of Thomas Hobbes, *Leviathan* (Harmondsworth: Penguin, 1981), who also introduces the idea of obligations *in foro interno*. For Kant's statements of it, see Reiss, ed., pp. 75, 81, 144–45. The dogma maintained its hold well into the twentieth century, when it declined together with the Austinian conception of jurisprudence. [John Austin (1790–1859), English legal theorist, associated with "legal positivism."—eds.] See Geoffrey Marshall, *Parliamentary Sovereignty and the Commonwealth* (Oxford: Oxford University Press, 1957), pt. 1; S. I. Benn and R.S. Peters, *Social Principles and the Democratic State* (London: Allen & Unwin, 1959), chaps. 3, 12; and Herbert L.A. Hart, *The Concept of Law* (Oxford: Oxford University Press, 1961).

of powers: we have learned that such crises need not be frequent or irresolvable. From a practical point of view, we know that constitutional democracies can endure and can ensure a robust juridical state.

This same point applies in the vertical dimension as well: just as it is nonsense to suppose that (in a juridical state) sovereignty must rest with one of the branches of government, it is similarly nonsensical to think that in a multilayered scheme sovereignty must be concentrated on one level exclusively. As the history of federalist regimes clearly shows, a vertical division of sovereignty can work quite well in practice, even while it leaves some conflicts over the constitutional allocation of powers without a legal path of authoritative resolution.

Objections of type 2 oppose, more specifically, a vertical dispersal of sovereignty: there are certain vertically indivisible governmental functions that form the core of sovereignty. Any political unit exercising these core functions must be dominant—free to determine the extent to which smaller units within it may engage in their own local political decision making, even while its own political process is immune to regulation and review by more inclusive units. Vertical distributions of sovereignty, if they are to exist at all, must therefore be lopsided (as in current federal regimes).

To be assessable, such a claim stands in need of two clarifications, which are rarely supplied. First, when one thinks about it more carefully, it turns out to be surprisingly difficult to come up with examples of indivisible governmental functions. Eminent domain, economic policy, foreign policy, judicial review; the control of raw materials, security forces, education, health care, and income support; the regulation and taxation of resource extraction and pollution, of work and consumption can all be handled at various levels and indeed are so handled in existing federal regimes and confederations. So what are the governmental functions that supposedly are vertically indivisible? Second, is their indivisibility supposed to be derived from a conceptual insight, from empirical exigencies, or from moral desiderata? And which ones?

Since I cannot here discuss all possible type 2 objections, let me concentrate on one paradigm case: Walzer's claim that the authority to fix membership, to admit and exclude, is at least part of an indivisible core of sovereignty: "At some level of political organization something like the sovereign state must take shape and claim the authority to make its own admissions policy, to control and sometimes to restrain

the flow of immigrants."[1] Walzer's "must" does not reflect a conceptual or empirical necessity, for in those senses the authority in question quite obviously can be divided—for example, by allowing political units on all levels to veto immigration. It is on moral grounds that Walzer rejects such an authority for provinces, towns, and neighborhoods: it would "create a thousand petty fortresses."[2] But if smaller units are to be precluded from controlling the influx of new members, then immigration must be controlled at the state level: "Only if the state makes a selection among would-be members and guarantees the loyalty, security, and welfare of the individuals it selects, can local communities take shape as "indifferent" associations, determined only by personal preference and market capacity."[3] The asserted connection is again a moral one: it is certainly factually possible for local communities to exist as indifferent associations even while no control is exercised over migration at all; as Walzer says, "The fortresses too could be torn down, of course."[4] Walzer's point is, then, that the insistence on openness (to avoid a thousand petty fortresses) is asking too much of neighborhoods, unless the state has control over immigration: "The distinctiveness of cultures and groups depends upon closure....If this distinctiveness is a value, ... then closure must be permitted somewhere."[5]

But is the conventional model, with this rationale, really morally necessary? To be sure, Walzer is right to claim that the value of protecting cohesive neighborhood cultures is better served by national immigration control than by no control at all.[6] But it would be much better served still if the state were constrained to admit only immigrants who are planning to move into a neighborhood that is willing to accept them. Moreover, since a neighborhood culture can be as effectively destroyed by the influx of fellow nationals as by that of immigrants, neighborhoods would do even better, if they had some authority to select from among prospective domestic newcomers or to limit their number. Finally, neighborhoods may often want to bring in new members from abroad—persons to whom they have special ethnic, religious, or cultural ties—and they would therefore benefit

---

1   "At some level ... flow of immigrants" Walzer, "Distribution," p. 10.

2   "create a thousand petty fortresses" Ibid., p. 9.

3   "Only if the state ... market capacity" Ibid.

4   "The fortresses too could be torn down, of course." Ibid.

5   "The distinctiveness of cultures ... closure must be permitted somewhere." Ibid., pp. 9–10.

6   To be sure ... no control at all Ibid., p. 9.

from a role in the national immigration control process that would allow them to facilitate the admission of such persons. Thus there are at least three reasons for believing that Walzer's rationale—cohesive neighborhood cultures ought to be protected without becoming petty fortresses—is actually better served by a division of the authority to admit and exclude than by the conventional concentration of this authority at the level of the state.

Some Main Reasons for a Vertical Dispersal of Sovereignty

Having dealt with some preliminary obstacles, let me now sketch four main reasons favoring, over the status quo, a world in which sovereignty is widely distributed vertically.

1. *Peace/security.*—Under the current regime, interstate rivalries are settled ultimately through military competition, including the threat and use of military force. Moreover, within their own territories, national governments are free to do virtually anything they like. Such governments therefore have very powerful incentives and very broad opportunities to develop their military might. This is bound to lead to the further proliferation of nuclear, biological, chemical, and conventional weapons of mass destruction. And in a world in which dozens of competing national governments control such weapons, the outbreak of devastating wars is only a matter of time. It is not feasible to reduce and eliminate national control over weapons of mass destruction through a program that depends upon the voluntary cooperation of each and every national government. What is needed, therefore, is the centrally enforced reduction and elimination of such weapons—in violation of the prevalent idea of state sovereignty. Such a program, if implemented soon, is much less dangerous than continuing the status quo. It could gain the support of most peoples and governments, if it increases the security of all on fair terms that are effectively adjudicated and enforced.

2. *Reducing oppression.*—Under the current global regime, national governments are effectively free to control "their" populations in whatever way they see fit. Many make extensive use of this freedom by torturing and murdering their domestic opponents, censoring information, suppressing and subverting democratic procedures, prohibiting emigration, and so forth. This problem could be reduced through a vertical dispersal of sovereignty over various layers of political units that would check and balance one another as well as publicize one another's abuses.

3. *Global economic justice.*—The magnitude and extent of current economic deprivations—over 20 million persons die every year from poverty-related causes—calls for some modification in the prevailing scheme of economic cooperation. One plausible reform would involve a global levy on the use of natural resources to support the economic development in the poorest areas.[1] Such a levy would tend to equalize per capita endowments and also encourage conservation. Reforms for the sake of economic justice would again involve some centralization—though without requiring anything like a global welfare bureaucracy.

Global economic justice is an end in its own right, which requires, and therefore supports, a reallocation of political authority. But it is also important as a means toward the first two purposes. War and oppression result from the contest for power within and among political units, which tends to be the more intense the higher the stakes. In fights to govern states, or to redraw their borders, far too much is now at stake by way of control of people and resources. We can best lower the stakes by dispersing political authority over several levels and institutionally securing economic justice at the global level.

This important point suggests why my first three considerations—though each supports some centralization—do not on balance support a world state. While a world state could lead to significant progress in terms of peace and economic justice, it also poses significant risks of oppression. Here the kind of multilayered scheme I propose has the great advantages of affording plenty of checks and balances and of assuring that, even when some political units turn tyrannical and oppressive, there will always be other, already fully organized political units (above, below, or on the same level) which can render aid and protection to the oppressed, publicize the abuses, and, if necessary, fight the oppressors.

There are two further important reasons against a world state. Cultural and social diversity are likely to be much better protected when the interests of cultural communities at all levels are represented (externally) and supported (internally) by coordinate political units. And the scheme I propose could be gradually reached from where we are now (through what I have called second-order decentralization), while a world state—involving, as it does, the annihilation

---

1   *One plausible reform ... in the poorest areas*   For further discussion of such a reform—backed perhaps by the idea that the world's resources should be owned or controlled by all its inhabitants as equals—see Beitz, *Political Theory*, pp. 136–43; and Pogge, *Realizing Rawls*, pp. 250–52, 263–65.

of existing states—would seem reachable only through revolution or in the wake of some global catastrophe.

4. *Ecology.*—Modern processes of production and consumption are liable to generate significant negative externalities that, to a large and increasing extent, transcend national borders. In a world of competing autonomous states, the internalization of such externalities is generally quite imperfect because of familiar isolation, assurance, and coordination problems. Treaties among a large number of very differently situated actors require difficult and time-consuming bargaining and negotiations, which often lead to only very slight progress, if any. And even when treaties are achieved, doubts about the full compliance of other parties tend to erode each party's own commitment to make good-faith efforts toward compliance.

Now one might think that this fourth reason goes beyond my institutional cosmopolitanism because there is no recognized human right to a clean environment. Why should people not be free to live in a degraded natural environment if they so choose? In response, perhaps they should be, but for now they won't have had a choice. The degradation of our natural environment ineluctably affects us all. And yet, most people are effectively excluded from any say about this issue which, in the current state-centric model, is regulated by national governments unilaterally or through intergovernmental bargaining heavily influenced by huge differentials in economic and military might.

This response suggests replacing *ecology* with a deeper and more general fourth reason, which might be labeled *democracy*: persons have a right to an institutional order under which those significantly and legitimately[1] affected by a political decision have a roughly equal opportunity to influence the making of this decision—directly or through elected delegates or representatives.[2] Such a human right

to political participation also supports greater local autonomy in matters of purely local concern than exists in most current states or would exist in a world state, however democratic. In fact, it supports just the kind of multilayered institutional scheme I have proposed.

Before developing this idea further, let me consider an objection. One might say, against a human right to political participation, that what matters about political decisions is that they be correct, not that they be made democratically by those concerned. But this objection applies, first of all, only to political choices that are morally closed and thus can be decided correctly or incorrectly. I believe that we should reject a view on which almost all political choices are viewed as morally closed (with the correct decision determined, perhaps, through utility differentials), but I have no space here to defend this belief. Second, even when political choices are morally closed, the primary and ultimate responsibility for their being made correctly should lie with the persons concerned. Of course, some other decision procedure—such as a group of experts—may be more reliable for this or that kind of decision, and such procedures (judges, parliaments, cabinets, etc.) should then be put in place. This should be done, however, by the people delegating, or abstaining from, such decisions. It is ultimately up to them, and not to self-appointed experts, to recognize the greater reliability of, and to institutionalize, alternative decision-making procedures.

Given the postulated human right to political participation, the proper vertical distribution of sovereignty is determined by three sets of considerations. The first favor decentralization, the second centralization, while the third may correct the resulting balance in either direction.

First, decision making should be decentralized as far as possible. This is desirable in part, of course, in order to minimize the decision-making burdens upon individuals.

---

1   *legitimately* The qualification "legitimately" is necessary to rule out claims such as this: "I should be allowed a vote on the permissibility of homosexuality, in all parts of the world, because the knowledge that homosexual acts are performed anywhere causes me great distress." I cannot enter a discussion of this proviso here, except to say that the arguments relevant to its specification are by and large analogous to the standard arguments relevant to the specification of Mill's no-harm principle.

2   *directly or through elected delegates or representatives* I understand opportunity as being impaired only by (social) disadvantages—not by (natural) handicaps. This is plausible only on a narrow construal of "handicap." Although being black and being female are natural features, they reduce a person's chances to affect political decisions only in certain social settings (in a racist/sexist culture). Such

reductions should therefore count as disadvantages. By contrast, those whose lesser ability to participate in public debate is due to their low intelligence are not disadvantaged but handicapped. They do not count as having a less-than-equal opportunity. The postulated human right is not a group right. Of course, the inhabitants of a town may appeal to this right to show that it was wrong for the national government, say, to impose some political decision that affects only them. In such a case, the townspeople form a group of those having a grievance. But they do not have a grievance as a group. Rather, each of them has such a grievance of not having been given her due political weight—just the grievance she would have had, had the decision been made by other townspeople with her excluded.

But there are more important reasons as well. Insofar as decisions are morally closed, outsiders are more likely to lack the knowledge and sensitivities to make responsible judgments—and the only practicable and morally acceptable way of delimiting those who are capable of such judgments is by rough geographical criteria. Insofar as decisions are morally open, the end must be to maximize each person's opportunity to influence the social conditions that shape her life—which should not be diluted for the sake of enhancing persons' opportunities to influence decisions of merely local significance elsewhere. At least persons should be left free to decide for themselves to what extent to engage in such exchanges. The first consideration does not then rule out voluntary creation of central decision-making mechanisms (even though their structure—dependent upon unanimous consent—would tend to reflect the participants' bargaining power). Such centralization may be rational, for example, in cases of conflict between local and global rationality (tragedy-of-the-commons cases: fishing, grazing, pollution) and also in regard to desired projects that require many contributors because they involve coordination problems or economies of scale, for example, or because they are simply too expensive (construction and maintenance of transportation and communication systems, research and technology, space programs, and so forth).

The second consideration favors centralization insofar as this is necessary to avoid excluding persons from the making of decisions that significantly (and legitimately) affect them. Such decisions are of two—possibly three—kinds. Inhabiting the same natural environment and being significantly affected by what others do to it, we have a right to participate in regulating how it may be used. And since the lives each of us can lead are very significantly shaped by prevailing institutions—such as marriage, reproduction and birth control, property, money, markets, and forms of political organization—we have a right to participate in their choice and design. These two kinds of decision arise directly from Kant's point that human beings cannot avoid influencing one another: through direct contact and through their impact upon the natural world in which they coexist. A right to participate in decisions of the third kind is more controversial. There are contexts, one might say, in which we act as a species and thus should decide together how to act. Examples might be our conduct toward other biological species (extinction, genetic engineering, cruelty), ventures into outer space, and the preservation of our human heritage (ancient skeletons and artifacts, great works of art and architecture, places of exceptional natural beauty). In all these cases it would seem wrong for one person or group to take irremediable steps unilaterally.

The significance of the second consideration depends heavily upon empirical matters, though it does so in a rather straightforward and accessible way. It is obvious upon minimal reflection that the developments of the past few centuries have greatly increased the significance of this consideration in favor of centralization. This is so partly because of rising population density, but much more importantly because of our vastly more powerful technologies and the tremendously increased level of global interdependence. Concerning technologies, the fact that what a population does within its own national borders—stockpiling weapons of mass destruction, depleting nonrenewable resources, cutting down vegetation essential for the reproduction of oxygen, emitting pollutants that are destroying the ozone layer and cause global warming—now often imposes very significant harms and risks upon outsiders brings into play the political human rights of these outsiders, thereby morally undermining the conventional insistence on absolute state autonomy. Global interdependence is best illustrated by the emergence of truly global capital and commodity markets (as dramatically illustrated by the stock market crash of October 1987): a change in Japanese interest rates, or a speculative frenzy of short-selling on the Chicago Futures Exchange, can literally make the difference between life and death for large numbers of people half a world away—in Africa, for example, where many countries depend upon foreign borrowing and cash crop exports. Such interdependence is not bad as such (it can hardly be scaled back in any case), but it does require democratic centralization of decision making: as more and more persons are significantly affected by certain institutions, more and more persons have a right to a political role in shaping them. The possibility of free bargaining over the design of such institutions does not satisfy the equal-opportunity principle, as is illustrated in the case of commodity markets by the fact that African populations simply lack the bargaining power that would allow them significantly to affect how such markets are organized. (This argument withstands the communitarian claim that we must reject supranational democratic processes for the sake of the value of national autonomy. Such rejection does indeed enhance the national autonomy of the advantaged First World populations. But their gain is purchased at the expense of poorer populations who, despite fictional or de jure state sovereignty, have virtually no control over the most basic parameters that shape their lives—a problem heightened by the fact that even their own, rather impotent governments face strong incentives to cater to foreign interests rather than to those of their constituents.)

The first two considerations by themselves yield the result that the authority to make decisions of some particular kind should rest with the democratic political process of a unit that (i) is as small as possible but still (ii) includes as equals all persons significantly and legitimately affected by decisions of this kind. In practice, some trading-off is required between these two considerations because there cannot always be an established political process that includes as equals all and only those significantly affected. A matter affecting the populations of two provinces, for example, might be referred to the national parliament or might be left to bargaining between the two provincial governments. The former solution caters to (ii) at the expense of (i): involving many persons who are not legitimately affected. The latter solution caters to (i) at the expense of (ii): giving the persons legitimately affected not an equal opportunity to influence the matter but one that depends on the relative bargaining power of the two provincial governments.

The first two considerations would suffice on the ideal-theory assumption that any decisions made satisfy all moral constraints with regard to both procedure (the equal-opportunity requirement) and output (this and other human rights). This assumption, however, could hardly be strictly true in practice. And so a third consideration must come into play: what would emerge as the proper vertical distribution of sovereignty from a balancing of the first two considerations alone should be modified—in either direction—if such modification significantly increases the democratic nature of decision making or its reliability (as measured in terms of human rights fulfillment). Let me briefly discuss how this third consideration might make a difference.

On the one hand, one must ask whether it would be a gain for human rights fulfillment on balance to transfer decision-making authority "upward" to larger units—or (perhaps more plausibly) to make the political process of smaller units subject to regulation and/or review by the political process of more inclusive units. Such authority would allow the larger unit, on human rights grounds,[1] to

require revisions in the structure of the political process of the smaller one and/or to nullify its political decisions and perhaps also to enforce such revisions and nullifications.

Even when such interventions really do protect human rights, this regulation and review authority has some costs in terms of the political human rights of the members of the smaller unit. But then, of course, the larger unit's regulation and review process may itself be unreliable and thus may produce human rights violations either by overturning unobjectionable structures or decisions (at even greater cost to the political human rights of members of the smaller unit) or by forcing the smaller unit to adopt structures and decisions that directly violate human rights.

On the other hand, there is also the inverse question: whether the third consideration might support a move in the direction of decentralization. Thus one must ask to what extent the political process of a larger unit is undemocratic or unreliable, and whether it might be a gain for human rights fulfillment on balance to transfer decision-making authority "downward" to smaller units—or to invest the political process of such subunits with review authority. Such an authority might, for example, allow provincial governments, on human rights grounds, to block the application of national laws in their province. This authority is justified if and only if its benefits (laws passed in an undemocratic manner or violating human rights are not applied) outweigh its costs (unobjectionable laws are blocked in violation of the political rights of members of the larger unit).

How such matters should be weighed is a highly complex question, which I cannot here address with any precision. Let me make two points nevertheless. First, a good deal of weight should be given to the actual views of those who suffer abridgments of their human rights and for whose benefit a regulation and/or review authority might thus be called for. If most blacks in some state would rather suffer discrimination than see their state government constrained by the federal government, then the presumption against such an authority should be much weightier than if the opposition came only from the whites. This is not to deny that victims of injustice may be brainwashed or may suffer from false consciousness of various sorts. It may still be possible to make the case for a regulation and/or review authority. But it should be significantly more difficult to do so.

---

1   *human rights grounds*   Though not in defense of other procedural or substantive constraints to which the smaller unit may have chosen to commit itself. Compare here the situation in the United States, where federal courts may review whether laws and decisions at the state level accord with superordinate federal requirements, but not whether they accord with superordinate requirements of that state itself.

Second, commonalities of language, religion, ethnicity, or history are strictly irrelevant. Such commonalities do not give people a claim to be part of one another's political lives, nor does the lack of such commonalities argue against restraints. The presence or absence of such commonalities may still be empirically significant, however. Thus suppose that the members of some smaller unit share religious or ethnic characteristics that in the larger unit are in the minority (e.g., a Muslim province within a predominantly Hindu state). Our historical experience with such cases may well support the view that a regulation and review authority by the larger unit would probably be frequently abused or that a review authority by the smaller unit would tend to enhance human rights fulfillment overall. The relevance of such information brings out that the required weighings do not depend on value judgments alone. They also depend on reasonable expectations about how alternative arrangements would actually work in one or another concrete context.

The third consideration must also play a central role in a special case: the question of where decisions about the proper allocation of decision making should be made. For example, should a dispute between a provincial parliament and a national legislature over which of them is properly in charge of a particular decision be referred to the provincial or the national supreme court? Here again one must present arguments to the effect that the preferred locus of decision making is likely to be more reliable than its alternative.

Nothing definite can be said about the ideal number of levels or the exact distribution of legislative, executive, and judicial functions over them. These matters might vary in space and time, depending on the prevailing empirical facts to be accommodated by my second and third considerations (externalities, interdependence; unreliabilities) and on persons' preferences as shaped by the historical, cultural, linguistic, or religious ties among them. The human right to political participation also leaves room for a wide variety, hence regional diversity, of decision-making procedures—direct or representative, with or without political parties, and so on. Democracy may take many forms.

The Shaping and Reshaping of Political Units

One great advantage of the proposed multilayered scheme is, I have said, that it can be reached gradually from where we are now. This requires moderate centralizing and decentralizing moves involving the strengthening of political units above and below the level of the state. In some cases, such units will have to be created, and so we need some ideas about how the geographical shape of new political units is to be determined. Or, seeing that there is considerable dissatisfaction about even the geographical shape of existing political units, we should ask more broadly: What principles ought to govern the geographical separation of political units on any level?

Guided again by the cosmopolitan ideal of democracy, I suggest these two procedural principles as a first approximation:

1. The inhabitants of any contiguous territory of reasonable shape may decide—through some majoritarian or supermajoritarian procedure—to join an existing political unit whose territory is contiguous with theirs and whose population is willing—as assessed through some majoritarian or supermajoritarian procedure—to accept them as members.[1] This liberty is conditional upon the political unit or units that are truncated through such a move either remaining viable (with a contiguous territory of reasonable shape and sufficient population) or being willingly incorporated, pursuant to the first clause, into another political unit or other political units.

2. The inhabitants of any contiguous territory of reasonable shape, if sufficiently numerous, may decide—through some majoritarian or supermajoritarian procedure—to form themselves into a political unit of a level commensurate with their number. This liberty is subject to three constraints: there may be subgroups whose members, pursuant to their liberty under 1, are free to reject membership in the unit to be formed in favor of membership in another political unit. There may be subgroups whose members, pursuant to their

---

1 *The inhabitants of any contiguous territory ... to accept them as members* I won't try to be precise about "reasonable shape." The idea is to rule out areas with extremely long borders, or borders that divide towns, integrated networks of economic activity, or the like. Perhaps the inhabitants in question should have to be minimally numerous; but I think the threshold could be quite low. If a tiny border village wants to belong to the neighboring province, why should it not be allowed to switch? The contiguity condition needs some relaxing to allow territories consisting of a small number of internally contiguous areas whose access to one another is not controlled by other political units. The United States of America would satisfy this relaxed condition through secure access among Puerto Rico, Alaska, Hawaii, and the remaining forty-eight contiguous states.

liberty under 2, are free to reject membership in the unit to be formed in favor of forming their own political unit on the same level.[1] And the political unit or units truncated through the requested move must either remain viable (with a contiguous territory of reasonable shape and sufficient population) or be willingly incorporated, pursuant to the first clause of 1, into another political unit or other political units.

It will be said that acceptance of such principles would trigger an avalanche of applications. It is surely true that a large number of existing groups are unhappy with their current membership status; there is a significant backlog, so to speak, that might pose a serious short-term problem. Once this backlog will have been worked down, however, there may not be much redrawing activity as people will then be content with their political memberships, and most borders will be supported by stable majorities.

Moreover, as the advocated vertical dispersal of sovereignty is implemented, conflicts over borders will lose much of their intensity. In our world, many such conflicts are motivated by morally inappropriate considerations—especially the following two. There is competition over valuable or strategically important territories and groups because their possession importantly affects the distribution of international bargaining power (economic and military potential) for the indefinite future. And there are attempts by the more affluent to interpose borders between themselves and the poor in order to circumvent widely recognized duties of distributive justice among compatriots.[2] Under the proposed multilayered scheme—in which the political authority currently exercised by national governments is both constrained and dispersed over several layers, and in which economic justice is institutionalized at the global level and thus inescapable—territorial disputes on any level would be only slightly more intense than disputes about provincial or county lines are now. It is quite possible that my two principles are not suitable for defining a right to secession in our present world of excessively sovereign states.[3] But their plausibility will increase as the proposed second-order decentralization progresses.[4]

Finally, the incidence of applications can be reduced through two reasonable amendments. First, the burden of proof, in appealing to either of the two principles, should rest with the advocates of change, who must map out an appropriate territory, organize its population, and so forth. This burden would tend to discourage frivolous claims. Second, it may be best to require some supermajoritarian process (e.g., proponents must outnumber opponents plus nonvoters in three consecutive referenda over a two-year period). Some such provision would especially help prevent areas changing back and forth repeatedly (with outside supporters moving in, perhaps, in order to tip the scales).

Let me briefly illustrate how the two principles would work in the case of nested political units. Suppose the Kashmiris agree that they want to belong together as one province but are divided on whether this should be a province of India or of Pakistan. The majority West Kashmiris favor affiliation with Pakistan, the East Kashmiris favor affiliation with India. There are four plausible outcomes: a united Kashmiri province of Pakistan (P), a united Kashmiri province of India (I), a separate state of Kashmir (S), and a divided Kashmir belonging partly to Pakistan and partly to India (D). Since the East Kashmiris can, by principle 2, unilaterally insist on D over P, they enjoy some protection against the West Kashmiri majority. They can use this protection for bargaining, which may result in outcome S (if this is the second preference on both sides) or even

---

1   *There may be subgroups ... on the same level*   What if minority subgroups are geographically dispersed (like the Serbs in Croatia)? In such cases, there is no attractive way of accommodating those opposed to the formation of the new political unit. My second principle would let the preference of the majority within the relevant territory prevail nevertheless. This is defensible, I think, so long as we can bracket any concern for human rights violations. Where justice is not at stake, it seems reasonable, if legitimate preferences are opposed and some must be frustrated, to let the majority prevail.

2   *And there are attempts by the more affluent ... justice among compatriots*   See Alan Buchanan, *Secession* (Boulder, Colo.: Westview, 1991), pp. 114–25; and Thomas W. Pogge, "Loopholes in Moralities," *Journal of Philosophy* 89 (1992): 79–98, pp. 88–90.

3   *It is quite possible ... excessively sovereign states*   That topic is extensively discussed by Buchanan. While he takes the current states system for granted and adjusts his theory of secession accordingly, I am arguing that a more appealing theory of secession would be plausible in the context of a somewhat different global order. I thereby offer one more reason in favor of the latter.

4   *But their plausibility ... decentralization progresses*   For example, as European states will increasingly become subject to global and regional constraints—regarding military might, pollution, exploitation of resources, treatment of its citizens, etc.—the importance of whether there is one state (Czechoslovakia) or two states (one Czech, one Slovak) would tend to decline: for the Slovaks, for the Czechs, and for any third parties in the vicinity.

in outcome I (if that is the second preference of the West Kashmiris while the East Kashmiris prefer D or S over P).[1]

The conventional alternatives to my cosmopolitan view on settling the borders of political units reserve a special role either for historical states and their members (compatriots) or for nations and their members (fellow nationals). The former version is inherently conservative, the latter potentially revisionist (by including, e.g., the Arab, Kurdish, and Armenian nations and by excluding multinational states like the Soviet Union or the Sudan). The two key claims of such a position are: (a) Only (encompassing) groups of compatriots/fellow nationals have a right to self-government. (b) Such government may be exercised even over unwilling geographical subgroups of compatriots/fellow nationals (who at most have a liberty of individual emigration).[2] Those who hold such a conventional position are liable to reject my cosmopolitan view as excessively individualist, contractarian, or voluntaristic. Examples of this sentiment are easy to find: "The more important human groupings need to be based on shared history, and on criteria of nonvoluntaristic (or at least not wholly contractarian) membership to have the value that they have."[3] Insofar as this is an empirical claim— about the preconditions of authentic solidarity and mutual trust, perhaps—I need not disagree with it.[4] If indeed a political unit is far more valuable for its members when they share a common descent and upbringing (language, culture, religion), then people will recognize this fact and will themselves seek to form political units along these lines. I don't doubt that groups seeking to change their political status under the two principles would for the most part be groups characterized by such unchosen commonalities.

But would I not give any other group, too, the right to change its political status, even if this means exchanging a more valuable for a less valuable membership? Margalit and Raz ridicule this idea through their examples of "the Tottenham Football Club supporters," "the fiction-reading public," and "the group of all the people whose surnames begin with a 'g' and end with an 'e.'"[5] Yet these examples—apart from being extremely farfetched—are ruled out by the contiguity requirement, which a "voluntarist" can and, I believe, should accept in light of the key function of government: to support shared rules among persons who cannot avoid influencing one another through direct interaction and through their impact upon their common environment. A more plausible example would then be that of the inhabitants of a culturally and linguistically Italian border village who prefer an (ex hypothesi) less valuable membership in France over a more valuable membership in Italy. Here I ask, Do they not, France willing, have a right to err? Or should they be forced to remain in, or be turned over to, a superordinate political unit against their will?

This example brings out the underlying philosophical value conflict. My cosmopolitanism is committed to the freedom of individual persons and therefore envisions a pluralist global institutional scheme. Such a scheme is compatible with political units whose membership is

---

1 *(if that is the second preference ... East Kashmiris prefer D or S over P)* Obviously, this story is not meant to reflect the actual situation on the Indian subcontinent.

2 *(who at most ... individual emigration)* While the precise definition of 'nation' and 'nationality' is not essential to my discussion, I do assume that nationality is not defined entirely in voluntaristic terms (e.g., "a nation is a group of persons all of whom desire to constitute one political unit of which they are the only members"), in which case the two claims would become trivial. The definition may still contain significant voluntaristic elements, as in Renan's proposal: "A nation is a grand solidarity constituted by the sentiment of sacrifices which one has made and those one is disposed to make again. It supposes a past" (quoted in Brian Barry, "Self-Government Revisited," in *The Nature of Political Theory*, ed. David Miller and Larry Siedentop [Oxford: Clarendon, 1983], p. 136). So long as some nonvoluntaristic element is present, at least one of the two claims can get off the ground: those who want to belong together as one political unit may be prevented from doing so when they lack an appropriate history of solidarity and sacrifices.

3 *"The more important human groupings ... value that they have"* Avishai Margalit and Joseph Raz, "National Self-Determination," *Journal of Philosophy* 57 (1990): 439–61, p. 456.

4 *I need not disagree with it* Though one should ask how this claim squares with the history of the United States, in the nineteenth

century, say. Those who enjoyed the rights of citizenship were highly heterogeneous in descent and upbringing, and they came as immigrants, through sheer choice. I do not believe these facts significantly reduced the level of solidarity and mutual trust they enjoyed, compared to the levels enjoyed in the major European states of that period. A careful study of this case might well show that people can be bound together by a common decision to follow the call of a certain constitution and ideology as well as the promise of opportunities and adventure. If so, this would suggest that what matters for solidarity and mutual trust is the will to make a political life together and that such will is possible without unchosen commonalities. This result would hardly be surprising, seeing how easily the closest friendships we form transcend such commonalities of facial features, native language, cultural background, and religious convictions.

5 *"the Tottenham Football Club supporters," ... surnames begin with a 'g' and end with an 'e'"* Margalit and Raz, pp. 443, 456.

homogeneous with respect to some partly unchosen criteria (nationality, ethnicity, native language, history, religion, etc.), and it would certainly engender such units. But it would do so only because persons choose to share their political life with others who are like themselves in such respects—not because persons are entitled to be part of one another's political lives if and only if they share certain unchosen features.

One way of supporting the conventional alternative involves rejecting the individualist premise that only human beings are ultimate units of moral concern.[1] One could then say that, once the moral claims of states/nations are taken into account alongside those of persons, one may well find that, all things considered, justice requires institutional arrangements that are inferior, in human rights terms, to feasible alternatives—institutional arrangements, for example, under which the interest of Italy in its border village would prevail over the expressed interest of the villagers.

This justificatory strategy faces two main problems. It is unclear how states/nations can have interests or moral claims that are not reducible to interests and moral claims of their members (which can be accommodated within a conception of human rights). This idea smacks of bad metaphysics[2] and also is dangerously subject to political/ideological manipulation (as exemplified by Charles de Gaulle who was fond of adducing the interests of la nation against those of his French compatriots). Moreover, it is unclear why this idea should work here, but not in the case of other kinds of (sub- and supranational) political units, nor in that of religious, cultural, and athletic entities. Why need we not also take into account the moral claims of Catholicism, art, or baseball?

These problems suggest the other justificatory strategy, which accepts the individualist premise but then formulates the political rights of persons with essential reference to the state/nation whose members they are. This strategy has been defended, most prominently, by Michael Walzer, albeit in a treatise that focuses on international ethics (interactions) rather than international justice (institutions). Walzer approvingly quotes Westlake: "The duties and rights of states are nothing more than the duties and rights of the men who compose them," adding "the rights ... [to] territorial integrity and political sovereignty ... belong to states, but they derive ultimately from the rights of individuals, and from them they take their force.... States are neither organic wholes nor mystical unions."[3]

The key question is, of course, how such a derivation is supposed to work. There are two possibilities. The direct route would be to postulate either a human right to be governed by one's compatriots/fellow nationals[4] or a human right to participate in the exercise of sovereignty over one's compatriots/fellow nationals. The former of these rights is implausibly demanding upon others (the Bavarians could insist on being part of Germany, even if all the other Germans wanted nothing to do with them) and would still fail to establish b, unless it were also unwaivable—a duty, really. The latter right is implausibly demanding upon those obligated to continue to abide by the common will merely because they have once (however violently) been incorporated into a state or merely because they have once shared solidarity and sacrifices.

The indirect, instrumental route would involve the empirical claim that human rights (on a noneccentric definition) are more likely to be satisfied, or are satisfied to a greater extent, if there is, for each person, one political unit that decisively shapes her life and is dominated by her compatriots/fellow nationals. This route remains open on my cosmopolitan conception (via the third consideration), though the relevant empirical claim would not seem to be sustainable on the historical record.

Supposing that this sort of argument fails on empirical grounds, my institutional cosmopolitanism would favor a global order in which sovereignty is widely distributed vertically, while the geographical shape of political units is determined by the autonomous preferences of situated individuals in accordance with principles 1 and 2.

---

1 *ultimate units of moral concern* For an example, see Brian Barry, "Do Countries Have Moral Obligations?" in *The Tanner Lectures on Human Value*, vol. 2, ed. S.M. McMurrin (Salt Lake City: University of Utah Press, 1981), pp. 27–44.

2 *bad metaphysics* Rawls makes this point: "We want to account for the social values, for the intrinsic good of institutional, community, and associative activities, by a conception of justice that in its theoretical basis is individualistic. For reasons of clarity among others, we do not want to ... suppose that society is an organic whole with a life of its own distinct from and superior to that of all its members in their relations with one another" (p. 264).

3 *"The duties and rights of states ... neither organic wholes nor mystical unions"* Michael Walzer, *Just and Unjust Wars* (New York: Basic, 1977), p. 53; cf. Walzer. "The Moral Standing of States," in Beitz et al., eds., p. 219.

4 *governed by one's compatriots/fellow nationals* Walzer suggests this tack: "Citizens of a sovereign state have a right, insofar as they are to be ravaged and coerced at all, to suffer only at one another's hand" (*Wars*, p. 86).

HARRY BRIGHOUSE
(1961–)
and ADAM SWIFT
(1963–)

Harry Brighouse and Adam Swift are at the forefront of a group of philosophers who have begun to deepen and clarify the rights of children and the rights and obligations that join parents and children. Brighouse is Professor of Philosophy and Affiliate Professor of Educational Policy Studies at University of Wisconsin, Madison. Swift is CUF University Lecturer in Politics and Director of the Centre for the Study of Social Justice at Balliol College. Individually, they have contributed widely to debates on liberal theory, social justice, educational reform, social choice theory, and egalitarianism. They are joint authors of a number of important works, including the forthcoming book *Family Values* (2009).

The idea that children have rights is of quite recent origins; it did not gain widespread prominence until the 1970s. Generally, if children were thought to have rights at all, they were thought to possess them derivatively in virtue of their relationship to their parents. Today, it is widely agreed that children possess both legal and human rights. The General Assembly of the United Nations adopted the *Convention on the Rights of the Children* in November of 1989; 193 countries have ratified it, with the United States a notable exception. The *Convention* extends to children the rights to be protected from abuse and exploitation, and to be provided with

an adequate standard of living, health care and education. Much more controversially, it also guarantees children's rights to freedom of thought, conscience, and religion; the right to freedom of association; and the right to protection from arbitrary interference with privacy.

The *Convention* is a welcome legal response to the appalling conditions under which many of the world's children live. It is, however, in need of philosophical clarification. The status of children poses challenges for liberal thinkers, especially those who emphasize the importance of agency and ground their liberalism on a notion of the moral equality of persons. Theories of rights are typically based either upon autonomy or interest (or both). It is relatively uncontroversial to argue that many of the *Convention* rights can be justified because they safeguard children's fundamental interests –children who are abused, forced to work long hours, malnourished, or deprived of basic education surely fall below the minimal threshold for a decent life.

At the same time, children require paternalistic supervision and are thus only potentially autonomous agents who possess full moral equality. Parents typically restrict their children's freedom of association, sometimes with good reason. Moreover, rights to freedom of thought, conscience, and religion protect agents' autonomy. It is difficult to know what they imply for agents who are not yet fully autonomous and these rights raise difficult questions about the role of parenting. Children's consciences are not fully developed and require parental guidance. It is also widely accepted that parents have a right to exercise a significant influence on children's values, including religious values; exerting such influence may in some cases reduce their children's future capacity for autonomy.

In "Parents' Rights and the Value of the Family," Brighouse and Swift address the vexing question of the rights that parents have over their children. Two ideas about the relationship between parents and children have predominated throughout the history of political thought. First, philosophers from Aristotle to Hobbes have held that children are their parents' property. In some cases, ownership is thought to give parents complete license over their offspring—to work, to sell, or even to kill. Other thinkers have maintained that, though children are property, parents also have the obligation to further their children's interests or, in some cases, the interests of society as a whole. Second, philosophers have seen children as potential adults who require parental supervision until they mature.

Few social and political theorists today believe that parents own their children. But the notion that parents are simply guarantors of their children's interests raises its own puzzles. If we base parents' rights over their children on the need to safeguard children's *interests*, a counterintuitive possibility arises. In at least some circumstances, the state would be justified in taking children away from perfectly adequate parents and giving them to adults who are in a better position to further their interests. It also might be the case that parents have no right to take actions that might undermine their children's autonomy (actions such as raising them in a particular religious or cultural tradition).

What is lacking in interest-based accounts of children's rights is a justification of the parental relationship itself; an account of why parents do have a right to have an intimate relationship with their own children is needed. Brighouse and Swift provide one of the most recent and promising accounts of the right to this relationship, pointing toward new directions in social and political thought around children's and parents' rights.

◆ ◆ ◆ ◆ ◆

Parents' Rights and the Value of the Family (2006)

1. Liberalism and Rights

Fundamental to the many varieties of liberalism is some version of the idea that individuals have rights to control over their own lives, rights that may not be overridden except, perhaps, when they conflict with those of others, or to avert very great disasters. Variants of liberalism differ on exactly what these rights are and under what conditions they can properly be overridden. But the basic idea is undisputed.

Most liberals have made at least one exception. Children, especially when they are very young, do not have rights to control over their own lives. Some adult, or some combination of adults, may properly control their lives. Usually, in societies in which liberal ideals are prominent in the public culture, the adults authorized to exert control are the children's parents, either biological or adoptive. These adults do not have the power of life and death over the children—other adults hold them in check in various ways—but they are the primary bearers of authority over and responsibility for the children.

It is natural to describe these adults as having rights over their children. They are legally authorized to exercise a great deal of discretion over the conditions in which their children are raised, the kind of education they will receive, what they will eat and do with their "spare time," with whom they will play, and so on. But do they have rights in a more fundamental sense? If, for example, the state decided to redistribute children at, or soon after, birth, from what it deemed less suitable to what it deemed more suitable parents, would it be violating the rights of parents (as opposed to merely harming them or doing some wrong to the child)? If it interfered with parents' ability to transmit their values to their children, would it be violating their rights? What if it prevented them from transmitting their wealth to their children?

In this article we argue that parents do indeed have rights with respect to their children.[1] This claim has two components. First, it is morally permissible for parents to pursue certain of their own interests at some cost to their children's interests; it is wrong for the state (or anyone else) to prevent them from exercising that permission. Second, there are things that it is permissible for them to do to, for, and with their children that it is not permissible for anyone else to do; this exclusive situation is justified not merely by

---

1   *their children*   [Unless otherwise indicated, all notes to this selection are by the authors of this selection.] Describing the children with respect to whom parents have rights as "their children" does not commit us to the view that parents have such rights specifically with respect to their biological children (see Sec. VI). The rights in question are held by adults with respect to the children they parent. One question at stake in the article concerns what principles should determine the distribution of parenting relationships.

reference to the interests of the children but by reference to the interests of the parents themselves.

This claim may seem obviously true. We think that its truth is not obvious and that, though true, it supports far less than most people take for granted in thinking about parents' rights. It does not, for example, imply that parents have a fundamental right to confer their wealth on their children, nor that they have extensive rights in transmitting their values to their children.[1] Furthermore, their rights are conditional on their succeeding in protecting their children's interests up to a fairly high threshold. So although parents' rights are, indeed, fundamental, they are conditional and limited.

2. *Children and the Tension in Liberalism*

Liberals have reason to be suspicious of the idea that parents have fundamental rights to direct the lives of their children. Liberalism takes individuals to be the fundamental objects of moral concern and takes the primary attributions of rights to be to individuals over themselves. Corporate entities are sometimes ascribed rights, and sometimes those rights are not in any straightforward sense reducible to the rights of the individuals who compose the corporate entity, but in liberal theory such attributions are usually taken to be in some sense secondary.[2] Furthermore, such attributions usually try to avoid ascribing to some members of the corporate entity rights over other members. When such rights are ascribed, we are typically concerned that they be limited and that those subject to control have realistic options of exit from the corporate entity in question. But parental rights are rights over others, and they are rights over others who have no realistic exit option.

The standard model of thinking about rights sees them as instruments for protecting people's abilities to make what they can of their own lives. Usually, then, rights over others are justified only by appeal to the interests of those others. So, for example, elderly parents sometimes give power of attorney to their adult children for various purposes, but the person with power of attorney is charged with pursuing the interests of the elderly parent. The relationship is purely fiduciary. The agent directs the affairs of the principal but has been appointed, and usually briefed by, that principal and is guided by the principal's best interests. Liberalism has no other example than the relationship between parents and children where rights over others are considered fundamental, in the sense that they are justified, at least in part, by the interest of the right holder.

Young children are entirely dependent and incapable of having formulated or previously expressed views about what their interests are. So the oddness of ascribing rights over them to parents cannot be decisive. The standing of children reveals tensions between two values to which liberals are committed, and which are usually congruent.[3] The principle of toleration says that we should not interfere with the moral beliefs and practices of others, as long as the practices that emanate from those beliefs do no harm to nonconsenting others. The principle of autonomy says that every individual should have the internal resources and skills necessary rationally to evaluate and revise her own commitments and practices.[4]

Tolerating people in the sense described usually expresses respect for their autonomy; coercing them, without justification in terms of harm to nonconsenting others, violates both their autonomy and the prohibition on intolerance. But the claim of parents to raise their children as they see fit, even in ways that will inhibit the development of their children's capacity for autonomy, throws the tension into sharp relief.

Three strategies are available. One is to decide straightforwardly in favor of autonomy. Children are, obviously,

---

1 *It does not ... their values to their children* There may be other, efficiency-based, reasons for allowing parents to confer their wealth on their children and to invest in their human capital, in ways that violate fair equality of opportunity (as, e.g., Rawls understands it), but these reasons do not support considering this permission as a right. See Harry Brighouse and Adam Swift, "Equality, Priority and Positional Goods," *Ethics* 116 (2006): 471–97.

2 *Corporate entities ... in some sense secondary* For accounts of group rights that nonetheless subscribe to ethical individualism, see, e.g., Joseph Raz, *The Morality of Freedom* (Oxford: Oxford University Press, 1986); Will Kymlicka, *Liberalism, Community and Culture* (Oxford: Oxford University Press, 1989).

3 *The standing ... usually congruent* This is not to say that all liberals accept both. William Galston, e.g., explicitly argues against the commitment to autonomy in "Two Concepts of Liberalism" (*Ethics* 105 [1995]: 516–34).

4 *The principle of autonomy ... commitments and practices* This commitment is elaborated in, among many others, Eamonn Callan, *Creating Citizens* (Oxford: Oxford University Press, 1997); Amy Gutmann, *Democratic Education* (Princeton, NJ: Princeton University Press, 1987); Steven Macedo, "Liberal Civic Education and Religious Fundamentalism: The Case of God v. John Rawls?" *Ethics* 105 (1995): 468–96; Harry Brighouse, "Civic Education and Liberal Legitimacy," *Ethics* 108 (1998): 719–45.

nonconsenting others. The principle of toleration does not extend to tolerating practices that are harmful to nonconsenting others. So we can regulate child rearing to promote autonomy without being intolerant. Although this is the strategy that we will ourselves pursue, it is problematic because it is so hard to prize apart the lives of parents from the lives of children while children are being raised, and because (as we will argue) the specific interest parents have in having a certain kind of relationship with their children is extremely powerful.

The second strategy, deciding in favor of toleration, is also problematic. One version simply denies that children have a fundamental interest in developing their capacity for personal autonomy. Loren Lomasky, for example, claims that we have a fundamental interest only in becoming independent project pursuers. Children therefore have an interest only in becoming nonservile, which does not support the principle of autonomy. Proponents of this variant of the strategy must deny that the principle of autonomy is required to support the principle of toleration—so Lomasky uses an apparently weaker idea of nonservility to support it. Another version accepts the fundamental interest in developing the capacity for autonomy but claims that the interest of parents in being tolerated trumps this interest of children when they conflict.[1]

The most promising variants of this strategy recognize the separateness of parent from child. But they face two problems. First, it is hard to give a full enough account of nonservility and autonomy to show how, exactly, they are distinct. More seriously, they do not in fact give any explanation of what rights parents have, why they have them, or what weight they should be given when they come into conflict with other principles. They tell us that when parental control conflicts with the value of nonservility, parental control must give way, and that when autonomy comes into conflict with parental control, autonomy must yield, but not what happens when parental control conflicts, for example, with fair equality of opportunity.

A third strategy denies the conflict. Proponents of this strategy point out (rightly) that autonomy can only be learned and practiced by children who have the emotional security provided by loving and caring parents, and these proponents argue that the deeply religious ways of life that most trouble liberals in fact contain ample opportunity to learn the skills associated with autonomy.[2] There may well be something to this strategy in many cases, but it cannot always succeed. Conflicts can and do arise, and a full liberal theory of the family needs to have something to say about how to resolve them when and if they do.

We are not satisfied with the accounts offered by those pursuing any of these strategies. In order to determine what rights, if any, parents have, a substantive investigation of the goods at stake in the parent-child relationship is needed. What is it about the value of the family, and the parent-child relationship in particular, that makes it so important to protect it with rights, and what rights are needed to protect it? Only after answering these questions can one know the appropriate scope of toleration (with respect to parents) and the appropriate weight to give it relative to the principle of autonomy (with respect to children).

3. Non-Parent-Centered Arguments for Parental Rights

A familiar, and powerful, argument for granting parents extensive permission to direct their children's lives, and for protecting them from interference by the state, focuses on the interests of children. The argument runs as follows. The nuclear family, or something like it, is the institution best suited to meeting children's interests. In order for the institution to work well for children, people must have incentives to be parents and to be the kind of parents who will do well by their children. The more regulation, monitoring, and outside control parents face, the less they will enjoy parenting and will have a sense that it is serving their own flourishing and well-being. It will therefore be less appealing, and children may suffer relative to a regime in which

---

1   *Another version ... when they conflict*   William Galston equivocates between this strategy and the one described in the next paragraph. Though he rejects the principle of autonomy, Galston ingratiates himself with the proponent of autonomy by giving evidence that his favored policy of granting parents extensive rights to control their children's moral and religious development will have less deleterious effects on the children's prospective autonomy than secularists usually suppose. See William Galston, *Liberal Purposes* (Cambridge: Cambridge University Press, 1991).

2   *A third strategy ... associated with autonomy*   This is the strategy pursued by Shelley Burtt, and, insofar as Rawls has a strategy, it seems to be his as well. See Shelley Burtt, "What Children Really Need: Toward a Critical Theory of Family Structure," in *The Moral and Political Status of Children*, ed. David Archard and Colin MacLeod (Oxford: Oxford University Press, 2002), pp. 231–52, and "Religious Parents, Secular Schools: A Liberal Defense of an Illiberal Education," *Review of Politics* 56 (1994): 51–70.

parenting is a less regulated and monitored activity.[1] One variant of this view conjectures that people will invest more in meeting the interests of children who are biologically their own, and so argues that redistributing children from their biological parents to other "more suitable" parents will not be an effective policy. For some, then, the biological nuclear family, with parents having extensive rights over their children's lives, is important as an institution for promoting children's interests.[2]

A second kind of argument appeals to the public goods created by good parenting. Well-raised children are public goods in many senses. Taxing their future income helps us to provide for the retirements of parents and nonparents alike. Their future participation in the economy as workers and consumers secures the long-term planning of the current generation of workers and consumers. Their future participation in public affairs contributes to goals that current adults have for the future. Some versions of this argument focus on how parental rights help to secure parental investment in children. Others conjecture that, without extensive powers and freedoms, parents will be unable, even if willing, to raise their children well. Still others focus on less tangible public goods than economic benefits and social order. Veronique Munoz-Darde, for example, develops an argument, which she attributes to Bertrand Russell, that the family (with the substantial array of parental rights that it involves) is necessary for maintaining the background of diversity against which people can make a wide range of choices about how to live.[3] Another variant claims that the family is causally necessary for, if not itself constitutive of, a just society. One might, for example, regard personal liberty

as the central value of political justice and regard the family as necessary for the kind of moral development that will produce citizens capable of respecting the liberties of others. Parental rights, then, are not owed to parents in their own right but must be granted them in order to reproduce justice over generations.[4]

We mention these arguments not to reject them—they may indeed provide good reasons to give parents legal rights and powers with respect to their children—but simply to distinguish them from our own. These arguments fail to show that parents have any fundamental rights with respect to their children, because they focus exclusively on the ways that the family benefits children or third parties. Interference in family life, in what parents do to and with their children, is bad, on these accounts, but it is, ultimately, bad for children, or for other people, not for parents. Our argument gives parents' interests the kind of status that these arguments rightly give to the interests of children and third parties. On our view, the interests of parents count, too, and justify some prohibitions on state intervention even when that intervention would reliably promote the interests of children or society in general.

4. Restoring the Parents to the Picture

The child-centered and public-goods accounts of the status of parents both leave open the possibility that it could be legitimate to redistribute children en masse. Consider the child-centered account; if all that matters is ensuring that children's interests are met as well as possible, then children should be distributed to those people judged most likely to raise them best. If parents' interests play no justificatory role, what would there be to impugn a well-intentioned and efficient government agency that distributed the children, who under a laissez-faire system would be reasonably well raised, to adults who would be better parents, thus leaving some adequately good parents childless? The analogous question arises with respect to the public-goods account. State institutions might be better than parents at raising economically productive good citizens. Reasonable skepticism about the efficiency and good will of the hypothetical

1   *A familiar ... monitored activity*   Examples of this child-centered approach include Robert Noggle, "Special Agents: Children's Autonomy and Parental Authority," in Archard and MacLeod, *The Moral and Political Status of Children*, pp. 97–117; Samantha Brennan and Robert Noggle, "The Moral Status of Children: Children's Rights, Parents' Rights, and Family Justice," *Social Theory and Practice* 23 (1997): 1–25; Ian Shapiro, *Democratic Justice* (New Haven, CT: Yale University Press, 1998), chap. 4; and perhaps John Locke, *The Second Treatise of Government*, ed. Peter Laslett (Cambridge: Cambridge University Press, 1988), chap. 6.

2   *One variant ... children's interests*   This is an empirical conjecture, not an established fact, and it would be hard to establish it without doing morally impermissible experiments. Our argument in this article shows why the necessary experiments would be impermissible.

3   *Veronique Munoz-Darde ... how to live*   Veronique Munoz-Darde, "Is the Family to Be Abolished, Then?" *Proceedings of the Aristotelian Society* 99 (1999): 37–56.

4   *Another variant ... justice over generations*   This is Jennifer Robak Morse's view in "No Families, No Freedom: Human Flourishing in a Free Society," *Social Philosophy and Policy* 16 (1999): 290–314, and also in *Love and Economics: Why the Laissez-Faire Family Doesn't Work* (New York: Spence, 2001).

agency does not settle the moral question. Would there be fundamental moral reasons for objecting?

We think that there would. In our view, children have a fundamental interest in developing the capacity to be autonomous and have other temporary and developmental interests that the state is obliged to guarantee. We agree, too, that there is a legitimate public interest in the way that children are raised. But these interests leave room for parental rights that are genuinely fundamental, though both limited and conditional. We will give an account of the parental interest in the parent-child relationship that we believe justifies some such rights. The parent child relationship is, indeed, a fiduciary relationship, but it is not exclusively fiduciary, and parents, as well as children, have an interest in its fiduciary character. Coming down on the autonomy side of the tension between autonomy and toleration does not require that we deny that there are (fundamental) parental rights; conversely, granting parental rights does not require denying the child's interest in autonomy.

We have said twice that parental rights are fundamental, conditional, and limited. What is it to say that a right is fundamental? We shall define a right as fundamental if it is owed to a person in virtue of their simply being a person, and its justification is grounded in the benefits it will bring to that person and not to others. The obvious examples, uncontroversial among liberals, would be the rights to freedom of conscience and of association. More controversial would be the right to vote in free and fair elections.[1] The contrast here is with rights that are merely instrumental: a right the recognition of which is desirable because it helps to protect some other rights that are fundamental, or because it benefits someone other than the right holder. We suspect that the right to a jury trial is like this; it is not fundamental but is desirable because it is the best way of protecting the (fundamental) right to due process. The theories mentioned in the previous section make parents' rights merely instrumental in this way. Our claim is that, although there may be sound instrumental justifications for parents' rights, these

do not exhaust the case for them: there is a parent-centered case for some parents' rights.[2]

Any liberal theory is going to have to make parental rights conditional in some way on the interests of the child being sufficiently protected (though liberals will differ over what counts as sufficient protection). This seems to have led some theorists to think that there cannot be fundamental parental rights—because fundamental rights must always be unconditional.[3] But there are many rights, normally regarded as fundamental in our sense, that are held conditionally. The rights to vote, to freedom of association, and to free expression are all conditional on the individual claiming them not having committed a serious crime. Some kinds of criminal forfeit many rights, at least temporarily. Not all rights are forfeited (e.g., the right against cruel and unusual punishment and the right to freedom of conscience), but this is not usually thought of as evidence that these are the only fundamental rights we have. To be sure, the conditionality of parental rights is somewhat different from that of other fundamental rights. The threshold is different. Mere non-feloniousness is usually a much easier condition to realize than is ensuring that one's children's interests are met to some high threshold.[4] But the difference seems appropriate. It seems reasonable to give great weight to the interests of vulnerable people who are involuntarily in the care of others.

Finally, we have said that the rights are limited in scope. Views about the content of parental rights fall along a continuum, granting parents less or more extensive bundles of

1 *The obvious examples ... fair elections* John Rawls seems to regard these rights as fundamental; see his *A Theory of Justice* (Cambridge, MA: Harvard University Press, 1971), pp. 224–27. Richard Arneson is against seeing them as fundamental in "Democracy Rights at National and Workplace Levels," in *The Idea of Democracy*, ed. David Copp, Jean Hampton, and John Roemer (Cambridge: Cambridge University Press, 1994), pp. 118–48, and in "Democracy Is Not Intrinsically Just," in *Justice and Democracy*, ed. Carole Pateman, Keith Dowding, and Robert Goodin (Cambridge: Cambridge University Press 2004), pp. 40–58.

2 *The contrast here ... some parents' rights* Our use of "fundamental" does not imply that the right, itself, is of fundamental importance, relative to other rights. Among fundamental rights there may be some that really are fundamentally important in the more intuitive sense of fundamental (such as the right to life) and others that are not (such as the right to vote in free and fair elections). There may also be rights that, though not fundamental in our sense, are of extreme moral importance and urgency. Furthermore, in saying that some rights are fundamental we do not mean to imply a rights-based political morality. Our use is consistent with the theories of rights on which they are moral constructs designed to protect interests, which are the truly fundamental moral considerations.

3 *This seems to have led ... always be unconditional* See James Dwyer, *Religious Schools versus Children's Rights* (Ithaca, NY: Cornell University Press, 1999), chap. 4.

4 *Mere non-feloniousness ... high threshold* We say "usually" because an editor pointed out to us that the relative ease is dependent on context; the social environment could be so constructed to make it extremely difficult for at least some people to resist felonies.

rights. A nice example concerns schooling. Some liberals believe that parents have extensive rights with respect to what kind of schooling their children should receive and even whether they should receive it at all. They are apparently supported in this by various international human rights documents, such as the International Covenant on Economic, Social and Cultural Rights, which asserts that parents have the liberty to "ensure the religious and moral education of their children in conformity with their own convictions," and U.S. Supreme Court decisions such as *Wisconsin v. Yoder*.[1] Other liberals deny such extensive rights over education, claiming that no parental right is violated when children are required to attend public schools and to learn from a curriculum designed to teach them substantive values, possibly in conflict with those of their parents, and to facilitate their personal autonomy.[2]

The view that parental rights are fundamental is commonly coupled with the view that such rights are extensive. In fact, some theorists appear to believe that establishing the former means establishing the latter. Charles Fried's comment that the right to "form one's child's values, one's child's life plan, and...to lavish attention on that child" is grounded in the "basic right not to be interfered with in doing these things for oneself" suggests this.[3] But fundamentalness and extensiveness are quite distinct. It is possible to think that parents should be granted quite extensive rights over their children, but for reasons that are entirely instrumental. It is also possible to hold that parents' interests justify some conditional, fundamental rights over their children but that these rights are quite limited, that more extensive rights can only be justified instrumentally, and that there are quite strict limits even on instrumental parents' rights. Indeed, that is the view for which we will argue.

5. The Parent's Interest in Intimacy

Our argument for fundamental parents' rights draws on a paper by Ferdinand Schoeman. In this section we outline

his argument and explain why it fails. In the next section we correct it.

Schoeman's argument proceeds in two stages. He argues first, and generally, that the state should facilitate our interest in having intimate relationships with others. He then argues, in particular, that this interest must be facilitated by the state's not interfering with parents' having intimate relationships with their children. The argument for the first conclusion seems sound. While we agree with the second conclusion, his argument for it seems wrong, and even if it worked it would not be the kind of argument that would support the claim that parents' rights are fundamental.

Schoeman claims that relationships involving personal commitments to others give meaning to our lives. They constitute, as he says, our "roots in life." Intimacy is, in turn, a necessary part of any such relationships.[4] But intimate sharing presupposes that the parties to the relationship have (admittedly limited) sovereignty over the terms of the relationship. If outsiders control the terms of the relationship, then the conditions for intimacy are jeopardized. If you think that an outside agent is monitoring, or dictating the terms of, a relationship, you cannot be sure of your own views or motives, or those of the person the relationship is with. So without privacy and autonomy, the relationship would be neither secure nor "on the parties' own terms."[5] But deep and authentic attachments between parents and children are vital for the well-being of both parties. Since intimacy is central to the significance of the family relationship, the state should absent itself (except where some threshold of treatment is not met).[6]

The argument so far provides a child-centered reason to ensure that children have adults with whom to have intimate relationships (their well-being is at stake). It also provides adult- and child-centered reasons to ensure that already established parent-child relationships be permitted (disruption would damage the well-being of both parents and children). But it provides no reason to ensure that such relationships are permitted to develop in the first place. As we have pointed out, child-centered reasons could justify distributing children to the most suitable parents, and

1 *Some liberals ... Wisconsin v. Yoder*   For this view, see William Galston, *Liberal Pluralism* (Cambridge: Cambridge University Press, 2003), chaps. 8 and 9. For the International Covenant, see http://www.unhchr.ch/html/menu3/b/a_cescr.htm.

2 *Other liberals ... personal autonomy*   See Callan, *Creating Citizens*, chap. 6.

3 *Charles Fried's comment ... suggests this*   Charles Fried, *Right and Wrong* (Cambridge, MA: Harvard University Press, 1976), p. 152.

4 *Schoeman claims ... such relationships*   Ferdinand Schoeman, "Rights of Children, Rights of Parents, and the Moral Basis of the Family," *Ethics* 91 (1980): pp. 6–19, 14.

5 *So without privacy ... the parties' own terms*"   Ibid., pp. 14–15.

6 *Since intimacy ... is not met)*   Ibid., pp. 15–16. For another account of the value of intimacy leading to a similar conclusion, see Schrag, "Justice and the Family."

adult- and child-centered reasons converge on justifying the maintenance of whatever relationship thereby occurs. But there is no adult-centered reason here to justify allowing adults (who might not, from the child-centered or public good perspectives, be the most suitable adults) to develop parental relationships with children.

If it is just intimacy per se that gives vital meaning to our lives, then adults could secure this through intimate relationships with other adults. Children could be redistributed at birth to other, perhaps more suitable or qualified, adults with whom they could have equally or more beneficial intimate relationships. So why should adults be allowed to establish intimate parental relationships specifically with children? Schoeman's answer is essential to his case: the redistribution of children suggested "does or may preclude such kinds of intimacy [with children] for those who are determined by social criteria to be not maximally fit or maximally competent to really provide children with all that they need or can use."[1] He later puts it a different way: "To set terms for emotional parenting more stringent than required for the protection of children from abuse and neglect constitutes an interference in a person's claim to establish intimate relations except on society's terms."[2]

This argument trades on an equivocation. Schoeman says that individuals' opportunities for intimate relationships must not be conducted on "society's terms" or in line with "social criteria." But the liberal who regards parental rights as instrumental does not seek to regulate parenting by "society's terms" if what is meant by that is "the standards a society would democratically adopt." The issue of parental discretion is, for liberals anyway, what Ronald Dworkin would characterize as a "choice-insensitive issue."[3] Parents and democratic decisions must both be judged against objective standards. The liberal will share revulsion at the idea of society having license to determine democratically the terms on which people can associate with their children but will nevertheless claim that there are firm and binding standards given by justice and that society should set those standards, and not any other, in law.

Schoeman's problem, then, is this. The child-centered liberal justification for extensive intervention in the family is not based on standards that are choice sensitive, but on objective standards, grounded in the developmental and (sometimes) temporary interests of the children. Schoeman is right in saying that it would be wrong for society to intervene on its own standards, if those standards are arbitrarily chosen. But the child-centered argument for redistribution does not propose arbitrary standards, and if redistribution left some adequate would-be parents bereft of children, their interest in having intimate relationships on their own terms could still be fulfilled through relationships with other adults.

6. Fundamental Parents' Rights

How might an argument appealing to the value of intimate relationships succeed in vindicating parental rights as fundamental? Schoeman's account fails to note the differences in quality between the intimate relationship adults can have with each other and those that they can have with the children they parent. He is driven to the second, flawed, part of his argument by observing, correctly, that adults can have intimacy with other consenting adults and so, it seems, do not need to have intimate relationships with children in order to have the intimacy so important to human flourishing. Schoeman is not alone in this. James Rachels's defense of modest parental partiality toward children similarly appeals to the idea that "loving relationships are personal goods of great importance. To love other people, and to be loved in return, is part of what is involved in having a rich and satisfying human life."[4] John Cottingham defends partiality toward loved ones on the grounds that "it is an essential ingredient in one of the highest human goods."[5] In addition, it makes no distinction between relationships with children and relationships with "wives, husbands, brothers, sisters, close friends, and lovers."[6]

But the relationships that adults have with the children they parent are not merely additional intimate valuable rela-

---

1   *Schoeman's answer ... or can use."* Schoeman, "Rights of Children, Rights of Parents, and the Moral Basis of the Family," 16.

2   *He later ... society's terms."* Ibid., p. 17. And even later: "It must not be up to society in general, without there being some special cause, to decide whom one can relate to and on what terms. Other things being equal, parents consequently are entitled to maintain their offspring and seek meaning with and through them" (17).

3   *what Ronald Dworkin ... "choice-insensitive issue"* Ronald Dworkin, *Sovereign Virtue* (Cambridge, MA: Harvard University Press, 2000), p. 198.

4   *James Rachels's ... human life"* James Rachels, *Can Ethics Provide Answers?* (Lanham, MD: Rowman & Littlefield, 1997), p. 223.

5   *John Cottingham ... human goods."* John Cottingham, "Partiality, Favouritism and Morality," *Philosophical Quarterly* 36 (1984): pp. 357–73, 369.

6   *In addition ... friends and lovers"* Ibid., p. 369.

tionships, which contribute to their flourishing in the same way as their relationships with other adults. They have a different moral quality, make a different kind of contribution to their flourishing, and so are not interchangeable with other relationships. It is not because people have a right generally to determine relationships on their own terms that the government is wrong to intervene to prevent parent-child relationships. They do not have this right; in fact the relationships between parents and children are governed by stringent and nondiscretionary moral norms. It is wrong to intervene, instead, because this is a different kind of relationship from those with adults, and one to which parents can claim a right.

Let us look at the relevant ways in which the relationships differ. First, obviously, they are not relationships among people with equal power or standing even in the minimal Hobbesian sense. Children are vulnerable to the decisions and choice making of their primary caretakers and, initially, wholly dependent on them for their well-being. Parents have power of life or death over their children, and this is not, at least when the child is young, reciprocated. But, more importantly, and less spectacularly, they have the power to make their children's lives miserable or enjoyable (within limits, at least at the enjoyable end). We do have these powers over those with whom we engage in adult relationships, but they are usually, to some extent, reciprocal.

How reciprocal depends, of course, on the dynamics of the relationship and the background against which it is played out, but in adult-adult relationships with very unequal power, the less powerful person usually has, or should have, the power to exit the relationship by his or her own choice. Where they do not, we usually think that there is something quite wrong. So this leads us to a second difference between intimate relationships between adults and those between an adult and a child: the power to exit the relationship. Whereas adults have the power to leave relationships with other adults, children lack this power with respect to their primary caretakers, at least until they reach sufficient age to escape (which age will be culturally sensitive, since different societies will monitor and enforce parental power with different levels of enthusiasm and effectiveness). Whether parents have the power to exit the parent-child relationship depends, of course, on social arrangements and also on how closely they bond to the child. But, as Anne Alstott points out, although we think that parents have a powerful obligation not to exit the relationship,

our social arrangements in contemporary liberal democracies typically give them considerable powers of exit, because the social steps required to block the option of exit would be extremely costly if not impossible (though typically, in modern societies, fathers have had considerable de facto powers of exit, mothers much less).[1] Again, we do not mean to suggest that all adult-adult relationships are characterized by equal power to exit, or even that in all such relationships there is one person who has the power to exit. The difference between the relationships is that young children have no resources whatsoever to exit, whereas adults usually have, or should have, some resources to execute departure from their intimate involvement with other adults.

These two features are not unique to this relationship. The prisoner is vulnerable to the warder in a way that the warder is not to the prisoner, and the powers of exit are similarly asymmetrical.[2] So it is only in combination with other facts about the relationship that they shape its character so as to make it a distinctive and vital contributor to our well-being.

The third feature concerns the quality of the intimacy of the relationship. The love one receives from one's children, again especially in the early years, is spontaneous and unconditional and, in particular, outside the rational control of the child. She shares herself unself-consciously with the parent, revealing her enthusiasms and aversions, fears and anxieties, in an uncontrolled manner. She trusts the parent until the parent betrays the trust, and her trust must be betrayed consistently and frequently before it will be completely undermined. Adults do not share themselves with each other in this way: intimacy requires a considerable act of will on the part of adults interacting together.

---

1   *But, as Anne Alstott ... much less)*   Anne Alstott, *No Exit: What Parents Owe Their Children and Society Owes Parents* (Oxford: Oxford University Press, 2004), p. 45: "Society only has limited means at its disposal to secure continuity. Our laws and institutions can encourage continuity, but they cannot compel the intimacy and care that are its foundation." Our claim that men have considerably more power to exit the relationship does not imply any legal asymmetry; men and women typically have the same legal rights of exit. But we believe that more fathers than mothers have the internal resources that enable them to break the relationships with their children (or, to put it more contentiously, more women than men have the emotional capacity to maintain such relationships) and that more men than women who abandon their children are able to find ways of doing so that avoid social stigma.

2   *The prisoner ... similarly asymmetrical*   We are grateful to Rob Reich for this analogy.

But with children, while parents are prone to spontaneity and intimacy, their fiduciary obligations often require them to be less than wholly spontaneous and intimate (despite the child's unconditional intimacy with the parent). The good parent masks sometimes her disappointment with, sometimes her pride in, her child, and often her frustration with other aspects of her life. She does not inflict on the child, as the child does on her, all her spontaneous reactions or all her emotional responses.

So far we have outlined the moral burden on the parent imposed by these differences between parent-child and adult-adult intimacy. It is valuable to meet this distinctive moral burden. But along with the moral burden come distinctive sources of satisfaction of a much less complicated kind. There is the enjoyment of the love (both the child's for oneself and one's own for the child) and the delight in the observations the child makes about the world: the pleasure (and sometimes dismay) of seeing the world from the child's perspective; enjoyment of her satisfaction in her successes, and of being able to console her in her disappointments.

The final difference concerns the moral quality of the relationship. The parent is charged with responsibility for both the immediate well-being of the child and the development of the child's capabilities. This is the fiduciary relationship emphasized by the child-centered argument for parental power. The child has immediate interests in being kept safe, enjoying herself, being sheltered and well nourished, having loving relationships with others, and so on. She has future interests in many of these same things, but also in becoming the kind of person who is not entirely dependent on others for having her interests met and the kind of person who can judge well and act on her interests.[1] The parent's fiduciary obligations are to guarantee the child's immediate well-being and to oversee and ensure her cognitive, emotional, physical, and moral development.[2] Meeting these obligations often involves the parent in co-

ercing the child to act against her own will, and often in manipulating her will so that it accords with her interests. The parent might, for example, lock away the bleach so the child cannot get at it, even though she has displayed great interest in it, or prevent her from having a third helping of ice cream, on the grounds that neither the bleach nor the ice cream will serve her interests. The parent might persistently serve whole grain pasta in the face of the child's frequent (and reasonable) complaints that it is tasteless, in order to habituate her to frequent intake of whole grains. The parent might engineer the child's social life in order to diminish the significance of a destructive friendship. Although in relationships with other adults we are obliged to take their interests into account, we do not have fiduciary responsibilities of this kind toward them. Indeed, if one saw one's relationship with, say, one's spouse, in this way, one could reasonably be accused of being overbearing, disrespectful, or unloving. One advises one's spouse, and one's friends, and even argues with them, but one does not routinely coerce and manipulate them, even in their own interests. To do so would be to fail as a spouse or friend, just as to refrain from doing so with one's children would be to fail as a parent.

The parent's fiduciary role has been widely acknowledged since Locke.[3] The point we are making here, however, is parent-centered. Parents have an interest in being in a relationship of this sort. They have a nonfiduciary interest in playing this fiduciary role. The role enables them to exercise and develop capacities the development and exercise of which are, for many (though not, certainly, for all), crucial to their living fully flourishing lives. Through exercising these capacities in the specific context of the intimately loving parent-child relationship, a parent comes to learn more about herself, she comes to develop as a person, and she

---

1   *The child has … her interests*   For an elaboration of these interests, see Harry Brighouse, "What Rights (If Any) Do Children Have?" in Archard and MacLeod, *The Moral and Political Status of Children*, pp. 31–52.

2   *The parent's … moral development*   The precise content of the obligations the parent has to the child is hard to specify independently of social context. What constitutes adequate care for a child's cognitive development, e.g., depends on how much cognitive development is needed in a particular society in order to have a successful life in that context. Parents in preliterate societies may have less to do in this respect than parents in complex modern societies.

3   *The parent's fiduciary role … since Locke*   Locke says that "parents were, by the Law of Nature, under an obligation to preserve, nourish, and educate the Children they had begotten; [though] not as their own Workmanship, but as the Workmanship of their own Maker, the Almighty to whom they were to be accountable for them" (Locke, *Second Treatise*, par. 56). Contemporary theorists who emphasize the fiduciary interest, despite giving otherwise different accounts of the relationships, include Rob Reich, *Bridging Liberalism and Multiculturalism in American Education* (Chicago: University of Chicago Press, 2002), p. 148–51; Galston, *Liberal Pluralism*, pp. 101–06; Callan, *Creating Citizens*, chap. 6; Dwyer, *Religious Schools versus Children's Rights*; Brennan and Noggle, "The Moral Status of Children"; David Archard, *Children: Rights and Childhood* (1991; repr., London: Routledge, 2004), and *Children, Family and the State* (Aldershot: Ashgate, 2002).

derives satisfactions that otherwise would be unavailable. The successful exercise of this role contributes to, and its unsuccessful exercise detracts from, the success of her own life as a whole.[1]

The other features of the relationship that distinguish it from other intimate relationships also shape the fiduciary role. If children could easily exit the relationship into another that would adequately meet their needs, then that would reduce their parents' level of responsibility. If they were not vulnerable to parental decisions, then fulfilling the fiduciary obligations would demand less of the parent and play less of a role in the development of her character. So, while the non-fiduciary interest in playing a fiduciary role is a key interest, the other features of the relationship are significant for the importance of that interest. Our suggestion is that no other relationship contains all of these features and that these features contribute to well-being in a quite distinctive way.

The intimacy one can have with one's children is quite different from the intimacy one can have with other adults.[2] It makes a contribution to one's flourishing of a different kind and, for many, is not substitutable by relationships of other kinds. The challenge of parenting is something adults have an interest in facing, and it is that interest that grounds fundamental parental rights over their children. The justification is parent-centered, so it is the right kind of justification for the claim that parental rights are fundamental. But it does not disregard the interests of children, and, as will be explained in the next section, a proper interpretation of the justification makes parents' rights both limited and conditional.[3]

Contrast the justification we have given with Veronique Munoz-Darde's non-parent-centered justification. She imagines a world in which well-run state orphanages would meet children's needs just as well as families do, and in which they, additionally, do a better job than families of implementing fair equality of opportunity. The reason that the well-run orphanages do better with regard to fair equality of opportunity is that

> since the state has overall control, it is able to equally guarantee to all children whichever conditions and principles are considered optimum for their upbringing as long as these conditions are compatible with such an overall control. It could be imagined as a generalized boarding school, with...well qualified teachers able to devote individualized attention to children. These teachers could take pride in the achievement of their pupils, but would probably not have the sort of personal investments that parents generally have.... Teachers would also be explicitly bound by a principle of impartiality, or at least fairness, between their pupils.[4]

Munoz-Darde's case for the family, despite the greater fairness of the well-run orphanage, is that "the diversity of families makes it possible for the worth of different ways of life to be available as options, and hence creates the conditions necessary for pluralism."[5] In her view, the state would inevitably use orphanages to foster uniformity. Our answer is different. Even if a state successfully used orphanages to foster diversity and fulfill children's needs excellently, there would be a serious loss of value and flourishing. Many adults would be unable to engage in activities and relationships that make an ineliminable and great contribution to their ability to flourish. They could not get access to the full package of these activities and relationships by becoming "teachers" at the orphanages, because, in the role of teacher, they could not enjoy the relevant kind of intimacy with, or exercise the relevant kind of legitimate partiality with

---

1 *The successful exercise ... as a whole* This explains why "success or failure in the task [of parenting], as measured by whatever standards we take to be relevant, is likely to affect profoundly our overall sense of how well or badly our lives have gone" (see Callan, *Creating Citizens*, p. 142). We're especially grateful to Victor Seidler and Larry Blum for suggesting that we think through the fiduciary aspect of the parental role.

2 *The intimacy ... other adults* An account somewhat similar to ours can be found in Colin MacLeod's "Liberal Equality and the Affective Family," in Archard and MacLeod, *The Moral and Political Status of Children*, pp. 212–30.

3 *a proper interpretation ... limited and conditional* The justification we have offered appeals to a cluster of interests parents have in parenting that cannot be fulfilled outside the role of parenthood. It does not constitute a full moral account of the parenting role, or of the interests people do, in fact, fulfill through parenthood. For many people parenting provides a vital link with, and stake in, the future of the world. But we are not certain that anyone has the kind of interest in such a link or stake that would support a right, and, given the variety of nonparental activities, roles,

and relationships that can contribute to the fulfillment of that interest (teaching, friendship with and mentoring of children and adults younger than oneself, architecture, horticulture, creative endeavor, political activity, etc.), we are doubtful that this interest will support any specifically parental right.

4 *since the state ... between their pupils* Munoz-Darde, "Is the Family to Be Abolished, Then?" 45.

5 *Munoz-Darde's case ... for pluralism* Ibid., p. 49.

respect to, a small number of particular children.[1] Such a society would be unacceptably diminished even if children were well "reared."[2]

Schoeman's argument was an attempt to show that children should not be redistributed to the parents who would best parent them, as the child-centered account would allow. The redistribution scenario has two features. The first is that children are routinely redistributed away from their biological parents (except in those cases in which they happen to be born to the adults who will parent them best). The second is that some adults who would be adequately good parents would be left childless, because the supply of children is exhausted by demand from people who will be better parents. We claim that Schoeman's argument fails to address both problems, but we should emphasize that our own argument succeeds only in addressing the second. We have shown why no one who will do an adequately good job of raising a child should be prevented from being a parent. But we have not shown that the child they should be allowed to raise should be their own biological child. This is not because we believe that there is no weighty interest in raising one's own biological child but because we do not have an argument establishing that there is such an interest. In this, we are not alone. Such an interest is frequently asserted, but we are not aware of any convincing arguments for it.[3] Furthermore, the interest we have described can, at least for many, be realized in a relationship with a child who is not biologically related to one. So, absent an argument

that the interest in having a biological connection to the child one raises is very powerful indeed, we do not claim that the interest in being a parent impugns redistribution at birth. What we do claim is that it impugns redistribution away from people who would be adequately good parents (though not as good as others).[4]

Consider a natural objection to the idea that parents' rights are fundamental. Rights claims are very strong claims. One can have an interest in something that does not support one's having a right to it. James Dwyer objects to the account of parental rights that grounds them in very intense desires to have and raise children because, as he points out, the intensity of a desire never, in itself, justifies a right. The desires for "marriage to a particular person, great wealth, political office," for example, however intense, do not plausibly ground rights to the objects of those desires.[5]

But neither Schoeman's nor our account grounds parents' rights in mere desires, however intense.[6] In order to ground a rights claim we have to show that the object of the right fulfills a very weighty interest: that, for example, it makes a very important contribution to their well-being or flourishing. Can this argument be made?

The above account of the distinctive value of the relationship between parents and children helps to provide the argument. Relationships of the specified kind make a distinctive and important contribution to the flourishing of the adults involved. Now, two caveats are necessary. First, it is obviously not the case (for the vast majority of adults) that it is impossible for them to flourish at all without relationships of this kind. People do indeed go to great lengths in order to have and raise children, but some cannot, and few (if any) of them regard their lives as worthless. Nevertheless, many regard themselves as having missed out on

---

1   *the relevant kind ... particular children*   We explore the extent of legitimate parental partiality and its connection to our justification of parents' rights in "Legitimate Parental Partiality" (unpublished manuscript, Department of Philosophy, University of Wisconsin–Madison).

2   *Such a society ... well "reared."*   Although the emphasis in this article is on the parent-centered case for parents' rights, we regard the child-centered case for many such rights as entirely plausible. It is thus worth pointing out that, since no adult could have a parental relationship with a child in the orphanage, no child can be on the other end of such a relationship, and we doubt the plausibility of the hypothetical that children will have their interests well met.

3   *Such an interest ... arguments for it*   Among those who assert the interest, see Mary Warnock, *Making Babies: Is There a Right to Have Children?* (Oxford: Oxford University Press: 2002), p. 40; Allen Buchanan, Dan W. Brock, Norman Daniels, and Daniel Wikler, *From Chance to Choice: Genetics and Justice* (Cambridge: Cambridge University Press, 2000), p. 200. For an argument against there being such an interest, see Neil Levy and Mianna Lotz, "Reproductive Cloning and a (Kind of) Genetic Fallacy," *Bioethics* 19 (2005): 232–50.

4   *This is not because ... as good as others)*   To be clear, we are confident that we could provide many arguments for maintaining the general practice of presuming that parents should raise their own biological children. Our point here is simply that the arguments we have in mind are not parent centered.

5   *James Dwyer objects ... those desires*   Dwyer, *Religious Schools versus Children's Rights*, p. 91.

6   *But neither ... desires, however intense*   The language used to ground parental rights sometimes suggests a desire interpretation; see, e.g., James Rachels: "A loving relationship with one's children is, for many parents, a source of such happiness that they would sacrifice almost anything else to preserve it" (*Can Ethics Provide Answers?*, 223). In context, however, it is clear that Rachels's justification is appealing to the relationship itself as a distinctive source of flourishing, rather than the desire for the relationship.

an experience that would have been necessary for them to have counted their life as fully flourishing. Second, a significant proportion of people have no desire to have and raise children, and for many of them the absence of this desire is not an epistemic failing but a response to the fact that, indeed, having and raising children is not essential for their flourishing, and perhaps would contribute nothing to it. So the claim that the relevant "relationship goods" make a powerful contribution to the flourishing of the rights holder does not commit us to the claim that those goods are good for everybody. In this respect the contribution of this kind of relationship is like the contribution of a romantic sexual relationship. Many, if not most, people are such that they could not flourish fully without it: it contributes something to their flourishing that nothing else could contribute. But there are two other classes of people: those who, although they might really enjoy parenting, could indeed flourish fully without it and those whose lives would actually be diminished by being a parent. Noting this does not contradict the general claim about the significance of the relationship.

It might be objected, further, that many parents seem to get along perfectly well with minimal relationships with their children. Some parents abandon their children and have little contact. Indeed, even in the nuclear family that emerged after industrialization, fathers have often had very limited time and intimacy with their children. These observations, however, do not show that people can get along well without relationships with their children, for we can ask whether those parents really have enjoyed fully flourishing lives. Not only have they, in many cases, failed to deliver on their obligations to their children, but, on our account, their own lives have been impoverished by their absence from their children's lives.[1] Our most urgent moral concern is, of course, with their children, but that should not obscure our sense that the parents' lives too have been diminished.

Another objection to our account might go as follows. We have said that the parent-child relationship has certain features and that being involved in this sort of relationship as a parent makes a crucial contribution to the flourishing of the adult. But some parent-child relationships lack some of these features, and some other relationships contain many of them. So, for example, the parent of a child with severe cognitive impairments might enjoy the intimacy and the joy in seeing the world reflected through her child's eyes, but her fiduciary obligations do not include preparing her child to become an autonomous adult. Pet owners (especially, we suspect, dog owners) take on fiduciary obligations and experience pride in the achievements of their pets; so do many carers for adults with severe cognitive impairments. So not only does our sketch of the relationship at stake fail to capture every parent-child relationship, but the contrast between it and other caring relationships is not as stark as we seem to suggest.[2]

We accept the truth of this observation. Our paradigm of the parent-child relationship is supposed to describe something that many adults have a very strong interest in participating in. Other relationships that resemble it to a greater or lesser degree will yield some of the same benefits, but not all; similarly, some of those other relationships will yield other benefits for some of the carers that are not yielded by the paradigm parent-child relationship.[3] Our claim is only that there is something distinctive about this kind of relationship and that for many people nothing will fully substitute.

A related challenge, and the last we will consider, would accuse us of acquiescence in, and perhaps even glorification of, the nuclear family. That conception of the family is subject to much criticism, not only as an accurate descriptive model of much family life today but in normative terms also. What about the interest in caring relationships—re-

---

1   *their own lives ... their children's lives*   For a startling real-life account of this phenomenon, see Martin Amis, *Experience* (London: Vintage, 2001). We are grateful to Donald Hubin for pointing us to a considerable amount of empirical evidence on the damage to psychological well-being suffered by parents who do not enjoy full relationships with their children, including Rosalind C. Barnett, Nancy Marshall, and Joseph Pleck, "Men's Multiple Roles and Their Relationship to Men's Psychological Distress," *Journal of Marriage and the Family* 54 (1992): 358–67; Robert E. Fay, "The Disenfranchised Father," *Advanced Pediatrics* 36 (1989): 407–30; Kirby Deater-Deckard, Sandra Scarr, Kathleen McCartney, and Marlene Eisenberg, "Paternal Separation Anxiety: Relationships with Parenting Stress, Child-Rearing Attitudes, and Maternal Anxieties," *Psychological Science* 5 (1994): 341–46.

2   *the contrast ... seem to suggest*   We're grateful to Jaime Ahlberg for this observation and for help in thinking about what is at stake.

3   *Other relationships ... parent-child relationship*   Think of Eva Feder Kittay's account of her relationship with her severely cognitively disabled daughter, which is clearly a source of flourishing for Kittay in many of the ways that the paradigm relationship we have outlined would be, but also in other ways that our account does not try to capture. See Eva Feder Kittay, *Love's Labour* (London: Routledge 1999), chap. 6.

lationships that involve at least some of the elements that are central to our account of parental interests—of grandparents, uncles and aunts, and neighbors or family friends? What about children's interests in intimate relationships with people other than their parents?[1]

Here, too, we acknowledge that there is much more to be said. The fact that our account gives central place to parents' interest in having fiduciary responsibility for their children makes it difficult to work out the implications of giving other people any kind of direct (rather than delegated by the parent) authoritative role in the upbringing of children. Our argument has been that adults do have an interest in enjoying a particular kind of relationship with "their" children and that that relationship involves not only the enjoyment of intimacy with but also the exercise of certain kinds of authority over those children. We believe that the interest in question is sufficiently important that not only the state but also other members of the community should facilitate, and not interfere with, that relationship. But the account of the content of parents' rights we have given in this section leaves open both that other adults might have a claim to having continuing and close relationships with children and that children might have a claim to continuing and close relationships with adults other than their parents. It also leaves open the possibility that the fiduciary responsibility might be enjoyed by a single parent or shared between more than two.

7. What Rights Do Parents Have Over Children?

The account offered so far supports the claim that the right to raise children is fundamental. But establishing the fundamental status of this right does little to establish its content. That content matters partly because it is normally assumed that parental rights act as a constraint on liberalism's redistributive ambitions. So, for example, Rawls is explicit that even though the family frustrates the implementation of fair equality of opportunity, it should not be abolished; he treats the family, in effect, as covered by the Liberty Prin-

ciple.[2] In a recent paper arguing a nonneutral case for egalitarian redistribution, Richard Miller posits "an appropriate valuing of parental nurturance" that "entails respect for the privacy of home-life and enduring family ties which ensure the transmission of skills and attitudes within families even when family differences reflect past differences in success and tend to create differences in life prospects."[3] Although we have not argued for giving family life such importance, we think that our case for parents' rights fits well with giving them priority over certain other principles, such as Rawls's fair equality of opportunity. But until we know the precise content of parents' rights, or of the "appropriate valuing of parental nurturance," we do not know how much, or what kind, of a limit it places on permissible redistribution. Our comments in this section provide the beginnings of an answer to this question.[4]

As we have said, it is sometimes assumed that if the right is fundamental it is also extensive. But, though the interest in the relationship supports the conclusion that parents should be allowed to raise their children, it does not establish that there are no limits on how they should raise them. The fundamental right to control one's own sexual behavior gives one discretion over whom to choose as a sexual partner, but the right to raise one's child yields no discretion whatsoever over whom to choose as the child's sexual partner. The right to suicide appears to follow from the right to self-governance, but clearly the right to infanticide does not follow from the right to raise a child. Suppose a drug that would produce firm and unshakable belief in the divine right of kings were available. The right to self-governance might give one the right to administer that drug to oneself, but it would not justify giving it to one's children.

The sketch of the distinctive value of the parent-child relationship supporting the claim that parental rights are fundamental also helps us to establish more precisely the content of parental rights. Insofar as the purpose of parental rights is to protect the parental interest in having and maintaining a relationship of that kind, parental rights are

---

1 *What about the interest ... their parents?* See Claudia Card, "Against Marriage and Motherhood," *Hypatia* 11 (1996): 1–23; Martha Minow, "All in the Family and In All Families," in *Sex, Preference and the Family,* ed. David Estlund and Martha Nussbaum (New York: Oxford University Press, 1997), pp. 249–76. We are grateful to Sally Haslanger for discussion on this issue.

2 *Rawls is explicit ... the Liberty Principle* Rawls, *A Theory of Justice,* p. 511 (447–48 in rev. ed. [Cambridge, MA: Harvard University Press, 1999]).

3 *In a recent paper ... life prospects"* Richard Miller, "Too Much Inequality," *Social Philosophy and Policy* 19 (2002): pp. 275–313, 284.

4 *Our comments ... this question* For a fuller answer, see Brighouse and Swift, "Legitimate Parental Partiality."

justified only insofar as they are required for protecting that relationship.

What parents fundamentally have a right to is an intimate relationship of a certain kind with their children. We suggest that this right unpacks into a series of associational rights, because these are what is required to protect that relationship. As Rob Reich explains, "Raising a child is never merely a service rendered to another person but is the collective sharing of a life."[1] This has implications for the character of the permissions that parents must have to share aspects of their lives with their children. Parents have the right to determine whether the child will attend a church, a mosque, or neither; they have the right to live with the child and spend a substantial part of the day with her. They have the right to share their enthusiasms with their children, including, for example, their enthusiasms regarding their own particular cultural heritage. These rights are not connected to or derived from their independent rights to freedom of religion, association, or expression, or to their expressive interests more generally, but directly to the right to a relationship of a certain kind. Furthermore, as long as they are ensuring that the child's interests are being well-enough served, parents are not under an obligation to be considering the child's best interests as they exercise these rights.

Our view thus contrasts with those that give great weight to the parental interest in the reproduction of her values or conception of the good. Charles Fried's claim, quoted earlier, that one has the right to "form one's child's values, one's child's life plan" suggests this, as does William Galston's claim that "the ability of parents to raise their children in a manner consistent with their deepest commitments is an essential element of expressive liberty."[2] Our account has not appealed to this interest. It does not deny that parents have an interest in forming their children's values or life plan, but it subordinates that interest to the child's interests and the parent's interests in acting as a fiduciary for, and enjoying an intimate relationship with, the child. The kind of proximity that parents must have as a consequence of granting them parental rights will give them, in consequence, some of the powers that Galston and Fried seek to ensure. But they are charged with using these powers to protect their child's interests in the first instance, including the interest

in developing the capacity to form one's own values and life plan. Furthermore, our account is indifferent as to whether parents use their power to promote their own conception of the good (or something consistent with it) in the child or some other, possibly conflicting, conception of the good. It does not privilege the parents' values in the ways that Fried's and Galston's accounts do. It is thus consistent with giving priority to the child's interest in autonomy over the impulse to tolerate parental behavior which conflicts with the child's prospective autonomy.

Associational rights contrast with control rights. Parents must indeed be given license to control certain aspects of their children's lives for the sake of the children's interests, and their fundamental associational rights will involve granting them some degree of control over their children. But if children's interests in general are best served by a division of authority between parents and some other agency, then that division is preferable to giving parents exclusive authority, as long as this division does not infringe the fundamental rights of parents to intimate relations with their children. So if parents, such as those in the Tennessee case of *Mozert v. Hawkins*, have the right to withdraw their children from a civic educational curriculum that conflicts with their religious beliefs, this is not a fundamental right, but one that must be justified by its benefit to those children or to third parties.[3] Similarly, if the parents in the case of *Wisconsin v. Yoder* have the right to deprive their children of formal education over age fourteen, that is because it is better for those children that the parents have this right than not.[4] Such rights might be justified in our terms, but they would not be fundamental.

Of course, associational rights involve control rights of a sort, especially when the children involved are very

---

1   *As Rob Reich explains … sharing of a life"* Reich, *Bridging Liberalism and Multiculturalism in American Education*, p. 149.

2   *William Galston's claim … expressive liberty"* Galston, *Liberal Pluralism*, p. 102.

3   *But if children's interests … third parties* Brighouse makes an argument for moderate parental deference in non-parent-centered terms in *On Education* (London: Routledge, 2006), chap. 5, and in "Religious Belief, Religious Schooling, and the Demands of Reciprocity," in *Deliberative Democracy: Theory and Practice*, ed. David Kahane and Daniel Weinstock (Vancouver: University of British Columbia Press, 2007).

4   *Mozert v. Hawkins … than not* For details of *Mozert v. Hawkins*, see Stephen Bates, *Battleground: One Mother's Crusade, the Religious Right, and the Struggle for Control of Our Classroom* (New York: Poseidon/Simon & Schuster, 1993); for details of *Wisconsin v. Yoder*, see *Wisconsin v. Yoder* 406 U.S. 205 (1972). For useful discussions, see Amy Gutmann, "Civic Education and Social Diversity," *Ethics* 105 (1995): 557–79; Galston, "Two Concepts of Liberalism."

young, so the distinction between associational and control rights is not very clean. But the control rights involved in associational rights are concerned with the moment, not with the future. The distinction is also unclean because parents who exercise their immediate control rights can use them to exert control over the shape of their children's future development—it is impossible to allow people to take their children to church without allowing them to use that right to try to indoctrinate their children in their faith. But the latter power is something they have no fundamental right to, even though, given the importance of unmonitored intimacy, there is no practicable way of depriving them of it without depriving them of something they do have a right to.

For reasons that go beyond the scope of this article, we side with liberals who assert that children have a fundamental interest in prospective autonomy.[1] Parents may not legitimately indoctrinate their children, but they do have a legitimate interest in being able deliberately to influence their children's values and beliefs insofar as they can do so without compromising the child's prospective autonomy. This follows partly from their duty to foster the moral development of their children. But they also have an interest in a continuing relationship, which interest depends on at least some shared interests and values. It is hard for us to imagine that two people can maintain intimacy without having some distinctive enthusiasms and interests in common. These shared enthusiasms provide for the interactions which to a considerable extent constitute the intimacy of the relationship and allow for the relationship to be pursued in a way that is not constantly self-conscious. After the child leaves home, as many do, shared interests provide much of the content for the interactions between the participants in the relationship. Of course, there is no reason why, as children grow up and start to develop interests and enthusiasms of their own, it should be parents rather than children who continue to determine the content of, or agenda for, familial interactions. That is another way in which our account does not privilege parents' values (here, as contrasted with the children's). But for the earlier years, as the child is only gradually forming its own ideas about what is and is not interesting or important in life, our account renders it

permissible for parents deliberately to present children with their views on such matters.

The bar on indoctrination extends to attempting to force their child into the family business or the family career (army, law), or manipulating an exclusive enthusiasm for cricket or folk music. But it does not bar deliberately ensuring that the child is exposed (albeit not exclusively) to the parents' values and enthusiasms. (That said, a good parent should be able to sustain a successful relationship without any particular shared interest or values. On our view, the parent who cuts off a child for marrying out of the faith, for refraining from joining the military, for entering a religious order, or for apostasy fails as a parent.) So while there is no right to "form one's children's values," and certainly none that is the corollary of the right to do so for oneself, there is a right to have distinctive influence over the formation of those values, if one that is limited by one's fiduciary obligations to the children, including the obligation to safeguard their prospective autonomy.

We have said both that parents' rights are limited and that they are conditional on parents' protecting certain of the children's interests. Failure to protect those interests amounts to a forfeiture of the right, in the same way that failure to obey just laws implies forfeiting one's right to freedom of association. All accounts of parental rights, in order to be plausible, have to make them conditional on parents' meeting certain of their children's interests adequately. It is standard to include an "abuse and neglect" clause as a condition on parents' rights attributions. We believe that this sets the bar too low, but to explain why would take another paper.[2] We want to make two points here. The first is simply that disagreements about where to set the bar are disagreements about the weight children's interests have relative to parental interests, not disagreements about whether parents' interests count fundamentally. The second is that the higher the bar is set, the more plausible will tend to be the case for leaving the children in the custody and care of the parent, even when he is currently failing to meet that threshold. Even modern welfare states have been notoriously bad at providing superior child-rearing arrangements for children who are in abusive and neglectful situations. But from the mere fact that there is no superior alternative (in child-centered terms) for the child, it does not follow that parents retain fundamental rights. They enjoy only the privilege

---

1   *For reasons that go ... prospective autonomy*   For some of those reasons, see Brighouse, "Civic Education and Liberal Legitimacy"; and Matthew Clayton, *Justice and Legitimacy in Upbringing* (Oxford: Oxford University Press, 2006), chap. 3.

2   *to explain why would take another paper*   That other paper is Brighouse, "What Rights (If Any) Do Children Have?" 31–52.

that is justified by appeal to the state's failure to provide a better alternative. This is different from the case of the parent who, having succeeded in meeting the conditions for parents' rights, would be entitled to exercise those rights even if the state could indeed provide a superior arrangement for the child.

8. Parenting, Policy, and Perfectionism

Suppose that our argument to this point is sound. Two questions naturally arise. First, what are the policy implications? We have an argument against the forcible redistribution of children from adequately good parents to others (or to state institutions) that might do better by them, but does our account of the parental interest in the parent-child relationship yield any other guidance for public policy? Second, to what extent do such policies as are justified by appeal to the parental interest we have outlined count as "perfectionist"? We have made several claims about aspects of the parenting experience that contribute distinctively to the flourishing of the parent, in a way that might seem to violate the (alleged) liberal commitment to the view that the state should eschew actions based on controversial claims of that kind. To do justice to either of these questions would require another paper, but it may be helpful at least to set out some of the issues that they raise.

First, it is important to be clear that many policies that would serve the parental interest in the relationship goods we identify can be justified without appeal to that interest. They can be justified by appealing, less controversially, to the interests of children (and, to some extent, of third parties). We believe, for example, that poverty is a major barrier to adults' capacity to participate in the relationships we have described. The conscientious parent, living in poverty, doing her best to provide her child with a decent start in life, may find herself working longer hours, or trying to hold down two or more jobs, in a way that makes it very difficult for her to enjoy an intimate relationship with them.[1]

We believe, also, that even many affluent parents in wealthy societies face significant barriers to enjoying relationships of the kind we have described. Professional and nonprofessional jobs, especially in the United States, frequently lack the kind of employment protection that enables parents to negotiate their hours of work to fit with the demands of parenting, and jobs are often structured in such a way that wholehearted involvement in them is strongly in tension with wholehearted involvement in family life. Policies to combat poverty and to help even affluent parents achieve a better work-life balance do, on our account, serve the interests of parents, but of course they serve children's interests too. Children's interests in growing up well parented (and other people's interest in their growing up that way) may be quite sufficient—and less "perfectionist"—justifications of many of the policies that we would advocate. In that sense, we can be thought of as pointing out the additional benefits that would accrue to parents from policies that might be justified in more straightforward terms.

We should be clear on the extent to which parents' and children's interests are intertwined. On our account, the parental interest is in large part an interest in acting as the fiduciary for the child. We don't believe that the parent has a duty to promote the child's best interests—there is some room for the parent to purse her own interest even where that may not be best for the child—but much of the value of parenting comes precisely from being able to look after children's interests well, being there to give them what they need to develop into the kind of people it is good for them to become. Policies aimed at tackling those aspects of poverty most damaging to a flourishing parent-child relationship, or at enabling even affluent parents to achieve a better work-life balance, help parents in large part by helping them do what parents should be able to do for their children. If it is good for the parent to be home from work in time to read bedtime stories to her children, that is in large part (though not entirely) because it is good for children to have bedtime stories read to them by the parent. We contribute to parents' flourishing indirectly, as it were,

---

[1] *The conscientious parent ... relationship with them* A phenomenon that looks particularly tragic in the light of our account is that of impoverished mothers who relinquish their day-to-day relationships with their children in order to earn money for them by taking care of other people's children. This is a case where fulfilling one's obligations to one's children requires, or appears to require, that one refrain from enjoying the intimate relationship with them (and providing that relationship for them). The relationship with the children one cares for instead is not an adequate substitute, on our account, because a nanny is vulnerable to other people's authority over the relationship. The terms of the relationship are set by a third party—the parent—and both parties are subject to monitoring and interference, and to sudden and arbitrary termination, by the parent. See the essays collected in Barbara Ehrenreich and Arlie Russell Hochschild, *Global Woman: Nannies, Maids, and Sex Workers in the New Economy* (New York: Holt, 2003), especially the first three chapters.

by policies justified primarily on child-centered, and less controversial, grounds.

It remains possible, of course, that children's interests will not justify all the policies that our parent-centered account would lead us to endorse. The parental interest in the relationship is not exhausted by its fiduciary aspect, and we could imagine, perhaps, that children would grow up well enough with a parenting relationship that was thinner or weaker than that which would be valuable for parents. This leads us to our second point. Insofar as policy prescriptions did appeal to claims about parents' interests, they might be conceived and presented as correcting or compensating for biases that make it unduly difficult, given current incentive structures, for adults to experience the kind of relationships that we have identified as distinctively valuable. Of course it is a complicated question how we should conceive the baseline against which to assess any claim about bias, and one would need to do a good deal of work to show that, say, existing arrangements were biased against parenting in a way that would justify profamily policies as consistent with an egalitarian or neutralist conception of distributive justice.[1] Still, especially where fertility rates are falling, it is important to keep in mind the possibility that we live in societies that have tilted the balance against parenthood. Most analyses, of course, think about falling fertility rates as an economic problem, and in what we have called public good terms. Our approach suggests a different kind of worry. People whose lives would go better were they to become parents may be missing out. Insofar as their decision to remain childless reflected our having made the costs of parenting unduly high, efforts to correct the imbalance could be justified without any appeal to perfectionist considerations.

Of course, one might want to go further, advocating proparenting policies on avowedly nonneutral grounds that appealed directly to the value, for parents, of parenting relationships. We do not mean to rule out such arguments. We simply mean to point out that the way in which proparenting policies can be justified on child-centered grounds, and, more speculatively, the possibility of conceiving such policies as corrections for existing biases against the enjoyment, on the part of parents, of valuable parent-child relationships, may go a long way toward justifying policies that would serve the interests that we have identified in this article.[2]

---

1 *one would need ... distributive justice* For examples of the kind of work we have in mind, see Paula Casal and Andrew Williams, "Equality of Resources and Procreative Justice," in *Dworkin and His Critics*, ed. Justine Burley (Oxford: Blackwell, 2004), pp. 150–69; Clayton, *Justice and Legitimacy in Upbringing*, pp. 61–75. Because these contributions deal with the issue at the level of ideal theory, their claims would need to be combined with complex empirical assessments to yield concrete policy implications here and now.

2 We are grateful to audiences at Bowling Green State University, the annual conference of the Philosophy of Education Society of Great Britain (PESGB; 2001); the Glasgow branch of the PESGB; the Nuffield Political Theory Workshop; Queens University, Kingston; the Graduate Conference on Political Theory at the University of Warwick; the University of Birmingham; Massachusetts Institute of Technology; the St. Catherine's College, Oxford, Political Thought Conference; and the University of Wisconsin Institute of the Humanities. Because the article has had such a long incubation period, we are certain that we have forgotten some of our debts, but we remember learning from comments from and discussion with Jaime Ahlberg, Larry Blum, the late Jim Childs, Matthew Clayton, David Copp, Geert Demuijnck, Sally Haslanger, Loren Lomasky, Emily McRae, Marina Oshana, Rob Reich, Miriam Ronzoni, Debra Satz, Victor Seidler, Christine Sypnowich, Leigh Vicens, Matt Waldren, Andrew Williams, Bekka Williams, Erik Olin Wright, an anonymous referee, and the editors of *Ethics*, especially Donald Hubin. We're particularly indebted to Dan Hausman for suggesting writing the article, and to Francis Schrag, for numerous conversations and for writing "Justice and the Family," (*Inquiry* 19 [1976]: 193–208), which inspired the argumentative strategy of the current article.

Sources/Permission Acknowledgments

The list below includes source information and copyright acknowledgments for all texts in the anthology that are in copyright, and all texts in translation, whether in copyright or in the public domain. Texts originally written in English and in the public domain are generally not included in the list below; unless otherwise noted the annotations to all such texts appearing in this anthology may be presumed to have been prepared for the anthology, and to be copyright © Broadview Press.

◆ ◆ ◆ ◆ ◆

ARENDT, Hannah
- Excerpt from *The Human Condition*. Chicago: University of Chicago Press, 1958. pp. 178–86. Copyright © 1958 by the University of Chicago. All rights reserved. Reprinted by permission of the University of Chicago.
- "On the Nature of Totalitarianism: An Essay in Understanding," from *Essays in Understanding 1930–1954*. Edited by Jerome Kohn. New York: Harcourt Brace & Company, 1994. pp. 328–60. Copyright © 1994, 1954, 1953, 1950, 1946, 1945, 1944 by The Literary Trust of Hannah Arendt Bluecher. Reprinted by permission of Georges Borchardt, Inc., on behalf of The Literary Trust of Hannah Arendt Bluecher.

BEAUVOIR, Simone de
- "Introduction (Woman as Other)" and "On the Social Construction of Reality (One is Not Born, One Becomes a Woman)," from *The Second Sex*. Translated by H.M. Parshley. Copyright © 1952 and renewed 1980 by Alfred A. Knopf, a division of Random House, Inc. Reprinted by permission of Georges Borchardt, Inc. for Éditions Gallimard and of Alfred A. Knopf, a division of Random House, Inc.

BERLIN, Isaiah
- "Two Concepts of Liberty," from *Four Essays on Liberty*. Edited by Henry Hardy. Oxford: Oxford University Press, 2002. pp. 166–217. Copyright © Isaiah Berlin 1959. Reprinted by permission of Curtis Brown Group, Ltd. on behalf of The Isaiah Berlin Literary Trust.

BRIGHOUSE, Harry, and Adam Smith
- "Parents' Rights and the Value of the Family," from *Ethics* 117.1 (October 2006): 80–108. Published by The University of Chicago Press. Copyright © 2006 by The University of Chicago. All rights reserved. Reprinted by permission of The University of Chicago Press.

COHEN, G.A.
- "Robert Nozick and Wilt Chamberlain: How Patterns Preserve Liberty," from *Self-Ownership, Freedom, and Equality: Studies in Marxism and Social Theory*. Cambridge: Cambridge University Press, 1995. pp. 19–37. Copyright © Maison des sciences de l'Homme and Cambridge University Press 1995. Reprinted by permission of Cambridge University Press.

DEWEY, John
- "Means and Ends: Their Interdependence and Leon Trotsky's Essay On 'Their Morals and Ours,'" from *The Collected Works of John Dewey: The Later Works, Volume 13: 1938–39*. Copyright © 1988 by the Board of Trustees, Southern Illinois University. Reprinted by permission of the publisher.

FANON, Frantz
- Excerpts from *The Wretched of the Earth/Frantz Fanon*. Translated by Richard Philcox. Introductions by Jean-Paul Sartre and Homi K. Bhabha. New York: Grove Press, 2004. pp. 01–08, 10, 21–24, 47–52, 170–80. Copyright © 2004 Grove/Atlantic Press. Reprinted by permission of Grove/Atlantic, Inc. and of HarperCollins Publishers, Ltd., UK.

FOUCAULT, Michel
- Excerpt from *The Foucault Reader*. Edited by Paul Rabinow. New York: Pantheon, 1984. pp. 78–108. Copyright © 1984 by Paul Rabinow. Originally appeared in *Power/Knowledge: Selected and Other Writings by Michel Foucault 1972–1977*. Edited by Colin Gordon. Copyright © 1972, 1975, 1976, 1977 by Michel Foucault. Reprinted by permission of Georges Borchardt, Inc. and of Pantheon Books, a division of Random House, Inc.
- Excerpt from *Discipline and Punish: The Birth of the*

OKIN, Susan Moller

- "Chapter 5: Justice as Fairness: For Whom?," from *Justice, Gender, and the Family*. New York: Basic Books, 1989. pp. 89–109. Copyright © 1989 by Basic Books, Inc. Reprinted by permission of Basic Books, a member of Perseus Books Group.

POGGE, Thomas W.

- "Cosmopolitanism and Sovereignty," from *Ethics* 103.1 (October 1992): 48–75. Published by The University of Chicago Press. Copyright © 1992, The University of Chicago Press. Reprinted by permission of The University of Chicago Press.

RAWLS, John

- Excerpts from *A Theory of Justice*. Cambridge, Mass.: The Belknap Press of Harvard University Press, 1971. pp. 10–25, 52–56, 73–81, 86–93, 118–123. Copyright © 1971, 1999 by the President and Fellows of Harvard College. Reprinted by permission of the publisher.
- "The Idea of an Overlapping Consensus," from *Oxford Journal of Legal Studies* 7.1 (Spring 1987): 1–25. Reprinted by permission of Oxford University Press.

SANDEL, Michael J.

- "The Procedural Republic and the Unencumbered Self," from *Political Theory* 12.1 (1984): 81–96. Copyright © 1984 by SAGE Publications. Reprinted by Permission of SAGE Publications, Inc.

SCHMITT, Carl

- Excerpts from *The Concept of the Political*. Translation, introduction and notes by George Schwab. New Brunswick, N.J.: Rutgers University Press, 1976. pp. 19–22, 25–28, 29–37, 58, 60–61, 63–66, 66–67, 68, 69–73, 73–76, 78-79. Reprinted by permission of George Schwab and Duncker & Humbolt.

SEN, Amartya Kumar

- "Chapter 1: The Perspective of Freedom," from *Development as Freedom*. 1st edition. New York: Knopf, 1999. pp. 13–34. Copyright © 1999 by Amartya Sen. Reprinted by permission of Lyn Nesbit for the author and of Alfred A. Knopf, a division of Random House, Inc.

TAYLOR, Charles

- "What's Wrong with Negative Liberty?," from *Philosophy and the Human Sciences*. New York: Cambridge University Press, 1985. pp. 211–29. Copyright © Cambridge University Press 1985. Reprinted by permission of Cambridge University Press.

WALZER, Michael

- Excerpts from *Spheres of Justice: A Defense of Pluralism and Equality*. New York: Basic Books, 1983. pp. 3–30. Copyright © 1983 by Basic Books, Inc. Reprinted by permission of Basic Books, a member of Perseus Books Group.

WEBER, Max

- "Politics as a Vocation," from *Max Weber: Selections in Translation*. Translated by E. Matthews. New York: Cambridge University Press, 1978. pp. 212–25. Reprinted by permission of Cambridge University Press.

YOUNG, Iris Marion

- "Chapter 1: Displacing the Distributive Paradigm," from *Justice and the Politics of Difference*. Princeton, N.J.: Princeton University Press, 1990. pp. 15–38. Copyright © 1990 Princeton University Press. Reprinted by permission of Princeton University Press.
- "Impartiality and the Civic Public: Some Implications of Feminist Critiques of Moral and Political Theory," from *Throwing Like a Girl and Other Essays in Feminist Philosophy and Social Theory*. Bloomington, Indiana: Indiana University Press, 1990. pp. 92–113. Originally published in *Feminism as Critique*. Edited by Seyla Benhabib and Drucilla Cornell. Copyright © 1987 University of Minnesota Press. Reprinted by permission of University of Minnesota Press and of Blackwell Publishers, Oxford, for Polity Press.

◆ ◆ ◆ ◆ ◆

Index of Authors and Titles